DICTIONARY

OF

INTERNATIONAL

TRADE

5th Edition

This book is dedicated to the memory of my father
Allen Joseph Hinkelman
who taught me the meaning of many words.

DICTIONARY
OF
INTERNATIONAL
TRADE
5th Edition

Handbook of the Global Trade Community
Includes 19 Key Appendices

Edward G. Hinkelman

with contributions by:
Karla Shippey, J.D. • Sibylla Putzi
Myron Manley • Paul Denegri • Philip Auerbach
John O'Conor • U.S. Department of Commerce
International Chamber of Commerce (ICC) • Sea Land Shipping
IATA (International Air Transport Association)
Air Transport Association (of the U.S.) • CIGNA Worldwide
Insurance Company of North America • World Bank
Swiss Bank Corporation • Wells Fargo HSBC Trade Bank

WORLD TRADE PRESS®
Professional Books for International Trade

World Trade Press
1450 Grant Avenue, Suite 204
Novato, California 94945 USA
Tel: [1] (415) 898-1124; Fax: [1] (415) 898-1080
Order Line (U.S. credit card sales only) [1] (800) 833-8586
E-mail: sales@worldtradepress.com
www.worldtradepress.com
www.globalroadwarrior.com
Edward G. Hinkelman E-mail: egh@worldtradepress.com

Disclaimer
This publication is designed to provide information concerning the terminology used in international trade and the businesses that support international trade. It is sold with the understanding that the publisher is not engaged in rendering legal or any other professional service. If legal advice or other expert assistance is required, the services of a competent professional should be sought.

Library of Congress Cataloging-in-Publication Data:

Hinkelman, Edward G., 1947—
     Dictionary of international trade : handbook of the global trade community, includes 19 key appendices / Edward G. Hinkelman ; with contributions by Karla Shippey ... [et al.]. -- 5th ed.
        p. cm.
     Includes bibliographical references.
     ISBN 1-885073-90-9
     1. International trade--Dictionaries. 2. United States--Commerce Dictionaries.
I. Shippey, Karla c., 1957 - II Title.
HF1373 .H55 2002
382'.03--dc21   2002071317

Printed in the United States of America

Table of Contents

A

abandonment
(shipping/insurance) (a) The act of refusing delivery of a shipment so badly damaged in transit that it is worthless. (b) Damage to a vessel that is so severe that it is considered a constructive total loss. *See* constructive total loss.

abatement
(shipping) A deduction or discount given as a result of damage to a shipment or an overcharge in the payment of a bill.

abbrochment
(law) The purchase at wholesale of all merchandise that is intended to be sold in a particular retail market for the purpose of controlling that market.

aboard
(shipping/logistics) (a) The placement or lading of cargo on any conveyance. (b) Cargo that has been placed or laden on any means of conveyance.

about
(banking) In connection with letters of credit, "about" means a tolerance of plus/minus 10% regarding the letter of credit value, unit price or the quantity of the goods, depending on the context in which the tolerance is mentioned.

absolute advantage
(economics) An advantage of one nation or area over another in the costs of manufacturing an item in terms of used resources.

absorption
(economics) Investment and consumption purchases by households, businesses and governments, both domestic and imported. When absorption exceeds production, the excess is the country's current account deficit. *See* current account.
(shipping) The assumption by one carrier of the special charges of another carrier generally without increasing charges to the shipper.

accelerated tariff elimination
(customs) The gradual reduction of import duties over time. Accelerated tariff elimination is often a feature of free trade agreements. The North American Free Trade Agreement (NAFTA) is an example of a trade agreement with accelerated tariff elimination.

acceptance
(law) (a) An unconditional assent to an offer. (b) An assent to an offer conditioned on only minor changes that do not affect any material terms of the offer. *See* counteroffer; offer.
(shipping) Receipt by the consignee of a shipment thus terminating the common carrier liability.

(banking) A time draft (bill of exchange) on the face of which the drawee has written "accepted" over his signature. The date and place payable are also indicated. The person accepting the draft is known as the acceptor. Note: The drawee's signature alone is a valid acceptance and is usually made across the left margin of the bill of exchange. *See* bank acceptance, bill of exchange.

acceptance letter of credit
(banking) A letter of credit which, in addition to other required documents, requires presentation of a term draft drawn on the bank nominated as the accepting bank under the letter of credit. *See* acceptance; bank acceptance; letter of credit.

accepted draft
(banking) A bill of exchange accepted by the drawee (acceptor) by putting his signature (acceptance) on its face. In doing so, he commits himself to pay the bill upon presentation at maturity. *See* acceptance; bank acceptance; bill of exchange.

accepting bank
(banking) A bank who by signing a time draft accepts responsibility to pay when the draft becomes due. In this case the bank is the drawee (party asked to pay the draft), but only becomes the acceptor (party accepting responsibility to pay) upon acceptance (signing the draft). *See* acceptance; bill of exchange.

acceptor
(banking) The party that signs a draft or obligation, thereby agreeing to pay the stated sum at maturity. *See* acceptance; bill of exchange.

accession
The process by which a country becomes a member of an international agreement, such as the World Trade Organization (WTO), the GATT or the European Community (EC). Accession to the WTO involves negotiations to determine the specific obligations a nonmember country must undertake before it will be entitled to membership benefits. *See also* accessions.

accessions
(law) (a) Goods that are affixed to and become part of other goods. Examples include semiconductors that are inserted into computers, parts that are added onto vehicles and dials that are used in watches. (b) A nation's acceptance of a treaty already made between other countries. *See also* accession.

accessorial charges
(shipping) Charges made for additional, special, or supplemental services, normally over and above the line haul services.

A

accessorial services
(shipping) Services performed by a shipping line or airline in addition to the normal transportation service. Common accessorial services include advancement of charges, pickup, delivery, C.O.D. service, signature service and storage.

accommodation
(law) An action by one individual or legal entity (the accommodation party) that is taken as a favor, without any consideration, for another individual or legal entity (the accommodated party). An **accommodation note or paper** is a commercial instrument of debt that is issued by or for an accommodated party (who is expected to pay the debt) and that contains the name of the accommodation party. A person may make an accommodation, for example, to help another party raise money or obtain credit. An accommodation party is usually treated like a surety, who is responsible for the performance of the accommodated party. The distinction between an accommodation and a surety is that an accommodation is made without consideration, that is, it is freely given. *See* surety.

accord and satisfaction
(law) A means of discharging a contract or cause of action by which the parties agree (the accord) to alter their obligations and then perform (the satisfaction) the new obligations. A seller who cannot, for example, obtain red fabric dye according to contract specifications and threatens to breach the contract may enter into an accord and satisfaction with the buyer to provide blue-dyed fabric for a slightly lower price.

account number
(shipping) An identifying number issued by a carrier's accounting office to identify a shipper and/or consignee. The number helps ensure accurate invoicing procedures and customer traffic activity.

account party
(banking) The party that instructs a bank (issuing bank) to open a letter of credit. The account party is usually the buyer or importer. *See* letter of credit.

accounts payable
(accounting) A current liability representing the amount owed by an individual or a business to a creditor(s) for merchandise or services purchased on an open account or short-term credit. *See also* accounts receivable.

accounts receivable
(accounting) Money owed a business enterprise for merchandise or services bought on open account. *See also* accounts payable.

accrual of obligation
(law) The time at which an obligation matures or vests, requiring the obligor to perform. In a contract between a buyer and seller, for example, the seller's obligation to deliver goods may accrue when the buyer tenders payment in full. Alternatively, if the contract specifies a date for delivery of the goods, the seller's obligation accrues at that date, even if the buyer tenders payment before or after that date.

acquisition
The purchase of complete or majority ownership in a business enterprise, usually by another business enterprise.

ACROSS
(Canada) Accelerated Commercial Release Operations Support System. An electronic data interchange (EDI) system offered by the Canada Customs and Revenue Agency (CCRA) allowing traders and brokers to file documents and transfer data to the CCRA 24 hours a day, 7 days a week. The system increases efficiency, decreases paperwork and speeds the release of shipments from Canadian Customs. Information at Web: www.ccra-adrc.gc.ca.

Act of God
An act of nature beyond man's control such as lightning, flood, earthquake or hurricane. Many shipping and other performance contracts include a "force majeure" clause which excuses a party who breaches the contract due to Acts of God. *See* force majeure.

action ex contractu
(law) A legal action for breach of a promise stated in an express or implied contract.

action ex delicto
(law) (a) A legal action for a breach of a duty that is not stated in a contract but arises from the contract. A seller of goods, for example, who represents that the goods can be used for a certain purpose has a duty to furnish goods that can be so used, even if that duty is not stated in the contract. If the seller fails to provide such goods, the seller breaches that duty and the buyer has an action ex delicto based on the seller's fraudulent representation. (b) A legal action that arises from a wrongful act, such as fraud.

activity-based costing (ABC)
(logistics) An accounting methodology that measures all the costs associated with a specific business activity regardless of organizational structure. The business activity can be the production, delivery or maintenance of a product or service.

added-value tax
See value-added tax.

address of record
(law) The official or primary location for an individual, company, or other organization.

adhesion contract
(law) Contract with standard, often printed, terms for sale of goods and services offered to consumers who usually cannot negotiate any of the terms and cannot acquire the product unless they agree to the terms.

adjustment

(general) The refund or replacement of lost or damaged goods by either the seller or by an insurance carrier.

(insurance) The settlement of an insurance claim.

(U.S. government) The negative impact of increased import competition to U.S. businesses. *See* adjustment assistance.

adjustment assistance

(U.S. law) Financial, training and reemployment technical assistance to workers and technical assistance to firms and industries, to help them cope with adjustment difficulties arising from increased import competition. The objective of the assistance is usually to help an industry become more competitive in the same line of production, or to move into other economic activities. The aid to workers can take the form of training (to qualify the affected individuals for employment in new or expanding industries), relocation allowances (to help them move from areas characterized by high unemployment to areas where employment may be available) or unemployment compensation (to tide them over while they are searching for new jobs). The aid to firms can take the form of technical assistance through Trade Adjustment Assistance Centers located throughout the United States. Industry-wide technical assistance also is available through the Trade Adjustment Assistance program. The benefits of increased trade to an importing country generally exceed the costs of adjustment, but the benefits are widely shared and the adjustment costs are sometimes narrowly—and some would say unfairly—concentrated on a few domestic producers and communities. Adjustment assistance can also be designed to facilitate structural shifts of resources from less productive to more productive industries, contributing further to greater economic efficiency and improved standards of living. Trade Adjustment Assistance Centers: E-mail: info@taacenters.org; Web: www.taacenters.org. *See* Trade Adjustment Assistance Centers.

Administrative Protective Order (APO)

(U.S. law) An Administrative Protective Order, APO, is used to protect proprietary data that is obtained during an administrative proceeding. Within the U.S. Department of Commerce, APO is most frequently used in connection with antidumping and countervailing duty investigations to prohibit opposing counsel from releasing data. The term is also applied in connection with civil enforcement of export control laws to protect against the disclosure of information provided by companies being investigated for violations. *See* dumping; countervailing duties.

admiralty

(law/shipping) Any civil or criminal issue having to do with maritime law.

admiralty court

(law/shipping) A court of law that has jurisdiction over maritime legal issues. These generally include ocean shipping, collisions of vessels, charters, contracts and damage to cargo.

admission temporaire

(customs) The free entry of goods normally dutiable. *See* ATA Carnet.

Admission Temporaire/Temporary Admission Carnet

See ATA Carnet.

ad valorem

Literally: according to value.

(general) Any charge, tax, or duty that is applied as a percentage of value.

(taxation) A tax calculated on the value of the property subject to the tax.

(shipping) A freight rate set at a certain percentage of the declared value of an article.

(U.S. Customs) Ad valorem duty. A duty assessed as a percentage rate or value of the imported merchandise. For example 5% ad valorem. *See* compound rate of duty; specific rate of duty; tariff.

advance against collection

(banking) A short term loan or credit extended to the seller (usually the exporter) by the seller's bank once a draft has been accepted by the buyer (generally the importer) of the seller's goods. Once the buyer pays, the loan is paid off. If the buyer does not pay the draft, the seller must still make good on the loan. *See* bill of exchange.

advance arrangements

(shipping) The shipment of certain classes of commodities—examples: gold, precious gems, furs, live animals, human remains and oversized shipments—require arrangements in advance with carriers.

advance shipment notice (ASN)

(logistics) A document transmitted (by courier, fax or e-mail) to a consignee in advance of delivery detailing the contents and particulars of a shipment. The particulars may include such items as shipment date, method of transport, carrier, expected date and time of arrival and a full listing of contents.

Advanced Technology Products (ATP)

(U.S. trade law) About 500 of some 22,000 commodity classification codes used in reporting U.S. merchandise trade are identified as "advanced technology" codes and they meet the following criteria: (1) The code contains products whose technology is from a recognized high technology field (e.g., biotechnology); (2) These products represent leading edge technology in that field; and (3) Such products constitute a significant part of all items covered in the selected classification code.

A

advancement of charges
(shipping) A service under which a shipping line or airline, in some instances, pays incidental charges arising before or after a shipment or airhaul. Examples include cartage and warehousing costs. These charges can be in advance for the convenience of either the shipper or the receiver.

advice
(banking) The term "advice" connotes several types of forms used on the banking field. Generally speaking, an advice is a form of letter that relates or acknowledges a certain activity or result with regard to a customer's relations with a bank. Examples include credit advice, debit advice, advice of payment and advice of execution. In commercial transactions, information on a business transaction such as shipment of goods.
(banking/letters of credit) The forwarding of a letter of credit, or an amendment to a letter of credit to the seller, or beneficiary of the credit, by the advising bank (seller's bank).
See issuance; letter of credit; amendment.

advice of fate
(banking) A bank's notification of the status of a collection which is still outstanding.

advised credit
(banking) A letter of credit whose terms and conditions have been confirmed by a bank. *See* letter of credit; confirmed letter of credit.

advising bank
(banking) The bank (also referred to as the seller's or exporter's bank) which receives a letter of credit or amendment to a letter of credit from the issuing bank (the buyer's bank) and forwards it to the beneficiary (seller/exporter) of the credit. *See* letter of credit; confirming bank; issuing bank.

Advisory Committee on Export Policy
(U.S. government) The ACEP is an interagency dispute resolution body that operates at the Assistant Secretary level. ACEP is chaired by the U.S. Department of Commerce; membership includes the Departments of Defense, Energy and State, the Arms Control and Disarmament Agency and the intelligence community. Disputes not resolved by the ACEP must be addressed by the cabinet-level Export Administration Review Board within specific time frames set forth under National Security Directive #53. *See* National Security Directive #53; Export Administration Review Board.

Advisory Committee on Trade Policy and Negotiations (ACTPN)
(U.S. government) The ACTPN is a group (membership of 45; two-year terms) appointed by the president to provide advice on matters of trade policy and related issues, including trade agreements. The 1974 Trade Act requires the ACTPN's establishment and broad representation of key economic sectors af-

fected by trade. Below the ACTPN are seven policy committees: SPAC (Services Policy Advisory Committee), INPAC (Investment Policy Advisory Committee), IGPAC (Intergovernmental Policy Advisory Committee), IPAC (Industry Policy Advisory Committee), APAC (Agriculture Policy Advisory Committee), LPAC (Labor Policy Advisory Committee) and DPAC (Defense Policy Advisory Committee). Below the policy committees are sectoral, technical and functional advisory committees. Information at Web: www.ustr.gov/outreach/advise.shtml.
See Industry Consultations Program.

affiliate
A business enterprise located in one country which is directly or indirectly owned or controlled by a person of another country.
(U.S.) A business enterprise located in one country which is directly or indirectly owned or controlled by a person of another country to the extent of 10 percent or more of its voting securities for an incorporated business enterprise, or an equivalent interest for an unincorporated business enterprise, including a branch. For outward investment, the affiliate is referred to as a "foreign affiliate"; for inward investment, it is referred to as a "U.S. affiliate." *See* direct foreign investment; foreign direct investment in the United States; affiliated foreign group.

affiliated foreign group
(U.S.) An affiliated foreign group means (a) the foreign parent, (b) any foreign person, proceeding up the foreign parent's ownership chain, which owns more than 50 percent of the person below it up to and including that person which is not owned more than 50 percent by another foreign person and (c) any foreign person, proceeding down the ownership chain(s) of each of these members, which is owned more than 50 percent by the person above it. *See* direct foreign investment; foreign direct investment in the United States; affiliate; foreign-owned affiliate in the U.S.

affreightment
(shipping) The hiring or chartering of all or part of a vessel for the transport of goods.

affreightment contract
(shipping/law) A contract with a shipowner to hire all or part of a ship for transporting goods.

afghani
The currency of Afghanistan. 1 Af = 100 puls.

afloat
(shipping) Refers to a shipment of cargo which is currently onboard a vessel between ports (as opposed to on land).

African, Caribbean and Pacific Countries (ACP)
Developing countries which are designated beneficiaries under the Lome Convention. *See* Lome Convention.

African Development Bank (AfDB)

The AfDB, established in 1963, provides financing through direct loans to African member states to cover the foreign exchange costs incurred in Bank-approved development projects in those countries. Fifty-one African countries are members and ordinarily receive loans. The Republic of South Africa is currently the only African country not a member. Address: African Development Bank, Rue Joseph Anoma, 01 BP 1387, Abidjan 01, Cote d'Ivoire; Tel: [225] 20-20-44-44; Fax: [225] 20-20-49-59; Web: www.afdb.org.

African Development Foundation

An independent, nonprofit U.S. government corporation established to provide financial assistance to grassroots organizations in Africa. ADF became operational in 1984. Address: African Development Foundation, 1400 Eye Street NW, 10th Floor, Washington, DC 20005 USA; Tel: [1] (202) 673-3916; Fax: [1] (202) 673-3810; Web: www.adf.gov.

aft

(shipping) Direction toward the stern of the vessel (ship or aircraft).

after date

(banking) A notation used on financial instruments (such as drafts or bills of exchange) to fix the maturity date as a fixed number of days past the date of drawing of the draft. For example, if a draft stipulates "60 days after date," it means that the draft is due (payable) 60 days after the date it was drawn. This has the effect of fixing the date of maturity of the draft, independent of the date of acceptance of the draft. *See* acceptance; drawee; bill of exchange.

after sight

(banking) A notation on a draft that indicates that payment is due a fixed number of days after the draft has been presented to the drawee. For example, "30 days after sight" means that the drawee has 30 days from the date of presentation of the draft to make payment. *See* acceptance; drawee; bill of exchange.

agency

(law) A relationship between one individual or legal entity (the agent) who represents, acts on behalf of, and binds another individual or legal entity (the principal) in accordance with the principal's request or instruction. In some countries, agency is more narrowly defined as a relationship created only by a written agreement or a power of attorney, entered into by a principal and a person who is designated to act for the principal within the limits of the written document creating the agency. *See* agent; principal; power of attorney.

(a) An **express agency** is established by a written or oral agreement between the parties. An express agency is created, for example, when a seller orally contracts with a sales representative to sell products or when a company makes a written power of attor-ney to authorize a person to act on its behalf. (b) An **implied agency** arises as a result of the conduct of the parties. If a seller's assistant, for example, sometimes deals with customers, a court may determine from that conduct that an implied agency exists between the seller and the assistant. (c) An **agency by estoppel** is imposed by law when an agent acts without authority, but the principal leads a third person to conclude reasonably that the agent had authority and to rely on that conclusion. If a seller, for example, informs a buyer that the seller's representative is authorized to negotiate any contract terms for the seller, a court may decide that an agency by estoppel existed, that the contract should be enforced and that the seller cannot avoid performing the contract by claiming that the representative in fact had no authority. (d) An **agency del credere** arises when a principal entrusts goods, documents, or securities to an agent who has broad authority to collect from a buyer and who may be liable for ensuring that the buyer is solvent. A sales representative, for example, who is given goods and who is authorized to receive payment from buyers is an agent del credere. (e) An **exclusive agency** is an arrangement with an agent under which the principal agrees not to sell property to a purchaser found by another agent. If a seller of green and red shoes, for example, gives a sales representative an exclusive agency to sell the green shoes in a particular country, the seller is not permitted to sell those shoes through any other representative in the same country. The seller may, however, authorize other agents to sell red shoes in that country. (f) A **universal agency** authorizes the agent to do every transaction that a principal can legally delegate. A principal who will be traveling for some time may, for example, give an agent authority to deal with all business and personal transactions for the principal during that absence. (g) A **general agency** authorizes an agent to do all acts related to the principal's business, which may include negotiating contracts, establishing credit, advertising, arranging for shipping and setting up overseas offices and outlets. (h) A **special agency** gives an agent limited powers to conduct one transaction or a specific series of transactions. A contract with a representative to secure the sale of certain components to a particular factory creates a special agency. *See* agent; principal; power of attorney.

agency by estoppel

See agency.

agency del credere

See agency.

Agency for International Development

(U.S. government) Formerly a unit of the now defunct United States International Development Cooperation Agency, in 1999 the AID was transferred to the Department of State and reports directly to the Secretary of State. AID administers U.S. foreign eco-

A

nomic and humanitarian assistance programs in the developing world, Central and Eastern Europe and the Commonwealth of Independent States. Among the economic programs are those that foster employment growth and that promote use of clean and efficient energy and environmental technologies. Maintains economic, social and demographic statistics for many developing countries. AID has field missions and representatives in approximately 70 developing countries in Africa, Latin America, the Caribbean and the Near East. Address: Agency for International Development, Ronald Reagan Building, 1300 Pennsylvania Avenue, NW; Washington, DC 20523 USA; Tel: [1] (202) 712-4320; Fax: [1] (202) 216-3524; Web: www.info.usaid.gov. *See* Center for Trade and Investment Services.

agent
(law) An individual or legal entity authorized to act on behalf of another individual or legal entity (the principal). An agent's authorized actions will bind the principal. A sales representative, for example, is an agent of the seller. *See* agency; principal; power of attorney.

agent ad litem
(shipping/law) An agent who acts on behalf of a principal in prosecuting or defending a lawsuit.

agent bank
(banking) (a) Bank acting for a foreign bank. (b) Bank handling administration of a loan in a syndicated credit.

aggregated shipments
(shipping) Numerous shipments from different shippers to one consignee that are consolidated and treated as a single consignment.

aggregate tender rate
(shipping) A reduced rate given to a shipper who tenders two or more shipments of the same or similar class at the same time and place. *See* class or kind (of merchandise); tender.

agreed valuation
(shipping) The value of a shipment agreed upon by the shipper and carrier to secure a specific rate and/or liability.

agriculture export connections
(U.S. government) The U.S. Foreign Agriculture Service through AgExport Connections (formerly Agriculture Information and Marketing Services) provides services designed to help U.S. exporters of agricultural products make direct contact with foreign buyers. Services include: Trade Leads—compiled by overseas offices and retrievable from the STAT-USA/Internet service at Web: www.stat-usa.gov; Buyer Alert—publication for U.S. exporters to advertise their products; and Foreign Buyer Lists. Contact: AgExport Connections, Foreign Agriculture Service, 1400 Independence Avenue, Ag Box 1052, Washington, DC 20250-1052 USA; Tel:

[1] (202) 690-3421; Fax: [1] (202) 690-4374; Web: www.fas.usda.gov.

airbill
See air waybill.

air cargo
(shipping) Any property (freight, mail, express) carried or to be carried in an aircraft. Does not include passenger baggage.

aircraft pallet
(shipping) A platform or pallet (in air freight usually from 3/4" to 2" thick) upon which a unitized shipment rests or on which goods are assembled and secured before being loaded as a unit onto an aircraft. Most carriers offer container discounts for palletized loads.

Palletization results in more efficient use of space aboard freighter aircraft and better cargo handling, particularly when used as part of mechanized systems employing such other advances as pallet loaders and pallet transporters. The **pallet loader** is a device employing one or more vertical lift platforms for the mechanical loading or unloading of palletized freight at planeside.

The **pallet transporter** is a vehicle for the movement of loaded pallets between the aircraft and the freight terminal or truck dock. Sometimes the functions of both the pallet loader and pallet transporter are combined into a single vehicle. *See also* pallet.

air express
(shipping) A term used to describe expedited handling of air freight service. *See* priority air freight; air freight.

air freight
(shipping) A service providing for the air transport of goods. The volume of air freight has been increasing significantly due to: (1) decreased shipping time, (2) greater inventory control for just-in-time manufacturing and stocking, (3) generally superior condition of goods upon arrival, and (4) for certain commodities, lower shipping costs.

air freight forwarder
(shipping) A freight forwarder for shipments by air. Air freight forwarders serve a dual role. The air freight forwarders are, to the shipper, an indirect carrier because they receive freight from various shippers under one tariff, usually consolidating the goods into a larger unit, which is then tendered to an airline. To the airlines, the air freight forwarder is a shipper. An air freight forwarder is ordinarily classed as an indirect air carrier; however, many air freight forwarders operate their own aircraft. *See* freight forwarder.

airmail
(shipping) The term "airmail" as a class of mail is used only in international postal service. Within the United States, the U.S. Postal Service moves all first

class mail, priority mail and express mail by air where doing so will expedite delivery.

air parcel post

(shipping) A term commonly used for priority mail which consists of first class mail weighing more than 13 ounces. Priority mail is another economical and expedited service for the shipping of parcels by air.

airport mail facility (AMF)

(shipping) A U.S. Postal Service facility located on or adjacent to an airport. AMFs are primarily engaged in the dispatch, receipt and transfer of mail directly with air carriers.

air waybill (airbill)

(shipping) A shipping document used by the airlines for air freight. It is a contract for carriage that includes carrier conditions of carriage including such items as limits of liability and claims procedures. The air waybill also contains shipping instructions to airlines, a description of the commodity and applicable transportation charges. Air waybills are used by many truckers as through documents for coordinated air/truck service.

Air waybills are not negotiable. The airline industry has adopted a standard formatted air waybill that accommodates both domestic and international traffic. The standard document was designed to enhance the application of modern computerized systems to air freight processing for both the carrier and the shipper. *See* bill of lading; negotiable.

airworthiness certification

(shipping) Documentation to show that an aircraft or components comply with all the airworthiness requirements related to its use as laid down by the regulatory authorities for the country in which the aircraft is registered.

Aksjeselskap (A/S)

(Norway) Designation for a joint stock company with limited personal liability to shareholders. See Business Entities Appendix.

Aktiebolag (AB)

(Finland, Sweden) Designation for a joint stock company with limited personal liability to shareholders. See Business Entities Appendix.

Aktiengesellschaft (AG)

(Austria, Germany, Switzerland, Liechtenstein) Designation for a joint stock company with limited personal liability to shareholders. See Business Entities Appendix.

Aktieselskab (A/S)

(Denmark) Designation for a joint stock company with limited personal liability to shareholders.

Alcohol, Tobacco and Firearms (ATF)

See Bureau of Alcohol, Tobacco and Firearms.

alienable

(law) The capacity to be transferred or conveyed. Interests in real or personal property, for example, are alienable.

aliquot

(law) A fractional share. A court, for example, may award damages aliquot against several parties who breached a contract, meaning that each must pay a proportionate share of the damages. Aliquot liability differs from joint and several liability, in that the latter refers to whether the breaching parties may be sued and held liable together or individually. *See* joint and several liability.

all-cargo aircraft

(shipping) An aircraft for the carriage of cargo only, rather than the combination of passengers and cargo. The all-cargo aircraft will carry cargo in bulk or container in the main deck as well as in the lower deck of the aircraft. It may include a scheduled and/or nonscheduled service.

all risk

(insurance) Extensive insurance coverage of cargo, including coverage due to external causes such as fire, collision, pilferage etc., but usually excluding "special" risks such as those resulting from acts of war, labor strikes, the perishing of goods, and from internal damage due to faulty packaging, decay or loss of market.

All risk insurance covers only physical loss or damage from external cause(s) and specifically affirms the exclusion of war risks and strikes and riots unless covered by endorsement. These losses are excluded, either by expressed exclusions, conditions or warranties written into the policy or by implied conditions or warranties that are read into every marine policy by legal interpretation.

An "all risks" policy may expressly exclude certain types of damage such as marring and scratching of unboxed automobiles or bending and twisting entirely or unless amounting to a specified percentage or amount.

Also, certain perils such as war and strikes, riots and civil commotions are commonly excluded, but these perils can be and usually are reinstated, at least in part, by special endorsement or by a separate policy.

The "all risk" clause is a logical extension of the broader forms of "with average" coverage. The all risk clause generally reads:

"To cover against all risks of physical loss or damage from any external cause irrespective of percentage, but excluding, nevertheless, the risk of war, strikes, riots, seizure, detention and other risks excluded by the F.C.&S. (Free of Capture and Seizure) Warranty and the S.R.&C.C. (Strikes, Riots and Civil Commotion) Warranty in this policy, excepting to the extent that such risks are specifically covered by endorsement."

(air shipments) All risk insurance of air shipments usually excludes loss due to cold or changes in atmospheric pressure. *See* average; with average; free of particular average; inherent vice, war risk; strikes, riots and civil commotion.

allowance

An amount paid or credited by a seller as a refund or reimbursement due to any one of a number of causes including: faulty packaging, shipment of goods which do not meet buyer's specifications, a late shipment, etc.

alongside

(shipping) A phrase referring to the side of a ship. (a) Goods to be delivered "alongside" are to be placed on the dock or lighter within reach of the transport ship's tackle so that they can be loaded aboard the ship. (b) Goods delivered to the port of embarkation, but without loading fees.

alternative tariff

(shipping) A tariff containing two or more rates from and to the same points, on the same goods, with authority to use the one which produces the lowest charge.

amendment

(law/general) An addition, deletion, or change in a legal document.

(banking/letters of credit) A change in the terms and conditions of a letter of credit (e.g., extension of the letter of credit's validity period, shipping deadline, etc.), usually to meet the needs of the seller. The seller requests an amendment of the buyer who, if he agrees, instructs his bank (the issuing bank) to issue the amendment. The issuing bank informs the seller's bank (the advising bank) who then notifies the seller of the amendment. In the case of irrevocable letters of credit, amendments may only be made with the agreement of all parties to the transaction. *See* letter of credit.

American Arbitration Association

A private not-for-profit organization formed in 1926 to encourage the use of arbitration in the settlement of disputes. Address: American Arbitration Association, 1633 Broadway, 10th Floor, New York NY 10019 USA; Tel: [1] (212) 484-4181; Fax: [1] (212) 246-7274; Web: www.adr.org. *See* arbitration.

American Association of Exporters and Importers

(U.S.) A trade association which advises members of legislation regarding importing and exporting, and fights against protectionism. Also hosts seminars and conferences for importers and exporters. Address: American Association of Exporters and Importers, P.O. Box 7813, Washington, DC 20044 USA; Tel: [1] (202) 661-2181; Fax: [1] (202) 661-2185; Web: www.aaei.org.

American Institute in Taiwan

A nonprofit corporation that represents U.S. interests in Taiwan in lieu of an embassy. In 1979, the United States terminated formal diplomatic relations with Taiwan when it recognized the People's Republic of China as the sole legal government of Taiwan. The AIT was authorized to continue commercial, cultural and other relations between the U.S. and Taiwan. Address: American Institute in Taiwan, 7, Section 3, Lane 134, Hsin Yi Road, Taipei, 106, Taiwan; Tel: [886] (2) 2720-1550; Fax: [886] (2) 2757-7162; http://ait.org.tw/.

American National Standards

A set of product standards established by the American National Standards Institute (ANSI). *See* American National Standards Institute. *See also* International Standards Organization.

American National Standards Institute (ANSI)

An organization that develops and publishes a set of voluntary product standards called the American National Standards. In addition to product standards, ANSI publishes a guide to unit-load and transportation package sizes for containers. ANSI is also an influential member of the ISO (International Standards Organization). Address: American National Standards Institute, 25 West 43rd Street, New York, NY 10036 USA; Tel: [1] (212) 642-4900; Fax: [1] (212) 398-0023; Web: www.ansi.org. *See also* International Standards Organization.

American option

(banking/foreign exchange) A foreign exchange option containing a provision to the effect that it can be exercised at any time between the date of writing and the expiration date. *See also* European option.

American Traders Index (ATI)

A compilation of individual U.S. & Foreign Commercial Service (US&FCS) domestic client files, for use by overseas posts to generate mailing lists. *See* United States and Foreign Commercial Service.

amidships

(shipping) At or in the middle of a vessel. Because a ship's movement is less in the middle of the vessel, shippers will sometimes specify that fragile freight be placed amidships.

amortization

(banking) (a) The gradual extinguishment of any amount over a period of time (e.g., the retirement of a debt). (b) A reduction of the book value of a fixed asset.

analysis certificate

See certificate of analysis.

ancillary

(logistics) Supplemental or additional. For example, an ancillary charge.

ancillary equipment

(shipping) Equipment used to build up a palletized load or to convey a unit load device outside an aircraft. *See* aircraft pallet.

Andean Group

An alliance of Latin American countries formed in 1969 to promote regional economic integration among medium-sized countries. Members include Bolivia, Colombia, Ecuador, Peru and Venezuela. Address: Andean Group, Avenida Paseo de la Republica 3895, Casilla Postal 18-1177, Lima 27, Peru; Tel: [51] (14) 11-1400; Fax: [51] (12) 21-3329; Web: www.comunidadandina.org.

Andean Trade Initiative (ATI)

(obsolete) A former U.S. government initiative providing for assistance for alternative economic development to the drug producing countries of Bolivia, Colombia, Ecuador and Peru. The program provided ten years of duty-free treatment for most goods produced in one or a combination of these four countries.

Animal and Plant Health Inspection Service (APHIS)

(U.S. government) A U.S. government agency attached to the U.S. Department of Agriculture which has the responsibility of inspecting and certifying animals, plants and related products for import to or export from the United States. APHIS is also responsible for the inspection of animal and plant product processing facilities both in the United States and in countries that export to the United States. Address: Animal and Plant Health Inspection Service, 4700 River Road, Riverdale, MD 20737 USA; Tel: [1] (301) 734-7799; Fax: [1] (301) 734-5221; Web: www.aphis.usda.gov. *See also* phytosanitary inspection certificate.

animal containers

(shipping) The use of air freight as a means of transporting household pets led to the development of special containers designed to provide adequate protection and air circulation. Such containers may be purchased or rented from many air carriers.

annual basis

(accounting) Statistical shifting of data that are for a period less than 12 months in order to estimate the full results for an entire year. To be accurate the processing should consider the effect of the seasonal variation.

ANSI

See American National Standards Institute.

ANSI 12

(logistics/data interchange) The most widely accepted standards for EDI (Electronic Data Interchange) in the United States. *See* American National Standards Institute, EDI, UN/EDIFACT.

antidumping

(customs) Antidumping, as a reference to the system of laws to remedy dumping, is defined as the converse of dumping. *See* dumping; antidumping duties; General Agreement on Tariffs and Trade; Antidumping Act of 1974.

Antidumping Act of 1974

(U.S. law) Legislation designed to prevent the sales of goods at a lower price than exists in the goods' country or origin. The U.S. Treasury Department determines whether imported products are being sold at a "less than fair value" in the United States. Should it be determined that the domestic industry is harmed by the imports, extra duties can be imposed. *See* countervailing duties; dumping.

Antidumping/Countervailing Duty System

(U.S. Customs) A part of the U.S. Customs' Automated Commercial System, containing a case reference database and a statistical reporting system to capture data for International Trade Commission reports on antidumping and countervailing duties assessed and paid. *See* dumping; countervailing duties.

antidumping duties

(customs) Duties assessed on imported merchandise of a class or kind that is sold at a price less than the fair market value. Fair market value of merchandise is defined as the price at which it is normally sold in the manufacturer's home market. *See* dumping; countervailing duties.

antidumping petition

(customs) A claim filed on behalf of a U.S. industry alleging that imported merchandise is being sold in the United States at "less than fair value," and that sales of such merchandise is causing or threatening injury to, or retarding the establishment of a U.S. industry. *See* dumping; countervailing duties.

any quantity

(shipping) A cargo rating that applies to an article regardless of weight (i.e., in any quantity).

apparent good order and condition

(shipping) A statement, on a bill of lading or other shipping document, indicating that the shipment is available for shipment or delivery with no apparent damage.

appraiser, customs

(U.S. Customs) An individual authorized by the U.S. Customs Service (Department of Treasury) to examine and determine the value of imported merchandise.

appreciation

(foreign exchange) An increase in the value of the currency of one nation in relation to the currency of another nation.

approval basis

(banking/letters of credit) If documents containing discrepancies are presented to the nominated bank

A

under a letter of credit, the bank can forward the documents to the issuing bank for approval, with the beneficiary's agreement. Because of the risk of loss in transit and delays resulting in interest loss, however, it is recommended that the beneficiary first try to correct the documents; but, if that is not possible, the beneficiary asks the nominated bank to contact the issuing bank for authorization to accept the discrepancies.

approximately
See about.

appurtenance
(law) An accessory that is connected to primary property, that is adapted to be used with that property and that generally is intended to be permanently affixed to that property. Appurtenances to a ship, for example, may include cranes attached to the ship for loading and unloading cargo. An easement for access to land is considered an appurtenance to that land. Industrial machinery that is affixed to a factory facility is an appurtenance to the building.

apron
(shipping) The area of an airport where aircraft are parked for loading and unloading of cargo or passengers.

Arab League
A regional alliance established in March 1945 which aims to improve relations among Arab nations. Headquarters are located in Cairo, Egypt. Members include: Algeria, Bahrain, Djibouti, Egypt, Iraq, Jordan, Kuwait, Lebanon, Libya, Mauritania, Morocco, Oman, Qatar, Saudi Arabia, Somalia, Sudan, Syria, Tunisia, United Arab Emirates and Yemen. Address: Arab League, P.O. Box 11642, Tahrir Square, Cairo, Egypt; Tel: [20] (2) 575-0511; Telex: 92111 ALS UN; Fax: [20] (2) 574-0331; Web: www.leagueofarabstates.org.

Arab Maghreb Union (AMU)
A regional alliance established in February 1989 with the goal of joining the Gulf Cooperation Council and other states in a common market. AMU members include: Algeria, Morocco, Tunisia, Libya and Mauritania. Address: Union du Maghreb Arabe, 14 Rue Zalagh Agdal, Rabat, Morocco; Tel: [212] (37) 671 274; Fax: [212] (37) 671 253; Web: www.maghrebarabe.org.

arbiter
See arbitration.

arbitrage
(banking/finance/foreign exchange) The simultaneous buying and selling (or borrowing and lending) of identical securities, currencies, or commodities in two or more markets in order to take advantage of price differentials. *See also* hedging.

arbitrage, space
(banking/finance/foreign exchange) The simultaneous buying and selling (or borrowing and lending) of identical securities, currencies, or commodities in two or more locations in order to take advantage of price differentials.

arbitrage, time
(banking/finance/foreign exchange) The simultaneous buying and selling (or borrowing and lending) of identical securities, currencies, or options at different maturity dates in order to take advantage of price differentials.

arbitrageur
(finance) A person systematically engaged in arbitrage dealing.

arbitration
(law) The resolution of a dispute between two parties through a voluntary or contractually required hearing and determination by an impartial third party. The impartial third party is called the arbiter or arbitrator and is chosen by a higher or disinterested body, or by the two parties in dispute. In the United States, the main arbitration body is the American Arbitration Association, 1633 Broadway, Floor 10, New York, NY 10019 USA; Tel: [1] (212) 484-4181; Fax: [1] (212) 246-7274; Web: www.adr.org. Internationally, the main arbitration body is the International Chamber of Commerce (ICC), 38 Cours Albert 1er, 75008 Paris, France; Tel: [33] 49-53-28-28; Fax: [33] 49-53-28-59; Web: www.iccwbo.org. For the U.S. representative of the ICC, contact: U.S. Council for International Business, 1212 Avenue of the Americas, New York, NY 10036 USA; Tel: [1] (212) 354-4480; Fax: [1] (212) 575-0327. *See* arbitration clause; American Arbitration Association; International Chamber of Commerce.

arbitration clause
(law) A contract clause included in many international contracts stating for example:
"Any controversy or claim arising out of or relating to this contract, or the breach thereof, shall be settled by arbitration in accordance with the Commercial Arbitration Rules of the American Arbitration Association and judgment upon the award rendered by the arbitrator(s) may be entered in any court having jurisdiction thereof." *See* arbitration; American Arbitration Association; International Chamber of Commerce.

Arms Control and Disarmament Agency
(U.S.) An independent agency within the U.S. State Department which reviews dual-use license applications from a nonproliferation perspective—anything that could impact on the proliferation of missiles, chemical and biological weapons, and nuclear weapons. The agency was created in 1961, has about 200 to 250 staff and has a fairly substantial and growing technology transfer and export control function. The director is the principal arms control adviser to the secretary of state, the president and the NSC on: conventional arms transfer; commercial sales of mu-

nitions; nuclear, missile, chemical and biological warfare; East-West military munitions issues; and negotiating Memorandums of Understanding (MOUs) with the Third World on strategic trade. *See* United States Department of State.

arrival notice
(shipping) A notice furnished to consignee and shipping broker alerting them to the projected arrival of freight and availability of freight for pickup.

arrivals
(customs) Imported goods which have been placed in a bonded warehouse for which duty has not been paid.

articles of extraordinary value (AEV)
(shipping) Commodities identified as high value items, requiring special care in shipping.

articulated lorry
(UK) British term for a truck with trailer or semi-trailer.

Asian Development Bank (ADB)
The ADB was formed in 1966 to foster economic growth and cooperation in Asia and to help accelerate economic development of members. Address: Asian Development Bank, PO Box 789, Manila Central Post Office, 0980 Manila, Philippines; Tel: [63] (2) 632-4444; Fax: [63] (2) 636-2444; Web: www.adb.org.

Asia Pacific Economic Cooperation (APEC)
An informal grouping of Asia Pacific countries that provides a forum for ministerial level discussion of a broad range of economic issues. APEC includes the six ASEAN countries (Brunei, Indonesia, Malaysia, Philippines, Singapore and Thailand), plus: Australia, Canada, China, Hong Kong, Japan, South Korea, Taiwan and the United States. The Secretariat is located in Singapore. Address: 438 Alexandra Road, #14-00, Alexandra Point, Singapore 119958; Tel: [65] 276-1880; Fax: [65] 276-1775; Web: www.apecsec.org.sg/.

as is
(law) A term indicating that goods offered for sale are without warranty or guarantee. The purchaser has no recourse to the vendor for quality of the goods.

ask(ed) price; market price
(finance) The price at which a security or commodity is quoted or offered for sale.

assailing thieves
(insurance) A reference to an insurance policy clause covering the forcible taking rather than the clandestine theft or mere pilferage of goods.

assembly service
(shipping) A service under which an airline assembles shipments from many shippers and transports them as one shipment to one receiver.

assessment
(customs) The imposition of antidumping duties on imported merchandise. *See* dumping; antidumping duties; countervailing duties.

assign
(law) To transfer or make over to another party.

assignee
(law) One to whom a right or property is transferred. *See also* assignor; assignment.

assignment
(law/shipping/banking) The transfer of rights, title, interest and benefits of a contract or financial instrument to a third party.

(banking/letters of credit) The beneficiary of a letter of credit is entitled to assign his/her claims to any of the proceeds that he/she may be entitled to, or portions thereof, to a third party. Usually the beneficiary informs the issuing or advising bank that his/her claims or particle claims under the letter of credit were assigned and asks the bank to advise the assignee (third party) that it has acknowledged the assignment. The validity of the assignment is not dependent on bank approval. In contrast, the transfer requires the agreement of the nominated bank. An assignment is possible regardless of whether the letter of credit is transferable. *See* letter of credit.

assignment of proceeds
See assignment.

assignor
(law) One by whom a right or property is transferred. *See also* assignee; assignment.

assist
(U.S. Customs) Any of a number of items that an importer provides directly or indirectly, free of charge, or at a reduced cost, for use in the production or sale of merchandise for export to the United States.

Assists are computed as part of the transaction value upon which duty is charged, when the duty rate is a percentage of the value of the merchandise.

Examples of assists are: materials, components, parts and similar items incorporated in the imported merchandise; tools, dies, molds and similar items used in producing the imported merchandise; engineering, development, artwork, design work and plans and sketches that are undertaken outside the United States. Engineering is not treated as an assist if the service or work is: (1) performed by a person domiciled within the United States, (2) performed while that person is acting as an employee or agent of the buyer of the imported merchandise, and (3) incidental to other engineering, development, artwork, design work, or plans or sketches undertaken within the United States. *See* valuation; transaction value; deductive value; computed value.

A

Association of Southeast Asian Nations (ASEAN)

ASEAN was established in 1967 to promote political, economic and social cooperation among its six member countries: Indonesia, Malaysia, Philippines, Singapore, Thailand and Brunei. Address: Association of Southeast Asian Nations, 70A Jalan Sisingamangaraja, Jakarta-12110, Indonesia; Tel: [62] (21) 726-2991; Fax: [62] (21) 739-8234; Web: www.aseansec.org.

assumpsit

(law) An assumption or undertaking by one person (the promisor) to perform an act for, or to pay a sum to, another person (the promisee), often without express agreement from the promisee to perform an act or remit consideration in return. An assumpsit is created, for example, when one person employs another without any written agreement as to compensation. In such an arrangement, the law will imply a duty to pay reasonable wages. An assumpsit also arises when one person receives money that belongs to another, in which event the law implies a duty to remit the sum to the owner.

(a) An **express assumpsit** is one in which the promisor states the assumption in distinct and definite language. A person who agrees to work for another on certain tasks for a specified time has made an express assumpsit.

(b) An **implied assumpsit** is one in which a promise is inferred by law from the conduct of a party or the circumstances of the case. If, without any express statement, a person begins working for another who knows and does not object to that work, a court may find that an implied assumpsit has arisen.

(c) An **action in assumpsit** is a court action to recover damages for breach of an oral or other informal contract. A seller who delivers goods to a buyer based on an oral contract and who does not receive payment may recover the proceeds in an action in assumpsit.

assurance

(insurance) British term for insurance.

assurance of performance

(law) A declaration intended to induce one contracting party to have full confidence in the other's performance. Pledges and sureties are forms of assurances.

assured

(insurance) The individual, company or entity which is insured.

astern

(shipping) (a) Behind a ship or aircraft, (b) Toward the back of a ship or aircraft, (c) Backward, as in the movement of a ship.

ATA Carnet

(customs) ATA stands for the combined French and English words "Admission Temporair/Temporary Admission." An ATA Carnet is an international customs document which may be used for the temporary duty-free admission of certain goods into a country in lieu of the usual customs documents required. The carnet serves as a guarantee against the payment of customs duties which may become due on goods temporarily imported and not reexported. Quota compliance may be required on certain types of merchandise. ATA textile carnets are subject to quota and visa requirements.

The ATA Convention of 1961 authorized the ATA Carnet to replace the ECS ("Echantillons Commerciaux/Commercial Samples") Carnet that was created by a 1956 convention sponsored by the Customs Cooperation Council.

ATA Carnets are issued by National Chambers of Commerce affiliated with the Paris-based International Chamber of Commerce (ICC). These associations guarantee the payment of duties to local customs authorities should goods imported under cover of a foreign-issued carnet not be reexported.

The issuing and guaranteeing organization in the United States is: U.S. Council, International Chamber of Commerce, 1212 Avenue of the Americas, New York, NY 10036 USA; Tel: [1] (212) 354-4480; Fax: [1] (212) 575-0327.

Additional information can be obtained from The Roanoke Companies, agents for the U.S. Council for International Business. Address: The Roanoke Companies, 1930 Thoreau Drive, Suite 101, Schaumburg, IL 60173 USA; Tel: [1] (800) ROANOKE, [1] (847) 490-5940.

See also International Chamber of Commerce; carnet.

athwartships

(shipping) Across a vessel from side to side.

at sight

(banking) Terms of a financial instrument which is payable upon presentation or demand. A bill of exchange may be made payable, for example, at sight or after sight, which (respectively) means it is payable upon presentation or demand, or within a particular period after demand is made. *See* bill of exchange.

attachment

(law) Legal process for seizing property before a judgment to secure the payment of damages if awarded. A party who sues for damages for breach of contract may request, for example, that the court issue an order freezing all transfers of specific property owned by the breaching party pending resolution of the dispute.

attendant accompanying shipments

(shipping) Sometimes attendants accompany cargo shipments as when grooms or veterinarians accompany race horses or other live animals. This service requires advance arrangements with a shipping company or airline.

at-the-money
(foreign exchange/finance) A call or put option is at-the-money when the price of the underlying instrument is equivalent or very near to the strike price. *See* option; call option; put option.

attorn
(law) To agree to turn over or transfer money or goods to an individual or legal entity other than the party who was to originally receive them. A company that has bought out another legal entity may seek an attornment from a supplier who had an outstanding contract with the former entity, and if the supplier attorns, the company can obtain goods on the same terms as were agreed to with the former entity.

attorney-in-fact
(law) A person authorized to transact business generally or to perform a designated task of a nonlegal nature on behalf of another individual or legal entity. An attorney-in-fact is a type of agent. In many countries, this authority must be conferred by a written power of attorney. If a company buys goods from a foreign firm, for example, and agrees to place sufficient funds for the purchase in an escrow account, the buyer may authorize an attorney-in-fact in that foreign country to disburse the escrow funds on receiving verification from the buyer that the goods are satisfactory. A business enterprise may also authorize an attorney-in-fact to testify to facts on the company's behalf in arbitration or legal proceedings held in a foreign country. *See* agent; agency; power of attorney.

audit
(general) A formal examination of records or documents—usually financial documents.
(shipping) The formal examination of freight bills to determine their accuracy.

Australia Group (AG)
An informal forum through which 20 industrialized nations cooperate to curb proliferation of chemical and biological weapons through a supply approach. The AG's first meeting, held at the Australian Embassy in Paris in June 1986, was attended by Australia, Canada, Japan, New Zealand, the United States, and the ten member nations of the European Community. Membership has expanded to include Norway, Portugal, Spain, Switzerland, Austria, and representatives of the European Commission, the European Community's executive arm.

austral
The currency of Argentina. 1A=100 centavos.

authentication
(law) The act of certifying that a written document is genuine, credible, and reliable. An authentication is performed by an authorized person who attests that the document is in proper legal form and is executed by a person identified as having authority to do so. In many countries, persons authorized to authenticate documents include consulate officials, notaries public, and judicial officers.

Automated Broker Interface (ABI)
(U.S. Customs) ABI, a part of U.S. Customs' Automated Commercial System, permits transmission of data pertaining to merchandise being imported into the U.S. directly to U.S. Customs. Qualified participants include customs brokers, importers, carriers, port authorities, and independent data processing companies referred to as service centers. To use ABI, send a letter of intent to the District Director of Customs or to your nearest district Customs Office. *See* Automated Commercial System.

Automated Clearinghouse (ACH)
(U.S. Customs) ACH is a feature of the Automated Broker Interface which is a part of Customs' Automated Commercial System. The ACH combines elements of bank lock box arrangements with electronic funds transfer services to replace cash or check for payment of estimated duties, taxes, and fees on imported merchandise. *See* Automated Commercial System.

Automated Commercial System
(U.S. Customs) The ACS is a joint public-private sector computerized data processing and telecommunications system linking customhouses, members of the import trade community, and other government agencies with the Customs computer.
Trade users file import data electronically, receive needed information on cargo status, and query Customs files to prepare submissions. Duties, taxes, and fees may be paid by electronic statement, through a Treasury-approved clearinghouse bank. ACS contains the import data used by Census to prepare U.S. foreign trade statistics. ACS began operating in February 1984 and includes: (1) the Automated Broker Interface, (2) the Census Interface System, (3) the Automated Manifest Systems, (4) the Bond System, (5) the In-Bond System, (6) the Cargo Selectivity System, (7) the Line Release System, (8) the Collections System, (9) the Security System, (10) the Quota System, (11) the Entry Summary Selectivity System, (12) the Entry Summary System, (13) the Automated Information Exchange, (14) the Antidumping/Countervailing Duty System, (15) the Firms System, (16) the Liquidation System, (17) the Drawback System, (18) the Fines, Penalties, and Forfeitures System, and (19) the Protest System. *See* United States Customs Service.

automated guided vehicle system (AGVS)
(logistics) A materials handling system that utilizes computer-controlled, battery-powered, driverless vehicles that move along guided paths. These systems are utilized in manufacturing plants and warehouses, may be automatically or manually loaded and unloaded and are designed for applications with load capacities ranging from 20 to 120,000 kilograms (10-55,000 pounds). For example, a manufacturing

plant might utilize an AGVS with an automated storage and retrieval system (ASRS) to automatically retrieve component parts from a warehouse just as they are needed for assembly on the shop floor. *See* automated storage and retrieval system (ASRS).

Automated Information Exchange (AIES)

(U.S. Customs) AIES, a part of Customs' Automated Commercial System, allows for exchange of classification and value information between field units and headquarters. *See* Automated Commercial System.

Automated Manifest Systems (AMS)

(U.S. Customs) AMS, a part of Customs' Automated Commercial System (ACS), controls imported merchandise from the time a carrier's cargo manifest is electronically transmitted to Customs until control is relinquished to another segment of the ACS. *See* Automated Commercial System.

automated storage and retrieval system (ASRS or AS/RS)

(logistics) A computer-controlled robotic storage, retrieval and shipment system used in manufacturing plants and warehouses for materials, component parts and finished products. These systems utilize specially designed automated guided vehicles, computer-controlled guideways and storage bin and rack systems. Advanced systems are capable of delivering materials and component parts to the shop floor, loading robotic manufacturing equipment, taking finished or partially finished goods to storage and delivering goods to a loading dock.

Automotive Parts Advisory Committee (APAC)

(U.S.) A working committee established by an amendment to the Trade Act to set up an advisory committee to the U.S. Department of Commerce for dealing with U.S.-Japan trade issues involving the auto parts industry. Address: U.S. Department of Commerce, International Trade Administration, Office of Automotive Affairs, Room 4036, Washington, DC 20230 USA; Tel: [1] (202) 482-0554; Fax: [1] (202) 482-0719.

availability

(banking/letters of credit) In letters of credit, refers to the availability of documents in exchange for payment of the amount stated in the letter of credit. Availability options are:

(1) By **sight payment**: payment on receipt of the documents by the issuing bank or the bank nominated in the letter of credit.

(2) By **deferred payment**: payment after a period specified in the letter of credit, often calculated as number of days after the date of presentation of the documents or after the shipping date.

(3) By **acceptance**: acceptance of a draft (to be presented together with other documents) by the issuing bank or by the bank nominated in the letter of credit, and the payment thereof at maturity.

(4) By **negotiation**: meaning the giving of value by the nominated bank to the beneficiary for the documents presented, subject to receipt of cover from the issuing bank.

See letter of credit; bill of exchange; negotiation.

aval

(banking) Payment of a bill of exchange, which is the responsibility of the drawee, can be either completely or partially guaranteed via an aval (joint and several guarantee), where the guarantor places his/her signature on the draft either alone or with corresponding explanation "per aval" or "as guarantor." If other information is lacking, the guarantor commits him/herself on behalf of the issuer. *See* bill of exchange.

average

(insurance) A loss to a shipment of goods that is less than a total loss. It comes from the French word avarie, which means "damage to ship or cargo," (and ultimately from the Arabic word awarijah, which means "merchandise damaged by sea water").

(a) A **particular average** is an insurance loss that affects specific interests only.

(b) A **general average** is an insurance loss that affects all cargo interests on board the vessel as well as the ship herself.

See also particular average; general average; with average; free of particular average; deductible average.

average inventory

(logistics) (a) The average quantity or volume of an inventory item held over a specified period of time (e.g., monthly, annually). (b) The average value of an inventory item held over a specified period of time.

avoidance of contract

(law) The legal cancellation of a contract because an event occurs that makes performance of the contract terms impossible or inequitable and that releases the parties from their obligations. *See* commercial frustration; commercial impracticability; force majeure.

avoirdupois

(measure) (a) French for "having weight." (b) A system of weight measurement based on the pound of 16 ounces and the ounce of 16 drams. Refer to Weights and Measures in the Appendix.

B

Background Notes

A series of publications by the U.S. State Department providing an overview of a country's history, people, political conditions, economy, and foreign relations. Also includes map of country and travel notes. Available from: Superintendent of Documents, U.S. Government Printing Office, Washington, DC 20402; P.O. Box 371954, Pittsburgh, PA 15250-7954 USA; Web: www.access.gpo.gov/su_docs. To receive catalog, contact U.S. Fax Watch: [1] (202) 512-1716.

back haul

(logistics) (a) The return movement of a transport vehicle from its original destination to its original point of departure. (b) The load carried by a transport vehicle all or part of the way from its original destination to its original point of departure.

back order

(logistics/commerce) A customer order for a material, component part or finished good that cannot be filled from current inventory.

back-to-back borrowing

(banking) The process whereby a bank brings together a borrower and a lender so that they agree on a loan contract.

back-to-back letter of credit

(banking) A new letter of credit opened in favor of another beneficiary on the basis of an already existing, nontransferable letter of credit. For example, a British merchant agrees to buy cotton in Egypt for sale to a Belgian shirtmaker. The Belgian establishes a nontransferable letter of credit for payment to the British merchant who then uses the strength of the letter of credit as a security with his bank for opening a letter of credit to finance payment to the Egyptian. *See* letter of credit.

back-to-back loan

(banking) Operations whereby a loan is made in one currency in one country against a loan in another currency in another country (e.g., a U.S. dollar loan in the U.S. against a pounds sterling loan in the U.K.).

bad faith

(law) The intent to mislead or deceive (mala fides). It does not include misleading by an honest, inadvertent or uncalled-for misstatement.

bagged cargo

(shipping) Goods shipped in sacks.

baht

The currency of Thailand. 1B=100 satangs.

bailment

(law) A delivery of goods or personal property by one person (the bailor) to another (the bailee) on an express or implied contract and for a particular purpose related to the goods while in possession of the bailee, who has a duty to redeliver them to the bailor or otherwise dispose of them in accordance with the bailor's instructions once the purpose has been accomplished. A bailment arises, for example, when a seller delivers goods to a shipping company with instructions to transport them to a buyer at a certain destination.

(a) A **bailment for hire** is a bailment contract in which the bailor agrees to compensate the bailee. A shipping contract is usually a bailment for hire because the shipper transports the goods for a fee. (b) A **special bailment** is one in which the law imposes greater duties and liabilities on the bailee than are ordinarily imposed on other bailees. Common carriers, for example, are special bailees, because the law imposes extra duties of due care with regard to the property and persons transported than are required of private carriers. *See* carrier.

balanced economy

(economics) A condition of national finances in which imports and exports are equal.

balance of payments

(economics) A statement identifying all the economic and financial transactions between companies, banks, private households and public authorities of one nation with those of other nations of the world over a specific time period. A transaction is defined as the transfer of ownership of something that has an economic value measurable in monetary terms from residents of one country to residents of another.

The transfer may involve: (1) goods, which consist of tangible and visible commodities or products; (2) services, which consist of intangible economic outputs, which usually must be produced, transferred, and consumed at the same time and in the same place; (3) income on investments; and (4) financial claims on, and liabilities to, the rest of the world, including changes in a country's reserve assets held by the central monetary authorities. A transaction may also involve a gift, which is the provision by one party of something of economic value to another party without something of economic value being received in return.

International transactions are recorded in the balance of payments on the basis of the double-entry principle used in business accounting, in which each transaction gives rise to two offsetting entries of equal value so that, in principle, the resulting credit and debit entries always balance. Transactions are generally valued at market prices and are, to the extent possible, recorded when a change of ownership occurs.

B

These transactions are divided into two broad groups: current account and capital account. The **current account** includes exports and imports of goods, services (including investment income) and unilateral transfers. The **capital account** includes financial flows related to international direct investment, investment in government and private securities, international bank transactions and changes in official gold holdings and foreign exchange reserves.

(IMF) The International Monetary Fund (IMF), which strives for international comparability, defines the balance of payments as "a statistical statement for a given period showing (1) transactions in goods, services and income between an economy and the rest of the world, (2) changes of ownership and other changes in that economy's monetary gold, special drawing rights (SDRs) and claims on and liabilities to the rest of the world, and (3) unrequited transfers and counterpart entries that are needed to balance, in the accounting sense, any entries for the foregoing transactions and changes which are not mutually offsetting."

(U.S.) The six balances that are currently published quarterly concerning the U.S. balance of payments are:

(1) The **balance on merchandise trade**, which measures the net transfer of merchandise exports and imports (which differs in some ways from the trade balance published monthly by the Bureau of the Census);

(2) The **balance on services**, which measures the net transfer of services, such as travel, other transportation, and business, professional, and other technical services (this balance was redefined in 1990 to exclude investment income);

(3) The **balance on investment income**, which measures the net transfer income on direct and portfolio investments;

(4) The **balance on goods, services and income**, which measures the net transfer of merchandise plus services and income on direct and portfolio investment (this balance is equivalent to the pre-1990 balance on goods and services; it is also conceptually comparable to net exports of goods and services included in GNP);

(5) The **balance on unilateral transfers** (net), which measures the net value of gifts, contributions, government grants to foreign countries and other unrequited transfers;

(6) The **balance on current account** (widely used for analysis and forecasting), which measures transactions in goods, services, income and unilateral transfers between residents and nonresidents.

balance of trade

(economics) The difference between a country's imports and exports over a set period. (a) A **balance of trade deficit** is when a country imports more than it

exports. (b) A **balance of trade surplus** is when a country exports more than it imports.

balance on ...

See balance of payments.

balboa

The currency of Panama. 1B=100 centesimos.

bale

(shipping) A large bundle of compressed, bound and usually wrapped goods, such as cotton.

bale cargo

(shipping) Bulky cargo shipped in bales, usually of burlap.

ballast

(shipping) Heavy material strategically placed on a ship to improve its trim or stability. In most vessels water is used as ballast.

bandwidth

(computers/Internet) The data transmission capacity of an electric communications channel or connection. The more bandwidth, the more data can be transferred in a given period of time. Bandwidth is measured in bits per second (bps). The technical definition of bandwidth refers to the difference between the highest and lowest frequency that a connection can transmit and is measured in hertz (Hz) or cycles per second. The greater the difference between these two values the more data can be sent in a given period of time. Bandwidth differs greatly depending upon a number of factors. LANs (local area networks) as used in many office environments are much faster than WANs (wide area networks) such as dial-up modems, DSL and T1-3 lines as used in most Internet connections. The following chart gives a sampling of bandwidth for the most common network configurations.

WAN Connections   Bandwidth
Switched Services
Dial-up modems 9.6, 14.4, 28.8, 33.6
    and 56 Kbps
ISDN BRI   64-128 Kbps
        PRI   1.544 Mbps
Unswitched Private Lines
T1 1.5 Mbps
T3 44.7 Mbps
DSL   144 Kbps to 52 Mbps
LAN Connections   Bandwidth
Ethernet (10 BaseT)   10 Mbps
Fast Ethernet (100 BaseT) 100 Mbps
Gigabit Ethernet   1,000 Mbps
Token Ring 4, 16 Mbps
ATM 25, 45, 155, 622,
    and 2,488 Mbps+

bank acceptance

(banking) A bill of exchange drawn on or accepted by a bank to pay specific bills for one of its customers when the bill become due. Depending on the bank's creditworthiness, the acceptance becomes a financial instrument which can be discounted for immediate payment. *See* bill of exchange.

bank affiliate export trading company

(U.S.) An export trading company partially or wholly owned by a banking institution as provided under the U.S. Export Trading Company Act. *See* export trading company; Export Trading Company Act.

bank draft

(banking) A check drawn by one bank against funds deposited to its account in another bank.

bank holiday

(UK) British term for a legal holiday where banks and government offices are closed.

banker's bank

(banking) A bank that is established by mutual consent by independent and unaffiliated banks to provide a clearinghouse for financial transactions.

banker's draft

(banking) A draft payable on demand and drawn by, or on behalf of, a bank upon itself. A banker's draft is considered cash and cannot be returned unpaid.

Bank for International Settlements (BIS)

(banking) Established in 1930, this organization was designed to foster cooperation among world central banks, to seek opportunities for development of financial activity among governments and to serve as an agent involving the transfer of payments. Address: Bank for International Settlements, Central-bahnplatz 2, CH-4002 Basel, Switzerland; Tel: [41] (61) 280-8080; Fax: [41] (61) 280-9100; Web: www.bis.org.

bank guarantee

(banking) Unilateral contract between a bank as guarantor and a beneficiary as warrantee in which the bank commits itself to pay a certain sum if a third party fails to perform or if any other specified event resulting in a default fails to take place. *See* letter of credit.

bank holding company

(banking) Any company which directly or indirectly owns or controls, with power to vote, more than five percent of voting shares of each of one or more other banks.

bank holiday

(banking) A day on which banks are closed.

bank note

(banking) Paper issued by the central bank, redeemable as money and considered to be full legal tender.

bank note rate

(banking/foreign exchange) Exchange rate used in bank note dealing.

bank release

(banking) A document issued by a bank, after it has been paid or given an acceptance, giving authority to a person to take delivery of goods.

bankruptcy

(law) (a) The status of an individual or legal entity who does not have the financial resources needed to pay debts as they come due. (b) The legal proceedings for declaring bankruptcy and discharging or restructuring debts. Laws related to these proceedings vary greatly among different countries. In the United States, bankruptcy proceedings are brought before bankruptcy courts. In some countries, a bankruptcy is dealt with through administrative agencies and a bankrupt person must first attempt to make a composition with creditors. *See* composition with creditors.

Bank Wire Service

(banking) A private wire service linking over 250 banks through the facilities of Western Union. This service serves as a message system for transfer of funds and information for the member banks.

banque d'affaires

(banking) A French bank involved in long-term financing and in the ownership of companies, usually industrial firms. Synonymous with merchant bank.

bar code

(logistics) A series of precisely printed parallel lines and spaces of varying widths used to represent data when "read" by a bar code scanner. Bar codes are used in many applications in industry to identify products, shipping units, assets, locations and services at every stage in the logistics chain. The most commonly seen are the EAN barcodes printed on virtually every commercially distributed product in the world from books to packaged food. If you have a World Trade Press edition of this book (all are published by World Trade Press, but thousands are sold in bulk with custom covers), you will see two bar codes on the lower right corner of the back cover. The one on the left identifies the ISBN (International Standard Book Number) while the one on the right identifies the price. *See* bar code character, bar code scanner, European Article Number Association International (EAN).

bar code character

(logistics) Within a bar code, a series of bars and spaces that identify a specific letter, number or other data. A series of bar code characters makes up the entire bar code. *See* bar code, bar code scanner.

bar code scanner

(logistics) A computer data input device designed to optically "read" the bars and spaces of a printed bar code and send the data to a computing device. Bar code scanners are used extensively in the entire logistics chain and can be stationary (as at most supermarket cash registers), or portable (as used by the major courier services at package pick-up). *See* bar code, bar code character.

bareboat charter
(shipping) A charter of a vessel where the charter party has the right to use his own master and crew on the vessel.

barge
(shipping) A flat bottomed inland cargo vessel with or without propulsion usually used on rivers and canals.

barratry
(shipping) The willful misconduct of ship's master or crew including theft, intentional casting away of vessel, or any breach of trust with dishonest intent.

barter
The direct exchange of goods for other goods without the use of money as a medium of exchange and without the involvement of a third party. *See also* countertrade.

Basel Convention
The Basel Convention restricts trade in hazardous waste, some nonhazardous wastes, solid wastes and incinerator ash. It was adopted in 1989 by a United Nations-sponsored conference of 116 nations in Basel, Switzerland. Twenty nations must ratify the treaty before it goes into effect. Contact at: Secretariat of the Basel Convention (SBC), International Environment House; 11-13 chemin des Anémones, Building D; 1219 Châtelaine; Geneva Switzerland; Tel: [41] (22) 917-8218; Fax: [41] (22) 797-3454; E-mail: sbc@unep.ch; Web: www.basel.int.

basing point
(shipping) A point (location) which is used in constructing through rates between other points.

basing rate
(shipping) A rate used only for the purpose of constructing other rates.

basket of currencies
(banking/foreign exchange) A means of establishing value for a composite unit consisting of the currencies of designated nations. Each currency is represented in proportion to its value in relation to the total. The European Currency Unit (now obsolete due to introduction of the Euro), for example, was a weighted average of the currencies of the European Community member nations, used as a unit of value in transactions among businesses in the member countries. *See* European Currency Unit.

battens
(shipping) The protruding fixtures of the inside walls of a vessel's hold which keep cargo away from the walls of the vessel, or to fasten the cargo to the walls of the vessel.

baud
(Internet) The measurement of the transmission speed of a computer modem expressed in bits per second.

bearer
(general) The person in possession.
(banking/finance/law/shipping) A person who possesses a bearer document and who is entitled to payment of funds or transfer of title to property on presentation of the document to the payee or transferor. A buyer, for example, who presents bearer documents of title (such as a bill of lading) to a shipper that transported the goods is entitled to receive the shipment. A seller who presents to a bank a negotiable instrument, such as a check, that is payable to the bearer is entitled to payment of the funds. *See* bearer document; endorsement.

bearer document
(banking/finance/law/shipping) A negotiable instrument, commercial paper, document of title, or security that is issued payable or transferable on demand to the individual who holds the instrument, or one that is endorsed in blank. A bearer document authorizes the payment of funds or the transfer of property to the bearer when the bearer presents the document to the person, such as a bank or a shipper, that is holding the funds or property. *See* bearer; endorsement.

bearer instrument
See bearer document.

beggar-thy-neighbor policy
(economics) A course of action through which a country tries to reduce unemployment and increase domestic output by raising tariffs and instituting non-tariff barriers that impede imports, or by accomplishing the same objective through competitive devaluation. Countries that pursued such policies in the early 1930s found that other countries retaliated by raising their own barriers against imports, which, by reducing export markets, tended to worsen the economic difficulties that precipitated the initial protectionist action. The Smoot-Hawley Tariff Act of 1930 is often cited as a conspicuous example of this approach.

Belgium, Netherlands, Luxembourg Economic Union (BENELUX)
A cooperative organization formed by Belgium, The Netherlands and Luxembourg to encourage economic activity among the three nations. It has eight committees addressing such areas as economic relations, agriculture, commerce, industry, customs and social affairs. Address: BENELUX, 39 rue de la Régence, 1000 Brussels, Belgium; Tel: [32] (2) 519-38-11; Fax: [32] (2) 513-42-06.

belly pits or holds
(shipping) Compartments located beneath the cabin of an aircraft and used for the carriage of cargo and passenger baggage.

beneficiary
(banking/letter of credit) The individual or company in whose favor a letter of credit is opened.

(insurance) The person or legal entity named to receive the proceeds or benefits of an insurance policy.

BENELUX
See Belgium, Netherlands, Luxembourg Economic Union.

Berne Convention for the Protection of Literary and Artistic Works
Formal name: The International Union for the Protection of Literary and Artistic Works. Also called the Berne Union. A part of the World Intellectual Property Organization. An international agreement that was concluded in Berne, Switzerland, by representatives of participating countries which provides copyright, patent, trademark and other intellectual property protection to countries that are signatories to the convention. *See* World Intellectual Property Organization; copyright; patent; trademark; service mark.

berth
(shipping/logistics) (a) The place where a ship lies secured to a wharf, pier or quay and can be loaded or unloaded of its cargo. (b) The distance or space required to safely maneuver a ship. (c) The place where a truck or motor vehicle is loaded or unloaded.

Besloten Vennootschap met Beperkte Aansprakelijkheid (B.V.B.A.)
(Belgium/Netherlands) Designation for a private limited liability corporation with limited liability to shareholders.

bid bond
Guarantee established in connection with international tenders. Guarantees fulfillment of the offer, i.e. that the contract will be signed if awarded. *See* bond; tender.

bilateral investment treaty (BIT)
(foreign investment) A treaty between two countries with the goals of ensuring investments abroad of national or most favored nation treatment; prohibiting the imposition of performance requirements; and allowing the investor to engage top management in a foreign country without regard to nationality. BITs ensure the right to make investment-related transfers and guarantee that expropriation takes place only in accordance with accepted international law. BITs also guarantee access by an investing party to impartial and binding international arbitration for dispute settlement.

bilateral steel agreements
(trade agreement) Agreements between governments to reduce or eliminate state intervention—that is, domestic subsidies and market barriers, in the production and sale of steel. The U.S. has negotiated ten BSAs with major steel trading partners.

bilateral trade
(economics) The commerce between two countries.

bilateral trade agreement
A formal or informal agreement involving commerce between two countries. Such agreements sometimes list the quantities of specific goods that may be exchanged between participating countries within a given period.

bill
(law) (a) A written statement of contract terms. (b) A listing of items in a transaction or demand. (c) A promissory obligation for the payment of money. (d) An account for goods sold, services, rendered, or work completed.
See bill of . . .; bill of lading.

billed weight
(shipping) The weight shown in a waybill or freight bill.

billing third party
(shipping) The invoicing of transportation charges to other than shipper or consignee.

bill of adventure
(law) A written certificate used if goods are shipped under the name of a merchant, shipmaster, or shipowner. It certifies that the property and risk in the goods belong to a person other than the shipper and that the shipper is accountable to that other person for only the proceeds.

bill of credit
(law) A written statement, commonly used by business travelers, given by one individual or legal entity to another, to authorize the recipient to receive or collect money from a foreign correspondent, such as a bank in the recipient's country. *See also* letter of credit.

bill of exchange
(banking) An unconditional order in writing, signed by a person (drawer) such as a buyer, and addressed to another person (drawee), typically a bank, ordering the drawee to pay a stated sum of money to yet another person (payee), often a seller, on demand or at a fixed or determinable future time.
The most common versions of a bill of exchange are:
(a) A **draft**, wherein the drawer instructs the drawee to pay a certain amount to a named person, usually in payment for the transfer of goods or services. **Sight drafts** are payable when presented. **Time drafts** (also called usance drafts) are payable at a future fixed (specific) date or determinable (30, 60, 90 days etc.) date. Time drafts are used as a financing tool (as with Documents against Acceptance, D/A terms) to give the buyer time to pay for his purchase.
(b) A **promissory note**, wherein the issuer promises to pay a certain amount.

bill of health
(general) A certificate issued by port or customs authorities attesting to the health of the crew and pas-

B

sengers of a vessel or airplane upon arrival or departure from the port.

(a) A **clean bill of health** is issued by authorities when no contagious disease(s) has been found,

(b) A **suspected bill of health** is issued when no contagious disease(s) has been found, but authorities fear that one may develop, and

(c) A **foul bill of health** is issued when a contagious disease has been found.

In the cases of issuance of a suspected bill of health or a foul bill of health, the vessel, airplane, or its passengers must enter a quarantine. *See* quarantine.

bill of lading

(shipping) A document issued by a carrier to a shipper, signed by the captain, agent, or owner of a vessel, furnishing written evidence regarding receipt of the goods (cargo), the conditions on which transportation is made (contract of carriage), and the engagement to deliver goods at the prescribed port of destination to the lawful holder of the bill of lading.

A bill of lading is, therefore, both a receipt for merchandise and a contract to deliver it as freight. There are a number of different types of bills of lading.

(a) A **straight bill of lading** indicates that the shipper will deliver the goods to the consignee. The document itself does not give title to the goods (nonnegotiable). The consignee need only identify himself to claim the goods. A straight bill of lading is often used when payment for the goods has been made in advance.

(b) A **shipper's order bill of lading** is a title document to the goods, issued "to the order of" a party, usually the shipper, whose endorsement is required to effect its negotiation. Because it is negotiable, a shipper's order bill of lading can be bought, sold, or traded while goods are in transit and is commonly used for letter-of-credit transactions. The buyer usually needs the original or a copy as proof of ownership to take possession of the goods.

(c) An **air waybill** is a form of bill of lading used for the air transport of goods and is not negotiable. *See* air waybill for a fuller explanation.

(d) A **clean bill of lading** is a bill of lading where the carrier has noted that the merchandise has been received in apparent good condition (no apparent damage, loss, etc.) and which does not bear such notations as "Shipper's Load and Count," etc.

(e) A **claused bill of lading** is a bill of lading which contains notations which specify deficient condition(s) of the goods and/or packaging.

bill of parcels

(law) A statement that lists the descriptions and prices of goods in a parcel and that is sent to the buyer with the goods. This bill is often referred to as a packing slip.

bill of sale

(law) A written document by which an individual or legal entity assigns or transfers title to goods to another.

bill of sight

(U.S. Customs) A document used by U.S. Customs that permits a consignee of goods to see them before paying duties.

bill-to party

(shipping) Refers to the party designated on a bill of lading as the one responsible for payment of the freight charges; this can be the shipper, freight forwarder, consignee, or another person.

binder

(insurance) A document certifying temporary insurance coverage. A binder is issued by an insurance company or its agent pending the issuance of an insurance policy.

binding decisions

(U.S. Customs) A binding tariff classification ruling (decision), which can be relied upon for placing or accepting orders or for making other business determinations. May be obtained by writing to a local Customs district director; a list of addresses can be found at: Web: www.faa.gov/ats/aat/ifim/ifim0302.htm. The rulings will be binding at all ports of entry unless revoked by the Customs Service's Office of Regulations and Rulings. Note that while the port and district offices of Customs are, for many purposes, your best sources of information, informal information obtained on tariff classification is not binding.

biological agents

A biologically active material. Several classes of biological agents have been identified according to their degree of pathogenic hazard, and are unilaterally controlled by various governments. In the United States applications to export certain biological agents are referred to the Department of State and the intelligence community on a case-by-case basis.

biomedical materials

(shipping) Items that can cause human disease (infectious/etiological agent). (UN CLASS 6) Examples are live virus vaccines and etiologic agents. Hazards/precautions are: may be ignited if carrier is flammable; contact may cause infection/disease; and damage to outer container may not affect inner container.

birr

The currency of Ethiopia. 1Br (or 1E$)=100 cents.

black market

Buying or selling of products and commodities, or engaging in exchange of foreign currencies in violation of government restrictions.

B

blank back

(documentation) A form that does not have the terms and conditions printed on the reverse (back) of the form. For example, a blank back bill of lading, also called a short form bill of lading, does not have the terms and conditions of carriage printed on the reverse. Instead, they are listed in another document. Unless otherwise stipulated in a letter of credit, a blank back bill of lading is acceptable in most transactions. Note that the more common term is short form.

blank endorsement

(law/banking/shipping) The signature or endorsement of a person or firm on any negotiable instrument (such as a check, draft or bill of lading), usually on the reverse of the document, without designating another person to whom the endorsement is made. The document therefore becomes bearer paper. In shipping, for example, the holder of a blank endorsed bill of lading can take possession of the merchandise. *See* endorsement; bearer document.

blanket rate

(shipping) (a) A rate applicable from and/or to a group of points; (b) A special single rate applicable to different articles in a single shipment.

blockade

The act of preventing commercial exchange with a country or port, usually during wartime, by physically preventing carriers from entering a specific port or nation. *See also* embargo.

blocking or bracing

(shipping) Wood or metal supports to keep shipments in place in or on containers.

board foot (fbm, BF, bd ft)

(measurement) A unit of measurement used for lumber. One board foot is 12 inches by 12 inches by 1 inch, or one square foot of lumber one inch thick.

bolivar

The currency of Venezuela. 1B=100 centimos.

boliviano

The currency of Bolivia. 1$b=100 centavos.

bona fide

(law) In or with good faith, honesty and sincerity. A bona fide purchaser, for example, is one who buys goods for value and without knowledge of fraud or unfair dealing in the transaction. Knowledge of fraud or unfair dealing may be implied if the facts are such that the purchaser should have reasonably known that the transaction involved deceit, such as when goods that are susceptible to copyright piracy are provided without product documentation as to their origin.

bond

(general) An interest-bearing certificate of debt, usually issued in series, by which the issuer obligates itself to pay the principal amount at a specified time and to pay interest periodically.

(banking) An instrument used as proof of a debt.

(finance) The obligation to answer for the debt of another person.

(insurance) A contract between a principal and a surety (insurance company or their agent) which is obtained to insure performance of an obligation (often imposed by law or regulation).

(U.S. Customs) A bond required by the federal government in connection with the payment of duties or to produce documentation. U.S. Customs entries must be accompanied by evidence that a surety bond is posted with Customs to cover any potential duties, taxes and penalties which may accrue. Bonds may be secured through a resident U.S. surety company, but may also be posted in the form of United States money or certain United States government obligations. In the event that a customs broker is employed for the purpose of making entry, the broker may permit the use of his or her bond to provide the required coverage. *See* bond system; surety; in bond.

bonded

(U.S. Customs) Goods stored under supervision of customs until the import duties are paid or the goods are exported.

bonded exchange

(foreign exchange) Foreign exchange which cannot be freely converted into other currencies. *See* foreign exchange.

bonded stores

(customs) A place (usually a secured storeroom) on a vessel or airplane where non-customs-entered goods are placed under seal until the vessel leaves the port or country.

bonded terminal

(customs) An airline terminal approved by the U.S. Treasury Department for storage of goods until Customs duties are paid or the goods are otherwise properly released.

bonded warehouse

(U.S. Customs) A warehouse owned by persons approved by the Treasury Department, and under bond or guarantee for the strict observance of the revenue laws of the United States; utilized for storing goods until duties are paid or goods are otherwise properly released. Payment of customs duties is deferred until the goods enter the Customs Territory of the United States. The goods are not subject to duties if reshipped to foreign points. *See* bond; in bond.

bond of indemnity

(shipping) An agreement made with a carrier relieving it from liability for any action on its part for which it would otherwise be liable.

bond system

(U.S. Customs) A part of the U.S. Customs' Automated Commercial System, provides information on

B

bond coverage. A Customs bond is a contract between a principal, usually an importer, and a surety which is obtained to insure performance of an obligation imposed by law or regulation. The bond covers potential loss of duties, taxes, and penalties for specific types of transactions. Customs is the contract beneficiary. *See* Automated Commercial System.

booking
(shipping) The act of recording arrangements for the movement of goods by vessel.

bordereau
(insurance) (a) A method of reporting shipments to an insurance company under an open insurance policy. (b) An insurance form, similar to a declaration, which provides for insurance coverage of multiple shipments within a prescribed reporting period, usually a month.
This form calls for the name of the vessel and sailing date, points of shipment and destination, nature of commodity, the amount of insurance desired, and the number of the open policy under which the shipment is made. The bordereau form is prepared by the assured and is forwarded within a prescribed reporting period, usually monthly. The forms are forwarded to the insurance agent or broker for transmission to the insurance company. The premium is billed monthly in accordance with the schedule of rates provided by the policy.
The bordereau is generally not used in cases where evidence of insurance must be supplied to a customer, to banks or to other third parties in order to permit collection of claims abroad. This calls for a special marine policy, occasionally referred to as a certificate. The bordereau, therefore, is mainly used for import shipments, not export shipments.
See special marine policy. *See also* declaration.

bounties or grants
Payments by governments to producers of goods, often to strengthen their competitive position.

bow
(shipping) The front of a vessel.

box
(shipping) Colloquial term referring to a trailer, semi-trailer or container.

box car
(shipping) A closed freight car.

boycott
A refusal to deal commercially or otherwise with a person, firm or country.

breakage
(a) A monetary allowance or credit that a manufacturer agrees to give a buyer to compensate for damage caused to goods during transit or storage. (b) A fractional amount due as part of a payment to a party, such as pennies that result from a computation of interest on a loan or deposit.

breakbulk
(shipping) To unload and distribute a portion or all of the contents of a consolidated shipment for delivery or reconsignment.

breakbulk cargo
(shipping) Cargo which is shipped as a unit but which is not containerized. Examples are any unitized cargo placed on pallets, or in boxes.

breakbulk vessel
(shipping) A general cargo vessel designed to efficiently handle breakbulk loads. Breakbulk cargo vessels are usually self-sustaining in that they have their own loading and unloading machinery.

break-even point
(banking/foreign exchange) The price of a financial instrument at which the option buyer recovers the premium, meaning that he makes neither a loss nor a gain. In the case of a call option, the break-even point is the exercise price plus the premium, and in the case of a put option, the exercise price minus the premium. *See* option; call option; put option.

Bretton-Woods Agreement of 1944
(banking/foreign exchange) Articles of agreement adopted by the international monetary conference of 44 nations which met at Bretton Woods, New Hampshire in 1944. The International Monetary Fund and the International Bank for Reconstruction and Development were created as a result of this agreement. The Fund's major responsibility was to maintain orderly currency practices in international trade, while the Bank's function was to facilitate extension of long-term investments for productive purposes.
See Bretton-Woods System; International Monetary Fund; International Bank for Reconstruction and Development.

Bretton-Woods System
(banking/foreign exchange) The system of fixed exchange rates with fluctuation grids, in which every member of the International Monetary Fund (IMF) set a specific parity for its currency relative to gold or the dollar, and undertook to keep fluctuations within ±1% of parity by central bank market interventions. This system was in operation from the end of WWII through the early 1970s.
See Bretton-Woods Agreement of 1944; International Monetary Fund; International Bank for Reconstruction and Development.

bribe
A payment resulting in the payer's receiving some right, benefit, or preference to which he has no legal right and which he would not have obtained except with the payment of the money. A bribe is a criminal offense in most countries, but may not be a criminal offense in a home country if committed in a foreign country. *See* Foreign Corrupt Practices Act.

British High Commission (BHC)

(diplomacy) The term British High Commission (BHC, or High Commission, HC, or Her Majesty's High Commission, HMHC) is used in lieu of "embassy" in Commonwealth countries.

broken cross rates; triangular arbitrage

(banking/foreign exchange) A forward foreign exchange arrangement which is not for a standard maturity period. Standard periods are: 1 week; 2 weeks; 1, 2, 3, 6 and 12 months.

(banking/foreign exchange) In foreign exchange, disparity among three or more rates; e.g., if DM 1=30 cents and FF 1.5 while FF 1=22 cents, a deutsch mark will bring 30 cents if converted directly but 33 cents if converted first into francs and then into dollars.

broker

An individual or firm that acts as an intermediary, often between a buyer and seller, usually for a commission. Often an agent.

(a) **Customs broker**—An individual or firm licensed to enter and clear goods through Customs for another individual or firm. *See* customs broker.

(b) **Insurance broker**—An individual or firm which acts as an intermediary between an insurance company and the insured. *See* insurance broker.

brokerage license, domestic

(U.S.) Authority granted by the U.S. Interstate Commerce Commission to persons to engage in the business of arranging for transportation of persons or property in interstate commerce.

browser

(Internet) A computer program used to access and search the Internet (World Wide Web).

Brussels Tariff Nomenclature

(customs) A once widely used international tariff classification system which preceded the Customs Cooperation Council Nomenclature (CCCN) and the Harmonized System Nomenclature (HS). *See* Harmonized Tariff Schedule; Customs Cooperation Council Nomenclature.

buffer stock

(logistics) Raw materials, component parts or finished goods maintained in inventory specifically in anticipation of unforeseen shortages of materials or component parts or unusual demand for finished goods. The volume of buffer stock held in inventory is typically determined by such factors as order fulfillment time from the supplier, delivery time from its point of origin, the potential for problems with supply and the potential for unusual increases in demand for finished products.

building society

(UK) British term for a savings and loan banking institution.

bulk cargo

(shipping) Cargo that consists entirely of one commodity and is usually shipped without packaging. Examples of bulk cargo are grain, ore and oil.

bulk carrier

(shipping) A vessel specifically designed to transport bulk cargo. There are two types of bulk carriers: those designed to transport dry bulk cargo such as grain or ore, and those designed to transport liquid bulk cargo such as oil.

bulk container

(shipping) An ocean or air freight container designed to ship dry bulk cargo such as malt. Bulk fluid cargo such as chemicals and fruit juices are shipped in tank containers. Bulk cargo such as ore, grain, and crude oil are generally shipped in specialized bulk cargo ships rather than in containers.

bulk freight

(shipping) Freight not in packages or containers. For example: grain, ore, timber.

bulkhead

(shipping) (a) A partition separating one part of a ship between decks from another. (b) A structure to resist the pressure of earth or water.

bulk liquids

(shipping) Liquid cargo shipped in intermodal tank containers.

bulk sale or transfer

(law) A transfer of substantially all of the inventory or property of an enterprise to one individual or legal entity in a single transaction not in the ordinary course of the business of the enterprise. In some countries, bulk sales and transfers are regulated by law in an effort to reduce the potential for defrauding creditors through this type of transaction.

bulk solids

(shipping) Dry cargo shipped loose in containers.

Bundesbank

(banking) Established in 1875, the central bank of Germany, located in Frankfurt.

bundling

(commerce/logistics) The combining of two or more usually related products or services for sale at the same time for a single price. For example, the bundling of a computer scanner and image-manipulation software for one price.

bunker

(shipping) A compartment on a ship for storage of fuel.

bunker adjustment factor (BAF)

(shipping) An adjustment in shipping charges to offset price fluctuations in the cost of bunker fuel.

bunker charge

See bunker adjustment factor.

B

bunker fuel
(shipping) The fuel used to power a ship.

Bureau of Alcohol, Tobacco and Firearms (ATF)
(U.S. government) An agency of the U.S. Department of Treasury, the ATF regulates the alcohol, firearms and explosives industry, ensures the collection of federal taxes imposed on alcohol and tobacco, investigates violations of federal firearms, explosives and tobacco laws. Address: Bureau of Alcohol, Tobacco and Firearms, Department of the Treasury, 650 Massachusetts Ave. NW, Washington, DC 20226 USA; Tel: [1] (202) 927-8500; Fax: [1] (202) 927-8868; Web: www.atf.treas.gov.

Bureau of Customs
See United States Customs Service.

Bureau of Export Administration
(U.S. government) As of April 18, 2002 the Bureau of Export Administration is now called the Bureau of Industry and Security. *See* Bureau of Industry and Security.

Bureau of Industry and Security
(U.S. government) Responsible for control of exports for reasons of national security, foreign policy and short supply. Licenses on controlled exports are issued and seminars on U.S. export regulations are held domestically and overseas. The Bureau of Industry and Security provides an Internet-based export license application program free of charge called the Simplified Network Application Process (SNAP) at Web: www.snapbxa.gov. Telephone support for SNAP is also available at [1] (202) 482-4811. Address: Bureau of Industry and Security, Office of Public Affairs, Room 3895, 14th Street and Constitution Avenue NW, Washington, DC 20230 USA; Tel: [1] (202) 482-4811; Fax: [1] (202) 482-3617; Web: www.bxa.doc.gov.

Bureau International des Expositions
(international organization) International Bureau of Expositions. An international organization established by the Paris Convention of 1928 to regulate the conduct and scheduling of international expositions in which foreign nations are officially invited to participate. The BIE divides international expositions into different categories and types and requires each member nation to observe specified minimum time intervals in scheduling each of these categories and types of operations. Under BIE rules, member nations may not ordinarily participate in an international exposition unless the exposition has been approved by the BIE. The U.S. became a member of the BIE in April 1968. Federal participation in a recognized international exposition requires specific authorization by the Congress, based on the president's finding that participation is in the national interest. Contact at Bureau; 56 Avenue Victor Hugo; 75783 Paris Cedex 16; France; Tel: [33] (45) 00 38 63; Fax: [33] (45) 00 96 15; Web: www.bie-paris.org.

Business Executive Enforcement Team
(U.S. government) A channel for private sector U.S. business executives to discuss export control enforcement matters with the Bureau of Export Administration. *See* Bureau of Export Administration. Information at Web: www.bxa.doc.gov/Enforcement/beets.htm.

Buy American acts
U.S. federal and state government statutes that give a preference to U.S. produced goods in government contracts. These statutes are designed to protect domestic industry and labor, but tend to increase the price paid for goods and services government agencies buy. *See also* non-tariff barriers or measures; trade barriers.

buyback
(economics) A form of countertrade that involves the exportation of technological know-how, specialized machinery and the construction of an entire factory in exchange for a set percentage of the factory's production over a five to twenty-five year period. Buyback is also known as compensation trading. *See* countertrade.

buying rate (bid rate)
(banking/foreign exchange) Rate at which a bank is prepared to buy foreign exchange or to accept deposits. The opposite of selling (or asked) rate.

C

cabotage

(shipping) Coast-wide water transportation, navigation or trade between ports of a nation. Many nations, like the U.S., have cabotage laws which require domestic owned vessels to perform domestic interport water transportation service.

CADEX

(Canada) An electronic data interchange (EDI) system offered by the Canada Customs and Revenue Agency (CCRA) allowing importers and brokers to file customs accounting documents (B3) form electronically. Information at Web: www.ccra-adrc.gc.ca.

Cairns Group

An informal association of agricultural exporting countries established in August 1986. Members include Argentina, Australia, Brazil, Canada, Chile, Colombia, Hungary, Indonesia, Malaysia, New Zealand, Philippines, Thailand and Uruguay. Web: www.cairnsgroup.org.

call

(banking) A demand of payment on a loan, often as a result of noncompliance on the part of the borrower to the terms and conditions of the loan.

call in a contract

(law) (a) Demanding payment on a contract. A seller, for example, may be entitled under the contract terms to demand payment at the time the goods are ready to ship. (b) Submitting a formal, usually written, notice to collect payment on a contract. A seller who has not received payment, for example, may send a written letter to the buyer demanding remittance of the funds owed—that is calling in the contract.

call money

(banking/finance/foreign exchange) Currency lent by banks on a very short-term basis, which can be called the same day, at one day's notice or at two days' notice. Called overnight money in Great Britain and Federal funds in the United States.

call option

(banking/finance/foreign exchange) The right (but not the obligation) to buy a fixed amount of a commodity, security or currency from the option writer (option seller) at a predetermined rate and/or exercise price within a specified time limit. *See* option; put option; American Option; European Option.

Calvo Doctrine

(foreign investment) The Calvo Doctrine (or principle) holds that jurisdiction in international investment disputes lies with the country in which the investment is located; thus, the investor has no recourse but to use the local courts. The principle, named after an Argentinian jurist, has been applied throughout Latin America and other areas of the world.

Canadian Commercial Corporation

(Canada) The prime contractor in government-to-government sales transactions, facilitating exports of a wide range of goods and services from Canadian sources. In response to requests from foreign governments and international agencies for individual products or services, CCC identifies Canadian firms capable of meeting the customer's requirements, executes prime as well as back-to-back contracts, and follows through with contract management, inspection, acceptance, and payment. Address: Canadian Commercial Corporation (CCC), 1100-50 O'Connor St., Ottawa, ON K1A 0S6, Canada; Tel: [1] (613) 996-0034; Fax: [1] (613) 995-2121; Web: www.ccc.ca.

cap

(banking/finance/foreign exchange) On borrowed funds with an interest rate which is tied to the market rate, an upside limit or cap can be agreed upon, i.e. against payment of a premium, an upper interest rate limit is agreed upon, which will not be exceeded even if the market rate rises above the stated level.

capacity to contract

(law) Legal competency to make a contract. A party has capacity to contract if he or she has attained the age required by law and has the mental ability to understand the nature of contract obligations.

capital account

(economics) Juxtaposition of the long- and short-term capital imports and exports of a country. *See* balance of payments.

capital flight

(economics) The transfer of money or other financial resources from one country to another as a hedge against inflation or poor economic or political conditions.

capital goods

(economics) Manufactured goods that are for productive industrial use. For example: machine tools. *See also* consumer goods.

capital market

(finance) The market for buying and selling long-term loanable funds, in the form of bonds, mortgages and the like. Unlike the money market, where short-term funds are traded, the capital market tends to center on well-organized institutions such as the stock exchange. However, there is no clear-cut distinction between the two other than that capital market loans are generally used by businesses, financial institutions and governments to buy capital goods whereas money-market loans generally fill a temporary need for working capital.

capital movements
(economics) (a) The international payments of a nation. (b) A nation's short- and long-term claims and liabilities, which are entered into vis-a-vis foreign countries, including repayment of foreign debt, direct investments, portfolio investments and purchase of private real estate.

captain's protest
(shipping) A document prepared by the captain of a vessel on arrival at port, showing unusual conditions encountered during voyage. Generally, a captain's protest is prepared to relieve the ship owner of any liability for any loss to cargo, thus requiring cargo owners to look to insurance companies for reimbursement.

cargo
(shipping) Merchandise hauled by transportation lines.

cargo agent
(shipping) An agent appointed by an airline or shipping line to solicit and process international air and ocean freight for shipments. Cargo agents are paid commissions by the airline or shipping line.

cargo aircraft
See all-cargo aircraft.

cargo manifest
(shipping) A list of a ship's cargo or passengers, but without a listing of charges.

cargo, N.O.S.
(shipping) Articles not otherwise specifically provided for. In determining the freight rate, a general category of articles for shipment.

cargo selectivity system
(U.S. Customs) A part of U.S. Customs' Automated Commercial System, specifies the type of examination (intensive or general) to be conducted for imported merchandise. The type of examination is based on database selectivity criteria such as assessments of risk by filer, consignee, tariff number, country of origin, and manufacturer/shipper. A first time consignee is always selected for an intensive examination. An alert is also generated in cargo selectivity the first time a consignee files an entry in a port with a particular tariff number, country of origin, or manufacturer/shipper. *See* Automated Commercial System.

cargo tonnage
(shipping) The weight of a shipment or of a ship's total cargo expressed in tons.

Caribbean Basin Economic Recovery Act (CBERA)
(U.S.) The CBERA affords nonreciprocal tariff preferences by the United States to developing countries in the Caribbean Basin area to aid their economic development and to diversify and expand their production and exports. The CBERA applies to merchandise entered, or withdrawn from warehouse for consumption, on or after January 1, 1984. This tariff preference program has no expiration date. *See* Caribbean Basin Initiative.

Caribbean Basin Initiative (CBI)
(U.S.) A program providing for the duty-free entry into the United States of merchandise from designated beneficiary countries or territories in the Caribbean Basin.

This program was enacted by the United States as the Caribbean Basin Economic Recovery Act and became effective January 1, 1984.

The purpose of the program is to increase economic aid and trade preferences for twenty-eight states of the Caribbean region. The Caribbean Basin Economic Recovery Act provided for twelve years of duty-free treatment of most goods produced in the Caribbean region. The Initiative was extended permanently (CBI II), by the Customs and Trade Act of August 1990. The 23 countries include Antigua and Barbuda, the Bahamas, Barbados, Belize, the British Virgin Islands, Costa Rica, Dominica, the Dominican Republic, El Salvador, Grenada, Guatemala, Guyana, Honduras, Jamaica, Montserrat, the Netherlands Antilles, Nicaragua, Panama, St. Christopher-Nevis, St. Lucia, St. Vincent and the Grenadines, Trinidad and Tobago. The following countries may be eligible for CBI benefits but have not formally requested designation: Anguilla, Cayman Islands, Suriname, and the Turks and Caicos Islands.

Caribbean Common Market (CARICOM)
A regional trade alliance composed of 13 English speaking Caribbean nations. Its purpose is to further economic development and increase social and cultural cooperation among member nations. Members include Antigua and Barbuda, the Bahamas, Barbados, Belize, Dominica, Grenada, Guyana, Jamaica, Montserrat, St. Kitts-Nevis, St. Lucia, St. Vincent and the Grenadines, and Trinidad and Tobago. Address: Caribbean Common Market, Bank of Guyana Building, PO Box 10827, Georgetown, Guyana; Tel: [592] (2) 26-9281; Fax: [592] (2) 26-7816; Web: www.caricom.org.

carnet
(customs) A customs document permitting the holder to carry or send merchandise temporarily into certain foreign countries (for display, demonstration, or similar purposes) without paying duties or posting bonds. *See* ATA Carnet.

Carriage and Insurance Paid To (...named place of destination) (CIP)
(Incoterms 2000) An international trade term of sale in which, for the quoted price, the seller/exporter clears the goods for export, delivers them to the carrier, and is responsible for paying for carriage and

insurance to the named place of destination. However, once the goods are delivered to the carrier, the buyer is responsible for all additional costs.

In Incoterms 2000 the seller is also responsible for the costs of unloading, customs clearance, duties, and other costs if such costs are included in the cost of carriage such as in small package courier delivery. The seller is responsible for procuring and paying for insurance cover.

The CIP term is valid for any form of transport including multimodal.

The "named place of destination" in CIP and all "C" Incoterms 2000 is domestic to the buyer, but is not necessarily the final delivery point.

The Carriage and Insurance Paid To term is often used in sales where the shipment is by air freight, containerized ocean freight, courier shipments of small parcels, and in "ro-ro" (roll-on, roll-off) shipments of motor vehicles.

A "carrier" can be a shipping line, airline, trucking firm, railway or also an individual or firm who undertakes to procure carriage by any of the above methods of transport including multimodal. Therefore, a person, such as a freight forwarder, can act as a "carrier" under this term.

If subsequent carriers are used for the carriage to the agreed destination, the risk passes when the goods have been delivered to the first carrier.

See Guide to Incoterms 2000 Appendix.

Carriage of Goods by Sea Act of 1936

(U.S. shipping law) A U.S. law which, among other provisions, establishes statutory responsibility for the carrier's liability for certain types of damage. Where the COGSA applies, generally speaking, the vessel or carrier is responsible for damage resulting from negligence in the loading, stowing and discharge of cargo. It is not responsible for damage resulting from errors of navigation or management of the ship, from unseaworthiness of the vessel (unless caused by lack of due diligence to make it seaworthy), or from perils of the sea, fire, and a number of other listed causes. The burden of proof in establishing fault will rest at times upon the shipper and at times upon the carrier.

The degree to which a steamship company can be held responsible for damage sustained by a specific shipment is frequently difficult to determine. COGSA applies to import and export shipments and, by agreement, to much U.S. coast-wise and intercoastal business as well.

Carriage Paid To (...named place of destination) (CPT)

(Incoterms 2000) An international trade term of sale in which, for the quoted price, the seller/exporter/ manufacturer clears the goods for export, delivers them to the carrier, and is responsible for paying for carriage to the named place of destination. However, once the seller delivers the goods to the carrier, the buyer becomes responsible for all additional costs.

In Incoterms 2000 the seller is also responsible for the costs of unloading, customs clearance, duties, and other costs if such costs are included in the cost of carriage such as in small package courier delivery. The seller is not responsible for procuring and paying for insurance cover.

The CPT term is valid for any form of transport including multimodal.

The "named place of destination" in CPT and all "C" Incoterms 2000 is domestic to the buyer, but is not necessarily the final delivery point.

The Carriage Paid To term is often used in sales where the shipment is by air freight, containerized ocean freight, courier shipments of small parcels, and in "ro-ro" (roll-on, roll-off) shipments of motor vehicles.

A "carrier" can be a shipping line, airline, trucking firm, railway or also an individual or firm who undertakes to procure carriage by any of the above methods of transport including multimodal. Therefore, a person, such as a freight forwarder, can act as a "carrier" under this term.

If subsequent carriers are used for the carriage to the agreed destination, the risk passes when the goods have been delivered to the first carrier.

See Guide to Incoterms 2000 Appendix.

carrier

(law/shipping) An individual or legal entity that is in the business of transporting passengers or goods for hire. Shipping lines, airlines, trucking companies, and railroad companies are all carriers.

Note: The worldwide acceptance of Incoterms 1990 (and now Incoterms 2000) has resulted in an expanded definition of "carrier." In the older and more limited definition, only shipping lines, airlines, trucking companies and railroad companies are carriers. However, the significant increase in multimodal transport and integrated logistics has placed freight forwarders into the position of "carrier." In the definition above, a freight forwarder is a "legal entity that is in the business of transporting goods." The ICC (International Chamber of Commerce) has established the following definition:

(ICC definition) "Carrier means any person who, in a contract of carriage, undertakes to perform or to procure the performance of transport by rail, road, air, sea, inland waterway or by combination of such modes." Within the context of this definition, when a buyer nominates a freight forwarder to receive the goods, such as in the FCA (Free Carrier) Incoterm, the seller fulfills his obligation to deliver the goods by delivering to that person.

(a) A **common carrier** is one that by law must convey passengers or goods without refusal, provided the party requesting conveyance has paid the charge for transport.

(b) A **private or contract carrier** is one that transports only those persons or goods that it selects.

(U.S. shipping) By U.S. government regulation a common carrier publishes stated rates for carriage and must accept any passengers or goods for transport so long as space is available and the published rate is paid.

carrier's certificate

(U.S. Customs) A document issued by a shipping company, addressed to a District Director of Customs, which certifies that a named individual is the owner or consignee of the articles listed in the certificate. This document is often the "evidence of right to make entry" required by U.S. Customs for an individual to clear goods through Customs. *See also* evidence of right to make entry.

cartage

(logistics) (a) The movement of goods for short distances, usually by truck. (b) The charge to pick up, move and deliver goods short distances.

cartage agent

(shipping) A ground service operator who provides pickup and delivery of freight in areas not served directly by an air or ocean carrier.

cartage/drayage

(shipping) (a) The local transport of goods. (b) The charge(s) made for hauling freight on carts, drays or trucks.

cartel

An organization of independent producers formed to regulate the production, pricing, or marketing practices of its members in order to limit competition and maximize their market power.

casco

(insurance) Marine insurance coverage on the hull of a ship.

cash against documents (CAD)

(commerce/banking) A method of payment where a seller, or an intermediary for a seller, delivers title documents for a shipment to the purchaser/buyer/consignee only upon payment for the shipment. This payment method holds less risk for the seller as title to the shipment does not pass until payment has been made. This is also called documents against payment. *See* documentary collection.

cash in advance (CIA)

(commerce) A method of payment where the seller requires payment for a shipment from the buyer prior to shipment or delivery. This method is advantageous to the seller, but disadvantageous to the buyer, who is subject to the risk that the seller may not ship or deliver as promised. *See* cash against documents, documentary collection.

cash with order (CWO)

(commerce) A method of payment where the buyer makes payment at the time the order is placed. This payment method is common for small orders (such as ordering a clothing item from a catalog company), where the buyer is unknown to an established seller or where the seller is known to the buyer and needs funds to produce the order. It is the same as the cash in advance payment method. *See* cash in advance.

casus major

(law/shipping) A major casualty that is usually accidental, such as a flood or shipwreck.

catalog & video; catalog exhibitions

(U.S.) A U.S. International Trade Administration program promoting low-cost exhibits of U.S. firms' catalogs and videos, offering small, less-experienced companies an opportunity to test overseas markets for their products without travel. The International Trade Administration promotes exhibitions, provides staff fluent in the local language to answer questions, and forwards all trade leads to participating firms. Contact: Trade Information Center; Tel: [1] (800) USA-TRADE. *See also* International Trade Administration.

category groups

Groupings of controlled products. *See* export control classification number.

cause of action

(law) Facts that give a party a right to seek a judicial remedy against another individual or legal entity.

caveat emptor

(law) Latin for "Let the buyer beware." The purchaser buys at his own risk.

cedi

The currency of Ghana. 1¢=100 pesewas.

cell

(shipping) The on board stowage space for one shipping container on a ship.

cells

(shipping) The modular construction system on board a cellular shipping vessel designed to allow containers to be stowed securely one on top of another with vertical bracing at the four corners.

cellular vessel

(shipping) A special use shipping vessel designed for the efficient stowage of ocean containers one on top of the other with vertical bracing at the four corners.

Census Interface System

(U.S. Customs) A part of U.S. Customs' Automated Commercial System, which includes edits and validations provided by the Bureau of the Census to allow for the accurate and timely collection and submission of entry summary data. Census Interface is accomplished through Automated Broker Interface entry summary transmissions. *See* Automated Commercial System.

Center for Trade and Investment Services

(U.S.) CTIS is the focal point in the Agency for International Development (AID) for the collection and dissemination of information on the agency's programs and activities that support international private enterprise in the developing countries where AID operates. CTIS is a full service, comprehensive "one-stop-shop" for information about AID's trade and investment programs and business opportunities in countries served by AID. The center's objective is to further economic development abroad by facilitating increased business activity between the private sectors of AID-assisted countries and the U.S. Address: Global Technology Network, 1301 Pennsylvania Ave., NW, Suite 925, Washington, DC 20004 USA; Tel: [1] (202) 628-9750; Fax: [1] (202) 628-9740; general AID information: Web: www.info.us-aid.gov; Global Network Technology: Web: www.usgtn.net.

Central American Common Market

A regional trade alliance established in July 1991 comprised of Honduras, Guatemala, El Salvador, Nicaragua and Costa Rica. The common market covers all products traded within the region as of 1992. A second step toward regional integration will be the establishment of a common external tariff. Panama is becoming progressively more involved in the regional integration discussions. Address: Central American Common Market, 4A Avda 10-25, Zona 14, Apdo Postal 1237, 01901, Guatemala City, Guatemala; Tel: [502] (3) 682-151; Telex: 5676; Fax: [502] (3) 681-071.

Central and Eastern Europe Business Information Center (CEEBIC)

(U.S. government) A Department of Commerce facility that was opened in January 1990 to provide information on trade and investment opportunities in Eastern Europe. Address: CEEBIC, 1401 Constitution Avenue, NW, Washington, DC 20230 USA; Tel: [1] (202) 482-2645; Fax: [1] (202) 482-3898; Web: www.mac.doc.gov/ceebic.

central bank

(banking) The only institution which has the right to issue banknotes and which constitutes the monetary and credit policy authority of a currency zone. Apart from this, it supplies the economy with money and credit, regulates domestic and foreign payments transactions and maintains internal and external monetary stability.

certificate of analysis

A document issued by a recognized organization or governmental authority confirming the quality and composition of goods listed in the certificate. Certificates of analysis are often required by authorities in importing countries for animal and plant products for consumption and for pharmaceuticals. *See* certificate of inspection; phytosanitary inspection certificate.

certificate of inspection

A document certifying that merchandise (such as perishable goods) was in good condition at the time of inspection, usually immediately prior to shipment. Pre-shipment inspection is a requirement for importation of goods into many developing countries. Often used interchangeably with certificate of analysis. *See* phytosanitary inspection certificate; certificate of analysis.

certificate of insurance

See insurance certificate.

certificate of manufacture

A document (often notarized) in which a producer of goods certifies that the manufacturing has been completed and the goods are now at the disposal of the buyer.

certificate of origin

(customs) A document attesting to the country of origin of goods. A certificate of origin is often required by the customs authorities of a country as part of the entry process. Such certificates are usually obtained through an official or quasi-official organization in the country of origin such as a consular office or local chamber of commerce. A certificate of origin may be required even though the commercial invoice contains the information.
Certificate of Origin Form A. A document required by customs in the United States and other developed countries to prove eligibility of merchandise under duty-free import programs such as the Generalized System of Preferences and the Caribbean Basin Initiative.

certificate of weight

(shipping) A document stating the weight of a shipment.

certification; legalization

Official certification of the authenticity of signatures or documents in connection with letter of credits, such as certificates of origin, commercial invoices, etc. by chambers of commerce, consulates and similar recognized government authorities.

Certified Trade Fair Program

(trade event) The U.S. Department of Commerce Certified Trade Fair Program is designed to encourage private organizations to recruit new-to-market and new-to-export U.S. firms to exhibit in trade fairs overseas. To receive certification, the organization must demonstrate: (1) the fair is a leading international trade event for an industry and (2) the fair organizer is capable of recruiting U.S. exhibitors and assisting them with freight forwarding, customs clearance, exhibit design and setup, public relations, and overall show promotion. The show organizer must agree to assist new-to-export exhibitors as well as small businesses interested in exporting.
In addition to the services the organizer provides, the Department of Commerce will:

(1) Assign a Washington coordinator.

(2) Operate a business information office, which provides meeting space, translators, hospitality, and assistance from U.S. exhibitors and foreign customers.

(3) Help contact buyers, agents, distributors, and other business leads and provide marketing assistance.

(4) Provide a press release on certification.

Contact the U.S. Department of Commerce, 14th St. at Constitution Ave. NW, Room H2116, Washington, DC 20230 USA; Tel: [1] (202) 482-2525; Web: www.usatrade.gov.

See new-to-market; new-to-export.

Certified Trade Missions Program

(U.S.) Former name: state/industry organized, government approved (S/IOGA). The U.S. Department of Commerce, through its Certified Trade Missions Program, offers guidance and assistance to federal, state and local development agencies, chambers of commerce, industry trade associations, and other export-oriented groups that are interested in becoming more actively involved in export promotion. Certified Trade Missions open doors to government and business leaders in promising export markets around the world.

Once the sponsoring organization has selected the countries to be considered, proposed an itinerary, and outlined its mission goals and objectives, the Department of Commerce coordinates the mission itinerary with its commercial staff at U.S. embassies and consulates overseas. These posts help to arrange the mission's activities to make the most productive use of each member's time at each stop on the itinerary. Some missions also include informational or technical seminars specifically designed to exhibit and promote sales of sophisticated products, technology, or services in targeted markets. Address: Certified Trade Missions, U.S. Department of Commerce, 14th St. and Constitution Ave. NW, Room H2116, Washington, DC 20230 USA; Tel: [1] (202) 482-4663; Web: www.usatrade.gov.

cession of goods

(law) A surrender of goods. A relinquishment of a debtor's property to creditors when the debtor cannot pay his or her debts.

C&F

See Cost and Freight; Incoterms.

chaebol

(Korea) Korean conglomerates which are characterized by strong family control, authoritarian management, and centralized decision making. Chaebol dominate the Korean economy, growing out of the takeover of the Japanese monopoly of the Korean economy following World War II. Korean government tax breaks and financial incentives emphasizing industrial reconstruction and exports provided continuing support to the growth of Chaebols during

the 1970s and 1980s. In 1988, the output of the 30 largest chaebol represented almost 95% of Korea's gross national product.

chandlery

See ship chandlery.

chargeable weight

(shipping) The weight of a shipment used in determining air or ocean freight charges. The chargeable weight may be the dimensional weight or on container shipments the gross weight of the shipment less the tare weight of the container.

chargé d'affaires

(diplomacy) A subordinate diplomat who takes charge in the absence of the ambassador.

charges advanced

See advancement of charges.

charges collect

(shipping) The total transportation charges which may include pickup and/or delivery charges which are entered on the ocean or air waybill to be collected from the consignee. Equivalent terms are "freight collect" or "charges forward."

charter

(law) (a) An instrument issued by a government to the governed people, a specific part of the people, a corporation, a colony, or a dependency confirming or conferring described rights, liberties, or powers. (b) A legislative act that creates a business corporation or that creates and defines a corporate franchise. (shipping) (a) A **charter party** or **charter agreement** is a lease or agreement to hire an airplane, vessel, or other means of conveyance to transport goods on a designated voyage to one or more locations. (b) A **gross charter** is a charter agreement by which the shipowner furnishes personnel and equipment and incurs other expenses, such as port costs. (c) A **bareboat charter** is a charter agreement under which an individual or legal entity charters a vessel without a crew, assumes full possession and control of the vessel, and is generally invested with temporary ownership powers.

chartered bank

(Canada) Financial institution licensed by the Canadian Parliament under the Bank Act to operate as a bank.

chartered ship

(shipping) A ship leased by its owner or agent for a stated time, voyage or voyages.

charter party bill of lading

(shipping) A bill of lading issued by a charter party. Charter party bills of lading are not acceptable by banks under letters of credit unless they are specifically authorized in the credit. *See* bill of lading.

charter party contract

(shipping) Contract according to which the precisely designated freight room of a ship or the whole ship is leased by the owner to a charterer for a specific period, specific voyage or voyages. If a ship is chartered without crew this is a bareboat charter. The freight documents issued by the current charterer or his authorized party are called charter party bills of lading.

charter service
(shipping) The temporary hiring of an aircraft, usually on a trip basis, for the movement of cargo or passengers.

chassis
(shipping) A special trailer or undercarriage on which containers are moved over the road. Chassis comes in skeletal types, parallel frame, perimeter frame and goose neck types, among others.

chattel
(law) An item of personal property.

chattel lien
(law) A lien on chattel in favor of a person who has expended labor, skill, or materials on the chattel or has furnished storage for it at the request of the owner, an agent, or a party who legally possesses it.

chattel paper
(law) A writing or a group of writings that constitute a security interest in, or a lease of, specific goods for a monetary obligation.

check digit number
(shipping) A single digit of an air waybill number used to insure that the air waybill number is correctly entered into a computer system.

chemical/biological weapons
(U.S.) The Department of Commerce maintains foreign policy export controls on certain chemical precursors useful in chemical warfare. Through the Australia Group (AG), the United States cooperates with other nations in controlling chemical weapons proliferation. The AG has developed a Core List of nine chemicals considered essential to the development of chemical weapons. The AG also developed a Warning List which identifies 41 precursors which are useful for chemical weapons development. The AG also provides the forum in which the member countries share information concerning the activities of nonmember countries where the proliferation of these weapons is of concern, including entities that are seeking chemical precursors and related items.

The United States controls all 50 chemical precursors designated by the AG as useful in chemical weapons production. The nine core list chemicals are controlled worldwide, except to the members of the AG and NATO. The remaining 41 chemicals are controlled to selected countries.

The U.S. also maintains unilateral controls on certain biological organisms and requires an individual validated license to all destinations except Canada. U.S. Department of Commerce regulations are designed in the form of a "negative" list. The list iden-

tifies those organisms that have been determined to be of no or minimal level of hazard. Any organism that is not included on the list is controlled. The U.S. Department of Commerce requires individual validated licenses for the export of Class 2, 3, and 4 organisms to all destinations except Canada. (The higher the class, the greater the toxicity.) License applications are referred to the U.S. State Department for review and recommendation. Approval or denial is determined by analysis of the application and intelligence input.
See Australia Group.

chill a sale
(law) Combining or conspiring (of buyers or bidders) to suppress competition at a sale, in order to acquire property at less than fair value.

chose in action
See thing in action.

CIF
See Cost, Insurance, Freight; Incoterms.

CIFCI
See Cost, Insurance, Freight, Commission and Interest; Incoterms.

CIM
(shipping) An internationally standardized freight document issued in rail transport. CIM stands for "Convention Internationale concernant le transport des Marchandises par chemin de fer." The agreement has been in force since January 1, 1965, and constitutes the legal basis for the conclusion of freight contracts in international rail goods transport using one freight document.

CISG
See United Nations Convention on Contracts for the International Sale of Goods.

city bank
(Japan) A major Japanese commercial bank, located in a city, dealing with corporations and major accounts (as compared to a local bank).

city terminal service
(shipping) A service provided by some airlines to accept shipments at the terminals of their cartage agents or other designated in-town terminals or to deliver shipments to these terminals at lower rates than those charged for the door-to-door pickup and delivery service.

Civil Aeronautics Board (CAB)
(U.S.) A U.S. federal agency created by Congress in 1938 to promote the development of the U.S. air transport system, to award air routes, and to regulate passenger fares and cargo rates. Legislation passed by the U.S. Congress in 1978 terminated the CAB, effective January 1, 1985. Many of the CAB functions such as certificates, air carrier fitness, consumer protection, international rates and services were transferred to the U.S. Department of Trans-

portation (DOT). *See* U.S. Department of Transportation.

civil law

(law) A body of law created by statutes and other enactments of legislatures and by rules and regulations adopted to give effect to those statutes and enactments. *See also* common law.

claim

(shipping) A demand made upon a transportation line for payment on account of a loss sustained through its negligence.

(insurance) A demand made upon an insurance company for payment on account of an insured loss.

claim tracer

(shipping) A request for an advice concerning the status of a claim.

classification

(general) The categorization of merchandise.

(shipping) The assignment of a category to a specific cargo for the purpose of applying class rates, together with governing rules and regulations.

(U.S. Customs) The categorization of merchandise according to the Harmonized Tariff Schedule of the United States (HTS or HTSUS). Classification affects the duty status of imported merchandise.

Classification and valuation of imported merchandise must be provided by commercial importers when an entry is filed. In addition, classification under the statistical suffixes of the tariff schedules must also be furnished even though this information is not pertinent to duitable status. Accordingly, classification is initially the responsibility of an importer, customs broker or other person preparing the entry papers. *See* Harmonized Tariff Schedule of the United States. *See also* valuation.

class or kind (of merchandise)

(customs) A term used in defining the scope of an antidumping investigation. Included in the "class or kind" of merchandise is merchandise sold in the home market which is "such or similar" to the petitioned product. "Such or similar" merchandise is that merchandise which is identical to or like the petitioned product in physical characteristics. *See* dumping.

class rates

(shipping) Shipping rates that apply to cargo covered in a single class of goods as defined in a cargo classification table. Cargo classification tables and rates are usually based on criteria such as weight, bulk, value, perishability, hazard/danger and method of packing. *See* class or kind (of merchandise).

claused bill of lading

(shipping) Notations on bills of lading which specify deficient condition(s) of the goods and/or the packaging. *See* bill of lading.

clean bill of exchange

(banking) A bill of exchange having no other documents, such as a bill of lading affixed to it.

clean bill of lading

(shipping) A bill of lading receipted by the carrier for goods received in "apparent good order and condition," without damages or other irregularities, and without the notation "Shippers Load and Count."

clean collection

(banking) A collection in which the demand for payment (such as a draft) is presented without additional documents. *See* bill of exchange.

clean draft

(banking) A sight or time draft which has no other documents attached to it. This is to be distinguished from documentary draft. *See* bill of exchange.

clean letter of credit

(banking) A letter of credit against which the beneficiary of the credit may draw a bill of exchange without presentation of documents. *See* letter of credit.

clean on board bill of lading

(shipping) A document evidencing cargo laden aboard a vessel with no exceptions as to cargo condition or quantity.

clearance

(customs) The completion of customs entry formalities resulting in the release of goods from customs custody to the importer.

close corporation

See closely held corporation.

closed conference

(shipping) A shipping conference that reserves the right to refuse membership to applying carriers. *See* conference. *See also* carrier.

closed-end transaction

(finance) A credit transaction that has a fixed amount and time for repayment.

closely held corporation

(law) A corporation with a small number of shareholders, who usually directly operate the corporation and have limited liability. A maximum number of shareholders is usually fixed by law. The minimum capitalization for a closely held corporation is less than that for a public corporation, and fewer formalities are required for managing it. The requirements for closely held corporations vary among jurisdictions. *See* corporation.

coastal trade

(shipping) Trade between ports of one nation.

Code of Federal Regulations (CFR)

(U.S. law) A compilation of the administrative rules adopted and followed by departments and agencies of the United States federal government. Copies of the CFR are available at major public libraries in the United States and for purchase from the Superintendent of Documents, U.S. Government Printing Office, PO Box 371954, Pittsburgh, PA 15250-7954; Web: www.access.gpo.gov/su_docs; to receive catalog, contact U.S. FAX Watch: [1] (202) 512-1716.

codes of conduct
International instruments that indicate standards of behavior by nation states or multi-national corporations deemed desirable by the international community. Several codes of conduct were negotiated during the Tokyo Round of the General Agreement on Tariffs and Trade (GATT) that liberalized and harmonized domestic measures that might impede trade.
The United Nations has also encouraged the negotiation of several "voluntary" codes of conduct, including one that seeks to specify the rights and obligations of transnational corporations and of governments.

coin silver
Coin or "German" silver is an alloy of silver that is 800/1000 pure. An article of coin or German silver is often marked "800."

collar
(banking) An agreement to put upper and lower (cap and floor) limits on an interest rate which will be adhered to even if the market rate lies outside this range.

collect charges
(shipping) The transportation practice under which the receiver of the goods pays charges.

collecting bank
(banking) The bank that acts as agent for the seller and seller's bank in collecting payment or a time draft from the buyer to be forwarded to the remitting bank (usually the seller's bank).

collection
(general) The presentation for payment of an obligation and the payment thereof.
(banking) The receipt of money for presentation of a draft or check for payment at the bank on which it was drawn, or presentation of any item for deposit at the place at which it is payable.

collection endorsement
See endorsement.

collection papers
(banking) All documents (invoices, bills of lading, etc.) submitted to a buyer for the purpose of receiving payment for a shipment.
See documents against payment; documents against acceptance.

collections system
(U.S. Customs) A part of U.S. Customs' Automated Commercial System, controls and accounts for the billions of dollars in payments collected by Customs each year and the millions in refunds processed each year. Daily statements are prepared for the auto-

mated brokers who select this service. The Collections System permits electronic payments of the related duties and taxes through the Automated Clearinghouse capability. Automated collections also meets the needs of the importing community through acceptance of electronic funds transfers for deferred tax bills and receipt of electronic payments from lockbox operations for Customs bills and fees.
See Automated Commercial System.

collective mark
(law) A trademark or service mark that a cooperative, association, or other collective group uses in commerce. A mark used to indicate membership in a union, association, or other organization.

collect on delivery (COD)
(shipping) A transportation service under which the purchase price of goods is collected by the carrier from the receiver at the time of delivery, and subsequently, payment is transmitted by the carrier to the shipper. Carriers charge a nominal fee for this service. As the term COD implies payment is due upon delivery. There are no credit provisions in COD service. Also called Cash On Delivery.

colón
The currency of:
Costa Rica, 1¢=100 centimos;
El Salvador, 1¢=100 centavos.

colorable imitation
(law) A mark that is so similar to another registered trademark or service mark that it may be considered as calculated to deceive an ordinary person.

colorable transaction
(law) A transaction that in appearance does not correspond to the actual transaction and that is usually intended to conceal or deceive.

column 1 rates
(U.S. Customs) The Harmonized Tariff Schedules of the United States (HTS) is an organized listing of goods and their import duty rates which is used as the basis of classifying products for entry into the United States. Column 1 duty rates in the HTS are low and apply to imports from countries that have achieved Most Favored Nation (MFN) trading status with the United States. *See* Harmonized Tariff Schedule of the United States; column 2 rates.

column 2 rates
(U.S. Customs) The Harmonized Tariff Schedules of the United States (HTS) is an organized listing of goods and their import duty rates which is used as the basis of classifying products for entry into the United States. Column 2 duty rates in the HTS apply to imports from countries that do not have Most Favored Nation (MFN) trading status with the United States. *See* Harmonized Tariff Schedule of the United States; column 1 rates.

combi aircraft
See combination aircraft.

C

combination aircraft

(shipping) An aircraft capable of transporting both passengers and cargo on the same flight. Such a plane will generally carry unitized cargo loads on the upper deck of the aircraft forward of the passenger compartment. Some cargo is carried on virtually all scheduled passenger flights in the belly pits below the passenger cabin.

combination in restraint of trade

(law) An understanding or agreement between two or more individuals or legal entities to do the following: (1) restrict competition; (2) monopolize trade; (3) control production, distribution, and price; and (4) otherwise interfere with freedom of trade.

combined bill of lading

(shipping) A bill of lading covering a shipment of goods by more than one mode of transportation. *See* bill of lading.

combined transport

(shipping) Consignment sent by means of various modes of transport, such as by rail and by ocean.

combined transport bill of lading

(shipping) A bill of lading covering a shipment of goods by more than one mode of transportation. *See* bill of lading.

comity

(law) Courtesy, respect, and goodwill. Government agencies or courts in one jurisdiction, for example, may agree out of comity to give effect to court judgments or arbitration awards of other jurisdictions.

command economy

(economics) An economic system where resources and decisions about production are controlled by a central government authority.

Commanditaire Vennootschap (C.V.)

(Netherlands) Designation for a limited partnership in which at least one of the partners has general personal liability and at least one of the other partners has limited liability.

Commerce Business Daily

(publication) A daily newspaper published by the U.S. Department of Commerce which lists government procurement invitations and contract awards, including foreign business opportunities and foreign government procurements. Available from: U.S. Department of Commerce, 14th St. at Constitution Ave., Washington, DC 20230 USA; Tel: [1] (202) 482-0633; Web: www.doc.gov.

Commerce Control List (CCL)

(U.S.) A list of all items—commodities, software, and technical data—subject to U.S. Bureau of Industry and Security (formerly the Bureau of Export Administration) export controls. Incorporates items controlled for foreign policy and other reasons. The list adopts a totally new method of categorizing commodities and is divided into 10 general catego-ries: (1) materials, (2) materials processing, (3) electronics, (4) computers, (5) telecommunications and cryptography, (6) sensors, (7) avionics and navigation, (8) marine technology, (9) propulsion systems and transportation equipment, and (10) miscellaneous. Replaced the former Commodity Control List as of September 1, 1991. Address: Bureau of Industry and Security, Office of Public Affairs, Room 3895, 14th Street and Constitution Avenue NW, Washington, DC 20230 USA; Tel: [1] (202) 482-4811; Fax: [1] (202) 482-3617; Web: www.bxa.doc.gov; *see also* export control classification number.

commercial bank

(banking) A bank that specializes in accepting demand deposits (deposits that can be withdrawn on demand by the depositor) and granting loans.

commercial bill of exchange

See bill of exchange.

commercial credit

(banking) A letter of credit used to facilitate a sale of goods by insuring that the seller will be paid once the seller has complied with the terms of credit that the buyer obtains. A letter of credit is usually issued by a bank (the issuer) on the request of its client (the buyer) to assure the seller that the buyer will pay for the goods sold. *See* letter of credit.

commercial frustration

(law) A legal theory that implies a condition or term into a contract, if no express provision was made, to excuse the parties when performance becomes impossible because an event occurs that the contracting parties could not have reasonably foreseen or controlled. Commercial frustration may arise, for example, if a seller's shipment is lost in a shipwreck or if a manufacturer cannot obtain raw materials because war has broken out in the country supplying them. *See* force majeure.

commercial impracticability

(law) A legal theory that implies a condition or term into a contract, if no express provision was made, to excuse either party when performance becomes impossible in practice because of the occurrence of a contingency, the nonoccurrence of which was a basic assumption for making the contract. A manufacturer, for example, who contracts to sell goods at a specific price in reliance on a subcontractor's bid to provide certain components at a low price may claim commercial impracticability if the subcontractor defaults and the manufacturer can only procure comparable components at a much higher price.

Commercial Information Management System (CIMS)

(U.S.) CIMS is a trade-related application using National Trade Data Bank CD-ROMs to disseminate market research and international economic data to U.S. & Foreign Commercial Service (US&FCS) domestic offices and overseas posts. The system includes data on U.S. and foreign traders and supports local collection and update of information on business contacts. Not available to the public.

commercial invoice

(general) A document identifying the seller and buyer of goods or services, identifying numbers such as invoice number, date, shipping date, mode of transport, delivery and payment terms, and a complete listing and description of the goods or services being sold including prices, discounts and quantities. (customs) A commercial invoice is often used by governments to determine the true (transaction) value of goods for the assessment of customs duties and also to prepare consular documentation. Governments using the commercial invoice to control imports often specify its form, content, number of copies, language to be used, and other characteristics.

(U.S. Customs) U.S. Customs requires that a commercial invoice provide the following information: (1) The port of entry, (2) If merchandise is sold or agreed to be sold, the time, place and names of buyer and seller; if consigned, the time and origin of shipment, and names of shipper and receiver, (3) Detailed description of the merchandise, including the name by which each item is known, the grade or quality, and the marks, numbers, and symbols under which sold by the seller or manufacturer to the trade in the country of exportation, together with the marks and numbers of the packages in which the merchandise is packed, (4) The quantities in weights and measures, (5) If sold or agreed to be sold, the purchase price of each item in the currency of the sale, (6) If consigned, the value for each item, in the currency in which the transactions are usually made or, in the absence of such value, the price in such currency that the manufacturer, seller, shipper, or owner would have received, or was willing to receive, for such merchandise if sold in the ordinary course of trade and in the usual wholesale quantities in the country of exportation, (7) The kind of currency, (8) All charges upon the merchandise, itemized by name and amount including freight, insurance, commission, cases, containers, coverings, and cost of packing; and, if not included above, all charges, costs, and expenses incurred in bringing the merchandise from alongside the carrier at the first U.S. port of entry. The cost of packing, cases, containers, and inland freight to the port of exportation need not be itemized by amount if included in the invoice price and so identified. Where the required information does not appear on the invoice as originally prepared, it shall be shown on an attachment to the invoice, (9) All rebates, drawbacks, and bounties, separately itemized, allowed upon the exportation of the merchandise, (10) The country of origin, and (11) All goods or services furnished for the production of the merchandise not included in the invoice price. The invoice and all attachments must be in the English language.

commercial letter of credit

(banking) An instrument by which a bank lends its credit to a customer to enable him to finance the purchase of goods. Addressed to the seller, it authorizes him to draw drafts on the bank under the terms stated in the letter. *See* letter of credit.

Commercial News USA (CNUSA)

(publication) A U.S. & Foreign Commercial Service fee-based magazine, published 10 times per year. CNUSA provides exposure for U.S. products and services through an illustrated catalog. The catalog is distributed through U.S. embassies and consulates to business readers in 140 countries. Copies are provided to international visitors at trade events around the world.

The CNUSA program covers about 30 industry categories and focuses on products that have been on the U.S. market for no longer than three years. To be eligible, products must be at least 51 percent U.S. parts and 51 percent U.S. labor. The service helps U.S. firms identify potential export markets and make contacts leading to representation, distributorships, joint venture or licensing agreements, or direct sales.

To order Commercial News USA, contact: Associated Business Publishers International, 317 Madison Avenue, Suite 1900, New York, NY 10017-5391 USA; Tel: [1] (212) 490-3999; Fax: [1] (212) 986-7864; Web: www.cnewsusa.com.

commercial officers

(diplomacy) Embassy officials who assist businesses through arranging appointments with local business and government officials, providing counsel on local trade regulations, laws, and customs; identifying importers, buyers, agents, distributors, and joint venture partners; and other business assistance. *See* economic officers.

commercial paper

(banking/law) Negotiable instruments used in commerce. Examples of commercial paper are bills of exchange, promissory notes, and bank checks. *See* negotiable instrument; bill of exchange.

commercial risk

(economics) Economic risk resulting from the normal course of operating a business. Commercial risk includes financial risk, legal risk, production risk, market risk and even the risk of failure to adapt to changing markets and technology. *See* political risk.

commercial set

(law) The primary documents for a shipment of goods. A commercial set usually includes, for example, an invoice, bill of lading, bill of exchange, and certificate of insurance.

commercial treaty

An agreement between two or more countries setting forth the conditions under which business between the countries may be transacted. May outline tariff privileges, terms on which property may be owned, the manner in which claims may be settled, etc.

commercial zone
(shipping/logistics) The area immediately surrounding a town or city that is subject to the same shipping rates as the city itself. *See* rate basis point.

commingling
The packing or mingling of various articles subject to different rates of duty in such a way that the quantity or value of each class of articles cannot readily be ascertained by Customs without the physical segregation of the shipment or the contents of any package thereof. Commingled articles are subject to the highest rate of duty applicable to any part of the commingled lot, unless the consignee or his agent segregates the articles under Customs supervision.

commission
(general) The amount paid to an agent, which may be an individual, a broker, or a financial institution, for consummating a transaction involving sale or purchase of assets or services.
(banking) Agents and brokers are usually compensated by being allowed to retain a certain percentage of the premiums they produce, known as a commission.

Commission on Security and Cooperation in Europe
An economic and defense alliance whose members include all recognized countries of Europe, Canada, the USA, and the former republics of the USSR. Included are: Albania, Armenia, Austria, Azerbaijan, Belgium, Bulgaria, Belarus, Canada, Cyprus, Czech Republic, Denmark, Estonia, Finland, France, Germany, Greece, the Holy See, Hungary, Iceland, Ireland, Italy, Kazakhstan, Kyrgyzstan, Latvia, Liechtenstein, Lithuania, Luxembourg, Malta, Moldova, Monaco, Netherlands, Norway, Poland, Portugal, Romania, Russia, San Marino, Slovakia, Spain, Sweden, Switzerland, Tajikistan, Turkey, Turkmenistan, Ukraine, the United Kingdom, the United States, Uzbekistan and Yugoslavia. Note: The Federal Republic of Yugoslavia (Serbia & Montenegro) was suspended in July 1992. Address: Commission on Security and Cooperation in Europe, 234 Ford House Office Building, 3rd and D Streets, SW, Washington, DC 20515 USA; Tel: [1] (202) 225-1901; Fax: [1] (202) 226-4199; Web: www.csce.gov.

Committee on Foreign Investment in the United States (CFIUS)
(U.S.) Created in 1975 to provide guidance on arrangements with foreign governments for advance consultations on prospective major foreign governmental investments in the United States, and to consider proposals for new legislation or regulation relating to foreign investment.

The authority of the Committee was amended by Section 5021 (the Exon-Florio provision) of the Omnibus Trade and Competitiveness Act of 1988 (Section 721 of the Defense Production Act), which gives the president authority to review mergers, acquisitions, and takeovers of U.S. companies by foreign interests and to prohibit, suspend, or seek divestiture in the courts of investments that may lead to actions that threaten to impair the national security.

By Executive Order in December 1988, the U.S. Treasury has authority to implement the Exon-Florio provision. CFIUS has eight members: Treasury (the chair), State, Defense, Commerce, the Council of Economic Advisors, the U.S. Trade Representative, the Attorney General, and the Office of Management and Budget.

The Office of Strategic Industries and Economic Security serves as Commerce's representative to CFIUS. Address: Committee on Foreign Investment in the United States, Room 3876, BXA, 14th and Constitution Avenues, NW, Washington, DC 20230 USA; Tel: [1] (202) 482-4811; Web: www.bxa.doc.gov.

commodity
Broadly defined, any article exchanged in trade, but most commonly used to refer to raw materials, including such minerals as tin, copper and manganese, and bulk-produced agricultural products such as coffee, tea and rubber.

commodity code
(shipping) A system for identifying a given commodity by a number in order to establish its commodity rate in freight transport. *See* Harmonized System.

commodity control list
See Commerce Control List.

Commodity Credit Corporation
(U.S.) A U.S. government corporation controlled by the Department of Agriculture that provides financing and stability to the marketing and exporting of agricultural commodities. Address: Commodity Credit Corporation, USDA, 1400 Independence Avenue, SW, Stop 0581, Washington, DC 20250-0581 USA; Tel: [1] (703) 305-1386; Web: www.fsa.usda.gov/dam/fmd/ccc.

commodity rate
(shipping) The rate (charges) applicable to shipping a specific commodity between certain specified points.

common agricultural policy (CAP)
(European Union) A set of regulations by which member states of the European Union (EU) seek to merge their individual agricultural programs into a unified effort to promote regional agricultural development, raise standards of living for the farm population, stabilize agricultural markets, increase

agricultural productivity, and establish methods of dealing with food supply security. Two of the principal elements of the CAP are the variable levy (an import duty amounting to the difference between EU target farm prices and the lowest available market prices of imported agricultural commodities) and export restitutions, or subsidies, to promote exports of farm goods that cannot be sold within the EU at the target prices.

common carrier
See carrier.

common external tariff (CXT)
(customs) A uniform tariff rate adopted by a customs union or common market such as the European Community, to imports from countries outside the union. For example, the European Common Market is based on the principle of a free internal trade area with a common external tariff (sometimes referred to in French as the Tarif Exterieur Commun—TEC) applied to products imported from nonmember countries. "Free trade areas" do not necessarily have common external tariffs.

common law
(law) The body of law derived from usages, customs, and judicial decisions, as distinguished from statutes. *See* civil law; stare decisis.

common market
(economics) A common market (as opposed to a free trade area) has a common external tariff and may allow for labor mobility and common economic policies among the participating nations. The European Community is the most notable example of a common market.

Common Monetary Agreement
A regional economic alliance of South Africa, Lesotho, and Swaziland under which member states apply uniform exchange control regulations to ensure monetary order in the region. Funds are freely transferable among the three countries, and Lesotho and Swaziland have free access to South African capital markets. Lesotho also uses the South African currency, the rand. The CMA was formed in 1986 as a result of the renegotiation of the Rand Monetary Agreement (RMA), which was originally formed in 1974 by the same member countries.

common point
(shipping) A point (location) serviced by two or more transportation lines.

common tariff
(shipping) A tariff published by or for the account of two or more transportation lines as issuing carriers. *See* tariff.

commonwealth
A free association of sovereign independent states that has no charter, treaty, or constitution. The association promotes cooperation, consultation, and mutual assistance among members. The British Commonwealth, the most notable example, included 54 states at the beginning of 2002.

Commonwealth of Independent States (CIS)
An association of 11 republics of the former Soviet Union established in December 1991. The members include: Russia, Ukraine, Belarus (formerly Byelorussia), Moldova (formerly Moldavia), Armenia, Azerbaijan, Uzbekistan, Turkmenistan, Tajikistan, Kazakhstan, and Kyrgystan (formerly Kirghiziya). Georgia is presently an "observer"; the Baltic states did not join.

Communications Satellite Corporation
(U.S.) COMSAT was established in 1963 under provision of the Communications Satellite Act of 1962. The legislation directed that COMSAT establish the world's first commercial international satellite communications system. The Act also stipulated that the company operate as a shareholder-owned "for-profit" corporation. COMSAT represents the U.S. in the International Telecommunications Satellite Organization. Contact through Lockheed Martin's Web site at: Web: www.lmgt.com.

commuter airline
(shipping/logistics) An air carrier with a prescribed time schedule for a specific route. A commuter airline generally operates over short distances and serves remote locations and small airports.

Compagnie (Cie.)
(France, Luxembourg) General designation for a business organization.

Company (Co.)
(South Africa, United States) General designation for a business organization.

comparative advantage
(economics) A central concept in international trade theory which holds that a country or a region should specialize in the production and export of those goods and services that it can produce relatively more efficiently than other goods and services, and import those goods and services in which it has a comparative disadvantage. This theory was first propounded by David Ricardo in 1817 as a basis for increasing the economic welfare of a population through international trade. The comparative advantage theory normally favors specialized production in a country based on intensive utilization of those factors of production in which the country is relatively well endowed (such as raw materials, fertile land or skilled labor); and perhaps also the accumulation of physical capital and the pace of research.

compensatory trade
(economics) A form of countertrade where any combination of goods and services are bartered. *See* countertrade.

C

competitive rate

(shipping) Rate established by a transportation line to meet competition of another transportation line.

complementary imports

(economics) Imports of raw materials or products which a country itself does not possess or produce.

compliance

Conformity in satisfying official requirements. *See* informed compliance.

composition with creditors

(law) An agreement between an insolvent debtor and one or more creditors under which the creditors consent to accept less than the total amount of their claims in order to secure immediate payment. Creditors will usually prefer a composition if a debtor threatens to declare bankruptcy, because otherwise the creditors are likely to incur costs in making a legal claim against the debtor in a bankruptcy proceeding, payment of debts will be delayed during the proceeding, and the amount paid to each creditor will depend on the judicial decision in that proceeding.

compound rate of duty

(customs) A combination of both a specific rate of duty and an ad valorem rate of duty. For example: 0.7 cents per pound plus 10 per cent ad valorem. *See also* duty; ad valorem; specific rate of duty.

compradore

An intermediary, agent or advisor in a foreign country employed by a domestic individual or company to facilitate transactions with local individuals or businesses in the foreign country.

compressed gases

(shipping) Items requiring storage and handling under pressure in compressed gas cylinders. (UN CLASS 2.) Examples are acetylene and chlorine. Hazards/precautions are container may explode in heat or fire; contact with liquid may cause frostbite; may be flammable, poisonous, explosive, irritating, corrosive or suffocating; may be EXTREMELY HAZARDOUS.

COMPRO

(information system) An on-line trade data retrieval system maintained by the International Trade Administration within the U.S. Department of Commerce. The system is exclusively for use within the federal government trade community (ITA, USTR, ITC, and other executive branch agencies). COMPRO includes:
(1) U.S. foreign trade data (detailed U.S. merchandise trade statistics compiled by Census);
(2) UN trade data (trade statistics of 170 countries;
(3) International Monetary Fund and World Bank databases (international finance, direction of trade, and developing country debt). COMPRO also maintains gateways to LABSTAT, a product of the Bureau of Labor Statistics.

computed value

(U.S. Customs) Generally, the Customs value of all merchandise exported to the United States is the transaction value for the goods. If the transaction value cannot be used, then certain secondary bases are considered. The secondary bases of value, listed in order of precedence for use, are:

(1) Transaction value of identical merchandise, (2) Transaction value of similar merchandise, (3) Deductive value, and (4) Computed value. The order of precedence of the last two values can be reversed if the importer so requests.

Computed value consists of the sum of the following items:

(1) Materials, fabrication, and other processing used in producing the imported merchandise, (2) Profit and general expenses, (3) Any assist, if not included in items 1 and 2, (4) Packaging costs.

See valuation; transaction value; identical merchandise; similar merchandise; assist; deductive value.

concealed damage

(shipping) Damage to the contents of a package which is in good order externally. *See also* inherent vice.

concealed loss

(shipping) Loss from a package bearing concealed damage. *See also* inherent vice.

concord

(law) An agreement between two parties that states the terms of a settlement of a right of action for a breach or wrongdoing that one of the parties has against the other. A buyer who has paid for goods but has not received them, for example, may agree to forgo the right to sue the seller for breach if the seller agrees to return the money paid. *See* accord and satisfaction.

conditional endorsement

See endorsement.

conditions of carriage

See contract of carriage.

conference

(shipping) A group of ocean freight carriers banding together, voluntarily, for the purpose of limiting and regulating competition among themselves. It may establish uniform tariff freight charges and terms and conditions of service. Conference establishment in the United States requires Federal Maritime Commission approval. Conferences in the United States are exempt from antitrust regulation. *See* open conference; closed conference.

conference carrier

(shipping) A member of an association of ocean cargo carriers that has agreed to standardize services, practices, rates and tariffs. *See* carrier, conference.

conference line

(shipping) Ocean shipping companies whose ships travel according to firmly established schedules along fixed routes. Uniform transport rates are established between the shipping lines. Such agreements are usually called conferences. The conference lines are therefore the shipping routes agreed by the conferences. *See* conference; open conference; closed conference.

conference rate

(shipping) Rates arrived at by conference of carriers applicable to transportation—generally water transportation. *See* conference.

confirmation

(law) A contract or written memorandum that ratifies, renders valid, and makes binding an agreement that was difficult to prove, invalid, or otherwise unenforceable. Parties who orally agree to a sale of goods, for example, may formalize that agreement by signing a written confirmation that contains all of the oral terms. *See* contract.

confirmed letter of credit

(banking) A letter of credit which contains a guarantee on the part of both the issuing and advising banks of payment to the seller so long as the seller's documentation is in order and the terms of the letter of credit are met.

Confirmation is only added to irrevocable letters of credit, usually available with the advising bank. If confirmation of the letter of credit is desired, the applicant must state this expressly in his/her letter of credit application. The confirming bank assumes the credit risk of the issuing bank as well as the political and transfer risks of the purchaser's country.

If a letter of credit does not contain a confirmation request by the issuing bank, in certain circumstances the possibility exists of confirming the letter of credit "by silent confirmation," i.e. without the issuing bank's knowledge. Without confirmation of the letter of credit, the advising bank will forward the letter of credit to the beneficiary without taking on its own commitment. *See* letter of credit.

confirming

A financial service in which an independent company confirms an export order in the seller's country and makes payment for the goods in the currency of that country. Among the items eligible for confirmation are the goods; inland, air, and ocean transportation costs; forwarding fees; custom brokerage fees; and duties. Confirming permits the entire export transaction from plant to end user to be fully coordinated and paid for.

confirming bank

(banking) In letter of credit transactions, the bank that assumes responsibility to the seller (usually exporter) for payment from the issuing bank (buyer's bank) so long as the terms and conditions of the letter of credit have been met by the seller/exporter. *See* letter of credit.

conflict of laws

(law) Differences between the laws of different countries or other jurisdictions that become significant in determining which law will apply when individuals or legal entities have acquired rights, incurred obligations, suffered injuries or damages, or made contracts in two or more jurisdictions. The rules that courts apply to resolve conflicts of laws vary among countries. In addition, different rules apply depending on the subject matter of a controversy—that is, whether a controversy involves property or personal rights. *See* governing law clause; lex loci actus; lex loci solutionis.

connecting carrier

(shipping) A carrier which has a direct physical connection with another carrier or forms a connecting link between two or more carriers.

consideration

(law) The price or other motivation that induces a party to make a contract. A buyer may agree, for example, to pay a sum of money or to furnish certain products as consideration for receiving the seller's goods. A contracting party may also promise to forgo a legal right, such as a right to sue for breach of contract, as consideration for the other party's promise to pay damages that resulted from the breach.

consignee

(shipping) The person or firm named in a freight contract to whom goods have been shipped or turned over for care. *See also* consignor.

consignee marks

(shipping) A symbol placed on packages for export, generally consisting of a square, triangle, diamond, circle, cross, etc., with designed letters and/or numbers for the purpose of identification.

consignment

(shipping) Shipment of one or more pieces of property, accepted by a carrier for one shipper at one time, receipted for in one lot, and moving on one bill of lading.

(commerce) Delivery of merchandise from an exporter (the consignor) to an agent (the consignee) under agreement that the agent sell the merchandise for the account of the exporter. The consignor retains title to the goods until sold. The consignee sells the goods for commission and remits the net proceeds to the consignor.

consignment contract

(law) An agreement by a seller (consignor) to deliver goods to an individual or legal entity (consignee) who will pay the seller for any goods sold, less a commission, and will return goods not sold. *See* consignment.

consignor

(shipping) The individual, company or entity that ships goods, or gives goods to another for care. The consignor is usually the exporter or his agent. *See also* consignee; consignment.

consolidated container

(shipping) A shipping container containing cargo from a number of shippers for delivery to a number of different consignees.

consolidation

(shipping) The combining of less than truckload (LTL) shipments of cargo from a number of shippers at a centrally located point of origin by a freight consolidator, and transporting them as a single shipment to a destination point. Consolidation of cargo often results in reduced shipping rates.

consolidator

(shipping) A company that provides consolidation services. Freight forwarders perform the functions of a consolidator. *See* consolidation.

consolidator's bill of lading

(shipping) A bill of lading issued by a consolidating freight forwarder to a shipper. *See also* bill of lading; house air waybill.

constructed value

(U.S. Customs) In customs valuation, a means of determining fair or foreign market value when sales of such or similar merchandise do not exist or, for various reasons, cannot be used for comparison purposes. The "constructed value" consists of the cost of materials and fabrication or other processing employed in producing the merchandise, general expenses of not less than 10 percent of material and fabrication costs, and profit of not less than 8 percent of the sum of the production costs and general expenses. To this amount is added the cost of packing for exportation. *See* valuation; transaction value.

constructive total loss

(insurance) An insurance loss where the expense of recovering or repairing the insured goods would exceed their value after this expenditure had been incurred.

In the adjustment of constructive total losses, the value of any remaining salvage abandoned to underwriters may, by agreement, be taken into consideration, with payment to the assured upon a net basis. Otherwise, underwriters pay full insured value and may then dispose of the salvage for their own account, provided they have elected to accept abandonment.

If the loss was due to sea peril, a "master's protest" (also called "captain's protest") will usually be required. This certifies the fact that unusually heavy weather or other exceptional circumstance was encountered during the voyage and is extended to confirm the loss of the shipment in question. In claims for total loss, it is especially necessary that a full set

of insurance certificates and bills of lading be submitted to the insurance company representative. *See* abandonment; captain's protest.

consular declaration

A formal statement, made in a country of export by the consul of an importing country, describing goods to be shipped to the importing country. *See* consular invoice.

consular invoice

(customs) An invoice covering a shipment of goods certified (usually in triplicate) by the consul of the country for which the merchandise is destined. This invoice is used by customs officials of the country of entry to verify the value, quantity, and nature of the merchandise imported. *See also* commercial invoice.

consular officers

(diplomacy) Embassy officials who extend the protection of their home government to their country's citizens and property abroad. They maintain lists of local attorneys, act as liaison with police and other officials and have the authority to notarize documents.

consular visa

(travel/customs) Any one of several official endorsements by a consul of a country. A consular visa can be issued for travel, consular invoices, certificates of origin, shipping documents and other legal documents.

consulate

(diplomacy) The offices representing the commercial interests of the citizens of one country in another country.

consumer goods

(economics) Any goods produced to satisfy the needs of individuals rather than those produced for the manufacturing or production of other goods. Examples of consumer goods are food, clothing and entertainment products. *See also* capital goods.

consumption entry

(general) (a) A customs entry where the importer pays applicable duty and merchandise is released from customs custody at a port, foreign trade zone or from a customs bonded warehouse. (b) The formal process for entering commercial shipments of goods into the customs territory of a country. A "formal entry."

(U.S. Customs) (a) A U.S. Customs entry where the importer pays applicable duty and merchandise is released from customs custody at a U.S. port, foreign trade zone or from a customs bonded warehouse. (b) The formal U.S. Customs process for entering commercial shipments of goods into the Customs territory of the United States. A "formal entry."

The entry of goods is a two-part process consisting of (1) filing the documents necessary to determine whether merchandise may be released from Customs custody, and (2) filing the documents which contain information for duty assessment and statistical purposes. In certain instances, such as the entry of merchandise subject to quotas, all documents must be filed and accepted by Customs prior to the release of goods. *See* entry.

container
(shipping/logistics) A single rigid, sealed, reusable metal box in which merchandise is shipped by vessel, truck or rail.

All containers have construction fittings, or fastenings able to withstand, without permanent distortion, all stresses that may be applied in normal service use of continuous transportation.

Ocean shipping containers are generally 10, 20, 30 or 40 feet (3.029, 6.058, 9.087 or 12.192m) long and 8 or 8.5 feet (2.423 or 2.575m) tall, and conform to International Standards Organization (ISO) standards. (40-foot containers are generally able to hold about 40,000 pounds or 18,000 kilos.) Ocean freight container types include: standard, high cube, hardtop, open top, flat, platform, ventilated, insulated, refrigerated and bulk (dry or wet).

Air freight containers (ULDs or unit load devices) come in a multitude of sizes and shapes to fit the unique requirements of airplane holds and conform to standards established by the International Airline Transport Association (IATA).

See International Standards Organization; International Air Transport Association; unit load device (ULD); and appendices for Ocean Freight Containers and Air Freight Containers.

container freight charge
(shipping) Charge made for the packing or unpacking of cargo into or from ocean freight containers.

container freight station
(shipping) A facility used by ocean carriers to load/unload cargo to and from containers. Most less-than-container-load lots of cargo are either packed into or devanned at a container freight station.

containerization
(shipping) The practice or technique of using a box-like device (container) in which a number of packages are stored, protected, and handled as a single unit in transit. Advantages of containerization include: less handling of cargo, more protection against pilferage, less exposure to the elements, and reduced cost of shipping.

(air freight) Container descriptions have been broadened to include a unitized load on a carrier-owned pallet, loaded by shippers, and unloaded by receivers at places other than on airline premises, and restrained and contoured so as to permit proper positioning and tiedown aboard the aircraft.

container load
(shipping) A shipment of cargo that fills a given container either by bulk or maximum weight.

container number
(shipping) An up to seven-digit number (six plus a check digit) used to identify the size and type of container; usually preceded by a four-letter alpha (letter) code prefix designating container ownership.

container on flatcar
(shipping) A container without wheels put on railcars for transport.

container part load
(shipping) A shipment of cargo that in either volume or weight is not sufficient to fill any one of many standard containers.

container terminal
(shipping/logistics) An area at the end of a rail, ship, air or truck line which serves as a loading, unloading and transfer point for cargo and containers. Container terminals often include loading equipment, storage facilities, repair facilities and management offices.

container vessel
(shipping) An oceangoing vessel designed specifically to easily handle the loading, stowage and off-loading of ocean freight containers. Containers may be stowed either below deck or on deck.

container yard
(shipping) The area adjacent to the vessel berth where containers are delivered to and received from the vessel, and delivered to and received from inland carriers.

contango
(banking/finance/foreign exchange) The amount (generally a percentage) a buyer pays a seller to delay transfer of a stock, security or foreign exchange to the next or any future day. The opposite of backwardation.

contingency insurance
(insurance) Also called difference in conditions insurance. Insurance which protects the interests of the insured in the event another party's insurance fails or falls short. Commonly used in both import and export situations:

Example 1: Exporting
There are several countries whose laws require that marine insurance on shipments to those countries be placed with local insurance companies. This has the effect of requiring the importer to furnish the insurance. The quality and extent of coverage of this insurance, however, may be in question. If the exporter feels that he has insurable interest he can still protect himself by the purchase of contingency or difference in conditions insurance which protects his own interests in the event the importer's insurance fails or falls short. While the cost of this is naturally less than the cost of primary insurance, it must be borne by the exporter.

Example 2: Importing
A domestic buyer on CIF (Cost, Insurance, Freight) terms must rely upon foreign underwriters, since the

C

insurance will have been placed by the seller in the country of origin. Once again, the quality and extent of coverage of this insurance may be in question. If the importer feels that he has insurable interest he can still protect himself by the purchase of "contingency" or "difference in conditions" insurance which protects his own interests in the event the exporter's insurance fails or falls short. Note: By purchasing on FOB, C & F or similar terms, the domestic importer can control his own insurance. He will then be able to deal with his own underwriters in case of loss or in case of demand for general average security. *See* insurable interest.

continuous replenishment planning (CRP)

(logistics) A supply management system of regular or automatic shipments of raw materials, component parts or finished goods based upon a user's determined or projected needs over specific units of time. For example, a hospital might have an automated inventory system that feeds into a vendor's order system on a real-time basis via a computer link. If the current inventory of an item falls below a specified minimum based upon mutually defined stock level indicators, the vendor may either automatically send a set volume of the required item or automatically send a request for a purchase order to the hospital for the required item. Such systems are based upon formal supply contracts and enable purchasers to both negotiate a lower price as well as maintain smaller average inventories at their place of business.

contra; contra account

(banking) An account with an offsetting credit or debit entry. In accounting, a contra account is generally the right-hand or credit side of a balance sheet in which the liabilities appear.

contraband

(customs) Any product which a nation has deemed to be unsuitable to produce, possess or transport. Any product that a country has deemed to be unsuitable for entry into that country. Contraband is subject to interdiction, possible forfeiture and possible destruction by customs authorities. Examples of contraband are narcotic drugs (most countries), alcohol (certain Islamic countries), seditious literature (many countries), sexually oriented goods and literature (many countries).

contract

(law) An agreement made between two or more parties who promise to perform or not to perform specified acts, which agreement creates for each party a legal duty and the right to seek a remedy for breach of that duty.
(a) A **constructive or implied contract** is an agreement that is implied by law from the circumstances of a business dealing and in accordance with the common understanding between reasonable persons in order to carry out the intent of the parties and do justice between them. (b) An **express contract** is an

oral or written agreement the terms of which are explicitly declared when the contract is made. (c) An **executory contract** is one that has not been performed.

contract carrier

(shipping) Any person not a common carrier who under special and individual contracts or agreements, transports passengers or property for compensation. *See also* carrier.

contracting parties

(law) Two or more individuals, companies or groups who are signatories to an agreement or contract.

contract manufacturing

(a) An agreement whereby a company agrees to manufacture a product to the specifications of another company or individual. This can be on an exclusive or nonexclusive sales basis. (b) An agreement by two companies to manufacture separate components of a product and jointly manufacture and sell the finished product in their respective markets.

contract of carriage

(shipping) The contract between the shipper (consignor) and carrier (shipping firm) for the transport of freight, including the terms and conditions of carriage and costs to the shipper. These conditions are printed on the bill of lading or air waybill and include such items as limits of liability, claims limitations, indemnity and dimensional weight rules. *See* bill of lading.

conventional arms transfer

The transfer of nonnuclear weapons, aircraft, equipment, and military services from supplier states to recipient states.

(U.S.) U.S. arms are transferred by grants as in the U.S. Military Assistance Program (MAP); by private commercial sales; and by government-to-government sales under Foreign Military Sales (FMS). MAP provides defense articles and defense services to eligible foreign governments on a grant basis.

FMS provides credits and loan repayment guarantees to enable eligible foreign governments to purchase defense articles and defense services.

Convention on Contracts for the International Sale of Goods

(law) A United Nations convention which establishes uniform legal rules governing formation of international sales contracts and the rights and obligations of the buyer and seller. The CISG applies automatically to all contracts for the sale of goods between traders from two different countries that have both ratified the CISG, unless the parties to the contract expressly exclude all or part of the CISG or expressly stipulate a law other than the CISG. The CISG became the law of the United States in January 1988.

Convention on International Trade in Endangered Species of Wild Fauna and Flora (CITES)

An international convention that controls and/or prohibits trade in endangered and threatened species of fauna and flora. Over 100 nations participate in the treaty that took effect in May 1977. The United States is a signatory to the treaty.

convertibility

(banking/foreign exchange) Ease of exchanging one currency for that of another nation or for gold.

convertible currency

(foreign exchange) Currency that can be easily exchanged, bought and sold for other currencies.

conveyancing

(UK) British term for buying and selling properties.

coordinated movement

(shipping) The extending of freight transportation systems to intermediate and smaller size communities through the use of interline agreements and the use of combined services of truck/air, helicopters, regional, and commuter airlines. In many cases such traffic moves under a joint freight rate. The success of such combined service hinges on preplanning on the part of the carriers, and often on the part of shippers, with regard to production and distribution schedules.

Coordinating Committee on Multilateral Export Controls (CoCom)

(obsolete) CoCom was an informal organization established in 1951 by NATO member countries to cooperatively restrict strategic exports (products and technical data) to controlled countries. CoCom has been replaced with the Wassenaar Arrangement. *See* Wassenaar Arrangement.

copyright

(law) An intangible right granted by law to the creator of a literary, musical, or artistic production to prevent any other person from copying, publishing, and selling those works. A copyright owner holds the sole and exclusive privilege to copy, publish, and sell the copyrighted work for the period specified by law. In general, copyright protection is available only after the work is fixed in a tangible medium, such as on paper, tape, canvas, or other materials, from which the work can be seen, reproduced, or otherwise communicated. It is not available to protect an idea, concept, procedure, process, system, operation method, principle, or discovery, but only the work as presented in a tangible medium. The works that can be copyrighted, the requirements for claiming a copyright, the extent of enforcement, and the time during which a copyright is effective varies from country to country. In the United States, for example, a copyright remains effective until 50 years after the death of the creator. In an effort to standardize copyright protection worldwide, many countries have become members of several international conventions on copyrights, including the Berne Convention for the Protection of Literary and Artistic Works, the Universal Copyright Convention, the UNESCO Treaty, the Convention for Protection of Producers of Phonograms against Unauthorized Duplication of Their Phonograms, and the International Convention for the Protection of Performers, Producers of Phonograms and Broadcasting Organizations. *See* Berne Convention for the Protection of Literary and Artistic Works; Universal Copyright Convention.

córdoba

The currency of Nicaragua. 1C$=100 centavos.

core inflation

(economics) The basic level of inflation over a period of time (e.g., a decade) as opposed to temporary fluctuations in the rate.

corporate dumping

The practice of exporting banned or out-of-date products from a domestic market to another national market where they are not banned or where regulations are more lax than in the domestic market. Out-of-date pharmaceuticals, for example, might be shipped from the U.S. to an Asian country that does not impose the same restrictions on the product.

corporation

(law) An association or entity created by persons under the authority of the laws of a particular jurisdiction. A corporation is treated as distinct from the persons (referred to as shareholders) who created it, and therefore the shareholders enjoy limited liability and the corporation has certain legal rights, such as the right to own property, enter contracts, and bring suit, similar to those given to individuals. *See* person.

correspondent bank

(banking) A bank that acts as a depository for another bank, accepting deposits and collecting items (such as drafts) on a reciprocal basis. Correspondent banks are often in different countries.

corrosives

(shipping) Items include materials that cause destruction to human tissue and corrode metal (i.e. steel) upon contact. (UN CLASS 8.) Examples are sodium hydroxide, hydrochloric acid, alkaline liquid. Hazards/precautions are contact causes burns to skin and eyes; may be harmful if breathed; fire may produce poisonous fumes; may react violently with water; may ignite combustibles; and explosive gasses may accumulate.

Cost and Freight (...named port of destination) (CFR)

(Incoterms 2000) An international trade term of sale in which, for the quoted price, the seller/exporter/manufacturer clears the goods for export and is responsible for delivering the goods past the ship's rail at the port of shipment (not destination).

The seller is also responsible for paying for the costs associated with transport of the goods to the named port of destination. However, once the goods pass the ship's rail at the port of shipment, the buyer assumes responsibility for risk of loss or damage as well as any additional transport costs.

The Cost and Freight term is used only for ocean or inland waterway transport.

The "named port of destination" in Cost and Freight and all "C" Incoterms 2000 is domestic to the buyer. The Cost and Freight term is commonly used in the sale of oversize and overweight cargo that will not fit into an ocean freight container or exceeds weight limitations of such containers. The term is also used for LCL (less than container load) cargo and for the shipment of goods by rail in boxcars to the ocean carrier.

See Guide to Incoterms 2000 Appendix.

Cost, Insurance and Freight (...named port of destination) (CIF)

(Incoterms 2000) An international trade term of sale in which, for the quoted price, the seller/exporter/manufacturer clears the goods for export and is responsible for delivering the goods past the ship's rail at the port of shipment (not destination).

The seller is responsible for paying for the costs associated with transport of the goods to the named port of destination. However, once the goods pass the ship's rail at the port of shipment, the buyer assumes responsibility for risk of loss or damage as well as any additional transport costs.

The seller is also responsible for procuring and paying for marine insurance in the buyer's name for the shipment.

The Cost and Freight term is used only for ocean or inland waterway transport.

The "named port of destination" in Cost and Freight and all "C" Incoterms 2000 is domestic to the buyer. *See* Guide to Incoterms 2000 Appendix.

Cost, Insurance, Freight, Commission, and Interest (CIFCI)

(trade term) The same as CIF (cost, insurance and freight), plus commission and interest.

cost of goods sold

(economics/accounting) The purchase price of goods sold during a specified period, including transportation costs.

cost of production

(economics) The sum of the cost of materials, fabrication and/or other processing employed in producing the merchandise sold in a home market or to another country together with appropriate allocations of general administrative and selling expenses. COP is based on the producer's actual experience and does not include any mandatory minimum general expense or profit as in "constructed value." *See* valuation; constructed value.

cost plus

A pricing method whereby the purchaser agrees to pay the vendor an amount determined by the costs incurred by the vendor to produce the goods or services purchased, plus a fixed percentage of that cost for profit.

costs of manufacture (COM)

(U.S. Customs) In the context of dumping investigations, the costs of manufacture, COM, is equal to the sum of the materials, labor and both direct and indirect factory overhead expenses required to produce the merchandise under investigation. *See* dumping.

cottage industry

(economics) An industry dependent upon a labor force that works out of their own homes and often with their own equipment.

Council of Economic Advisers

(U.S. government) A three-member executive office of the president which analyzes the U.S. economy, advises the president on economic developments, appraises programs and policies, and recommends policies for economic growth to the president. Address: Council of Economic Advisers, Old Executive Office Building, 17th St. & Pennsylvania Ave. NW, Washington, DC 20502 USA; Web: www.whitehouse.gov/cea.

Council of Europe

A regional alliance established in May 1949 to encourage unity and social and economic growth among members, which currently include: Austria, Belgium, Bulgaria, Cyprus, Denmark, Finland, France, Germany, Greece, Hungary, Iceland, Ireland, Italy, Liechtenstein, Luxembourg, Malta, the Netherlands, Norway, Poland, Portugal, San Marino, Spain, Sweden, Switzerland, Turkey, and the United Kingdom. Address: The Council of Europe, Point 1, F67075 Strasbourg Cedex, France. Tel: [33] (3) 88-41-20-00; Fax: [33] (3) 88-41-27-81; Web: www.coe.fr/index.asp.

Council of Logistics Management (CLM)

(logistics) A not-for-profit organization of logistics professionals dedicated to the improvement of logistics management skills. The CLM works in cooperation with industry and other NGOs (nongovernmental organizations) to further the understanding and development of the logistics concept. The organization focuses on three main areas: 1) improving communication between members of the logistics profession, 2) conducting research into logistics and 3) building awareness of the importance of logistics in the world economy. The CLM promotes various activities and seminars throughout the year. Membership is open to any individual and its 15,000 members hail from countries all around the world. Council of Logistics Management; 2805

Butterfield Road, Suite 200; Oak Brook, IL 60521 USA; Tel: [1] (630) 574-0985; Fax: [1] (630) 574-0989; E-mail: clmadmin@clm1.org; Web: www.clm1.org/default.htm.

counteroffer
(law) A reply to an offer that adds to, limits, or modifies materially the terms of the offer. A seller, for example, who accepts a buyer's offer, but informs the buyer that the goods will be of a different color has made a counteroffer. *See* acceptance; offer.

counterpurchase
See countertrade.

countertrade
An umbrella term for several sorts of trade in which the seller is required to accept goods or other instruments or trade, in partial or whole payment for its products.

Countertrade transactions include barter, buy-back or compensation, counterpurchase, offset requirements, swap, switch, or triangular trade, evidence or clearing accounts.

The main types are:

(a) **Counterpurchase** (one of the most common forms of countertrade), where an exporter agrees to purchase a quantity of unrelated goods or services from a country in exchange for and in approximate value to the goods he has sold.

(b) **Offset**, where the exporter agrees to use goods and services from the buyer's country in the product being sold. Offsets may be direct or indirect, depending on whether the goods and services are integral parts of the product. In a **direct offset**, a U.S. manufacturer selling a product in a country uses a component that is made in the purchasing country. In an **indirect offset**, the exporter would buy products made in the purchasing country that are peripheral to the manufacture of its product.

(c) **Compensation** or **buy-back**, where exporters of heavy equipment, technology, or even entire facilities agree to purchase a certain percentage of the output of the new facility once it is in production.

(d) **Barter**, which is a simple swap of one good for another. Two parties directly exchange goods deemed to be of approximately equivalent value without any flow of money taking place.

(e) **Switch** trading is a more complicated form of barter that involves a chain of buyers and sellers in different markets. A switch arrangement permits the sale of unpaid balances in a **clearing account** to be sold to a third party, usually at a discount, that may be used for producing goods in the country holding the balance.

(f) **Swap**, where products from different locations are traded to save transportation costs. For example, Russian oil may be "swapped" for oil from a Latin American producer, so the Russian oil can be shipped to a country in South Asia, while the Latin American oil is shipped to Cuba.

(g) **Reverse countertrade,** where an importer (a U.S. buyer of machine tools from Poland, for example) is required to export goods equivalent in value to a specified percentage of the value of the imported goods—an obligation that can be sold to an exporter in a third country.

(h) **Clearing** agreements between two countries, which is an agreement to purchase specific amounts of each other's products over a specified period of time, using a designated "clearing currency" in the transactions.

countervailing duties
(customs) Special duties imposed on imports to offset the benefits of subsidies to producers or exporters in the exporting country.

(WTO) The World Trade Organization (WTO) "Agreement on Subsidies and Countervailing Measures" permits the use of such duties if the importing country can prove that the subsidy would cause injury to domestic industry.

(U.S.) The Executive Branch of the U.S. government has been legally empowered since the 1890s to impose countervailing duties in amounts equal to any "bounties" or "grants" reflected in products imported into the United States. Under U.S. law and WTO rules a wide range of practices are recognized as constituting subsidies that may be offset through the imposition of countervailing duties. The Trade Agreements Act of 1979, through amendments to the Tariff Act of 1930 (both U.S. laws) established rigorous procedures and deadlines for determining the existence of subsidies in response to petitions filed by interested parties such as domestic producers of competitive products and their workers. In all cases involving subsidized products from countries recognized by the United States as signatories to the Agreement on Subsidies and Countervailing Duties, or countries which have assumed obligations substantially equivalent to those under the Agreement, U.S. law requires that countervailing duties may be imposed only after the U.S. International Trade Commission has determined that the imports are causing or threatening to cause material injury to an industry in the United States.

Countervailing duties in the U.S. can only be imposed after the International Trade Commission has determined that the imports are causing or threatening to cause material injury to a U.S. industry.

See dumping; General Agreement on Tariffs and Trade; International Trade Commission.

country desk officers
(U.S. government) Country-specific export trade specialists working at the U.S. Department of Commerce in Washington, DC. Country desk officers provide assistance to U.S. exporters on a country-specific, rather than commodity-specific basis. Their responsibility is to remain current on any issues that would affect U.S. exporters and travelers in the spe-

C

cific country. For information call the United States Department of Commerce, Tel: [1] (202) 482-2000, or the Trade Information Center, Tel: [1] (800) USA-TRADE. *See* U.S. Department of Commerce.

country marketing plan

(U.S.) An analysis of a country's business and economic climate, giving emphasis to marketing and trade issues. Usually prepared by the U.S. embassy in the subject country and published by the U.S. Department of Commerce, International Trade Administration. Also available on CD-ROM in the National Trade Data Bank, and available from the U.S. Department of Commerce, 14th Street and Constitution Ave., Washington, DC 20230 USA; Tel: [1] (202) 482-2000.

country of departure

(shipping) The country from which a ship or shipment has or is scheduled to depart.

country of destination

(shipping) The country that is the ultimate destination for a ship or shipment of goods.

country of dispatch

(shipping) The country from which cargo was shipped.

country of exportation

(shipping) Usually, but not necessarily, the country in which merchandise was manufactured or produced and from which it was first exported. For example, merchandise made in Switzerland and shipped to the United States through Frankfurt, Germany, has as the country of exportation Switzerland.

country of export destination

The country where the goods are to be consumed, further processed, or manufactured, as known to the shipper at the time of exportation. If the shipper does not know the country of ultimate destination, the shipment is credited for statistical purposes to the last country to which the shipper knows that the merchandise will be shipped in the same form as when exported.

country of origin

The country where merchandise was grown, mined, or manufactured.
(U.S. Customs) In instances where the country of origin cannot be determined, transactions are credited to the country of shipment. Certain foreign trade reports show country subcodes to indicate special tariff treatment afforded some imported articles. *See* certificate of origin.

country risk

(economics) The financial risks of a transaction which relate to the political, economic or social instability of a country.

courier

(shipping) (a) An attendant who accompanies a shipment (generally of documents). (b) A company that provides full transportation service, without an accompanying attendant, offering door-to-door air service for time-sensitive documents or small packages on a same-day or next-day basis. Examples are DHL, FedEx (Federal Express) and UPS (United Parcel Service).

Courier LVS

(Canada) Low Value Shipment. A Canada Customs and Revenue Agency (CCRA) program that speeds the release of low-value entries of up to C$1,600 for commercial imports by approved carriers. Information at Web: www.ccra-adrc.gc.ca.courtage

courtage

(banking) A European term for brokerage fee.

cover; coverage

See insurance coverage.

cover note

(insurance) Often also called "broker's cover note." Document issued by insurance companies or insurance brokers in lieu of insurance policies or insurance certificates which serves as proof of usual insurance notification and represents cover approval. Cover notes may be accepted under letters of credit only when they are expressly permitted.

credit arrangements

A series of programs under which service providers (such as ocean and air carriers, trucking companies, customs brokers and freight forwarders) extend credit to shippers and consignees for the payment of charges.

creditor nation

(economics) A nation that is owed more foreign currency obligations than it owes other nations. *See also* debtor nation.

credit risk insurance

(insurance) Insurance designed to cover risks of nonpayment for delivered goods.

creeping nationalization

(economics/law) A continuing sequence of small but material changes to a firm's status that leads to nationalization. *See* nationalization.

critical circumstances

(U.S. Customs) A determination made by the Assistant Secretary for Import Administration as to whether there is a reasonable basis to believe or suspect that there is a history of dumping in the United States or elsewhere of the merchandise under consideration, or that the importer knew or should have known that the exporter was selling this merchandise at less than fair value, and there have been massive imports of this merchandise over a relatively short period. This determination is made if an allegation of critical circumstances is received from the petitioner. *See* dumping.

cross-currency exchange risk
(banking/foreign exchange) The exchange risk inherent in carrying out foreign exchange transactions in two or more currencies.

cross-docking
(logistics) The immediate transfer of cargo from one transport vehicle to another eliminating the intervening steps of receiving and shipping, thus facilitating the flow of product and reducing costs.

crossed check
(banking) A check that bears on its face two parallel transverse lines and that cannot be presented for cash. A bank that accepts the check may pay the proceeds only to another bank, which will credit the money to the account of the payee of the check. A crossed check may also include the words "and company." A specially crossed check contains in the crossing lines the name of the bank that will honor the check.

cross rate
(foreign exchange) Exchange rate parities which are not quoted against the dollar.

cruzeiro real
The currency of Brazil. 1Cr$=100 centavos.

cube out
(shipping/logistics) When a shipping container has been filled by volume but has not reached its maximum weight limit.

cubic capacity
(shipping) The carrying capacity of a container according to measurement in cubic feet, cubic centimeters or cubic meters.

cubic foot
(measurement) A unit of volume measurement equal to 1,728 cubic inches.

currency
(banking/foreign exchange) Name given to the material form of a country's payment medium, for example, "Swiss francs, divided into 100 centimes."

currency adjustment factor (CAF)
(logistics) A freight surcharge or adjustment factor imposed by an international carrier to offset foreign currency fluctuations. In some cases an emergency currency adjustment factor (ECAF) may be applied when a charge or rate has been originally published in a currency that is experiencing sustained or rapid decline. The CAF is charged as a percentage of the published rate. *See* emergency currency adjustment factor.

currency area
See currency zone.

currency basket
(banking/foreign exchange) A means of establishing value for a composite unit consisting of the currencies of designated nations. Each currency is represented in proportion to its value in relation to the total. The European Currency Unit (ecu) which is now obsolete, for example, was a weighted average of the currencies of the European Union member nations, used as a unit of value in transactions among businesses in the member countries. The ecu has been replaced by the European Union euro.

currency of the contract
(commerce/law/banking) The required currency of payment as stated in a sales contract. The currency of a contract is generally a hard currency such as the U.S. dollar, Japanese yen, British pound or EU euro. (Note that as of January 1, 2002, the euro replaced the Austrian schilling, Belgium franc, Dutch guilder, Finnish markka, French franc, German mark, Irish punt, Italian lira, Luxembourg franc, Portuguese escudo and Spanish peseta.) Choosing the currency of the contract is a point of negotiation and can be a significant economic factor, especially if the time from contract to delivery (or billing) is great, or if fluctuations in the currencies of the buyer and seller are anticipated over the course of the contract.

currency snake
See snake system.

currency swap
(banking/foreign exchange) System whereby an institution with funds in one currency converts them into another and enters into a forward exchange contract to recover the currency borrowed.

currency (term) of insurance
(insurance) A statement of insurance coverage expressed either in time, or for transit from two physical points. For example: one year commencing on a specific date and time, or, from point a to point b.
Formerly, the marine insurance policy covered only from the time goods were actually loaded on board an ocean vessel at the port of shipment until they were "discharged and safely landed" at the port of destination. This was later extended by adding the words "including transit by craft, raft and/or lighter to and from the vessel."
More recently, insurance coverage has included risks to a shipment of goods from the time the goods leave the warehouse for commencement of transit and continue during ordinary course of transit until delivered to final warehouse (warehouse-to-warehouse coverage) at destination, or until the expiration of 15 days (30 if destination is outside the limits of the port), whichever shall first occur. In the case of delay in excess of the time limit specified, if it arises from circumstances beyond his control, the assured is "held covered" if he gives prompt notice and pays additional premium. *See also* all risk; Marine Extension Clause 1943 & 1952.

currency translation
(accounting/foreign exchange) The recording in accounts of assets (or liabilities) in one currency when they are actually in another. No actual exchange of

C

funds takes place. The World Bank, for example, translates all their assets and liabilities into U.S. dollar amounts, regardless of the actual currency in which they are denominated.

currency zone
(banking/foreign exchange) A geographic area where one currency is valid. A currency zone normally, but not always coincides with the national frontiers of a country. A **supranational currency zone** arises when different currencies are connected either through convertibility or fixed exchange rates. An example is the Sterling zone.

current account
(economics) That portion of a country's balance of payments that records current (as opposed to capital) transactions, including visible trade (exports and imports), invisible trade (income and expenditures for services), profits earned from foreign operations, interest and transfer payments.
(UK) British term for a bank checking account.
See balance of payments.

current balance
(economics) The value of all exports (goods plus services) less all imports of a country over a specific period of time, equal to the sum of the trade (visible) and invisible balances plus net receipts of interest, profits and dividends from abroad. *See* balance of payments.

custody bill of lading
(shipping) A bill of lading issued by U.S. warehouses as a receipt for goods stored. *See* bill of lading.

customer automation
(shipping) The use of carrier automation equipment on the customer's premises that aids in the processing of shipments, i.e., airbill preparations, invoicing, weighing, and tracing.

customhouse
(customs) The government office where duties, tolls, or taxes placed on imports or exports are paid and vessels entered or cleared.

Customized Market Analysis
(U.S.) A fee-based International Trade Administration service that provides firms with key marketing, pricing, and foreign representation information about their specific products. Overseas staff conduct on-site interviews to provide data in nine marketing areas about the product, such as sales potential in the market, comparable products, distribution channels, going price, competitive factors, and qualified purchasers. Information on pricing and on contacting a trade specialist near you can be found at: Web: www.usatrade.gov (click "Contact Us").

customs
(a) A government authority designated to regulate flow of goods to/from a country and to collect duties levied by a country on imports and exports. The term also applies to the procedures involved in such collection. (b) The United States Customs Service. *See* United States Customs Service. (c) Taxes imposed by a government on the import or export of products or services. *See also* tariff.

customs bond
See bond; surety.

customs bonded warehouse
(customs) A federal warehouse where goods remain until duty has been collected from the importer. Goods under bond are also kept here. *See* surety; bond; in bond; bonded warehouse.

customs broker
(U.S. Customs) An individual or firm licensed by the U.S. Customs Service to act for importers in handling the sequence of custom formalities and other details critical to the legal and speedy exporting and importing of goods.

customs classification
(customs) The particular category in a tariff nomenclature in which a product is classified for tariff purposes; or, the procedure for determining the appropriate tariff category in a country's nomenclature system used for the classification, coding and description of internationally traded goods. *See* Harmonized System; Harmonized Tariff Schedule of the United States.

Customs Cooperation Council (CCC)
An intergovernmental organization created in 1953 and headquartered in Brussels, through which customs officials of participating countries seek to simplify, standardize, and conciliate customs procedures. The Council has sponsored a standardized product classification, a set of definitions of commodities for customs purposes, a standardized definition of value and a number of recommendations designed to facilitate customs procedures. *See* Harmonized System.

Customs Cooperation Council Nomenclature
A customs tariff system formerly used by many countries, including most European nations but not the United States. It has been superseded by the Harmonized System Nomenclature to which most major trading nations, including the U.S., adhere. *See* Harmonized System; Harmonized Tariff Schedule of the United States.

customs court
(U.S. Customs) A U.S. Customs Service court based in New York, NY, consisting of three 3-party divisions to which importers may appeal or protest classification and valuation decisions and certain other actions taken by the U.S. Customs Service.

customs declaration
(U.S. Customs) An oral or written statement attesting to the correctness of description, quantity, value,

etc., of merchandise offered for importation into the United States. *See* entry.

customs duty

(customs) A tax levied and collected by custom officials in discharging the tariff regulations on imports. *See also* tariff.

customs harmonization

(customs) International efforts to increase the uniformity of customs nomenclatures and procedures in cooperating countries. The Customs Cooperation Council has developed an up-to-date and internationally accepted "Harmonized Commodity Coding and Description System" for classifying goods for customs, statistical, and other purposes. *See* Customs Cooperation Council; Harmonized System; Harmonized Tariff Schedule of the United States.

customshouse broker

See customs broker.

Customs House Guide

See United States Customs House Guide.

customs import value

(U.S. Customs) U.S. Customs Service appraisal value of merchandise. Methodologically, the Customs value is similar to Free Alongside Ship (FAS) value since it is based on the value of the product in the foreign country of origin, and excludes charges incurred in bringing the merchandise to the United States (import duties, ocean freight, insurance, and so forth); but it differs in that the U.S. Customs Service, not the importer or exporter, has the final authority to determine the value of the good. *See* valuation.

Customs Information Exchange

A clearinghouse of information for U.S. Customs Service officers. *See* United States Customs Service.

customs invoice

(customs) An invoice made out on a special form prescribed by the customs authorities of the importing country. Used only in a few countries. *See also* commercial invoice.

customs tariff

(customs) A schedule of charges assessed by government on imported or exported goods. *See* Harmonized System; Harmonized Tariff Schedule of the United States.

customs territory

The geographic territory upon which a sovereign nation imposes its import and export regulations and duties. Certain territorial possessions and special economic zones (such as foreign trade zones) are often considered outside the customs territory of a nation.

(U.S. Customs) The customs territory of the United States consists of the 50 states, the District of Columbia, and Puerto Rico. Foreign trade zones are not considered customs territory of the United States. *See* United States Customs Service; foreign trade zone.

customs union

(customs) An agreement by two or more trading countries to dissolve trade restrictions such as tariffs and quotas among themselves, and to develop a common external policy or trade (e.g., trade agreement).

cycle inventory

(logistics) An inventory-taking methodology where the counting of items occurs continuously but at different intervals for different items. Thus, some items may be inventoried monthly, quarterly, biannually or yearly. In some cases a cycle inventory eliminates the need for an annual inventory. *See* inventory.

cycle time

(general) The interval of time required to complete an activity or a succession of related events.

(sales) The time it takes to make a sale, measured from the identification of the opportunity or prospect to the receipt of a purchase order.

(logistics) (a) The time required to fill an order, measured from the receipt of the order to the delivery of the product to the customer. Once measured in weeks and months, cycle time is now measured in days and even hours. (b) The time required to replenish stock of a raw material, component part or finished product, expressed as the sum of the time required to secure a purchase order plus the time required to obtain delivery from the supplier.

D

D/A
See documentary collection.

dalasi
The currency of Gambia. 1D=100 butut.

damages
(law) (a) A loss or harm to a person or his or her property. (b) An award given to a person (usually as a result of a court action) as compensation for a loss.

dangerous goods
(air transport) Articles or substances which are capable of posing a significant risk to health, safety, or property when transported by air and which are classified according to the most current editions of the International Civil Aviation Organization (ICAO) Technical Instructions for the Safe Transport of Dangerous Goods by Air and the IATA (International Air Transport Association) Dangerous Goods Regulations. Dangerous goods may be transported domestically and internationally by air. *See* hazardous materials.

dangerous when wet
(shipping) These items include flammable solids that are reactive with water. (UN CLASS 4.) Examples: magnesium; aluminum phosphide; lithium hydride; calcium carbide. Hazards: may ignite in presence of moisture; contact with water produces flammable gas; may reignite after fire is extinguished; contact may cause burns to skin and eyes; skin contact may be poisonous; inhalation or vapors may be harmful. Precautions: prohibit flames or smoking in area.

Data Interchange Standards Association (DISA)
(e-commerce) An international organization dedicated to the development of cross-industry electronic data interchange standards that provide the foundation to enable individuals, companies and organizations to participate in global e-business. The organization provides technical and administrative support for e-commerce and conducts training and seminars on XML and EDI. DISA publishes standards such as ASC X12, UN/EDIFACT, ANSI and offers EC/EDI publications.
Data Interchange Standards Association; 333 John Carlyle Street, Suite 600; Alexandria, VA 22314 USA; Tel: [1] (703) 548-7005; Fax: [1] (703) 548-5738; Web: www.disa.org.

Data Universal Numbering System (DUNS or D-U-N-S) Number
(commerce) A company numbering and identification system developed and maintained by Dunn & Bradstreet Corporation (Web: www.dnb.com). The standard DUNS nine-digit universal identification number is particular to a specific listed company. The DUNS+4 number uniquely identifies an affiliate, subsidiary or division of a listed company.
DUNS number company identifiers are recognized, recommended or required by more than 50 global, industry and trade associations, including the United Nations, the U.S. Federal Government, the Australian Government and the European Commission. For more information and to register a company go to Web: www.dnb.com/duns.

date draft
(banking) A draft which matures a specified number of days after the date it is issued, without regard to the date of acceptance.
See acceptance; bill of exchange.

dating
The practice of granting extended credit terms by the seller to induce buyers to receive goods in advance of required delivery dates.

dead heading
(trucking) Operating a motor vehicle or vessel without a load of cargo. The term most commonly applies to the trucking industry and refers to either the return trip from delivering a cargo, or driving empty to a location in order to pick up cargo. Dead heading is considered a waste of resources and avoided whenever possible.

deadweight
(shipping) The maximum carrying capacity of a ship, expressed in tons, of cargo, stores, provisions and bunker fuel. Deadweight is used interchangeably with deadweight tonnage and deadweight carrying capacity. A vessel's capacity for cargo is less than its total deadweight tonnage.

deadweight cargo
(shipping) Cargo of such weight and volume that a long ton (2,240 pounds) is stowed in an area of less than 70 cubic feet.

dealer
An individual or firm who acts as a principal in the sale of merchandise.

debt-for-export swap; debt-for-products swap
(banking/trade) Swap whereby a bank arranges to export a variety of domestic products and commodities to offset part of its outstanding claims in the country.

debt-for-nature swap
(banking/trade) Swap arranged by private conservation group to use the proceeds of debt conversions to finance conservation projects relating to parkland or tropical forests.

debtor nation

(economics) A nation that is owed less foreign currency obligations than it owes other nations. *See also* creditor nation.

deck cargo

(shipping) Cargo shipped on the deck of a vessel rather than in holds below deck. Cargo shipped on deck is more likely to be adversely affected by heat, cold, rain, seawater and movement of the ship. Some shippers require that their cargo not be shipped on deck. On the other hand, certain dangerous cargo, such as explosives are required to be shipped on deck.

declaration

(insurance) A method of reporting shipments to an insurance company under an open insurance policy. This "short form" calls for the name of the vessel and sailing date, points of shipment and destination, nature of commodity, description of units comprising the shipment, the amount of insurance desired and the number of the open policy under which the declaration is made. The declaration forms are prepared by the assured and are forwarded daily, weekly, or as shipments are made. The forms are forwarded to the insurance agent or broker for transmission to the insurance company. When full information is not available at the time a declaration is made, a provisional report may be sent in. The "provisional" is closed when value is finally known. The premium is billed monthly in accordance with the schedule of rates provided by the policy. The declaration is generally not used in cases where evidence of insurance must be supplied to a customer, to banks or to other third parties in order to permit collection of claims abroad. This calls for a special marine policy, occasionally referred to as a certificate. Declarations, therefore, are usually used for import shipments, not export shipments. *See* open policy; special marine policy; bordereau.

declared value for carriage

(shipping/insurance) The value of goods declared to the carrier by the shipper for the purposes of determining charges, or of establishing the limit of the carrier's liability for loss, damage, or delay. *See* valuation charges.

declared value for customs

(U.S. Customs) The selling price of a shipment or the replacement cost if the shipment is not for resale. The amount must be equal to or greater than the declared value. *See* valuation.

deductible average

(insurance) The deductible amount that is subtracted from each covered average loss whereby the assured always bears part of the loss. *See also* average; particular average; general average; with average; free of particular average.

deductive value

(U.S. Customs) In valuation of merchandise for customs purposes, deductive value is the resale price of imported merchandise in the United States with deductions for certain items. Generally, the deductive value is calculated by starting with a unit price and making certain additions to and deductions from that price.

Unit Price: One of three prices constitutes the unit price in deductive value. The price used depends on *when* and in *what condition* the merchandise concerned is sold in the United States.

(1) *Time and Condition*: The merchandise is sold in the condition as imported at or about the date of importation of the merchandise being appraised. *Price*: The price used is the unit price at which the greatest aggregate quantity of the merchandise concerned is sold at or about the date of importation.

(2) *Time and Condition*: The merchandise concerned is sold in the condition as imported but not sold at or about the date of importation of the merchandise being appraised. *Price*: The price used is the unit price at which the greatest aggregate quantity of the merchandise concerned is sold after the date of importation of the merchandise being appraised, but before the close of the 90th day after the date of importation.

(3) *Time and Condition*: The merchandise concerned is not sold in the condition as imported and not sold before the close of the 90th day after the date of importation of the merchandise being appraised. *Price*: The price used is the unit price at which the greatest aggregate quantity of the merchandise being appraised, after further processing, is sold before the 180th day after the date of the importation.

The third price is also known as the "further processing price" or "superdeductive."

Additions: Packing costs for the merchandise concerned are added to the price used for deductive value, provided these costs have not otherwise been included. These costs are added regardless of whether the importer or the buyer incurs the cost.

Deductions: Certain items are not part of the deductive value and must be deducted from the unit price. These items include:

(1) Commissions or profits and general expense,

(2) Transportation and insurance costs,

(3) Customs duties and federal taxes,

(4) Value of further processing.

If an assist is involved in a sale, that sale cannot be used in determining deductive value.

See valuation; transaction value; identical merchandise; similar merchandise; computed value.

defective goods inventory (DGI)

(commerce/logistics) Inventory of damaged or defective goods. Specifically, goods that were damaged during handling in the warehouse, damaged during delivery and returned or damaged during de-

D

livery where a credit was issued to the buyer and that have an outstanding freight claim. *See* inventory.

defense memoranda of understanding (MOU)
(U.S.) Defense cooperation agreements between the U.S. and allied nations. MOUs are signed by the U.S. Department of Defense (DOD) with allied nations and are related to research, development, or production of defense equipment or reciprocal procurement of defense items.

Defense Threat Reduction Agency
(U.S. government) DTRA is the Department of Defense (DOD) organization which reviews applications for the export of items that are subject to the dual-use license controls of the U.S. Commerce Department. DTRA is located in the Office of the Secretary of Defense, and administers DOD technology security policy so that the U.S. is not technologically surprised on the battlefield. Address: Defense Threat Reduction Agency, 45045 Aviation Drive, Dulles, VA 20166-7517 USA; Tel: [1] (800) 701-5096; Fax: [1] (703) 767-4450; Web: www.dtra.mil.

Defense Trade Controls (DTC)
(U.S.) DTC (formerly the Office of Munitions Control, OMC) at the U.S. Department of State administers licenses for the export of items that are exclusively, or primarily, of munitions significance. These items are listed in the International Traffic in Arms Regulations (ITAR) and the U.S. Munitions List. In circumstances in which an item may be considered either dual-use or subject to the ITAR, the State Department has the option to assert jurisdiction. In some cases, decisions about jurisdiction are made after an item has been subject to a dual-use license application sent to the Commerce Department. Commerce is never involved in State's process, unless there are matters involving dual-use or issues involving jurisdiction. Address: PM/DTC, SA-1, 13th Floor, Office of Defense Trade Controls, Bureau of Political and Military Affairs, U.S. Department of State, Washington, DC 20522-0112 USA; Tel: [1] (202) 663-2700; Fax: [1] (202) 261-8264; Web: www.pmdtc.org.

Defense Trade Working Group
(U.S.) A committee of officials from the U.S. Departments of Commerce, Defense, State and the United States Trade Representative (USTR) was established in 1990 to coordinate agency policies and resources in areas concerned with defense expenditures. The group works with industry to identify ways to target industry needs and increase the success of industry export efforts by minimizing government impediments, streamlining procedures, and improving the availability of market information. The DTWG includes three subgroups: (1) The **Defense Export Market Opportunity Subgroup**, chaired by the U.S. Department of Commerce, which helps implement Administration defense export policy and enhances U.S. government support for U.S. defense exporters; (2) The **European Defense Cooperation Subgroup**, chaired by the U.S. Department of State, which coordinates interagency input to U.S.-NATO International Staff for the NATO Council on National Armaments Directors (CNAD) study on defense trade; and (3) The **Technology Transfer/Third Country Reexport Subgroup**, chaired by the U.S. Department of Defense, which works with industry to define a more proactive technology transfer regime that could be implemented within the limits of U.S. national security and industrial competitiveness interests.

deferred air freight
(shipping) Air freight of a less time sensitive nature, with delivery provided over a period of days.

deferred payment letter of credit
(banking) A letter of credit which enables the buyer to take possession of the title documents and the goods by agreeing to pay the issuing bank at a fixed time in the future. *See* letter of credit.

delay clause
(insurance) An insurance policy clause which excludes claims for loss of market and for loss, damage or deterioration arising from delay. This exclusion appears in almost every marine cargo insurance policy.

Insurance underwriters are exceedingly reluctant to assume any liability for loss of market, which is generally considered a "trade loss" and uninsurable. A market loss, furthermore, is an indirect or consequential damage. It is not a "physical loss or damage." *See* special marine policy.

del credere risk
(law) Risk that a counterparty is either unable or unwilling to fulfill his payment obligations.

Delivered At Frontier (...named place) (DAF)
(Incoterms 2000) An international trade term of sale in which, for the quoted price, the seller/exporter/manufacturer clears the goods for export and is responsible for making them available to the buyer at the named point and place at the frontier, not unloaded, and not cleared for import.

In the DAF term, naming the precise point, place, and time of availability at the frontier is very important as the buyer must make arrangements to unload and secure the goods in a timely manner.

Frontier can mean any frontier including the frontier of export.

The DAF term is valid for any mode of shipment, so long as the final shipment to the named place at the frontier is by land.

The seller is not responsible for procuring and paying for insurance cover.

See Guide to Incoterms 2000 Appendix.

Delivered Duty Paid (...named place of destination) (DDP)

(Incoterms 2000) An international trade term of sale in which, for the quoted price, the seller/exporter/manufacturer clears the goods for export and is responsible for making them available to the buyer at the named place of destination, cleared for import, but not unloaded from the transport vehicle.

The seller, therefore, assumes all responsibilities for delivering the goods to the named place of destination, including all responsibility for import clearance, duties, and other costs payable upon import. The DDP term can be used for any mode of transport.

The DDP term is used when the named place of destination (point of delivery) is other than the seaport or airport.

See Guide to Incoterms 2000 Appendix.

Delivered Duty Unpaid (...named place of destination) (DDU)

(Incoterms 2000) An international trade term of sale in which, for the quoted price, the seller/exporter/manufacturer clears the goods for export and is responsible for making them available to the buyer at the named place of destination, not cleared for import.

The seller, therefore, assumes all responsibilities for delivering the goods to the named place of destination, but the buyer assumes all responsibility for import clearance, duties, administrative costs, and any other costs upon import as well as transport to the final destination.

The DDU term can be used for any mode of transport. However, if the seller and buyer desire that delivery should take place on board a sea vessel or on a quay (wharf), the DES or DEQ terms are recommended.

The DDU term is used when the named place of destination (point of delivery) is other than the seaport or airport.

See Guide to Incoterms 2000 Appendix.

Delivered Ex Quay (...named port of destination) (DEQ)

(Incoterms 2000) An international trade term of sale in which, for the quoted price, the seller/exporter/manufacturer clears the goods for export and is responsible for making them available to the buyer on the quay (wharf) at the named port of destination, not cleared for import.

The buyer, therefore, assumes all responsibilities for import clearance, duties, and other costs upon import as well as transport to the final destination. (This is new for Incoterms 2000.)

The DEQ term is used only for shipments of goods arriving at the port of destination by ocean or by inland waterway.

See Guide to Incoterms 2000 Appendix.

Delivered Ex Ship (...named port of destination) (DES)

(Incoterms 2000) An international trade term of sale in which, for the quoted price, the seller/exporter/manufacturer clears the goods for export and is responsible for making them available to the buyer on board the ship at the named port of destination, not cleared for import.

The seller is thus responsible for all costs of getting the goods to the named port of destination prior to unloading.

The DES term is used only for shipments of goods by ocean or inland waterway or by multimodal transport where the final delivery is made on a vessel at the named port of destination.

See Guide to Incoterms 2000 Appendix.

delivery

(shipping/law) The act of transferring physical possession, such as the transfer of property from consignor to carrier, one carrier to another, or carrier to consignee.

delivery carrier

(shipping) The carrier (transport company) whose responsibility is to place a shipment at the disposal of the consignee at the address stated on the bill of lading. *See* carrier; bill of lading.

delivery instructions

(shipping) Specific delivery instructions for the freight forwarder or carrier (transport company) stating exactly where the goods are to be delivered, the deadline, and the name, address, and telephone number of the person to contact if delivery problems are encountered. *See also* delivery order.

delivery order

(shipping) (a) A document from the consignee, shipper, or owner of freight ordering a terminal operator, carrier, or warehouseman to deliver freight to another party. (b) An order from a steamship company to the terminal superintendent for the release of goods to a consignee following payment of freight charges. (c) Order to deliver specified packages out of a combined consignment covered by one single bill of lading.

delta

(general/statistics) An increment of a variable.

(finance/foreign exchange) Measure of the relationship between an option price and the underlying futures contract or stock price.

The delta ratio indicates by how many units the premium on an option changes for a one unit change in the value of the underlying instrument. An at-the-money option has a delta of about 0.5. The deeper the option is in-the-money, the closer the delta gets to 1 and the deeper the option is out-of-the-money, the more the delta approaches 0.

delta hedging

(banking/foreign exchange) A method used by options writers to hedge risk exposure of written op-

D

tions by purchase or sale of the underlying instrument in proportion to the delta. Example: the writer of a call option with a delta of 0.5 would have to buy half the amount of the instrument underlying the option (e.g., US$), which he might eventually be forced to deliver upon expiry of the option.

Delta Nu Alpha (DNA)
(logistics) An international nonprofit organization of logistics professionals that encourages education in the field of transportation and logistics. The organization provides mentoring and financial assistance for students, continuing education for professionals in the field, and vigilance in communicating changes in regulations that affect the industry. Contact at Web: www.deltanualpha.org.

demand
(banking/law) (a) A request for the payment of a debt or other amount due. (b) A demand clause is a term in a note by which the note holder can compel full payment if the maker of the note fails to meet an installment.

demand chain
(logistics) The concept that consumer demand can "pull" products through the logistics chain. Demand chain logistics is a counterpoint to supply chain logistics where products are "pushed" through the logistics system to the ultimate consumer by the actions of the producer and marketing and logistics professionals.
In demand chain logistics, however, it is the producers who are responding to the demands of customers in the marketplace. In demand chain logistics producers and logistics professionals must have a thorough understanding of their customers, an unimpeded flow of information and the ability to respond quickly to changing demand. *See* supply chain.

demise
(law) A lease of property. A demise charter is a bareboat charter. *See* bareboat charter.

demurrage
(shipping) (a) The detention of a freight car or ship by the shipper beyond time permitted (grace period) for loading or unloading, (b) The extra charges a shipper pays for detaining a freight car or ship beyond time permitted for loading or unloading. Used interchangeably with detention. Detention applies to equipment. Demurrage applies to cargo. *See* detention.

denar
The currency of Macedonia. 1 denar=100 deni.

Denied Parties List (DPL)
(U.S. trade law) A set of lists maintained by the U.S. Bureau of Industry and Security (formerly the U.S. Bureau of Export Administration) (Web: www.bxa.doc.gov/DPL/Default.shtm) of individuals and firms denied export privileges, specifically for strategic and controlled materials, components and products.

density
(shipping) (a) The weight of an article or container per cubic foot. (b) The ratio of mass to bulk or volume.

Department of Agriculture (DOA)
See United States Department of Agriculture.

Department of Commerce (DOC)
See United States Department of Commerce.

Department of Defense (DOD)
See United States Department of Defense.

Department of Energy (DOE)
See United States Department of Energy.

Department of Labor (DOL)
See United States Department of Labor.

Department of State
See United States Department of State.

Department of the Interior (DOI)
See United States Department of the Interior.

Department of the Treasury
See United States Department of the Treasury.

Department of Transportation (DOT)
See United States Department of Transportation.

deposit dealings
(banking) Money market operations.

deposit money
(banking) Also known as bank or giro money. Bank, giro and postal giro account credit balances which can be converted at any time into notes and coinage, but which are normally used for cash-less payment transactions.

deposit of estimated duties
(U.S. Customs) This refers to antidumping duties which must be deposited upon entry of merchandise into the United States which is the subject of an antidumping duty order for each manufacturer, producer or exporter equal to the amount by which the foreign market value exceeds the United States price of the merchandise. *See* antidumping duties; dumping.

depreciation
(economics/accounting) (a) The charges against earnings to write-off the purchase price of an asset over its useful life. (b) The decline in the value of a property or asset.
(foreign exchange) The decline in value of one currency in relation to another currency.

deputy chief of mission (DCM)
(diplomacy) Position second-in-command to ambassador in an embassy. The DCM is responsible for managing the daily operations of all departments in an embassy. Also serves as acting ambassador during the absence of the ambassador.

D

destination
(shipping) The place to which a shipment is consigned.

detention
(shipping) (a) Holding a carrier's driver and/or trailer beyond a certain stated period of "free time," often resulting in the assessment of detention charges. (b) The delay in clearing goods through customs resulting in storage and other charges. *See* demurrage.

detention charges
(shipping) Charges assessed by a carrier against the consignor or consignee as compensation for holding a carrier's driver and/or trailer beyond a certain stated period of "free time." Detention is an accessorial service and charge. *See also* demurrage.

detention insurance
(insurance) Insurance coverage to pay for the costs resulting in the storage or maintenance of goods delayed in the clearance of customs at a foreign port.

devaluation
(economics) The lowering of the value of a national currency in terms of the currency of another nation. Devaluation tends to reduce domestic demand for imports in a country by raising their prices in terms of the devalued currency and to raise foreign demand for the country's exports by reducing their prices in terms of foreign currencies. Devaluation can therefore help to correct a balance of payments deficit and sometimes provide a short-term basis for economic adjustment of a national economy.
In a fixed exchange rate situation, devaluation occurs as the result of an administrative action taken by a government to reduce the value of its domestic currency in terms of gold or foreign monies.
In a free exchange rate situation, devaluation occurs as a result of the action of the foreign exchange market where the value of the domestic currency drops by market forces against a specific unit of foreign currency.

devanning
(shipping) The unloading of cargo from a container. Also called stripping.

developed countries
(economics) A term used to distinguish the more industrialized nations—including all Organization for Economic Cooperation and Development (OECD) member countries as well as the Soviet Union and most of the socialist countries of Eastern Europe—from "developing"—or less developed countries. The developed countries are sometimes collectively designated as the "North," because most of them are in the Northern Hemisphere. *See also* developing countries.

developing countries
(economics) A broad range of countries that generally lack a high degree of industrialization, infrastructure and other capital investment, sophisticated technology, widespread literacy, and advanced living standards among their populations as a whole. The developing countries are sometimes collectively designated as the "South," because a large number of them are in the Southern Hemisphere. All of the countries of Africa (except South Africa), Asia and Oceania (except Australia, Japan and New Zealand), Latin America, and the Middle East are generally considered "developing countries" as are a few European countries (Cyprus, Malta, Turkey and countries of the former Yugoslavia, for example). Some experts differentiate four subcategories of developing countries as having different economic needs and interests: (1) A few relatively wealthy Organization of Petroleum Exporting Countries (OPEC) countries— sometimes referred to as oil exporting developing countries—share a particular interest in a financially sound international economy and open capital markets; (2) Newly Industrializing Countries (NICs) have a growing stake in an open international trading system; (3) A number of middle income countries—principally commodity exporters—have shown a particular interest in commodity stabilization schemes; and (4) More than 30 very poor countries ("least developed countries") are predominantly agricultural, have sharply limited development prospects during the near future, and tend to be heavily dependent on official development assistance.

difference in conditions insurance
See contingency insurance.

differential
(shipping) An amount added to or deducted from a shipping base rate between two established points to make a rate to or from some other points or via another route.

dimensional weight
(shipping) Dimensional weight refers to density, i.e., weight per cubic foot of a shipment of cargo. The weight of a shipment per cubic foot is one of its most important transportation characteristics. Some commodities, such as machinery, have a relatively high density. Others, like hats, have a relatively low density. Hence, the **dimensional weight rule** was developed as a practice applicable to low density shipments under which the transportation charges are based on a cubic dimensional weight rather than upon actual weight. Examples: one pound for each 194 cubic inches of the shipment in the case of most domestic air freight, one pound for each 266 cubic inches of cut flowers or nursery stock shipments, and one pound for each 194 cubic inches of most international shipments.

dinar
The currency of:
Algeria, 1DA=100 centimes;
Bahrain, 1BD=1,000 fils;
Bosnia-Herzegovina, (no symbol available, no subcurrency);

D

Croatia, HrD (no subcurrency in use);
Iraq, 1ID=1,000 fils;
Jordan, 1JD=1,000 fils;
Kuwait, 1 KD=1,000 fils;
Libya, 1LD=100 dirhams;
Tunisia, 1D=1,000 fils;
Yugoslavia, Yun (no subcurrency in use).

direct foreign investment (DFI)

(economics) Investment that is made to acquire a lasting interest in an enterprise operating in an economy other than that of the investor.

(U.S.) In the United States, direct investment is defined for statistical purposes as the ownership or control, directly or indirectly, by one person of 10 percent of more of the voting securities of an incorporated business enterprise, or an equivalent interest in an unincorporated business enterprise. Direct investment transactions are not limited to transactions in voting securities. The percentage ownership of voting securities is used to determine if direct investment exists, but once it is determined that it does, all parent-affiliate transactions, including those not involving voting securities, are recorded under direct investment. *See* affiliate; affiliated foreign group; foreign direct investment in the United States.

direct store delivery (DSD)

(logistics) A logistics strategy where products sold in large volume on a regular basis are shipped directly from the producer or manufacturer to a store, eliminating the store's need to warehouse and handle the product in its own facilities. When store stocks fall below a prescribed level, orders are placed electronically either through an automated inventory system or manually and then are delivered directly to the store location. In DSD the producer or manufacturer handles both warehousing and delivery on a just-in-time delivery basis. Large volume products like beer or bread that are bulky and/or heavy are best candidates for DSD.

dirham

The currency of:
Morocco, 1DH=100 centimes;
United Arab Emirates, 1Dh (or 1UD)=1,000 fils.

dirty floating

See floating.

discharge

(shipping) The unloading of passengers or cargo from a vessel, vehicle or aircraft.

disclosure meeting

(U.S.) An informal meeting at which the International Trade Administration (ITA) discloses to parties the proceeding methodology used in determining the results of an antidumping investigation or administrative review. *See* dumping.

discounting

(general) The sale at less than original price value of a commodity or monetary instrument, often for immediate payment.

(banking/letters of credit) The beneficiary under a usance/term letter of credit has the possibility of discounting his claim for immediate payment. The bank credits the beneficiary with the value of the documents, less the discount, but on an unconfirmed credit, reserves the right of recourse. (*See* recourse.) In the case of a confirmed letter of credit the discount would be without recourse.

discount/markdown

(foreign exchange) In foreign exchange, refers to a situation where currency can be bought more cheaply at a future date than for immediate delivery. For example, if US$1 buys £1.55 for delivery now, while it buys £1.6 for delivery twelve months hence, then the pound sterling is said to be at a discount against the U.S. dollar.

discount rate

(banking) (a) Annualized rate of discount applied to debt securities issued below par (e.g., U.S. Treasury bills). (b) Rate at which a central bank (Federal Reserve System in the U.S.) (re)discounts certain bills for financial institutions.

discrepancies

(banking/letters of credit) The noncompliance of documents with the terms and conditions of a letter of credit. Information (or missing information or missing documents/papers, etc.) in the documents submitted under a letter of credit, which: (1) is not consistent with its terms and conditions; (2) is inconsistent with other documents submitted; (3) does not meet the requirements of the Uniform Customs and Practice for Documentary Credits (UCPDC).

If the documents show discrepancies of any kind, the issuing bank is no longer obliged to pay and, in the case of a confirmed letter of credit, neither is the confirming bank (strict documentary compliance). *See* letter of credit; Uniform Customs and Practice.

discrimination

(shipping) The granting of preferential rates or other privileges to some shippers or receivers which are not accorded to others under practically the same conditions. In the U.S., laws regulating common carriers prohibit discrimination.

dishonor

(banking) The refusal of the maker of a promissory note to pay upon presentation of the note.

dismissal of petition

(U.S.) A determination made by the U.S. Office of Administration that an antidumping petition does not properly allege the basis on which antidumping duties may be imposed, does not contain information deemed reasonably available to the petitioner supporting the allegations, or is not filed by an appropriate interested party. *See* dumping.

dispatch

(shipping) (a) An amount paid by a vessel's operator to a charter if loading or unloading is completed in less time than stipulated in the charter agreement. (b) The release of a container to an interline carrier.

displacement of vessel

(shipping) The weight of the quantity of water displaced by a vessel without stores, bunker fuel or cargo. Displacement "loaded" is the weight of the vessel, plus cargo and stores.

disposable income

(economics) Personal income minus income taxes and other taxes paid by an individual, the balance being available for consumption or savings.

dispute settlement

(general) Resolution of a conflict, usually through a compromise between opposing claims, sometimes facilitated through the efforts of an intermediary such as an arbiter.

distrain

(law) The detention or seizure of the property of an individual or legal entity to secure that party's performance of a particular act. A court may order that property be distrained, for example, to ensure that an individual or legal entity will appear or be represented before the court at a hearing.

distribution license

(U.S.) A license that allows the holder to make multiple exports of authorized commodities to foreign consignees who are approved in advance by the U.S. Bureau of Industry and Security (formerly the U.S. Bureau of Export Administration). The procedure also authorizes approved foreign consignees to reexport among themselves and to certain approved countries. *See* Bureau of Industry and Security.

distribution requirements planning (DRP)

(logistics) A logistics strategy designed to manage a distribution network and link it with manufacturing. DRP involves planning for future stock requirements at various distribution points and determining the process by which these requirements will be met. DRP systems are based on manufacturing resources planning (MRP) technology and can span a whole logistics chain from remote warehouses to the factory floor. *See* MRP (manufacturing resources planning).

distribution service

(shipping) A service under which an airline accepts one shipment from one shipper and, after transporting it as a single shipment, separates it into a number of parts at destination and distributes them to many receivers. *See* assembly service.

distributor

An agent who sells directly for a supplier and maintains an inventory of the supplier's products.

District Export Councils

(U.S.) A voluntary auxiliary of the United States and Foreign Commercial Service (US&FCS) district offices to support export expansion activities. There are 51 DECs with 1,800 members which help with workshops and also provide counseling to less experienced exporters. *See* United States and Foreign Commercial Service.

diversion

(shipping) (a) Any change in the billing of a shipment after it has been received by the carrier at point of origin and prior to delivery at destination. (b) The diverting of a shipment of goods from the original port of destination to another port due to circumstances such as a storm at sea, breakdown of the vessel or other factors generally out of the control of the shipping line. *See also* reconsignment.

diversionary dumping

(customs) The sale of foreign products to a third country market at less than fair value where the product is further processed and shipped to another country. *See* dumping.

dobra

The currency of Sao Tomé and Principe. 1Db=100 centimos.

dock

(shipping) (a) Loading or unloading platform at an industrial location or carrier terminal. (b) The space or waterway between two piers or wharves for receiving a ship.

dock examination

(U.S. Customs) A U.S. Customs examination during which a container is opened for a thorough inspection, as opposed to a tailgate examination, which requires only a visual inspection at the exit gate. It may be necessary to devan the container in order for customs to make its inspection.

dock receipt

(shipping) A receipt issued by a warehouse supervisor or port officer certifying that goods have been received by the shipping company. The dock receipt is used to transfer accountability when an export item is moved by the domestic carrier to the port of embarkation and left with the international carrier for movement to its final destination.

documentary collection

(banking) A method of effecting payment for goods whereby the seller/exporter ships goods to the buyer, but instructs his bank to collect a certain sum from the buyer/importer in exchange for the transfer of title, shipping and other documentation enabling buyer/importer to take possession of the goods. The two types of documentary collection are:

(a) **Documents against Payment (D/P)** where the bank releases the documents to the buyer/importer only against a cash payment in a prescribed currency; and

(b) **Documents against Acceptance (D/A)** where the bank releases the documents to the buyer/importer against acceptance of a bill of exchange (draft) guaranteeing payment at a later date.

In documentary collections, banks act in a fiduciary capacity and make every effort to ensure that payment is received, but are liable only for the correct execution of the collection instructions, and do not make any commitment to pay the seller/exporter themselves.

Documentary collections are subject to the Uniform Rules of Collections, Brochure No. 322, revised 1978, of the International Chamber of Commerce (ICC) in Paris.

See Uniform Rules for Collections; International Chamber of Commerce.

documentary credit
documentary letter of credit

(banking) The formal terminology for letter of credit. *See* letter of credit.

documentary instructions

(banking) The formal list and description of documents (primarily shipping documents) a buyer requires of the seller, especially in a documentary letter of credit. *See* documentation; letter of credit.

documentation

(general) All or any of the financial and commercial documents relating to a transaction.

Documents in an international trade transaction may include commercial invoice, consular invoice, customs invoice, certificate of origin, bill of lading, inspection certificates, bills of exchange and others.

(banking) The documents required for a letter of credit or documentary collection (documents against payment or documents against acceptance) transaction. *See* letter of credit; documentary collection.

(customs) The documents required by the customs authority of a country to effect entry of merchandise into the country. *See* entry.

(shipping) The function of receiving, matching, reviewing, and preparing all the paperwork necessary to effect the shipment of cargo. This includes bills of lading, dock receipts, export declarations, manifests, etc.

documents against acceptance (D/A)

See documentary collection.

documents against payment (D/P)

See documentary collection.

dollar

The currency of:
American Samoa (uses U.S. dollar)
Anguilla, 1EC$=100 cents;
Antigua and Barbuda, 1EC$=100 cents;
Australia, 1$A=100 cents;
Bahamas, 1B$=100 cents;
Barbados, 1Bds$=100 cents;
Belize, 1Bz$=100 cents;
Bermuda, 1Ber$=100 cents;
British Virgin Islands (uses U.S. dollar);
Brunei, 1B$=100 cents;
Canada, 1Can$=100 cents;
Cayman Islands, 1CI$=100 cents;
Dominica, 1EC$-100 cents;
Fiji, 1F$=100 cents;
Grenada, 1EC$=100 cents;
Guam (uses U.S. dollar);
Guyana, 1G$=100 cents;
Hong Kong, 1HK$=100 cents;
Jamaica, 1J$=100 cents;
Kiribati (uses Australian dollar);
Liberia, 1$=100 cents;
Montserrat, 1EC$=100 cents;
Nauru (uses Australian dollar);
New Zealand, 1$NZ=100 cents;
Puerto Rico (uses U.S. dollar);
St. Christopher, 1EC$=100 cents;
St. Kitts-Nevis, 1EC$=100 cents;
St. Lucia, 1EC$=100 cents;
St. Vincent and the Grenadines, 1EC$=100 cents;
Singapore, 1S$=100 cents;
Solomon Islands, 1SI$=100 cents;
Taiwan, 1NT$=100 cents;
Trinidad and Tobago, 1TT$=100 cents;
Turks and Caicos Islands (uses U.S. dollar);
Tuvalu (uses Australian dollar);
United States, 1US$=100 cents;
Virgin Islands, U.S. & British (use U.S. dollar);
Zimbabwe, 1Z$=100 cents.

dolly

(shipping) A piece of equipment with wheels used to move containers, pallets or freight with or without the aid of a tractor.

domestic exports

(U.S.) Exports of commodities which are grown, produced, or manufactured in the United States, and commodities of foreign origin which have been changed in the United States, including U.S. foreign trade zones, from the form in which they were imported, or which have been enhanced in value by further manufacture in the United States.

domestic international sales corporation (DISC)

(U.S.) A special U.S. corporation authorized by the U.S. Revenue Act of 1971, as amended by the Tax Reform Act of 1984, to borrow from the U.S. Treasury at the average one-year Treasury bill interest rate to the extent of income tax liable on 94 percent of its annual corporate income. To qualify, the corporation must derive 95 percent of its income from U.S. exports; also, at least 95 percent of its gross assets, such as working capital, inventories, building and equipment, must be export-related. Such a corporation can buy and sell independently, or can operate as a subsidiary of another corporation. It can maintain sales and service facilities outside the

United States to promote and market its goods. DISCs can now provide a tax deferral on up to $10 million of exports so long as the funds remain in export-related investments.

domestic trunk line carrier

(U.S. logistics) The now obsolete designation for air carriers that operate between major population centers. The new classification term is major carriers.

domicile

(banking) The place where a draft or acceptance is made payable. *See* bill of exchange.

dong

The currency of Vietnam. 1D=100 xu.

door-to-door

(shipping) Shipping service from shipper's door to consignee's door. Originating carrier spots (places) empty container at shipper's facility at carrier's expense for loading by and at expense of shipper. The delivering carrier spots the loaded container at consignee's facility at carrier's expense for unloading by and at expense of consignee.

double bottoms

(trucking) The combination of a tractor pulling two trailers, in tandem connected by a converter dolly. *See* tractor, trailer.

double-column tariff

(customs) An import tariff schedule listing two rates. The rates in one column are for products imported from preferred trading partner countries, while the rates in the second column are for products imported from non-preferred trading countries. *See* column 1 rates; column 2 rates; Harmonized Tariff Schedules of the United States.

downstream dumping

(customs) The sale of products by a manufacturer below cost to a secondary producer in its domestic market where the product is then further processed and shipped to another country. *See* dumping.

D/P

See documentary collection.

drachma

The currency of Greece. 1Dr=100 lepta.

draft; draft bill of exchange

See bill of exchange.

draft or draught

(shipping) The vertical distance between the waterline and the bottom of the keel of a vessel. The draft of a vessel determines the minimum depth of water in a channel or waterway required for the vessel to travel safely. *See also* plimsoll mark.

drawback—refund of duties

(U.S. Customs) The refund of all or part of customs duties, or domestic tax paid on imported merchandise which was subsequently either manufactured into a different article or reexported.

The purpose of drawback is to enable a domestic manufacturer to compete in foreign markets without the handicap of including in his costs, and consequently in his sales price, the duty paid on imported raw materials or merchandise used in the subsequent manufacture of the exported goods.

There are several types of drawback:

(a) **Direct identification drawback** provides a refund of duties paid on imported merchandise that is partially or totally used in the manufacture of an exported article. Identification of the imported merchandise from import to export is required by proper record-keeping procedures. The imported merchandise must be used in the manufacturing process and exported within 5 years from date of importation of merchandise.

(b) **Substitution drawback** provides for a refund of duties paid on designated imported merchandise upon exportation of articles manufactured or produced with use of substituted domestic or imported merchandise that is of the same kind or quality as the designated imported merchandise. Same kind and quality means merchandise that is interchangeable in a specific manufacturing process. The imported materials must be used in a manufacturing process within 3 years after receipt by manufacturer, the domestic material of same kind and quality as imported materials must be used in manufacturing process within 3 years of receipt of the imported material and the exported products must be manufactured within 3 years after receipt of imported material by manufacturer, and exported within 5 years of date of importation of designated material.

(c) **Rejected merchandise drawback** is a 99 percent refund of duties paid on imported merchandise found not to conform to sample or specification, or shipped without the consent of the consignee, if returned to Customs custody within 90 days of its original Customs release (unless an extension is granted) for examination and exportation under Customs supervision.

Questions regarding the legal aspects of drawback should be addressed to: Chief, Drawback Unit, Office of Field Operations, U.S. Customs Service, 1300 Pennsylvania Avenue, NW, Washington, DC 20229 USA; Tel: [1] (202) 927-0100; Web: www.customs.ustreas.gov.

drawback system

(U.S. Customs) A part of U.S. Customs' Automated Commercial System, provides the means for processing and tracking of drawback claims. *See* Automated Commercial System; drawback.

drawee

(banking) The individual or firm on whom a draft is drawn and who owes the indicated amount. In a documentary collection, the drawee is the buyer. *See* drawer; bill of exchange.

drawer

(banking) The individual or firm that issues or signs a draft and thus stands to receive payment of the indicated amount from the drawee. In a documentary collection, the drawer is the seller. *See* drawee; bill of exchange.

dray

(shipping) A vehicle used to haul cargo or goods.

drayage

(shipping) The charge made for hauling freight or carts, drays or trucks.

driving-time regulations

(U.S. trucking) U.S. Department of Transportation (U.S. DOT) rules that limit the number of consecutive daily and weekly hours that a driver can operate a motor vehicle in interstate commerce. Details of other regulations can be found at the Federal Motor Carrier Safety Administration Web site at Web: www.fmcsa.dot.gov/rulesregs/fmcsrhome.htm.

droit moral

(law) Moral right doctrine, which is a European legal theory that gives artists certain rights with respect to their works, including to create, disclose, and publish a work; to withdraw it from publication; to be identified as its creator; and to prevent alteration of it without permission.

drop

(logistics) To place an unloaded or full trailer, boxcar or container at a client facility where it can be loaded or unloaded by the client.

(marketing) To deliver a bulk mailing to the postal services (or courier) for mailing. *See* drop date.

drop date

(marketing) The date a bulk mailing is handed over to the postal services (or courier). *See* drop.

dropoff

(shipping) The delivery of a shipment by a shipper to a carrier for transportation.

dropoff charge

(shipping) A charge made by a transportation company for delivery of a container.

drop shipment

(shipping) A shipment of goods from a manufacturer directly to a dealer or consumer, avoiding shipment to the wholesaler (drop shipper). The wholesaler, however, is compensated for taking the order.

dry-bulk container

(shipping) A container designed to carry any of a number of free-flowing dry solids such as grain or sand.

dry-cargo container

(shipping) Any shipping container designed to transport goods other than liquids.

dry cargo/freight

(shipping) Cargo which does not require temperature control.

dual exchange rate

(foreign exchange) The existence of two or more exchange rates for a single currency.

dual operation

(logistics/trucking) A motor carrier that is registered to operate as both a common carrier and contract carrier.

dual pricing

The selling of identical products in different markets for different prices. This often reflects dumping practices. *See* dumping.

dual-rate system

(shipping) A conference carrier pricing system that allows ocean shippers who sign exclusive shipping agreements to receive discounted services.

dumping

(customs) The sale of a commodity in a foreign market at less than fair value, usually considered to be a price lower than that at which it is sold within the exporting country or to third countries.

"Fair value" can also be the constructed value of the merchandise, which includes cost of production plus a mandatory 8 percent profit margin.

Dumping is generally recognized as an unfair trade practice because it can disrupt markets and injure producers of competitive products in an importing country.

(a) With **price-price dumping**, the foreign producer can use its sales in the high-priced market (usually the home market) to subsidize its sales in the low-priced export market. The price difference is often due to protection in the high-priced market.

(b) **Price-cost dumping** indicates that the foreign supplier has a special advantage. Sustained sales below cost are normally possible only if the sales are somehow subsidized.

(c) **Diversionary dumping** is the sale of foreign products to a third country at less than fair value where the product is further processed and shipped to another country.

(d) **Downstream dumping** is the sale of products below cost to a secondary producer in the original producer's domestic market who then further processes the product and ships it to a foreign country.

(U.S.) The U.S. Antidumping Law of 1921, as amended, considered dumping as constituting "sales at less than fair value," combined with injury, the likelihood of injury, or the prevention of the establishment of a competitive industry in the United States. The Trade Act of 1974 added a "cost of production" provision, which required that dumping determinations ignore sales in the home market of the exporting country or in third country markets at prices that are too low to "permit recovery of all costs within a reasonable period of time in the normal course of trade." The Trade Agreements Act of 1979 repealed the 1921 act, but reenacted most of its substance in Title VII of the Tariff Act of 1930. *See* countervailing duties; antidumping duties; constructed value; dumping margin; fair value.

dumping margin
(customs) The amount by which imported merchandise is sold in a country below the home market or third country price or the constructed value (that is, at less than its "fair value"). For example, if the U.S. "purchase price" of an imported article is $200 and the fair value is $220, the dumping margin is $20. This margin is expressed as a percentage of the import country price. In this example, the margin is 10 percent. *See* dumping; fair value.

dunnage
(shipping) Material placed around cargo to prevent damage or breakage by preventing movement. The material is normally furnished by the shipper and its weight is charged for in the rating of the shipment.

durable goods
(economics) Any product which is not consumed through use. Examples are automobiles, furniture, computers and machinery.

dutiable list
(customs) Items listed in a country's tariff schedule for which it charges import duty. *See* Harmonized System; Harmonized Tariff Schedule of the United States.

duty
(customs) A tax levied by a government on the import, export or consumption of goods. Usually a tax imposed on imports by the customs authority of a country. Duties are generally based on the value of the goods (ad valorem duties), some other factors such as weight or quantity (specific duties), or a combination of value and other factors (compound duties). *See* ad valorem; specific rate of duty; compound rate of duty.
(U.S. Customs) All goods imported into the United States are subject to duty or duty-free entry in accordance with their classification under the applicable items in the Harmonized Tariff Schedule of the United States (HTS or HTSUS). An annotated, loose-leaf edition of the HTS may be purchased from the Superintendent of Documents, U.S. Government Printing Office, Washington, DC 20402 USA; Tel: [1] (202) 512-1800.
Note that duty rates are subject to the classification of goods by Customs. Articles that appear to be similar may have significantly different rates of duty. *See* classification.
Note also that the actual duty paid is also determined by how Customs values the merchandise. *See* Harmonized Tariff Schedule; valuation.

duty drawback
See drawback.

E

easement
(law) A right to use another person's property. A property owner who, to enter and exit the property, is given a right to cross another person's adjoining property holds an easement. The right to use an easement is a servitude against the property burdened. *See* servitude.

East-South trade
(economics) Trade between developing countries (South) with non-market economies (East).

East-West trade
(economics) Trade between countries with developed market economies (West) and countries with nonmarket economies (East).

ECB
See European Central Bank.

Economic Bulletin Board (EBB)
(U.S.) The EBB, which was a personal computer-based economic bulletin board operated by the U.S. Department of Commerce, has been replaced by services available through the Department's fee-based STAT-USA/Internet service at Web: www.stat-usa.gov or at [1] (800) STAT-USA. *See* STAT-USA.

Economic Community of West African States (ECOWAS)
Established in May 1975 by the Treaty of Lagos, the ECOWAS brought together 16 West African countries in an economic association aimed at creating a full customs union (not yet achieved). Members include: Benin, Burkina Faso, Cape Verde, Cote d'Ivoire, Gambia, Ghana, Guinea, Guinea-Bissau, Liberia, Mali, Mauritania, Niger, Nigeria, Senegal, Sierra Leone, and Togo. Contact at: 60 Yakubu Gowon Crescent; Asokoro District P.M.B.; 401 Abuja, Nigeria; Tel: [234] (9) 31 47 647-9; Fax: [234] (9) 31 43 005, 31 47 646; E-mail: info@ecowasmail.net; Web: www.ecowas.int.

economic officers
(U.S.) Embassy officials who analyze and report on macroeconomic trends and trade policies and their implications for U.S. policies and programs. Economic officers represent U.S. interests and arrange and participate in economic and commercial negotiations. *See* commercial officers; Foreign Service.

economic order quantity (EOQ)
(logistics) The optimum order size that achieves the best possible balance between meeting customer needs and minimizing ordering and inventory holding costs.

economy of scale

(economics) The decrease in unit cost as a result of increasing production so that fixed costs may be spread out over a greater number of units produced.

ecu or ECU

See European Currency Unit.

Edge Act corporations

(banking) Banks that are subsidiaries either to bank holding companies or other banks established to engage in foreign business transactions.

EDI

(logistics/computers) Acronym for Electronic Data Interchange. (a) The transfer of structured data, by agreed message standards, from one computer application to another by electronic means and with a minimum of human intervention. (b) The electronic exchange of documents between businesses and organizations, or between businesses and government agencies.

Documents routinely sent by EDI include purchase orders, commercial invoices, inquiries, price sheets, shipping documents, test results, payment documents and compliance documents for government agencies. The trend is for more and more documentation to be sent by EDI. For example, a number of government agencies worldwide, including import and export authorities, now require that compliance documents be sent exclusively by EDI. The key issue in EDI today relates to establishing international and industry-specific standards for document transmittal. *See* UN/EDIFACT, American National Standards Organization; International Standards Organization.

EDIFACT

See UN/EDIFACT.

effective exchange rate

(banking/foreign exchange) Any spot exchange rate actually paid or received by the public, including any taxes or subsidies on the exchange transaction as well as any applicable banking commissions.

efficient consumer response (ECR)

(logistics) A demand-driven stock replenishment system that links point-of-sale data with all points in the logistics chain for the purpose of satisfying customer demand quickly, efficiently and at least cost.

Electronic Data Interchange

See EDI.

Electronic Data Interchange for Administration, Commerce and Transportation

See UN/EDIFACT

electronic funds transfer (EFT)

(banking) System of transferring funds from one account to another by electronic impulses rather than transfer of paper (such as a check).

embargo

A prohibition upon exports or imports, either with respect to specific products or specific countries. Historically, embargoes have been ordered most frequently in time of war, but they may also be applied for political, economic or sanitary purposes. Embargoes imposed against an individual country by the United Nations—or a group of nations—in an effort to influence its conduct or its policies are sometimes called "sanctions." *See also* sanction.

emergency currency adjustment factor (ECAF)

(logistics) A freight surcharge or adjustment factor imposed by an international carrier to compensate for sustained or rapid fluctuations in foreign currency exchange rates. The ECAF is charged as a percentage of the published rate. *See* currency adjustment factor.

emphyteusis

(law) A tenant's right to enjoy property owned by another individual or legal entity for a lengthy time and for rent as if the tenant owned it. The tenant may, and is usually expected to, improve the property. The tenant may also demise, assign, or otherwise transfer his or her interest in the property, but the tenant must preserve the property from destruction.

enabling clause

(WTO) A part of the World Trade Organization (WTO) framework which permits developed country members to give more favorable treatment to developing countries and special treatment to the least developed countries, notwithstanding most-favored-nation provisions.

endorsement

(banking/law) (In U.K., indorsement) The act of a person who is the holder of a negotiable instrument in signing his or her name on the back of that instrument, thereby transferring title or ownership. An endorsement may be made in favor of another individual or legal entity, resulting in a transfer of the property to that other individual or legal entity.

(a) An **endorsement in blank** is the writing of only the endorser's name on the negotiable instrument without designating another person to whom the endorsement is made, and with the implied understanding that the instrument is payable to the bearer.

(b) A **collection endorsement** is one that restricts payment of the endorsed instrument to purposes of deposit or collection.

(c) A **conditional endorsement** is one that limits the time at which the instrument can be paid or further transferred or that requires the occurrence of an event before the instrument is payable.

(d) A **restrictive endorsement** is one that directs a specific payment of the instrument, such as for deposit or collection only, and that precludes any other transfer of it.

Enhanced Proliferation Control Initiative (EPCI)

(U.S.) A series of measures to tighten export controls on goods and technologies useful in the production of chemical and missile weapons systems. EPCI allows the U.S. Department of Commerce greater authority to deny exports of low-level goods and technologies to nations of proliferation concern. *See* U.S. Department of Commerce.

en route

(shipping) In transit (referring to goods, passengers or vessel).

Enterprise for the Americas Initiative (EAI)

The EAI, which was launched in June 1990, is intended to develop a new economic relationship of the U.S. with Latin America. The EAI has trade investment, debt, and environment aspects. With regard to trade, the EAI involves an effort to move toward free trade agreements with markets in Latin America and the Caribbean, particularly with groups of countries that have associated for purposes of trade liberalization.

To begin the process of creating a hemispheric free trade system, the U.S. seeks to enter into "framework" agreements on trade and investment with interested countries or groups of countries. These agreements set up intergovernmental councils to discuss and, where appropriate, to negotiate the removal of trade and investment barriers.

enterprise resource planning

See ERP.

entrepôt

(shipping) An intermediary storage facility where goods are kept temporarily for distribution within a country or for reexport.

entrepôt trade

The import and export of goods without the further processing of the goods. Usually refers to a country, locale or business that buys and sells (imports and exports) as a middleman.

entry

(customs) A statement of the kinds, quantities and values of goods imported together with duties due, if any, and declared before a customs officer or other designated officer.

(U.S. Customs) The process of, and documentation required for securing the release of imported merchandise from Customs.

See also entry for consumption; entry for warehouse; mail entry; entry documents.

entry documents

(customs) The documents required to secure the release of imported merchandise.

(U.S Customs) Within five working days of the date of arrival of a shipment at a U.S. port of entry, entry documents must be filed at a location specified by the district/area director, unless an extension is granted. These documents consist of:

(1) Entry Manifest, Customs Form 7533; or Application and Special Permit for Immediate Delivery, Customs Form 3461, or other form of merchandise release required by the district director.

(2) Evidence of right to make entry.

(3) Commercial invoice or a pro-forma invoice when the commercial invoice cannot be produced.

(4) Packing lists if appropriate.

(5) Other documents necessary to determine merchandise admissibility.

If the goods are to be released from Customs custody on entry documents, an entry summary for consumption must be filed and estimated duties deposited at the port of entry within 10 working days of the time the goods are entered and released. *See* entry.

entry for consumption

(U.S. Customs) The process of effecting entry of goods into the United States for use in the United States. The entry of merchandise is a two-part process consisting of: (1) filing the documents necessary to determine whether merchandise may be released from Customs custody and (2) filing the documents which contain information for duty assessment and statistical purposes. In certain instances, such as the entry of merchandise subject to quotas, all documents must be filed and accepted by Customs prior to the release of the goods. *See* entry; entry documents.

entry for warehouse

(U.S. Customs) A type of U.S. Customs entry where the release of goods (and payment of duty) is postponed by having them placed in a Customs bonded warehouse, where they may remain for up to five years from the date of importation. At any time during that period the goods may be reexported without the payment of duty, or they may be withdrawn for consumption upon the payment of duty at the rate of duty in effect on the date of withdrawal. If the goods are destroyed under Customs' supervision, no duty is payable. *See* entry; customs bonded warehouse; entry for consumption.

entry summary selectivity system

(U.S. Customs) A part of U.S. Customs' Automated Commercial System, provides an automated review of entry data to determine whether team or routine review of entry is required. Selectivity criteria include an assessment of risk by importer, tariff number, country of origin, manufacturer, and value. Summaries with Census warnings, as well as quota, antidumping and countervailing duty entry summaries are selected for team review. A random sample of routine review summaries is also automatically selected for team review. *See* Automated Commercial System.

E

Environmental Protection Agency (EPA)
(U.S. government) An independent agency in the executive branch whose mandate is to control and abate pollution in the areas of air, water, solid waste, pesticides, radiation, and toxic substances. This is achieved through a combination of research, monitoring, standard setting and enforcement activities. Address: Environmental Protection Agency, 401 M St. SW, Washington, DC 20460 USA; E-mail: Public-Access@epa.gov; Web: www.epa.gov.

equalization
(shipping) A monetary allowance to the customer for picking up or delivering cargo to/from a point which is not the origin/destination shown on the bill of lading. Example, when the bill of lading destination indicates "San Francisco" and cargo is discharged in "Oakland," if the customer picks up the cargo in Oakland, he is allowed the difference in cost between the Oakland pickup to the customer's place of business and the projected actual cost if pickup had been made in San Francisco and drayed to the customer's place of business in San Francisco. This provision is covered by tariff publication.

equitable assignment
(law) An assignment that does not meet statutory requirements but that a court may nevertheless recognize and enforce in equity, that is, to do justice between the parties. If parties make an oral assignment that by statute must be in writing to be enforced, for example, a court may still enforce it as an equitable assignment, particularly if one party has acted in reliance on the assignment and would be harmed if it were not enforced. *See* assignment.

ERP
(logistics) Acronym for Enterprise Resource Planning. A resource planning methodology (and application software) that integrates all aspects of forecasting, distribution and manufacturing for the purpose of efficiently allocating resources. It is the next generation of MRP II (Manufacturing Resources Planning) and includes additional functionality such as quality process operations management and regulatory reporting. *See* MRP (Manufacturing Resources Planning).

errors & omissions excepted (E&OE)
(shipping) A notation adjacent to a signature on a document signifying that the signor is disclaiming responsibility for typographical errors or unintentional omissions.

escape clause
A provision in a bilateral or multilateral commercial agreement permitting a signatory nation to suspend tariff or other concessions (temporarily violate their obligations) when imports threaten serious harm to the producers of competitive domestic goods.
(U.S.) Section 201 of the U.S. Trade Act of 1974 requires the U.S. International Trade Commission to investigate complaints formally known as "petitions" filed by domestic industries or workers claiming that they have been injured or are threatened with injury as a consequence of rapidly rising imports, and to complete any such investigation within six months. Section 203 of the Act provides that if the Commission finds that a domestic industry has been seriously injured or threatened with serious injury, it may recommend that the president grant relief to the industry in the form of adjustment assistance or temporary import restrictions in the form of tariffs, quotas, or tariff quotas. The president must then take action pursuant to the Commission's recommendations within 60 days, but he may accept, modify or reject them, according to his assessment of the national interest. The Congress can, through majority vote in both the Senate and the House of Representatives within 90 legislative days, override a presidential decision not to implement the Commission's recommendations. The law permits the president to impose import restrictions for an initial period of five years and to extend them for a maximum additional period of three years. *See* adjustment assistance.

escudo
The currency of:
Cape Verde, 1C.V.Esc=100 centavos;
The former currency of Portugal, 1Esc=100 centavos. The new currency of Portugal is the European Union euro. 1 € = 100 cents.

estate agent
(UK) British term for real estate agent.

estimated time of arrival (ETA)
(shipping) The expected date and time of arrival of a shipment, passenger or vessel at a port, airport or terminal.

estimated time of departure (ETD)
(shipping) The estimated date and time of departure of a shipment, passenger or vessel from a port, airport or terminal.

EUR 1
(shipping) Goods transport certificate and proof of preference for export in countries and regions associated with the European Union (EU) and European Economic Area (EEA) through free trade agreements, association or preferential agreements, as long as the goods concerned are included in the tariffs preferences.

euro
The currency of the European Union. 1 € = 100 cents. As of January 1, 2002, the euro became the official currency of Austria, Belgium, Finland, France, Germany, Ireland, Italy, Luxembourg, Netherlands, Portugal and Spain.

Eurobond

(finance) A bond issued in a currency other than that of the market or markets in which it is sold. The issue is handled by an international syndicate.

Eurobond market

(finance) Euromarket for international long-term bonds (Eurobonds).

Eurocard

(banking) A European credit card developed by the West German banking system that is accepted in most western European countries.

Eurocheque

(banking) A credit card (in the form of a check) for purchasing goods in several western European countries.

Eurocredit market

(finance) Euromarket for medium-term credits.

Eurocurrency

(banking) A currency deposit held outside the country which issued the currency.

Eurodollars

(banking) U.S. dollar-denominated deposits in banks and other financial institutions outside of the United States. Originating from, but not limited to, the large quantity of U.S. dollar deposits held in western Europe.

Euromarket

(finance) An international capital market on which deposits and claims are traded in currencies outside the sovereign territory of the states in question. Euromoney markets exist in the major financial hubs of western Europe but are focused on London and Luxembourg. Exists alongside the national money markets.

European Article Number Association International (EAN)

(international standards) A not-for-profit international organization whose mission is to develop a set of standards enabling the efficient management of global, multi-industry supply chains by uniquely identifying products, shipping units, assets, locations and services. Individuals worldwide see EAN bar codes on virtually all consumer products. Worldwide consistency in identification practices enables the sharing of electronic data and streamlines the supply chain. Founded in 1977 to form a Universal Product Code (UPC), EAN aimed to facilitate the development of such standards. It seized a lead role in encouraging and propagating standards and achieved worldwide acceptance. Today 97 member organizations from 99 countries support its activities and disseminate information to about 850,000 member companies who benefit from using the EAN-UPC system. The main activities of member organizations include the allocation of unique numbers, distribution of specialized publications, training on EDI and bar coding and supplying information on the contin-

ued development of EAN standards. Contact at Web: www.ean-int.org.

European Bank for Reconstruction and Development (EBRD)

(banking) The EBRD provides assistance through direct loans. The loans are designed to facilitate the development of market-oriented economies and to promote private and entrepreneurial initiatives. EBRD began financing operations in June 1991. Address: European Bank for Reconstruction and Development, One Exchange Square, London EC2A 2JN, UK; Tel: [44] (207) 338-6000; Telex: 8812161; Fax: [44] (207) 338-6100; Web: www.ebrd.com.

European Central Bank (ECB)

(banking) The central bank of the European Union (EU), which, along with the ESCB (European System of Central Banks), sets monetary policy for EU countries in the single currency (the euro or €). Contact at Web: www.ecb.int.

European Coal and Steel Community

See European Community.

European Commission

One of the five major institutions of the European Union (EU), the Commission is responsible for ensuring the implementation of the Treaty of Rome and EU rules and obligations; submission of proposals to the Council of Ministers; execution of the Council's decisions; reconciliation of disagreements among Council members; administration of EC policies, such as the Common Agricultural Policy and coal and steel policies; taking necessary legal action against firms or member governments; and representing the EU in trade negotiations with nonmember countries. Address: European Commission, 200 rue de la Loi, 1049 Brussels, Belgium; http://europa.eu.int. *See* European Community; European Union; Treaty of Rome; common agricultural policy.

European Committee for Electrotechnical Standardization (CENELEC)

CENELEC is a nonprofit international organization under Belgian law. CENELEC seeks to harmonize electrotechnical standards published by the national member organizations and to remove technical barriers to trade that may be caused by differences in standards. CENELEC members include Austria, Belgium, Denmark, Finland, France, Germany, Greece, Iceland, Ireland, Italy, Luxembourg, Netherlands, Norway, Portugal, Spain, Sweden, Switzerland, and the United Kingdom. Address: CENELEC (Comite European Normalization Electrotechnical), rue de Stassart 35, B-1050 Brussels, Belgium; Tel: [32] (2) 519-68-71; Fax: [32] (2) 519-6819; Web: www.cenelec.org.

The National Institute of Standards and Technology of the United States Department of Commerce operates an EC Hotline, which provides information on directives and draft CEN and CENELEC standards. Tel: [1] (301) 921-4164.

European Committee for Standardization (CEN)

The CEN (Comité European de Normalisation) is an association of the national standards organizations of 18 countries of the European Community (EC) and of the European Free Trade Association (EFTA). CEN membership is open to the national standards organization of any European country which is, or is capable of becoming, a member of the EC or EFTA. CEN develops voluntary standards in building, machine tools, information technology, and in all sectors excluding the electrical ones covered by the European Committee for Electrotechnical Standardization. CEN is involved in accreditation of laboratories and certification bodies as well as quality assurance. Address: CEN (Comité European de Normalisation), rue de Stassart 36, B-1050 Brussels, Belgium; Tel: [32] (2) 550-0811; Fax: [32] (2) 550-0819; Web: www.cenorm.be.

The National Institute of Standards and Technology of the United States Department of Commerce operates an EU Hotline, which provides information on directives and draft CEN and CENELEC standards. Tel: [1] (301) 921-4164.

European Community (EC)

A popular term for the European Communities that resulted from the 1967 "Treaty of Fusion" that merged the secretariat (the "Commission") and the intergovernmental executive body (the "Council") of the older European Economic Community (EEC) with those of the European Coal and Steel Community (ECSC) and the European Atomic Energy Community EURATOM, which was established to develop nuclear fuel and power for civilian purposes. The European Community has since been renamed the European Union (EU). *See* European Union.

European Conference of Postal and Telecommunications Administrations (CEPT)

Founded in 1959 to strengthen relations between postal and telecommunications administrations and to improve their technical services. Address: CEPT Information Desk, European Radio Communications Office, Midtermolen 1, DK-2100 Copenhagen, Denmark; Tel: [45] (35) 25-03-00; Fax: [45] (35) 25-03-30; Web: www.cept.org.

European Currency Unit (ecu or ECU)

(banking/foreign exchange-obsolete) The ecu was a "basket" of specified amounts of each European Union (EU) member state currency used as an internal accounting unit. Amounts were determined according to the economic size of each EU member. The ecu was conceived by the European Economic Community (EEC), the predecessor of the European

Union. The ecu has been replaced by the European Union euro (€). *See* currency basket.

European Economic Community

See European Union.

European Free Trade Association (EFTA)

A regional trade organization established in 1960 by the Stockholm Convention, as an alternative to the Common Market. EFTA was designed to provide a free trade area for industrial products among member countries. Unlike the European Community (now the European Union), however, EFTA members did not set up a common external tariff and did not include agricultural trade.

The EFTA is headquartered in Geneva, and comprises Austria, Iceland, Norway, Sweden, and Switzerland. Finland is an Associate Member. Denmark and the United Kingdom were formerly members, but they withdrew from EFTA when they joined the European Community in 1973. Portugal, also a former member, withdrew from EFTA in 1986 when it joined the EC (now the EU).

EFTA member countries have gradually eliminated tariffs on manufactured goods originating and traded within EFTA. Agricultural products, for the most part, are not included on the EFTA schedule for internal tariff reductions. Each member country maintains its own external tariff schedule and each has concluded a trade agreement with the European Community that provides for the mutual elimination of tariffs for most manufactured goods except for a few sensitive products. As a result, the European Community and EFTA form a de facto free trade area. Contact: EFTA; 9-11, rue de Varembé; CH-1211 Geneva 20, Switzerland; Tel: [41] (22) 749 11 11; Fax: [41] (22) 733 92 91; E-mail: efta-mailbox@efta.int; Web: www.efta.int. *See* European Union.

European Investment Bank (EIB)

(banking) The EIB is an independent public institution set up by the Treaty of Rome to contribute to balanced and steady development in the European Community. The EIB provides loans and guarantees to companies and public institutions to finance regional development, structural development, and achieve cross-border objectives. The EIB has emphasized regional development and energy, with Italy, Greece, and Ireland receiving major support. Address: European Investment Bank, 100 blvd. Konrad Adenauer, L-2950 Luxembourg; Tel: [352] 43 79 01; Fax: [352] 43 77 04; Web: www.eib.org.

European Monetary System (EMS)

(banking/foreign exchange-obsolete) The former monetary system of the European Community (EC) member states (now the European Union-EU) which led to the creation of a zone of currency stability as the forerunner of the single European currency (the euro or €).

The goal of the EMS was to move Europe toward closer economic integration and avoid the disruptions in trade that resulted from fluctuations in currency exchange rates. The EMS member countries deposited gold and dollar reserves with the European Monetary Cooperation Fund in exchange for the issuance of European Currency Units (ecu). Established in 1979; all EC (now EU) members except Greece and the United Kingdom participated in the exchange rate mechanism of the EMS. Note that as of January 1, 2002, the ecu has been replaced by the euro (€).
See European Currency Unit; European Monetary Union; European Community, euro.

European option
(banking/foreign exchange) An option containing a provision to the effect that it can only be exercised on the expiry or maturity date. *See also* American option; option.

European Organization for Conformity Assessment (EOTC)
The EOTC (the organization has retained its old acronym for European Organization for Testing and Certification) was created in October 1990 by the European Community Commission under a memorandum of agreement with the European Committee for Standardization/European Committee for Electrotechnical Standardization (CEN/CENELEC) and the European Free Trade Association countries. The EOTC promotes mutual recognition of tests, test and certification procedures, and quality systems within the European private sector for product areas or characteristics not covered by European Community legislative requirements. Contact: EOTC; European Organization for Conformity Assessment; Rue d'Egmont 15; B-1000 Brussels, Belgium; Tel: [32] (2) 502-41-41; Fax: [32] (2) 502-42-39; E-mail: help-desk@eotc.be; Web: www.eotc.be.

European Patent Convention (EPC)
An agreement between European nations to centralize and standardize patent law and procedure. The EPC, which took effect in 1977, established a single "European patent" through application to the European Patent Office in Munich. Once granted, the patent matures into a bundle of individual patents—one in each member country. Address: European Patent Office, Erhardtstrasse 27, 80331 Munich, Germany; Tel: [49] (89) 2399-0; Fax: [49] (89) 2399-4465; Web: www.european-patent-office.org.

European Patent Office
See European Patent Convention.

European (style) option
See European option.

European Telecommunications Standards Institute (ETSI)
ETSI was established in March 1988 in response to the inability of the Council of European Post and Telecommunications Administration (CEPT) to keep up with the schedule of work on common European standards and specifications agreed to in the 1984 Memorandum of Understanding between CEPT and the European Community (EC). ETSI has a contractual relationship with the EC to pursue standards development for telecommunications equipment and services, and it cooperates with other European standards bodies such as the European Committee for Standardization/European Committee for Electrotechnical Standardization (CEN/CENELEC). ETSI membership includes the telecommunications administrations that constitute the CEPT as well as manufacturers, service providers, and users. Address: European Telecommunications Standards Institute (ETSI), 650 route des Lucioles, 06291 Sophia-Antipolis Cedex, France; Tel: [33] (4) 92 94 42 00; Fax: [33] (4) 93 65 47 16; E-mail: infocentre@etsi.org; Web: www.etsi.org.

European Union (EU)
A regional economic, monetary, social and political association of European states founded for the purpose of the elimination of intraregional customs duties and other internal trade barriers, the establishment of a common external tariff against other countries, the establishment of a common monetary policy and common currency, the gradual adoption of other integrating measures, including a Common Agricultural Policy and guarantees of free movement of labor and capital.
The EU was originally established by the Maastricht Treaty in 1993. The Treaty extended the previous Treaties establishing the three European Communities, i.e., the European Coal and Steel Community (ECSC), the European Atomic Energy Community (Euratom), and the European Economic Community.
The EU is the result of a process of cooperation and integration which began in 1951 between six countries (Belgium, Germany, France, Italy, Luxembourg and the Netherlands). After nearly 50 years, with four waves of accessions (1973: Denmark, Ireland and the United Kingdom; 1981: Greece; 1986: Spain and Portugal; 1995: Austria, Finland and Sweden), the EU today has fifteen Member States and is preparing for its fifth enlargement, this time toward eastern and southern Europe.
Objectives
The European Union's mission is to organize relations between the Member States and between their peoples in a coherent manner and on the basis of solidarity.
The main objectives are:
1) to promote economic and social progress (the single market was established in 1993; the single currency was launched in 1999);
2) to assert the identity of the European Union on the international scene (through European humanitarian

aid to non-EU countries, common foreign and security policy, action in international crises; common positions within international organizations);
3) to introduce European citizenship (which does not replace national citizenship but complements it and confers a number of civil and politic rights on European citizens);
4) to develop an area of freedom, security and justice (linked to the operation of the internal market and more particularly the freedom of movement of persons);
5) to maintain and build on established EU law (all the legislation adopted by the European institutions, together with the founding treaties).

Institutions
There are five institutions involved in running the European Union: the European Parliament (elected by the peoples of the Member States), the Council (representing the governments of the Member States), the Commission (the executive and the body having the right to initiate legislation), the Court of Justice (ensuring compliance with the law), and the Court of Auditors (responsible for auditing the accounts). These institutions are supported by other bodies: the Economic and Social Committee and the Committee of the Regions (advisory bodies which help to ensure that the positions of the EU's various economic and social categories and regions respectively are taken into account), the European Ombudsman (dealing with complaints from citizens concerning maladministration at European level), the European Investment Bank (EU financial institution) and the European Central Bank (responsible for monetary policy in the euro-area).
Contact: European Union, 62 rue Belliard; 1040 Brussels, Belgium; Tel: [32] (2) 233-21-11; Fax: [32] (2) 231-10-75; Web: www.europa.eu.int.

evidence of right to make entry
(U.S. Customs) Goods may be entered into the Customs territory of the United States only by the owner, purchaser, or a licensed customs broker acting on behalf of the owner or purchaser. Customs requires evidence of right to make entry as part of the entry documentation.
When the goods are consigned "to order," the bill of lading properly endorsed by the consignor may serve as evidence of the right to make entry. An air waybill may be used for merchandise arriving by air. In most instances, entry is made by a person or firm certified by the carrier bringing the goods to the port of entry and is considered the "owner" of the goods for customs purposes. For example, a customs broker with a valid power of attorney signed by the owner of a shipment may present documents to customs as evidence of right to make entry. The document issued by the carrier is known as a "carrier's certificate." In certain circumstances, entry may be made by means of a duplicate bill of lading or a shipping receipt. *See* entry.

ex ... (named point of origin)
(trade term) A term of sale where the price quoted applies only at the point of origin and the seller agrees to place the goods at the disposal of the buyer at the specified place on the date or within the period fixed. All other charges are for the account of the buyer. For a more complete definition, *see* Ex Works. *See also* Incoterms.

exaction
(law) A fee or contribution demanded or levied by a government entity or by an individual or group in a position of power. Examples of exactions can include illegal "tolls" on public roads by outlaw police and army units in Third World countries, to harbor maintenance fees and antidumping fees collected by government authorities in First World industrialized countries.

exception rate
(logistics/shipping) A deviation or exception to the published class rate for a shipment of cargo. Exception rates are often applied to unusual cargo that is difficult to transport, extremely heavy and/or bulky or that requires special handling, such as live animals, human remains, or motor vehicles. *See* class or kind (of merchandise).

excess valuation
See declared value.

exchange control(s)
(foreign exchange) The rationing of foreign currencies, bank drafts, and other monetary instruments for settling international financial obligations by countries seeking to ameliorate acute balance of payments difficulties. When such measures are imposed, importers must apply for prior authorization from the government to obtain the foreign currency required to bring in designated amounts and types of goods. Since such measures have the effect of restricting imports, they are considered nontariff barriers to trade. *See* balance of trade.

exchange rate
(foreign exchange) The price of one currency expressed in terms of another, i.e., the number of units of one currency that may be exchanged for one unit of another currency. For example, $/SFr = 1.50, means that one U.S. dollar costs 1.50 Swiss francs.
(a) In a system of **free exchange rates**, the actual exchange rate is determined by supply and demand on the foreign exchange market.
(b) In a system of **fixed exchange rates**, the exchange rate is tied to a reference (e.g., gold, US$, etc.).
Influences on exchange rates include differences between interest rates and other asset yields between countries; investor expectations about future changes in a currency's value; investors' views on the overall quantity of assets in circulation; arbitrage; and central bank exchange rate support. *See also* floating.

excise tax

A selective tax—sometimes called a consumption tax—on certain goods produced within or imported into a country. An example is a tax on the import of crude oil, or a tax on certain luxury goods.

exclusive agency

See agency.

exclusive economic zone (EEZ)

(international law) EEZ refers to the rights of coastal states to control the living and nonliving resources of the sea for 200 miles off their coasts while allowing freedom of navigation to other states beyond 12 miles, as agreed at the sixth session of the Third UN Conference on the Law of the Sea (UNCLOS). The EEZ also gives the coastal states the responsibility for managing the conservation of all natural resources within the 200-mile limit.

exclusive patronage agreements

(logistics/shipping) An agreement whereby a company agrees to ship cargo exclusively with a particular carrier and in return receives a preferred rate.

exclusive use

(logistics) Vehicles assigned by a carrier to serve the exclusive needs of a particular shipper.

exculpatory clause

(law) A contract clause by which a party is released from liability for wrongful acts committed by the other party. A seller may agree to release a buyer, for example, from liability for all or specified defects in the design, packaging, or manufacture of a product.

ex dock

(trade term) A term of sale where the buyer takes title to the goods only when they are unloaded on his/her dock. *See* Ex Works; Incoterms.

execution

(law) (a) A signature on a document. (b) A legal process for enforcing a judgment for damages, usually by seizure and sale of the debtor's personal property. If a court awards damages in a breach of contract action, for example, but the breaching party has failed to remit such sum, the party awarded damages may request the court to order seizure and sale of the breaching party's inventory or property to the extent necessary to satisfy the award.

exempt carrier

(U.S. logistics) A for-hire carrier that operates with an exemption from economic regulations.

exercise price

See strike price.

ex factory

(trade term) A term of sale where the buyer takes title to the goods when they leave the vendor's dock. *See* Ex Works; Incoterms.

exhibit

(law) (a) A document or object given or produced as evidence, often in a court of law. (b) A document that serves as an addendum to a contract.

EXIM Bank

See Export-Import Bank of the United States.

ex parte

(law) By one party or side only. An application ex parte, for example, is a request that is made by only one of the parties involved in a legal action. A hearing ex parte is a court proceeding at which the persons present represent only one side of the controversy. *See* letter of credit.

expiration date

(banking) In letter of credit transaction, the final date the seller (beneficiary of the credit) may present documents and draw a draft under the terms of the letter of credit. Also called expiry date. *See* letter of credit.

expiry day

(banking/foreign exchange) In foreign exchange options business, the last day on which an option can be exercised.

explosives

(shipping) (UN CLASS 1.) EXPLOSIVE A: Items are capable of exploding with a small spark, shock, or flame and spreading the explosion hazard to other packages. EXPLOSIVE B: Items are very rapidly combustible. EXPLOSIVE C: Items are a low hazard but may explode under high heat when many are tightly packed together. Examples: A—dynamite; B—propellants or flares; C—common fireworks. Hazards/precautions: no flares, smoking, flames, or sparks in the hazard area; may explode if dropped, heated or sparked.

export

To ship an item away from a country for sale to another country.

Export Administration Act (EAA)

(U.S. law) Authorizes the president to control exports of U.S. goods and technology to all foreign destinations, as necessary for the purpose of national security, foreign policy, and short supply.

As the basic export administration statute, the EAA is the first big revision of export control law since enactment of the Export Control Act of 1949. The EAA is not permanent legislation; it must be reauthorized—usually every three years. There have been reauthorizations of the EAA in 1982, 1985 (the Export Administration Amendments Act), and 1988 (Omnibus Amendments of 1988) which have changed provisions of the basic Act. The Export Administration Act of 1990 was pocket vetoed by the president, charging that provisions involved micromanagement.

E

Export Administration Regulations (EAR)

(U.S. law) Provides specific instructions on the use and types of export licenses required and the types of commodities and technical data under export control. The text of the regulations, as well as other government documents pertaining to the regulations, are available from the U.S. Government Printing Office's Web site at http://w3.access.gpo.gov/bxa; E-mail: gpoaccess@gpo.gov.

Export Administration Review Board (EARB)

(U.S. government) A U.S. cabinet-level export licensing dispute resolution group. The EARB was originally established in June 1970 under Executive Order 11533. Under Executive Order 12755 of March 1991, EARB membership includes the Departments of Commerce (as chair), State, Defense, and Energy, the Arms Control and Disarmament Agency and, as nonvoting members, the Joint Chiefs of Staff and the Central Intelligence Agency. The EARB is the final review body to resolve differences among agency views on the granting of an export license. Preceding EARB review are: (1) Operating Committees, and (2) the Advisory Committee on Export Policy. National Security Directive #53 requires escalation of disputes regarding an export license to the Advisory Committee on Export Policy (ACEP) not later than 100 days from the filing date of the applicant's application. Any cases not resolved at the ACEP level must be escalated to the EARB within 35 days of the date of the ACEP meeting. Cases not resolved by the EARB must be escalated to the president for resolution. Address: Export Administration Review Board, 14th and Constitution Avenue NW, Herbert Hoover Building, Room 2639, Washington, DC 20230 USA; Tel: [1] (202) 482-5863.

export broker

An individual or firm that brings together buyers and sellers for a fee but does not take part in actual sales transactions.

export commodity classification number

See export control classification number.

export control

(U.S. Customs) To exercise control over exports for statistical and strategic purposes, Customs enforces export control laws for the U.S. Department of Commerce and other federal agencies. *See* United States Customs Service.

Export Control Automated Support System (ECASS)

(U.S.) ECASS was implemented by the U.S. Department of Commerce in 1985 to automate a paper-based system. The system currently provides:

(1) electronic submission of export application forms directly by exporters;

(2) optical character recognition of applications submitted on paper;

(3) paperless workstations for all licensing officers to review the application, route it to other officers, branches, or external agencies, and to enter their final action along with riders and conditions;

(4) automated audit of all export licenses issued; and

(5) real-time management reporting on Licensing Officer workloads, average processing times, counts and times by license type, destination country, commodity code, and other data. The U.S. Department of Commerce's Bureau of Industry and Security (formerly the Bureau of Export Administration) is expanding ECASS to include export enforcement activities.

See United States Department of Commerce; Bureau of Industry and Security.

export control classification number (ECCN)

(U.S.) Every product has an export control classification number (formerly export commodity classification number) within the Commerce Control List. The ECCN consists of a five-character number that identifies categories, product groups, strategic level of control, and country groups. *See* Commerce Control List.

export credit agencies (ECAs)

Government agencies or programs providing government loans, guarantees or insurance to finance exports. In the U.S., the Export/Import Bank is the government's general purpose credit agency, while the Commodity Credit Corporation is the export credit agency for agricultural exports. *See* Export-Import Bank of the United States; Commodity Credit Corporation.

Export Credit Enhanced Leverage Program (EXCEL)

The EXCEL program was developed in 1990 by the World Bank in conjunction with a working group of the International Union of Credit and Investment Insurers (the Berne Union). The objective of EXCEL is to provide export credits at consensus rates for private sector borrowers in highly indebted countries, which would previously have been too great a risk for most agencies to cover.

export credit insurance

(insurance) Special insurance coverage for exporters to protect against commercial and political risks of making an international sale. Export credit insurance is available from insurance underwriters as well as from government agencies. *See* export credit agencies.

export declaration

(trade documentation) A document required of the exporter by the export authority of a country identifying the particulars of a specific export shipment, including the seller, buyer, goods shipped, quantities and description of the goods and other details.

(U.S. trade documentation) A document required by the U.S. Department of Treasury for the export of goods from the United States. Also known as the Shipper's Export Declaration (SED), this form includes complete particulars on an individual export shipment and is required by the U.S. Department of Commerce to control exports and act as a source document for export statistics. *See* shipper's export declaration.

Export Development Corporation (EDC)

(Canada) Canada's official export credit agency, responsible for providing export credit insurance, loans, guarantees, and other financial services to promote Canadian export trade. Address: Export Development Corporation, 151 O'Connor Street, Ottawa, ON K1A 1K3, Canada; Tel: [1] (613) 598-2500; Fax: [1] (613) 237-2690; Web: www.edc.ca.

Export Development Office (EDO)

(U.S. government) Export Development Offices (EDOs) in seven cities (Tokyo, Sydney, Seoul, Milan, London, Mexico City, and São Paulo) provide services to U.S. exporters, including market research to identify specific marketing opportunities and products with the greatest sales potential; and to organize export promotion events. EDOs are staffed by U.S. and Foreign Commercial Service officers. When not in use for trade exhibitions, EDOs with exhibit and conference facilities are made available to individual firms or associations. *See* U.S. and Foreign Commercial Service.

export draft

(banking) An unconditional order that is drawn by an exporting seller and that directs an importing buyer to pay the amount stated on the order to the seller or the seller's bank.

(a) A **sight export draft** is one that is payable when presented. (b) A **time export draft or usance** is one that is payable at a specified future date. *See* bill of exchange.

export duty

(customs) A tax imposed on exports of some nations. *See* duty; tariff.

Export Enhancement Program (EEP)

(U.S). A U.S. Department of Agriculture program that assists exporters who are shipping U.S. agricultural products to countries that subsidize agricultural products. Address: Operations Division, Export Credits, Foreign Agricultural Service, USDA, Stop 1035, 1400 Independence Ave., SW, Washington, DC 20250-1035 USA; Tel: [1] (202) 720-6211; Fax: [1] (202) 720-0938.

exporter

An individual or company that transports goods or merchandise from one country to another in the course of trade.

exporter identification number (EIN)

(U.S.) An identification number required on the Shipper's Export Declaration for all export shipments. U.S. corporations may use their federal Employer Identification Number issued by the IRS. Individuals and companies that are not incorporated may use the Social Security number of the exporter. *See* shipper's export declaration.

exporters sales price (ESP)

(U.S.) A statutory term used to refer to the United States sales prices of merchandise which is sold or likely to be sold in the United States, before or after the time of importation, by or for the account of the exporter. Certain statutory adjustments are made to permit a meaningful comparison with the foreign market value of such or similar merchandise, e.g., import duties, United States selling and administrative expenses, and freight are deducted from the United States price.

Export-Import Bank of the United States (Eximbank)

(U.S.) A public corporation created by executive order of the president in 1934 and given a statutory basis in 1945. The Bank makes guarantees and insures loans to help finance U.S. exports, particularly for equipment to be used in capital improvement projects. The Bank also provides short-term insurance for both commercial and political risks, either directly or in cooperation with U.S. commercial banks.

Eximbank offers four major export finance support programs: loans, guarantees, working capital guarantees, and insurance. Eximbank undertakes some of the risk associated with financing the production and sale of U.S.-made goods; provides financing to overseas customers for U.S. goods when lenders are not prepared to finance the transactions; and enhances a U.S. exporter's ability to match foreign government subsidies by helping lenders meet lower rates, or by giving financing incentives directly to foreign buyers. The Export-Import Bank will consider aiding in the export financing of U.S. goods and services when there is a reasonable assurance of repayment. Eximbank is not to compete with private financing, but to supplement it when adequate funds are not available in the private sector. Address: Export-Import Bank of the United States, 811 Vermont Avenue NW, Washington, DC 20571 USA; Tel: [1] (800) 565-3946; Fax: [1] (202) 565-3380; Web: www.exim.gov.

Export Legal Assistance Network (ELAN)

(U.S.) A nationwide group of attorneys with experience in international trade who provide free initial consultations to small businesses on export-related matters. This service is available through the U.S. Small Business Administration (SBA). For the address and phone number of your nearest Small Business Administration District Office, call [1] (800) U-

E

ASK-SBA. Address: National Coordinator Judd Kessler, Porter, Wright, Morris, & Arthur, 1667 K Street NW, Suite 1100, Washington, DC 20006-1605 USA; Tel: [1] (202) 778-3080; Fax: [1] (202) 778-3063; Web: www.fita.org/elan/.

export license

A document prepared by a government authority, granting the right to export a specified quantity of a commodity to a specified country. This document may be required in some countries for most or all exports and in other countries only under special circumstances.

(U.S.) A document issued by the U.S. government authorizing the export of commodities for which written export authorization is required by law. For more information on export licensing in general, call Exporter Assistance at [1] (202) 482-4811. Address: Bureau of Industry and Security (formerly the Bureau of Export Administration), U.S. Department of Commerce, 14th St. and Constitution Ave. NW, Washington, DC 20230 USA; Tel: [1] (202) 482-4811; Fax: [1] (202) 482-3617; Web: www.bxa.doc.gov.

Export License Application and Information Network (ELAIN)

(U.S.) ELAIN is a Bureau of Industry and Security (formerly the Bureau of Export Administration) 24-hour on-line service which allows exporters to submit license applications. Contact: Bureau of Industry and Security, 14th and Constitution Ave. NW, Washington, DC 20230; Tel: [1] (202) 482-4811; Web: www.bxa.doc.gov.

export management company

A private firm that serves as the export department for several manufacturers, soliciting and transacting export business on behalf of its clients in return for a commission, salary, or retainer plus commission.

export merchant

A company that buys products directly from manufacturers, then packages and marks the merchandise for resale under its own name.

export processing zone (EPZ)

Industrial parks designated by a government to provide tax and other incentives to export firms.

export quotas

Specific restrictions or ceilings imposed by an exporting country on the value or volume of certain exports, designed to protect domestic producers and consumers from temporary shortages of the materials or goods affected, or to bolster their prices in world markets. Some International Commodity Agreements explicitly indicate when producers should apply such restraints. Export quotas are also often applied in orderly marketing agreements and voluntary restraint agreements, and to promote domestic processing of raw materials in countries that produce them. *See* international commodity agreement; orderly marketing agreements; voluntary restraint agreements.

export restraint agreements

See voluntary restraint agreements.

export restraints

Quantitative restrictions imposed by exporting countries to limit exports to specified foreign markets, usually pursuant to a formal or informal agreement concluded at the request of the importing countries. *See* voluntary restraint agreements.

export revolving line of credit (ERLC)

(U.S.) Financial assistance provided by the U.S. Small Business Administration (SBA) to exporters of U.S. products. The ERLC guarantees loans to U.S. firms to help bridge the working capital gap between the time inventory and production costs are disbursed until payment is received from a foreign buyer. SBA guarantees 85 percent of the ERLC subject to a $750,000 guarantee limit. The ERLC is granted on the likelihood of a company satisfactorily completing its export transaction. The guarantee covers default by the exporter, but does not cover default by a foreign buyer; failure on the buyer's side is expected to be covered by letters of credit or export credit insurance.

Under the SBA's ERLC program, any number of withdrawals and repayments can be made as long as the dollar limit on the line of credit is not exceeded and disbursements are made within the stated maturity period (not more than 18 months). Proceeds can be used only to finance labor and materials needed for manufacturing, to purchase inventory to meet an export order, and to penetrate or develop foreign markets. Examples of eligible expenses for developing foreign markets include professional export marketing advice or services, foreign business travel, and trade show participation. Under the ERLC program, funds may not be used to purchase fixed assets. Contact: SBA Answer Desk, 200 North College Street, Suite A-2015, Charlotte, NC 28202 USA; Tel: [1] (800) 827-5722; Web: www.sba.gov. *See also* letter of credit.

export service

(shipping) Shipping lines, airlines and freight forwarders perform, at the request of shippers, many services relating to the transfer, storage, and documentation of freight destined for export. The same is true of imports. Some carriers have a tariff on such traffic, which sets forth a rate covering the air transportation from airport of origin to seaport and all relevant transfer and documentation procedures. On freight arriving in the United States, via an ocean vessel and having a subsequent movement by air, some airlines have a similar tariff program known as "Import Service."

export statistics
(U.S.) Export statistics measure the total physical quantity or value of merchandise (except for shipments to U.S. military forces overseas) moving out of the United States to foreign countries, whether such merchandise is exported from within the U.S. Customs territory or from a U.S. Customs bonded warehouse or a U.S. Foreign Trade Zone.

export subsidies
Government payments, economic inducements or other financially quantifiable benefits provided to domestic producers or exporters contingent on the export of their goods or services.
(WTO) The World Trade Organization (WTO) recognizes that subsidies in general, and especially export subsidies, distort normal commercial activities and hinder the achievement of WTO objectives. An Agreement on Subsidies and Countervailing Measures rules on export subsidies and provides for an outright prohibition of export subsidies by developed countries for manufactured and semi-manufactured products. Under certain conditions, the Agreement allows developing countries to use export subsidies on manufactured and semi-manufactured products, and on primary products as well, provided that the subsidies do not result in more than an equitable share of world exports of the product for the country. *See also* subsidy.

export trading company
A corporation or other business unit organized and operated principally for the purpose of exporting goods and services, or of providing export related services to other companies. An ETC can be owned by foreigners and can import, barter, and arrange sales between third countries, as well as export.
(U.S.) The Export Trading Company Act of 1982 exempts authorized trading companies from certain provisions of U.S. antitrust laws. *See* Export Trading Company Act.

Export Trading Company Act
(U.S. law) The Export Trading Company Act of 1982 initiates the Export Trade Certificate of Review program that provides antitrust preclearance for export activities; permits bankers' banks and bank holding companies to invest in Export Trading Companies; and establishes a Contact Facilitation Service within the U.S. Department of Commerce designed to facilitate contact between firms that produce exportable goods and services and firms that provide export trade services.

express agency
See agency.

expropriation
(economics/law) The forcible acquisition, usually for compensation, of private property by a sovereign government. For example, a national government might expropriate real estate from private owners in order to construct a highway or government building. *See* nationalization.

ex quay
See Delivered Ex Quay; Incoterms.

ex ship
See Delivered Ex Ship; Incoterms.

external value
(economics/foreign exchange) The purchasing power of a currency abroad, converted using the exchange rate.

extradition
The surrender by one country of an alleged criminal to the authorities of the country that has jurisdiction to try the charge. Extradition usually occurs under the provisions of a treaty between the two countries.

ex warehouse
See Ex Works; Incoterms.

Ex Works (...named place) (EXW)
(Incoterms 2000) An international trade term of sale in which, for the quoted price, the seller/exporter/manufacturer merely makes the goods available to the buyer at the seller's "named place" of business. This trade term places the greatest responsibility on the buyer and minimum obligations on the seller.
The seller does not clear the goods for export and does not load the goods onto a truck or other transport vehicle at the named place of departure. The parties to the transaction, however, may stipulate that the seller be responsible for the costs and risks of loading the goods onto a transport vehicle. Such a stipulation must be made within the contract of sale. If the buyer cannot handle export formalities the Ex Works term should not be used. In such a case Free Carrier (FCA) is recommended.
The Ex Works term is often used when making an initial quotation for the sale of goods. It represents the cost of the goods without any other costs included. *See* Guide to Incoterms 2000 Appendix.

F

facilitation

Any of a number of programs designed to expedite the flow of international commerce through modernizing and simplifying customs procedures, duty collection, and other procedures to which international cargo and passengers are subject. Examples of progress in facilitation include the elimination of certain export declaration requirements, more expeditious release of cargo from customs, and clearance of cargo at point of origin.

facsimile (fax)

(a) An office machine used to transmit a copy of a document (including graphic images) via telephone lines. (b) The physical paper output of a fax machine which is a copy of the document transmitted. Facsimile use has grown significantly in the past few years. Note that in some countries some facsimile documents are not considered legal documents.

factor

(a) An agent who receives merchandise under a consignment or bailment contract, who sells it for the principal or in the factor's own name, and who is paid a commission for each sale. (b) A firm, such as a finance company, that purchases another company's receivables at a discount and processes and collects the remaining account balances.

factorage

The commission or other compensation paid to a factor.

factoring

The discounting of an account receivable in order to receive immediate payment. In international trade factoring is the discounting of a foreign account receivable that does not involve a draft. The exporter transfers title to its foreign accounts receivable to a factoring house (an organization that specializes in the financing of accounts receivable) for cash at a discount from the face value. Factoring is often done without recourse to the exporter. Factoring of foreign accounts receivable is less common than with domestic receivables.

factoring houses

Certain companies which purchase domestic or foreign accounts receivables (e.g., the as yet unpaid invoices to domestic and foreign buyers) at a discounted price, usually about 2 to 4 percent less than their face value. *See* factor; factoring.

factor's lien

The right of a factor to retain the principal's merchandise until the factor receives full compensation from the principal.

fair trade

The social, economic and political theory that individuals and societies in producer nations should 1) gain a greater share of the final market value of the raw materials and products they produce, 2) have better working conditions and 3) benefit from better environmental polices.

fair value

(U.S. Customs) The reference against which U.S. purchase prices of imported merchandise are compared during an antidumping investigation. Generally expressed as the weighted average of the exporter's domestic market prices, or prices of exports to third countries during the period of investigation.

In some cases fair value is the constructed value. Constructed value is used if there are no, or virtually no, home market or third country sales, or if the number of such sales made at prices below the cost of production is so great that remaining sales above the cost of production provide an inadequate basis for comparison. *See* dumping; constructed value.

FAK

(shipping) Freight all kinds. Usually refers to consolidated cargo.

family corporation

See closely held corporation.

FAS

See Free Alongside Ship; Incoterms.

fast track

(U.S.) Fast track procedures for approval of trade agreements were included by the U.S. Congress in trade legislation in 1974, in 1979, and again in the 1988 Trade Act. Fast track provides two guarantees essential to the successful negotiation of trade agreements: (1) a vote on implementing legislation within a fixed period of time, and (2) a vote, yes or no, with no amendments to that legislation.

Provisions in the Omnibus Trade and Competitiveness Act of 1988 include that the foreign country request negotiation of a Free Trade Agreement (FTA) and that the president give the Congress a 60-legislative-day notice of intent to negotiate an FTA. During the 60-legislative-day period, either committee can disapprove fast track authority by a majority vote. Disapproval would likely end the possibility of FTA negotiations. The 60-legislative-days can translate into five to ten months of calendar time, depending on the congressional schedule. Formal negotiations would begin following this 60-day congressional consideration period.

fathom

(measurement) A unit of length equal to six feet. Used primarily to measure the depth of water.

fax

See facsimile.

Federal Aviation Administration (FAA)

(U.S.) Created under the Federal Aviation Act of 1958 as the Federal Aviation Agency and charged with the responsibility of promulgating operational standards and procedures for all classes of aviation in the United States. With the creation of the cabinet level Department of Transportation in 1966, FAA became a unit within the new Department and received the new designation Federal Aviation Administration. The FAA Administrator, however, continues to be a presidential appointee and the FAA remains a separate entity with most of its former functions. In the field of air cargo FAA promulgates certain stress standards which must be met in the tiedown of cargo in flight. For information: Federal Aviation Administration, 800 Independence Avenue, Washington, DC 20591 USA; Tel: [1] (202) 366-4000; Web: www.faa.gov.

federally chartered bank

(U.S. banking) In the United States, a bank that has been chartered by the comptroller of currency, that belongs to the Federal Reserve System and meets the requirements for a national bank as defined under the National Bank Act. In the U.S. only federally and state chartered banks and other authorized institutions may receive deposits.

Federal Maritime Commission (FMC)

(U.S.) The U.S. federal agency responsible for overseeing rates and practices of ocean carriers who handle cargo to or from U.S. ports. Address: Federal Maritime Commission, 800 North Capitol St. NW, Washington, DC 20573-0001 USA; Tel: [1] (202) 523-5911; Web: www.fmc.gov.

Federal Reserve System

(U.S. banking) The central banking system of the U.S. It has twelve Federal Reserve Banks divided up by geographical regions. The Board of Governors supervises the operations of the regional banks and coordinates monetary policy through its Federal Open Market Committee.

Federal Trade Commission (FTC)

(U.S.) Plays a key role in ensuring that consumers are protected against unfair methods of competition in the marketplace. Address: Federal Trade Commission, Pennsylvania Avenue and 6th Street NW, Washington, DC 20580 USA; Tel: [1] (202) 326-2222; Web: www.ftc.gov.

feeder vessel

(shipping) A vessel used to connect with a line vessel to service a port which is not served directly by the line vessel. *See* line haul vessel.

FEU

(shipping) Forty foot equivalent units. Two 20 ft. containers equal one FEU.

field warehouse

(logistics/finance) A warehouse operated by a third-party warehouse firm, but located on the property or premises of the owner of the goods. Field warehouses are used in special financing agreements where inventory pledged as collateral is physically separated from a company's other inventories and placed under the custody, control and supervision of a third-party warehouse firm.

fieri facias writ

(law) A judicial order issued to "cause to be done," which generally orders an officer of law or another authorized person to satisfy a judgment by seizure and sale of a debtor's property. *See* execution.

fill rate

(logistics) The percentage of order items that are picked and readied for shipment in a specified amount of time.

final determination

(U.S.) In antidumping investigations a final determination is made after the investigation of sales at "less than fair value" and the receipt of comments from interested parties. This determination usually is made within 75 days after the date a preliminary determination is made. However, if the preliminary determination was affirmative, the exporters who account for a significant proportion of the merchandise under consideration may request, in writing, a postponement of this determination. If the preliminary determination was negative, the petitioner may likewise request a postponement. In neither case can this postponement be more than 135 days after the date of the preliminary determination. If the final determination is affirmative and follows a negative preliminary determination, the matter is referred to the International Trade Commission (ITC) for a determination of the injury caused or threatened by the sales at less than fair value. (Had the preliminary determination been affirmative, the ITC would have begun its investigation at that time.) Not later than 45 days after the date the International Trade Administration makes an affirmative final determination, in a case where the preliminary determination also was affirmative, the International Trade Commission must render its decision on injury. Where the preliminary determination was negative, the ITC must render a decision not later than 75 days after the affirmative final determination. A negative final determination by the Assistant Secretary for Import Administration terminates an antidumping investigation. *See* dumping; International Trade Commission.

financial instrument

(banking/finance) A document which has monetary value, or is evidence of a financial transaction. Examples of financial instruments are: checks, bonds, stock certificates, bills of exchange, promissory notes and bills of lading.

financial market
(banking/finance) Market for the exchange of capital and credit in an economy. It is divided into money markets, and capital market(s).

Financial Times (of London)
(publication) Considered by professionals as one of the best English-language newspapers for business and financial news.

Fines, Penalties, and Forfeitures System (FPFS)
(U.S. Customs) A part of the U.S. Customs' Automated Commercial System, is used to assess, control, and process penalties resulting from violations of law or Customs regulations. FPFS provides retrieval of case information for monitoring case status. *See* Automated Commercial System.

finished goods inventory (FGI)
(logistics) Inventory of products that have been manufactured, packed and stored and are ready for distribution.

fire insurance
(insurance) Marine insurance coverage that includes both direct fire damage and also consequential damage, as by smoke or steam, and loss resulting from efforts to extinguish a fire. Includes explosion caused by fire.

firm planned order
(logistics) In distribution requirements planning (DRP) or manufacturing resources planning (MRP) systems, an order whose status has been fixed in the computer system with regard to quantity and time. This is an issue in DRP and MRP systems as the software program, under certain circumstances, has the ability to change a planned order's status with regard to quantities and time. Firm planned orders are an aid in establishing a master production schedule. *See* planned order.

FIRST
(Canada) A system operated by the Canada Customs and Revenue Agency (CCRA) that allows pre-authorized quick release of repetitive low-risk shipments for frequent importers. Information at Web: www.ccra-adrc.gc.ca.

First World Countries
(economics) Western, industrialized, noncommunist countries.

five dragons
See five tigers; five dragons.

five tigers; five dragons
Terms used to describe the emerging economies of Hong Kong, Singapore, South Korea, Taiwan and Thailand.

fixed charges
(general) Charges which do not vary with an increase in production or sales volume.

(shipping) Charges which do not vary with an increase or decrease in traffic.

fixed exchange
(foreign exchange) An administratively fixed exchange rate. With rate fixed exchange rates, no rate fluctuations are possible.

fixed exchange rate
See exchange rate; fixed exchange.

fixed quantity inventory model
(logistics) An inventory control, maintenance and reorder system that specifies that a fixed quantity of a product be reordered whenever inventory of that item falls below a preestablished minimum.

fixing
(foreign exchange) Establishing of the official exchange rate of a domestic currency against other negotiable currencies.

flag
(shipping) A reference to the country of registry of a vessel. A vessel flying the flag of the country of its registry.

flag of convenience
(shipping) The national flag flown by a ship that is registered in a country other than that of its owners (e.g., to escape taxes and high domestic wages).

flammable
(shipping) Any substance capable of catching fire. *See* flammable liquid; flammable solid.

flammable liquid
(shipping) Liquids with a flash point less than 100°F. (UN CLASS 3) Examples are ether, acetone, gasoline, toluene and pentane. Hazards/precautions are no flares, smoking, flames, or sparks in the hazard area; vapors are an explosion hazard; can be poisonous; check labels; if it is poisonous, it can cause death when inhaled, swallowed or touched.

flammable solid
(shipping) Any solid material which, under certain conditions, might cause fires or which can be ignited readily and burns vigorously. (UN CLASS 4) Examples are calcium resinate; potassium, sodium amide. Hazards/precautions are may ignite when exposed to air or moisture, may reignite after extinguishing; fires may produce irritation or poisonous gases; contact may cause burns to skin or eyes.

flexible-path equipment
(logistics) Non automated materials handling equipment used to move goods around a warehouse (e.g., pallet jacks, forklifts and hand trucks).

flight of capital

(banking/finance) The movement of capital, which has usually been converted into a liquid asset, from one place to another to avoid loss or to increase gain.

floating

(foreign exchange) (a) **Clean floating**: Free determination of exchange rates without intervention on the part of the central bank. Correspondingly, exchange rates are determined by supply and demand on the foreign exchange market. (b) **Dirty floating**: Monetary policy which in principle recognizes floating exchange rates, but which tries to influence the exchange rate level through more or less frequent interventions. *See* floating currency.

floating currency

(banking/foreign exchange) One whose value in terms of foreign currency is not kept stable (on the basis of the par value or a fixed relationship to some other currency) but instead is allowed, without a multiplicity of exchange rates, to be determined (entirely or to some degree) by market forces. Even where a currency is floating, the authorities may influence its movements by official intervention; if such intervention is absent or minor, the expression "clean float" is sometimes used. *See* floating.

floor

(banking/finance) With cash investments, where the rate of interest is subject to adjustment to the market rate, a so-called floor can be agreed upon, i.e., for a premium, a minimum interest rate is stipulated and remains valid even if the market interest rate is lower.

florin

The currency of Aruba. 1F=100 cents.

flotsam

(shipping) Floating debris or wreckage of a ship or a ship's cargo. *See also* jetsam.

flow rack

(logistics) A point-of-use storage and picking system where parts or products are loaded at one end of a gravity flow rack and picked for use or distribution from the other.

FOB

(trade term) *See* Free On Board, Guide to Incoterms 2000 Appendix.

FOB Airport

(trade term) An incorrect use of the trade term Free On Board. *See* Free on Board, Guide to Incoterms 2000 Appendix.

FOB Destination, Freight Collect

(trade term) An incorrect use of the trade term Free On Board. *See* Free on Board, Guide to Incoterms 2000 Appendix.

FOB Destination, Freight Prepaid

(trade term) An incorrect use of the trade term Free On Board. *See* Free on Board, Guide to Incoterms 2000 Appendix.

FOB Origin, Freight Collect

(trade term) An incorrect use of the trade term Free On Board. *See* Free on Board, Guide to Incoterms 2000 Appendix.

FOB Origin, Freight Prepaid and Charged

(trade term) An incorrect use of the trade term Free On Board. *See* Free on Board, Guide to Incoterms 2000 Appendix.

Food and Agricultural Organization (FAO)

A specialized agency of the United Nations established in 1945 to combat hunger and malnutrition. The FAO serves as a coordinating body between government representatives, scientific groups, and non-governmental organizations to carry out development programs relating to food and agriculture. Address: Food and Agriculture Organization, Viale delle Terme di Caracalla, 00100 Rome, Italy; Tel: [39] 065-7051; Telex: 610181; Fax: [39] 065-705-3152; E-mail: FAO-HQ@fao.org; Web: www.fao.org.

Food and Drug Administration (FDA)

U.S. governmental agency which enforces the Federal Food Drug and Cosmetic Act, the Fair Packaging and Labeling Act, and sections of the Public Health Service Act. Address: Food and Drug Administration, Public Relations, 5600 Fishers Lane, Rockwell, MD 20857; Tel: [1] (888) 463-6332; Web: www.fda.gov.

FOR

(trade term) Abbreviation for "free on rail" used in connection with transportation by rail, indicating that the price covers the goods loaded on the railcar. *See* Free On Board; Guide to Incoterms 2000 Appendix.

force majeure

(shipping) Any condition or set of circumstances, such as earthquakes, floods, or war, beyond the carrier's control that prevents the carrier from performing fulfillment of their obligations.

force majeure clause

(law/insurance/shipping) A contract clause, which usually excuses a party who breaches the contract because that party's performance is prevented by the occurrence of an event that is beyond the party's reasonable control. A force majeure clause may excuse performance on the occurrence of such events as natural disasters, labor strikes, bankruptcy, or failure of subcontractors to perform. If a force majeure clause is not expressly included in a contract, a legal action may be brought on the basis that such a clause should be implied under the doctrine of commercial frustration or commercial impracticability.

See commercial frustration; commercial impracticability.

foreign affiliate
See affiliate.

foreign affiliate of a foreign parent
(U.S.) Any member of an affiliated foreign group owning a U.S. affiliate that is not a foreign parent of the U.S. affiliate. *See* affiliate.

Foreign Agricultural Service (FAS)

(U.S.) An agency of the U.S. Department of Agriculture (USDA). FAS maintains a global network of agricultural officers as well as a Washington-based staff to analyze and disseminate information on world agriculture and trade, develop and expand export markets, and represent the agricultural trade policy interests of U.S. producers in multilateral forums. FAS also administers USDA's export credit and concessional sales programs. Address: Information Staff, Foreign Agriculture Service, Department of Agriculture, Washington, DC 20250 USA; Tel: [1] (202) 720-7115; Web: www.fas.usda.gov.

Foreign Assets Control (FAC)
(U.S.) An agency of the U.S. Treasury Department that administers sanctions programs involving specific countries and restricts the involvement of U.S. persons in third country strategic exports. Address: Office of Foreign Assets Control, Department of Treasury, 1500 Pennsylvania Avenue NW, Washington, DC 20220 USA; Tel: [1] (202) 622-2480; Fax-on-demand: [1] (202) 622-0077 to request licensing; Web: www.treas.gov/ofac.

Foreign Assistance Act of 1991
(U.S.) This Act replaced the Support for East European Democracy (SEED) Act. The Foreign Assistance Act allows support to 26 countries, including all eastern European nations and most of the former Soviet republics.

foreign availability
(U.S.) The U.S. Bureau of Industry and Security (formerly the Bureau of Export Administration) conducts reviews to determine the foreign availability of selected commodities or technology subject to U.S. export control. The reviews use four criteria to determine foreign availability: comparable quality, availability-in-fact, foreign source, and adequacy of available quantities that would render continuation of the U.S. control ineffective in meeting its intended purpose. A positive determination of foreign availability means that a non-U.S. origin item of comparable quality may be obtained by one or more proscribed countries in quantities sufficient to satisfy their needs so that U.S. exports of such item would not make a significant contribution to the military potential of such countries. A positive determination may result in the decontrol of a U.S. product that has been under export control, or

the approval of an export license. However, the control may be maintained if the president invokes the national security override provision. Beginning with the 1977 amendments to the Export Administration Act, the Congress directed that products with foreign availability be identified and decontrolled unless essential to national security. In January 1983, a program to assess the foreign availability of specific products was established within the Office of Export Administration, now the Bureau of Industry and Security. Further, 1985 amendments to the Act directed that an Office of Foreign Availability be created. *See* Bureau of Industry and Security.

foreign bills
(banking) Bills of exchange or drafts drawn on a foreign party and denominated in foreign currency. *See* bill of exchange.

foreign bond
(banking/finance) An international bond denominated in the currency of the country where it is issued.

Foreign Buyer Program
See International Buyer Program.

foreign commerce
(trade) Trade between individuals or legal entities in different countries.

Foreign Corrupt Practices Act (FCPA)
(U.S. law) The FCPA makes it unlawful for any United States citizen or firm (or any person who acts on behalf of a U.S. citizen or firm) to offer, pay, transfer, promise to pay or transfer, or authorize a payment, transfer, or promise of money or anything of value to any foreign appointed or elected government official, foreign political party, or candidate for a foreign political office for a corrupt purpose, (that is, to influence a discretionary act or decision of the official) and for the purpose of obtaining or retaining business.

It is also unlawful for a U.S. business owner to make such an offer, promise, payment, or transfer to any person if the U.S. business owner knows, or has reason to know, that the person will offer, give, or promise directly or indirectly all or any part of the payment to a foreign government official, political party, or candidate. For purposes of the FCPA, the term knowledge means *actual knowledge*—the business owner in fact knew that the offer, payment, or transfer was included in the transaction—and *implied knowledge*—the business owner should have known from the facts and circumstances of a transaction that the agent paid a bribe, but failed to carry out a reasonable investigation into the transaction.

The provisions of the FCPA do not prohibit payments made to facilitate a routine government action. A facilitating payment is one made in connection with an action that a foreign official must perform as part of the job. In comparison, a corrupt payment is made to influence an official's discretionary decision. For example, payments are not generally considered corrupt if made to cover an official's overtime required to expedite the processing of export documentation for a legal shipment of merchandise, or to cover the expense of additional crew to handle a shipment.

Any person may request the Department of Justice to issue a statement of opinion on whether specific proposed business conduct would be considered a violation of the FCPA. The opinion procedure is detailed in 28 C.F.R. Part 77. If the Department of Justice issues an opinion stating that certain conduct conforms with current enforcement policy, conduct in accordance with that opinion is presumed to comply with FCPA provisions. Contact: United States Department of Justice, Washington, DC.

Foreign Credit Insurance Association

(U.S.) An agency established in 1961 to offer insurance covering political and commercial risks on U.S. export receivables in partnership with the Export-Import Bank (Eximbank) of the United States.

The FCIA was founded in 1961 as a partnership of the Eximbank and a group of private insurance companies. Eximbank is responsible for the political risk and may underwrite or reinsure the commercial risk. The FCIA acts as an agent responsible for the marketing and daily administration of the program. Address: F.C.I.A. Management Co., Inc., 40 Rector St., 11th Floor, New York, NY 10006 USA; Tel: [1] (212) 306-5000; Fax: [1] (212) 513-4704; E-mail: service@fcia.com; Web: www.fcia.com. *See* Export-Import Bank of the United States.

foreign currency

(banking) The currency of any foreign country which is the authorized medium of circulation and the basis for record keeping in that country. Foreign currency is traded in by banks either by the actual handling of currency or checks, or by establishing balances in foreign currency with banks in those countries.

foreign currency account

(banking) An account maintained in a foreign bank in the currency of the country in which the bank is located. Foreign currency accounts are also maintained by banks in the United States for depositors. When such accounts are kept, they usually represent that portion of the carrying bank's foreign currency account that is in excess of its contractual requirements.

foreign direct investment in the United States (FDIUS)

(foreign investment) Foreign direct investment in the United States is the ownership or control, directly or indirectly, by a single foreign person (an individual, or related group of individuals, company, or government) of 10 percent or more of the voting securities

of an incorporated U.S. business enterprise or an equivalent interest in an unincorporated U.S. business enterprise, including real property. Such a business is referred to as a U.S. affiliate of a foreign direct investor. *See* Committee on Foreign Investment in the United States; foreign person; portfolio investment; affiliate; United States Affiliate.

foreign draft

(banking) A draft drawn by an individual (drawer) or bank in one country on another individual (drawee) or bank in another country. *See* bill of exchange.

Foreign Economic Trends

(publication) Reports prepared by U.S. embassies abroad to describe foreign country economic and commercial trends and trade and investment climates. The reports describe current economic conditions; provide updates on the principal factors influencing development and the possible impacts on U.S. exports; review newly announced foreign government policies as well as consumption, investment, and foreign debt trends. Available from: Superintendent of Documents, U.S. Government Printing Office, Washington, DC 20402 USA; Tel: [1] (202) 512-1800.

foreign exchange

(banking/foreign exchange) Current or liquid claims payable in foreign currency and in a foreign country (bank balances, checks, bills of exchange). Not to be confused with foreign bank notes and coin, which are not included in this definition. *See also* bank notes.

foreign exchange auctions

(foreign exchange) Auctions of foreign currency, as used in some developing countries, whereby the price obtained for the foreign currency at the auction is the rate of exchange applied till the next auction.

foreign exchange contract

(foreign exchange) A contract for the sale or purchase of foreign exchange specifying an exchange rate and delivery date.

foreign exchange control

(foreign exchange) Governmental control and supervision of: transactions within the country involving its currency, foreign exchange for imports and exports, capital movements of any currency or monetary instruments into and out of the country, and expenditures of currency by its own citizens traveling abroad.

foreign exchange desk

(Federal Reserve Bank) The foreign exchange trading desk at the New York Federal Reserve Bank. The desk undertakes operations in the exchange markets for the account of the Federal Open Market Committee, as agent for the U.S. Treasury and as agent for foreign central banks.

foreign exchange holdings
(foreign exchange) Holdings of current or liquid foreign exchange claims denominated in the currency of another country.

foreign exchange market
(foreign exchange) (a) The worldwide system of contacts, either by telephone, teleprinter or in writing, which take place between nonbank foreign exchange dealers and foreign exchange traders at banks as well as foreign exchange traders amongst themselves, where the monies of different countries are bought and sold. (b) Wherever foreign exchange rates are determined.

foreign exchange rate
(foreign exchange) The price of one currency in terms of another.

foreign exchange trader
(foreign exchange) An individual engaged in the business of buying and selling foreign exchange on his own account or as an employee of a bank or other business authorized to deal in foreign exchange.

foreign exchange trading
(foreign exchange) Buying and selling of foreign exchange, holding of currency positions, foreign exchange arbitrage, and foreign exchange speculation on the foreign exchange market.

foreign exchange transactions
(foreign exchange) The purchase or sale of one currency with another. Foreign exchange rates refer to the number of units of one currency needed to purchase one unit of another, or the value of one currency in terms of another.

foreign exports
(U.S.) The U.S. export of foreign merchandise (re-exports), consisting of commodities of foreign origin which have entered the United States for consumption or into Customs bonded warehouses or U.S. Foreign Trade Zones, and which, at the time of exportation, are in substantially the same condition as when imported. *See* re-export.

foreign flag
(shipping) A reference to a carrier not registered in a country, but which flies that country's flag. The term applies to both air and sea transportation.

foreign freight forwarder
See freight forwarder.

foreign income
(economics) Income earned from work performed in another country.
(U.S.) Income earned by U.S. citizens from work performed in another country. Under the Tax Reform Act of 1976, the amount of annual income that can be excluded from taxable income by U.S. citizens working abroad was reduced from $20,000 (in some cases from $25,000) to $15,000. Foreign employees

of U.S. charitable organizations are able to exclude $20,000 each year.

foreign investment
(banking) The purchase of assets from abroad.

foreign investments
(economics) The flow of foreign capital into U.S. business enterprises in which foreign residents have significant control.

Foreign Labor Trends
(publication) Published by U.S. Department of Labor, provides an overview of the labor sector of a country's economy. Includes information on labor standards, conditions of employment, human resource development and labor relations. Can be purchased from: Superintendent of Documents, U.S. Government Printing Office, Washington, DC 20402 USA; Tel: [1] (202) 512-1800 or the U.S. Government Printing Office online at http://bookstore.gpo.gov; Tel: [1] [866] 512-1800.

foreign market value
The price at which merchandise is sold, or offered for sale, in the principal markets of the country from which it is exported.
(U.S.) In U.S. dumping investigations, if information on foreign home market sales is not available, the foreign market value is based on prices of exports to third countries or constructed value. Adjustments for quantities sold, circumstances of sales, and differences in the merchandise can be made to those prices to ensure a proper comparison with the prices of goods exported to the United States. *See* dumping; constructive value.

foreign military sales (FMS)
See conventional arms transfer.

foreign-owned affiliate in the U.S.
(U.S.) A business in the United States in which there is sufficient foreign investment to be classified as direct foreign investment. To determine fully the foreign owners of a U.S. affiliate, three entities must be identified: the foreign parent, the ultimate beneficial owner, and the foreign parent group. All these entities are "persons" in the broad sense: thus, they may be individuals; business enterprises; governments; religious, charitable, and other nonprofit organizations; estates and trusts; or associated groups.
A U.S. affiliate may have an ultimate beneficial owner (UBO) that is not the immediate foreign parent; moreover, the affiliate may have several ownership chains above it, if it is owned at least 10 percent by more than one foreign person. In such cases, the affiliate may have more than one foreign parent, UBO, and/or foreign parent group.
See also United States Affiliate; foreign parent group; person; ultimate beneficial owner; affiliate; foreign parent.

foreign parent

(U.S.) The first foreign person or entity outside the United States in an affiliate's ownership chain that has direct investment in the affiliate. The foreign parent consists only of the first person or entity outside the United States in the affiliate's ownership chain; all other affiliated foreign persons are excluded.

foreign parent group (FPG)

(U.S.) Consists of: (a) the foreign parent, (b) any foreign person or entity, proceeding up the foreign parent's ownership chain, that owns more than 50 percent of the party below it, up to and including the ultimate beneficial owner (UBO), and (c) any foreign person or entity, proceeding down the ownership chain(s) of each of these members, that is owned more than 50 percent by the party above it. A particular U.S. affiliate may have several ownership chains above it, if it is owned at least 10 percent by more than one foreign party. In such cases, the affiliate may have more than one foreign parent, UBO, and/or foreign parent group. *See also* United States Affiliate; affiliate; ultimate beneficial owner.

foreign person

A person who is resident outside a particular country or subject to the jurisdiction of another country.

(U.S. law) Any person resident outside the United States or subject to the jurisdiction of a country other than the United States. "Person" is any individual, branch, partnership, association, associated group, estate, trust, corporation, or other organization (whether or not organized under the laws of any state), and any government (including a foreign government, the U.S. government, a state or local government, and any agency, corporation, financial institution, or other entity or instrumentality thereof, including a government sponsored agency.)

foreign policy controls

(U.S.) U.S. export controls that are distinct from national security controls (such as the Coordinating Committee in Multilateral Export Controls or other international agreements) and are imposed to further U.S. foreign policy. The controls are typically imposed in response to developments in a country or countries—such as considerations regarding terrorism and human rights—or to developments involving a type or types of commodities and their related technical data. Foreign policy controls expire annually, unless extended.

foreign remittances

(banking) The transfer of any monetary instrument across national boundaries.

foreign sales agent

An individual or firm that serves as the foreign representative of a domestic supplier and seeks sales abroad for the supplier.

Foreign Service (U.S.)

(U.S. diplomacy) The Foreign Service supports the president of the United States and the secretary of state in pursuing U.S. foreign policy objectives. Foreign service functions include: representing U.S. interests; operating U.S. overseas missions; assisting U.S. citizens abroad; public diplomacy and reporting; and communicating and negotiating political, economic, consular, administrative, cultural, and commercial affairs. The Foreign Service comprises officers from the Departments of State, Commerce, and Agriculture and the United States Information Service. *See* commercial officers; economic officers.

Foreign Service Institute

(U.S. government) The FSI was founded in 1946 to train U.S. foreign and civil service officials. Training courses cover administrative, consular, economic, commercial, and political work; foreign languages; and diplomatic life overseas. Address: Foreign Service Institute, National Foreign Affairs Training Center, 4000 Arlington Blvd., Arlington, VA 22204-1500 USA; Tel: [1] (703) 302-6729.

foreign status merchandise

(U.S. foreign trade zones) Imported merchandise which has not been released from U.S. Customs custody. Also refers to domestically produced merchandise which has been exported and later reimported into the U.S.

See foreign trade zone; Foreign Trade Zones Board; Foreign Trade Zone Act; grantee; operator; zone user; subzone.

foreign trade zone (FTZ)

FTZs (or free zones, free ports, or bonded warehouses) are special commercial and industrial areas in or near ports of entry where foreign and domestic merchandise, including raw materials, components, and finished goods, may be brought in without being subject to payment of customs duties. Merchandise brought into these zones may be stored, sold, exhibited, repacked, assembled, sorted, graded, cleaned, or otherwise manipulated prior to reexport or entry into the national customs territory.

(U.S.) FTZs are restricted-access sites in or near ports of entry, which are licensed by the Foreign-Trade Zones Board and operated under the supervision of the U.S. Customs Service. Zones are operated under public utility principles to create and maintain employment by encouraging operations in the U.S. which might otherwise have been carried on abroad.

Subzones are a special-purpose type of ancillary zone authorized by the Board for companies unable to operate effectively at public zone sites. Subzones may be approved when it can be demonstrated that the activity to be performed there will result in significant public benefit and is in the public interest.

F

A **Foreign Trade Zones Board**, created by the Foreign Trade Zones Act of 1934, reviews and approves applications to establish, operate, and maintain foreign trade zones.
See free trade area; grantee; operator; zone user; subzones; free trade agreement.
Location of and general information on U.S. Foreign Trade Zones may be obtained from Foreign Trade Zones Board, Department of Commerce, Washington, DC 20230 USA; Tel: [1] (202) 482-2862; Fax: [1] (202) 482-0002.
Questions relating to operational aspects of such responsibilities should be addressed to the appropriate district/area director of U.S. Customs.
The Foreign Trade Zones Manual, for grantees, operators, users, Customs brokers, may be purchased from the Superintendent of Documents, U.S. Government Printing Office, Washington, DC 20402; Tel: [1] (866) 512-1800; Web: www.access.gop.gov.
Additional information may be obtained from the National Association of Foreign Trade Zones, 1000 Connecticut Ave. NW, Suite 1001, Washington, DC 20036; Tel: [1] (202) 331-1950; Fax: [1] (202) 331-1994; E-mail: info@naftz.org; Web: www.naftz.org.

Foreign Trade Zone Act (FTZA)
(U.S. law) The principal statute governing foreign trade zones is the Foreign Trade Zones Act of 1934 (FTZA), which has been codified in the United States Code as Title 19, Sections 81a through 81u. The FTZA has been periodically amended. The FTZA generally covers how and where zones are established, how they are administered and what may and may not be done in them. *See* foreign trade zone; Foreign Trade Zones Board.

foreign trade zone entry
(U.S. Customs) The transfer of goods into a foreign trade zone. *See* foreign trade zone; entry.

Foreign Trade Zones Board
(U.S. Customs) The administrative group responsible for the establishment, maintenance and administration of foreign trade zones in the United States under the Foreign Trade Zone Act. The Foreign Trade Zones Board consists of the U.S. Secretary of Commerce who is chairman and executive officer of the Board, the Secretary of the Treasury, and the Secretary of the Army. Address: Foreign Trade Zones Board, Department of Commerce, Room 3716, Washington, DC 20230 USA; Tel: [1] (202) 482-2862; Fax: [1] (202) 482-0002; www.ita.doc.gov/import_admin/records/fgzpage/. *See* foreign trade zone.

Foreign Traders Index (FTI)
(publication) The Foreign Traders Index, which is part of the National Trade Data Bank (NTDB), identifies foreign firms that are interested in importing U.S. products. The FTI includes background information on foreign companies, address, contact person, sales figures, size of company, and products by SIC code. Information in the NTDB is available from the Department of Commerce's STAT-USA/Internet service at Web: www.stat-usa.gov or at [1] (800) STAT-USA. Address: U.S. Department of Commerce, HCHB Room 4885, Washington, DC 20230 USA; Tel: [1] (202) 482-1986; Fax: [1] (202) 482-2164; Web: www.stat-usa.gov.

forex
Abbreviation for foreign exchange. *See* foreign exchange.

forfaiting
(trade/finance) The selling, at a discount, of medium to longer term accounts receivable or promissory notes of a foreign buyer (including those arising out of a letter of credit transaction) for immediate payment. These instruments may also carry the guarantee of the foreign government. Forfaiting emerged after the Second World War to expedite finance transactions between Eastern and Western European countries. More recently, it has become popular in Asian and Third World countries. Both U.S. and European forfaiting houses, which purchase the instruments at a discount from the exporters, are active in the U.S. market. *See also* factoring.

forint
The currency of Hungary. 1Ft=100 fillér.

forklift truck
(logistics) A highly maneuverable utility vehicle designed to move loaded pallets or skids in warehouses and manufacturing plants. Forklift trucks feature two long prongs (forks) that extend from the front of the vehicle and fit under or into openings at the bottom of a pallet or skid. These prongs can be raised, lowered or tilted to secure, move, raise, lower and position the loaded pallet in warehouse racks, containers, trucks or other vehicles. Special forklifts can handle very heavy weights and access high shelving. *See* pallet; skid.

Form A
See Certificate of Origin Form A.

forward contract
(trade/finance) Purchase or sale of a specific quantity of a commodity, security, currency or other financial instrument at a predetermined rate with delivery and settlement at a specified future date.

forwarder
See freight forwarder.

forwarder's bill of lading
(shipping) A bill of lading issued by a forwarding agent. *See* bill of lading.

forward foreign exchange
(foreign exchange) An agreement to purchase foreign exchange (currency) at a future date at a predetermined rate of exchange. Forward foreign exchange contracts are often purchased by international buyers of goods who wish to hedge against

foreign exchange fluctuations between the time the contract is negotiated and the time payment is to be made.

forwarding agent's bill of lading
(shipping) A bill of lading issued by a forwarding agent. *See* bill of lading.

forwarding agent's receipt
(shipping) Receipt issued by a forwarding agent for goods received.

forward market
(foreign exchange) The market for the purchase and sale of forward foreign exchange. Forward dates are usually one, three, six or twelve months in the future. *See* forward foreign exchange.

forward operations
(foreign exchange) Foreign exchange transactions, on which the fulfillment of the mutual delivery obligations is made on a date later than the second business day after the transaction was concluded.

forward rate
(foreign exchange) A contractually agreed upon exchange rate for a forward foreign exchange contract.

forward rate agreements (FRA)
(banking) With forward rate agreements (also known as future rate agreements) two counterparties can hedge themselves against future interest rate changes. They agree upon an interest rate for a future period within a specific currency segment, which is valid for a predetermined amount. In contrast to futures, FRA's are not standardized and are not traded on exchanges but are used in interbank trading.

FOT
See free on rail; free on truck; Incoterms.

foul bill of lading
(shipping) A receipt for goods issued by a carrier with an indication that the goods were damaged or short in quantity when received. *See* bill of lading.

four tigers; four dragons
A term used to describe the emerging economies of Hong Kong, Singapore, South Korea and Taiwan.

fractional currency
(banking) Any currency that is smaller than a standard money unit (e.g., any coin worth less than $1).

framework agreement
(a) (GATT/WTO): The Tokyo Round of the GATT called for consideration to be given "to improvements in the international framework for the conduct of world trade." Four separate agreements make up what is known as the "framework agreement." They concern: (1) differential and more favorable treatment for, and reciprocity by, developing countries in the international framework for trade; (2) trade measures taken for balance of payments purposes; (3) safeguard actions for development

purposes; and (4) an understanding on notification, consultation, dispute settlement, and surveillance in the GATT.
(b) Under the umbrella of the Enterprise for the Americas Initiative the United States and interested Western Hemisphere countries are negotiating bilateral "framework agreements" which establish agreed upon stages for eliminating counterproductive barriers to trade and investment. They also provide a forum for bilateral dispute settlement.
Generally, bilateral framework agreements contain similar objectives. They are based on a statement of agreed principles regarding the benefits of open trade and investment, increased importance of services to economies, the need for adequate intellectual property rights protection, the importance of observing and promoting internationally recognized worker rights, and the desirability of resolving trade and investment problems expeditiously. The parties establish a Council on Trade and Investment to monitor trade and investment relations, hold consultations on specific trade and investment matters of interest to both sides, and work toward removing impediments to trade and investment flows. Framework agreements do not bind signatories to implement specific trade liberalization measures. *See* General Agreement on Tariffs and Trade.

franc
The currency for:
Benin, CFAF;
Burkina Faso, 1CFAF=100 centimes;
Burundi, 1 FBu=100 centimes;
Cameroon, 1 CFAF=100 centimes;
Central African Republic, 1CFAF=100 centimes;
Chad, CFAF (centime eliminated);
Comoros, CFAF (centime eliminated);
Congo, CFAF (centime eliminated);
Djibouti, 1DF=100 centimes;
Equatorial Guinea, CFAF (centime eliminated);
French Pacific Islands, 1CFPF=100 centimes;
Gabon, CFAF (centime eliminated);
Guadeloupe, 1F=100 centimes;
Guinea, 1GFr=100 centimes;
Ivory Coast, CFAF (centime eliminated);
Liechtenstein (uses Swiss franc);
Madagascar, 1FMG=100 centimes;
Mali, CFAF (centime eliminated);
Niger, CFAF (centime eliminated);
Rwanda, 1RF=100 centimes;
St. Pierre, 1F=100 centimes;
Senegal, CFAF (centime eliminated);
Switzerland, 1SwF=100 centimes;
Togo, CFAF (centime eliminated).
The former currencies of: Andorra, Belgium, France, French Guiana, Guadeloupe, Luxembourg, Martinique, Monaco, Reunion Island and St. Pierre. The new currency of these countries is the European Union euro. 1 € = 100 cents.

F

franco
(trade term) Free from duties, transportation charges and other levies. Used also as delivery condition, e.g., franco ... (named place of delivery), which means that the seller must bear all transportation charges and duties up to the named place. *See also* Incoterms.

fraud
(law) An intentional deception or false representation made to induce another person to act in reliance on that representation with the result that the person incurs damages. A buyer acts fraudulently, for example, by promising to pay for goods on delivery even though the buyer does not have the funds needed, accepting the goods as satisfactory, but not paying for them.

Free Alongside Ship (...named port of shipment) (FAS)
(Incoterms 2000) An international trade term of sale in which, for the quoted price, the seller/exporter/manufacturer clears the goods for export and then places them alongside the vessel at the "named port of shipment." (The seller's clearing the goods for export is new to Incoterms 2000.)

The parties to the transaction, however, may stipulate in their contract of sale that the buyer will clear the goods for export.

The Free Alongside Ship term is used only for ocean or inland waterway transport.

The "named place" in Free Alongside Ship and all "F" Incoterms 2000 is domestic to the seller.

The Free Alongside Ship term is commonly used in the sale of bulk commodity cargo such as oil, grains, and ore.

See Guide to Incoterms 2000 Appendix.

free astray
(shipping) A shipment miscarried or unloaded at the wrong station is billed and forwarded to the correct station, free of charges, on account of being astray, hence the term free astray.

Free Carrier (...named place) (FCA)
(Incoterms 2000) An international trade term of sale in which, for the quoted price, the seller/exporter/manufacturer clears the goods for export and then delivers them to the carrier specified by the buyer at the named place.

If the named place is the seller's place of business, the seller is responsible for loading the goods onto the transport vehicle. If the named place is any other location, such as the loading dock of the carrier, the seller is not responsible for loading the goods onto the transport vehicle.

The Free Carrier term may be used for any mode of transport, including multimodal.

The "named place" in Free Carrier and all "F" Incoterms 2000 is domestic to the seller.

"Carrier" has a specific and somewhat expanded meaning. A carrier can be a shipping line, an airline, a trucking firm, or a railway. The carrier can also be an individual or firm who undertakes to procure carriage by any of the above methods of transport including multimodal. Therefore, a person, such as a freight forwarder, can act as a "carrier" under this term. In such a case, the buyer names the carrier or the individual who is to receive the goods.

The Free Carrier term is often used when making an initial quotation for the sale of goods.

See Guide to Incoterms 2000 Appendix.

free domicile (door to door)
(trade term/logistics) A trade term that specifies that the shipper is responsible for all costs of delivery of a shipment, including customs clearance fees, directly to the door of the consignee. *See* Incoterms.

free exchange rate
See exchange rate; floating.

freehold
(law) Fee simple, fee tail or life estate tenure in real property. (a) Fee simple means that an individual has tenure without limitation or restriction on transfer of ownership by sale or inheritance. (b) Fee tail means that only a specified individual or group of heirs is granted tenure. (c) Life estate means that tenure is granted to a specific individual during his or her lifetime or to an individual during the lifetime of the person in whose name the life estate is granted.

free in
(shipping) A pricing term indicating that the loading charges are for the account of the supplier.

free in and out (FIO)
(shipping) A pricing term indicating that the charterer of a vessel is responsible for the cost of loading and unloading goods from the vessel.

free list
(customs) A statement, prepared by the customs department of a country, of items that are not liable to the payment of duties.

freely negotiable
(banking) When a letter of credit is stated as "freely negotiable," the beneficiary of the letter of credit has the right to present his documents at a bank of his choice for negotiation. *See* letter of credit.

free market
(economics) Describes the unrestricted movement of items in and out from the market, unhampered by the existence of tariffs or other trade barriers.

free of capture and seizure (F.C.&S.)
(insurance) An insurance policy provision stating that the policy does not cover warlike operations or its consequences, whether before or after the actual declaration of war. Currently, most open policies omit war perils from its insuring conditions and in all cases will include a F.C.&S. clause. War coverage is customarily furnished in conjunction with an open cargo policy and is written under a separate, distinct

policy—the War Risk Only Policy. *See* war risk; all risk; special marine policy.

free of particular average (FPA)

(insurance) A clause in an insurance policy that provides that in addition to total losses, partial losses resulting from perils of the sea are recoverable, but only in the event that the carrying vessel has stranded, sunk, burnt, been on fire or been in collision. *See also* average; particular average; general average; with average; deductible average.

Free On Board (...named port of shipment) (FOB)

(Incoterms 2000) An international trade term of sale in which, for the quoted price, the seller/exporter/manufacturer clears the goods for export and is responsible for the costs and risks of delivering the goods past the ship's rail at the named port of shipment.

The Free On Board term is used only for ocean or inland waterway transport.

The "named place" in Free On Board and all "F" Incoterms 2000 is domestic to the seller.

The Free On Board term is commonly used in the sale of bulk commodity cargo such as oil, grains, and ore where passing the ship's rail is important. However, it is also commonly used in shipping container loads of other goods.

The key document in FOB transactions is the "On Board Bill of Lading."

Sellers and buyers often confuse the Free On Board term with Free Carrier. Free On Board (FOB) does not mean loading the goods onto a truck at the seller's place of business. Free On Board is used only in reference to delivering the goods past a ship's rail in ocean or inland waterway transport. Free Carrier, on the other hand, is applicable to all modes of transport.

See Guide to Incoterms 2000 Appendix.

free on rail; free on truck (FOR/FOT)

(trade terms) These terms are synonymous, since the word "truck" relates to the railway wagons. The terms should only be used when the goods are to be carried by rail. *See* Free Carrier; Incoterms.

free out

(shipping) A pricing term indicating that unloading charges are for the account of the receiver.

free port

An area, such as a port city, into which imported merchandise may legally be moved without payment of duties. *See also* foreign trade zone.

free time

(shipping) The time allowed shippers or receivers to load or unload cars before demurrage, detention, or storage charges accrue. *See* demurrage; detention.

free trade

(economics) A theoretical concept that assumes international trade unhampered by government measures such as tariffs or nontariff barriers. The objective of trade liberalization is to achieve "freer trade" rather than "free trade," it being generally recognized among trade policy officials that some restrictions on trade are likely to remain in effect for the foreseeable future.

free trade agreement (FTA)

An FTA is an arrangement which establishes unimpeded exchange and flow of goods and services between trading partners regardless of national borders. An FTA does not (as opposed to a common market) address labor mobility across borders or other common policies such as taxes. Member countries of a free trade area apply their individual tariff rates to countries outside the free trade area.

free trade area

A group of two or more countries that have eliminated tariff and most nontariff barriers affecting trade among themselves, while each participating country applies its own independent schedule of tariffs to imports from countries that are not members. A free trade area allows member countries to maintain individually separate tariff schedules for external countries; members of a customs union employ a common external tariff. The best known example is the European Free Trade Association (EFTA) and the free trade area for manufactured goods that has been created through the trade agreements that have been concluded between the European Community and the individual EFTA countries. The World Trade Organization (WTO) spells out the meaning of a free trade area and specifies the applicability of other WTO provisions to free trade areas. *See* European Community; European Free Trade Association; common market.

free trade zone

See foreign trade zone; free zone.

free zone

An area within a country (a seaport, airport, warehouse or any designated area) regarded as being outside its customs territory. Importers may therefore bring goods of foreign origin into such an area without paying customs duties and taxes, pending their eventual processing, transshipment or reexportation. Free zones are also known as "free ports," "free warehouses," and "foreign trade zones."

freight

(shipping) All merchandise, goods, products, or commodities shipped by rail, air, road, or water, other than baggage, express mail, or regular mail.

freight all kinds (FAK)

(shipping/logistics) A carrier's rate classification that usually refers to a consolidated cargo shipment where items of different classes (weight, bulk or value) are shipped in a single container, but charged at a single rate. This rate classification is used only for establishing shipping rates and is not acceptable on customs documents, which must detail the specific contents of a shipment. *See* class or kind (of merchandise).

freight bill

(shipping) (a) **Destination freight bill**—A bill rendered by a transportation line to consignee, giving a description of the freight, the name of shipper, point or origin, weight and amount of charges (if not prepaid).

(b) **Prepaid freight bill**—A bill rendered by a transportation line to shipper, giving a description of the freight, the names of consignee and destination, weight and amount of charges.

freight carriage ... and insurance paid to

See Cost, Insurance, Freight; Incoterms.

freight carriage ... paid to

See Carriage Paid To; Incoterms 2000.

freight charge

(shipping) The charge assessed for transporting freight.

freight claim

(shipping) A demand upon a carrier for the payment of overcharge or loss or damage sustained by shipper or consignee.

freighter

(shipping) A ship or airplane used primarily to carry freight.

freight forwarder

(shipping) A person engaged in the business of assembling, collection, consolidating, shipping and distributing less-than-carload or less-than-truckload freight. Also, a person acting as agent in the transshipping of freight to or from foreign countries and the clearing of freight through customs, including full preparation of documents, arranging for shipping, warehousing, delivery and export clearance.

full container load (FCL)

(logistics) A shipment of cargo that fills a given container either by bulk or maximum weight.

full set

All the originals of a particular document (usually the bill of lading). The number of originals is usually indicated on the document itself.

full truck load (FTL)

(logistics) A shipment of cargo that fills a given truck either by bulk or maximum weight.

fundamental analysis

(economics) Analysis of basic economic data in a market (supply and demand), in order to be able to make assertions as to the future price trend of a traded commodity. Fundamental exchange rate analysis is based on the economic and business cycle data of the country in question and leads to longer-term exchange rate forecasts.

fungibles

(law) Goods that are identical with other goods of the same nature. A merchant who is unable to deliver a specific load of grain, for example, may negotiate to replace that grain with fungibles, that is another load of grain of the same nature and quality.

future exchange contract

See futures contract.

futures contract

(finance/foreign exchange) A contract for the future delivery of a specified commodity, currency or security on a specific date at a rate determined in the present. Standardized forward contracts are officially traded on an exchange such as the Chicago Board of Trade (CBOT), London International Financial Futures Exchange (LIFFE), Commodity Exchange Inc. (COMEX), or New York Mercantile Exchange (NYMEX). The contract is valid for a specific amount of a commodity or a fixed amount of a financial instrument.

future trading

The sale or purchase of a commodity, currency or security for future delivery.

G

gamma
(statistics/banking/foreign exchange) The rate of change of an option's delta with respect to a marginal change in the price of the underlying instrument.

gang
(shipping) A group of usually four to six stevedores with a supervisor who are assigned to the loading or unloading of a portion of a vessel.

gangway
(shipping) (a) The opening through which a ship is boarded, (b) Either of the sides of the upper deck of a ship.

gantry crane
(shipping) A specialized machine for the raising or lowering of cargo mounted on a structure spanning an open space on a ship. The hoisting device travels back and forth along the spanning structure from port to starboard, while the spanning structure itself is often mounted on a set of rails which enables it to move from fore to aft.

gateway
(general) A major airport or seaport.
(customs) The port where customs clearance takes place.
(shipping) A point at which freight moving from one territory to another is interchanged between transportation lines.

GATT
See General Agreement on Tariffs and Trade.

geisha bond
(finance/banking) Bond issued on the Japanese market in currencies other than yen. Yen-denominated bonds are known as Samurai bonds.

general agency
See agency.

General Agreement on Tariffs and Trade (GATT)
[The General Agreement on Tariffs and Trade has been superseded by the World Trade Organization (WTO). The following entry remains for historical purposes. See World Trade Organization (WTO).]
Both a multilateral trade agreement aimed at expanding international trade and the organization which oversees the agreement. The main goals of GATT are to liberalize world trade and place it on a secure basis thereby contributing to economic growth and development and the welfare of the world's people. GATT is the only multilateral instru-

ment that lays down agreed rules for international trade, and the organization is the principal international body concerned with negotiating the reduction of trade barriers and with international trade relations.

One hundred and seventeen countries accounting for approximately 90 percent of world trade are Contracting Parties to GATT, while some other countries apply GATT rules on a de facto basis. Approximately 2/3 of GATT's membership consists of developing countries.

The GATT was signed in 1948 by 23 nations as a response to the trade conflicts which contributed to the outbreak of World War II. Originally looked upon as an interim agreement, it has become recognized as the key institution concerned with international trade negotiations. An important element which contributed to GATT's importance early on came with the United States' refusal to ratify the Havana Charter of 1948, which would have created an International Trade Organization (ITO) as a Specialized Agency of the United Nations system, similar to the International Monetary Fund and the World Bank. The Interim Commission of the ITO (ICITO), which was established to facilitate the creation of the ITO, subsequently became the GATT Secretariat. One result of the recent Uruguay Round was the decision to replace the GATT Secretariat with a Multilateral Trading Organization (MTO), which will have more authority to enforce free trade rules, as through the assessment of trade penalties. In December, 1993, agreements were reached at the conclusion of the Uruguay Round to revise the framework of GATT. Member nations will sign the agreement in April, 1994, and it will go into effect July 1, 1995.

The purpose of the GATT organization, headquartered in Geneva, is to provide a forum for discussion of world trade issues that allows for the disciplined resolution of trade disputes, based on the founding principles of GATT which include nondiscrimination, national treatment, transparency, and most-favored-nations (MFN) treatment. International negotiations known as "Rounds" are conducted to lower tariffs and other barriers to trade, and a consultative mechanism that may be invoked by governments seeking to protect their trade interests.

A few of the fundamental principles and aims of GATT:

(1) **Trade without discrimination**—The first principle embodied in the famous "most-favored nation" clause is that trade must be conducted on the basis of non-discrimination. No country is to give special trading advantages to another or to discriminate against it; all are on an equal basis and all share the benefits of any moves towards lower trade barriers.

(2) **Protection through tariffs**—Ensures that if protection to a domestic industry is given, it should be extended through the customs tariff, and not through other commercial measures.

(3) **A stable basis for trade**—Provided partly by the binding of the tariff levels negotiated among contracting parties. These bound items are listed, for each country, in tariff schedules which form an integral part of the General Agreement.

(4) **Promoting fair competition**—Concerns over dumping and subsidies are addressed by the "Antidumping Code" which provides rules under which governments may respond to dumping in their domestic market by overseas competitors, and rules for the application of "countervailing" duties which can be imposed to negate the effects of export subsidies.

(5) **Quantitative restrictions on imports**—A basic provision of GATT is a general prohibition of quantitative restrictions (import quotas). The main exception to the general rule against these restrictions allows their use in balance-of-payments difficulties under Article XII.

(6) **The "waiver" and the possible emergency action**—Waiver procedures allow a country to seek release from particular GATT obligations, when its economic or trade circumstances so warrant. The "safeguards" rule of GATT (Article XIX) permits members, under carefully defined circumstances, to impose import restrictions or suspend tariff concessions on products which are being imported in such increased quantities and under such conditions that they cause serious injury to competing domestic producers.

(7) **Regional trading arrangements**—Regional trade groupings, as an exception to the general most-favored-nations treatment, are permitted in the form of a customs union or free trade area. Article XXIV recognizes the value of such agreements, which foster free trade by abolishing or reducing barriers against imports from countries in a particular region.

(8) **Settling trade disputes**—Consultation, conciliation, and dispute settlement are fundamental aspects of GATT's work. Countries can petition GATT for a fair settlement of cases in which they feel their rights under the General Agreement are being withheld or compromised by other members. Bilateral consultations are emphasized, but if necessary, unresolved cases go before a GATT panel of experts.

(U.S.) For the United States, the GATT came into existence as an executive agreement, which, under the U.S. Constitution does not require Senate ratification.

See also rounds; Tokyo Round; Uruguay Round; multilateral trade negotiations; rollback; standstill; safeguards; special and different treatment.

See also World Trade Organization (WTO).

general average

(shipping) A loss that affects all cargo interests on board a vessel as well as the ship herself. These include the owner of the hull and the owners of all the cargoes aboard for their respective values plus the owner or charterer who stands to earn a specific income from freight charges for the voyage.

A general average loss may occur whether goods are insured or not. It is one that results from an intentional sacrifice (or expenditure) incurred by the master of a vessel in time of danger for the benefit of both ship and cargo. The classic example of this is jettison to lighten a stranded vessel. From the most ancient times, the maritime laws of all trading nations have held that such a sacrifice shall be borne by all for whose benefit the sacrifice was made, and not alone by the owner of the cargo thrown overboard.

The principles of general average have been refined over the years, and they have inevitably come to reflect the increasing complexity of present day commerce. A vessel owner may and does declare his vessel under general average whenever, for the common good in time of danger an intentional sacrifice of ship or cargo has been made, or an extraordinary expenditure has been incurred. In actual practice, general averages result mainly from strandings, fires, collisions and from engaging salvage assistance or putting into a port of refuge following a machinery breakdown or other peril.

As the name implies, general average claims affect all the interests which stand to suffer a financial loss if a particular voyage is not successfully completed.

(insurance) Insurance coverage for a general average loss.

See also average; particular average; with average; free of particular average; deductible average.

general cargo rate

(shipping) The rate a carrier charges for the shipment of cargo which does not have a special class rate or commodity rate.

general cargo vessels

(shipping) A vessel designed to handle break-bulk cargo such as bags, cartons, cases, crates and drums, either individually or in unitized or palletized loads. *See* breakbulk vessel.

general commodity rate

(shipping) A freight rate applicable to all commodities except those for which specific rates have been filed. Such rates are based on weight and distance and are published for each pair of ports or cities a carrier serves.

general imports

(U.S. Customs) The total physical arrivals of merchandise from foreign countries, whether such merchandise enters consumption channels immediately or is entered into bonded warehouses or Foreign Trade Zones under U.S. Customs custody.

Generalized System of Preferences (GSP)

A program providing for free rates of duty for merchandise from beneficiary developing independent countries and territories to encourage their economic growth.

GSP is one element of a coordinated effort by the industrial trading nations to bring developing countries more fully into the international trading system.

The GSP reflects international agreement, negotiated at the United Nations Conference on Trade and Development II (UNCTAD-II) in New Delhi in 1968, that a temporary and non-reciprocal grant of preferences by developed countries to developing countries would be equitable and, in the long term, mutually beneficial.

(U.S.) The U.S. GSP scheme is a system of nonreciprocal tariff preferences for the benefit of these countries. The U.S. conducts annual GSP reviews to consider petitions requesting modification of product coverage and/or country eligibility. United States GSP law requires that a beneficiary country's laws and practices relating to market access, intellectual property rights protection, investment, export practices, and workers rights be considered in all GSP decisions.

The GSP eligibility list includes a wide range of products classifiable under approximately 3,000 different subheadings in the Harmonized Tariff Schedule of the United States (HTS or HTSUS). These items are identified either by an "A" or "A*" in the "Special" column 1 of the tariff schedule. Note that the eligible countries and eligible items change from time-to-time over the life of the program.

Eligible merchandise will be entitled to duty-free treatment provided the following conditions are met: (1) The merchandise must be destined for the United States without contingency for diversion at the time of exportation from the beneficiary developing country. (2) The UNCTAD (United Nations Conference on Trade and Development) Certificate of Origin Form A must be properly prepared, signed by the exporter and either be filed with the customs entry or furnished before liquidation or other final action on the entry if requested to do so by Customs. (3) The merchandise must be imported directly into the United States from the beneficiary country. (4) The cost or value of materials produced in the beneficiary developing country and/or the direct cost of processing performed there must represent at least 35 percent of the appraised value of the goods.

See Certificate of Origin Form A; Harmonized Tariff Schedule of the United States.

general liability

(law) Unlimited responsibility for an obligation, such as payment of the debts of a business. *See* joint and several liability; limited liability.

general license (GL)

(U.S.) [*Obsolete as of January 1997; information provided for historical reference only.*] Licenses, authorized in the past by the U.S. Bureau of Export Administration (now the Bureau of Industry and Security), that permitted the export of non-strategic goods to specified countries without the need for a validated license. No prior written authorization was required and no individual license was issued for these categories

There were over twenty different types of general licenses, each represented by a symbol. These licenses included:
(a) General license BAGGAGE
(b) General license CREW
(c) General license GATS
(d) General license GCG
(e) General license G-COCOM
(f) General license GCT
(g) General license G-DEST
(h) General license GFW
(i) General license GIFT
(j) General license GIT
(k) General license GLR
(l) General license GLV
(m) General license G-NNR
(n) General license GTDA
(o) General license GTDR
(p) General license G-TEMP
(q) General license GTF-U.S.
(r) General license GUS
(s) General license PLANE STORES
(t) General license RCS
(u) General license SAFEGUARDS
(v) General license SHIP STORES

Former contact: Bureau of Industry and Security, Office of Public Affairs, Room 3895, Fourteenth Street and Constitution Avenue NW, Washington, DC 20230 USA; Tel: [1] (202) 482-2721; Web: www.bxa.doc.gov.

general order (GO)

(U.S. Customs/shipping) Merchandise not entered within 5 working days after arrival of the carrier and then stored at the risk and expense of the importer. *See* general order warehouse.

general order warehouse

(U.S. Customs) A customs bonded warehouse to which customs sends goods (at the owner's expense and risk) which have not been claimed within five days of arrival.

general partnership

(law) A partnership in which all of the partners have joint and several liability for the partnership obligations. *See* joint and several liability.

general tariff

A tariff that applies to countries that do not enjoy either preferential or most-favored-nation tariff treatment. Where the general tariff rate differs from the most-favored-nation rate, the general tariff rate is usually the higher rate.

"German" silver

"German," or coin silver is an alloy of silver that is 800/1000 pure. An article of German or coin silver is often marked "800".

G

Gesellschaft mit beschrankter Haftung (GmbH)
(Austria, Germany, Switzerland) Designation for a private limited liability corporation with limited liability to shareholders.

giro
See deposit money.

global bond
(banking/finance) A bond that can be traded immediately in any United States capital market and in the Euromarket.

globalization
(economics) The internationalization of business, communications and culture. The term has come to refer to the interdependence of the world economy and the fact that activities or events in one country can have far-reaching effects across the globe.

global quota
(customs) A quota on the total imports of a product from all countries.

gnomes of Zurich
(banking) Those financial and banking people of Zurich, Switzerland, involved in foreign exchange speculation. The term was coined by Great Britain's Labor ministers during the 1964 sterling crisis.

godown
(Chinese) A warehouse where goods are stored.

Golden Share
(finance/economics/politics) (a) The right of a government to exercise veto power over a company's wishes to materially change its articles of association. This term came into use in the 1980s to refer to France's and Spain's continued control of companies they had privatized.
(b) A holding of voting stock in a company sufficient to exercise control of the company. Usually, this means 51% of the voting stock. However, if the balance of the voting stock is evenly divided over an issue, control of as little as 10 percent of the voting stock can control a company.

gold exchange standard
(banking/foreign exchange) An international monetary agreement according to which money consists of fiat national currencies that can be converted into gold at established price ratios.

gold fixing
(banking/commodity markets) In London, Paris and Zurich, at 10:30 a.m. and again at 3:30 p.m., gold specialists or bank officials specializing in gold bullion activity determine the price for the metal.

Gold Key Service
(U.S.) An International Trade Administration, U.S. Department of Commerce service that provides customized information for U.S. firms visiting a country—market orientation briefings, market research, introductions to potential business partners, an interpreter for meetings, assistance in developing a market strategy, and help in putting together a follow-up plan. Trade specialists design an agenda of meetings, screen and select the right companies, arrange meetings with key people, and go with U.S. representatives to ensure that no unforeseen difficulties occur. For further information, in the U.S. call [1] (800) USA-TRADE or on the Web at Web: www.usa-trade.gov.

gold reserves
(banking/foreign exchange) Gold, retained by a nation's monetary agency, forming the backing of currency that the nation has issued.

gold standard
(economics) A monetary agreement whereby all national currencies are backed 100 percent by gold and the gold is utilized for payments of foreign activity.

gold tranche position in International Monetary Fund
(banking) Represents the amount that a member country can draw in foreign currencies virtually automatically from the International Monetary fund if such borrowings are needed to finance a balance-of-payments deficit.
(U.S.) In the case of the U.S., the gold tranche itself is determined by the U.S. quota paid in gold minus the holdings of dollars by the fund in excess of the dollar portion of the U.S. quota. Transactions of the fund in a member country's currency are transactions in monetary reserves. When the fund sells dollars to other countries to enable them to finance their international payments, the net position of the United States in the fund is improved. An improvement in the net position in the gold tranche is similar to an increase in the reserve assets of the United States. On the other hand, when the United States buys other currencies from the fund, or when other countries use dollars to meet obligations to the fund, the net position of the United States in the fund is reduced.

gondola car
(shipping) An open railway car with sides and ends, used principally for hauling coal, sand, etc.

goods
(law) (a) Merchandise, supplies, raw materials, and completed products. (b) All things that are movable and are designated as sold to a particular buyer. (c) **Durable goods** are ones that last a relatively long time and that are not dissipated or depleted when used generally, such as machinery and tools. (d) **Consumer goods** are ones that are purchased primarily for the buyer's personal, family, or household use. (e) **Hard goods** are consumer durable goods, such as appliances. (f) **Soft goods** are consumer goods that are not durable, such as clothing.

gourde
The currency of Haiti. 1G=100 centimes.

governing law clause

(law) A contract clause by which the parties agree that their contract should be interpreted in accordance with the law of a designated jurisdiction. A court may decide not to follow the choice made by the parties, because the parties cannot deprive a court of jurisdiction, but courts will often agree to apply the law that the parties have specified.

government bill of lading (GB/L)

(U.S. logistics) A special bill of lading used for shipments made by the U.S. government. The U.S. Government Bill of Lading (GB/L) and the U.S. Government Bill of Lading - Privately Owned Personal Property (PPGBL) are the primary documents used by the U.S. government to procure freight, express transportation and other related services from commercial carriers.

Government Printing Office

See Superintendent of Documents.

government procurement policies and practices

The means and mechanisms through which official government agencies purchase goods and services. Government procurement policies and practices may be considered to be non-tariff barriers to trade, involving the discriminatory purchase by official government agencies of goods and services from domestic suppliers, despite their higher prices or inferior quality as compared with competitive goods that could be imported.

(U.S.) The United States pressed for an international agreement during the Tokyo Round (of the General Agreement on Tariffs and Trade, GATT) to ensure that government purchase of goods entering into international trade should be based on specific published regulations that prescribe open procedures for submitting bids, as had been the traditional practice in the United States. Most governments had traditionally awarded such contracts on the basis of bids solicited from selected domestic suppliers, or through private negotiations with suppliers that involved little, if any, competition. Other countries, including the United States, gave domestic suppliers a specified preferential margin, as compared with foreign suppliers. The Government Procurement Code negotiated during the Tokyo Round sought to reduce, if not eliminate, the "Buy National" bias underlying such practices by improving transparency and equity in national procurement practices and by ensuring effective recourse to dispute settlement procedures. The Code became effective Jan. 1, 1981.

See General Agreement on Tariffs and Trade; Tokyo Round, World Trade Organization (WTO).

graduation

The presumption that individual developing countries are capable of assuming greater responsibilities and obligations in the international community— within the WTO or the World Bank, for example— as their economies advance, as through industrialization, export development, and rising living standards. In this sense, graduation implies that donor countries may remove the more advanced developing countries from eligibility for all or some products under the Generalized System of Preferences. Within the World Bank, graduation moves a country from dependence on concessional grants to non-concessional loans from international financial institutions and private banks.

Granger Laws

(U.S. law) State laws passed in the late 1800s in the western and mid-western states of the U.S. that sought to regulate railroads, warehouses and grain elevators and eliminate discriminatory rates and charges. The name came from an organization of farmers established in 1867 called the National Grange of the Patrons of Husbandry (commonly called the Grange). While the group was fundamentally nonpolitical, it urged state legislation to regulate railroad rates and practices. Although most of these laws were eventually repealed or drastically changed, they served as a basis for later regulation of utilities and railroads.

grandfather clause

(law) A contract clause in a legal document granting a formal exemption to a rule or law based on previously existing conditions or circumstances.

(WTO) A World Trade Organization (WTO) provision that allows the original contracting parties to exempt from general WTO obligations mandatory domestic legislation which is inconsistent with WTO provisions, but which existed before the WTO/GATT was signed. Newer members may also "grandfather" domestic legislation if that is agreed to in negotiating the terms of accession.

grantee

(U.S. foreign trade zones) A public or private corporation to which the privilege of establishing, operating or maintaining a foreign trade zone has been given. *See* foreign trade zone; Foreign Trade Zone Board; Foreign Trade Zone Act; operator; zone user; subzones.

green card

(U.S. immigration) An identity card (visa) issued by the U.S. Immigration and Naturalization Service entitling a foreign national to enter and reside in the United States as a permanent resident.

green line

See China green line.

grey list

(U.S.) A list of disreputable end users in nations of concern for missile proliferation from the U.S. intelligence community. Licensing officials in the U.S. Departments of Commerce and State use this list as a cross-reference when reviewing export license applications for commodities listed in the Missile

Technology Control Regime (MTCR) Equipment and Technology Annex.

grid
(foreign exchange) Fixed margin within which exchange rates are allowed to fluctuate.

gross
(general) 12 dozen or 144 articles.
(finance) The total amount before any deductions have been made.

gross axle weight rating (GAWR)
(logistics) An axle manufacturer's maximum weight rating for a truck axle and the proportion of the truck's weight that may be carried by that axle. *See* gross vehicle weight rating.

gross domestic product (GDP)
(economics) A measure of the market value of all goods and services produced within the boundaries of a nation, regardless of asset ownership. Unlike gross national product, GDP excludes receipts from that nation's business operations in foreign countries, as well as the share of reinvested earning in foreign affiliates of domestic corporations. *See also* gross national product.

gross national product (GNP)
(economics) A measure of the market value of all goods and services produced by the labor and property of a nation. Includes receipts from that nation's business operation in foreign countries, as well as the share of reinvested earnings in foreign affiliates of domestic corporations. *See also* gross domestic product.

gross vehicle weight
(logistics) The total weight of a vehicle and its load.

gross vehicle weight rating (GVWR)
(logistics) A truck manufacturer's stated maximum loaded weight of a vehicle including the vehicle itself, fuel, fluids and a full load of cargo. *See* gross axle weight rating.

Group of Five (G-5)
Similar to the Group of Seven (G-7), with the exception of Canada and Italy.

Group of Seven (G-7)
Group comprising the major industrialized nations in economic terms, which in view of the global economic importance of the member states have made it their objective to coordinate domestic economic policies. The coordination of economic, exchange rate and monetary policy aims is achieved both at government, central bank and also on other institutionalized levels. Member states are the USA, France, Great Britain, Germany, Japan, Canada, and Italy.

Group of Ten (G-10)
A group of originally 10 countries (following Switzerland's accession, 11) comprising Belgium, Germany, France, Great Britain, Italy, Japan, Canada, Holland, Sweden and the United States, who within the framework of the General Arrangements to Bor-

row (GAB) have decided to put the equivalent of 17 billion in Special Drawing Rights (SDRs) in their various currencies at the International Monetary Fund's (IMF) disposal for granting loans. The Group of Ten plays an important role in discussions concerning international monetary policy. The Group of Ten is also called the Paris Club.

Group of Fifteen (G-15)
The G-15, established in 1990, consists of relatively prosperous or large developing countries. The G-15 discusses the benefits of mutual cooperation in improving their international economic positions. Members include: Algeria, Argentina, Brazil, Egypt, India, Indonesia, Jamaica, Malaysia (a very active member), Mexico, Nigeria, Peru, Senegal, Venezuela, Yugoslavia, and Zimbabwe.

Group of Twenty-Four (G-24)
A grouping of finance ministers from 24 developing country members of the International Monetary Fund. The Group, representing eight countries from each of the African, Asian, and Latin American country groupings in the Group of 77, was formed in 1971 to counterbalance the influence of the Group of Ten.

Group of Seventy-Seven (G-77)
A grouping of developing countries which had its origins in the early 1960s. This numerical designation persists, although membership had increased to more than 120 countries. The G-77 functions as a caucus for the developing countries on economic matters in many forums including the United Nations.

gross ton
(measure) A unit of mass or weight measure equal to 2,240 pounds.

gross tonnage
(shipping) The capacity of a vessel (not cargo) expressed in vessel tons. It is determined by dividing by 100 the contents, in cubic feet, of the vessels closed-in spaces. (A vessel ton is 100 cubic feet.) The register of a vessel states both gross and net tonnage.

gross weight
(shipping) The full weight of a shipment, including goods and packaging. *See also* tare weight.

GSP
See Generalized System of Preferences.

GST
(Canada) Goods and Services Tax. A Canadian tax that is payable on most goods and services (imported and domestic) at the rate of 7.0 percent.

guanxi
(China) Chinese for relationships. More specifically, the network of business and personal relationships that support success in an endeavor. Includes connections, clout, favors given and favors owed, trust, courtesy, and gifts (not bribery).

G

guarani

The currency of Paraguay. 1G=100 centesimos.

guarantor

(law) An individual or legal entity that makes a guaranty, by which the guarantor agrees to be held liable for another's debt or performance. *See* guaranty.

guaranty

(law) A contract by which one person (the guarantor) agrees to pay another's debt or to perform another's obligation only if that other individual or legal entity fails to pay or perform. A guaranty is usually a separate contract from the principal agreement, and therefore the guarantor is secondarily liable to the third person. *See* guarantor; surety.

Guidelines for Trade Data Interchange (GTDI)

(computers/data interchange) A set of trade data interchange rules first published in 1981 in Europe and enhanced at later dates with the goal of achieving wider acceptance. GTDI and other standards (such as American National Standards Institute ANSI X12) seek to facilitate Electronic Data Interchange (EDI), which is the direct transfer of business data between computers. GTDI led to the UN/EDIFACT standards. Uniformity in international rules for trade data interchange, however, remains an unfulfilled goal. Competing standards and legacy systems have led to the failure of countries and companies to adopt a single standard. *See* American National Standards Institute, EDI, UN/EDIFACT.

guilder

The currency of:

Aruba, 1 Af = 100 cents.

Netherlands Antilles, 1 Naf = 100 cents;

Suriname, 1Sf = 100 cents.

The former currency of the Netherlands. The new currency of the Netherlands is the European Union euro. 1 € = 100 cents.

Gulf Cooperation Council (GCC)

The six member countries (Saudi Arabia, Kuwait, the United Arab Emirates, Bahrain, Qatar, and Oman) of the Gulf Cooperation Council (GCC) control half the proven oil reserves outside the Soviet Union, and account for about 40 percent of all the oil moving in international trade. The GCC was created in 1981, largely in response to the outbreak of the Iran-Iraq war. In creating the GCC, the members tried to maintain the balance of power in the Gulf by strengthening multilateral cooperation in security and economic matters. As regards trade, the GCC is only a policy-coordinating forum; the Council cannot impose policies on the members. GCC headquarters are in Riyadh, Saudi Arabia. The presidency of the GCC rotates yearly among the rulers of the member countries. Address: Gulf Cooperation Council, PO Box 7153, Riyadh 11462, Saudi Arabia; Tel: [966] (1) 482-7777; Telex: (1) 403635; Fax: [966] (1) 482-9089; Web: www.gcc-sg.org

H

hallmark

An impression made on gold and silverware introduced in the beginning of the fourteenth century in England to identify the quality of the metal used.

handling costs

(logistics) Costs related to moving, transferring, and preparing inventory for shipment, but not the shipping charges themselves.

harbor fees

(shipping) Charges assessed to users for use of a harbor, used generally for maintenance of the harbor. *See* users fees.

harbor master

(shipping) An officer who attends to the berthing, etc. of ships in a harbor.

hard loan

(banking) A foreign loan that must be paid in hard money.

hard money (currency)

(general) (a) Currency of a nation having stability in the country and abroad. Refers to currency that is accepted internationally and freely convertible. (b) Coins, in contrast with paper currency, or soft money.

(finance) Describes a situation in which interest rates are high and loans are difficult to arrange. synonymous with dear money.

hard top container

(shipping/logistics) A shipping container that has a roof which can be opened on hinges or lifted off. These two features facilitate loading through the top of the container, especially of awkward-sized cargo.

Harmonized System (HS)

A multipurpose international goods classification system designed to be used by manufacturers, transporters, exporters, importers, customs, statisticians, and others in classifying goods moving in international trade under a single commodity code.

Developed under the auspices of the Customs Cooperation Council (CCC), an international Customs organization in Brussels, this code is a hierarchically structured product nomenclature containing approximately 5,000 headings and subheadings describing the articles moving in international trade. It is organized into 99 chapters arranged in 22 sections with the sections generally covering an industry (e.g., Section XI, Textiles and Textile Articles) and the chapters covering the various materials and products of the industry (e.g., Chapter 50—Silk; Chapter 55—Man-made Staple Fibers; Chapter 57—Carpets). The basic code contains 4-digit headings and 6-digit subheadings.

(U.S.) The United States has added digits for tariff and statistical purposes. In the United States, duty rates are in the 8-digit level; statistical suffixes at the 10-digit level. The Harmonized System (HS) supplanted the U.S. Tariff Schedule (TSUSA) in January 1989.

For the United States, the HS numbers are the numbers that are entered on the actual export and import documents. Any other commodity code classification number (SIC, SITC, end-use, etc.) are just rearrangements and transformations of the original HS numbers.

See also Harmonized Tariff Schedule of the United States.

Harmonized Tariff Schedule of the United States (HTS or HTSUS)

(U.S.) An organized listing of goods and their duty rates which is used by U.S. Customs as the basis for classifying imported products and therefore establishing the duty to be charged and providing the U.S. Census with statistical information about imports and exports. The categorization of product listings in the HTSUS is based on the international Harmonized Commodity Description and Coding System developed under the auspices of the Customs Cooperation Council (Harmonized System, HS).

Familiarity with the organization of the HTSUS facilitates the classification process. The tariff schedule is divided into various sections and chapters dealing separately with merchandise in broad product categories. These categories, for example, separately cover animal products, vegetable products, products of various basic materials such as wood, textiles, plastics, rubber, and steel and other metal products in various stages of manufacture. Other sections encompass chemicals, machinery and electrical equipment, and other specified or non-enumerated products. The last section, Section XXII, covers certain exceptions from duty and special statutory exceptions.

In Sections I through XXI, products are classifiable (1) under items or descriptions which name them, known as an eo nomine provision; (2) under provisions of general description; (3) under provisions which identify them by component material; or (4) under provisions which encompass merchandise in accordance with its actual or principal use. When two or more provisions seem to cover the same merchandise, the prevailing provision is determined in accordance with the legal notes and the General Rules of Interpretation for the tariff schedule. Also applicable are tariff classification principles contained in administrative precedents or in the case law of the U.S. Court of International Trade (formerly the U.S. Customs Court) or the U.S.Court of Appeals for the Federal Circuit Court (formerly the U.S. Court of Customs and Patent Appeals).

The Harmonized Tariff Schedules of the United States also contain two rates of duty for each commodity listed. Column 1 duty rates are low and apply to imports from countries that have achieved Most Favored Nation (MFN) trading status with the United States. Column 2 duty rates apply to imports from countries that do not have Most Favored Nation (MFN) trading status with the United States. The Office of Tariff Affairs and Trade Agreements of the U.S. International Trade Commission is responsible for publishing the Schedule. The latest edition can be found online at http://dataweb.usitc.gov/SCRIPTS/tariff/toc.html. Adobe Acrobat PDF versions, including those of prior years, are downloadable at Web: www.usitc.gov/taffairs.htm. Print and CD-ROM versions are available from the U.S. Government Printing office at http://bookstore.gpo.gov; Tel: [1] [866] 512-8000. *See also* classification; Harmonized System.

Harter Act

(shipping) Legislation protecting a ship's owner against claims for damage resulting from the behavior of the vessel's crew, provided the ship left port in a seaworthy condition, properly manned and equipped.

hatch

(shipping) The opening in the deck of a vessel which gives access to the cargo hold.

haulage

(shipping) The local transport of goods. Also the charge(s) made for hauling freight on carts, drays or trucks. Also called cartage or drayage.

hawala

(banking) An informal worldwide network of businesses that offer foreign exchange and international funds transfer services to clients, but operate outside of traditional western banking channels.

Originating in India (*hawala* means "providing a code" in Hindi), the hawala system is often the only means of currency exchange and funds transfer in countries and regions where no banking services are offered to individuals and small businesses.

Hawala transactions are often simply legitimate transfers of funds from overseas workers to their families back home. However, the system is coming under scrutiny as it is also a favored conduit of funds by money launderers, drug dealers, arms dealers and terrorists.

In extremely bureaucratic countries such as India, a bank transfer might be illegal or could take as long as a month to complete. Hawala transactions, on the other hand, are often completed in as little as three days, regardless of official regulations.

Hawala dealers are often able to offer more favorable foreign exchange rates and quicker turnaround time because they typically operate outside of government control, do not use standard banking records and do not pay taxes.

As a result, hawala operations are legal and subject to government control in some countries, but entirely illegal in others. In 1994 the U.S. required hawala dealers to register with the government. The hawala system operates primarily in the Middle East, North Africa and Central, South and East Asia, but the network is worldwide.

How it works

An individual gives a local hawala dealer cash and asks that it be transferred to a named individual in a foreign country. The dealer charges the remitter a transfer fee of from 1 to 4 percent for large transactions and from 5 to 20 percent for small transactions. The hawala dealer than calls, faxes or e-mails (in code) a counterpart in another part of the world with instructions to give the funds to the named individual who uses a password or code as identification when collecting the money. In India the codes typically involve animals, (e.g., "five pigs" or "twelve hens.")

Unlike typical western banking, the hawala dealer does not forward the funds to his counterpart. Both dealers make a record in their ledgers with the assumption that a counterbalancing transaction will occur at a later date. If one dealer has paid out a substantial sum over time to another dealer, a compensating shipment of valuable or saleable goods may be made. Such a shipment might include gold jewelry (such as 22-24 karat gold) that has an internationally known market value, or merchandise that the dealer can easily sell in his local market.

Hawley-Smoot Act

See Smoot-Hawley Tariff Act of 1930.

hazardous materials

(shipping) A substance or material which has been determined to be capable of posing a risk to health, safety, and property when transported in commerce. (U.S.) A substance or material which has been determined by the U.S. Secretary of Transportation to be capable of posing an unreasonable risk to health, safety, and property when transported in commerce and which has been so designated. Title 49, Code of Federal Regulations (U.S.) Transportation—Parts 100-199, govern the transportation of hazardous materials. Hazardous materials may be transported domestically, but they may be classified as Dangerous Goods when transported internationally by air. *See also* restricted article; dangerous goods.

hazmat

(logistics) An abbreviation for hazardous materials. *See* hazardous materials.

heavy lift

(shipping) Articles too heavy to be lifted by a ship's tackle.

heavy lift charge

(shipping) A charge made for lifting (onloading or offloading) articles too heavy to be lifted by a ship's tackle. Usually requiring the use of heavy lift equipment at a port.

heavy lift vessel

(shipping) A vessel with heavy lift cranes and other equipment designed to be self-sustaining in the handling of heavy cargo.

hedge

To offset. Also, a security that has offsetting qualities. Thus one attempts to "hedge" against inflation by the purchase of securities whose values should respond to inflationary developments. Securities having these qualities are "inflation hedges." *See* hedging; delta hedging.

hedge ratio

(finance/foreign exchange) The amount of an underlying instrument or the number of options which are needed to hedge a covered option. The hedge ratio is determined by the size of the delta. *See* delta; delta hedging.

hedging

(finance/foreign exchange) A type of economic insurance used by dealers in commodities, foreign exchange and securities, manufacturers, and other producers to prevent loss due to price fluctuations. Hedging consists of counterbalancing a present sale or purchase by a purchase or sale of a similar commodity or of a different commodity, usually for delivery at some future date. The desired result is that the profit or loss on a current sale or purchase be offset by the loss or profit on the future purchase or sale. *See also* arbitrage; delta hedging.

high density

(shipping) The compression of flat or standard bales of cotton to high density of approximately 32 pounds. This compression usually applies to cotton exported or shipped coast to coast.

hitchment

(shipping) The marrying of two or more portions of one shipment that originate at different geographical locations, moving under one bill of lading, from one shipper to one consignee. Authority for this service must be granted by tariff publication.

hold

(shipping) The space below deck in a vessel used to carry cargo.

holder in due course

(law) An individual or legal entity (holder) who possesses a negotiable instrument, document of title, or similar document, and who took possession for value, in good faith, and without notice of any other individual's or legal entity's claim or defense against the instrument or document. A buyer, for example, who receives title to goods after remitting the contract price to the seller is a holder in due course, provided the buyer has no notice of any lien or other claim against the goods. A holder in due course is generally protected from the claims of third parties

H

against the item transferred, and thus the only recourse of a third party is against the person that transferred the title, instrument, or other item to the holder in due course.

hold for pickup
(shipping) Freight to be held at the carrier's destination location for pickup by the recipient.

hold harmless contract
(law) An agreement by which one party accepts responsibility for all damages and other liability that arise from a transaction, relieving the other party of any such liability. A commercial tenant, for example, may agree to hold a landlord harmless for all liabilities that could arise from injuries to customers who enter the premises. A guarantor may agree to guaranty a person's debt only if that person agrees to hold the guarantor harmless from all damages that may arise if the person fails to pay the debt. A hold harmless contract provides complete indemnity. *See* guaranty; indemnity; surety.

honor
(banking) To pay or to accept a draft complying with the terms of credit. *See* bill of exchange.

hopper cars
(railroads/logistics) A rail car designed for top-loading and bottom-unloading of dry bulk commodities such as iron ore. Some hopper cars have hatched or sliding roofs for protection of cargo from the elements.

horizontal export trading company
An export trading company which exports a range of similar or identical products supplied by a number of manufacturers or other producers. Webb-Pomerene Organizations, trade-grouped organized export trading companies, and an export trading company formed by an association of agricultural cooperatives are prime examples of horizontally organized export trading companies.

horizontal integration
(economics/management) The expansion, acquisition or merger of firms or business activities that produce or deliver similar products to similar markets. For example, a supermarket chain that purchases another supermarket chain. *See* vertical integration.

house air waybill (HAWB)
(shipping) A bill of lading issued by a freight forwarder for consolidated air freight shipments. In documentary letter of credit transactions HAWBs are treated exactly the same as conventional air waybills, provided they indicate that the issuer itself assumes the liability as carrier or is acting as the agent of a named carrier, or if the credit expressly permits the acceptance of a HAWB. *See* air waybill; bill of lading.

house-to-house
(shipping) A term usually used to indicate a container yard to container yard (CY/CY) shipment.

hub and spoke routing
(shipping) Aircraft routing service pattern that feeds traffic from many cities into a central hub designed to connect with other flights to final destinations. The system maximizes operating flexibility by connecting many markets through a central hub with fewer flights than would be required to connect each pair of cities in an extensive system.

hull
(shipping) The outer shell of a vessel usually made of steel.

hump
(shipping) That part of a rail track which is elevated so that when a car is pushed up on "the hump" and uncoupled it runs down on the other side by gravity.

hundredweight pricing
(shipping) Special pricing for multiple-piece shipments traveling to one destination which are rated on the total weight of the shipment (usually over 100 pounds) as opposed to rating on a per package basis.

I

identical merchandise

(U.S. Customs) In establishing the customs value of merchandise exported to the United States, identical merchandise is merchandise that is: (1) Identical in all respects to the merchandise being appraised, (2) Produced in the same country as the merchandise being appraised, and (3) Produced by the same person as the merchandise being appraised.

If merchandise meeting all these criteria cannot be found, then identical merchandise is merchandise satisfying the first two criteria but produced by a different person than the producer of merchandise being appraised.

Note: Merchandise can be identical to the merchandise being appraised and still show minor differences in appearance.

Exclusion: Identical merchandise does not include merchandise that incorporates or reflects engineering, development, artwork, design work, and plans and sketches provided free or at reduced cost by the buyer and undertaken in the United States.

See valuation; transaction value; computed value; similar merchandise.

igloo

(air freight/logistics) An air freight cargo container (unit load device or ULD) designed to fit the interior contours (usually of an upper deck) of a specific airplane. The name comes from the fact that many of these containers are in the shape of an igloo. *See* unit load device and the appendix "Guide to Air Freight Containers."

immediate delivery

(U.S. Customs) An alternate U.S. Customs entry procedure which provides for immediate release of a shipment in certain cases. Application must be made to Customs for a Special Permit for Immediate Delivery on Customs Form 3461 prior to the arrival of the merchandise. If the application is approved, the shipment is released expeditiously following arrival. An entry summary must then be filed in proper form and estimated duties deposited within 10 working days of release. *See* entry.

immediate transportation entry

(U.S. Customs) A form of U.S. Customs entry which allows imported merchandise to be forwarded from the port of original entry to another final destination for customs clearance. Merchandise travels in bond, without appraisal, from the original port of entry to the final destination, where it is then inspected by customs. *See* entry.

immigration

The entry of foreign nationals into a country for the purpose of establishing permanent residence. *See also* green card.

implied agency

See agency.

implied conditions

(insurance) Certain implied conditions are not written into marine insurance policies, but they are so basic to understanding between underwriter and assured that the law gives them much the same effect as if written. Thus, it is implied: (1) that the assured will exercise the utmost good faith in disclosing to his underwriter all facts material to the risk when applying for insurance; (2) that the generally established usages of trade applicable to the insured subject matter are followed; and (3) that the assured shall not contribute to loss through willful fault or negligence. *See* special marine policy.

implied volatility

See volatility.

implied warranties

(insurance) Legal decisions have established two important implied warranties in marine insurance policies, that of legality of the venture and that of seaworthiness. The latter is of little concern today since insurance policies commonly waive the warranty of seaworthiness by stating that seaworthiness is admitted as between the assured and the insurer. The insurer is not at liberty, however, to waive the implied warranty of legality. Such a waiver would be against public policy and the law of the land. *See* special marine policy.

import

(a) To receive goods and services from abroad. (b) An imported item.

import credit

(banking) A commercial letter of credit issued for the purpose of financing the importation of goods. *See* letter of credit.

import duty

(customs) Any tax on items imported. *See also* tariff; Harmonized Tariff Schedule of the United States.

import license

(customs) A document required and issued by some national governments authorizing the importation of goods.

import quota

(customs) A protective ruling establishing limits on the quantity of a particular product that can be imported. Quotas are a means of restricting imports by the issuance of licenses to importers, assigning each a quota, after determination of the total amount of any commodity which is to be imported during a period. Import licenses may also specify the country from which the importer must purchase the goods. *See* quota; tariff quotas.

import quota auctioning

(customs) The process of auctioning the right to import specified quantities of quota-restricted goods.

import relief

Any of several measures imposed by a government to temporarily restrict imports of a product or commodity to protect domestic producers from competition.

import restrictions

Any one of a series of tariff and non-tariff barriers imposed by an importing nation to control the volume of goods coming into the country from other countries. May include the imposition of tariffs or import quotas, restrictions on the amount of foreign currency available to cover imports, a requirement for import deposits, the imposition of import surcharges, or the prohibition of various categories of imports. *See* tariff; non-tariff barriers.

import sensitive producers

Domestic producers whose economic viability is threatened by competition (quality, price or service) from imported products.

import service

See export service.

import substitution

A strategy which emphasizes the replacement of imports with domestically produced goods, rather than the production of goods for export, to encourage the development of domestic industry.

importer

The individual, firm or legal entity that brings articles of trade from a foreign source into a domestic market in the course of trade.

importer number

(U.S. Customs) An identification number assigned by the U.S. Customs Service to each importer, used to track entries and other transactions.

Importers Manual USA

(publication) A reference book detailing specific requirements for importing each of the 99 Chapters (categories of goods) of the Harmonized Tariff Schedule of the United States, plus extensive sections on banking, letters of credit, foreign exchange, packing, shipping, insurance, and U.S. Customs Entry. Published by World Trade Press, 1450 Grant Ave., Novato, CA 94945 USA; Tel: [1] (415) 898-1124; Fax: [1] (415) 898-1080; Web: www.worldtradepress.com.

imports

Commodities of foreign origin as well as goods of domestic origin returned to the producing country with no change in condition, or after having been processed and/or assembled in other countries.

(U.S.) For statistical purposes, imports to the U.S. are classified by type of transaction:

(a) Merchandise entered for immediate consumption. ("duty free" merchandise and merchandise on which duty is paid on arrival);

(b) Merchandise withdrawn for consumption from U.S. Customs bonded warehouses, and U.S. Foreign Trade Zones;

(c) Merchandise entered into U.S. Customs bonded warehouses and U.S. Foreign Trade Zones from foreign countries.

imports for consumption

(U.S. Customs) The total of merchandise that has physically cleared through U.S. Customs either entering domestic consumption channels immediately or entering after withdrawal for consumption from bonded warehouses under U.S. Customs custody or from U.S. Foreign Trade Zones. Many countries use the term "special imports" to designate statistics compiled on this basis. *See also* consumption entry.

imports of goods and services (U.S.)

(economics) Represent the sum of all payments for merchandise imports, military expenditures, transportation and travel costs, other private and U.S. government services, and income and service payments to foreign parent companies by their affiliates operating in the United States. By far the largest component of this category is merchandise imports, which includes all goods bought or otherwise transferred from a foreign country to the United States.

impost

A tax, usually an import duty. *See also* tariff.

impound

(law/customs) (a) To seize or hold. (b) To place in protective custody by order of a court (e.g., impounded property, impounded records).

in bond

(U.S. Customs) A procedure under which goods are transported or warehoused under customs supervision until they are either formally entered into the customs territory of the United States and duties paid, or until they are exported from the United States.

The procedure is so named because the cargo moves under the carrier's bond (financial liability assured by the carrier) from the gateway sea port or airport and remains "in bond" until customs releases the cargo at the inland customs point.

This procedure is used in several ways:

(1) To postpone the payment of import duties on high duty merchandise, (such as alcoholic beverages), until they are needed,

(2) To hold goods that may or may not meet a requirement of customs until a determination is made and the importer decides to enter the goods or re-export them,

(3) To effect the transport of goods originating in one foreign country through the United States for export to a third country without having to pay customs duties. *See also* temporary importation under bond.

in bond goods
See in bond.

in bond shipment
(customs) An import or export shipment which has not been cleared by U.S. Customs officials. *See* in bond.

in-bond system
(U.S. Customs) A part of U.S. Customs' Automated Commercial System, controls merchandise from the point of unloading at the port of entry or exportation. The system works with the input of departures (from the port of unlading), arrivals, and closures (accountability of arrivals). *See* Automated Commercial System; in bond.

incentive
(economics) A motivational force that stimulates people to greater activity or increased efficiency.

incentive rate
(logistics) A special lower freight rate applied to large or heavy loads to encourage larger volume shipments.

Inchmaree Clause
(insurance) An insurance policy extension to cover loss resulting from a latent defect of the carrying vessel's hull or machinery which is not discoverable by due diligence. (So-called for a celebrated legal decision involving a vessel of that name.) Latent defect is not, by law, recoverable from the vessel owner, and the Inchmaree Clause thus plugs a gap that would otherwise exist in complete insurance protection. Loss resulting from errors of navigation or management of the vessel by the master or the crew, and for which the vessel owner is likewise relieved of liability by law, is also covered by the Inchmaree Clause. *See* special marine policy.

income
(economics) Money or its equivalent, earned or accrued, arising from the sale of goods or services.

Incorporated (Inc.)
(South Africa) Designation for a private limited liability corporation with limited liability to shareholders but with joint and several liability to the directors.
(United States) Designation for a corporation with limited liability to shareholders.

Incoterms
A codification of international rules for the uniform interpretation of common contract clauses in export/import transactions involving goods. Developed and issued by the International Chamber of Commerce (ICC) in Paris. The version which is currently valid is from 2000. The thirteen Incoterms 2000 are:

(1) Ex Works (EXW),
(2) Free Carrier (FCA),
(3) Free Alongside Ship (FAS),
(4) Free On Board FOB),
(5) Cost and Freight CFR),
(6) Cost, Insurance and Freight (CIF),
(7) Carriage Paid To (CPT),
(8) Carriage and Insurance Paid To (CIP),
(9) Delivered At Frontier (DAF),
(10) Delivered Ex Ship (DES),
(11) Delivered Ex Quay (DEQ),
(12) Delivered Duty Unpaid (DDU), and
(13) Delivered Duty Paid (DDP).
Refer to individual listings for definitions of these terms. Also refer to the Appendix Guide to Incoterms 2000. For a book fully describing responsibilities of the seller and the buyer in each term, contact: International Chamber of Commerce (ICC), 38, Cours Albert 1er, 75008 Paris, France; Tel: [33] (1) 49-53-28-28; Fax: [33] (1) 49-53-28-59; Web: www.iccwbo.org; In U.S. contact: ICC Publishing, Inc., 156 Fifth Avenue, Suite 417, New York, NY 10010 USA; Tel: [1] (212) 206-1150; Fax: [1] (212) 633-6025.

indemnify
(insurance/law) To compensate for actual loss sustained. Many insurance policies and all bonds promise to "indemnify" the insureds. Under such a contract, there can be no recovery until the insured has actually suffered a loss, at which time he or she is entitled to be compensated for the damage that has occurred (i.e. to be restored to the same financial position enjoyed before the loss).

indemnity
(insurance/law) An agreement to reimburse another individual or legal entity who incurs a loss that is covered by the agreement. An indemnity against loss may be partial or whole. A buyer may obtain indemnity insurance, for example, to insure against damage to or destruction of goods that may occur after title has passed to the buyer.
(finance) A bond protecting the insured against losses from others failing to fulfill their obligations.
(investments) An option to buy or sell a specific quantity of a stock at a state price within a given time period.
(law) An act of legislation, granting exemption from prosecution to certain people.

independent action
(shipping) The right of a conference member to depart from the common freight rates, terms or conditions of the conference without the need for prior approval of the conference. *See* conference.

indexed currency borrowings
(banking/finance) Borrowings in a foreign currency where the rate of interest is linked to an agreed scale.

indexed currency option note
(banking/finance) Note denominated and paying interest in one currency but whose redemption value is linked to an exchange rate for another currency. Also called Heaven and Hell Bond.

individual validated license
(U.S.) Written approval by the U.S. Department of Commerce granting permission, which is valid for 2 years, for the export of a specified quantity of products or technical data to a single recipient. Individual validated licenses also are required, under certain circumstances, as authorization for re export of U.S.-origin commodities to new destinations abroad. *See* United States Department of Commerce.

indorsement
See endorsement.

industrial list
The Coordinating Committee for Multilateral Export Controls (CoCom) industrial list contains dual-use items whose export are controlled for strategic reasons. *See* Coordinating Committee for Multilateral Export Controls.

industrial policy
(economics) Encompasses traditional government policies intended to provide a favorable economic climate for the development of industry in general or specific industrial sectors. Instruments of industrial policy may include tax incentives to promote investments or exports, direct or indirect subsidies, special financing arrangements, protection against foreign competition, worker training programs, regional development programs, assistance for research and development, and measures to help small business firms. Historically, the term industrial policy has been associated with some degree of centralized economic planning or indicative planning, but this connotation is not always intended by its contemporary advocates.

Industry Consultations Program
(U.S.) An advisory committee structure created by the Trade Act of 1974, expanded by the Trade Agreements Act of 1979, and amended by the Omnibus Trade and Competitiveness Act of 1988. Jointly sponsored by the U.S. Department of Commerce and the U.S. Trade Representative, the program includes over 500 industry executives who provide advice and information to the U.S. government on trade policy matters. The advisors focus on objectives and bargaining positions for multilateral trade negotiations, bilateral trade negotiations, and other trade-related matters. Members of the committees are appointed by the Secretary of Commerce and the U.S. Trade Representative.

The present structure consists of 17 Industry Sector Advisory Committees (ISACs), 3 Industry Functional Advisory Committees (IFACs), a Committee of Chairs, and an Industry Policy Advisory Committee (IPAC). The focus of the 3 Functional Advisory Committees are: (1) Customs Matters, (2) Standards, and (3) Intellectual Property Rights.

The focus of the 17 Industry Sector Advisory Committees are: (1) Aerospace Equipment, (2) Capital Goods, (3) Chemicals and Allied Products, (4) Consumer Goods, (5) Electronics and Instrumentation, (6) Energy, (7) Ferrous Ores and Metals, (8) Footwear, Leather, and Leather Products, (9) Building Products and Other Materials, (10) Lumber and Wood Products, (11) Nonferrous Ores and Metals, (12) Paper and Paper Products, (13) Services, (14) Small and Minority Business, (15) Textiles and Apparel, (16) Transportation, Construction, and Agricultural Equipment, (17) Wholesaling and Retailing.
See Advisory Committee on Trade Policy and Negotiations.

Industry Functional Advisory Committee
See Industry Consultations Program.

Industry Policy Advisory Committee
See Industry Consultations Program.

Industry Sector Advisory Committee
See Industry Consultations Program.

Industry Subsector Analysis
(U.S.) Overseas market research for a given industry subsector (such as cardiological equipment for the medical equipment industry) that presents basic information about a foreign market such as market size, the competitive environment, primary end users, best prospect products, and market access information. Available as individual reports from the U.S. Department of Commerce, or on the National Trade Data Bank, U.S. Dept. of Commerce, Office of Business Analysis, HCHB Room 4885, Washington, DC 20230 USA; Tel: [1] (202) 482-1986.

infant industry argument
(economics) The view that "temporary protection" for a new industry or firm in a particular country through tariff and non-tariff barriers to imports can help it to become established and eventually competitive in world markets. Historically, new industries that are soundly based and efficiently operated have experienced declining costs as output expands and production experience is acquired. However, industries that have been established and operated with heavy dependence on direct or indirect government subsidies have sometimes found it difficult to relinquish that support. The rationale underlying the Generalized System of Preferences is comparable to that of the infant industry argument. *See* Generalized System of Preferences.

inflammable
See flammable.

inflammable liquids
See flammable liquids.

inflation

(economics) Loss of purchasing power of money, caused by growth of the amount of money in circulation which, if the supply of goods stays the same or only increases at a slower rate, leads to an increase in prices.

in-flight survey (IFS)

(U.S.) A survey of U.S. and foreign travelers departing the U.S. as a means of obtaining data on visitor characteristics, travel patterns and spending habits, and for supplying data on the U.S. international travel dollar accounts as well as to meet balance of payments estimation needs. The IFS covers about 70 percent of U.S. carriers and 35 percent of foreign carriers, who voluntarily choose to participate. Sample results are expanded to universe estimates to account for non response of passengers on each sampled flight, for coverage of all flights on each major airline route, and for all international routes. The basis for the expansion is the number of passengers departing the United States, obtained from the Immigration and Naturalization Service.

informal entry

(U.S. Customs) A simplified import entry procedure accepted at the option of Customs for any noncommercial shipment (baggage) and any commercial shipment not over $1,000 in value. *See* entry.

informed compliance

(US Customs) A shared responsibility wherein the US Customs Service effectively communicates its requirements to the trade, and the people and businesses subject to those requirements conduct their regulated activities in conformance with US laws and regulations.

infrastructure

(economics) The basic structure of a nation's economy, including transportation, communications, and other public services, on which the economic activity relies.

inherent vice

(shipping/insurance) Damage to goods which one can foresee is bound to occur during any normal transit, and which arises solely because of the nature or condition of the goods shipped. Such damage is said to arise from "inherent vice" which may be defined as an internal cause rather than an external cause of damage. An example of damage from inherent vice is deterioration of imperfectly cured skins.

Exclusion of insurance coverage for inherent vice is implied in every cargo policy. This type of exclusion is reinforced by the words "from any external cause" in the "all risks" coverage. The word "risk" itself implies that only fortuitous losses are intended to be covered. Insurance protects against hazards, not certainties.

initial margin

(finance/foreign exchange) The amount of margin which has to be deposited with the clearing house both by the buyer and the seller through the respective broker and/or bank in order to establish a position in a futures contract.

initial negotiating right (INR)

(WTO) A right held by a World Trade Organization (WTO) country to seek compensation for an impairment of a given bound tariff rate by another WTO country. INRs stem from past negotiating concessions and allow the INR holder to seek compensation for an impairment of tariff concessions regardless of its status as a supplier of the product in question. *See* World Trade Organization (WTO).

injury

(U.S.) A finding by the U.S. International Trade Commission that imports are causing, or are likely to cause, harm to a U.S. industry. An injury determination is the basis for a Section 201 case. It is also a requirement in all antidumping and most countervailing duty cases, in conjunction with Commerce Department determinations on dumping and subsidization. *See* dumping; countervailing duty; Section 201.

inland bill of lading

(shipping) A bill of lading used in transporting goods overland to the exporter's international carrier. Although a through bill of lading can sometimes be used, it is usually necessary to prepare both an inland bill of lading and an ocean bill of lading for export shipments. *See* bill of lading.

inland carrier

(shipping) A transportation line which hauls import/export traffic between ports and inland points.

in personam

(law) Against the person. In personam jurisdiction, for example, is a court's authority in a legal action to subject a person to its order or judgment.

in rem

(law) Against the thing. In rem jurisdiction, for example, is a court's authority in a legal action to determine title to, or affect interests in, property of the parties.

insolvency

See bankruptcy.

insourcing

(logistics) The sourcing of raw materials, component parts and finished goods from within a business organization. The opposite of outsourcing. *See* outsourcing.

inspection certificate

A document confirming that goods have been inspected for conformity to a set of industry, customer, government or carrier specifications prior to shipment. Inspection certificates are generally obtained from independent, neutral testing organizations.

instrument
(law) Any written document that gives formal expression to a legal agreement or act. *See also* financial instrument.

insulated container
(logistics) A shipping container designed to protect sensitive cargo from extremes in temperature. These containers are not heated or refrigerated, but can, for a limited time, keep inside temperatures from exceeding certain limits. Such containers are often used to transport electronics, electronic equipment, ammunition, some foods and other sensitive goods. *See* container, and the appendix "Guide to Ocean Freight Containers."

insurable interest
(insurance) The financial interest of an individual or business in property, even if that individual is not the owner of the property.

A typical case of insurable interest is where title to goods has passed from the seller to the buyer, but where the seller has yet to receive payment, and still has exposure for loss.

Example 1: When a seller sells on FOB inland point terms, he transfers the title to the buyer before the commencement of the ocean voyage. In this case the obligation to place marine and war risk insurance rests, strictly speaking, with the buyer. However, it is customary in many trades for the seller on FOB terms (or similar terms), to obtain insurance, as well as ocean freight space, for account of the buyer.

This is, in effect, an agency relationship. It can be provided for by a policy clause reading: "to cover all shipments made by or to the assured for their own account as principals, or as agents for others and in which they have an insurable interest, or for the account of others from which written instructions to insure them have been received prior to any known or reported loss, damage or accident prior to sailing of vessel."

Example 2: The seller on FOB or other terms, under which the title passes to the buyer at some inland point of departure, will have a financial interest in the goods until payment has been received. This situation arises when the terms of payment call for sight draft against documents, or for acceptance at 30-60-90 days sight, or for open account. Under such circumstances, the seller will be well advised to place his own insurance to protect himself in the event that the loss or damage to the shipment impairs the buyer's desire to make payment as originally contemplated. For example, the buyer may be uninsured, or the buyer's coverage may be inadequate because of under-insurance or restricted conditions. The buyer's insurance company may be less liberal in loss adjustments than would the insurer of the seller or,

because of currency restrictions, a foreign company may be hampered in its ability to transmit funds. *See* contingency insurance.

insurance
(general) A method whereby those concerned about some form of hazard contribute to a common fund usually an insurance company, out of which losses sustained by the contributors are paid.

(law) A contractual relationship that exists when one party (the insurer), for a consideration (the premium), agrees to reimburse another party (the insured) for loss to a specified subject (the risk) caused by designated contingencies (hazards or perils), or to pay in behalf of the insured all reasonable sums for which he may be liable to a third party (the claimant).

insurance broker
(insurance) An individual or firm who represents buyers of insurance and deals with insurance companies or their agents in arranging for insurance coverage for the buyer.

An insurance agent represents a single insurance company whereas an insurance broker is free to obtain insurance coverage from any insurance company.

insurance certificate
(insurance) A document indicating the type and amount of insurance coverage in force on a particular shipment. Used to assure the consignee that insurance is provided to cover loss of or damage to the cargo while in transit.

In some cases a shipper may issue a document that certifies that a shipment has been insured under a given open policy, and that the certificate represents and takes the place of such open policy, the provisions of which are controlling.

Because of the objections that an instrument of this kind did not constitute a "policy" within the requirements of letters of credit, it has become the practice to use a special marine policy. A special marine policy makes no reference to an open policy and stands on its own feet as an obligation of the underwriting company.

See special marine policy; declaration; bordereau; open policy.

insurance company
(insurance) An organization chartered under state or provincial laws to act as an insurer. In the United States, insurance companies are usually classified as fire and marine, life, casualty, and surety companies and may write only the kinds of insurance for which they are specifically authorized by their charters.

insurance coverage
(insurance) The total amount of insurance that is carried.

insurance document
See insurance certificate.

insurance policy

(insurance) Broadly, the entire written contract of insurance. More specifically, it is the basic written or printed document, as well as the coverage forms and endorsement added to it.

insurance premium

(insurance) The amount paid to an insurance company for coverage under an insurance policy.

insured

(insurance) The person(s) protected under an insurance contract (policy).

insured value

(insurance) The combined value of merchandise, inland freight, ocean freight, cost of packaging, freight forwarding charges, consular fees, and insurance cost, for which insurance is obtained.

insurer

(insurance) The party to the insurance contract who promises to indemnify losses or provide service; the insurance company.

integrated cargo service

(shipping) A blend of all segments of the cargo system providing the combined services of carrier, forwarder, handlers and agents.

integrated carriers

(shipping) Carriers that have both air and ground fleets; or other combinations, such as sea, rail, and truck. Since they usually handle large volumes, they are often less expensive and offer more diverse services than regular carriers.

integrated logistics

(shipping/management) The management of logistics operations as a system rather than as individual activities. Relates to the integration of the entire supply chain management process from just-in-time manufacturing/warehousing through final distribution to the ultimate consumer. Includes the merging of warehousing, packaging, local transportation, international transportation, local market warehousing and final distribution. *See* logistics.

integrated logistics support (ILS)

(logistics) The process of ensuring that all requirements for a logistics system are met. This encompasses all aspects of the supply chain and includes planning, funding, facilities, personnel, hardware and software.

intellectual property

(law) An original work that can be copyrighted, patented, or registered as a trademark or service mark. Ownership conferring the right to possess, use, or dispose of products created by human ingenuity, including patents, trademarks and copyrights. *See* copyright; patent; service mark; trademark.

intellectual property rights

(law) The ownership of the right to possess or otherwise use or dispose of products created by human in-

genuity. See copyright; patent; service mark; trademark.

INTELSAT

See International Telecommunications Satellite Organization.

intended

(shipping) A reference which may appear on marine/ocean bills of lading, non-negotiable sea waybills and multimodal transport documents where the carrier reserves the right to change the port of loading, the ship or the port of discharge. Examples: "intended port of shipment Hamburg," "intended ocean vessel MV Swissahoi," "intended port of discharge Hong Kong."

inter absentee

(law) Among absent parties. An inter absentee contract, for example, is made between parties who do not meet face-to-face.

Interagency Group on Countertrade

(U.S.) Established in December 1988 under Executive Order 12661, reviews policy and negotiates agreements with other countries on countertrade and offsets. The IGC operates at the Assistant Secretary level, with the Department of Commerce as chair. Membership includes 11 other agencies: the Departments of Agriculture, Defense, Energy, Justice, Labor, State, Treasury, the Agency for International Development, the Federal Emergency Management Agency, the U.S. Trade Representative, and the Office of Management and Budget. Contact: Assistant Secretary of Trade Development, U.S. Department of Commerce, 14th Street and Constitution Ave. NW, Washington, DC 20230 USA; Tel: [1] (202) 482-1461. *See* countertrade; offsets.

Inter-American Development Bank

A regional financial institution established in 1959 to advance the economic and social development of 27 Latin American member countries. Address: Inter-American Development Bank, 1300 New York Avenue NW, Washington, DC 20577; Tel: [1] (202) 623-1000; Web: www.iadb.org.

interbank dealings

(banking) Dealings between the banks.

interbank offered rate (IBOR)

(banking/finance) Rate of interest offered by banks for their loans to the most creditworthy banks for a large loan, for a specific period and in a specific currency. The best known one is the London Interbank Offered Rate (LIBOR), but they also exist for Abu Dhabi (ADIBOR), Amsterdam (AIBOR), Bahrein (BIBOR), Brussels (BRIBOR), Hong Kong (HIBOR) or (HKIBOR), Kuwait (KIBOR), Luxembourg (LUXIBOR), Madrid (MIBOR), Paris (PIBOR) (occasionally known as taux interbancaire offert à Paris - TIOP), Saudi Arabia (SAIBOR), Singapore (SIBOR), 6 month SDRs (SDRIBOR), Zurich (ZIBOR) and other financial centers.

interchange

(logistics) (a) The transfer of freight from one carrier to another. (b) The transfer of transportation equipment from one carrier to another.

(data/computers) The transfer of electronic data from one computer to another. *See* EDI, UN/EDIFACT.

interchange agreement

(shipping) An agreement which fixes specific accountability for use and maintenance of carrier-owned equipment. It formalizes terms and conditions under which equipment will be leased, in order to protect the carrier's financial and legal interest in the operation of the leased equipment.

interchange point

(transportation/logistics) A location where one carrier delivers freight or freight transportation equipment to another carrier. *See* interchange, interchange agreement, interchange receipt.

interchange receipt

(logistics) A document that states the condition of equipment at the time of interchange. *See* interchange agreement, interchange point.

intercoastal carrier

(shipping) A carrier that transports cargo between ports of one nation.

(U.S. shipping) A carrier that transports cargo between U.S. east and west coast ports. Refers specifically to water carriers that travel through the Panama Canal.

intercorporate hauling

(logistics) The act of a carrier transporting cargo for a subsidiary and charging a fee.

(U.S. logistics) Intercorporate hauling is legal in the U.S. if the subsidiary is wholly owned by the carrier or if the carrier has common-carrier authority.

Interessantelskab (I/S)

(Denmark, Norway) Designation for a general partnership, in which all partners have joint and several liability.

interest arbitrage

(banking) The attempt to make a profit out of differing interest rates for various maturities and/or various instruments. *See* arbitrage.

interline shipping

(shipping) The movement of a single shipment of freight via two or more carriers. *See* intermodal; coordinated movement; intermodal compatibility.

interlocutory

(law) Temporary or interim. An interlocutory injunction, for example, may be granted pending trial as a temporary restraint against a party before final judgment is rendered.

intermediate consignee

A bank, forwarding agent, or other intermediary (if any) which acts in a foreign country as an agent for the exporter, the purchaser, or the ultimate consignee, for the purpose of effecting delivery of the export to the ultimate consignee.

intermodal transport

(shipping) The coordinated transport of freight, especially in connection with relatively long-haul movements using any combination of freight forwarders, piggyback, containerization, air-freight, ocean freight, assemblers, motor carriers.

intermodal compatibility

(shipping) The capability which enables a shipment to be transferred from one form of transport to another, as from airplane to highway truck, to railway freight car, to ocean vessel.

intermodal marketing company (IMC)

(logistics) A shipping intermediary that acts as a broker by arranging, buying and selling intermodal freight services. IMCs are not carriers.

International Air Transport Association (IATA)

A trade association serving airlines, passengers, shippers, travel agents, and governments. Address: International Air Transport Association, 800 Place Victoria, P.O. Box 113, Montreal, Quebec H4Z 1M1 Canada; Tel: [1] (514) 874-0202; Fax: [1] (514) 874-9632; Web: www.iata.org.

International Anticounterfeiting Coalition

A non-profit organization located in Washington, DC that seeks to advance intellectual property rights protection on a worldwide basis by promoting laws, regulations, and directives designed to render theft of intellectual property rights unattractive and unprofitable. Address: International Anticounterfeiting Coalition, 1725 K Street, NW, Suite 1101, Washington, DC 20006 USA; Tel: [1] (202) 223-6667; Fax: [1] (202) 223-6668; Web: www.iacc.org.

International Atomic Energy Agency (IAEA)

The primary international organization that enforces a system of safeguards to ensure that non-nuclear weapons states do not divert shipments of sensitive equipment from peaceful applications to the production of nuclear weapons. Before a supplier state of nuclear materials or equipment may approve an export to a non-nuclear weapons NPT (Nuclear Non-Proliferation Treaty) signatory state, it must receive assurances that the recipient will place the material under IAEA safeguards. Subsequent to shipment, the recipient state must allow IAEA officials to verify the legitimate end use of the exported materials or equipment.

IAEA, established in July 1957, gives advice and technical assistance to developing countries on nuclear power development, nuclear safety, radioactive waste management, and related efforts. Safeguards are the technical means applied by the IAEA to verify that nuclear equipment or materials are used exclusively for peaceful purposes. Address: International Atomic Energy Agency, Vienna International Centre, Wagramerstrasse 5, Postfach 100, A-1400 Vienna, Austria; Tel: [43] (1) 26-000; Fax: [43] (1) 26-007; Web: www.iaea.org.

International Bank for Reconstruction and Development (The World Bank)

(banking) The International Bank for Reconstruction and Finance (IBRF) was proposed at Bretton Woods on July 1944, commencing operation in June 1946. Originally established to help countries reconstruct their economies after World War II. IBRD, commonly referred to as the World Bank, now assists developing member countries by lending to government agencies, or by guaranteeing private loans for such projects as agricultural modernization or infrastructural development. Address: International Bank for Reconstruction and Development, 1818 H Street NW, Washington, DC 20433 USA; Tel: [1] (202) 477-1234. *See also* International Monetary Fund; World Bank; World Bank Group; Web: www.worldbank.org.

international banking facility (IBF)

(U.S.) One of four categories of foreign banking in the United States. An IBF is a set of asset and liability accounts that is segregated and limited to financing international trade.

International Buyer Program

(U.S.) (Formerly Foreign Buyer Program) A joint industry-U.S. International Trade Administration program to assist exporters in meeting qualified foreign purchasers for their product or service at trade shows held in the United States. ITA selects leading U.S. trade shows in industries with high export potential. Each show selected for the FBP receives promotion through overseas mailings, U.S. embassy and regional commercial newsletters, and other promotional techniques. ITA trade specialists counsel participating U.S. exhibitors. Contact: International Buyer Program, International Trade Administration, Department of Commerce, Washington, DC 20230 USA; Web: www.usatrade.gov/Website/Website.nsf/Web-BySubj/TradeEvents_InternationalBuyerProgram

International Center for Settlement of Investment Disputes (ICSID)

(banking) A separate organization of the World Bank which encourages greater flows of investment capital by providing facilities for the conciliation and arbitration of disputes between governments and foreign investors. The ICSID also conducts and publishes research in foreign-investment law. Address: International Center for Settlement of Investment Disputes, 1818 H Street NW, Washington, DC 20433 USA; Tel: [1] (202) 458-1534; Fax: [1] (202) 522-2615; Web: www.worldbank.org/icsid.

International Chamber of Commerce (ICC)

A non-governmental organization serving as a policy advocate for world business. Members in 110 countries comprise tens of thousands of companies and business organizations. The ICC aims to facilitate world trade, investment, and an international free market economy through consultation with other inter-governmental organizations.

The ICC was founded in Atlantic City in 1919. It now encompasses associations and companies from all branches of industry. As an institution of international economic self-administration, it operates through expert commissions, sub-committees and working groups to address questions which are of importance for the international business community. These include, for example, contract and delivery clauses (Incoterms); standardization of means of payment, (Uniform Rules for Collection, Uniform Customs and Practice for Documentary Credits, Uniform Rules for Demand Guarantees); arbitral jurisdiction (Rules of Conciliation and Arbitration); questions relating to such issues as competition, foreign investments, and transportation.

The ICC also offers various services to the business community such as the ATA Carnet system. The ICC publishes many books and references which are valuable to the international trade community. Address: International Chamber of Commerce, 38 Cours Albert 1er, 75008 Paris, France; Tel: (1) 49-53-28-28; Fax: (1) 49-53-28-59; Web: www.uscib.org; For U.S. representative, contact: U.S. Council for International Business, 1212 Avenue of the Americas, New York, NY 10036; Tel: [1] (212) 354-4480, or, for ICC publications in the U.S. contact ICC Publishing, Inc., 156 Fifth Avenue, New York, NY 10010 USA; Tel: [1] (212) 206-1150; Fax: [1] (212) 633-6025. Refer to the Appendix for a list of ICC publications.

International Cocoa Agreement

See international commodity agreement.

International Coffee Agreement

See international commodity agreement.

international commodity agreement

An international understanding, usually reflected in a legal instrument, relating to trade in a particular basic commodity, and based on terms negotiated and accepted by most of the countries that export and import commercially significant quantities of the commodity. Some commodity agreements (such as exists for coffee, cocoa, natural rubber, sugar, and tin) center on economic provisions intended to defend a price range for the commodity through the use of buffer stocks or export quotas or both. Other commodity agreements (such as existing agreements for jute and jute products, olive oil, and wheat) promote cooperation among producers and consumers through improved consultation, exchange of information, research and development, and export promotion.

International Communications Satellite Organization (Intelsat)

The organization formed under a multilateral agreement which owns, maintains, and operates the global satellite system used by over 100 participating countries. COMSAT is the United States' representative to and participant in Intelsat. Address: International Communications Satellite Organization (Intelsat), 3400 International Drive NW, Washington, DC 20008-3098 USA; Tel: [1] (202) 944-6800; Fax: [1] (202) 944-7898; Web: www.intelsat.com.

International Company Profile (ICP)

(U.S. Dept. of Commerce) A fee-based service that provides a background report on a specific foreign firm, prepared by U.S. commercial officers overseas. ICPs provide information about the type of organization, year established, relative size, number of employees, general reputation, territory covered, language preferred, product lines handled, principal owners, financial references, and trade references. ICPs include narrative information about the reliability of the foreign firm. Cost is $100 per report. Issued by the ITA. To obtain an International Company Profile, contact the nearest Department of Commerce district office, or call [1] (800) USA-TRADE; Web: www.usatrade.gov.

International Dairy Agreement

See international commodity agreement.

International Development Association (IDA)

An affiliate of the World Bank Group that was created in 1959 to lend money to developing countries at no interest and for a long repayment period. By providing development assistance through soft loans, IDA meets the needs of many developing countries that cannot afford development loans at ordinary rates of interest and in the time span of conventional loans. Address: International Development Association, World Bank, 1818 H Street NW, Washington, DC 20433 USA; Tel: [1] (202) 477-1234; Fax:[1] (202) 477-6391.

International Electrotechnical Commission (IEC)

The IEC was established in 1906 to deal with questions related to international standardization in the electrical and electronic engineering fields. The members of the IEC are the national committees, one for each country, which are required to be as representative as possible of all electrical interests in the country concerned: manufacturers, users, governmental authorities, teaching, and professional bodies. They are composed of representatives of the various organizations which deal with questions of electrical standardization at the national level. Most of them are recognized and supported by their governments. Address: International Electrotechnical Commission, 3 rue de Varembé, PO Box 131, 1211 Geneva 20, Switzerland; Tel: [41] (22) 919-02-11; Fax: [41] (22) 919-03-00; Web: www.iec.ch.

International Emergency Economic Powers Act (IEEPA)

(U.S. law) The IEEPA was enacted in 1977 to extend emergency powers previously granted to the president by the Trading with the Enemy Act of 1917 (which still authorized the president to exercise extraordinary powers when the United States is at war). IEEPA enables the president, after declaring that a national emergency exists because of a threat from a source outside the United States, to investigate, regulate, compel or prohibit virtually any economic transaction involving property in which a foreign country or national has an interest.

International Energy Agency (IEA)

The IEA was founded in 1974 as a forum for energy cooperation among 21 member nations. The IEA helps participating countries prepare to reduce the economic risks of oil supply disruptions and to reduce dependence on oil through coordinated and cooperative research efforts. Headquarters address: International Energy Agency, 9 rue de la Federation, 75739 Paris Cedex 15, France; Tel: [33] (1) 40 57 65 51; Web: www.iea.org.

International Federation of Freight Forwarders Associations (FIATA)

(logistics) The world's largest non-governmental trade organization in the field of transportation and logistics. FIATA's objectives are to unite the freight-forwarding industry worldwide, represent and promote the interests of the industry with other international organizations, disseminate information, offer publications about the industry to members and to the public, promote uniform forwarding documents, assist in vocational training, help develop tools for electronic commerce including electronic data interchange (EDI) and promote standard trading conditions. Contact: FIATA Secretariat; Baumackerstrasse 24; CH-8050 Zurich; Switzerland; Tel: [44] (1) 311 65 11; Fax: [44] (1) 311 90 44; Web: www.fiata.com.

International Finance Corporation (IFC)

The IFC was established in 1956 as a member of the World Bank Group. The IFC promotes capital flow into private investment in developing countries. Address: International Finance Corporation, 2121 Pennsylvania Ave. NW, Washington, DC 20433 USA; Tel: [1] (202) 473-7711; Fax: [1] (202) 974-4384; Web: www.ifc.org. *See* World Bank Group.

International Frequency Registration Board (IFRB)

An organizational entity under the International Telecommunication Union (ITU). Located in Geneva, IFRB is composed of five full-time elected officials with a rotating chairmanship. IFRB maintains the International Frequency Register, monitors and analyzes all ITU records of frequency use around the world, and makes determinations as to whether or not certain systems are in compliance with the Radio Regulations. *See* International Telecommunications Union.

international investment

See foreign direct investment in the U.S.

International Jute Agreement

See international commodity agreement.

International Labor Organization (ILO)

The ILO, set up in 1919, became a specialized agency of the United Nations in 1946. The ILO seeks to promote improved working and living conditions by establishing standards that reduce social injustice. Address: International Labor Organization, 4, rue des Morillons, CH-1211, Geneva 22, Switzerland; Tel: [41] (22) 799-6111; Fax: [41] (22) 798-8685; Web: www.ilo.org.

International Maritime Organization (IMO)

The International Maritime Organization, IMO, was established as a specialized agency of the United Nations in 1948. The IMO facilitates cooperation on technical matters affecting merchant shipping and traffic. It publishes "Guidelines for Packing and Securing Cargoes in Containers for Transport by Land or Sea" (Container Packing Guidelines). Address: International Maritime Organization, 4 Albert Embankment, London SE1 7SR, England; Tel: [44] (207) 735-7611; Fax: [44] (207) 587-3210; Web: www.imo.org.

International Maritime Satellite Organization (IMSO or INMARSAT)

An international partnership of signatories from 62 nations. The partnership provides mobile satellite capacity to its signatories, who, in turn, use the capacity to provide worldwide mobile satellite services to their maritime, aeronautical and land-mobile customers—including shipping, cruise, fishing, research and offshore exploration industries, and airlines. INMARSAT began service in 1976. COMSAT is the U.S. signatory to INMARSAT. Address: International Maritime Satellite Organization, 99 City Road, London EC1Y 1AX, UK; Tel: [44] (207) 728-1000; Fax: [44] (207) 728-1044; Web: www.imso.org.

International Market Insights (IMI)

(U.S.) Reports prepared by staff at American embassies and consulates covering developments in a single country that are of interest to traders and investors. Topics may include: new laws, policies and procedures, new trade regulations, and marketplace changes. Available from the National Trade Data Bank CD-ROM, online through the Department of Commerce's STAT-USA/Internet service at Web: www.stat-usa.gov, or as individual reports from the Department of Commerce. For address information, *see* National Trade Data Bank; STAT-USA; United States Department of Commerce. Tel: [1] (800) STAT-USA.

international market research

See Industry Subsector Analysis.

International Monetary Fund (IMF)

(banking/finance/foreign exchange) An international financial institution proposed at the 1944 Bretton Woods Conference and established in 1946 that seeks to stabilize the international monetary system as a sound basis for the orderly expansion of international trade. Specifically, among other things, the Fund monitors exchange rate policies of member countries, lends them foreign exchange resources to support their adjustment policies when they experience balance of payments difficulties, and provides them financial assistance through a special "compensatory financing facility" when they experience temporary shortfalls in commodity export earnings. Membership in the fund is a prerequisite to membership in the International Bank for Reconstruction and Development.

Address: International Monetary Fund, 700 19th Street NW, Washington, DC 20431 USA; Tel: [1] (202) 623-7000; Fax: [1] (202) 623-4661; Web: www.imf.org.

See Bretton-Woods Agreement; International Bank for Reconstruction and Development; World Bank Group.

International Olive Oil Agreement

See international commodity agreement.

International Organization for Standardization.

See International Standards Organization.

International Partner Search (IPS)

(U.S. government) An International Trade Administration (ITA) fee-based service which locates foreign import agents and distributors for U.S. exporters. IPS provides a custom search overseas for interested and qualified foreign representatives on behalf of a U.S. exporter. Officers abroad conduct the search and prepare a report identifying up to six foreign prospects that have examined the U.S. firm's product literature and have expressed interest in representing the U.S. firm's products. Contact the nearest Department of Commerce District Office or call [1] (800) USA-TRADE. To obtain more information or to order an International Partner Search, visit Web: www.usatrade.gov. *See* United States Department of Commerce.

International POW WOW

(U.S.) An annual trade fair, coordinated by the Travel Industry Association of America (TIA) to promote foreign tourism to the United States, which brings together over 1,200 international buyers (tour operators and wholesalers) from 55 countries. The buyers are chosen through international selection criteria and purchase packages which they sell to their respective travel retailers.

Each non-U.S. country has a chairman and the chairman has a selection committee. Each country has a quota of buyers they can send to either the U.S. or the European POW WOW. If a buyer wants to go and hasn't already been selected, they can try contacting the selection committee via the chairman. One way to find out who this is, would be to contact the Travel Industry Association of America (see address below.) U.S. sellers do not need to go through such a process. However, to have a booth at the European POW WOW they must be TIA members. They do not have to be TIA members to participate in the U.S. POW WOW. Organizer: Travel Industry Association of America, 1100 New York Ave. NW, Suite 450, Washington, DC 20005-3934 USA; Tel: [1] (202) 408-8422; Fax: [1] (202) 408-1255; Web: www.tia.org. The TIA coordinates the POW WOW with the U.S. Travel and Tourism Administration of the U.S. Department of Commerce.

International Rubber Agreement (IRA)

An international agreement among natural rubber exporting and importing nations whose purpose is to stabilize the price of rubber through import quotas, thereby protecting rubber exporting countries in the developing world from the effects of extreme price fluctuations. *See* international commodity agreement.

International Standard Audiovisual Number (ISAN)

(international standard) An internationally recognized voluntary numbering system for the identification of audiovisual works. The ISAN is similar to the ISBN (International Standard Book Number) system for the identification of books.

The ISAN is a 16-digit number consisting of a 12-digit root segment and a 4-digit segment for the identification of episodes or parts when applicable. A check digit is added whenever the ISAN is presented in human-readable form.

The ISAN identifies the work rather than the content of the work or actual publications. There is no relation between the ISAN and copyright registration. The standard was developed by the International Standards Organization (ISO).

Contact: Web: www.nlc-bnc.ca/iso/tc46sc9, clicking specifically on WG 1 (ISAN).

International Standard Book Number (ISBN)

(international standard) The internationally-recognized standard numbering system for the identification of publications of all kinds.

The ISBN is a 10-digit number that identifies both the publisher and the publication. The numbering system was defined by the International Organization for Standardization (ISO) in 1970 as ISO 2108. Numbers are assigned by agencies in the U.S. and Germany.

U.S. ISBN Agency; 121 Chanlon Road; New Providence, NJ 07974 USA; Tel: 877-310-7333; Fax: 908-665-2895; isbn-san@bowker.com.

International Standard Book Number Agency; Staatsbibliothek zu Berlin; Preussischer Kulturbesitz; D-10772 Berlin, Germany; Tel: [49] 30 266 23 38; Fax: [49] (30) 266 28 14, 266 23 78; E-mail: isbn@sbb.spk-Berlin.de; Web: www.isbn.spk-berlin.de; also Web: www.isbn.org.

International Standard Industrial Classification

(classification system) A United Nations business enterprise classification system based upon the economic activity of the enterprise. The currently valid version is Revision 3. Contact at UNSD (United Nations Statistical Division); Web: www.un.org.

International Standard Musical Work Code (ISWC)

(international standard) The internationally recognized standard numbering system for the identification of musical works.

An ISWC for musical works consists of a letter followed by nine digits and a check digit, as follows:

distinguishing element (1 letter); work identifier (9 digits) and check digit (1 digit). The distinguishing element for musical works is the letter «T». In printed form the ISWC is preceded by a label and may include hyphens and dots between the elements for ease of reading. Example ISWC T-034.524.680-1

Arrangements, adaptations and translations are all given separate ISWCs. These are known collectively as versions. The system is based on the International Standards Organization ISO 15707. The International ISWC Agency is provided by CISAC (International Confederation of Societies of Authors and Composers).

Numbers may be obtained through rights societies or directly by individuals. Works in the public domain may also have a number allocated.

Contact: ISWC Administrator; International ISWC Agency; CISAC; 20-26, Boulevard du Parc; 92200 Neuilly sur Seine France; Tel: [33] 1 55 62 08 50; Fax: [33] 1 55 62 08 60; E-mail: info@iswc.org; Web: www.iswc.org.

International Standard Music Number (ISMN)

(international standard) An internationally recognized code used in the identification of music publications. The ISMN is similar to the ISBN (International Standard Book Number) system for the identification of books. The ISMN identifies all printed music publications, whether available for sale, hire or free of charge—whether a part, a score or an element in a multi-media kit.

The ISMN consists of four elements comprising ten digits: 1) a constant <M>, to distinguish it from other standard numbers, 2) a publisher prefix which identifies a certain music publisher, 3) a title number which identifies a certain publication and 4) a check digit which validates the number on a mathematical basis.

Items to be given an ISMN include:

Scores, miniature (study) scores, vocal scores, sets of parts, individual parts when available separately, pop folios, anthologies, multimedia when printed music is a part of the kit, song texts or lyrics when published with the music, song books (optional), microform publications, braille music publications and electronic publications.

Items not to be given ISMNs include:

Books on music, stand-alone sound or video recordings and serials.

Benefits of the ISMN system include:

Fast and unique identification, allows quick and efficient ordering and tele-ordering, speeded up distribution, creation of a music trade directory, Music in Print, support for bar coding and electronic point-of-sale systems and support for a variety of computer applications.

The International Agency is responsible for the maintenance of the ISMN system, the standard and its application. Publishers prefixes are distributed on a national or regional level by ISMN agencies. Publishers usually administer their own contingents of title numbers as received from the ISMN agency.

ISO Standard 10957 gives basic rules of the ISMN system. A more explicit ISMN Users's Manual is available free of charge from the International ISMN Agency. International ISMN Agency; Berlin, Germany; Web: www.ismn-international.org.

International Standard Recording Code (ISRC)

(international standard) The internationally recognized standard code system used to identify sound and audio-visual recordings and individual tracks on compact disks (CDs), music videos and other media, primarily to ensure royalty payments. The ISRC is contained in the subcode (Q-channel) and is unique to each track of the recording. Note that the ISRC identifies the track and not the physical product.

Each ISRC is comprised of 12 characters as follows: 2 characters to identify the country of residence of the registrant of the recording (such as FR for France); 3 characters or digits to identify the first owner (as allocated by Phonographic Performance Ltd. for audio); 2 digits to identify the year of recording (represented as the last two digits of the year); and a 5 digit Designation Code assigned by the first owner.

The ISRC was developed by the International Standards Organization (ISO) in 1986 and is also known as ISO 3901.

U.S. Contact: RIAA (Recording Industry Association of America); Web: www.riaa.org/index.cfm.

International Standard Serial Number (ISSN)

(international standard) The internationally recognized standard numbering system used to identify serial publications (such as newspapers, annuals, magazines and journals).

Each ISSN is comprised of two groups of 4 digits separated by a hyphen. The eighth character is a control digit calculated using the preceding 7 digits. If the calculation equals "10" the control digit is "X" (e.g., ISSN 1234-567X).

The ISSN is simply an identifier of a specific serial. The ISSN does not identify the serial's country of origin, language, contents, frequency of publication or copyright.

The ISSN was originally established by the International Standards Organization (ISO) and is currently administered from over 60 national centers. The International Center in Paris handles central distribution of ISSNs and takes care of countries that do not have their own national center.

ISSN International Center; 20, rue Bachaumont; 75002 Paris France; Tel: [33] (1) 40 26 32 43; Fax: [33] (1) 44 88 60 96; E-mail: issnic@issn.org; Web: www.issn.org

International Standards Organization (ISO)

The ISO, established in 1947, is a worldwide federation of national bodies, representing approximately 90 member countries. The scope of the International Standards Organization covers standardization in all fields except electrical and electronic engineering standards, which are the responsibility of the International Electrotechnical Commission (IEC). Together, the ISO and IEC form the specialized system for worldwide standardization—the world's largest nongovernmental system for voluntary industrial and technical collaboration at the international level.

The result of ISO technical work is published in the form of International Standards. There are, for example, ISO standards for the quality grading of steel; for testing the strength of woven textiles; for storage of citrus fruits; for magnetic codes on credit cards; for automobile safety belts; and for ensuring the quality and performance of such diverse products as surgical implants, ski bindings, wire ropes, and photographic lenses.

ISO 9000 is a new series of voluntary international quality standards. Its formal name is ISO 9000 Series of Standards. Adoption of ISO standards has become a virtual prerequisite for doing business internationally. Address: International Standards Organization, 1 rue de Varembé, PO Box 56, CH-1211 Geneva 20, Switzerland; Tel: [41] (22) 749-0111; Fax: [41] (22) 733-3430; Web: www.iso.ch. In the United States contact: International Organization for Standards, The American National Standards Institute, 25 West 43rd Street, 4th Floor, New York, NY 10036 USA; Tel: [1] (212) 642-4900; Web: www.ansi.org.

International Sugar Agreement

See international commodity agreement.

International Telecommunications Satellite Organization (INTELSAT)

Created in 1964 under a multilateral agreement, INTELSAT was originally a nonprofit cooperation of countries from around the world that jointly owned and operated a global communications satellite system serving the world. Currently, INTELSAT is a private corporation with a global fleet of 21 satellites (with plans to launch an additional seven), and offers wholesale Internet, broadcast, telephony and corporate network solutions to leading service providers in more than 200 countries and territories worldwide. Contact: Intelsat Global Service Corporation, 3400 International Drive, NW, Washington, D.C. 20008 USA; Tel: [1] (202) 944-6800; Fax: [1] (202) 944-7898; Web: www.intelsat.com.

International Telecommunications Union

A specialized agency of the United Nations with responsibilities for developing operational procedures and technical standards for the use of the radio frequency spectrum, the satellite orbit, and for the international public telephone and telegraph network. There are over 160 member nations of the ITU. The Radio Regulations that result from ITU conferences have treaty status and provide the principal guidelines for world telecommunications. In the case of the U.S., they are the framework for development of the U.S. national frequency allocations and regulations. The ITU has four permanent organs: the General Secretariat, the International Frequency Registration Board (IFRB), the International Radio Consultative Committee (CCIR), and the International Telegraph and Telephone and Consultative Committee (ITTCC). Address: International Telecommunications Union, Place des Nations, CH-1211 Geneva 20, Switzerland; Tel: [41] (22) 730-5111; Fax: [41] (22) 733-7256; Web: www.itu.int.

International Tin Agreement

See international commodity agreement.

International Trade Administration (ITA)

(U.S.) The trade unit of the U.S. Department of Commerce, ITA was established in 1980 to carry out the U.S. government's nonagricultural foreign trade activities and support the policy negotiations of the U.S. Trade Representative. It encourages and promotes U.S. exports of manufactured goods, administers U.S. statutes and agreements dealing with foreign trade, and advises on U.S. international trade and commercial policy. An important arm of the ITA is the United States and Foreign Commercial Service. Address: International Trade Administration, 14th Street and Constitution Avenue NW, Washington, DC 20230 USA; Tel: [1] (202) 482-2867. *See also* United States Department of Commerce; United States and Foreign Commercial Service; United States Trade Representative.

International Trade Commission (ITC)

(U.S.) An independent U.S. government fact-finding agency with six commissioners who review and make recommendations concerning countervailing duty and antidumping petitions submitted by U.S. industries seeking relief from imports that benefit unfair trade practices. Known as the U.S. Tariff Commission before its mandate was broadened by the Trade Act of 1974. Address: U.S. Department of Commerce, International Trade Commission, 500 E. Street SW, Washington, DC 20436 USA; Tel: [1] (202) 205-2000; Web: www.usitc.gov. *See* dumping; countervailing duty.

International Traffic in Arms Regulations

(U.S.) Regulations administered in the United States by the U.S. State Department to control the export of weapons and munitions.

International Union for the Protection of Literary and Artistic Works

See Berne Convention; World Intellectual Property Organization.

International Wheat Agreement

See international commodity agreement.

interstate carrier

(shipping-U.S.) A common carrier whose business extends beyond the boundaries of one state. *See* carrier; common carrier.

interstate commerce

(U.S.) Trade between or among several states of the United States. A seller that uses a telephone or facsimile across state lines in its transactions, or transports goods by rail or interstate roads is using interstate commerce.

Interstate Commerce Act of 1887

(U.S. law) Federal legislation regulating the practices, rates, and rules of transportation for carriers engaged in handling interstate shipments or the movement for a fee of people across state lines.

intervention
(banking/foreign exchange) Efforts by central banks and national governments to influence the exchange rates for its currency. Intervention is usually done in one of two ways: (1) The purchase of large amounts of a currency in order to bolster the price, or (2) The sale of large amounts of a currency to lower the price of the currency. Central banks can also raise interest rates in order to attract capital into the country or lower interest rates to discourage the flow of capital into the country.

intervention currency
(banking/foreign exchange) The foreign currency a country uses to ensure by means of official exchange transactions that the permitted exchange rate margins are observed. Intervention usually takes the form of purchases and sales of foreign currency by the central bank or exchange equalization fund in domestic dealings with commercial banks.

in-the-money
(foreign exchange) An option is in-the-money in the following cases: (1) Call option: market price is greater than the strike price; and (2) Put option: market price less than the strike price. For European options, replace the market price by the forward price of the underlying instrument on the expiry date of the option. *See also* call option; put option; strike price; European option; out-of-the-money.

intrinsic value
(commerce/economics) The value of an item independent of location or ownership.
(banking/finance/foreign exchange) The difference between the strike price of an option and the forward price of the underlying security up to maturity, as long as the option is in-the-money. The premium of an option is made up of the time value and the intrinsic value.

in trust (goods/documents)
(banking) In documentary collections, when a bank releases documents to the importer/buyer to allow him to inspect them prior to payment.

inventory
(commerce/accounting/logistics) (a) A listing of raw materials, component parts, work in progress and finished goods on hand at any given moment. (b) The value of raw materials, component parts, work in progress and finished goods on hand at any given moment. *See* cycle inventory, defective goods inventory, inventory deployment, inventory in transit, inventory turns.

inventory carrying costs
(commerce/accounting/logistics) The costs associated with maintaining goods in inventory. These include the time value of money invested in producing or purchasing the inventory, warehousing, insurance,

depreciation of warehouse and equipment, obsolescence, taxes, utilities and administrative costs.

inventory deployment
(logistics) The strategic management of inventory to minimize stock and storage levels (and thus costs) while meeting customer demand. This is achieved by dynamically monitoring supply, demand, inventory at rest and inventory in transit.

inventory in transit
(logistics/accounting) (a) Inventory that is in the possession of carriers. (b) The value of inventory that is in the possession of carriers. Value can be defined as the either the cost or the sales value.

inventory turns
(logistics) The number of times an inventory is replaced over a stated period of time. The annual unit calculation is: total number of units sold during a year divided by the average number of units kept in inventory during the year.

investment climate statements
(U.S.) Reports prepared occasionally by the commercial sections of U.S. embassies for the U.S. and Foreign Commercial Service, covering 67 individual countries. The ICSs provide statistics and analysis of policies and issues effecting the climate for direct investment in the individual country. *See* United States and Foreign Commercial Service.

investment performance requirements
(foreign investment) Special conditions imposed on direct foreign investment by recipient governments, sometimes requiring commitments to export a certain percentage of the output, to purchase given supplies locally, or to ensure the employment of a specified percentage of local labor and management.

invisible balance
See invisible trade balance.

invisible barriers to trade
Government regulations that do not directly restrict trade, but indirectly impede free trade by imposing excessive or obscure requirements on goods sold within a country, especially imported goods. These regulations are often known to business owners within the country, because they may be required to comply with them, but are often not known by foreign businesses seeking to export their products, and therefore such regulations are "invisible." Examples include labelling requirements, sanitary standards, and size or measurement standards.

invisibles; invisible trade
(economics) Non-merchandise items such as freight, insurance, and financial services that are included in a country's balance of payments accounts (in the "current" account), even though they are not re-

corded as physically visible exports and imports. *See* balance of trade.

invisible trade balance

(economics) As contrasted with the import and export of goods—the trade balance created by the import and export of services, including consulting and advisory services, transportation services, income and expenditure on travel services, insurances, licenses, earnings and interest income from international capital movements. *See* balance of trade.

invoice

A document identifying the seller and buyer of goods or services, identifying numbers such as invoice number, date, shipping date, mode of transport, delivery and payment terms, and a complete listing and description of the goods or services being sold including prices, discounts and quantities. *See* commercial invoice.

inward foreign manifest (IFM)

(U.S. Customs) A U.S. Customs mandated document requiring the complete listing by bill of lading numbers of an arriving ship's freight being imported into the United States.

ipso jure

(law) By operation of law. Contract terms that are implied by a court from the conduct of the parties, for example, are enforceable ipso jure.

irregular route carrier

(logistics) A motor carrier that does not follow a set route.

irrevocable letter of credit

(banking) A letter of credit which cannot be amended or canceled without prior mutual consent of all parties to the credit. Such a letter of credit guarantees payment by the bank to the seller/exporter so long as all the terms and conditions of the credit have been met.

Documentary letters of credit issued subject to the Uniform Customs and Practice for Documentary Credits (UCPDC) Publication No. 500 are deemed to be irrevocable unless expressly marked as revocable. *See* letter of credit.

irritating material

(shipping) Items capable of causing discomfort such as tearing, choking, vomiting and skin irritation. (UN CLASS 6.) Examples are tear gas and riot control agents. Hazards/precautions are: may cause difficulty in breathing; may burn but do not ignite readily; exposure in enclosed areas may be harmful; may cause tearing of the eyes, choking, nausea or skin irritation.

ISIC

See International Standard Industrial Classification.

ISO 1400

A family of voluntary *generic management system standards* established by the ISO (International Standards Organization) that are concerned with "environmental management." ISO 14000 is not a product or service standard. Generic means that the same standards may be applied to any organization, whether public or private, non-profit or profit-making, regardless of its size or whether it deals in a products or services. Management system means that the organization has a systematic written procedure for managing its activities. Standards means that the organization is following an internationally recognized model for setting up and operating the management system. Environmental management is what an organization does to make sure that its products and/or services will have the least harmful impact on the environment, either during production or disposal, either by pollution or by depleting natural resources.

Adoption of ISO standards has become a virtual prerequisite for doing business internationally. See International Standards Organization.

ISO 9000

A family of voluntary *generic management system standards* established by the ISO (International Standards Organization) that are concerned with "quality management." ISO 9000 is not a product or service standard. Generic means that the same standards may be applied to any organization, whether public or private, non-profit or profit-making, regardless of its size or whether it deals in a products or services. Management system means that the organization has a systematic written procedure for managing its activities. Standards means that the organization is following an internationally recognized model for setting up and operating the management system. Quality management is what an organization does to make sure that its products and/or services conform to customer requirements.

Its formal name is ISO 9000 Series of Standards. Adoption of ISO standards has become a virtual prerequisite for doing business internationally. *See* International Standards Organization.

ISRC

See International Standard Recording Code.

issuance

(banking) The establishment of a letter of credit by the issuing bank (buyer's bank) based on the buyer's application and credit relationship with the bank. *See* letter of credit; advice; amendment.

issuance date of the documents

(shipping) Unless otherwise stipulated in a transport document, the date of issuance is deemed to be the date of shipment or loading on board of the goods.

(banking) Unless prohibited by the documentary letter of credit, documents bearing a date of issuance prior to that of the letter of credit are acceptable.

issuing bank

(banking) The buyer's bank which establishes a letter of credit at the request of the buyer, in favor of the beneficiary (seller/exporter). Also called the buyer's bank or the opening bank. *See also* advising bank; negotiating bank.

issuing carrier

(logistics) The carrier that issues the bill of lading. Specifically, the carrier that establishes the contract for carriage.

J

Japan Bank for International Cooperation (JBIC)

(Japan) Japan's official provider of export credits. Address: Japan Bank for International Cooperation, 4-1, Otemachi 1-chome, Chiyoda-ku, Tokyo 100-8144, Japan; Tel: [81] (3) 3287-9101; Telex: 23728; Fax: [81] (3) 3287-9539; Web: www.jbic.go.jp.

Japan, Development Bank of (DBJ)

(Japan) The Development Bank of Japan was founded in 1951 to aid in developing and diversifying the Japanese economy. The DBJ is a non-profit organization owned entirely by the Japanese Government. U.S. companies may participate in DBJ funding activity under the Bank's Loan Division in the International Department. The International Department disburses loans to foreign companies under two primary loan programs: Promotion of Foreign Direct Investment in Japan and Facilities for Import Products. The other loan programs of DBJ are also available to foreign-owned companies under the principle of equal treatment of clients regardless of nationality. Contact: Development Bank of Japan; 9-1, 1-chome, Otemachi; Chiyoda-ku, Tokyo 100-0004, Japan; Tel: [81] (3) 3244-1900; Web: www.dbj.go.jp (in Japanese)

Japan Export Information Center (JEIC)

(U.S.) Provides information on doing business in Japan, market entry alternatives, market information and research, product standards and testing requirements, tariffs and non-tariff barriers. The Center maintains a commercial library and participates in private- and government-sponsored seminars on doing business in Japan. JEIC is operated by the International Trade Administration of the U.S. Department of Commerce, 14th Street and Constitution Ave. NW, Washington, DC 20230 USA; Tel: [1] (202) 482-2425 and [1] (202) 482-4524; Fax: [1] (202) 482-0469;

Japan External Trade Organization (JETRO)

(Japan) Although legally under the aegis of the Ministry of International Trade and Industry (MITI), JETRO administers the export programs of the Japanese Government independently. The MITI subsidizes about 60 percent of JETRO's total annual expenditures and, technically, has final decision-making authority over JETRO management and programs. Originally established to help Japanese firms export, JETRO also assists American companies seeking to export to Japan and promotes Japanese direct investment in the United States and U.S. direct investment in Japan. JETRO offices in the U.S. have excellent trade libraries open to the public. There are seven branches throughout the U.S. Headquarters are in Tokyo: Japan External Trade Organization, 2-5 Toranomon, 2-chome, Minato-ku, Tokyo 105, Japan; Tel: [81] (3) 3582-5522; New York branch Tel: [1] (212) 997-0400; San Francisco branch Tel: [1] (415) 392-1333; Fax: (415) 788-6927; Web: www.jetro.go.jp.

Japan International Cooperation Agency (JICA)

Established in August 1974 to administer the bilateral grant portion of Japan's Official Development Assistance (ODA). JICA covers both: (1) grant aid cooperation (offered without the obligation of repayment) and (2) technical cooperation (offering trainees, experts, equipment, project-type technical cooperation, and development studies). Address: Japan International Cooperation Agency, 6-13F, Shinjuku Maynds Tower, 1-1, Yoyogi 2-chome, Shibuyaku, Tokyo 151; Tel: [81] (3) 5352-5311; Web: www.jica.go.jp.

jetsam

(shipping) Articles from a ship or ship's cargo which are thrown overboard, usually to lighten the load in times of emergency or distress and that sinks or is washed ashore. *See also* flotsam.

jettison

(shipping) To unload or throw overboard at sea a part of a ship's paraphernalia or cargo to lighten the ship in time of emergency.

joint agent

(shipping) A person having authority to transact business for two or more transportation lines.

joint and several guarantee

See aval.

joint and several liability

(law) Liability for damages imposed on two or more individuals or legal entities who are responsible together and individually, allowing the party harmed to seek full remedy against all or any number of the wrongdoers. The availability of joint and several liability varies among countries, and some jurisdictions have placed limitations on the amount of damages for which a single person can be held liable when multiple parties could be responsible.

joint rate

(shipping) A single through-rate on cargo moving via two or more carriers.

joint stock company

(law) An unincorporated business association with ownership interests represented by shares of stock. These companies have characteristics of both corporations and partnerships. They are created under authority of law and are treated differently from jurisdiction to jurisdiction. *See* corporation; partnership.

joint venture

(law) (a) A combination of two or more individuals or legal entities who undertake together a transaction for mutual gain or to engage in a commercial enterprise together with mutual sharing of profits and losses. (b) A form of business partnership involving joint management and the sharing of risks and profits as between enterprises based in different countries. If joint ownership of capital is involved, the partnership is known as an equity joint venture.

Jones Act

(U.S. maritime law) The U.S. Merchant Marine Act of 1920 and related statutes, commonly known as the Jones Act, require that vessels used to transport passengers or cargo between U.S. ports be built in U.S. shipyards, owned by U.S. citizens, and manned by U.S. crews. The purpose and argument for the Jones Act is to maintain a national shipbuilding and repair base as well as jobs and training for U.S. mariners, and to provide maritime assets in times of national emergencies. The argument against The Jones Act is that it is discriminatory and anti-competitive. As expected, from time-to-time the Jones Act becomes a hot political issue. The Jones Act is similar to cabotage laws in place in some 50 other nations around the world that protect domestic shipping and reserve immediate coastal activity for home fleets. *See* cabotage.

jurat

(law) A statement signed by a person authorized to take oaths certifying to the authenticity of a document or affidavit. *See* authentication; notary public.

juridical person

See person, as defined by law.

juristic act

(law) Action intended to, and capable of having, a legal effect, such as the creation, termination, or modification of a legal right. Signing a power of attorney, for example, is a juristic act because it gives legal authority to an agent.

juristic person

See person, as defined by law.

just in time

(economics/manufacturing) The principle of production and inventory control that prescribes precise controls for the movement of raw materials, component parts and work-in-progress. Goods arrive when needed (just in time) for production for use rather than becoming expensive inventory that occupies costly warehouse space.

K

K&R insurance
(insurance) Acronym for kidnapping and ransom insurance. Insurance coverage against the threat of kidnapping or ransom of staff working in another country.

Kabushiki Kaisha (KK)
(Japan) Designation for a joint stock company with limited personal liability to shareholders.

Kaizen
(Japanese management) A Japanese word meaning gradual, orderly and continuous improvement. Specifically a management theory defined in the book *Kaizen: The key to Japan's Competitive Success*, by Mr. Masaaki Imai, that promotes a personal and business culture of sustained continuous improvement. For information connect at Web: www.kaizen-institute.com.

Kanban system
(Japanese logistics) A just-in-time inventory and production flow system developed in Japan that uses a card to signal when refurbishment is needed. It is a demand-oriented system whose purpose is to minimize raw materials and work-in-progress inventory. Kanban is a Japanese word that defines a communication signal or card.

karbovanet
The currency of Ukraine. The abbreviation is Uak. No subcurrency is in use.

keelage
(shipping) The charges paid by a ship entering or remaining in certain ports.

Keidanren
(Japan) Keidanren (the Japanese Federation of Economic Organizations) was established in 1946 as a private, non-profit economic organization representing virtually all branches of economic activity in Japan. Address: Japan Federation of Economic Organizations (Keidanren), 9-4, Otemachi 1-chome, Chiyoda-ku, Tokyo 100, Japan; Tel: [81] (3) 3279-1411; Fax: [81] (3) 5255-6250; Web: www.keidanren.or.jp.

keiretsu
(Japan) Keiretsu refers to the horizontally and vertically linked industrial structure of post-war Japan. The horizontally linked groups include a broad range of industries linked via banks and general trading firms. There are eight major industrial groups, sometimes referred to as "Kigyo Shudan": Mitsubishi, Mitsui, Sumitomo, Fuyo, DKB, Sanwa, Tokai, and IBJ. The vertically linked groups (such as Toyota, Matsushita, and Sony) are centered around parent companies, with subsidiaries frequently serving as suppliers, distributors, and retail outlets. Common characteristics among the groups include crossholding of company shares, intra-group financing, joint investment, mutual appointment of officers, and other joint business activities. The keiretsu system emphasizes mutual cooperation and protects affiliates from mergers and acquisitions. Ties within groups became looser after the oil shocks of the 1970s as a result of decreasing dependence on banks for capital.

key currency
(foreign exchange) A major currency in the global economy. Small countries, which are highly dependent on exports, orientate their exchange rate to major currencies in the global economy, the so-called key currencies. Key currencies include the U.S. dollar, the British pound sterling, the European Union euro, the Swiss franc, the Japanese yen and the Canadian dollar.

kidnapping and ransom insurance
See K&R insurance.

kilogram
(measure) A unit of mass or weight measure equal to 2.2046 lbs. Abbreviated as k, K, KS, kg, KG, kgs, or KGS.

kilo ton (metric ton)
(measure) A unit of mass or weight measure equal to 2,204.6 pounds.

kina
The currency of Papua New Guinea. 1K=1 toea.

kind or quality
See drawback—refund of duties.

kip
The currency of Laos. 1K=100 at.

kitting
(logistics) The assembly or packaging of components, parts or finished products into a new single item. This light assembly operation is sometimes performed in foreign trade zones or special economic zones. The term refers to the making of a kit (a collection of items).

kiwi bond
(banking/finance) Bond issued in New Zealand dollars on the New Zealand market by non New Zealand borrowers.

knocked down (K.D.)
An article taken apart and folded or telescoped in such a manner as to reduce its bulk at least 66 2/3 percent from its normal shipping cubage when set up or assembled.

knot
(measure) A unit of measurement of speed of a vessel in water or an airplane in air equal to one nautical mile (6082.66 feet) per hour.

known loss
(shipping/insurance) A loss discovered before or at the time of delivery of a shipment.

Kokusai Denshin Denwa
(Japan) The Kokusai Denshin Denwa Company, KDD, was established in 1953 but traces its history back to 1871 and the establishment of its predecessor organizations. For more than a century, the company was Japan's sole supplier of international telecommunications services and today remains Japan's leading international carrier. KDD is Japan's signatory to INTELSAT and INMARSAT.

Kommanditgesellschaft (KG)
(Austria, Germany, Switzerland) Designation for a limited partnership in which at least one of the partners has general liability and at least one of the other partners has limited liability.

Kommanditselskab (K/S)
(Denmark) Designation for a limited partnership in which at least one of the partners has general liability and at least one of the other partners has limited liability.

koruna
The currency of the Czech and the Slovak Republics. 1Kcs=100 halers.

krona
The currency of:
Iceland, 1IKr=100 aurar;
Sweden, 1SKr=100 öre.

krone
The currency of:
Denmark, 1DKr=100 öre;
Norway, 1NKr=100 öre;
Greenland (*see* Denmark).

kroon
The currency of Estonia. 1Eek=100 senti.

kwacha
The currency of:
Malawi, 1MK=100 tambala;
Zambia, 1K=100 ngwee.

kwanza
The currency of Angola. 1Kz=100 lwei.

kyat
The currency of Myanmar (Burma). 1K=100 pyas.

L

lading
(logistics) (a) The act of loading cargo or freight onto a conveyance. (b) Cargo or freight.

laissez-faire
(economics) A term used to describe minimal governmental involvement in an economy, allowing market forces and individuals to make their own decisions, with little or no regulation.

land
(shipping) A cargo vessel that operates on the Great Lakes of the U.S. and Canada.

lakh
(South Asia term) The quantity 100,000 of any item, but especially rupees (currency).

land
(shipping/logistics) To place cargo on shore (land) from a ship.

landbridge
(shipping) The movement of containers from a foreign country by vessel, transiting a country by rail or truck, and then being loaded aboard another vessel for delivery to a second foreign country. An example would be a container from Shanghai which arrives in the U.S. at Tacoma, Washington and is carried by rail to New Jersey where it is shipped by ocean to London (water-rail-water operation).

landed cost
(shipping) The total cost of a shipment delivered to a named location. Specifically, the cost of the goods plus the cost of transportation. See Incoterms.

landed price (named location)
See Incoterms.

Lanham Act of 1947
(U.S. law) Federal legislation governing trademarks and other symbols for identifying goods sold in interstate commerce. As amended, it allows a manufacturer to protect his brand or trademark in the United States by having it recorded on a government register in the U.S. Patent Office. Also provides for the legal right to register any distinctive mark.

lash
See lighter aboard ship.

lashing device
(logistics) A rope, cable or other tie-down device designed to secure cargo to its transport and provide minimal shifting during its journey. Typical lashing arrangements may secure a container by running across the middle or with four individual lashing devices one attached to each corner of the top face of the container.

LASH Vessel
(shipping/logistics) A ship of at least 820 feet specially designed with an onboard deck crane capable of loading and unloading lighters (barges) through a stern section of the ship that projects out over the water. Lighters are generally used in shallow water ports or where the port does not have container facilities. LASH vessels usually handle breakbulk cargo. *See* lighter aboard ship, lighter.

lat
The currency of Latvia. 1LvL=100 sintim.

Latin American Free Trade Association (LAFTA)
See Latin American Integration Association.

Latin American Integration Association (LAIA)
(regional trade alliance) LAIA was created by the 1980 Montevideo Treaty as a replacement to the Latin American Free Trade Association (LAFTA). LAFTA was rejected because members felt its rules governing integration trends were too rigid. LAIA, an association involving Argentina, Bolivia, Brazil, Chile, Colombia, Ecuador, Mexico, Paraguay, Peru, Uruguay, and Venezuela, since has declined as a major Latin American integration effort in favor of regional efforts, such as Mercosur. *See* Mercosur.

lay order
(customs) The period during which imported merchandise may remain at the place of unlading without some action being taken for its disposition, i.e., beyond the 5-day General Order period. *See* general order.

lead inventory
(logistics) The volume of inventory necessary to satisfy demand during the cycle time required to obtain a new shipment from a supplier. *See* inventory.

League of Arab States
See Arab League.

leasehold
(law) The temporary right to possess land. Technically a lease on land which reverts to the owner at the end of the lease term. *See* freehold.

least developed countries (LDC's)
(economics) Some 36 of the world's poorest countries. considered by the United Nations to be the least developed of the less developed countries. Most of them are small in terms of area and population, and some are land-locked or small island countries. They are generally characterized by low: per capita incomes, literacy levels, and medical standards; subsistence agriculture; and a lack of exploitable minerals and competitive industries. Many suffer from aridity, floods, hurricanes, and excessive animal and plant pests, and most are situated in the zone 10 to 30 degrees north latitude. These countries have little prospect of rapid economic development in the foreseeable future and are likely to remain heavily dependent upon official development assistance for many years. Most are in Africa, but a few, such as Bangladesh, Afghanistan, Laos, and Nepal, are in Asia. Haiti is the only country in the Western Hemisphere classified by the United Nations as "least developed." *See* developing countries; less developed country.

legal entity
(law) Any individual, proprietorship, partnership, corporation, association, or other organization that has, in the eyes of the law, the capacity to make a contract or an agreement, and the abilities to assume an obligation and to discharge an indebtedness. A legal entity is a responsible being in the eyes of the law and can be sued for damages if the performance of a contract or agreement is not met. *See also* person.

legal person
See person; legal entity.

legal tender
(banking/currency/law) Any money that is recognized as being lawful for use by a debtor to pay a creditor, who must accept same in the discharge of a debt unless the contract between the parties specifically states that another type of money is to be used.

lek
The currency of Albania. 1L=100 qintars.

lempira
The currency of Honduras. 1L=100 centavos.

lender of last resort
(banking) One of the functions and a major raison d'être of a modern central bank; whereby the bank has to provide liquid assets to the banking system when the existing liquid assets of the banking system threaten to deplete.

leone
The currency of Sierra Leone. 1Le=100 cents.

less developed country (LDC)
(economics) A country showing: (1) a poverty level of income, (2) a high rate of population increase, (3) a substantial portion of its workers employed in agriculture, (4) a low proportion of adult literacy, (5) high unemployment, and (6) a significant reliance on a few items for export.

Terms such as third world, poor, developing nations, and underdeveloped have also been used to describe less developed countries.

lesser developed country (LLDC)
(economics) The classification LLDC was developed by the United Nations to give some guidance to donor agencies and countries about an equitable allocation of foreign assistance. The criteria for designating a country an LLDC, originally adopted by the UN Committee for Development Planning in 1971, have been modified several times. Criteria have included low: per capita income, literacy, and manu-

facturing share of the country's total gross domestic product. There is continuing concern that the criteria should be more robust and less subject to the possibility of easy fluctuation of a country between less developed and least developed status.

less than container load (LCL)

(shipping) A shipment of cargo that does not fill a container and is merged with cargo for more than one consignee or from more than one shipper. A container may be packed with LCL cargo at a container freight station for LCL delivery.

less than truckload (LTL)

(shipping) A shipment weighing less than the weight required for the application of the truckload rate.

letter of assignment

A document with which the assignor assigns rights to a third party. *See* assignment.

letter of credit (L/C)

(banking) Formal term: Documentary credit or documentary letter of credit.

A letter of credit is a document issued by a bank stating its commitment to pay someone (supplier/exporter/seller) a stated amount of money on behalf of a buyer (importer) so long as the seller meets very specific terms and conditions. Letters of credit are more formally called documentary letters of credit because the banks handling the transaction deal in documents as opposed to goods.

The terms and conditions listed in the credit all involve presentation of specific documents within a stated period of time, hence the formal name—documentary credits.

The documents the buyer requires in the credit may vary, but at a minimum include an invoice and a bill of lading. Other documents the buyer may specify are certificate of origin, consular invoice, insurance certificate, inspection certificate and others.

Letters of credit are the most common method of making international payments, because the risks of the transaction are shared by both the buyer and the supplier.

Documentary letters of credit are subject to the Uniform Customs and Practice for Documentary Credits (UCPDC), Brochure No. 500, of the International Chamber of Commerce (ICC) in Paris. *See* Uniform Customs and Practice.

Basic Letters of Credit

There are two basic forms of a letter of credit: the Revocable Credit and the Irrevocable Credit. There are also two types of irrevocable credit: the Irrevocable Credit not Confirmed, and the Irrevocable Confirmed Credit. Each type of credit has advantages and disadvantages for the buyer and for the seller. Also note that the more the banks assume risk by guaranteeing payment, the more they will charge for providing the service.

(a) **Revocable credit**—This credit can be changed or canceled by the buyer without prior notice to the

supplier. Because it offers little security to the seller, revocable credits are generally unacceptable and are rarely used.

(b) **Irrevocable credit**—The irrevocable credit is one which the issuing bank commits itself irrevocably to honor, provided the beneficiary complies with all stipulated conditions. This credit cannot be changed or canceled without the consent of both the buyer and the seller. As a result, this type of credit is the most widely used in international trade. Irrevocable credits are more expensive because of the issuing bank's added liability in guaranteeing the credit. There are two types of irrevocable credits:

(1) **The Irrevocable credit not confirmed (Unconfirmed credit)**. This means that the buyer's bank which issues the credit is the only party responsible for payment to the supplier, and the supplier's bank is obliged to pay the supplier only after receiving payment from the buyer's bank. The supplier's bank merely acts on behalf of the issuing bank and therefore incurs no risk.

(2) **The Irrevocable, confirmed credit.** In a confirmed credit, the advising bank adds its guarantee to pay the supplier to that of the issuing bank. If the issuing bank fails to make payment, the advising bank will pay. If a supplier is unfamiliar with the buyer's bank which issues the letter of credit, he may insist on an irrevocable confirmed credit. These credits may be used when trade is conducted in a high risk area where there are fears of outbreak of war or social, political, or financial instability. Confirmed credits may also be used by the supplier to enlist the aid of a local bank to extend financing to enable him to fill the order. A confirmed credit costs more because the bank has added liability.

Special Letters of Credit

There are numerous special letters of credit designed to meet specific needs of buyers, suppliers, and intermediaries. Special letters of credit usually involve increased participation by banks, so financing and service charges are higher than those for basic letters of credit. The following is a brief description of some special letters of credit.

(a) **Standby letter of credit**—This credit is primarily a payment or performance guarantee. It is used primarily in the United States because U.S. banks are prevented by law from giving certain guarantees. Standby credits are often called non-performing letters of credit because they are only used as a backup payment method if the collection on a primary payment method is past due.

Standby letters of credit can be used, for example, to guarantee the following types of payment and performance:

- repayment of loans,
- fulfillment by subcontractors,
- securing the payment for goods delivered by third parties.

The beneficiary to a standby letter of credit can draw from it on demand, so the buyer assumes added risk.

(b) **Revolving letter of credit**—This credit is a commitment on the part of the issuing bank to restore the credit to the original amount after it has been used or drawn down. The number of times it can be utilized and the period of validity is stated in the credit. The credit can be cumulative or noncumulative. Cumulative means that unutilized sums can be added to the next installment, whereas noncumulative means that partial amounts not utilized in time expire.

(c) **Deferred payment letter of credit**—In this credit the buyer takes delivery of the shipped goods by accepting the documents and agreeing to pay the bank after a fixed period of time. This credit gives the buyer a grace period for payment.

(d) **Red clause letter of credit**—This is used to provide the supplier with some funds prior to shipment to finance production of the goods. The credit may be advanced in part or in full, and the buyer's bank finances the advance payment. The buyer, in essence, extends financing to the seller and incurs ultimate risk for all advanced credits.

(e) **Transferable Letter of Credit**—This credit allows the supplier to transfer all or part of the proceeds of the letter of credit to a second beneficiary, usually the ultimate supplier of the goods. This is a common financing tactic for middlemen and is used extensively in the Far East.

(f) **Back-to-Back Letter of Credit**—This is a new credit opened on the basis of an already existing, nontransferable credit. It is used by traders to make payment to the ultimate supplier. A trader receives a letter of credit from the buyer and then opens another letter of credit in favor of the supplier. The first letter of credit is used as collateral for the second credit. The second credit makes price adjustments from which come the trader's profit. *See* Guide to Letters of Credit Appendix.

letter of indemnity (LOI)

(shipping) A document which serves to protect the carrier/owner financially against possible repercussions in connection with the release of goods without presentation of an original bill of lading. A letter of indemnity (usually as an indemnity for missing bill of lading) is used in cases in which the goods arrive at the port of destination before the original bills of lading. The issuance of the letter of indemnity allows the purchaser to take immediate delivery of the goods, thus saving himself time, additional demurrage, storage expenses, insurance costs, etc.

letter of intent

(law) A document, such as a written memorandum, that describes the preliminary understanding between parties who intend to make a contract or join together in another action, such as a joint venture or a corporate merger.

leu

The currency of Romania. 1L=100 bani.

lev

The currency of Bulgaria. 1Lv=100 stotinki.

leverage

(finance/foreign exchange) In options terminology, this expresses the disproportionately large change in the premium in terms of the relative price movement of the underlying instrument.

lex loci actus

(law) A legal rule to apply the law of the place where a wrongful act occurred. A court may apply this law in a legal action if the parties have not expressly agreed to the law that will govern their contract and if the laws of more than one jurisdiction could apply. If a buyer and seller, for example, are located in different countries and the buyer breaches the contract, under the rule of lex loci actus the court will apply the law of the buyer's country in interpreting the contract. This rule is usually applied when the wrongful act has a greater effect in the jurisdiction where it occurred than in any other jurisdiction. *See* conflict of laws; nexus; lex loci solutionis.

lex loci solutionis

(law) A legal rule to apply the law of the place where payment is to be made or a contract is to be performed. A country may apply this law in a legal action if the parties have not expressly agreed to the law that will govern their contract and if the laws of more than one jurisdiction could apply. If a buyer and seller, for example, are located in different countries and the buyer breaches the contract, under the rule of lex loci solutionis the court will apply the law of the seller's country, which is where payment is to be made. This rule is usually applied when performance of the contract has a greater effect in the jurisdiction where it is to occur than in any other jurisdiction. *See* conflict of laws; nexus; lex loci actus.

liberal

(economics) When referring to trade policy, "liberal" usually means relatively free of import controls or restraints and/or a preference for reducing existing barriers to trade, often contrasted with the protectionist preference for retaining or raising selected barriers to imports.

LIBID

See London Interbank Bid Rate.

LIBOR

See London Interbank Offered Rate.

licensing agreement

(law) A contract whereby the holder of a trademark, patent, or copyright transfers a limited right to use a process, sell or manufacture an article, or furnish specialized services covered by the trademark, patent or copyright to another firm.

life-cycle processing
(economics/accounting) An accounting approach in which a company sets product prices based on recovering costs over the life cycle of the product.
(U.S.) In antidumping cases, U.S. authorities dispute the validity of this approach because projections of future yield improvements cannot be verified at the time of dumping calculations. *See* dumping.

lift on, lift off (Lo/Lo)
(shipping) the loading and unloading of cargo from a ship using a crane.

lift van
(shipping) A wooden or metal container used for packing household goods and personal effects. A lift van must be at least 100 cubic feet and be suitable for lifting by mechanical device.

lighter
(shipping) An open or covered barge towed by a tugboat and used mainly in harbors and inland waterways for the transport of cargo. Lighters are used in situations where shallow water prevents the ocean going vessel from coming close to shore.

lighter aboard ship (LASH)
(shipping) A floatable large container (lighter) used in the combined ocean and inland waterway transport of goods. Lighters are transported on specially constructed ships.

lighterage
(shipping) (a) The loading or unloading of a ship by means of a lighter. (b) Charges assessed for lighter service.

lilangeni
The currency of Swaziland. 1L=100 cents. The plural of lilangeni is emalangeni (E).

LIMEAN
(banking/finance) The calculated average of the London Interbank Bid Rate (LIBID) and the London Interbank Offered Rate (LIBOR).
See London Interbank Bid Rate; London Interbank Offered Rate.

Limitada (Ltda.)
(Brazil, Portugal) Designation for a private limited liability corporation with limited liability to shareholders. *See* Sociedad por Quota.

limitation period
(law) A maximum period set by statute within which a legal action can be brought or a right enforced. A statute may prohibit, for example, any individual or legal entity from bringing an action for breach of contract more than one year after the breach occurred.

Limited (Ltd.)
(United Kingdom) Designation for a private limited liability corporation with limited liability to shareholders.
(South Africa, United States) Designation for a public corporation with limited liability to shareholders.

limited appointment
(diplomacy) Limited appointees to the U.S. & Foreign Commercial Service (or to other foreign services) are persons from the private sector or from the federal government who are non-career officers assigned overseas for a limited time.

limited liability
(law) Restricted liability for the obligations of a business. Liability may be limited, for example, to the amount of a partner's or shareholder's contribution to the capital of partnership or corporation.

limited partnership
(law) A partnership in which at least one partner has general liability and at least one of the other partners has limited liability.

Limitée (Ltée.)
(Canada) Designation for a public corporation with limited liability to shareholders.

line haul
(shipping) The direct movement of freight between two major ports by a single ship.

line haul vessel
(shipping) A vessel which is on a regularly defined schedule.

liner
(shipping) A vessel carrying passengers and cargo that operates on a route with a fixed schedule.

line release system
(U.S. Customs) A part of the U.S. Customs' Automated Commercial System, is designed for the release and tracking of shipments through the use of personal computers and bar code technology. To qualify for line release, a commodity must have a history of invoice accuracy, and be selected by local Customs districts on the basis of high volume. To release the merchandise, Customs reads the bar code into a personal computer, verifies that the bar code matches the invoice data, and enters the quantity. The cargo release is transmitted to the Automated Commercial System, which establishes an entry and the requirement for an entry summary, and provides the Automated Broker Interface system participants with release information. *See* Automated Commercial System.

liner terms
(shipping) Conditions under which a shipping company will transport goods, including the amount payable for carriage of the goods (freight) and the cost both for loading and discharge of the vessel.

liquidated damages
(law) A sum of money that a contracting party agrees to pay to the other party for breaching an agreement, particularly important in a contract in which damages for breach may be difficult to assess. A manufacturer, for example, that agrees to develop, produce, and sell unique products to a buyer may in-

sist on a contract clause for liquidated damages in the event that the buyer rejects the goods without justifiable reason because the market for resale of the unique goods will be so limited that damages will be difficult to assess.

liquidation

(U.S. Customs) The final review of a U.S. Customs entry, and determination of the rate of duty and amount of duty by Customs. Liquidation is accomplished by Customs posting a notice on a public bulletin board at the customshouse. An importer may receive an advance notice on Customs Form 4333A "Courtesy Notice" stating when and in what amount duty will be liquidated. This form is not the liquidation, and protest rights do not accrue until the notice is posted. Time limits for protesting do not start to run until the date of posting, and a protest cannot be filed before liquidation is posted.

The Customs Service may determine that an entry cannot be liquidated as entered for one reason or another. For example, the tariff classification may not be correct or may not be acceptable because it is not consistent with an established and uniform classification practice. If the change required by this determination results in a rate of duty more favorable to an importer, the entry is liquidated accordingly and a refund of the applicable amount of the deposited duties is authorized. On the other hand, a change may be necessary which imposes a higher rate of duty. For example, a claim for an exemption from duty under a duty-free provision or under a conditional exemption may be found to be insufficient for lack of the required supporting documentation. In this situation, the importer will be given an advance notice of the proposed duty rate advancement and an opportunity to validate the claim for a free rate or more favorable rate of duty.

If the importer does not respond to the notice or if the response is found to be without merit, duty is liquidated in accordance with the entry as corrected and the importer is billed for the additional duty. The port or district may find that the importer's response raises issues of such complexity that resolution by a Customs Headquarters decision through the internal advise procedure is warranted. Internal advice from Customs Headquarters may be requested by the local Customs officers on their own initiative or in response to a request by the importer.

Public Law 95-410 (Customs Procedural Reform and Simplification Act of 1978) requires that all liquidations be performed within one year from the date of consumption entry or final withdrawal on a warehouse entry. Three one-year extensions are permitted. *See* protest; entry; classification; valuation.

liquidation system

(U.S. Customs) A part of U.S. Customs' Automated Commercial System, closes the file on each entry and establishes a batch filing number which is essen-

tial for recovering an entry for review or enforcement purposes. An entry liquidation is a final review of the entry. Public Law 95-410 (Customs Procedural Reform and Simplification Act of 1978) requires that all liquidations be performed within one year from the date of consumption entry or final withdrawal on a warehouse entry. Three one-year extensions are permitted. *See* liquidation; Automated Commercial System.

liquidity

(economics) (a) A company's ability to meet its obligations at all times. (b) The availability of liquid funds in an economy. (c) The possibility of being able to carry out financial transactions without influencing the market.

lira

The currency of:
Malta, 1£M (or 1 LM)=100 cents;
San Marino (uses Italian lira);
Turkey, 1T£=100 kurus;
Vatican, 1VLit=100 centesimi.
The former currency of Italy. The new currency of Italy is the European Union euro. 1 € = 100 cents.

litas

The currency of Lithuania. 1Lit=100 centai.

Lloyds (of London)

(insurance) An association of English insurance underwriters, the oldest of its kind in the world. Not in itself an insurance company. The Corporation of Lloyds also provides a daily newspaper.

Lloyd's Registry

(shipping) An organization maintained for the surveying and classifying of ships so that insurance underwriters and other interested parties may know the quality and condition of the vessels offered by insurance or employment.

loading

(shipping) The physical placing of cargo into carrier's container, or onto a vessel.

localization

A broad term used to describe the modification, preparation and/or translation of products, services, media or advertising for use or sale in a local market. Localization can include changes to product or service specifications, additions of content that are more appropriate for a local market, deletion of content deemed insensitive or not applicable to a local market, checking content for cultural insensitivity and the translation of books, operational manuals and advertising into a local language or dialect. Examples include converting a U.S.-made, left-hand drive automobile to right-hand drive for the Japanese market; changing the cutting patterns for clothing to reflect different body shapes (not just sizes) for another culture; making sure that translations of marketing materials are not incorrect, insensitive or contrary to the goals of the advertiser; adding coverage of local issues to Web sites; and deleting or changing references that imply that the reader or user is from a country or culture other than the "target" country or culture.

locus
(law) A place. The locus of arbitration, for example, is the place where arbitration proceedings are held.

logistics
The process of planning, implementing and controlling the flow of personnel, materials and information from the point of origin to the point of destination at the required time and in the desired condition.
(shipping) The process of planning and controlling the flow of raw materials, work in progress or finished products from the point of origin to the point of destination (either to a factory for further processing, to a warehouse for storage or to the marketplace for sale) at the required time and in the desired condition.

logistics data interchange (LDI)
(logistics) The electronic exchange of logistics data through a computer system. LDI is similar to electronic data interchange (EDI). *See* EDI.

logistics resource management (LRM)
"A new class of software for supply chain execution that provides visibility and control of integrated transportation and import export processes and delivers cost savings, trade security, and supply chain advantages to Global 2000 companies." (Definition by Arzoon, Inc., Web: www.arzoon.com.)

Lombard rate
(banking/finance-Germany) The interest rate applied to loans backed by collateral in the form of movable, easily-sold assets (goods or securities). Particularly used with reference to the German Bundesbank, which normally maintains its Lombard rate at about 1/2 percent above its discount rate.

Lomé Convention
A 1975 agreement between the European Community (EC) and 62 African, Caribbean, and Pacific (ACP) states (mostly former colonies of the EC members). The agreement covers some aid provisions as well as trade and tariff preferences for the ACP countries when shipping to the EC. The Lome Convention grew out of the 1958 Treaty of Rome's "association" with the 18 African colonies/countries that had ties with Belgium and France.

London Interbank Bid Rate (LIBID)
(banking/finance) The bid in a quotation representing the interest rate at which U.S. dollar deposits are retraded in London. *See* London Interbank Offered Rate; LIMEAN.

London Interbank Offered Rate (LIBOR)
(banking/finance) The interest rate at which banks in London are prepared to lend funds to first-class banks. It is used to determine the interest rate payable on most Eurocredits. *See* London Interbank Bid Rate; LIMEAN.

London Metal Exchange
(banking/finance) A commodity exchange whose members, approximately 110 in number, deal in copper, lead, zinc, and tin. Address: London Metal Exchange, 56 Leadenhall Street, London EC3A 2 DX, UK; Tel: [44] (0) 207 264-5555; Fax: [44] (0) 207 680-0505; Web: www.lme.co.uk.

long form
A form (document) that has terms and conditions printed on the reverse (back) of the form. For example, a long form bill of lading has the terms and conditions of carriage printed on the reverse. The long form bill of lading is preferred in international transactions. *See also* short form.

long of exchange
(banking/foreign exchange) When a trader in foreign currency holds foreign bills in an amount exceeding the bills of his or her own that have been sold and remain outstanding, the trader is long of exchange.

longshoreman
(shipping) A laborer who loads and unloads ships at a seaport. *See also* stevedore; gang.

long ton
(measure) A unit of mass or weight measurement equal to 2,240 pounds. A short ton is 2,000 pounds.

lorry
(UK term) British for truck.

loss of specie
(insurance) A loss when goods arrive so damaged as to cease to be a thing of the kind insured. Examples of "loss of specie" are cement arriving as rock, or textiles as rags. *See also* total loss.

loti
The currency of Lesotho. 1L=100 lisente. Plural of loti is maloti (M).

lot labels
(shipping) Labels attached to each piece of multiple lot shipment for identification purposes.

lower deck
(logistics) The lower cargo holding area of an airplane or a ship.

lower deck containers
(shipping) Carrier owned containers specially designed as an integral part of the aircraft to fit in the cargo compartments (lower deck) of a wide body aircraft.

lumper
(logistics/trucking) A laborer who assists a motor carrier or truck driver in the loading or unloading of cargo. *See* lumping.

lumping
(logistics/trucking) The assistance given to a motor carrier, specifically a truck driver, in the loading and unloading of cargo. This practice occurs most commonly in the food and produce industries. The labor-

ers (lumpers) may be paid by the terminal operator or by the driver. See lumper.

lump of labor fallacy

(economics) The fallacious theory that an ever-increasing population leads to an ever-increasing rate of unemployment because there are only a fixed number of jobs to go around. The resurgence of this theory is the effort by some European nations to reduce the legal workweek as a means of reducing unemployment.

LVS (Courier LVS)

(Canada) Low Value Shipment. A Canada Customs and Revenue Agency (CCRA) program that speeds the release of low-value entries of up to C$1,600 for commercial imports by approved carriers. Information at Web: www.ccra-adrc.gc.ca.

M

Maastricht (Treaty)

(European Union) The popular name for the European Treaty for Economic Union. A treaty, signed in the Dutch city of Maastricht on February 7, 1992, that changed the name of the European Community (EC) to the European Union (EU) and paved the way for further European integration. In addition to the change in name, the major aims of the treaty were: 1) Monetary union. To abolish existing European currencies and replace them with the euro. (This was achieved as of January 1, 2002.) In addition, to create a European Central Bank (ECB) to assume the various functions of the central banks of the member states in establishing monetary policy. 2) Political and military integration. To work towards a common foreign policy and a joint military force. (These goals have proved to be more controversial than monetary union as they have been seen to infringe upon the very core of national sovereignty.) And 3) Common citizenship. To establish common EU citizenship for nationals of all member states.

The ratification of the treaty was a sometimes dramatic affair during the course of 1992 and 1993. National referendums were held in France, Spain, and Ireland and twice in Denmark. The Danes initially voted to reject the treaty prompting the UK and Italy to withdraw from the European Exchange Rate Mechanism. The French voted narrowly in favor in September 1992.

Low-income countries such as Spain and Ireland, however, voted clearly for ratification as they stood to benefit the greatest from the treaty. By November 1992 all member states except Denmark and Great Britain had ratified the treaty. At a summit meeting in Edinburgh in December 1992, compromises were made which led to Danish ratification in a second referendum in May 1993 and to ratification in the UK in July 1993. The treaty was formally ratified by all member states on November 1, 1993.

See European Union.

Maatschappij (Mij.)

(Netherlands) Designation for a combination of two or more persons who enter into a joint arrangement to conduct certain business activities.

macroeconomics

(economics) (a) The study of statistics (e.g., total consumption, total employment) of the economy as a whole rather than as single economic units. (b) Synonymous with aggregate economics. *See also* microeconomics.

mail entry

(U.S. Customs) A means of shipping and entering goods into the Customs Territory of the United States. Mail entry has several advantages as well as several limitations.

(1) Duties on parcels valued at US$1,200 or less are collected by the letter carrier delivering the parcel to the addressee.

(2) No formal entry paperwork is required on duty-free merchandise not exceeding US$1,200 in value.

(3) There is no need to clear shipments personally if under US$1,200 in value.

Joint Customs and postal regulations provide that all international parcel post packages must have a Customs declaration securely attached giving an accurate description and the value of the contents. This declaration is obtained at post offices. Commercial shipments must also be accompanied by a commercial invoice enclosed in the parcel bearing the declaration.

Parcels and packages not labeled or endorsed properly and found to contain merchandise subject to duty or taxes are subject to forfeiture.

If the value of a mail importation exceeds US$1,250, the addressee is notified to prepare and file a formal Customs entry (consumption entry) for it at the nearest Customs port.

A mail entry limit of US$250 has been set for a number of articles classified in sub-chapters III and IV, chapter 99, of the Harmonized Tariff Schedule of the U.S. as an exception to the above US$1,250 limit. Items on this list include billfolds, feathers, flowers, footwear, fur, gloves, handbags, headwear, leather, luggage, millinery, pillows, plastics, skins, rubber, textiles, toys, games, sports equipment and trimmings.

Unaccompanied shipments of made-to-measure suits from Hong Kong require a formal entry regardless of value.

See entry; consumption entry.

mala fide

(law) In bad faith. A seller's representation that goods are usable for a particular purpose when in fact the seller knows that the goods are not is a representation made mala fide.

manifest

(shipping) A document giving the description of a ship's cargo or the contents of a car or truck.

Manufactured Imports Promotion Organization (MIPRO)

(Japan) A non-profit organization, established in 1978 by the joint efforts of the Japanese Government and the private sector to promote imports of foreign manufactured products by hosting exhibitions and providing a wide range of market information. MIPRO's activities are broadly classified into three categories: (1) holding imported product trade exhibitions for buyers and the general public; (2) disseminating information regarding imported products and the Japanese market; and (3) promoting sales of foreign products to Japanese consumers to promote recognition of the quality of imported goods. Address: Manufactured Imports Promotion Organization, 1-3, Higashi Ikebukuro 3-chome, Toshima-ku, Tokyo 170, Japan; Tel: [81] (3) 3988-2791; Fax: [81] (3) 3988-1629.

manufacturing resources planning

See MRP.

maquiladora

(Mexico) A program which allows foreign manufacturers to ship components into Mexico duty-free for assembly and subsequent reexport. Industry established under the maquiladora program is Mexico's second largest source of foreign revenue (following oil exports).

In December 1989, the Mexican government liberalized the maquiladora program to make it a more attractive and dynamic sector of the economy. As a result, maquiladora operations may import, duty and import license free, products not directly involved in production, but that support production, including computers and other administrative materials and transportation equipment.

The maquiladora program may decline in importance over time as provisions of the North American Free Trade Agreement take effect. See North American Free Trade Agreement.

margin

(general) The difference between the cost of sold items and the total net sales income.

(finance) The difference between the market value of collateral pledged to secure a loan and the face value of the loan itself.

(investments—U.S.) The amount paid by the customer when he or she uses a broker credit to buy a security under Federal Reserve regulations, the initial margin required in past decades has ranged from 50 to 100 percent of the purchase price.

(finance) The spread between bid and asked rates

(foreign exchange) The good faith deposit which the writer of an option or the buyer of a forward or futures contract has to put up to cover the risk of adverse price movements.

marginal cost

(economics) The increase in the total cost of production that results from manufacturing one more unit output.

marine cargo insurance

(insurance) Broadly, insurance covering loss of, or damage to, goods at sea. Marine insurance typically compensates the owner of merchandise for losses in excess of those which can be legally recovered from the carrier that are sustained from fire, shipwreck, piracy, and various other causes. See special marine policy; all risk.

Marine Extension Clause 1943 & 1952

(insurance) An insurance extension which broadens warehouse-to-warehouse insurance coverage by eliminating the requirement that ordinary course of transit be maintained as well as the 15- or 30-day time limit at destination. Moreover, continuation of coverage is provided when certain conditions necessitate discharge of goods from vessel at a port other than the original destination. The most recent form of Marine Extension Clause was developed in 1952. It too provides for extensions as does the 1943 version, and adds that the assured will act with reasonable dispatch. The Warehouse-to-Warehouse Clause is now found in practically all open cargo policies. *See also* warehouse-to-warehouse.

marine insurance

See marine cargo insurance.

marine protection and indemnity insurance

(insurance) Insurance against legal liability of the insured for loss, damage, or expense arising out of or incident to the ownership, operation, chartering, maintenance, use, repair, or construction of any vessel, craft, or instrumentality in use in ocean or inland waterways, including liability of the insured for personal injury or death, and for loss of or damage to the property of another person.

maritime

Business pertaining to commerce or navigation transacted upon the sea or in seaports in such matters as the court of admiralty have jurisdiction over, concurrently with the courts of common law.

mark

The former currency of Germany. 1DM=100 pfennig. The new currency of Germany is the European Union euro. 1 € = 100 cents.

market access

(economics) The openness of a national market to foreign products. Market access reflects a government's willingness to permit imports to compete relatively unimpeded with similar domestically produced goods.

Market Access Program (MAP)

(U.S.) A U.S. government program authorized by the U.S. Food, Agriculture, Conservation, and Trade Act of 1990 and administered by the U.S. Department of Agriculture's Foreign Agricultural Service. Under the MPP, surplus stocks or funds from the Commodity Credit Corporation are used to partially reimburse agricultural organizations conducting specific foreign market development projects for eligible products in specified countries. Proposals for MPP programs are developed by trade organizations and private firms. Activities financed by the programs vary from commodity to commodity, and include activities such as market research, construction of a three-story wood demonstration building, construction of a model feed mill, and consumer promotion activities. (MPP is similar to the Targeted Export Assistance (TEA) program which was repealed by the 1990 Farm Bill.) Contact: U.S. Department of Agriculture, Foreign Agriculture Service, Marketing Operations Staff, 1400 Independence Ave., Washington, DC 20250 USA; Tel: [1] (202) 720-4327; Fax: [1] (202) 720-9361; Web: www.fas.usda.gov/mos/programs/mapprog.html.

market disruption

(economics) The situation created when a surge of imports in a given product area causes sales of domestically produced goods in a particular country to decline to such an extent that the domestic producers and their employees suffer major economic hardship.

market economy

(economics) An economic system where resources are allocated and production of products determined by market forces rather than by government decree.

Market-Oriented Cooperation Plan

(U.S./Japan) A U.S. Japan trade agreement aimed at improving long-term business relations between Japan's automotive manufacturers and U.S. auto parts suppliers.

Market-Oriented Sector-Selective

(U.S./Japan) Bilateral trade discussions between the U.S. and Japan begun in January 1985 in an effort to remove many trade barriers at once in a given sector. MOSS talks have focused on five sectors: (1) telecommunications, (2) medical equipment and pharmaceuticals, (3) electronics, (4) forest products, and (5) auto parts. Overall, the talks focus high-level attention on reducing certain market obstacles opening communication channels to resolve follow-up disputes.

market price

(economics) (a) The price established in the market where buyers and sellers meet to buy and sell similar products. (b) The price determined by factors of supply and demand rather than by decisions made by management.

marking: country of origin

The physical markings on a product that indicate the country of origin where the article was produced.

(U.S. Customs) U.S. Customs laws require each imported article produced abroad to be marked in a conspicuous place as legibly, indelibly, and permanently as the nature of the article permits, with the English name of the country of origin, to indicate to the ultimate purchaser in the United States the name of the country in which the article was manufactured or produced. Articles which are otherwise specifically exempted from individual marking are an exception to this rule. *See* United States Customs Service.

markka

The former currency of Finland. 1Fmk=100 pennia. The new currency of Finland is the European Union euro. 1 € = 100 cents.

marks

(shipping) Information placed on outer surface of shipping containers or packages such as address labels, identifying numbers, box specifications, caution, or directional warnings.

markup

See premium.

master air waybill (MAWB)

(logistics) An air waybill of lading that covers a consolidated shipment of goods and lists the consolidator as the shipper. *See* bill of lading, air waybill.

master's protest

See captain's protest.

matador bond

(banking/finance) Bond issued on the Spanish market, denominated in currencies other than the peseta.

Matchmaker Program

(U.S.) Matchmaker trade delegations are organized and led by the U.S. International Trade Administration to help new-to-export and new-to-market firms meet prescreened prospects who are interested in their products or services in overseas markets. Matchmaker delegations usually target two major country markets in two countries and limit trips to a week or less. This approach is designed to permit U.S. firms to interview a maximum number of prospective overseas business partners with a minimum of time away from their home office. The program includes U.S. embassy support, briefings on market requirements and business practices, and interpreters' services. Matchmaker events, based on specific product themes and end-users, are scheduled for a limited number of countries each year. Contact: International Trade Administration, Department of Commerce, 14th and Constitution Ave. NW, Washington, DC 20230 USA; Tel: [1] (202) 482-2000. *See* new-to-export; new-to-market.

material contract terms

(law) Terms that are necessary to the agreement. Clauses that describe the goods, fix the price, and set the delivery date are examples of material contract terms.

mate's receipt

(shipping) A declaration issued by an officer of a vessel in the name of the shipping company stating that certain goods have been received on board his vessel. A mate's receipt is not a title document. Used as an interim document until the bill of lading is issued.

maximum payload

(logistics) The maximum weight limit of cargo that a particular transportation vehicle can carry.

measurement cargo

(shipping) A cargo on which the transportation charge is assessed on the basis of measurement.

measurement ton

(shipping) Also known as a cargo or freight ton. A space measurement usually 40 cubic feet or one cubic meter. The cargo is assessed a certain rate for every 40 cubic feet of space it occupies.

medium of exchange

(economics) Any commodity (commonly money) which is widely accepted in payment for goods and services and in settlement of debts, and is accepted without reference to the standing of the person who offers it in payment.

memorandum bill of lading

(shipping) The duplicate copy of a bill of lading. *See* bill of lading.

memorandum of understanding (MOU)

(general) An informal record, document or instrument that serves as the basis of a future contact.

(U.S.) A very detailed document devised by executive branch agencies of the government in areas such as aviation and fisheries that serve as agreements between nations.

memorandum tariff

(shipping) Publications which contain rule and rate information extracted from official tariffs. Memorandum tariffs are published by many carriers and are available from these carriers upon request. *See* tariff.

mercantilism

(economics) A prominent economic philosophy in the 16th and 17th centuries that equated the accumulation and possession of gold and other international monetary assets, such as foreign currency reserves, with national wealth. Although this point of view is generally discredited among 20th century economists and trade policy experts, some contemporary politicians still favor policies designed to create trade "surpluses," such as import substitution and tariff protection for domestic industries, as essential to national economic strength.

merchandise trade balance

See balance of payments.

merchant bank

(banking) A term used in Great Britain for an organization that underwrites securities for corporations, advises such clients on mergers, and is involved in the ownership of commercial ventures.

merchant's credit

(banking) A letter of credit issued by the buyer himself. Contains no commitment whatever on the part of a bank. *See* letter of credit.

merchant's haulage
(shipping) The inland move from or to a port that has all arrangements made by the cargo interests (seller/exporter).

Mercosur
(regional trade alliance) Mercosur (Spanish; Mercosul in Portuguese) or Southern Common Market, is comprised of Argentina, Brazil, Paraguay, and Uruguay. Mercosur is scheduled to enter into force in December 1994 for Argentina and Brazil and to enter into force in December 1995 for Paraguay and Uruguay. Mercosur, modeled similarly to the European Community's Treaty of Rome, will establish a common external tariff and eliminate barriers to trade in services. Chile has not sought entry to Mercosur, but does have an agreement with Argentina which will provide for some similar benefits.

merry-go-round
(banking/finance/foreign exchange) The circulation of money through various sources, ending up where it started. For instance the German Central Bank recycles excess capital by selling U.S. dollars to banks under a repurchase agreement and the banks place the U.S. dollars in the Euromarket. As the financial institutions could run up a U.S. dollar debt on the Euromarket, the Central Bank must buy back the U.S. dollars and sell domestic currency to avoid an excessive increase in the mark.

meter
(measure) A unit of linear measure equal to 39.37 inches (approximately). *See* Weights and Measures in the Appendix.

metical
The currency of Mozambique. 1Mt=100 centavos.

metric system
(measurement) A decimal system of weights and measures based on the meter of approximately 39.37 inches and the kilogram of approximately 2.2046 pounds. *See* Weights and Measures in the Appendix.

metric ton
(measure) A unit of mass or weight measure equal to 2,204.6 pounds or 1,000 kilograms preferably called kiloton.

microbridge
(shipping) A landbridge movement in which cargo originating/destined to an inland point is railed or trucked to/from the water port for a shipment to/from a foreign country. Carrier is responsible for cargo and costs from origin to destination.

microeconomics
(economics) The examination of the economic behavior of individual units in the economy, such as households or corporations. *See also* macroeconomics.

Military Critical Technologies List
(U.S.) A document listing technologies that the U.S. Defense Department considers to have current or future utility in military systems. The MCTL describes arrays of design and manufacturing know-how; keystone manufacturing, inspection, and test equipment; and goods accompanied by sophisticated operation, application, and maintenance know-how. Military justification for each entry is included in a classified version of the list. *See* United States Department of Defense.

minibridge
(shipping) Movement of cargo from a port over water, then over land to a port on an opposite coast.

minimum bill of lading
(shipping) Ocean bills of lading are known as minimum because they contain a clause which specifies the least charge that the carrier will make for the issuance of a lading. The charge may be a definite sum, or the current charge per ton or for any specified quantity of cargo. *See* bill of lading.

minimum charge
(shipping) The lowest rate applicable on each type of cargo service no matter how small the shipment.

Ministry of Economy, Trade and Industry (METI)
(Japan) METI occupies a central position in Japan's "economic bureaucracy" and is regarded as one of the three most powerful and prestigious ministries of the central government (along with the Ministry of Finance and the Ministry of Foreign Affairs). In formulating and implementing Japan's trade and industrial policies, METI is responsible for funding most of Japan's export promotion programs (although operation of these programs is left to JETRO). The Ministry also supervises the export financing programs of Japan's Export-Import Bank, operates several types of export insurance programs, supports research organizations, and facilitates various types of overseas technical and cooperation training programs. Lately, METI has assumed a role in encouraging imports of foreign products into Japan. Address: Ministry of International Trade and Industry, 3-1, Kasumigaseki 1-chome, Chiyoda-ku, Tokyo 100, Japan; Tel: [81] (3) 3501-1511; Web: www.meti.go.jp.

Ministry of Foreign Economic Relations and Trade (MOFERT)
Renamed Ministry of Foreign Economic Trade and Economic Cooperation. *See* Ministry of Foreign Economic Trade and Economic Cooperation.

Ministry of Foreign Economic Trade and Economic Cooperation
(China) The People's Republic of China (PRC) Ministry of Foreign Economic Trade and Economic Cooperation implements national trade policies through administrative actions, drafting laws and issuing for-

eign trade regulations. It does not engage in foreign trade transactions but facilitates the foreign trading corporations (FTCs) which do. Address: Ministry of Foreign Trade & Economic Cooperation (MOFTEC), 2 Dongchangan Ave., Beijing 100731, CHINA; Tel: [86] (10) 651-98114; Fax: [86] (10) 651-98039; Web: www.moftec.gov.cn.

Ministry of Posts and Telecommunications (MPT)

(Japan) MPT is Japan's telecommunications regulatory agency. The Ministry is authorized to adjust supply and demand among service providers to ensure that there is not excessive competition in a given market. To do so, MPT issues "administrative guidance" to the industry and recommends "unification" when there appears to be excessive competition in a given market. Contact at E-mail: feedback_e@mpt.go.jp; Web: www.yusei.go.jp/index-e.html.

Minitel

(France) The still used, but now outdated, French online telephone directory and information source.

mitigation of damages

(law/insurance) A legal doctrine that charges a party who suffers contract damages with a duty to use reasonable diligence and ordinary care in attempting to minimize damages or avoid aggravating the injury. If a seller of oranges, for example, is entitled to prepayment before shipment and the buyer fails to pay, the seller should make a reasonable attempt to sell the oranges to another buyer before they spoil so as to mitigate the seller's damages. The seller may then recover from the breaching buyer the difference between the contract price and the price at which the oranges were sold to the other buyer.

The concept also applies to insurance where the insured has the responsibility to minimize damages to an insured cargo shipment.

mixed credit

(banking) The combining of concessional (liberal) and market-rate export credit as an export promotion mechanism.

mixed load

(logistics) A shipment of goods that includes regulated and exempt commodities in the same vehicle at the same time.

modal split

(logistics) A measure of an individual company's or organization's use of different modes of transport. Modal split can be expressed in terms of numbers of shipments, tonmiles/kilometers, expenses or revenues. For example, modal split in percentages by cost: air 34%, sea 47%, truck 19%.

monetary instrument

See financial instrument.

monetary system

(banking) The authority of the state in matters of establishing monetary policy, including determining the monetary unit, the monetary authorities, and the ways in which money is issued and the way the money supply is controlled.

money

(banking) Any denomination of coin or paper currency of legal tender that passes freely as a medium of exchange; anything that is accepted in exchange for other things (e.g., precious metals). Major characteristics of money include easy recognition, uniformity in quality, easy divisibility, and a relatively high value within a small area.

money creation

(banking) The increase in money supply by the central or commercial banks.

money market

(banking/finance) The market for short-term financial instruments, such as certificates of deposit, commercial paper, banker's acceptances, Treasury bills, discount notes and others. These instruments are all liquid and tend to be safe. *See* capital market, financial market.

money market operations

(banking) Comprises the acceptance and re-lending of deposits (*see* time deposits) on the money market.

money supply

(economics/banking) The amount of domestic cash and deposit money available in an economy.

moor

(shipping) To secure a vessel to an anchor, buoy or pier.

moorage

(shipping) Charges assessed for mooring a vessel to a pier or wharf.

Most Favored Nation (MFN)

A non-discriminatory trade policy commitment on the part of one country to extend to another country the lowest tariff rates it applies to any other country.

(WTO) All contracting parties to the World Trade Organization (WTO) undertake to apply such treatment to one another under Article I of the treaty.

Under MFN principles, when a country agrees to cut tariffs on a particular product imported from one country, the tariff reduction automatically applies to imports of this product from any other country eligible for most-favored nation treatment. This principle of nondiscriminatory treatment of imports appeared in numerous bilateral trade agreements prior to establishment of the WTO. A country is under no obligation to extend MFN treatment to another country unless both are bilateral contracting parties of the World Trade Organization or MFN treatment is specified in a bilateral agreement.

(U.S.) The most favored nation principle was a feature of U.S. trade policy as early as 1778. Since 1923 the United States has incorporated an "unconditional" Most Favored Nation clause in its trade agreements, binding the contracting governments to confer upon each other all the most favorable trade concessions that either may grant to any other country subsequent to the signing of the agreement. The United States now applies this provision to its trade with all of its trading partners except for those specifically excluded by law. As a result of the controversy around granting China MFN status, the U.S. has changed MFN to "Normal Trade Relations." *See* normal trade relations, Harmonized Tariff Schedule of the United States.

motor carrier's terminal

(shipping) The place where loaded or empty shipping containers are received or delivered by a motor carrier and where the motor carrier maintains an equipment pool.

motor vehicle

(shipping) Any vehicle, machine, tractor, trailer or semi-trailer propelled or drawn by mechanical power and used upon the highways in the transportation of passengers or property.

MRP

(manufacturing/logistics) Acronym for Manufacturing Resources Planning. A materials procurement planning system that uses the production plan for finished goods to determine what raw materials and component parts will be required to make the product. MRP involves planning for the collection, stocking and distribution of raw materials and component parts in the manufacturing process. MRP focuses on materials and inventories rather than personnel and equipment. MRP software is available from a number of firms. *See* MRP II, ERP.

MRP II

(logistics) Acronym for Manufacturing Resources Planning II. A further development of MRP which includes production planning and scheduling, shop-floor control, financial management, forecasting, order processing and performance measurement. MRP II software is available from a number of firms. *See* MRP.

multicurrency clause

(banking) a clause in a loan agreement stating that more than one currency may be used in paying or redeeming the loan.

Multi-Fiber Arrangement, textiles (MFA)

(WTO) An international compact under the World Trade Organization (WTO) that allows an importing signatory country to apply quantitative restrictions on textiles imports when it considers them necessary to prevent market disruption.

The MFA provides a framework for regulating international trade in textiles and apparel with the objectives of achieving "orderly marketing" of such products, and of avoiding "market disruption" in importing countries. It provides a basis on which major importers, such as the United States and the European Community, may negotiate bilateral agreements or, if necessary, impose restraints on imports from low-wage producing countries. It provides, among other things, standards for determining market disruption, minimum levels of import restraints, and annual growth of imports.

The MFA provides that such restrictions should not reduce imports to levels below those attained during the preceding year. Bilateral agreements usually allow for import growth tied to anticipated greater demand.

Since an importing country may impose such quotas unilaterally to restrict rapidly rising textiles imports, many important textiles-exporting countries consider it advantageous to enter into bilateral agreements with the principal textiles-importing countries.

The MFA went into effect on Jan. 1, 1974, was renewed in December 1977, in December 1981, and again in July 1986. It succeeded the Long-term Agreement on International Trade in Cotton Textiles ("The LTA"), which had been in effect since 1962. Whereas the LTA applied only to cotton textiles, the MFA now applies to wool, man-made (synthetic) fiber, silk blend and other vegetable fiber textiles and apparel. Note: The MFA will eventually be phased out as a result of the Uruguay Round of the General Agreement on Tariffs and Trade. *See also* quotas; bilateral trade agreement; Uruguay Round; General Agreement on Tariffs and Trade.

multilateral agreement

An international compact involving three or more parties. For example, the World Trade Organization (WTO), has been seeking to promote trade liberalization through multilateral negotiations. *See also* bilateral trade agreement.

Multilateral Investment Fund

Under the Enterprise for the Americas Initiative, the fund complements the Inter-American Development Bank. The fund provides program and project grants to advance specific, market-oriented investment policy initiatives and reforms, and encourages domestic and foreign investment in Latin America and the Caribbean. Contact: InterAmerican Development Bank, 1300 New York Avenue NW, Washington, DC 20577 USA; Tel: [1] (202) 623-1000; Web: www.iadb.org.

Multilateral Investment Guarantee Agency (MIGA)

A part of the World Bank Group. MIGA encourages equity investment and other direct investment flows to developing countries through the mitigation of noncommercial investment barriers. The agency offers investors guarantees against noncommercial

M

risks; advises developing member governments on the design and implementation of policies, programs, and procedures related to foreign investments; and sponsors a dialogue between the international business community and host governments on investment issues. Address: Multilateral Investment Guarantee Agency, World Bank, 1818 H Street NW, Washington, DC 20433 USA; Tel: [1] (202) 473-6168; Web: www.miga.org.

multilateral trade negotiations
(GATT/WTO) A term describing the multilateral rounds of negotiations held under the auspices of the General Agreement on Tariffs and Trade (GATT) and World Trade Organization (WTO) since 1947. Each Round represented a discrete and lengthy series of interacting bargaining sessions among the participating Contracting Parties in search of mutually beneficial agreements looking toward the reduction of barriers to world trade. The agreements ultimately reached at the conclusion of each Round became new commitments and thus amounted to an important step in the evolution of the world trading system. *See* General Agreement on Tariffs and Trade; rounds; Tokyo Round; Uruguay Round, World Trade Organization (WTO).

multimodal transport
(shipping) Shipping which includes at least two modes of transport, such as shipping by rail and by sea.

multinational corporation
(economics) A corporation having subsidiaries in more than one country.

multiple-car/trailer load rate
(logistics) A special lower freight rate that applies to a bulk shipment that requires multiple trailers or rail cars.

mutatis mutandis
(law) Meaning changing what needs to be changed; used when cases are nearly the same except for minor details. A statute that governs one type of transaction, for example, may also be applied to another transaction with minor exceptions, in which event the statute applies mutatis mutandis. A country may apply its trademark law mutatis mutandis to service marks, in which event the same law will apply except for changes to account for such details as the use of the mark to distinguish services instead of goods.

N

Naamloze Vennotschap (N.V.)
(Belgium, Netherlands) Designation for a joint stock company with limited personal liability to shareholders.

NAFTA
See North American Free Trade Agreement.

naira
The currency of Nigeria. 1N=100 kobo.

named insured
(insurance) Any person or firm or corporation or any of its members, specially designated by name as insured(s) in a policy, as distinguished from others who, although unnamed, are protected under some circumstances.

National Association of Export Companies
(U.S.) A non-profit organization established in 1965 to act as the information provider, support clearinghouse forum, and advocate for those involved in exporting and servicing exporters. Provides networking opportunities, counseling, publications, seminars, etc. Address: National Association of Export Companies, 205 Bergen Turnpike, Suite 2L, Ridgefield Park, NJ 07660 USA; Tel: [1] (201) 814-0336; Fax: [1] (201) 440-1216; Web: www.nexco.org.

National Association of State Development Agencies (NASDA)
(U.S.) NASDA was formed in 1946 to provide a forum for directors of state economic development agencies to exchange information, compare programs, and deal with issues of mutual interest. NASDA's organization includes International Trade and Foreign Investment components. Trade activities include maintenance of a State Export Program Database. Address: NASDA, 750 First Street NE, Suite 1100, Washington, DC 20002 USA; Tel: [1] (703) 490-6777; Fax: [1] (703) 492-4404; Web: www.nasda.com.

National Customs Brokers and Forwarders Association of America
A non-profit organization founded in 1897 which serves as the trade organization of customs brokers and international freight forwarders in the U.S. Through ongoing communications with industry trade publications and the general media, the Association projects the industry's interests and objectives. Membership includes brokers and freight forwarders in 32 affiliated associations located at major ports throughout the U.S. Address: National Customs Brokers and Forwarders Association of America, 1200 18th Street, NW, #901 Washington, DC 20036 USA;

Tel: [1] (202) 466-0222; Fax: [1] (202) 466-0226; E-mail: staff@ncbfaa.org; Web: www.ncbfaa.org.

nationalization

(economics/law) The forcible acquisition, with or without compensation, of private property such as real estate, a business enterprise or an entire industry by a sovereign nation. In nationalization, social or economic equality is often stated as the motive. Nationalization is most common in socialistic and communistic countries, but also in less-developed nations where there is resentment of foreign control of major industries. Famous examples of nationalizations include: Mexico's nationalization of oil producing properties owned by U.S. firms in 1938, Great Britain's nationalization of the coal, steel and transportation industries between 1945 and 1951, Iran's nationalization of the Anglo-Iranian Oil Company in 1951, Egypt's nationalization of the Suez Canal in 1956 and Chile's nationalization of foreign-owned copper mines in 1971. *See* privatization.

National Motor Freight Classification (NMFC)

(U.S. logistics) A freight classification schedule of tariffs applicable to less-than-truck-load (LTL) freight shipments. This tariff divides products into one of 18 classes and provides a standard for the pricing of domestic shipments throughout the United States. Information at Web: www.nmfta.org.

national security controls

(U.S.) National security controls restrict exports of U.S. goods and technology which would make a significant contribution to the military potential of another country and thus be detrimental to national security.

National Security Directive #53

(U.S.) NSD-53 deals with the export licensing process and sets specified time periods for resolving disputes on both national security and foreign policy export license applications. Under NSD-53, exports controlled on both of these grounds are subject to explicit timetables for interagency dispute resolution at the Sub-Cabinet level by the Advisory Committee on Export Policy (ACEP), and at the cabinet level by the Export Administration Review Board (EARB). The Directive requires escalation to the ACEP not later than 100 days from the filing date of the applicant's application, and if the disagreement cannot be resolved by the ACEP, for review and resolution by the EARB within 35 days of the date of the ACEP meeting. Cases not resolved by the EARB must be escalated to the president for resolution. The new procedures also permit an agency to refer a case at any stage of the dispute resolution process to the NSC for a 30 day policy review. *See* National Security Directives.

National Security Directives (NSD)

(U.S.) NSDs provide policy or procedural guidance and are signed by the president. In 1989, the president reorganized the national security council committee process (separate from the Export Administration Review Board (EARB)). As reorganized, under the National Security Council (NSC), there are committees for Coordinating Committee for Multilateral Export Controls (CoCom), terrorism, nonproliferation, etc. NSDs were known as National Security Decision Directives, NSDDs, before President Bush's reorganization. NSD-1 reorganized the process; NSD-10 established the committees; NSD-53 deals with export licensing. The scope of coverage and the players are about the same under the NSD and NSDD processes.

National Security Override (NSO)

(U.S.) In some cases of U.S. export law, despite a finding of foreign availability of a controlled commodity, control is maintained over exporting the commodity because it is deemed a national security sensitive item. The term national security override is used to describe this circumstance.

The term has also been used in other contexts. For example, under a November 16, 1990 directive, the president instructed the interagency control groups to move as many dual use items from the U.S. State Department's International Munitions List to the Commerce Department's Commerce Control List. In some circumstances, a national security override is applied to prevent transfer of a particular item.

See also International Munitions List; Commerce Control List.

National Tourism Policy Act

(U.S. law) Legislation passed in 1981 that created the U.S. Travel and Tourism Administration and required the establishment of the Tourism Policy Council and the Travel and Tourism Advisory Board.

National Trade Data Bank (NTDB)

(CD-ROM publication/Internet service) The NTDB is an electronic database available on CD-ROM and on the World Wide Web through the U.S. Department of Commerce's fee-based STAT-USA/Internet service at Web: www.stat-usa.gov. The NTDB contains international economic and export promotion information supplied by various U.S. governmental agencies. The NTDB provides world trade data from several hundred thousand documents taken from over 20 Federal sources. Topics include: export opportunities by industry, country, and product; foreign companies or importers looking for specific products; how-to market guides; and demographic, political, and socio-economic conditions in hundreds of countries. Source: U.S. Department of Commerce, Office of Economic Analysis, HCHB Room 4885, Washington, DC 20230 USA; Tel: [1] (202) 482-1986, [1] (800) STAT-USA; Web: www.stat-usa.gov.

National Trade Estimates Report

(U.S.) An annual report by the United States Trade Representative (USTR) that identifies significant foreign barriers to and distortions of trade. Contact: Office of the United States Trade Representative, Executive Office of the President, 600 17th Street NW, Washington, DC 20508 USA; Tel: [1] (888) 473-8787; Web: www.ustr.gov.

national treatment

(trade policy) A requirement in World Trade Organization (WTO) trade policy that member nations regulate imports in the same way they regulate domestic goods. Specifically, member nations cannot impose more stringent regulations on imports as a "non-tariff barrier" in an effort to exclude such imports. National treatment affords individuals and firms of foreign countries the same competitive opportunities, including market access, as are available to domestic parties.

natural advantage

(economics) Economic theory that states that a country has a competitive advantage in the production of certain products as a result of access to natural resources, transportation or climatic conditions.

NDA

See non-disclosure agreement.

near-bank

(banking-Canada) A financial institution, excluding standard commercial bank, such as savings bank, credit union, etc.

negligence

(law) Failure to do that which an ordinary, reasonable, prudent person would do, or the doing of some act that an ordinary, prudent person would not do. Reference is made of the situation, circumstances, and awareness of the parties involved.

negotiable

(general) Anything that can be sold or transferred to another for money or as payments of a debt. In international trade, usually refers to the transferability of a title document—such as a negotiable bill of lading. (investments) Refers to a security, title to which is transferable by delivery.
See negotiable instrument.

negotiable bill of lading

(shipping) Bill of lading transferred by endorsement. There are three possibilities: (1) to XY & Co. or their order; (2) to the order of XY & Co.; and (3) to order, without the name of the party. In the latter case the bill remains to the order of the shipper until he endorses it.

These types of bills of lading are usually endorsed on the reverse. The opposite of a negotiable bill of lading is the straight bill of lading *See* bill of lading; endorsement.

negotiable instrument

(law/banking/shipping) A written document (instrument) that can be transferred merely by endorsement (signing) or delivery. Checks, bills of exchange, bills of lading and warehouse receipts (if marked negotiable), and promissory notes are examples of negotiable instruments.

(U.S.) The Uniform Negotiable Instruments Act states: "An instrument, to be negotiable, must conform to the following requirements: (1) it must be in writing and signed by the maker or drawer; (2) it must contain an unconditional promise or order to pay a certain sum in money; (3) it must be payable on demand, or at a fixed or determinable future time; (4) it must be payable to order or to bearer; and (5) where the instrument is addressed to a drawee, he must be named or otherwise indicated therein with reasonable certainty."

negotiable warehouse receipt

(shipping) A certificate issued by an approved warehouse that guarantees the existence and the grade of a commodity held in store. *See* negotiable instrument.

negotiating bank

(banking) In a letter of credit transaction, the bank that (1) receives and examines the seller's documents for adherence to the terms and conditions of the letter of credit, (2) gives value to the seller, so long as the terms of the credit have been met, and (3) forwards them to the issuing bank (the buyer's or importer's bank). Depending upon the type of credit, the negotiating bank will either credit or pay the seller/exporter immediately under the terms of the letter of credit, or credit or pay the exporter once it has received payment from the issuing bank. *See* advising bank; issuing bank.

negotiation

(banking) (a) The action by which a negotiable instrument is circulated (bought and sold) from one holder to another. (b) In letter of credit transactions, (1) the examination of the seller's documentation by the negotiating bank to determine if they comply with the terms and conditions of the letter of credit and (2) the giving of value for draft(s) and/or document(s) by the bank authorized to negotiate. Mere examination of the documents without giving value does not constitute a negotiation. *See* letter of credit.

negotiation credit

(banking) A documentary letter of credit available by negotiation. *See* letter of credit.

NES

See not elsewhere specified.

nested

(shipping) Packed one within another.

net cash
Payment for goods sold usually within a short period of time with no deduction allowed from the invoice price.

net export of goods and services
(economics) The excess of exports of goods and services (domestic output sold abroad, and the production abroad credit to U.S.-owned resources) over imports (U.S. purchases of foreign output, domestic production credit to foreign-owned resources, and net private cash remittances to creditors abroad).

net foreign investment
(economics/foreign investment) The net change in a nation's foreign assets and liabilities, including the monetary gold stocks, arising out of current trade, income on foreign investment, and cash gifts and contributions. It measures the excess of: (1) exports over imports, (2) income on U.S. public and private investment abroad over payments on foreign investment in the U.S., and (3) cash gifts and contributions of the U.S. (public and private) to foreigners over cash gifts and contributions received from abroad.

Net foreign investment may also be viewed as the acquisition of foreign assets by that country's residents, less the acquisition of that country's assets by foreign residents.

net income
(economics) The remains from earnings after all costs, expenses and allowances for depreciation and probable loss have been deducted.

net loss
(economics) The excess of expenses and losses during a specified period over revenues and gains in the same time frame.

net national product
(economics) Gross national product minus capital consumption (depreciation). The market value of the net output of goods and services produced by the nation's economy.

net price
Price after all discounts, rebates, etc., have been allowed.

net ton (N.T.)
(measure) A unit of mass or weight measurement equal to 2,000 pounds. Also called short ton (S.T.).

net tonnage
(shipping) A vessel's gross tonnage minus deductions for space occupied by accommodations for crew, machinery for navigation, the engine room, and fuel. A vessel's net tonnage represents the space available for the accommodation of passengers and the stowage of cargo.

net weight
(general) The weight of goods without packaging.

(shipping) The weight of merchandise without the shipper container. Also the weight of the contents of a freight car.

neutral air waybill
(shipping) A standard air waybill without identification of issuing carrier. *See* air waybill; bill of lading.

neutral body
(shipping) A regulatory entity operating within the framework of a shipping conference, established by the member carriers to act as a self-policing force to ferret out malpractices and other tariff violations. The neutral body has authority to scrutinize all documents kept by the carriers and the carriers' personnel with right of entry to all areas of the carrier's facilities including desks, briefcases, etc. Violations found are reported to the membership with significant penalties being assessed. Repeated offenses are subject to escalating penalty amounts. Revenue from penalties are used to support the cost of the neutral body activity. *See* carrier; conference.

newly industrializing countries (NICs)
(economics) Relatively advanced developing countries whose industrial production and exports have grown rapidly in recent years. Examples include Brazil, Hong Kong, Korea, Mexico, Singapore, and Taiwan. The term was originated by the Organization for Economic Cooperation and Development (OECD).

new-to-export (NTE)
(U.S.) As defined by the United States Department of Commerce, a new-to-export action is one that results from documented assistance to a company that assists the client's first verifiable export sale. Either the company has not exported to any destination during the past 24 months or prior exports have resulted from unsolicited orders or were received through a U.S.-based intermediary. *See* United States Department of Commerce.

new-to-market (NTM)
(U.S.) As defined by the U.S. Department of Commerce, a reportable new-to-market export action is one that results from documented assistance to an exporter that facilitates a verifiable sale in a new foreign market. Either the company has not exported to that market during the past 24 months or previous exports to that market have resulted from unsolicited orders or were received through a U.S. based intermediary. *See* United States Department of Commerce.

nexus
(law) A party's connection with, or presence in, a place that is sufficient enough that it would be fair to subject the party to the jurisdiction of the court or government located there.

NGO
Acronym for non-government organization.
a) A private sector profit or non-profit organization.

(b) A private sector non-profit organization that "pursues activities to relieve suffering, promote the interests of the poor, protect the environment, provide basic social services or undertake community development." (World Bank NGO criteria.)

ngultrum

The currency of Bhutan. 1Nu=100 chetrum.

Nippon Telegraph and Telephone Corporation (NTT)

(Japan) NTT is Japan's largest telecommunications enterprise and was converted from a public corporation to a private enterprise in April 1985. Although competition has been allowed, the Japanese Government still owns the majority of NTT stock and postponement of a decision in NTT divestiture is an issue of considerable importance to market access by foreign companies. NTT was established in 1952. Address: Nippon Telegraph and Telephone Corporation, 3-1, Otemachi 2-chome, Chiyoda-ku, Tokyo 100, Japan; Tel: [81] (3) 3509-5111; Web: www.ntt.co.jp.

non-disclosure agreement (NDA)

(law) An agreement between two or more parties not to disclose trade secrets, trade practices, business or marketing plans or other proprietary or confidential information. A non-disclosure agreement is often signed by parties entering into a business negotiation or business relationship where such information is likely to be revealed.

non-government organization

See NGO.

non-market economy

(economics) A national economy or a country in which the government seeks to determine economic activity largely through a mechanism of central planning, as formerly in the Soviet Union, in contrast to a market economy that depends heavily upon market forces to allocate productive resources. In a "non-market" economy, production targets, prices, costs, investment allocations, raw materials, labor, international trade, and most other economic aggregates are manipulated within a national economic plan drawn up by a central planning authority, and hence the public sector makes the major decisions affecting demand and supply within the national economy.

non-negotiable

(law) Not transferable from one person to another. Usually refers to the transferability of a title document (e.g., non-negotiable bill of lading). Possession of a non-negotiable title document alone does not entitle the holder to receive the goods named therein (e.g., non-negotiable sea waybill, air waybill, forwarder's receipt, etc.). *See also* negotiable; negotiable instrument.

nonperforming assets

(banking) Assets which have no financial return.

nonperforming debt

(banking) A debt which has no financial return (i.e. no interest is paid on it).

nonperforming loan; nonaccruing loan

(banking) Loan where payment of interest has been delayed for more than 90 days.

nonstructural container

(shipping) A unit load device composed of a bottomless rigid shell used in combination with a pallet and net assembly. Note: The expression "nonstructural container" is also used to refer to the shell part of a device.

non-tariff barriers or measures

(economics) Any number of import quotas or other quantitative restrictions, non-automatic import licensing, customs surcharges or other fees and charges, customs procedures, export subsidies, unreasonable standards or standards-setting procedures, government procurement restrictions, inadequate intellectual property protection and investment restrictions which deny or make market access excessively difficult for goods or services of foreign origin.

(GATT) Participants in the Tokyo Round of the General Agreement on Tariffs and Trade attempted to address these barriers through the negotiations of a number of GATT codes, open for signature to all GATT members. Seven codes were negotiated during the Tokyo Round, covering customs valuations, import licensing, subsidies and countervailing duties, antidumping duties, standards, government procurement and trade in civil aircraft. Although the Tokyo Round codes had alleviated some of the problems caused by non-tariff measures, overall use of NTMs has increased since conclusion of the Tokyo Round.

See also import restrictions; non-tariff barriers; Tokyo Round; General Agreement on Tariffs and Trade, World Trade Organization.

non-vessel operating common carrier (NVOCC)

(shipping) A carrier issuing bills of lading for carriage of goods on vessels which it neither operates nor owns. NVOCCs purchase large blocks of space at discounted rates from shipping lines and resell them in smaller blocks to other shippers at a profit. NVOCCs often consolidate and transport shipments under a single bill of lading.

(U.S.) A "carrier" defined by maritime law offering an international cargo transport service through the use of underlying carriers and under their own rate structure in accordance with tariffs filed with the Federal Maritime Commission in Washington, DC. The rates filed are required only to port-to-port portion. Specific authority for the NVOCC is given in the code of Federal Regulations, Title 46, Chapter IV, Federal Maritime Commission Sub-Part B, entitled "Regulations Affecting Maritime Carriers and

Related Activities." General Order 4, Amendment i, Section 510.2 (d) states:

"The term 'non-vessel operating common carrier by water' means a person who holds himself out by the establishment and maintenance of tariffs, by advertisement, solicitation, or otherwise, to provide transportation for hire by water in interstate commerce as defined in the Act, and in commerce from the United States as defined in paragraph (b) of the section; assumes responsibility or has liability imposed by law for safe transportation of shipments; and arranges in his own name with underlying water carriers for the performance of such transportation whether or not owning or controlling the means by which such transportation is affected."

Nordic Council

(regional alliance) The Nordic Council, established in 1952, supports cooperation among Nordic countries in communications, cultural, economic, environmental, fiscal, legal and social areas. Members include: Denmark, Finland, Iceland, Norway and Sweden. Address: Nordic Council, P.O. Box 3043, DK-1021 Copenhagen K, Denmark; Tel: [45] (33) 96-04-00; Fax: [45] (33) 11-18-70; Web: www.norden.org.

normal trade relations (NTR)

(trade policy) The new designation for Most Favored Nation (MFN) trading status. Although the name has changed, the privileges remain the same. (U.S. trade policy) With controversy surrounding giving Most Favored Nation status to China, it was decided that for political reasons the designation would change to Normal Trade Relations. Countries with MFN/NTR status enjoy preferred import tariff rates on goods exported to the U.S.

North American Free Trade Agreement (NAFTA)

A free trade agreement that comprises Canada, the U.S. and Mexico. The objectives of the Agreement are to eliminate barriers to trade, promote conditions of fair competition, increase investment opportunities, provide protection for intellectual property rights and establish procedures for the resolution of disputes.

NAFTA eliminates all tariffs on goods originating in Canada, Mexico and the United States over a transition period. Rules of origin are necessary to define which goods are eligible for preferential tariff treatment.

NAFTA contains special provisions for market access, customs administration, automotive goods, textiles and apparel, energy and petrochemicals, agriculture, sanitary and phytosanitary measures, technical standards, emergency action, antidumping and countervailing duty matters, government procurement, trade in services, land transportation, telecommunications, investment, financial services, intellectual property, temporary entry for business persons, dispute settlement, administration of law and the environment.

NAFTA will produce a market exceeding 360 million consumers and a combined output of more than $6 trillion—20 percent larger than the European Community. The agreement took effect January 1, 1994.

The Commerce Department's Office of NAFTA & Inter-American affairs has its Web site at Web: www.mac.doc.gov/nafta/. This site contains the full text of the treaty, as well as resources, news items, items from the Federal Register, ways to contact this office for assistance, and links to other NAFTA-related sites on the Web. The entire text of NAFTA is also available from the U.S. Government Printing Office, Washington, DC 20402-9325 USA; Tel: [1] (866) 512-1800; or on the National Trade Data Bank on CD-ROM, Tel: [1] (202) 482-1986.

North-South trade

(economics) Trade between developed countries (North) and developing countries (South). *See* developed countries; developing countries.

no show

(shipping) Freight that has been booked to a ship, but has not physically arrived in time to be loaded to that ship.

nostro account

(banking) "Our" account. An account maintained by a bank with a bank in a foreign country. Nostro accounts are kept in foreign currencies of the country which the monies are held, with the equivalent dollar value listed in another column for accounting purposes.

notary public

(law-U.S.) A person commissioned by a state for a stipulated period (with the privilege of renewal) to administer certain oaths and to attest and certify documents, thus authorizing him or her to take affidavits and depositions. A notary is also authorized to "protect" negotiable instruments for nonpayment or nonacceptance.

The role of a notary public varies from country to country. In some countries they take on many of the responsibilities which in the U.S. an attorney would assume, while in other countries they do not exist at all.

not elsewhere specified (N.E.S.)

(shipping) The abbreviation N.E.S. often appears in air freight tariffs. For example: "advertising matter, N.E.S.," "printed matter, N.E.S.," indicating that the rate stated in the tariff applies to all commodities within the commodity group except those appearing under their own rate. The abbreviation N.E.S., as used in air freight tariffs, is comparable to the abbreviation N.O.I.B.N. (not otherwise indexed by number) and N.O.S. (not otherwise specified) which appear in tariffs published by the surface modes.

notify address
(shipping) Address mentioned in the transport document (bill of lading or an air waybill), to which the carrier is to give notice when goods are due to arrive.

notify party
(shipping) Name and address of a party in the transport document (bill of lading or air waybill), usually the buyer or his agent, to be notified by the shipping company of the arrival of a shipment.

NTR
See normal trade relations.

Nuclear Energy Agency (NEA)
Promotes the safe and effective use of nuclear energy through the exchange of information among technical experts, the sharing of analytical studies, and undertaking joint research and development projects by member countries. Headquarters are in Paris, France. Address: Nuclear Energy Agency, Le Seine-Saint Germain, 12 blvd. des Iles, 92130 Issy-les-Moulineaux, France; Tel: [33] (1) 45-24-82-00; Fax: [33] (1) 45-24-11-10; Web: www.nea.fr.

Nuclear Non-Proliferation Act
(U.S. law) Among other actions, this Act made the U.S. Energy Department responsible for approving arrangements for nuclear exports and transfers. Each arrangement requires U.S. State Department concurrence, as well as consultations with the Arms Control and Disarmament Agency, the Nuclear Regulatory Commission, and the Departments of Defense and Commerce.

Nuclear Non-Proliferation Treaty
The NPT became effective in 1970 and was intended to limit the number of states with nuclear weapons to five: the U.S., the Soviet Union, Britain, France, and China. In doing so, the NPT attempts to: (1) prevent nuclear weapons sales by not assisting other nations with nuclear weapons development; (2) halt the nuclear weapons development programs of non-nuclear weapons states; and (3) promote nuclear disarmament and the peaceful use of nuclear technologies and materials. Over 140 states have pledged not to acquire nuclear weapons and to accept the safeguards of the International Atomic Energy Agency over all their nuclear materials. The treaty, however, is not of indefinite duration. One of the provisions of the treaty was to convene a conference 25 years after entry to decide whether the treaty would continue indefinitely or be extended for a specified time.

Nuclear Referral List
See Nuclear Regulatory Commission.

Nuclear Regulatory Commission (NRC)
(U.S.) The NRC regulates the transfer of nuclear facilities, materials and parts with uniquely nuclear applications (such as items associated with nuclear reactors). The U.S. Department of Energy regulates the transfer of information relating to nuclear technology. The U.S. State Department controls defense articles and services, such as nuclear weapons design and test equipment. The U.S. Department of Commerce controls a range of dual-use items with potential nuclear application. Validated licensing controls are in effect for commodities and technical data identified to be useful in the design, development, production or use of nuclear weapons or nuclear explosive purposes. These commodities compose the "Nuclear Referral List" (NRL). Any item under national security-based licensing requirements and intended for a nuclear-related end-use/end-user is also subject to review. In addition, any commodity that will be used in a sensitive nuclear activity is also subject to validated licensing controls. License applications for U.S. export of NRL items as well as applications that may involve possible nuclear uses are reviewed by the U.S. Department of Commerce in consultation with the Department of Energy. When either Department believes that the application requires further review, the application is referred to the Subgroup on Nuclear Export Coordination (SNEC). The SNEC is comprised of representatives from State, Defense, ACDA, and the NRC. Contact: U.S. Nuclear Regulatory Commission, Office of Public Affairs (OPA), Washington, D.C. 20555 USA; Tel: [1] (800) 368-5642; E-mail: opa@nrc.gov; Web: www.nrc.gov. *See* Nuclear Suppliers Group; Zangger Committee.

Nuclear Suppliers Group
An organization of nuclear supplier nations which coordinates exports of nuclear materials and equipment with the International Atomic Energy Agency (IAEA) inspectorate regime. The reason for creating the NSG was to allow member states some flexibility (which they do not enjoy in the Zangger Committee) in controlling items to non-nuclear weapons states.

The NSG's independence from the Nuclear Non-Proliferation Treaty (NPT) enables NSG to enlist the cooperation of supplier states that are not signatories to the NPT and thus not involved in the nuclear export control activities of the Zangger Committee. The NSG's control list is more comprehensive than the Zangger Committee's "trigger list"; it requires the imposition of safeguards on exports of nuclear technology in addition to nuclear materials and equipment.
See Nuclear Non-Proliferation Treaty; Zangger Committee; Nuclear Regulatory Commission.

O

ocean bill of lading (B/L)

(shipping) A receipt for the cargo and a contract for transportation between a shipper and the ocean carrier. It may also be used as an instrument of ownership (negotiable bill of lading) which can be bought, sold, or traded while the goods are in transit. To be used in this manner, it must be a negotiable "Order" Bill-of-Lading.

(a) A **clean bill of lading** is issued when the shipment is received in good order. If damaged or a shortage is noted, a clean bill of lading will not be issued.

(b) An **on board bill of lading** certifies that the cargo has been placed aboard the named vessel and is signed by the master of the vessel or his representative. In letter of credit transactions, an on board bill of lading is usually necessary for the shipper to obtain payment from the bank. When all bills of lading are processed, a ship's manifest is prepared by the steamship line. This summarizes all cargo aboard the vessel by port of loading and discharge.

(c) An **inland bill of lading** (a waybill on rail or the "pro forma" bill of lading in trucking) is used to document the transportation of the goods between the port and the point of origin or destination. It should contain information such as marks, numbers, steamship line, and similar information to match with a dock receipt.

See also bill of lading.

ocean transport intermediary (OTI)

(shipping) An ocean freight forwarders and NVOCC (Non Vessel Operating Common Carriers) that acts as an intermediary between shippers and shipping lines. In the U.S. OTI's are licensed according to provisions in the Ocean Shipping Reform Act of 1998 which include the responsibility to publish tariffs (charges) in an electronically accessible automated tariff system.

OEM

Acronym for original equipment manufacturer. (a) A manufacturer who sells equipment to a reseller for the purpose of repackaging, bundling, rebranding or co-branding. (b) (popular) The reseller of repackaged, bundled, rebranded or co-branded equipment. In both cases, the reseller can simply repackage and resell the equipment, add value to the equipment or bundle the equipment with other products for resale. *See* VAR (value-added reseller).

Offene Handelsgesellschaft (OHG)

(Austria) Designation for a general partnership, in which all partners have joint and several liability.

offer

(law) A proposal that is made to a certain individual or legal entity to enter into a contract, that is definite in its terms, and that indicates the offeror's intent to be bound by an acceptance. For example, an order delivered to a seller to buy a product on certain terms is an offer, but an advertisement sent to many potential buyers is not. *See* acceptance; counteroffer.

Office of Export Licensing (OEL)

(U.S.) Under the Commerce Department's Bureau of Export Administration, the OEL administers export licenses. The Bureau of Industry and Security (formerly the Bureau of Export Administration) provides an Internet-based export license application program free of charge called the Simplified Network Application Process (SNAP) at Web: www.snapbxa.gov. Telephone support for SNAP is also available at [1] (202) 482-4811. Address: Office of Export Licensing, U.S. Department of Commerce, 14th and Pennsylvania NW, Washington, DC 20230 USA; Web: www.bxa.doc.gov. See Bureau of Export Administration.

Office of Management and Budget (OMB)

(U.S.) An executive office of the president which evaluates, formulates and coordinates management procedures and program objectives within and among federal departments and agencies. It also controls the administration of the federal budget. Address: Office of Management and Budget, New Executive Office Building, 725 17th Street NW, Washington, DC 20503 USA; Tel: [1] (202) 395-7254; Web: www.omb.gov.

Office of Munitions Control

See Defense Trade Controls.

official development assistance

(U.S.) Financial flows to developing countries and multilateral institutions provided by official agencies of national, state, or local governments. Each transaction must be:

(1) administered with the promotion of the economic development and welfare of developing countries as its main objective; and

(2) concessional in character and contain a grant element of at least 25 percent.

offset(s)

(general) In non-defense trade, governments sometimes impose offset requirements on foreign exporters, as a condition for approval of major sales agreements in an effort to either reduce the adverse trade impact of a major sale or to gain specified industrial benefits for the importing country. In these circumstances, offset requirements generally take one of two forms. In one formulation, an exporter may be required to purchase a specified amount of locally-produced goods or services from the importing country. For example, a commercial aircraft manufacturer seeking sales to an airline in another country might be required to purchase products as different from airplanes as canned hams. In other instances, an exporter might be required to establish manufacturing facilities in the importing country or to secure a specified percentage of the components used in manufacturing his product from established local manufacturers. *See* countertrade.

(defense related–U.S.) In trade of defense items, "offsets" are industrial compensation practices mandated by many foreign governments when purchasing U.S. defense systems. Types of offsets include mandatory coproduction, subcontractor production, technology transfer, countertrade, and foreign investment. Countries require offsets for a variety of reasons: to ease (or "offset") the burden of large defense purchases on their economies, to increase domestic employment, to obtain desired technology, or to promote targeted industrial sectors. *See* countertrade.

offshore
(banking) Refers to financial operations transacted outside the country in question.

offshore bank
(banking) Bank located outside the country in question.

offshore banking center
(banking) Financial center where many of the financial institutions have little connection with that country's financial system. Usually established for purposes of tax avoidance. Examples are the Cayman Islands, where many of the corporations are engaged in business in the U.S. and Europe, and London, where many of the financial institutions are engaged in Eurodollar trading.

offshore banking unit (OBU)
(banking) Department within a bank that, in certain countries (e.g., Bahrain), is permitted to engage in specific transactions (usually Euromarket business) that ordinary domestic banks are not allowed to do.

old-to-market (OTM)
(U.S.) A committed to export, experienced, larger-scale firm. A significant portion of manufacturing capability may be foreign sourced. Export sales volume is often in excess of 15 percent of total sales.

on board
(shipping) Notation on a bill of lading indicating that the goods have been loaded on board or shipped on a named ship. In the case of received for shipment bills of lading, the following four parties are authorized to add this "on board" notation: (1) the carrier, (2) the carrier's agent, (3) the master of the ship, and (4) the master's agent. *See* ocean bill of lading; bill of lading; negotiable bill of lading.

on deck
(shipping) Notation on a bill of lading which indicates that the goods have been loaded on the deck of the ship. In letter of credit transactions documents

with an "on deck" notation will only be accepted if expressly authorized in the credit. *See* ocean bill of lading.

on deck bill of lading
(shipping) Bill of lading containing the notation that goods have been placed on deck.
See ocean bill of lading; bill of lading.

online receiving
(logistics) A freight management system where operators enter goods received information directly into computer terminals as shipments occur.

on their face
(banking) In letter of credit and other documentary operations banks must examine documents with reasonable care to ascertain whether or not they appear, on their face, to be in compliance with the terms or conditions of the documentary letter of credit. *See* letter of credit; documentary collection.

open account
Credit extended that is not supported by a note, mortgage, or other formal written evidence of indebtedness (e.g., merchandise for which a buyer is billed later). Because this method poses an obvious risk to the supplier, it is essential that the buyer's integrity be unquestionable.

open conference
(shipping) A shipping conference in which there are no restrictions upon membership other than ability and willingness to serve the trade. U.S. law requires all conferences serving the U.S. to be open. *See* conference; closed conference.

open economy
(economics) An economy free of trade restrictions.

open-end contract
(law) An agreement by which the buyer may purchase goods from a seller for a certain time without changes in the price or the contract terms.

open policy
(insurance) An insurance contract (policy) which remains in force until cancelled and under which individual successive shipments are reported or declared and automatically covered on or after the inception date. The open policy saves time and expense for all concerned, whether underwriter, agent or assured. The shipper gains many advantages from the use of an open policy.

(1) He or she has automatic protection (up to the maximum limits stated in the policy) from the time shipments leave the warehouse at the place named in the policy for the commencement of transit. The policyholder warrants that shipments will be declared as soon as practicable, but unintentional failure to report will not void the insurance, since the goods are "held covered," subject to policy conditions. In effect, this is errors and omissions coverage, and it forestalls the possibility that, because of the press of

O

business, goods may commence transit without being insured.

(2) The open policy provides a convenient way to report shipments. It also relieves the shipper from the necessity of arranging individual placings of insurance for each shipment.

(3) Under an open policy the shipper has prior knowledge of the rate of premium that will be charged and thus can be certain of the cost. This in turn facilitates his quoting a landed sales price.

(4) The use of the open policy creates a business relationship that may exist over a long period of time. This permits the insurer to learn the special requirements of its assureds and so to provide them with individualized protection, tailor-made to fit the specific situation. This may be an important factor in the case of loss adjustments at out-of-the-way ports around the world, or in overcoming problems peculiar to a given commodity.

Some letter of credit transactions require evidence of an individual "policy" covering the specified shipment. In such cases it has become the practice to use a special marine policy.

See bordereau; declaration; special marine policy.

open-top container
(logistics/shipping) A shipping container that is designed to open from the top so that cargo too large to be loaded from the side can be lowered in through the roof. This type of container is especially suitable for machinery. Once loaded the container is covered with rigid panels or a tarpaulin.

operating committees
(U.S.) There are four operating committees (OCs), which are the first step in resolving interagency disputes over the disposition of export license applications. The operating committees are: (1) the State Department's Subgroup on Nuclear Export Coordination (SNEC), (2) the State Department's working group on Missile Technology, (3) the State Department's working group on Chemical and Biological Warfare, and (4) the Department of Commerce's operating committee on all other dual-use items. Operating committees must make recommendations within 90 days of the date of the filing of an export license application. Operating committees generally meet a couple of times per month. *See* United States Department of Commerce; United States Department of State.

Operating Differential Subsidy (ODS)
(U.S. shipping) A subsidy paid to an American flag carrier by the U.S. government to offset the higher costs of operating a U.S. flag vessel than a foreign flag vessel.

Operation Exodus
(U.S.) A U.S. Customs Service export enforcement program that was developed in 1981 to help stem the flow of the illegal export of U.S.-sourced arms and technology to the Soviet bloc and other prohibited destinations. These enforcement activities are currently coordinated by the U.S. Customs Service's Exodus Command Center. Information on this Center can be found online at Web: www.customs.ustreas.gov/impoexpo/tools/exodus.htm. *See* United States Customs Service.

operator
(U.S. foreign trade zones) A corporation, partnership or person that operates a foreign trade zone under the terms of an agreement with a foreign trade zone grantee. If there is no operator agreement and the grantee operates his own zone, the grantee is considered the operator for Customs Regulations purposes. *See* foreign trade zone; Foreign Trade Zone Board; Foreign Trade Zone Act; grantee; zone user; subzones.

option
(general) (a) A right to take up an offer. (b) The right to choose from several different possibilities. (c) A privilege to buy or sell, receive, or deliver property, given in accordance with the terms stated, with a consideration for price. This privilege may or may not be exercised at the option holder's discretion. Failure to exercise the option leads to forfeiture of the option.

(securities) A contract giving the holder the right to buy or sell a stated number of shares of a particular security at a fixed price within a predetermined period.

(foreign exchange) The contractually agreed upon right to buy (call option) or sell (put option) a specific amount of an underlying instrument at a predetermined price on a specific date (European option) or up to a future date (American option).

See call option; put option; American option; European option.

order
(law/banking/shipping) A request to deliver, sell, receive, or purchase goods or services.

order bill
(law) A bill of lading that states that goods are consigned to the order of the person named in the bill. *See* bill of lading; ocean bill of lading.

order cycle
(logistics) The total time and process required for the placement of an order and its final receipt by a customer. This includes order placement, order processing, production and transportation to the final destination.

orderly marketing agreements
International agreements negotiated between two or more governments, in which the trading partners agree to restrain the growth of trade (limit exports) in specified "sensitive" products, usually through the imposition of import quotas. Orderly Marketing Agreements are intended to ensure that future trade increases will not disrupt, threaten or impair competitive industries or their workers in importing countries.

order notify

(shipping) A bill of lading term to provide for surrender of the original bill of lading before freight is surrendered; usually handled through a bank. *See* letter of credit; bill of lading; ocean bill of lading; documentary collection.

order picking

(logistics) The process of retrieving goods from storage to fill shop or customer orders.

order processing

(logistics) The process of fulfillment of a customer order. This includes the entire process from order receiving, invoicing and other documentation, picking, packing and shipping.

Organization for Economic Cooperation and Development (OECD)

The OECD is the primary forum for the discussion of common economic and social issues confronting the U.S., Canada, Western Europe, Japan, Australia, and New Zealand. It was founded in 1960 as the successor to the Organization for European Economic Cooperation which oversaw European participation in the Marshall Plan. The OECD's fundamental objective is "to achieve the highest sustainable economic growth and employment and a rising standard of living in member countries while maintaining financial stability and thus contribute to the world economy." Members currently include: Australia, Austria, Belgium-Luxembourg, Canada, Denmark, Finland, France, Germany, Greece, Iceland, Ireland, Italy, Japan, the Netherlands, New Zealand, Norway, Portugal, Spain, Sweden, Switzerland, Turkey, the United Kingdom, and the United States. Address: Organization for Economic Cooperation and Development, 2 rue Andre Pascal, F-75775 Paris Cedex 16, France; Tel: [33] (1) 45-24-82-00; Web: www.oecd.org.

Organization of African Unity (OAU)

The OAU was founded in May 1963 with 32 African countries as original members; it had 51 members in 1990. The Organization aims to further African unity and solidarity, to coordinate political, economic, cultural, scientific, and defense policies; and to eliminate colonialism in Africa. Address: Organization of African Unity, PO Box 3243, Addis Ababa, Ethiopia; Tel: [251] (1) 517700; Telex: OAU 21046; Fax: [251] (1) 513036; Web: www.oau-oua.org.

Organization of American States (OAS)

The OAS is a regional organization established in April 1948 which promotes Latin American economic and social development. Members include the United States, Mexico, and most Central American, South American, and Caribbean nations. Members include: Antigua and Barbuda, Argentina, the Bahamas, Barbados, Belize, Bolivia, Brazil, Canada, Chile, Colombia, Costa Rica, Cuba (participation suspended), Dominica, Dominican Republic, Ecua-

dor, El Salvador, Grenada, Guatemala, Guyana, Haiti, Honduras, Jamaica, Mexico, Nicaragua, Panama, Paraguay, Peru, St. Christopher-Nevis, St. Lucia, St. Vincent and the Grenadines, Suriname, Trinidad and Tobago, the United States, Uruguay, and Venezuela. Address: Organization of American States, 17th Street and Constitution Avenue NW, Washington, DC 20006; Tel: [1] (202) 458-3000; Web: www.oas.org.

Organization of Arab Petroleum Exporting Countries (OAPEC)

OAPEC was established in 1968 to safeguard the interests of its members and to provide a forum for cooperation in the petroleum industry. Approximately 25% of the annual world petroleum production is from the member states of OAPEC. OAPEC members include: Algeria, Bahrain, Egypt, Iraq, Kuwait, Libya, Qatar, Saudi Arabia, Syria, and the United Arab Emirates. Address: Organization of Arab Petroleum Exporting Countries, P.O. Box 20501, SAFAT 13066 Kuwait; Tel: [96] (5) 484-4500; Fax: [96] (5) 481-5747; Web: www.oapecorg.org.

Organization of Petroleum Exporting Countries (OPEC)

An association of the world's oil-producing countries, formed in 1960. The chief purpose of OPEC is to coordinate oil production and pricing policies of its members: Algeria, Ecuador, Gabon, Indonesia, Iran, Iraq, Kuwait, Libya, Nigeria, Qatar, Saudi Arabia, the United Arab Emirates, and Venezuela. Address: Organization of Petroleum Exporting Countries, Obere-Donaustrasse 93, A-1020 Vienna, Austria; Tel: [43] (1) 211-12-279; Fax: [43] (1) 214-98-27; Web: www.opec.org.

Organization of the Islamic Conference (OIC)

The OIC, established in May 1971, promotes cooperation in cultural, economic, scientific and social areas among Islamic nations. Headquarters are located in Jeddah, Saudi Arabia. Members include: Afghanistan, Algeria, Bahrain, Bangladesh, Benin, Brunei, Burkina Faso, Cameroon, Chad, Comoros, Cyprus, Djibouti, Egypt, Gabon, the Gambia, Guinea, Guinea-Bissau, Indonesia, Iran, Iraq, Jordan, Kuwait, Lebanon, Libya, Malaysia, Maldives, Mali, Mauritania, Morocco, Niger, Nigeria, Oman, Pakistan, Qatar, Saudi Arabia, Senegal, Sierra Leone, Somalia, Sudan, Syria, Tunisia, Turkey, Uganda, the United Arab Emirates, and Yemen. Web: www.oic-oci.org.

original documents

(banking/letters of credit) Unless otherwise stated in the letter of credit, the requirement for an original document may also be satisfied by the presentation of documents produced or appearing to have been produced:

(1) reprographically,

(2) by automated or computerized systems, or

(3) as carbon copies,

and marked as "originals" and where necessary appearing to be signed. *See* letter of credit.

original equipment manufacturer (OEM)
See OEM.

ORM (other regulated material)
See hazardous materials; restricted articles; ORM; ORM-A, B, C, D, E.

ORM-A
(shipping) Material with an anesthetic, irritating, noxious, toxic or other properties that can cause discomfort to persons in the event of leakage. Examples are trichloroethylene, 1,1,1-trichloroethane, dry ice, chloroform, carbon tetrachloride.

ORM-B
(shipping) Material specifically named or capable of causing significant corrosion damage from leakage. Examples are lead chloride, quicklime, metallic mercury, barium oxide.

ORM-C
(shipping) Material specifically named and with characteristics which make it unsuitable for shipment unless properly packaged. Examples are bleaching powder, lithium batteries (for disposal), magnetized materials, sawdust, asbestos.

ORM-D
(shipping) Material such as consumer commodities which present a limited hazard due to form, quantity and packaging. They must be materials for which exceptions are provided. Examples are chemical consumer commodities (e.g., hair spray and shaving lotion) and small arm ammunition (reclassified because of packaging).

ORM-E
(shipping) Material that is not included in any other hazard class, but is regulated as ORM. Examples are hazardous waste and hazardous substances.

other regulated materials
See ORM.

ouguiya
The currency of Mauritania. 1UM=5 khoums.

outbound consolidation
See consolidation.

out-of-the-money
(foreign exchange) An option is out-of-the-money in the following cases:
(1) Call option: market price less than the strike price.
(2) Put option: market price greater than the strike price.
For European options, replace the market price by the forward price of the underlying instrument on the expiry date of the option. *See also* call option; put option; option; in-the-money.

output contract
(law) An agreement by which one party agrees to sell his or her entire production to the other, who agrees to purchase it.

outright
(foreign exchange) A forward purchase or sale of foreign exchange which is not offset by a corresponding spot transaction, i.e. which has not been contracted through swaps. *See* foreign exchange.

outsourcing
(logistics) The sourcing of raw materials, component parts and finished goods from outside a business organization. The opposite of insourcing. *See* insourcing.

outward swap
(foreign exchange) Spot purchase of foreign exchange and forward resale of the same currency against domestic currency. *See* foreign exchange.

overland common point (OCP)
(shipping) A special rate concession made by shipping lines, rail carriers, and truckers serving the U.S. West Coast for export and import traffic intended to benefit midwest shippers and importers by equalizing rates to and from other coastal areas, and offering these Midwest companies a comparable alternative. The steamship companies lower their rates and their inland carriers pick up the terminal charges, which consist of handling charges, wharfage charges, and carloading or unloading charges. OCP rates apply to cargo shipped from or consigned to the states of North Dakota, South Dakota, Nebraska, Colorado, New Mexico and all states east thereof. OCP rates in Canada apply to the provinces of Manitoba, Ontario and Quebec.

overnight
(foreign exchange) Swap from settlement date until the following business day, i.e., one day or three days over the weekend. *See* foreign exchange.

Overseas Private Investment Corporation (OPIC)
(U.S.) A self-sustaining U.S. agency, whose purpose is to promote economic growth in developing countries by encouraging U.S. private investment in those nations. The Corporation assists American investors in three principal ways: (1) financing investment projects through direct loans and/or guaranties; (2) insuring investment projects against a broad range of political risks; and (3) providing a variety of investor services including investor counseling, country and regional information kits, computer-assisted project and investor matching, and investment missions. OPIC does not support projects that will result in the loss of domestic jobs or have a negative impact on the host country's environment or worker's rights. Address: Overseas Private Investment Corporation, 1100 New York Ave. NW, Washington, DC 20527 USA; Tel: [1] (202) 336-8799; Web: www.opic.gov.

overs, short, and damaged (OSD)
(logistics) A report that details discrepancies between a bill of lading and a shipment at hand. Extra goods are "overs," missing goods are "short," and damaged goods are listed as "damaged."

over the counter (OTC)
(finance) Securities trading which takes place outside the normal exchanges. In contrast to normal exchanges, it is not tied to a central set-up in any one place but is conducted mainly by telephone and telex between traders, brokers and customers.

over the counter small package service
See small package service.

oxidizing material
(shipping) These items are chemically reactive and will provide both heat and oxygen to support a fire. (UN CLASS 5.) Examples are calcium permanganate, calcium hypochlorite, barium perchlorate, hydrogen peroxide and ammonium nitrate. Hazards/precautions are: may ignite combustibles (wood, paper, etc.); reaction with fuels may be violent; fires may produce poisonous fumes; vapors and dusts may be irritating; contact may burn skin and eyes; and peroxides may explode from heat or contamination.

P

pa'anga
The currency of Tonga. 1T$=100 seniti.

Pacific Rim
Refers to countries and economies bordering the Pacific ocean. Pacific Rim is an informal, flexible term which generally has been regarded as a reference to East Asia, Canada, and the United States. At a minimum, the Pacific Rim includes Canada, Japan, the People's Republic of China, Taiwan, and the United States. It may also include Australia, Brunei, Cambodia, Hong Kong/Macau, Indonesia, Laos, North Korea, South Korea, Malaysia, New Zealand, the Pacific Islands, the Philippines, Russia (or the Commonwealth of Independent States), Singapore, Thailand, and Vietnam. As an evolutionary term, usage sometimes includes Mexico, the countries of Central America, and the Pacific coast countries of South America.

packing credit
(banking) A monetary advance granted by a bank in connection with shipments of storable goods guaranteed by the assignment of the payment expected later on under a documentary letter of credit.

packing list
(shipping) A document prepared by the shipper listing the kinds and quantities of merchandise in a particular shipment. A copy is usually sent to the consignee to assist in checking the shipment when received. Also referred to as a bill of parcels.

pallet
(shipping) A shallow portable platform with or without sides used to store, handle or move materials and goods in factories, warehouses, containers or vessels. Pallets are usually constructed of wood and are designed so that the prongs of a fork-lift truck can lift the pallet and its load. *See* skid, forklift truck.

(air freight) A platform with a flat metal framed undersurface on which goods are assembled and secured by nets and straps. *See also* aircraft pallet.

Palletization results in more efficient use of space and better cargo handling, particularly when used as part of mechanized loading systems.

palletizing
(shipping) The loading and securing of a number of sacks, bags, boxes or drums on a pallet base.

pallet loader
(shipping) A device employing one or more vertical lift platforms for the mechanical loading or unloading of palletized freight at planeside.

pallet transporter
(shipping) A vehicle for the movement of loaded pallets between the aircraft and the freight terminal or truck dock.

parcel post air freight
(shipping) An airline service through which a shipper can consolidate a number of parcel post packages (with destination postage affixed by the shipper) for shipment as air freight to the postmaster at another city for subsequent delivery within local postal zones or beyond.

parent bank
(banking) A bank in a major industrial country that sets up a subsidiary in a developing country.

Pareto Principle/Postulate
(business theory) The concept that when a large number of individuals or organizations contribute to a result, the major part of the result comes from a minority of the contributors. The Pareto Postulate is that 20% of your effort or clients will generate 80% of your results or business. This is commonly referred to as the 80/20 rule. An actual percentage can be calculated by ranking customers or contributors by volume or any other factor. The Pareto Principle is based on the work and writings of the 19th century Italian economist Vilfredo Pareto.

par exchange rate
(foreign exchange) The free market price of one country's money in terms of the currency of another.

pari passu
(law) On an equal basis without preference. Creditors who receive payment pari passu, for example, are paid in proportion to their interests without regard to whether any of the claims would have taken priority over others.

Paris Club
Under the International Monetary Fund's (IMF) General Agreements to Borrow (GAB), established in 1962, 10 of the wealthiest industrial members of the IMF agreed to lend funds to the IMF, up to specified amounts "when supplementary resources are needed." The finance ministers of these countries comprise the Paris Club (also called the Group of 10).

The Paris Club has become a popular designation for meetings between representatives of a developing country that wishes to renegotiate its "official" debt (normally excluding debts owed by and to the private sector without official guarantees) and representatives of the relevant creditor governments and international institutions. These meetings usually occur at the request of a debtor country that wishes to consolidate all or part of its debt service payments falling due over a specified period. Meetings are traditionally chaired by a senior official of the French Treasury Department. Comparable meetings occasionally take place in London and in New York for countries that wish to renegotiate repayment terms for their debts to private banks. These meetings are sometimes called "creditor clubs." *See* International Monetary Fund; Group of Ten.

Paris Convention
The Paris Convention for the Protection of Industrial Property, first adopted in 1883, is the major international agreement providing basic rights for protecting industrial property. It covers patents, industrial designs, service marks, trade names, indications of source, and unfair competition. The U.S. ratified this treaty in 1903. The treaty provides two fundamental rights:

(1) The **principle of national treatment** provides that nationals of any signatory nation shall enjoy in all other countries of the union the advantages that each nation's laws grant to its own nationals.

(2) The **right of priority** enables any resident or national of a member country to, first, file a patent application in any member country and, thereafter, to file a patent application for the same invention in any of the other member countries within 12 months of the original filing and receive benefit of the original filing date.

See patent; trademark; copyright; World Intellectual Property Organization; Patent Cooperation Treaty.

Paris Union
See World Intellectual Property Organization.

parity
(general) Equality in amount or value. For example, if the price for goods sold in two different markets is the same, the price is in parity.

(foreign exchange) Exchange relationship of a currency to a legally binding reference, i.e., to a specific amount of gold, to Special Drawing Rights (SDRs) or to other currencies. *See also* special drawing right(s).

(foreign exchange/official parity) Predetermined exchange rate relationship between two currencies.

par of exchange
(foreign exchange) The market price of money in one national currency that is exchanged at the official rate for a specific amount in another national currency, or another commodity of value (gold, silver, etc.).

parol
(law) Oral expression. A parol contract, for example, is one that is verbal only and that has not be put into writing by the parties.

PARS
(Canada) A Canada Customs and Revenue Agency (CCRA) electronic data interchange (EDI) system that allows importers and brokers to gain shipment release information prior to the arrival of the goods in Canada. Information at Web: www.ccra-adrc.gc.ca.

particular average
(insurance) An insurance loss that affects specific interests only. There are two kinds of particular aver-

age losses: the total loss of a part of the goods, and the arrival of goods at destination in a damaged condition.

In the first situation, it is necessary to determine how much of the total amount insured is applicable to the missing item. In homogeneous or fungible cargo—that is, cargo which is capable of mutual substitution, like oil or coal—it is frequently a matter of simple arithmetic. The value of the unit of measurement of the cargo is found by dividing the amount of insurance by the total number of units in the shipment. This value multiplied by the number of missing units gives the value of the loss.

Where a normal or trade loss is to be expected, as in cargo subject to leakage, slackage or loss of moisture during the voyage, the method of calculation is slightly different. The value of the insurance is divided by the number of units in the "expected outturn," that is, the expected arrived quantity rather than the shipped quantity. This can be determined either by the normal percentage of trade loss for similar shipments or by examinations of sound arrived cargo forming part of the shipment in question. While this method will produce a somewhat higher insured value per unit, it naturally requires the normal or trade loss to be deducted in calculating the actual shortage sustained.

See also average; general average; with average; free of particular average; deductible average; trade loss.

parties to the credit

(banking) At least the following three parties are involved in a documentary letter of credit transaction:
(1) Applicant (buyer/importer),
(2) Issuing bank (buyers bank), and
(3) Beneficiary (seller/exporter).
As a rule, however, the issuing bank will entrust a correspondent bank with the task of advising and authenticating the credit and, if applicable, with payment, acceptance or negotiation. The issuing bank may also request the advising bank to add its confirmation.
See letter of credit; confirmation; issuing bank; advising bank.

partnership

(law) An unincorporated business owned and operated by two or more persons (partners), who may have general or limited liability in accordance with the partnership agreement. Note: The definition of status of partnership varies from country to country, and is not recognized as a business entity in some countries. See general partnership; limited partnership.

par value

(foreign exchange) The official fixed exchange rate between two currencies or between a currency and a specific weight of gold or a basket of currencies. *See* foreign exchange.

passengermile/kilometer

(logistics) A passenger load factor equal to the transportation of one passenger for one mile/kilometer. A measure of a carrier's total passenger miles/kilometers in the course of a year would be the total number of passengers carried during a year multiplied by the average number of miles/kilometers each passenger traveled

pataca

The currency of Macao. 1P=100 avos.

patent

(law) A grant by law to an inventor of a device of the right to exclude other persons from making, using, or selling the device. The patent holder has the right to license to another person the right to make, use, or sell the device. A patent is available only for devices that embody a new idea or principle and that involve a discovery. Patent protection varies from country to country, and may not be available in some jurisdictions. A country that is a member the Paris Convention for the Protection of Industrial Property may recognize patents held in other jurisdictions. *See* copyright; service mark; trademark; Paris Convention; World Intellectual Property Organization.

Patent Cooperation Treaty (PCT)

The PCT, is a worldwide convention, open to any Paris Convention country. The PCT entered into force in 1978. Unlike the Paris Convention, which addresses substantive intellectual property rights, the PCT addresses procedural requirements, aiming to simplify the filing, searching, and publication of international patent applications. *See* Paris Convention.

payable in exchange

(foreign exchange) The requirement that a negotiable instrument be paid in the funds of the place from which it was originally issued.

payee

(banking) The person or organization to whom a check or draft or note is made payable. The payee's name follows the expression "pay to the order of." *See also* payer; negotiable; negotiable instrument.

payer

(banking) The party primarily responsible for the payment of the amount owed as evidenced by a given negotiable instrument. *See also* payee; negotiable; negotiable instrument.

payments surplus

(economics) The excess of the value of a nation's exports over its imports. *See also* balance of trade.

penalties

(customs) The charges assessed or action taken by customs in response to a violation of a customs-enforced regulation or law.

P

per diem
(general) Latin for "per day." A charge or allowance based upon a rate or cost per day.
(travel) The monetary cost or allowance given an employee to pay expenses while traveling or living at another location.
(logistics) Payment or charges based on a daily rate.

perfect competition
(economics) A description for an industry or market unit consisting of a large number of purchasers and sellers all involved in the buying and selling of a homogeneous good, with awareness of prices and volume, no discrimination in buying and selling, and a mobility of resources.

performance
(law) The proper fulfillment of a contract or obligation.

performance bond
(insurance) A bond which guarantees proper fulfillment of the terms of a contract. In practice, the beneficiary of the bond (usually the buyer of services and/or goods), will claim financial restitution under the bond if the principal (supplier of the services and/or goods) fails to comply with the terms and conditions of the contract. *See* bond; surety.

peril point
(economics) A hypothetical limit beyond which a reduction in tariff protection would cause serious injury to a domestic industry.
(U.S.) U.S. legislation in 1949 that extended the Trade Agreements Act of 1934 required the Tariff Commission to establish such "peril points" for U.S. industries, and for the president to submit specific reasons to Congress if and when any U.S. tariff was reduced below those levels. This requirement, which was an important constraint on U.S. negotiating positions in early General Agreement on Tariffs and Trade (GATT) tariff-cutting Rounds, was eliminated by the Trade Expansion Act of 1962.

perils of the sea
(shipping) Causes of loss to cargo resulting from a shipment by sea.
(insurance) Marine insurance coverage that includes unusual action of wind and waves (often described as "stress of weather" or "heavy weather"), stranding, lightning, collision and damage by sea water when caused by insured perils such as opening of the seams of the vessel by stranding or collision. *See also* special marine policy; all risk.

perishable freight
(shipping) Freight subject to decay or deterioration.

permanent normalized trade relations
See normal trade relations (NTR).

person
(law) An individual or legal entity recognized under law as having legal rights and obligations. In the United States, for example, corporations and partnerships are examples of legal entities that are recognized as persons under the law. In countries that allow the formation of limited and unlimited liability companies, those companies are recognized as persons under the law.

personal income
(economics) National income less various kinds of income not actually received by individuals, nonprofit institutions, and so on (e.g., undistributed corporate profits, corporate taxes, employer contributions for social insurance), plus certain receipts that do not arise from production (i.e., transfer payments and government interest).

peseta
The currency of:
Andorra (uses Spanish peseta);
The former currency of Spain, 1Pts=100 centimos.
The new currency of Spain is the European Union euro. 1 € = 100 cents.

peso
The currency of:
Argentina, 1$a=100 centavos;
Chile, 1Ch$=100 centavos;
Columbia, 1Col$=100 centavos;
Cuba, 1$=100 centavos;
Dominican Republic, 1RD$=100 centavos;
Guinea-Bissau, 1PG=100 centavos;
Mexico, 1Mex$=100 centavos;
Philippines, 1P=100 centavos;
Uruguay, 1UR$=100 centesimos.

petrodollars
(foreign investment/banking) Huge sums of money from oil-producing nations other than the United States or Great Britain. These funds are initially converted into Eurocurrency and deposited with international banks to be used for future investment and for paying debts. These banks traditionally set limits on the sum they will accept from any one country.

physical distribution
(logistics) The storage and movement of finished products from manufacturing facilities through the logistics chain to the ultimate consumer. *See* logistics.

phytosanitary inspection certificate
A document indicating that a shipment of cargo has been inspected and is free from harmful pests and plant diseases. Phytosanitary inspection certificates are often required by import authorities for shipments containing plant products.

pick/pack
(logistics) The selection of component parts or finished products from inventory and their subsequent packing for shipment.

pickup and delivery service
(shipping) An optional service for the surface transport of shipments from shipper's door to originating

carrier's terminal and from the terminal of destination to receiver's door. Pickup service, at an additional charge, is provided upon shipper's request. In air cargo shipments delivery service is provided automatically by the air carrier at an additional charge unless the shipper requests otherwise. PU&D service is provided between all airports and all local points of such airports. For service beyond the terminal area *See* truck/air service.

pickup order
(shipping) An order from a broker (working as the agent of a consignee) to a carrier to pick up freight at a location.

pier-to-pier
(shipping) Shipment of cargo by carrier from origin pier to discharge pier. Applies to container yard (CY) cargo. Drayage to/from pier is borne by customer.

piggyback
(shipping) The transportation of truck trailers and containers on specially equipped railroad flat-cars. Also called trailer on flatcar.

pilferage
(shipping/insurance) The loss of goods due to steady theft in small amounts.

pilot
(shipping) A person whose office or occupation is to steer ships, particularly along a coast, or into and out of a harbor.

pips
(foreign exchange) In foreign exchange dealing, the last decimal places of a price quotation are called pips for purposes of simplicity (1/100th of 1 percent or 0.0001 of a unit). In futures trading the smallest possible price fluctuation upwards or downwards (1 pip) is called a tick.

place utility
(economics/logistics) The added value given a raw material, component part or finished good as a result of a change in its location. For example, iron ore brought to the smelter is more valuable that iron ore at the mine.

planned order
(logistics) In MRP (Materials Requirements Planning) and DRP (Distribution Requirements Planning) computer software systems, an order that the system automatically creates based upon projected demand, but which may be amended based upon changing demand. *See* MRP, DRP.

plimsoll mark
(shipping) The depth to which a vessel may safely load as identified by a horizontal line painted on the outside of the ship. This "plimsoll mark" must remain above the surface of the water. Named after English shipping reformer Samuel Plimsoll. *See also* draft or draught.

PNTR
Acronym for permanent normal trade relations. *See* normal trade relations (NTR).

point of origin
(shipping) The location at which a shipment is received by a transportation line from the shipper.

point-to-point; door-to-door
(shipping) Designates service and rates for shipments in door-to-door service. Originating carrier spots (places) empty container at shipper's facility at carrier's expense for loading by and at expense of shipper, the delivering carrier spots the loaded container at consignee's facility at carrier's expense for unloading by and at expense of consignee. *See also* demurrage; detention.

poisonous material
(shipping) Items that are extremely toxic to man and animals. (UN CLASS 6.) Examples are cyanogen gas, lead cyanide and parathion. Hazards/precautions are: may cause death quickly if breathed, swallowed or touched; may be flammable, explosive, corrosive or irritating; may be EXTREMELY HAZARDOUS. Look for the "Skull and Crossbones" on the label; degree of hazard key words: poison, danger, warning, highly toxic, moderately toxic, least toxic; and read the label carefully for storage and safety information.

political risk
(economics) Economic risk resulting from the political decisions of sovereign governments as well as political and social events in a country. Political risks includes confiscation, expropriation, nationalization, currency inconvertibility, contract frustration, war, civil unrest, revolution and annexation. Political risk can lead to the inability of a debtor to comply with a contract or to the loss, confiscation or damage to goods belonging to an exporter. An exporter may be able to cover this risk by utilizing a confirmed letter of credit or by applying for cover from export credit agencies. *See* commercial risk.

political risk insurance
(economics) Insurance coverage against political risk. Political risk insurance is typically provided by insurance companies, government entities and organizations such as the Inter-American Development Bank, (Web: www.iadb.org) and the Multilateral Investment Guarantee Agency (Web: www.miga.org).

pooling
(logistics) An agreement among a group of carriers to share freight, customers, revenues and/or profits.

(U.S. law) The U.S. Interstate Commerce Act outlaws pooling; however, the Civil Aeronautics Board allows air carriers, during strikes, to enter into profit-pooling agreements.

P

port

(shipping) (a) A harbor or haven where ships may anchor and discharge or receive cargo. (b) The left side of a ship when one is facing the bow.

port charge

(shipping) A charge made for services performed at ports.

portfolio investment

(foreign investment) In general, any foreign investment that is not direct investment is considered portfolio investment. Foreign portfolio investment includes the purchase of voting securities (stocks) at less than a 10 percent level, bonds, trade finance, and government lending or borrowing, excluding transactions in official reserves.

port of discharge

(shipping) The port at which a shipment is off-loaded by a transportation line, not to be confused with destination which may be a point further inland.

port of embarkation

See port of export.

port of entry

(shipping/customs) A port at which foreign goods are admitted into the receiving country. Ports of entry are officially designated by the importing country's government.

(U.S. Customs) Any place designated by act of U.S. Congress, executive order of the President of the United States, or order of the U.S. Secretary of the Treasury, at which a U.S. Customs officer is assigned with authority to accept entries of merchandise, to collect duties, and to enforce the various provisions of the U.S. Customs laws.

port of export

(shipping) The port, airport or customs point from which an export shipment leaves a country for a voyage to a foreign country.

port-of-origin air cargo clearance

(shipping) For the convenience of exporters moving goods by air from inland U.S. cities, certain U.S. Customs formalities can now be handled at the originating airport city. This avoids delaying such procedures until the export reaches a gateway point sometimes hundreds of miles from the exporter's business.

postdated check

(banking) A check bearing a date that has not yet arrived. Such a check cannot be paid by a bank before the date shown and must be returned to the maker or to the person attempting to use it. If presented on or after the date shown, the same check will be honored if the account contains sufficient funds.

positive-sum

(economics) The concept that a business transaction or negotiation can result in additional benefits or profits to both or all parties to the transaction. ALso referred to as win-win. Compare to zero-sum.

post-shipment verifications (PSV)

(U.S.) An inspection to determine that an exported strategic commodity is being used for the purposes for which its export was licensed. Firms or individuals representing the end user, intermediate consignees, or the purchaser may be subject to inquiries pertaining to the post-shipment verification. As part of the PSV process, the Bureau of Industry and Security (formerly the Bureau of Export Administration) forwards a cable to the U.S. embassy or consulate in the respective geographical location to conduct an on-site inspection to ensure that the commodity is physically present and used as stated in the application. Post-shipment verifications are usually conducted six-to-eight months subsequent to export of the commodity. *See* Bureau of Industry and Security.

pound

The currency for:

Cyprus, 1£C=100 cents;

Egypt, 1LE (or 1E£)=100 piasters=1,000 milliemes;

Falkland Islands, 1£F=100 pence;

Lebanon, 1LL (or 1L£) =100 piasters;

St. Helena (uses U.K. pound);

Syria, 1S£=100 piasters;

United Kingdom, 1£=100 pence.

The former currency of Ireland (pound or punt). The new currency of Ireland is the European Union euro. 1 € = 100 cents.

power of attorney

(law) A written legal document by which one person (principal) authorizes another person (agent) to perform stated acts on the principal's behalf. For example: to enter into contracts, to sign documents, to sign checks, and spend money, etc.

A principal may execute a **special power of attorney** authorizing an agent to sign a specific contract or a **general power of attorney** authorizing the agent to sign all contracts for the principal.

(U.S. Customs) Importers often give a limited power of attorney to their customs broker to conduct business with U.S. Customs on their behalf.

Tip: When you set up a power of attorney, make sure that it is broad enough in its language to cover the types of situations likely to arise, but not so broad that it gives more power to that individual than you intend. Power of attorney falls under "agency" law, which varies from country to country. Before giving someone power of attorney in a foreign country, be sure you understand what the local legal ramifications are. *See* agent; agency.

POW WOW

See International POW WOW.

pre-advice

(banking/letters of credit) At the request of an applicant to a letter of credit, the issuing bank may give a pre-advice of issuance and/or amendment of the letter of credit. A pre-advice is usually marked with a reference such as "Full details to follow." Unless otherwise stated, the pre-advice irrevocably commits the issuing bank to issue/amend the credit in a manner consistent with said pre-advice. *See* letter of credit; advice; advising bank; issuing bank; amendment.

preferences

(law) A creditor's right to be paid before other creditors of the same debtor. A creditor who holds a secured note, for example, generally has preference over one who holds an unsecured note.

Preferential Trade Agreement for Eastern and Southern Africa

PTA was founded in 1981 in order to improve commercial and economic cooperation in Eastern and Southern Africa; transform the structure of national economies in the region; promote regional trade; support inter-country cooperation, cooperation in agricultural development, and improvement of transport links. Accomplishments include: tariff reductions, multilateral trade, common travellers checks, a federation of chambers of commerce, a federation of commercial banks, and a commercial Arbitration board. The PTA Trade and Development Bank is in Burundi. Current goals include monetary harmonization and the establishment of a commodity futures market and stock exchange.

The PTA's members are: Burundi, Comoros, Djibouti, Ethiopia, Kenya, Lesotho, Malawi, Mauritius, Rwanda, Somalia, Swaziland, Tanzania, Uganda, Zambia, and Zimbabwe. Address: Preferential Trade Area for Eastern and Southern Africa, PO Box 30051, Lotti House, Cairo Rd., Lusaka 10101, Zambia; Tel: [260] (1) 229726; Telex: 40127; Fax: [260] (1) 225107; Web: www.mbendi.co.za/orgs/co4s.htm.

pre-license checks (PLC)

(U.S.) Pre-license checks are conducted to determine that a request for a license to export a controlled commodity represents a legitimate order. Firms or individuals representing the licensee (the applicant), a consignee, the purchaser, an intermediate consignee, or the end user may be subject to inquiries pertaining to the pre-license check. As part of the process, the Bureau of Industry and Security (formerly the Bureau of Export Administration) forwards a cable to the U.S. embassy or consulate in the respective geographical location to conduct an inspection or meet with company representatives to conduct inquiries on BXA's behalf. *See* Bureau of Industry and Security.

preliminary determination

(U.S.) The determination announcing the results of a dumping investigation conducted within 160 days (or, in extraordinarily complicated cases, 210 days) after a petition is filed or an investigation is self-initiated by the International Trade Administration (ITA). If it is determined that there is a reasonable basis to believe or suspect that the merchandise under consideration is being sold or is likely to be sold at less than fair value, liquidation of all affected entries is suspended, and the matter is referred to the International Trade Commission. "Preliminary determination" also refers to the decision by the ITC where there is a reasonable indication that an industry in the United States is materially injured, or threatened with material injury, or the establishment of an industry in the United States is materially retarded by reason of the imports of the merchandise which is the subject of the petition. The ITC must make its decision within 45 days after the date on which the petition is filed or an investigation is self-initiated by the International Trade Administration. If this determination is negative, the investigation is terminated. *See* dumping; International Trade Administration; fair value.

premium

(general) The amount above a regular price, paid as an incentive to do something. For example, a buyer might pay a premium for quick delivery. Opposite of discount.

(insurance) The amount paid to an insurance company for coverage under an insurance policy.

(foreign exchange) (a) Premium, markup (forward premium) or contango of a forward rate against the spot rate. (b) The price at which an option sells.

prepaid

(shipping) (a) A notation on a shipping document indicating that shipping charges have already been paid by the shipper or his agent to the carrier. (b) Also, that shipping charges are to be paid by the consignee or his agent prior to release of the shipment.

prepaid charges

See prepaid freight.

prepaid freight

(logistics) Freight for which transportation charges have been paid by the consignor (shipper) at the time of shipment. Prepaid freight charges are generally not refundable.

prescription period

See limitation period.

President's Export Council (PEC)

(U.S.) Advises the president on government policies and programs that affect U.S. trade performance; promotes export expansion; and provides a forum for discussing and resolving trade-related problems among the business, industrial, agricultural, labor, and government sectors.

The Council was established by Executive Order of the president in 1973 and was originally composed only of business executives. The Council was reconstituted in 1979 to include leaders of the labor and agricultural communities, Congress, and the Executive branch.

Twenty-eight private sector members serve "at the pleasure of the president" with no set term of office. Other members include five U.S. Senators and five Members of the House, the Secretaries of Agriculture, Commerce, Labor, State, and Treasury, the Chairman of the Export-Import Bank, and the U.S. Trade Representative. The Council reports to the president through the Secretary of Commerce.

price support

(economics) Subsidy or financial aid offered to specific growers, producers, or distributors, in accordance with governmental regulations to keep market prices from dropping below a certain minimum level.

pricing (of a loan)

(banking/finance) Fixing the cost of a loan, i.e., the interest rate and any other charges, such as front end fees.

prima facie

(law) A presumption of fact as true unless contradicted by other evidence. For example, unless an agreement assigning contract rights clearly states that outstanding interest payments are retained by the assignor, the right to collect such payments is deemed transferred prima facie to the assignee.

primary-business test

(U.S. law/trucking) A test used by the U.S. Interstate Commerce Commission (ICC) to determine if a trucking operation is a bona fide private transportation firm. The test was designed as a response to certain trucking operators who had been using phony "buy and sell" arrangements to avoid interstate trucking regulations.

principal

(law) An individual or legal entity who authorizes another party (agent) to act on the principal's behalf. *See* agency; agent; power of attorney.

priority air freight

(shipping) Reserved air freight or air express service wherein shipments have a priority after mail and the small package services. Any size or weight allowed within air freight service limits is acceptable. Advanced reservations are permitted for movement on a given flight and in some cases a partial refund is paid the shipper if the shipment is not moved on the flight specified.

priority foreign countries

See Special 301.

priority logistics management

(shipping) The application of the just in time transportation theory. *See* just in time.

priority watchlist

See Special 301.

private corporation

(law) (a) A business corporation with shares that are not traded among the general public. (b) A corporation that is established by individuals to conduct business or other activities and that does not perform government functions. *See* corporation; close corporation; public corporation.

Private Export Funding Corporation (PEFC)

(U.S.) PEFCO works with the Export-Import Bank in using private capital to finance U.S. exports. PEFCO acts as a supplemental lender to traditional commercial banking sources by making loans to public and private borrowers located outside of the United States who require medium and/or longer-term financing of their purchases of U.S. goods and services. Contact: PEFCO, 280 Park Avenue, New York, NY 10017 USA; Tel: [1] (212) 916-0300; Fax: [1] (212) 286-0304; Web: www.pefco.com. *See* Export-Import Bank of the United States.

Private Limited (Pte. Ltd.)

(India, Rhodesia, Singapore) Designation for a private limited liability corporation with limited liability to shareholders.

private limited liability corporation

See closely held corporation.

private sector

(economics) That part of an economy not under direct government control and that functions within the market. Private enterprise. *See* public sector

privatization

(economics/law) The sale of state owned and operated enterprises and assets to private individuals or groups of individuals. Privatization is the opposite of nationalization and is an effort by governments to allow market forces determine the fate of the enterprise. *See* nationalization, expropriation.

procurement and lead time

The time required by the buyer to select a supplier and to place and obtain a commitment for specific quantities of material at specified times.

product groups

(U.S.) Commodity groupings used for export control purposes. *See* export control classification number.

productivity

(economics) A measurement of the efficiency of production. A ratio of output to input (e.g., 10 units per man-hour).

profit, gross

(economics/accounting) (gross profit/gross margin) Net sales less cost of goods sold (before consideration of selling and administrative expenses). Gross profit is expressed in dollar figures; gross margin is expressed as a percentage of net sales.

(U.S. Customs) For the purposes of constructed value in an antidumping duty investigation or review, the profit used is the profit normally earned by a producer, from the country of export, of the same or similar product as that under investigation. By statute, the amount of profit shall not be less than 8 percent of the sum of general expenses and cost. *See* dumping; countervailing duty.

pro forma

When coupled with the title of another document (pro forma invoice, pro forma manifest), it means an informal document presented in advance of the arrival or preparation of the required document in order to satisfy a requirement, usually a customs requirement.

pro forma invoice

An invoice provided by a supplier prior to a sale or shipment of merchandise, informing the buyer of the kinds and quantities of goods to be sent, their value, and important specifications (weight, size, and similar characteristics). A pro forma invoice is used: (1) as a preliminary invoice together with a quotation; (2) for customs purposes in connection with shipments of samples, advertising material, etc.

(U.S. Customs) An invoice provided by the importer in lieu of a commercial invoice when a commercial invoice is not available at the time of merchandise entry. In such cases the importer must present a bond to Customs guaranteeing production of the required commercial invoice not later than 120 days from the date of entry. If the invoice is needed by Customs for statistical purposes, it must generally be produced within 50 days from the date the entry summary is required to be filed.

If the required commercial invoice is not presented to Customs before the expiration of the 120-day period, the importer incurs a liability under his bond for failure to file.

See also invoice; commercial invoice; entry; bond.

project license

(U.S.) A license which authorizes large-scale exports of a wide variety of commodities and technical data for specified activities. Those activities can include capital expansion, maintenance, repair or operating supplies, or the supply of materials to be used in the production of other commodities for sale. *See* Bureau of Export Administration.

promissory note

(banking) (a) Any written promise to pay. (b) A negotiable instrument that is evidence of a debt contracted by a borrower from a creditor, known as a lender of funds. If the instrument does not have all the qualities of a negotiable instrument, it cannot legally be transferred. *See* negotiable instrument.

promoter of corporation

(law) Individual or entity that organizes a corporation.

promotional rate

(shipping) A rate applying to traffic under special conditions and usually confined to movement between a limited number of cities. Early rates on fresh farm produce which helped develop increased air freight volumes from the West Coast to eastern cities are examples of promotional rates. *See* special rates.

proof of delivery

(shipping) Information provided to payor containing name of person who signed for the package with the date and time of delivery.

Proprietary Limited (Pty. Ltd.)

(Australia, South Africa) Designation for a private limited liability corporation with limited liability to shareholders.

proprietor

(law) A person who has an exclusive right or interest in property or in a business.

proprietorship

(law) A business owned by one person. The individual owner has all the rights to profits from the business as well as all the liabilities and losses. Synonymous with "individual proprietorship."

protectionism

(economics) The deliberate use or encouragement of restrictions on imports to enable relatively inefficient domestic producers to compete successfully with foreign producers.

protective order

(U.S. Customs) With regard to antidumping cases, a term for the order under which most business proprietary information is made available to an attorney or other representative of a party to the proceeding. *See* dumping.

protective service

(shipping) Many airlines offer a protective service where shippers can arrange to have their shipments under carrier surveillance at each stage of transit from origin to destination. This service can be extended to pickup and delivery. Shippers can also arrange for armed guard protection. There is usually an extra charge for various levels of protective service. *See* signature service.

protective tariff

(customs/economics) A duty or tax imposed on imported products for the purpose of making them more expensive in comparison to domestic products, thereby giving the domestic products a price advantage. *See* tariff.

protest

(U.S. Customs) The means by which an importer, consignee, or other designated party may challenge decisions, (usually regarding the duitable status of imported goods) made by a District Director of Customs. The importer files a protest and an application for further review on Customs Form 19 within 90 days after liquidation. If the Customs Service denies a protest, an importer has the right to litigate the matter by filing a summons with the U.S. Court of International Trade within 180 days after denial of the protest. The rules of the court and other applicable statutes and precedents determine the course of Customs litigation.

While the Customs ascertainment of duitable status is final for most purposes at the time of liquidation, a liquidation is not final until any protest which has been filed against it has been decided. Similarly, the administrative decision issued on a protest is not final until any litigation filed against it has become final.

Entries must be liquidated within one year of the date of entry unless the liquidation needs to be extended for another one-year period not to exceed a total of four years from the date of entry. The Customs Service will suspend liquidation of an entry when required by statute or court order. A suspension will remain in effect until the issue is resolved. Notifications of extensions and suspensions are given to importers, surety companies and customs brokers who are parties to the transaction.

See entry; liquidation.

(banking) Legal procedure noting the refusal of the drawee to accept a bill of exchange (protest for non-acceptance) or to pay it (protest for non-payment). Essential in order to preserve the right of recourse on the endorser.

protest system

(U.S. Customs) A part of U.S. Customs' Automated Commercial System, tracks protests from the date they are received through final action. *See* Automated Commercial System.

protocol

(diplomacy) (a) A preliminary document or memorandum signed by diplomatic or commercial negotiators which is used as a basis for final negotiations, agreements conventions or treaties. (b) The etiquette and ranking of diplomatic personnel.

(U.S.) U.S. diplomatic ranking is as follows: (1) Ambassadors-at-large have a higher rank than a regular Ambassador and are higher ranked on protocol than, say, the head of the C.I.A.; (2) The Deputy Chief of Mission, almost always a career officer, has the personal rank of Minister which is one rank down from Ambassador; (3) The rank of Minister-Counselor is just a little step below Minister; (4) The Chargé d'Affaires may either be acting, or indefinite, and is regarded as the acting Ambassador when the Ambassador is out of the country or when, for political reasons, an Ambassador is not appointed to a country; (5) An Attaché may be either fairly high or fairly low; in terms of rank an Attaché can be anything; a Military Attaché is of at least medium rank, but the military hold no diplomatic rank; (6) A consulate is not a diplomatic mission, nor is it autono-

mous; it is established by an international organization (such as U.S. Mission to the European Communities (USEC) or NATO) or is used for reasons of diplomatic snobbery or pique.

Protocol of Provisional Application

(GATT/WTO) A legal device that enabled the original contracting parties to accept General Agreement on Tariffs and Trade (GATT) obligations and benefits, despite the fact that some of their existing domestic legislation at that time discriminated against imports in a manner that was inconsistent with certain GATT provisions. Although meant to be "temporary," the Protocol has remained in effect; and countries that signed the PPA in 1947 continue to invoke it to defend certain practices that are otherwise inconsistent with their GATT/WTO obligations. Countries that acceded to the GATT/WTO after 1947 have also done so under the terms of the Protocol. *See* General Agreement on Tariffs and Trade, World Trade Organization (WTO).

PTT

Acronym for Post Telephone Telegraph. The national monopoly agency or authority that provides postal, telephone and telegraph services in certain countries. Most western economies have deregulated at least their telecommunications systems and rigid monopolies rarely exist.

publication

(law) (a) Offering or distributing information or materials to the public generally. (b) Communicating defamatory information to a third person.

public corporation

(law) (a) A business corporation with shares traded among the general public, such as through a stock exchange. (b) A corporation created by a government to administer its operations. *See* corporation; close corporation; private corporation.

Public Limited Company (PLC)

(United Kingdom) Designation for a public corporation with limited liability to shareholders.

public sector

(economics) That part of an economy that is not privately owned, either because it is owned by the state or because it is subject to common ownership. Includes the national government, local authorities, national industries and public corporations. *See* private sector.

public warehouse receipt

(logistics) A document issued by a public warehouse manager for receipt of goods into a warehouse. Public warehouse receipts can be either negotiable or non-negotiable.

published rate

(shipping) The charges for a particular class of cargo as published in a carrier's tariff.

pula
The currency of Botswana. 1P=100 thebe.

pull ordering system
(logistics) A stocking and warehousing order system where a stocking location places orders for inventory based upon its own individual needs. A pull ordering system is based upon actual demand for the product, service or component. *See* push ordering system, push strategy, pull strategy, push/pull strategy.

pull strategy
(logistics) A production and distribution strategy based on specific customer demand. In a pure pull strategy only goods and services actually ordered by customers are produced and shipped; there is no inventory of completed products. The term is used in many other fields to describe decision making by demand of the marketplace rather than by a central authority. *See* push ordering system, push strategy, pull ordering system, push/pull strategy.

punt
The former currency of Ireland. The new currency of Ireland is the European Union euro. 1 € = 100 cents.

purchase order
A purchaser's written offer to a supplier formally stating all terms and conditions of a proposed transaction.

purchase price
(U.S. Customs) A statutory term used in dumping investigations to refer to the United States sales price of merchandise which is sold or likely to be sold prior to the date of importation, by the producer or reseller of the merchandise for exportation to the United States. Certain statutory adjustments (e.g., import duties, commissions, freight) are made, if appropriate, to permit a meaningful comparison with the foreign market value of such or similar merchandise. *See* dumping.

purchaser
(U.S.) Within the context of export controls, the purchaser is that person abroad who has entered into the export transaction with the applicant to purchase the commodities or technical data for delivery to the ultimate consignee.

purchasing agent
(law) An agent who purchases goods in his/her own country on behalf of foreign buyers such as government agencies and private businesses. *See* agent; agency.

pure market economy
(economics) A competitive economic system of numerous buyers and sellers, where prices are determined by the free interaction of supply and demand.

push ordering system
(logistics) A stocking and warehousing order system based on inventory deployment decisions being made by a centralized authority rather than by field locations. *See* pull ordering system, pull strategy, push strategy, push/pull strategy.

push strategy
(logistics) A production and distribution strategy based upon forecasts rather than on specific customer demand. The term is used in many other fields to describe centralized decision-making authority without the immediate input of data from the marketplace. *See* pull strategy, pull ordering system, push ordering system, push/pull strategy.

push/pull strategy
(logistics) A production and distribution strategy based upon a combination of forecasts and specific customer demand. For example, a manufacturer might purchase component parts based upon sales forecasts, but manufacture finished products only upon actual customer orders. *See* pull strategy, pull ordering system, push strategy, push ordering system.

put
(banking/finance) A right to redeem a debt instrument before maturity at par under specific circumstances outlined in the original agreement. *See* option; put option; call; call option.

put option
(banking/finance) A contract which entitles one party, at his option, to sell a specified amount of a commodity, security or foreign exchange to another party, at the price fixed in the contract, during the life of the contract. *See* option; call option; American Option; European Option.

quadrilateral meetings

Meetings involving trade ministers from the U.S., the European Community, Canada, and Japan to discuss trade policy matters.

quantitative restrictions (QRs)

(customs) Explicit limits, or quotas, on the physical amounts of particular commodities that can be imported or exported during a specified time period, usually measured by volume but sometimes by value. The quota may be applied on a "selective" basis, with varying limits set according to the country of origin, or on a quantitative global basis that only specifies the total limit and thus tends to benefit more efficient suppliers. Quotas are frequently ministered through a system of licensing.

(WTO) The World Trade Organization (WTO) generally prohibits the use of quantitative restrictions, except under conditions specified by other WTO articles.

See quotas; General Agreement on Tariffs and Trade (GATT) , World Trade Organization (WTO).

quarantine

(shipping) (a) The term during which an arriving ship or airplane, including its passengers, crew and cargo, suspected of carrying a contagious disease, is held in isolation to prevent the possible spread of the disease. (b) The place where a ship, airplane, individual or cargo is detained during quarantine.

quay

(shipping) A structure built for the purpose of mooring a vessel. Also called a pier.

quetzal

The currency of Guatemala. 1Q=100 centavos.

queue

(a) A line or group of people waiting for service, such as a line of people waiting in a teller line at a bank. (b) Paperwork in a stack waiting for processing. (c) Items on a waiting list waiting for processing or repair.

quick response

(logistics) A logistics strategy designed to lower costs and increase response to customer demand by shortening the lead time for order fulfillment and increasing the frequency of deliveries.

quid pro quo

(law/business) "Something for something" (Latin). A mutual consideration; securing an advantage or receiving a concession in return for a similar favor.

quota

(customs) A limitation on the quantity of goods that may be imported into a country from all countries or from specific countries during a set period of time.

(a) **Absolute quotas** permit a limited number of units of specified merchandise to be entered or withdrawn for consumption in a country during specified periods.

(b) **Tariff-rate quotas** permit a specified quantity of merchandise to be entered or withdrawn in a country at a reduced rate during a specified period.

(U.S. Customs) In the United States, quotas are established by Presidential Proclamations, Executive Orders, or other legislation. *See also* quantitative restrictions; quota system; visa.

quota system

(U.S. Customs) A part of the U.S. Customs' Service Automated Commercial System, controls quota levels (quantities authorized) and quantities entered against those levels. Visas control exports from the country of origin. Visa authorizations are received from other countries and quantities entered against those visas are transmitted back to them. Control of visas and quotas simplify reconciliation of other countries' exports and U.S. imports.

See Automated Commercial System; visa.

quotation

(foreign exchange) The price quotation of a currency can be made either directly or indirectly. (a) The **direct quotation** gives the equivalent of a certain amount of foreign currency (normally in units of 100 or 1) in domestic currency. (b) In an **indirect price quotation** (less common) the domestic currency is valued in units of foreign currency.

R

radioactive materials
(shipping) Degree of hazard will vary depending on type and quantity of material. (UN CLASS 7.) Examples are thorium 232, carbon 14 and radium 226. Hazards/precautions are: avoid touching broken or damaged radioactive items; persons handling damaged items must wear rubber or plastic gloves; damaged items will be monitored and safely packaged under the surveillance of the radiological monitor; and persons having come in direct contact with damaged or broken radioactive items must move away from the spill site (but stay in the area) to be monitored and decontaminated.

rail waybill
(shipping) Freight document that indicates goods have been received for shipment by rail. A duplicate is given to the shipper as a receipt for acceptance of the goods (also called duplicate waybill). *See* bill of lading.

rand
The currency of:
Namibia, 1R=100 cents.
South Africa, 1R=100 cents;

rate basis
(logistics) The economic factors considered when establishing a freight transportation rate. These factors at the very least include weight, bulk, packaging, equipment depreciation, freight handling by personnel, fuel, port charges, insurance and management costs.

rate basis number
(logistics) The distance between two rate basis points. Used to determine tariff rates from a table. *See* rate basis point.

rate basis point
(logistics) The formally named point (such as Houston, Texas) in a geographic area (such as greater Houston Texas) that serves as the identifier on a freight rate table for all departures or arrivals in that area. Carriers consider all points in the immediate geographic area to be the rate basis point.

rate bureau
(logistics) A group of carriers that have organized for the purpose of establishing joint rates, dividing joint revenues and liabilities and publishing tariffs for participating carriers.
(U.S. law) Rate bureaus were legalized under the Reed-Bullwinkle Act for the purpose of establishing joint rates. *See* Reed-Bullwinkle Act.

rate of exchange
(banking/foreign exchange) The amount of funds of one nation that can be bought, at a specific date, for a sum of currency of another country. Rates fluctuate often because of economic, political and other forces. *See* foreign exchange.

realignment
(foreign exchange) Simultaneous and mutually coordinated re- and devaluation of the currencies of several countries. The concept was first used in 1971 for the exchange rate corrections made in a number of countries within the framework of the Smithsonian Agreement. Since then, it has mainly been used to describe the exchange rate corrections within the European Monetary System.

real rights
(law) Rights in real estate or in items attached to real estate.

reasonable person standard
(law) A legal test that is used to determine whether a person is liable for damages. It is based on a comparison of the person's conduct with the actions or conduct expected of a reasonable person of the same characteristics in similar circumstances.

receipt
(law) Any written acknowledgment of value received.

receipt point
(logistics) The place where freight or cargo enters into the care and custody of a carrier for either storage or shipment.

received for shipment bill of lading
(shipping) A bill of lading which confirms the receipt of goods by the carrier, but not their actual loading on board. *See* bill of lading.
(banking/letters of credit) A received for shipment bill of lading can be accepted under letters of credit only if this is expressly permitted in the letter of credit, or if the credit stipulates a document covering multimodal transport. Otherwise, "received for shipment" bills of lading must show an additional "On board" notation in order to be accepted as an ocean bill of lading. *See* bill of lading; ocean bill of lading.

receiving papers
(shipping) Paperwork that accompanies a shipment when it is brought to the dock. Usual information listed is name and address of shipper, number of pieces, commodity, weight, consignee, booking number and any special requirements, such as label cargo or temperature control.

reciprocal defense procurement memoranda of understanding
(NATO/USA) Reciprocal memoranda of understanding (MOU) are broad bilateral umbrella MOUs that seek to reduce trade barriers on defense procurement. They usually call for the waiver of "buy national" restrictions, cus-

toms and duties to allow the contractors of the signatories to participate, on a competitive basis, in the defense procurement of the other country. These agreements were designed in the late 1970's to promote rationalization, standardization, and interoperability of defense equipment within NATO. At that time, the MOUs were also intended to reduce the large defense trade advantage the United States possessed over the European allies. The first agreements were signed in 1978. *See* memorandum of understanding.

reciprocal trade agreement

(trade) An international agreement between two or more countries to establish mutual trade concessions that are expected to be of equal value.

reciprocity

(general) The mutual exchange of privileges or benefits. Also called "mutuality of benefits," "quid pro quo," and "equivalence of advantages."

(international trade) The practice by which governments extend similar concessions to each other, as when one government lowers its tariffs or other barriers (non-tariff barriers) impeding its imports in exchange for equivalent concessions from a trading partner on barriers affecting its exports (a "balance of concessions"). Reciprocity has traditionally been a principal objective of negotiators in the World Trade Organization (WTO) "Rounds."

In practice, this principle applies only in negotiations between developed countries. Because of the frequently wide disparity in their economic capacities and potential, the relationship between developed and developing countries is generally not one of equivalence.

The concept of "relative reciprocity" has emerged to characterize the practice by developed countries to seek less than full reciprocity from developing countries in trade negotiations.

reconsignment

(shipping) A change in the name of the consignor or consignee; a change in the place of delivery; a change in the destination point; or relinquishment of shipment at point of origin.

recourse

(banking) Right of claim against the joint and several guarantors (e.g., endorsers, drawers) of a bill of exchange or cheque. *See* protest; bill of exchange.

red clause (letter of credit)

(banking) A special clause included in a documentary letter of credit which allows the seller to obtain an advance on an unsecured basis from the correspondent bank to finance the manufacture or purchase of goods to be delivered under the documentary letter of credit. Liability is assumed by the issuing bank rather than the corresponding bank. It is called red clause because red ink used to be used to draw attention to the clause. *See* letter of credit.

Reed-Bullwinkle Act

(U.S. law/shipping) Legislation originally passed by the U.S. Congress in 1948 authorizing the creation of rate bureaus which would provide a sanctioned forum for domestic railroads to set agreements on rates. In the 1970 revision of the Act, Congress expressly granted railroads antitrust immunity for any collective rate-making activity accomplished in accordance with the procedures described in the Act. *See* rate bureau.

redeliver

(U.S. Customs) A demand by the U.S. Customs Service to return previously released merchandise to Customs custody for reexamination, reexport or destruction.

reefer container

(shipping) A controlled temperature refrigerated shipping container.

reefer vessel

(shipping) A vessel with refrigerated cargo holds.

re-engineering

(management) (a) The radical change of processes on all levels within an organization. (b) The way a company performs radical changes to processes. As opposed to gradual improvements over time, re-engineering seeks to create breakthrough changes in the way a business operates. Re-engineering is often sought by senior managers as a means of dramatically reducing labor costs, increasing productivity and increasing responsiveness to customer demand.

re-export

(general) The export of imported goods without added value.

(U.S.) For U.S. export control purposes: the shipment of U.S. origin products from one foreign destination to another.

For U.S. statistical reporting purposes: exports of foreign-origin merchandise which have previously entered the United States for consumption or into Customs bonded warehouses for U.S. Foreign Trade Zones.

refrigerated container

(logistics) An insulated container with a refrigeration unit attached designed to maintain a constant low temperature for temperature-sensitive cargo. *See* container.

refund

(shipping) An amount returned to the consignor or consignee as a result of the carrier having collected charges in excess of the originally agreed upon, or legally applicable, charges.

(customs) Refund of import duties. *See* drawback.

regional carrier

(logistics) (a) A carrier that operates regionally rather than nationally or internationally. (b) A carrier that transports passengers or cargo between small cities or between major cities and small cities or towns.

R

reimbursing bank

(banking) The bank named in a documentary credit (letter of credit) from which the paying, accepting or negotiating bank may request cover after receipt of the documents in compliance with the documentary credit. The reimbursing bank is often, but not always, the issuing bank. If the reimbursing bank is not the issuing bank, it does not have a commitment to pay unless it has confirmed the reimbursement instruction. The issuing bank is not released from its commitment to pay through the nomination of a reimbursing bank. If cover from the reimbursing bank should not arrive in time, the issuing bank is obliged to pay (also any accrued interest on arrears).

re-insurance

(insurance) The insurance of insurance companies by other insurance companies for excessive losses. For example, an insurance company might obtain insurance coverage for losses exceeding US$50 million in a single catastrophe in order to limit its maximum liability. Furthermore, reinsurance coverage is often spread out among a group of insurance companies so as to further distribute potential liabilities for losses.

rejected merchandise drawback

See drawback.

relative reciprocity

See reciprocity.

relay

(shipping) A shipment that is transferred to its ultimate destination port after having been shipped to an intermediate point.

released-value rate

(logistics) A reduced transportation rate given on a high-value shipment based upon the shipper's agreement to accept a set maximum carrier liability in the case of loss or damage that is less than the actual or declared value.

relief from liability

(U.S. Customs) In cases where articles imported under temporary importation under bond (TIB), relief from liability under bond may be obtained in any case in which the articles are destroyed under Customs supervision, in lieu of exportation, within the original bond period. However, in the case of articles imported solely for testing or experimentation, destruction need not be under Customs supervision where articles are destroyed during the course of experiments or tests during the bond period or any lawful extension, but satisfactory proof of destruction shall be furnished to the district or port director with whom the customs entry was filed. *See* temporary importation under bond; drawback; in bond.

remittance

(banking) Funds forwarded from one person to another as payment for bought items or services.

remittance following collection

(shipping) In instances when the shipper has performed services incident to the transportation of goods a carrier will collect payment for these services from the receiver and remit such payment to the shipper. Carriers charge nominal fees for this service.

remitter

(banking) In a documentary collection, an alternate name given to the seller who forwards documents to the buyer through banks. *See* documentary collection.

remitting

(banking) Paying, as in remitting a payment; also canceling, as in remitting a debt.

remitting bank

(banking) In a documentary collection, a bank which acts as an intermediary, forwarding the remitter's documents to, and payments from the collecting bank. *See* documentary collection.

renminbi (RMB)

(People's Republic of China) Literally "people's currency." The official currency of China, issued by the Central Bank of China. As of January 1, 1994, China's dual currency system of RMB and FEC (Foreign Exchange Certificate) was united in a step toward making the RMB more freely convertible and bringing its exchange rate closer to market value.

reorder point

(logistics) A predetermined inventory level at or below which a replenishment order is made. The reorder point inventory quantity must be sufficient to respond to customer demand for the time required to order and receive additional stock.

reparation

(general) Repairing or keeping in repair.

(ethics/law) The making of amends or giving satisfaction to a wronged party.

(logistics) A compensation paid by a carrier to a shipper that has been overcharged.

(U.S. law) Compensation ordered by the Interstate Commerce Commission (ICC) in situations where a carrier (specifically a railroad) has charged a shipper more than is allowable by law.

Reparation claims are differentiated from overcharge claims in that they refer to an illegal amount being charged as opposed to a legal charge: the overcharge.

replevin

(law) A legal action for recovering property brought by the owner or party entitled to repossess the property against a party who has wrongfully kept it. A seller that furnishes products to a sales representative on consignment, for example, may sue for replevin if the sales representative wrongfully retains products not sold at the end of the term of the consignment agreement.

request for quotation (RFQ)

A negotiating approach whereby the buyer asks for a price quotation from a potential seller/suppler for specific quantities of goods (or services) to specifications the buyer establishes in the request for quotation letter.

requirement contract

(law) An agreement by which a seller promises to supply all of the specified goods or services that a buyer needs over a certain time and at a fixed price, and the buyer agrees to purchase such goods or services exclusively from the seller during that time.

rescind

(law) To cancel a contract. A contract may, for example, give one party a right to rescind if the other party fails to perform within a reasonable time.

rescission

See rescind.

reserved freight space

(shipping) A service by some airlines enabling shippers to reserve freight space on designated flights. *See* priority air freight.

residual restrictions

(GATT/WTO) Quantitative restrictions that have been maintained by governments before they became contracting parties to the General Agreement on Tariffs and Trade (GATT) and the World Trade Organization (WTO) and, hence, permissible under the GATT/WTO "grandfather clause." Most of the residual restrictions still in effect are maintained by developed countries against the imports of agricultural products. *See* grandfather clause; General Agreement on Tariffs and Trade, World Trade Organization (WTO).

restitution

(law) A legal remedy for a breach of contract by which the parties are restored to their original positions before the contract was made or the breach occurred. Damages are distinguished from restitution in that damages compensate for a party who has suffered a loss. If a buyer, for example, partially pays for merchandise in advance and the seller delivers merchandise that fails to meet the buyer's specifications, the buyer may file a legal action seeking restitution, that is, a return of the advance payment to the buyer and of the goods to the seller. Alternatively, the buyer may accept the goods and may sue for damages in the amount by which the worth of the goods is less than the original contract price.

restricted articles

(shipping) An airline term meaning a hazardous material as defined by Title 49, Code of Federal Regulations (U.S.) and Air Transport Restricted Articles Circular 6-D. Restricted articles may be transported domestically and be classified dangerous goods when transported internationally by air. *See* dangerous goods; hazardous material.

restricted letter of credit

(banking) A letter of credit, the negotiation of which is restricted to a bank specially mentioned. See letter of credit.

restrictive business practices

(economics) Actions in the private sector, such as collusion among the largest suppliers, designed to restrict competition so as to keep prices relatively high.

restrictive endorsement

See endorsement.

retaliation

Action taken by a country to restrain its imports from a country that has increased a tariff or imposed other measures that adversely affect its exports.

(WTO) The World Trade Organization, in certain circumstances, permits retaliation, although this has very rarely been practiced. The value of trade affected by such retaliatory measures should in theory, approximately equal the value affected by the initial import restriction.

retaliatory duty

See retaliation.

returned without action

(U.S.) For export control purposes, the return of an export license application without action because the application is incomplete, additional information is required, or the product is eligible for a general license. *See* Bureau of Export Administration; general license.

revaluation

(economics) The increase of the value (restoration) of a nation's currency (that had once been devalued) in terms of the currency of another nation.

reverse logistics

(logistics) The act of, and management systems associated with, the recovery of discarded products and packaging from the end user. Reverse logistics is based upon a heightened environmental consciousness, public policy and law. The concept is that reusable packaging, as well as outdated, damaged or defective products, can best be recycled or reused by the original manufacturer. Reverse logistics, however, is much more than recycling. It involves both product and systems designs that make recovery and reuse possible, efficient and even profitable. In reverse logistics a measure of what gets thrown away is a measure of the failure of the product design and recovery process.

reverse preferences

Tariff advantages once offered by developing countries to imports from certain developed countries that granted them preferences. Reverse preferences characterized trading arrangements between the European Community and some developing countries prior to the advent of the Generalized System of Preferences (GSP) and the signing of the Lome Convention.

reverse swap

(banking/trade) A swap which offsets the interest rate or currency exposure on an existing swap. It can be written with the original counterparty or with a new counterparty. In either case, it is typically executed to realize capital gains.

Revised American Foreign Trade Definitions

A set of foreign trade terms which are considered obsolete, but still sometimes used in domestic U.S. trade. The most widely accepted international trade terms are Incoterms 2000. *See* Incoterms 2000.

revocable letter of credit

(banking) A letter of credit which can be cancelled or altered by the drawee (buyer) after it has been issued by the drawee's bank. Due to the low level of security of this type of credit, they are extremely rare in practice. *See* letter of credit.

revocation of antidumping duty order & termination of suspended investigation

(U.S. Customs) An antidumping duty order may be revoked or a suspended investigation may be terminated upon application from a party to the proceeding. Ordinarily the application is considered only if there have been no sales at less than fair value for at least the two most recent years. However, the Department of Commerce may on its own initiative revoke an antidumping duty order or terminate a suspended investigation if there have not been sales at less than fair value for a period of 3 years. *See* dumping.

revolving letter of credit

(banking) A letter of credit which is automatically restored to its full amount after the completion of each documentary exchange.

The number of utilizations and the period of time within which these must take place are specified in the documentary letter of credit. The revolving letter of credit is used when a purchaser wishes to have certain partial quantities of the ordered goods delivered at specified intervals (multiple delivery contract) and when multiple documents are presented for this purpose. Such credit may be cumulative or non-cumulative. *See* letter of credit.

rial

The currency of:
Iran, 1Rl=100 dinars;
Oman, 1RO=1,000 baiza;
Yemen, 1YR=100 fils.

riel

The currency of Kampuchea. 1CR=100 sen.

ringgit

The currency of Malaysia. 1M$=100 sen.

risk position

(banking/finance/foreign exchange) An asset or liability, which is exposed to fluctuations in value through changes in exchange rates or interest rates.

riyal

The currency of:
Qatar, 1QR=100 dirhams;
Saudi Arabia, 1SR=100 halala.

RNS

(Canada) Release Notification System. A Canada Customs and Revenue Agency (CCRA) electronic data interchange (EDI) system that notifies importers, brokers, warehouse operators, and carriers of customs releases.

road waybill

(shipping) Transport document that indicates goods have been received for shipment by road haulage carrier. *See* bill of lading.

rollback

(GATT) Refers to an agreement among Uruguay Round participants to dismantle all trade-restrictive or distorting measures that are inconsistent with the provisions of the General Agreement on Tariffs and Trade (GATT). Measures subject to rollback would be phased out or brought into conformity within an agreed timeframe, no later than by the formal completion of the negotiations. The rollback agreement is accompanied by a commitment to "standstill" on existing trade-restrictive measures. Rollback is also used as a reference to the imposition of quantitative restrictions at levels less than those occurring in the present.

See standstill; General Agreement on Tariffs and Trade; rounds; Tokyo Round; Uruguay Round.

roll-on, roll-off (RoRo)

(shipping) A broad category of ships designed to load and discharge cargo which rolls on wheels. Broadly interpreted, this may include train ships, trailer ships, auto, truck and trailer ferries, and ships designed to carry military vehicles.

rollover

(finance/foreign exchange) (a) Extension of a maturing financial instrument, such as a loan or certificate of deposit. (b) Extension of a maturing foreign exchange operation through the conclusion of a swap agreement (e.g., tom/next swap). (c) Variability of an interest rate according to the appropriate, currently prevailing rates on the Euromarket (normally LIBOR) for a medium-term loan.

rollover credit

(banking) Any line of credit that can be borrowed against up to a stated credit limit and into which repayments go for crediting. *See* letter of credit.

rouble

The currency of Russia and throughout the Commonwealth of Independent States. 1R=100 kopecks.

R

rounds (of trade negotiations)

(GATT/WTO) Cycles of multilateral trade negotiations under the General Agreement on Tariffs and Trade (GATT) and the successor World Trade Organization (WTO), culminating in simultaneous agreements among participating countries to reduce tariff and non-tariff trade barriers.

1st Round: 1947, Geneva (creation of the GATT);
2nd Round: 1949, Annecy, France (tariff reduction);
3rd Round: 1951, Torquay, England (accession & tariff reduction);
4th Round: 1956, Geneva (accession and tariff reduction);
5th Round: 1960-62, Geneva ("Dillon" Round; revision of GATT; addition of more countries);
6th Round: 1964-67, Geneva ("Kennedy" Round);
7th Round: 1973-79, Geneva ("Tokyo" Round);
8th Round: 1986-93, Geneva ("Uruguay" Round);
9th Round: 9th round: Launched 11/14/01 by the WTO's 142 members in a Ministerial Declaration at the Doha (Qatar) Ministerial Conference, with a target completion date of January 2005.

See General Agreement on Tariffs and Trade; Tokyo Round; Uruguay Round, World Trade Organization.

route

(shipping) (a) The course or direction that a shipment moves. (b) To designate the course or direction a shipment shall move.

royalty

(law) Compensation for the use of a person's property based on an agreed percentage of the income arising from its use (e.g., to an author on sale of his book, to a manufacturer for use of his machinery in the factory of another person, to a composer or performer, etc.). A royalty is a payment, lease or similar right, while a residual payment is often made on properties that have not been patented or are not patentable.

rufiyaa

The currency of Maldives. 1Rf=100 larees.

rule of law

(law) Equal protection and equal punishment under the law for all individual in a society. Equal protection includes protection of human rights as well as property and other rights. The concept is that the rule of law reigns over government, protecting citizens against arbitrary state action, and over society generally, governing relations among private interests. It ensures that all citizens are treated equally and are subject to the law rather than the whims of the powerful. The rule of law is an essential precondition for accountability and predictability in both the public and private sector.

rulings on imports

(U.S. Customs) An exporter, importer, or other interested party may get advance information on any matter affecting the dutiable status of merchandise by writing the District Director of Customs where the merchandise will be entered, or to the Regional Commissioner of Customs, New York Region, New York, NY 10048 USA, or to the U.S. Customs Service, Office of Regulations and Rulings, Washington, DC 20229 USA. Detailed information on the procedures applicable to decisions on prospective importations is given in 19 Code of Federal Regulations part 177.

Tip: Do not depend on a small "trial" or "test" import shipments since there is no guarantee that the next shipment will receive the same tariff treatment. Small importations may slip by, particularly if they are processed under informal procedures which apply to small shipments or in circumstances warranting application of a flat rate.

rupee

The currency of:
India, 1Re=100 paise;
Mauritius, 1MauRe=100 cents;
Nepal, 1NRe=100 paise;
Pakistan, 1PRe=100 paisas;
Seychelles, 1Re=100 cents;
Sri Lanka, 1R=100 cents.

rupiah

The currency of Indonesia. 1Rp=100 sen.

R

S

safeguards

(WTO) The World Trade Organization (WTO) permits two forms of multilateral safeguards: (1) a country's right to impose temporary import controls or other trade restrictions to prevent commercial injury to domestic industry, and (2) the corresponding right of exporters not to be deprived arbitrarily of access to markets.

Article XIX permits a country whose domestic industries or workers are adversely affected by increased imports to withdraw or modify concessions the country had earlier granted, to impose, for a limited period, new import restrictions if the country can establish that a product is "being imported in such increased quantities as to cause or threaten serious injury to domestic producers," and to keep such restrictions in effect for such time as may be necessary to prevent or remedy such injury. *See* General Agreement on Tariffs and Trade, World Trade Organization.

safety stock

(logistics) (a) (technical) The average volume of inventory on hand when a new order is received. (b) (general) Raw materials, component parts or finished goods maintained in inventory specifically in anticipation of unforeseen shortages of materials or component parts or unusual demand for finished goods. The volume of safety stock held in inventory is determined by such factors as instability in supplier markets, supplier production time, order fulfillment and delivery time from the point of origin and the potential for unusual increases in demand for finished product. *See* buffer stock.

said to contain (s.t.c.); said to weigh (s.t.w.); shipper's load and count

(shipping) Clauses in transport documents which exclude liability of the carrier for the consistency of the description of the goods or the weight of the goods actually loaded, e.g., goods in containers. This provides protection to the carrier against claims by the consignee.

sales agreement

(law) A written document by which a seller agrees to convey property to a buyer for a stipulated price under specified conditions. *See also* contract.

sales representative

An agent who distributes, represents, services, or sells goods on behalf of sellers. *See also* agent; agency.

sales tax

A tax placed by a state or municipality on items at the time of their purchase. It may be a tax on the sale of an item every time it changes hands (value added tax, VAT), or only upon its transfer of ownership at one specific time.

In the case of a VAT, the sales of manufacturers are taxed when the items are considered to be completed goods; the sales of wholesalers are taxed when their goods are sold to retailers; and retail sales are taxed when the goods are purchased by consumers. *See* value added tax.

salvage

(insurance) (a) Compensation paid for the rescue of a ship, its cargo or passengers from a loss at sea, (b) The act of saving a ship or its cargo from possible loss, (c) Property saved from a wreck or fire.

salvage loss

(insurance) A method of insurance adjustment where the underwriter pays the difference between the amount of insurance and the net proceeds of the sale of damaged goods. It is sometimes incorrectly assumed that when damaged goods are sold to determine the extent of loss, the underwriter is obligated to pay the difference between the amount of insurance and the net proceeds of the sale. The salvage loss method is regularly used only if goods are justifiably sold short of destination.

samurai bond

(banking/finance) Bond issued on the Japanese market in yen outside Japan.

sanction

(economics) An embargo imposed against an individual country by the United Nations—or a group of nations—in an effort to influence its conduct or its policies. *See also* embargo.

sanitary certificate

A document attesting to the absence of disease or pests in a shipment of animal or plant products, especially foodstuffs. *See* phytosanitary inspection certificate.

Saudi Arabian Standards Organization

(Saudi Arabia) SASO was established in April 1972 as the sole Saudi Arabian government organization to promulgate standards and measurements in the kingdom. Primarily, SASO promulgates standards for electrical equipment and some food products. Some of these standards have been adopted by the Gulf Cooperation Council. Contact: Saudi Arabian Standards Organization, P.O. Box 3437, Riyadh 1147 Saudi Arabia; Tel: [966] (1) 452-0000; Fax: [966] (1) 452-0133; E-mail: sasoinfo@saso.org; Web: www.saso.org. *See also* International Standards Organization.

scanner

See bar code scanner.

schilling

The currency of:

Austria, 1S=100 groschen.

SDR

See special drawing rights.

seal

(law) A mark or sign that is used to witness and authenticate the signing of an instrument, contract, or other document. A corporation, for example, uses a seal to authenticate its contracts and records of its corporate acts.

(shipping) A small metal strip and lead fastener used for fastening or locking the doors of a container, which is usually numbered and which provides proof that a container has not been opened since the seal was applied.

seal number

(logistics) A number located on the plastic or metal tamper seal or tag affixed to a loaded container or truck. Seals and seal numbers are not reused. A new seal and therefore a new seal number are used each time a container or truck is sealed. *See* container.

sea waybill

(banking) A transport document which is not a document of title/negotiable document. The sea waybill indicates the "on board" loading of the goods and can be used in cases where no ocean bill of lading, i.e. no document of title is required. For receipt of the goods, presentation of the sea waybill by the consignee named therein is not required, which can speed up processing at the port of destination. *See* bill of lading; ocean bill of lading.

seaworthiness

(shipping) The fitness or safety of a vessel for its intended use.

Section 201

(U.S.) Section 201, the "escape clause" provision of the Trade Act of 1974, permits temporary import relief, not to exceed a maximum of eight years, to a domestic industry which is seriously injured, or threatened with serious injury, due to increased imports. Import relief, granted at the president's discretion, generally takes the form of increased tariffs or quantitative restrictions. To be eligible for section 201 relief, the International Trade Commission (ITC) must determine that: (1) the industry has been seriously injured or threatened to be injured and (2) imports have been a substantial cause (not less than any other cause) of that injury. Industries need not prove that an unfair trade practice exists, as is necessary under the antidumping and countervailing duty laws. However, under section 201, a greater degree of injury—"serious" injury— must be found to exist, and imports must be a "substantial" cause (defined as not less than any other cause) of that injury.

If the ITC finding is affirmative, the president's remedy may be a tariff increase, quantitative restrictions, or orderly marketing agreements. At the conclusion of any relief action, the Commission must report on the effectiveness of the relief action in facilitating the positive adjustment of the domestic industry to import competition. If the decision is made not to grant relief, the president must provide an explanation to the Congress. *See* escape clause; unfair trade advantage; orderly marketing agreements; adjustment assistance; International Trade Administration. *See also* quantitative restrictions; International Trade Commission.

Section 232

(U.S.) Under Section 232 of the Trade Expansion Act of 1962, as amended, the U.S. Department of Commerce determines whether articles are being imported into the U.S. in quantities or circumstances that threaten national security. Based on the investigation report, the president can adjust imports of the article(s) in question.

The U.S. Department of Commerce must report on the effects these imports have on national security and make recommendations for action or inaction within 270 days after starting an investigation. Within 90 days of the report, the president decides whether to take action to adjust imports on the basis of national security. The president must notify Congress of his decision within 30 days.

Section 301

(U.S.) Under Section 301 of the Trade Act of 1974, firms can complain about a foreign country's trade policies or practices that are harmful to U.S. commerce. The section empowers the United States Trade Representative (USTR) to investigate the allegations and to negotiate the removal of any trade barriers. The section requires that the World Trade Organization (WTO) dispute resolution process be invoked where applicable and, if negotiations fail, to retaliate within 180 days from the date that discovery of a trade agreement violation took place.

This provision enables the president to withdraw concessions or restrict imports from countries that discriminate against U.S. exports, subsidize their own exports to the United States, or engage in other unjustifiable or unreasonable practices that burden or discriminate against U.S. trade. *See* Super 301; Special 301.

Section 337

(U.S.) Section 337 of the Tariff Act of 1930 requires investigations of unfair practices in import trade. Under this authority, the International Trade Commission (ITA) applies U.S. statutory and common law of unfair competition to the importation of products into the United States and their sale. Section 337 prohibits unfair competition and unfair importing practices and sales of products in the U.S., when these threaten to: (1) destroy or substantially injure a

S

domestic industry, (2) prevent the establishment of such an industry, or (3) restrain or monopolize U.S. trade and commerce. Section 337 also prohibits infringement of U.S. patents, copyrights or registered trademarks.

secured
(law/banking) Guaranteed as to payment by the pledge of something valuable.

security
(general) Property pledged as collateral.
(investments) Stocks and bonds placed by a debtor with a creditor, with authority to sell for the creditor's account if the debt is not paid.
(law) (a) Any evidence of debt or right to a property.
(b) An individual who agrees to make good the failure of another to pay.

seizure
(law) The act of taking possession of property.

self-insurance
(insurance) A system whereby a firm or individual, by setting aside an amount of monies, provides for the occurrence of losses that would ordinarily be covered under an insurance program. The monies that would normally be used for premium payments are added to this special fund for payment of losses incurred.

seller's market
Exists when goods cannot easily be secured and when the economic forces of business tend to cause goods to be priced at the vendor's estimate of value.

selling, general and administrative (expenses)
(U.S. Customs) In establishing valuation of an import shipment, the sum of:
(1) General and administrative expenses (such as: salaries of non-sales personnel, rent, heat, and light);
(2) Direct selling expenses (that is, expenses that can be directly tied to the sale of a specific unit, such as: credit, warranty, and advertising expenses); and
(3) Indirect selling expenses (that is, expenses which cannot be directly tied to the sale of a specific unit but which are proportionally allocated to all units sold during a certain period, such as: telephone, interest, and postal charges).
See valuation.

selling rate
(banking/foreign exchange) Rate at which a bank is willing to sell foreign exchange or to lend money.

semi
See semitrailer.

Semiconductor Trade Arrangement
The U.S.-Japan Semiconductor Trade Arrangement is a bilateral agreement which came into effect on August 1, 1991, replacing the prior 1986 Semiconductor Trade Arrangement. The new Arrangement contains provisions to: (1) increase

foreign access to the Japanese semiconductor market; and (2) deter dumping of semiconductors by Japanese suppliers into the U.S. market, as well as in third country markets. In evaluating market access improvement, both governments agreed to pay particular attention to market share. The expectation of a 20 percent foreign market share by the end of 1992 is included in the Arrangement. The Arrangement explicitly states, however, that the 20 percent figure is not a guarantee, a ceiling, or a floor on the foreign market share.

semitrailer
(logistics/trucking) A non-motorized cargo vehicle designed to be supported at one end by wheels and the other by a motorized vehicle such as a tractor. *See* trailer, tractor.

senior commercial officer (SCO)
(U.S. diplomacy) The SCO is the senior U.S. and Foreign Commercial Officer at an embassy and reports in-country to the Ambassador. At major posts, this position carries the title of Commercial Counselor; in key posts, Minister Counselor. Usually reporting to the SCO are a Commercial Attaché and Commercial Officers. The latter are sometimes assigned to subordinate posts throughout the country.

separable cost
(logistics) A cost that can be assigned to a specific portion of a business activity or operation.

sequestration
See attachment.

service a loan
(banking) To pay interest due on a loan.

service commitments
(shipping) Pickup and/or delivery commitments agreed to by carrier and shipper.

service mark
(law) A mark used in sales or advertising to identify a service offered by an individual or legal entity and to distinguish that service from services offered by others. A service mark is distinguished from a trademark in that the former identifies services, while the later identifies goods. Protection for service marks varies from country to country, and may not be available in some jurisdictions. Service marks are often, but not necessarily, regulated by the same laws that govern trademarks. A country that is a member the Paris Convention for the Protection of Industrial Property may recognize service marks held in other jurisdictions. *See* trademark; patent; Paris Convention; World Intellectual Property Organization.

services
(economics) Economic activities—such as transportation, banking, insurance, tourism, space launching telecommunications, advertising, entertainment, data processing, consulting and the li-

censing of intellectual property—that are usually of an intangible character and often consumed as they are produced. Service industries have become increasingly important since the l920s. Services now account for more than two-thirds of the economic activity of the United States and about 25 percent of world trade.

servitude

(law) A charge against or burden on property that benefits a person with an interest in another property. An owner of property may grant another person, for example, a right to travel over that property to reach adjoining land, in which case the owner has created a servitude against the property. *See* easement.

settlement date

(banking) The date on which payment for a transaction must be made.

severability clause

(law) A contract term that provides that each portion of the agreement is independent of the others, allowing a court to invalidate a clause of the contract without voiding the entire agreement.

shared foreign sales corporation

(U.S.) A foreign sales corporation consisting of more than one and less than 25 unrelated exporters. *See* foreign sales corporation.

shekel

The currency of Israel. 1IS=100 agorot.

shilling

The currency of:
Kenya, 1KSh=100 cents;
Somalia, 1 SoSh=100 cents;
Tanzania, 1 TSh=100 cents;
Uganda, 1USh=100 cents.
The former currency of Austria, The new currency of Austria is the European Union euro. 1 € = 100 cents.

ship agent

(shipping) A port-based representative for a shipping line or tramp operation who handles ship arrival and departure formalities, port clearance, payment of fees, loading and unloading and local provisioning.

ship broker

(logistics) An individual or company that acts as an intermediary between a shipper and a ship owner or operator, especially tramp ship owners and operators.

ship chandlery

(shipping) A business that sells ships' provisions, supplies and equipment.
(general) A dealer and/or maker of wax, tallow, candles and soap.
Historic note: In the days of sailing ships, a ship's crew would collect the residual grease (called slush)

from empty barrels of fried salt pork and sell it to chandlers once in port. The money so earned was called the *slush fund* and was used to purchase small necessities such as razors, soap, mirrors and tobacco. Chandlers eventually came to be suppliers of ships' provisions.

shipment

(shipping) Except as otherwise provided, cargo tendered by one shipper, on one bill of lading, from one point of departure, for one consignee, to one destination, at one time, via a single port of discharge.

shipment record

(shipping) A repository of information for each shipment that reflects all activity throughout each step of the shipment life cycle.

shipped on deck

(shipping) Annotation in a bill of lading stating that the goods have been shipped on the deck of a ship. *See* bill of lading.

shipper

(shipping) The company or person who ships cargo to the consignee.

shipper's export declaration

(documentation) A form required by the export authorities of many countries to document an export of goods.
(U.S. documentation) Form required for all U.S. export shipments by mail valued at more than $500 and for non-mail shipments with declared value greater than $2,500. Also required for shipments requiring a U.S. Department of Commerce validated export license or U.S. Department of State license regardless of value of goods. Prepared by a shipper indicating the value, weight, destination, and other basic information about the shipment. The shipper's export declaration is used to control exports and compile trade statistics.

shipper's letter of instruction

(shipping) A form used by a shipper to authorize a carrier to issue a bill of lading or an air waybill on the shipper's behalf. The form contains all details of shipment and authorizes the carrier to sign the bill of lading in the name of the shipper. *See* bill of lading.

shipper's load and count

(shipping) A clause in, or notation on, a transport document noting that the contents of a container were loaded and counted by the shipper and not checked or verified by the carrier. Such a notation provides protection to the carrier against claims by the consignee.

shipping point

(logistics) The physical place where cargo begins moving aboard a vessel toward its destination.

shipping instructions

(shipping) Information supplied by the shipper/exporter providing detailed instructions pertaining to the shipment (e.g., shipper, consignee, bill-to party, commodity, pieces, weight, cube, etc.).

shipping order

(shipping) Instructions of shipper to carrier for forwarding of goods; usually the triplicate copy of the bill of lading.

shipping weight

(shipping) The total weight usually expressed in kilograms of shipments, including the weight of moisture content, wrappings, crates, boxes, and containers (other than cargo vans and similar substantial outer containers).

ship's manifest

(shipping) A list, signed by the captain of a ship, of the individual shipments constituting the ship's cargo. *See* manifest.

ship's papers

(shipping) The documents a ship must carry to meet the safety, health, immigration, commercial and customs requirements of a port of call or of international law.

ship's stores

(shipping) The food, medical supplies, spare parts and other provisions carried for the day-to-day running of a vessel.

shogun bond

(finance) Non-resident bond issues denominated in foreign currencies on the Tokyo market. Started June 1985.

shortage

(shipping) A deficiency in quantity shipped.

short form bill of lading

(shipping) A bill of lading that does not have the detailed terms and conditions of carriage printed on (usually) the reverse of the form. A deviation from a regular (long form) bill of lading since it only refers to the contract terms but does not include them. *See* bill of lading, blank back, long form.

short of exchange

(banking/foreign exchange) The position of a foreign exchange trader who has sold more foreign bills than the quantity of bills he or she has in possession to cover sales.

short supply

(U.S.) Commodities in short supply may be subject to export controls to protect the domestic economy from the excessive drain of scarce materials and to reduce the serious inflationary impact of satisfying foreign demand. Two commodities which the U.S. controls for short supply purposes are crude oil and unprocessed western red cedar.

short ton

(measure) A unit of mass or weight measurement equal to 2,000 pounds. A long ton is 2,240 pounds.

short weight

(shipping) Notation of a shipment's weight as less than that noted on the original bill of lading, indicating loss during shipment.

sight draft

(banking) A financial instrument payable upon presentation or demand. A bill of exchange may be made payable, for example, at sight or after sight, which means it is payable upon presentation or demand, or within a particular period after demand is made. *See* bill of exchange.

signature service

(shipping) A service designed to provide continuous responsibility for the custody of shipments in transit, so named because a signature is required from each person handling the shipment at each stage of its transit from origin to destination.

silent confirmation

(banking/letters of credit) In addition to the commitment of the issuing bank of a letter of credit, the advising bank can, by silent confirmation, enter into its own, independent commitment to pay or accept. In contrast to the confirmed letter of credit, in this case there is no confirmation instruction given by the issuing bank. Silent confirmations are thus purely agreements between the beneficiary and the "silently confirming" bank. In order to enforce its claim, the "silently confirming" bank requires the assignment of all the rights of the beneficiary under the letter of credit. *See* letter of credit.

similar merchandise

(U.S. Customs) For purposes of establishing the customs value of imported merchandise, similar merchandise is merchandise that is:

(1) Produced in the same country and by the same person as the merchandise being appraised,

(2) Like merchandise being appraised in characteristics and component materials,

(3) Commercially interchangeable with the merchandise being appraised.

If merchandise meeting all these criteria cannot be found, then similar merchandise is merchandise having the same country of production, like characteristics and component materials, and commercially interchangeability, but produced by a different person.

In determining whether goods are similar, some of the factors to be considered are the quality of the goods, their reputation, and existence of a trademark.

Exclusion: Similar merchandise does not include merchandise that incorporates or reflects engineering, development, artwork, design work, and plans and sketches provided free or at reduced

S

cost by the buyer and undertaken in the United States.
See valuation; transaction value; computed value; identical merchandise.

simple average
(insurance) Particular average. *See* particular average.

Single European Act
The SEA, which entered into force in July 1987, provided the legal and procedural support for achievement of the single European Market by 1992. The SEA revised the European Economic Community (EEC) Treaty and, where not already provided for in the Treaty, majority decisions were introduced for numerous votes facing the Council of Ministers, particularly those affecting establishment of the single European Market and the European financial common market. The role of the European Parliament was strengthened; decisions on fiscal matters remained subject to unanimity.

Single Internal Market Information Service
SIMIS, run by the the European Community Affairs Office under the United States International Trade Administration (ITA), is a clearinghouse for information on European Community activities. Contact: European Community Affairs Office, United States Department of Commerce, 14th and Constitution Ave. NW, Room 3036, Washington, DC 20230 USA; Tel: [1] (202) 482-5823.

SITC
See standard international trade classification.

skid
(logistics/transportation) A portable platform supported by two parallel runners that elevate the platform so that the prongs of a forklift truck can fit underneath. Skids are used to store, handle and move materials and goods in factories, warehouses, containers and vessels. A skid is different from a pallet in that it is generally higher and does not have additional cross member support beneath the runners. *See* pallet, forklift.

sling
(shipping) A contrivance into which freight is placed to be hoisted into or out of a ship.

slip
(shipping) A vessel's berth between two piers.

slip seat
(logistics) The replacement of a driver who has, by regulation, reached maximum driving time, by a fresh driver.

slip sheet
(logistics) A durable sheet of plastic or cardboard upon which goods are stacked and used as an alternative to a traditional pallet.

slurry
(logistics/transportation) The substance that results when dry commodities (such as coal) are liquefied by the addition of a fluid for the purpose of transmission through a pipeline.

Small Business Administration (SBA)
(U.S. government) An independent government organizations which acts as an advocate to small business, providing aid, counseling, assistance and protection. The SBA's Office of International Trade plans, develops and implements programs to encourage small business participation in international trade. The Office also coordinates the Administrations' International Trade Program with the Departments of Commerce and Agriculture, the Export-Import Bank of the United States, the Agency for International Development, and with other Federal and State agencies with private organizations concerned with international trade. Address: Small Business Administration, 1110 Vermont Ave. NW, 9th Floor, Washington, DC 20416 USA; Web: www.sba.gov. The SBA provides an answer desk at: SBA Answer Desk, 200 North College Street, Suite A-2015, Charlotte, NC 28202 USA; Tel: [1] (800) 827-5722; E-mail: answerdesk@sba.gov.

small package service
(shipping) A specialized service to guarantee the delivery of small parcels within specified express time limits, e.g., same day or next day. This traffic is subject to size and weight limitations. Air carriers that also transport passengers often accept these packages at airport ticket counters with delivery at destination baggage claim area. Many carriers provide door-to-door service on a 24-hour basis.

Smoot Hawley Tariff Act of 1930
(U.S.) The Tariff Act of 1930, also commonly known as the Smoot Hawley Tariff, was protectionist legislation that raised tariff rates on most articles imported by the United States, triggering comparable tariff increases by U.S. trading partners.

smuggling
(customs) Conveying goods or persons, without permission, across the borders of a country or other political entities (e.g., cigarette smuggling across state lines).

snake system
(banking/foreign exchange-obsolete) The former agreement between Belgium, The Netherlands, Luxembourg, Denmark, Sweden, Norway, and West Germany, linking the currencies of these countries together in an exchange system. The signatories agreed to limit fluctuations in exchange rates among their currencies to 2.25 percent above or below set median rates. The snake was designed to be the first stage in forming a uni-

form Common Market currency which was finally achieved January 1, 2002. See euro.

Sociedad Anónima (S.A.)
(Latin America, Mexico, Spain) Designation for a joint stock company with limited personal liability to shareholders.

Sociedad a Responsabilidad Limitada (S.R.L.)
(Latin America, Mexico, Spain) Designation for a private limited liability corporation with limited liability to shareholders.

Sociedad por Quota (S.Q.)
(Portugal) Designation for a private limited liability corporation with limited liability to shareholders. *See* Limitada.

Società a Garanzia Limitata (S.G.L.)
(Switzerland) Designation for a private limited liability corporation with limited liability to shareholders.

Società Cooperativa a Responsabilità (SCaRL)
(Italy, Switzerland) Designation for an incorporated association with limited liability for its members, unless its articles provide otherwise.

Società in Accomandita Semplice (S.A.S.)
(Italy) Designation for a limited partnership in which at least one of the partners has general liability and at least one of the other partners has limited liability.

Società per Azioni (S.p.A.)
(Italy) Designation for a joint stock company with limited personal liability to shareholders.

Société (Sté.)
(France, Luxembourg, Switzerland) General designation for a corporation, partnership, or association.

Société Anonyme (S.A.)
(Belgium, France, Luxembourg, Switzerland) Designation for a joint stock company with limited personal liability to shareholders.

Société à Responsabilité Limitée (S.R.L.)
(France, Luxembourg, Switzerland) Designation for a private limited liability corporation with limited liability to shareholders.

Société Cooperative (Sté. Cve.)
(Belgium, Switzerland) Designation for an incorporated association with limited liability for its members, unless its articles provide otherwise.

Société de Personnes à Responsabilité Limitée (S.P.R.L.)
(Belgium) Designation for a private limited liability company with limited liability to shareholders.

Société en Commandité par Actions (S.C.)
(France, Luxembourg) Designation for a limited partnership in which the partners have limited liability.

Société en Commandité Simple (S.C.S.)
(France, Luxembourg) Designation for a limited partnership in which at least one of the partners has general personal liability and at least one of the other partners has limited liability.

Société en Nom Collectif (S.N.C.)
(France, Luxembourg) Designation for a general partnership, in which all partners have joint and several liability.

soft clause
(banking) Clauses in a documentary letter of credit which make it impossible for the beneficiary (seller) to meet the conditions of the documentary letter of credit on his own and independently of the purchaser.
Example: "The goods must be accepted prior to shipment by a representative of the purchaser." The name of the representative is made known via an amendment in the documentary letter of credit at a later stage when it is either too late or very inconvenient to follow through on the requirement. It is not recommended for exporters to agree to this type of request.

soft currency
(banking/foreign exchange) The funds of a country that are controlled by exchange procedures, thereby having limited convertibility into gold and other currencies.

soft loan
(general) A loan made with easy or generous terms such as low or no interest and long payback.
(banking) This term refers to the no-interest loans granted to developing countries by the International Development Association. Such a "soft loan" carries no interest (although there is a small annual service charge), is payable in 50 years, and has an amortization rate of 1% repayable annually for the 10 years following an initial 10-year grace period, followed by 3% repayable annually for the remaining 30 years.

sogo bank
(banking/finance) Regional finance institutions in Japan, dealing chiefly with smaller enterprises.

sol
The currency of Peru. 1S=100 centavos.

Southern Africa Development Community (SADC)
A regional economic pact comprising Angola, Botswana, Lesotho, Malawi, Mozambique, Namibia, Swaziland, Tanzania, Zambia, and Zimbabwe. Note: The Southern Africa Development Coordinating Conference (SADCC) became the Southern Africa Development Community (SADC) in August, 1992, when the 10 member countries signed a treaty to establish it and replace the SADCC. The SADC placed binding obligations on member countries with the aim of promoting economic integration

towards a fully developed common market. Address: Southern Africa Development Community, Private Bag 0095, Gaborone, Botswana; Tel: [267] (35) 1863; Fax: [267] (37) 2848; Web: www.saep.org/sadc, Web: www.sadcreview.com.

Southern Africa Development Coordination Conference

Note: The Southern Africa Development Coordinating Conference (SADCC) became the Southern Africa Development Community (SADC) in August, 1992, when the 10 member countries signed a treaty to establish it and replace the SADCC. *See* Southern Africa Development Community.

Southern African Customs Union

SACU, established in 1910, includes Botswana, Lesotho, Namibia, South Africa, and Swaziland. SACU provides for the free exchange of goods within the area, a common external tariff, and a sharing of custom revenues. External tariffs, excise duties, and several rebate and refund provisions are the same for all SACU members. SACU's revenues are apportioned among its members according to a set formula. These funds constitute a significant contribution to each member's government revenues.

Southern Common Market

See Mercosur.

southern cone

The southern cone consists of Argentina, Brazil, Chile, Paraguay, and Uruguay. With the exception of Chile, these countries also comprise the Southern Common Market.

sovereign credit

(finance) A borrowing guaranteed by the government of a sovereign state.

sovereign risk

(finance) The risk to a lendor that the government of a sovereign state may default on its financial obligations.

sovereignty

The rights of a nation to self determination over all that transpires within its boundaries, especially concerning the rights of its people, immigration policy, business dealings, and jurisdiction over airspace, land and maritime matters.

space and equipment reservation

(logistics) A carrier's setting aside of cargo space and equipment for a shipper's specific future shipment.

space arbitrage

See arbitrage, space.

space request (space and equipment request)

(logistics) A shipper's asking a carrier for availability of cargo space and the equipment required to effect a shipment at a future date. This is generally the first contact a shipper makes with a carrier concerning a shipment.

Special 301

(U.S.) The Special 301 statute requires the United States Trade Representative (USTR) to review annually the condition of intellectual property protection among U.S. trading partners. Submissions are accepted from industry after which the USTR, weighing all relevant information, makes a determination as to whether a country presents excessive barriers to trade with the United States by virtue of its inadequate protection of intellectual property. If the USTR makes a positive determination, a country may be named to the list of: (1) Priority Foreign Countries (the most egregious), (2) the Priority Watch List, or (3) the Watch List. *See* Section 301; Super 301.

special agency

See agency.

Special American Business Internship Training Program (SABIT)

(U.S. government agency) SABIT, formerly the Soviet-American Business Internship Training Program, is a program in which American companies give managers from the Confederation of Independent States (CIS) an opportunity to work in a U.S. corporate setting for up to six months. CIS business managers are referred by the U.S. Department of Commerce to sponsoring U.S. companies, which make the final selection of their interns. The SABIT program matches U.S. corporate sponsors with CIS business executives from the same industries. The CIS provides transportation; the companies provide living expenses and training in management techniques (production, distribution, marketing, accounting, wholesaling, and publishing). SABIT is funded by the U.S. Agency for International Development. Contact: U.S. Department of Commerce, SABIT, 14th and Constitution NW, Washington, DC 20230 USA; Tel: [1] (202) 482-0073; Web: www.mac.doc.gov/sabit/sabit.html.

special and differential treatment

(GATT/WTO) The principle, enunciated in the Tokyo Declaration, that the Tokyo Round of the General Agreement on Tariffs and Trade (GATT) negotiations should seek to accord particular benefits to the exports of developing countries, consistent with their trade, financial, and development needs. Among proposals for special or differential treatment are reduction or elimination of tariffs applied to exports of developing countries under the Generalized System of Preferences (GSP), expansion of product and country coverage of the GSP, accelerated implementation of tariff cuts agreed to in the Tokyo Round for developing country exports, substantial reduction or elimination of tariff escalation, special provisions for developing country exports in any new codes of conduct covering nontariff measures, assurance that any new multilateral safeguard system will contain special provisions for developing country exports, and the principle that developed countries will expect less than full reciprocity for trade concessions they grant developing countries.

See General Agreement on Tariffs and Trade; Generalized System of Preferences, World Trade Organization.

special commodities carrier

(logistics/trucking) A common carrier that is authorized to haul certain regulated items, such as household goods, petroleum products and hazardous materials.

special commodity warehouse

(logistics) A warehouse designed with special facilities and authorized to store unique products such as chemicals (in tanks), grain (in elevators) and tobacco (in barns).

special customs invoice

(customs) A country-of-import required document, similar to a commercial invoice, that contains particular information required for entry of goods into that country. Special customs invoices often itemize freight and insurance charges when a country bases import duties on the landed cost (CIF or Cost, Insurance and Freight) of a shipment.

special drawing right(s) (SDR)

(banking) Reserve assets of the member states of the International Monetary Fund, (IMF) (Bretton-Woods system), for which they can draw an amount of SDRs proportional to their predetermined quota in the IMF. The value of an SDR is based on a currency basket (the last realignment in January 2001: U.S.$=45%, euro=29%, Yen=15%, GB£ = 11%.) Some countries define the parity of their currencies in SDRs.

(banking/foreign exchange) The amount by which each member state of the IMF is permitted to have its international checking account with the International Monetary Fund go negative before the nation must ask for additional loans.

SDRs were established at the Rio de Janeiro conference of 1967. SDRs are available to governments through the Fund and may be used in transactions between the Fund and member governments.

IMF member countries have agreed to regard SDRs as complementary to gold and reserve currencies in settling their international accounts. The unit value of an SDR reflects the foreign exchange value of a "basket" of currencies of several major trading countries (the U.S. dollar, the European Union euro, the Japanese yen, and the British pound). The SDR has become the unit of account used by the IMF and several national currencies are pegged to it. Some commercial banks accept deposits denominated in SDR's (although they are unofficial and not the same units transacted among governments and the fund). *See* International Monetary Fund.

special marine policy

(insurance) An insurance policy which is issued to cover a single shipment. The special marine policy form calls for the name of the vessel and sailing date, points of shipment and destination, nature of commodity, description of units comprising the shipment, and the amount of insurance desired. In addition, it calls for the marks and numbers of the shipment, the name of the party to whom loss shall be payable (usually the assured "or orders" thus making the instrument negotiable upon endorsement by the assured), and the applicable policy provisions. Some of these provisions are standard clauses and are incorporated by reference only, while others are specific and apply to the individual shipment in question.

A special marine policy is usually utilized on export shipments when the sale is financed through a bank by letter of credit and evidence of insurance is a part of the required documentation.

The special marine policy is generally prepared in four or more copies. The original (and duplicate if necessary) is negotiable and is forwarded with the shipping documents to the consignee. The remaining documents serve as office copies for the assured and for the insurance company.

The terms "special marine policy" and "certificate" are often used interchangeably. The practical effect of the two is the same, but a word as to their difference will be of interest.

In former years the use of "certificate" was customary. This, as the name implies, certifies that a shipment has been insured under a given open policy, and that the certificate represents and takes the place of such open policy, the provisions of which are controlling.

Because of the objections that an instrument of this kind did not constitute a "policy" within the requirements of letters of credit, it has become the practice to use a special marine policy. This makes no reference to an open policy and stands on its own feet as an obligation of the underwriting company.

In some cases, exporters insure through freight forwarders when arranging for forwarding, warehousing, documentation, ocean freight space and the other requirements of overseas trade. While this method may have the merit of simplicity, it should be emphasized that there are definite advantages in having one's own policy and that this need not entail burdensome clerical detail.

See open policy; declaration; bordereau.

special rates

(shipping) Rates that apply to cargo traffic under special conditions and usually at a limited number of cities. Examples of such rates are container rates, exception ratings, surface-air rates, and import rates.

specific commodity rate

(shipping) Rate applicable to certain classes of commodities, usually commodities moving in volume shipments. Hence, specific commodity rates are usually lower than the general commodity rate between the same pair of cities.

specific rate of duty

(customs) A specified amount of duty per unit of weight or other quantity. For example 5.9 cents per pound, or 8 cents per dozen. *See also* ad valorem; compound rate of duty.

spot

See spot operations.

spot cash

(banking) Immediate cash payment in a transaction, as opposed to payment at some future time.

spot exchange

(foreign exchange) The purchase and sale of foreign exchange for delivery and payment at the time of the transaction.

spot exchange rate

(foreign exchange) The price of one currency expressed in terms of another currency at a given moment in time.

spot market

(foreign exchange) The market (or exchange) for a commodity or foreign exchange available for immediate delivery (usually one or two days after the transaction date).

spot/next

(foreign exchange) Swap transaction, the spot side of which has the normal spot value date while the forward side becomes due one business day later.

spot operations

(foreign exchange) Foreign exchange dealing in which settlement of the mutual delivery commitments is made at the latest two days (normally on the second business day) after the transaction was carried out.

spot price

A price quotation for immediate sale and delivery of a commodity or currency.

spot rate

The rate for purchase or sale of a commodity for immediate delivery.

spotting

(shipping) The placing of a container where required to be loaded or unloaded.

spot trading

See spot market; spot operations.

squaring (positions)

(finance/foreign exchange) Covering an open position (securities, foreign exchange or commodities) by means of corresponding contra business.

spur track

(logistics/rail transport) A section of railroad track that connects a manufacturing plant or warehouse to the main railroad line. The cost of the spur and its maintenance is borne by the connected facility.

stage

(logistics) Positioning and preparing freight for shipment at a specific location.

stanchion

(shipping) An upright bar or post used as a tie-down point or to support a shipping container or railcar roof.

standard industrial classification (SIC)

(U.S.) The classification standard underlying all establishment-based U.S. economic statistics classified by industry.

Standard International Trade Classification, Revision 3 (SITC, Rev. 3)

(international classification system) A United Nations-established and maintained classification and coding system developed for the compilation of international trade statistics and the promotion of international comparability of international trade statistics. The SITC code reflects: 1) the materials used in production, 2) the processing stage, 3) market practices and uses of the products, 4) the importance of the commodities in terms of world trade, and 5) technological changes. The latest revision was Revision 3 in 1986. The SITC corresponds to the following other international classifications: Classification by Broad Economic Categories (BEC), The Harmonized Commodity Description and Coding System (HS), Central Product Classification (CPC), and the International Standard Industrial Classification (ISIC). Contact at UNSD (United Nations Statistics Division); International Trade Statistics Branch; Fax: [1] (212) 963-9851; e-mail: civitello@un.org; Web: www.un.org/depts/unsd.
See Harmonized System, International Standard Industrial Classification.

standard of living

(economics) The level of material affluence of a nation as measured by per capita output.

standards

As defined by the Multilateral Trade Negotiations "Agreement on Technical Barriers to Trade" (Standards Code), a standard is a technical specification contained in a document that lays down characteristics of a product such as levels of quality, performance, safety, or dimensions. Standards may include, or deal exclusively with, terminology, symbols, testing and test methods, packaging, marking, or labeling requirements as they apply to a product. *See* International Standards Organization; American National Standards Institute.

standby commitment

(banking) A bank commitment to loan money up to a specified amount for a specific period, to be used only in a certain contingency.

standby letter of credit

(banking) The standby letter of credit is very similar in nature to a guarantee. The beneficiary can claim payment in the event that the principal does not comply with its obligations to the beneficiary. Payment can usually be realized against presentation of a sight draft and written statement that the principal has failed to fulfill his obligations.

With this instrument the following payments and performances, among others, can be supported:

(1) repay funds borrowed or advanced,

(2) fulfill subcontracts, and

(3) undertake payment of invoices made on open account. *See* letter of credit.

standing to sue

(law) A party's interest in a controversy that is sufficient to allow the party to request a judicial resolution. A buyer who suffers damages because of the seller's breach of contract, for example, has standing to sue, but a friend of the buyer who was not a party to the contract and who has not suffered damages from the breach has no standing to sue.

standstill

(GATT) Standstill refers to a commitment of the General Agreement on Tariffs and Trade (GATT) contracting parties not to impose new trade-restrictive measures during the Uruguay Round negotiations. *See* rollback; General Agreement on Tariffs and Trade; Uruguay Round.

starboard

(shipping) The right side of a ship when one is facing the bow.

stare decisis

(law) A legal doctrine under which courts, in resolving current disputes, follow cases decided previously. This doctrine is followed in countries that adhere to common law principles. *See* common law.

State Export Program Database

(U.S.) The SEPD is a trade lead system maintained by the National Association of State Development Agencies (NASDA). The SEPD includes information on state operated trade lead systems. The SEPD can be purchased on CD-ROM for $225.00 directly from the NASDA's Web site at Web: www.nasda.com. *See* National Association of State Development Agencies.

state/industry-organized, government approved (S/IOGA)

The name of this program has recently been changed to Certified Trade Missions Program. *See* Certified Trade Missions Program.

state trading enterprises

Entities established by governments to import, export and/or produce certain products. Examples include: government-operated import/export monopolies and marketing boards, or private companies that receive special or exclusive privileges from their governments to engage in trading activities.

STAT-USA

(U.S. Dept. of Commerce) STAT-USA is a fee-funded office in the U.S. Department of Commerce that develops and operates electronic information systems to deliver government economic, business, statistical, and foreign trade information to the public, primarily through subscription online services. STAT-USA's flagship product, STAT-USA/Internet (Web: www.stat-usa.gov), is a subscription based Internet site that contains all of the information in the National Trade Data Bank (NTDB) as well as an extensive collection of domestic economic data. Customers can view, print and download trade opportunity leads, market reports, economic releases and more from the State Department, the Bureau of Export Administration, the Federal Reserve Board, the U.S. Census Bureau, and others. USA Trade Online, a joint venture with the U.S. Census Bureau and a private partner, is the latest STAT-USA product, offering trade statistics to subscribers within minutes of release. Tel: [1] (800) STAT-USA; E-mail: statmail@mail.doc.gov; Web: www.stat-usa.gov.

strategic alliance

(commerce/management) An agreement made between two or more individuals, organizations or legal entities, within the same or complimentary industries, to accomplish one or more specific goals such as: increase market share, reduce costs, create new products or enter new markets. *See* joint venture.

state trading nations

(economics) Countries such as the former Soviet Union, the People's Republic of China, and nations of Eastern Europe that rely heavily on government entities, instead of the private sector, to conduct trade with other countries. Some of these countries, (e.g., Cuba) have long been Contracting Parties to the General Agreement on Tariffs and Trade (GATT) and now the World Trade Organization (WTO), whereas others (e.g., Poland, Hungary, and Romania), became Contracting Parties later under special Protocols of Accession. The different terms and conditions under which these countries acceded to GATT and the WTO were designed in each case to ensure steady expansion of the country's trade with other GATT/WTO countries taking into account the relative insignificance of tariffs on imports into state trading nations.

statute of frauds
(U.S. law) A law that requires designated documents to be written in order to be enforced by a court. Contracting parties, for example, may orally agree to transfer ownership of land, but a court may not enforce that contract, and may not award damages for breach, unless the contract is written.

steamship indemnity
(shipping) An indemnity received by an ocean carrier issued by a bank indemnifying him for any loss incurred for release of goods to the buyer without presentation of the original bill of lading.

sterling
(a) The money of Great Britain. (b) An article made from sterling silver. Sterling silver is an alloy of silver that is 925/1000 pure. An article of sterling silver is generally marked "925".

stern
(shipping) The rear part of a ship, boat or airplane.

stevedore
(shipping) A person having charge of the loading and unloading of ships in port. *See also* longshoreman; gang.

stock on hand
(logistics) Inventory of raw materials, component parts or finished goods available for shipment at any given moment in time. The term generally refers to stock of finished goods.

stop loss order
(foreign exchange) An order to buy (on a short position) or to sell (on a long position) foreign exchange if the rate rises above or falls below a specific limit. As soon as the rate reaches the prescribed limit, the order will be carried out at the next rate. Depending on the market situation, this rate can differ considerably from the limit rate.

storage
(shipping) The keeping of goods in a warehouse.

storage demurrage
(shipping) A charge made on property remaining on the dock past the prescribed "free-time period." *See* demurrage.

storage in transit
(shipping) The stopping of freight traffic at a point located between the point of origin and destination to be stored and reforwarded at a later date.

store-door delivery
(shipping) The movement of goods to the consignee's place of business, customarily applied to movement by truck.

stores
See ship's stores.

stowage
(shipping) The arranging and packing of cargo in a vessel for shipment.

stowage instructions
(shipping) Specific instructions given by the shipper or his agent concerning the way in which cargo is to be stowed. For example, a shipper may require that his shipment be placed below deck if it may be damaged by exposure to the elements above deck, or midships if it may be damaged by the greater movement of the vessel in fore and aft sections.

stowplan or stowage plan
(shipping) A diagram showing how cargo or containers have been placed on a vessel.

straight bill of lading
(shipping) A nonnegotiable bill of lading that designates a consignee who is to receive the goods and that obligates the carrier to deliver the goods to that consignee only. A straight bill of lading cannot be transferred by endorsement. *See* bill of lading; negotiable instrument; ocean bill of lading.

strategic level of controls
(U.S.) Commodity groupings used for export control purposes. *See* export control classification number.

strike clause
(insurance) An insurance clause included in policies to cover against losses as a result of strikes.

strike price
(finance/foreign exchange) Price at which the option buyer obtains the right to purchase (call option) or sell (put option) the underlying security or currency.

strikes, riots and civil commotion
(insurance) An insurance policy endorsement, usually referred to as S.R.&C.C. (strikes, riots and civil commotion) coverage, which extends the insurance policy to cover damage, theft, pilferage, breakage or destruction of the insured property directly caused by strikers, locked-out workmen or persons taking part in labor disturbances, riots or civil commotions.
Destruction of and damage to property caused by vandalism, sabotage and malicious acts of person(s) regardless of (political/ideological/terroristic) intent be it accidental or otherwise is also held covered under S.R.&C.C. unless so excluded in the F.C.&S. (free of capture and seizure) warranty in the policy.
The S.R.&C.C. endorsement excludes coverage for any damage or deterioration as a result of delay or loss of market, change in temperature/humidity, loss resulting from hostilities or warlike operations, absence/shortage/withholding power, fuel, labor during a strike (riot or civil commotion) or weapons of war that employ atomic or nuclear fusion/fission.
In order to eliminate the war cover from the marine policy it became customary to add a "free of

capture and seizure" clause, stating that the policy did not cover warlike operations or its consequences, whether before or after the actual declaration of war. Currently, most open policies omit war perils from its insuring conditions and in all cases will include a F.C.&S. clause. War coverage is customarily furnished in conjunction with an open cargo policy and is written under a separate, distinct policy-the War Risk Only Policy.
See war risk; war risk insurance; open policy.

striking price; exercise price
See strike price.

stripping
(shipping) The unloading of cargo from a container. Also called devanning.

Structural Impediments Initiative (SII)
(U.S./Japan) The SII was started in July 1989 to identify and solve structural problems that restrict bringing two-way trade between the U.S. and Japan into better balance.
Both the U.S. and Japanese governments chose issues of concern in the other's economy as impediments to trade and current account imbalances. The areas which the U.S. government chose included: (1) Japanese savings and investment patterns, (2) land use, (3) distribution, (4) keiretsu, (5) exclusionary business practices, and (6) pricing. Areas which the Japanese Government chose included: (1) U.S. savings and investment patterns, (2) corporate investment patterns and supply capacity, (3) corporate behavior, (4) government regulation, (5) research and development, (6) export promotion, and g) workforce education and training.
In a June 1990 report, the U.S. and Japan agreed to seven meetings in the following three years to review progress, discuss problems, and produce annual joint reports.

stuffing
(shipping) The loading of cargo into a container.

subrogation
(insurance) The right of the insurer, upon payment of a loss, to the benefit of any rights against third parties that may be held by the assured himself. This usually involves recoveries from carriers that handled the shipment.

subsidiary
(law) Any organization more than 50 percent of whose voting stock is owned by another firm.

subsidy
(economics) A bounty, grant or economic advantage paid by a government to producers of goods for the manufacture, production, or export of an article, often to strengthen their competitive position. Export subsidies are contingent on exports; domestic subsidies are conferred on production without reference to exports.

The subsidy may be direct (a cash grant), or indirect, low-interest export credits guaranteed by a government agency, for example), or take a less direct form (R&D support, tax breaks, loans on preferential terms, and provision of raw materials at below-market prices).
(WTO) The payment of subsidies by a national government to export producers in a major trade issue. *See* World Trade Organization.

subzone
(U.S. foreign trade zones) A special purpose foreign trade zone established as part of a foreign trade zone project for a limited purpose that cannot be accommodated within an existing zone. Subzones are often established to serve the needs of a specific company and may be located within an existing facility of the company. *See* foreign trade zone; Foreign Trade Zone Board; Foreign Trade Zone Act; operator; grantee; zone user.

sucre
The currency of Ecuador. 1S/=100 centavos.

sue and labor
(insurance) The responsibility of the assured to act to keep his insured loss at a minimum. The sue and labor clause of the open cargo policy reads essentially as follows:
"In case of any loss or misfortune it shall be lawful and necessary to and for the assured, his or their factors, servants and assigns to sue, labor, and travel, for, in and about the defense, safeguard and recovery of the goods and merchandise or any part thereof ... to the charges whereof this company will contribute according to the rate and quantity of the sum herein insured."
Reasonable charges incurred for this purpose are generally collectible under the insurance policy. For example, when a shipment of canned goods arrives with some leaking cans in each of several cartons, the leaking cans must be taken out if rusting and label damage are to be minimized. The expense insured in this operation may be recovered under the insurance policy.

summary investigation
(U.S.) A 20-day investigation conducted immediately following filing of an antidumping petition to ascertain if the petition contains sufficient information with respect to sales at "less than fair value" and the injury or threat of material injury to a domestic industry caused by the alleged sales at "less than fair value" to warrant the initiation of an antidumping investigation. *See* dumping.

summit conference
(diplomacy) An international meeting at which heads of government are the chief negotiators, major world powers are represented, and the meeting serves substantive rather than ceremonial purposes.

The term first came into use in reference to the Geneva Big Four Conference of 1955.

Super 301

(U.S.) This provision was enacted due to U.S. Congressional concern that the regular Section 301 procedures narrowly limit U.S. attention to the market access problems of individual sectors or companies. Super 301 sets procedures to identify and address within three years certain "priority," systemic trade restriction policies of other nations. Super 301 authority expired May 30, 1990. *See* Section 301; Special 301.

superdeductive

See deductive value.

superficies

(law) A right to build on the surface of real property. A landowner may transfer a superficies right, for example, to a developer who agrees to build on the property in exchange for an annual rent to the landowner.

Superintendent of Documents

(U.S.) Official supplier of U.S. government documents, publications, books, etc. Government Periodicals and Subscription Services is a catalog of products and prices. Address: Superintendent of Documents, U.S. Government Printing Office, Washington, DC 20402 USA; Tel: [1] (202) 512-1800.

supplemental carrier

(logistics) A for-hire air carrier that operates without a set schedule or designated route. Service is provided on a charter or contract basis.

supply access

(economics/customs) Assurances that importing countries will, in the future, have fair and equitable access at reasonable prices to supplies of raw materials and other essential imports. Such assurances should include explicit constraints against the use of the export embargo as an instrument of foreign policy.

supply chain logistics

The series of physical facilities, equipment, management and technology that supply goods or services from source to the ultimate consumer. For products these minimally include manufacturing plants, warehouses, distribution centers, conveyances (such as trucks, cargo aircraft, ships and trains), sales locations or methodologies (such as retail stores or Internet Web sites), computer systems and software. The processes, systems and links between these facilities are the subject of ever evolving theory, debate and great technological change. For example, computers and the Internet are part of the supply chain through inventory information systems and e-commerce ordering systems as well as Web-based delivery of information and services.

See supply chain management.

supply chain management

(logistics) The efficient integration of the processes, facilities and technologies involved in the movement of goods or services from source to the ultimate consumer. Modern supply chain management involves the linking of all parties in the supply chain to effectively coordinate the production of the right products or services and their delivery to the right place at the right time for the least cost. Supply chain management refers to the aggregate of the following processes: customer ordering or obtaining sales data, raw material and component parts procurement, coordination of the manufacturing process, warehousing, distribution, invoicing, shipping, receiving, inventory control and order fulfillment. *See* supply chain.

surcharge

(shipping) A charge above the usual or customary charge.

surety

(insurance) A bond, guaranty, or other security that protects a person, corporation, or other legal entity in cases of another's default in the payment of a given obligation, improper performance of a given contract, malfeasance of office, and others.

(law) A surety is usually a party to the contract with the principal debtor and the third person, making the surety equally liable with the debtor. In contrast, a guarantor is usually not a party to the contract between the debtor and the third person.

(U.S. Customs) Surety Bond—U.S. Customs entries must be accompanied by evidence that a bond is posted with Customs to cover any potential duties, taxes, and penalties which may accrue. Bonds may be secured through a resident U.S. surety company, but may be posted in the form of United States money or certain United States government obligations. In the event that a customs broker is employed for the purpose of making entry, the broker may permit the use of his bond to provide the required coverage. *See* bond; guaranty.

survey

(shipping) To examine the condition of a vessel for purposes of establishing seaworthiness and/or value.

(insurance) To inspect goods as to their condition, weight and/or value in order to establish the extent of an insured loss.

survey report

Report of an expert, issued by an independent party. *See* inspection certificate.

sushi bond

(banking/finance) Eurodollar bonds issued by Japanese corporations on the Japanese market for Japanese investors.

suspension of investigation

(U.S.) A decision to suspend an antidumping investigation if the exporters who account for substantially all of the imported merchandise agree to stop exports to the U.S. or agree to revise their prices promptly to eliminate any dumping margin. An investigation may be suspended at any time before a final determination is made. No agreement to suspend an investigation may be made unless effective monitoring of the agreement is practicable and is determined to be in the public interest. *See* dumping.

suspension of liquidation

(U.S. Customs) When a preliminary determination of dumping or subsidization, or final determination after a negative preliminary determination is affirmative, there is a provision for suspension of liquidation of all entries of merchandise subject to the determination which are entered, or withdrawn from warehouse, for consumption, on or after the date of the publication of the notice in the Federal Register. Customs is directed to require a cash deposit, or the posting of a bond or other security, for each entry affected equal to the estimated amount of the subsidy or the amount by which the fair value exceeds the U.S. price. When an administrative review is completed, Customs is directed to collect the final subsidy rate or amount by which the foreign market value exceeds the U.S. price, and to require for each entry thereafter a cash deposit equal to the newly determined subsidy rate or margin of dumping. *See* liquidation; dumping.

swap (transaction)

(banking/finance/foreign exchange) A spot purchase of foreign exchange (currency swaps), fixed or floating rate funds (interest rate swaps) or assets (asset swaps) with simultaneous forward sale or vice versa.

Pase financiero is an Argentinian system, related to the swap system, whereby persons or institutions making capital investments are given an "exchange guarantee," which guarantees that the funds can be reexchanged at a predetermined exchange rate on a specific date. The French government is recommending the term *crédit croisé* but it is fighting a losing battle.

(foreign exchange) Sale of one currency against another currency at a specific maturity and the simultaneous repurchase from the same counterparty at a different maturity. Normally, one of the maturity dates will be that of spot operations.

See also countertrade.

switch

(railroads/logistics) (a) To move railway cars around a railyard or terminal. (b) To detach a railway car from one train and attach it to another.

switch arrangements

(commerce/banking) A form of countertrade in which the seller sells on credit and then transfers the credit to a third party. *See* countertrade.

switch engine

(railroads/logistics) A railroad engine used to move railway cars around a railyard or terminal.

switching and terminal company

(logistics) A company that provides specialized terminal services to carriers including switching, terminal trackage, bridges or ferries. These firms sometimes operate cargo and passenger services.

System for Tracking Export License Applications (STELA)

(U.S.) STELA is a U.S. Department of Commerce, Bureau of Industry and Security (formerly the Bureau of Export Administration) computer-generated voice unit that provides callers with the status of their license and classification applications. STELA enables a caller to check on an export license by making a telephone call to [1] (202) 482-2752. *See* Bureau of Industry and Security.

T

table of denial orders

(U.S.) A list of individuals and firms which have been disbarred from shipping or receiving U.S. goods or technology. Firms and individuals on the list may be disbarred with respect to either controlled commodities or general destination (across-the-board) exports.

taka

The currency of Bangladesh. 1Tk=100 paise.

tala

The currency of Western Samoa. 1WS$=100 sene.

tally sheet

(logistics) A record of the particulars of freight being loaded or unloaded, including quantities, descriptions and marks.

tandem

(trucking) A vehicle, such as a tractor or semitrailer, with a close coupled pair of rear axles.

tank car

(trucking/rail transport) A tank carried on a railway car frame for carriage by rail or by road. Tank cars are used for the shipment of bulk liquids or gases. *See* tank container.

tank container

(logistics) A receptacle used for holding, storing or transporting liquid or gas in bulk. The typical tank container consists of a tank encased in a framework of a standard 10-, 20-, or 40-foot length container. Some tank containers are divided into separate internal sections. *See* tank car.

tapering rate

(logistics) A cargo shipping rate that increases with distance traveled, but not in as great a proportion as the distance traveled. For example, the rate for cargo shipped 2,000 km might only be 60 percent greater than the rate for shipping the same cargo 1,000 km.

tare or tare weight

(shipping) The weight of a container and/or packing materials, but without the goods being shipped. The gross weight of a shipment less the net weight of the goods being shipped.

tariff

(general) A comprehensive list or "schedule" of merchandise with applicable rates to be paid or charged for each listed article.

(shipping) A schedule of shipping rates charged, together with governing rules and regulations. A tariff sets forth a contract of carriage for the shipper, the consignee, and the carrier. Individual carriers also publish their own tariffs covering special services.

International tariffs containing freight rates of the U.S. international carriers are published by the U.S. flag carriers.

(customs) A schedule of duties or taxes assessed by a government on goods as they enter (or leave) a country. Tariffs may be imposed to protect domestic industries from imported goods and/or to generate revenue. Types include ad valorem, specific, variable, or compound. In the United States, the imposition of tariffs is made on imported goods only.

Tariffs raise the prices of imported goods, thus making them less competitive within the market of the importing country. Tariffs are much less important measures of protection than they used to be.

See ad valorem; specific rate of duty; variable rate of duty; compound rate of duty.

tariff anomaly

(customs) A tariff anomaly exists when the tariff on raw materials or semi-manufactured goods is higher than the tariff on the finished product.

tariff escalation

(customs) A situation in which tariffs on manufactured goods are relatively high, tariffs on semi-processed goods are moderate, and tariffs on raw materials are nonexistent or very low.

tariff quotas

(customs) Application of a higher tariff rate to imported goods after a specified quantity of the item has entered the country at a lower prevailing rate. *See* quota.

tariff schedule

(customs) A comprehensive list of the goods which a country may import and the import duties applicable to each product. *See* Harmonized System; Harmonized Tariff Schedule of the United States.

Tariff Schedule of the United States

See Harmonized Tariff Schedule of the United States.

tariff trade barriers

See trade barriers.

tariff war

When one nation increases the tariffs on goods imported from, or exported to another country, and that country then follows by raising tariffs itself in a retaliatory manner.

tau

(foreign exchange) The price change of a foreign exchange option for a 1 percent change in the implied volatility.

tax haven

(trade) A nation offering low tax rates and other incentives for individuals and businesses of other countries.

Tax Information Exchange Agreement

An agreement concluded between the U.S. and a beneficiary country designated pursuant to the Caribbean Basin Economic Recovery Act of 1983. This agreement generally involves an expanded version of the standard exchange of information article usually included in a bilateral income tax treaty. The U.S. has similar agreements with most major trading partners. Like the standard tax treaty exchange of information article, a TIEA imposes on the agreeing countries a mutual and reciprocal obligation to exchange information relating to the enforcement of their respective tax laws.

Technical Advisory Committee(s)

(U.S.) Voluntary groups of industry and government representatives who provide guidance and expertise to the U.S. Department of Commerce on technical and export control matters, including evaluation of technical issues; worldwide availability, use and production of technology; and licensing procedures related to specific industries. TACs have been set up for: (1) materials, (2) biotechnology, (3) computer systems, (4) electronics (formerly "semiconductors"), (5) sensors (formerly "electronic instrumentation"), (6) materials processing equipment (formerly "automated manufacturing equipment"), (7) military critical technologies, (8) telecommunications equipment, and (9) transportation and related equipment. *See* United States Department of Commerce.

technical analysis

(economics/foreign exchange) The analysis of past price and volume trends–often with the help of chart analysis–in a market, in order to be able to make forecasts about the future price developments of the commodity being traded. Technical exchange rate analysis is often used in professional dealing for short-term foreign exchange rate forecasts.

technical barrier to trade

A specification which sets forth stringent standards a product must meet (such as levels of quality, performance, safety, or dimensions) in order to be imported. A technical barrier to trade has the effect of adding to the cost of an imported article, thereby making it less competitive in the marketplace when compared to domestically produced articles.

technical data

Information of any kind that can be used, or adapted for use, in the design, production, manufacture, utilization, or reconstruction of articles or materials. All software is technical data. Technical data can be either "tangible" or "intangible." Models, prototypes, blueprints or operating manuals (even if stored on recording media) are examples of tangible technical data. Intangible technical data consists of technical services, such as training, oral advice, information, guidance and consulting.

technology transfer

The transfer of knowledge generated and developed in one place to another, where is it is used to achieve some practical end. Technology may be transferred

in many ways: by giving it away (technical journals, conferences, emigration of technical experts, technical assistance programs); by industrial espionage; or by sale (patents, blueprints, industrial processes, and the activities of multinational corporations).

temperature controlled ground handling

(air freight) Many of the commodities moving in air freight must be protected against sudden changes in temperatures. The temperature of a jet freighter's cabin is ideal to maintain perishables in peak condition; but the increase in the shipment of perishables by air required new strides in ground handling to protect cargoes from spoilage induced by marked differences in temperatures often encountered on the ground at points of origin and destination. To meet these needs the airlines have, at some cities, special equipment and facilities ranging from heated vans to temperature controlled holding rooms in which 100,000 pounds of perishables can be held at one time.

temporary importation under bond (TIB)

(U.S. Customs) Temporary admission into the United States under a conditional bond for articles not imported for sale or for sale on approval.

Certain classes of goods may be admitted into the United States without the payment of duty, under bond, for their exportation within one year from the date of importation when they are not imported for sale, or for sale on approval. Generally, the amount of the bond is double the estimated duties. The one-year period for exportation may, upon application to the district or port director of Customs, be extended for one or more further periods which, when added to the initial one year, shall not exceed a total of three years. There is an exception in the case of automobiles or any parts thereof which are subject to a total period of six months which may not be extended.

Merchandise entered under TIB must be exported before expiration of the bond period, or any extension, to avoid assessment of liquidated damages in the amount of the bond.

Classes of goods which may be entered under a TIB include a wide range of merchandise. Some examples are: (1) merchandise to be repaired or altered; (2) wearing apparel for use as samples; (3) articles imported by illustrators or photographers for use solely as models; (4) samples for use in taking orders; (5) articles solely for examination with a view to reproduction; (6) articles intended solely for testing; (7) automobiles and other motor vehicles, boats, balloons, racing shells etc. and the usual equipment of the forgoing, imported by non-residents for the purposes of taking part in races; (8) locomotives and railway equipment for use in clearing obstructions; (9) containers for holding merchandise; (10) articles of special design for temporary use in connection with the manufacture of articles for export; (11) animals brought into the United States for the purposes of breeding; (12) theatrical scenery, properties and costumes; (13) works of fine art brought in by lecturers; (14) automobiles, other motor vehicles, and parts thereof brought in for show purposes.

Relief from Liability. Relief from liability under bond may be obtained in any case in which the articles are destroyed under Customs supervision, in lieu of exportation, within the original bond period. However, in the case of articles imported solely for testing or experimentation, destruction need not be under Customs supervision where articles are destroyed during the course of experiments or tests during the bond period or any lawful extension, but satisfactory proof of destruction shall be furnished to the district or port director with whom the customs entry was filed. *See* ATA Carnet; bond; in bond.

tender
(shipping) (a) A small vessel which serves a larger vessel in a port for the purpose of supplying provisions and carrying passengers from ship to shore. (b) A vessel that supplies provisions to a ship at sea.
(law) (a) An offer or proposal submitted for acceptance. (b) A public offer to purchase a minimum number of shares of a publicly-traded stock for a fixed price per share. (c) An offer of money in satisfaction of a debt or obligation.

tenor
(law/banking) The period between the formation of a debt and the date of expected payment.

terminal
(shipping) An area at the end of a rail, ship, air or truck line which serves as a loading, unloading and transfer point for cargo or passengers, and often includes storage facilities, management offices and repair facilities.

terminal charge
(logistics) A charge made for services performed at a terminal. Terminal charges can include those for loading, unloading, stevedores, warehousing and drayage.

terminal delivery allowance
(logistics) A reduction in freight charges or a reduced freight rate based upon the consignor/shipper's agreement to deliver or pick up a shipment at the carrier's terminal.

terminal handling charge (THC)
(logistics/shipping) A charge made to a shipper for moving a container from within a terminal to an ocean vessel.

terminal operator
(logistics) The business entity responsible for the operation of a terminal and its facilities.

terminal pass
(logistics) A document allowing a delivering or receiving carrier to enter a terminal.

terminal receipt
(logistics) A document that evidences proof of delivery (for the delivering carrier) and verification of receipt (for the terminal operator) of cargo or equipment at a terminal.

terms of trade
(economics) The volume of exports that can be traded for a given volume of imports. Changes in the terms of trade are generally measured by comparing changes in the ratio of export prices to import prices. The terms of trade are considered to have improved when a given volume of exports can be exchanged for a larger volume of imports.

TEU
(logistics) Acronym for twenty-foot equivalent unit. (a) A standard 20-foot international ocean shipping container. (b) A measure of a shipping container's capacity using a standard 20-foot international ocean shipping container as a measuring unit. A 40-foot container is therefore equal to two TEUs. (c) A measure of a container vessel's capacity using a standard 20-foot international ocean shipping container as the measuring unit. d) A measure of a container vessel's load using a standard 20-foot international ocean shipping container as the measuring unit.

theta
(statistics/foreign exchange) A ratio expressing the price change of an option (i.e. the change in the premium) over a period of time (per time unit). Mathematically, this corresponds to the 1st derivative of the option premium according to the time factor.

thing in action
(law) A right to bring a legal action to recover personal property, money, damages, or a debt. A seller, for example, who has a right to recover payment for goods and who is not in possession of the buyer's payment has a thing in action, that is, a right to procure payment by lawsuit.

Third Country Meat Directive
A regulation by which the European Community (EC) controls meat imports based on sanitary requirements. The TCMD requires individual inspection and certification by EC veterinarians of meat plants wishing to export to the EC. *See* European Community.

third-party beneficiary
(law) An individual or legal entity that benefits from, but is not a contracting party of, a contract between two or more other individuals or legal entities. A bank, for example, that loans a business owner funds to purchase specific property is a third-party beneficiary to the sales contract between the business owner and seller.

third party documents
(banking) In letter of credit operations, documents which indicate a party other than the beneficiary of the credit as the consignor of the goods. Banks ac-

T

cept third party transport documents. *See* transport documents; letter of credit.

third-party insurance
(insurance) Liability insurance.

third-party logistics
(logistics) A company that provides logistics and logistics management services to other companies. *See* logistics.

third world countries
(economics) Developing countries, especially in Asia, Africa and Latin America, but excluding communist countries and industrial non-communist countries.

through bill of lading
(shipping) A single bill of lading covering receipt of the cargo at the point of origin for delivery to the ultimate consignee, using two or more modes of transportation. *See* bill of lading; ocean bill of lading.

throughput
(logistics) (a) A measure of the number of units or tonnage of shipping containers that pass through a container facility or port in a given period of time. The measure is a function of units received, units shipped and units that remain in the facility. (b) A measure of the number of units of materials or products that pass through a warehouse in a given period of time. The measure is a function of units received, units shipped and units that remain in the facility.
(computers) A measure of the processing power of a computer system based on transactions, batches or other criteria.

through rate
(shipping) A shipping rate applicable from point of origin to destination. A through rate may be either a joint rate or a combination of two or more rates.

tick
See pips.

tied aid credit
The practice of providing grants and/or concessional loans, either alone or combined with export credits, linked to procurement from the donor country.

tied loan
(banking) A loan made by a government agency that requires a foreign borrower to spend the proceeds in the lender's country.

time arbitrage
See arbitrage, time.

time definite services
(logistics) A freight, cargo or courier service standard specifying or guaranteeing delivery either on a specific day or time or within a set number of days or time from receipt.

time deposits
(banking) Funds invested in a bank for a pre-determined time and at a specific interest rate. For large amounts, conditions can be freely negotiable (maturity, interest rate).

time draft
(banking) A financial instrument that is payable at a future fixed or determinable date. *See* bill of exchange.

time value
(finance) The value of an option if the intrinsic value is zero. It merely reflects possible price fluctuations of the underlying instrument, so that at a later point in time the option could achieve an intrinsic value.

title
(law) A document evidencing legal ownership in goods or real estate (deed). Title can also refer to non-paper documentary rights to legal possession.

Tokyo Round
(GATT) The seventh round of multilateral negotiations concerning the General Agreement on Tariffs and Trade (GATT). Begun in 1973, it concluded November 1979, with agreements covering the following: (1) an improved legal framework for the conduct of world trade (which includes preferential tariff and non-tariff treatment in favor of, and among, developing countries as a permanent legal feature of the world trading system); (2) non-tariff measures (subsidies and countervailing measures; technical barriers to trade; government procurement; customs valuation; import licensing procedures; a revision of the 1967 GATT anti-dumping code); (3) bovine meat; (4) dairy products; (5) tropical products; and (6) an agreement on free trade in civil aircraft.
Participating countries (99) also agreed to reduce tariffs on thousands of industrial and agricultural products. These cuts were gradually implemented over a period of eight years ending January 1, 1987. The total value of trade affected by Tokyo Round most-favored-nation (MFN) tariff reductions, and by bindings of prevailing tariff rates, amounted to more than US$300 billion, measured on MFN imports in 1981. As a result of these cuts, the weighted average (the average tariff measured against actual trade flows) on manufactured products in the world's nine major industrial markets declined 7.0 to 4.7 percent, representing a 34 percent reduction of customs collection. This can be contrasted with the average tariff of around 40 percent at the time of GATT's establishment in the late 1940's. Since the tariff-cutting formula adopted by most industrialized countries resulted in the largest reductions generally being made in the highest duties, the customs duties of different countries were brought closer together or "harmonized."
See also General Agreement on Tariffs and Trade; rounds; Uruguay Round; World Trade Organization.

tolar
The currency of Slovenia. 1SiT=100 stotinev.

tom/next
(foreign exchange) Swap transaction where the spot side becomes due on the business day following the day on which the contract was concluded and where the forward side becomes due on the day after, i.e. on the normal spot value date.

ton
(measure) A unit of mass or weight equal to 1.1016 metric tons, 2,240 pounds, or 1,016.06 kilograms.

ton mile
(shipping) The transport of one ton of cargo for one mile. Used most often in air cargo services.

to order
(law/banking/shipping) A term on a financial instrument or title document indicating that it is negotiable and transferable. For example, on a bill of lading "to order" means that it is negotiable and transferable by the person or entity whose name appears on the document.

total average inventory
(logistics) (a) (general) The average of total stock on hand over a specified period of time. (b) (technical) Average normal use inventory plus average lead inventory plus buffer stock inventory.

total cost analysis
(logistics) A systems approach to assessing the costs and interrelationships of transportation, warehousing, inventory and customer service in relation to providing logistics services.

total cost of distribution
(shipping) The sum total of all the costs incurred in the distribution of goods. The total cost of distribution includes such items as: (1) Transportation charges, (2) Inventory carrying costs, (3) Warehousing expenses, (4) Packaging, (5) Insurance, (6) Product obsolescence while en route or in storage, and (7) Pilferage.

total loss
(insurance) An actual total loss occurs when the goods are destroyed, when the assured is irretrievably deprived of their possession or when they arrive so damaged as to cease to be a thing of the kind insured. Examples of this last, which is spoken of as a "loss of specie," are cement arriving as rock or textiles as rags. Disasters likely to give rise to total loss include fire, sinking or stranding of the vessel, collision and loss overboard in the course of loading or discharge.

tracer
(shipping) (a) A request upon a transportation line to trace a shipment for the purpose of expediting its movement or establishing delivery;
(general/banking) (b) A request for an answer to a communication, or for advice concerning the status of a subject.

tracking; tracing
(shipping) A carrier's system of recording movement intervals of shipments from origin to destination.

tractor
(shipping) A vehicle with four or more wheels designed and used primarily for drawing other vehicles such as a trailer or semitrailer and not designed to carry a load itself other than part of the weight of the vehicle and load being drawn.

Trade Act of 1974
(U.S. law) Legislation enacted late in 1974 and signed into law in January 1975, granting the president broad authority to enter into international agreements to reduce import barriers. Major purposes were to: (1) stimulate U.S. economic growth and to maintain and enlarge foreign markets for the products of U.S. agriculture, industry, mining and commerce; (2) strengthen economic relations with other countries through open and non-discriminatory trading practices; (3) protect American industry and workers against unfair or injurious import competition; and (4) provide "adjustment assistance" to industries, workers and communities injured or threatened by increased imports. The Act allowed the president to extend tariff preferences to certain imports from developing countries and set conditions under which Most-Favored-Nation Treatment could be extended to non-market economy countries and provided negotiating authority for the Tokyo Round of multilateral trade negotiations. *See* trade adjustment assistance; most favored nation; Tokyo Round.

trade adjustment assistance (TAA)
(U.S.) TAA for firms and workers is authorized by the 1974 Trade Act. TAA for firms is administered by the U.S. Department of Commerce; TAA for workers is administered by the U.S. Department of Labor.
Eligible firms must show that increased imports of articles like or directly competitive with those produced by the firm contributed importantly to declines in its sales and/or production and to the separation or threat of separation of a significant portion of the firm's workers. These firms receive help through Trade Adjustment Assistance Centers (TAACs), primarily in implementing adjustment strategies in production, marketing, and management.
Eligible workers must be associated with a firm whose sales or production have decreased absolutely due to increases in like or directly competitive imported products resulting in total or partial separation of the employee and the decline in the firm's sales or production. Assistance includes training, job search and relocation allowances, plus reemployment services for workers adversely affected by the increased imports.

See United States Department of Commerce; United States Department of Labor.

Trade Adjustment Assistance Centers

(U.S.) TAACs are nonprofit, nongovernment organizations established to help firms qualify for and receive assistance in adjusting to import competition. TAACs are funded by the U.S. Department of Commerce as a primary source of technical assistance to certified firms. Trade Adjustment Assistance Centers; E-mail: info@taacenters.org; Web: www.taacenters.org. *See* trade adjustment assistance; United States Department of Commerce.

Trade Agreements Act of 1979

(U.S.) Legislation authorizing the U.S. to implement trade agreements dealing with non-tariff barriers negotiated during the Tokyo Round of the General Agreement on Tariffs and Trade (GATT), including agreements that required changes in existing U.S. laws, and certain concessions that had not been explicitly authorized by the Trade Act of 1974. The Act incorporated into U.S. law the Tokyo Round (GATT) agreements on dumping, customs valuation, import licensing procedures, government procurement practices, product standards, civil aircraft, meat and dairy products, and liquor duties. The Act also extended the president's authority to negotiate trade agreements with foreign countries to reduce or eliminate non-tariff barriers to trade. *See* General Agreement on Tariffs and Trade; Tokyo Round.

Trade and Development Agency (TDA)

(U.S.) Initially started as the Trade and Development Program within the Agency for International Development, the TDA was spun off as an independent agency in 1981. TDA offers tied aid and resembles Japan's tied aid funding. The program provides project planning funding only for projects that are priorities of the host country and present a good opportunity for sales of U.S. goods and services. Contact: Trade and Development Agency; 1621 North Kent Street, Suite 200; Arlington, VA 22209-2131 USA; Tel: [1] (703) 875-4357; Fax: [1] (703) 875-4009; E-mail: info@tda.gov; Web: www.tda.gov.

trade balance

See current balance; balance of payments.

trade barriers

Any one or group of tariff or non-tariff barriers to trade often classified into eight general categories: (1) import policies (tariffs and other import charges, quantitative restrictions, import licensing, and customs barriers); (2) standards, testing, labeling, and certification; (3) government procurement; (4) export subsidies; (5) lack of intellectual property protection; (6) service barriers; (7) investment barriers; and (8) other barriers (e.g., barriers encompassing more than one category or barriers affecting a single sector). *See* technical barrier to trade; tariff; quota.

trade concordance

Trade concordance refers to the matching of Harmonized System (HS) codes to larger statistical definitions, such as the Standard Industrial Classification (SIC) code and the Standard International Trade Classification (SITC) system. The U.S. Bureau of the Census, the United Nations, as well as individual U.S. Federal and private organizations, maintain trade concordances for the purpose of relating trade and production data. *See* Harmonized System.

trade credit

(commerce) (a) Credit extended to a customer (e.g., a businesses, a government or government agency, non-profit organization or individual) for the sale of goods or services. (b) Credit extended by one government to another for the purchase of exports. (c) The accounts receivable and/or trade acceptances of a business purchased by a bank or financial institution, at a discount for immediate payment.

trade deficit

(economics) A nation's excess of imports over exports over a period of time.

trade event

A promotional activity that may include a demonstration of products or services and brings together in one viewing area the principals in the purchase and sale of the products or services. As a generic term, trade events may include trade fairs, trade missions, trade shows, catalog shows, matchmaker events, foreign buyer missions, and similar functions.

Trade Expansion Act of 1962

(U.S. law) The Act provided authority for U.S. participation in the Kennedy Round of the General Agreement on Tariffs and Trade (GATT). The legislation granted the president general authority to negotiate, on a reciprocal basis, reductions of up to 50 percent in U.S. tariffs. The Act explicitly eliminated the "Peril Point" provision that had limited U.S. negotiating positions in earlier GATT Rounds, and instead called on the Tariff Commission, the U.S. International Trade Commission, and other federal agencies to provide information regarding the probable economic effects of specific tariff concessions. This Act superseded the Trade Agreements Act of 1934, as amended. *See* General Agreement on Tariffs and Trade; peril point.

trade fair

A stage-setting event in which firms of several nationalities present their products or services to prospective customers in a pre-formatted setting (usually a booth of a certain size which is located adjacent to other potential suppliers). A distinguishing factor between trade fairs and trade shows is size. A trade fair is generally viewed as having a larger number of participants than other trade events, or as an event bringing together related industries.

Trade Fair Certification Program

(U.S.) The U.S. Department of Commerce Trade Fair Certification program was started in 1983 to promote selected privately organized trade shows. The program helps private sector organizations in mounting certified international fairs. The Department of Commerce assistance includes promoting the fair among foreign customers and helping exhibitors to make commercial contacts. *See* United States Department of Commerce.

Trade Information Center

(U.S.) A U.S. government one-stop source for information on Federal programs to assist U.S. exporters; Tel: [1] (800) USA-TRADE, [1] (800) 872-8723). Address: Trade Information Center, U.S. Department of Commerce, 14th St. and Constitution Ave. NW, Washington, DC 20230 USA; Web: www.ita.doc.gov/td/tic.

trade lane

(logistics) A carrier route between a point of origin and a point of destination.

trade loss

(insurance) The ordinary and unavoidable loss of weight caused by evaporation as in ore shipments. May also include shortages due to other causes which are considered normal and unavoidable. These losses are generally uninsurable.

trademark

(law) A distinctive identification of a manufactured product or of a service taking the form of a name, logo, motto, and so on; a trademarked brand has legal protection and only the owner can use the mark. A trademark is distinguished from a servicemark in that the former identifies products while the later identifies services.

Trademark protection varies from country to country, and may not be available in some jurisdictions. If trademark protection is available under the laws of a particular country, a trademark may usually be registered only if it is distinguishable from other registered trademarks and if it contains a name, brand, label, signature, word, letter, numeral, device, or any combination of these items. A country that is a member the Paris Convention for the Protection of Industrial Property may recognize trademarks held in other jurisdictions.

(U.S.) Organizations that file an application at the U.S. Patent Office and use the brand for five years may be granted a trademark. A firm may lose a trademark that has become generic. Generic names are those which consumers use to identify the product, rather than to specify a particular brand (e.g., escalator, aspirin and nylon).

See copyright; service mark; patent; World Intellectual Property Organization; Patent Cooperation Treaty.

trade mission

Generically, a trade mission is composed of individuals who are taken as a group to meet with prospective customers overseas. Missions visit specific individuals or places with no specific stage setting other than appointments. Appointments are made with government and/or commercial customers, or with individuals who may be a stepping stone to customers.

(U.S.) International Trade Administration (ITA) trade missions are scheduled in selected countries to help participants find local agents, representatives, and distributors, to make direct sales, or to conduct market assessments. Some missions include technical seminars to support sales of sophisticated products and technology in specific markets. ITA missions include planning and publicity, appointments with qualified contacts and with government officials, market briefings and background information on contacts, as well as logistical support and interpreter service. Trade missions also are frequently organized by other Federal, State, or local agencies.

trade name

(law) The name under which an organization conducts business, or by which the business or its goods and services are identified. It may or may not be registered as a trademark.

Trade Negotiations Committee

(WTO/GATT) The steering group that historically has managed the GATT and WTO trade negotiation rounds. For information on the Trade Negotiations Committee for the 9th (current) round of negotiations, go to the WTO's Web site at Web: www.wto.org/english/tratop_e/dda_e/tnc_e.htm. *See* rounds (of trade negotiations), General Agreement on Tariffs and Trade, World Trade Organization.

tradeoffs

(shipping) Interaction between related activities such as the offsetting of higher costs in one area with reduced costs or other benefits in another. In air freight, for example, the classic "tradeoff" is one of time (quick delivery) versus money (greater expense).

Trade Opportunities Program (TOP)

(U.S.) An International Trade Administration service which provides sales leads from overseas firms seeking to buy or represent U.S. products and services. Through overseas channels, U.S. foreign commercial officers gather leads and details, including specifications, quantities, end use, and delivery deadlines. TOP leads can be obtained in an electronic format from the Commerce Department's STAT-USA hotline at [1] (800) STAT-USA or through the Department's STAT-USA/Internet service at Web: www.stat-usa.com.

Trade Policy Committee (TPC)

(U.S.) A cabinet-level, interagency trade committee established by the Trade Expansion Act of 1962 (chaired by the U.S. Trade Representative) to provide broad guidance on trade issues. Members include the Secretaries of Commerce, State, Treasury, Agriculture, and Labor. The Committee was renewed by an Executive Order at the end of the Carter Administration. Toward the end of the first Reagan Administration, with much dissension over Japan policy between the TPC, the Senior Interagency Group (chaired by Treasury), and the other groups, the White House created the Economic Policy Council (EPC) in 1985 as a single forum to reduce tensions. *See* Economic Policy Council.

Trade Policy Review Mechanism

The TPRM was created at the General Agreement on Tariffs and Trade (GATT) Uruguay Round midterm ministerial meeting in Montreal. Under the TPRM, the trade policies of any GATT contracting party were subject to regularly scheduled review by the GATT Council. Reviews led to recommendations on ways to improve a contracting party's trade policies. *See* General Agreements on Tariffs and Trade; Uruguay Round.

Trade Promotion Coordinating Committee

(U.S.) The president established the TPCC in May 1990 to unify and streamline the government's decentralized approach to export promotion. TPCC members include Departments of Commerce (as chair), State, Treasury, Agriculture, Defense, Energy, and Transportation, the Office of Management and Budget, the U.S. Trade Representative, the Council of Economic Advisers, Eximbank, the Overseas Private Investment Corporation, the U.S. Information Agency, the Agency for International Development, the Trade and Development Program, and the Small Business Administration. The TPCC chair office is at the U.S. Department of Commerce. 19 agencies are on the committee. The Trade Information Center was created as one of the main missions of the TPCC. The TPCC is not a body which would be contacted by the general public. If you have questions about what they do, or how it works, call [1] (800) USA-TRADE or visit http://tradecenter.ntis.gov/tpcc.htm.

trade-related aspects of intellectual property rights (TRIPs)

(WTO) TRIPs refers to intellectual property rights objectives in the General Agreement on Tariffs and Trade (GATT) Uruguay Round and the successor World Trade Organization (WTO). These objectives include achieving a comprehensive agreement that would include: (1) substantive standards of protection for all areas of intellectual property (patents, trademarks, copyrights, etc.); (2) effective enforcement measures (both at the border and internally);

and (3) effective dispute settlement provisions. *See* Uruguay Round, World Trade Organization.

trade show

A trade show is a stage-setting event in which firms present their products or services to prospective customers in a pre-formatted setting (usually a booth of a certain size which is located adjacent to other potential suppliers). The firms are generally in the same industry but not necessarily of the same nationality. A distinguishing factor between trade fairs and trade shows is size. A trade show is generally viewed as a smaller assembly of participants.

trade surplus

(economics) A nation's excess of exports over imports over a period of time.

Trade Tariff Act of 1930

(U.S. law) U.S. statutes originally enacted in 1930 and amended periodically that impose duties payable for the importation of articles into the United States and that contain schedules of the duties for specific merchandise. The Act is found at 19 United States Code, sections 1202, et seq.

trade terms

(a) The terms of a sale. The setting of responsibilities of the buyer and seller in a sale, including: sale price, responsibility for shipping, insurance and customs duties. (b) One of the several recognized sets of definitions of trade terms. The most widely used trade terms are Incoterms 2000, which are published by the International Chamber of Commerce, which have replaced the now obsolete Revised American Foreign Trade Definitions. *See* Incoterms; International Chamber of Commerce.

trade-weighted revaluation rate

(foreign exchange) The change in value of a currency is ascertained in terms of an index against a basket of currencies. The make-up of the currencies in the basket and their weighting are determined according to the percentage of exports of the country whose currency is to be valued with its trading partners.

trailer

(logistics/trucking) A non-motorized cargo vehicle supported by wheels at each of four corners and designed to be drawn by a motorized vehicle such as a tractor. *See* semitrailer, tractor.

trailer on flatcar (TOFC)

(logistics/trucking/rail transport) A truck trailer or semitrailer transported on a rail flatcar. This is a multi-modal form of transportation often used when the rail leg of the route is less costly than transportation by roadway. Also called piggyback. *See* trailer.

tramp line

(shipping) A transportation line operating tramp steamers.

tramp steamer

(shipping) A steamship which does not operate under any regular schedule from one port to another, but calls at any port where cargo may be obtained.

transaction value

(general) The price actually paid or payable for merchandise.

(U.S. Customs) U.S. Customs officers are required by law to determine the value of imported merchandise. Valuation is necessary for statistical purposes as well as to determine the amount of import duty which must be paid if the duty rate is stated as a percentage of value (ad valorem duty).

The transaction value of imported merchandise is the price actually paid or payable for the merchandise when sold for exportation to the United States, plus amounts for the following items if not included in the price:

(1) The packing costs incurred by the buyer.

(2) Any selling commission incurred by the buyer,

(3) The value of any assist,

(4) Any royalty or license fee that the buyer is required to pay as a condition of the sale, and

(5) The proceeds, accruing to the seller, of any subsequent resale, disposal, or use of the imported merchandise.

The amounts for the above items are added only to the extent that each is not included in the price actually paid or payable and information is available to establish the accuracy of the amount. If sufficient information is not available, then the transaction value cannot be determined and the next basis of value, in order of precedence, must be considered for appraisement.

If the transaction value cannot be used, then certain secondary bases are considered. The secondary bases of value, listed in order of precedence for use, are:

(1) Transaction value of identical merchandise,

(2) Transaction value of similar merchandise,

(3) Deductive value, and

(4) Computed value.

The order of precedence of the last two values can be reversed if the importer so requests.

See valuation; identical merchandise; similar merchandise; computed value; deductive value; assist.

transferable letter of credit

(banking) A letter of credit where the beneficiary specified in the credit has the option of instructing his bank to transfer the credit fully or in part to another beneficiary.

A letter of credit can only be transferred if it is expressly designated as "transferable" by the issuing bank. This type of letter of credit enables intermediaries (first beneficiaries) to offer security in the form of a letter of credit to their suppliers (second beneficiaries). *See* letter of credit.

transfer of technology

The movement of modern or scientific methods of production or distribution from one enterprise, institution or country to another, as through foreign investment, international trade licensing of patent rights, technical assistance or training.

transfer pricing

(law/customs) The overpricing of imports and/or underpricing of exports between affiliated companies in different countries for the purpose of transferring profits, revenues or monies out of a country in order to evade taxes.

transfer risk

(banking) Currency measures of foreign governments which make it impossible for the debtor to allocate and transfer foreign exchange abroad. Transfer risks can be covered through use of bank guarantees, confirmed letters of credits, export credit agencies, etc.

transfers (mail, wire, cable)

(banking) Transfers are the remittance of money by a bank to be paid to a party in another town or city. If the instruction to pay such funds is transmitted by regular mail, the term "mail transfer" is used. Wire transfer is used to designate a transfer of funds from one point to another by wire or telegraph. Cable transfer is used to designate a transfer of funds to a city or town located outside the United States by cable. Commissions or fees are charged for all typed of transfers. When transfers are made by wire or cable, the cost of transmitting the instructions to pay by wire or cable is charged to the remitter in addition to the commission.

Transit Air Cargo Manifest

(shipping-U.S.) Procedures under which air cargo imports move through a gateway city to the city of final U.S. Customs destination for the collection of duty and other import processing, thereby expediting shipment movements, reducing gateway congestion, and saving expense for importers, the U.S. Customs Service, and the airlines.

transit zone

(shipping) A port of entry in a coastal country that is established as a storage and distribution center for the convenience of a neighboring country lacking adequate port facilities or access to the sea. A zone is administered so that goods in transit to and from the neighboring country are not subject to the customs duties, import controls or many of the entry and exit formalities of the host country. A transit zone is a more limited facility then a free trade zone or a free port.

transmittal letter

(shipping) A list of the particulars of a shipment and a record of the documents being transmitted together with instructions for disposition of documents. Any special instructions are also included.

T

Trans-Pacific Stabilization Agreement (TSA)

(logistics) An organization of twelve ocean freight carriers controlling approximately 85 percent of Pacific Ocean freight trade who seek a platform for discussing and sharing mutual concerns. The TSA is not in itself a conference and does not publish rates. The TSA enjoys antitrust immunity although the U.S. Ocean Shipping Reform Act (OSRA) of 1998 has curtailed a significant amount of the group's influence. The TSA consists of the Japan-United States Eastbound Freight Conference (JUSEFC), the Asia North America Eastbound Freight Rate Agreement (ANAERA) and four major non-conference carriers. The twelve members are: APL, Mark Island, NYK, P&O, Hapag-Lloyd, Hyundai, Hanjin, Evergreen, Yang Ming, Orient Overseas Container Lines (OOCL), Cosco and MOL (Mitsui OSK Lines).

transparency

The extent to which laws, regulations, agreements, and practices affecting international trade are open, clear, measurable, and verifiable.

(GATT/WTO) Some of the codes of conduct negotiated during the Tokyo Round of the General Agreement on Tariff and Trade sought to increase the transparency of non-tariff barriers that impede trade. *See* General Agreement on Tariff and Trade, World Trade Organization.

Transparency International

A non-profit, non-governmental organization dedicated to counter corrupt international business and government practices. The organization's stated concerns include: 1) humanitarian, as corruption undermines and distorts development and leads to increasing levels of human rights abuse, 2) democratic, as corruption undermines democracies and in particular the achievements of many developing countries and countries in transition, 3) ethical, as corruption undermines a society's integrity, and 4) practical, as corruption distorts the operations of markets and deprives ordinary people of the benefits which should flow from them. The organization is headquartered in Germany and has chapter offices around the world. Transparency International; Otto-Suhr-Allee 97/99; 10585 Berlin; Germany; Tel: [49] (30) 343 8200; Fax: [49] (30) 3470 3912; E-mail: ti@transparency.org; Web: www.transparency.org.

transportation and exportation entry

(U.S. Customs) Customs entry used when merchandise arrives in the U.S. and is destined for a foreign country. Under a transportation and exportation entry, merchandise may be transported in bond through U.S. territory. For example, a transportation and exportation entry would be used for merchandise destined for Canada, arriving in Seattle, from Japan. *See* entry; in bond.

transport documents

(shipping) All types of documents evidencing acceptance, receipt and shipment of goods. Examples: bill of lading; ocean bill of lading; air waybill; rail waybill; dock receipt; etc.

transship

(logistics) The transfer of freight from one conveyance or carrier to another, or from one ship to another of different ownership.

(economics/commerce) The transfer of merchandise from the country-of-origin to an intermediary country prior to shipment to the destination country for purposes of 1) achieving a lower transport cost, 2) legally or illegally achieving new country of origin status for the merchandise or 3) circumventing the foreign trade policies of the country of origin or the country of destination.

Travel Advisories

(U.S.) Reports by the U.S. Department of State to inform traveling U.S. citizens of conditions abroad which may affect them adversely. Travel advisories are generally about physical dangers, unexpected arrests or detention, serious health hazards, and other conditions abroad with serious consequences for traveling U.S. citizens. Travel advisories are available at any of the U.S. passport agencies, field offices of the U.S. Department of Commerce and U.S. Embassies and consulates abroad. They are also available at the Bureau of Consular Affairs, Room 4811, N.S., U.S. Department of State, Washington, DC 20520 USA; Tel: [1] (202) 647-5225; http://travel.state.gov.

traveler

(U.S.) A traveler is a person who stays for a period of less than 1 year in a country of which he or she is not a resident. Military and other government personnel and their dependents stationed outside their country of residence are not considered travelers, regardless of the length of their stay abroad; they are considered to have remained within the economy of their home country. The definition of travelers also excludes owners or employees of business enterprises who temporarily work abroad in order to further the enterprise's business, but intend to return to their country of residence within a reasonable period of time.

traveler's checks

(banking) A form of check especially designed for travelers, including persons on vacation and business trips. These checks are usually preprinted in denominations of US$10, 20, 50, and 100, as well as in other currencies such as the euro and British pounds Sterling. They can be cashed and used to purchase goods and services at businesses that accept them.

traveler's letter of credit

(banking) A letter of credit issued by a bank to a customer preparing for an extended trip. The customer pays for the letter of credit, which is issued for a specified period of time in the amount purchased. The bank furnishes a list of correspondent banks or its own foreign branches at which drafts drawn against the letter of credit will be honored. *See* letter of credit.

Travel Industry Association of America (TIA)

Organizer of the International POW WOW. Address: Travel Industry Association of America, 2 Lafayette Center, 1100 New York Ave. NW, Suite 450, Washington, DC 20005-3934 USA; Tel: [1] (202) 408-8422; Fax: [1] (202) 408-1255; Web: www.tia.org. *See* International POW WOW.

travel mission

See trade mission.

Treaty of Fusion

See European Community.

Treaty of Rome

The 1957 Treaty of Rome was intended to create a single market for the European Community, with free movement of goods, persons, services, and capital. Article 30 of the Treaty prohibited not only quantitative restrictions on imports but also all measures having an equivalent effect. *See* European Community.

triangular trade

(trade) Trade between three countries, in which an attempt is made to create a favorable balance for each.

trigger price mechanism

(U.S.) System for monitoring imported goods (particularly steel) to identify imports that are possibly being "dumped" in the United States or subsidized by the governments of exporting countries. The minimum price under this system is based on the estimated landed cost at a U.S. port of entry of the product produced by the world's most efficient producers.

Imported products entering the United States below that price may "trigger" formal anti-dumping investigations by the Department of Commerce and the U.S. International Trade Commission. The TPM was first used to protect the U.S. steel industry and was in effect between early 1978 and March 1980. It was reinstated in October 1980 and suspended for all products except for stainless steel wire in January 1982. *See* dumping.

tri-temp

(shipping) A container that can maintain three exact temperature zones in difference compartments simultaneously.

tropical products

Traditionally, agricultural goods of export interest to developing countries in the tropical zones of Africa, Latin America, and East Asia (coffee, tea, spices, bananas, and tropical hardwoods).

truck/air service

(shipping) The surface movement of air freight to and from airports and origin and destination points beyond the terminal area of pickup and delivery service. A directory listing cities served is available through your local airline office.

truck bill of lading

(logistics) A non-negotiable bill of lading used for domestic shipments by truck. This bill of lading is issued in either a short or long form but with freight rates and charges not shown. Any party may sign to verify receipt of goods unless the bill is marked as "signature service," which requires that the party named by the shipper sign to confirm delivery of goods. *See* bill of lading.

truck load

A shipment of cargo that fills a given truck either by bulk or maximum weight.

truckload (TL) carrier

(logistics/trucking) A trucking company that specializes in hauling a trailerload or more of freight at a time for individual shippers, typically delivering to a final destination location directly rather than to a terminal. Compare to an LTL (less than truckload) carrier that carries consolidated cargo for a number of shippers on the same truck and typically delivers the entire load to a terminal before making individual deliveries.

trust bank (shintaku ginko)

(banking-Japan) Japanese bank involved in both lending and money management.

trust receipt

(banking) A declaration by a client to a bank that ownership in goods released by the bank are retained by the bank, and that the client has received the goods in trust only.

Release of merchandise by a bank to a buyer in which the bank retains title to the merchandise. The buyer, who obtains the goods for manufacturing or sales purposes, is obligated to maintain the goods (or the proceeds from their sale) distinct from the remainder of his/her assets and to hold them ready for repossession by the bank.

Trust receipts are used under letters of credit or collections so that the buyer may receive the goods before paying the issuing bank or collecting bank. *See* documentary collection; letter of credit.

tugrik

The currency of Mongolia. 1Tug=100 mongos.

turnkey

A method of construction whereby the contractor assumes total responsibility from design through completion of the project (and then hands over the "key" to the owner).

turnkey contract

An agreement under which a builder agrees to complete a facility so that it is ready for use when delivered to the other contracting party. A contractor may agree, for example, to build a fully equipped and operational factory under a turnkey contract. The responsibility of the contractor ends when he hands the completed installation over to the client.

twenty-foot equivalent unit

See TEU.

two-tier market

(foreign exchange) An exchange rate regime which normally insulates a country from the balance of payments effects of capital flows while it maintains a stable exchange rate for current account transactions. Capital transactions are normally required to pass through a "financial" market while current transactions go through an "official" market, though other arrangements are possible. Examples are found in Belgium and the United Kingdom, though France and Italy have experimented with such systems.

tying arrangement

(law) A condition that a seller imposes on a buyer, requiring that if the buyer desires to purchase one product (tying product), the buyer must also agree to purchase another product (tied product), which the buyer may or may not want. The laws of some countries prohibit certain tying arrangements.

U

ULD

See unit load device.

ultimate beneficial owner (UBO)

(U.S.) The UBO of a U.S. affiliate is that person, proceeding up the affiliate's ownership chain beginning with and including the foreign parent, that is not owned more than 50 percent by another person. The UBO consists of only the ultimate owner, other affiliated persons are excluded. If the foreign parent is not owned more than 50 percent by another person, the foreign parent and the UBO are the same. A UBO, unlike a foreign parent, may be a U.S. person.

ultimate consignee

(shipping) The person who is the true party in interest, receiving goods for the designated end-use.

ultimo day

(finance/foreign exchange) The last business day or last stock trading day of a month.

ultra vires

(law) An act performed without authority to do so. If a contract provision, for example, requires both parties to approve an assignment of the contract but one party agrees to an assignment without obtaining the other's consent, the assignment is ultra vires.

umbrella rate

(logistics) A shipping rate system that establishes artificially high minimum rates in order to protect less competitive carriers and carrier modes.

unclean bill of lading

See claused bill of lading; bill of lading; ocean bill of lading.

unconfirmed

(banking) A documentary letter of credit where the advising bank makes no commitment to pay, accept or negotiate. *See* letter of credit; silent confirmation.

unconscionable

(law) Unfair or oppressive. A contract with unconscionable terms, for example, favors one party over the other to such an extent that it is unjust, and if the oppressed party made the contract under duress or without meaningful negotiation as to the terms, a court may refuse to enforce it against that party.

underdeveloped country

(economics) A nation in which per capita real income is proportionately low when contrasted with the per capita real income of nations where industry flourishes. *See also* less developed countries; least developed country; lesser developed country.

Underwriters Laboratory Inc. (UL)

(international standards) An independent not-for-profit product safety testing and certification organization. Founded in 1894 in the U.S., UL has developed more than 740 product safety standards and a reputation as the leader in U.S. product safety and certification. The organization is also rapidly becoming one of the most recognized conformity assessment providers in the world. Each year 16 billion UL Marks are applied to products worldwide. Contact at Web: www.ul.com.

UN/EDIFACT

(logistics) Acronym for United Nations [rules for] Electronic Data Interchange for Administration, Commerce and Transportation. A set of standards, directories and guidelines for the electronic interchange, between computer systems, of structured data and documents, especially those that relate to the international trade in goods and services. For information: Web: www.unece.org/trade/untdid/welcome/htm. *See* EDI.

unfair trade practice

(general) Unusual government support to firms— such as export subsidies to certain anti-competitive practices by firms themselves—such as dumping, boycotts or discriminatory shipping arrangements— that result in competitive advantages for the benefiting firms in international trade.

(U.S.) Any act, policy, or practice of a foreign government that: (1) violates, is inconsistent with, or otherwise denies benefits to the U.S. under any trade agreement to which the United States is a party; (2) is unjustifiable, unreasonable, or discriminatory and burdens or restricts United States commerce; or (3) is otherwise inconsistent with a favorable Section 301 determination by the U.S. Trade Representative. *See* Section 301; dumping.

Uniform Code Council (UCC)

(international standards) An independent not-for-profit standards organization dedicated to the development and distribution of integrated business standards. The UCC administers the Universal Product Code (UPC) and provides other open and global standards for supply chain and business processes in its partnership with EAN (European Article Number) International. The UCC is a primary resource for businesses and provides publications and training in all aspects of identification numbers, bar coding, and electronic commerce. Uniform Code Council; Web: www.uc-council.org.

Uniform Commercial Code (UCC)

(U.S. law) A set of statutes purporting to provide some consistency among states' commercial laws. It includes uniform laws dealing with bills of lading, negotiable instruments, sales, stock transfers, trust receipts, and warehouse receipts.

Uniform Customs and Practice (UCP)

(banking) Full name: Uniform Customs and Practice for Documentary Credits (UCPDC). The internationally recognized codification of rules unifying banking practice regarding documentary credits (letters of credit).

The UCPDC was developed by a working group attached to the International Chamber of Commerce (ICC) in Paris, France. It is revised and updated from time to time and the current valid version as of January 1, 1994 is ICC Publication 500 which is the 1993 edition.

It is highly recommended that all documentary credits (letters of credit) specify that they are subject to the UCPDC. *See* letter of credit; International Chamber of Commerce; and the Appendix for a listing of ICC publications that relate to the UCPDC.

Uniform Rules for Collections (URC)

(banking) The internationally recognized codification of rules unifying banking practice regarding collection operations for drafts, their payment or non-payment, protest and for documentary collections, (documents against payment, D/P, and documents against acceptance, D/A).

The URC was developed by a working group attached to the International Chamber of Commerce (ICC) in Paris, France. It is revised and updated from time to time and the current valid version as of January 1, 1994 is ICC Publication 322.

See documentary collection; International Chamber of Commerce; and the Appendix for a listing of ICC publications that relate to the URC.

Uniform Warehouse Receipts Act

(U.S. logistics) An act establishing management responsibilities and documentation requirements for public warehouses.

unit cost

(logistics) (a) The total of all costs associated with the production of a single unit of a product or service. (b) The total of all costs associated with a production run of a product or service divided by the total number of units produced.

United Nations Conference on Trade and Development (UNCTAD)

UNCTAD was set up in December 1964 as a permanent organ of the UN General Assembly. UNCTAD promotes international trade and seeks to increase trade between developing countries and countries with different social and economic systems. UNCTAD also examines problems of economic development within the context of principles and policies of international trade and seeks to harmonize trade, development, and regional economic policies. The Conference was first convened (UNCTAD-1) in Geneva in 1964.

United Nations Convention on Contracts for the International Sale of Goods (CISG)

(law) A United Nations-sponsored multilateral treaty containing a commercial code that governs the rights and responsibilities of buyers and sellers in international sales contracts. The CISG was designed to foster international trade by establishing a unified legal framework for the sale of goods internationally. The CISG was finalized at a United Nations conference held in Vienna in 1980 and as a result is sometimes referred to as the Vienna Sales Convention.

There are many similarities between the U.S. UCC (Uniform Commercial Code) and the UN CISG which both serve to avoid misunderstandings when one set of rules govern the buyer and another set of rules govern the seller. The U.S. UCC is designed to avoid differences in the laws of the fifty U.S. states while the CISG is designed to avoid misunderstandings in the laws of the countries of the world.

The CISG specifically does not apply to the sale of services or labor and as a result agreements involving distribution, licensing, leasing, transportation, carriage, insurance and financing are generally not covered. The CISG does not apply to the sale of goods for consumption directly by consumers; goods sold at auction; securities or negotiable instruments; ships, vessels or aircraft; or electricity. The CISG also does not cover liabilities or injuries caused by goods.

Transactions for the sale of computer software, the sale of both goods and services, or sales of leases with purchase options are considered gray areas where the validity of the CISG is in question and subject to legal challenge. For a list of related Web resources see Web: www.uncitral.org/english/links.htm and scroll down to the CISG heading.

United Nations Industrial Development Organization (UNIDO)

Established in 1967, under the UN Secretariat, UNIDO serves as a specialized agency to foster industrial development in lesser developed countries through offering technical assistance in the form of expert services, supplying equipment and/or training. Address: United Nations Industrial Development Organization, PO Box 300, 1400 Vienna, Austria; Tel: [43] (1) 26-026; Fax: [43] (1) 26-92-669; Web: www.unido.org.

United States Affiliate

(U.S. foreign investment) A U.S. business enterprise in which there is foreign direct investment–that is, in which a single foreign person owns or controls, directly or indirectly, 10 percent or more of its voting securities if the enterprise is incorporated or an equivalent interest if the enterprise is unincorporated. The affiliate is called a U.S. affiliate to denote that the affiliate is located in the U.S. (although it is owned by a foreign person). *See* foreign person; affiliate.

United States and Foreign Commercial Service (US&FCS)

(U.S.) An agency of the U.S. Department of Commerce that helps U.S. firms compete more effectively in the global marketplace. The US&FCS (more commonly known as the U.S. Commercial Service) has a network of trade specialists in 68 U.S. cities and 66 countries worldwide. US&FCS offices provide information on foreign markets, agent/distributor location services, trade leads, and counseling on business opportunities, trade barriers and prospects abroad. Contact: Tel: [1] (800) USA-TRADE; E-mail: TIC@ita.doc.gov; Web: www.usa-trade.gov.

United States-Canada Free Trade Agreement (FTA)

The provisions of the U.S./Canada Free Trade Agreement were adopted by the U.S. with the enactment of the FTA Implementation Act of 1988. The FTA not only reduced tariffs on imported merchandise between Canada and the U.S., but opened up new areas of trade in investment services, agriculture, and business travel. In order to be eligible for FTA treatment, goods must not enter the commerce of a third country, or, if shipped through a third country, must remain under customs control.

Several publications about the United States-Canada Free Trade Agreement are available from: the National Technical Information Service (NTIS), Springfield, VA 22161; Tel: [1] (703) 605-6000; Web: www.ntis.gov.

Other sources of information about the agreement can be obtained from the Office of North American Affairs, Office of the United States Trade Representative (USTR), 600 17th St. NW, Washington, DC 20508 USA; Tel: [1] (888) 473-8787.

United States Code (USC)

(U.S. law) A set of volumes containing the official compilation of U.S. law. A new edition of the USC is printed every six years with supplemental volumes issued every year. The USC is found in larger public libraries and is available for purchase from the Superintendent of Documents, U.S. Government Printing Office, Washington, DC 20402 USA; Tel: (866) 512-1800, and at Web: www.access.gpo.gov. There are also local offices of the U.S. Government Printing Office in major U.S. cities.

United States Customs House Guide

(publication) A comprehensive resource for importing goods to the U.S., covering three major topics: 1) Ports of Entry (U.S. and Canadian) and U.S. Import Regulations, 2) the U.S. Harmonized Tariff Schedule and 3) Trade Services Directory and Guide. Available as a print product and as an online service. Contact: Commonwealth Business Media, Inc.; 400

Windsor Corporate Center; 50 Millstone Road, Suite 200; East Windsor, New Jersey 08520 USA; Tel: [1] (800) 221-5488; Fax: [1] (609) 371-7718; Web: www.cbizmedia.com.

United States Customs Service

(U.S. Customs) U.S. governmental agency, whose major responsibility is to administer the Tariff Act of 1930, as amended. Primary duties include the assessment and collection of all duties, taxes and fees on imported merchandise, and the enforcement of customs and related laws and treaties. As a major enforcement organization, the Customs Service combats smuggling and fraud on the revenue and enforces the regulations of numerous other federal agencies at ports of entry and along the land and sea borders of the U.S.

The customs territory of the United States consists of the 50 states, the District of Columbia, and Puerto Rico. The Customs Service, an agency under the Department of Treasury, has its headquarters in Washington, DC and is headed by a Commissioner of Customs. The field organization consists of seven geographical regions further divided into districts with ports of entry within each district. These organizational elements are headed respectively by regional commissioners, district directors (or area directors in the case of the New York Region), and port directors. The Customs Service is also responsible for administering the customs laws of the Virgin Islands of the United States.

Address: U.S. Customs Service Headquarters, 1300 Pennsylvania Avenue NW, Washington, DC 20229 USA; Tel: [1] (202) 927-1770; Web: www.customs.ustreas.gov.

U.S. Customs regional and district offices are in Boston, Massachusetts; New York, NY; Miami, Florida; New Orleans, Louisiana; Houston, Texas; Los Angeles, California; and Chicago, Illinois.

The U.S. Customs Service also has offices in Austria, Belgium, Canada, France, Hong Kong, Italy, Japan, Korea, Mexico, The Netherlands, Panama, Singapore, Thailand, The United Kingdom, Uruguay, and Germany. These offices are a part of the U.S. Embassy complex in each country.

United States Department of Agriculture (DOA)

(U.S. government) An executive department which serves as the principal adviser to the president on agricultural policy. The Department works to improve and maintain farm income, implement nutrition programs and develop and expand markets abroad for U.S. agricultural products. It is also charged with inspecting and grading food products for safe consumption. Organizations within the Department of Agriculture include: Agricultural Marketing Service, Agricultural Stabilization and Conservation Service, Animal and Plant Inspection Service, the Commodity Credit Corporation, the Extension Service, the Farmers Home Administration, Federal Grain Inspection Service, the Food and Inspection Service, the Food Safety and Inspection Service, the Foreign Agricultural Service, Forest Service, Rural Electrification Administration, Soil Conservation Service. Address: United States Department of Agriculture, 14th St. and Independence Ave. SW, Washington, DC 20250 USA; Tel: [1] (202) 720-2791; Web: www.usda.gov. Foreign Agricultural Service; Tel: [1] (202) 720-7115.

United States Department of Commerce (DOC)

(U.S. government) An executive department which encourages and promotes the United States' economic growth, international trade, and technological advancement. The Department provides a wide variety of programs to increase American competitiveness in the world economy and to assist business. The DOC also: works to prevent unfair foreign trade competition, provides social and economic statistics and analyses, supports the increased use of scientific engineering and technological development, grants patents and registers trademarks, and provides assistance to promote domestic economic development. Organizations within the DOC include the Bureau of Export Administration, Tel: [1] (202) 482-2000; the Census Bureau, Web: www.census.gov; the Economic Development Administration, Tel: [1] (202) 482-2000; the International Trade Administration, Tel: [1] (202) 482-2000; the Minority Business Development Agency, Tel: [1] (202) 482-2000; the National Institute of Standards and Technology, Tel: [1] (301) 975-6478; the National Oceanic and Atmospheric Administration, E-mail: answers@noaa.gov; the Patent and Trademark Office, Tel: [1] (703) 308-4357 (Public Affairs) or [1] (800) 786-9199; and the Technology Administration, E-mail: Public_Affairs@ta.doc.gov. Address: United States Department of Commerce, 14th Street & Constitution Ave. NW, Washington, DC 20230 USA; Tel: [1] (202) 482-2000; Web: www.doc.gov. *See also* Bureau of Export Administration; International Trade Administration.

United States Department of Defense

(U.S. government) A civilian executive department providing the military forces needed to deter war and protect the security of the U.S. There are three departments within the Department of Defense: the Air Force, Army, and Navy. Address: United States Department of Defense, The Pentagon, Washington, DC 20301 USA; Tel: [1] (703) 697-5737; Web: www.defenselink.mil.

United States Department of Energy (DOE)

(U.S. government) An executive department created in 1977 to consolidate all major Federal energy functions into one department. The principal programmatic missions are energy programs, weapons and waste clean-up programs, and science and technology programs. Organizations under the department include the Economic Regulatory Administration, the Energy Information Administration, and the Federal Energy Regulatory Commission. Address: United States Department of Energy, 1000 Independence Ave. SW, Washington, DC 20585 USA; Tel: [1] (800) dial-DOE; Web: www.energy.gov.

United States Department of Labor (DOL)

(U.S. government) An executive department which promotes and develops the welfare of U.S. wage earners, improves working conditions, and advances opportunities for profitable employment. The DOL keeps track of changes in employment, prices, and other national economic measures. Organizations under the Department include the Bureau of Labor Statistics, the Employment and Training Administration, the Employment Standards Administration, Labor-Management Standards, the Mine Safety and Health Administration, Occupational Safety and Health, and the Pension and Welfare Benefits Administration. Address: United States Department of Labor, 200 Constitution Ave. NW, Washington, DC 20210 USA; Tel: [1] (800) 4-USA-DOL; Web: www.dol.gov.

United States Department of State

(U.S. government) An executive department which directs U.S. foreign relations and negotiates treaties and agreements with foreign nations. Activities of the State Department are coordinated with foreign activities of other U.S. departments and agencies. Organizations within the Department include the Bureau of Consular Affairs, the Bureau of Economic and Business Affairs, the Bureau of Intelligence and Research, the Bureau of International Organization Affairs, and the Bureau of Oceans. Address: United States Department of State, 2201 C St. NW, Washington, DC 20520 USA; Tel: [1] (202) 647-4000; Web: www.state.gov.

United States Department of the Interior (DOI)

(U.S. government) An executive department that has responsibility for most U.S. federal government owned public lands and natural resources; the principal U.S. conservation agency. The office of Territorial and International Affairs oversees activities pertaining to U.S. territorial lands and the Freely Associated States and coordinates the international affairs of the Department. Organizations under the DOI include: the Bureau of Indian Affairs, the Bureau of Land Management, the Bureau of Mines, the Bureau of Reclamation, the Minerals Management Service, the National Park Service, the U.S. Fish and Wildlife Service, and the U.S. Geological Survey. Address: United States Department of the Interior, 1849 C St. NW, Washington, DC 20240 USA; Tel: [1] (202) 208-3171; Web: www.doi.gov.

United States Department of the Treasury

(U.S. government) An executive department which performs four basic functions: formulating and recommending economic, financial, tax and fiscal policies; serving as financial agent for the U.S. government; enforcing the law; and manufacturing coins and currency. The International Affairs unit is responsible for Department activities in international monetary affairs, trade and investment policy, international debt strategy, and U.S. participation in international financial institutions. The Under Secretary of the International Affairs unit acts as the U.S. Group of Seven (G-7) Deputy. Organizations within the Department include the Bureau of Alcohol, Tobacco and Firearms; the Bureau of Engraving and Printing; the Comptroller of the Currency; the Internal Revenue Service; the Office of Thrift Supervision; the U.S. Customs Service; the U.S. Mint; the U.S. Secret Service. Address: United States Department of the Treasury, 1500 Pennsylvania Ave. NW, Washington, DC 20220 USA; Tel: [1] (202) 622-1502; Web: www.ustreas.gov. *See also* Group of Seven (G-7); United States Customs Service; Bureau of Alcohol, Tobacco and Firearms.

United States Department of Transportation (DOT)

(U.S. government) An executive department of the U.S. government established by the Department of Transportation Act of 1966 (80 Stat 931) for the purpose of developing national transportation policies. Organizations within the Department of Transportation include the Federal Aviation Administration, the Federal Highway Administration, the Federal Railroad Administration, the Federal Transit Administration, the Maritime Administration, the National Highway Traffic Safety Administration, the Research and Special Programs Administration, the St. Lawrence Seaway Development Corporation, and the U.S. Coast Guard. Address: United States Department of Transportation, 400 7th Street SW, Washington, DC 20590 USA; Tel: [1] (202) 366-4000; Web: www.dot.gov.

United States Foreign Trade Definitions

An obsolete standard of trade terms, although they are sometimes specified in U.S. domestic contracts. The international standard of trade terms is Incoterms 2000. *See* Incoterms 2000.

United States International Trade Commission

(U.S. government) Formerly the U.S. Tariff Commission, which was created in 1916 by an Act of Congress. Its mandate was broadened and its name changed by the Trade Act of 1974. It is an independent fact-finding agency of the U.S. government that studies the effects of tariffs and other restraints to trade on the U.S. economy. It conducts public hearings to assist in determining whether particular U.S. industries are injured or threatened with injury by dumping, export subsidies in other countries, or rapidly rising imports. It also studies the probable economic impact on specific U.S. industries of proposed reductions in U.S. tariffs and non-tariff barriers to imports. Its six members are appointed by the president with the advice and consent of the U.S. Senate for nine-year terms (six-year terms prior to 1974). Address: International Trade Commission, 500 E Street SW, Washington, DC 20436 USA; Tel: [1] (202) 205-2000; Web: www.usitc.gov.

United States-Japan Semiconductor Trade Arrangement

See Semiconductor Trade Arrangement.

United States Munitions List

(U.S.) The USML identifies those items or categories of items considered to be defense articles and defense services subject to export control. The USML is similar in coverage to the International Munitions List (IML), but is more restrictive in two ways. First, the USML currently contains some dual-use items that are controlled for national security and foreign policy reasons (such as space-related or encryption-related equipment). Second, the USML contains some nuclear-related items. Under Presidential directive, most dual-use items are to be transferred from the USML to the Commerce Department's dual-use list. The Department of State, with the concurrence of Defense, designates which articles will be controlled under the USML. Items on the Munitions List face a stricter control regime and lack the safeguards to protect commercial competitiveness that apply to dual-use items. *See* International Munitions List; United States Department of State.

United States price

(U.S.) In the context of dumping investigations, this term refers to the price at which goods are sold in the U.S. compared to their foreign market value. The comparisons are used in the process of determining whether imported merchandise is sold at less than fair value. *See* dumping.

United States Trade and Development Agency

(U.S. government) An independent agency within the executive branch. Its mandate is to promote economic development in, and simultaneously export U.S. goods and services to, developing and middle-income countries. The Agency conducts feasibility studies and orientation visits, and provides trade-related training to assist U.S. firms in becoming involved in developing projects with substantial U.S. export potential. It also coordinates government-to-government technical assistance. Address: United States Trade and Development Agency, 1621 North Kent Street, Suite 200, Arlington, VA 22209-2131 USA; Tel: [1] (703) 875-4357; Web: www.tda.gov.

United States Trade Representative

(U.S. government) A cabinet-level official with the rank of Ambassador who is the principal adviser to the president on international trade policy, and has responsibility for setting and administering overall trade policy. The U.S. Trade Representative is concerned with the expansion of U.S. exports; U.S. participation in the World Trade Organization (WTO), commodity issues; East-West and North-South trade; and direct investment related to trade. As Chairman of the U.S. Trade Policy Committee he is also the primary official responsible for U.S. participation in all international trade negotiations. Prior to the Trade Agreements Act of 1979, which created the Office of the U.S. Trade Representative, the comparable official was known as the President's Special Representative for Trade Negotiations (STR), a position first established by the Trade Expansion Act of 1962. Address: United States Trade Representative, 600 17th St. NW, Washington, DC 20508 USA; Tel: [1] (888) 473-8787; Web: www.ustr.gov.

unitization

(shipping) The practice or technique of consolidating many small pieces of freight into a single unit for easier handling.

unit load

(shipping) The strapping or banding together of a number of individual cartons, packages, sacks, drums or other cargo, often on a pallet, in order to create a single unit.

unit load device (ULD)

(logistics/air freight) (a) Any type of container or pallet used to load or transport cargo. (b) Any type of container or pallet used to load or transport cargo in the hold of an aircraft. ULDs vary in size and shape to fit specific vessels. *See* the appendix Guide to Air Freight Containers (ULDs).

universal agency

See agency.

Universal Copyright Convention

An international agreement that was concluded to afford copyright protection to literary and artistic works in all countries that voluntarily agree to be bound by the Convention terms. *See* copyright; trademark; service mark.

unloading

(shipping) The physical removal of cargo from carrier's container.

unrestricted letter of credit

(banking) A letter of credit which may be negotiated through any bank of the beneficiary's choice. *See* letter of credit.

upper deck

(logistics) The upper cargo holding area of an airplane or ship.

Uruguay Round

(GATT) The eighth round of multilateral trade negotiations concerning the General Agreement on Tariffs and Trade (GATT). The Uruguay Round (so named because meetings began in Punta del Este, Uruguay in 1987) concluded in December, 1993 after seven years of talks with 117 member nations. The major goals of the Uruguay Round were to reduce barriers to trade in goods; to strengthen the role of GATT and improve the multilateral trading system; to increase the responsiveness of GATT to the evolving international economic environment; to encourage cooperation in strengthening the inter-relationship between trade and other economic policies affecting growth and development; and the establishment of a multilateral framework of principles and rules for trade in services, including the elaboration of possible disciplines for individual service sectors. Key provisions of the Uruguay Round agreements were: a reduction of import tariffs, with an overall cut of more than 33 percent of global tariffs; a gradual reduction of 36 percent of government subsidies for farmers; a phasing-out of import protection for textile producers in industrialized countries allowing more open markets for entry of cheaper products from Third World countries; stricter anti-dumping rules; greater global protection of intellectual property rights, including patents and copyrighted goods such as films and music. Although agriculture and other industries were brought under GATT for the first time, certain industries (such as the entertainment industry) were, in the end, excluded from the Round negotiations in order for negotiators to reach a final agreement. Particularly disappointing to many was the lack of progress in opening access to the trade of financial services, such as banking, accounting, and insurance. Most aspects of the agreement went into effect July 1, 1995.

Agreements reached at the Uruguay Round covered:

(1) **Market Access for Goods**—Tariffs to be reduced by an average of one-third, with the U.S. and other major industrial nations eliminating tariffs altogether on some products, by one-half on others, while cutting tariffs much less in the rest of the world.

(2) **Agriculture**—Strengthened long-term rules for agricultural trade and assures reduction of specific policies that distort agricultural trade. Addressed export subsidies, domestic subsidies, and market access. Agricultural export subsidies and some farm subsidies made subject to multilateral disciplines, and to be bound and reduced. Many non-tariff measures, including quotas to be converted to low tariffs over time.

(3) **Textiles and Clothing**—The Multi-Fiber Arrangement (MFA), a system of quotas that limits imports of textiles and apparel to the U.S. and other developed countries, to be phased out over a 10 year period. The quotas will eventually be replaced by tariffs.

(4) **Safeguards**—Provided incentives for countries to use GATT safeguard rules when import-related, serious injury problems occur.

(5) **Antidumping**—Revised the 1979 Antidumping Code, by improving provisions to define, deter, and discourage the use of dumping practices. Disputes between GATT members to be settled by binding dispute settlement.

(6) **Subsidies and Countervailing Measures**—Established clearer rules and stronger disciplines in the subsidies area while also making certain subsidies non-actionable.

(7) **Trade-related Investment Measures** (TRIMs)—Limited the ability of countries to favor domestically owned factories at the expense of foreign-owned ones. Prohibits local content and trade balancing requirements. Established a 5 to 7-year transition period for developing and least-developed countries.

(8) **Import Licensing Procedures**—More precisely defined automatic and non-automatic licensing. Signatories that adopt new procedures to notify the Import Licensing Committee within 60 days and provide information about it.

(9) **Customs Valuation**—Amendments to the Customs Valuation Code to help stem fraud, retain established minimum values, and encourage developing countries to study areas of concern in customs valuation.

(10) **Preshipment Inspection**—Regulated activities of Preshipment Inspection companies and reduced impediments to international trade resulting from the use of such companies, particularly in developing countries where they may supplement or replace national customs services.

(11) **Rules of Origin**—A program to be implemented to harmonize rules for determination of the origin of goods. Established a GATT Committee on Rules of Origin and a Customs Cooperation Council Technical Committee on Rules of Origin.

(12) **Technical Barriers to Trade**—Updated and improved rules respecting standards, technical regulations and conformity assessment procedures.

(13) **Sanitary and Phytosanitary Measures**—Established rules for the development of measures which are taken to protect human, animal or plant life or health in food safety or agriculture. Included quarantine procedures, food processing measures, meat inspection rules, procedures for approval of food additives or use of pesticides.

(14) **Services**—The General Agreement on Trade in Services (GATS) was the first multilateral, legally enforceable agreement covering trade investment in the service sectors. Principal elements included most-favored-nation treatment, national treatment, market access, transparency, and the free flow of payments and transfers.

(15) **Trade-Related Intellectual Property Rights** (TRIPs)—Established improved standards for the

protection of a full range of property rights and the enforcement of those standards both internally and at the border. Covered: copyrights, patents, trademarks, industrial designs, trade secrets, integrated circuits, and geographical indications. Provided for a 20-year term of protection for most of these rights.

(16) **Dispute Settlement**—The Dispute Settlement Understanding (DSU) created new procedures for settlement of disputes arising under any of the Uruguay Round agreements.

(17) **World Trade Organization** (WTO)—Established a new organization available only to countries that were contracting parties to the GATT and that agreed and adhered to all of the Uruguay Round agreements. Encompassed and extended the then current GATT structure. The intention was for the new WTO to have a stature similar to that of the Bretton Woods financial institutions, the World Bank, and the International Monetary Fund.

(18) **GATT Articles**—Updated articles relating to balance-of-payment reform, state trading enterprises, regional trading arrangements, and waivers of obligation.

(19) **Trade Policy Review Mechanism**—Provided for regular examination of national trade policies and other economic policies bearing on international trading.

(20) **Ministerial Decisions and Declaration**—Stated the views and objectives of the Uruguay Round participants on a number of issues relating to the operation of the global trading system.

(21) **Government Procurement**—A new Agreement on Government Procurement replaced the existing agreement. Included procurement of services and construction and some coverage of subcentral governments and government-owned utilities.

See also General Agreement on Tariffs and Trade; rounds; Tokyo Round, World Trade Organization

U.S. ...
See United States ....

usance letter of credit
(banking) A documentary letter of credit which is not available by sight payment and which is therefore available against:

(1) acceptance of a term bill of exchange,

(2) or in certain usages by deferred payment. *See* letter of credit.

users fees
(U.S. Customs) Assessments collected by the U.S. Customs Service as part of the entry process to help defray various costs involved in the importation of goods to the United States.

(a) The **harbor maintenance fee** is an ad valorem fee assessed on cargo imports and admissions into foreign trade zones. The fee is 0.125 percent of the value of the cargo and is paid quarterly, except for imports which are paid at the time of entry. Customs deposits the harbor maintenance fee collections into the Harbor Maintenance Trust Fund. The funds are made available, subject to appropriation, to the Army Corps of Engineers for the improvement and maintenance of U.S. ports and harbors.

(b) The **merchandise processing fee** sets a fee schedule for formal entries (generally, those valued over US$1,250) at a minimum of US$21 per entry and a maximum of US$400 per entry, with an ad valorem rate of 0.17 percent. The fee for informal entries (those valued at under US$1,250) is US$2 for automated entries, US$5 for manual entries not prepared by Customs, and US$8 for manual entries prepared by Customs.

usuance
(banking) The time allowed for payment of an international obligation. A usuance credit is a credit available against time drafts. *See* letter of credit; usance letter of credit.

U

V

validated export license

(U.S.) A document issued by the U.S. government authorizing the export of commodities for which written export authorization is required by law. For more information on export licensing in general, call Exporter Assistance at: [1] (202) 482-4811. Address: Bureau of Export Administration, U.S. Department of Commerce, 14th St. and Constitution Ave. NW, Washington, DC 20230 USA; Tel: [1] (202) 482-4811; Fax: [1] (202) 482-3617; Web: www.bxa.doc.gov.

validity

(banking) The time period for which a letter of credit is valid. After receiving notice of a letter of credit opened in his behalf, the seller/exporter/beneficiary must meet all the requirements of the letter of credit within the period of validity. *See* letter of credit.

valuation

The fixing of value to anything.

(customs) The appraisal of the worth of imported goods by customs officials for the purpose of determining the amount of duty payable in the importing country. The WTO Customs Valuation Code obligates governments that sign it to use the "transaction value" of imported goods—or the price actually paid or payable for them—as the principal basis for valuing the goods for customs purposes.

(U.S. Customs) U.S. Customs officers are required by law to determine the value of imported merchandise. Valuation is necessary for statistical purposes as well as to determine the amount of import duty which must be paid if the duty rate is stated as a percentage of value (ad valorem duty). Generally, the Customs value of all merchandise exported to the United States is the transaction value for the goods. The transaction value of imported merchandise is the price actually paid or payable for the merchandise when sold for exportation to the United States, plus amounts for the following items if not included in the price:

(1) The packing costs incurred by the buyer.
(2) Any selling commission incurred by the buyer,
(3) The value of any assist,
(4) Any royalty or license fee that the buyer is required to pay as a condition of the sale, and
(5) The proceeds, accruing to the seller, of any subsequent resale, disposal, or use of the imported merchandise.

The amounts for the above items are added only to the extent that each is not included in the price actually paid or payable and information is avail-

able to establish the accuracy of the amount. If sufficient information is not available, then the transaction value cannot be determined and the next basis of value, in order of precedence, must be considered for appraisement.

The secondary bases of value, listed in order of precedence for use, are:
(1) Transaction value of identical merchandise,
(2) Transaction value of similar merchandise,
(3) Deductive value, and
(4) Computed value.

The order of precedence of the last two values can be reversed if the importer so requests.

See transaction value; deductive value; computed value.

valuation charges

(shipping) Transportation charges assessed shippers who declare a value of goods higher than the value of carriers' limits of liability. *See* declared value for carriage.

valuation clause

(insurance) A clause in an insurance policy stating the value of the policy. A valuation clause commonly in use reads:

"valued premium included at amount of invoice, including all charges in the invoice and including prepaid and/or advanced and/or guaranteed freight, if any, plus _____%." (This is usually 10% on exports.)

value added

(economics) That part of the value of produced goods developed in a company. It is determined by subtracting from sales the costs of materials and supplies, energy costs, contract work, and so on, and it includes labor expenses, administrative and sales costs, and other operating profits. *See also* value-added tax.

value added counseling

Assessing a company's current international business operations and assisting in one or more of the following: (1) identifying and selecting the most viable markets; (2) developing an export market strategy; (3) implementing the export market strategy; and (4) increasing market presence.

value-added tax (VAT)

(taxation) An indirect tax on consumption that is assessed on the increased value of goods at each discrete point in the chain of production and distribution, from the raw material stage to final consumption. The tax on processors or merchants is levied on the amount by which they increase the value of items they purchase and resell.

value-added reseller

Acronym for value-added reseller. A company that combines products and/or services from several sources to produce a new product for sale. For example, a VAR might purchase computer systems from a manufacturer at a discount, add their own proprietary medical billing software and sell the resulting system to medical offices as a complete solution.

value date
(banking) Fixing of a value date for accounting purposes on banking operations, i.e. the date on which the interest accrual for the respective accounting entry begins or ends.

VAR
See value-added reseller.

variable rate of duty
(customs) A tariff subject to alterations as world market prices change, the alterations are designed to assure that the import price after payment of the duty will equal a predetermined "gate" price.

vatu
The currency of Vanuatu. 1VT=100 centimes.

vega
(statistics/foreign exchange) The price change of a foreign exchange option for a 1 percent change in the implied volatility.

vendor
A company or individual that supplies goods or services.

Vennootschap onder firma
(Netherlands) Designation for a general partnership, in which all partners have joint and several liability.

ventilated container
(logistics) A weather-proof cargo container with protected small openings in the top and/or sides to allow for free movement of air.

vertical export trading company
An export trading company that integrates a range of functions taking products from suppliers to consumers.

vertical integration
(economics/management) The expansion, acquisition or merger of firms or business activities into different points of the same production and/or distribution path. For example, a leather shoe manufacturer who acquires a leather manufacturer and a retail shoe store chain.
See horizontal integration.

vessel ton
(shipping/measurement) A unit of measurement in the shipping industry assuming that 100 cubic feet of cargo equals one ton.

videoconferencing
A conference between two or more individuals at different locations using telephone lines or computer networks to transmit and receive audio and video of the participants in real time.

Vienna Sales Convention
See United Nations Convention on Contracts for the International Sale of Goods (CISG).

visa
(general) A certificate or stamp placed in a passport by a foreign government's embassy, consular office or other representative. It permits the holder to either visit (tourist visa) conduct business in (business visa), work (work permit or visa) in, or immigrate (residency or immigration visa) to the issuing country for a specified time.
(customs) A license issued by the government of an exporting country for the export to a specific importing country of a certain quantity of a quota controlled commodity (such as textiles) subject to a voluntary export restriction or a voluntary restraint agreement.

visa waiver
A program of selected countries to eliminate their visa requirement on a test basis.

vis major
(law) A major force or disturbance, usually a natural cause, that a person cannot prevent despite exercise of due care. Floods and labor strikes are examples of vis major events.

void ab initio
(law) Invalid from the time of initiation. A contract, for example, that violates law or public policy is void ab initio, that is, it is invalid when it is made.

voidable contract
(law) An agreement that is valid but that one party may declare invalid because of a defect or illegality in making it. A contract that is entered into in reliance on a fraudulent misrepresentation, for example, will be enforced against the party that committed the fraud, but the party harmed by the misrepresentation may elect to void the contract.

void contract
(law) An agreement that has no legal effect and that cannot be ratified or otherwise made effective. A contract that requires the performance of an illegal act, for example, is void and cannot become effective.

volatility
(foreign exchange) The measure of the relative deviation of a price from the mean.

volume rate
(shipping) A rate applicable in connection with a specified volume of freight.

voluntary export restriction
An understanding between trading partners in which the exporting nation, in order to reduce trade friction, agrees to limit its exports of a particular good. Also called voluntary restraint agreement. *See* voluntary restraint agreements.

voluntary restraint agreements (VRA's)
Informal bilateral or multilateral arrangements through which exporters voluntarily restrain certain exports, usually through export quotas to avoid eco-

nomic dislocation in an importing country and to avert the possible imposition of mandatory import restrictions.

These arrangements do not involve an obligation on the part of the importing country to provide "compensation" to the exporting country, as would be the case if the importing country unilaterally imposed equivalent restraints on imports. *See* voluntary export restriction; quota; visa.

war clause

(insurance) An insurance clause included in policies to cover against losses as a result of war. *See* war risk.

warehouse

(logistics) A secured, weatherproof building where raw materials, component parts, finished products and/or freight and cargo can be stored. There are many different types of warehouses including:

customs bonded warehouse: A warehouse where goods may be stored under the direct or indirect supervision of a country's import or export authorities.

public warehouse: A warehouse subject to government regulation where a number of different firms may store goods.

private warehouse: A warehouse operated by a manufacturing or trading firm, often adjacent to a manufacturing plant or port, used solely to store that firm's goods.

special commodities warehouse: A warehouse designed with special facilities and authorized to store unique products such as chemicals (in tanks), grain (in elevators) and tobacco (in barns).

temperature controlled warehouse: A warehouse that has either heating and/or refrigeration to maintain goods at a specified constant temperature.

U.S. Customs bonded warehouse: A federal warehouse where goods remain until duty has been collected from the importer. Goods under bond are also kept here. *See* surety; bond; in bond.

warehouse receipt

(shipping) An instrument (document) listing the goods or commodities deposited in a warehouse. It is a receipt for the commodities listed, and for which the warehouse is the bailee. Warehouse receipts may be either non-negotiable or negotiable.

warehouse-to-warehouse

(insurance) Insurance coverage of risks to a shipment of goods from the time the goods leave the warehouse for commencement of transit and continue during ordinary course of transit until delivered to final warehouse at destination, or until the expiration of 15 days (30 if destination is outside the limits of the port), whichever shall first occur. In the case of delay in excess of the time limit specified, if it arises from circumstances beyond his control, the assured is "held covered" if he gives prompt notice and pays additional premium.

W

See Marine Extension Clause 1943 & 1952; currency (term) of insurance.

warehousing

(logistics) The storing, securing and managing of raw materials, component parts or finished goods in a secure location. *See* warehouse, bonded warehouse.

warranty

(law) A promise by a contracting party that the other party can rely on certain facts or representations as being true. A seller, for example, may warrant that certain products will meet a list of specifications furnished by the buyer.

war risk

(insurance) The risk to a vessel, its cargo and passengers by aggressive actions of a hostile nation or group. *See* war risk insurance.

war risk insurance

(insurance) Insurance coverage against war risks as outlined in detail in some dozen rather specific paragraphs of an insurance policy. The policy conditions must be read for complete understanding. In general, they cover risks of capture and seizure, destruction or damage by warlike operations in prosecution of hostilities, civil wars and insurrections or in the application of sanctions under international agreements. Delay or loss of market is excluded. Loss or expense arising from detainments, nationalization of the government to or from which the goods are insured or seizure under quarantine or customs regulations is also excluded.

War risk insurance generally attaches as goods are first loaded on board a vessel at the port of shipment, and it ceases to attach as goods are landed at the intended port of discharge or on expiry of 15 days from arrival of the overseas vessel whichever first occurs. It includes transshipment and intermediate overland transit to an on-carrying overseas vessel, if any, but in no case for more than 15 days counting from midnight of the day of arrival of the overseas vessel at the intended port of discharge. If in transshipment, the 15-day period is exceeded, the insurance re-attaches as the interest is loaded on the on-carrying vessel. In case the voyage is terminated and the goods are discharged at a port or place other than the original port of discharge, such port or place shall be deemed the intended port of discharge.

The war risk policy is subject to 48 hours cancellation by either party. However, it cannot be cancelled on shipments upon which insurance has already attached. Since the cancellation provision is used at times for changing the conditions of insurance the current coverage should be studied for exact understanding of the war risk policy.

War risk insurance is routinely obtained for protection against mines and other implements of war from former wars.

Warsaw Convention

(shipping) Formal name: The Convention for the Unification of Certain Rules Relating to International Carriage by Air, signed in Warsaw in 1929. An international multilateral treaty which regulates, in a uniform manner, the conditions of international transportation by air. Among other things it establishes the international liability of air carriers and establishes the monetary limits for loss, damage, and delay.

Wassenaar Arrangement

An understanding between thirty-three nations promoting voluntary export control guidelines, as well as transparency and greater responsibility in the transfer of conventional arms and dual-use goods and technologies. Contact: Wassenaar Arrangement; Vienna Austria; Tel: [43] (1) 960 03; Web: www.wassenaar.org.

Watch List

See Special 301.

waterway use tax

(shipping) A usage fee for vessels operating on inland waterways. The fee is generally assessed as a tax on fuel used in vessels operating on the waterway.

waybill

(shipping) A document prepared by a transportation line at the point of a shipment, showing the point or origin, destination, route, consignor, consignee, description of shipment and amount charged for the transportation service, and forwarded with the shipment, or direct by mail, to the agent at the transfer point or waybill destination. *See* bill of lading; air waybill; ocean bill of lading.

Webb-Pomerene Act of 1918

(U.S. law) Federal legislation exempting exporters' associations from the antitrust regulations.

Webb-Pomerene Association

(U.S.) Associations engaged in exporting that combine the products of similar producers for overseas sales. These associations have partial exemption from U.S. anti-trust laws but may not engage in import, domestic or third country trade, or combine to export services.

weight break

(shipping) Levels at which the freight rate per 100 pounds decreases because of substantial increases in the weight of the shipment. Examples of levels at which weight breaks occur (in pounds) are 100, 500, 1,000, 3,000, 5,000 and 10,000.

weights and measures

See the Weights and Measures Appendix.

weight ton

(measurement) (a) Short ton = 2,000 pounds, (b) Long ton = 2,240 pounds, (c) Metric ton = 2,204.68 pounds.

weight unit qualifier

(logistics) (a) The unit of weight measure specified for use in a contract. (b) A symbol or code that represents the unit of weight measure to be used in a contract.

West Africa Economic Community

A regional alliance CEAO (French for Communauté Economique de l'Afrique), created in 1974, includes: Benin, Burkina Faso, Cote d'Ivoire, Mali, Mauritania, Niger, and Senegal. (Togo has observer status). The CEAO operates as a free trade area for agricultural products and raw materials and as a preferential trading area for approved industrial products, with a regional cooperation tax (TCR) replacing import duties and encouraging trade among member states. In order to ensure that benefits of the regional grouping flow to all members, especially the least developed ones (Mali, Mauritania, Niger, and Burkina Faso), the CEAO has established a fund to provide financial services and guarantees to development lenders in both public and private sectors for projects in member states. In addition, CEAO has the long-term objective of creating a customs union with extensive harmonization of fiscal policies between member states, though no concrete achievements in this direction have been recorded. Address: Communauté économique de l'Afrique de l'ouest (CEAO), rue Agostino Neto, 01 BP 634, Ouagadougou 01, Burkina Faso; Tel: 226-30-6189.

West African Economic and Monetary Union

A regional alliance, WAMU (French: Union Monetaire Ouest Africaine, UMOA) was created by treaty signed in May 1962. WAMU comprises seven French-speaking African countries: Benin, Burkina Faso, Cote d'Ivoire, Mali, Niger, Senegal, and Togo. Within WAMU, these countries share a common currency (CFA Franc) now freely convertible into the European Union euro (€) at a fixed parity (under special arrangement with the French government), and a common Central Bank (BCEAO) responsible for the conduct of the Union's monetary and credit policies. There is also a common regional development bank. West African Economic and Monetary Union; 01 B.P. 543, Ouagafdougou 01; Burkina Faso; Tel: [226] 31-88-73; Fax: [226] 31-88-72.

wharfage

(shipping) (a) A charge assessed by a pier or dock owner for handling incoming or outgoing cargo, (b) The charge made for docking vessels at a wharf.

with average (WA)

(insurance) Insurance coverage which gives the assured protection for partial damage by sea perils, if the partial damage amounts to 3% (or other percentage as specified) or more of the value of the whole shipment or of a shipping package. If the vessel has stranded, sunk, been on fire or in collision, the percentage requirement is waived and losses from sea perils are recoverable in full.

Additional named perils may be added to the WA Clause. Theft, pilferage, nondelivery, fresh water damage, sweat damage, breakage and leakage are often covered. The combination of perils needed by a particular assured will naturally depend upon the commodity being shipped and the trade involved.

In its standard form a typical with average clause may read:

Subject to particular average if amounting to 3%, unless general or the vessel and/or craft is stranded, sunk, burnt, on fire and/or in collision, each package separately insured or on the whole."

The "all risk" clause is a logical extension of the broader forms of "With Average" coverage. This clause reads:

To cover against all risks of physical loss or damage from any external cause irrespective of percentage, but excluding, nevertheless, the risk of war, strikes, riots, seizure, detention and other risks excluded by the F.C.&S. (Free of Capture and Seizure) Warranty and the S.R.&C.C. (Strikes, Riots and Civil Commotion) Warranty in this policy, excepting to the extent that such risks are specifically covered by endorsement."

Some types of loss are commonly excluded and others not recoverable, even under the "all risk" clauses. *See also* average; particular average; general average; free of particular average; deductible average; all risk; special marine policy.

without reserve

(shipping) A term indicating that a shipper's agent or representative is empowered to make definitive decisions and adjustments abroad without approval of the group or individual represented.

with particular average

(insurance) Insurance covering also the loss of single cases or partial quantities (as opposed to free from particular average, fpa). *See also* average; particular average; deductible average; all risk.

won

The currency of:

North Korea, 1W=100 jun;

South Korea, 1W=100 jeon.

work in progress (WIP)

(logistics) Raw materials and component parts that have entered a production cycle or process that has not been completed.

World Administrative Radio Conference

WARC refers to the conference convened regularly by the United Nations' International Telegraphic Union (ITU) to allocate and regulate radio frequencies for the purposes of television and radio broadcasting, telephone data communications, navigation, maritime and aeronautical communication, and satellite broadcasting. *See* International Telecommunications Union.

World Bank

(banking) The International Bank for Reconstruction and Development (IBRD), commonly referred to as the World Bank, is an intergovernmental financial institution located in Washington, DC. Its objectives are to help raise productivity and incomes and reduce poverty in developing countries. It was established in December 1945 on the basis of a plan developed at the Bretton Woods Conference of 1944. The Bank loans financial resources to credit worthy developing countries. It raises most of its funds by selling bonds in the world's major capital markets. Its bonds have, over the years, earned a quality rating enjoyed only by sound governments and leading corporations. Projects supported by the World Bank normally receive high priority within recipient governments and are usually well planned and supervised. The World Bank earns a profit, which is plowed back into its capital. Address: World Bank, 1818 H Street NW, Washington, DC 20433 USA; Tel: [1] (202) 477-1234; Fax: [1] (202) 477-6391. *See* International Bank for Reconstruction and Development; World Bank Group.

World Bank Group

(banking) An integrated group of international institutions that provides financial and technical assistance to developing countries. The group includes the International Bank for Reconstruction and Development, the International Development Association, and the International Finance Corporation. Address: World Bank Group, 1818 H Street NW, Washington, DC 20433; Tel: [1] (202) 477-1234; Fax: [1] (202) 477-6391; Web: www.worldbank.org.

World Intellectual Property Organization

A specialized agency of the United Nations system of organizations that seeks to promote international cooperation in the protection of intellectual property around the world through cooperation among states, and administers various "Unions," each founded on a multilateral treaty and dealing with the legal and administrative aspects of intellectual property.

WIPO administers the International Union for the Protection of Industrial Property (the "Paris Union"), which was founded in 1883 to reduce discrimination in national patent practices, the International Union for the Protection of Literary and Artistic Works (the "Bern Union"), which was founded in 1886 to provide analogous functions with respect to copyrights, and other treaties, conventions and agreements concerned with intellectual property. Address: World Intellectual Property Organization, 34, chemin des Colombettes, CH-1211 Geneva 20, Switzerland; Tel: [41] (22) 338-9111; Fax: [41] (22) 733-5428; E-mail: wipo.mail@wipo.int; Web: www.wipo.int. *See also* patent; copyright; service mark; trademark; Patent Cooperation Treaty.

World Meteorological Organization

The WMO facilitates worldwide cooperation in establishing a network for meteorological, hydrological, and geophysical observations, for exchanging meteorological and related information, and for promoting standardization in meteorological measurements. Address: World Meteorological Organization, Case Postale 2300, CH-1211 Geneva 2, Switzerland; Tel: [41] (22) 730-8111; Fax: [41] (22) 730-8181; Web: www. wmo.ch

World Tourism Organization (WTO)

An intergovernmental technical body dealing with all aspects of tourism. The WTO promotes and develops tourism as a means of contributing to economic development, international understanding, peace, and prosperity. Headquarters address: World Tourism Organization, Calle Capitan Haya 42, E-28020 Madrid, Spain; Tel: [34] (91) 567-8100; Fax: [34] (91) 571-3733; Web: www.world-tourism.org.

world trade clubs / centers

Local or regional based organizations in the United States and around the world of importers, exporters, customs brokers, freight forwarders, attorneys, bankers, manufacturers and shippers.

Each world trade club provides different services and activities, but many provide: information services including data bases and libraries, educational services including seminars and regularly scheduled classes, meeting space, club atmosphere, dining, exhibit facilities, and trade missions. Most major cities in the world have world trade clubs. For a list of world trade clubs internationally contact: World Trade Center Association, 60 East 42nd Street, Suite 1901, New York, NY 10165 USA; Tel: [1] (212) 599-3444; Fax: [1] (212) 599-1950; http://iserve.wtca.org.

World Trade Institute

One of the world's foremost educational institutions and resources for the international business and financial community. Its programs include conferences and seminars, the School of International Trade & Commerce (SITC), the WTI Language Center, international training programs and academic partnership programs. Contact: World Trade Institute; 551 5th Avenue, 8th Floor; New York, NY 10176; E-mail: wti@pace.edu.

World Trade Organization (WTO)

The WTO is the premier international organization seeking to deal with the global rules of trade between nations. Created by the Uruguay Round of trade negotiations (1986-1994) of the GATT (General Agreement on Tariffs and Trade), the WTO was established 1 January 1995, and is comprised of 134 nations with others actively seeking membership.

WTO Objective

The WTO's stated objective is to help trade flow smoothly, freely, fairly and predictably. It does this by administering WTO trade agreements, acting as a forum for international trade negotiations, settling trade disputes, monitoring national trade policies, assisting developing countries in trade policy issues through technical assistance and training programs, and cooperation with other international organizations.

The activities of the WTO are based on the implementation of multilateral trade agreements which have been negotiated and signed by a majority of the world's trading nations, and ratified by their parliaments. These agreements are contracts guaranteeing member countries important trade rights. They also bind governments to keep their trade policies within agreed limits to the benefit of the whole.

WTO Structure

The WTO is run by its member governments. Major decisions are made by the membership as a whole, either by ministers (who meet every two years at a ministerial conference) or by officials (who meet regularly in Geneva). Decisions are normally made by consensus.

The ministerial conference can make decisions on all matters under any of the multilateral trade agreements. Day-to-day work in between the ministerial conferences is handled by three bodies: 1) The General Council, 2) The Dispute Settlement Body, and 3) The Trade Policy Review Body. All three are called The General Council, although they meet under different terms of reference.

Three more councils, each handling a different broad area of trade, report to the General Council. These are: 1) The Council for Trade in Goods (Goods Council), 2) The Council for Trade in Services (Services Council), and 3) The Council for Trade-Related Aspects of Intellectual Property (TRIPS Council).

Additional groups report to the General Council. The scope of their coverage is smaller, so they are called "committees." These committees cover such issues as trade and development, the environment, regional trading agreements, investment and competition policy, government procurement, trade facilitation, and others.

Each of the higher level councils has subsidiary bodies. For example, the Goods Council has 11 committees dealing with specific subjects such as agriculture, market access, subsidies, anti-dumping, and others.

The most difficult issues are not resolved in these upper level councils, but rather in much smaller meetings with representatives from as many as 40 countries to as few as two countries.

Successes

The WTO (and its predecessor GATT) has played a major role in the following areas: the reduction of tariffs on manufactured goods and agricultural products, the opening of banking, insurance and telecommunications markets to foreign competition, standards for the protection of intellectual property rights, food safety regulations, and bans on local preferences for government purchasing.

Challenges

With all its successes, the WTO is challenged by disputes by member nations to: 1) tariffs—lower or eliminate tariffs on agricultural, aquaculture and forest products, scientific, environmental and medical equipment, and chemicals, 2) agricultural subsidies—eliminate government subsidies to agriculture that set artificially low prices for agricultural products (thus hurting exporters), 3) intellectual property rights—either strengthen intellectual property rights (primarily proposed by advanced western nations that are home to major pharmaceutical companies) or establish exemptions from such rules (primarily proposed by developing nations that desire cheap access to drugs to treat HIV/AIDS and other health problems), 4) environment—establish more stringent rules designed to protect the environment, 5) services—continue to open up such service industries such as banking, insurance and medical technology, as well as maintain a tax-free status on Internet commerce, 6) genetically modified food products—give nations more latitude in their ability to exclude genetically altered food products based on public health or environmental concerns, 7) labor—open discussions on how international trade affects labor and possibly to establish international labor standards in the areas of child labor, health, and safety issues, and 8) transparency—make the WTO more transparent by eliminating secretive practices.

World Trade Organization; Centre William Rappard; Rue de Lausanne 154; CH-1211 Geneva 21; Switzerland; Tel: [41] (22) 739-51-11; Web: www.wto.org. WTO Information and Media Relations Division; Tel: [41] (22) 739-50-07; Fax: [41] (22) 739-54-58; E-mail: enquiries@wto.org. WTO Publications; Tel: [41] (22) 739-52-08 / 739-53-08; Fax: [41] (22) 739-57-92; E-mail: publications@wto.org.

See also General Agreement on Tariffs and Trade, Uruguay Round.

World Wide Web (Web: www)

(Internet) The international network of electronic links that connect personal computers with computer servers. Also referred to as 'the Web'.

writ

(law) A judicial order to a person, often a sheriff, judge, or another officer of the law, to perform a specified act or to have the act performed. Writs of attachment, execution, and replevin are examples of writs that courts issue to require officials to carry out court judgments. *See* attachment; execution; replevin.

writer

(foreign exchange) The party which writes an option (also known as the option seller). The writer undertakes the obligation to carry out the conditions of the options contract according to the choice of the option buyer during the whole life to maturity of the option. For this he receives a premium which is paid to him by the buyer of the option.

WTO

See World Trade Organization (WTO).

Web: www

See World Wide Web

X-Y-Z

yen

The currency of Japan. 1¥=100 sen.

yuan

The currency of China. 1¥=100 fen.

zaire

The currency of Zaire. 1Z=100 makuta.

Zangger Committee

Examines controls enacted pursuant to the Nuclear Nonproliferation Treaty by refining the list of items requiring nuclear safeguards. The Zangger Committee consists of 23 Nuclear Non-Proliferation Treaty (NPT) nuclear supplier nations and includes all nuclear weapons states except France and China. Through a series of consultations in the early 1970's, the countries of the Zangger Committee compiled a "trigger list" of nuclear materials and equipment. The shipment of any item on the list to a non-nuclear weapons state "triggers" the requirement of International Atomic Energy Agency (IAEA) safeguards. Since the Zangger Committee is associated with the NPT, its members are obligated to treat all non-nuclear weapons parties to the treaty alike. For fear of discrediting the NPT, the Zangger countries cannot target strict nuclear controls toward certain nations with questionable proliferation credentials; the NPT binds them to assist non-nuclear weapons states with peaceful atomic energy projects. *See* International Atomic Energy Agency; Nuclear Non-Proliferation Treaty.

zero-sum

(economics) The concept that one side's gains are directly offset by the other side's losses in business or negotiations. When all the gains and losses from each side are totalled, the sum is zero. Compare to positive-sum.

zip code

(shipping) A numerical code, established by the U.S. Postal Service, used for the purpose of routing and to identify delivery zones. Some U.S. carriers apply this code for freight in the same manner.

zloty

The currency of Poland. 1Zl=100 groszy.

zone

(shipping) Any one of a number of sections or districts of the United States or of the world used for the purpose of establishing proper rates for parcels, mail, and pickup and delivery.

zone price

(logistics) The price or rate to transport mail, cargo or freight to any location within a zone. *See* zone.

zone status

(U.S. foreign trade zones) The legal status of merchandise which has been admitted to a U.S. foreign trade zone, thereby becoming subject to the provisions of the Foreign Trade Zone Act (FTZA). *See* foreign trade zone; Foreign Trade Zone Board; Foreign Trade Zone Act; grantee; operator; zone user; subzones.

zone user

(U.S. foreign trade zones) A corporation, partnership or party that uses a U.S. foreign trade zone for storage, handling, processing, or manufacturing merchandise in zone status, whether foreign or domestic. Usually, the zone user is the party which requests a Customs permit to admit, process or remove zone status merchandise. In subzones, the operator and zone user are usually the same party. Users pay the grantee or operator for services such as rent on facilities, storage, handling, promotion and similar services. *See* foreign trade zone; Foreign Trade Zone Board; Foreign Trade Zone Act; operator; zone user; subzones; zone status.

X
Y
Z

Acronyms and Abbreviations[1]

A

AAA
American Arbitration Association

AAB
Arab-African Bank

AAEI
American Association of Exporters and Importers

AAR
Against All Risks (insurance)

AB
Aktiebolag. company limited by shares. *See* Business Entities Appendix.

ABI
Automated Broker Interface
American Business Initiative

ABTA
Association of British Travel Agents

A/C
Account Current

ACC
Arab Cooperation Council

ACDA
Arms Control and Disarmament Agency

ACE
Agrupamento Complementar de Empresas, *See* Business Entities Appendix.

ACEP
Advisory Committee on Export Policy

ACH
Automated Clearinghouse

ACP
African, Caribbean, and Pacific

ACS
Automated Commercial System

ACTPN
Advisory Committee on Trade Policy and Negotiations

a/d
After date

AD
Aktzionerno Drouzestvo. *See* Business Entities Appendix.

ADB
Asian Development Bank

ADF
African Development Foundation

ADS
Agent Distributor Service

Ad Val (or A.V.)
Ad Valorem

AE
Anonymos Eteria. *See* Business Entities Appendix.

AECA
Arms Export Control Act

AEIE
Agrupamento Europeu de Interêsse Econômico. *See* Business Entities Appendix.

AEN
Administrative Exception Note

AEV
Articles of Extraordinary Value

AFDB
African Development Bank

AFT
Bureau of Alcohol, Tobacco, and Firearms

AG
Aktiengesellschaften. *See* Business Entities Appendix.
Australia Group

AGX
Agriculture Export Connections

AID
Agency for International Development

AIES
Automated Information Exchange System

AIMS
Agriculture Information and Marketing Services

AIT
American Institute in Taiwan

AL
Arab League

AMB
Ambassador

AMF
Airport Mail Facility

AMS
Automated Manifest System

AMU
Arab Maghreb Union

ANSI
American National Standards Institute

A/O
Account Of

AOSIS
Alliance of Small Island States

APAC
Agriculture Policy Advisory Committee
Auto Parts Advisory Committee

APEC
Asian-Pacific Economic Cooperation

APHIS
Animal and Plant Health Inspection Service

---

1. Most acronyms are written in upper case letters without periods (.). However, due to different customs and practice they may be written in uppercase and/or lowercase, and with or without various punctuation. Some examples: Facsimile may be abbreviated as Fax, fax, Fax:, fax., or telefax. Foreign Exchange may be abbreviated as FX or F/X. United States of America may be abbreviated as U.S.A., U.S., USA or US.

ACRONYMS

APO
Administrative Protective Order

a.s.
Akciova Spolecnost, *See* Business
  Entities Appendix.

A.S.
Anonim Sirket. *See* Business
  Entities Appendix.

A/S
Aktieselskab. *See* Business
  Entities Appendix.
Aksjeselskap

ASEAN
Association of Southeast Asian
  Nations

ASIC
Application-Specific Integrated
  Circuit

ATA Carnet
"Admission Temporaire-
  Temporary Admission" Carnet

ATI
American Traders Index
Andean Trade Initiative

ATP
Advanced Technology Products

ATPI
Andean Trade Preference
  Initiative

AT&T
American Telephone & Telegraph

AUTOVON
Automatic Voice Network

avdp.
avoirdupois (weight)

A.V. (or Ad Val)
Ad Valorem

B

B.A.
Buenos Aires (Argentina)

B/A
Bill of Adventure

BAF
Bunker Adjustment Factor

BATF
Bureau of Alcohol, Tobacco, and
  Firearms

Bbl
Barrel

B/C
Bill of Credit

B/D
Bank Draft

B./Dft.
Bank Draft

Bd. Ft. (also fbm)
Board Foot

Bdl
Bundle

B/E
Bill of Exchange

BENELUX
Belgium, Netherlands,
  Luxembourg Economic Union

BF
Board Foot

BFP
Bona Fide Purchaser

B.H.
Bill of Health

BHC
Bank Holding Company
British High Commission

Bhd.
Berhad. *See* Business Entities
  Appendix.

BIE
Bureau of International
  Expositions

BIS
Bank for International Settlements

BIT(s)
Bilateral Investment Treaty(ies)

B/L
Bill of Lading

BLEU
Belgium-Luxembourg Economic
  Union

Bls
Bales

B/M
Board measure

B.O.
Bad order

BOP
Balance of Payments

BOT
Balance of Trade

B/P
Bill of Parcels
Bills Payable

B/R
Bills Receivable

BRITE
Basic Research in Industrial
  Technologies in Europe

B.S.
Bill of Sale

BSA
Bilateral Steel Agreement

BSP
Business Sponsored
Between Show Promotion

Bt
Betéti Társaság. *See* Business
  Entities Appendix.

BTN
Brussels Tariff Nomenclature

B/V
Book Value

B.V.B.A.
Besloten Vennootschap met
  Beperkte Aansprakelijkheid.
  See Business Entities Appendix.

BWS
Bank Wire Service
Bretton-Woods System

Bx
Box

BXA
Bureau of Export Administration

C

C
Consulate

C.A.
Compainía Anómima. *See*
Business Entities Appendix.

CAB
Civil Aeronautics Board

CACM
Central American Common
Market

CAD/CAM
Computer Aided Design/
Computer Aided Manufacturing

C.A.F.
Currency Adjustment Factor

CAP
Common Agricultural Policy
Country Action Plan

CAR
Commercial Activity Report

CARICOM
Caribbean Common Market

CASE
Council of American States in
Europe

CBD
Commerce Business Daily

CBERA
Caribbean Basin Economic
Recovery Act

CBI
Caribbean Basin Initiative

Cbm/ (or C.B.M.)
Cubic Meter

CBW
Chemical and Biological
Weapons

CCC
Canadian Commercial
Corporation
Commodity Credit Corporation
Customs Cooperation Council

CCCN
Customs Cooperation Council
Nomenclature

CCL
Commerce Control List.
(Commodity Control List)

C.D.
Carried Down
Certificate of Deposit

CD-R
Compact Disc—Rewritable

CD-ROM
Compact Disc—Read Only
Memory

CDT
Center for Defense Trade

CEA
Council of Economic Advisors

CEAO
West Africa Economic
Community (Communauté
Economique de l'Afrique)

Celsius
centigrade

CEN
European Committee for
Standardization

C. en C.
Compainía en Comandita. *See*
Business Entities Appendix.

C. en C. por A.
Compainía en Comandita por
Acciones. *See* Business Entities
Appendix.

CENELEC
European Committee for
Electrotechnical
Standardization

CEO
Chief Executive Officer

CEPT
European Conference of Postal
and Telecommunications
Administrations

CERN
European Center for Nuclear
Research (Centre Européen de
Recherche Nucléaire)

CET
Common External Tariff

C&F
Cost and Freight

CFIUS
Committee on Foreign Investment
in the U.S.

CFO
Chief Financial Officer

CFR
Code of Federal Regulations
Cost and Freight

CFS
Country Focused Seminar

Cft. (or CuFt.)
Cubic Foot (Feet)

CFTA
Canadian Free Trade Agreement

CG
Consul General, Consulate
General

CHG
Charge d'Affairs

C.I.
Cost and insurance

Cía
Sociedad Colectiva. *See* Business
Entities Appendix.

CIB
Council for International Business

Cie
Compagnie
Offene Handelsgesellschaft. *See*
Business Entities Appendix.

CIF
Cost, Insurance and Freight

C.I.F.& C.
Cost, insurance, freight and
commission.

C.I.F.C.I.
Cost, insurance, freight, collection
and interest.

C.I.F.I.&E.
Cost, insurance, freight, interest,
and exchange.

CIM
Convention Internationale
Concernant le Transport des
Marchandises par Chemin de
Fer (The International
Convention for Transport of
Merchandise by Rail)

ACRONYMS

ACRONYMS

CIMS
Commercial Information Management System

CIO
Congress of Industrial Organizations

CIP
Carriage and Insurance Paid To
Commodity Import Program

CIS
Census Interface System
Commonwealth of Independent States

CISG
Convention on Contracts for the International Sale of Goods

CIT
Court of International Trade

CITA
Committee for the Implementation of Textile Agreements

CITES
Convention on International Trade in Endangered Species in Wild Fauna and Flora

C.K.D.
Completely Knocked Down

C.L.
Carload

CL
Containerload

CLS
Company Limited by Shares. *See* Business Entities Appendix.

C. Ltda.
Compainía de Responsabilidad Limitada. *See* Business Entities Appendix.

C.M.
Cubic Meter (capital letters);

cm
cm (small letters) centimeter

CMA
Common Monetary Agreement

CMEA
Council for Mutual Economic Assistance

CMP
Country Marketing Plan

C/N
Circular Note
Credit Note

CNUSA
Commercial News USA

C/O
In Care Of
Carried Over
Cash Order

Co.
Company. *See* Business Entities Appendix.
Offene Handelsgesellschaft. *See* Business Entities Appendix.
S Corporation. *See* Business Entities Appendix.

COCOM
Coordinating Committee on Multilateral Export Controls

C.O.D.
Collect (cash) on delivery

COE
Council of Europe

C.O.F.C.
Container on flatcar

COGSA
Carriage of Goods by Sea Act

COM
Chief of Mission
Cost of Manufacture

COMECON
Council for Mutual Economic Assistance

COMEX
Commodity Exchange Inc. (futures contracts)

COMSAT
Communications Satellite Corporation

Conc'd.
Concluded

Cont'd.
Continued

COO
Chief Operating Officer

COP
Cost of Production

Corp.
Corporation, *See* Business Entities Appendix.
Stock Corporation. *See* Business Entities Appendix.

CPE
Centrally Planned Economy

C. por A.
Companía por Acciones. *See* Sociedad Anónima in Business Entities Appendix.

c.p.t.
Cuideachta Phoibli Theoranta. *See* Business Entities Appendix.

CPT
Carriage Paid To

C.S.C.
Container Service Charge

CSCE
Conference on Security and Cooperation in Europe

CSIS
Center for Strategic and International Studies

CSP
Common Standard Level of Effective Protection

CSS
Cargo Selectivity System
Comparison Shopping Service

CT
Countertrade

CTD
Committee on Trade and Development

CTF
Certified Trade Fair (Certified Event)

CTIS
Center for Trade and Investment Services

CTM
Certified Trade Mission

CTP
Composite Theoretical Performance

Ctr
Container

Cu.
Cubic (measure)

CV
Constructed Value

C.V.
Commanditaire Vennootschap.
See Business Entities Appendix.

CVD
Countervailing Duty

Cwt.
(measure) Hundredweight
(U.S.A. is 100 lbs., United
Kingdom 112 lbs.)

CXT
Common External Tariff

C.Y.
Container Yard.

D

D/A
Documents Against Acceptance

DAF
Delivered at Frontier

D.B.A.
Doing Business As

DCM
Deputy Chief of Mission

D/D
Delivered

DDP
Delivered Duty Paid

DDU
Delivered Duty Unpaid

DEC
District Export Council

DEQ
Delivered Ex Quay

DES
Delivered Ex Ship

DISC
Domestic International Sales
Corporation

DISCO
Defense Industrial Security
Clearing Office

DL
Distribution License

D/O
Delivery Order

DOA
Department of Agriculture

DOC
Department of Commerce (U.S.)

DOD
Department of Defense (U.S.)

DOE
Department of Energy (U.S.)

DOL
Department of Labor (U.S.)

DOT
Department of Transportation

D/P
Documents Against Payment

DPAC
Defense Policy Advisory
Committee

D-RAM
Dynamic Random Access
Memory

DTC
Defense Trade Controls

DSL
Digital Subscriber Line

DTSA
Defense Technology Security
Administration

DTWG
Defense Trade Working Group

E

Ea or ea.
each

EAA
Export Administration Act

EAAA
Export Administration
Amendments Act

EAC
Export Assistance Center

EAEC
European Atomic Energy
Community

EAI
Enterprise for the Americas
Initiative

EAN
Except as otherwise noted

EAR
Export Administration
Regulations

EARB
Export Administration Review
Board

EBB
Economic Bulletin Board

EBRD
European Bank for
Reconstruction and
Development

EC
European Community

ECAs
Export Credit Agencies

ECASS
Export Control Automated
Support System

ECCN
Export Control Classification
Number; formerly: Export
Commodity Classification
Number

ECLS
Export Contact List Service

ECO/COM
Economic/Commercial Section

ECOWAS
Economic Community of West
African States

ECSC
European Coal and Steel
Community

ECU
European Currency Unit

EDC
Export Development Corporation

EDI
Electronic Data Interchange

EDIFACT
Electronic Data Interchange for
Administration, Commerce, and
Transportation

EDO
Export Development Office

A C R O N Y M S

EE
Eterorythmos Eteria. *See* Business Entities Appendix.

EEA
European Economic Area

EEBIC
Eastern Europe Business Information Center

EEC
European Economic Community

EEP
Export Enhancement Program

EEPROM
Electronically Erasable Programmable Read-Only Memory

EEZ
Exclusive Economic Zones

EFT
Electronic Funds Transfer

EFTA
European Free Trade Association

EIB
European Investment Bank

E.I. de R.L.
Empresa Individual de Responsibilidad Limitada. *See* Business Entities Appendix.

EIN
Employer Identification Number
Exporter Identification Number

EIRL
Eestabelecimento Individual de Responsabildade Limitada. *See* Business Entities Appendix.

ELAIN
Electronic License Application and Information Network

ELAN
Export Legal Assistance Network

ELP
Exempted Limited Partnership. *See* Business Entities Appendix.

ELVIS
Export License Voice Information System

EMC
Export Management Company

EMS
European Monetary System

EMU
European Monetary Union

E&OE
Errors and Omissions Excepted

EOTC
European Organization for Testing and Certification

EP
European Parliament

EPA
Environmental Protection Agency

EPC
Economic Policy Council
European Patent Convention

EPCI
Enhanced Proliferation Control Initiative

EPE
Eteria Periorismenis Efthinis. *See* Business Entities Appendix.

EPROM
Erasable Programmable Read-Only Memory

EPS
Export Promotion Services

EPZ
Export Processing Zone

ERLC
Export Revolving Line of Credit

ERM
Exchange Rate Mechanism

ESA
European Space Agency

ESP
Exporter's Sale Price

ESPRIT
European Strategic Program for Research and Development in Information Technologies

ESSS
Entry Summary Selectivity System

ETA
Estimated Time of Arrival

etc.
etcetra

ETC
Export Trading Company

ETD
Estimated Time of Departure

ETSI
European Telecommunications Standards Institute

EU
European Union

EUCLID
European Cooperation for the Long-term in Defense

EURAM
European Research in Advanced Materials

EURATOM
European Atomic Energy Community

EUREKA
European Research Coordination Agency

E.U.R.L.
Entreprise Unipersonnelle à Responsabilité Limitée. *See* Business Entities Appendix.

EXCEL
Export Credit Enhanced Leverage

EXIMBANK
Export-Import Bank of the U.S.A.

EXW
Ex Works

F

F
Fahrenheit

FAA
Federal Aviation Administration
Foreign Assistance Act

FAAS
Foreign Affairs Administrative Support

FAC
Foreign Assets Control

F.A.K.
Freight All Kinds

FAO
Food and Agricultural Organization

FAS
Foreign Agricultural Service
Free Alongside Ship

fax
facsimile (fax machine or fax letter)

FBIS
Foreign Broadcast Information Service

fbm (also Bd.Ft.)
Board Foot

FBP
Foreign Buyer Program

FBT
Flatbed Trailer

FCA
Free Carrier

FCIA
Foreign Credit Insurance Association

FCPA
Foreign Corrupt Practices Act

F.C.&S.
Free of Capture and Seizure Warranty

FDA
Food and Drug Administration

FDIC
Federal Deposit Insurance Corporation

FDIUS
Foreign Direct Investment in the United States

FEMA
Federal Emergency Management Agency

FET
Foreign Economic Trends

FEU
Forty Foot Equivalent Units

FFP
Food For Progress

FI
Free In

FIO
Free In and Out

F.I.O.S.
Free In, Out and Stow

FIT
Foreign Independent Tour

F.M.C. (or FMC)
Federal Maritime Commission

FMS
Foreign Military Sales

FMV
Foreign Market Value

FO
Free Out

FOB
Free on Board

FOR/FOT
Free on Rail/Free on Truck

FOREX
Foreign Exchange

FPA
Free of Particular Average

FPFS
Fines, Penalties, and Forfeitures System

FPG
Foreign Parent Group

FR
Flat Rack

FRA
Forward/Future Rate Agreement

FSC
Foreign Sales Corporation

FSI
Foreign Service Institute

FSN
Foreign Service National

FSO
Foreign Service Officer

ft
Foot/Feet (measure)

FTA
Free Trade Agreement
Free Trade Area

FTC
Federal Trade Commission (U.S.)

FTI
Foreign Traders Index

FTO
Foreign Trade Organization

FTZ
Foreign Trade Zone

FTZA
Foreign Trade Zone Act

FTZB
Foreign Trade Zone Board

FTZ-SZ
Foreign Trade Zone-Subzone

F/X
Foreign Exchange

G

G-5
Group of Five

G-7
Group of Seven

G-10
Group of Ten

G-24
Group of Twenty-Four

G-77
Group of Seventy-Seven

G/A
General Average

GAB
General Agreements to Borrow (Paris Club)

GATS
General License - Aircraft on Temporary Sojourn

GATT
General Agreement on Tariffs and Trade

G-BAGGAGE
General License - Baggage

GCC
Gulf Cooperation Council

GCG
General License - Shipments to Agencies of Cooperating Governments

G-COCOM
General License - COCOM

G-DEST
General License - Destination

GDP
Gross Domestic Product

GEM
Global Export Manager

GFW
General License - Free World

GIT
General License - In Transit
Shipments

GL
General License

GLR
General License - Return
(Replacement)

GLV
General License - Shipments of
Limited Value

GmbH
Gesellschaft mit beschränkter
Haftung. *See* Business Entities
Appendix.

G-NNR
General License - Non-Naval
Reserve

GNP
Gross National Product

GO
General Order

GPO
Government Printing Office
(U.S.)

G.R.I.
General Rate Increase

GSP
Generalized System of
Preferences

GTDA
General License - Technical Data

GTDR
General License - Technical Data
Restricted

G-TEMP
General License - Temporary
Export

GTF-U.S.
General License - Goods
Imported for Display at U.S.
Exhibitions or Trade Fairs

GUS
General License - Shipments to
Personnel and Agencies of the
U.S. Government

H

H
Height

HAWB
House Air Waybill

HC
High Commission (British)

H/H
House to House

HMHC
Her Majesty's High Commission

H.P.
Horsepower

H/P
House to Pier

HS
Harmonized System

HTS
Harmonized Tariff Schedule

HTSUS
Harmonized Tariff Schedule of
the U.S.

HTWG
High Technology Working Group

I

IACC
International Anticounterfeiting
Coalition

IAEA
International Atomic Energy
Agency

IAEL
International Atomic Energy List

IATA
International Air Transport
Association

IBF
International Banking Facility

IBOR
Interbank Offered Rate

IBM
International Business Machines
(Company)

IBRD
International Bank for
Reconstruction and
Development

IC
Import Certificate
Integrated Circuit

ICA
International Cocoa Agreement
International Coffee Agreement
International Commodity
Agreement

ICAO
International Civil Aviation
Organization

ICC
International Chamber of
Commerce (Paris)
Interstate Commerce Commission

ICO
International Congress Office

ICP
Industry Consultations Program

ICS
Investment Climate Statement

ICSID
International Center for the
Settlement for Investment
Disputes

ICSU
International Council of Scientific
Unions

I.D.
Inside Diameter

IDA
International Development
Association

IDB
Inter-American Development
Bank

IDCA
International Development
Cooperation Agency

IEA
International Energy Agency

IEC
International Electrotechnical
Commission

IEEPA
International Emergency
  Economic Powers Act

IEPG
Independent European Program
  Group

IESC
International Executive Service
  Corps

IFAC
Industry Functional Advisory
  Committee

IFAD
International Fund for
  Agricultural Development

IFC
International Finance Corporation

IFM
Inward Foreign Manifest

IFRB
International Frequency
  Registration Board

IFS
Industry Focused Seminar
In-Flight Survey

IGC
Interagency Group on
  Countertrade

IGPAC
Intergovernmental Policy
  Advisory Committee

IJA
International Jute Agreement

IL
Industrial List

ILO
International Labor Organization

IMF
International Monetary Fund

IMI
International Market Insight

IML
International Munitions List

IMO
International Maritime
  Organization

IMSO
International Maritime Satellite
  Organization

In.
Inch

Inc. or Corp.
Incorporated
Corporation
C corporation, *See* Business
  Entities Appendix.
Close Corporation, *See* Business
  Entities Appendix.
Stock Corporation. *See* Business
  Entities Appendix.

info.
Information

INMARSAT
International Maritime Satellite
  Organization

INPAC
Investment Policy Advisory
  Committee

INR
Initial Negotiating Right

INS
Immigration and Naturalization
  Service

INTELSAT
International Telecommunications
  Satellite Organization

IOGA
Industry-Organized, Government-
  Approved Mission

IPAC
Industry Policy Advisory
  Committee

IPO
Initial Public Offering (stock)

IPR
Intellectual Property Rights

IRA
International Rubber Agreement

IRS
Internal Revenue Service

I/S
Interessantelskab

ISA
Industry Sub-Sector Analysis
International Sugar Agreement

ISAC
Industry Sector Advisory
  Committee

ISBN
International Standard Book
  Number (publishing)

ISC
Intermodal Service Charge

ISDN
Integrated Services Digital
  Network

ISO
International Standards
  Organization

ITA
International Tin Agreement
International Trade
  Administration

ITAR
International Traffic in Arms
  Regulations

ITC
International Trade Commission

ITT
International Telephone &
  Telegraph

ITU
International Telecommunication
  Union

IVL
Individual Validated License

IWC
International Whaling
  Commission

J

JCIT
Joint Committee for Investment
  and Trade

JDB
Japan Development Bank

JEIC
Japan Export Information Center

JETRO
Japan External Trade
  Organization

JEXIM
The Export-Import Bank of Japan

JICA
Japan International Cooperation
  Agency

ACRONYMS

ACRONYMS

K

K.D.
Knocked Down

KDD
Kokusai Denshin Denwa

K.D.F.
Knocked Down Flat

KEG
Kommandit Erwerbsgesellschaft.
See Business Entities Appendix.

Kft
Korlátolt Felelosségu Társaság.
See Business Entities Appendix.

KG
Kommanditgesellschaft

KGS or Kilo(s)
Kilogram(s)

KK
Kabushiki Kaisha

Kkt
Közkereseti Társaság. See
Business Entities Appendix.

k.s.
Komanditní Spolecnost. See
Business Entities Appendix.

K/S
Kommanditselskab

L

L
Length

LAFTA
Latin American Free Trade
Association

LAIA
Latin American Integration
Association

LASH
Lighter Aboard Ship

Lb (s)
Pound(s) (weight measure)

L/C
Letter of Credit

LCL
Less Than Container Load

Lda.
Sociedade por Quota. See
Business Entities Appendix.

LDC
Least (Less, Lesser) Developed
Country
Limited Duration Companies. See
Business Entities Appendix.

LIBID
London Interbank Bid Rate

LIBOR
London Interbank Offered Rate

LIFFE
London International Financial
Futures Exchange

LIMEAN
London Interbank Mean

LLC
Limited Liability Company. See
Business Entities Appendix.

LLP
Limited Liability Partnership. See
Business Entities Appendix.

L.O.A.
Length Overall

LOI
Letter of Indemnity

L.S.
Lump Sum

L.T.
Long Ton (2,240 Pounds)

Ltd.
Limited
Corporation, See Business Entities
Appendix.
Private Company. See Business
Entities Appendix.

Ltda.
Sociedad de Responsabilidad
Limitada. See Business Entities
Appendix.
Limitada

Ltée.
Corporation, See Business Entities
Appendix.
Limitée

L.T.L.
Less than truckload

M

M
Measurement
Thousand (1,000 units)

max.
Maximum

MBF or MBM
One Thousand Board Feet

MC
Minister Counsellor

MCTL
Militarily Critical Technologies
List

M/D
Month's Date

MD
Managing Director

MDB
Multilateral Development Bank

MFA
Multi-Fiber Arrangement

MFN
Most Favored Nation

MFT
Per Thousand Feet

MHW
Ministry of Health and Welfare

MIF
Multilateral Investment Fund

MIGA
Multilateral Investment Guarantee
Agency

Mij.
Maatschappij

min.
Minimum

MIPRO
Manufactured Imports Promotion
Organization

MITI
Ministry of International Trade
and Industry

MKR
Matchmaker Program

M.O.
Money Order

ACRONYMS

MOCP
Market-Oriented Cooperation Plan

MOFERT
Ministry of Foreign Economic Relations and Trade

MOFTEC
Ministry of Foreign Economic Trade and Economic Cooperation

MOSS
Market-Oriented, Sector-Selective

MOU
Memorandum of Understanding

MPA
Major Projects Agreement

MPP
Market Promotion Program

MPT
Ministry of Posts and Telecommunications

MRA
Mutual Recognition Agreement

MT
Marine Terminal

MTAG
Missile Technology Advisory Group

MTCR
Missile Technology Control Regime

MTEC
Missile Technology Export Control Group

MTN
Multilateral Trade Negotiations

MTO
Multilateral Trade Organization

N

N/A
Not Applicable

NAEC
National Association of Export Companies

NAFTA
North American Free Trade Agreement

NASDA
National Association of State Development Agencies

NATO
North Atlantic Treaty Organization

N.B.
Note Below

NCC
National Chambers of Commerce

NEA
Nuclear Energy Agency

N.E.S.
Not Elsewhere Specified

NICs
Newly Industrializing Countries

NIPA
National Income and Product Accounts

NMEs
Nonmarket Economies

NNPA
Nuclear Non-Proliferation Act

NNPT
Nuclear Non-Proliferation Treaty

No
Number

N.O.I.B.N.
Not Otherwise Indexed by Number

N.O.S.
Not Otherwise Specified

NPT
Nuclear Non-Proliferation Treaty

NRC
Nuclear Regulatory Commission

NRL
Nuclear Referral List

NRPB
Natural Resource Based Products

N/S (also NSF)
Not Sufficient Funds

NS
Not Subject To

NSC
National Security Council

NSD
National Security Directive

NSF (also N/S)
Not Sufficient Funds

NSG
Nuclear Suppliers Group

NSO
National Security Override

NT
Net Ton

NTBs
Non-Tariff Barriers

NTDB
National Trade Data Bank

NTE
National Trade Estimates Report
New-To-Export

NTM
New-To-Market

NTMs
Non-Tariff Measures

NTT
Nippon Telegraph and Telephone Corporation

N.V.
Naamloze Vennootschap. *See* Business Entities Appendix.

NVOCC
Non-Vessel Operating Common Carrier

NYMEX
New York Mercantile Exchange

NYSE
New York Stock Exchange

O

OAPEC
Organization of Arab Petroleum Exporting Countries

OAS
Organization of American States

OAU
Organization of African Unity

O.B.L.
Ocean bill of lading

OBR
Overseas Business Report

OBU
Offshore Banking Unit

O/C
Overcharge

OC
Operating Committee

OCP
Overland Common Point

O.D.
Outside Diameter

ODA
Official Development Assistance

OE
Omorythmos Eteria. *See* Business
Entities Appendix.

OECD
Organization for Economic
Cooperation and Development

OEG
Offene Erwerbsgesellschaft. *See*
Business Entities Appendix.

OEL
Office of Export Licensing

OFAC
Office of Foreign Assets Control

OHG
Offene Handelsgesellschaft. *See*
Business Entities Appendix.

OIC
Organization of the Islamic
Conference

OIEC
Organization for Economic
Cooperation

OMA
Orderly Marketing Agreement

OMB
Office of Management and
Budget

OMC
Office of Munitions Control

OOD
Drouzestvo s Ogranichena
Otgovornost. *See* Business
Entities Appendix.

OPEC
Organization of Petroleum
Exporting Countries

OPIC
Overseas Private Investment
Corporation

ORM
Other Regulated Materials

O/S
Out of Stock

OSHA
Occupational Safety and Health
Administration

OT
Open Top

O/T
Overtime

OTC
Over the Counter

OTM
Old-To-Market

OWC
On Wheels Charge

Oy
Osakeyhtiö. *See* Business Entities
Appendix.

P

P/A
Power of Attorney

PC
Per Container
Personal Computer

P/C
Prices Current
Petty Cash

PCS
Piece(s)

PCT
Patent Cooperation Treaty

PEC
President's Export Council

PEFCO
Private Export Funding
Corporation

P/H
Pier to House

P&I
Principal and Interest

PIP
Post-Initiated Promotion

Pkg(s)
Package(s)

P&L
Profit and Loss

P.L.C.
Public Company. *See* Business
Entities Appendix.

PLC
Pre-License Check
Public Limited Company

P/N
Promissory Note

PP
Purchase Price

P.P.
Prepaid (Freight Prepaid)

P/P
Pier to Pier

PPA
Protocol of Provisional
Application

P.R.C.
People's Republic of China

PSV
Post-Shipment Verification

p/t
Part-time
Pte. Ltd.
Private Limited

PT
Per Trailer

PT 20
Per 20 Foot Trailer/Container

PT 40
Per 40 Foot Trailer/Container

PTA
Preferential Trade Agreement for
Eastern and Southern Africa

PU&D
Pick Up and Delivery

Pvt. Ltd.
Private Company. *See* Business
Entities Appendix.

Q

QRs
Quantitative Restrictions

R

R
Rail Ramp

RACE
Research in Advanced
  Communications in Europe

RAM
Random Access Memory

RBPs
Restrictive Business Practices

RCS
Regular Catalog Show

R&D
Research and Development

RFP
Request for Proposal

RFQ
Request for Quotation

ROM
Read Only Memory

RoRo
Roll-on, Roll-off

R.R.
Railroad

Rt
Részvénytársaság. *See* Business
  Entities Appendix.

RWA
Returned Without Action

S

S.A.
Sociedad Anónima. *See* Business
  Entities Appendix.
Sociedade Anónima. *See* Business
  Entities Appendix.
Società per Azioni. *See* Business
  Entities Appendix.
Société Anonyme. *See* Business
  Entities Appendix.
Spólka Akcyjna. *See* Business
  Entities Appendix.

SABIT
Special American Business
  Internship Training Program

SADC
Southern Africa Development
  Community

SACU
Southern African Customs Union

SADCC
Southern Africa Development
  Coordination Conference

S.A. de C.A.
Sociedad Anónima de Capital
  Abierto. *See* Business Entities
  Appendix.

S.A.R.L.
Société à Responsabilité Limitée.
  See Business Entities Appendix.

S.A.S.
Società in Accomandita Semplice.
  See Business Entities Appendix.
Société par Actions Simplifée. *See*
  Business Entities Appendix.

SASO
Saudi Arabian Standards
  Organization

SBA
Small Business Administration

S.C.
Sociedad Colectiva. *See* Business
  Entities Appendix.
Société en Commandite. Société
  Coopérative. *See* Business
  Entities Appendix.

S.C.A.
Sociedad en Comandita por
  Acciones. *See* Business Entities
  Appendix.

SCaRL
Società Cooperativa a
  Responsabilità. *See* Business
  Entities Appendix.

S.C.I.
Sociedad de Capital e Industria.
  See Business Entities Appendix.

SCM
Southern Common Market

SCO
Senior Commercial Officer

S.C. par A.
Société en Commandite par
  Actionss. *See* Business Entities
  Appendix.

SCRL
Sociedade Cooperativa. *See*
  Business Entities Appendix.

S.C.S.
Société en Commandite Simple.
  See Business Entities Appendix.

S&D
Special and Differential Treatment

S. de R.L. (also Ltda.)
Sociedad de Responsabilidad
  Limitada. *See* Business Entities
  Appendix.

Sdn. Bhd.
Sendirian Berhard. *See* Business
  Entities Appendix.

SDRs
Special Drawing Rights (banking)

SEA
Single European Act

SEC
Securities and Exchange
  Commission
Special Equipment Compensation

SED
Shipper's Export Declaration

SEED
Support for East European
  Democracy

SEM
Seminar Mission

S. en C.
Sociedad en Comandita. *See*
  Business Entities Appendix.
Société en Commandite Simple.
  See Business Entities Appendix.

S. en C.S.
Société en Commandite Simple.
  See Business Entities Appendix.

SEPD
State Export Program Database

SFO
Solo Fair (overseas procured)

SFSC
Shared Foreign Sales Corporation

ACRONYMS

A C R O N Y M S

SFW
Solo Fair (Washington procured)

SGA
Selling, General, and
Administrative (Expenses)

S.G.L.
Società a Garanzia Limitata. *See*
Business Entities Appendix.

SIC
Standard Industrial Classification

SII
Structural Impediments Initiative

SIMIS
Single Internal Market
Information Service

SIMS
Single Internal Market Service

S/IOGA
State/Industry-Organized,
Government-Approved

SITC
Standard International Tariff
Classification

SLI
Shipper's Letter of Instruction

SM (or sm)
Service Mark

SMSA
Standard Metropolitan Statistical
Area

SNC
Société en Nom Collectif. *See*
Business Entities Appendix.

SNEC
Sub-Group on Nuclear Export
Coordination

s/o (or S.O.)
Ship's Option, (rate yielding
greater revenue; must be
charged)

SOD
Shipped on Deck

SOGA
State-Organized, Government-
Approved Mission

S.p.A.
Società per Azioni. *See* Business
Entities Appendix.

SPAC
Services Policy Advisory
Committee

spol. s r.o.
Spolecnost s Rucením
Omezenym. *See* Business
Entities Appendix.

S.P.R.L.
Société Privée a Reponsabilité
Limitéeprivate. *See* Business
Entities Appendix.

S.P.R.L.
Société de Personnes à
Responsabilité Limitée. *See*
Business Entities Appendix.

Sp. z o.o.
Spólka z Ograniczona Odpowied
Zialnóscia. *See* Business
Entities Appendix.

S.Q.
Sociedad por Quota

S.R.&C.C.
Strikes, Riots and Civil
Commotion Warranty (all risk
insurance)

S.R.L.
Sociedad de Responsabilidad
Limitada. *See* Business Entities
Appendix.
Società a Responsabilità Limitata.
See Business Entities Appendix.
Société à Responsabilité Limitée.
See Business Entities Appendix.

s.r.o.
Spolecnost s Rucením
Omezenym. *See* Business
Entities Appendix.

SSA
Sub-Saharan Africa

STA
Semiconductor Trade Agreement

S.T.C.
Said to Contain

Sté.
Société

Ste. Cve.
Société Cooperative. *See* Business
Entities Appendix.

STELA
System for Tracking Export
License Applications

STEs
State Trading Enterprises

STM
State Trade Mission

S.T.W.
Said to Weigh

S.U.
Set Up

T

T.
Ton of 2,240 lbs

TA
Trade Assistant

TAA
Trade Adjustment Assistance

TAAC
Trade Adjustment Assistance
Center

TAC
Technical Advisory Committee

TACM
Transit Air Cargo Manifest

TAPO
Trade Assistance and Planning
Office

TCI
Third Country Initiative

TCMD
Third Country Meat Directive

TDO
Table of Denial Orders

TDP
Trade and Development Program

TEC or CXT
Tarif Extérieur Commun
(common external tariff)

Tel.
Telephone

Teo.
Steoranta. *See* Business Entities
Appendix.

TEU
Twenty foot equivalent unit. A forty foot container is equal to two (2) TEU'S.

TFC
Trade Fair Certification

TFO
Trade Fair (Overseas-Recruited)

TFW
Trade Fair (Washington-Recruited)

THC
Terminal Handling Charge

TIA
Travel Industry Association of America

TIB
Temporary Importation under Bond

TIC
Trade Information Center

TIEA
Tax Information Exchange Agreement

TIFTs
Trade and Investment Facilitation Talks

TIMS
Textiles Information Management System

T.L.
Total Loss (shipping)
Truckload

T.L.S.
Türk Limited Sirket. *See* Business Entities Appendix.

T.M.
Traffic Manager

TM
Trademark
Trade Mission

TNC
Trade Negotiations Committee

T.O.F.C.
Trailer (On Wheels) Flat Car

TOP
Trade Opportunities Program

TPC
Trade Policy Committee

TPCC
Trade Promotion Coordinating Committee

TPIS
Trade Policy Information System

TPM
Trigger Price Mechanism

TPRG
Trade Policy Review Group

TPRM
Trade Policy Review Mechanism

TPSC
Trade Policy Staff Committee

TRA
Trade Reference Assistant

TRIMs
Trade-Related Investment Measures

TRIPs
Trade-Related Aspects of Intellectual Property Rights

TRO
Temporary Restraining Order

TS
Trade Specialist

TSB
Textile Surveillance Body

TSUSA
Tariff Schedules of the United States Annotated. Usually referred to as HTSUS or Harmonized Tariff Schedules of the United States

T.T.S.
Telegraphic transfer selling rate

TWEA
Trading With the Enemy Act

U

U.A.E.
United Arab Emirates

UBO
Ultimate Beneficial Owner

UCC
Uniform Commercial Code

UCP
Uniform Customs and Practices

UCPDC
Uniform Customs and Practice for Documentary Credits

U.K.
United Kingdom

ULD
Unit Load Device

UMOA
West African Monetary Union (Union Monétaire Ouest Africaine)

UN
United Nations

UNCDF
United Nations Capital Development Fund

UNCSTD
United Nations Conference on Science and Technology for Development

UNCTAD
United Nations Conference on Trade and Development

UNDP
United Nations Development Program

UNDRO
United Nations Disaster Relief Organization

UNEP
United Nations Environment Program

UNESCO
United Nations Educational, Scientific, and Cultural Organization

UNFPA
United Nations Fund for Population Activities

UNGA
United Nations General Assembly

UNHCR
United Nations High Commissioner for Refugees

UNICEF
United Nations International Children's Emergency Fund

ACRONYMS

UNIDO
United Nations Industrial
Development Organization

UNITAR
United Nations Institute for
Training and Research

UNRISD
United Nations Research Institute
for Social Development

UNRWA
United Nations Relief and Works
Agency

URC
Uniform Rules for Collection

U.S. or U.S.A.
United States of America

USC
United States Code

USCS
United States Customs Service

USD (also US$)
United States Dollar

USDA
U.S. Department of Agriculture

USDIA
U.S. Direct Investment Abroad

USEC
U.S. Mission to the European
Communities

US&FCS
United States and Foreign
Commercial Service

USGPO
U.S. Government Printing Office

USIA
U.S. Information Agency

USIS
United States Information Service

USITC
United States International Trade
Commission

U.S.M.C
United States Maritime
Commission

USML
U.S. Munitions List

USP
United States Price

USSR
Union of Soviet Socialist
Republics

USTDA
U.S. Trade and Development
Agency

USTR
United States Trade
Representative

USTTA
United States Travel and Tourism
Administration

USUN
U.S. Mission to the United
Nations

V

VAT
Value-Added Tax

VER
Voluntary Export Restriction

VHF
Very High Frequency

Viz
Namely

VL
Variable Levy

VOA
Voice of America

v.o.s.
Verejná Obchodní Spolecnost. *See*
Business Entities Appendix.

VP
Vice President

VRA
Voluntary Restraint Agreement

W-X-Y-Z

W
Width

W
Ton of 1000 kilos

w/ (also W/)
With

WA
With Average

WAMU
West African Monetary Union

WARC
World Administrative Radio
Conference

W/B
Waybill

WFG
Wharfage

WIPO
World Intellectual Property
Organization

WLL
Sharika That Massouliyyah
Mahdoodah. *See* Business
Entities Appendix.

WMO
World Meteorological
Organization

W/O
Without

W.P.A.
With Particular Average
(insurance)

WTDR
World Traders Data Report

WTO
World Tourism Organization
World Trade Organization

WWW
World Wide Web

Country Codes (ISO 3166)

The following two tables list ISO (International Organization for Standardization) 2-letter, 3-letter and numeric codes for countries of the world. ISO codes are used in communications to identify countries where a code or abbreviation is helpful. These *are not* currency or dialing codes.
Table 1 is sorted by country and then codes.
Table 2 is sorted by 2-letter code, then country.

Table 1: COUNTRY ☞ Country Code

Country	2-letter	3-letter	Numeric
Afghanistan	AF	AFG	4
Albania	AL	ALB	8
Algeria	DZ	DZA	12
American Samoa	AS	ASM	16
Andorra	AD	AND	20
Angola	AO	AGO	24
Anguilla	AI	AIA	660
Antarctica	AQ	ATA	10
Antigua and Barbuda	AG	ATG	28
Argentina	AR	ARG	32
Armenia	AM	ARM	51
Aruba	AW	ABW	533
Australia	AU	AUS	36
Austria	AT	AUT	40
Azerbaijan	AZ	AZE	31
Bahamas	BS	BHS	44
Bahrain	BH	BHR	48
Bangladesh	BD	BGD	50
Barbados	BB	BRB	52
Belarus	BY	BLR	112
Belgium	BE	BEL	56
Belize	BZ	BLZ	84
Benin	BJ	BEN	204
Bermuda	BM	BMU	60
Bhutan	BT	BTN	64
Bolivia	BO	BOL	68
Bosnia-Herzegovina	BA	BIH	70
Botswana	BW	BWA	72
Bouvet Island	BV	BVT	74
Brazil	BR	BRA	76

Table 2: COUNTRY CODE ☞ Country

2-letter	Country	3-letter	Numeric
AD	Andorra	AND	20
AE	United Arab Emirates	ARE	784
AF	Afghanistan	AFG	4
AG	Antigua and Barbuda	ATG	28
AI	Anguilla	AIA	660
AL	Albania	ALB	8
AM	Armenia	ARM	51
AN	Netherlands Antilles	ANT	530
AO	Angola	AGO	24
AQ	Antarctica	ATA	10
AR	Argentina	ARG	32
AS	American Samoa	ASM	16
AT	Austria	AUT	40
AU	Australia	AUS	36
AW	Aruba	ABW	533
AZ	Azerbaijan	AZE	31
BA	Bosnia-Herzegovina	BIH	70
BB	Barbados	BRB	52
BD	Bangladesh	BGD	50
BE	Belgium	BEL	56
BF	Burkina Faso	BFA	854
BG	Bulgaria	BGR	100
BH	Bahrain	BHR	48
BI	Burundi	BDI	108
BJ	Benin	BEN	204
BM	Bermuda	BMU	60
BN	Brunei Darussalam	BRN	96
BO	Bolivia	BOL	68

COUNTRIES

Table 1: COUNTRY ☞ Country Code

Country	2-letter	3-letter	Numeric
British Indian Ocean Territory	IO	IOT	86
Brunei Darussalam	BN	BRN	96
Bulgaria	BG	BGR	100
Burkina Faso	BF	BFA	854
Burundi	BI	BDI	108
Cambodia	KH	KHM	116
Cameroon	CM	CMR	120
Canada	CA	CAN	124
Cape Verde	CV	CPV	132
Cayman Islands	KY	CYM	136
Central African Republic	CF	CAF	140
Chad	TD	TCD	148
Chile	CL	CHL	152
China	CN	CHN	156
Christmas Island	CX	CXR	162
Cocos (Keeling) Islands	CC	CCK	166
Colombia	CO	COL	170
Comoros	KM	COM	174
Congo	CG	COG	178
Cook Islands	CK	COK	184
Costa Rica	CR	CRI	188
Croatia	HR	HRV	191
Cuba	CU	CUB	192
Cyprus	CY	CYP	196
Czech Republic	CZ	CZE	203
Denmark	DK	DNK	208
Djibouti	DJ	DJI	262
Dominica	DM	DMA	212
Dominican Republic	DO	DOM	214
East Timor	TP	TMP	626
Ecuador	EC	ECU	218
Egypt	EG	EGY	818
El Salvador	SV	SLV	222
Equat. Guinea	GQ	GNQ	226

Table 2: COUNTRY CODE ☞ Country

2-letter	Country	3-letter	Numeric
BR	Brazil	BRA	76
BS	Bahamas	BHS	44
BT	Bhutan	BTN	64
BV	Bouvet Island	BVT	74
BW	Botswana	BWA	72
BY	Belarus	BLR	112
BZ	Belize	BLZ	84
CA	Canada	CAN	124
CC	Cocos (Keeling) Islands	CCK	166
CD	Zaire	COD	180
CF	Central African Republic	CAF	140
CG	Congo	COG	178
CH	Switzerland	CHE	756
CI	Ivory Coast	CIV	384
CK	Cook Islands	COK	184
CL	Chile	CHL	152
CM	Cameroon	CMR	120
CN	China	CHN	156
CO	Colombia	COL	170
CR	Costa Rica	CRI	188
CU	Cuba	CUB	192
CV	Cape Verde	CPV	132
CX	Christmas Island	CXR	162
CY	Cyprus	CYP	196
CZ	Czech Republic	CZE	203
DE	Germany	DEU	276
DJ	Djibouti	DJI	262
DK	Denmark	DNK	208
DM	Dominica	DMA	212
DO	Dominican Republic	DOM	214
DZ	Algeria	DZA	12
EC	Ecuador	ECU	218
EE	Estonia	EST	233
EG	Egypt	EGY	818
EH	Western Sahara	ESH	732
ER	Eritrea	ERI	232

Table 1: COUNTRY ☞ Country Code

Country	2-letter	3-letter	Numeric
Eritrea	ER	ERI	232
Estonia	EE	EST	233
Ethiopia	ET	ETH	231
Falkland Islands	FK	FLK	238
Faroe Islands	FO	FRO	234
Fiji	FJ	FJI	242
Finland	FI	FIN	246
France	FR	FRA	250
France (Metro)	FX	FXX	249
French Guiana	GF	GUF	254
French Polynesia	PF	PYF	258
French Southern Territories	TF	ATF	260
Gabon	GA	GAB	266
Gambia	GM	GMB	270
Georgia	GE	GEO	268
Germany	DE	DEU	276
Ghana	GH	GHA	288
Gibraltar	GI	GIB	292
Greece	GR	GRC	300
Greenland	GL	GRL	304
Grenada	GD	GRD	308
Guadeloupe	GP	GLP	312
Guam	GU	GUM	316
Guatemala	GT	GTM	320
Guinea	GN	GIN	324
Guinea-Bissau	GW	GNB	624
Guyana	GY	GUY	328
Haiti	HT	HTI	332
Heard and McDonald Isl.	HM	HMD	334
Honduras	HN	HND	340
Hong Kong	HK	HKG	344
Hungary	HU	HUN	348
Iceland	IS	ISL	352
India	IN	IND	356
Indonesia	ID	IDN	360
Iran	IR	IRN	364

Table 2: COUNTRY CODE ☞ Country

2-letter	Country	3-letter	Numeric
ES	Spain	ESP	724
ET	Ethiopia	ETH	231
FI	Finland	FIN	246
FJ	Fiji	FJI	242
FK	Falkland Islands	FLK	238
FO	Faroe Islands	FRO	234
FR	France	FRA	250
FX	France (Metropolitan)	FXX	249
GA	Gabon	GAB	266
GB	United Kingdom	GBR	826
GD	Grenada	GRD	308
GE	Georgia	GEO	268
GF	French Guiana	GUF	254
GH	Ghana	GHA	288
GI	Gibraltar	GIB	292
GL	Greenland	GRL	304
GM	Gambia	GMB	270
GN	Guinea	GIN	324
GP	Guadeloupe	GLP	312
GQ	Equatorial Guinea	GNQ	226
GR	Greece	GRC	300
GS	S. Georgia & South Sandwich Islands	SGS	239
GT	Guatemala	GTM	320
GU	Guam	GUM	316
GW	Guinea-Bissau	GNB	624
GY	Guyana	GUY	328
HK	Hong Kong	HKG	344
HM	Heard and McDonald Islands	HMD	334
HN	Honduras	HND	340
HR	Croatia	HRV	191
HT	Haiti	HTI	332
HU	Hungary	HUN	348
ID	Indonesia	IDN	360
IE	Ireland	IRL	372
IL	Israel	ISR	376
IN	India	IND	356

COUNTRIES

COUNTRIES

Table 1: COUNTRY ☞ Country Code

Country	2-letter	3-letter	Numeric
Iraq	IQ	IRQ	368
Ireland	IE	IRL	372
Israel	IL	ISR	376
Italy	IT	ITA	380
Ivory Coast	CI	CIV	384
Jamaica	JM	JAM	388
Japan	JP	JPN	392
Jordan	JO	JOR	400
Kazakhstan	KZ	KAZ	398
Kenya	KE	KEN	404
Kiribati	KI	KIR	296
Kuwait	KW	KWT	414
Kyrgyzstan	KG	KGZ	417
Laos	LA	LAO	418
Latvia	LV	LVA	428
Lebanon	LB	LBN	422
Lesotho	LS	LSO	426
Liberia	LR	LBR	430
Libya	LY	LBY	434
Liechtenstein	LI	LIE	438
Lithuania	LT	LTU	440
Luxembourg	LU	LUX	442
Macau	MO	MAC	446
Macedonia	MK	MKD	807
Madagascar	MG	MDG	450
Malawi	MW	MWI	454
Malaysia	MY	MYS	458
Maldives	MV	MDV	462
Mali	ML	MLI	466
Malta	MT	MLT	470
Marshall Islands	MH	MHL	584
Martinique	MQ	MTQ	474
Mauritania	MR	MRT	478
Mauritius	MU	MUS	480
Mayotte	YT	MYT	175
Mexico	MX	MEX	484
Micronesia	OF	FM	FSM
Moldova	MD	MDA	498

Table 2: COUNTRY CODE ☞ Country

2-letter	Country	3-letter	Numeric
IO	British Indian Ocean Territory	IOT	86
IQ	Iraq	IRQ	368
IR	Iran	IRN	364
IS	Iceland	ISL	352
IT	Italy	ITA	380
JM	Jamaica	JAM	388
JO	Jordan	JOR	400
JP	Japan	JPN	392
KE	Kenya	KEN	404
KG	Kyrgyzstan	KGZ	417
KH	Cambodia	KHM	116
KI	Kiribati	KIR	296
KM	Comoros	COM	174
KN	Saint Kitts and Nevis	KNA	659
KP	North Korea	PRK	408
KR	South Korea	KOR	410
KW	Kuwait	KWT	414
KY	Cayman Islands	CYM	136
KZ	Kazakhstan	KAZ	398
LA	Laos	LAO	418
LB	Lebanon	LBN	422
LC	Saint Lucia	LCA	662
LI	Liechtenstein	LIE	438
LK	Sri Lanka	LKA	144
LR	Liberia	LBR	430
LS	Lesotho	LSO	426
LT	Lithuania	LTU	440
LU	Luxembourg	LUX	442
LV	Latvia	LVA	428
LY	Libya	LBY	434
MA	Morocco	MAR	504
MC	Monaco	MCO	492
MD	Moldova	MDA	498
MG	Madagascar	MDG	450
MH	Marshall Islands	MHL	584
MK	Macedonia	MKD	807

Table 1: COUNTRY ☞ Country Code

Country	2-letter	3-letter	Numeric
Monaco	MC	MCO	492
Mongolia	MN	MNG	496
Montserrat	MS	MSR	500
Morocco	MA	MAR	504
Mozambique	MZ	MOZ	508
Myanmar	MM	MMR	104
Namibia	NA	NAM	516
Nauru	NR	NRU	520
Nepal	NP	NPL	524
Netherlands	NL	NLD	528
Netherlands Antilles	AN	ANT	530
New Caledonia	NC	NCL	540
New Zealand	NZ	NZL	554
Nicaragua	NI	NIC	558
Niger	NE	NER	562
Nigeria	NG	NGA	566
Niue	NU	NIU	570
Norfolk Island	NF	NFK	574
North Korea	KP	PRK	408
Northern Marianas	MP	MNP	580
Norway	NO	NOR	578
Oman	OM	OMN	512
Pakistan	PK	PAK	586
Palau	PW	PLW	585
Palestinian Territory, Occup.	PS	PSE	275
Panama	PA	PAN	591
Papua New Guinea	PG	PNG	598
Paraguay	PY	PRY	600
Peru	PE	PER	604
Philippines	PH	PHL	608
Pitcairn Islands	PN	PCN	612
Poland	PL	POL	616
Portugal	PT	PRT	620
Puerto Rico	PR	PRI	630
Qatar	QA	QAT	634

Table 2: COUNTRY CODE ☞ Country

2-letter	Country	3-letter	Numeric
ML	Mali	MLI	466
MM	Myanmar	MMR	104
MN	Mongolia	MNG	496
MO	Macau	MAC	446
MP	Northern Marianas	MNP	580
MQ	Martinique	MTQ	474
MR	Mauritania	MRT	478
MS	Montserrat	MSR	500
MT	Malta	MLT	470
MU	Mauritius	MUS	480
MV	Maldives	MDV	462
MW	Malawi	MWI	454
MX	Mexico	MEX	484
MY	Malaysia	MYS	458
MZ	Mozambique	MOZ	508
NA	Namibia	NAM	516
NC	New Caledonia	NCL	540
NE	Niger	NER	562
NF	Norfolk Island	NFK	574
NG	Nigeria	NGA	566
NI	Nicaragua	NIC	558
NL	Netherlands	NLD	528
NO	Norway	NOR	578
NP	Nepal	NPL	524
NR	Nauru	NRU	520
NU	Niue	NIU	570
NZ	New Zealand	NZL	554
OF	Micronesia	FM	FSM
OM	Oman	OMN	512
PA	Panama	PAN	591
PE	Peru	PER	604
PF	French Polynesia	PYF	258
PG	Papua New Guinea	PNG	598
PH	Philippines	PHL	608
PK	Pakistan	PAK	586
PL	Poland	POL	616
PM	Saint Pierre and Miquelon	SPM	666

COUNTRIES

Table 1: COUNTRY ☛ Country Code

Country	2-letter	3-letter	Numeric
Reunion	RE	REU	638
Romania	RO	ROM	642
Russian Federation	RU	RUS	643
Rwanda	RW	RWA	646
Saint Kitts and Nevis	KN	KNA	659
Saint Lucia	LC	LCA	662
Saint Helena and Dependencies	SH	SHN	654
Saint Pierre and Miquelon	PM	SPM	666
Saint Vincent and Grenadines	VC	VCT	670
Samoa	WS	WSM	882
San Marino	SM	SMR	674
Sao Tome and Principe	ST	STP	678
Saudi Arabia	SA	SAU	682
Senegal	SN	SEN	686
Seychelles	SC	SYC	690
Sierra Leone	SL	SLE	694
Singapore	SG	SGP	702
Slovakia	SK	SVK	703
Slovenia	SI	SVN	705
Solomon Islands	SB	SLB	90
Somalia	SO	SOM	706
South Africa	ZA	ZAF	710
S. Georgia and S. Sandwich Isl.	GS	SGS	239
South Korea	KR	KOR	410
Spain	ES	ESP	724
Sri Lanka	LK	LKA	144
Sudan	SD	SDN	736
Suriname	SR	SUR	740
Svalbard and Jan Mayen Islands	SJ	SJM	744
Swaziland	SZ	SWZ	748
Sweden	SE	SWE	752
Switzerland	CH	CHE	756

Table 2: COUNTRY CODE ☛ Country

2-letter	Country	3-letter	Numeric
PN	Pitcairn Islands	PCN	612
PR	Puerto Rico	PRI	630
PS	Palestinian Territory, Occupied	PSE	275
PT	Portugal	PRT	620
PW	Palau	PLW	585
PY	Paraguay	PRY	600
QA	Qatar	QAT	634
RE	Reunion	REU	638
RO	Romania	ROM	642
RU	Russian Federation	RUS	643
RW	Rwanda	RWA	646
SA	Saudi Arabia	SAU	682
SB	Solomon Islands	SLB	90
SC	Seychelles	SYC	690
SD	Sudan	SDN	736
SE	Sweden	SWE	752
SG	Singapore	SGP	702
SH	Saint Helena and Dependencies	SHN	654
SI	Slovenia	SVN	705
SJ	Svalbard and Jan Mayen Islands	SJM	744
SK	Slovakia	SVK	703
SL	Sierra Leone	SLE	694
SM	San Marino	SMR	674
SN	Senegal	SEN	686
SO	Somalia	SOM	706
SR	Suriname	SUR	740
ST	Sao Tome and Principe	STP	678
SV	El Salvador	SLV	222
SY	Syria	SYR	760
SZ	Swaziland	SWZ	748
TC	Turks and Caicos Islands	TCA	796
TD	Chad	TCD	148
TF	French Southern Territories	ATF	260

Table 1: COUNTRY ☞ Country Code

Country	2-letter	3-letter	Numeric
Syria	SY	SYR	760
Taiwan	TW	TWN	158
Tajikistan	TJ	TJK	762
Tanzania	TZ	TZA	834
Thailand	TH	THA	764
Togo	TG	TGO	768
Tokelau	TK	TKL	772
Tonga	TO	TON	776
Trinidad & Tobago	TT	TTO	780
Tunisia	TN	TUN	788
Turkey	TR	TUR	792
Turkmenistan	TM	TKM	795
Turks and Caicos Islands	TC	TCA	796
Tuvalu	TV	TUV	798
Uganda	UG	UGA	800
Ukraine	UA	UKR	804
United Arab Emirates	AE	ARE	784
United Kingdom	GB	GBR	826
United States	US	USA	840
US Minor Outlying Islands	UM	UMI	581
Uruguay	UY	URY	858
Uzbekistan	UZ	UZB	860
Vanuatu	VU	VUT	548
Vatican City	VA	VAT	336
Venezuela	VE	VEN	862
Vietnam	VN	VNM	704
Virgin Is. (UK)	VG	VGB	92
Virgin Is. (US)	VI	VIR	850
Wallis & Futuna	WF	WLF	876
Western Sahara	EH	ESH	732
Yemen	YE	YEM	887
Yugoslavia	YU	YUG	891
Zaire	CD	COD	180
Zambia	ZM	ZMB	894
Zimbabwe	ZW	ZWE	716

Table 2: COUNTRY CODE ☞ Country

2-letter	Country	3-letter	Numeric
TG	Togo	TGO	768
TH	Thailand	THA	764
TJ	Tajikistan	TJK	762
TK	Tokelau	TKL	772
TM	Turkmenistan	TKM	795
TN	Tunisia	TUN	788
TO	Tonga	TON	776
TP	East Timor	TMP	626
TR	Turkey	TUR	792
TT	Trinidad and Tobago	TTO	780
TV	Tuvalu	TUV	798
TW	Taiwan	TWN	158
TZ	Tanzania	TZA	834
UA	Ukraine	UKR	804
UG	Uganda	UGA	800
UM	United States Minor Outlying Islands	UMI	581
US	United States	USA	840
UY	Uruguay	URY	858
UZ	Uzbekistan	UZB	860
VA	Vatican City	VAT	336
VC	Saint Vincent and the Grenadines	VCT	670
VE	Venezuela	VEN	862
VG	Virgin Islands (UK)	VGB	92
VI	Virgin Islands (US)	VIR	850
VN	Vietnam	VNM	704
VU	Vanuatu	VUT	548
WF	Wallis and Futuna	WLF	876
WS	Samoa	WSM	882
YE	Yemen	YEM	887
YT	Mayotte	MYT	175
YU	Yugoslavia	YUG	891
ZA	South Africa	ZAF	710
ZM	Zambia	ZMB	894
ZW	Zimbabwe	ZWE	716

COUNTRIES

International Dialing Guide

This Dialing Guide and the table that follows have been designed to be useful for anyone, regardless of the country of origin or the country of destination of their call.

For each country, the country dialing code, the capital city (when applicable), the city (or area) code, and time zone information are provided. The capital city is indicated with a ◉.

HOW TO DIAL INTERNATIONAL CALLS

International direct dialing from most countries is quite easy. An international call simply consists of dialing a sequence of numbers as follows:
1. The International Access Code (IAC),
2. The country code,
3. The city/area code, and
4. The local telephone number.

Each step routes your call a step closer to the person or business you are calling.

The International Access Code (IAC). The IAC is a prefix used to get an international line. For example, if you are calling from the United States, the IAC is '011'. The IAC differs from country to country. For Brazil it is '00'. Some countries do not allow direct dialing for international calls and require an operator. The table on the next page lists IAC prefixes for most countries. You may need to wait for a dial tone after dialing the IAC.

The Country Code. Next comes the code of the country you are calling. Refer to "International Dialing Codes" on page 235 for a list of country codes.

The Area Code. This is the regional or city dialing code. Refer to "International Dialing Codes" on page 235 for a listing of many area codes. Note that some countries have done away with area codes, incorporating them into individual subscriber numbers.

The Local Telephone Number. This is also called the subscriber number.

Points of Confusion

1. When you get someone's phone number, you may also get the IAC, country code and area code along with the actual subscriber number. This can cause confusion, especially when they give you *their* country's IAC rather than *your* IAC.

2. Many business cards have the country's long-distance prefix added to the number. This is *not* the IAC and is only used when making long-distance calls within their country. For example, "0" is the long-distance, direct-dial-prefix for

Germany. This prefix is not added to an international call to Germany.

3. The country code for the North American Numbering Plan (USA, Canada and much of the Caribbean nations) is '1'. Calls between these countries are treated simply as long-distance calls within the same country; you do not use the IAC, but use '1' as the long distance prefix.

Example 1
A call from London, U.K. ➔ Chicago, USA:
> **010 + [1] + (312) + (local number)**

UK's IAC is '010', the U.S.' country code is [1] and Chicago's area code is (312).

Example 2
A call from Denmark ➔ Sydney, Australia:
> **00 + [61] + (2) + (local number)**

Denmark's IAC is '00', Australia's country code is [61] and Sydney's area code is (2).

Example 3
A call from the USA ➔ Vancouver, Canada:
> **1 + (604) + (the local number)**

The prefix '1' is used for long-distance calls in Canada, the U.S., and the Caribbean. Vancouver's area code is (604).

Example 4
A call from Hong Kong ➔ Delhi, India:
> **001 + [91] + (11) + (local number).**

Hong Kong's IAC is '001', India's country code is [91], and Delhi's city code is (11).

Example 5
A call from the USA ➔ Hong Kong:
> **011 + [852] + (local number)**

The U.S.' IAC is '011', Hong Kong's country code is [852], and there are no city/area codes.

Example 6
A call from the USA ➔ anywhere in the Dominican Republic:
> **1+ (809) + (local number)**

The prefix '1' is used for long-distance calls within the North American Numbering Plan (Canada, the U.S., and much of the Caribbean) and (809) is the area code for the Dominican Republic.

D
I
A
L
I
N
G

INTERNATIONAL ACCESS CODES (IAC)

When making an international call *from* a country listed below, dial its IAC prior to the country code of the country you are calling. See "How to Dial International Calls" on the preceding page.

*Denotes a pause (e.g., 8*10 means dial 8, wait for tone, then dial 10).

Afghanistan 00	Georgia 8*10	New Zealand 00
Albania 00	Germany 00	Nicaragua 00
Algeria 00*	Greece 00	Niger 00
Angola 00	Guam 011	Nigeria 009
Argentina 00	Guatemala 00	Norway 00
Armenia................................... 00	Guinea 00	Oman....................................... 00
Australia 0011	Guyana 001	Pakistan 00
Austria 00	Haiti 00	Panama 0
Austria fax calls 0015	Honduras 00	Papua New Guinea.............. 05
Azerbaijan 8*10	Hong Kong 001	Paraguay................................. 00
Bahamas 011	Hungary 00	Peru 00
Bahrain 0	Iceland 00	Philippines 00
Bangladesh 00	India 00	Poland 0*0
Belarus.................................... 8	Indonesia 001	Portugal 00
Belgium 00	Iran 00	Qatar 0
Belize..................................... 00	Iraq 00	Romania 00
Bermuda................................ 011	Ireland 00	Russia 8*10
Bolivia 00	Israel 00	Rwanda 00
Bosnia & Herzegovina 00	Italy 00	Saudi Arabia 00
Brazil 0021	Ivory Coast 00	Senegal 00
Brunei 00	Jamaica 011	Sierra Leone 00
Burkina Faso 00	Japan 001	Singapore 001
Burundi.................................. 90	Jordan 00	Slovakia 00
Bulgaria 00	Kazakhstan 8*10	Slovenia.................................. 00
Cambodia 00	Kenya 000	Somalia 19
Cameroon 00	Korea, South 001	South Africa 09
Canada 011	Korea, North 00	Spain 00
Central African Rep. 19	Kuwait 00	Sri Lanka 00
Chad 00	Kyrgyzstan 00	Sudan 00
Chile 00	Laos....................................... 14	Suriname 00
China (PRC) 00	Latvia 00	Swaziland 00
Colombia 009	Lebanon 00	Sweden 00
Congo, Dem. Rep. of	Lesotho 00	Switzerland 00
(formerly Zaire) 00	Liberia 00	Syria....................................... 00
Costa Rica 00	Libya 00	Taiwan 002
Côte d'Ivoire 00	Liechtenstein 00	Tajikistan 8*10
Croatia................................... 00	Lithuania 8*10	Tanzania 000
Cuba 119	Luxembourg 00	Thailand 001
Cuba	Macau 00	Thailand to Malaysia 007
(Guantánamo Bay) 00	Madagascar 00	Trinidad & Tobago.............. 011
Cyprus 00	Malawi 101	Tunisia 00
Czech Republic 00	Malaysia 00	Turkey 00
Denmark 00	Mali 00	Turkmenistan 8
Djibouti 00	Malta 00	Uganda 00
Dominican Republic 011	Mauritius 00	Ukraine................................ 8*10
Ecuador 00	Mexico 00	United Arab Emirates 00
Egypt 00	Moldova 8*10	United Kingdom 00
El Salvador 0	Monaco 00	United States 011
Estonia 00	Mongolia 00	Uruguay 00
Ethiopia 00	Morocco 00*	Uzbekistan 8
Fiji... 05	Mozambique 00	Venezuela 00
Finland 00	Myanmar 00	Vietnam 00
France 00	Namibia 09	Yugoslavia 99
French Antilles 00	Nepal 00	Zambia 00
French Guiana 00	Netherlands 00	Zimbabwe 00
Gabon 00	Netherlands Antilles 00	

TIME ZONES

Time differences, that is, how many hours the given city or country is ahead or behind the four major U.S. time zones and Greenwich Mean Time, have been given in the right-hand columns in the table on the following pages. All cities in a given country or territory are in one time zone unless a †† symbol appears next to the country name. Find the city you wish to call, and the column which corresponds to the time zone from which you are calling. Add or subtract the number shown to your own current time to find the time in that city.

Example: You are calling France from New York. +6 appears in the New York column for France, which means France is 6 hours *ahead* of New York. Thus, when it is 9 a.m. Monday in New York, it is 3:00 p.m. Monday in France.

Example: You are calling Japan from San Francisco. +17 appears in the Los Angeles column for Japan, which means Japan is also 17 hours ahead of San Francisco. Thus, when it is 4:00 p.m. Monday in San Francisco, it is 9:00 a.m. Tuesday in Japan.

DAYLIGHT SAVINGS TIME

The time differences in the table are based on Standard Time and may require adjustment if either you or the country you are calling is following Daylight Savings Time (DST) at the time you place the call.

Most of the United States is in DST from the first Sunday in April until the last Sunday in October. Many, but not all, countries north of the Tropic of Cancer also use DST during a similar period. DST is not used in most tropical areas. Countries in the southern hemisphere that follow a daylight savings period normally use it from mid-March through mid-October, their summertime.

The dates used for DST vary considerably from country to country and even from year to year. Also, in a few larger countries like the United States, Australia, and Brazil, some regions of the country may follow daylight savings while others do not.

If you are in DST, and the country you are calling is not, *subtract* one hour from the time shown. If you are in Standard Time, and the country you are calling is currently following DST, *add* one hour to the time shown. If you and the country you are calling are both using DST the time difference shown in the table will be correct.

Example: You are calling Japan from San Francisco in June. California follows DST in the summer, while Japan does not. The PST (Pacific Standard Time) column for Japan shows +17. Subtract one hour from this, to find that Japan is 16 hours ahead of San Francisco. Thus, when it is 4:00 p.m. Monday in San Francisco, it is 8:00 a.m. Tuesday in Japan.

FOR FURTHER INFORMATION

Listed information was current as of March 2002. City codes and dialing systems are changing rapidly as the need for more telephone numbers increases worldwide.

For codes not listed here, or for the current time anywhere in the world, call your international operator. In the United States, dial '00' for AT&T information.

The most comprehensive source for international communications data is *Global Connect!*, also by World Trade Press. It contains telecommunications, cell communications, mobile connectivity and Internet connectivity information for 161 countries of the world, plus a series of key appendices on all aspects of communications issues including "25 Problems and Solutions for Mobile Connectivity."

On the Internet, world time listed by country is at www.globaltimeclock.com. World time and dialing codes at www.whitepages.com.au/wp/search/time.html. A list of International Dialing Codes is at www.kropla.com/dialcode.htm, and the AmeriCom Long Distance Area Decoder at www.areadecoder.com will allow you to look up both U.S. and international country codes, city codes, and area codes.

International Dialing Codes

Country	Code	City Code Area Code	Cities in Column 3 are X Hours Ahead (+) or Behind (-):					
			Los Angeles	New York	London (GMT)	Paris/ Berlin	Hong Kong	Tokyo/ Seoul
Afghanistan	[93]	✪Kabul (20) Herat (40) Jalalabad (60) Kandahar (30) Kunduz (56) Mazar-i-Sherif (50)	+12₁/₂	+9₁/₂	+4₁/₂	+3₁/₂	-3₁/₂	-4₁/₂
Albania (DST)	[355]	✪Tirana (4)	+9	+6	+1	0	-7	-8
Algeria	[213]	✪Algiers (21) Mascara (Oran) (45)	+9	+6	+1	0	-7	-8
American Samoa	[684]	✪Pago Pago*	-3	-6	-11	-12	-19	-20
Andorra (DST)	[376]	✪Andorra la *	+9	+6	+1	0	-7	-8
Angola	[244]	✪Luanda (2) Huambo (41)	+9	+6	+1	0	-7	-8
Anguilla	[1]	✪ The Valley (264)** (7-digit numbers)	+4	+1	-4	-5	-12	-13
Antigua & Barbuda	[1]	✪St. John's (268)** (7-digit numbers)	+4	+1	-4	-5	-12	-13
Argentina††	[54]	✪Buenos Aires (11) Cordoba (351) La Plata (221) Mendoza (261) Rosario (341)	+5	+2	-3	-4	-11	-12
Armenia (DST)	[374]	✪Yerevan (1) Ararat (38)	+11	+8	+3	+2	-5	-6
Aruba	[297]	✪ Oranjestad (8)**	+4	+1	-4	-5	-12	-13
Australia†† (DST)	[61]	✪Canberra (2) Adelaide (8) Brisbane (7) Cairns (7) Melbourne (3) Perth (9) Sydney (2)	+18 +17₁/₂ +18 +18 +18 +16 +18	+15 +14₁/₂ +15 +15 +15 +13 +15	+10 +9₁/₂ +10 +10 +10 +8 +10	+9 +8₁/₂ +9 +9 +9 +7 +9	+2 +1₁/₂ +2 +2 +2 0 +2	+1 +1/₂ +1 +1 +1 -1 +1
DST Note: Queensland, Northern Territory, and Western Australia do not use DST.								
Austria (DST)	[43]	✪Vienna (1) Graz (316) Innsbruck (512) Linz (732) Salzburg (662)	+9	+6	+1	0	-7	-8
Azerbaijan (DST)	[994]	✪Baku (12) Gandja (222)	+11	+8	+3	+2	-5	-6

D I A L I N G

Country	Code	City Code Area Code	Cities in Column 3 are X Hours Ahead (+) or Behind (-):					
			Los Angeles	New York	London (GMT)	Paris/ Berlin	Hong Kong	Tokyo/ Seoul
Bahamas (DST)	[1]	✪Nassau (242)** (7-digit numbers)	+3	0	-5	-6	-13	-14
Bahrain	[973]	✪Manama*	+11	+8	+3	+2	-5	-6
Bangladesh	[880]	✪Dhaka (2) Barisal (431) Chittagong(31)	+14	+11	+6	+5	-2	-3
Barbados	[1]	✪Bridgetown (246)**	+4	+1	-4	-5	-12	-13
Belarus (DST)	[375]	✪Mensk (17) Gomel (23) Gorki (22)	+10	+7	+2	+1	-6	-7
Belgium (DST)	[32]	✪Brussels*	+9	+6	+1	0	-7	-8
In 2000, area code plus local number = new national number.								
Belize	[501]	✪Belmopan (8)	+2	-1	-6	-7	-14	-15
Benin	[229]	✪Porto-Novo*	+9	+6	+1	0	-7	-8
Bermuda (DST)	[1]	✪Hamilton (441)** (7-digit numbers)	+4	+1	-4	-5	-12	-13
Bhutan	[975]	✪Thimphu*	+14	+11	+6	+5	-2	-3
Bolivia	[591]	✪La Paz (2) ✪Sucre (4) Cochabamba (4) Santa Cruz (3)	+4	+1	-4	-5	-12	-13
Bosnia & Herzegovina(DST)	[387]	✪Sarajevo (33) Tuzla (35)	+9	+6	+1	0	-7	-8
Botswana	[267]	✪Gaborone*	+10	+7	+2	+1	-6	-7
Brazil†† (DST)	[55]	✪Brasilia (61)	+5	+2	-3	-4	-11	-12
		Belém (91)	+5	+2	-3	-4	-11	-12
		Belo Horizonte (31)	+5	+2	-3	-4	-11	-12
		Curitiba (41)	+5	+2	-3	-4	-11	-12
		Manaus (92)	+4	+1	-4	-5	-12	-13
		Porto Alegre (51)	+5	+2	-3	-4	-11	-12
		Recife (81)	+5	+2	-3	-4	-11	-12
		Rio de Janeiro (21)	+5	+2	-3	-4	-11	-12
		Salvador (71)	+5	+2	-3	-4	-11	-12
		Sao Paulo (11)	+5	+2	-3	-4	-11	-12
		Vitoria (27)	+5	+2	-3	-4	-11	-12
Brunei	[673]	✪Bandar Seri Begawan	+16	+13	+8	+7	0	-1
Bulgaria (DST)	[359]	✪Sofia (2)	+10	+7	+2	+1	-6	-7
Burkina Faso	[226]	✪Ouagadougou*	+8	+5	0	-1	-8	-9
Burundi	[257]	✪Bujumbura (2)	+10	+7	+2	+1	-6	-7

✪ Capital city   †† More than one time zone in this country.
(DST) = Uses Daylight Savings Time   * City/area codes not used in this country
Code = Country Dialing Code   ** This area code used for entire country

D I A L I N G

Country	Code	City Code Area Code	Cities in Column 3 are X Hours Ahead (+) or Behind (-):					
			Los Angeles	New York	London (GMT)	Paris/ Berlin	Hong Kong	Tokyo/ Seoul
Cambodia	[855]	✪Phnom Penh (23)	+15	+12	+7	+6	-1	-2
		Angkor Wat (63)						
Cameroon	[237]	✪Yaoundé*	+9	+6	+1	0	-7	-8
Canada†† (DST)	[1]	✪Ottawa, ON (613)	+3	0	-5	-6	-13	-14
		Calgary, AB (403)	+1	-2	-7	-8	-15	-16
		Edmonton,AB (780)	+1	-2	-7	-8	-15	-16
		Fredericton, NB (506)	+4	+1	-4	-5	-12	-13
		Halifax, NS (902)	+4	+1	-4	-5	-12	-13
		London, ON (519)	+3	0	-5	-6	-13	-14
		Montreal, PQ (514)	+3	0	-5	-6	-13	-14
		Quebec City, PQ (418)	+3	0	-5	-6	-13	-14
		Regina, SK (306)	+1	-2	-7	-8	-15	-16
		Saskatoon, SK (306)	+1	-2	-7	-8	-15	-16
		St. John's, NF (709)	+4 1/2	+1 1/2	-3 1/2	-4 1/2	-11 1/2	-12 1/2
		Toronto, ON Metro (416, 647)	+3	0	-5	-6	-13	-14
		Toronto Vicinity (905)	+3	0	-5	-6	-13	-14
		Vancouver, BC (604)	0	-3	-8	-9	-16	-17
		Victoria, BC (250)	0	-3	-8	-9	-16	-17
		Winnipeg, MB (204)	+2	-1	-6	-7	-14	-15
Cape Verde Isl.	[238]	✪Praia*	+7	+4	-1	-2	-9	-10
Cayman Islands	[1]	✪George Town (345)**	+3	0	-5	-6	-13	-14
Central African Republic	[236]	✪Bangui* (6-digit numbers)	+9	+6	+1	0	-7	-8
Chad	[235]	✪N'Djamena*	+9	+6	+1	0	-7	-8
Chagos Archipelago	[246]	✪Diego Garcia*	+13	+10	+5	+4	-3	-4
Chile (DST)	[56]	✪Santiago (2)	+4	+1	-4	-5	-12	-13
		Concepcion (41)						
		Punta Arenas (61)						
		Valparaiso (32)						
China, People's Republic of	[86]	✪Beijing (10)	+16	+13	+8	+7	0	-1
		Fuzhou (591)						
		Guangzhou (20)						
		Harbin (451)						
		Nanjing (25)						
		Nanjing Fujian (596)						
		Shanghai (21)						
		Shenzhen (755)						
		Tianjin (22)						
		Wuhan (27)						
		Xiamen (592)						
		Xian (29)						

DIALING

Country	Code	City Code Area Code	Cities in Column 3 are X Hours Ahead (+) or Behind (-):					
			Los Angeles	New York	London (GMT)	Paris/ Berlin	Hong Kong	Tokyo/ Seoul
Colombia	[57]	✪Bogota (1) Barranquilla (5) Cali (23) Medellin (4)	+3	0	-5	-6	-13	-14
Comoros	[269]	✪Moroni*	+11	+8	+3	+2	-5	-6
Congo, Dem. Rep. of	[243]	✪Kinshasa (12) Lubumbashi (2)	+9	+6	+1	0	-7	-8
Congo	[242]	✪Brazzaville*	+9	+6	+1	0	-7	-8
Cook Islands	[682]	✪Avarua*	-2	-5	-10	-11	-18	-19
Costa Rica	[506]	✪San José* (7-digit numbers)	+2	-1	-6	-7	-14	-15
Côte d'Ivoire	[225]	✪Yamoussoukro* Abidjan* (8-digit numbers)	+8	+5	0	-1	-8	-9
Croatia (DST)	[385]	✪Zagreb (1) Dubrovnik (20) Split (21)	+9	+6	+1	0	-7	-8
Cuba (DST)	[53]	✪Havana (7) Santiago (22)	+3	0	-5	-6	-13	-14
Cyprus (DST)	[357]	✪Nicosia (2) (8-digit numbers)	+10	+7	+2	+1	-6	-7
Czech Republic (DST)	[420]	✪Prague (2) Brno (5) Ostrava (69)	+9	+6	+1	0	-7	-8
In September 2002, area code plus local number = new 9-digit national number.								
Denmark (DST)	[45]	✪Copenhagen* (8-digit numbers)	+9	+6	+1	0	-7	-8
Djibouti	[253]	✪Djibouti* (6-digit numbers)	+11	+8	+3	+2	-5	-6
Dominica	[1]	✪Roseau (767)**	+4	+1	-4	-5	-12	-13
Dominican Republic	[1]	✪Santo Domingo (809)**	+4	+1	-4	-5	-12	-13
Ecuador	[593]	✪Quito (2) Guayaquil (4)	+3	0	-5	-6	-13	-14
Egypt (DST	[20]	✪Cairo (2) Alexandria (3) Aswan (97) Luxor (95) Port Said (66)	+10	+7	+2	+1	-6	-7

✪ Capital city
(DST) = Uses Daylight Savings Time
Code = Country Dialing Code

†† More than one time zone in this country.
* City/area codes not used in this country
** This area code used for entire country

DIALING

Country	Code	City Code Area Code	Cities in Column 3 are X Hours Ahead (+) or Behind (-):					
			Los Angeles	New York	London (GMT)	Paris/ Berlin	Hong Kong	Tokyo/ Seoul
El Salvador	[503]	✪San Salvador*	+2	-1	-6	-7	-14	-15
Equatorial Guinea	[240]	✪Malabo (9) Bata (8)	+9	+6	+1	0	-7	-8
Estonia (DST)	[372]	✪Tallinn (2)	+10	+7	+2	+1	-6	-7
Ethiopia	[251]	✪Addis Ababa (1)	+11	+8	+3	+2	-5	-6
Faeroe Isl (DST)	[298]	✪Tórshavn*	+8	+5	0	-1	-8	-9
Falkland Islands	[500]	✪Stanley* (5-digit numbers)	+4	+1	-4	-5	-12	-13
Fiji (DST	[679]	✪Suva*	+20	+17	+12	+11	+4	+3
Finland (DST)	[358]	✪Helsinki (9)	+10	+7	+2	+1	-6	-7
France (DST)	[33]	✪Paris*	+9	+6	+1	0	-7	-8
		Old area codes plus local number = new 9-digit national number.						
French Antilles	[590]	Guadeloupe*	+4	+1	-4	-5	-12	-13
French Guiana	[594]	✪Cayenne* (9-digit numbers)	+5	+2	-3	-4	-11	-12
French Polynesia††	[689]	✪Papeete, Tahiti*	-2	-5	-10	-11	-18	-19
Gabon	[241]	✪Libreville*	+9	+6	+1	0	-7	-8
Gambia, The	[220]	✪Banjul*	+8	+5	0	-1	-8	-9
Georgia (DST)	[995]	✪Tbilisi (32)	+11	+8	+3	+2	-5	-6
Germany (DST)	[49]	✪Berlin (30) Bonn (228) Bremen (421) Cologne (221) Dresden (351) Dusseldorf (211) Essen (201) Frankfurt am Main (69) Freiburg (761) Hamburg (40) Hannover (511) Heidelberg (6221) Leipzig (341) Munich (89) Postdam (331) Stuttgart (711) Wiesbaden (611)	+9	+6	+1	0	-7	-8
Ghana	[233]	✪Accra (21) Kumasi (51)	+8	+5	0	-1	-8	-9
Gibraltar (DST)	[350]	✪Gibraltar* (5-digit numbers)	+9	+6	+1	0	-7	-8

DIALING

Country	Code	City Code Area Code	Cities in Column 3 are X Hours Ahead (+) or Behind (-):					
			Los Angeles	New York	London (GMT)	Paris/ Berlin	Hong Kong	Tokyo/ Seoul
Greece (DST)	[30]	✪Athens*	+10	+7	+2	+1	-6	-7
		In 2002, the trunk prefix '2' ('0' until October 2002) plus an area code plus a local number = new 10-digit national number. As of October 2002, the prefix '2' is required even for international calls to Greece.						
Greenland†† (DST)	[299]	✪Nuuk (Godthaab)*	+5	+2	-3	-4	-11	-12
Grenada	[1]	✪St. George's (473)** (7-digit numbers)	+4	+1	-4	-5	-12	-13
Guadeloupe	[590]	✪Basse-Terre (81) (10-digit numbers)	+4	+1	-4	-5	-12	-13
Guam	[1]	✪Agana (671)** (7-digit numbers)	+18	+15	+10	+9	+2	+1
Guatemala	[502]	✪Guatemala City* (7-digit numbers)	+2	-1	-6	-7	-14	-15
Guinea	[224]	✪Conakry*	+8	+5	0	-1	-8	-9
Guinea-Bissau	[245]	✪Bissau* (6-digit numbers)	+8	+5	0	-1	-8	-9
Guyana	[592]	✪Georgetown* (7-digit numbers)	+5	+2	-3	-4	-11	-12
Haiti	[509]	✪Port-au-Prince (6-digit numbers)	+3	0	-5	-6	-13	-14
Honduras	[504]	✪Tegucigalpa (7-digit numbers)	+3	0	-5	-6	-13	-14
Hong Kong	[852]	✪Hong Kong* (8-digit numbers)	+16	+13	+8	+7	0	-1
Hungary (DST)	[36]	✪Budapest (1) Miskolc (46)	+9	+6	+1	0	-7	-8
Iceland	[354]	✪Reykjavik (7-digit numbers)	+8	+5	0	-1	-8	-9
India	[91]	✪New Delhi (11) Ahmadabad (79) Bangalore (80) Calcutta (33) Hyderabad (40) Jaipur (141) Kanpur (512) Lucknow (522) Madras (44) Mumbai (Bombay) (22)	+13 1/2	+10 1/2	+5 1/2	+4 1/2	-2 1/2	-3 1/2

✪ Capital city
(DST) = Uses Daylight Savings Time
Code = Country Dialing Code

†† More than one time zone in this country.
* City/area codes not used in this country
** This area code used for entire country

DIALING

Country	Code	City Code Area Code	Cities in Column 3 are X Hours Ahead (+) or Behind (-):					
			Los Angeles	New York	London (GMT)	Paris/ Berlin	Hong Kong	Tokyo/ Seoul
Indonesia††	[62]	✪Jakarta (21)	+15	+12	+7	+6	-1	-2
		Bandung (22)	+15	+12	+7	+6	-1	-2
		Denpasar, Bali (361)	+16	+13	+8	+7	0	-1
		Padang (751)	+15	+12	+7	+6	-1	-2
		Palu (451)	+16	+13	+8	+7	0	-1
		Palembang (711)	+15	+12	+7	+6	-1	-2
		Semarang (24)	+15	+12	+7	+6	-1	-2
		Sinjai (482)	+16	+13	+8	+7	0	-1
		Surabaya (31)	+15	+12	+7	+6	-1	-2
		Yogyakarta (274)	+15	+12	+7	+6	-1	-2
Iran (DST)	[98]	✪Tehran (21)	+12	+9	+4	+3	-4	-5
		Esfahan (311)						
		Mashhad (511)						
		Shiraz (71)						
		Tabriz (41)						
Iraq (DST)	[964]	✪Baghdad (1)	+11	+8	+3	+2	-5	-6
		Basra (40)						
		Erbil (66)						
		Sulayamaniyah (53)						
Ireland (DST)	[353]	✪Dublin (1)	+8	+5	0	-1	-8	-9
		Cork (21)						
		Galway (91)						
		Limerick (61)						
		Waterford (51)						
Israel (DST)	[972]	✪Jerusalem (2)	+10	+7	+2	+1	-6	-7
		Haifa (4)						
		Holon (3)						
		Petah Tikva (3)						
		Tel Aviv (3)						
Italy (DST)	[39]	✪Rome*	+9	+6	+1	0	-7	-8
	'0' plus area codes plus local numbers = new 9-digit national numbers.							
Ivory Coast	[225]	✪Yamoussoukro* ✪Abidjan*	+8	+5	0	-1	-8	-9
Jamaica	[1]	✪Kingston (876)**	+3	0	-5	-6	-13	-14
Japan	[81]	✪Tokyo (3)	+17	+14	+9	+8	+1	0
		Fukuoka (92)						
		Hiroshima (82)						
		Kobe (78)						
		Kyoto (75)						
		Nagasaki (958)						
		Nagoya (52)						
		Osaka (66)						
		Sapporo (11)						
		Yamaguchi (839)						
		Yokohama (45)						

DIALING

Country	Code	City Code Area Code	Cities in Column 3 are X Hours Ahead (+) or Behind (-):					
			Los Angeles	New York	London (GMT)	Paris/ Berlin	Hong Kong	Tokyo/ Seoul
Jordan (DST)	[962]	✪Amman (6) Irbid (2) Zerqua (9)	+11	+8	+3	+2	-5	-6
Kazakhstan(DST)	[7]	✪Almaty (3272) Chimkent (325) Karaganda (3212)	+14	+11	+6	+5	-2	-3
Kenya	[254]	✪Nairobi (2) Mombasa (11)	+11	+8	+3	+2	-5	-6
Korea, North	[850]	✪Pyongyang (2)	+17	+14	+9	+8	+1	0
Korea, South	[82]	✪Seoul (2) Cheju (64) Inchon (32) Kwangju (62) Pusan (51) Taegu (53)	+17	+14	+9	+8	+1	0
Kuwait	[965]	✪Kuwait*	+11	+8	+3	+2	-5	-6
Kyrgyzstan(DST)	[996]	✪Bishkek (312) Jalal-Abad (3722) Osh (3222)	+13	+10	+5	+4	-3	-4
Laos	[856]	✪Vientiane (21) Luang Prabang (71) Svannakhet (41)	+15	+12	+7	+6	-1	-2
Latvia (DST)	[371]	✪Riga (2) Daugavpils (54) Liepaja (34)	+10	+7	+2	+1	-6	-7
Lebanon (DST)	[961]	✪Beirut (1) Tripoli (6)	+10	+7	+2	+1	-6	-7
Lesotho	[266]	✪Maseru*	+10	+7	+2	+1	-6	-7
Liberia	[231]	✪Monrovia*	+8	+5	0	-1	-8	-9
Libya	[218]	✪Tripoli (21) Benghazi (61) Misratah (51)	+10	+7	+2	+1	-6	-7
Liechtenstein(DST)	[423]	✪Vaduz*	+9	+6	+1	0	-7	-8
Lithuania	[370]	✪Vilnius (2) Kaunas (7)	+10	+7	+2	+1	-6	-7
		By 2003, area codes plus local number = new 8-digit national numbers						
Luxembourg(DST)	[352]	✪Luxembourg*	+9	+6	+1	0	-7	-8
Macau	[853]	✪Macau* (6-digit numbers)	+16	+13	+8	+7	0	-1

✪ Capital city	†† More than one time zone in this country.
(DST) = Uses Daylight Savings Time	* City/area codes not used in this country
Code = Country Dialing Code	** This area code used for entire country

DIALING

Country	Code	City Code Area Code	Cities in Column 3 are X Hours Ahead (+) or Behind (-):					
			Los Angeles	New York	London (GMT)	Paris/ Berlin	Hong Kong	Tokyo/ Seoul
Macedonia (DST)	[389]	✪Skopje (2)	+9	+6	+1	0	-7	-8
Madagascar	[261]	✪Antananarivo* (7-digit numbers)	+11	+8	+3	+2	-5	-6
Malawi	[265]	✪Lilongwe* (6-digit numbers)	+10	+7	+2	+1	-6	-7
Malaysia	[60]	✪Kuala Lumpur (3) Johor Bahru (7) Kota Bahru (9) Melaka (6) Penang (4)	+16	+13	+8	+7	0	-1
Maldives	[960]	✪Malé* (6-digit numbers)	+13	+10	+5	+4	-3	-4
Mali	[223]	✪Bamako* (6-digit numbers)	+8	+5	0	-1	-8	-9
Malta (DST)	[356]	✪Valletta* (8-digit numbers)	+9	+6	+1	0	-7	-8
Marshall Islands	[692]	✪Majuro* (7-digit numbers)	+20	+17	+12	+11	+4	+3
Martinique	[596]	✪Fort-De-France* (10-digit numbers)	+4	+1	-4	-5	-12	-13
Mauritania	[222]	✪Nouakchott* (7-digit numbers)	+8	+5	0	-1	-8	-9
Mauritius	[230]	✪Port Louis* (7-digit numbers)	+12	+9	+4	+3	-4	-5
Mexico†† (DST)	[52]	✪Mexico City (55)	+2	-1	-6	-7	-14	-15
		Acapulco (744)	+2	-1	-6	-7	-14	-15
		Cuidad Juarez (656)	+2	-1	-6	-7	-14	-15
		Durango (618)	+2	-1	-6	-7	-14	-15
		Ensenada (646)	0	-3	-8	-9	-16	-17
		Guadalajara (33)	+2	-1	-6	-7	-14	-15
		Leon (477)	+1	-2	-7	-8	-15	-16
		Mazatlan (669)	0	-3	-8	-9	-16	-17
		Mexicali (686)	+2	-1	-6	-7	-14	-15
		Monterrey (81)	+2	-1	-6	-7	-14	-15
		Nuevo Laredo (867)	0	-3	-8	-9	-16	-17
		Puebla (222)	+2	-1	-6	-7	-14	-15
		Tijuana (664)	0	-3	-8	-9	-16	-17
		Veracruz (229)	+2	-1	-6	-7	-14	-15
Midway Islands	[808]		-3	-6	-11	-12	-19	-20
Moldova (DST)	[373]	✪Kishinev (2) Tiraspol (33)	+10	+7	+2	+1	-6	-7
Monaco (DST)	[377]	✪Monaco*	+9	+6	+1	0	-7	-8
Mongolia (DST)	[976]	✪Ulan Bator (1)	+16	+13	+8	+7	0	-1

D I A L I N G

Country	Code	City Code Area Code	Cities in Column 3 are X Hours Ahead (+) or Behind (-):					
			Los Angeles	New York	London (GMT)	Paris/ Berlin	Hong Kong	Tokyo/ Seoul
Montenegro & Serbia (DST)	[381]	✪Belgrade (11) Nis (18) Novi Sad (21)	+9	+6	+1	0	-7	-8
Montserrat	[1]	✪Plymouth (664)** (7-digit numbers)	+4	+1	-4	-5	-12	-13
Morocco	[212]	✪Rabat (3) Casablanca (2) Fez (5) Marrakech (4) Tangiers (3)	+8	+5	0	-1	-8	-9
Mozambique	[258]	✪Maputo (1) Nampula (6)	+10	+7	+2	+1	-6	-7
Myanmar (Burma)	[95]	✪ Yangon (1) Mandalay (2)	+14$_{1/2}$	+11$_{1/2}$	+6$_{1/2}$	+5$_{1/2}$	-1$_{1/2}$	-2$_{1/2}$
Namibia (DST)	[264]	✪Windhoek (61)	+10	+7	+2	+1	-6	-7
Nepal	[977]	✪Kathmandu (1)	+13$_{3/4}$	+10$_{3/4}$	+5$_{3/4}$	+4$_{3/4}$	-2$_{1/4}$	-3$_{1/4}$
Netherlands(DST)	[31]	✪Amsterdam (20) ✪The Hague (70) Eindhoven (40) Rotterdam (10) Utrecht (30)	+9	+6	+1	0	-7	-8
Netherlands Antilles	[599]	✪Willemstad (9) St. Maarten (5)	+4	+1	-4	-5	-12	-13
New Caledonia	[687]	✪Nouméa*	+19	+16	+11	+10	+3	+2
New Zealand (DST)	[64]	✪Wellington (4) Auckland (9) Christchurch (3) Telecom Mobile Phones (25)	+20	+17	+12	+11	+4	+3
Nicaragua	[505]	✪Managua (2) Leon (311)	+2	-1	-6	-7	-14	-15
Niger Republic	[227]	✪Niamey* (6-digit numbers)	+9	+6	+1	0	-7	-8
Nigeria	[234]	✪Abuja (9) ✪Lagos (1) Ibadan (22) Kano (64) Cell Phones (90)	+9	+6	+1	0	-7	-8
Northern Mariana Isl.	[1]	✪Saipan (670)**	+18	+15	+10	+9	+2	+1

✪ Capital city
(DST) = Uses Daylight Savings Time
Code = Country Dialing Code

†† More than one time zone in this country.
* City/area codes not used in this country
** This area code used for entire country

DIALING

Country	Code	City Code Area Code	Cities in Column 3 are X Hours Ahead (+) or Behind (-):					
			Los Angeles	New York	London (GMT)	Paris/ Berlin	Hong Kong	Tokyo/ Seoul
Norway (DST)	[47]	✪Oslo* (8-digit numbers)	+9	+6	+1	0	-7	-8
Oman	[968]	✪Muscat*	+12	+9	+4	+3	-4	-5
Pakistan (DST)	[92]	✪Islamabad (51) Faisalabad (41) Karachi (21) Lahore (42) Rawalpindi (51)	+13	+10	+5	+4	-3	-4
Palau	[680]	✪Koror*	+17	+14	+9	+8	+1	0
Panama	[507]	✪Panama City* (7-digit numbers)	+3	0	-5	-6	-13	-14
Papua New Guinea	[675]	✪Port Moresby*	+18	+15	+10	+9	+2	+1
Paraguay (DST)	[595]	✪Asuncion (21)	+4	+1	-4	-5	-12	-13
Peru	[51]	✪Lima (1) Arequipa (54) Callao (1) Trujillo (44)	+3	0	-5	-6	-13	-14
Philippines	[63]	✪Manila (2) Cebu (32) Davao (82) Quezon City (2)	+16	+13	+8	+7	0	-1
Poland (DST)	[48]	✪Warsaw (22) Gdansk (58) Kraków (12) Lodz (42)	+9	+6	+1	0	-7	-8
Portugal (DST)	[351]	✪Lisbon*	+8	+5	0	-1	-8	-9
		Are a codes plus local numbers to make uniform 9-digit national numbers.						
Puerto Rico	[1]	✪San Juan (787)**	+4	+1	-4	-5	-12	-13
Qatar	[974]	✪Doha*	+11	+8	+3	+2	-5	-6
Reunion Island	[262]	✪St. Denis* (10-digit numbers)	+12	+9	+4	+3	-4	-5
Romania (DST)	[40]	✪Bucharest (21) Constanta (241) Iasi (232)	+10	+7	+2	+1	-6	-7
Russia†† (DST)	[7]	✪Moscow (095) & mobile (096)	+11	+8	+3	+2	-5	-6
		Novgorod (816)	+11	+8	+3	+2	-5	-6
		Novosibirsk (3832)	+14	+11	+6	+5	-2	-3
		St. Petersburg (812)	+11	+8	+3	+2	-5	-6
Rwanda	[250]	✪Kigali*	+10	+7	+2	+1	-6	-7
St. Kitts & Nevis	[1]	✪Basseterre (869)**	+4	+1	-4	-5	-12	-13

Country	Code	City Code Area Code	Cities in Column 3 are X Hours Ahead (+) or Behind (-):					
			Los Angeles	New York	London (GMT)	Paris/ Berlin	Hong Kong	Tokyo/ Seoul
St. Lucia	[1]	✪Castries (758)**	+4	+1	-4	-5	-12	-13
St. Vincents & Grenadines	[1]	✪Kingstown (784)**	+4	+1	-4	-5	-12	-13
San Marino(DST)	[378]	✪San Marino*	+9	+6	+1	0	-7	-8
São Tomé & Principe	[239]	✪São Tomé*	+8	+5	0	-1	-8	-9
Saudi Arabia	[966]	✪Riyadh (1) Jeddah (2) Makkah (Mecca) (2)	+11	+8	+3	+2	-5	-6
Senegal	[221]	✪Dakar* (7-digit numbers)	+8	+5	0	-1	-8	-9
Seychelles	[248]	✪Victoria (6-digit numbers)	+12	+9	+4	+3	-4	-5
Sierra Leone	[232]	✪Freetown (22)	+8	+5	0	-1	-8	-9
Singapore	[65]	✪Singapore* (8-digit numbers)	+16	+13	+8	+7	0	-1
Slovak Republic (DST)	[421]	✪Bratislava (2) Kosice (55)	+9	+6	+1	0	-7	-8
Slovenia (DST)	[386]	✪Ljubljana (1) Maribor (2)	+9	+6	+1	0	-7	-8
Solomon Islands	[677]	✪Honiara*	+19	+16	+11	+10	+3	+2
Somalia	[252]	✪Mogadishu (1)	+11	+8	+3	+2	-5	-6
South Africa	[27]	✪Cape Town* ✪Pretoria	+10	+7	+2	+1	-6	-7
		Area codes plus local numbers = new 9-digit national numbers.						
Spain (DST)	[34]	✪Madrid*	+9	+6	+1	0	-7	-8
		Area codes plus local numbers = new 9-digit national numbers.						
Sri Lanka	[94]	✪Colombo (1)	+13 1/2	+10 1/2	+5 1/2	+4 1/2	-2 1/2	-3 1/2
Sudan	[249]	✪Khartoum (11) Omdurman (11) Port Sudan (311)	+10	+7	+2	+1	-6	-7
Suriname	[597]	✪Paramaribo*	+5	+2	-3	-4	-11	-12
Swaziland	[268]	✪Mbabane* ✪Lobamba*	+10	+7	+2	+1	-6	-7

D
I
A
L
I
N
G

✪ Capital city
(DST) = Uses Daylight Savings Time
Code = Country Dialing Code

†† More than one time zone in this country.
* City/area codes not used in this country
** This area code used for entire country

Country	Code	City Code Area Code	Cities in Column 3 are X Hours Ahead (+) or Behind (-):					
			Los Angeles	New York	London (GMT)	Paris/ Berlin	Hong Kong	Tokyo/ Seoul
Sweden (DST)	[46]	✪Stockholm (8) Goteberg (31) Malmö (40) Uppsala (18)	+9	+6	+1	0	-7	-8
Switzerland(DST)	[41]	✪Bern*	+9	+6	+1	0	-7	-8
		As of March 2002, area codes plus local numbers = new national numbers.						
Syria (DST)	[963]	✪Damascus (11) Aleppo (21)	+10	+7	+2	+1	-6	-7
Taiwan	[886]	✪Taipei (2) Kaohsiung (7) Taichung (4) Tainan (6)	+16	+13	+8	+7	0	-1
Tajikistan	[992]	✪Dushanbe (37) Khujand (34)	+13	+10	+5	+4	-3	-4
Tanzania	[255]	✪Dar es Salaam (22) Dodoma (26)	+11	+8	+3	+2	-5	-6
Thailand	[66]	✪Bangkok*	+15	+12	+7	+6	-1	-2
		Area codes plus local numbers = new 8-digit national numbers.						
Togo	[228]	✪Lomé* (7-digit numbers)	+8	+5	0	-1	-8	-9
Tonga	[676]	✪Nukualofa**	-3	-6	-11	-12	-19	-20
Trinidad & Tobago	[1]	✪Port-of-Spain (868)** (7-digit numbers)	+4	+1	-4	-5	-12	-13
Tunisia	[216]	✪Tunis (1) Ariana (1) Sfax (4)	+9	+6	+1	0	-7	-8
Turkey (DST)	[90]	✪Ankara (312) Istanbul (212), (216) Adana (322) Bursa (224) Izmir (232)	+10	+7	+2	+1	-6	-7
Turkmenistan	[993]	✪Ashgabat (12)	+13	+10	+5	+4	-3	-4
Turks & Caicos Islands (DST)	[1]	✪Grand Turk (649)**	+3	0	-5	-6	-13	-14
Tuvalu	[688]	✪Funafuti* (5-digit numbers)	+20	+17	+12	+11	+4	+3
Uganda	[256]	✪Kampala (41)	+11	+8	+3	+2	-5	-6
Ukraine (DST)	[380]	✪Kiev (44) Odessa (48)	+10	+7	+2	+1	-6	-7
		In addition to the trunk prefix '8', long-distance calls within Ukraine add the prefix '0' to the area code (e.g., *8 (044) + number* for Kiev)						

DIALING

Country	Code	City Code Area Code	Cities in Column 3 are X Hours Ahead (+) or Behind (-):					
			Los Angeles	New York	London (GMT)	Paris/ Berlin	Hong Kong	Tokyo/ Seoul
United Arab Emirates	[971]	✪Abu Dhabi (2)	+12	+9	+4	+3	-4	-5
		Dubai (4)						
United Kingdom (DST)	[44]	✪London (20)	+8	+5	0	-1	-8	-9
		Belfast (1232)						
		Birmingham (121)						
		Bristol (117)						
		Edinburgh (131)						
		Glasgow (141)						
		Leeds (113)						
		Liverpool (151)						
		Manchester (161)						
		Sheffield (114)						
United States †† (DST)	[1]	✪Washington, DC	+3	0	-5	-6	-13	-14
		(202)	+3	0	-5	-6	-13	-14
		Atlanta (404)	+3	0	-5	-6	-13	-14
		Baltimore (410)	+3	0	-5	-6	-13	-14
		Boston (617)	+3	0	-5	-6	-13	-14
		Chicago (312) (773)	+2	-1	-6	-7	-14	-15
		Cleveland (216)	+2	-1	-6	-7	-14	-15
		Dallas (214) (972)	+2	-1	-6	-7	-14	-15
		Denver (303)	+1	-2	-7	-8	-15	-16
		Detroit (313)	+3	0	-5	-6	-13	-14
		Honolulu (808)	-2	-5	-10	-11	-18	-19
		Houston (713) (281)	+2	-1	-6	-7	-14	-15
		Los Angeles (213) &	0	-3	-8	-9	-16	-17
		(310)	0	-3	-8	-9	-16	-17
		Miami (305)	+3	0	-5	-6	-13	-14
		Minneapolis (612)	+2	-1	-6	-7	-14	-15
		New Orleans (504)	+2	-1	-6	-7	-14	-15
		New York (212), (718)	+3	0	-5	-6	-13	-14
		Philadelphia (215) &	+3	0	-5	-6	-13	-14
		(610)	+3	0	-5	-6	-13	-14
		Phoenix (602)	+1	-2	-7	-8	-15	-16
		Sacramento (916) &	0	-3	-8	-9	-16	-17
		(530)	0	-3	-8	-9	-16	-17
		St. Louis (314)	+2	-1	-6	-7	-14	-15
		Salt Lake City (801)	+1	-2	-7	-8	-15	-16
		San Antonio (210)	+2	-1	-6	-7	-14	-15
		San Diego (619)	0	-3	-8	-9	-16	-17
		San Francisco (415)	0	-3	-8	-9	-16	-17
		San Jose (408)	0	-3	-8	-9	-16	-17
		Seattle (206)	0	-3	-8	-9	-16	-17
Uruguay	[598]	✪Montevideo (2)	+5	+2	-3	-4	-11	-12

✪ Capital city
(DST) = Uses Daylight Savings Time
Code = Country Dialing Code

†† More than one time zone in this country.
* City/area codes not used in this country
** This area code used for entire country

DIALING

Country	Code	City Code Area Code	Cities in Column 3 are X Hours Ahead (+) or Behind (-):					
			Los Angeles	New York	London (GMT)	Paris/ Berlin	Hong Kong	Tokyo/ Seoul
Uzbekistan	[998]	✪Tashkent (71) Namangan (69) Samarkandy (66)	+13	+10	+5	+4	-3	-4
Vanuatu	[678]	✪Port Vila* (5-digit numbers)	+20	+17	+12	+11	+4	+3
Venezuela	[58]	✪Caracas (212) Maracaibo (261) Valencia (241)	+4	+1	-4	-5	-12	-13
Vietnam	[84]	✪Hanoi (4) Ho Chi Minh City (8)	+15	+12	+7	+6	-1	-2
Virgin Islands, British	[1]	✪Road Town (284)**	+4	+1	-4	-5	-12	-13
Virgin Islands, U.S.	[1]	✪Charlotte Amalie (340)** St. Thomas (340)	+4	+1	-4	-5	-12	-13
Western Samoa	[685]	✪Apia*	-3	-6	-11	-12	-19	-20
Yemen	[967]	✪Sana'a (1)	+11	+8	+3	+2	-5	-6
Yugoslavia	[381]	✪Belgrade (11)	+9	+6	+1	0	-7	-8
Zaire †† See Congo	[243]	✪Kinshasa (12)	+9	+6	+1	0	-7	-8
Zambia	[260]	✪Lusaka (1)	+10	+7	+2	+1	-6	-7
Zimbabwe	[263]	✪Harare(4)	+10	+7	+2	+1	-6	-7

D
I
A
L
I
N
G

✪ Capital city	†† More than one time zone in this country.
(DST) = Uses Daylight Savings Time	* City/area codes not used in this country
Code = Country Dialing Code	** This area code used for entire country

Currencies of the World

The table below lists the currencies and subcurrencies in use in more than 200 countries and territories around the world.

Country Name
We have used the popular rather than the formal names of countries and territories. For example, we list Korea, South, rather than Republic of Korea.

Currency Name
In many cases a number of countries share the same currency name, but not the same currency. To lessen confusion, we have included the country name in the currency column (e.g., Australian Dollar, U.S. Dollar, Hong Kong Dollar).

ISO Codes
The International Organization for Standardization (ISO, not IOS) has established alpha and numeric codes for all currencies. These are the formal codes that banks and currency dealers use.

Symbols
Most every currency in the world has a symbol or abbreviation that is more commonly used than the formal ISO codes. For example, $, £ and ¥.

The Euro
On January 1, 2002, the Euro replaced the national currencies of 12 European Union (EU) countries including Austria, Belgium, Finland, France, Germany, Greece, Ireland, Italy, Luxembourg, the Netherlands, Portugal and Spain. At the same time,

many other countries and territories that used the former currencies of these countries converted as well. For example, French Guiana used the French franc but now also uses the Euro.

Hard vs. Soft Currencies
Some currencies are "soft," meaning they are either legally inconvertible, or simply undesirable because they are not stable. "Hard" currencies, on the other hand, are convertible and stable and, therefore, most often used in international transactions. Hard currencies include the EU Euro, U.S. dollar, British Pound Sterling, Japanese Yen and Swiss Franc.

Exchange Rate and Currency Information
Exchange rates can and do fluctuate, sometime wildly. The traditional method for learning about rates used to include the Monday edition of the Wall Street Journal, other major newspapers, banks and foreign exchange firms like Thomas Cook. Now, of course, instant information is available on the Internet at services such as:
Oanda (www.oanda.com),
Bloomberg (www.bloomberg.com), and
Universal Currency Converter (www.xe.com).
Two other great sources of currency information include the **Pacific Exchange Rate Service** at: http://pacific.commerce.ubc.ca/xr/currency_table.html and the **UN Operational Rates of Exchange** at gopher://gopher.undp.org/00/uncurr/exch_rates.
The information below is current as of March 2002.

| Country | Currency | ISO 4217 Codes | | Symbol | Sub-Currency |
		Alpha	Numeric		
Afghanistan	Afghani	AFA	4	Af	Af 1 = 100 puls
Albania	Lek	ALL	8	L	L1 = 100 qintars
Algeria	Algerian Dinar	DZD	12	DA	DA1= 100 centimes
American Samoa	U.S. Dollar	USD	840	US$	US$1 = 100 cents
Andorra	European Union Euro	EUR	978	€	€ 1 = 100 cents
Angola	Kwanza	AOA	24	Kz	
Angola	New Kwanza	AON	24	Kz	Kz1 = 100 lwei
Anguilla	East Caribbean Dollar	XCD	951	EC$	EC$1 = 100 cents
Antigua and Barbuda	East Caribbean Dollar	XCD	951	EC$	EC$1 = 100 cents
Argentina	Argentinian Peso	ARS	32	$	$1 = 100 centavos
Armenia	Dram	AMD	51	n/a	1 Dram = 100 looma
Aruba	Aruban Guilder	AWG	533	Af.	Af.1 = 100 cents

Country	Currency	ISO 4217 Codes		Symbol	Sub-Currency
		Alpha	Numeric		
Australia	Australian Dollar	AUD	36	A$	A$1 = 100 cent
Austria	European Union Euro	EUR	978	€	€ 1 = 100 cents
Austria (pre-2002)	Schilling	ATS	40	S	S1 = 100 groschen
Azerbaijan	Manat	AZM	31	n/a	1 Manat = 100 gopik
Bahamas	Bahamian Dollar	BSD	44	B$	B$1 = 100 cents
Bahrain	Bahrain Dinar	BHD	48	BD	BD1 = 100 filses
Bangladesh	Taka	BDT	50	Tk	TK1 = 100 poisha
Barbados	Barbados Dollar	BBD	52	Bds$	Bds$ = 100 cents
Belarus	Belarussian Ruble	BYB	112	BR	BR1 = 100 kopeks
Belgium	European Union Euro	EUR	978	€	€ 1 = 100 cents
Belgium (pre-2002)	Belgium Franc	BEF	56	BF	BF1 = 100 centimes
Belize	Belize Dollar	BZD	84	BZ$	BZ$1 = 100 cents
Benin	CFA Franc BCEAO	XOF	952	CFAF	CFAF 1 = 100 centimes (discontinued)
Bermuda	Bermudian Dollar	BMD	60	Bd$	Bd$1 = 100 cents
Bhutan	Ngultrum	BTN	64	Nu	Nu1 = 100 chetrums
Bolivia	Boliviano	BOB	68	Bs	Bs1 = 100 centavos
Bosnia-Herzegovina	Convertible Mark	BAM	977	KM	KM1 = 100 pfennigs
Botswana	Pula	BWP	72	P	P1 = 100 thebe
Bouvet Island	Norwegian Krone	NOK	578	NKr	NKr1 = 100 Øre
Brazil	Real	BRL	986	R$	R$1 = 100 centavos
British Indian Ocean Territory	Pound Sterling	GBP	826	£	£1 = 100 pence
Brunei Darussalam	Brunei Dollar	BND	96	B$	B$1 = 100 sen
Bulgaria	Lev	BGL	100	Lv	Lv1 = 100 stotinki
Burkina Faso	CFA Franc BCEAO	XOF	952	CFAF	CFAF1 = 100 centimes (discontinued)
Burundi	Burundi Franc	BIF	108	FBu	FBu1 = 100 centimes
Cambodia	Riel	KHR	116	CR	CR1 = 100 sen
Cameroon	CFA Franc BEAC	XAF	950	CFAF	CFAF1 = 100 centimes (discontinued)
Canada	Canadian Dollar	CAD	124	Can$	Can$1 = 100 cents
Cape Verde	Escudo Caboverdiano	CVE	132	C.V.Esc.	C.V.Esc.1 = 100 centavos
Cayman Islands	Cayman Islands Dollar	KYD	136	CI$	CI$1 = 100 cents
Central African Republic	CFA Franc BEAC	XAF	950	CFAF	CFAF1 = 100 centimes (discontinued)

CURRENCY

Country	Currency	ISO 4217 Codes		Symbol	Sub-Currency
		Alpha	Numeric		
Chad	CFA Franc BEAC	XAF	950	CFAF	CFAF1 = 100 centimes (discontinued)
Chile	Chilean Peso	CLP	152	Ch$	Ch$1 = 100 centavos
China	Renminbi Yuan	CNY	156	Y	Y1 = 10 jiao, 100 fen
Christmas Island	Australian Dollar	AUD	36	A$	A$1 = 100 cents
Cocos (Keeling) Islands	Australian Dollar	AUD	36	A$	A$1 = 100 cents
Colombia	Colombian Peso	COP	170	Col$	Col$1 = 100 centavos
Comoros	Comorian Franc	KMF	174	CF	CF1 = 100 centimes (discontinued)
Congo-Brazzaville	CFA Franc BEAC	XAF	950	CFAF	CFAF1 = 100 centimes (discontinued)
Congo-Kinshasa (Democratic Republic of the Congo)	New Zaïre	ZRN	186		1New Zaïre = 100 makuta
Cook Islands	New Zealand Dollar	NZD	554	NZ$	NZ$1 = 100 cents
Costa Rica	Costa Rican Colón	CRC	188		1 Colón = 100 centimos
Côte d'Ivoire	CFA Franc BCEAO	XOF	952	CFAF	CFAF1 = 100 centimes (discontinued)
Croatia	Kuna	HRK	191	HRK	HRK1 = 100 lipa
Cuba	Cuban Peso	CUP	192	Cu$	Cu$1 = 100 centavos
Cyprus	Cypriot Pound	CYP	196	£C	£C1 = 100 cents
Cyprus, Northern	Turkish Lira	TRL	792	TL	TL1 = 100 kurus
Czech Republic	Czech Koruna	CZK	203	K	K1 = 100 halers
Denmark	Danish Krone	DKK	208	Dkr	Dkr1 = 100 Øre
Djibouti	Djibouti franc	DJF	262	DF	DF1 = 100 centimes
Dominica	East Caribbean Dollar	XCD	951	EC$	EC$1 = 100 cents
Dominican Republic	Dominican Republic Peso	DOP	214	RD$	RD$1 = 100 centavos
East Timor	U.S. Dollar	USD	840	US$	US$1 = 100 cents
Ecuador	U.S. Dollar	USD	840	US$	US$1 = 100 cents
Ecuador (pre-9/02)	Sucre	ECS	218	S/	S/1 = 100 centavos
Egypt	Egyptian Pound	EGP	818	£E	£E1 = 100 piasters, 1,000 milliemes
El Salvador	El Salvadorian Colón	SVC	222	¢	¢1 = 100 centavos
Equatorial Guinea	CFA Franc BEAC	XAF	950	CFAF	CFAF1 = 100 centimes (discontinued)
Eritrea	Nakfa	ERN	232	Nfa	Nfa1 = 100 cents
Estonia	Estonia Kroon	EEK	233	KR	KR1 = 100 senti

Country	Currency	ISO 4217 Codes		Symbol	Sub-Currency
		Alpha	Numeric		
Ethiopia	Birr	ETB	230	Br	Br1 = 100 cents
European Union	European Union Euro	EUR	978	€	€ 1 = 100 cents
Falkland Islands	Falkland Pound	FKP	238	£F	£F1 = 100 pence
Faroe Islands	Danish Krone	DKK	208	Dkr	Dkr1 = 100 Øre
Fiji	Fiji Dollar	FJD	242	F$	F$1 = 100 cents
Finland	European Union Euro	EUR	978	€	€ 1 = 100 cents
Finland (pre-2002)	Markka	FIM	246	mk	mk1 = 100 penniä
France	European Union Euro	EUR	978	€	€ 1 = 100 cents
France (pre-2002)	French Franc	FRF	250	F	F1 = 100 centimes
French Guiana	European Union Euro	EUR	978	€	€ 1 = 100 cents
French Polynesia	CFP Franc	XPF	953	CFPF	CFPF1 = 100 centimes
French Southern Territories	European Union Euro	EUR	978	€	€ 1 = 100 cents
Gabon	CFA Franc BEAC	XAF	950	CFAF	CFAF1 = 100 centimes (discontinued)
Gambia	Dalasi	GMD	270	D	D1 = 100 bututs
Gaza	New Shekel (Israel) Jordanian Dinar	ILS JOD	376 400	NIS JD	NIS1 = 100 agorot JD1 = 1,000 fils
Georgia	Lari	GEL	268		1 Lari = 100 tetri
Germany	European Union Euro	EUR	978	€	€ 1 = 100 cents
Germany (pre-2002)	Deutsche Mark	DEM	276	DM	DM1 = 100 pfennigs
Ghana	Cedi	GHC	288	¢	¢1 = 100 psewas
Gibraltar	Gibraltar Pound	GIP	292	£G	£G1 = 100 pence
Greece	European Union Euro	EUR	978	€	€ 1 = 100 cents
Greece (pre-2002)	Drachma	GRD	300	Dr	Dr1 = 100 lepta
Greenland	Danish Krone	DKK	208	Dkr	Dkr1 = 100 Øre
Grenada	East Caribbean Dollar	XCD	951	EC$	EC$1 = 100 cents
Guadeloupe	European Union Euro	EUR	978	€	€ 1 = 100 cents
Guam	U.S. Dollar	USD	840	US$	US$1 = 100 cents
Guatemala	Quetzal	GTQ	320	Q	Q1 = 100 centavos
Guinea	Guinea Franc	GNF	324		1 Franc = 100 centimes
Guinea-Bissau	CFA Franc BCEAO	XOF	952	CFAF	CFAF1 = 100 centimes (discontinued)
Guyana	Guyana Dollar	GYD	328	G$	G$1 = 100 cents
Haiti	Gourde	HTG	332	G	G1 = 100 centimes
Heard and McDonald Islands	Australian Dollar	AUD	36	A$	A$1 = 100 cents

CURRENCY

Country	Currency	ISO 4217 Codes		Symbol	Sub-Currency
		Alpha	Numeric		
Honduras	Lempira	HNL	340	L	L1 = 100 centavos
Hong Kong	Hong Kong Dollar	HKD	344	HK$	HK$1 = 100 cents
Hungary	Forint	HUF	348	Ft	Ft1 = 100 fillérs
Iceland	Króna	ISK	352	Ikr	Ikr1 = 100 aurar
India	Rupee	INR	356	Rs	Rs1 = 100 paise
Indonesia	Rupiah	IDR	360	Rp	Rp1 = 100 sen
Iran	Rial	IRR	364	Rls	1 toman=10 rials =1000 dinars
Iraq	Iraqi Dinar	IQD	368	ID	ID1 = 20 dirhams, 1000 filses
Ireland	European Union Euro	EUR	978	€	€ 1 = 100 cents
Ireland (pre-2002)	Irish Pound	IEP	372	IR£	IR£1 = 100 pence
Israel	New Shekel	ILS	376	NIS	NIS1 = 100 agorot
Italy	European Union Euro	EUR	978	€	€ 1 = 100 cents
Italy (pre-2002)	Italian Lira	ITL	380	Lit	Lit1 = 100 centesimi (not used)
Jamaica	Jamaican Dollar	JMD	388	J$	J$1 = 100 cents
Japan	Yen	JPY	392	¥	¥1 = 100 sen (not used)
Jordan	Jordanian Dinar	JOD	400	JD	JD1 = 100 piasters, 1000 filses
Kazakhstan	Tenge	KZT	398	n/a	1 Tenge = 100 tiyn
Kenya	Kenyan Shilling	KES	404	K Sh	K Sh1 = 100 cents
Kiribati	Australian Dollar	AUD	36	A$	A$ 1 = 100 cents
Kuwait	Kuwaiti Dinar	KWD	414	KD	KD1 = 1000 filses
Kyrgyzstan	Kyrgyzstan Som	KGS	417	n/a	1 Som = 100 tyyn
Laos	Kip	LAK	418	KN	KN1 = 100 at
Latvia	Lat	LVL	428	Ls	Ls1 = 100 santim
Lebanon	Lebanese Pound	LBP	422	L.L.	L.L.1 = 100 piasters
Lesotho	Loti	LSL	426	L (sing.) M (plu.)	1L = 100 lisente
Liberia	Liberian Dollar	LRD	430	$	$1 = 100 cents
Libya	Libyan Dinar	LYD	434	LD	LD1 = 1000 dirhams
Liechtenstein	Swiss Franc	CHF	756	SwF	SwF1 = 100 centimes
Lithuania	Litas	LTL	440	n/a	1 Litas = 100 centai
Luxembourg	European Union Euro	EUR	978	€	€ 1 = 100 cents
Luxembourg (pre-2002)	Luxembourg Franc	LUF	442	LuxF	LuxF1 = 100 centimes
Macau	Pataca	MOP	446	P	P1 = 100 avos

CURRENCY

Country	Currency	ISO 4217 Codes		Symbol	Sub-Currency
		Alpha	Numeric		
Macedonia	Denar	MKD	807	MKD	MKD1 = 100 deni
Madagascar	Malagasy Franc	MGF	450	FMG	1 ariayry = 5 francs 1 franc = 100 centimes
Malawi	Kwacha	MWK	454	MK	MK1 = 100 tambala
Malaysia	Ringgit	MYR	458	RM	RM1 = 100 sen
Maldives	Rufiyaa	MVR	462	Rf	Rf1 = 100 laari
Mali	CFA Franc BCEAO	XOF	952	CFAF	CFAF1 = 100 centimes (discontinued)
Malta	Maltese Lira	MTL	470	Lm	Lm1 = 100 cents
Marshall Islands	U.S. Dollar	USD	840	US$	US$1 = 100 cents
Martinique	European Union Euro	EUR	978	€	€ 1 = 100 cents
Mauritania	Ouguiya	MRO	478	UM	UM1 = 5 khoums
Mauritius	Mauritius Rupee	MUR	480	Mau Rs	Mau Rs1 = 100 cents
Mayotte	European Union Euro	EUR	978	€	€ 1 = 100 cents
Mexico	Mexican Peso	MXN	484		1 Peso = 100 centavos
Micronesia	U.S. Dollar	USD	840	US$	US$1 = 100 cents
Midway Islands	U.S. Dollar	USD	840	US$	US$1 = 100 cents
Moldova	Leu	MDL	498	n/a	1 Leu = 100 bani
Monaco	European Union Euro	EUR	978	€	€ 1 = 100 cents
Mongolia	Tugrik	MNT	496	Tug	Tug1 = 100 mongos
Montserrat	Pound Sterling	GBP	826	EC$	EC$1 = 100 pence
Morocco	Morrocan Dirham	MAD	504	DH	DH1 = 100 centimes
Mozambique	Metical	MZM	508	Mt	Mt1 = 100 centavos
Myanmar (Burma)	Kyat	MMK	104	K	K1 = 100 pyas
Namibia	Namibian Dollar	NAD	516	N$	N$1 = 100 cents
Nauru	Australian Dollar	AUD	36	A$	A$1 = 100 cents
Nepal	Nepalese Rupee	NPR	524	NRs	NRs1 = 100 paise
Netherlands	European Union Euro	EUR	978	€	€ 1 = 100 cents
Netherlands (pre-2002)	Dutch Guilder (florin or gulden)	NLG	528	f.	f.1 = 100 cents
Netherlands Antilles	Netherlands Antilles Guilder (florin or gulden)	ANG	532	Ant.f. or NAf.	Ant.f. or NAf.1 = 100 cents
New Caledonia	CFP Franc	XPF	953	CFPF	CFPF1 = 100 centimes
New Zealand	New Zealand Dollar	NZD	554	NZ$	NZ$1 = 100 cents
Nicaragua	Córdoba	NIC	558	C$	C$1 = 100 centavos
Niger	CFA Franc BCEAO	XOF	952	CFAF	CFAF1 = 100 centimes (discontinued)

CURRENCY

Country	Currency	ISO 4217 Codes		Symbol	Sub-Currency
		Alpha	Numeric		
Nigeria	Naira	NGN	566		1 Naria = 100 kobo
Niue	New Zealand Dollar	NZD	554	NZ$	NZ$1 = 100 cents
Norfolk Island	Australian Dollar	AUD	36	A$	A$1 = 100 cents
North Korea	North Korean Won	KPW	408	Wn	Wn1 = 100 chon
Northern Marianas	U.S. Dollar	USD	840	US$	US$1 = 100 cents
Norway	Norwegian Krone	NOK	578	NKr	NKr1 = 100 Øre
Oman	Rial Omani	OMR	512	RO	RO1 = 1000 baizas
Pakistan	Pakistani Rupee	PKR	586	Rs	Rs1 = 100 paisa
Palau	U.S. Dollar	USD	840	US$	US$1 = 100 cents
Palestinian Territory, Occupied	Israel Shekel	ILS	376		1 Shekel = 100 agorots
Panama	Balboa	PAB	590	B	B1 = 100 centesimos
Panama Canal Zone	U.S. Dollar	USD	840	US$	US$1 = 100 cents
Papua New Guinea	Kina	PGK	598	K	K1 = 100 toeas
Paraguay	Guarani	PYG	600		1 Guarani = 100 centimos
Peru	New Sol	PEN	604	S/.	S/.1 = 100 centimos
Philippines	Philippine Peso	PHP	608		1 Peso = 100 centavos
Pitcairn Islands	Pound Sterling	GBP	826	NZ$	NZ$1 = 100 pence
Poland	New Zloty	PLN	985		1 Zloty = 100 groszy
Portugal	European Union Euro	EUR	978	€	€ 1 = 100 cents
Portugal (pre-2002)	Portuguese Escudo	PTE	620	Esc	Esc1 = 100 centavos
Puerto Rico	U.S. Dollar	USD	840	US$	US$1 = 100 cents
Qatar	Qatari Riyal	QAR	634	QR	1 = 100 dirhams
Reunion	European Union Euro	EUR	978	€	€ 1 = 100 cents
Romania	Leu	ROL	642	L	L1 = 100 bani
Russian Federation	Ruble	RUB	810	R	R1 = 100 kopeks
Rwanda	Rwanda Franc	RWF	646	RF	RF1 = 100 centimes
Saint Kitts and Nevis	East Caribbean Dollar	XCD	951	EC$	EC$1 = 100 cents
Saint Helena and Dependencies	St. Helena Pound	SHP	654	£S	£S1 = 100 pence
Saint Lucia	East Caribbean Dollar	XCD	951	EC$	EC$1 = 100 cents
Saint Pierre and Miquelon	European Union Euro	EUR	978	€	€ 1 = 100 cents
Saint Vincent and the Grenadines	East Caribbean Dollar	XCD	951	EC$	EC$1 = 100 cents
Samoa, Western	Tala	WST	882	WS$	WS$1 = 100 sene

Country	Currency	ISO 4217 Codes		Symbol	Sub-Currency
		Alpha	Numeric		
San Marino	European Union Euro	EUR	978	€	€ 1 = 100 cents
Sao Tome and Principe	Dobra	STD	678	Db	Db1 = 100 centimos
Saudi Arabia	Saudi Riyal	SAR	682	SRls	SRls1 = 20 qursh, 100 Halalas
Senegal	CFA Franc BCEAO	XOF	952	CFAF	CFAF1 = 100 centimes (discontinued)
Seychelles	Seychelles Rupee	SCR	690	SR	SR1 = 100 cents
Sierra Leone	Leone	SLL	694	Le	Le1 = 100 cents
Singapore	Singapore Dollar	SGD	702	S$	S$1 = 100 cents
Slovakia	Slovak Koruna	SKK	703	Sk	Sk1 = 100 haliers
Slovenia	Tolar	SIT	705	SIT	SIT1 = 100 stotins
Solomon Islands	Solomon Islands Dollar	SBD	90	SI$	SI$1 = 100 cents
Somalia	Somali Shilling	SOS	706	So. Sh.	So. Sh.1 = 100 cents
South Africa	Rand	ZAR	710	R	R1 = 100 cents
South Georgia and South Sandwich Islands	Pound Sterling	GBP	826	£	£1 = 100 pence
South Korea	South Korean Won	KRW	410	W	W1 = 100 chon
Spain	European Union Euro	EUR	978	€	€ 1 = 100 cents
Spain (pre-2002)	Peseta	ESP	724	Ptas	Ptas1 = 100 centimos
Sri Lanka	Sri Lankan Rupee	LKR	144	SLRs	SLRs1 = 100 cents
Sudan	Sudanese Dinar	SDD	736	n/a	1 Dinar = 100 piasters
Suriname	Suriname Guilder (florin or gulden)	SRG	740	Sur.f. or Sf.	Sur.f. or Sf.1 = 100 cents
Svalbard and Jan Mayen Islands	Norwegian Krone	NOK	578	Nkr	Nkr1 = 100 Øre
Swaziland	Lilangeni Emalangeni	SZL	748	SwF	SwF1 = 100 cents
Sweden	Swedish Krona	SEK	752	Sk	Sk1 = 100 Öre
Switzerland	Swiss Franc	CHF	756	SwF	SwF1 = 100 centimes
Syria	Syrian Pound	SYP	760	£S	£S1 = 100 piasters
Taiwan	Taiwan Dollar	TWD	901	NT$	NT$1 = 100 cents
Tajikistan	Tajikistan Ruble	TJR	762	n/a	1 Ruble = 100 kopeks
Tajikistan	Somoni	TJS	762	n/a	1 Somoni = 100 dirams
Tanzania	Tanzanian Shilling	TZS	834	TSh	TSh1 = 100 cents
Thailand	Baht	THB	764	Bht or Bt	Bht or Bt1 = 100 satang

CURRENCY

Country	Currency	ISO 4217 Codes		Symbol	Sub-Currency
		Alpha	Numeric		
Togo	CFA Franc BCEAO	XOF	952	CFAF	CFAF1 = 100 centimes (discontinued)
Tokelau	New Zealand Dollar	NZD	554	NZ$	NZ$1 = 100 cents
Tonga	Palanga	TOP	776	PT or T$	PT or T$1 = 100 seniti
Trinidad and Tobago	Trinidad and Tobago Dollar	TTD	780	TT$	TT$1 = 100 cents
Tunisia	Tunisian Dinar	TND	788	TD	TD1 = 100 millimes
Turkey	Turkish Lira	TRL	792	TL	TL1 = 100 kurus
Turkmenistan	Manat	TMM	795	n/a	1 Manat= 100 tenge
Turks and Caicos Islands	U.S. Dollar	USD	840	US$	US$1 = 100 cents
Tuvalu	Australian Dollar	AUD	36	A$	A$1 = 100 cents
Uganda	Ugandian Shilling	UGX	800	USh	USh1 = 100 cents
Ukraine	Hryvna	UAH	980	n/a	1 Hryvna = 100 kopiyka
United Arab Emirates	UAE Dirham	AED	784	Dh	Dh1 = 100 filses
United Kingdom	Pound Sterling	GBP	826	£	£1 = 100 pence
United States	U.S. Dollar	USD	840	US$	US$1 = 100 cents
United States Minor Outlying Islands	U.S. Dollar	USD	840	US$	US$1 = 100 cents
Uruguay (to 1975)	Uruguayan Peso	UYP	858	Ur$	Ur$1 = 100 centésimos
Uruguay	Uruguayan New Peso	UYN	858	NUr$	NUr$1 = 100 centésimos
Uzbekistan	Uzbek Som	UZS	860	n/a	1 Som = 100 tiyin
Vanuatu	Vatu	VUV	548	VT	VT1 = 100 centimes
Vatican City	European Union Euro	EUR	978	€	€ 1 = 100 cents
Venezuela	Venezuela Bolivar	VEB	862	Bs	Bs1 = 100 centimos
Vietnam	New Dong	VND	704	D	D1 = 100 hao, 100 xu
Virgin Islands (British)	U.S. Dollar	USD	840	US$	US$1 = 100 cents
Virgin Islands (U.S.)	U.S. Dollar	USD	840	US$	US$1 = 100 cents
Wallis and Futuna	European Union Euro	EUR	978	€	€ 1 = 100 cents
Western Sahara	Morrocan Dirham Euro (Spain) Ouguiya (Mauritania)	MAD EUR MRO	504 978 478	DH € UM	DH1=100 centimes € 1 = 100 cents UM1 = 5 khoums
Yemen	Yemen Rial	YER	886	YRis	YRis1 = 100 filses
Yugoslavia	Yugoslavian Dinar	YUM	891	Din	Din1 = 100 paras
Zambia	Kwacha	ZMK	894	ZK	ZK1 = 100 ngwee
Zimbabwe	Zimbabwe Dollar	ZWD	716	Z$	Z$1 = 100 cents

Business Entities Worldwide

The following is a list of the most common business entities worldwide. It is not intended to be exhaustive of all enterprises in the world. Nonprofit enterprises and informal associations have generally not been included, unless they are in common use among traders. Emphasis has been given to private enterprises, as opposed to government or civil enterprises.

The detailed legal requirements for enterprises are numerous, complex, and different from country to country. Moreover, they usually have little meaning within a general definition or comparison of enterprises. The following definitions include some of these details for purposes of giving a general idea of the relative size and complexity of the enterprises, but it is beyond the scope of this work to list and explain every single characteristic, legal nuance, and exception to the exception. For more detailed information, advice should be sought from legal counsel in the relevant country. Another source is the "Martindale-Hubbell International Law Guide." See Resources Appendix for source information.

In many countries, the words "company", "association", and "venture" have special meanings, and therefore the word "enterprise" has been used as a generic term for the concept of a group of persons who join together for purposes of conducting business for profit. Similarly, the word "incorporate" in many countries refers to the procedure for registration of a business, even a partnership; therefore usage of this word has been avoided.
Note: Several definitions are useful at this time:

corporate person
An enterprise whether incorporated or not.

entity
An individual or an enterprise, having an organizational presence separate from the owner, recognized by law as having rights and obligations.

natural person
An individual.

joint liability
Liability for the obligations of an enterprise imposed on two or more owners of an enterprise.

person
An individual or legal entity recognized under law as having legal rights and obligations.

share or stock
An ownership interest in an enterprise. Stock usually refers to an ownership interest evidenced by a formal document issued by the enterprise. Share has a broader meaning in that it can describe a formal interest (such as stock) as well as a less formal interest such as in a partnership. Shares can have different characteristics depending upon the type of enterprise and country of the enterprise. For example: shares can be of equal or unequal value, be voting or non-voting, or can convey limited or unlimited liability for its owner(s).

several liability
Liability for the full obligations of an enterprise imposed on a single owner when other owners who also share responsibility cannot or do not pay.

---

additional liability company
(Russian Federation)
An enterprise with ownership interests divided into "parts" or "shares," formed to conduct business activities, and owned by one or more natural or corporate persons (members) who are jointly and severally liable for enterprise obligations in the percentage of their respective contributions to the enterprise.

agrupamento complementar de empresas
(ACE) (association of business entities) **(Portugal)**
An association of natural or corporate persons in Portugal formed to facilitate and develop the economic activities of the association members for their mutual benefit. Members have unlimited liability for association obligations.

agrupamento Europeu de interêsse econômico
(AEIE) (European economic interest group) **(Portugal)**
An association of natural or corporate persons from different European Community countries, formed to facilitate and develop the economic activities of the association members for their mutual benefit. Members have unlimited liability for association obligations.

Akciova Spolecnost
(a.s.) (joint stock company) **(Czech Republic)**
An enterprise with ownership interests in the form of shares and minimal capitalization of Kc 1,000,000, formed to undertake business activities,

ENTITIES

and owned by a single entity or by two or more individuals or entities (shareholders) whose liability for enterprise obligations is limited to the price of the shares.

Aktiebolag
(AB) (company limited by shares)
(Finland, Sweden)
An enterprise with ownership interests in the form of shares and minimum capital of SEK 100,000 (private company) or SEK 500,000 (public company), owned by one or more natural or corporate persons (shareholders) who receive dividends and whose liability for enterprise obligations is limited to the price of the shares.

Aktiengesellschaft
(AG) (corporation limited by shares)
(Germany, Liechtenstein)
An enterprise with ownership interests in the form of shares, owned by one or more natural or corporate persons (shareholders) who receive dividends and whose liability for enterprise obligations is limited to the price of the shares.

Aktiengesellschaften
(AG) (joint stock corporation) **(Austria)**
An enterprise with ownership interests in the form of shares and having minimal capital of ATS 1,000,000, formed for commercial purposes, and owned by natural or corporate persons (stockholders) whose liability for enterprise obligations is limited to the price of the shares.

Aktieselskab
(A/S) (joint stock company) **(Denmark)**
An enterprise with ownership interests in the form of shares and minimum capital of DKK 500,000, formed to conduct business activities, and owned by three or more natural or corporate natural or corporate persons (shareholders) whose liability for enterprise obligations is limited to the price of the shares.

Aktzionerno Drouzestvo
(AD) (public limited company) **(Bulgaria)**
An enterprise with ownership interests in the form of stock, formed to conduct any business, and owned by two or more natural or corporate persons (stockholders) who receive dividends, but whose liability for enterprise obligations is limited to the price of the stock.

anonim sirket
(A.S.) (public company) **(Turkey)**
An enterprise with ownership interests in the form of shares that are traded publicly, formed for any lawful purpose, and owned by five or more natural or corporate persons (shareholders) who receive

dividends but whose liability for enterprise obligations is limited to the price of the shares.

anonymos eteria
(AE) (joint stock company) **(Greece)**
An enterprise with ownership interests in the form of shares which may be traded publicly or privately, formed for any lawful purpose, and owned by one or more natural or corporate persons (shareholders) who receive dividends but who are liable only for the price of the shares.

Anpartsselskaber
(private company) **(Denmark)**
An enterprise with ownership interests in the form of shares and minimum capital of DKK 125,000, owned by one or more natural or corporate persons whose liability for enterprise obligations is limited to the price of the shares.

Anstalt
(establishment) **(Liechtenstein)**
An enterprise in which ownership interests are placed in an undivided fund, usually formed as a holding or investment company, and owned by one or more natural or corporate members who share profits in accordance with contractual provisions in the founding documents.

Ansvarlig Selskap
(unlimited partnership) **(Norway)**
An enterprise with ownership interests stated by contract and formed for commercial purposes by two or more natural or corporate natural or corporate persons who have unlimited and joint liability for enterprise obligations.

Artel
(production cooperative) **(Russian Federation)**
An enterprise with ownership interests combined into a single fund, formed by individuals to produce goods or engage in business activities jointly for their mutual benefit. The owners contribute labor and property to the enterprise, profits are divided in accordance with the labor contributed, and liability for enterprise obligations is stated in the enterprise bylaws.

Associazione in Partecipazione
(participation in association) **(Italy)**
An enterprise with ownership interests determined by contract and formed by a combination of individuals who contribute capital funds and individuals who provide only services. The partners who provide services have unlimited and joint liability for enterprise obligations, while the liability of partners who contribute capital is limited to the amount

of their contribution. Profit-sharing is fixed by the partnership agreement.

Berhad
(Bhd.) (public limited liability company) **(Malaysia)**
An enterprise with ownership interests in the form of shares that are publicly traded, owned by one or more natural or corporate persons who receive dividends and whose liability for enterprise obligations is limited to the price of the shares.

Besloten Vennootschap met Beperkte Aansprakelijkheid
(B.V.B.A.) (private limited company) **(Belgium, Netherlands)**
An enterprise with ownership interests in the form of shares that are not publicly traded, owned by one or more natural or corporate persons who receive dividends and whose liability for enterprise obligations is limited to the price of the shares.

Betéti Társaság
(Bt) (limited partnership) **(Hungary)**
An enterprise with ownership interests determined by contract and owned by one or more general partners and one or more limited partners. General partners have unlimited and joint liability for enterprise obligations, while limited partners have liability only to the amount of funds they have agreed to invest in the enterprise.

C corporation
(inc. or corp.) **(United States)**
A name derived from United States tax laws to refer to a corporation. *See* corporation.

Chusik-Hosea
(stock companies) **(Korea, Republic of)**
An enterprise with ownership interests in the form of shares, owned by one or more natural or corporate natural or corporate persons who receive dividends and whose liability for enterprise obligations is limited to the price of the shares.

Close Corporation
(Inc.) **(Canada, South Africa, United States)**
An enterprise with ownership interests in the form of shares, formed for purposes of conducting business, and owned by one or more persons (shareholders) who usually restrict the power of the managing directors to operate the enterprise. The shares are usually not traded publicly and the number of shareholders is usually less than 30. In some countries, the owners must be natural persons only, while in other countries corporate or natural persons may own shares in a close corporation.

Closed Company
(private company) **(Brazil)**
A sociedade anonima having shares traded privately. *See* Sociedade Anonima.

closed joint stock company
(Russian Federation)
An enterprise with ownership interests in the form of stock that can be transferred by private sale only, owned by one to fifty natural or corporate persons (stockholders) who receive dividends and whose liability for enterprise obligations is limited to the price of the stock.

Commanditaire Vennootschap
(special partnership) **(Belgium, Netherlands)**
An enterprise with ownership interests determined by written contract, and owned by one or more general partners and one or more special partners. General partners have unlimited and joint liability for enterprise obligations, while special partners have liability only to the amount of capital they have agreed to invest in the company.

Compainía Anómima
(C.A.) (corporation)
(Dominican Republic, Ecuador, Venezuela)
See Sociedad Anónima.

Compainía de Responsabilidad Limitada
(C. Ltda.) (limited liability company) **(Ecuador)**
An enterprise with ownership interests divided in shares of equal value known as participations, formed for any commercial purpose, and owned by at least 3 but no more than 25 members. Liability of each member for enterprise obligations is limited to the amount that the member agrees to invest in the enterprise.

compainía en comandita
(C. en C.) (limited partnership)
(Dominican Republic, Ecuador, Venezuela)
An enterprise with ownership interests in the form of "parts" and formed for commercial purposes by two or more general and limited partners. General partners have unlimited and joint liability for enterprise obligations, while limited partners are liable only to the capital that the partner has agreed to invest in the enterprise.

compainía en comandita por acciones
(C. en C. por A.) (limited partnership with shares)
(Dominican Republic, Ecuador, Venezuela)
A compaiñía en comandita with ownership interests in the form of shares instead of "parts". *See* compaiñía en comandita.

compainía por acciones
(C. por A.) (corporation) **(Dominican Republic)**
See Sociedad Anónima.

Company

(Co.) **(Australia, England, Papua New Guinea)**
An enterprise having ownership interests in the form of shares owned by natural or corporate persons whose liability is limited to the price of the shares. *See* public company; private company.

company limited by guarantee

(Papua New Guinea, South Africa)
An enterprise with ownership interests in the form of shares and owned by members who are liable for enterprise obligations in the amount stated in the formation documents.

Company Limited by Shares

(CLS) **(China)**
An enterprise with ownership interests in the form of shares and having minimum capital of RMB 10,000,000, formed for commercial purposes, and owned by natural or corporate persons (shareholders) whose liability for enterprise obligations is limited to the price of the shares. Shares may be sold privately or offered to the public at large.

Compaõnía en Nombre Colectivo

(Compaõnía) (general partnership)
(Dominican Republic, Ecuador, Venezuela)
An enterprise with ownership interests stated by contract and formed for commercial purposes by two or more natural or corporate persons who have unlimited and joint liability for enterprise obligations.

Corporation

(Inc. or Corp. or Ltd. or Ltée.)
(Bahamas, Canada, United States)
An enterprise with ownership interests in the form of shares, formed to do business for gain, and owned by one or more natural or corporate persons (shareholders) who receive dividends but whose liability for enterprise obligations is limited to the price of the shares.

Cuideachta Phoibli Theoranta

(c.p.t.) **(Ireland)**
See Private Company.

Drouzestvo s Ogranichena Otgovornost

(OOD) (private limited company) **(Bulgaria)**
An enterprise with ownership interests in the form of shares and with minimum capital of 50,000 leva, formed for business purposes, and owned by one or more natural or corporate persons (shareholders) who receive dividends but whose liability for enterprise obligations is limited to the price of the shares. New members may be admitted only by approval of the existing members.

Empresa Individual de Responsibilidad Limitada

(E.I. de R.L.) (individual limited liability company) **(Costa Rica, El Salvador)**
An enterprise with ownership interests stated in the formation documents, formed for any lawful purpose, and owned by a single individual who may withdraw profits and whose liability for enterprise obligations is limited to the enterprise property.

Entreprise Unipersonnelle à Responsabilité Limitée

(E.U.R.L.) (individual limited liability company) **(France)**
A société à responsabilité limitée formed and owned by one person (associé unique) who receives dividends and whose liability for enterprise obligations is limited to the price of the participations. *See* société à responsabilité limitée.

Eshamli Komandit Sirket

(special partnership with shares) **(Turkey)**
An enterprise with ownership interests in the form of shares and formed for commercial purposes by two or more general and special partners. General partners have unlimited and joint liability for enterprise obligations, while special partners are liable only to the funds that the partner has agreed to invest in the enterprise.

estabelecimento individual de responsabildade limitada

(EIRL) (individual limited liability company) **(Portugal)**
An enterprise with ownership interests stated in the formation documents, formed for any lawful purpose, having minimum capital of Esc 400,000 and owned by a single individual who may withdraw profits and whose liability for enterprise obligations is limited to the enterprise property.

eteria periorismenis efthinis

(EPE) (limited liability company) **(Greece)**
An enterprise with ownership interests in the form of shares that are transferred privately and owned by one or more natural or corporate persons (shareholders) whose liability for enterprise obligations is limited to the price of the shares.

eterorythmos eteria

(EE) (limited partnership) **(Greece)**
An enterprise with ownership interests and profit-sharing determined by written contract, formed to undertake business activities, and owned by general and limited partners. Each general partner has unlimited and joint liability for enterprise obligations,

while each limited partner is liable only for the funds that the partner has agreed to invest in the enterprise.

Exempted Limited Partnership
(ELP) **(Bahamas)**
An enterprise that is formed and operated similarly to a limited partnership, but that is exempt from business licensee fees and government-imposed taxes for 50 years. General partners have unlimited and joint liability for enterprise obligations, while limited partners incur no liability except for the purchase of their interests.

General Partnership
(Australia, Bahamas, Canada, Channel Islands, China, Cyprus, England, Hong Kong, India, Israel, Russian Federation, South Africa, Turkey, United States, Zimbabwe)
An enterprise with ownership interests and profit-sharing fixed by contract and formed to carry on business for gain by the partners, all of whom have unlimited and joint personal liability for enterprise obligations.

Gesellschaft mit beschränkter Haftung
(GmbH) (limited liability company)
(Austria, Germany, Liechtenstein)
An enterprise with ownership interests in the form of shares that are transferred privately and owned by one or more natural or corporate persons (shareholders) whose liability for enterprise obligations is limited to the price of the shares.

Gomei Kaisha
(partnership corporation) **(Japan)**
An enterprise with ownership interests in the form of shares and formed for commercial purposes by two or more partners.

Goshi Kaisha
(limited partnership corporation) **(Japan)**
An enterprise with ownership interests in the form of shares, owned by one or more general partners and one or more special partners. General partners have unlimited and joint liability for enterprise obligations, while special partners have liability only to the amount of funds they have agreed to invest in the enterprise.

Handelsbolag
(general partnership) **(Sweden)**
An enterprise with ownership interests stated by contract and formed for commercial purposes by two or more natural or corporate persons who have unlimited and joint liability for enterprise obligations.

Hapcha-Hosea
(limited partnership) **(Korea, Republic of)**
An enterprise with ownership interests determined by contract, and owned by one or more general partners and one or more special partners. General partners have unlimited and joint liability for enterprise obligations, while special partners have liability only to the amount of funds they have agreed to invest in the enterprise.

Hapmyong-Hosea
(partnership) **(Korea, Republic of)**
An enterprise with ownership interests stated by contract and formed for commercial purposes by two or more natural or corporate persons who have unlimited and joint liability for enterprise obligations.

Is Ortakligi
(business partnership) **(Turkey)**
An enterprise with ownership interests stated by contract and formed for commercial purposes by two or more natural or corporate persons who have unlimited and joint liability for enterprise obligations.

Julkinen Osakeyhtiö-oyj
(public limited liability company) **(Finland)**
An enterprise with ownership interests in the form of shares and minimum capital of Fmk 500,000, formed to conduct any business, and owned by one or more natural or corporate persons (shareholders) whose liability for enterprise obligations is limited to the price of the shares.

Kollektif Sirket
(general partnership) **(Turkey)**
An enterprise with ownership interests stated by contract and formed for commercial or other lawful purposes by two or more natural or corporate persons who have unlimited and joint liability for enterprise obligations.

Kollektivgesellschaft
(general partnership) **(Liechtenstein)**
An enterprise with ownership and profit-sharing interests stated by contract and formed for commercial purposes by two or more natural or corporate persons who have unlimited and joint liability for enterprise obligations.

Komandit Sirket
(special partnership) **(Turkey)**
An enterprise with ownership interests determined by contract, and owned by one or more general partners and one or more special partners. General partners have unlimited and joint liability for enterprise obligations, while special partners have liability only to the amount of funds they have agreed to invest in the enterprise.

Komanditní Spolecnost
(k.s.) (limited partnership) **(Czech Republic)**
An enterprise with ownership interests and profit-

sharing determined by written contract, formed to undertake business activities, and owned by general and limited partners. Each general partner has unlimited and joint liability for enterprise obligations, while each limited partner is liable only to the amount of the funds that the partner has agreed to invest in the enterprise.

Komanditno Druzestvo
(limited partnership) (**Bulgaria**)
An enterprise with ownership interests determined by written contract and formed to conclude commercial transactions by two or more individuals who decide to act in concert, but at least one of whom has unlimited liability for enterprise obligations and at least one of whom has liability limited in accordance with the partnership contract.

Kommandit Erwerbsgesellschaft
(KEG) (limited professional association) (**Austria**)
An enterprise with ownership interests determined by contract, formed to provide professional or business services that require special regulatory licenses, and owned by partners who have limited liability for enterprise obligations.

Kommanditbolag
(limited partnership) (**Sweden**)
An enterprise with ownership interests determined by contract, and owned by one or more general partners and one or more limited partners. General partners have unlimited and joint liability for enterprise obligations, while limited partners have liability only to the amount of the funds they have agreed to invest in the enterprise.

Kommanditgesellschaft
(limited partnership)
(**Austria, Germany, Liechtenstein**)
An enterprise with ownership interests determined by contract, formed to carry on trade or production, and owned by two or more partners. At least one partner (Komplementaer) has unlimited liability for enterprise obligations, while at least one other partner (Kommanditist) is liable only to the amount of the funds that the partner has invested in the enterprise.

Kommanditselskap
(limited partnership) (**Norway**)
An enterprise with ownership interests determined by contract, and owned by one or more general partners and one or more limited partners. General partners have unlimited and joint liability for enterprise obligations, while limited partners have liability only to the amount of the funds they have agreed to invest in the enterprise.

korlátolt felelosségu társaság
(Kft) (limited liability company) (**Hungary**)
An enterprise with ownership interests in the form of "parts" and minimum capital of HUF 1,000,000, formed to conduct business for profit, owned by one or more natural or corporate persons who receive dividends and whose liability for enterprise obligations is limited to the price of the parts.

közkereseti társaság
(Kkt) (general partnership) (**Hungary**)
An enterprise with ownership interests stated by contract and formed to conduct business for profit by two or more natural or corporate persons who have unlimited and joint liability for enterprise obligations.

közös vállalat
(joint venture) (**Hungary**)
An enterprise formed for profit from commercial activities by two or more natural or corporate persons who are liable for enterprise obligations in proportion to their respective contributions to the enterprise.

Limited Duration Companies
(LDC) (**Bahamas**)
An enterprise with a limited duration of 30 years or less, formed to allow for automatic termination of the enterprise when the period of existence has elapsed. The formation documents determine whether ownership interests are in the form of shares or otherwise, and liability of the shareholders may be limited or unlimited.

limited liability company
(LLC)
(**China, Russian Federation, United States**)
An enterprise with ownership interests in the form of shares, formed for commercial purposes, and owned by one or more natural or corporate persons (shareholders) but no more than the statutory maximum (usually 50 shareholders). The liability of the shareholders for enterprise obligations is limited to the price of the shares.

limited liability partnership
(LLP) (**United States**)
An enterprise with ownership interests determined by written contract among the partners, all of whom must be professionals licensed or otherwise specially qualified to offer services regulated by law and must be permitted to offer services through a limited liability partnership. The partners remain personally liable for their own obligations, jointly and severally liable for partnership obligations, but have no liability for the actions of other partners.

limited partnership
(Bahamas, Canada, Channel Islands, Cyprus, England, India, Israel, South Africa, United States, Zimbabwe)
An enterprise with ownership interests and profit-sharing fixed by contract among the partners and formed to carry on business for gain by two or more partners. At least one partner has unlimited liability for enterprise obligations, while at least one other partner is liable only to the amount of the funds that the partner has invested in the enterprise, provided that the limited partner contributes no services and takes no part in controlling the day-to-day partnership business.

Maatschap
(partnership) **(Netherlands)**
An enterprise with ownership interests stated by contract and formed to conduct business or to offer services for profit by two or more natural or corporate persons who contribute labor, funds, and property to the enterprise and who have unlimited and joint liability for enterprise obligations. The formation contract may limit a partner's liability to the partner's percentage of contribution to the enterprise.

Naamloze Vennootschap
(N.V.) (public joint stock company)
(Belgium, Netherlands)
An enterprise with ownership interests in the form of shares that are publicly traded, owned by one or more natural or corporate persons who receive dividends and whose liability for enterprise obligations is limited to the price of the shares.

Offene Erwerbsgesellschaft
(OEG) (general professional association) **(Austria)**
An enterprise with ownership interests determined by contract, formed to provide professional or business services that require special regulatory licenses, and owned by partners who have unlimited and joint liability for enterprise obligations.

Offene Handelsgesellschaft
(Co. or Cie.) (general partnership)
(Austria, Germany)
An enterprise with ownership interests determined by contract, formed to carry on a trade or production, and owned by partners who are jointly and severally liable for enterprise obligations.

omorythmos eteria
(OE) (general partnership) **(Greece)**
An enterprise with ownership interests stated by contract and formed for commercial purposes by two or more natural or corporate persons (partners) who have unlimited and joint liability for enterprise actions.

Open Company
(public company) **(Brazil)**
A sociedade anonima having shares traded publicly through a stock exchange or otherwise in an over-the-counter market. *See* Sociedade Anonima.

open joint stock company
(Russian Federation)
An enterprise with ownership interests in the form of stock sold to the public, owned by one or more natural or corporate persons (stockholders) who receive dividends and whose liability for enterprise obligations is limited to the price of the stock.

Ordinary Partnership
(England, Hong Kong, Zimbabwe)
See General Partnership.

Osakeyhtiö
(Oy) (private limited liability company) **(Finland)**
An enterprise with ownership interests in the form of shares and minimum capital of Fmk 50,000, owned by one or more natural or corporate persons whose liability for enterprise obligations is limited to the price of the shares.

osuuskunta
(osuus) (cooperative association) **(Finland)**
An enterprise with ownership and profit-sharing interests determined by contract, formed by five or more members who contribute their property and labor for purposes of carrying on business to their mutual benefit. The liability of the members for enterprise obligations is determined by the formation contract.

Partnership
(England, United States)
An enterprise with ownership interests determined by contract between the owners (partners) who join together for purposes of acting in concert to attain common goals. *See* general partnership, limited partnership, and limited liability partnership.

partnership in commendam
(limited partnership) **(Russian Federation)**
An enterprise with ownership interests and profit-sharing fixed by contract among the partners and formed to carry on business for gain by two or more partners. At least one partner has unlimited liability for enterprise obligations, while at least one other partner is liable only to the amount of the funds that the partner has agreed to invest in the enterprise.

Private Company
(Ltd. or Pvt. Ltd.) **(Australia, Bahamas, Channel Islands, Cyprus, England, Hong Kong, India, Israel, Nigeria, Pakistan, Zimbabwe)**
An enterprise with ownership interests in the form of

shares that are not sold to the public at large, owned by natural or corporate persons (shareholders) who receive dividends but whose liability for enterprise obligations is limited to the price of the shares.

Public Company
(P.L.C.) **(Australia, Bahamas, Channel Islands, Cyprus, England, Hong Kong, India, Israel, Nigeria, Pakistan, Zimbabwe)**
An enterprise having ownership interests in the form of shares that are sold to the public at large and owned by natural or corporate persons (shareholders) who receive dividends but whose liability for enterprise obligations is limited to the price of the shares.

Publikt Aktiebolag-abp
(public limited liability company) **(Finland)**
See Julkinen Osakeyhtiö-oyj.

Részvénytársaság
(Rt) (corporation limited by shares) **(Hungary)**
An enterprise with ownership interests in the form of shares and minimum capital of HUF 10,000,000, owned by one or more natural or corporate persons (shareholders) who receive dividends and whose liability for enterprise obligations is limited to the price of the shares.

S Corporation
(Inc. or Co.) **(United States)**
An enterprise with special tax features, having ownership interests in the form of shares, owned by one to thirty-five natural or corporate persons (shareholders) who receive a share of annual net profits as determined by their respective share percentages, and whose liability for enterprise obligations is limited to the funds they agree to invest in the enterprise.

Sendirian Berhard
(Sdn. Bhd.) (private limited liability company) **(Malaysia)**
An enterprise with ownership interests in the form of shares that are privately traded only, owned by one or more natural or corporate persons who receive dividends and whose liability for enterprise obligations is limited to the price of the shares.

sharika mossahmah
(joint stock company) **(Bahrain, Egypt, Qatar)**
An enterprise with ownership interests in the form of stock or shares, formed for commercial purposes, and owned by natural or corporate persons (stockholders or shareholders) who receive dividends but whose liability for enterprise obligations is limited to the price of the stock or shares.

sharika tadhamun
(general partnership) **(Bahrain, Egypt, Qatar)**
An enterprise with ownership interests stated by contract and formed for commercial purposes by two or more natural or corporate persons (partners) who have unlimited and joint liability for enterprise actions.

sharika tawsiyah baseetah
(limited partnership) **(Bahrain, Egypt, Qatar)**
An enterprise with ownership interests and profit-sharing fixed by contract among the partners and formed to carry on business for gain by two or more partners. At least one partner has unlimited liability for enterprise obligations, while at least one other partner is liable only to the amount of the funds that the partner has agreed to invest in the enterprise.

sharika tawsiyah biel-ash-nam
(partnership limited by shares)
(Bahrain, Egypt, Qatar)
An enterprise with ownership interests in the form of shares and formed for commercial purposes by two or more general and limited partners. General partners have unlimited and joint liability for enterprise actions, while limited partners are liable only to the price of the shares.

sharika that massouliyyah mahdoodah
(WLL) (limited liability company)
(Bahrain, Egypt, Qatar)
An enterprise with ownership interests divided in shares that cannot be sold publicly, formed for any commercial purpose, having limited duration of no more than 25 years, and owned by at least two natural or corporate persons but no more than the number of members permitted by law (usually 50 or fewer). Liability of members for enterprise obligations is limited to the amount stated in the formation documents.

Sociedad Anónima
(S.A.) (stock company)
(Argentina, Bahamas, Bolivia, Chile, Columbia, Costa Rica, Denmark, Dominican Republic, Ecuador, El Salvador, Guatemala, Honduras, Mexico, Paraguay, Peru, Spain, Uruguay)
An enterprise with ownership interests in the form of stock or shares, formed to sell goods or services, and owned by natural or corporate persons (stockholders or shareholders) who receive dividends based on enterprise net profits but whose liability for enterprise obligations is limited to the price of the stock or shares.

Sociedad Anónima de Capital Abierto
(S.A. de C.A.) (public corporation) **(Costa Rica)**
A sociedad anónima registered on the Costa Rican

stock exchange, having at least 50 stockholders none of whom own more than 10 percent of the shares, and with at least 10 percent of its shares transferred annually through the stock exchange. *See* Sociedad Anónima.

Sociedad Colectiva

(S.C. or Cía) (general partnership) **(Argentina, Bolivia, Chile, Columbia, El Salvador, Guatemala, Honduras, Peru, Uruguay)**
An enterprise with ownership interests stated by contract and formed for commercial purposes by two or more natural or corporate persons who have unlimited and joint liability for enterprise obligations.

Sociedad Commanditaria

(limited partnership) **(Spain)**
An enterprise with ownership interests determined by contract, and owned by one or more general partners and one or more limited partners. General partners have unlimited and joint liability for enterprise obligations, while limited partners have liability only to the amount of the funds they have agreed to invest in the enterprise.

Sociedad de Capital e Industria

(S.C.I.) (capital and industry partnership) **(Argentina)**
An enterprise with ownership interests determined by contract and formed by a combination of individuals who contribute funds and individuals who provide only services. The partners who contribute funds have unlimited liability, while the other partners are not liable personally for enterprise obligations. Profit-sharing is fixed by the partnership agreement.

Sociedad de Responsabilidad Limitada

(S.R.L. or S. de R.L. or Ltda.) (limited liability company) **(Argentina, Bolivia, Brazil, Chile, Columbia, El Salvador, Honduras, Mexico, Spain)**
An enterprise with ownership interests divided in shares of equal value known as quotas, formed for any commercial purpose, and owned by no more than the number of members permitted by law (usually 50 or fewer). Liability of members for enterprise obligations is limited to the amount stated in the enterprise contract.

Sociedad en Comandita

(S. en C.) (limited partnership) **(Argentina, Bolivia, Chile, Columbia, El Salvador, Guatemala, Honduras, Mexico, Peru, Uruguay)**
An enterprise with ownership interests stated by contract and formed for commercial purposes by two or more active and silent partners. Active partners have unlimited and joint liability for enterprise obliga-

tions, while silent partners are liable only to the funds that the partner has invested in the enterprise.

Sociedad en Comandita por Acciones

(S.C.A.) (joint stock company) **(Argentina, Columbia, Guatemala, Honduras, Mexico)**
An enterprise having attributes of both a stock company and partnership, with ownership interests in the form of stock, and owned by active and silent partners. Active partners are liable for enterprise obligations and obligations to the same degree as in a general partnership. The liability of each silent partner is limited to the funds that the partner has agreed to invest in the enterprise.

Sociedad en Nombre Colectivo

(general partnership) **(Mexico)**
An enterprise with ownership interests stated by contract and formed for commercial purposes by two or more natural or corporate persons who have unlimited and joint liability for enterprise obligations.

Sociedad Regular Colectiva

(general partnership) **(Spain)**
An enterprise with ownership interests stated by contract and formed for commercial purposes by two or more natural or corporate persons who have unlimited and joint liability for enterprise obligations.

sociedade anónima

(S.A.) (stock company) **(Brazil, Portugal)**
An enterprise with ownership interests in the form of shares, formed for any object or gain not contrary to law or public order, and owned by two or more natural or corporate persons (shareholders) who receive dividends and whose liability for enterprise obligations is limited to the price of the shares.

sociedade cooperativa

(SCRL) (cooperative) **(Portugal)**
An enterprise with ownership interests in the form of shares and minimum capitalization of Esc 50,000, formed for commercial purposes, and owned by ten or more natural or corporate persons (shareholders) who share profits in relation to their labor contributions to the business and whose liability for enterprise obligations may be limited or unlimited as stated in the formation documents.

sociedade em comandita por acções

(partnership with shares) **(Portugal)**
An enterprise with ownership interests in the form of shares and formed for commercial purposes by two or more general and limited partners. General partners have unlimited and joint liability for enterprise actions, while limited partners are liable only to the funds that they have agreed to invest in the enterprise.

sociedade em commandita simple
(limited partnership) (**Portugal**)
An enterprise with ownership interests in the form of "quotas" and formed for commercial purposes by two or more active and silent partners. Active partners have unlimited and joint liability for enterprise actions, while silent partners are liable only to the amount of funds that the partner has invested in the enterprise.

sociedade em nome colectivo
(general partnership) (**Portugal**)
An enterprise with ownership interests stated by contract and formed for commercial purposes by two or more natural or corporate persons who have unlimited and joint liability for enterprise actions.

sociedade por quota
(Lda.) (limited liability companyl) (**Portugal**)
An enterprise with ownership interests in the form of "quotas", formed for any commercial purpose, and owned by no more than the number of members permitted by law (usually 50 or fewer). Liability of members for enterprise obligations is limited to the amount stated in the enterprise contract.

Società a Responsabilità Limitata
(S.R.L.) (limited liability company) (**Italy**)
An enterprise with ownership interests in the form of "quotas", having limits on the transfer of quotas, and owned by one or more natural or corporate persons (quotaholders) whose liability for enterprise obligations is limited to the price of the shares, except that a sole quotaholder that is a corporate entity has unlimited liability for enterprise obligations if the enterprise becomes insolvent.

Società in Accomandita per Azioni
(company with liability limited per share) (**Italy**)
An enterprise with ownership interests in the form of shares, owned by one or more natural or corporate persons (partners) whose liability for enterprise obligations is limited to the price of the shares.

Società in Accomandita Semplice
(unlimited liability share company) (**Italy**)
An enterprise with ownership interests in the form of shares, owned by one or more natural or corporate persons (partners) who have unlimited and joint liability for enterprise obligations.

Società in Nome Collettivo
(general partnership) (**Italy**)
A enterprise with ownership interests stated by contract and formed for commercial purposes by two or more natural or corporate persons (partners) who have unlimited and joint liability for enterprise obligations.

Società per Azioni
(S.A.) (corporation) (**Italy**)
An enterprise with ownership interests in the form of shares and minimum capital of 200,000,000 lire, owned by one or more natural or corporate persons who receive dividends and whose liability for enterprise obligations is limited to the price of the shares, except that a sole shareholder has unlimited liability for enterprise obligations in the event the enterprise becomes insolvent.

Società Semplice
(simple partnership) (**Italy**)
An enterprise with ownership interests stated by written or verbal contract, formed other than for industrial or commercial purposes by two or more individuals who act severally but have unlimited and joint liability for enterprise obligations.

Societate cu Raspundere Limitata
(limited liability company) (**Romania**)
An enterprise with ownership interests in the form of "shares" or "parts", owned by one or more natural or corporate persons whose liability for enterprise obligations is limited to the price of the shares.

Societate in Comandita pe Actiuni
(limited joint stock company) (**Romania**)
An enterprise with ownership interests in the form of shares that are privately traded, owned by one or more natural or corporate persons who receive dividends and whose liability for enterprise obligations is limited to the price of the shares.

Societate in Comandita Simpla
(limited partnership) (**Romania**)
An enterprise with ownership interests determined by contract, and owned by one or more general partners and one or more limited partners. General partners have unlimited and joint liability for enterprise obligations, while limited partners have liability only to the amount of the funds they have agreed to invest in the enterprise.

Societate in Nume Colectiv
(general partnership) (**Romania**)
An enterprise with ownership interests stated by contract and formed for commercial purposes by two or more natural or corporate persons who have unlimited and joint liability for enterprise obligations.

Societate pe Actiuni
(joint stock company) (**Romania**)
An enterprise with ownership interests in the form of shares that are publicly traded, owned by one or more natural or corporate persons who receive dividends and whose liability for enterprise obligations is limited to the price of the shares.

Société à Responsabilité Limitée
(S.A.R.L.) (limited liability company)
(France, Luxembourg, Morocco)
An enterprise with ownership interests in the form of "participations", having a maximum duration of 99 years, and owned by one to fifty natural or corporate persons (associés) who receive dividends and whose liability for enterprise obligations is limited to the price of the participations.

Société Anonyme
(S.A.) (joint stock company) **(Bahamas, Belgium, France, Lebanon, Luxembourg, Morocco)**
An enterprise with ownership interests in the form of shares, formed for any lawful purpose, and owned by natural or corporate persons (shareholders) who receive dividends but who are liable only for the price of the shares.

Société Coopérative
(S.C.) (cooperative company) **(Belgium)**
An enterprise with ownership interests in the form of shares and minimum capitalization of BF 750,000, formed for commercial purposes, and owned by three or more natural or corporate persons (shareholders) who share profits in relation to the amount of business with the enterprise and whose liability for enterprise obligations may be limited or limited as stated in the enterprise formation documents.

Société en Commandite
(S. en C.) (special partnership)
(France, Lebanon, Morocco)
See Société en Commandite Simple.

Société en Commandite par Actions
(S.C. par A.) (special partnership by shares)
(France, Morocco)
An enterprise with ownership interests in the form of shares and formed for commercial purposes by two or more general and limited partners. General partners have unlimited and joint liability for enterprise obligations, while limited partners are liable only to the funds that the partner has agreed to invest in the enterprise.

Société en Commandite Simple
(S. en C.S.) (special partnership)
(France, Lebanon, Morocco)
An enterprise with ownership interests determined by public deed or private written contract, and owned by one or more general partners and one or more special partners. General partners have unlimited and joint liability for enterprise obligations, while special partners have liability only to the amount of the funds they have agreed to invest in the company.

Société en Nom Collectif
(SNC) (general partnership)
(Belgium, France, Lebanon, Morocco)
An enterprise with ownership interests determined by public deed or private written contract, and owned by two or more partners who have unlimited and joint liability for all enterprise obligations.

société en participation
(joint venture) **(France)**
An enterprise formed by written or verbal contract by natural or corporate persons who agree to act in concert for a particular purpose. Partners conduct business in their own names and are personally liable for enterprise obligations.

Société par Actions Simplifée
(S.A.S.) (simplified shares company) **(France)**
An enterprise with ownership interests in the form of shares and minimum capital of FF 250,000, formed by companies for the purpose of conducting business jointly, and owned by two or more corporations (shareholders) that receive dividends and that have liability for enterprise obligations limited to the price of the shares.

Société Privée a Reponsabilité Limitée
(S.P.R.L.) (private limited company) **(Belgium)**
An enterprise with ownership interests in the form of shares and minimum capitalization of BEF 750,000, and owned by two or more members with liability limited to the amount of the funds they agreed to invest in the enterprise.

Spolecnost s Rucením Omezenym
(s.r.o. or spol. s r.o.) (limited liability company)
(Czech Republic)
An enterprise with ownership interests in the form of investments agreed by the members in advance, formed to undertake business activities, and owned by one or more natural or corporate persons, to a maximum of 50. Liability of members for enterprise obligations is limited to the investment amount stated in the founding documents for the enterprise.

spólka akcyjna
(S.A.) (joint stock company) **(Poland)**
An enterprise with ownership interests in the form of shares and minimum capital of Zl 1 billion, owned by one or more natural or corporate persons (shareholders) who receive dividends and whose liability for enterprise obligations is limited to the price of the shares.

spólka cywilna
(civil partnership) **(Poland)**
An enterprise with ownership interests determined by private written or verbal contract, formed for

business purposes but not registered nationally, and owned by two or more partners who have unlimited and joint liability for all enterprise obligations.

spólka jawna
(registered general partnership) **(Poland)**
An enterprise with ownership interests determined by written or verbal contract, formed for commercial purposes and registered nationally, and owned by two or more partners who have unlimited and joint liability for all enterprise obligations.

spólka komandytowa
(limited partnership) **(Poland)**
An enterprise with ownership interests determined by contract, and owned by one or more general partners and one or more special partners. General partners have unlimited and joint liability for enterprise obligations, while special partners have liability only to the amount of funds they have agreed to invest in the enterprise.

spólka z ograniczona odpowied zialnóscia
(Sp. z o.o.) (limited liability company) **(Poland)**
An enterprise with ownership interests in the form of shares that are transferred privately, having minimum capital of Zl 40 million, and owned by one or more natural or corporate persons (shareholders) whose liability for enterprise obligations is limited to the price of the shares.

Stock Corporation
(Inc. or Corp.) **(Philippines)**
An enterprise with ownership interests in the form of shares, owned by one or more natural or corporate persons who receive dividends and whose liability for enterprise obligations is limited to the price of the shares.

Subiratelno Druzestvo
(sudrudzie) (general partnership) **(Bulgaria)**
An enterprise with ownership interests determined by written contract and formed to conclude commercial transactions by two or more individuals who decide to act in concert and who have unlimited and joint liability for enterprise obligations.

Teoranta
(Teo.) **(Ireland)**
See Public Company.

Trading Company
(Brazil)
An enterprise with ownership interests in the form of stocks, formed to manufacture goods for export only, and owned by natural or corporate persons (stockholders) whose liability is limited to the purchase of the shares.

Treuunternehmen
(business trust) **(Liechtenstein)**
An enterprise that has both corporate and trust attributes because a natural or corporate person (trustor) places property into the trust, and the trust property is then invested or otherwise utilized to conduct the business stated in the trust documents. The trust is administered by an trustee on behalf of the trust beneficiaries.

türk limited sirket
(T.L.S.) (limited liability company) **(Turkey)**
An enterprise with ownership interests in the form of shares that are transferred privately only, having minimum capital of TL 10,000, and owned by two to 50 natural or corporate persons (shareholders) whose liability for enterprise obligations is limited to the price of the shares.

Vennootschap Onder Firma
(general partnership) **(Belgium, Netherlands)**
An enterprise with ownership interests stated by contract, registered to conduct business, and formed for commercial purposes by two or more natural or corporate persons who have unlimited and joint liability for enterprise obligations.

Verejná Obchodní Spolecnost
(v.o.s.) (general commercial partnership) **(Czech Republic)**
An enterprise with ownership interests and profit-sharing determined by written contract, formed to undertake business activities, and owned by two or more partners who have unlimited and joint liability for enterprise obligations.

Yugen Kaisha
(joint stock corporation) **(Japan)**
An enterprise with ownership interests in the form of shares that are publicly traded, owned by one or more natural or corporate persons who receive dividends and whose liability for enterprise obligations is limited to the price of the shares.

Yuhan-Hosea
(limited companies) **(Korea, Republic of)**
An enterprise with ownership interests in the form of "shares" that are privately transferred, owned by one or more natural or corporate persons whose liability for enterprise obligations is limited to the price of the shares.

Weights and Measures

LINEAR MEASURES

U.S. CUSTOMARY LINEAR MEASURES

Many of these measures are based on those developed in medieval England, when a yard was a measure of King Edward I's waist, a rod was an actual 10-foot pole and a furlong was the width of 32 plowed rows. The mile began with the Romans measuring it as 1,000 paces. The United States is one of the few countries which still uses many of them. Our yard is now officially 3600/3937 of a meter (exactly 0.9144 meter), while a survey foot is 1200/3937 of a meter (approximately 0.3048 meter).

1000 mil	= 1 inch	= 2.54 centimeters
12 inches (in)	= 1 foot (ft)	= 30.48 centimeters
3 feet	= 1 yard (yd)	= 0.9144 meter
5-1/2 yards	= 1 rod (rd), pole, or perch = 16-1/2 ft	= 5.029 meters
40 rods	= 1 furlong (fur) = 220 yds = 660 ft	= 0.201 kilometers
8 furlongs	= 1 statute mile (mi) = 1,760 yds = 5,280 ft	= 1.609 kilometers
3 statute miles	= 1 league* = 5,280 yds = 15,840 ft	= 4.82 kilometers

* A league is an imprecise measure that may range from approximately 2.4 to 4.6 statute miles, but in most English-speaking countries it refers to 3 statute miles.

GUNTER'S OR SURVEYOR'S CHAIN MEASURES

These measures are based on a 17th century British surveyor's tool that was, in fact, a 66-foot long chain composed of 100 links. They fit in with the rod and furlong already in use.

7.92 inches	= 1 link (li)	= 20.12 centimeters
25 links	= 1 rod (rd) = 16-1/2 feet	= 5.029 meters
100 links	= 1 chain (ch) = 4 rods = 66 ft	= 20.11 meters
10 chains	= 1 furlong (fur) = 660 ft	= 0.201 kilometers
80 chains	= 1 statute mile = 320 rods = 5,280 ft	= 1.609 kilometers

NAUTICAL MEASURES

A nautical mile is based on the circumference of the earth, but the precise definition of it has varied considerably through the centuries. Most recently, a nautical mile has meant a minute (1/60) of a degree. The current International Nautical Mile, defined in 1929 and adopted by U.S. in 1954 is slightly shorter than the U.S. Nautical Mile, which is no longer used.

6 feet	= 1 fathom	= 1.82 meters
120 fathoms	= 1 cable = 720 feet	= 219.45 meters
8.44 cables	= 1 International Nautical Mile	= 1.852 kilometers
1.15 statute mi	= 1 Int'l Nautical Mile = 6,076.11549 feet	= 1.852 kilometers

METRIC LINEAR MEASURES

A meter is the length of the path traveled by light in a vacuum during the time interval of 1/299,794,458 second. Originally, it was one 10-millionth of a line running from the equator, through Paris to the North Pole. The metric system is also called SI (Systèm Internationale).

10 millimeters (mm)	= 1 centimeter (cm)	= 0.39 inch
10 centimeters	= 1 decimeter (dm) = 100 millimeters	= 3.94 inches
10 decimeters	= 1 meter (m) = 1000 millimeters	= 39.37 inches
10 meters	= 1 dekameter (dam)	= 32.81 feet
10 dekameters	= 1 hectometer (hm) = 100 meters	= 328.1 feet
10 hectometers	= 1 kilometer (km) = 1000 meters	= 0.62 mile

W & M

AREA MEASURES

Squares and cubes of units are sometimes abbreviated by using "superior" figures. For example, ft^2 means square foot, and m^3 means cubic meter.

U.S. CUSTOMARY AREA MEASURES

144 square inches	$= 1$ sq ft (ft^2)	$= 0.093$ sq meter
9 square feet	$= 1$ sq yd (yd^2) $= 1,296$ sq in	$= 0.836$ sq meter
30-1/4 square yards	$= 1$ sq rd (rd^2) $= 272$-1/4 sq ft	$= 25.29$ square meters
160 square rods	$= 1$ acre $= 4,840$ yd^2 $= 43,560$ ft^2	$= 0.405$ hectare
640 acres	$= 1$ square mile (mi^2)	$= 2.590$ sq kilometers
1 square mile	$= 1$ section (of land)	$= 2.590$ sq kilometers
6 square miles	$= 1$ township* $= 36$ sections $= 36$ square mi.	$= 93.24$ sq kilometers

W & M

* 6 square miles is a somewhat imprecise measure of a township, but one which is used for many practical purposes. In actuality, the east and west borders follow the meridians, making the north or south border slightly less than 6 miles long due to the curve of the earth.

METRIC AREA MEASURES

100 square millimeters (mm^2)	$= 1$ square centimeter (cm^2)	$= 0.155$ square inch
10,000 square centimeters	$= 1$ square meter (m^2) $= 1,000,000$ mm^2	$= 1.19$ square yards
100 square meters	$= 1$ are (a)	$= 119.60$ square yards
100 ares	$= 1$ hectare (ha) $= 10,000$ m^2	$= 2.471$ acres
100 hectares	$= 1$ square kilometer (km^2) $= 1,000,000$ m^2	$= 0.3861$ square miles

CAPACITY MEASURES

The American method of measuring volume is based on an Ancient Egyptian measure, a 12th century British measure and a custom of doubling each measure to find the next. Some measures dropped along the way, so this is no longer apparent. There are two official sets of volume measures in the U.S., wet and dry.

U.S. CUSTOMARY LIQUID MEASURES

The gallon is now officially defined in terms of cubic inches, which, in turn, are defined in terms of the meter. When necessary to distinguish the liquid pint or quart from the dry pint or quart, the word "liquid" or the abbreviation "liq" should be used in combination with the name or abbreviation of the liquid unit.

8 fluid drams	$= 1$ fluid ounce	$= 29.57$ milliliters
4 fluid ounces (oz)	$= 1$ gill	$= 0.118$ liter
4 gills (gi)	$= 1$ pint (pt) $= 28.875$ in^3	$= 0.473$ liter
2 pints	$= 1$ quart (qt) $= 57.75$ in^3	$= 0.946$ liter
4 quarts	$= 1$ gallon (gal) $= 231$ in^3 $= 8$ pts $= 32$ gills	$= 3.785$ liters

U.S. CUSTOMARY DRY MEASURES

The bushel is now officially defined in terms of cubic inches, which, in turn, are defined in terms of the meter. When necessary to distinguish the dry pint or quart from the liquid pint or quart; the word "dry" should be used in combination with the name or abbreviation of the dry unit.

2 dry pints (pt)	$= 1$ dry quart (qt) $= 67.2006$ in^3	$= 1.101$ liters
8 dry quarts	$= 1$ peck (pk) $= 537.605$ in^3 $= 16$ pt	$= 8.81$ liters
4 pecks	$= 1$ bushel (bu)* $= 2,150.42$ in^3 $= 32$ dry qt	$= 35.239$ liters

* This is also called a bushel, struck measure. One bushel, heaped measure is frequently recognized as 1-1/4 bushels, struck measure. More precisely, one bushel, heaped is equal to 1.278 bushels, struck.

APOTHECARIES' FLUID MEASURES

These units were once widely used in the U.S. for pharmaceutical purposes, but have largely been replaced by metric units. These measures are actually the same as those for U.S. customary wet measure (above), with some additional subdivisions.

60 minims (min)	= 1 fluid dram (fl dr) = 0.2256 in^3	= 3.888 grams
8 fluid drams	= 1 fluid ounce (fl oz) = 1.8047 in^3	= 31.103 grams
16 fluid ounces	= 1 pint (pt) = 28.875 in^3 = 128 fl drs	= 0.473 liter
2 pints	= 1 quart (qt) = 57.75 in^3 = 32 fl oz = 256 fl drs	= 0.946 liter
4 quarts	= 1 gallon (gal) = 231 in^3 = 128 fl oz = 1,024 fl drs	= 3.785 liters

U.S. COOKING MEASURES

76 drops	= 1 teaspoon = 1-1/3 fl drams	= 4.9288 milliliters
3 teaspoons	= 1 tablespoon = 4 fl drams	= 14.786 milliliters
16 tablespoons	= 1 cup = 8 fl ounces	= 0.2366 liter
2 cups	= 1 pint = 16 fl ounces	= 0.4732 liter
2 pints	= 1 quart = 32 fl ounces	= 0.9463 liter

BRITISH IMPERIAL LIQUID AND DRY MEASURES

The British changed their definitions of capacity measures slightly in the 19th century, so that British Imperial measures having the same names as U.S. measures are slightly larger than their U.S. counterparts.

British imperial		cubic inches	U.S. equiv.	Metric
60 minims	= 1 fluidram (fl dr)	= 0.216734 in^3	= 0.961 fl dr	= 3.552 milliliters
8 fluidrams	= 1 fluidounce (fl oz)	= 1.7339 in^3	= 0.961 fl oz	= 28.412 milliliters
5 fluidounces	= 1 gill	= 8.669 in^3	= 4.805 fl oz	= 142.066 milliliters
4 gills	= 1 pint	= 34.678 in^3	= 1.201 fl pt	= 0.5683 liters
2 pints	= 1 quart	= 69.355 in^3	= 1.201 fl qt, 1.032 dry qt	= 1.136 liters
4 quarts	= 1 gallon	= 277.420 in^3	= 1.201 fl gal	= 4.546 liters
2 gallons	= 1 peck	= 554.84 in^3	= 1.0314 pecks	= 9.087 liters
4 pecks	= 1 bushel	= 2219.36 in^3	= 1.032 bushels	= 36.369 liters

METRIC MEASURES OF CAPACITY

The liter was derived from the kilogram, originally the volume occupied by a kilogram of water. It is now officially defined as a cubic decimeter of pure water, which is nearly the same. This one set of measures is used for all capacity measures.

10 milliliters (ml)	= 1 centiliter (cl)	= 0.338 fluid ounce
10 centiliters	= 1 deciliter (dl) = 100 milliliters	= 0.21 pint
10 deciliters	= 1 liter (l) = 1000 milliliters	= 1.057 quarts
10 liters	= 1 dekaliter (dal)	= 2.6417 gallons
10 dekaliters	= 1 hectoliter (hl) = 100 liters	= 26.417 gallons
10 hectoliters	= 1 kiloliter (kl) = 1,000 liters	= 264.17 gallons

CUBIC MEASURES

U.S. CUSTOMARY CUBIC MEASURES

1,728 cubic inches (in^3)	= 1 cubic foot (ft^3)	= 0.028 cubic meter
27 cubic feet	= 1 cubic yard (yd^3)	= 0.765 cubic meter

METRIC

1,000 cubic millimeters (mm^3)	= 1 cubic centimeter (cm^3)	= 0.061 cubic inch
1,000 cubic centimeters	= 1 cubic decimeter (dm^3)	= 61.023 cubic inches
1,000 cubic decimeters	= 1 cubic meter (m^3) = 1 stere	= 1.307 cubic yards

WEIGHTS

When necessary to distinguish avoirdupois units from troy or apothecaries' units, the word "avoirdupois" or the abbreviation "avdp" should be used in combination with the name or abbreviation of the unit.

AVOIRDUPOIS WEIGHT

This is the weight system in everyday use in the U.S. Historically, it is a rearrangement of the troy system. The word avoirdupois is French, meaning goods of weight. The avoirdupois pound is now officially defined as 0.45359237 kilogram.

27-11/32 grains	= 1 dram (dr)	= 1.1772 grams
16 drams	= 1 ounce (oz) = 437-1/2 grains	= 28.35 grams
16 ounces	= 1 pound (lb) = 256 drams = 7,000 grains	= 0.454 kilogram
100 pounds	= 1 hundredweight (cwt)*	= 45.359 kilograms
112 pounds	= 1 gross or long hundredweight (cwt)*	= 50.802 kilograms
20 hundredweights	= 1 short ton (tn) = 2,000 lbs*	= 0.907 metric ton
20 gross or long hundredweights	= 1 gross or long ton = 2,240 lbs*	= 1.016 metric tons

*When the terms "hundredweight" and "ton" are used unmodified, they are commonly understood to mean the 100-pound hundredweight and the 2,000-pound (short) ton, respectively; these units may be designated "net" or "short" when necessary to distinguish them from the corresponding units in gross of long measure.

TROY WEIGHT

The troy system began in Ancient Egypt and was modified over the years by Europeans. The British used the troy as the official weight system for currency, while the U.S. mint adopted it in America. These units are still used for over-the-counter sales of precious metals, although they have largely fallen into disuse, in favor of the metric system.

24 grains (gr)	= 1 pennyweight (dwt)	= 1.555 grams
20 pennyweights	= 1 ounce troy (oz t) = 480 grains	= 31.103 grams
12 ounces troy	= 1 pound troy (lb t) = 240 dwt = 5,760 gr	= 0.373 kilogram

APOTHECARIES' WEIGHT

While one pound apothecaries' is equivalent to 1 pound troy, the apothecaries' system differs in its subdivisions. These units were once widely used in the United States for pharmaceutical purposes, but have largely been replaced by metric units, although they are still legal standards.

20 grains (gr)	= 1 scruple (s ap)	= 1.296 grams
3 scruples	= 1 dram apothecaries' (dr ap) = 60 gr	= 3.888 grams
8 drams apothecaries	= 1 ounce apothecaries' (oz ap) = 24 s ap = 480 gr	= 31.103 grams
12 ounces apothecaries	= 1 pound apothecaries' (lb ap) = 96 dr ap	= 373.24 grams
	= 288 s ap = 5,760 grains	

METRIC WEIGHT (MASS)

A kilogram was originally defined as the mass of one cubic decimeter of water at the temperature of maximum density, but is now a cylinder of platinum-iridium alloy of the same size.

10 milligrams (mg)	= 1 centigram (cg)	= 0.154 grain
10 centigrams	= 1 decigram (dg) = 100 milligrams	= 1.543 grains
10 decigrams	= 1 gram (g) = 1,000 milligrams	= 0.035 ounce
10 grams	= 1 dekagram (dag)	= 0.353 ounce
10 dekagrams	= 1 hectogram (hg) = 100 grams	= 3.527 ounces
10 hectograms	= 1 kilogram (kg) = 1,000 grams	= 2.2046 pounds
1,000 kilograms	= 1 metric ton (t)	= 1.102 short tons

MISCELLANEOUS UNITS OF MEASURE

acre
A measure of area, used for surveying land. One acre is equal to 160 square rods or 43,560 square feet. The term originally referred to the area of land a yoke of oxen (two oxen) could plow in one day.

agate
A measure used in printing, especially for classified advertising, equivalent to 1/14 inch. An agate line is a space one column wide and 1/14 inch deep (1/14 of a column inch). Originally, a measure of type size of 5-1/2 points. *See also* point.

ampere (Amp)
A unit of electrical current in electrons per second. Equivalent to a flow of one coulomb per second or to the steady current produced by the pressure of one volt applied across a resistance of one ohm. *See also* ohm; volt.

assay ton (AT)
A unit of weight used in assaying. One assay ton is equal to 29.167 grams. The relationship between one assay ton to one milligram is the same as one net ton (2,000 pounds avoirdupois) to one ounce troy. Therefore, the weight in milligrams of precious metal from one assay ton gives the number of troy ounces to the net ton.

bale
An imprecise measure of a large bundle of goods, especially cotton or hay. The weight varies from country to country. In the U.S., the approximate weight of a bale of cotton is 500 pounds, while in Egypt it is approximately 750 pounds.

barrel (bbl)
A measure of volume, which varies according to the commodity, and can also vary from state to state. A barrel can be either a wet or dry volume measure. One barrel is generally between 31 and 42 gallons. One barrel of fermented liquors often means 31 gallons, one barrel of liquid is often 31-1/2 gallons, on barrel of beer is often 36 gallons, one barrel of "proof spirits" is 40 gallons by U.S. federal law, and one barrel of crude oil for statistical purposes is generally 42 gallons or 159 liters. Two common barrel measurements for dry commodities are:
1 barrel, standard for fruits, vegetables, and other dry commodities (except cranberries) = 105 dry quarts = 7,056 in3 = 3.281 bushels, struck measure.
1 barrel, standard, cranberries = 86-45/64 dry quarts = 5,826 in3 = 2.709 bushels, struck measure.

board foot (fbm, BF, bd ft)
A unit of measurement used for lumber. One board foot is 12 inches by 12 inches by 1 inch, or one square foot of lumber one inch thick. Rough lumber is often sold by the board foot.

bolt
A unit of measurement used for fabric. One bolt is 40 yards long.

British thermal unit (Btu)
A unit used to describe heating capacity. One Btu is the amount of energy needed to raise the temperature of one pound of water one degree Fahrenheit. 1 Btu = 252 Calories. *See also* calorie.

caliber
A unit for measuring the diameter of the bore of a gun. In the U.S. and Britain, this has traditionally been expressed in hundredths or thousandths of an inch and written as a decimal fraction (i.e., .22 or .465). It has become more common for caliber to be expressed in millimeters. Naval gun caliber is the number by which one multiplies the bore diameter to find the barrel length.

caliper
A unit used to measure the thickness of paper or board. One caliper is equal to one mil, or 1/1,000 of an inch.

calorie
A measurement of heat used in place of British thermal units (Btu) by countries using the metric system. One small calorie is the amount of energy needed to raise the temperature of one gram of water by one degree Celsius, from 14.5°C to 15.5°C, or 4.1840 joules. One big calorie (kilocalorie) = 1,000 small Calories. *See also* British thermal unit; joule.

carat
A unit for measuring the weight of precious stones. One international carat is 200 milligrams (approximately 3.086 grains). Originally, a carat was the weight of a locust tree seed, about 1/142 of an ounce. *See also* karat.

cord
A unit of volume used for firewood. One cord is a stack of wood that measures 8 feet by 8 feet by 2 feet, or 128 cubic feet. A face cord (or short cord) is a stack of logs measuring 8 feet by 4 feet by whatever the length of the logs happens to be.

cubit
An ancient unit of length based on the length of the forearm, from the elbow to the tip of the middle finger. One cubit is not a precise length, although it is usually figured between 17 and 21 inches, and most often at 18 inches.

decibel

Not an actual unit of measurement, but a comparison between one sound an another to show the level of a sound's energy. 0 decibels is the softest sound audible to the human ear, and 130 decibels is painful to the human ear. The decibel scale is logarithmic, so that a 10 decibel increase doubles the loudness.

displacement ton

A unit used for measuring the weight of water displaced by a ship, in place of weighing the ship itself. One displacement ton is equal to a long ton, or 2,240 pounds. It is calculated by finding the number of cubic feet of water displaced and figuring the weight of the water. Loaded displacement tonnage refers to the displacement tonnage of a ship when it is carrying its usual cargo, fuel and crew load. Light displacement tonnage is the displacement tonnage of an unloaded ship, while the dead weight tonnage is the weight that the ship can carry, or the difference between the loaded displacement and the light displacement tonnage. Different types of ships are more commonly described according to one type of displacement tonnage or another.

ell

A unit of length used for measuring fabric. An English term, an ell is 45 inches, or 1/32 of a bolt. Bolts of fabric are often sold in the United States and England in 45 inch widths. *See also* bolt.

em

A unit of length used in printing. An em is equal to the point size of the type in use, that is, a 6-point em is 6 points wide. An en is equal to one half of an em. Nut is another printer's term for an en.

freight ton (also called measurement ton)

A unit of volume used most often for sea freight. One freight ton is usually equal to 40 cubic feet of merchandise. A freight ton may also refer to a unit of volume for freight that weighs one ton, varying depending on the commodity.

gauge

A measure of shotgun bore diameter. Gauge numbers originally were determined by finding the number of lead balls with a diameter equal to that of the bore that made up a pound (i.e., a 12 gauge shotgun), so that the smaller the gauge number, the bigger the shotgun bore. Today an international agreement assigns millimeter measures to each gauge. *See also* caliber.

great gross

A numerical figure used for counting commercial items. One great gross is a dozen gross, or 1,728 items. *See also* gross.

gross

A numerical figure used for counting commercial items. One gross is a dozen dozen, or 144 items. *See also* great gross.

hand

A unit of length, usually used for measuring horses at withers. One hand is 4 inches or 10.16 cm. It was derived from the width of the hand.

hertz

Measurement unit for the frequency of electromagnetic waves. One hertz is equal to one cycle per second.

hogshead (hhd)

A liquid measurement for a large cask or barrel. One hogshead is 63 U.S. gallons, or 238 liters. A hogshead may also refer to a large cask containing anywhere from 63 to 140 gallons.

horsepower (hp)

A unit used to measure the power of engines. One horsepower is equal to 746 watts or to 2,546.0756 Btu per hour. It was derived from the power needed by a horse to lift 33,000 pounds a distance of 1 foot in 1 minute or to lift 550 pounds 1 foot in 1 second. *See also* British thermal unit, Watt.

joule

A unit of energy. One joule is equal to the amount of work done by a force of one newton when its point of application moves through a distance of one meter in the direction of the force.

karat

A measure of the purity of gold in an alloy. Each karat represents a ratio of 1/24 purity, indicating how many parts out of 24 are pure. 24 karat gold is pure, while 18 karat gold is 3/4 gold and 1/4 alloy. The system was derived from a time when a karat was used to describe 1/24 of a troy pound and 24 karat was one full troy pound.

knot

A rate of travel used to measure a ship's speed, but also used for airplanes and other vehicles. One knot is the rate of one nautical mile (1,852 meters) per hour.

league

A unit of distance. One league is usually estimated at 3 statute miles in English-speaking countries, but it can range anywhere from about 2.4 to 4.6 statute miles. The league was originally a Gaulish unit of distance equal to 1.5 Roman miles.

light-year

A unit of distance used by astronomers. One light year is 5,880,000,000,000 miles, which is the distance light travels in a vacuum in a year at the rate of 186,281.7 miles (299,792 kilometers) per second.

magnum
A unit of volume for liquid, most often for wine. A magnum is not a precise unit, but may refer to 1.5 liters, 2/5 of a gallon or two quarts. It also refers to the bottle itself.

ohm
A unit of electrical resistance which slow the flow of amps. A circuit in which a potential difference of one volt produces a current of one ampere has a resistance of one ohm. *See also* ampere; volt.

parsec
A unit of measure used by astronomers. One parsec is approximately 3.26 light-years or 19.2 trillion miles. The term is derived from a combination of first syllables of parallax and second. A parsec is the distance is a distance having a heliocentric parallax of one second (1/3600 degree). *See also* light-year.

pi (π)
The ratio of the circumference of a circle to its diameter. The value of pi is approximately 3.1416.

pica
A unit of length used in printing to describe the width of a line of type. One pica is usually calculated as 1/6 inch or 12 points. *See also* point.

pipe
A unit of liquid measure, most often used for wine or oil. One pipe is equal to two hogsheads, or 126 gallons. *See also* hogshead.

point
A unit of measurement for the height of type in printing. One point is approximately .013837, 1/72 inch, or 1/12 pica. Used in printing for measuring type size. Originally one point was 1/72 of a French inch. European and American point sizes are slightly different. A point can also a unit of measurement used in printing and binding equal to 1/1,000 of an inch. *See also* pica.

ream
The numerical unit used for measuring pieces of paper. One ream is 20 quires, which is now usually 500 sheets, but can be 480 sheets, and occasionally is 516 sheets of paper.

register tons
A unit of volume, and not weight, used to express the total capacity of a ship, called gross register tonnage, gross tonnage, or gross weight. One register ton is equal to 100 cubic feet. Most often used for passenger ships, but may be applied to other types of ships.

roentgen
An unit to measure radiation exposure produced by X-rays. One roentgen is equal to the amount of radiation produced in one cubic centimeter of dry air at 0°C and standard atmospheric pressure ionization equal to one electrostatic unit of charge.

score
A numerical figure. One score is 20 units.

sound, speed of
A rate of speed, which varies depending on temperature, altitude and the media through which the sound is traveling. In general terms, the "speed of sound" is usually placed at 1,088 feet per second, or about 750 miles per hour at 32°F at sea level.

span
A British unit of length, now little used. One span is equivalent to 9 inches or 22.86 cm. It is derived from the distance between the end of the thumb and the end of the little finger of a spread hand.

square
A unit of square measure used in the building trade. One square is equal to 100 square feet. It often refers to roofing materials.

stone
A unit of weight still in use in the United Kingdom. One stone is equal to 14 pounds avoirdupois, or approximately 6.3 kilograms.

therm
A unit of heat, although it may be defined in different ways. One therm is equal to 100,000 Btu's or to 1,000 large calories. *See also* British thermal unit; calorie.

ton mile
(shipping) The transport of one ton of cargo for one mile. Used most often in air cargo services.

township
A unit of land measurement used in the U.S. One township is almost 36 square miles. The south border is 6 miles long. The east and west borders, also 6 miles long, follow the meridians, making the north border slightly less than 6 miles long.

tun
A unit of liquid measurement, used for wine and other liquids. One tun is equal to two pipes, or four hogsheads, or 252 gallons. In practice a tun may be more than 252 gallons. *See also* hogsheads; pipes.

volt
A measure of electrical potential difference. Volts are the pressure that moves the amps along a wire. Normal household voltage in the U.S. is 120 volts.

watt
A unit of power which is a measure of the amount of work an appliance is capable of. A watt is the power used by a current of one ampere across a potential difference of one volt.

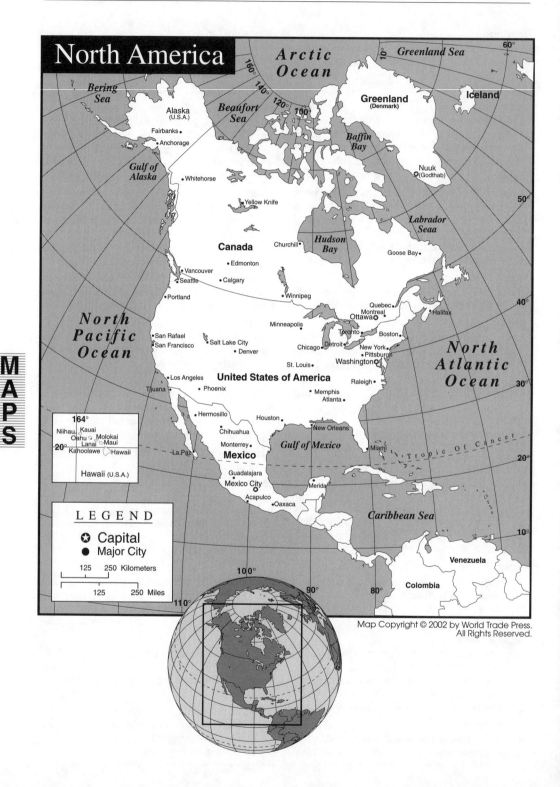

North America

Arctic Ocean

Greenland Sea

60°

Greenland
(Denmark)

Iceland

Bering Sea

Alaska
(U.S.A.)

Beaufort Sea

Fairbanks •

• Anchorage

Baffin Bay

Gulf of Alaska

• Whitehorse

Nuuk
(Godthab)

50°

Yellow Knife •

Labrador Seaa

Canada

Churchill •

Hudson Bay

Goose Bay •

• Edmonton

North Pacific Ocean

• Vancouver

• Seattle

• Calgary

• Winnipeg

Quebec •

Montreal •

Ottawa ✪

Halifax •

40°

• Portland

Minneapolis •

Toronto •

Boston •

• San Rafael

• Salt Lake City

Chicago •

Detroit •

New York •

Pittsburgh •

North Atlantic Ocean

San Francisco •

• Denver

St. Louis •

Washington ✪

• Los Angeles

United States of America

Raleigh •

30°

Tijuana •

• Phoenix

• Memphis
Atlanta •

MAPS

164°

Niihau Kauai
Oahu Molokai
Lanai Maui
20° Kahoolawe Hawaii

Hawaii (U.S.A.)

• Hermosillo

Houston •

New Orleans •

Chihuahua •

Monterrey •

Gulf of Mexico

Miami •

Tropic Of Cancer

20°

La Paz •

Mexico

Guadalajara •

Mexico City ✪

Merida •

Acapulco •

• Oaxaca

Caribbean Sea

10°

LEGEND

✪ Capital
● Major City

Venezuela

125   250 Kilometers

100°

Colombia

80°

125   250 Miles

110°

90°

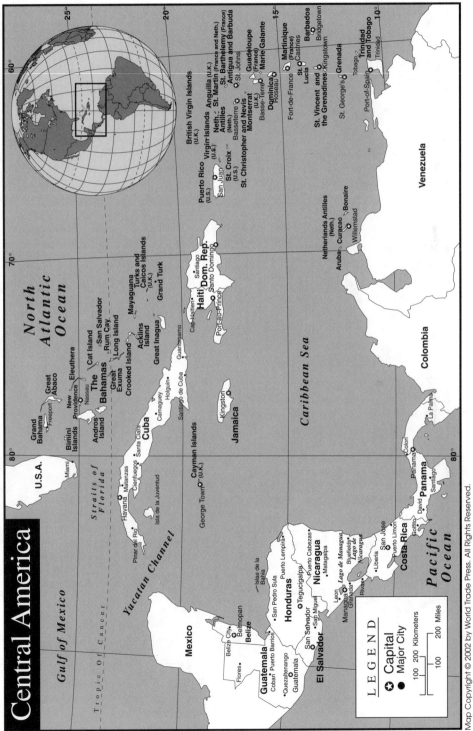

Central America

MAPS

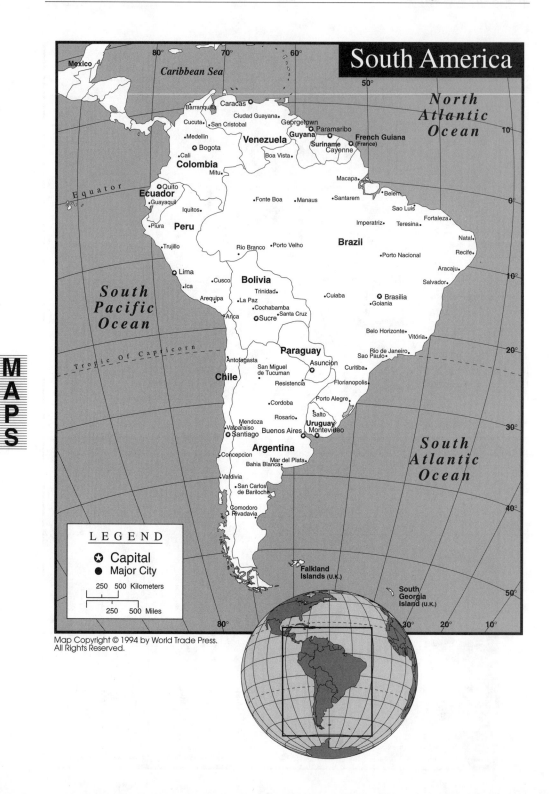

South America

Mexico
Caribbean Sea
North Atlantic Ocean

Barranquilla
Caracas
Ciudad Guayana
Cucuta
Georgetown
San Cristobal
Paramaribo
French Guiana (France)
Medellin
Venezuela
Guyana
Suriname
Cayenne
Bogota
Boa Vista
Cali
Colombia
Mitu
Macapa
Equator
Quito
Ecuador
Fonte Boa
Manaus
Santarem
Belem
Guayaquil
Sao Luis
Iquitos
Fortaleza
Piura
Peru
Imperatriz
Teresina
Natal
Trujillo
Rio Branco
Porto Velho
Brazil
Recife
Lima
Cusco
Bolivia
Porto Nacional
Aracaju
Ica
Trinidad
Cuiaba
Brasilia
Salvador
South Pacific Ocean
Arequipa
La Paz
Goiania
Arica
Cochabamba
Santa Cruz
Sucre
Belo Horizonte
Vitória
Tropic Of Capricorn
Antofagasta
Paraguay
Rio de Janeiro
Sao Paulo
South Atlantic Ocean
San Miguel de Tucuman
Asuncion
Curitiba
Chile
Resistencia
Florianopolis
Cordoba
Porto Alegre
Rosario
Salto
Mendoza
Uruguay
Valparaiso
Buenos Aires
Montevideo
Santiago
Argentina
Concepcion
Mar del Plata
Bahia Blanca
Valdivia
San Carlos de Bariloche
Comodoro Rivadavia
Falkland Islands (U.K.)
South Georgia Island (U.K.)

LEGEND
✪ Capital
● Major City
250 500 Kilometers
250 500 Miles

M
A
P
S

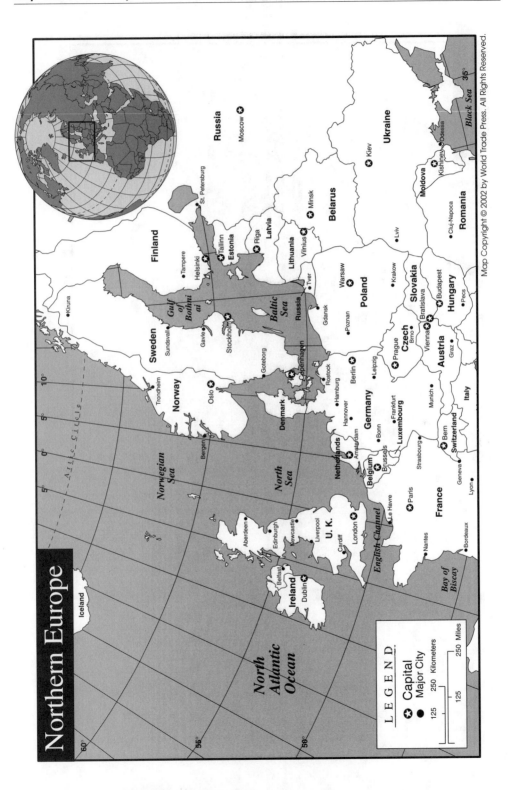

Northern Europe

M A P S

LEGEND
✪ Capital
● Major City

125   250 Kilometers
125   250 Miles

Iceland

North
Atlantic
Ocean

Norwegian
Sea

North
Sea

Arctic Circle

Bay of
Biscay

English Channel

Ireland
● Belfast
✪ Dublin

U. K.
● Aberdeen
● Edinburgh
● Newcastle
● Liverpool
● Cardiff
✪ London

Norway
● Trondheim
● Bergen
✪ Oslo

Sweden
● Kiruna
● Sundsvall
● Gavle
✪ Stockholm
● Goteborg

Gulf
of
Bothnia

Finland
● Tampere
✪ Helsinki

Baltic
Sea

St. Petersburg

Russia
✪ Moscow

Estonia
✪ Tallinn

Latvia
✪ Riga

Lithuania
✪ Vilnius

Russia
● Tver

Belarus
✪ Minsk
● Lviv

Ukraine
✪ Kiev

Moldova
● Kishinev
● Odessa

Romania
● Cluj-Napoca

Black Sea

35°

Denmark
✪ Copenhagen
● Rostock

Germany
● Hamburg
● Hannover
● Berlin
● Bonn
● Leipzig
● Frankfurt
● Munich

Netherlands
✪ Amsterdam

Belgium
✪ Brussels

Luxembourg ✪

Poland
● Gdansk
● Poznan
✪ Warsaw
● Krakow

Czech
✪ Prague
● Brno

Slovakia
✪ Bratislava

Austria
✪ Vienna
● Graz

Hungary
✪ Budapest
● Pecs

Switzerland
✪ Bern
● Geneva

France
● Le Havre
✪ Paris
● Nantes
● Lyon
● Bordeaux
● Strasbourg

Italy

60°

55°

50°

10°

5°

0°

5°

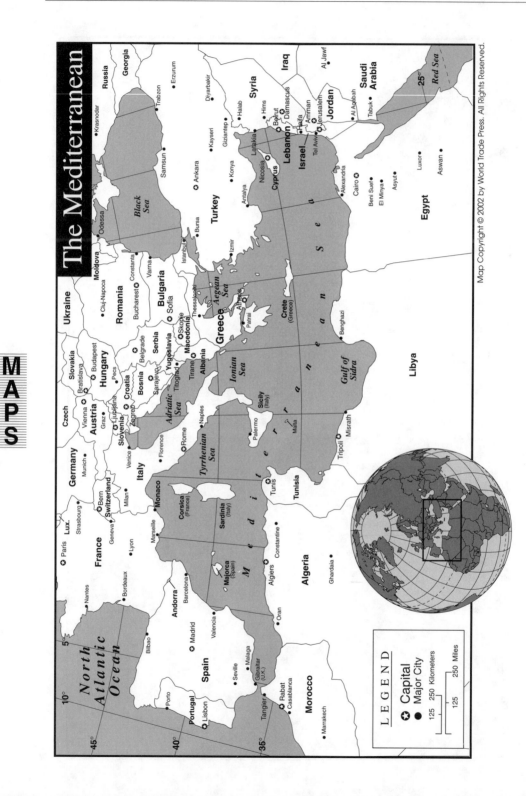

The Mediterranean

LEGEND
✪ Capital
● Major City

125   250 Kilometers
125   250 Miles

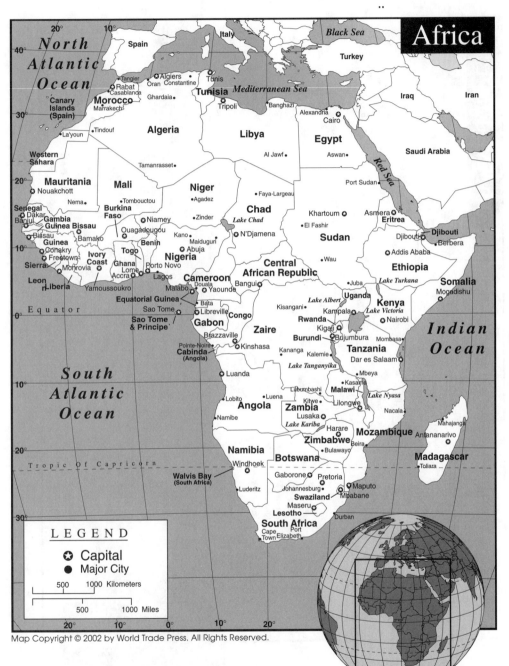

Africa

North Atlantic Ocean

20°   10°

Spain   Italy

Black Sea

Turkey

40°

Tangier   Algiers   Tunis   Mediterranean Sea

Oran   Constantine

Rabat   Casablanca

Morocco   Ghardaia

Marrakech

Canary Islands (Spain)

30°

Iraq   Iran

Tripoli   Banghazi

Alexandria

Cairo

La'youn   Tindouf

Algeria   **Libya**   **Egypt**

Saudi Arabia

Western Sahara

Al Jawf   Aswan

Red Sea

Tamanrasset

20°

Mauritania   **Mali**   **Niger**

Port Sudan

Nouakchott

Nema   Tombouctou   Agadez   Faya-Largeau

Burkina Faso

Khartoum   Asmera

Eritrea

Senegal   Dakar   **Chad**

Banjul   **Gambia**   Niamey   Zinder   Lake Chad   El Fashir

Djibouti

Berbera

Guinea Bissau   Ouagadougou   N'Djamena

Sudan

Djibouti

Bissau   Kano   Maidugun

Addis Ababa

10°

Guinea   Bamako   **Benin**

Conakry   **Togo**   Abuja

Freetown   **Ivory Coast**   **Nigeria**   Wau

Ethiopia

Sierra   Monrovia   **Ghana**   Porto Novo

Leon   Accra   Lome   Lagos

Central African Republic

Lake Turkana

Somalia

Liberia   Yamoussoukro   **Cameroon**   Bangui

Mogadishu

Malabo   Douala   Yaounde

Juba

Equatorial Guinea   Bata   Lake Albert   **Uganda**

Sao Tome   Libreville   **Congo**   Kisangani   Kampala   **Kenya**

Sao Tome & Principe   **Gabon**   **Rwanda**   Lake Victoria

Equator   0°

Indian Ocean

Brazzaville   **Zaire**   Kigali   Nairobi

Burundi   Bujumbura

Pointe-Noire   Kinshasa   Kananga   Mombasa

Cabinda (Angola)   Kalemie   **Tanzania**

Dar es Salaam

Lake Tanganyika

Luanda   Mbeya

10°

South Atlantic Ocean

Lubumbashi   Kasama

Lobito   Luena   **Malawi**   Lake Nyasa

Kitwe   Lilongwe   Nacala

Angola   **Zambia**   Lusaka

Namibe   Mahajanga

Lake Kariba   Harare

Mozambique   Antananarivo

Zimbabwe   Beira

20°

Namibia   **Botswana**   Bulawayo

Madagascar

Windhoek   Toliara

Tropic Of Capricorn

Gaborone   Pretoria

Walvis Bay (South Africa)   Maputo

Luderitz   Johannesburg   Mbabane

Swaziland

Maseru

Lesotho

South Africa   Durban

Cape   Port

30°   Town   Elizabeth

LEGEND

⊛ Capital

● Major City

500   1000 Kilometers

500   1000 Miles

20°   10°   0°   10°   20°

M A P S

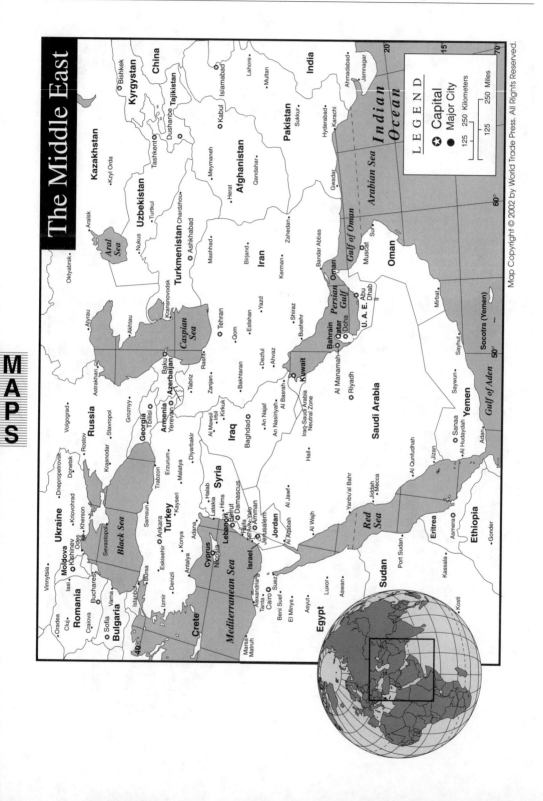

The Middle East

MAPS

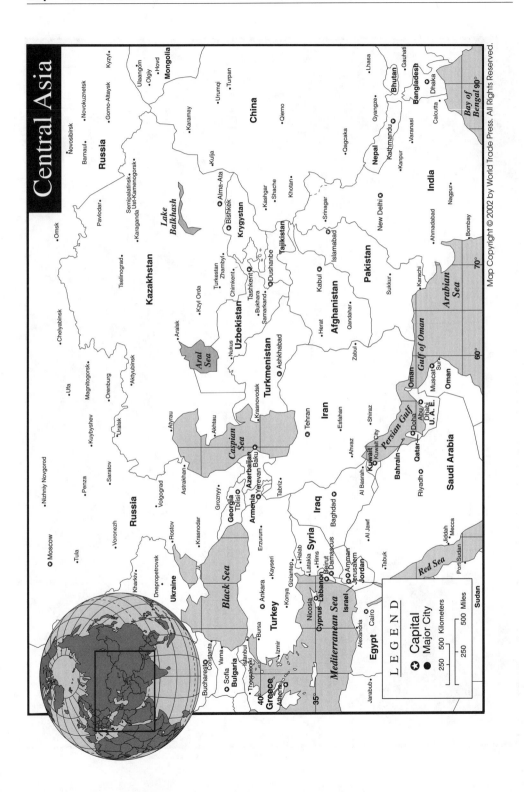

Central Asia

M A P S

L E G E N D
⊛ Capital
● Major City

250   500 Kilometers
250   500 Miles

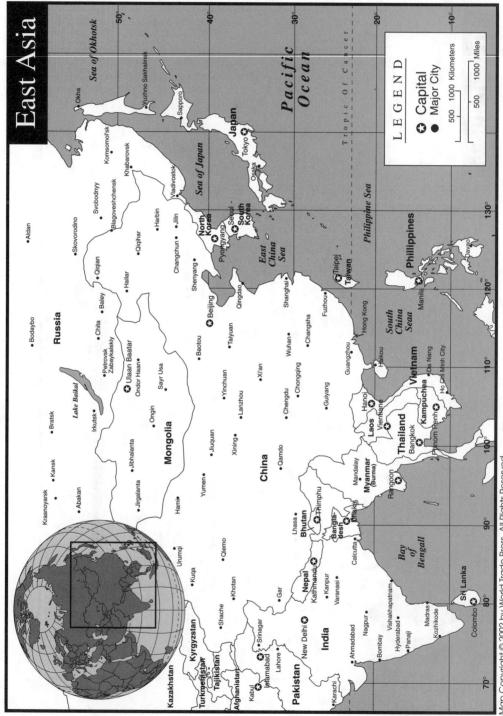

East Asia

MAPS

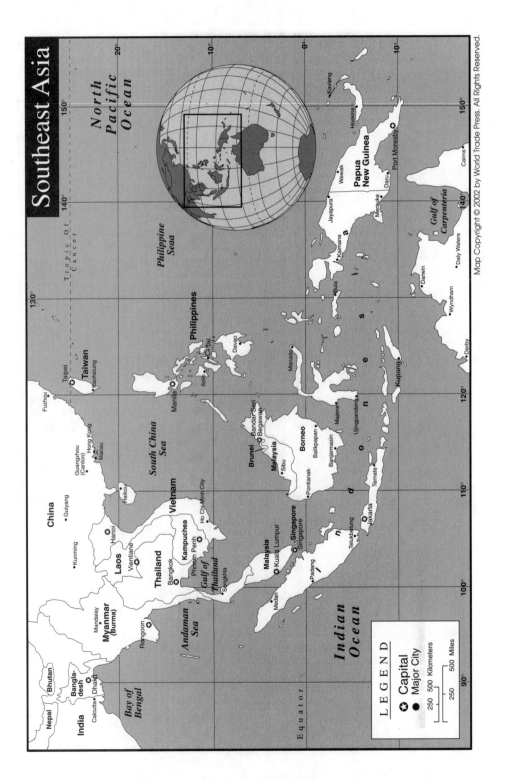

Southeast Asia

M
A
P
S

North Pacific Ocean

Philippine Sea

Tropic of Cancer

China
Guiyang
Fuzhou
Kunming
Guangzhou (Canton)
Hong Kong
Macau

Taipei
Taiwan
Kaohsiung

Philippines
Cebu
Iloilo
Manila
Davao

Manado

Nepal
Bhutan
Bangla-desh
Dhaka
Calcutta
India
Bay of Bengal

Mandalay
Myanmar (Burma)
Rangoon

Andaman Sea

Thailand
Bangkok
Songkhla
Gulf of Thailand
Kampuchea
Phnom Penh
Laos
Vientiane
Hanoi
Haikou
Vietnam
Ho Chi Minh City

South China Sea

Brunel
Bandar Seri Begawan
Malaysia
Sibu
Borneo
Pontianak
Balikpapan
Banjarmasin
Majene

Ujungpandang
Ternate

Indonesia

Singapore
Singapore
Malaysia
Kuala Lumpur
Padang
Medan
Jakarta
Telukbetung

Indian Ocean

Equator

Kavieng
Hoskins
Port Moresby
Papua New Guinea
Wewak
Daru
Jayapura
Merauke
Kaimana
Bula

Gulf of Carpenteria
Darwin
Daly Waters
Wyndham
Derby
Cairns

Kupang

90°
100°
110°
120°
130°
140°
150°
0°
10°
20°
10°

LEGEND
✪ Capital
● Major City

250   500 Kilometers
250   500 Miles

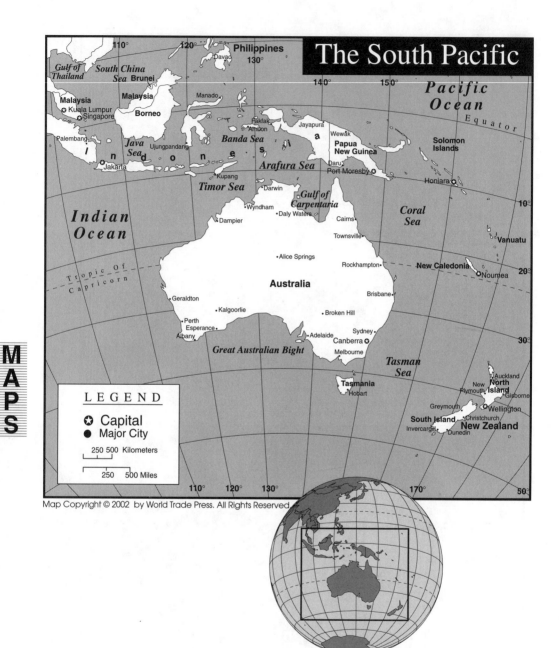

The South Pacific

MAPS

LEGEND

✪ Capital
● Major City

250 500 Kilometers

250 500 Miles

Guide to Ocean Freight Containers

Introduction

The following Guide to Ocean Freight Container Specifications is provided courtesy of Hapag-Lloyd America Inc. The container specifications listed are virtually standardized world-wide. However, the possibility exists that individual container manufacturers and shipping lines will have container specifications which vary somewhat from those listed in this section. Be certain to inquire about precise specifications from your shipping line or forwarder when you arrange for a shipment.

Values / Details

All values listed in the tables are given in metric. Ft and lbs values are for easy reference only.

All details listed are nominal figures. Apart from the tolerances given on internal dimensions below the tare weight can vary +/- 2%.

General Information

External and Minimum Internal Dimensions

The following table gives the overall external dimensions as standardized in ISO 668 and the minimum internal dimensions and door openings for General Purpose Containers as standardized in ISO 1496-1.

	Length		Width		Height	
Dimensions	20' 6,058 mm	40' 12,192 mm	8' 2,438 mm	8'6" 2,438 mm	8'6" 2,438 mm	9'6" 2,896 mm
Minimum Internal Dimensions	5,867 mm 19'3"	11,998 mm 39' 4 3/8"	2,330 mm 7'7 3/4"	2,197 mm 7'2 1/2"	2,350 mm 7'8 1/2"	2,655 mm 8'8 1/2"
Minimun Door Opening Dimensions	-	-	2,286 mm 7'6"	2,134 mm 7'	2,261 mm 7'5"	2,566 mm 8'5"

Internal Dimensions

The internal dimensions and door openings of most containers exceed the above given dimensions. However, the dimensions mentioned on the following pages are nominal figures. Because of production tolerances a difference in measurements is possible:

Tolerances	Length	Width	Height
Maximum Difference	10 mm 3/8"	10 mm 3/8"	10 mm 3/8"

Maximum Gross Weights

20' containers:
24,000 kg (52,910 lbs) according to the latest issue of ISO 668;
30, 480 kg (67,200 lbs) valid for most Hapag-Lloyd 20' containers; exceeds ISO minimum standards.
40' containers:
30,480 kg (67,200 lbs).

Floor Loads

A container floor is capable of carrying a fork-lift truck with a maximum axle load of 5,460 kg (12,040 lbs), if the contact area per wheel is at least 142 cm2 (22 sq.in) (ISO 1496/I).

Concentrated Loads

When stowing heavy cargo in containers other than flats or platforms due care has to be taken that concentrated loads will not exceed the strength of the bottom construction of the container.
The maximum spreaded load should not exceed
—for 20' containers 4 ts per running meter in length (3' 3.5")
—for 40' containers 3 ts per running meter in length.

Gooseneck Tunnel on 40' Containers

All Hapag-Lloyd 40' containers are fitted with a Gooseneck tunnel to enable the transport on Gooseneck chassis.

Timber Treatment

Exposed timber is treated according to Australian requirements (exceptions: 40' flats and platforms).

General Purpose Container   20'

- Suitable for any general cargo.
- Containers may be equipped with liner bags suitable for bulk cargo, e.g. malt.
- Fork-lift pockets on a number of containers.
- Various lashing devices on the top and bottom longitudinal rails and the corner posts.
  Lashing devices have a permissible load of 1,000 kg (2,205 lbs) each.
- Note permissable weight limits for road and rail transport.

General Purpose Container   20'

O
C
E
A
N

Construction	Inside Dimensions			Door Opening		Weights			Capacity
	Length	Width	Height	Width	Height	Max. Gross	Tare	Max. Payload	
	mm	mm	mm	mm	mm	kg	kg	kg	m³
	ft	ft	ft	ft	ft	lbs	lbs	lbs	cu.ft.

8'6" high

Construction	Length	Width	Height	Width	Height	Max. Gross	Tare	Max. Payload	Capacity
Steel container with corrugated walls and wooden floor	5,895	2,350	2,392	2,340	2,292	30,480	2,250	28,230	33.2
	19'4¹/₈"	7'8¹/₂"	7'10¹/₈"	7'8¹/₈"	7'6¹/₄"	67,200	4,960	62,240	1,172
	5,895	2,350	2,385	2,338	2,292	24,000	2,250	21,750	33.2
	19'4"	7'8¹/₂"	7'9⁷/₈"	7'8"	7'6¹/₄"	52,910	4,960	47,950	1,172
	5,879	2,330	2,370	2,330	2,290	24,000	2,250	21,750	33.0
	19'3³/₈"	7'7³/₄"	7'9¹/₄"	7'7³/₄"	7'6¹/₈"	52,910	4,960	47,950	1,165
	5,889	2,346	2,372	2,330	2,272	24,000	2,360	21,640	32.8
	19'3⁷/₈"	7'8³/₈"	7'9³/₈"	7'7³/₄"	7'5¹/₂"	52,910	5,200	47,710	1,158
	5,885	2,350	2,403	2,338	2,292	24,000	2,150	21,850	33.15
	19'4"	7'8¹/₂"	7'10⁵/₈"	7'8"	7'6¹/₄"	52,910	4,740	48,170	1,170
	5,884	2,335	2,390	2,335	2,292	24,000	2,200	21,800	33.1
	19'3⁵/₈"	7'8"	7'10"	7'8"	7'6¹/₄"	52,910	4,850	48,060	1,169
	5,899	2,350	2,394	2,338	2,280	24,000	2,180	21,820	33.2
	19'4¹/₄"	7'8¹/₂"	7'10¹/₄"	7'8"	7'5³/₄"	52,910	4,810	48,100	1,172
	5,891	2,330	2,376	2,330	2,272	24,000	2,300	21,700	33.0
	19'3⁷/₈"	7'7³/₄"	7'9¹/₂"	7'7³/₄"	7'5¹/₂"	52,910	5,070	47,840	1,165
	5,880	2,330	2,380	2,330	2,275	24,000	2,300	21,700	33.0
	19'3¹/₂"	7'7³/₄"	7'9⁵/₈"	7'7³/₄"	7'5¹/₂"	52,910	5,070	47,840	1,165

**O
C
E
A
N**

General Purpose Container   40'

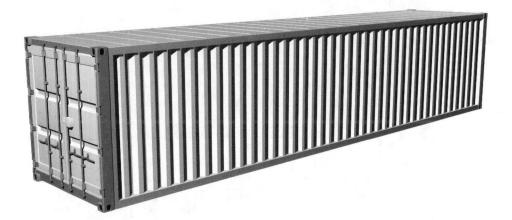

- Suitable for any general cargo.
- Various lashing devices on the top and bottom longitudinal rails and the corner posts.
  Lashing devices have a permissible load of 1,000 kg (2,205 lbs) each.

- Note permissable weight limits for road and rail transport.

General Purpose Container   40'

Construction	Inside Dimensions			Door Opening		Weights			Capacity
	Length	Width	Height	Width	Height	Max. Gross	Tare	Max. Payload	
	mm ft	mm ft	mm ft	mm ft	mm ft	kg lbs	kg lbs	kg lbs	m³ cu.ft.

8'6" high

Construction	Length	Width	Height	Width	Height	Max. Gross	Tare	Max. Payload	Capacity
Steel container with corrugated walls and wooden floor	12,029 39'5½"	2,350 7'8½"	2,392 7'10⅛"	2,340 7'8½"	2,292 7'6¼"	30,480 67,200	3,780 8,330	26,700 58,870	67.7 2,390
	12,024 39'5⅜"	2,350 7'8½"	2,387 7'10"	2,340 7'8⅛"	2,292 7'6¼"	30,480 67,200	3,810 8,400	26,670 58,800	67.7 2,390
	12,033 39'5¾"	2,350 7'8½"	2,394 7'10¼"	2,338 7'8"	2,280 7'5¾"	30,480 67,200	3,800 8,377	26,680 58,823	67.7 2,390

High Cube General Purpose Container   40'

OCEAN

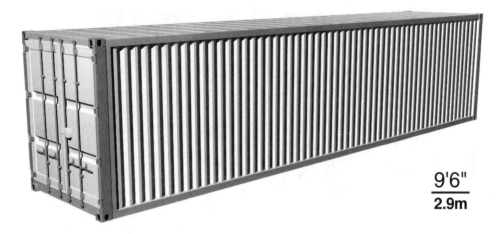

9'6"
2.9m

- Especially for light, voluminous cargo and overheight cargo up to maximum 2.70 m (8'10¼") (see table).
- Numerous lashing devices on the top and bottom longitudinal rails and the corner posts.

- Lashing devices have a permissible load of 1,000 kg (2,205 lbs) each.
- Consider overheight for inland transportation.
- Note permissable weight limits for road and rail transport.

High Cube General Purpose Container   40'

Construction	Inside Dimensions			Door Opening		Weights			Capacity
	Length	Width	Height	Width	Height	Max. Gross	Tare	Max. Payload	
	mm ft	mm ft	mm ft	mm ft	mm ft	kg lbs	kg lbs	kg lbs	m³ cu.ft.
9'6" high									
Steel container with corrugated walls and wooden floor	12,024 39'5⅜"	2,350 7'8½"	2,697 8'10⅛"	2,340 7'8⅛"	2,597 8'6¼"	30,480 67,200	4,020 8,860	26,460 58,340	76.3 2,694
	12,024 39'5⅜"	2,350 7'8½"	2,697 8'10⅛"	2,338 7'8"	2,585 8'5¾"	30,480 67,200	4,020 8,860	26,460 58,340	76.3 2,694

O
C
E
A
N

Hardtop Container   20'

- This container type has been especially designed and developed for
  —heavy loads
  —high and excessively high loads
  —loading, e.g. by crane, through roof opening and door side.
- The steel roof of some series is lifted with fork-lift rings so that it can be removed by using a fork-lift. The weight of the steel roof is approx. 450 kg (990 lbs).
- With the roof removed and the door header swung out, it is much easier to load cargo using a crane via the door side.
- In case your cargo is overheight, the roof sections can be lashed to a sidewall inside the container using only some 13 cm (5 1/8") of space.
- If required, disposable tarpaulins can be provided for the transport which can be fastened to the walls on the outside using lashing devices.
- The capacity of the container floor exceeds the ISO 1496/1 standard by 33%, so that a fork-lift whose front axle weight does not exceed 7,280 kg (16,000 lbs) can be used inside.
- The hardtop container provides many lashing devices to fasten goods. The lashing devices on the corner posts and on the longitudinal rails of the roof and floor are capable of bearing loads of up to 2,000 kg (4,410 lbs) each, and those in the middle of the side walls up to 500 kg (1,100 lbs) each. Lashing to the side walls can only be done after the roof has been closed.
- This container type has been designed for heavy loads. While considering the technical data (including the permissible spreaded load limitations) please bear in mind the prevalent weight restrictions for land transport.
- Note permissable weight limits for road and rail transport.

Hardtop Container   20'

Construction	Inside Dimensions				Weights			Capacity
	Length	Width	Height		Max.	Tare	Max.	
			Middle	Side	Gross		Payload	
	mm ft	mm ft	mm ft	mm ft	kg lbs	kg lbs	kg lbs	m³ cu.ft.

8'6" high

Construction	Length	Width	Middle	Side	Gross	Tare	Payload	Capacity
Steel container with corrugated walls and wooden floor	5,886 19'3³/₄"	2,342 7'8¹/₈"	2,388 7'10"	2,313 7'7"	30,480 67,200	2,700 5,950	27,780 61,250	32.8 1,160
	5,886 19'3³/₄"	2,342 7'8¹/₈"	2,388 7'10"	2,313 7'7"	30,480 67,200	2,700 5,950	27,780 61,250	32.8 1,160
	5,886 19'3³/₄"	2,342 7'8¹/₈"	2,375 7'9¹/₂"	2,330 7'7³/₄"	30,480 67,200	2,590 5,710	27,890 61,490	32.8 1,160
	5,871 19'3¹/₈"	2,338 7'8"	2,390 7'10"	2,335 7'8"	24,000 52,910	2,580 5,690	21,420 47,220	32.8 1,158

Roof Opening   Door Opening

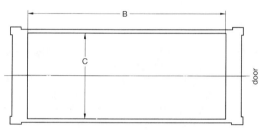

Hardtop Container   Roof Openings   20'

Roof Openings		Door Openings					Roof Inside Container		
Length	Width	Width			Height		Reduced Width		
B Between Gusset Plates mm ft	C Max. Width mm ft	F Max. Width mm ft	G At Door Header mm ft	H Between Top Longitudinal Rails mm ft	I Up to Door Header mm ft	K Up to Top Longitudinal Rail mm ft	Inside Width mm ft	Width of Roof Opening mm ft	Width of Door Opening mm ft
5,590 18'4"	2,208 7'2⁷/₈"	2,336 7'8"	1,896 6'2⁵/₈"	2,208 7'2⁷/₈"	2,276 7'5⁵/₈"	2,220 7'³/₈"	2,209 7'3"	2,142 7'¹/₄"	2,206 7'2⁷/₈"
5,590 18'4"	2,208 7'2⁷/₈"	2,336 7'8"	1,896 6'2⁵/₈"	2,208 7'2⁷/₈"	2,292 7'6¹/₄"	2,220 7'³/₈"	2,209 7'3"	2,142 7'¹/₄"	2,206 7'2⁷/₈"
5,590 18'4"	2,208 7'2⁷/₈"	2,336 7'8"	1,896 6'2⁵/₈"	2,208 7'2⁷/₈"	2,280 7'5³/₄"	2,231 7'3³/₄"	2,215 7'3¹/₈"	2,148 7'¹/₂"	2,212 7'3"
5,616 18'5¹/₈"	2,206 7'2⁷/₈"	2,335 7'8"	1,890 6'2³/₈"	2,206 7'2⁷/₈"	2,292 7'6¹/₄"	2,225 7'3¹/₂"	2,250 7'4¹/₂"	2,180 7'1³/₄"	2,250 7'4¹/₂"

Hardtop Container   40'

- The 40' hardtop container has particularly been constructed for:
  —long loads which cannot be transport-ed in the 20' hardtop container
  —heavy loads
  —high and excessively high loads
  —loading, e.g. by crane, through roof opening and door side.
- The roof can be removed by using a fork-lift. The weight of the steel roof is approx. 450 kg (990 lbs) each section.
- With the roof removed and the door-header swung out, it is much easier to load cargo using a crane via the door side.
- In case your cargo is overheight, the roof sections can be lashed to a sidewall inside the container using only some 13 cm (5 $^1/_8$") of space.
- If required, disposable tarpaulins can be provided for the transport which can be fastened to the walls on the outside using lashing devices.
- The capacity of the container floor exceeds the ISO 1496/1 standard by 33%, so that a fork-lift whose front axle weight does not exceed 7,280 kg (16,000 lbs) can be used inside.

- The hardtop container provides many lashing devices to fasten goods. The lashing devices on the corner posts and on the longitudinal rails of the roof and floor are capable of bearing loads of up to 2,000 kg (4,410 lbs) each, and those in the middle of the side walls up to 500 kg (1,100 lbs) each. Lashing to the side walls can only be done after the roof has been closed.
- The roof can easily be raised by about 70 mm (2 $^3/_4$"), using the roof locking devices so that the door-header can be swung out without removing the roof.
- This container type has been designed for heavy loads. While considering the technical data (including the permissible spreaded load limitations) please bear in mind the prevalent weight restrictions for land transport.
- Note permissable weight limits for road and rail transport.

Hardtop Container 40'

Construction	Inside Dimensions				Weights			Capacity
	Length	Width	Height		Max.	Tare	Max.	
	mm ft	mm ft	Middle mm ft	Side mm ft	Gross kg lbs	kg lbs	Payload kg lbs	m³ cu.ft.
8'6" high								
Steel container with corrugated walls and wooden floor	12,020 39'5 1/4"	2,342 7'8 1/8"	2,388 7'10"	2,313 7'7"	30,480 67,200	4,700 10,360	25,780 56,840	67.2 2,374
	12,020 39'5 1/4"	2,342 7'8 1/8"	2,388 7'10"	2,313 7'7"	30,480 67,200	4,700 10,360	25,780 56,840	67.2 2,374

Roof Opening

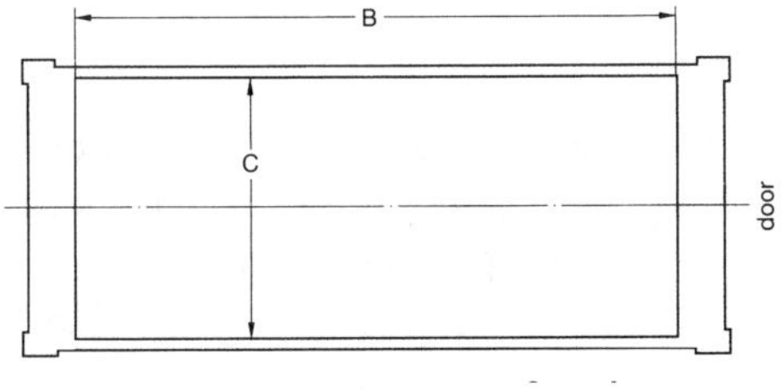

Door Opening

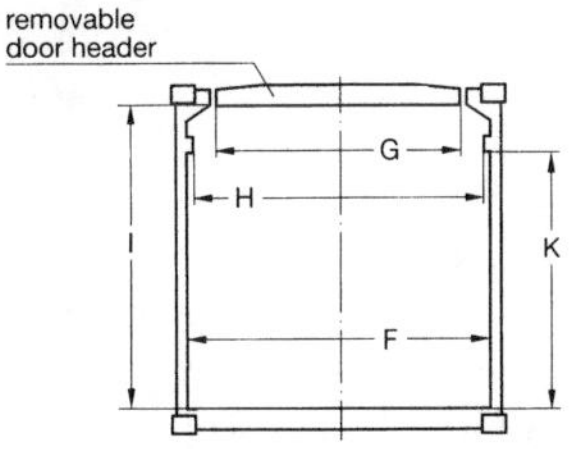

Hardtop Container 40'

Roof Openings		Door Openings					Roof Inside Container		
Length	Width	Width			Height		Reduced Width		
B Between Gusset Plates mm ft	C Max. Width mm ft	F Max. Width mm ft	G At Door Header mm ft	H Between Top Longitudinal Rails mm ft	I Up to Door Header mm ft	K Up to Top Longitudinal Rail mm ft	Inside Width mm ft	Width of Roof Opening mm ft	Width of Door Opening mm ft
11,724 38'5"	2,208 7'2 7/8"	2,336 7'8"	1,896 6'2 5/8"	2,208 7'2 7/8"	2,292 7'6 1/4"	2,220 7'3 3/8"	2,209 7'3"	2,142 7' 3/8"	2,206 7'2 7/8"
11,724 38'5"	2,208 7'2 7/8"	2,336 7'8"	1,896 6'2 5/8"	2,208 7'2 7/8"	2,276 7'5 5/8"	2,220 7'3 3/8"	2,209 7'3"	2,142 7' 3/8"	2,206 7'2 7/8"

OCEAN

Open Top Container   20'

- Especially for:
  —overheight cargo
  —loading from top side, e.g. by crane
  —loading from door side, e.g. with cargo hanging from overhead tackle.
- Door header can be swung out on all open top containers.
- If required, disposable tarpaulins can be provided. For fastening tarpaulins, lashing bars are available on the outside of the walls. Using one way tarpaulins requires the corner castings to be accessible.
- Fork-lift pockets on a number of containers (please see footnote 1).

- The capacity of the floor for use of fort-lift trucks exceeds the ISO standards by 33% on all 20' open top containers.
- Numerous lashing devices are located on the top and bottom longitudinal rails and the corner posts. Lashing devices have a permissible load of 1,000 kg (2,205 lbs) each.
- Dimensions of roof and door openings are on the next page.
- Note permissable weight limits for road and rail transport.

Open Top Container Dimensions   20'

Construction	Inside Dimensions				Weights			Capacity
	Length	Width	Height		Max.	Tare	Max.	
			Middle	Side	Gross		Payload	
	mm ft	mm ft	mm ft	mm ft	kg lbs	kg lbs	kg lbs	m³ cu.ft.
8'6" high								
Steel container with corrugated walls, removable tarpaulin and wooden floor	5,895 19'4"	2,350 7'8½"	2,394 7'10¼"	2,364 7'9"	24,000 52,910	2,100 4,630	21,900 48,280	32.45 1,146
	5,877 19'3⅜"	2,335 7'8"	2,369 7'9¼"	2,309 7'6⅞"	24,000 52,910	2,200 4,850	21,800 48,060	32.4 1,140
	5,895 19'4"	2,330 7'7¾"	2,329 7'7¾"	—	24,000 52,910	2,200 4,850	21,800 48,060	32.0 1,130
	5,888 19'3¾"	2,345 7'8⅛"	2,365 7'9"	2,315 7'7⅛"	30,480 67,200	2,250 4,960	28,230 62,240	32.0 1,130

Roof and Door Openings of Open Top Containers   20'

Types:

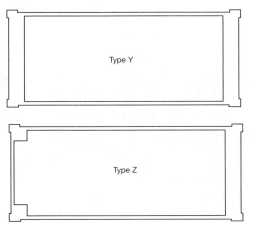

Type Y

Type Z

Door Openings:

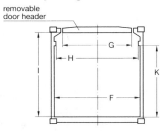

removable door header

Roof Openings:

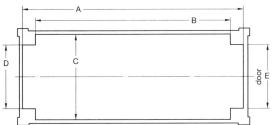

Roof and Door Openings of Open Top Containers   20'

	Roof Openings					Door Openings				
	Length		Width			Width			Height	
Type	A Max. Length	B Between Gusset Plates	C Max. Width	D Front End between Gusset Plates	E Door End, between Gusset Plates	F Max. Width	G At Door Header	H Between Top Longitudinal Rails	I Up to Door Header	K Up to Top Longitudinal Rail
	mm ft	mm ft	mm ft	mm ft	mm ft	mm ft	mm ft	mm ft	mm ft	mm ft
Z	5,583 18'3³/₄"	5,488 18"	2,230 7'3³/₄"	1,928 6'3⁷/₈"	—	2,335 7'8"	1,928 6'3⁷/₈"	2,230 7'3³/₄"	2,291 7'6¹/₄"	2,194 7'2³/₈"
Z	5,660 18'6⁷/₈"	5,440 17'10¹/₈"	2,208 7'2⁷/₈"	1,860 6'1¹/₄"	—	2,335 7'8"	1,848 6'¹⁹/₄"	2,208 7'2⁷/₈"	2,290 7'6¹/₈"	1,889 6'2³/₈"
Z	5,770 18'11¹/₈"	5,452 17'10⁵/₈"	2,232 7'3⁷/₈"	—	1,904 6'3"	2,305 7'6³/₄"	1,834 6'¹/₈"	2,208 7'3⁷/₈"	2,218 7'3¹/₄"	2,033 6'8"
Z	5,415 17'9¹/₈"	5,360 17'7"	2,205 7'2³/₄"	—	1,880 6'2"	2,335 7'8"	1,880 6'2"	2,205 7'2³/₄"	2,280 7'5³/₄"	2,125 6'11⁵/₈"

OCEAN

Open Top Container   40'

- Especially for:
  - —overheight cargo
  - —loading from top side, e.g. by crane
  - —loading from door side, e.g. with cargo hanging from overhead tackle.
- Door header can be swung out on all open top containers.
- If required, disposable tarpaulins can be provided. For fastening tarpaulins, lashing bars are available on the outside of the walls. Using one way tarpaulins requires the corner castings to be accessible.

- The capacity of the floor for use of fort-lift trucks exceeds the ISO standards by 33% on all 40' open top containers.
- Numerous lashing devices are located on the top and bottom longitudinal rails and the corner posts.
  Lashing devices have a permissible load of 1,000 kg (2,205 lbs) each.
- Dimensions of roof and door openings follow in two pages.
- Note permissable weight limits for road and rail transport.

O C E A N

Open Top Container Dimensions 40'

Construction	Inside Dimensions				Weights			Capacity
	Length	Width	Height		Max.	Tare	Max.	
			Middle	Side	Gross		Payload	
	mm ft	mm ft	mm ft	mm ft	kg lbs	kg lbs	kg lbs	m³ cu.ft.

8'6" high

Steel container with corrugated walls, removable tarpaulin and wooden floor	12,023 39'5³/₈"	2,335 7'8"	2,378 7'9⁵/₈"	2,318 7'7¹/₄"	30,480 67,200	3,800 8,380	26,680 58,820	66.7 2,354
	12,038 39'5⁷/₈"	2,338 7'8"	2,363 7'9"	2,313 7'7¹/₈"	30,480 67,200	3,650 8,050	26,830 59,150	66.7 2,354
	12,025 39'5¹/₂"	2,330 7'7³/₄"	2,360 7'8⁷/₈"	2,325 7'7¹/₂"	30,480 67,200	3,890 8,580	26,590 58,620	66.0 2,330
	12,038 39'5⁷/₈"	2,336 7'8"	2,370 7'9¹/₄"	2,320 7'7¹/₄"	30,480 67,197	3,700 8,157	26,780 59,040	65.3 2,306
	12,029 39'5¹/₂"	2,342 7'8¹/₈"	2,376 7'9¹/₂"	2,326 7'7¹/₂"	30,480 67,200	3,810 8,400	26,670 58,800	65.5 2,310
	12,022 39'5¹/₄"	2,346 7'8³/₈"	2,365 7'9¹/₈"	2,315 7'7¹/₈"	30,480 67,200	3,740 8,250	26,740 58,950	65.3 2,306
	12,007 39'4³/₄"	2,315 7'7¹/₈"	2,362 7'9"	2,317 7'7¹/₄"	30,480 67,200	3,950 8,710	26,530 58,490	65.0 2,295
	12,005 39'4⁵/₈"	2,330 7'7³/₄"	2,380 7'9⁵/₈"	2,340 7'8¹/₈"	30,480 67,200	4,350 9,590	26,130 57,610	65.5 2,315

**O
C
E
A
N**

Roof and Door Openings of Open Top Containers   **40'**

Types:

Door Openings:

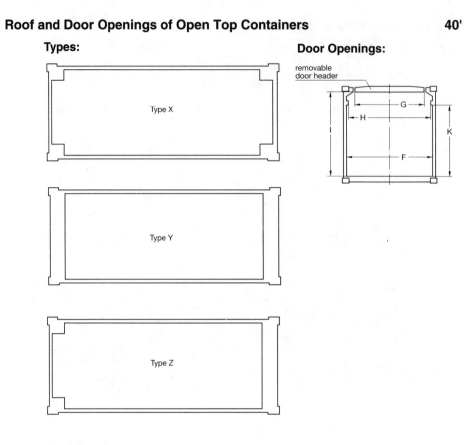

Roof Opening:

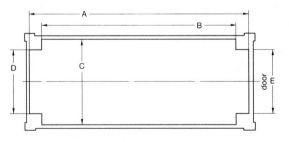

Roof and Door Openings of Open Top Containers 40'

Type	Roof Openings					Door Openings				
	Length		Width			Width			Height	
	A Max. Length mm ft	B Between Gusset Plates mm ft	C Max. Width mm ft	D Front End between Gusset Plates mm ft	E Door End, between Gusset Plates mm ft	F Max. Width mm ft	G At Door Header mm ft	H Between Top Longitudinal Rails mm ft	I Up to Door Header mm ft	K Up to Top Longitudinal Rail mm ft
Z	11,800 38'8 5/8"	11,317 37'1 1/2"	2,205 7'2 3/4"	1,728 5'8"	—	2,335 7'8"	1,840 6'1/2"	2,205 7'2 3/4"	2,287 7'6"	1,889 6'2 3/8"
Z	11,787 38'8"	11,563 37'11 1/4"	2,208 7'2 7/8"	1,850 6'7/8"	—	2,335 7'8"	1,844 6'5/8"	2,208 7'2 7/8"	2,287 7'6"	1,896 6'2 5/8"
X	11,917 39'1 1/8"	10,837 35'6 5/8"	2,128 6'11 3/4"	1,600 5'3"	1,816 5'11 1/2"	2,330 7'7 3/4"	1,816 5'11 1/2"	2,128 6'11 7/8"	2,201 7'2 5/8"	1,957 6'5"
Y	—	11,550 37'10 5/8"	2,220 7'3 3/8"	—	—	2,336 7'8"	1,845 6'5/8"	2,220 7'3 3/8"	2,292 7'6 1/4"	2,125 6'11 5/8"
Z	11,544 37'10 1/2"	11,444 37'6 1/2"	2,230 7'3 3/4"	—	1,885 6'2 1/8"	2,336 7'8"	1,885 6'2 1/8"	2,230 7'3 3/4"	2,280 7'5 3/4"	2,146 7'1/2"
Z	11,550 37'10 3/4"	11,515 37'9 3/8"	2,205 7'2 3/4"	—	1,880 6'2"	2,335 7'8"	1,880 6'2"	2,205 7'2 3/4"	2,280 7'5 3/4"	2,125 6'11 5/8"
Y	—	11,379 37'4"	2,205 7'2 3/4"	—	—	2,315 7'7 1/8"	1,855 6'1"	2,205 7'2 3/4"	2,266 7'5 1/4"	1,957 6'5"
X	11,825 38'9 1/2"	11,496 37'8 5/8"	2,100 6'10 5/8"	1,774 5'9 7/8"	1,774 5'9 7/8"	2,335 7'8"	1,750 5'8 7/8"	2,100 6'10 5/8"	2,180 7'1 3/4"	2180 7'1 3/4"

Flat   40'

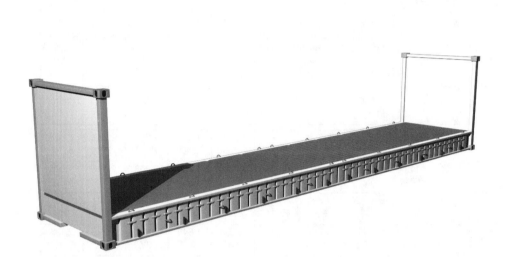

- Especially for heavy loads and overwidth cargo.
- Higher loadings possible.
- Strong bottom construction with fixed endwalls (which allow bracing and lashing of cargo as well as stacking).
- Gooseneck tunnel on both ends of 40' flats.
- Numerous very strong lashing devices on the corner posts, longitudinal rails and the floor. Lashing devices on the longitudinal rails and on the floor of 40' containers have a permissible load of 4,000 kg respectively (8,820 lbs) each.
- Maximum payload can only be used if distributed over the total floor area of the flat.
  If concentration of heavy load on a small part floor area is required please contact representative for stowage advice.
- Flats are delivered without stanchions. If stancions are required, please contact representative upon booking.
- Note permissable weight limits for road and rail transport.

Flat   40'

O C E A N

Construction	Inside Dimensions						Weights		
	Length of floor	Width between Corner Posts	Width of Floor	Width between Stanchions	Height	Height of Bottom	Max. Gross	Tare	Max. Payload
	mm ft	mm ft	mm ft	mm ft	mm ft	mm ft	kg lbs	kg lbs	kg lbs

8'6" high

Construction	Inside Dimensions						Weights		
Steelframe with fixed endwalls and softwood floor	12,008 39'4¾"	11,712 38'5⅛"	2,318 7'7¼"	2,232 7'3⅞"	1,981 6'6"	610 2'	30,480 67,200	4,750 10,470	25,730 56,730
	11,990 39'4"	11,722 38'5½"	2,400 7'10½"	2,202 7'2¾"	1,981 6'6"	610 2'	30,480 67,200	5,100 11,240	25,380 55,960
	11,990 39'4"	11,758 38'6⅞"	2,338 7'8"	2,228 7'3¾"	1,981 6'6"	610 2'	30,480 67,200	4,200 9,265	26,280 57,935
	12,010 39'4⅞"	11,832 38'9⅞"	2,228 7'3¾"	2,228 7'3¾"	1,981 6'6"	610 2'	30,480 67,200	4,200 9,265	26,280 57,935
	12,086 39'7⅞"	11,826 38'9⅝"	2,224 7'3½"	2,224 7'3½"	1,981 6'6"	610 2'	30,480 67,200	4,200 9,265	26,280 57,935
	12,010 39'4⅞"	11,826 38'9⅝"	2,244 7'4⅜"	2,204 7'2¾"	1,981 6'6"	610 2'	30,480 67,200	4,200 9,265	26,280 57,935

9'6" high

Construction	Inside Dimensions						Weights		
Steel container with collapsible endwalls and softwood floor	12,060 39'6¾"	11,660 38'3⅛"	2,365 7'9⅛"	2,200 7'2⅝"	2,245 7'4⅜"	648 2'1½"	45,000 99,210	5,700 12,570	39,300 86,640

OCEAN

Flat   20'

- Especially for heavy and overwidth cargo.
- Strong bottom construction with fixed endwalls (which allow bracing and lashing of cargo as well as stacking).
- Fork-lift pockets on a number of 20' flats
- Numerous very strong lashing devices on the corner posts, longitudinal rails and on the floor. Lashing devices on the longitudinal rails of 20' containers have a permissible load of 2,000 kg or 4,000 kg respectively (4,410 lbs or 8,820 lbs respectively) each.

- Maximum payload can only be used if distributed over the total floor area.
  If concentration of heavy load on a small part floor area is required please contact representative for stowage advice.
- Flats are delivered without stanchions. If stancions are required, please contact representative upon booking.
- Note permissable weight limits for road and rail transport.

Flat   20'

Construction	Inside Dimensions						Weights		
	Length of floor	Width between Corner Posts	Width of floor	Width between Stanchions	Height	Height of Bottom	Max. Gross	Tare	Max. Payload
	mm ft	mm ft	mm ft	mm ft	mm ft	mm ft	kg lbs	kg lbs	kg lbs
8' high									
Steelframe with fixed endwalls and softwood floor	5,918 19'5"	5,625 18'5³/₈"	2,398 7'10³/₈"	2,208 7'2⁷/₈"	2,172 7'1¹/₂"	265 10¹/₂"	24,000 52,910	2,800 6,170	21,200 46,740
8'6" high									
Steelframe with fixed endwalls and softwood floor	5,902 19'4³/₈"	5,700 18'8³/₈"	2,358 7'8⁷/₈"	2,235 7'4"	2,276 7'5⁵/₈"	315 1³/₈"	24,000 52,910	2,720 6,000	21,280 46,910
	5,980 19'7³/₈"	5,698 18'8³/₈"	2,230 7'3³/₄"	2,245 7'4³/₈"	2,255 7'4³/₄"	336 1¹¹/₄"	24,000 52,910	2,500 5,510	21,500 47,400
	5,962 19'6³/₄"	5,672 18'7¹/₄"	2,242 7'4¹/₄"	2,242 7'4¹/₄"	2,261 7'5"	330 1'1"	30,000 66,140	2,200 4,850	27,800 61,290
Steel container with collapsible endwalls and softwood floors.	5,956 19'6¹/₂"	5,658 18'6³/₄"	2,418 7'11¹/₈"	2,181 7'1⁷/₈"	2,320 7'7³/₈"	271 10⁵/₈"	33,050 72,860	3,045 6,710	30,005 66,150

Platform   20' / 40'

OCEAN

- Especially for heavy loads and oversized cargo.
- Strong bottom construction.
- Gooseneck tunnel on both ends of all 40' platforms.
- Numerous very strong lashing devices on the longitudinal rails. Lashing devices have a permissible load of 3,000 kg (6,615 lbs) each.
- Transport of heavy loads concentrated on a small load transfer area is possible. Contact your representative for details.

Platform Dimensions   20'

Construction	Dimensions			Weights		
	Length	Width	Height of bottom	Max. Gross	Tare	Max. Payload
	mm ft	mm ft	mm ft	kg lbs	kg lbs	kg lbs
1'1¼" high						
Steelframe with softwood floor	6,058 20'	2,438 8'	335 1'1¼"	24,000 52,910	2,100 4,630	21,900 48,280

Platform Dimensions   40'

Construction	Dimensions			Weights		
	Length	Width	Height of bottom	Max. Gross	Tare	Max. Payload
	mm ft	mm ft	mm ft	kg lbs	kg lbs	kg lbs
2' high						
Steelframe with softwood floor	12,192 40'	2,438 8'	610 2'	45,000 99,210"	4,200 9,260	40,800 89,950

OCEAN

Insulated Container   20' / 40'

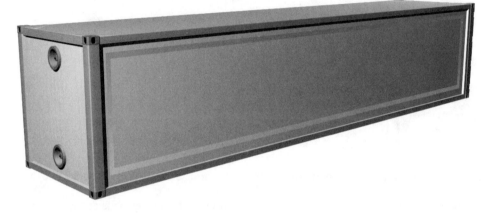

Porthole Type

- Especially for cargo which needs constant temperatures above or below freezing point.
- Walls in "sandwich-construction", with Polyurethane foam to provide maximum insulation.
- Temperature is controlled by ship's/terminal's cooling plant or "clip-on" unit.
- The air, delivered at the correct temperature, is circulated in the container through two aperatures in the front wall (supply air via the lower aperature, return air via the upper aperature).
- Possible temperatures inside the 20' containers, depending on specification of respective cooling device, from about +12˚C to -25˚C (+54˚F to -14˚F).

- Please note maximum stowage height in below table and as indicated by red line inside container in order to ensure proper ventilation.
- Possible temperatures inside the 40' containers, depending on specification of respective cooling device, from about +13˚C to -22˚C (+57˚F to -8˚F).
- Note permissable weight limits for road and rail transport.

Insulated Container   20'

Construction	Inside Dimensions			Door Opening		Weights			Capacity
	Length	Width	Max. Stowable Height	Width	Height	Max. Gross	Tare	Max. Payload	
	mm ft	mm ft	mm ft	mm ft	mm ft	kg lbs	kg lbs	kg lbs	m³ cu.ft.

8' high

Construction	Length	Width	Max. Stowable Height	Width	Height	Max. Gross	Tare	Max. Payload	Capacity
Steelframe. Walls: outside plywood, coated with GRP, inside GRP shell	5,652 18'6½"	2,235 7'4"	2,000 6'6¾"	2,235 7'4"	2,083 6'10"	20,320 44,800	2,500 5,510	17,820 39,290	26.35 930
	5,652 18'6½"	2,235 7'4"	2,000 6'6¾"	2,235 7'4"	2,083 6'10"	24,000 52,910	2,450 5,400	21,550 47,510	26.3 930
Steelframe. Walls outside and inside GRP.	5,652 18'6½"	2,235 7'8"	2,000 6'6¾"	2,218 7'3¼"	2,083 6'10"	20,320 44,800	2,633 5,800	17,687 39,000	26.3 930
Steelframe. Walls outside and inside stainless steel.	5,724 18'9⅜"	2,286 7'6"	2,014 6'7¼"	2,286 7'6"	2,067 6'9⅜"	24,000 52,910	2,550 5,620	21,450 47,290	26.4 933

Insulated Container   40'

Construction	Inside Dimensions			Door Opening		Weights			Capacity
	Length	Width	Max. Stowage Height	Width	Height	Max. Gross	Tare	Max. Payload	
	mm ft	mm ft	mm ft	mm ft	mm ft	kg lbs	kg lbs	kg lbs	m³ cu.ft.

8' high

Construction	Length	Width	Max. Stowage Height	Width	Height	Max. Gross	Tare	Max. Payload	Capacity
Steelframe. Walls: outside/ inside: stainless steel coated plywood/ stainless steel and aluminum/ aluminum	11,750 38'6⅝"	2,250 7'4½"	2,080 6'9⅞"	2,250 7'4½"	2,180 7'1⅞"	30,480 67,200	4,650 10,250	25,830 56,950	58.4 2,060
	11,840 38'10⅛"	2,286 7'6"	2,120 6'11½"	2,286 7'6"	2,195 7'2⅜"	30,480 67,200	3,850 8,490	26,630 58,710	60.6 2,140

Ventilated Container   40'

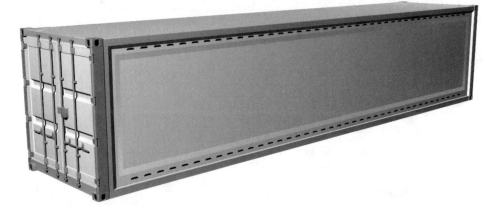

- Especially for cargo that needs ventilation.
- Natural ventilation is provided by openings in top and bottom longitudinal rails. The labyrinth construction of these ventilation openings ensures weather-proofness.
- Numerous lashing devices on the top and bottom longitudinal rails and the corner posts. Lashing devices have a permissible load of 1,000 kg (2,205 lbs) each.
- Note permissable weight limits for road and rail transport.

Ventilated Container   20'

Construction	Inside Dimensions			Door Opening		Weights			Capacity
	Length	Width	Height	Width	Height	Max. Gross	Tare	Max. Payload	
	mm ft	mm ft	mm ft	mm ft	mm ft	kg lbs	kg lbs	kg lbs	m³ cu.ft.

8'6" high

Construction	Length	Width	Height	Width	Height	Max. Gross	Tare	Max. Payload	Capacity
Steelframe. Walls: plywood, coated with GRP, wooden floor.	5,930 19'5¹/₂"	2,358 7'8⁷/₈"	2,375 7'9¹/₂"	2,335 7'8"	2,292 7'6¹/₄"	24,000 52,910	2,400 5,290	21,600 47,620	33.7 1,190
Steel container with corrugated walls and wooden floor.	5,888 19'3³/₄"	2,346 7'8³/₈"	2,392 7'10¹/₈"	2,334 7'7⁷/₈"	2,290 7'6¹/₈"	30,480 67,200	2,400 5,290	28,080 61,910	33.0 1,167

Bulk Container   20'

- Especially for dry bulk cargos, e.g. malt.
- Three manholes for top loading of each container. Distance centerline to centerline manhole 1.83 m (6').
- One discharge opening in each door wing. On demand, short discharge tubes can be installed to move the cargo in desired directions.
- Fastening of linerbag possible.

- Fork-lift pockets on a number of the containers.
- Lashing devices on the top longitudinal rails.
- Roof openings 455 mm (18") discharge door openings 340 x 380 mm (13.5" x 15").
- Note permissable weight limits for road and rail transport.

Bulk Container   20'

Construction	Inside Dimensions			Door Opening		Weights			Capacity
	Length	Width	Height	Width	Height	Max. Gross	Tare	Max. Payload	
	mm ft	mm ft	mm ft	mm ft	mm ft	kg lbs	kg lbs	kg lbs	m³ cu.ft.

8'6" high

Construction	Length	Width	Height	Width	Height	Max. Gross	Tare	Max. Payload	Capacity
Steelframe. Walls: plywood, coated with GRP.	5,934 19'5¹/₂"	2,358 7'8³/₄"	2,340 7'8¹/₈"	2,335 7'8"	2,292 7'6¹/₄"	24,000 52,910	2,450 5,400	21,550 47,510	32.9 1,162
	5,931 19'5¹/₂"	2,358 7'8³/₄"	2,326 7'7⁵/₈"	2,335 7'8"	2,292 7'6¹/₄"	24,000 52,910	2,370 5,220	21,630 47,690	32.9 1,162

OCEAN

Refrigerated Container   20'

Temperature Controlled Container

- Especially for cargo that needs constant temperatures above or below freezing point.
- Controlled fresh-air supply is possible. Containers are ATO-approved (formerly SPRENGER).
- Walls in "sandwich-construction", with Polyurethane foam to provide maximum insulation.
- The reefer unit is a compact-design compressor unit with aircooled condenser. It switches automatically from cooling to heating operation (and vice versa), if a change of the outside temperatures makes it necessary.
- Please note maximum stowage height in below table and as indicated by red line inside container in order to ensure proper ventilation.
- Possible voltages:
  380V/50 Hz to 460 V/60Hz
  200 V/50 Hz to 220 V/60 Hz
- Refer to technical specifications and illustrations of electric plugs on refrigerated containers on page 319.
- Note permissable weight limits for road and rail transport.
- Permissable temperature setting:
  +25°C to -25°C (+77°F to -13°F).
- The set temperatures can be kept as long as the difference between outside and cargo temperatures does not exceed the following limits:
  for heating 42°C (76°F)
  for cooling 65°C (117°F).

Refrigerated Container   20'

Construction	Inside Dimensions				Door Opening		Weights			Capacity
	Length	Width	Height	Max. Stowable Height	Width	Height	Max. Gross	Tare	Max. Payload	
	mm ft	mm ft	mm ft	mm ft	mm ft	mm ft	kg lbs	kg lbs	kg lbs	m³ cu.ft.

8'6" high

Construction	Length	Width	Height	Max. Stowable Height	Width	Height	Max. Gross	Tare	Max. Payload	Capacity
Steelframe. Walls: outside plywood, coated with GRP, inside GRP, inside stainless steel	5,340 17'6¼"	2,200 7'2⅝"	2,254 7'4¾"	2,154 7'1¾"	2,200 7'2⅝"	2,220 7'3⅜"	24,000 52,910	3,380 7,450	20,620 45,460	26.4 932
Steelframe. Walls outside and inside stainless steel	5,479 17'11⅝"	2,286 7'6"	2,257 7'4⅞"	2,157 7'7⅞"	2,286 7'6"	2,220 7'3⅜"	30,480 67,200	3,160 6,970	27,320 60,230	28.3 1,000
	5,459 17'10⅞"	2,295 7'6⅛"	2,268 7'6"	2,168 7'1⅜"	2,291 7'6⅛"	2,259 7'4⅞"	30,480 67,200	3,050 6,720	27,430 60,480	28.4 1,003
	5,448 17'10½"	2,290 7'6⅛"	2,264 7'5⅛"	2,164 7'1⅛"	2,286 7'6"	2,260 7'5"	30,480 67,200	3,060 6,750	27,420 60,450	28.3 1,000

OCEAN

Refrigerated Container   40'

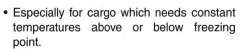

- Especially for cargo which needs constant temperatures above or below freezing point.
- Controlled fresh-air supply is possible. Containers are ATO-approved (formerly SPRENGER).
- Walls in "sandwich-construction", with Polyurethane foam to provide maximum insulation.
- The reefer unit is a compact-design compressor unit with aircooled condenser. It switches automatically from cooling to heating operation (and vice versa), if a change of the outside temperatures makes it necessary.
- Please note maximum stowage height in below table and as indicated by red line inside container in order to ensure proper ventilation.

- Possible voltages:
  380V/50 Hz to 460 V/60Hz
  200 V/50 Hz to 220 V/60 Hz
- Technical specifications and illustrations of electric plugs for refrigerated containers on page 319.
- Note permissable weight limits for road and rail transport.
- Possible temperature setting:
  +25°C to -25°C (+77°F to -13°F).
- Diesel generators are installed on some 40' containers to provide a power supply.
- The set temperatures can be kept as long as the difference between outside and cargo temperatures does not exceed the following limits:
  for heating 42°C (76°F)
  for cooling 60°C (108°F)

Refrigerated Container   40'

OCEAN

Construction	Inside Dimensions				Door Opening		Weights			Capacity
	Length	Width	Height	Max. Stowable Height	Width	Height	Max. Gross	Tare	Max. Payload	
	mm ft	mm ft	mm ft	mm ft	mm ft	mm ft	kg lbs	kg lbs	kg lbs	m³ cu.ft.

8' high

Construction	Length	Width	Height	Max. Stow. Height	Width	Height	Max. Gross	Tare	Max. Payload	Capacity
Steelframe. Walls: outside plywood, coated with GRP, inside GRP shell	11,141 36'4⁵/₈"	2,197 7'2¹/₂"	2,216 7'3¹/₄"	2,096 6'10¹/₂"	2,197 7'2¹/₂"	2,173 7'1¹/₂"	30,480 67,200	6,010 13,250	24,470 53,950	54.2 1,920
	11,141 36'4⁵/₈"	2,197 7'2¹/₂"	2,216 7'3¹/₄"	2,096 6'10¹/₂"	2,197 7'2¹/₂"	2,173 7'1¹/₂"	30,480 67,200	6,010 13,250	24,470 53,950	54.2 1,920
Steelframe. Walls: outside plywood coated with GRP, inside stainless steel	11,141 36'4⁵/₈"	2,197 7'2¹/₂"	2,216 7'3¹/₄"	2,096 6'10¹/₂"	2,197 7'2¹/₂"	2,173 7'1¹/₂"	30,480 67,200	6,010 13,250	24,470 53,950	54.2 1,920
	11,140 36'4⁵/₈"	2,226 7'3⁵/₈"	2,221 7'3³/₈"	2,101 6'10⁵/₈"	2,226 7'3⁵/₈"	2,173 7'1¹/₂"	30,480 67,200	6,010 13,250	24,470 53,950	55.0 1,945
Steelframe. Walls: outside aluminum, inside stainless steel	11,170 36'7³/₄"	2,286 7'6"	2,235 7'4"	2,115 6'11¹/₄"	2,286 7'6"	2,200 7'2⁵/₈"	30,480 67,200	5,200 11,460	25,280 55,740	57.3 2,023
	11,192 36'8⁵/₈"	2,286 7'6"	2,240 7'5¹/₄"	2,120 6'11¹/₂"	2,286 7'6"	2,195 7'2³/₈"	30,480 67,200	5,200 11,460	25,280 55,740	57.3 2,023
	11,572 37'11⁵/₈"	2,286 7'6"	2,254 7'4³/₄"	2,134 7'	2,286 7'6"	2,207 7'2⁷/₈"	30,480 67,200	4,400 9,700	26,080 57,500	59.64 2,106
Steelframe. Rails aluminum. Walls: outside aluminum, inside stainless steel	11,558 37'11"	2,286 7'6"	2,188 7'1⁷/₈"	2,068 6'9³/₈"	2,286 7'6"	2,161 7'1"	30,480 67,200	4,140 9,130	26,340 58,070	57.8 2,023

High Cube Refrigerated Container   40'

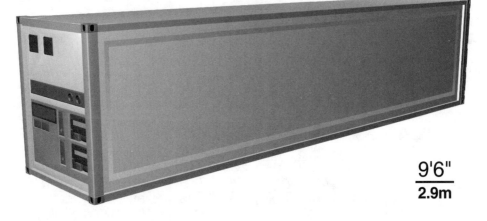

$$\frac{9'6''}{2.9m}$$

- Particularly suitable for voluminous light-weight cargoes (e.g., fruit, flowers, ferns).
- Especially for cargo that needs constant temperatures above or below freezing point.
- Controlled fresh-air supply is possible. Containers are ATO-approved (formerly SPRENGER).
- Walls in "sandwich-construction", with Polyurethane foam to provide maximum insulation.
- The reefer unit is a compact-design compressor unit with aircooled condenser. It switches automatically from cooling to heating operation (and vice versa), if a change of the outside temperatures makes it necessary.
- Possible voltages:
  380V/50 Hz to 460 V/60Hz

- Technical specifications and illustrations of electric plugs for refrigerated containers on page 319.
- Note permissable weight limits for road and rail transport.
- Permissable temperature setting:
  +25˚C to -25˚C (+77˚F to -13˚F).
- The set temperatures can be kept as long as the difference between outside and cargo temperatures does not exceed the following limits:
  for heating 42˚C (76˚F)
  for cooling 60˚C (108˚F)

High Cube Refrigerated Container   40'

OCEAN

Construction	Inside Dimensions				Door Opening		Weights			Capacity
	Length	Width	Height	Max. Stowage Height	Width	Height	Max. Gross	Tare	Max. Payload	
	mm ft	mm ft	mm ft	mm ft	mm ft	mm ft	kg lbs	kg lbs	kg lbs	m³ cu.ft.

9'6" high — without Diesel Generator Set

Construction	Length	Width	Height	Max. Stowage Height	Width	Height	Max. Gross	Tare	Max. Payload	Capacity
Steelframes. Rails: Aluminum. Walls: outside aluminum, inside stainless steel.	11,634 38'2"	2,288 7'6¹/₈"	2,498 8'2³/₈"	2,378 7'9⁵/₈"	2,288 7'6¹/₈"	2,517 8'3¹/₈"	30,480 67,200	4,180 9,220	26,300 57,980	66.5 2348
	11,568 37'11³/₈"	2,290 7'6¹/₈"	2,509 8'2³/₄"	2,389 7'10"	2,290 7'6¹/₈"	2,473 8'1³/₈"	32,480 71,600	4,240 9,350	28,240 62,250	66.4 2,345
	11,580 37'11¹/₈"	2,288 7'6¹/₈"	2,498 8'2³/₈"	2,378 7'9⁵/₈"	2,288 7'6¹/₈"	2,517 8'3¹/₈"	30,480 67,200	4,180 9,220	26,300 57,980	66.2 2370
	11,580 37'11⁷/₈"	2,290 7'6¹/₈"	2,513 8'3"	2,393 7'10¹/₄"	2,290 7'6¹/₈"	2,522 8'3¹/₄"	30,480 67,200	4,180 9,220	26,300 57,980	67.0 2,370
	11,580 37'11⁷/₈"	2,286 7'6"	2,528 8'1¹/₂"	2,408 7'10³/₄"	2,286 7'6"	2,545 8'4¹/₈"	30,480 67,200	4,000 8,820	26,480 58,380	67.0 2,366
	11,580 37'11⁷/₈"	2,286 7'6"	2,515 8'3"	2,395 7'10¹/₄"	2,286 7'6"	2,535 8'3³/₄"	30,480 67,200	4,150 9,150	26,330 58,050	67.0 2,366
	11,580 37'11⁷/₈"	2,286 7'6"	2,515 8'3"	2,395 7'10¹/₄"	2,286 7'6"	2,535 8'3³/₄"	30,480 67,200	6,000 13,230	24,480 53,970	67.0 2,366
Steelframe. Walls outside and inside GRP.	11,575 37'11⁵/₈"	2,294 7'6¹/₄"	2,560 8'4³/₄"	2,440 8'	2,286 7'6"	2,570 8'5¹/₈"	32,500 71,650	4,300 9,480	28,200 62,170	68.0 2,400
	11,575 37'11⁵/₈"	2,294 7'6¹/₄"	2,560 8'4³/₄"	2,440 8'	2,286 7'6"	2,570 8'5¹/₈"	32,500 71,650	4,240 9,350	28,260 62,300	68.0 2,400
	11,578 37'11³/₄"	2,295 7'6³/₈"	2,550 8'4³/₈"	2,425 7'11¹/₂"	2,290 7'6¹/₈"	2,560 8'4³/₄"	30,480 67,200	4,640 10,230	25,840 56,970	67.8 2,394
	11,578 37'11³/₄"	2,295 7'6³/₈"	2,550 8'4³/₈"	2,425 7'11¹/₂"	2,290 7'6¹/₈"	2,560 8'4³/₄"	30,480 67,200	4,580 10,100	25,900 57,100	67.8 2,394

Tank Container

20'

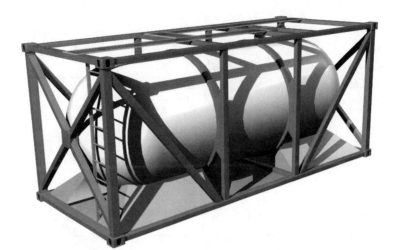

- Separate tank fleets are available for:
  CHEMICAL PRODUCTS, e.g.:
  —Flammables
  —Oxidising agents
  —Toxic substances
  —Corrosives
    FOODSTUFFS, e.g.:
  —Alcohols
  —Fruit juices
  —Edible oils
  —Food additives
- Tanks must be filled to not less than 80% of their capacity to avoid dangerous surg/ swells during transport.
  Tanks must not be filled to 100% of their capacity. Sufficient ullage space shall be left—which must be determined depending on the thermal expansion of the product to be carried.
- Certain dangerous products must be carried in tanks having no openings below the surface level of the liquid. Such tanks must be discharged through a syphon pipe by either pressure or pumping.
- National road/rail weight limitations have to be maintained when arranging land transport.
- For the cleaning of tanks and disposal of residues tariff rules apply. Tanks moving in a dedicated service are exempted from such rules until the dedication is terminated.
- For more details contact your representative.

Electric Plugs

The following are electric plug configurations
for refrigerated containers.

- Depending on power sources refrigerated
  containers are equipped with 1 or 2 plugs
  380V/50Hz to 460V/60Hz (32 A),
  200V/50Hz to 220V/60Hz (60A).
- There are fixed cables with a length of 15 m
  (49 ft).
- Couplings for adapters are available.
- Adapters are subject to corresponding
  safety regulations.

Earth Contact

all series

380/460 V plugs
- 4 poles according to CEE.
- According to ISO 1496-2 annex M.
- Earth contact in 3rd position according to
  socket.

Earth Contact

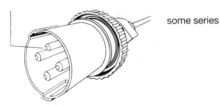

some series

200/220 V plugs
- 4 poles
- According to ISO 1496-2 annex O.
- Position of earth contact according to
  illustration.

OCEAN

NOTES

Guide to Air Freight Containers (ULDs)

Introduction
The following guide to air freight containers has been developed from materials supplied by the International Air Transport Association (IATA), air cargo carriers and container manufacturers. It should be noted that producing a truly comprehensive guide is a problematic task. While it would appear that there is a limited number of cargo aircraft operating the world, there are in fact, many aircraft types and many more aircraft cargo configurations. Each aircraft and configuration may require customized containers. The guide that follows contains illustrations and specifications of the most common containers in use today. Many of these containers can be used in multiple aircraft.

ULD (Unit Load Devices)
While in the ocean freight cargo business the word "container" is widely accepted, in the air freight cargo business the proper term is "unit load device", or more commonly ULD. However, both terms are used.

IATA
The International Air Transport Association (IATA) is the primary source of industry wide technical information for ULDs. Their "ULD Technical Manual" contains the specifications manufacturers usually follow in making containers for airlines. The book can be obtained from:

IATA
2000 Peel Street; Montreal, Quebec
Canada H3A 2R4
Tel: [1] (514) 985-6326; Fax: [1] (514) 844-7711
or
IATA
331 North Bridge Road; Suite 20-00;
Odeon Towers; Singapore 188720
Tel: [65] 331-0420; Fax: [65] 339-0855

Your Air Freight Forwarder
The practical source of information concerning ULDs for your shipment will most likely come from your air carrier or air freight forwarder. They will be best equipped to assist you in selecting the appropriate ULD for your needs.

Values / Details
All values listed in illustrations and tables are given in metric. Ft and lbs values are for easy reference only.

Openings / Doors
While airlines may be quite rigid about external dimensions and maximum gross weights, there are many styles of door openings that are permissible. ULD manufacturers produce products with hinged doors, folding aluminum panels as well as reinforced nylon curtains.

Pallets / Nettings
Pallets are in common use in most aircraft cargo configurations. All require the use of restraining devices. The most common type is a flexible netting of which there are numerous designs. Ask your air carrier or freight forwarder for details.

Maximum Gross Weights
Maximum gross weights vary from ULD type, ULD manufacturer, aircraft and air carrier. Be certain to confirm weight maximums.

ULD Markings
According to IATA all ULDs must carry the following marking information: 1) ULD Type Code, 2) Maximum Gross Weight (MGW) in kilograms and pounds and 3) The actual Tare Weight (TARE) in kilograms and pounds. Example:

UAK	1 2 3 4	XB
MGW	6,033 kg	13,300 lb
TARE	216 kg	476 lb

For marking non-structural aircraft containers MGW is optional. The actual TARE shall be the sum of the components aircraft pallet, net and container.

IATA ULD Identification Codes
Prior to October 1, 1993 the IATA Identification Code consisted of nine (9) alpha numeric elements in the following sequence:

Position	Character Type	Description
1	alphabetic	ULD Category
2	alphabetic	Base Dimensions
3	alphabetic	Contour or Compatibility
4,5,6,7	numeric	Serial Number
8,9	alpha-numeric	Owner/Registrant

Effective October 1, 1993 he IATA Identification Code consists of nine (9) or ten (10) alpha-numeric elements in the following sequence:

Position	Character Type	Description
1	alphabetic	ULD Category
2	alphabetic	Base Dimensions
3	alphabetic	Contour or Compatibility
4,5,6,7,8	(see Note below)	Serial Number
9, 10	alpha-numeric	Owner/Registrant

The serial number consists of four or five numerics.

ULD Type Code

IATA uses three letter codes (in upper case letters) to describe key characteristics of ULDs. Examples are AKE, DPN and RKE. Each of the three letter code positions describes particular characteristics of the ULD.

Position 1

The Position 1 letter describes the container as:

1. certified as to airworthiness or non-certified
2. structural unit or non-structural
3. fitted with equipment for refrigeration, insulation or thermal control (Thermal) or not fitted with refrigeration, insulation or thermal control
4. containers, pallets, nets, pallet/net/non-structural igloo assembly

The Code List for Position 1 is as follows:

A Certified Aircraft Container
D Non-Certified Aircraft Container
F Non-Certified Aircraft Pallet
G Non-Certified Aircraft Pallet Net
J Thermal Non-Structural Igloo
H Horse Stalls
K Cattle Stalls
M Thermal Non-Certified Aircraft Container
N Certified Aircraft Pallet Net
P Certified Aircraft Pallet
R Thermal Certified Aircraft Container
U Non-Structural Container
V Automobile Transport Equipment

The following are obsolete codes that are still found on some older ULDs.

(B) Certified Main Deck Aircraft Container
(C) Non-Aircraft Container
(E) Non-Certified Main Deck Aircraft Container
(S) Structural Igloo— Solid Doors
(T) Structural Igloo—Other Closures (other than solid doors)

Position 2

The Position 2 letter describes the base dimensions of the container. For containers manufactured after October 1, 1990 the following code letters are used:

A 2,235 x 3,175 mm (88 x 125 in)
B 2,235 x 2,743 mm (88 x 108 in)
E 1,346 x 2,235 mm (53 x 88 in)
F 2,438 x 2,991 mm (96 x 117 $\frac{3}{4}$ in)
G 2,438 x 6,058 mm (96 x 238 $\frac{1}{2}$ in)
H 2,438 x 9,125 mm (96 x 359 $\frac{1}{4}$ in)
J 2,438 x 12,192 mm (96 x 480 in)
K 1,534 x 1,562 mm (60.4 x 61.5 in)
L 1,534 x 3,175 mm (60.4 x 125 in)
M 2,438 x 3,175 mm (96 x 125 in)
N 1,562 x 2,438 mm (61.5 x 96 in)
P 1,198 x 1,534 mm (47 x 60.4 in)
Q 1,534 x 2,438 mm (60.4 x 96 in)
R 2,438 x 4,938 mm (96 x 196 in)
X Miscellaneous sizes largest dimension between 2,438 mm and 3,175 mm (between 96 in and 125 in)
Y Miscellaneous sizes largest dimension 2,438 mm (96 in)
Z Miscellaneous sizes largest dimension >3,175 (>125 in)

Position 3

The Position 3 letter describes the container's contour, fork lift capability, and in the case of pallets and nets, the restraint system into which the unit is classified. The Position 3 codes are extremely complex and are not within the scope of this publication. Refer to the IATA "ULD Technical Manual" for complete information.

Notes on ULD Guide

1. IATA (International Air Transport Association) and ATA (Air Transport Association of America) have different designations for air containers. For example: A US Type LD-3 is equivalent to the IATA Type 8 container. We list the IATA designation first and then the ATA designation second.

2. This guide lists and illustrates the primary air containers in use today. There are other types not listed that can be found in the IATA ULD Technical Manual.

3. Specifications listed in metric measures of kilos and millimeters (kg, mm) are official IATA specifications. Pounds and inches are listed only as a point of reference.

4. L x W x H = Length x Width x Height.

5. Specifications listed are taken from IATA's "ULD Technical Manual." In practice, these specifications (dimensions and weight) may vary according to special aircraft configurations and ULD manufacturers.

6. ULDs are generally classified as lower deck containers and upper deck containers. Lower deck containers generally have smaller base dimensions than upper deck containers as a result of the curvature of the airplane body.

7. Since a great deal of cargo is carried on commercial passenger flights, there are generally more lower deck than upper deck containers.

Main Deck Pallet with Net—IATA Type 1/1S—IATA Prefix: PG

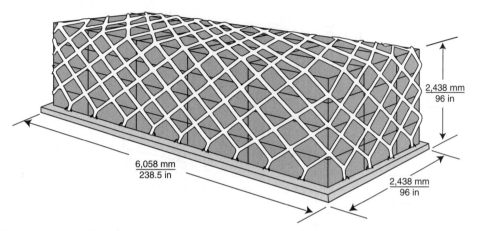

Maximum Gross Weight
13,608 kg / 30,000 lb

Volume
33.25 m³ / 1,174 ft³

Tare
400 kg / 882 lb

External Dimensions
(L x W x H)
6,058 mm x 2,438 mm x 2,438 mm
(238.5 in x 96 in x 96 in)

Aircraft Accepted For
DC10-30 Freighter, 747F

Main Deck Pallet with Net—IATA Type 2/2Q—IATA Prefix: PM

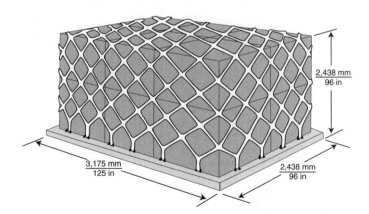

Maximum Gross Weight
6,804 kg / 15,000 lb

Volume
17.16 m³ / 606 ft³

Tare
130 kg / 287 lb

External Dimensions
(L x W x H)
3,175 mm x 2,438 mm x 2,438 mm
(125 in x 96 in x 96 in)

Aircraft Accepted For
DC10-30 Freighter, 747F

Main Deck Pallet with Net—IATA Type 2H—IATA Prefix: PM

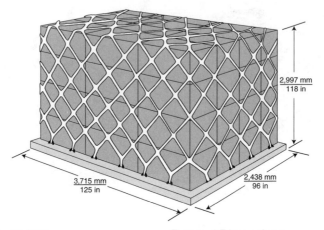

Maximum Gross Weight
6,804 kg / 15,000 lb

Volume
21.16 m³ / 747 ft³

Tare
130 kg / 287 lb

External Dimensions
(L x W x H)
3,715 mm x 2,438 mm x 2,997 mm
(125 in x 96 in x 118in)

Aircraft Accepted For:
DC10-30 Freighter, 747F

Pallet with Net—IATA Type 2WA—IATA Prefix: PM

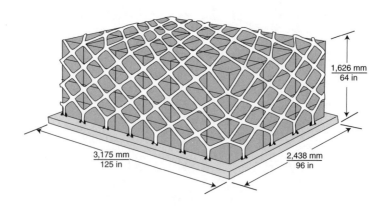

Maximum Gross Weight
5,035 kg / 11,100 lb

Volume
15.8 m³ / 557 ft³

Tare
130 kg / 287 lb

External Dimensions
(L x W x H)
3,715 mm x 2,438 mm x 1,626 mm
(125 in x 96 in x 64 in)

Aircraft Accepted For:
DC10-30, Freighter, DC10-30, 747, 747F

Pallet with Net—IATA Type 5—IATA Prefix: PA

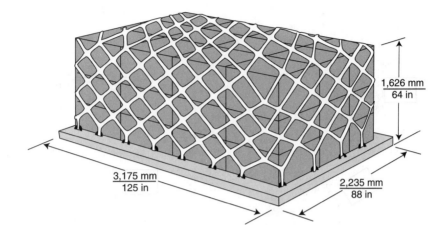

1,626 mm
64 in

3,175 mm
125 in

2,235 mm
88 in

Maximum Gross Weight
4,626 kg / 10,200 lb

Volume
9.91 m³ / 350 ft³

Tare
120 kg / 264 lb

External Dimensions
(L x W x H)
3,715 mm x 2,235 mm x 1,626 mm
(125 in x 88 in x 64 in)

Aircraft Accepted For:
DC10-30 Freighter, DC10-30
747, 747F, 777, 767-300

Lower Deck Pallet with Net—IATA Type 6—IATA Prefix: PL

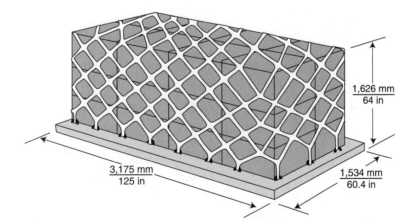

1,626 mm
64 in

3,175 mm
125 in

1,534 mm
60.4 in

Maximum Gross Weight
3,175 kg / 7,000 lb

Volume
6.94 m³ / 245 ft³

Tare
90 kg / 198 lb

External Dimensions
(L x W x H)
3,175 mm x 1,534 mm x 1,626 mm
(125 in x 60.4 in x 64 in)

Aircraft Accepted For:
DC10, DC10-30 Freighter, 747, 777

A
I
R

A I R

Lower Deck Container—IATA Type 2BG—IATA Prefix: AMU

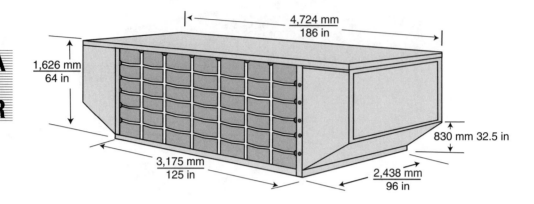

Maximum Gross Weight
6,033 kg / 13,300 lb

Volume
13.7 m³ / 480 ft³

Tare
200 kg / 440 lb

External Dimensions
(L x W x H)
3,175 mm x 2,438 mm x 1,626 mm
(125 in x 96 in x 64 in)

Aircraft Accepted For:
747, 747F

Main Deck Container—IATA Type 2/2Q—IATA Prefix: AMA

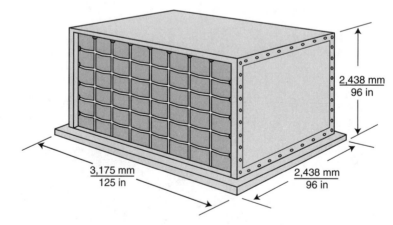

Maximum Gross Weight
6,804 kg / 15,000 lb

Volume
17.16 m³ / 606 ft³

Tare
260 kg / 572 lb

External Dimensions
(L x W x H)
3,175 mm x 2,438 mm x 2,438 mm
(125 in x 96 in x 96 in)

Aircraft Accepted For:
747F

Upper Deck Container—IATA Type 5—IATA Prefix AAK—ATA: LD-7

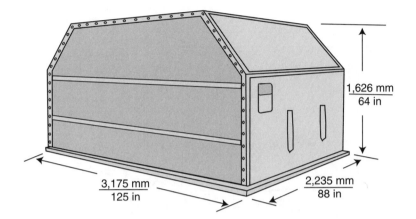

1,626 mm
64 in

3,175 mm
125 in

2,235 mm
88 in

Maximum Gross Weight
6,033 kg / 13,300 lb

Volume
9.91 m³ / 350 ft³

Tare
200 kg / 440 lb

External Dimensions
(L x W x H)
3,175 mm x 2,235 mm x 1,626 mm
(125 in x 88 in x 64 in)

Aircraft Accepted For

Container—IATA Type 5—IATA Prefix AAP—ATA: LD-9

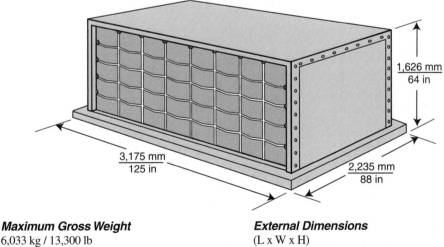

1,626 mm
64 in

3,175 mm
125 in

2,235 mm
88 in

Maximum Gross Weight
6,033 kg / 13,300 lb

Volume
9.91 m³ / 350 ft³

Tare
200 kg / 440 lb

External Dimensions
(L x W x H)
3,175 mm x 2,235 mm x 1,626 mm
(125 in x 88 in x 64 in)

Aircraft Accepted For:
747, 747F, L1011

A
I
R

Lower Deck Container—IATA Type 6B—IATA Prefix: AQ—ATA: LD-8

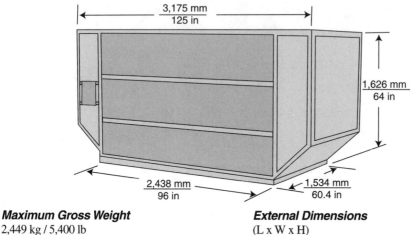

Maximum Gross Weight
2,449 kg / 5,400 lb

Volume
6.94 m³ / 245 ft³

Tare
120 kg / 264 lb

External Dimensions
(L x W x H)
2,438 mm x 1,534 mm x 1,626 mm
(96 in x 60.4 in x 64 in)

Aircraft Accepted For:
777, 767

Lower Deck Container—IATA Type 6—IATA Prefix: ALF—ATA: LD-6

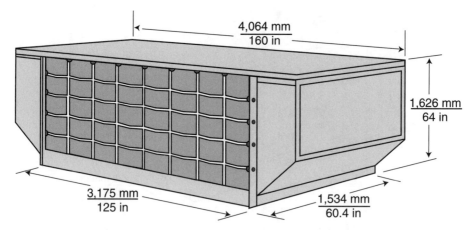

Maximum Gross Weight
3,175 kg / 7,000 lb

Volume
6.94 m³ / 245 ft³

Tare
180 kg / 397 lb

External Dimensions
(L x W x H)
3,175 mm x 1,534 mm x 1,626 mm
(125 in x 60.4 in x 64 in)

Aircraft Accepted For:
747, 747F, L1011

Lower Deck Container—IATA Type 8—IATA Prefix AK—ATA: LD-3

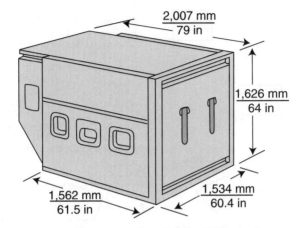

Maximum Gross Weight
1,588 kg / 3,500 lb

Volume
4.53 m³ / 160 ft³

Tare
70 kg / 154 lb

External Dimensions
(L x W x H)
1,562 mm x 1,534 mm x 1,626 mm
(61.5 in x 60.4 in x 64 in)

Aircraft Accepted For:
DC10-30 Freighter, DC10, 747, 777, 767

Lower Deck Container—IATA Type 8D—Prefix: APA—APA: LD-2

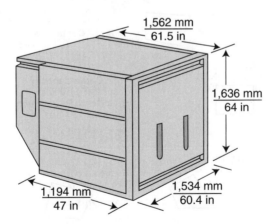

Maximum Gross Weight
1,225 kg / 2,700 lb

Volume
3.4 m³ / 120 ft³

Tare
60 kg / 132 lb

External Dimensions
(L x W x H)
1,194 mm x 1,534 mm x 1,626 mm
(47 in x 60.4 in x 64 in)

Aircraft Accepted For:
777, 767

A
I
R

Cargo Aircraft Specifications

DC 10-30 Freighter
Total Cargo Capacity   **Total Cargo Volume**
73,182 kg / 161,000 lb   452 m³ / 15,972 ft³
Main Deck Cargo Door (w x h)
350 cm x 255 cm / 140 in x 102 in
Lower Forward Cargo Door (w x h)
175 cm x 165 cm / 70 in x 66 in
Lower Rear Cargo Door (w x h)
175 cm x 165 cm / 70 in x 66 in
Types of Containers
Main Deck Pallet, LD-7, P9A, LD-11, LD-3

747 (400 Series)
Total Cargo Capacity   **Total Cargo Volume**
53,091 kg / 116,800 lb   159 m³ / 5,634 ft³
Bulk Cargo Door Dimensions (w x h)
111 cm x 119 cm / 44 in x 47in
Types of Containers
LD-7, P9A, LD-11, LD-3

747 (200 Series)
Total Cargo Capacity   **Total Cargo Volume**
48,091 kg / 105,800 lb   144 m³ / 5,123 ft³
Bulk Cargo Door Dimensions (w x h)
111 cm x 119 cm / 44 in x 47in
Types of Containers
LD-7, P9A, LD-11, LD-3

747 (100 Series)
Total Cargo Capacity   **Total Cargo Volume**
32,521 kg / 71,546 lb   115 m³ / 3,843 ft³
Bulk Cargo Door Dimensions (w x h)
111 cm x 119 cm / 44 in x 47in
Types of Containers
LD-7, P9A, LD-11, LD-3

767 (300 Series)
Total Cargo Capacity   **Total Cargo Volume**
33,062 kg / 72,736 lb   114 m³ / 4,030 ft³
Bulk Cargo Door Dimensions (w x h)
91 cm x 119 cm / 36 in x 47in
Types of Containers
LD-7, LD-8, LD-4, LD-3, LD-2

767 (200 Series)
Total Cargo Capacity   **Total Cargo Volume**
26,165 kg / 57,562 lb   92 m³ / 3,070 ft³
Bulk Cargo Door Dimensions (w x h)
91 cm x 119 cm / 36 in x 47in
Types of Containers
LD-8, LD-4, LD-3, LD-2

777
Total Cargo Capacity   **Total Cargo Volume**
54,685 kg / 120,306 lb   160 m³ / 5,720 ft³
Bulk Cargo Door Dimensions (w x h)
90 cm x 114 cm (left) x 122 cm (right)
35.7 in x 45.3 in (left) x 48.5 in (right)
Types of Containers
LD-7, LD-8, LD-4, LD-3, LD-2

757
Total Cargo Capacity   **Total Cargo Volume**
11,273 kg / 24,800lb   48 m³ / 1,698 ft³
Bulk Cargo Door Dimensions (w x h)
139 cm x 106 cm / 55 in x 42 in
Types of Containers

A 320
Total Cargo Capacity   **Total Cargo Volume**
9,125 kg / 20,074 lb   36 m³ / 1,270 ft³
Bulk Cargo Door Dimensions (w x h)
149 cm x 119 cm / 59 in x 47 in
Types of Containers

A 319
Total Cargo Capacity   **Total Cargo Volume**
6,800 kg / 14,960 lb   27 m³ / 975 ft³
Bulk Cargo Door Dimensions (w x h)
142 cm x 116 cm / 56 in x 46 in
Types of Containers

DC 10 (10 Series)
Total Cargo Capacity   **Total Cargo Volume**
43,636 kg / 96,000 lb   132 m³ / 4,678 ft³
Bulk Cargo Door Dimensions (w x h)
76 cm x 91 cm / 30 in x 36 in
Types of Containers
P9A, LD-11, LD-3

DC 10 (30 Series)
Total Cargo Capacity   **Total Cargo Volume**
27,727 kg / 61,000 lb   92 m³ / 3,280 ft³
Bulk Cargo Door Dimensions (w x h)
76 cm x 91 cm / 30 in x 36 in
Types of Containers
LD-7, P9A, LD-11, LD-3

727
Total Cargo Capacity   **Total Cargo Volume**
7,727 kg / 17,000 lb   40 m³ / 1,435 ft³
Bulk Cargo Door Dimensions (w x h)
139 cm x 106 cm / 55 in x 42 in

737 (300 Series)
Total Cargo Capacity   **Total Cargo Volume**
5,750 kg / 12,650 lb   30 m³ / 1,068 ft³
Bulk Cargo Door Dimensions (w x h)
114 cm x 86 cm / 45 in x 34 in

737 (200 Series)
Total Cargo Capacity   **Total Cargo Volume**
4,766 kg / 10,486 lb   24 m³ / 875 ft³
Bulk Cargo Door Dimensions (w x h)
114 cm x 86 cm / 45 in x 34 in

737 (500 Series)
Total Cargo Capacity   **Total Cargo Volume**
4,471 kg / 9,836 lb   23 m³ / 822 ft³
Bulk Cargo Door Dimensions (w x h)
114 cm x 86 cm / 45 in x 34 in

Guide to INCOTERMS 2000

While the terms of sale in international business often sound similar to those commonly used in domestic contracts, they often have different meanings. Confusion over these terms can result in a lost sale or a financial loss on a sale. Thus, it is essential that you understand what terms you are agreeing to before you finalize a contract.

Incoterms 2000[1]

By the 1920s, commercial traders had developed a set of trade terms to describe their rights and liabilities with regard to the sale and transport of goods. These trade terms consisted of short abbreviations for lengthy contract provisions. Unfortunately, there was no uniform interpretation of them in all countries, and therefore misunderstandings often arose in cross-border transactions.

To improve this aspect of international trade, the International Chamber of Commerce (ICC) in Paris developed INCOTERMS (INternational COmmercial TERMS), a set of uniform rules for the interpretation of international commercial terms defining the costs, risks, and obligations of buyers and sellers in international transactions. First published in 1936, these rules have been periodically revised to account for changing modes of transport and document delivery. The current version is Incoterms 2000.

Use of Incoterms

Incoterms are not implied into contracts for the sale of goods. If you desire to use Incoterms, you must specifically include them in your contract. Further, your contract should expressly refer to the rules of interpretation as defined in the latest revision of Incoterms, for example, *Incoterms 2000*, and you should ensure the proper application of the terms by additional contract provisions. Also, Incoterms are not "laws." In case of a dispute, courts and arbitrators will look at: 1) the sales contract, 2) who has possession of the goods, and 3) what payment, if any, has been made. See *International Contracts*, also by World Trade Press.

Illustrated Guide to Incoterms

This guide was designed to give a graphic representation of the buyer's and seller's risks and costs under each Incoterm. The material on each facing page gives a summary of seller and buyer responsibilities.

Incoterms Do . . .

Incoterms 2000 may be included in a sales contract if the parties desire the following:
1. To complete a sale of goods.
2. To indicate each contracting party's costs, risks, and obligations with regard to delivery of the goods as follows:
   a. When is the delivery completed?
   b. How does a party ensure that the other party has met that standard of conduct?
   c. Which party must comply with requisite licenses and government-imposed formalities?
   d. What are the mode and terms of carriage?
   e. What are the delivery terms and what is required as proof of delivery?
   f. When is the risk of loss transferred from the seller to the buyer?
   g. How will transport costs be divided between the parties?
   h. What notices are the parties required to give to each other regarding the transport and transfer of the goods?
3. To establish basic terms of transport and delivery in a short format.

Incoterms Do Not . . .

Incoterms 2000 are not sufficient on their own to express the full intent of the parties. They will not:
1. Apply to contracts for services.
2. Define contractual rights and obligations other than for delivery.
3. Specify details of the transfer, transport, and delivery of the goods.
4. Determine how title to the goods will be transferred.
5. Protect a party from his/her own risk of loss.
6. Cover the goods before or after delivery.
7. Define the remedies for breach of contract.

Tip: Incoterms can be quite useful, but their use has limitations. If you use them incorrectly, your contract may be ambiguous, if not impossible to perform. It is therefore important to understand the scope and purpose of Incoterms—when and why you might use them—before you rely on them to define such important terms as mode of delivery, customs clearance, passage of title, and transfer of risk.

I
N
C
O
T
E
R
M
S

---

1. INCOTERMS 2000 are Copyright © 1999 by ICC Publishing S.A. All rights reserved. The actual text of INCOTERMS 2000 is contained in ICC publication No. 560. Contact: ICC Publishing, Inc.; 156 Fifth Avenue; New York, New York 10010; Tel: +1 (212) 206-1150. ICC Publishing S.A.; 38 Cours Albert, 1er; 75008 Paris, France; Tel: +[33] (1) 49 53 29 23; e-mail: pub@iccbo.org; www.iccbooks.com.
2. This Illustrated Guide to Incoterms 2000 is © Copyright 2000-2002 by World Trade Press. All Rights Reserved. World Trade Press; 1450 Grant Avenue; Suite 204, Novato, CA 94945 USA; Tel: (415) 898-1124

Organization of Incoterms

Incoterms are grouped into four categories:

1. **The "E" term (EXW)**—The only term where the seller/exporter makes the goods available at his or her own premises to the buyer/importer.
2. **The "F" terms (FCA, FAS and FOB)**—Terms where the seller/exporter is responsible to deliver the goods to a carrier named by the buyer.
3. **The "C" terms (CFR, CIF, CPT and CIP)**—Terms where the seller/exporter/manufacturer is responsible for contracting and paying for carriage of the goods, but not responsible for additional costs or risk of loss or damage to the goods once they have been shipped. C terms evidence "shipment" (as opposed to "arrival") contracts.
4. **The "D" terms (DAF, DES, DEQ, DDU and DDP)**—Terms where the seller/exporter/manufacturer is responsible for all costs and risks associated with bringing the goods to the place of destination. D terms evidence "arrival" contracts.

The following table sets out these categories.

INCOTERMS 2000

Group E Departure	EXW	Ex Works (...named place)
Group F Main Carriage Unpaid	FCA	Free Carrier (...named place)
	FAS	Free Alongside Ship (...named port of shipment)
	FOB	Free On Board (...named port of shipment)
Group C Main Carriage Paid	CFR	Cost and Freight (...named port of destination)
	CIF	Cost, Insurance and Freight (...named port of destination)
	CPT	Carriage Paid To (...named place of destination)
	CIP	Carriage and Insurance Paid To (...named place of destination)
Group D Arrival	DAF	Delivered at Frontier (...named place)
	DES	Delivered Ex Ship (...named port of destination)
	DEQ	Delivered Ex Quay (...named port of destination)
	DDU	Delivered Duty Unpaid (...named port of destination)
	DDP	Delivered Duty Paid (...named port of destination)

Mode of transport

Not all Incoterms are appropriate for all modes of transport. Some terms were designed with sea vessels in mind while others were designed to be applicable to all modes. The following table sets out which terms are appropriate for each mode of transport.

INCOTERMS 2000

All modes of transport including multimodal	EXW	Ex Works (...named place)
	FCA	Free Carrier (...named place)
	CPT	Carriage Paid To (...named place of destination)
	CIP	Carriage and Insurance Paid To (...named place of destination)
	DAF	Delivered at Frontier (...named place)
	DDU	Delivered Duty Unpaid
	DDP	Delivered Duty Paid
Sea and inland waterway transport only	FAS	Free Alongside Ship (...named port of shipment)
	FOB	Free On Board (...named port of shipment)
	CFR	Cost and Freight (...named port of destination)
	CIF	Cost, Insurance and Freight (...named port of destination)
	DES	Delivered Ex Ship (...named port of destination)
	DEQ	Delivered Ex Quay (...named port of destination)

Helpful Definitions

Pre-carriage—The initial transport of goods from the seller's premises to the main port of shipment. Usually by truck, rail or on inland waterways.

Main carriage—The primary transport of goods, generally for the longest part of the journey and generally from one country to another. Usually by sea vessel or by airplane, but can be by truck or rail as well.

On-carriage—Transport from the port of arrival in the country of destination to the buyer's premises. Usually by truck, rail or on inland waterways.

Notes on Incoterms

1. **Underlying Contract**—Incoterms were designed to be used within the context of a written contract for the sale of goods. Incoterms, therefore, refer to the contract of sale, rather than the contract of carriage of the goods. Buyers and sellers should specify that their contract be governed by Incoterms 2000.

2. **EXW and FCA**—If you buy Ex Works or Free Carrier you will need to arrange for the contract of carriage. Also, since the shipper will not receive a bill of lading, using a letter of credit requiring a bill of lading will not be possible.

3. **EDI: Electronic Data Interchange**—It is increasingly common for sellers to prepare and transmit documents electronically. Incoterms provides for EDI so long as buyers and sellers agree on their use in the sales contract.

4. **Insurable Interest**—Note that in many cases either the buyer or the seller is not *obligated* to provide insurance. In a number of cases neither party is obligated to provide insurance. However, both the seller and buyer should be aware that they may have insurable interest in the goods and prudence dictates purchase of insurance coverage.

5. **Customs of the Port or Trade**—Incoterms are an attempt to standardize trade terms for all nations and all trades. However, different ports and different trades have their own customs and practices. It is best if specific customs and practices are specified in the sales contract.

6. **Precise Point of Delivery**—In some cases it may not be possible for the buyer to name the precise point of delivery at contract. However, if the buyer does not do so in a timely manner, it may give the seller the option to make delivery within a range of places that is within the terms of the contract. For example, the original terms of sale may state CFR Port of Rotterdam. The Port of Rotterdam is huge and the buyer may find that a particular point within the port is best and should so state in the sales contract and in the trade term. Also, since the buyer becomes liable for the goods once they arrive, he or she may be responsible for unloading, storage and other charges once the goods have been made available at the place named.

7. **Export and Import Customs Clearance**—It is usually desirable that export customs formalities be handled by the seller and import customs formalities be handled by the buyer. However, some trade terms require that the buyer handle export formalities and others require that the seller handle import formalities. In each case the buyer and seller will have to assume risk from export and import restrictions and prohibitions. In some cases foreign exporters may not be able to obtain import licenses in the country of import. This should be researched before accepting final terms.

8. **Added Wording**—It is possible, and in many cases desirable, that the seller and buyer agree to additional wording to an Incoterm. For example, if the seller agrees to DDP terms, agreeing to pay for customs formalities and import duties, but not for VAT (Value Added Taxes) the term "DDP VAT Unpaid" may be used.

9. **Packing**—It is the responsibility of the seller to provide packaging unless the goods shipped are customarily shipped in bulk (usually commodities such as oil or grain). In most situations it is best if the buyer and seller agree in the sales contract on the type and extent of packing required. However, it may not be possible to know beforehand the type or duration of transport. As a result, it is the responsibility of the seller to provide for safe and appropriate packaging, but only to the extent that the buyer has made the circumstances of the transport known to the seller beforehand.

   If the seller is responsible for packing goods in an ocean or air freight container it is also his responsibility to pack the container properly to withstand shipment.

10. **Inspection**—These are several issues related to inspections: a) the seller is responsible for costs of inspection to make certain the quantity and quality of the shipment is in conformity with the sales contract, b) pre-shipment inspections as required by the export authority are the responsibility of the party responsible for export formalities, c) import inspections as required by the import authority are the responsibility of the party responsible for import formalities, and d) third-party inspections for independent verification of quality and quantity (if required) are generally the responsibility of the buyer. The buyer may require such an inspection and inspection document as a condition of payment.

11. **Passing of Risks and Costs**—The general rule is that risks and costs pass from the seller to the buyer once the buyer has delivered the goods to the point and place named in the trade term.

INCOTERMS

INCOTERMS

EXW
Ex Works (. . . named place)

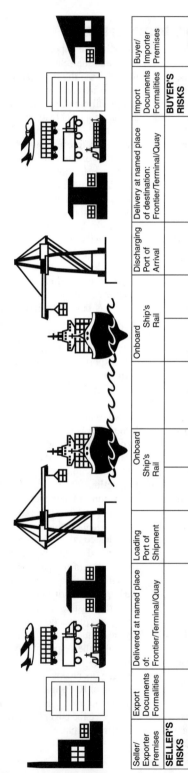

	SELLER	BUYER

Seller/Exporter Premises	Export Documents Formalities	Delivered at named place of: Frontier/Terminal/Quay	Loading Port of Shipment	Onboard Ship's Rail	Onboard Ship's Rail	Discharging Port of Arrival	Delivery at named place of destination: Frontier/Terminal/Quay	Import Documents Formalities	Buyer/Importer Premises
SELLER'S RISKS								**BUYER'S RISKS**	
SELLER'S COSTS								**BUYER'S COSTS**	

EXW, Ex Works (...named place)

In Ex Works, the seller/exporter/manufacturer merely makes the goods available to the buyer at the seller's "named place" of business. This trade term places the greatest responsibility on the buyer and minimum obligations on the seller. The seller does not clear the goods for export and does not load the goods onto a truck or other transport vehicle at the named place of departure.

The parties to the transaction, however, may stipulate that the seller be responsible for the costs and risks of loading the goods onto a transport vehicle. Such a stipulation must be made within the contract of sale.

If the buyer cannot handle export formalities the Ex Works term should not be used. In such a case Free Carrier (FCA) is recommended.

The Ex Works term is often used when making an initial quotation for the sale of goods. It represents the cost of the goods without any other costs included. Normal payment terms for Ex Works transactions are generally cash in advance and open account.

Examples
EXW Ex Works ABC Factory Paris, France
EXW Ex Works XYZ Printing Plant Singapore

EXW
Ex Works (. . . named place)

Incoterm Category

EXW is the only "E" Incoterm. The "E" Incoterm is where the seller/exporter makes the goods available to the buyer/importer at the seller/exporter's premises/factory/warehouse.

Modes of Transport Covered

All modes of transport including multimodal.

Seller's Responsibilities (summary)

1. **Goods**—Provide the goods, commercial invoice or electronic message, and other documentation as required by the sales contract.

2. **Licenses and Customs Formalities**—Provide the buyer at the buyer's request, risk and cost, every assistance in obtaining any license, authorization or documentation required for export of the goods.

3. **Carriage and Insurance**—The seller has no obligation to provide carriage of goods or insurance.

4. **Delivery**—Make the goods available to the buyer, unloaded, at the named place and on the date stipulated in the sales contract.

5. **Risk Transfer**—Assume all risks to the goods (loss or damage) until they have been made available to the buyer as above in # 4 above.

6. **Costs**—Pay all costs until the goods have been made available to the buyer in accordance with #4 above.

7. **Notice to the Buyer**—Provide sufficient notice to the buyer of the location and time of availability of the goods.

8. **Proof of Delivery, Transport Documents**—The seller has no obligation to provide the buyer with a proof of delivery or a transport document.

9. **Checking, Packing, Marking**—Pay all costs associated with checking the quality and quantity of the goods to be in conformity with the sales contract. Provide appropriate packing (unless the goods are traditionally delivered unpackaged) as required for the transport of the goods, to the extent that the buyer has made transport circumstances known to the seller prior to the execution of the sales contract. Provide marking appropriate to the packaging.

10. **Other**—Provide the buyer, at the buyer's request, risk and expense, assistance in securing documentation originating in the country of origin or of export as required for export and import. Provide the buyer at the buyer's request information necessary to obtain insurance.

Buyer's Responsibilities (summary)

1. **Payment**—Pay for the goods as provided in the sales contract.

2. **Licenses and Customs Formalities**—Obtain at own risk and cost all export and import licenses and authorizations. Carry out all export and import formalities at own risk and cost.

3. **Carriage and Insurance**—The buyer has no obligation to the seller to provide contract of carriage or insurance.

4. **Taking Delivery**—Take delivery of the goods when they have been made available by the seller in accordance with the terms of the sales contract.

5. **Risk Transfer**—Assume all risks (loss or damage) from the time the goods have been made available by the seller in accordance with the terms of the sales contract. Pay all costs resulting from failure to take delivery at the named place and time. Pay all costs relating to export and import including duties, taxes, customs formalities and other charges including transshipment.Reimburse the seller for costs of providing assistance in obtaining export licenses and authorizations.

6. **Costs**—Pay all costs for carriage and insurance from the time the goods have been made available by the seller in accordance with the terms of the sales contract.

7. **Notice to Seller**—If, according to the sales contract, the buyer is able to specify a time within a stipulated period, and/or specify a place of taking delivery, to give the seller sufficient notice.

8. **Proof of Delivery**—Provide the seller with evidence of having taken delivery.

9. **Inspection(s)**—Pay for the costs of pre-shipment inspection(s) including inspections required by the country of export.

10. **Other**—Pay and/or reimburse the seller for all costs associated with securing documentation originating in the country of origin or export as required for export and import.

INCOTERMS

FCA
Free Carrier (. . . named place)

SELLER ⟶   BUYER ⟶

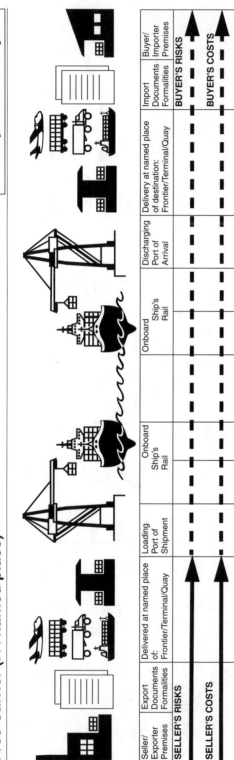

Seller/Exporter Premises	Export Documents Formalities	Delivered at named place of: Frontier/Terminal/Quay	Loading Port of Shipment	Onboard Ship's Rail	Onboard Ship's Rail	Discharging Port of Arrival	Delivery at named place of destination: Frontier/Terminal/Quay	Import Documents Formalities	Buyer/Importer Premises
SELLER'S RISKS							BUYER'S RISKS		
SELLER'S COSTS							BUYER'S COSTS		

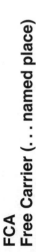

FCA, Free Carrier (...named place)

In Free Carrier, the seller/exporter/manufacturer clears the goods for export and then delivers them to the carrier specified by the buyer at the named place. If the named place is the seller's place of business, the seller is responsible for loading the goods onto the transport vehicle. If the named place is any other location, such as the loading dock of the carrier, the seller is not responsible for loading the goods onto the transport vehicle.

The Free Carrier term may be used for any mode of transport, including multimodal.

The "named place" in Free Carrier and all "F" terms is domestic to the seller.

"Carrier" has a specific and somewhat expanded meaning. A carrier can be a shipping line, an airline, a trucking firm, or a railway. The carrier can also be an individual or firm who undertakes to procure carriage by any of the above

methods of transport including multimodal. Therefore, a person, such as a freight forwarder, can act as a "carrier" under this term. In such a case, the buyer names the carrier or the individual who is to receive the goods. The Free Carrier term is often used when making an initial quotation for the sale of goods.

Normal payment terms for Free Carrier transactions are generally cash in advance and open account.

Examples

FCA Free Carrier ABC Shipping Lines Hamburg Germany
FCA Free Carrier XYZ Air Lines SFO (San Francisco International Airport)
FCA Free Carrier AZ Freight Forwarders Tokyo Japan

FCA
Free Carrier (. . . named place)

Incoterm Category

FCA is an "F" Incoterm where the seller/exporter delivers the goods export cleared to a carrier named by the buyer, but does not bear risk or costs once the goods have been handed over.

Modes of Transport Covered

All modes of transport including multimodal.

Seller's Responsibilities (summary)

1. **Goods**—Provide the goods, commercial invoice or electronic message, and other documentation as required by the sales contract.

2. **Licenses and Customs Formalities**—Obtain at own risk and cost all required export licenses, documentation and authorizations and carry out all export formalities and procedures.

3. **Carriage and Insurance**—The seller has no obligation to provide carriage of goods or insurance. However, if requested by buyer, the seller may contract for carriage on standard industry terms at the buyer's risk and cost. If so, the seller must notify buyer who may chose to decline the contract and notify the seller.

4. **Delivery**—Deliver the goods to the named carrier, freight forwarder or person at the named place and at the time stipulated in the sales contract. Requirements for delivery to the carrier vary depending upon the means of transport and the size of the shipment. In general, delivery is considered complete when the seller either loads the goods onto the vehicle provided, or delivers the goods to the carrier's terminal, unloaded

5. **Risk Transfer**—Assume all risks to the goods (loss or damage) until they have been delivered to the carrier.

6. **Costs**—Pay all costs until the goods have been delivered to the carrier as well as all costs relating to export including duties, taxes and customs formalities.

7. **Notices**—Provide sufficient notice to the buyer that the goods have been delivered to the carrier.

8. **Proof of Delivery, Transport Documents**—Provide the buyer with a proof of delivery (to the carrier) or a transport document, or to assist the buyer in obtaining a transport document.

9. **Checking, Packing, Marking**—Pay all costs associated with checking the quality and quantity of the goods to be in conformity with the sales contract. Provide appropriate packing (unless the goods are traditionally delivered unpackaged) as required for the transport of the goods, to the extent that the buyer has made transport circumstances known to the seller prior to the execution of the sales contract. Provide marking appropriate to the packaging.

10. **Other**—Provide the buyer, at the buyer's request, risk and expense, assistance in securing documentation originating in the country of origin or of export as required for import or transshipment through another country. Provide the buyer at the buyer's request information necessary to obtain insurance.

Buyer's Responsibilities (summary)

1. **Payment**—Pay for the goods as provided in the sales contract.

2. **Licenses and Customs Formalities**—Obtain all import licenses, documentation and authorizations and carry out all import formalities.

3. **Carriage and Insurance**—Provide for contract of carriage from the named place. No obligation to seller for insurance.

4. **Taking Delivery**—Take delivery of the goods as provided in the sales contract.

5. **Risk Transfer**—Assume all risk of loss or damage from the time the goods have been delivered to the carrier as provided in the sales contract.

6. **Costs**—Pay all costs for carriage and insurance from the time the goods have been delivered to the carrier as provided in the sales contract. Pay all costs resulting from failure to take delivery at the named place and time. Pay all costs relating to import formalities including duties, taxes and other charges including transshipment.

7. **Notice to Seller**—Give the seller sufficient notice of the name of the carrier, the time or period for delivery and the place of delivery.

8. **Proof of Delivery, Transport Document**—Accept the seller's proof of delivery or transport document.

9. **Inspection(s)**—Pay for the costs of pre-shipment inspection except inspections required by the country of export.

10. **Other**—Pay all costs associated with securing documentation originating in the country of origin or export as required for import. Reimburse seller for costs in providing documentation or assistance. Give the seller instructions regarding carriage.

INCOTERMS

FAS
Free Alongside Ship (. . . named port of shipment)

SELLER ➞　　BUYER ▸▸▸

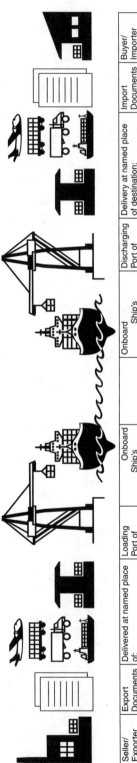

Seller/ Exporter Premises	Export Documents Formalities	Delivered at named place of: Frontier/Terminal/Quay	Loading Port of Shipment	Onboard Ship's Rail	Onboard Ship's Rail	Discharging Port of Arrival	Delivery at named place of destination: Frontier/Terminal/Quay	Import Documents Formalities	Buyer/ Importer Premises
SELLER'S RISKS								**BUYER'S RISKS**	
SELLER'S COSTS								**BUYER'S COSTS**	

FAS, Free Alongside Ship (...named port of shipment)

In Free Alongside Ship, the seller/exporter/manufacturer clears the goods for export and then places them alongside the vessel at the "named port of shipment." [The seller's clearing the goods for export is new to Incoterms 2000.] The parties to the transaction, however, may stipulate in their contract of sale that the buyer will clear the goods for export.

The Free Alongside Ship term is used only for ocean or inland waterway transport.

The "named place" in Free Alongside Ship and all "F" terms is domestic to the seller.

The Free Alongside Ship term is commonly used in the sale of bulk commodity cargo such as oil, grains, and ore.

Normal payment terms for Free Carrier transactions are generally cash in advance and open account, but letters of credit are also used.

Examples
FAS Free Alongside Ship Port Elizabeth South Africa
FAS Free Alongside Ship Le Havre France

FAS
Free Alongside Ship (... named port of shipment)

Incoterm Category

FAS is an "F" Incoterm where the seller/exporter delivers the goods, non-export cleared, alongside a ship, and does not bear risk or costs once the goods have been handed over.

Modes of Transport Covered

Used only for ocean or inland waterway transport.

Seller's Responsibilities (summary)

1. **Goods**—Provide the goods, commercial invoice or electronic message, and other documentation as required by the sales contract.

2. **Licenses and Customs Formalities**—Obtain at own risk and cost any export licenses and authorizations and carry out all export formalities and procedures.

3. **Carriage and Insurance**—The seller has no obligation to the buyer to provide carriage of goods or insurance.

4. **Delivery**—Deliver the goods on the quay alongside the named vessel at the named place and at the time stipulated in the sales contract.

5. **Risk Transfer**—Assume all risks of loss or damage to the goods until they have been delivered to the port at the named place and time as provided in the sales contract.

6. **Costs**—Pay all costs until the goods have been delivered alongside the named vessel and all costs related to export formalities.

7. **Notice to the Buyer**—Provide sufficient notice to the buyer that the goods have been delivered alongside the named vessel.

8. **Proof of Delivery, Transport Documents**—Provide the buyer with a proof of delivery (to the carrier) or a transport document, or to assist the buyer in obtaining a transport document.

9. **Checking, Packing, Marking**—Pay all costs associated with checking the quality and quantity of the goods to be in conformity with the sales contract. Provide appropriate packing (unless the goods are traditionally delivered unpackaged) as required for the transport of the goods, to the extent that the buyer has made transport circumstances known to the seller prior to the execution of the sales contract. Provide marking appropriate to the packaging.

10. **Other**—Provide the buyer at the buyer's request, risk and expense any and all assistance in securing documentation originating in the country of export or of origin required for import and transshipment through another country. Provide the buyer at the buyer's request information necessary to obtain insurance.

Buyer's Responsibilities (summary)

1. **Payment**—Pay for the goods as provided in the sales contract.

2. **Licenses and Customs Formalities**—Obtain at own risk and cost any import licenses and authorizations and carry out all import formalities.

3. **Carriage and Insurance**—Provide for contract of carriage from the named port of shipment. No obligation for insurance.

4. **Taking Delivery**—Take delivery of the goods as provided in the sales contract.

5. **Risk Transfer**—Assume all risk of loss or damage from the time the goods have been delivered alongside the ship as provided in the sales contract.

6. **Costs**—Pay all costs for carriage and insurance from the time the goods have been delivered alongside the vessel in accordance with the terms of the sales contract. Pay all costs resulting from failure of the named ship to arrive on time or to be able to take the goods. Pay all costs relating import formalities including duties, taxes and other charges including transshipment.

7. **Notice to Seller**—Give sufficient notice to the seller of the name of the vessel, the time or period for delivery and the place of delivery.

8. **Proof of Delivery, Transport Document**—Accept the seller's proof of delivery or transport document.

9. **Inspection(s)**—Pay for the costs of pre-shipment inspection except inspections required by the country of export.

10. **Other**—Pay all costs associated with securing documentation originating in the country of origin or export as required for import formalities. Reimburse seller for seller's costs in providing such documentation or assistance. Also, to give the seller instructions regarding contract for carriage.

INCOTERMS

INCOTERMS

FOB
Free On Board (. . . named port of shipment)

Seller/ Exporter Premises	Export Documents Formalities	Delivered at named place of: Frontier/Terminal/Quay	Loading Port of Shipment	Onboard Ship's Rail	Onboard Ship's Rail	Discharging Port of Arrival	Delivery at named place of destination: Frontier/Terminal/Quay	Import Documents Formalities	Buyer/ Importer Premises
SELLER'S RISKS								**BUYER'S RISKS**	
SELLER'S COSTS								**BUYER'S COSTS**	

SELLER →   BUYER

FOB, Free On Board (...named port of shipment)

In Free On Board, the seller/exporter/manufacturer clears the goods for export and is responsible for the costs and risks of delivering the goods past the ship's rail at the named port of shipment.

The Free On Board term is used only for ocean or inland waterway transport.

The "named place" in Free On Board and all "F" terms is domestic to the seller.

Normal payment terms for Free On Board transactions include cash in advance, open account, and letters of credit.

The Free On Board term is commonly used in the sale of bulk commodity cargo such as oil, grains, and ore where passing the ship's rail is important. However, it is also commonly used in shipping container loads of other goods.

The key document in FOB transactions is the "On Board Bill of Lading."

Sellers and buyers often confuse the Free On Board term with Free Carrier. Free On Board (FOB) does not mean loading the goods onto a truck at the seller's place of business. Free On Board is used only in reference to delivering the goods past a ship's rail in ocean or inland waterway transport. Free Carrier, on the other hand, is applicable to all modes of transport.

Examples

FOB Free on Board "Vessel ABC" Buenos Aires Argentina

FOB Free on Board Gdansk Poland

FOB
Free on Board (. . . named port of shipment)

Incoterm Category
FOB is an "F" Incoterm where the seller/exporter is responsible for delivering the goods, export cleared, on board a ship, and does not bear risk or costs afterwards.

Modes of Transport Covered
Used only for ocean or inland waterway transport.

Seller's Responsibilities (summary)
1. **Goods**—Provide the goods, commercial invoice or electronic message, and other documentation as required by the sales contract.
2. **Licenses and Customs Formalities**—Obtain at own risk and cost any export licenses and authorizations and carry out all export formalities and procedures.
3. **Carriage and Insurance**—The seller has no obligation to the buyer to provide carriage of goods or insurance.
4. **Delivery**—Deliver the goods on board the named vessel at the named port and place and at the time stipulated in the sales contract.
5. **Risk Transfer**—Assume all risks of loss or damage to the goods until they have passed the ship's rail on the named vessel as provided in the sales contract.
6. **Costs**—Pay all costs until the goods have passed the ship's rail on the named vessel as well as all costs relating to export including duties, taxes and customs formalities.
7. **Notice to the Buyer**—Provide sufficient notice to the buyer that the goods have been delivered on board the named vessel.
8. **Proof of Delivery, Transport Documents**—Provide the buyer with a proof of delivery or a transport document, or to assist the buyer in obtaining a transport document.
9. **Checking, Packing, Marking**—Pay all costs associated with checking the quality and quantity of the goods to be in conformity with the sales contract. Provide appropriate packing (unless the goods are traditionally delivered unpackaged) as required for the transport of the goods, to the extent that the buyer has made transport circumstances known to the seller prior to the execution of the sales contract. Provide marking appropriate to the packaging.
10. **Other**—Provide the buyer at the buyer's request, risk and expense any and all assistance in securing documentation originating in the country of export or of origin required for import and transshipment through another country. Provide the buyer at the buyer's request information necessary to obtain insurance.

5. **Risk Transfer**—Assume all risks of loss or damage from the time the goods have passed the ship's rail at the port of shipment.
6. **Costs**—Pay all costs for carriage and insurance from the time the goods have passed the ship's rail at the port of shipment in accordance with the terms of the sales contract. Pay all costs resulting from failure of the named ship to arrive on time or to be able to take the goods. Pay all costs relating to import formalities including duties, taxes and other charges including transshipment.
7. **Notice to Seller**—Give sufficient notice to the seller of the name of the vessel, the time or period for delivery and the place of delivery.
8. **Proof of Delivery, Transport Document**—Accept the seller's proof of delivery or transport document.
9. **Inspection(s)**—Pay for the costs of pre-shipment inspection except inspections required by the country of export.
10. **Other**—Pay all costs associated with securing documentation originating in the country of origin or export as required for import. Reimburse seller for seller's costs in providing such documentation or assistance.

Buyer's Responsibilities (summary)
1. **Payment**—Pay for the goods as provided in the sales contract.
2. **Licenses and Customs Formalities**—Obtain at own risk and cost any import licenses and authorizations and carry out all import formalities.
3. **Carriage and Insurance**—Provide for contract of carriage from the named port of shipment. No obligation for insurance.
4. **Taking Delivery**—Take delivery of the goods as provided in the sales contract.

INCOTERMS

INCOTERMS

CFR
Cost and Freight (. . . named port of destination)

SELLER   BUYER

Seller/ Exporter Premises	Export Documents Formalities	Delivered at named place of: Frontier/Terminal/Quay	Loading Port of Shipment	Onboard Ship's Rail	Onboard Ship's Rail	Discharging at Port of Arrival	Delivery at named place of destination: Frontier/Terminal/Quay	Import Documents Formalities	Buyer/ Importer Premises
SELLER'S RISKS								BUYER'S RISKS	
SELLER'S COSTS				SELLERS INSURABLE INTEREST*				BUYER'S COSTS	

CFR Cost and Freight (...named port of destination)

In Cost and Freight, the seller/exporter/manufacturer clears the goods for export and is responsible for delivering the goods past the ship's rail at the port of shipment (not destination).

The seller is also responsible for paying for the costs associated with transport of the goods to the named port of destination. However, once the goods pass the ship's rail at the port of shipment, the buyer assumes responsibility for risk of loss or damage as well as any additional transport costs.

The Cost and Freight term is used only for ocean or inland waterway transport. The "named port of destination" in Cost and Freight and all "C" terms is domestic to the buyer.

Normal payment terms for Cost and Freight transactions include cash in advance, open account, and letters of credit.

The Cost and Freight term is commonly used in the sale of oversize and over-weight cargo that will not fit into an ocean freight container or exceeds weight limitations of such containers. The term is also used for LCL (less than container load) cargo and for the shipment of goods by rail in boxcars to the ocean carrier.

*Insurance Note
While the seller may not be legally responsible for the goods once they pass the ship's rail in the port of shipment, he may have "insurable interest" during the voyage. Prudence may dictate purchase of additional insurance coverage.

Examples
CIF Cost and Freight Port-au-Prince Haiti
CIF Cost and Freight Bombay India

CFR
Cost and Freight (. . . named port of destination)

Incoterm Category

CFR is a "C" Incoterm where the seller is responsible for contracting and paying for carriage of the goods, but not responsible for additional costs or risk of loss or damage to the goods once they have been shipped. C terms evidence "shipment" (as opposed to "arrival") contracts.

Modes of Transport Covered

Used only for ocean or inland waterway transport.

Seller's Responsibilities (summary)

1. **Goods**—Provide the goods, commercial invoice or electronic message, and other documentation as required by the sales contract.

2. **Licenses and Customs Formalities**—Obtain at own risk and cost any export licenses and authorizations and carry out all export formalities and procedures.

3. **Carriage and Insurance**—Contract for and pay all costs of carriage by sea vessel to the named port of destination. No obligation to provide insurance.

4. **Delivery**—Deliver the goods on board the named vessel at the named port and on the date or within the time period stipulated in the sales contract.

5. **Risk Transfer**—Assume all risks of loss or damage to the goods until they have passed over the ship's rail at the port of shipment.

6. **Costs**—Pay all costs until the goods have been delivered to the named port of shipment and passed over the ship's rail plus costs of loading, carriage to the port of destination and normal un-

loading. Also to pay all costs relating to export including duties, taxes and customs formalities.

7. **Notice to the Buyer**—Provide sufficient notice to the buyer that the goods have been delivered on board the named vessel.

8. **Proof of Delivery, Transport Documents**—Provide the buyer with a transport document that will allow the buyer to claim the goods at the destination and (unless otherwise agreed) allow the buyer to sell the goods while in transit through the transfer of the transport document or by notification to the sea carrier.

9. **Checking, Packing, Marking**—Pay all costs associated with checking the quality and quantity of the goods to be in conformity with the sales contract. Provide appropriate packing (unless the goods are traditionally delivered unpackaged) as required for the transport of the goods, to the extent that the buyer has made transport circumstances known to the seller prior to the execution of the sales contract. Provide marking appropriate to the packaging.

10. **Other**—Provide the buyer at the buyer's request, risk and expense any and all assistance in securing documentation originating in the country of export or of origin required for import and transshipment (as necessary). Provide the buyer at the buyer's request information necessary to obtain insurance.

Buyer's Responsibilities (summary)

1. **Payment**—Pay for the goods as provided in the sales contract.

2. **Licenses and Customs Formalities**—Obtain and pay costs of all import licenses and authorizations and carry out all import formalities.

3. **Carriage and Insurance**—No obligation to the seller.

4. **Taking Delivery**—Take delivery of the goods at the port of destination as provided in the sales contract.

5. **Risk Transfer**—Assume all risk of loss or damage from the time the goods have passed over the ship's rail at the port of shipment.

6. **Costs**—Pay all additional costs for the goods once they have passed over the ship's rail at the port of shipment, including unloading, lighterage and wharfage at the port of destination. Pay all costs relating to import formalities including duties, taxes and other charges including transshipment.

7. **Notice to Seller**—If, according to the sales contract, the buyer is able to specify a time for shipping and/or specify a port of destination, to give the seller sufficient notice.

8. **Proof of Delivery, Transport Document**—Accept the seller's transport document so long as it is in conformity with the sales contract.

9. **Inspection(s)**—Pay for the costs of pre-shipment inspection except inspections required by the country of export.

10. **Other**—Pay all costs of securing documentation from the country of origin or export as required for import. Reimburse seller for costs in providing such documentation or assistance.

CIF
Cost, Insurance and Freight (... named port of destination)

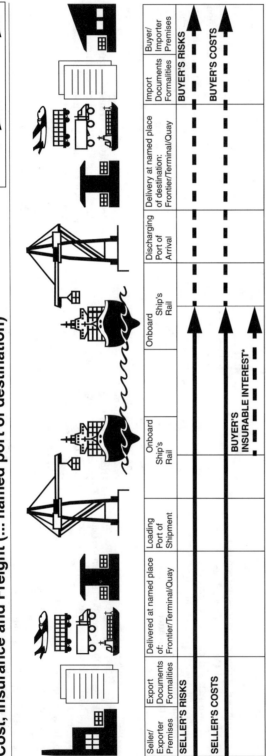

	SELLER	BUYER

Seller/ Exporter Premises	Export Documents Formalities	Delivered at named place of: Frontier/Terminal/Quay	Loading Port of Shipment	Onboard Ship's Rail	Onboard Ship's Rail	Discharging Port of Arrival	Delivery at named place of destination: Frontier/Terminal/Quay	Import Documents Formalities	Buyer/ Importer Premises
SELLER'S RISKS						**BUYER'S RISKS**			
SELLER'S COSTS						**BUYER'S COSTS**			
				BUYER'S INSURABLE INTEREST*					

CIF Cost, Insurance and Freight (...named port of destination)

In Cost, Insurance and Freight, the seller/exporter/manufacturer clears the goods for export and is responsible for delivering the goods past the ship's rail at the port of shipment (not destination).

The seller is responsible for paying for the costs associated with transport of the goods to the named port of destination. However, once the goods pass the ship's rail at the port of shipment, the buyer assumes responsibility for risk of loss or damage as well as any additional transport costs.

The seller is also responsible for procuring and paying for marine insurance in the buyer's name for the shipment.

The Cost and Freight term is used only for ocean or inland waterway transport.

The "named port of destination" in Cost and Freight and all "C" terms is domestic to the buyer.

Normal payment terms for Cost and Freight transactions include cash in advance, open account, and letters of credit.

*Insurance Note
While the seller is responsible for procuring and paying for insurance cover during the voyage to the named port of destination, the buyer may exercise prudence and purchase additional insurance coverage.

Examples
CIF Cost Insurance and Freight Hong Kong
CIF Cost, Insurance and Freight Port of New York

CIF
Cost, Insurance and Freight (. . . named port of destination)

Incoterm Category

CIF is a "C" Incoterm where the seller is responsible for contracting and paying for carriage and insurance of the goods, but not responsible for additional costs or risk of loss or damage to the goods once they have been shipped. C terms evidence "shipment" (as opposed to "arrival") contracts.

Modes of Transport Covered

Used only for ocean or inland waterway transport.

Seller's Responsibilities (summary)

1. **Goods**—Provide the goods, commercial invoice or electronic message, and other documentation as required by the sales contract.
2. **Licenses and Customs Formalities**—Obtain at own risk and cost any export licenses and authorizations and carry out all export formalities and procedures.
3. **Carriage and Insurance**—Contract for and pay costs of carriage by sea or inland waterway and insurance for 110 percent of the value of the contract to the named port of destination. The insurance policy must allow the buyer to make claim directly from the insurer. Deliver the insurance document to the buyer.
4. **Delivery**—Deliver the goods on board the named vessel at the named port and at the date or within the time period stipulated in the sales contract.
5. **Risk Transfer**—Assume all risks of loss or damage to the goods until they have passed over the ship's rail at the port of shipment.
6. **Costs**—Pay all costs of carriage and insurance until the goods have been delivered to the named port of shipment and passed over the ship's rail, plus costs of loading, carriage to the port of destination and normal unloading. Also to pay all costs relating to export including duties, taxes and customs formalities.
7. **Notice to the Buyer**—Provide sufficient notice to the buyer that the goods have been delivered on board the named vessel.
8. **Proof of Delivery, Transport Documents**—Provide the buyer with a transport document that will allow the buyer to claim the goods at the destination and (unless otherwise agreed) allow the buyer to sell the goods while in transit through the transfer of the transport document or by notification to the sea carrier.
9. **Checking, Packing, Marking**—Pay all costs associated with checking the quality and quantity of the goods to be in conformity with the sales contract. Provide appropriate packing (unless the goods are traditionally delivered unpackaged) as required for the transport of the goods, to the extent that the buyer has made transport circumstances known to the seller prior to the execution of the sales contract. Provide marking appropriate to the packaging.
10. **Other**—Provide the buyer at the buyer's request, risk and cost any and all assistance in securing documentation originating in the country of export or of origin required for import and for transshipment.

Buyer's Responsibilities (summary)

1. **Payment**—Pay for the goods as provided in the sales contract.
2. **Licenses and Customs Formalities**—Obtain and pay costs of all import licenses and authorizations and carry out all import formalities.
3. **Carriage and Insurance**—No obligation to the seller to pay for carriage or insurance.
4. **Taking Delivery**—Take delivery of the goods at the port of destination as provided in the sales contract.
5. **Risk Transfer**—Assume all risk of loss or damage from the time the goods have passed over the ship's rail at the port of shipment.
6. **Costs**—Pay all supplemental costs for the goods once they have passed over the ship's rail at the port of shipment, including unloading, lighterage and wharfage at the port of destination. Pay all costs relating to import formalities including duties, taxes and other charges including transshipment.
7. **Notice to Seller**—If, according to the sales contract, the buyer is able to specify a time for shipping and/or specify a port of destination, to give the seller sufficient notice.
8. **Proof of Delivery, Transport Document**—Accept the seller's transport document so long as it is in conformity with the sales contract.
9. **Inspection(s)**—Pay for the costs of pre-shipment inspection except inspections required by the country of export.
10. **Other**—Pay costs of securing documentation from the country of origin or export as required for import. Reimburse seller such costs. Provide information necessary to obtain insurance.

INCOTERMS

INCOTERMS

CPT
Carriage Paid To (. . . named place of destination)

SELLER ➤   BUYER ➤ (dashed)

Seller/Exporter Premises	Export Documents Formalities	Delivered at named place of: Frontier/Terminal/Quay	Loading Port of Shipment	Onboard Ship's Rail	Onboard Ship's Rail	Discharging Port of Arrival	Delivery at named place of destination: Frontier/Terminal/Quay	Import Documents Formalities	Buyer/Importer Premises
SELLER'S RISKS			BUYER'S RISKS						
SELLER'S COSTS				BUYER'S COSTS					
			BUYER'S and SELLER'S INSURABLE INTEREST*						

CPT Carriage Paid To (...named place of destination)

In Carriage Paid To, the seller/exporter/manufacturer clears the goods for export, delivers them to the carrier, and is responsible for paying for carriage to the named place of destination. However, once the seller delivers the goods to the carrier, the buyer becomes responsible for all additional costs.

In Incoterms 2000 the seller is also responsible for the costs of unloading, customs clearance, duties, and other costs if such costs are included in the cost of carriage such as in small package courier delivery.

The seller is not responsible for procuring and paying for insurance cover.

The CPT term is valid for any form of transport including multimodal.

The "named place of destination" in CPT and all "C" terms is domestic to the buyer, but is not necessarily the final delivery point.

The Carriage Paid To term is often used in sales where the shipment is by air freight, containerized ocean freight, courier shipments of small parcels, and in "ro-ro" (roll-on, roll-off) shipments of motor vehicles.

A "carrier" can be a shipping line, airline, trucking firm, railway or also an individual or firm who undertakes to procure carriage by any of the above methods of transport including multimodal. Therefore, a person, such as a freight forwarder, can act as a "carrier" under this term.

If subsequent carriers are used for the carriage to the agreed destination, the risk passes when the goods have been delivered to the first carrier.

*Insurance Note
While neither the buyer nor seller have obligation for providing insurance during the main voyage, both may have "insurable interest" and prudence may dictate purchase of insurance coverage.

CPT
Carriage Paid To (. . . named place of destination)

Incoterm Category
CPT is a "C" Incoterm where the seller is responsible for contracting and paying for carriage of the goods, but not responsible for additional costs or risk of loss or damage to the goods once they have been shipped. C terms evidence "shipment" (as opposed to "arrival") contracts.

Modes of Transport Covered
All modes of transport including multimodal.

Seller's Responsibilities (summary)
1. **Goods**—Provide the goods, commercial invoice or electronic message, and other documentation as required by the sales contract.
2. **Licenses and Customs Formalities**—Obtain at own risk and cost any export licenses and authorizations and carry out all export formalities and procedures.
3. **Carriage and Insurance**—Contract for and pay all costs of carriage to the agreed point at the named place of destination. No obligation to provide insurance.
4. **Delivery**—Deliver the goods to the carrier (or first of multiple carriers) for carriage to the named place of destination within the time period stipulated in the sales contract.
5. **Risk Transfer**—Assume all risks of loss or damage to the goods until they have been delivered to the carrier or first of multiple carriers.
6. **Costs**—Pay all costs until the goods have been delivered to the carrier plus costs of loading, carriage to the place of destination and normal unloading. Also to pay all costs related to ex-

port including duties, taxes and customs formalities. Pay the costs of unloading, customs clearance, duties, and other costs if such costs are included in the cost of carriage.
7. **Notice to the Buyer**—Provide sufficient notice to the buyer that the goods have been delivered to the carrier.
8. **Proof of Delivery, Transport Documents**—Provide the buyer with a transport document.
9. **Checking, Packing, Marking**—Pay all costs associated with checking the quality and quantity of the goods to be in conformity with the sales contract. Provide appropriate packing (unless the goods are traditionally delivered unpackaged) as required for the transport of the goods, to the extent that the buyer has made transport circumstances known to the seller prior to the execution of the sales contract. Provide marking appropriate to the packaging.
10. **Other**—Provide the buyer at the buyer's request, risk and expense any and all assistance in securing documentation originating in the country of export or of origin required for import and for transshipment (as necessary). Provide the buyer at the buyer's request information necessary to obtain insurance.

Buyer's Responsibilities (summary)
1. **Payment**—Pay for the goods as provided in the sales contract.
2. **Licenses and Customs Formalities**—Obtain and pay costs of all import licenses and authorizations and carry out all import formalities.

3. **Carriage and Insurance**—No obligation to the seller for either carriage or insurance.
4. **Taking Delivery**—Take delivery of the goods from the carrier at the place of destination as provided in the sales contract.
5. **Risk Transfer**—Assume all risk of loss or damage from the time the goods have been delivered to the carrier by the seller.
6. **Costs**—Pay all additional costs (not covered in the seller's contract of carriage in Seller's #6) for the goods once they have been delivered to the carrier, including unloading, lighterage and wharfage at the place of destination. Pay all costs relating to import formalities including duties, taxes and other charges including transshipment.
7. **Notice to Seller**—If, according to the sales contract, the buyer is able to specify a time for shipping and/or specify a place of destination, to give the seller sufficient notice.
8. **Proof of Delivery, Transport Document**—Accept the seller's transport document so long as it is in conformity with the sales contract.
9. **Inspection(s)**—Pay for the costs of pre-shipment inspection(s) except inspections required by the country of export.
10. **Other**—Pay all costs associated with securing documentation from the country of origin or export as required for import. Reimburse seller for costs in providing such documentation or assistance.

INCOTERMS

INCOTERMS

CIP
Carriage and Insurance Paid To (... named place of destination)

	Seller/ Exporter Premises	Export Documents Formalities	Delivered at named place of: Frontier/Terminal/Quay	Loading Port of Shipment	Onboard Ship's Rail	Onboard Ship's Rail	Discharging Port of Arrival	Delivery at named place of destination: Frontier/Terminal/Quay	Import Documents Formalities	Buyer/ Importer Premises
SELLER'S RISKS									BUYER'S RISKS	
SELLER'S COSTS									BUYER'S COSTS	
					BUYER'S INSURABLE INTEREST*					

CIP Carriage and Insurance Paid To (...named place of destination)

In Carriage and Insurance Paid To, the seller/exporter clears the goods for export, delivers them to the carrier, and is responsible for paying for carriage and insurance to the named place of destination. However, once the goods are delivered to the carrier, the buyer is responsible for all additional costs.

In Incoterms 2000 the seller is also responsible for the costs of unloading, customs clearance, duties, and other costs if such costs are included in the cost of carriage such as in small package courier delivery.

The seller is responsible for procuring and paying for insurance cover.

The CIP term is valid for any form of transport including multimodal.

The "named place of destination" in CIP and all "C" terms is domestic to the buyer, but is not necessarily the final delivery point.

The Carriage and Insurance Paid To term is often used in sales where the shipment is by air freight, containerized ocean freight, courier shipments of small parcels, and in "ro-ro" (roll-on, roll-off) shipments of motor vehicles.

A "carrier" can be a shipping line, airline, trucking firm, railway or also an individual or firm who undertakes to procure carriage by any of the above methods of transport including multimodal. Therefore, a person, such as a freight forwarder, can act as a "carrier" under this term.

If subsequent carriers are used for the carriage to the agreed destination, the risk passes when the goods have been delivered to the first carrier.

*Insurance Note
While the seller is responsible for insurance coverage during the main voyage, the buyer may have additional "insurable interest" and prudence may dictate purchase of additional coverage.

CIP
Carriage and Insurance Paid To (. . . named place of destination)

Incoterm Category

CIP is a "C" Incoterm where the seller is responsible for contracting and paying for carriage and insurance of the goods, but not responsible for additional costs or risk of loss or damage to the goods once they have been shipped. C terms evidence "shipment" (as opposed to "arrival") contracts.

Modes of Transport Covered

All modes of transport including multimodal.

Seller's Responsibilities (summary)

1. **Goods**—Provide the goods, commercial invoice or electronic message, and other documentation as required by the sales contract.
2. **Licenses and Customs Formalities**—Obtain at own risk and cost any export licenses and authorizations and carry out all export formalities and procedures.
3. **Carriage and Insurance**—Contract for and pay all costs of carriage and insurance to the named place of destination. The insurance policy or document must allow the buyer to make a claim directly from the insurer. Deliver the insurance document to the buyer.
4. **Delivery**—Deliver the goods to the carrier (or first of multiple carriers) for carriage to the named place of destination within the time period stipulated in the sales contract.
5. **Risk Transfer**—Assume all risks of loss or damage to the goods until they have been delivered to the carrier or first of multiple carriers.
6. **Costs**—Pay all costs until the goods have been delivered to the carrier, plus costs of loading, carriage, insurance to the named place of destination plus normal unloading. Also to pay all costs relating to export including duties, taxes and customs formalities. Pay the costs of unloading, customs clearance, duties, and other costs if such costs are included in the cost of carriage.
7. **Notice to the Buyer**—Provide sufficient notice to the buyer that the goods have been delivered to the carrier.
8. **Proof of Delivery, Transport Documents**—Provide the buyer with a transport document.
9. **Checking, Packing, Marking**—Pay all costs associated with checking the quality and quantity of the goods to be in conformity with the sales contract. Provide appropriate packing (unless the goods are traditionally delivered unpackaged) as required for the transport of the goods, to the extent that the buyer has made transport circumstances known to the seller prior to the execution of the sales contract. Provide appropriate marking to the packaging.
10. **Other**—Provide the buyer at the buyer's request, risk and expense any and all assistance in securing documentation originating in the country of export or of origin required for import and for transshipment (as necessary). Provide the buyer with information necessary to procure additional insurance.

Buyer's Responsibilities (summary)

1. **Payment**—Pay for the goods as provided in the sales contract.
2. **Licenses and Customs Formalities**—Obtain and pay costs of all import licenses and authorizations and carry out all import formalities.
3. **Carriage and Insurance**—No obligation to the seller for either carriage or insurance.
4. **Taking Delivery**—Take delivery of the goods from the carrier at the place of destination as provided in the sales contract.
5. **Risk Transfer**—Assume all risk of loss or damage from the time the goods have been delivered to the carrier by the seller.
6. **Costs**—Pay all additional costs (not covered in the seller's contract of carriage in Seller's #6) for the goods once they have been delivered to the carrier, including unloading, lighterage and wharfage at the place of destination. Pay all costs relating to import formalities including duties, taxes and other charges including transshipment.
7. **Notice to Seller**—If, according to the sales contract, the buyer is able to specify a time for shipping and/or specify a place of destination, to give the seller sufficient notice.
8. **Proof of Delivery, Transport Document**—Accept the seller's transport document so long as it is in conformity with the sales contract.
9. **Inspection(s)**—Pay for the costs of pre-shipment inspection(s) except inspections required by the country of export.
10. **Other**—Pay all costs associated with securing documentation from the country of origin or export required for import. Reimburse seller for costs in providing such documentation or assistance.

INCOTERMS

INCOTERMS

DAF
Delivered At Frontier (. . . named place)

SELLER ➤
BUYER ▪▪▶

Seller/Exporter Premises	Export Documents Formalities	Delivered at named place of: Frontier/Terminal/Quay	Loading Port of Shipment	Onboard Ship's Rail	Onboard Ship's Rail	Discharging Port of Arrival	Delivery at named place of destination: Frontier/Terminal/Quay	Import Documents Formalities	Buyer/Importer Premises
EXAMPLE 1 SELLER'S RISKS				NOT APPLICABLE			EXAMPLE 1 BUYER'S RISKS		
EXAMPLE 1 SELLER'S COSTS				NOT APPLICABLE			EXAMPLE 1 BUYER'S COSTS		
EXAMPLE 2 SELLER'S RISKS							EXAMPLE 2 BUYER'S RISKS		
EXAMPLE 2 SELLER'S COSTS							EXAMPLE 2 BUYER'S COSTS		

DAF Delivered At Frontier (...named place)

In Delivered At Frontier, the seller/exporter/manufacturer clears the goods for export and is responsible for making them available to the buyer at the named point and place at the frontier, not unloaded, and not cleared for import. In the DAF term, naming the precise point, place, and time of availability at the frontier is very important as the buyer must make arrangements to unload and secure the goods in a timely manner.

Frontier can mean any frontier including the frontier of export.

The DAF term is valid for any mode of shipment, so long as the final shipment to the named place at the frontier is by land.

The seller is not responsible for procuring and paying for insurance cover.

Example 1

DAF Laredo, Texas. Seller is in Dallas, Texas, buyer is in Mexico City, Mexico. The shipment travels by truck from Dallas to the frontier at Laredo, Texas USA where the buyer takes possession and trucks the goods to Mexico City.

Example 2

DAF Basel Switzerland. Seller is in Dallas, Texas, buyer is in Bern Switzerland. The shipment travels by truck from Dallas to Port Arthur, by ship to Le Havre, France and then by rail to the frontier in Basel where the buyer takes possession and transports the goods to the city of Bern.

DAF
Delivered at Frontier (. . . named place)

Incoterm Category

DAF is a "D" Incoterm where the seller is responsible for all costs associated with delivering the goods to the named point and place of destination. "D" terms evidence "arrival" (as opposed to "shipment") contracts.

Modes of Transport Covered

Used for all modes of transport so long as the final shipment to the named place at the frontier is by land.

Seller's Responsibilities (summary)

1. **Goods**—Provide the goods, commercial invoice or electronic message, and other documentation as required by the sales contract.
2. **Licenses and Customs Formalities**—a) Obtain at own risk and cost any export licenses and authorizations required to enable the buyer to deal with export formalities at the named frontier. And, if transshipped, b) Carry out all export formalities and procedures required to bring the goods to the named frontier.
3. **Carriage and Insurance**—Contract for and pay all costs of carriage and transshipment (if necessary) to the named place. No obligation to provide insurance.
4. **Delivery**—Make the goods available to the buyer unloaded at the frontier at the named point and place and on the date or period specified in the sales contract.
5. **Risk Transfer**—Assume all risks of loss or damage to the goods until they have been made available to the buyer at the named point place and time at the frontier.

6. **Costs**—Pay all costs until the goods have been delivered at the frontier, including carriage, and all prior to delivery export formalities.
7. **Notice to the Buyer**—Provide sufficient notice of dispatch and projected arrival that the buyer can take appropriate action to arrange pick-up of the goods.
8. **Proof of Delivery, Transport Documents**—Provide the buyer with documentary evidence of delivery at the frontier. At the buyer's request, risk and cost, provide a through document of transport to the named place of destination.
9. **Checking, Packing, Marking**—Pay all costs associated with checking the quality and quantity of the goods to be in conformity with the sales contract. Provide appropriate packing (unless the goods are traditionally delivered unpackaged) as required for the transport of the goods, to the extent that the buyer has made transport circumstances known to the seller prior to the execution of the sales contract. Provide marking appropriate to the packaging.
10. **Other**—Provide the buyer at the buyer's request, risk and expense any and all assistance in securing documentation originating in the country of export or of origin required for import. Provide the buyer with information necessary to obtain insurance.

Buyer's Responsibilities (summary)

1. **Payment**—Pay for the goods as provided in the sales contract.
2. **Licenses and Customs Formalities**—Obtain

and pay costs of all import licenses and authorizations and carry out all import formalities.
3. **Carriage and Insurance**—No obligation to the seller for either carriage or insurance.
4. **Taking Delivery**—Take delivery of the goods once they are made available at the frontier.
5. **Risk Transfer**—Assume all risk of loss or damage from the time the goods have been delivered at the named point, place and time at the frontier.
6. **Costs**—Pay all costs for the goods once they have been delivered to the frontier including unloading. Pay all costs relating to import formalities including duties, taxes and formalities. Pay for transport from the frontier to the final destination.
7. **Notice to Seller**—If, according to the sales contract, the buyer is able to specify a time for and/or a place of delivery, to give the seller sufficient notice.
8. **Proof of Delivery, Transport Document**—Accept the seller's transport document so long as it is in conformity with the sales contract.
9. **Inspection(s)**—Pay for the costs of pre-shipment inspection(s) except inspections required by the country of export.
10. **Other**—Pay all costs associated with securing documentation from the country of origin or export required for import. Reimburse seller for costs in providing such documentation or assistance. Provide the seller with any authorizations, permits, documents or other information required for obtaining a through transport document.

INCOTERMS

DES
Delivered Ex Ship (. . . named port of destination)

Seller/ Exporter Premises	Export Documents Formalities	Delivered at named place of: Frontier/Terminal/Quay	Loading Port of Shipment	Onboard Ship's Rail	Onboard Ship's Rail	Discharging Port of Arrival	Delivery at named place of destination: Frontier/Terminal/Quay	Import Documents Formalities	Buyer/ Importer Premises
SELLER'S RISKS							**BUYER'S RISKS**		
SELLER'S COSTS							**BUYER'S COSTS**		

DES Delivered Ex Ship (...named port of destination)

In Delivered Ex Ship, the seller/exporter/manufacturer clears the goods for export and is responsible for making them available to the buyer on board the ship at the named port of destination, not cleared for import.

The seller is thus responsible for all costs of getting the goods to the named port of destination prior to unloading.

The DES term is used only for shipments of goods by ocean or inland waterway or by multimodal transport where the final delivery is made on a vessel at the named port of destination.

All forms of payment are used in DES transactions.

Examples
DES Delivered Ex Ship Port of Calcutta
DES Delivered Ex Ship Port of New York

DES
Delivered Ex Ship (. . . named port of destination)

Incoterm Category

DES is a "D" Incoterm where the seller is responsible for all costs associated with delivering the goods to the named port of destination. "D" terms evidence "arrival" (as opposed to "shipment") contracts.

Modes of Transport Covered

Used only for ocean or inland waterway transport.

Seller's Responsibilities (summary)

1. **Goods**—Provide the goods, commercial invoice or electronic message, and other documentation as required by the sales contract.

2. **Licenses and Customs Formalities**—Obtain at own risk and cost any export licenses and authorizations and carry out all export formalities and procedures, including those associated with transshipment to the named port of destination.

3. **Carriage and Insurance**—Contract for and pay all costs of carriage and transshipment (if necessary) to the named place and port of destination. No obligation to provide insurance.

4. **Delivery**—Make the goods available to the buyer uncleared for import on board the vessel at the named place and port on the date or within the time period specified in the sales contract.

5. **Risk Transfer**—Assume all risks of loss or damage to the goods until they have been made available to the buyer at the named place and port.

6. **Costs**—Pay all costs until the goods have been delivered, including all export formalities, carriage and transshipment (if necessary) to the named place and port.

7. **Notice to the Buyer**—Provide sufficient notice of dispatch and projected arrival that the buyer can take appropriate action to arrange pick-up of the goods.

8. **Proof of Delivery, Transport Documents**—Provide the buyer with the delivery order and/or a transport document enabling the buyer to take delivery of the goods at the port of destination.

9. **Checking, Packing, Marking**—Pay all costs associated with checking the quality and quantity of the goods to be in conformity with the sales contract. Provide appropriate packing (unless the goods are traditionally delivered unpackaged) as required for the transport of the goods, to the extent that the buyer has made transport circumstances known to the seller prior to the execution of the sales contract. Provide appropriate marking to the packaging.

10. **Other**—Provide the buyer at the buyer's request, risk and expense any and all assistance in securing documentation originating in the country of export or of origin required for import. Provide the buyer with information necessary to obtain insurance.

Buyer's Responsibilities (summary)

1. **Payment**—Pay for the goods as provided in the sales contract.

2. **Licenses and Customs Formalities**—Obtain and pay costs of all import licenses and authorizations and carry out all import formalities.

3. **Carriage and Insurance**—No obligation to the seller for either carriage or insurance.

4. **Taking Delivery**—Take delivery of the goods once they are made available at the port.

5. **Risk Transfer**—Assume all risk of loss or damage from the time the goods have been made available at the port.

6. **Costs**—Pay all costs for the goods once they have been made available at the port including unloading. Pay all costs relating to import formalities including duties, taxes and other charges.

7. **Notice to Seller**—If, according to the sales contract, the buyer is able to specify a time for and/or a place of delivery, to give the seller sufficient notice.

8. **Proof of Delivery, Transport Document**—Accept the seller's transport document so long as it is in conformity with the sales contract.

9. **Inspection(s)**—Pay for the costs of pre-shipment inspection(s) except inspections required by the country of export.

10. **Other**—Pay all costs associated with securing documentation from the country of origin or export required for import. Reimburse seller for costs in providing such documentation or assistance.

INCOTERMS

INCOTERMS

DEQ
Delivered Ex Quay (. . . named port of destination)

SELLER   BUYER

Seller/ Exporter Premises	Export Documents Formalities	Delivered at named place of: Frontier/Terminal/Quay	Loading Port of Shipment	Onboard Ship's Rail	Onboard Ship's Rail	Quay at named place	On-carriage to final destination	Import Documents Formalities	Buyer/ Importer Premises
SELLER'S RISKS							BUYER'S RISKS		
SELLER'S COSTS							BUYER'S COSTS		

DEQ Delivered Ex Quay (...named port of destination)

In Delivered Ex Quay, the seller/exporter/manufacturer clears the goods for export and is responsible for making them available to the buyer on the quay (warf) at the named port of destination, not cleared for import.

The buyer, therefore, assumes all responsibilities for import clearance, duties, and other costs upon import as well as transport to the final destination. This is new for Incoterms 2000.

The DES term is used only for shipments of goods arriving at the port of destination by ocean or by inland waterway.

All forms of payment are used in DEQ transactions.

Examples

DEQ Delivered Ex Quay Alexandria Egypt
DEQ Delivered Ex Quay Stockholm Sweden

DEQ
Delivered Ex Quay (. . . named port of destination)

Incoterm Category

DEQ is a "D" Incoterm where the seller is responsible for all costs associated with delivering the goods to the quay (wharf) at the named port of destination. "D" terms evidence "arrival" (as opposed to "shipment") contracts.

Modes of Transport Covered

Used only for ocean or inland waterway transport.

Seller's Responsibilities (summary)

1. **Goods**—Provide the goods, commercial invoice or electronic message, and other documentation as required by the sales contract.

2. **Licenses and Customs Formalities**—Obtain at own risk and cost any export licenses and authorizations and carry out all export formalities and procedures, including those associated with transshipment to the named port of destination.

3. **Carriage and Insurance**—Contract for and pay all costs of carriage and transshipment (if necessary) to the named place, port and quay (wharf) of destination. No obligation to provide insurance.

4. **Delivery**—Make the goods available to the buyer at the named port and quay on the date or within the period specified in the sales contract.

5. **Risk Transfer**—Assume all risks of loss or damage to the goods until they have been made available to the buyer at the named port and quay (wharf).

6. **Costs**—Pay all costs until the goods have been delivered, including carriage, unloading, all export and import formalities, duties and taxes and transshipment (if necessary) to the named port and quay (wharf).

7. **Notice to the Buyer**—Provide sufficient notice of dispatch and projected arrival that the buyer can take appropriate action to arrange pick-up of the goods.

8. **Transport Documents**—Provide the buyer with the delivery order and/or a transport document enabling the buyer to take possession at the port of destination.

9. **Checking, Packing, Marking**—Pay all costs associated with checking the quality and quantity of the goods to be in conformity with the sales contract. Provide appropriate packing (unless the goods are traditionally delivered unpackaged) as required for the transport of the goods, to the extent that the buyer has made transport circumstances known to the seller prior to the execution of the sales contract. Provide marking appropriate to the packaging.

10. **Other**—Pay all costs associated with securing documentation originating in the country of importation required to for import clearance of the goods. Provide the buyer with information necessary to obtain insurance.

Buyer's Responsibilities (summary)

1. **Payment**—Pay for the goods as provided in the sales contract.

2. **Licenses and Customs Formalities**—Obtain and pay costs of all import licenses and autho-

rizations and carry out all import formalities.

3. **Carriage and Insurance**—No obligation to the seller for either carriage or insurance.

4. **Taking Delivery**—Take delivery of the goods once they are made available at the quay.

5. **Risk Transfer**—Assume all risk of loss or damage from the time the goods have been made available at the quay wharf).

6. **Costs**—Pay all costs for the goods once they have been made available at the quay (wharf).

7. **Notice to Seller**—If, according to the sales contract, the buyer is able to specify a time for and/or a place of delivery, to give the seller sufficient notice.

8. **Proof of Delivery, Transport Document**—Accept the seller's delivery order or transport document so long as it is in conformity with the sales contract.

9. **Inspection(s)**—Pay for the costs of pre-shipment inspection(s) except inspections required by the country of export.

10. **Other**—Pay all costs associated with securing documentation from the country of origin or export required for import. Reimburse seller for costs in providing such documentation or assistance.

INCOTERMS

DDU
Delivered Duty Unpaid (... named place of destination)

SELLER →   BUYER →

Seller/ Exporter Premises	Export Documents Formalities	Delivered at named place of: Frontier/Terminal/Quay	Loading Port of Shipment	Onboard Ship's Rail	Onboard Ship's Rail	Discharging Port of Arrival	Delivery at named place of destination: Frontier/Terminal/Quay	Import Documents Formalities	Buyer/ Importer Premises
SELLER'S RISKS								BUYER'S RISKS	
SELLER'S COSTS								BUYER'S COSTS	

DDU Delivered Duty Unpaid (...named place of destination)

In Delivered Duty Unpaid, the seller/exporter/manufacturer clears the goods for export and is responsible for making them available to the buyer at the named place of destination, not cleared for import.

The seller, therefore, assumes all responsibilities for delivering the goods to the named place of destination, but the buyer assumes all responsibility for import clearance, duties, administrative costs, and any other costs upon import as well as transport to the final destination.

The DDU term can be used for any mode of transport. However, if the seller and buyer desire that delivery should take place on board a sea vessel or on a quay (wharf), the DES or DEQ terms are recommended.

All forms of payment are used in DDU transactions.

The DDU term is used when the named place of destination (point of delivery) is other than the seaport or airport.

Examples

DDU Delivered Duty Unpaid New York New York USA

DDU Delivered Duty Unpaid Hamburg Germany

DDU
Delivered Duty Unpaid (. . . named place of destination)

Incoterm Category

DES is a "D" Incoterm where the seller is responsible for all costs associated with delivering the goods to the named point and place of destination. "D" terms evidence "arrival" (as opposed to "shipment") contracts.

Modes of Transport Covered

All modes of transport including multimodal.

Seller's Responsibilities (summary)

1. **Goods**—Provide the goods, commercial invoice or electronic message, and other documentation as required by the sales contract.

2. **Licenses and Customs Formalities**—Obtain at own risk and cost any export licenses and authorizations and carry out all export formalities and procedures, including those associated with transshipment to the named port of destination.

3. **Carriage and Insurance**—Contract for and pay all costs of carriage and transshipment (if necessary) to the named destination. No obligation to provide insurance.

4. **Delivery**—Make the goods available to the buyer at the named destination on the date or within the period specified in the sales contract.

5. **Risk Transfer**—Assume all risks of loss or damage to the goods until they have been made available to the buyer at the named destination.

6. **Costs**—Pay all costs until the goods have been delivered to the named destination, including carriage, all export formalities, export duties and taxes, and transshipment (if necessary) to the named destination.

7. **Notice to the Buyer**—Provide sufficient notice of dispatch and projected arrival that the buyer can take appropriate action to arrange pick-up of the goods.

8. **Proof of Delivery, Transport Documents**—Provide the buyer with the delivery order and/or a transport document enabling the buyer to take delivery at the named place of destination.

9. **Checking, Packing, Marking**—Pay all costs associated with checking the quality and quantity of the goods to be in conformity with the sales contract. Provide appropriate packing (unless the goods are traditionally delivered unpackaged) as required for the transport of the goods, to the extent that the buyer has made transport circumstances known to the seller prior to the execution of the sales contract. Provide marking appropriate to the packaging.

10. **Other**—Provide the buyer at the buyer's request, risk and expense any and all assistance in securing documentation originating in the country of export or of origin required for import. Provide the buyer with information necessary to obtain insurance.

Buyer's Responsibilities (summary)

1. **Payment**—Pay for the goods as provided in the sales contract.

2. **Licenses and Customs Formalities**—Obtain and pay costs of all import licenses, documen-

tation and authorizations and carry out all import formalities.

3. **Carriage and Insurance**—No obligation to the seller for either carriage or insurance.

4. **Taking Delivery**—Take delivery of the goods once they are made available at the named destination.

5. **Risk Transfer**—Assume all risk of loss or damage from the time the goods have been made available at the named place of destination.

6. **Costs**—Pay all costs for the goods once they have been made available at the named place of destination. Pay all costs relating to import formalities including duties, taxes and other charges.

7. **Notice to Seller**—If, according to the sales contract, the buyer is able to specify a time for and/or a place of delivery, to give the seller sufficient notice.

8. **Proof of Delivery, Transport Document**—Accept the seller's transport document so long as it is in conformity with the sales contract.

9. **Inspection(s)**—Pay for the costs of pre-shipment inspection(s) except inspections required by the country of export.

10. **Other**—Pay all costs associated with securing documentation from the country of origin or export required for import. Reimburse seller for costs in providing such documentation or assistance.

INCOTERMS

INCOTERMS

DDP
Delivered Duty Paid (. . . named place of destination)

SELLER →   BUYER ⇢

Seller/ Exporter Premises	Export Documents Formalities	Delivered at named place of: Frontier/Terminal/Quay	Loading Port of Shipment	Onboard Ship's Rail	Onboard Ship's Rail	Discharging Port of Arrival	Delivery at named place of destination: Frontier/Terminal/Quay	Import Documents Formalities	Buyer/ Importer Premises
SELLER'S RISKS →									**BUYER'S RISKS** →
SELLER'S COSTS →									**BUYER'S COSTS** →

DDP Delivered Duty Paid (...named place of destination)

In Delivered Duty Paid, the seller/exporter/manufacturer clears the goods for export and is responsible for making them available to the buyer at the named place of destination, cleared for import, but not unloaded from the transport vehicle.

The seller, therefore, assumes all responsibilities for delivering the goods to the named place of destination, including all responsibility for import clearance, duties, and other costs payable upon import.

The DDP term can be used for any mode of transport.

All forms of payment are used in DDP transactions.

The DDP term is used when the named place of destination (point of delivery) is other than the seaport or airport.

Examples
DDP Delivered Duty Paid Chicago USA
DDP Delivered Duty Paid VAT Unpaid Paris France

DDP
Delivered Duty Paid (. . . named place of destination)

Incoterm Category

DDP is a "D" Incoterm where the seller is responsible for all costs associated with delivering the goods to the named point and place of destination. "D" terms evidence "arrival" (as opposed to "shipment") contracts.

Modes of Transport Covered

All modes of transport including multimodal.

Seller's Responsibilities (summary)

1. **Goods**—Provide the goods, commercial invoice or electronic message, and other documentation as required by the sales contract.

2. **Licenses and Customs Formalities**—Obtain at own risk and cost any export and import licenses and authorizations and carry out all export and import formalities and procedures, including those associated with transshipment to the named port of destination.

3. **Carriage and Insurance**—Contract for and pay all costs of carriage and transshipment (if necessary) to the named destination. No obligation to provide insurance.

4. **Delivery**—Make the goods available to the buyer not unloaded at the named destination on the date or within the period specified in the sales contract.

5. **Risk Transfer**—Assume all risks of loss or damage to the goods until they have been made available to the buyer at the named destination.

6. **Costs**—Pay all costs until the goods have been delivered to the named destination, including

carriage, all export and import formalities and transshipment (if necessary) to the named destination.

7. **Notice to the Buyer**—Provide sufficient notice of dispatch and projected arrival that the buyer can take appropriate action to arrange unloading of the goods.

8. **Proof of Delivery, Transport Documents**—Provide the buyer with the delivery order and/or a transport document enabling the buyer to take delivery at the named place of destination.

9. **Checking, Packing, Marking**—Pay all costs associated with checking the quality and quantity of the goods to be in conformity with the sales contract. Provide appropriate packing (unless the goods are traditionally delivered unpackaged) as required for the transport of the goods, to the extent that the buyer has made transport circumstances known to the seller prior to the execution of the sales contract. Provide marking appropriate to the packaging.

10. **Other**—Pay all costs associated with securing documentation necessary for to make the goods available to the buyer at the named place of destination. Provide the buyer with information necessary to obtain insurance.

Buyer's Responsibilities (summary)

1. **Payment**—Pay for the goods as provided in the sales contract.

2. **Licenses and Customs Formalities**—Provide the seller at the seller's request, risk and cost any and all assistance in securing licenses, doc-

umentation and authorizations necessary to import the goods.

3. **Carriage and Insurance**—No obligation to the seller for either carriage or insurance.

4. **Taking Delivery**—Take delivery of the goods once they are made available at the named destination.

5. **Risk Transfer**—Assume all risk of loss or damage from the time the goods have been made available at the named place of destination.

6. **Costs**—Pay all costs for the goods once they have been made available at the named place of destination.

7. **Notice to Seller**—If, according to the sales contract, the buyer is able to specify a time for and/or a place of delivery, to give the seller sufficient notice.

8. **Proof of Delivery, Transport Document**—Accept the seller's transport document so long as it is in conformity with the sales contract.

9. **Inspection(s)**—Pay for the costs of pre-shipment inspection(s) except inspections required by the country of export.

10. **Other**—Provide the seller, at the seller's request, risk and cost any and all assistance in securing import and other documentation necessary for the seller to make the goods available to buyer at the named destination.

INCOTERMS

Guide to Letters of Credit[1]

Letters of Credit Defined

A documentary credit is the written promise of a bank, undertaken on behalf of a buyer, to pay a seller the amount specified in the credit provided the seller complies with the terms and conditions set forth in the credit. The terms and conditions of a documentary credit revolve around two issues: (1) the presentation of documents that evidence title to goods shipped by the seller, and (2) payment.

In simple terms, banks act as intermediaries to collect payment from the buyer in exchange for the transfer of documents that enable the holder to take possession of the goods.

Documentary credits provide a high level of protection and security to both buyers and sellers engaged in international trade. The seller is assured that payment will be made by a party independent of the buyer so long as the terms and conditions of the credit are met. The buyer is assured that payment will be released to the seller only after the bank has received the title documents called for in the credit.

Documentary credits are so named because of the importance of documents in the transaction. Letter of credit (L/C) is the historic and popular term used for a documentary credit because such credits were and are transmitted in the form of a letter from the buyer's bank. Both "documentary credit" and "letter of credit" will be used for our discussions.

Types of Credits

There are a number of different types of standard and special documentary credits. Each type contains a variety of features designed to meet the different needs of buyers, sellers, or the banks involved.

For example, standard documentary credits can be either revocable (may be cancelled by the buyer), or irrevocable (noncancellable by the buyer), or confirmed (a second bank, in addition to the buyer's bank, guarantees payment) or uncon-firmed (payment guaranteed only by the issuing bank). The most popular variation for sellers is the irrevocable confirmed credit because it cannot be cancelled by the buyer, and a second bank (usually the seller's bank) adds its guarantee of payment to that of the buyer's bank. Standard credits are discussed later in this section.

Specialized credits include revolving credits, red clause credits, standby credits, transferable credits, and back-to-back credits. These are also discussed later this section.

This section is designed as an introduction to letters of credit. It is not comprehensive. To learn more about letters of credit and other types of international payments see *A Short Course in International Payments*, also available from World Trade Press.

Limitations of Letters of Credit

Although documentary credits provide good protection and are the preferred means of payment in many international transactions, they do have limitations. They do not, for example, ensure that the goods actually shipped are as ordered nor do they insulate buyers and sellers from other disagreements or complaints arising from their relationship. It is up to the parties to settle questions of this nature between themselves.

Advantages, disadvantages, and issues for both buyer and seller will be discussed later in this section. Please note that these issues can have a significant impact on a given transaction. An incomplete understanding of the subject can be more dangerous than no knowledge at all.

Role of Banks

It is important to note, and not for the last time, that a fundamental principle of documentary credits is that banks deal in documents and not goods. Banks are responsible for issues relating to documents and the specific wording of the documentary credit as opposed to issues relating to the goods themselves.

Therefore, banks are not concerned if a shipment is in conformity with the documents, only that the documents are in conformity to the wording of the credit.

1. This section has been excerpted from the book *A Short Course in International Payments*, ISBN 1-885073-50-X, also by Edward G. Hinkelman and available from World Trade Press.

The Uniform Customs and Practice

Although documentary credits, in one form or another, have been in use for a long time, questions arose about how to effect transactions in a practical, fair, and uniform manner.

The Uniform Customs and Practice for Documentary Credits (UCP) is the internationally recognized codification of rules unifying banking practice regarding documentary credits. The UCP was developed by a working committee attached to the International Chamber of Commerce (ICC) in Paris. It is revised and updated from time to time; the current valid version is ICC publication No. 500. See the Resources Appendix for contact information for the ICC.

Parties to the Transaction

There are four main parties to a basic documentary letter of credit transaction. Note that each party has multiple names. The name used for each party to the transaction depends upon who is speaking. Businesspeople like to use the names buyer, seller, buyer's bank and seller's bank. The banks prefer to use the names applicant, beneficiary, issuing bank, and advising bank. The four parties are:

The Buyer (Applicant/Importer)

The buyer initiates the documentary credit process by applying to his bank to open a documentary credit naming the seller as the beneficiary. The buyer, therefore, may be called the buyer in commercial terms, the importer in economic terms, and the applicant in banking terms. They are all one and the same.

The Issuing (Buyer's) Bank

Upon instructions from the buyer, the issuing bank (typically the buyer's regular business bank) issues a documentary credit naming the seller as the beneficiary and sends it to the advising bank (typically the seller's bank).

The Advising (Seller's) Bank

Upon instructions from the issuing bank and the buyer, the advising bank (typically the seller's bank) advises the seller of the credit. The advising bank is typically the seller's regular business bank and is in the seller's country.

The Seller (Beneficiary/Exporter)

The seller receives notification (advice) of the credit from the advising bank, complies with the terms and conditions of the credit, and gets paid. The seller is the beneficiary of the documentary credit. The seller, therefore, may be called the seller in commercial terms, the exporter in economic terms, and the beneficiary in banking terms. They are all one and the same.

Basic Documentary Credit Procedure

Documentary credit procedure involves the step-by-step exchange of documents giving title to the goods for either cash or a contracted promise to pay at a later time. There are four basic steps in the procedure.

Issuance

Issuance describes the process of the buyer's applying for and opening a documentary credit at the issuing bank and the issuing bank's formal notification of the seller through the advising bank.

Amendment

Amendment describes the process whereby the terms and conditions of a documentary credit may be modified after the credit has been issued.

Utilization

This describes the procedure for the seller's shipping of goods, transfer of documents from the seller to the buyer through the banks, and transfer of payment from the buyer to the seller through the banks (settlement).

Settlement

Settlement (a subpart of utilization) describes the different ways in which payment may be effected to the seller from the buyer through the banks.

Note: Specific issues relating to applying for a credit, confirmed vs. unconfirmed credits, special types of credits, settlement, correspondent and confirming banks will be discussed later.

Issuance

Procedure

Refer to the diagram on the facing page for each numbered step.

Buyer and   Seller

1. The buyer and seller agree on the terms of sale: (a) specifying a documentary credit as the means of payment, (b) naming an advising bank (usually the seller's bank), and (c) listing required documents.

Buyer (Applicant/Importer)

2. The buyer applies to his bank (issuing bank) and opens a documentary credit naming the seller as beneficiary based on specific terms and conditions that are listed in the credit.

Issuing (Buyer's) Bank

3. The issuing bank sends the documentary credit to the advising bank named in the credit.

Advising (Seller's) Bank

4. The advising bank informs (advises) the seller of the documentary credit.

ISSUANCE

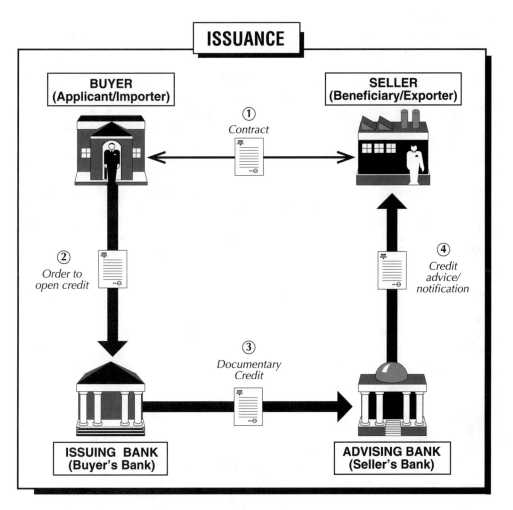

BUYER
(Applicant/Importer)

SELLER
(Beneficiary/Exporter)

① *Contract*

② *Order to open credit*

③ *Documentary Credit*

④ *Credit advice/ notification*

ISSUING BANK
(Buyer's Bank)

ADVISING BANK
(Seller's Bank)

Amendment

When the seller receives the documentary credit it must be examined closely to determine if the terms and conditions (1) reflect the agreement of the buyer and seller, and (2) can be met within the time stipulated.

Upon examination, the seller may find problems. Some examples:

1. The seller might disagree with the terms and conditions. For example, the transaction price listed in the credit may be lower than the originally agreed upon price, or perhaps the seller has specified that the total price is to include shipping, whereas the seller originally quoted a price without shipping.

2. The seller might find himself unable to meet specific requirements of the credit. For example, the time may be too short to effect shipment, or certain documents may not be available.

If the buyer still wants to proceed with the transaction, but with modification to the terms of the credit, he or she should contact the buyer immediately and request an amendment.

Amendments must be authorized by the buyer and issued by the issuing bank to the seller through the same channel as the original documentary letter of credit. This can be an involved undertaking so any amendments should be initiated only when necessary and as soon as a problem is identified.

Procedure

Refer to the diagram on the facing page for each numbered step.

 Seller

1. The seller requests that the buyer make an amendment to the credit. This can be effected by a telephone call, a fax letter, or by face-to-face negotiation.

 Buyer

2. If the buyer agrees, the buyer orders the issuing bank to issue the amendment.

  Issuing Bank

3. The issuing bank amends the credit and notifies the advising bank of the amendment.

Advising Bank

4. The advising bank notifies seller of the amendment.

AMENDMENT

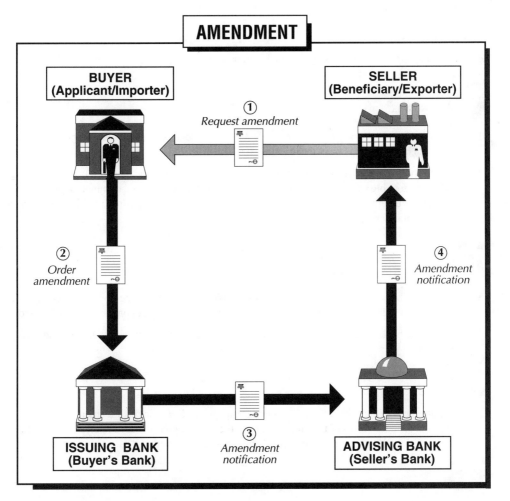

BUYER (Applicant/Importer)

SELLER (Beneficiary/Exporter)

① Request amendment

② Order amendment

④ Amendment notification

③ Amendment notification

ISSUING BANK (Buyer's Bank)

ADVISING BANK (Seller's Bank)

L/C

Utilization

Procedure

Refer to the diagram on the facing page for each numbered step.

 Seller

1. The seller (beneficiary) ships the goods to the buyer and obtains a negotiable transport document (negotiable bill of lading) from the shipping firm/agent.

2. The seller prepares and presents a document package to his bank (the advising bank) consisting of (a) the negotiable transport document, and (b) other documents (e.g., commercial invoice, insurance document, certificate of origin, inspection certificate, etc.) as required by the buyer in the documentary credit.

 Advising Bank

3. The advising bank (a) reviews the document package making certain the documents are in conformity with the terms of the credit and (b) pays the seller (based upon the terms of the credit).

4. The advising bank sends the documentation package by mail or by courier to the issuing bank.

 Issuing Bank

5. The issuing bank (a) reviews the document package making certain the documents are in conformity with the terms of the credit, (b) pays the advising bank (based upon the terms of the credit), and (c) advises the buyer that the documents have arrived.

 Buyer

6. The buyer (a) reviews the document package making certain the documents are in conformity with the terms of the credit, and (b) makes a cash payment (signs a sight draft) to the issuing bank, or if the collection order allows, signs an acceptance (promise to pay at a future date).

 Issuing Bank

7. The issuing bank sends the document package by mail or courier to the buyer who then takes possession of the shipment.

UTILIZATION

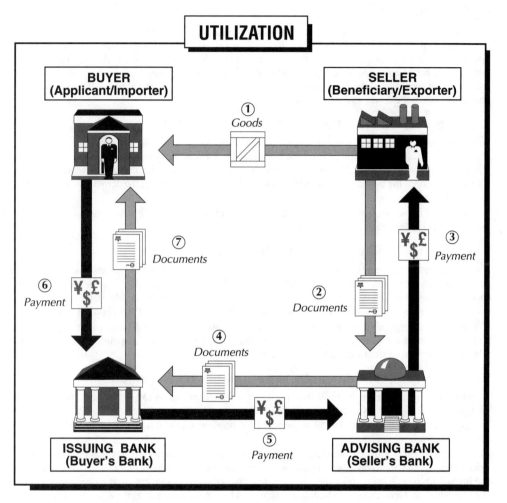

L/C

Settlement (Availability)

Settlement and availability refer to the availability of proceeds (funds) to the beneficiary (seller) after presentation of documents under the credit. Each of the following forms of payment availability must be specified in the original credit, and be accepted by the seller. For example, if the original agreement between the buyer and seller calls for a sight credit (immediate availability of funds to the seller) and a usance credit (funds available in 30, 60 or 90 days) is prescribed in the credit presented to the seller, the seller may reject the credit and the transaction.

The Sight Credit (Settlement by Payment)

In a sight credit (confirmed sight credit) the value of the credit is available to the beneficiary as soon as the terms and conditions of the credit have been met (as soon as the prescribed document package has been presented to and checked by the confirming bank). When foreign exchange is at issue, several days may pass between the time of beneficiary's presentation of documents and the actual transfer of funds to the beneficiary's account.

In a sight credit (unconfirmed), the value of the credit is made available to the beneficiary once the advising bank has received the funds from the issuing bank.

The Usance Credit (Settlement by Acceptance)

In a usance credit the beneficiary presents the required document package to the bank along with a time draft drawn on the issuing, advising, or a third bank for the value of the credit. Once the documents have made their way to the buyer and found to be in order, the draft is accepted by the bank upon which it is drawn (the draft is now called an acceptance) and it is returned to the seller who holds it until maturity.

The seller has the option of selling the acceptance by discounting its value. The discount charged will be in some proportion to the time to maturity of the draft and the perceived risk associated with its collection. The buyer pays the draft at maturity to its holder.

The Deferred Payment Credit (Settlement by Negotiation)

In a deferred payment credit the buyer accepts the documents and agrees to pay the bank after a set period of time. Essentially, this gives the buyer time (a grace period) between delivery of the goods and payment. The issuing bank makes the payment at the specified time, when the terms and conditions of the credit have been met.

Deferred payment credits are often used in transactions involving food or drugs that require inspection prior to import and approval by a government agency. In this case the bank will release the documents to the importer/buyer against a trust receipt. The bank holds the title documents to the goods and still owns the merchandise. Once the goods have been approved by the government agency, the bank transfers the titles documents to the buyer, charges the buyer's account, and pays the seller.

Opening a Documentary Credit

The Importance of Wording

The success or failure of a documentary credit transaction can turn upon the wording of the documentary credit itself. As such, the buyer (whose responsibility it is to open the credit) should adhere to the greatest extent possible to the terms and conditions of the original contractual agreement, keeping the specifications clear and concise and as simple as possible.

Refer to Documents

The buyer's instructions to the issuing bank should be given in clear, professional wording, and should pertain only to documentation, not to the goods themselves. It is very important to demand documents in the credit that clearly reflect the agreements reached.

Example 1: Require confirmation that goods are shipped by Conference vessel no more than twenty years old, rather than that the goods be shipped by Conference vessel no more than twenty years old.

Example 2: Require confirmation that the goods were packaged in double-strength, waterproof containers, rather than requiring that the goods be packaged in double-strength, waterproof containers.

Example 3: Require proof of notification to buyer (such as a copy of the cable or telex) that goods were shipped, rather than requiring that the buyer be notified that the goods were shipped.

Remember, the banks are concerned only with the documents presented, not with whether a party has complied with the contract clauses when they check compliance with the documentary credit terms.

Be Clear and Concise

The wording in a documentary credit should be simple but specific. The more detailed the documentary credit is, the more likely the seller will reject it as too difficult to fulfill. It is also more likely that the banks will find a discrepancy in the details, thus voiding the credit, even though simpler terms might have been found to be in compliance with the credit.

The buyer should, however, completely and precisely set forth the details of the agreement as it relates to credit terms and conditions and the presentation of documents.

Do Not Specify Impossible Documentation

The documentary credit should not require documents that the seller cannot obtain; nor should it call for details in a document that are beyond the knowledge of the issuer of the document. The documents specified should be limited to those required to smoothly and completely conclude an international sale of goods.

Documentary Credit Application

Procedure

Refer to the application form on the facing page for each numbered step.

 Buyer

1. **Beneficiary** Always write the seller's company name and address completely and correctly. A simple mistake here may result in the seller preparing inconsistent or improper documentation on the other end.

2. **Amount** State the actual amount of the credit. You may state a maximum amount in a situation where actual count or quantity is in question. You also may use the words APPROXIMATE, CIRCA, or ABOUT to indicate an acceptable 10 percent plus or minus amount from the stated amount. If you use such wording, you will need to be consistent and use it also in connection with the quantity as well.

3. **Validity Period** The validity and period for presentation of the documents following shipment of the goods should be sufficiently long to allow the exporter time to prepare the necessary documents and send them to the bank.

4. **Beneficiary's Bank** Either leave blank to indicate that the issuing bank may freely select the correspondent bank or name the seller's bank.

5. **Type of Payment Availability** Sight drafts, time drafts, or deferred payment may be used, as previously agreed to by the seller and buyer.

6. **Desired Documents** The buyer specifies which documents are needed. Buyer can list, for example, a bill of lading, a commercial invoice, a certificate of origin, certificates of analysis, and so on.

7. **Notify Address** An address is given for notification of the imminent arrival of goods at the port or airport of destination. This address can also be used for notification of damage to the shipment while en route. The buyer's business or shipping agent is most often used.

8. **Merchandise Description** A short, precise description of the goods is given, along with quantity. Note the comments in number two above concerning approximate amounts.

9. **Confirmation Order** If the foreign beneficiary (exporter) insists on having the credit confirmed by a bank in his or her country it will be so noted in this space.

Sender Argentine Trading Company Lavalle 1716, Piso 2 1048 Buenos Aires Argentina Our reference AB/02	**Instructions to open a Documentary Credit** Buenos Aires, 30th September 19.. Place / Date

Please open the following [X] irrevocable [ ] revocable documentary credit	**Argentine Bank Corporation** Documentary Credits P.O. Box 1040 Buenos Aires, Argentina

Beneficiary ① American Import-Export Co., Inc. 123 Main Street San Francisco, California USA	Beneficiary's bank (if known) ④ US Domestic Bank 525 Main Street San Francisco, CA 94105 USA

Amount ② US$1,250,000.--	
Date and place of expiry ③ 25th November 19.. in San Francisco	Please advise this bank [ ] by letter [X] by letter, cabling main details in advance [ ] by telex / telegram with full text of credit

Partial shipments	Transhipment	Terms of shipment (FOB, C & F, CIF)
[X] allowed [ ] not allowed	[ ] allowed [X] not allowed	CIF Buenos Aires

Despatch from / Taking in charge at	For transportation to	Latest date of shipment	Documents must be presented not later than
Oakland	Buenos Aires	10th Nov. 19..	③ 15 days after date of despatch

Beneficiary may dispose of the credit amount as follows [X] at sight upon presentation of documents ⑤ [ ] after ....days, calculated from date of	[ ] by a draft due .... drawn on [ ] you [ ] your correspondents which you / your correspondents will please accept

against surrender of the following documents ⑥ [X] invoice (.....3......copies) Shipping document [X] sea: bill of lading, to order, endorsed in blank [ ] rail: duplicate waybill [ ] air: air consignment note [ ]	[X] insurance policy, certificte (................. copies) covering the following risks: "all risks" including war up to [ ] Additional documents final destination in Argentina [X] Confirmation of the carrier that the ship is not more than 15 years old [X] packing list (3 copies)

Notify address in bill of lading / goods addressed to Argentine Trading Company ⑦ Lavalle 1716, Piso 2 1048 Buenos Aires Argentina	Goods insured by [ ] us [X] seller

Goods ⑧ 1,000 "Computers model 486 as per pro forma invoice no. 74/1853 dd 10th September 19.." at US$1,250.00 per unit

Your correspondents to advise beneficiary [ ] adding their confirmation [X] without adding their confirmation ⑨ Payments to be debited to our U.S. Dollars account no 10-326.791.50

NB. The applicable text is marked by [X]

Argentine Trading Company

Signature _____

For mailing please see overleaf

L/C

Details on Parties and Procedures

The Buyer (Importer/Applicant)

Since a documentary credit is a pledge by the bank to make payment to the seller, the bank will want to evaluate the creditworthiness of the buyer. If the buyer's credit and relationship with the bank is excellent, the bank will issue a credit for the full value. If the buyer's relationship is good, but perhaps not excellent, the bank will require that the buyer pledge a percentage of the value of the documentary credit in cash funds. If the buyer's relationship with the bank is less established, the bank will require that they buyer pledge 100 percent of the value of the documentary credit in cash funds in advance.

It is essential that the application for the documentary credit be in conformity with the underlying sales contract between the buyer and the seller. The buyer's instructions to the issuing bank must be clear with respect to the type of credit, the amount, duration, required documents, shipping date, expiration date, and beneficiary.

The Issuing (Buyer's) Bank

Upon receiving the buyer's application, the opening bank checks the credit of the applicant, determines whether cash security is necessary, and scrutinizes the contents of the application to see whether they generally are consistent with national and international banking and legal requirements. If the application is satisfactory to the bank, the buyer and the opening bank will sign an agreement to open a documentary credit. The credit must be written and signed by an authorized person of the issuing bank.

The issuing bank usually sends the original documentary credit to the seller (called the beneficiary) through an advising bank, which may be a branch or correspondent bank of the issuing (opening) bank. The seller may request that a particular bank be the advising bank, or the buyer's bank may select one of its correspondent banks in the seller's country.

The Advising (Seller's) Bank

Upon receipt of the credit from the issuing bank, the advising bank informs the seller that the credit has been issued.

The advising bank will examine the credit upon receipt. The advising bank, however, examines the terms of the credit itself; it does not determine whether the terms of the credit are consistent with those of the contract between the buyer and seller, or whether the description of goods is correctly stated in accordance with the contract. The advising bank then forwards the credit to the seller.

If the advising bank is simply "advising the credit," it is under no obligation or commitment to make payment, and it will so advise the seller. In some cases the advising bank confirms (adds its guarantee to pay) the seller. In this case it becomes the confirming bank.

If the advising bank confirms the credit it must pay without recourse to the seller when the documents are presented, provided they are in order and the credit requirements are met.

The Seller/Exporter/Beneficiary

In addition to assessing the reputation of the buyer prior to signing a sales contract, the seller should also assess the reputation of the buyer's (issuing) bank before agreeing to rely upon that bank for payment in a documentary credit. It is not unknown for sellers to receive fictitious documentary credits from non-existent banks and to realize their mistake after shipment.

The seller must carefully review all conditions the buyer has stipulated in the documentary credit. If the seller cannot comply with one or more of the provisions, or if the terms of the credit are not in accordance with those of the contract, the buyer should be notified immediately and asked to make an amendment to the credit.

The seller should also scrutinize the credit to make certain that it does not contain provisions that specify documents such as acceptance reports, progress reports, etc. that have to be signed or approved by the buyer. By refusing to sign such documents, the buyer can block payment.

After reaching agreement, the seller is well-advised to provide the buyer with a sample of the final product specified in the credit for confirmation of quality, suitability, etc.

Complying With the Documentary Credit

 Seller/Exporter/Beneficiary

Upon receipt of the documentary credit, the seller should immediately and carefully examine it to ensure it conforms with the original sales contract with the buyer and that all the conditions stated in the credit can be met. If any of its conditions have to be amended, which can be time-consuming, the seller should immediately contact the buyer.

Examining the Documentary Credit

The following is a checklist for the seller's examination of the credit:

1. The buyer's and seller's names and addresses are correct. ❑

2. The amount of the credit is in accordance with the contract, including unit prices, shipping charges, handling costs, and total invoice amounts. ❑

3. The merchandise description is consistent with the sales contract. ❑

4. The credit's payment availability agrees with the contract conditions. ❑

5. The shipping, expiration, and presentation dates allow sufficient time for processing the order, shipping the merchandise, and preparing the documents for presentation to the bank. ❑

6. Partial or transshipments are specified correctly. ❑

7. The point of dispatch, taking charge of the goods, loading on board, or of discharge at final destination are as agreed. ❑

8. Insurance coverage and party to pay charges are as agreed.

9. Instructions on whom the drafts are to be drawn, and in what tenor (maturity dates), are correct. ❑

10. The credit is confirmed or unconfirmed as agreed. ❑

11. There are no unacceptable conditions. ❑

12. The specified documents can be obtained in the form required. ❑

13. The issuing (or confirming) bank is known to the seller. ❑

Revocable vs. Irrevocable Documentary Credits

Documentary credits may be issued by the buyer and issuing bank as revocable or irrevocable. (The buyer must indicate either revocable or irrevocable on the application form to the issuing bank.) Each has a distinct advantage for buyers and sellers.

Revocable Credit

A revocable documentary credit gives the buyer and/or issuing bank the ability to amend or cancel the credit at any time right up to the moment of intended payment without approval by, or notice to, the seller. Revocable credits are, therefore, of great advantage to the buyer.

Revocable credits are, conversely, of great disadvantage to the seller as the credit may be canceled at any time, even while the goods are in transit, giving the seller no security whatsoever. Although revocable credits are sometimes used between affiliated firms, sellers are advised never to accept a revocable credit as a payment method.

Irrevocable Credit

An irrevocable documentary credit constitutes a firm contractual obligation on the part of the issuing bank to honor the terms of payment of the credit as issued. The buyer and issuing bank cannot amend or cancel the credit without the express approval of the seller.

Irrevocable credits are of advantage to the seller. As long as the seller complies with the terms of the credit, payment will be made by the issuing bank. Virtually all documentary credits issued today are irrevocable and so state on their face (on the face of the documentary credit itself). Sellers are advised to insist upon an irrevocable credit from the buyer.

Confirmed vs. Unconfirmed Documentary Credits

Payment under an irrevocable documentary credit is guaranteed by the issuing bank. However, from the seller's perspective, this guarantee may have limited value as the issuing bank may be (1) in a foreign country, (2) beholden to the buyer, (3) small and unknown to the seller, or (4) subject to unknown foreign exchange control restrictions. The seller, therefore, might wish that another, more local bank add its guarantee (confirmation) of payment to that of the issuing bank.

Within the category of irrevocable credits there are two further options for the buyer and seller. These are the irrevocable unconfirmed credit and the irrevocable confirmed credit. Once again, each has a distinct advantage for buyers and sellers.

Unconfirmed (or Advised) Documentary Credit

Under an unconfirmed documentary credit only the issuing bank assumes the undertaking to pay, thus payment is the sole responsibility of the issuing bank. An unconfirmed documentary credit will be communicated (advised) to the seller through a bank most likely located in the seller's country, and the related shipping and other documents will usually be presented to that bank for eventual payment. However, the final responsibility for payment rests with the issuing bank alone. The advising bank may or may not negotiate the seller's draft depending on the degree of political and financial risk anticipated in the issuing bank's country, as well as the credit standing of the issuing bank.

In dealing with a readily identifiable issuing bank in a developed country, an unconfirmed documentary credit is very probably an acceptable, safe instrument for most sellers. If you have any doubt about the issuing bank and its standing, you can check the name through a local bank with an international department.

Note: Some countries (most notably China) do not permit confirmation of letters of credit issued by their banks, deeming that the credit of their national financial institutions should not be questioned by others.

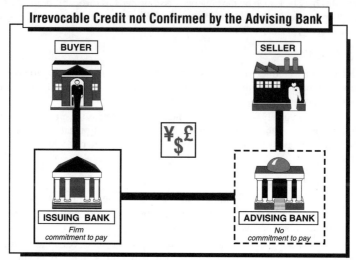

Confirmed Documentary Credit

Confirmed letters of credit carry the commitment to pay of both the issuing and the advising banks. The advising bank adds its undertaking to pay to that of the issuing bank, and its commitment is independent of that of the issuing bank. Therefore, when documents conforming to the requirements of the confirmed documentary credit are presented in a timely manner, the payment from the advising bank to the seller is final in all respects as far as the seller is concerned.

Confirmed, irrevocable letters of credit give the seller the greatest protection, since sellers can rely on the commitment of two banks to make payment. The confirming bank will pay even if the issuing bank cannot or will not honor the draft for any reason whatever. In accordance with the additional risk assumed by the banks, however, confirmed, irrevocable letters of credit are more expensive than unconfirmed letters of credit. Confirmed, irrevocable letters of credit are used most frequently in transactions involving buyers in developing countries.

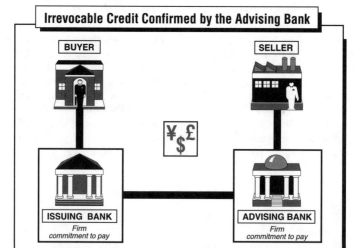

Special Letters of Credits

There are several special credits designed to meet the specific needs of buyers, suppliers, and intermediaries. Special credits involve increased participation by banks, so financing and service charges are higher. Each of the credits listed below is explained in greater detail in the pages that follow.

Standby Credit

Standby credits are often called nonperforming letters of credit because they are only used if the collection on a primary payment method is past due. Standby credits can be used to guarantee repayment of loans, fulfillment by subcontractors, and securing the payment for goods delivered by third parties.

Revolving Credit

This is a commitment on the part of the issuing bank to restore the credit to the original amount after it has been used or drawn down. This credit is used in cases where a buyer wishes to have certain quantities of the ordered goods delivered at specified intervals, such as in a multiple delivery contract.

Red Clause Credit

A red clause credit has a special clause (red clause) that authorizes the confirming bank to make advances to the beneficiary (seller) prior to the presentation of the shipping documents. In this credit the buyer, in essence, extends financing to the seller and incurs ultimate risk for all sums advanced under the credit.

Transferable Credit

A transferable credit is one where the original beneficiary transfers all or part of the proceeds of an existing credit to another party (typically the ultimate supplier of the goods). It is normally used by middlemen as a financing tool.

Back-to-Back Credit

This is a new credit opened on the basis of an already existing, nontransferable credit. It is used by traders to make payment to the ultimate supplier. A trader receives a documentary credit from the buyer and then opens another documentary credit in favor of the ultimate supplier. The first documentary credit is used as collateral for the second credit. The second credit makes price adjustments from which comes the trader's profit.

L
/
C

Notes

L/C

Computer Terms

**C
O
M
P
U
T
E
R
S**

Over the course of the past decade computers and computer technology have had a significant impact upon international trade. Some points: 1) Virtually every firm conducting trade uses computers, 2) Many firms now use specialized import/export document software, 3) Many countries require compliance documents to be filed electronically, and 4) The Internet has created a whole new field of cross-border trade.

This glossary of computer terms is not meant to be exhaustive. Rather, it is designed to offer the user a solid base in understanding the basic terms of computing with an emphasis upon Internet technology and e-commerce.

Note that many terms are listed by their acronym when common usage dictates. In some instances the full term is spelled out with a cross reference to the main entry.

For a comprehensive glossary/encyclopedia we recommend the Osborne/McGraw -Hill *Computer Desktop Encyclopedia*, by Alan Freedman. Contact at www.osborne.com.

---

access provider
(Internet) *See* ISP (Internet Service Provider).

Acrobat
(computers) Computer software from Adobe Systems, Inc. that allows documents to be sent from one computer to another and printed regardless of platform and without losing formatting, fonts or graphics, all of which are embedded in the transmitted document. The transmitted document is called a PDF (Portable Document Format). Acrobat Distiller is the software used to create a PDF, while Acrobat Reader is the software used to display and print *.pdf documents. Acrobat Reader can be downloaded for free from the Adobe Web site (www.adobe.com). *See* PDF, platform.

AltaVista
(computers/Internet) An Internet search engine. Connect at www.altavista.com. *See* keyword search, search engine.

American Standard Code for Information Interchange
See ASCII.

analog
The representation of data in continuous quantities, as opposed to digital, which is the representation of data in discrete units. The most common explanation of analog vs. digital uses clocks. An analog clock has hour, minute, and second hands that display time in a continuous manner. The information displayed is in a constant state of change. A digital clock, on the other hand, displays time in discrete units such as hour, minute, and second. It shows one second, then the next, and then the next.

(wireless) A voice transmission characterized by continuous change and flow achieved by modulating its frequency and amplitude. Analog wireless service is being replaced by digital, because digital signals are more secure, transmit and receive signals with less noise and interference, and importantly, are faster and more reliable for data communications, which is the future of wireless.

AOL
(Internet) Acronym for America Online. An online information service that combines access to the Internet, e-mail, databases, and other features to more than 20 million subscribers worldwide. Connect at www.aol.com.

applet
(computers/Internet) a) A small or simple computer application (program). b) Specifically, a small application program written in Java programming language. Applets are embedded into the HTML of a Web page and are downloaded to, and then executed by, the local computer's browser. Applets generally run faster than other Web applications because they do not need to send user requests back to the server. *See* Java.

application (software)
(computers) Short for "application program." Computer software designed to perform a specific function directly for the user. An application typically manipulates data and then supplies results to the user. Examples of common applications include: word processors, spreadsheets, accounting and database programs. Web browsers and graphics software are also considered to be applications. Compare to "systems software," which includes programming languages and op-

erating systems that are required to run applications software.

ASCII

(computers) Acronym for American Standard Code for Information Interchange. A binary data coding system developed by the American National Standards Institute (ANSI) to represent the letters of the Western alphabet, Arabic numbers and commonly used symbols (such as punctuation marks) with a value that can be manipulated by a computer for data communications and data processing. Not included are accents and letters not used in English. Pronounced "ask-ee," this coding system assigns a 7-digit binary number to represent each of these 128 alphanumeric characters.

attachment (e-mail)

(Internet) A text, graphic, audio, video, or other data file that is sent along with an e-mail on the Internet. In most e-mail systems one selects "Attach" from a menu and then selects a specific file or document to attach. Attachments are often compressed when the file size is large.

B2B

(commerce/e-commerce) Acronym for business-to-business. Commerce in goods, services, or information that takes place between business enterprises. Contrast to the exchange of goods, services, or information between businesses and private individuals (B2C or business-to-consumer). Business-to-business is a term associated with the pre-Internet "old" economy whereas B2B is a term associated with the "new" Internet economy. B2B sales on the Internet are expected to grow at a faster rate than the B2C sector.

B2C

(commerce/e-commerce) Acronym for business-to-consumer. Commerce in goods, services, or information that takes place between a business enterprise and a private individual. Contrast to the exchange of goods between companies (B2B or business-to-business). Business-to-consumer is a term associated with the pre-Internet "old" economy, whereas B2C is a term associated with the "new" Internet economy.

backup

(computers) A duplicate copy of a computer file such as a company database or application program. A backup is made for security purposes in case of loss of data because of an equipment fail-

ure, fire, theft, or other causes. Many businesses keep backup copies of important files off-site in a secure location such as a bank safety deposit box. Also used as a verb: to backup a file.

band

(wireless) A range of radio frequencies between two defined limits that are used for a specific purpose.

bandwidth

(computers/Internet) The data transmission capacity of an electric communications channel or connection. The more bandwidth, the more data can be transferred in a given period of time. Bandwidth is measured in bits per second (bps).

The technical definition of bandwidth refers to the difference between the highest and lowest frequency that a connection can transmit and is measured in hertz (Hz) or cycles per second. The greater the difference between these two values the more data can be sent in a given period of time. Bandwidth differs greatly depending upon a number of factors. LANs (local area networks) used in many office environments are much faster than WANs (wide area networks) such as dial-up modems, DSL, and T1-3 lines as used in most Internet connections. The following chart gives a sampling of bandwidth for the most common network configurations.

WAN Connections—Bandwidth
Switched Services
Dial-up modems: 9.6, 14.4, 28.8, 33.6
    and 56 Kbps.
ISDN: BRI 64-128 Kbps
        PRI 1.544 Mbps
Unswitched Private Lines
T1: 1.5 Mbps
T3: 44.7 Mbps
DSL: 144 Kbps to 52 Mbps.
LAN Connections—Bandwidth
Ethernet (10 BaseT): 10 Mbps
Fast Ethernet (100 BaseT): 100 Mbps
Gigabit Ethernet: 1,000 Mbps
Token Ring: 4, 16 Mbps
ATM: 25, 45, 155, 622, 2,488 Mbps+

banner ad

(Internet) A graphic image of generally 460 pixels wide by 60 pixels high (also 460 x 55 or 392 x 72 pixels) used on a Web page to advertise a product or service. Many banner ads are now animated and/or hot linked to an advertiser's Web site.

C
O
M
P
U
T
E
R
S

baud

(computers/Internet) a) (common usage) A measure of data transfer speed of a computer modem expressed as the number of bits the modem can send or receive per second. b) (technical) A unit of signaling speed related to the number of times per second that the carrier signal can shift value, expressed as the number of state-transitions or symbols that can be transmitted per second on a connection. This value can be different from the number of bits that can be moved per second. For example, a modem running at 300 baud can move 4 bits per baud or 1,200 bps. The true technical baud rate depends on the type of connection. *See* bandwidth.

beta version

(computer software) The final (or near final), pre-release version of computer hardware or software used for quality assurance testing. Beta testing is often conducted by individuals in real-world settings to help identify problems or "bugs" that still exist in the product. Final revisions are then made before the product is released to the general public.

binary

(computers) a) Two parts or things. b) A base-two system of representing data. In modern computing, all data (text, images, audio, and video) is stored, read, and processed by the computer in the form of ON and OFF electrical impulses. This binary system (ON or OFF) can also be represented as 1 (ON) or 0 (OFF), or as TRUE (1) or FALSE (0). Each byte of data is represented by a series of these ON, OFF electrical impulses. For example, the letter "A" is "01000001." The representation of data in binary form is the basis of modern digital computers, digital audio recordings, and digital wireless communications. *See* bit, byte.

bit

(computers) Contraction of binary digit. The smallest element of data storage on a computer. In a binary system (0 or 1, OFF or ON) a bit represents either 0 or 1, OFF or ON.

bookmark

(Internet) A hyperlink marker that serves as a shortcut to a particular Web site or a specific page of content within a Web site. Web browsers enable users to automatically bookmark favorite Web sites or pages for quick retrieval at a later date.

boot

(computers) To start a computer and its operating system software. To start application software, the term "launch" is used; as in "launch Microsoft Word."

bps

(computers) Acronym for bits per second. *See* bandwidth, bit.

bricks and clicks

(Internet) A business that combines a physical location open to the public (bricks and mortar) with an Internet e-commerce presence (click of a mouse).

bricks and mortar

(Internet) A business with a physical location (building) open to the public, especially retail locations, as opposed to a business that operates only on the Internet.

broadband

(computers/Internet) High-speed data transmission over a network. Broadband is generally considered to be a speed of 1.544 Mbps (T1 line) or faster. *See* bandwidth, DSL, ISDN, T1-3.

broadcast

(Internet) To transmit data to anyone with access to a receiver (radio, television or computer with Internet access). Radio and television are early examples of broadcast; their signals can be accessed by anyone with a radio or television receiver. A Web site can be considered a form of broadcast message as it is available to anyone with access to the Internet. Some consider e-mail sent in bulk to everyone on a network as broadcast, but others consider it to be a bulk point-to-point communication.

browser

See Web browser.

bug

(computers) An error or problem in computer software or hardware that cannot be fixed by the user.

business-to-business

See B2B.

business-to-consumer

See B2C.

byte

(computers) Contraction of binary table. A unit of computer storage that consists of 8 bits and that generally represents a single character (a, b, c, 1, 2, 3, $, %, etc.). Computer storage (either in

RAM, disk space, or file sizes) is generally stated in either kilobytes (KB or thousands of bytes), megabytes (MB or millions of bytes), or gigabytes (GB or billions of bytes). *See* bit.

carrier
(wireless) A company that provides telephone, wireless, and/or other communications services.

CD-R
(computers) Acronym for Compact Disk-Recordable. A recordable compact disk (CD) used for recording data or music that can be written (recorded) only once. Once recorded, a CD-R can be used (played) in a standard CD-ROM computer drive. CD-Rs are used for backup storage of data and as a pre-master for the replication of CD-ROMs in bulk. *See* CD-ROM, CD-RW, DVD.

CD-ROM
(computers) Compact Disk-Read Only Memory. A storage medium using the compact disk format and used to record data, text, graphics, and/or audio files. The most common data capacities for CD-ROM disks are 650 and 700 MB. Note that computer CD-ROM drives can play both CD-ROM and audio CDs but that audio CD players can play only audio CDs. CD-ROMs provide more stable data storage than floppy disks and other magnetic storage mediums and are used extensively for the distribution of computer software, games, and other data.

CD-RW
(computers) Acronym for Compact Disk-Re-Writeable. A recordable compact disk (CD) used for recording data or music that can be written (recorded) multiple times. Once recorded, a CD-RW can be used (played) in a standard CD-ROM computer drive. *See* CD-R, CD-ROM, DVD.

cellular
(wireless) A wireless communications system and technology that divides a service area into a multitude of cells, each with a cell site (base station). Cellular calls are transferred from cell site to cell site as the user travels from cell to cell.

cellular phone
(wireless) A wireless radiotelephone that operates within the service area of a cellular network.

central processing unit
See CPU.

chip
(computers) A set of miniaturized electronic circuits used to process or store data. There are many types of chips designed for specific functions. Chip, microchip, and integrated circuit are used interchangeably.

COMDEX
(computers) Contraction of Computer Dealers Exposition. The U.S.'s largest and most important trade show for computers and computer-related products and services. COMDEX/Fall is the original show and is about twice the size of COMDEX/Spring. Both take place in Las Vegas, Nevada, USA. The shows are produced by the Japanese-owned Softbank Corporation (www.comdex.com).

comma delimited
(computers) A database record format that separates data fields in a record with a comma. In some cases the data content of each field is surrounded with quotes. For example: "World Trade Press", "1450 Grant Avenue, Suite 204", "Novato", "CA", "94945", "USA", "Publisher". *See* tab delimited.

compression
(computers) The encoding of data to reduce storage space. There are different compression methods and programs but they all work on the same basis of finding repeatable patterns of binary data (0s and 1s) and replacing them with a code and marker system. Compression is especially popular in sending large files (attachments) by e-mail. WinZip (www.winzip.com) is one example of a popular compression utility.

CompuServe
(Internet) An online information service that combines access to the Internet, e-mail, databases, and other features. CompuServe is one of the oldest online services and is geared to business users, especially in the airline, insurance, and legal industries. CompuServe was acquired by AOL (www.aol.com) in 1998. Connect at www.compuserve.com.

CPU
(computers) Acronym for central processing unit. a) The processor or computing unit of a computer. In modern PCs the CPU is contained on a single small computer chip. b) (popular) The computer as opposed to the monitor, keyboard and mouse. *See* chip, hardware, Pentium, software.

crash
(computers) An event that renders a computer temporarily inoperable. Most computer crashes

are the result of 1) an overload of instructions or data, 2) a conflict in software, or 3) a hardware failure. Most computer crashes can be resolved by re-booting (restarting) the computer. Also called an abend (contraction of abnormal end).

cross platform
(computers) A computer application (software) that is able to operate on all or a variety of different computer hardware or software platforms. The ability of an application to run across various platforms has become a hot topic in the age of Internet and wireless technology.

cyberspace
(Internet) A popular term used to describe the aggregate of information available on the Internet and other computer networks. The term was originally coined by William Gibson in his 1984 novel *Neuromancer* and (interestingly) referred to a futuristic computer network comprised of the minds (not computers!) of all the people who were "plugged" in.

database
(general) An organization of related files in a structured format that enables easy access and manipulation. Examples range from a paper card file to a computer database.
(computer software) A computer application designed to organize, store and retrieve data from a database.
Modern computer databases can store any form of binary data including text, images, audio and video. Many data driven Web sites are built around powerful relational database software (such as Oracle, IBM's DB2 or Microsoft's SQL Server) and allow for dynamically updated information to be displayed on the Web site.

debug
(computers) To fix an error or problem in computer software or hardware. *See* bug.

default
(computers) The preestablished setting of a piece of computer hardware or software. For example, the default opening screen for a word-processing application might be a "New" document. Many default settings can be changed through user customization, often from a "Preferences," "User Preferences," or "Settings" menu.

digital
(computers) a) The representation of data in numerical form, usually in a binary system. b) Anything relating to numerical systems.

digital subscriber line
See DSL.

discussion group
See newsgroup.

domain name
See Internet domain name.

dot-com
(Internet) a) The period "." followed by the commercial (com) domain of an Internet domain name or e-mail address. b) Anything related to the Internet industry or economy. c) A company that does business on the Internet.

down
(computers/Internet) a) A computer that has not been turned on or that is not in operational condition. b) A Web site that is not operational. *See* up.

download
(Internet/computers) The transfer of computer documents or data files from a remote (host) computer to a local (client) computer over a network. To download means to receive and to upload means to transmit. *See* upload.

DSL
(Internet) Digital Subscriber Line. A technology that dramatically increases the data transmission capacity of telephone lines into homes and offices. DSL is one of the most popular forms of Internet access because it provides "always on" operation and uses existing telephone lines. DSL speeds, however, are a function of the distance between the subscriber and the telecom central office. The greater the distance, the slower the speed. There are many versions of DSL, but the two main groupings of service are Asymmetric DSL (including ADSL, RADSL, G.Lite, and VDSL) and Symmetric DSL (including HDSL, HDSL-2, SDSL, and IDSL). Asymmetric DSL features fast download and slow upload of data and is used primarily for Internet connections. Symmetric DSL features fast speeds in both directions but is used only where the distance from the telecom office is short. *See* bandwidth, E1, E3, ISDN, modem, T1-3.

dual band
(telecommunications) A mobile phone (handset) that is capable of sending and receiving signals in both 800 MHz cellular and 1900 MHz PCS frequencies. *See* dual mode, PCS.

COMPUTERS

dual mode

(wireless) A mobile phone (handset) that is capable of operating on analog and digital wireless networks. *See* dual band.

DVD

(computers) Acronym for Digital Video Disk. A portable storage medium used to store large volumes of data. DVDs are the same physical size as CDs, but are double-sided and hold from 2.6 GB to 17 GB of data (in contrast to the typical 650 MB capacity of CDs). Originally designed for video distribution, DVDs have become important in the computer industry for backup storage of large databases, computer graphics audio and video. DVDs come in a variety of formats and storage capacities. Many feel that DVDs will eventually replace CD-ROMs. *See* CD-ROM.

E1, E2, E3

(Internet, European standard) A dedicated digital circuit connection leased from a telecommunications provider that provides 2.048 Mbps (E1), 8.448 Mbps (E2) or 44.736 Mbps (E3) data transmission capacity. E1-E3 lines are used for high speed private networks and connections to the Internet. E3 lines can handle full-screen, full-motion video. *See also* T1, T2, T3.

e-business

(Internet) Short for electronic business. An umbrella term for doing business online. In addition to simply processing transactions online (e-commerce), e-business includes all aspects of conducting business online including: buying, selling, marketing, advertising, order tracking, shipment tracking, and customer service. *See* e-commerce.

e-commerce

(Internet) Short for electronic commerce. Business transactions conducted on the Internet. The sale of goods or services online. E-commerce is a subset of e-business and generally refers specifically to the ability to process a transaction online. E-commerce also includes electronic data interchange (EDI) which is the structured exchange of business documents (e.g., inquiries, purchase orders, invoices, compliance documents, etc.) between computers.

EDI

(computers/Internet) Acronym for Electronic Data Interchange. The electronic communication of business-transaction information and documentation between businesses and between busi-

nesses and governmental entities. EDI includes transmission of purchase orders, order confirmations, invoices and compliance documents. Modern EDI involves direct links into supplier ordering systems and government regulatory authorities.

Electronic Data Interchange (EDI)

See EDI.

e-mail

(Internet) Short for electronic-mail. The transmission of electronic messages over a network from one computer to another, especially over the Internet. *See* attachment, spam.

e-mail attachment

See attachment.

e-mail blast

(Internet) A large number of e-mail advertising messages sent at the same time. *See* attachment, spam.

encryption

(computers) The encoding of data for security while in transmission.

e-tailing

(Internet) Short for electronic retailing. Business-to-consumer (B2C) sales over the Internet. *See* B2C, e-business, e-commerce.

Ethernet

(computers) The most popular LAN (local area network) technology currently in use. Many PCs, most peripherals (such as laser printers), and all Macintosh computers come standard with an Ethernet port (RJ-45 connector) for connecting to a LAN or to a DSL or cable modem for Internet access.

Ethernet is available in three bandwidths:
Ethernet: 10BaseT (10 Mbps)
Fast Ethernet: 100BaseT (100 Mbps)
Gigabit Ethernet: 1,000BaseT (1,000 Mbps)
See bandwidth.

Excite

(computers/Internet) An Internet portal and search engine. Connect at www.excite.com. *See* search engine, keyword search.

Explorer

See Internet Explorer.

Extensible Markup Language

See XML.

extensions

See Internet domain name, top-level domain, URL.

COMPUTERS

extranet
(Internet) A Web site with limited access, designed and maintained specifically for communicating with clients and customers rather than with the general public. An extranet uses the Internet as its delivery system, but restricts access via passwords. An extranet can be used to deliver vendor inventory information, specialized content such as research, or any other private data. Access to an extranet site may be free or on a paid subscription basis.

FAQ
(Internet) Acronym for Frequently Asked Questions. A list of commonly asked questions, with answers, maintained on a Web site to assist users with fundamental content, navigation, and usage information. It is considered a breach of netiquette (etiquette of the Internet) to call or e-mail asking a question that is answered in the FAQ section.

fiber optics
(telecommunications) Wire or cable made from glass fiber and designed to transmit digital signals (audio, video, or other data) as pulses of light.

firewall
(Internet) Computer software, or more commonly, a combination of computer hardware, software, and security measures designed to keep a computer or computer network secure from intruders. *See* hacker, virus.

flame
(Internet) A critical, often abusive message that is delivered by e-mail. For example, a flame may be received by someone who has abused the netiquette (etiquette of the Internet) by using public forums for advertising.

floppy disk
(computers) A flexible magnetic storage medium housed in a paper envelope or plastic shell. Also called a "diskette," floppy disks come in a number of different physical sizes that each have varying storage capacity. The standard sizes are:
8" in a flexible envelope: 100-500KB storage
5.25" in a flexible envelope: 100KB-1.2MB storage
3.5" in a rigid case: 400KB-2.8MB storage
Today, only the 3.5" disk is still widely used and many predict that it too will disappear within a few years because of its limited storage capacity. *See* CD-ROM, DVD, hard disk.

frequently asked questions
See FAQ.

FTP
(Internet) File Transfer Protocol. A standard protocol for transferring computer files over the Internet. FTP is often used by Web developers to upload their files to a host server. An FTP transfer is generally performed with a utility program or from within a Web browser. *See* upload.

GB
See gigabyte.

gigabyte (GB)
(computers) One billion bytes. *See* byte.

Global Positioning System
See GPS.

Global System for Mobile Communications
See GSM.

Google
(computers/Internet) An Internet portal and search engine. Connect at www.google.com. *See* keyword search, search engine.

Gopher
(Internet) An application program that searches the Internet for file names and other information and presents its findings in a hierarchical format. Developed at the University of Minnesota (USA), home to the "Golden Gophers," Gopher was a big step forward in the development of the Internet and paved the way for the Hypertext Transfer Protocol (HTTP). It remains available at many universities and most recent Web browsers still incorporate support for the protocol. Note: Gopher is both the name of a burrowing animal and a slang term for "Go fer (for)" as in "go get it."

GPS
Acronym for Global Positioning System. A worldwide satellite-based radio navigation system consisting of 24 Earth orbit satellites operated by the U.S. Department of Defense and used to provide three- and four-dimensional position, time, and velocity information to military and civilian users who have GPS receivers. The system has two levels of service. **Standard Positioning Service** is available to anyone in possession of a GPS receiver (available for as little as US$100) and allows the user to establish their Earth location in latitude and longitude within a proximity of 10 meters. **Precise Positioning Service** is a highly accurate military positioning,

velocity and timing service available only to the U.S. military and other authorized users.

How GPS works: Each of the 24 satellites contains a computer, atomic clock, and radio. The strategic positioning of these satellites enables a GPS receiver on Earth to establish location by communicating with at least three of the orbiting satellites within its "field of view." If contact can be made from a fourth satellite, altitude data can also be obtained. GPS is used in various industries including navigation (ocean and land), energy exploration, and environment monitoring. GPS is the essential component in automobiles equipped with navigation systems.

graphic user interface
See GUI.

GSM
(wireless) Global System for Mobile Communications. The predominant worldwide standard for digital wireless service. GSM operates at either 900 or 1800 MHz and is used extensively in Europe and in more than 120 countries. GSM is a TDMA (Time Division Multiple Access) technology and allows a number of calls to take place on a single channel or frequency at the same time. For more information, contact GSM World at www.gsmworld.com.

GUI
(computers) Acronym for Graphical User Interface. Pronounced "goo-ey." A graphics-based as opposed to a text-based interface used to communicate with a computer. A text-based interface uses words and alphanumeric commands, whereas a GUI uses icons, pull-down menus and a computer mouse for navigation, giving commands and operating the machine. The three major operating system GUIs are Windows (for the PC), Mac OS (for the Macintosh) and Motif (for UNIX).

hacker
(computers) a) A highly-skilled and clever computer programmer who writes programs in assembly or systems-level languages. The term refers to the programmer's "hacking away" at tedious computer code when writing complex programs. b) (popular usage) A mischievous person who seeks unauthorized entry into computer systems. Such entry can be benign (simply for the satisfaction of succeeding) or malicious (for the purpose of doing harm). *See* virus.

Handheld Devices Markup Language
See HDML.

hard disk
(computers) A rigid magnetic storage medium that is fixed within a computer in a sealed compartment. A hard disk can also be contained in an external device or in a removable cartridge. In the mid-1980s hard disks for PCs had storage capacities of 5 to 20 MB. By the year 2000 most PCs came standard with 5 to 20 GB hard disks. *See* gigabyte, megabyte.

hardware
(computers/logistics) Machines and equipment. In the field of computers, hardware refers to physical equipment such as CPUs, keyboards, monitors, disk drives, modems, and cables. *See also* software.

HDML
(computers) Handheld Devices Markup Language. A computer language and coding system used to enable wireless devices such as cell phones, wireless pagers, and other handheld devices with small display screens to view information from the Internet. HDML is a version of HTML (HyperText Markup Language) and a subset of WAP (Wireless Application Protocol). *See* HTML, WAP.

home page
(Internet) The first page viewed (main access page) on an Internet Web site. All other pages are accessed from the home page. The home page of a well-designed Web site enables the user to intuitively understand and navigate through the content of the site.

HotBot
(computers/Internet) An Internet portal and search engine. Connect at www.hotbot.com. *See* search engine, keyword search.

Hotmail
(Internet) A Web-based e-mail provider that enables users to send and receive messages from any computer connected to the Internet. Users get a special Hotmail e-mail address (_____@hotmail.com) that they can use from home, an office, or from an Internet café anywhere in the world. This is a favorite of travelers as the e-mail address is permanent and has an inexpensive annual charge. In any browser type in *Hotmail*.

HTML
(Internet) HyperText Markup Language. The computer language used for creating hyperlinked

or hypertext documents on the World Wide Web. This computer language (also called a document format) enables users to view content in a Web browser and navigate within a Web site and to other Web sites by clicking hyperlinked text or graphics.

HTTP
(Internet) Acronym for HyperText Transfer Protocol. The communications protocol used by computers and Web browsers to connect to Web servers and move HTML files across the Internet. For example, to establish a connection with the World Trade Press Web server, one types http as a prefix to the Web domain name (http://www.worldtradepress.com) in the address field of a Web browser.

hyperlink
(Internet) A link between two text or graphic objects. Pointing with the computer's cursor and clicking a hyperlink will transfer you to a specified page, file (text, graphic, audio, or video), or Web site. Hyperlinks are generally identified in computer documents by underlined colored text (often blue) or by graphic buttons. Hyperlinks form the foundation for navigation on the World Wide Web. Hyperlink and hypertext are used interchangeably. *See* hypertext.

hypertext
(Internet) A single word or text passage on a Web page that has been hyperlinked to a related text occurrence, page, file (text, graphic, audio, or video), or Web site. Hypertext passages are often referred to as a "link" or "hyperlink." Hypertext links are generally identified in computer documents by underlined colored text (usually blue). Hypertext and hyperlink are used interchangeably. *See* hyperlink.

HyperText Markup Language
See HTML.

hypertext transfer protocol
See HTTP.

IE
(Internet) Acronym for Internet Explorer. *See* Internet Explorer.

Infoseek
(computers/Internet) An Internet portal and search engine. Connect at www.infoseek.com. *See* search engine, keyword search.

Integrated Services Digital Network
See ISDN.

Interface
(computers) a) The connection of two or more computer devices such as a computer and a printer, or a keyboard and a computer. b) The connection between an individual computer, its operating system software, application software, and the user. c) (popular usage) To work with another individual or organization.

Internet
(computers/Internet) The world's largest, fastest-growing, and most important computer network. Specifically, a worldwide network made up of smaller networks that provides access to all those connected to any part of the network.
The original Internet was started in 1969 as the ARPAnet and was designed as a series of high-speed links between educational and research institutions. By the 1990s commercial and other traffic increased exponentially and the Internet became an economic and cultural phenomenon. While the Internet's exact future is unclear, the following is generally understood to be true: 1) Internet use will continue to grow, 2) the Internet is by far the world's greatest source of information, and 3) the Internet holds untold opportunities for commerce and education. *See* World Wide Web.

Internet address
(Internet) a) An individual's e-mail address on the Internet. b) An individual Web site address (URL) on the Internet. *See* e-mail, Internet domain name, URL.

Internet discussion group
See newsgroup.

Internet domain name
(Internet) The address of an Internet Web site. Technically, an organization's domain name combined with a top-level domain (TLD). TLDs are extensions to the domain name such as ".com", ".org", ".net", etc. For example: www.worldtradepress.com. Note that no two organizations can hold the same Internet domain name and that trademarked names can only be used by the trademark holder. One can register an Internet domain name at any number of Web sites, but the most important register is Network Solutions (www.networksolutions.com). An Internet domain name is one of the components of a URL.

Internet Explorer
(Internet) The Web browser developed by Microsoft Corporation (www.microsoft.com), and referred to simply as Explorer or IE. Along with

C O M P U T E R S

Netscape Navigator, Explorer is one of the two most popular Web browsers, although Explorer has been gaining market share and is now dominant. *See* Netscape Navigator.

Internet Service Provider
See ISP.

intranet
(Internet) A private computer network designed for use by one company or organization. For example, a company might design and maintain an intranet to share databases and provide intra-company e-mail services for its employees. An intranet operates on the same principles as the Internet. *See* Internet, extranet.

ISDN
(Internet) Integrated Services Digital Network. A technology that dramatically increases the data transmission capacity of telephone lines into homes and offices. With ISDN one can send analog and digital data over the same network at transmission rates of up to 128 Kbps. *See* bandwidth, DSL, E1, E3, modem, T1-3.

ISP
(Internet) Internet Service Provider. A firm that provides clients with direct access to the Internet. ISPs may provide other services such as Web hosting and Web site design and building. An ISP provides a local telephone number for your computer to call to connect to the Internet. Online services such as AOL and CompuServe also provide Internet access as part of their service offering. For a directory of ISPs see Boardwatch Magazine's "Internet Service Providers" at www.boardwatch.com.

Java
(Internet) A programming language developed by Sun Microsystems (www.sun.com) designed to run on all computer operating systems, especially in Web applications. A Java "applet" is a Java program that is first downloaded from the host Web server to a user's local computer, where it runs after being called from a Web page. A Java "servlet" is a Java program that resides on and operates from a Web server. *See* applet.

KB
See kilobyte.

Kbps
(computers/Internet) Acronym for kilo (1,000) bits per second. *See* bandwidth, bit.

keyword search
(Internet) A search for information or documents on the World Wide Web based on use of a single word, phrase, or combination of words in a search engine. By modifying the keywords and their sequence one can often obtain different search results.

kilobyte (KB)
(computers) One thousand bytes. *See* byte.

LAN
(computers) Acronym for Local Area Network. A computer network that is shared by computers and devices within a relatively small area. A LAN may serve two or three users or it may be used by hundreds, but the geographic area served ranges typically from a single office to part or all of a single floor of a building.

laptop
(computers) A small, portable, battery-operated computer with integrated screen and keyboard.

link
See hyperlink.

Linux
(computers) A computer operating system based on UNIX that runs on PCs and UNIX-based computers. Linux is an "open system" and is gaining some popularity because of its stability in running servers, especially Web servers. UNIX and Windows, however, remain the dominant operating systems worldwide. The name Linux comes from its original creator Linus Torvalds. *See* Mac OS, operating system, UNIX, Windows.

local area network
See LAN.

Lycos
(computers/Internet) An Internet portal and search engine. Connect at www.lycos.com. *See* keyword search, search engine.

Mac OS
(computers) Short for Macintosh Operating System. The operating system used on Macintosh computers. The Mac OS is especially popular in desktop publishing, design, and graphics-related industries.

MB
See megabyte.

Mbps
(computers) Acronym for mega (1,000,000) bits per second. See bandwidth, bit.

COMPUTERS

megabyte (MB)
(computers) One million bytes. *See* byte.

menu
(computers) An on-screen list of computer functions or operations that may be selected by the user.

mobile e-commerce
(Internet) Electronic commerce that uses a wireless device as the access point (as opposed to a PC that is connected by landlines to the Internet). Examples of wireless devices used in mobile e-commerce include cellular telephones, beepers, and PDAs (Personal Digital Assistants) with Internet access.

mobile Web
(wireless) Access to the World Wide Web from a mobile wireless device such as a cellular phone, beeper, or PDA (Personal Digital Assistant). Mobile Web promises to be a huge area for growth because of users' ability to gain instant access to information and mobile e-mail.

modem
(computers/Internet) Contraction of Modulator-Demodulator. An electronic hardware device that connects a computer communications port to a telephone line or TV cable and thence to other computers or computer networks including the Internet. Technically, a modem is a digital-to-analog and analog-to-digital device that converts a computer's digital pulses to audio frequencies that can be transmitted over a telephone line and vice-versa. A modem is only one way in which a user can connect to the Internet. Modern modems connect to the Internet at speeds of up to 56,000 bps, slower than ISDN, DSL and T1, T2, and T3 lines.

Navigator
See Netscape Navigator.

Netscape Navigator
(Internet) The Web browser developed by Netscape Communications Corporation (www.netscape.com), now part of AOL Time Warner (www.aol.com). Along with Microsoft's Internet Explorer, Netscape is one of the two most popular Web browsers, although it has been losing worldwide market share to Internet Explorer, which since 1999 is the most widely used Web browser.

network
(computers) A group of linked computers. A network can link as few as two computers in a small office (a Local Area Network), several hundred or thousand computers in a company wide network (a Wide Area Network), or tens of millions of computers on the Internet. *See* extranet, Internet, intranet, LAN (Local Area Network), WAN (Wide Area Network).

New Economy
(Internet) The economy associated with the Internet. *See* B2B, B2C, e-commerce, Old Economy.

newsgroup
(Internet) A message board on an Internet Web site or portal. Also known as an Internet discussion group. A newsgroup is generally topic-specific and starts with a single user posting a query or comment that is followed by comments and queries by other users. Newsgroups have become an extremely popular addition to Web sites that wish to foster communications among and with members or users.

Northern Light
(computers/Internet) An Internet portal and search engine. Connect at www.northern-light.com. *See* keyword search, search engine.

offline
(Internet) Not connected to the Internet.
(computers) a) Describes a device (such as a laser printer) that is not connected to a computer. b) Describes a device that is not in ready mode.
(general) Not available for use.

Old Economy
(Internet) a) The pre-Internet economy. b) The economy associated with "bricks and mortar" businesses. *See* New Economy.

online
(Internet) Connected to the Internet.
(computers) a) Describes a device (such as a laser printer) that is connected to a computer. b) Describes a device that is in ready mode.
(general) Available for use.

online service
(Internet) A business entity that provides access to the Internet, proprietary databases and e-mail services to its users. Several of the largest online services include:
America Online (AOL) (www.aol.com)
CompuServe (www.compuserve.com)
DIALOG (online databases) (www.dialog.com)
Dow Jones Interactive (business, finance and news) (bis.dowjones.com)

COMPUTERS

LEXIS-NEXIS (legal and news information) (www.lexis-nexis.com)
Prodigy (www.prodigy.com)
WESTLAW (legal databases) (www.west-pub.com)

operating system (OS)
(computers) The primary software program that manages a computer's basic functions and controls the execution of application programs. All application software must conform to certain standards of a computer's operating system to function. Also called system software. The most common operating systems are Windows (for Intel/IBM PC-compatible computers), Mac OS (for Macintosh), and UNIX and Linux (for PC and UNIX computers).

OS
See operating system.

PC
(computers) a) Personal Computer. Specifically a personal computer (laptop or desktop) running Windows or DOS. b) Any laptop or desktop personal computer. c) Acronym for printed circuit.

PCS
(wireless) Personal Communication Services. A second-generation digital wireless two-way voice, messaging, and data communications service operating at 1900 MHz. PCS is usually packaged with call waiting, voice mail, and caller ID service features.

PDA
(computers) Personal Digital Assistant. A hand-held, battery-powered computing device used to store addresses, personal calendars, and notes. PDA and wireless technologies are merging to create combination PDA, wireless phone, and Internet-accessible devices.

PDF
Acronym for Portable Document Format. *See* Acrobat.

Pentium
(computers) The world's dominant series of 32-bit CPU microprocessor chips manufactured by the Intel Corporation (www.intel.com) and used in PCs (personal computers). Pentium can refer to either the chip or a computer that uses the chip.

personal digital assistant
See PDA.

PIN
(wireless) Personal Identity Number. A code number used as a security password by the authorized owner or user for accessing a wireless phone, bank accounts, and other services and accounts.

pixel
(computers) Contraction of Picture (slang "pix") Element. The smallest element of visual information that can be used to make an image on a computer monitor or TV screen. The more pixels, the higher the resolution of a monitor. A pixel on a color monitor is made up of red, blue, and green dots of varying intensity that converge at the same point.

platform
(computers) a) A specific computer hardware architecture. For example, the PC, Macintosh, or UNIX platforms. b) A specific computer software architecture. For example, the Windows platform, or the Mac OS platform. The terms "platform," "operating system," and "environment" are often used interchangeably. *See* cross platform, operating system.

plug and play
(computers) Specialized computer software that recognizes when a new hardware component has been plugged into the computer system and that initializes and installs the component for immediate use with the system.

portal
(Internet) A Web site that provides a wide variety of services to the user including Web search functionality, directories, news, e-mail, databases, discussion groups, online shopping, and links to other sites. The term was originally used to refer to all-purpose sites such as AOL and CompuServe, but is now more commonly used to refer to vertical market sites that cover specific industries or topics.

pull-down menu
(computers) An on-screen list of computer functions or operations accessed by selecting (clicking) a single main menu title.

RAM
(computers) Random Access Memory. Memory chips that plug into a computer's motherboard and that serve as the computer's primary but temporary workspace. Generally, the larger the files that are in use at one time, the more RAM a computer needs to operate. For example, a com-

puter needs more RAM to process graphics files than textual word-processing files. Most new computers (as of 2002) are made with a standard minimum of 128 MB (megabytes) of RAM and allow for additional upgrades. Note that storage of data in RAM is temporary and is lost when the computer is turned off. *See* ROM (Read Only Memory).

Random Access Memory
See RAM.

Read Only Memory
See ROM.

real time
(computers) a) A measure of computational time that relates to achieving a result in an external process. b) A computer system that interacts with and gives an immediate result to external input. Explanation: A computer will continue to perform a task until the task has been completed. However, some tasks must be performed very quickly to have any value. For example, a GPS (Global Positioning System) device held by a hiker in the remote wilderness could take as long as several seconds to compute location coordinates to the user and still be useful. However, a jet airplane traveling at 1,000 miles per hour (more than a mile every four seconds!) must make this calculation in much less time to be useful. In another example, a video-conferencing camera is considered to operate in real time, even though it takes a very small amount of time for the video image to move over the phone lines. In popular usage, a computational operation that takes "essentially" no time is considered to happen in real time.

re-boot
(computers) To restart (turn off, then turn on) a computer. This resets the computer, often resolving conflicts in the processing. *See* boot.

ROM
(computers) Read Only Memory. Memory chips built into the motherboard of a computer that permanently store data, instructions, and routines for the operation of the computer. ROM cannot be altered by the user and is not lost when the computer is turned off. *See* RAM.

search engine
(Internet) Computer software designed by a company and offered online to search the Internet for information based upon keywords entered by the user. Search engines do not reside on the user's computer, but rather at the online location of the respective company. Major search engines on the Web include:
AltaVista (www.altavista.com)
Excite (www.excite.com)
Google (www.google.com)
Hotbot (www.hotbot.com)
Infoseek (www.infoseek.com)
Lycos (www.lycos.com)
Northern Light (www.northernlight.com)
Overture (www.overture.com)
WebCrawler (www.webcrawler.com)
Yahoo! (www.yahoo.com)

server
(Internet) A computer connected to a network so its data and programs can be shared by multiple users of the other connected computers. Server can refer to either or both the hardware or the software that runs the computer itself. Some of the many types of servers include: Application Server (runs application software for multiple computers); Database Server (maintains a database accessed by multiple users); Remote Access Server (provides access to information to multiple remote users); and Web Server (provides World Wide Web access to the Internet).

software
(computers) A series of instructions that run on a computer. Software can be either "system software" that runs the computer itself, or "application software" that interacts with and performs specific tasks for the user. *See* application (software), system software, operating system.

spam
(Internet) Unsolicited e-mail, usually mass e-mail messages promoting a political or social message or advertising a product. Named after the canned meat by-product SPAM (which is a registered trademark of Hormel Corporation). The use of mass e-mailings is the subject of great controversy. Some feel that unsolicited e-mail is a violation of the basic values of the Internet, while others have built legitimate businesses on such "mailings." *See* e-mail.

streaming audio
(computers/Internet) Digital audio transmission over a data network such as the Internet. Streaming audio is a one-way data transmission.

COMPUTERS

streaming video
(computers/Internet) Digital video transmission over a data network such as the Internet. Streaming video is a one-way data transmission.

system
(computers) A group of computer components and peripherals that work together to perform a task.

system software
(computers) The primary software program that manages a computer's basic functions and controls the execution of application programs. All application software must conform to certain standards of a computer's operating system software to function. Also called operating system. The most common operating systems are Windows (for Intel/IBM PC-compatible computers), Mac OS (for Macintosh), and UNIX and Linux (for PC and UNIX computers).

T1
(Internet) A dedicated digital circuit connection leased from a telecommunications provider that provides 1.544 Mbps data transmission capacity. T1 lines are used for high speed private networks and connections to the Internet. *See* bandwidth, DSL, E1, E2, E3, ISDN, modem, T2, T3.

T2
(Internet) A dedicated digital circuit connection leased from a telecommunications provider that provides 3.152 Mbps data transmission capacity. T2 lines are used for high speed private networks and connections to the Internet. *See* bandwidth, DSL, E1, E2, E3, ISDN, modem, T1, T3.

T3
(Internet) A dedicated digital circuit connection leased from a telecommunications provider that provides 44.736 Mbps data transmission capacity. T3 lines are used for ultra high speed private networks and connections to the Internet. T3 lines can handle full-screen, full-motion video. The European equivalent is E3. *See* bandwidth, DSL, E1, E3, ISDN, modem, T1, T2.

tab delimited
(computers) A database record format that separates data fields in a record with a tab. Tab delimited formatting, unlike comma delimited formatting, does not use quotation marks around each field of data content. *See* comma delimited.

top-level domain
(Internet) The primary organizational category of a domain name. All domain names are orga-
nized into categories that are assigned and administered by ICANN (Internet Corporation for Assigned Names and Numbers). The top-level domain is indicated by the extension at the end of a domain name and is intended to describe the nature of the domain name owner. Top-level domains include:
.com —commercial (business entities)
.net —network
.org —organization (non-government organization)
.edu —U.S. educational institution
.gov —U.S. government (federal, state, or local)
.mil —U.S. military
The exponential surge in domain name registrations has led to the introduction of new top-level domains, some of which include:
.biz —business entity
.pro —professional
.museum —museum
.info —information service
.name —individual person
Many countries are permitted to have top-level domains, indicated by two-letter extensions. A few examples include:
.ca —Canada
.fr —France
.uk —United Kingdom

tri-band (mode) phone
(wireless) A mobile phone (handset) that is capable of operating on digital 800 MHz and 1900 MHz frequencies as well as analog 800 MHz frequency.

UNIX
(computers) A computer operating system used extensively in workstations and servers in scientific and academic environments and especially on the Internet. UNIX is especially popular because of its stability and ability to multitask. *See* Linux, Mac OS, operating system, Windows.

up
(computers/Internet) a) A computer that has been been turned on or that is in operational condition. b) A Web site that is operational. *See* down.

upload
(Internet/computers) The transfer of computer documents or files from a local (client) computer to a remote computer over a network. To download means to receive and to upload means to transmit. *See* download.

C O M P U T E R S

URL
(Internet) Acronym for Uniform Resource Locator. The address and/or route to a file, document, or Web site on the Internet. A URL is typed into the "address" window of a Web browser to access a particular Web domain or Web page on the Internet. For example:
http://www.worldtradepress.com
is the URL for World Trade Press.
Specifically, a URL is a series of letters, characters, and numbers that contain 1) a protocol prefix, 2) port number, 3) domain name, 4) subdirectory name, and 5) file name. The port number is almost always a default and does not need to be included. As a result, a user need only type in the protocol prefix and domain name to gain access to a Web site or page. There are more than 10 protocol prefixes, but the most common are:
http: —World Wide Web server
ftp: —file transfer protocol server
news: —Usenet newsgroups
mailto: —e-mail
gopher: —Gopher service
file: —file on local system
In many cases a specific page is stored in a subdirectory on the domain. For example:
http://www.worldtradepress.com/catalog/dictionary.html is the specific Web page for the World Trade Press Dictionary of International Trade. This URL can be broken up as follows:
http: —protocol prefix
// —separators
www.worldtradepress.com/ —domain name
catalog/ —subdirectory name
dictionary.html —document name
See Internet domain name, top-level domain.

Usenet
(Internet) Contraction of User Network. An Internet-based bulletin board network that provides access to newsgroups and group e-mail.

user interface
(computers) The means of communication between a user and a computer. This includes the computer keyboard, mouse, text commands (such as "Ctrl S" to save) and pull-down menus and other hyperlinked commands that enter data or tell the computer what to do. *See* GUI.

virus
(computers) A software program designed maliciously to infect and harm computer files. A computer virus is distinguished by its ability to attach itself to other programs and self-replicate. Typically, a virus arrives hidden within or attached to a file, program, e-mail, or e-mail attachment. Some viruses simply display a harmless message when activated, while others are designed to do severe damage to computer files and system software. A virus can be activated automatically or by a trigger event such as a date, time, or sequence of keyboard strokes. A number of anti-virus programs are available and can be especially helpful because many viruses operate on similar principles that can be detected by the anti-virus software. However, it is wise to regularly update this software (often with direct downloads from Web sites) as new viruses are invented and discovered daily. *See* hacker.

WAN
(computers) Wide Area Network. A data communications network that serves a very large geographic area such as a state, province, or country. *See* extranet, Internet, intranet, LAN (Local Area Network), network.

WAP
(computers/Internet) Wireless Application Protocol. A set of communications protocols designed to provide e-mail, Internet Relay Chat (IRC), and Web content to wireless devices such as cellular phones, beepers, and wireless PDAs (Personal Digital Assistants). The development of WAP was initially spurred by four major manufacturers of wireless products: Motorola, Nokia, Ericsson, and Unwired Planet. WAP technology is based on WML (Wireless Markup Language), which is a derivative of HDML and HTML designed for small screen displays. *See* HDML, HTML.

Web
See World Wide Web.

Web browser
(Internet) An application program that enables the user to access the World Wide Web on the Internet. To view a particular Web site or page, the user types its Internet address (URL) into the "Address" window of the Web browser. Today's popular browsers enable the user to view graphics and text as well as listen to audio files and see video files that reside on the World Wide Web. Technically a browser is a client application that uses the HyperText Transfer Protocol (HTTP) to enable the user to make requests of Web servers. Popular browsers include Microsoft Internet Explorer and Netscape Navigator, both of which

support e-mail. *See* Internet Explorer, Netscape Navigator.

Webcrawler
(computers/Internet) An Internet portal and search engine. Connect at www.webcrawler.com. *See* keyword search, search engine.

Web page
(Internet) A document on the World Wide Web. A Web page is maintained on a Web site. *See* Web site, home page.

Web server
(computers/Internet) A computer with an operating system and server software designed to provide World Wide Web (WWW) services on the Internet. After an organization's Web site data is loaded onto its Web server, it is accessible to anyone accessing the WWW. A Web server can be located in an organization's offices or at a third-party hosting service.

Web site
(Internet) A collection of files on a server that are accessible on the World Wide Web. The term is used both to denote the server that contains files and the collection of files that relate to a specific URL. A Web site is composed of a "home page" and other data files that can be accessed from the home page.

wide area network
See WAN.

Windows
(computers) The dominant IBM PC-compatible computer operating system developed by Microsoft Corporation (www.microsoft.com). Windows comes in a number of variations including Windows 95, Windows 98, Windows 2000 and Windows XP. *See* Linux, Mac OS, operating system,,PC, UNIX.

Wintel
(computers) Contraction of Windows Intel. A general reference to the dominant computing environment of PCs using Intel CPUs and Windows operating systems. *See* PC, Windows.

Wireless Application Protocol
See WAP.

World Wide Web (WWW) (Web)
(Internet) a) The aggregation of documents that can be accessed via the Internet. b) The aggregation of hypertext servers (HTTP servers) that can be accessed via the Internet. c) The system of accessing files and documents on the Internet using hypertext links.

The Web operates using the HTTP protocol and provides graphic capability. The Internet, on the other hand, is the network of computer networks and servers on which the Web resides and operates. The Web was developed at the European Center for Nuclear Research (CERN) between 1989 and 1991 as a means of sharing data on nuclear research.

WWW
See World Wide Web.

XML
(Internet) Acronym for Extensible Markup Language. An open standard computer language used for defining data elements on a Web page. XML is considered the successor language to HTML (HyperText Markup Language) because of its ability to define content and function as if it were a database. In HTML the Web developer defines how text and graphic elements are displayed, whereas in XML the developer defines what these text and graphic elements contain. In HTML the developer can use only predefined tags, whereas in XML the developer can create and define the tags.

Yahoo
(computers/Internet) An Internet portal and search engine. Connect at www.yahoo.com. *See* keyword search, search engine.

zip
(computers/Internet) A popular method of compressing a computer file or group of files. Compression of large documents makes them easier to store or send via e-mail as an attachment. After being "zipped" a file has the suffix ".zip" appended to its name. When extracted, the file returns to its normal size and can be opened using the original application program. Most computers and browsers come equipped with a zip utility and *.zip files can be extracted (uncompressed) simply by double-clicking the document icon or name.

Resources for International Trade

BOOKS & DIRECTORIES

Air Freight Directory

Directory of air freight motor carriers. Bimonthly. Suite$84.00 per year (six issues). Available from: Air Cargo, Inc., 1819 Bay Ridge Ave., Annapolis, MD 21403 USA; Tel: [1] (410) 280-5578, or (for subscription to the directory) [1] (410) 280-8949; Fax: [1] (410) 268-3154; Web: www.air-cargo-inc.com/aci.

Basic Guide to Exporting

Designed to help U.S. firms learn the costs and risks associated with exporting and to develop a strategy for exporting. Sources of assistance throughout the federal and state governments as well as the private sector. Available from: World Trade Press, 1450 Grant Ave., Suite 204, Novato, CA 94945 USA; Tel: [1] (415) 898-1124 or [1] (800) 833-8586; Fax: [1] (415) 898-1080; Web: www.worldtradepress.com.

Black's Law Dictionary

Considered a standard in the field. Lists over 10,000 entries updated to reflect recent developments in the law. Includes pronunciation guides. By Henry Campbell Black. $44.95 Softcover. Abridged 7th Edition. ISBN 0-314-88536-6. Available from: West Group, PO Box 64833, St. Paul, MN 55164-0833 USA; Tel: [1] (800) 328-4880; Fax: [1] (800) 340-9378; Web: www.westgroup.com.

Breaking into the Trade Game: A Small Business Guide to Exporting

An information tool to assist America businesses develop international markets. Both a comprehensive how-to manual and reference book providing the reader with the contacts and resources to ease entry into markets around the world. Also highlights export success stories of small businesses. The full text of the Guide is available on the SBA's Web Site at www.sba.gov/oit/info/Guide-To-Exporting. Print versions free of charge can be requested from the SBA Answer Desk, 200 North College Street, Suite A-2015, Charlotte, NC 28202 USA; Tel: [1] (800) UASK-SBA; E-mail: answerdesk@sba.gov.

19 Code of Federal Regulations (CFR)

Two volumes. Vol. 1 contains regulations of the U.S. Customs Services, Department of Treasury. Vol. 2 contains regulations of the International Trade Commission, International Trade Administration, Department of Commerce. Topics covered include packing and stamping, marking; customs financial and accounting procedure; customs bond; air commerce regulations; trademarks, trade names, and copyrights, etc. Available from the U.S. Government Printing Office at: Tel: [1] (866) 512-1800; Web: http://bookstore.gpo.gov.

Directory of United States Exporters

Directory of U.S. export firms, export executives, and products exported. Annual. $475.00. Available from Piers Publishing Group. Contact at: Tel: [1] (877) 203-5277; Fax: [1] (973) 848-7133; Web: http://pierspub.com. A CD-ROM version can be ordered from this Web site. *See* Directory of United States Importers/Exporters for a directory of both importers and exporters.

Directory of United States Importers

Directory of U.S. import firms, import executives, and products imported. Annual. $475.00. Available from Piers Publishing Group. Contact at: Tel: [1] (877) 203-5277; Fax: [1] (973) 848-7133; Web: http://pierspub.com. A CD-ROM version can be ordered from this Web site. *See* Directory of United States Importers/Exporters for a directory of both importers and exporters.

Directory of United States Importers/ Exporters

Directory of U.S. import and export firms, company executives, and products imported or exported on CD-ROM. Annual. $675.00 for print version and $995.000 for CD-ROM. Available from Piers Publishing Group. Contact at: Tel: [1] (877) 203-5277; Fax: [1] (973) 848-7133; Web: http://pierspub.com.

Europa World Year Book

Provides analytical, statistical, and directory information on each country's economic, social and political structure. Volume 1 covers international organizations and countries from A-J. Volume 2 covers countries from K-Z. ISBN: 1-85743-100-6. Annual. Available from: Europa Publications Ltd., 11 New Fetter Lane, London EC4P 4EE UK; Tel: [44] (20) 7842 2110; Fax: [44] (20) 7842 2249; E-mail: info.europa@tandf.co.uk; Web: www.europa-publications.co.uk.

Export Documentation, A Guide to

Describes the preparation of Export Documentation. Contains hundreds of samples of documents,

RESOURCES

By Donald Ewert. Available from: International Trade Institute, Inc., 5055 N. Main Street; Dayton, OH 45415 USA; Tel: [1] (800) 543-2453.

Export Reference Guide

A reference guide used by exporters and freight forwarders as a source of country specific shipping document and import information. CD-ROM version is updated monthly, and the Web version is updated weekly. Available from: BNA, 1231 25th Street NW; Washington, DC 20037 USA; Tel: [1] (800) 372-1033; Web: www.bna.com.

Export Sales and Marketing Manual

Step-by-step procedural manual for marketing U.S. products world-wide. The manual contains illustrations, flow charts, worksheets, and samples of export contracts, shipping documents, and effective international correspondence. By John Jagoe. $295.00 (print or CD-ROM). Available directly from Export Institute USA's Web site at www.exportinstitute.com. Address: Export Institute USA, 6901 West 84th St., Suite 359, P.O. Box 385883, Minneapolis, MN 55438 USA; Tel: (from within the U.S.) [1] (800) 943-3171, (from outside the U.S.) (952) 943-1505; Fax: [1] (952) 943-1535; E-mail: jrj@exportinstitute.com; Web: www.export-institute.com.

Exporters' Encyclopedia - Reference Book

A comprehensive reference manual detailing trade regulations, documentation requirements, transportation, key contacts, etc. for 200 world markets. Sections cover export order, markets and know-how, communication data, information sources and services, and transportation data. ISBN 1-56203-006-X. Available from: The D&B Corporation, 1 Diamond Hill Road, Murray Hill, N.J. 07974-1218 USA; Tel: (from within the U.S.) [1] (866) 719-7158, (from outside the U.S.) (512) 794-7768; Fax: [1] (512) 794-7670; E-mail: custserv@dnb.com; Web: http:www.dnb.com. Subscriptions include twice-monthly country-specific trade updates and access to free consultations with export specialists.

Foreign Trade Zone Manual

A U.S. government reference manual for grantees, operators, and users of U.S. Foreign Trade Zones and customs brokers. Available from the U.S. Government Printing Office at: Tel: [1] (866) 512-1800; Web: http://bookstore.gpo.gov. An Internet version of the manual is found at www.customs.ustreas.gov/impexp2/comm-imp/ftz/manual; a WordPerfect 5.0 version can also be downloaded from this site.

Gestures: The Do's and Taboo's of Body Language Around the World

A humorous and informative book on gestures and body language around the world. The first half of the book illustrates gestures and describes what each gestures means in different countries. The second half presents a country by country listing of gestures and body language. By Roger Axtell. ISBN: 0-471-18342-3. Other books by Roger Axtell: *Do's and Taboos Around the World*, 2nd Edition; *Do's and Taboos of International Trade: A Small Business Primer; Do's and Taboos of Hosting International Visitors*. Available in many bookstores, and also from the publisher at: John Wiley and Sons, Inc., Distribution Center, 1 Wiley Drive, Somerset, NJ 08875-1272 USA; Tel: [1] (800) 225-5945; Fax: [1] (732) 302-2300; E-mail: bookinfo@wiley.com; Web: www.wiley.com.

Global Road Warrior (book and CD-ROM)

95-country handbook for the international business traveler. Thousands of facts and tips for surviving and succeeding while "on the road internationally." Includes detailed "techno travel" information on Internet access, electrical requirements, and local support numbers for hardware and software vendors. Softcover, 850 pages, $65.00. Also available as a 161-country CD-ROM for both PC and Mac, for $65.00. Available from: World Trade Press, 1450 Grant Ave., Suite 204, Novato, CA 94945 USA; Tel: [1] (415) 898-1124 or (800) 833-8586; Fax: [1] (415) 898-1080; Web: www.globalroadwarrior.com, www.worldtradepress.com.

Harmonized Tariff Schedule of the United States (HTS or HTSUS)

(USA) An organized listing of goods and their duty rates which is used by U.S. Customs as the basis for classifying imported products and therefore establishing the duty to be charged and providing the U.S. Census with statistical information about imports and exports. The categorization of product listings in the HTSUS is based on the international Harmonized Commodity Description and Coding System developed under the auspices of the Customs Cooperation Council (Harmonized System, HS). Available from the U.S. Government Printing Office at: Tel: [1] (866) 512-1800; Web: http://bookstore.gpo.gov.

Importer's Manual USA (3rd Edition)

A comprehensive reference for importing to the United States. Topics include U.S. Customs Entry and Clearance; International Banking, Letters of Credit; Foreign Exchange; International Law; Packing, Shipping and Insurance; and Commodity Index.

Import how-to for 99 commodity groups. ISBN 1-885073-00-3. Hardbound, 860 pages, includes illustrations, photographs. $87.00. By Edward G. Hinkelman, Available from: World Trade Press, 1450 Grant Ave., Suite 204, Novato, CA 94945 USA; Tel: [1] (415) 898-1124 or [1] (800) 833-8586; Fax: [1] (415) 898-1080; Web: www.worldtradepress.com.

International Business Transactions

From the "In a Nutshell" series, a succinct exposition of the law for those who are not specialists in international trade. Traces legal aspects of an international business transaction from first idea to negotiated conclusion. By Ralph H. Folsom, Michael Wallace, John Spanogle, Jr. ISBN: 0314240934. 6th edition (449 pages) available for $23.00 from major online bookstores, such as Amazon (www.amazon.com) and Barnes & Noble (www.barnesandnoble.com).

Law Digest, The

Contains information on the legal systems of countries around the world. Included are the following:
• Up-to-date digests of the laws of the 50 states, the District of Columbia, Puerto Rico and the US Virgin Islands.
• English-language summaries of the laws of 80 countries
• The complete texts of over 50 Uniform and Model Acts and International Conventions.
• Useful information on the Federal Judiciary and the Rules of Conduct of the American Bar Association.
Annual. Available from: Martindale-Hubbell, Customer Relations Dept., 121 Chanlon Road, New Providence, NJ 07974 USA; E-mail: info@martindale.com; Tel: [1] (800) 526-4902; Fax: [1] (908) 771-8704; Web: www.martindale.com.
The Law Digest is also available through LEXIS®-NEXIS®. The Digest is found in the MARHUB library on the LEXIS®-NEXIS® service. Contact at: www.lexis.com.

Maritime Guide

Includes sections on dry and wet docks, a gazetteer, maps, postal and telecommunication addresses, call signs, and more, including shipbreakers listed by country. Annual. Can be purchased directly from Lloyd's Register "Fairplay" Web site at www.fairplay.co.uk; E-mail: sales@lrfairplay.com.

National Trade Data Bank (NTDB)

(CD-ROM/Internet) Contains international economic and export promotion information supplied by 15 U.S. agencies. Data are updated monthly. The NTDB contains data from the Departments of Agriculture (Foreign Agricultural Service), Commerce (Bureau of the Census, Bureau of Economic Analysis, Office of Administration, and National Institute for Standards and Technology), Energy, Labor (Bureau of Labor Statistics), the Central Intelligence Agency, Eximbank, Federal Reserve System, U.S. International Trade Commission, Overseas Private Investment Corporation, Small Business Administration, the U.S. Trade Representative, and the University of Massachusetts. Source: U.S. Department of Commerce, Office of Economic Analysis, HCHB Room 4885, Washington, DC 20230 USA; Tel: [1] (202) 482-1986; Web: www.stat-usa.gov.

Official Export Guide

Gives comprehensive export information from source to market for shippers, freight forwarders, and transportation companies. Features marketing, shipping, and documentation information. Includes country profiles with trade data to find new markets, surveys of major world ports, and Export Administration regulations. The Guide is available from Commonwealth Business Media, Inc. in a subscription service either online (at www.officialexportguide.com) or in print; changes are published in biweekly updates available to both online and print subscribers. E-mail: subscriptions@officialexportguide.com.

Paperboard Packaging Resource Directory

(Formerly, the Official Container Directory) The Paperboard Packaging Resource Directory is an annually-updated resource supporting the paperboard converting industry. Can be purchased directly at www.container-directory.com; credit card orders can be made at (from within the U.S.) [1] (800) 598-6008 or (from outside the U.S.) (218) 723-9180; Advanstar Marketing Services, Customer Service Dept., 131 W. 1st St., Duluth, MN 55802 USA; Fax: [1] (218) 723-9146.

Reference Book for World Traders

A looseleaf handbook covering information required for planning and executing exports and imports to and from all foreign countries; kept up to date by an amendment service. Includes sections covering exporting, free trade zones, and trade-related information on the countries of the world. Three volumes. $170.00 for master volume plus monthly supplements. Available from: Croner Publications, Inc., 10951 Sorrento Valley Rd., Suite 1D, San Diego, CA 92121-1613 USA; Tel: [1] (800) 441-4033; Fax: [1] (800) 809-0334; Web: www.croner.com.

RESOURCES

RESOURCES

Thompson Bank Directory, Intl. Edition
Lists banks located around the world with addresses of branches and other information. Included are Central Bank and trade association information for each country and each US state. 5 Volumes (includes Worldwide Correspondence Guide). Biannual. $575.00. Can be ordered directly at www.tfp.com. Available from: Thomson Financial Publishing; Tel: [1] (800) 321-3373 or [1] (847) 676-9600; E-mail: customerservice@tfp.com; Web: www.tfp.com.

Trade Shows Worldwide
Details of conventions, conferences, trade shows and expositions. Five-year date and location information provided. U.S., Canada, and 60 other countries. ISBN: 0-7876-5905-3. $335.00. Available from: Gale, P.O. Box 9187, Farmington Hills, MI 48333-9187 USA; Tel: [1] (800) 877-GALE (4253); Fax: [1] (800) 414-5043; E-mail: galeord@gale.com; Web: www.gale.com.

U.S. Customs House Guide
Comprehensive reference that provides information necessary to document, ship and distribute goods to market. Profiles of U.S. and Canadian ports. Updated harmonized tariff schedules, customs regulations and directories of services. Available in both online (www.cbizmedia.com) and print subscriptions. Subscriptions include free updates. Available from: Commonwealth Business Media, Inc., 400 Windsore Corporate Center, 50 Millstone Road Suite 200, East Windsor, NJ 08520-1415 USA; Tel: [1] (800) 221-5488 ext. 7782; Fax: [1] (609) 371-7718; Web: www.cbizmedia.com.

World Business Directory
Contains information on about 136,000 trade-oriented businesses in 180 countries. 10th edition. ISBN: 0-7876-3432-8. $630.00. Available from: Gale, P.O. Box 9187, Farmington Hills, MI 48333-9187 USA; Tel: [1] (800) 877-GALE (4253); Fax: [1] (800) 414-5043; E-mail: galeord@gale.com; Web: www.gale.com.

World Directory of Trade and Business Associations
Provides contact information and extensive details on the activities, publications and membership of more than 3,000 trade and business associations worldwide. Associations from all major sectors are covered, including finance, general business and industry, advertising and marketing, and major consumer markets. 3rd Edition. ISBN: 0-86338-939-2. $590.00. Available from: Gale, P.O. Box 9187, Farmington Hills, MI 48333-9187 USA; Tel: [1] (800) 877-GALE (4253); Fax: [1] (800) 414-5043; E-mail: galeord@gale.com; Web: www.gale.com.

World Trade Almanac
Detailed economic, marketing, trade, cultural, legal & business travel surveys for the world's top 100 countries. Hardbound, 844 pages, includes 100 maps. Available from: World Trade Press, 1450 Grant Ave., Suite 204, Novato, CA 94945 USA; Tel: [1] (415) 898-1124 or [1] (800) 833-8586; Fax: [1] (415) 898-1080; Web: www.worldtradepress.com.

Worldwide Corporate Tax Guide
Summarizes the corporate tax systems in over 130 countries. Revised annually. Available from: Ernst & Young Product Sales at [1] (800) 726-7339; Web: www.ey.com/global/gcr.nsf/EYPassport/EYPassport_Home. Also available as a downloadable Adobe Acrobat PDF file free of charge at this Web site.

International Chamber of Commerce Publications

ICC Publishing; International Chamber of Commerce (ICC); 38 Cours Albert 1er; 75008 Paris, France; Tel: [33] (1) 49-53-28-28; Fax: [33] (1) 49-53-29-42; U.S. address: ICC Publishing, Inc., 156 Fifth Avenue, Suite 417, New York, NY 10010 USA; Tel: [1] (212) 206-1150; Fax: [1] (212) 633-6025. Publications can be purchased directly at www.iccbooks.com. Web: www.iccwbo.org.

Export and Trade Finance

Designed specifically for the needs of trade finance professionals. This publication covers everything from organizational and tax considerations to payment mechanics to official programs intended to promote exports. 402 pages. ICC Publication 970.

Guide to the ICC Uniform Rules for Demand Guarantees

Intended to apply worldwide to the use of guarantees, bonds, and other payments arising on presentation of a written demand and other documents specified in the guarantee, and which are not conditional on proof of default by the principal in the underlying transaction. The Rules take into account the rights and obligations of all parties. 136 pages. ICC Publication No. 510.

Handbook of World Trade

A guide for business practitioners and adviser to review their companies' international trade strategies and current activities, and an authoritative reference source for anyone needing to understand the framework and mechanics of world trade. 486 pages. ICC Publication 638.

ICC Arbitration

Details the history and workings of the world's foremost arbitration institutions, the ICC International Court of Arbitration. By Craig, Park, and Paulsson. 800 pages. ICC Publication No. 594.

ICC Guide to Documentary Credit Operations

ICC's popular Guide to Documentary Credit Operations offers a total explanation of the documentary credit process. Each stage of the process is illustrated by colorful, easy-to-read diagrams and supported by concrete examples of how it applies in practice. 117 pages. ICC Publication No. 515.

ICC Model Commercial Agency Contract

New model form for negotiating agency agreements abroad which incorporates prevailing practice in international trade as well as principles generally recognized by domestic laws on agency agreements. 25 pages. ICC Publication No. 496.

ICC Uniform Rules for Collections

This publication describes the conditions governing collections, including those for the presentation, payment and the acceptance terms. The Articles also specify the responsibility of the bank regarding protest, case of need and actions to protect the merchandise. An aid to everyday banking operations. (A revised, updated edition was published in 1995). ICC Publication No. 522.

ICC Uniform Rules for Contract Guarantees

This short publication aims to achieve a fair balance between the legitimate interests of all three parties. They invest guarantee practice with a moral content by establishing the principle that a claim under a guarantee must be justified. By doing this, they encourage greater confidence in such guarantees and enable them to play a wider role in international commerce. 30 pages. ICC Publication 325.

Incoterms 2000

Defines the thirteen trading terms and specifies respective rights and obligations of buyer and seller in international transactions. 127 pages; ICC Publication No. 560.

International Commercial Transactions

Takes a detailed look at the vital sectors of commercial practice. This publication presents a legal framework within which rules of law, general principles, standard contracts and commercial practice are shown to interact to the benefit of the parties involved in international trade transactions. 516 pages. ICC Publication 624.

Key Words in International Trade

Contains more than 3000 business words and expressions, translated into English, German, Spanish, French, and Italian. Separate alphabetical indexes are also included for all languages. 450 pages. ICC Publication No. 417/4.

UP 500 and 400 Compared

This publication was developed as a vehicle from which to train managers, supervisors and practitioners of international trade in critical areas of the new UCP 500 Rules. It pays particular attention to those Articles that have been the source of litigation. 135 pages. Edited by Charles del Busto. ICC Publication No. 511.

PERIODICALS & REPORTS

Background Notes

A series of publications by the U.S. State Department providing an overview of a country's history, people, political conditions, economy and foreign relations. Each publication also includes map of country and travel notes. Available from the U.S. Government Printing Office at: Tel: [1] (866) 512-1800; Web: http://bookstore.gpo.gov.

Commercial News USA (CNUSA)

Provides exposure for U.S. products and services through the Commercial News USA export-magazine and Web site (www.cnewsusa.com). The catalog is distributed through U.S. embassies and consulates to business readers in 150 countries. Copies are provided to international visitors at trade events around the world. To be eligible for inclusion in the catalog, products must be at least 51 percent U.S. parts and 51 percent U.S. labor. The service helps U.S. firms identify potential export markets and make contacts leading to representation, distributorships, joint venture or licensing agreements, or direct sales. Published monthly. Contact: Associated Business Publications, International, 317 Madison Ave., Suite 1900, New York, NY 10017 USA; Tel: [1] (212) 490-3999; Fax: [1] (212) 986-7864; E-mail: cnusa@abpi.net; Web: www.abpi.net.

Economist, The

Current affairs and business magazine (the publishers call it a newspaper). Includes reports, analysis, and comments on key events in business, finance, science and technology. Special editorial surveys focus on specific countries, industries or markets. Available in a weekly print edition and an online edition. Contact at www.economist.com to subscribe to either the print or online editions.

Economist Intelligence Unit

A publishing company which sells research reports, country profiles, newsletters, and on-line information to help companies operate and expand abroad. Also sells individual country studies, quarterly country reports, and forecasts. Contact the Economist Intelligence Unit, Ltd. online at www.eiu.com for subscription and advertising information; Tel: (London) [44] (20) 7830-1007, (Hong Kong) [8] (52) 2802-7288, (New York) [1] (212) 554-0600.

Export America

The official U.S. government trade magazine presents international business news. Published monthly by the International Trade Administration of the U.S Department of Commerce. $55.00/year. Available from the U.S. Government Printing Office at: Tel: [1] (866) 512-1800; Web: http://bookstore.gpo.gov.

Exporter, The

Monthly reports on the business of exporting. Available from: The Exporter, 26 Broadway, Suite 776, New York, NY 10004 USA; Tel: [1] (212) 269-2016; Fax: [1] (212) 269-2740; Web: www.exporter.com.

Financial Times (of London)

Daily newspaper specifically for those in the economic and financial sector. Covers current news and information of financial and political issues. Also includes stock tables, graphs, and commentary. Contact the Financial Times online at www.ft-subs.com for subscription information specific to the country or continent of delivery.

Foreign Labor Trends

A series of reports on specific countries of the world, providing an overview of the labor sector of a country's economy. Includes information on labor standards, conditions of employment, human resource development and labor relations. Available from the U.S. Government Printing Office at: Tel: [1] (866) 512-1800; Web: http://bookstore.gpo.gov.

Foreign Traders Index (FTI)

The foreign traders index, which is part of the National Trade Data Bank (NTDB), identifies foreign firms that are interested in importing U.S. products. The FTI includes background information on foreign companies, address, contact person, sales figures, size of company, and products by SIC code. Contact: U.S. Department of Commerce, HCHB Room 4885, Washington, DC 20230 USA; Tel: [1] (202) 482-1986; Fax: [1] (202) 482-2164; Web: www.stat-usa.gov.

International Company Profiles (ICPs)

U.S. government fee-based service which provides a background report on a specific foreign firm, prepared by U.S. commercial officers overseas. ICPs provide information about the type of organization, year established, size, number of employees, reputation, language preferred, product lines, principal owners, financial and trade references. ICPs include narrative information about the reliability of the foreign firm. Issued by the International Trade Administration (U.S. Dept. of Commerce). To obtain an International Company Profile, contact your nearest Dept. of Commerce district office, or call [1] (800) USA-TRADE; Web: www.usatrade.gov.

Journal of Commerce (JoC Week)

The Journal of Commerce publishes the weekly magazine Joc Week in both print and online versions. Subscription to the print version includes full access to the online version, which contains an extensive archive of articles. JoC Week has information on domestic and foreign economic developments plus export opportunities, shipyards, agricultural trade leads, and trade fair information. Feature articles on tariff and non-tariff barriers, licensing controls, joint ventures, and trade legislation in foreign countries. Contact the Journal online at www.joc.com; Tel: [1] (800) 331-1341 or (from outside the U.S.) (973) 848-7259; E-mail: customersvs@joc.com.

OAG Cargo Guide

A basic reference publication for shipping freight by air. It contains current domestic and international cargo flight schedules, including pure cargo, wide body, and combination passenger-cargo flights. Each monthly issue also contains information on air carriers' special services, labeling, airline and aircraft decodings, air carrier and freight forwarders directory, cargo charter information, Worldwide City Directory, small package services, interline air freight agreements, aircraft loading charts and more. Includes the OAG Cargo Guide Rules Supplement with regulations by country, documentary requirements and aircraft-loading restrictions. $265.00 for annual subscription. Can be purchased from OAG Worldwide, Ltd. online at www.oag.com; Tel: (from within the U.S.) [1] (800) 525-1138, (from outside the U.S.) [44] (1582) 69 5050; E-mail: (in the U.S.) helpdesk@oag.com, (from outside the U.S.) ctech@oag.com.

Wall Street Journal

National and international finance and business. A more conservative tone. Also publishes a European and Asian edition as well as the Asian Wall Street Journal Weekly. Available in print and/or online subscriptions. Print subscription (subscribe directly at http://subscribe.wsj.com/wsjie): $175/year, published weekdays. Online subscription (go to http://interactive.wsj.com): $59/year ($29 for print subscribers). Available from: The Wall Street Journal; Tel: (from within the U.S.) [1] (800) JOURNAL (from outside the U.S., see listing of phone numbers at http://interactive.wsj.com); E-mail: wsj.service@dowjones.com; Web: www.wsj.com.

World Trade Magazine

Provides information to help exporters increase global sales. Targeted to U.S. executives shipping and sourcing worldwide. Available from: from World Trade Magazine, P.O. Box 8010, Laguna Hills, CA 92654-8010 USA; Tel: [1] (949) 830-1340 or [1] (800) 640-7071; Fax: [1] (949) 830-1328; Web: www.worldtrademag.com.

COUNTRY SERIES BOOKS

Business Profile Series

Booklets in electronic format prepared by the HSBC Group and covering more than 40 countries in the Asia-Pacific region, Middle East, Asia, and the Americas. Each provides an overview of the economy, facts and figures, business information, and information for visitors and residents. Downloadable free of charge as Adobe Acrobat PDF files at www.hsbc.com.hk/hk/corp/buspro.htm. Available from the HSBC Group; Web: www.hsbc.com.

Country Business Guides

Each book presents a comprehensive view of a country's business life, covering 25 topics important to international business. Included are chapters on the economy and natural resources, business formation, business entities, demographics, foreign investment, labor, business practices and etiquette, trade fairs, business law, industry reviews, business travel, personal and business taxation, opportunities, important addresses, maps and more. Available from: World Trade Press, 1450 Grant Ave., Suite 204, Novato, CA 94945 USA; Tel: [1] (415) 898-1124 or [1] (800) 833-8586; Fax: [1] (415) 898-1080; Web: www.worldtradepress.com.

Country Profiles

Detailed and continually updated analysis of the financial, political, and economic climate in 180 countries around the world. $235.00 subscription. Available from the Economist Intelligence Unit, Ltd. directly from their online bookstore at http://store.eiu.com (home page www.eiu.com).

Culture Shock Series

A series of roughly 50 country-specific books devoted to helping the business person visiting or working in a particular country to wisely handle various cultural situations. Provides survival guide for expatriates and suggestions on dealing with culture shock. Available from: Graphic Arts Center Publishing Company; 3019 NW Yeon; Portland, OR 97210 USA; Tel: [1] (800) 452-3032; Fax: [1] (800) 355-9685; E-mail: sales@gacpc.com; Web: www.gacpc.com. Also

RESOURCES

available from major online bookstores such as Amazon (www.amazon.com) and Barnes and Noble (www.barnesandnoble.com).

Doing Business in ... Guides

Comprehensive guides by PricewaterhouseCoopers on approximately 90 countries worldwide from Antigua to Zimbabwe. Chapters discuss investment climate, doing business, audits, accounting, and taxation, and include helpful appendix items. Each publication is $39.95. Entire set is available for $795.00. Can be ordered directly from the Web site at www.pwcglobal.com.

Passport to the World

Pocket-sized guides to the business, culture, etiquette and communication styles of a country. Designed to help businesspeople avoid cultural faux-pas, learn about a country's values and beliefs and develop an effective negotiating style. Twenty-four countries. Softcover, $6.95 each. Available from: World Trade Press, 1450 Grant Ave., Suite 204, Novato, CA 94945 USA; Tel: [1] (415) 898-1124 or [1] (800) 833-8586; Fax: [1] (415) 898-1080; Web: www.worldtradepress.com.

TRADE ASSOCIATIONS

Air Transport Association of America (ATA)

The trade and service organization for the U.S. scheduled airlines. ATA acts on behalf of the airlines in activities ranging from improvement in air safety to planning for the airlines' role in national defense. ATA works with the airlines, the Government, and shippers in developing standards and techniques in all phases of air cargo. ATA is a source of information on cargo matters ranging from air freight packaging practices, automation, and freight lift capacity, data on air freight growth, and statistical data on air cargo services. Contact: Air Transport Association of America, 1301 Pennsylvania Ave. NW, Suite 1100, Washington, DC 20004-1707 USA; Tel: [1] (202) 626-4000; E-mail: ata@airlines.org; Web: www.airlines.org.

American Association of Exporters and Importers (AAEI)

A trade association which advises members of legislation regarding importing and exporting. Provides information to the international trade community and fights against protectionism. Hosts seminars and conferences for importers and exporters. Contact: American Association of Exporters and Importers, P.O. Box 7813, Washington, DC 20044-7813 USA; Tel: [1] (202) 661-2181; Fax: [1] (202) 661-2185; Web: www.aaei.org.

Federation of International Trade Associations (FITA)

Can assist you in locating an international trade association in your geographic area. Contact: Federation of International Trade Associations, 11800 Sunrise Valley Drive, Suite 210, Reston, VA 20191 USA; [1] (800) 969-FITA (3482) or [1] (703) 620-1588; E-mail: info@fita.org; Fax: [1] (703) 620-4922; Web: www.fita.org.

International Air Transport Association

The trade and service organization for airlines of more than 100 countries serving international routes. IATA activities on behalf of shippers in international air freight include development of containerization programs, freight handling techniques and, for some airlines, uniform rates and rules. Contact: IATA, Route de l'Aeroport 33, PO Box 416, 15 Airport, CH-1215 Geneva Switzerland; Tel: [41] (22) 799-2525; Fax: [41] (22) 798-3553. Addresses and phone numbers for all offices can be found at www.iata.org/contacts.

International Civil Aviation Organization

The ICAO is an agency of the United Nations. It was organized to insure orderly worldwide technical development of civil aviation. Contact: ICAO, Public Information Office, 999 University Street, Montreal, Quebec H3C 5H7 Canada; Tel: [1] (514) 954-8219; Fax: [1] (514) 954 6077; E-mail: icaohq@icao.int; Web: www.icao.int.

National Association of Export Companies (NEXCO)

An information provider, support clearinghouse, forum, and advocate for those involved in exporting and servicing exporters. Provides networking opportunities, counseling, publications, seminars, etc. Contact: NEXCO, 205 Bergen Turnpike, Suite 2L, Ridgefield Park, NJ 07660 USA; Tel: [1] (201) 814-0336; Fax: [1] (201) 440-1216; Web: www.nexco.org.

National Association of Foreign Trade Zones

A U.S. based trade association of operators and users of U.S. Foreign Trade Zones. Contact: National Association of Foreign Trade Zones, 1000 Connecticut Ave. NW, Suite 1001, Washington, DC 20036 USA; Tel: [1] (202) 331-1950; Fax: [1] (202) 331-1994; E-mail: info@naftz.org; Web: www.naftz.org.

RESOURCES

National Customs Brokers & Forwarders Association of America

A non-profit organization which serves as the trade organization of customs brokers and international freight forwarders in the U.S. Through ongoing communications with industry trade publications and the general media, the Association projects the industry's interests and objectives. Membership includes brokers and freight forwarders in 32 affiliated associations located at major ports throughout the U.S. Contact: National Customs Brokers & Forwarders Association of America, Inc., 1200 18th Street NW, #901, Washington, DC 20036 USA: Tel: [1] (202) 466-0222; Fax: [1] (202) 466-0226; E-mail: staff@ncbfaa.org; Web: www.ncb-faa.org.

National Foreign Trade Council

Trade association that deals exclusively with U.S. public policy affecting international trade and investment. The Council consists of about 500 U.S. manufacturing and service corporations that have international operations of interest. Contact: National Foreign Trade Council, 1625 K St. NW, Suite 1090, Washington, DC 20006 USA; Tel: [1] (202) 887-0278; Fax: [1] (202) 452-8160; E-mail: nftcinformation@nftc.org; Web: www.nftc.org.

Small Business Exporters Association

A trade association representing small- and medium-size exporters. Contact: Small Business Exporters Association, 1156 15th Street, Washington, DC 20005 USA; Tel: [1] (202) 659-9320; Fax: [1] (202) 872-8543; E-mail: sbexporters@aol.com; Web: www.sbea.org.

U.S. Chamber of Commerce, International Division

Represents American business. It lobbies the U.S. Government for specific trade policies and sponsors a number of conferences. Contact: U.S. Chamber of Commerce, International Division, 1615 H Street NW, Washington, DC 20062-2000 USA; Tel: [1] (202) 659-6000; E-mail: intl@uschamber.com; Web: www.uschamber.com/International.

U.S. Council for International Business

A membership organization which is the official U.S. affiliate of the International Chamber of Commerce. The council also oversees the Interstate Commerce Commission's Temporary Admission Carnet System. Provides a number of programs available for members: Court of Arbitration; Counterfeiting Intelligence Bureau; Institute of International Business and Law Practice; International Environmental Bureau. Address: Contact: United States Council for International Business, 1212 Avenue of the Americas, New York, NY 10036 USA; Tel: [1] (212) 354-4480; E-mail: info@uscib.org; Web: www.uscib.org.

Washington International Trade Association (WITA)

A non-profit, voluntary organization dedicated to providing a neutral forum in the nation's capital for the open discussion of international trade issues. WITA has over 800 members consisting of business executives, consultants, lawyers, federal officials, diplomats and academics. Through an extensive series of programs, WITA keeps its members informed of the latest positions taken by the Administration and Congress on trade policy, rules and regulations governing international trade, and views of U.S. trade policy from abroad. Contact: Washington International Trade Association, 1300 Pennsylvania Ave., NW, Suite 350 Washington, DC 20004 USA; Tel: [1] (202) 312-1600; Fax: [1] (202) 312-1601; E-mail: wita@wita.org; Web: www.wita.org.

World Trade Centers Association

Located around the world. World Trade Center members receive office support services, consultant services, conferences and reciprocal membership services at WTCs globally. Administers NETWORK, a trade lead data bank system. Contact: World Trade Centers Association, 60 East 42nd Street, Suite 1901, New York, NY 10165 USA; Tel: [1] (212) 599-3444; Fax: [1] (212) 599-1950; Web: http://iserve.wtca.org.

RESOURCES

OTHER INFORMATION SOURCES

Air Cargo, Inc. (ACI)

A ground service corporation established and jointly owned by 17 U.S. scheduled airlines. In addition to its airline owners, ACI also serves over 53 air freight forwarders and international air carriers. One of ACI's major functions is to facilitate the surface movement of air freight by negotiating and supervising the performance of a nationwide series of contracts under which trucking companies provide both local pickup and delivery service at airport cities and over-the-road truck service to move air freight to and from points not directly served by the airlines. ACI also makes available, in many cities, low cost, disposable containers for shippers' use. Contact: Air Cargo, Inc., 1819 Bay Ridge Avenue, Annapolis, MD 21403 USA; Tel: [1] (410) 280-5578.

Boskage Commerce Publications

More than 100 policy and procedure guidelines written by the leading U.S. Customs compliance expert. Fine and penalty proof techniques for handling U.S. Customs business. Functional guide for training new and existing employees. Free customizable software included. Boskage Commerce Publications, Ltd., P.O. Box 337, Allegan, MI 49010 USA; Tel: [1] (616) 673-7242 or [1] (888) 880-4088; www.boskage.com.

STAT-USA

STAT-USA is a fee-funded office in the U.S. Department of Commerce that develops and operates electronic information systems to deliver government economic, business, statistical, and foreign trade information to the public, primarily through subscription on-line services. STAT-USA's flagship product, STAT-USA/Internet, is a subscription based Internet site that contains the international trade information of the National Trade Data Bank (NTDB) as well as an extensive collection of domestic economic data. Customers can view, print, and download trade opportunity leads, market reports, economic releases, and more from the State Department, the Bureau of Export Administration, the Federal Reserve Board, the US Census Bureau, and others. USA Trade On-line, a joint venture with the US Census Bureau and a private partner, is the latest STAT-USA product, offering trade statistics to subscribers within minutes of release. Contact STAT-USA online at www.stat-usa.gov.

World Trade Center Clubs

Local and regional based organizations around the world of importers, exporters, customs brokers, freight forwarders, attorneys, bankers, manufacturers and shippers. Each world trade club provides different services and activities, but many provide information services including data bases and libraries, educational services including seminars and regularly scheduled classes, meeting space, club atmosphere, dining, exhibit facilities, and trade missions. Most major cities in the world have World Trade Clubs. For a list of world trade clubs internationally, go online at http://iserve.wtca.org. World Trade Centers Association, 60 East 42nd Street, Suite 1901, New York, NY 10165 USA; Tel: [1] (212) 599-3444; Fax: [1] (212) 599-1950; Web: http://iserve.wtca.org.

Web Resources

The following are internet Web sites that may be of interest to individuals and organizations involved in international trade. We offer this as a starting point for your research rather than as a comprehensive listing. Please note that the Internet is a very fluid medium and Web siteaddresses are subject to change.

General Travel Sites

Business Traveler Online www.btonline.com
The online version of the monthly magazine for business travelers featuring country profiles, plus hotel, airline, and special perk information.

Center for Disease Control www.cdc.gov
The U.S. Government's site for disease control and global immunization information.

Consular Information Sheets http://travel.state.gov/travel_warnings.html
U.S. Department of State country information sheets apprising travelers of current events and dangers affecting international travel safety. Also contact information for US consulates abroad.

Embassies and Consulates http://travel.state.gov/links.html
Links to embassies and consulates worldwide.

Expedia Travel www.expedia.com
Microsoft's online travel service featuring a fare finder, discounts, destination information, vacation packages, maps, global guidebook search, accommodations, transportation and travel merchandise.

Foreign Language for Travelers www.travlang.com/languages
Foreign languages for travelers, dictionaries, worldwide hotels and currency exchange rates.

Global Road Warrior www.globalroadwarrior.com
A 174-country travel and business information resource for the international business communicator and traveler. Contains pragmatic information on communications, mobile connectivity, business services, technical support, business culture, travel facts, color maps and city centers for each country.

iGo.com www.igo.com
A major supplier of mobile connectivity and technology products for business travelers. Print catalog also available.

Konexx www.konexx.com
Comprehensive supplier of computer-telephone interface products and accessories. Also has online tech support for products.

Maps.com www.maps.com
Specializing in maps, Maps.com provides digital maps, travel guides and gear, an online map store, driving directions and an address locator.

Magellan's www.magellans.com
A major mail order supplier of tech and non-tech travel products. Many mobile connectivity products. They also have an excellent print catalog you can order through their Web site.

Lonely Planet Online www.lonelyplanet.com
A travel guide to many destinations around the world, mostly aimed at the budget and adventure traveler, but with many helpful tips and insights useful to the businessperson.

Port Incorporated www.port.com
Major supplier of mobile connectivity products.

TeleAdapt www.teleadapt.com
TeleAdapt is a major worldwide supplier of mobile connectivity products for the business traveler, such as electrical and telephone plug adapters and much more.

Travel Documents www.traveldocs.com
A country-by-country listing of required travel documents and customs information. Works closely with the U.S. Passport agency and the embassies of many countries worldwide.

Travelocity www.travelocity.com
Online travel service with air, hotel, and car reservations, maps, weather, currency converter, electronic ticketing, destination guide, consolidator fares, travel agency locator and travel headlines.

WEBSITES

Walkabout Travel Gear   www.walkabouttravelgear.com

Supplier of mobile connectivity products as well as useful items of travel gear. See photos of how the products work and order them online.

World Maps   www.mapquest.com

Create driving directions and maps, or purchase maps on this Web site.

World Time Information   www.worldtime.com

Features an interactive world atlas, information on local time worldwide and a public holiday database for countries around the world.

World Travel Guide   www.wtgonline.com

A extensive travel site with key information for most countries, including some business protocol and contact information. Contains separate guides relating to cities, weather, airports, events; also, has an on-line bookstore.

International Trade Related Sites

A to Z Freight Gateway   www.azfreight.com

An air freight industry Web site containing listings of airlines, cargo handling agents, sales agents, airports, cargo agents, freight forwarders, couriers, services and supplies.

Alibaba Trade Leads   www.alibaba.com

Big marketplace for global trade and a leading provider of online marketing services for importers and exporters. Headquartered in Hong Kong, the service covers more than 200 countries worldwide. Trade leads can be bought and sold; the leads are organized and searchable by business types and categories.

AllBusiness Global Directory   www.allbusiness.com/directory/index.jsp

Huge global business-to-business directory, with more than 1,000,000 business listings and 9,000 categories. Businesses can use the Directory to generate sales leads by sourcing companies that need their products or services, locate new vendors, and identify and assess their competitors.

BizEurope   www.bizeurope.com

A business portal providing trade leads, company information and contacts, import and export information, individual country guides, a directory of World Trade Centers, and more.

Business Wire   www.businesswire.com

A newswire service listing the day's business headlines in industry-specific categories.

Cargo Ports of the World   www.hal-pc.org/~nugent/port.html

Provides links to ports and terminals around the world and contains information on vessel traffic and cargo types that individual ports allow.

Centre for International Trade   www.centretrade.com

This helpful Web site for international trade includes rules, regulations, tariffs, trade opportunities, finance, management, transportation, resource and travel information. Also has a free newsletter.

Dow Jones & Company   www.dowjones.com

Website includes indexes, business publications, financial information services, investor relations, Wall Street Journal services, press releases and a directory.

Federation of Intl. Trade Associations   www.fita.org

Provides over 1,000 links to websites related to international trade. The site has a useful page called "The Trading Hub: Import and Export Trade Leads from Around the World."

Financial Professionals International   www.fpionline.com

Free, independent online news resource for banking and securities professionals.

Foreign Trade Online   www.foreign-trade.com

A global B2B trade portal that helps companies around the world expand their business beyond their own borders. The service helps manufacturers, exporters, and companies planning to export to market themselves cost-effectively on a global scale by providing qualified foreign buyers with information about their products and services. Also helps importers to locate their product sourcing from around the world. Trade leads can be posted on the site.

GlobalBiz Directory   www.globalbizdirectory.com

Can be used by purchasing agents and managers, acquisitions departments, company buyers, retail and wholesale buyers, and service purchasers to assist in purchasing decisions, marketing and direction, advisory information, and to perform research. Inclusion in the Directory is fee-based. Members have access to special Research and Publications sections and other services.

Global Board of Trade   **www.gbot.net**
Provides an integrated end-to-end B2B trade solution that integrates trade transaction documents, se-cured encrypted transmission and authentication, traditional trade finance mechanisms, and shipping/lo-gistics services. Use the "Trade Lead AutoSubmitter" to automatically post trade leads to various related bulletin boards on the Internet. Also contains: the Trade Accelerator - a global trade lead re-distribution service with significant market penetration; the Big Board Auction; and the GBOT Exchange, to search trade data by Keyword, HTS Code, Country and Lead Type (Offer or Demand).

Global Business Centre   **www.glreach.com/gbc**
A guide to Web sites around the world, arranged by language in topic-specific directories. Provides links to interesting Web sites, especially those not written in English. The site is organized according to sub-ject matter within each language: business, culture, online publications and e-zines (electronic maga-zines), index (lists of sites in this online language community), leisure, jobs, shopping and travel.

Global Business Information Network   **www.bus.indiana.edu/gbin/gbin.htm**
Part of the University of Indiana's Kelley School of Business. Helps companies, non-profit organiza-tions, and government agencies by gathering and analyzing information on international markets and global trade. Includes the Global Connector search engine, designed specifically for the needs of interna-tional businesspersons.

Global Business Network (GBN)   **www.gbn.org**
Membership-based organization made up of individuals and organizations worldwide. Through its WorldView service, GBN brings this network together through: meetings and events; learning journeys; the GBN Book Club; and publications, commentary, and conversations. Services also include consulting and customized offerings as well as scenario training.

Global Business Resources   **http://globaledge.msu.edu/ibrd/ibrd.asp**
Links to trade information. Includes regional and country information. Maintained by the Center for In-ternational Business Education and Research of Michigan State University (USA).

Global ConneXions   **www.globalcon.com**
Trade database directory and trade services, Internet access and Web site hosting. Search international world trade leads and a company product advertiser directory.

Global Index of Chambers of Commerce   **www.worldchambers.com**
A listing of chambers of commerce worldwide.

Global Industrial Buying Guide   **www.tgrnet.com**
Site of the Thomas Global Register, an extensive and regularly update directory of worldwide industrial product information. Visitors can search for over 500,000 industrial suppliers, organized by 10,500 in-dustrial product classifications, in 9 languages, and from 26 countries. Companies are listed free of charge.

Global Information Network   **www.ginfo.net**
A search engine and portal for global e-business.

International Chamber of Commerce (ICC) **www.icc-ibcc.org**
The ICC represents businesses and chambers of commerce worldwide and facilitates contacts with inter-governmental organizations and other international bodies. The ICC also is the source of extremely im-portant publications on international banking, letters of credit and mediation.

International Import Export Exchange   **www.imex.com**
Directory of trade associations, companies, products, import-export advice, and global markets.

International Monetary Fund (IMF)   **www.imf.org**
Official Web site of the IMF includes news releases, publications, fund rates, data standards and index.

Internet Service Providers   **www.thelist.com**
A listing of internet service providers (ISPs) and their service parameters within a specified country; list-ings include Web links to the individual ISP sites.

The Journal of Commerce   **www.joc.com**
The daily Journal of Commerce online. Includes a plenitude of information about trade.

Nafta Home Page   **www.mac.doc.gov/nafta**
Web site about the North American Free Trade Agreement provided by the U.S. Department of Commerce.

National Ass'n of Foreign Trade Zones   **www.naftz.org**
Official site of the National Association of FTZs, including descriptions of FTZs and how to establish one. Provides case studies, an event calendar, a member directory and a listing of zones and subzones.

W E B S I T E S

National Technical Information Service   **www.ntis.gov**
The National Technical Information Service is the Federal Government's central source for the sale of scientific, technical, engineering, and related business information produced by or for the U.S. Government and complementary material from international sources.

Pangea.Net   **www.pangea.net**
Comprehensive source and reference for international business activities -- from information collection and strategy development through tactical implementation. PANGAEA.NET is the online service of PANGAEAR, International Consultants, a global consultancy with expertise in strategic positioning, branding, competitive intelligence, multicultural advertising and consumer psychographics for the largest consumer products/services companies in the world.

Planet Business   **www.planetbiz.com**
Contains a directory organized by continent, trade zone, and name of business, with links to "gateway" business search/portal sites all over the world.

Seaports of the World   **www.seaportsinfo.com**
A directory with links for seaports, port authorities and port industry info. for the Western Hemisphere.

Shipping International   **www.shipint.com**
Free online publication for the maritime community. Includes late-breaking articles and press releases in maritime shipping covering: ports, shipyards, logistics, events, incidents and operation. Updated several times per week.

Tradecompass   **www.tradecompass.com**
Large resource for electronic products and services that facilitate international commerce over the internet. Helps companies and individuals investigate trade, importing and exporting, sales, marketing, logistics, research and e-business.

Tradeport   **www.tradeport.org**
An international trade Web site funded by the California Export Assistance Center and the U.S. Department of Commerce provides information on trade leads, market and industry research, events and trade shows, trade tutorial and other information.

United Nations Online   **www.un.org**
Official site of the United Nations.

Women's Global Business Alliance   **www.wgba-business.com**
Member-based organization for senior-level executive women worldwide. Provides executive women with direct and personal connections to an elite group of peers, thought leaders, and some of the world's most renowned business executives and change agents. Members exchange views on critical business issues and share tools that impact the bottom line.

World Trade Centers Association   **http://iserve.wtca.org**
A complete listing of world trade centers worldwide, their services and membership information.

World Trade Organization (WTO)   **www.wto.org**
Official Web site of the WTO contains trade topics, resources, and membership information.

World Trade Magazine   **www.worldtrademag.com**
Source of news and information for US companies doing business in the global marketplace. Targeted to U.S. executives shipping and sourcing worldwide. Core coverage areas include: banking, finance and insurance; cargo transportation and logistics; economic development; technology; international marketing and protocol; foreign exchange; tips on travel; cultural considerations; political risk analysis; and demographics.

World Trade Press   **www.worldtradepress.com**
Worldwide publisher of professional books, CD-ROMs and databases for international trade.

World Trade Zone   **www.tradezone.com**
Tradezone.com provides international trade services for manufacturers, importers/exporters, trade service businesses and opportunity seekers. Includes import-export trade leads, the International Traders Bulletin Board, traders Web sites (such as the Trade Opportunities Magazine Online) and Web site advertising services. Contains a Global Trade Lead database that can be searched for leads or in which company information can be placed free of charge.

W E B S I T E S

Country-Specific Sources

ARGENTINA

Fundacíon Invertir Argentina	**www.invertir.com**
The comprehensive Web site covering topics related to doing business in Argentina.

Grippo Argentina Directory	**www.grippo.com**
A search engine for Argentina with links to other search engines. Links are usually in Spanish.

Trade Leads Online	**www.tradeline.com.ar**
A Web site for companies interested in exporting to or importing from Argentina and Mercosur countries.

AUSTRALIA

Austrade World Direct	**www.austrade.gov.au**
The Australian Trade Commission online; includes export and investment information, international business guide, general information, supplier database, Austrade offices, trade shows, importing from Australia and a link to the Australian stock exchange.

Australia Department of Foreign Affairs	**www.dfat.gov.au**
and Trade
Searchable collection of detailed information on services, travel, trade policy, and foreign policy.

TradeData	**www.tradedata.net**
Marketing information service based on details of internationally traded goods. Up-to-date information on thousands of products, covering imports and exports for a wide range of countries. Offers reports providing a vast range of international trade statistics. TradeData reports assist you in identifying market opportunities, monitoring competitors, identifying new sources of cheaper material inputs, monitoring growth, volatility and seasonal behavior, assessing possible dumping of imported products, and monitoring price/quantity relationships.

Web Wombat	**www.webwombat.com.au/wombat**
An Australian search engine, with the largest online database of searchable information on Australia.

AUSTRIA

Austrian Worldport	**www.worldport.at/index.html**
An index of company names and Austrian business information, including: marketing, legal, investment, business travel, addresses and on-line services.

AustroNaut	**www.austronaut.at**
An Austrian Web search engine in German for various categories including business.

BELGIUM

Belgian and Luxembourg Exports	**www.belgiumexports.com**
Overview of exporting and importing companies, links to importers and detailed company profiles.

EuroCommerce	**www.eurocommerce.be**
News, conferences, publications, and manifesto of the retail, wholesale and international trade representation to the European Union.

Scoot, the Belgium Business Directory	**www.scoot.be**

A quick find guide (in French and Flemish) to companies, searchable by product, service, or company name, with identical local sites for the Netherlands and the United Kingdom.

Webwatch	**www.webwatch.be**
A comprehensive Belgian search engine and directory, available also in English.

BOLIVIA

Bolivian Law	**natlaw.com/bolivia/links.htm**
The National Law Center for Inter-American free trade provides links to Bolivia's Central Bank, Bolivian statistics, business information, country information, industrial and commercial information and law.

WEBSITES

Bolivia Web www.boliviaweb.com/
This Web site for Bolivia includes business, communications, government, and travel links, as well as a chat room and classifieds.

BRAZIL

Brazil InfoNet www.brazilinfo.net
A business directory with information and resources; includes economic statistics, government resources, trade shows, daily news, trade leads and trade zones.

BrazilBiz www.brazilbiz.com.br/english
A Brazilian business to business directory for products and services; includes a business center for companies interested in buying, business opportunities as well as an international business directory.

Brazil Exporters www.brazilexporters.com
This Web site has assisted hundreds of thousands of business people worldwide do business with Brazil. Contains an online directory of Brazilian exporters, plus other business resources.

Brazil Now Online www.brazilnow.com
English-language international magazine, published every two months. Provides high value information on business and investment opportunities and foreign trade. The international magazine of the Brazilian Foreign Trade Association.

BrazilTradeNet www.braziltradenet.gov.br
BrazilTradeNet is maintained by the Ministry of External Relations of Brazil to offer foreign enterprises easy contact with Brazilian companies wishing to export or to establish business ventures. Offers information on trade fairs and other events in Brazil.

Brazilian Web Resources www.brazilcham.com/brazweb.html
A member directory searchable by name or product/service description; includes government sites, financial institutions and media.

BULGARIA

Bulgaria.Com www.bulgaria.com
Business, services, travel, government, history, art, news, chat rooms and links are all included in this business and general information site.

Bulgarian Industrial Association www.bia-bg.com
Directory for regional associations, branch chambers, economic focus, legal framework, investments, calendar, regulations, customs, tariffs and a Bulgarian company directory.

CANADA

Canada Business Directory www.cdnbusinessdirectory.com
Directory of businesses organized by province.

**Department of Foreign Affairs
and International Trade** www.dfait-maeci.gc.ca
Official Web site of the Department of Foreign Affairs with links to trade, investment, market information, exporting programs and services, plus a directory.

Doing Business in Canada www.dbic.com
Includes the online Canadian Business Guide, which is a resource for companies planning to do business in Canada as well as companies already doing business in Canada.

Strategis http://strategis.ic.gc.ca/engdoc/main.html
This Web site includes company directories; industry and professional associations; sector analysis and statistics; information on international trade, legislation, regulation, financial management, provinces and territories.

CHINA

BLI Internet Center for Chinese Products www.buildlink.com
Build Link International provides listings of Chinese products, companies, investment opportunities, joint ventures, product bidding and general information.

**W
E
B
S
I
T
E
S**

China Company Database Register   www.wtdb.com/information/company.htm
Provides links to 4,000 import and export corporations and enterprises of ministries under state council; also lists the China offices of American companies.

China Economic Opportunity Trade Mission   http://china-inc.com
Provides trade leads from China and for China, as well as business and marketing resources. Investment and trade links, links on competitive zones for foreign investment, as well as an extensive business directory organized by business types and categories.

China Today   www.chinatoday.com
Provides links to banking and finance, culture, diplomatic missions, government agencies and services, health, international trade, investment and business opportunities, products, legal services and law, mass media and publications, real estate and more.

SinoSource   www.sinosource.com
Internet-based business info provider in China. Targets in helping foreign business, particularly small and middle-sized companies, to communicate directly with business in China.

COLOMBIA

Colombian Trade   www.coltrade.org
The Colombian Government Trade Bureau in Washington, DC USA supplies information on trade and economy, industrial sectors, commercial laws, trade agreements, trading with Colombia, news and events, trade shows. Also offers weblinks.

CUBA

CubaFirst   www.cubafirst.com
Comprehensive investment guide for Cuba. Categories include: How to do business in cuba; foreign investment in cuba; investment application; banking regulations; free zones and industrial parks; commercial relations with foreign firms; administrative tariffs; real estate & building; and a business consulting gallery.

LatinWorld - Cuba   www.latinworld.com/caribe/cuba
Links to Cuba including companies, exporters, organizations, products, services, economy, culture, government and politics, internet resources, news and travel.

CZECH REPUBLIC

Czech Information System   www.czis.cz/en
This site provides contacts to Czech companies, searchable by industry.

Czech Republic Business Guide   www.neweuropepromotions.com/czech
Provides information relating to real estate, human resources, banking, taxes and auditing, corporate legal issues, communications, transportation, health care, travel and tourism.

Czech Trading Center   www.czechtrading.com
Catalog of Czech companies, organized by industry and type of business.

DENMARK

Export Directory of Denmark   www.danishexporters.dk
An export directory and search engine; includes information about investing in Denmark, legal framework, organizations and media.

Invest in Denmark Agency   www.investindk.com
The Royal Danish Ministry of Foreign Affairs provides news and information, facts and figures, Denmark investment information, company profiles and business networks and links.

ECUADOR

Ecuador   www.ecuador.org
A general educational site on Ecuador, with specific sections on economy and trade.

WEBSITES

EGYPT

American Chamber of Commerce in Egypt   www.amcham.org.eg/Publications/
BusinessMonthly/Business_Monthly.htm
Online business monthly publication; covers chamber's activities, committees, events, meetings, trade missions and more. Highest circulation English language business magazine in Egypt.

Egyptian Exporters Association   www.expolink.org
Nonprofit organization providing services to exporters and assisting companies who want to import.

Egyptian Trading Directory   www.egtrade.com
Free service that can be used to locate factories, import and export companies, agents, banks, hotels, insurance companies, and maritime companies in Egypt. Visitors can sign up for regular e-mail with company listing updates for a specific field of interest.

World Trade Way   www.worldtradeway.com
Commisson-based global trade organization that links exporters and importers worldwide to Egypt.

FINLAND

Contact Finland   www.contactfinland.fi
A guide to Finnish business services, organizations and authorities.

The Nordic Pages   www.markovits.com/nordic
The Nordic Pages provide resource links for Scandinavian countries, including Finland.

FRANCE

Business-in-Europe   www.business-in-europe.com
An extensive Web directory of sites to assist in doing business in France. Includes: Ernst & Young report, Web site addresses, industry-by-industry guide, contacts in France as well as news.

France Companies   www.france-companies.com
Created in partnership with the French Ministry of Economy, Finance, and Industry, this Web site offers a directory of French companies, information on economic partners, business relations, international trade, job offers and searches and marketing in France. Has a search engine dedicated to French import/export companies.

French Food Finder   www.frenchfoodfinder.com
A French food and wine export market place. Products are classified by specialized area and by French departments. For international buyers, facilitates their research for suppliers on Internet and offers to its members: full access to 1000 most competitive French food and wine companies, free price quotations sent within 72 hours, sampling service, and a monthly newsletterS.

Invest in France   www.investinfrancena.org
Works with a vast global network to provide international firms with a wide range of services to make their operations in France a success and promote France to business leaders worldwide.

GERMANY

Business Links to Germany   www.integration.org/germany.htm
Economic news, databases, economic research, international economy, statistics, politics and public administration, economic organizations, trade fairs, basic facts, geography, travel information and dictionaries are all included on this extensive Web site.

DeTeMedien   www.teleauskunft.de
German Telekom posts a yellow-page directory comprising all of Germany.

Eule   www.eule.de
A German search engine and portal in the German language.

German Business Center   www.business-channel.de
Business news, stock market, politics, economy, and private business news from Germany (in German).

Globis   www.globis.de
A search engine and portal in German that offers a supplier database searchable by company, brand name, or product; also contains a business center with economic and business information, and trade fairs taking place at the Hannover Convention Center.

WEBSITES

BusinessLink **www.businesslink.ch**
A product and services search engine, convention guide and buyer contact list for Switzerland and Germany (in German).

GREECE

Hellenic Foreign Trade Board **www.hepo.gr**
Trade Board services, publications, economic and commercial offices, Greek investment information and Greek exports.

Go Greece **www.gogreece.com**
Internet directory of links to Greek travel, business, finance, education, news, government, and more.

GUATEMALA

Guatemalan Development Foundation **www.fundesa.guatemala.org**
The Guatemalan Development Foundation is a non-profit, non-partisan organization of businesspersons from all sectors of Guatemala which promotes foreign investment in Guatemala. Provides information about its activities, investment and trade, tourism, resources and news.

Guatemala Online **www.quetzalnet.com**
Website includes an exporter directory, newswatch, a phone-number converter, country profile, economic overview, Fundesa's business guidebook, traditional and non-traditional investment areas, business assistance and support institutions.

HONDURAS

Honduras Internet Directory **www.hondirectorio.com**
Links to all manner of Honduras related information, including business, industry, and technology.

Hondu-Web **www.marrder.com/hw**
Includes the online version of the Honduras This Week magazine, as well as content on travel and industry.

In-Honduras **www.in-honduras.com**
A search engine and portal for Honduras.

HONG KONG

Hong Kong Trade Development Council **www.tdc.org.hk**
The Hong Kong Trade Development Council (HKTDC) promotes Hong Kong's trade in goods and services. The Web site offers a products and services catalog, HKTDC business information, media information and more. Visitors can subscribe to a free newsletter.

Hong Kong and Chinese Stocks Live **www.int.quamnet.com**
This stock site includes daily quotes from the Hang Seng index with daily market reports. The mainland Chinese stock market is also covered.

HUNGARY

Access Hungary **www.access-hungary.hu**
An online guide to news and business information in Hungary.

Hungarian Yellowpages **www.yellowpages.hu**
Hungarian yellow page search directory in Hungarian, English, and German.

INDIA

Link India **www.link-india.com**
Comprehensive search engine and portal for India.

India Business Directory **www.india-invest.com/directory.htm**
Presents a directory of indian companies having a presence on the Web.

IndiaMart **www.indiamart.com**
A massive Web directory with links to 60,000 Indian businesses (manufacture and exporters, importers and buyers and service providers), including foreign business, apparel and textiles, travel and tourism.

WEBSITES

India Trade Zone   **www.indiatradezone.com**
Extensive site that lets you search products, companies and trade leads. Connects Indian exporters and importers to their counterparts across the world.

Trade India   **www.trade-india.com**
A major reference site containing an Exporters Yellow Pages, Indian Importers Directory, Top 1,000 Companies of India, Trade Leads, Newsletters, Forums, Links, Forex Watch and more.

INDONESIA

Indonesia Yellow Pages   **www.yellowpages.co.id**
Yellow-page listings of Indonesian companies and businesses.

National Agency for Export Development   **www.nafed.go.id**
The Ministry of Industry and Trade provides information on resources, trade fairs, offers, and links to other sources as well as maintaining a bulletin board dedicated to these topics.

IRAN

Neda Business Directory   **www.neda.net/business**
Presents Iranian resources available on the Internet, specifically targeted toward the needs of small business owners, professionals, and home office entrepreneurs.

Iranian Trade Association   **www.iraniantrade.org**
Daily updates, press releases, trade board publications, calendar, Iranian news, congressional directory, U.S. sanction watch, doing business with Iran, membership guest registry, advertising and other links provided by the U.S.-Iran Business Council.

IRELAND

Finfacts Irish Finance Portal   **www.finfacts.ie**
This Web site is a major portal to Irish business and financial sites, including those providing stock market analysis.

Investment and Development Agency   **www.idaireland.com**
Information on investment in Ireland, with profiles on a range of service and manufacturing based industries, a directory of overseas companies currently doing business in Ireland, and statistics and demographics on the Irish labor force and local business environment.

Irish Financial Sector   **http://ireland.iol.ie/~rclapham/finance.html**
An index for associations, banking, budgets and tax, government, investment, legal, life assurance, media and news, PLC's (corporations), securities, stock brokers, and travel.

Swift Guide to Ireland   **http://swift.kerna.ie**
A database of more than 3,000 sites sectioned by business category.

ISRAEL

Israeli Business Center   **http://aai.business.israel.net**
Channel for investment projects and business connections with companies, agencies and fine arts in Israel.

Globes Arena   **www.globes.co.il**
Israel's business in daily headlines, economic analysis and Tel Aviv stock exchange reports. Includes a Start-up Guide, which is a comprehensive directory of sources of information and assistance for those interested in Israel's high-tech industry.

U.S.-Israel Business Networking   **www.std.com/neicc/contents.html**
A resource guide to promote business between U.S. and Israel. Links to chambers of commerce, Israeli government, U.S. and local government programs, Israeli business and trade associations, development programs, finance and investments, academic institutions, research and reference materials and major trade fairs.

ITALY

ANIBO Italian Buyers   **http://anibo.com**
The National Association of Italian Buying Offices provides a listing of member Italian purchasing agents with contact information, e-mail links and some Web links.

Invest in Italy   **www.investinitaly.com/**
Site maintained by the Italian Trade Commission. Content includes incentives, location opportunities, and specific information for investors.

Italian Institute for Foreign Trade   **www.italtrade.com**
Public agency entrusted with promoting trade, business opportunities and industrial co-operation between Italian and foreign companies, mostly by organizing the participation of Italian firms in fairs, exhibitions, workshops and bilateral meetings in more than 100 countries. Comprehensive Web site.

Trade World Italy Industry   **www.italyindustry.com**
An index of Italian companies searchable by product or industry, with product specific sub sites and free URL submission.

JAPAN

Global Window   **www.anderson.ucla.edu/research/japan/ mainfrm.htm**
A guide to conducting business successfully in Japan, including information on business culture, consumers, economy, financial structure and institutions and legal and business travel tips.

Japan Export and Trade Consultants   **www.jetc.com**
Resources for developing your business in Japan; includes trade leads, directories of Japanese companies, business protocols, trade fairs, classifieds and business tips.

JETRO   **www.jetro.go.jp**
The Japan External Trade Organization is a non-profit, government-supported organization which promotes building trade and economic relationships; their Web site includes business information, useful links, publications, and latest developments.

KOREA

Business Korea Plaza   **www.bizkorea.com**
The Korean Exporters' Catalog; search for products offered by manufacturers and exporters from Korea. Visitors can ask for assistance over the Internet.

Korea International Trade Association   **www.kita.or.kr**
KITA's Web site includes trade opportunities, a company directory, a digital catalog, trade information and Korean business information; offered in Korean and English.

KOTRA   **www.kotra.or.kr**
The Korea Trade and Investment Promotion Agency Web site; links to Korean products, export, trade fairs, investment guide and opportunities and a directory.

Silkroad 21   **www.silkroad21.com**
Global import-export e-marketplace. Provides trade leads and online directory for Korean products.

LEBANON

Business@Lebanon.com   **www.lebanon.com/business**
A Web site which includes links to Lebanese weekly business reports, the Beirut stock exchange, real estate, financial information, import-export, tour and hotel guide and a business directory.

Lebanon Index   **www.lebindex.com**
A search engine and portal for Lebanon; categories include business, government, banking and finance, tourism, and industry and trade.

LIBYA

ArabNet   **www.arab.net/libya/libya_contents.html**
Overview, history, geography, business, culture, government and transport information about Libya.

Libya Business Directory   **http://daleel.libyaonline.com**
98 categories and more than 600 listings online.

MBendi   **http://mbendi.co.za**
A large electronic encyclopedia of business and communication information in Africa. Links to countries, companies, events, industries, organizations, personalities, stock exchanges, publications, projects, products and country-specific information.

WEBSITES

MALAYSIA

Malaysia Classified www.aseanbiz.com/malaysia/
Comprehensive online directory of Malaysian businesses, organized alphabetically and by category.

Malaysia Products www.malaysiaproducts.com
A site which includes a products directory, company index, market place and more.

MEXICO

Mexico Information Center www.bancomext.com
Export directory, business opportunities, export and investment offices in Mexico, trade leads, Mexican government agencies, resource centers, universities and research institutes, trade shows, news sources, NAFTA information, and regional information. Sponsored by the Mexican Export Bank.

Mexico Business Directory www.mexbusinessdirectory.com
Online directory of over 115,000 Mexican companies, organized by business category.

Mexico Connect www.mexconnect.com/mexbusboard/
Mexican Trade and Business Forum, listing Mexican products and services and providing a forum for business practices and problems of Mexican trade; refer to home page at www.mexconnect.com for general information on working and living in Mexico.

MOROCCO

ArabNet www.arab.net/morocco/
morocco_contents.html
General country information, with culture, business and government links.

MBendi http://mbendi.co.za
A large electronic encyclopedia of business and communication information in Africa. Links to countries, companies, events, industries, organizations, personalities, stock exchanges, publications, projects, products and country-specific information.

Morocco - Casanet www.casanet.net.ma
Index of Moroccan websites, e-mail addresses, classified ads, personal ads, events, business opportunities, Moroccan yellow pages and job offers (mostly in French).

NETHERLANDS

Dutch Yellow Pages www.dmo.com
Organized for quick location of businesses in the Netherlands.

Scoot, the Netherlands Business Directory www.scoot.nl
A quick find guide (in Dutch) to companies, searchable by product, service, or company name, with identical local sites for Belgium and the United Kingdom.

The Dutch Export Site www.export.nl
A yellow-page directory of nearly 7,000 Dutch exporting companies and their international business partners, including corporate identity, products, and services, searchable by country, business category or alphabetical name. Export information is also available.

NEW ZEALAND

National Business Review Online www.nbr.co.nz
A large business internet site. Includes instant news, share market, global update, politics and polls.

New Zealand Business Directory www.ubd.co.nz/
Online directory of New Zealand businesses.

Trade New Zealand www.tradenz.govt.nz
Information on importing, exporting and investing.

NICARAGUA

Centramerica Nicaragua   **www.directory.centramerica.com/
nicaragua_asp**
Includes a business directory and links to economy, government, laws, demographics, news services, maps, related sites and events in Nicaragua.

NIGERIA

MBendi   **http://mbendi.co.za**
A large electronic encyclopedia of business and communication information in Africa, searchable by country; includes information on companies, events, industries, organizations, personalities, stock exchanges, publications, projects, products and country information.

Nigerian Business.Com   **www.nigerianbusiness.com/index.html**
Nigerian Business includes business news, a daily list of Nigerian equities and bonds, company profiles, stock exchange, a matching service and business sector information.

NORWAY

Norway Online Information Service   **www.norway.org**
Business information on this Web site includes links to the Norwegian Trade Council in North America, industry attaches, products made in Norway, oil production, the fishing industry, Norwegian shipping, the stock exchange, exchange rates, statistics and yellow pages.

ODIN   **http://odin.dep.no**
Official Documentation and Information from Norway is the central Web server for the Norwegian government, the office of the Prime Minister and the ministries. An English language version can be linked-to from this page.

PAKISTAN

Trade Index of Pakistan   **www.PakistanBiz.com**
Hosted by the Government of Pakistan, Trade Index offers buy and sell information, export and investment guides, and a Pakistan business directory.

Vital Pakistan   **www.vitalpakistan.com/businesslinks.htm**
Detailed site containing exporter and importer directories, business guides, and links to government agencies and Web sites.

PANAMA

Centramerica Panama   **http://directory.centramerica.com
panama_asp**
Includes a business directory and links to economy, government, laws, demographics, news services, maps, related sites and events in Panama.

PARAGUAY

Latinworld - Paraguay   **www.latinworld.com/sur/paraguay**
Latinworld provides links to business information in Paraguay, as well as North, Central and South American countries, the Caribbean, and Spain.

PERU

Latinworld - Peru   **www.latinworld.com/sur/peru**
Latinworld provides links to business information in Peru, as well as North, Central and South American countries, the Caribbean, and Spain.

Peru Business and Economy Page   **www.latininvestor.com/country/peru.htm**
Links to Peruvian information sources: companies, economic and investment data, newspapers, government, financial, laws and regulations and Latin American news.

U.S. Embassy in Lima   **http://usembassy.state.gov/lima**
Links to USAID, agricultural service, consular section, commercial service and weekly topics.

WEBSITES

PHILIPPINES

Filipino Directory Online   **www.filipino-directory.com**
A large Web site providing links for everything related to the Philippines including business and investment opportunities.

Philexport   **http://philexport.org**
An export oriented site for importers of products made in the Philippines. The database includes information for most products made in the Philippines.

Edsa World Search Engine   **www.edsaworld.com**
A major Philippine search engine and portal. Includes business and economy as categories.

POLAND

Business Polska   **www.polska.net**
This site includes an investor's guide, business news on Poland, companies on the Web, organizations, Warsaw Stock Exchange, market reports and a partner's forum.

Embassy of Poland Commercial Office   **http://pw1.netcom.com/~brhusa/index.html**
Provides information on laws and regulations, business and economy, news, customs tariff, directory of Polish companies, sector information, business opportunities and contact by e-mail.

Polish Business   **business.poland.net**
A directory of Polish businesses, organizations, institutions, and resources.

PORTUGAL

Portugal.Com Business   **www.portugal.com/business**
Detailed site providing business directories as well as import, export, insurance, and real estate services.

Portugal Offer   **www.portugaloffer.com**
Helps you business directly with Portuguese companies; contacts, products and services offered by the nation's top 200 businesses so that you can find a supplier, customer, agent or partner in Portugal.

ROMANIA

Embassy of Romania   **www.roembus.org**
Information on consular services, embassy news, travel tips, trade and business, news and media, and links to other official Romanian sites.

Romanian Business Guide   **www.neweuropepromotions.com/romanian**
Provides information relating to real estate, human resources, banking, taxes and auditing, corporate legal issues, communications, transportation, health care, travel and tourism.

RUSSIA

Russia at Your Fingertips   **www.publications-etc.com/russia**
News, services, business FAQs, conferences, exhibitions, associations, and companies of Russia; the on-line version of the monthly magazine: Russian Business and Trade Connections.

Russia on the Net   **www.ru**
A Russian Web directory and search engine. The Business category includes companies, banks and finance, products and services, electronic commerce, news and references.

American Chamber of Commerce in Russia   **www.amcham.ru**
In addition to news, events, and marketing information, has detailed advice on various aspects of doing business Russia, with links to other Russian business-related sites.

Russia Today   **www.europeaninternet.com/russia**
Daily news and business updates concerning Russia and the CIS.

SAUDI ARABIA

ArabNet   **www.arab.net**
A large source of information for the Middle East, including Saudi Arabia.

WEBSITES

U.S.-Saudi Arabian Business Council   **www.us-saudi-business.org**
Basic facts about Saudi Arabia, economy, doing business in Saudi Arabia, business regulations and procedures, joint venture opportunities, key contacts and certification procedures.

SINGAPORE

Singapore Yellow Pages   **www.yellowpages.com.sg**
A yellow-page directory of businesses in Singapore, organized by business category. Also contains various "resource" links.

The Green Book   **www.thegreenbook.com**
The Singapore Industrial Directory directs users to chambers of commerce, news, the Singapore government, products and services, brand names, company information for 200,000 local companies and trade enquiries.

International Enterprise Singapore   **www.tdb.gov.sg**
The government trade promotion site of Singapore featuring business matching, trade promotion, import and export information, foreign market information, information services, trade statistics, trade news and trade policy watch.

SLOVAKIA

Guide to the Slovak Republic   **www.slovakia.org**
An internet-based information site dedicated to presenting objective and non-partisan information about Slovak politics, society, history, culture, economy and links to government sites.

Slovensko.com   **www.slovensko.com/business/**
Internet guide to Slovakia. Contains up-to-date news and business information. Numerous links to sites related to doing business in the Slovakia, including directories of businesses and consultants.

U.S. Embassy in Slovakia   **www.usis.sk**
The U.S. Embassy provides news, a daily Washington file, U.S. information service, commercial services, a contact list, USAID information, consular section and information about Slovakia.

SLOVENIA

Slovenia Yellow Pages   **http://yellow2.eunet.si/yellowpage/a/index.html**

An internet directory of Slovenian businesses.

SOUTH AFRICA

ExiNet   **www.exinet.co.za/business.htm**
Links to trade, travel, Web search, environment, events, professional services and yellow pages. Trade link includes manufacturers, exporters, importers and distributors, freight clearing and forwarding agents, investments and trade opportunities.

South African Business Directory   **http://iafrica.com/directories/business**
A business directory searchable by sector or business name.

SPAIN

Camerdata Online   **www.camerdata.es**
Spanish chambers of commerce, Euro chambers, a Spanish company directory, a business information area, commercial offers and a business guide. In Spanish.

SPAINDUSTRY   **www.spaindustry.com**
A search engine for companies, trade leads, exporters and importers; search by economic activity, exported or imported products or by company name in five languages.

SWEDEN

Swedish Web Sites   **http://katalogen.sunet.se/index-en.html**
A search engine of Swedish Web pages searchable by category or by key words. Contains an extensive business section.

**W
E
B
S
I
T
E
S**

The Swedish Page   **www.inetmedia.nu/sweden**
A directory of Swedish sites including business, economy, government, politics, and education. Also, an address book.

Swedish Trade Council   **www.swedishtrade.com/other**
An informative Web site for the foreign company wishing to do business in Sweden; offers company search, an export directory, sector information, business news, investment advice, legal information, and a listing of relevant publications.

SWITZERLAND

SwissInfo   **www.swissinfo.org**
General Swiss information in eight languages, including an alphabetical listing of Swiss companies.

Swisstrade   **www.swisstrade.com**
Links to Swiss export services and companies, manufacturing pool and the Federal Office for Economic Development and Labor.

Swiss Search Engine   **www.search.ch**
A search engine offered in German, English, French and Italian languages; search all of Switzerland or by specific region.

TAIWAN

China Productivity Center (CPC)   **www.cpc.org.tw**
Homepage for the CPC, a statutory body in Taiwan. The CPC assists Taiwan enterprises to upgrade quality and productivity, gives Taiwan's enterprises competitiveness information and promotes economic growth. The CPC also publishes directories in English and guides to international trade in Chinese.

TAIMEX Directory   **www.cens.com/cens/taimex.html**
Taiwan's Leading Manufacturers' and Exporters' Directory includes links to more than 8,000 participants of the China External Trade Development Council's trade shows.

Taiwan Commerce   **http://Taiwan-Commerce.com**
The Taiwan Commerce search engine includes global trade, a trade bulletin board, business service, technology, world news, financial services and trade exhibition information.

TransWorld Trade Net   **www.ttnet.net**
An extensive databank of matching trade opportunities and trade information; enter keywords of products or companies.

THAILAND

Department of Export Promotion   **www.thaitrade.com**
Information and links to business opportunities, trade fairs, pre-registration, trade associations, Thai exporters and special events.

Thai Trading   **www.thaitrading.com**
Includes an extensive Thai business directory.

Thailand Board of Investment   **www.boi.go.th**
Offers information about investing in Thailand.

Thailand Investment Gateway   **www.investmentthailand.com**
A site developed by the Thailand Board of Investment to be a gateway that domestic and foreign investors can use for investment decision making.

TURKEY

Turkey Business Center   **http://business.wec-net.com.tr**
This site is organized into Sector Lists, Companies, Import & Export, and Banking & Finance. News and a Turkish search feature are also provided.

TurkEx   **www.turkex.com**
The Turkish Foreign Trade Center provides a source of online information about Turkish importers, exporters, fairs and tourism.

W E B S I T E S

UKRAINE

UkraineBiz www.ukrainebiz.com
A free informational site describing services and products available for export to and from the Ukraine operated by the Center for Economic Initiatives. Companies are listed free of charge.

Welcome to Ukraine www.ukraine.org
General Ukraine information with business contacts searchable by category.

UNITED ARAB EMIRATES (U.A.E.)

Go Dubai www.godubai.com
A guide to Dubai and the United Arab Emirates, with information on travel facilities, a searchable database of companies, local business news, and more.

United Arab Emirates Internet Pages www.uae-pages.com
Comprehensive collection of links to UAE based business, arts, education, government, science, and local newspapers

UNITED KINGDOM

British Exporters www.export.co.uk
A database of British companies with listings by company name or business classification; users must register company data in order to use the directory.

British Promotional Merchandise Ass'n www.promotionalmerchandise.org.uk
A source directory of British promotional merchandise manufacturers and suppliers with listings by product category.

Scoot Business Directory www.scoot.co.uk
A quick find guide to companies, searchable by product, service, or company name, with identical local sites for Belgium and Holland.

The Business Information Zone www.thebiz.co.uk
Business information, products and services on the Internet as well as database listings for companies and organizations not yet on the internet. The extensive business directory is organized into business types.

UK Electronic Yellow Pages http://search.yell.com
A yellow-page directory of businesses in the United Kingdom.

UNITED STATES

Export Import Bank of the U.S. www.exim.gov
Provides information regarding loans for U.S. exporters and purchasers of U.S. goods and services, and insurance against foreign buyer defaults.

Foreign Trade Statistics www.census.gov/foreign-trade/www
The U.S. Census Bureau provides foreign trade statistics for the U.S.; includes country trade data, export classification assistance, profile of U.S. export companies, export seminars and more.

International Trade Administration www.ita.doc.gov
A Web site by the U.S. Department of Commerce providing leads to exporters, trade development information, market access and compliance as well as import regulations.

Library of International Trade Resources www.litr.com
Online service providing both interactive information access and customized consultation services. The providers have expertise in the areas of antidumping, the textile and apparel quota regime, import and export market research, and economic and statistical analysis.

Trade Information Center www.trade.gov/td/tic
Provides information about federal export assistance programs and country market information. Part of the International Trade Administration of the U.S. Department of Commerce.

U.S. Council for Intl. Business www.uscib.org
U.S. affiliate of the International Chamber of Commerce (ICC). Among the premier pro-trade, pro-market liberalization organizations. Membership includes over 300 multinational companies, law firms and business associations. Provides access to international policy makers and regulatory authorities.

WEBSITES

U.S. Customs Service　　　　　　**www.customs.ustreas.gov**
Importing and exporting, traveler information, enforcement activities and news.

U.S. Department of Commerce　　　　**www.doc.gov**
The gateway for links to all the main agencies and bureaus within the Department of Commerce.

VENEZUELA

Venezuela Export　　　　　　**www.venexport.com/**
A directory of exporters, searchable by name or sector.

Venezuela Business and Economy Page　　　**www.latinvestor.com/country/venezuela.htm**
Links to Venezuelan information sources: companies, economic and investment data, newspapers, government, financial, laws and regulations and Latin American news.

VIETNAM

Vietnam Access　　　　　　**www.vietnamaccess.com**
Resources for business news, directories, law, trade fairs, exhibitions, investors, travel, importers and exporters seeking opportunities, contacts and trading and investment in Vietnam.

Vietnam Business Center　　　　**www.usvietnam.com**
A resource for Vietnam market intelligence information. Provides news, market research, facts and figures. Visitors can find business partners and explore trade opportunities at the site's Trade Exchange Center, which is a destination for buyers and sellers, importers and exporters to find trade opportunities and promote business online. A search feature can locate hundreds of businesses in the Business Directory. Visitors can request custom market intelligence information.

VVG Vietnam　　　　　　**www.vvg-vietnam.com**
The Vietnam Venture Group site provides Web links related to business formation and investment advice, and provides access to business consultants, investment counselors, purchasing and export agents, and market entry service providers. Also contains articles on business and Investment.

**W
E
B
S
I
T
E
S**

Guide to Trade Documents[1]

Documents play a key role in international transactions. Both buyers and sellers need documents for bookkeeping, accounting, taxation, export and import formalities, as well as making payment using letters of credit and other documentary payment methods.

This section gives examples of the most common documents used in international trade. It is not an exhaustive listing. Specialized trades, special circumstances and different countries of origin and destination may require additional documentation. For more information contact your local logistics company representative or refer to *A Short Course in International Trade Documentation*, also by World Trade Press.

Following a general discussion of a) document categories, b) transport documents and c) documents and international payments; sample documents will be presented and defined, key elements listed, and cautions offered concerning important issues and common problems. Emphasis will be given to issues regarding letters of credit.

Document Categories

Documents for international trade fall into several overlapping categories:

Transaction Document(s)

The key transaction document is the invoice or commercial invoice. This document is used by all parties to the transaction for accounting and bookkeeping purposes. It is also required for export and import formalities as well as most banking and payment procedures.

Export Documents

These are documents required by the customs or national export authority of the country of export and vary greatly from country to country. Included are licenses, permits, export declarations, inspection certificates, commercial invoice and sometimes transport documents.

Transport Documents

These are documents issued by a shipping line, air cargo carrier, trucking company or freight forwarder that detail the terms of transport for cargo. The key transport document is the bill of lading.

Inspection Documents

These documents are generally issued by third party inspection firms at the request of the buyer to certify the quality and quantities of a shipment.

Inspection documents are also issued to satisfy country export and import requirements.

Insurance Documents

These documents evidence insurance coverage of a shipment and can be in the form of a policy or a certificate.

Banking / Payment Documents

Banking and payment documents include letters of credit, amendments to letters of credit, various advices, plus virtually all the other documents used in trade (bills of lading, commercial invoice, insurance document, inspection certificates, etc.).

Import Documents

These are documents required by the customs authority of the country of import and vary greatly from country to country. The minimum documentation requirement is an entry form and a commercial invoice. However, many other forms may be required, especially if the imported merchandise is sensitive (e.g., animals, weapons, drugs, food), if the importer is requesting special tariff treatment under an import program (e.g., GSP, NAFTA) or if the import comes from certain countries.

Transport Documents

Bills of lading

A bill of lading is a document issued by a carrier to a shipper, signed by the captain, agent, or owner of a vessel, furnishing written evidence regarding receipt of the goods (cargo), the conditions on which transportation is made (contract of carriage), and the engagement to deliver goods at the prescribed port of destination to the lawful holder of the bill of lading.

A bill of lading is, therefore, both a receipt for merchandise and a contract to deliver it as freight. There are a number of different types of bills of

1. This section has been excerpted from the book Short Course in International Trade Documentation, ISBN 1-885073-59-3, also by Edward G. Hinkelman and available from World Trade Press.

DOCUMENTS

lading and a number of issues that relate to them as a group of documents.

Straight bill of lading (non-negotiable)

A straight bill of lading indicates that the shipper will deliver the goods to the consignee. The document itself does not give title to the goods (making it "non-negotiable"). The consignee need only identify himself to claim the goods. A straight bill of lading is often used when payment for the goods has already been made in advance or in cases where the goods are shipped on open account. A straight bill of lading, therefore, cannot be transferred by endorsement.

Shipper's order bill of lading (negotiable)

A shipper's order bill of lading is a title document to the goods, issued "to the order of" a party, usually the shipper, whose endorsement is required to effect its negotiation. Because it is negotiable, it can be bought, sold, or traded while goods are in transit. These are highly favored for documentary credit transactions. The buyer usually needs the original or a copy as proof of ownership to take possession of the goods.

Blank endorsed negotiable bill of lading

A blank endorsed negotiable bill of lading is one that has been endorsed without naming an endorsee. In simple terms, the person in possession of the document may claim possession of the goods.

Air waybill

An air waybill is a form of bill of lading used for the air transport of goods and is not negotiable.

Clean bill of lading

A clean bill of lading is one where the carrier has noted that the merchandise has been received in apparent good condition (no apparent damage, loss, etc.) and that does not bear such notations as "Shipper's Load and Count," etc.

Most forms of documentary payment require a "clean" bill of lading in order for the seller to obtain payment. There are, however, some circumstances in some trades, in which transport documents with special clauses are acceptable.

Claused bill of lading

A claused bill of lading is one which contains notations that specify a shortfall in quantity or deficient condition of the goods and/or packaging. Opposite of clean bill of lading.

Originals

Some bills of lading are issued in "sets of originals." In documentary credit transactions the "full set" of original transport documents (one or more) must usually be presented for payment (especially if they are negotiable documents).

On board

An "on board" notation on a bill of lading means that the goods have in fact been loaded on board or shipped on a named vessel. This notation may be made by the carrier, his agent, the master of the ship, or his agent. Unless expressly authorized, the transport document issued by the carrier must reflect that it is "on board" in order for the seller to obtain payment under a documentary credit.

On deck

An "on deck" notation means that the goods have been secured on the deck of the vessel rather than in its hold, and therefore subject to wind and weather. Such a notation is generally not acceptable in documentary credit transactions unless specifically authorized. If the transport document shows that the goods are loaded on deck, any accompanying insurance document must show cover against "on deck" risks. Bear in mind, however, that certain dangerous cargo (including certain chemicals and live animals) are often carried on deck.

Documents and International Payments

Documents are an integral part of all international payment methods, including documentary letters of credit, documents against payment, and documents against acceptance.

The documents called for by a payment type will differ somewhat according to the nature of the goods and the countries of export and import. Some documents, however, such as the commercial invoice and a bill of lading, are specified in all transactions.

Consistency Among Documents

One of the major issues in the preparation, presentation, and verification of documentation by sellers, buyers, and banks in payment situations is consistency among the documents.

Example: In examining the documentation for a letter of credit transaction involving the sale of five pieces of machinery, the buyer noticed that the commercial invoice listed the net weight as 12,140 kilograms and the gross weight as 12,860

DOCUMENTS

kilograms. The bill of lading, however, listed the gross weight as 9,612 kilograms. What happened to the other 3,248 kilograms? Did the seller make a mistake in preparing the commercial invoice? Did the shipping company make a mistake in preparing the bill of lading? Did the seller forget to ship one or more pieces of machinery? Did the shipping company misplace some machinery? Did someone steal the machinery?

In the above example, the seller should have noticed the inconsistency before forwarding the documents to the advising bank. The advising bank should have noticed the inconsistency before forwarding the documents to the issuing bank. The issuing bank should have noticed the inconsistency before forwarding the documents to the buyer. The buyer will most certainly reject this documentation.

Documentation Consistency Checklist

The following is a list of points of consistency buyers, sellers, and banks should all be aware of when preparing, presenting, and checking documents for documentary payment transactions:

1. Name and address of shipper
2. Name and address of buyer/consignee
3. Issuer name and address
4. Description of the goods, quantities, units
5. Country of origin of the goods
6. Country of destination of the goods
7. Invoice numbers, documentary credit numbers
8. Certifications
9. Legalizations
10. Shipping marks and numbers
11. Net weight, gross weight, volume
12. Number of crates, cartons, or containers

Ambiguity as to issuers of documents

If terms such as "first class," "well-known," "qualified," "independent," "official," "competent," or "local" are used in a documentary credit to refer to the issuer of a required document (e.g., inspection certificate or certificate of origin), banks are authorized to accept whatever documents are presented, provided that on their face they appear to be in compliance with the credit and were not issued and signed by the seller (beneficiary).

Originals

The originals of specified documents should be provided unless copies are called for or allowed. If more than one set of originals is required, the buyer should specify in the credit how many are necessary.

Unless otherwise noted in the documentary credit, banks are authorized to accept documents as originals, even if they were produced or appear to have been produced on a copy machine, by a computerized system, or are carbon copies, provided they have the notation "Original" and are, when necessary, signed.

Named carrier

A transport document must appear on its face to have been issued by a named carrier, or his agent. This does not mean that the applicant must name the carrier in the documentary credit application. It merely means that the transport document must indicate the name of the carrier.

Authentication

Unless otherwise noted in the documentary credit, banks are authorized to accept documents that are authenticated, validated, legalized, visaed, or certified so long as the document appears on its face to satisfy the requirement. This means that the banks are not responsible for the verification of the certification or authorized signature. Certificates must usually bear the signature of the issuer.

Signature

Banks are authorized to accept documents that have been signed by facsimile, perforated signature, stamp, symbol, or any other mechanical or electronic method.

Unspecified issuers or contents of documents

If the credit does not name a specific issuer or specific contents of a document (other than transport documents, insurance documents, and the commercial invoice), banks are authorized to accept documents as presented so long as the data contained in the documents are consistent with the credit and other stipulated documents.

Issuance date vs. documentary credit date

Unless otherwise noted in the documentary credit, banks are authorized to accept documents dated prior to the issuance date of the credit, so long as all other terms of the credit have been satisfied.

DOCUMENTS

Commercial Invoice

Definition

The commercial invoice is the key accounting document describing the commercial transaction between the buyer and the seller.

✔ Key Elements

The commercial invoice includes the following elements:

1. Name and address of seller
2. Name and address of buyer
3. Date of issuance
4. Invoice number
5. Order or contract number
6. Quantity and description of the goods
7. Unit price, total price, other agreed upon charges, and total invoice amount stated in the currency of the contract or letter of credit (e.g., US$, DM, ¥, etc.)
8. Shipping details including: weight of the goods, number of packages, and shipping marks and numbers
9. Terms of delivery and payment
10. Any other information as required in the sales contract or letter of credit (e.g., country of origin)

Cautions & Notes for Documentary Letters of Credit

In transactions involving a documentary letter of credit it is vitally important that the description of the goods in the commercial invoice correspond precisely to the description of goods in the credit.

The invoice amount should match exactly (or at least should not exceed) the amount specified in the credit. Banks have the right to refuse invoices issued for amounts in excess of the amount stated in the credit. For this, as well as other reasons, the invoice should be made out in the same currency as the credit.

The exception: when a documentary credit specifies "about" in relation to the currency amount and quantity of merchandise, in which case the invoice may specify an amount equal to plus or minus 10 percent of the stipulated amount of the credit.

Unless otherwise stipulated in the documentary credit, the commercial invoice must be made out in the name of the applicant (buyer). The exception: In a transferable documentary credit the invoice may be made out to a third party.

The buyer, seller, and bank(s) should all carefully check for discrepancies in the invoice. The details specified therein should not be inconsistent with those of any other documents, and should exactly conform to the specifications of the credit.

DOCUMENTS

Indonesia Coffee Export Co.
Jalan Sudirman
Jakarta 10420, Indonesia

INVOICE

June 27, 1998
Invoice No. 98-123456

American Caffeine Import Company
125 Main Street
Seattle, Washington

Description of goods:
15 metric tons of 60-kilo bags of New Crop D.P. Sumatra Mandheling Arabica
Grade 1 - Green Coffee - As per buyer's purchase order No. 1234

TOTAL CIF Seattle, Washington, USA US$65,000.00

Payment:	By irrevocable documentary letter of credit No. 1234567 dated May 27, 1998 of The American Import Bank, Seattle, Washington USA
Payment Terms:	At 120 days' sight, draft drawn on San Francisco International Bank, San Francisco, California, USA
Country of Origin:	Indonesia
Number of bags:	250 bags
Weights:	Gross 15,000 kilo, Net 15,000 kilo
Marks/No.:	USA Made in Indonesia No. 12345.67
Dispatch:	Through ABC Freight Services, by sea from Jakarta via Sea Maritime Steamship Line to Seattle

Indonesia Coffee Export Co.

Indonesia Coffee Export Company

DOCUMENTS

Marine/Ocean/Port-to-Port Bill of Lading

Definition

A marine bill of lading is a transport document covering port-to-port shipments of goods (for carriage of goods solely by sea).

✔ Key Elements

A completed marine bill of lading contains the following elements:

1. Name of carrier with a signature identified as that of carrier, or ship's master, or agent for or on behalf of either the carrier or ship's master
2. An indication or notation that the goods have been loaded "on board" or shipped on a named vessel. Also, the date of issuance or date of loading
3. An indication of the port of loading and the port of discharge
4. A sole original, or if issued in multiple originals, the full set of originals
5. The terms and conditions of carriage or a reference to the terms and conditions of carriage in another source or document
6. In a documentary letter of credit, no indication that the document is subject to a charter party and/or an indication that the named vessel is propelled by sail only
7. Meets any other stipulations of the sales contract or documentary letter of credit

Cautions & Notes for Documentary Letters of Credits

If the document includes the notation "intended vessel" it must also contain an "on board" notation of a named vessel along with the date of loading, even if the named vessel is the same as the intended vessel.

If the document indicates a place where the goods were received by the carrier different from the port of loading, the document must also contain an "on-board" notation indicating the port of loading as named in the credit and the named vessel, along with the date.

If a documentary credit calls for a port-to-port shipment but does not call specifically for a marine bill of lading, the banks will accept a transport document, however named, that contains the above information. Banks will normally accept the following documents under this title: ocean bill of lading, combined transport bill of lading, short form bill of lading, or received for shipment bill of lading, provided it carries the notation "on board."

If the documents are drawn up "to the order of" the exporter or "to order" they must be endorsed.

If the documentary credit prohibits transshipment this document will be rejected if it specifically states that the goods will be transshipped.

Since this is a negotiable instrument, it may be endorsed and transferred to a third party while the goods are in transit.

D O C U M E N T S

Bill of Lading

Carrier:
Hapag-Lloyd Container Linie GmbH, Hamburg

Multimodal Transport or Port to Port Shipment   PAGE 2

Hapag-Lloyd

Shipper: WATSON/SHAKLEY RICE INTERNATIONAL 8176 WILLOW STREET WINDSOR, CALIFORNIA CA 95492-9305	**Hapag-Lloyd Reference:** 14013696	**B/L-No.:** HLCUOAK980300049

Export References:
SHPR REF: JFC(UK) LTD
FWDR REF: SF01078226
C.H.B.NO: 5118

Consignee or Order: TO THE ORDER BANK OF LLOYDS LONDON L/C# 3892XVGR012965	**Forwarding Agent:** F.M.C.NO: 0087 NALDUZAK ASSOCIATES, INC. 5088A DIAMOND HEIGHTS BLVD. SAN FRANCISCO, CA 94131-1605

Consignee's Reference:

Notify Address (Carrier not responsible for failure to notify; see clause 20 (1) hereof): CONNOLLY (UK) LIMITED #1 1000 NORTH CIRCLE ROAD EAST STAPLES CORNER LONDON NW2 7JP ENGLAND	**Place of Receipt:**

Pre-Carriage by:	**Place of Receipt by Pre-Carrier:**	**Place of Delivery:**

Ocean Vessel: 50E04 HEIDELBERG EXPRES	**Port of Loading:** OAKLAND, CA	

Port of Discharge: THAMESPORT	**Place of Delivery by On-Carrier:**	

Container Nos., Seal Nos., Marks and Nos.	**Number and Kind of Packages; Description of Goods**	**Gross Weight (kg)**	**Measurement (cbm)**
HLCU 2254295 SEAL: 136427	1 FCL/FCL 20' CONTAINER STC: 1420 PACKAGES MILLED RICE COMMODITY: 1006000000	43020# 19513K	

SHIPPED ON BOARD DATE: MAR/05/1998
PORT OF LOADING: OAKLAND, CA
VESSEL NAME: KOELN EXPRESS

SHIPMENT PURSUANT TO SC NO. 98-302
SHIPPER'S LOAD, STOWAGE AND COUNT
FREIGHT PREPAID - ORIGIN TERMINAL CHARGE PREPAID
NO S.E.D. REQUIRED, SECTION 30.39 FTSR, C.A.S. - JL.
THESE COMMODITIES, TECHNOLOGY OR SOFTWARE WERE EXPORTED FROM
THE UNITED STATES IN ACCORDANCE WITH THE EXPORT ADMINISTRATION
REGULATIONS.   DIVERSION CONTRARY TO U.S. LAW PROHIBITED. NLR

ORIGINAL

Above Particulars as declared by Shipper. Without responsibility or warranty as to correctness by carrier (see clause 11(1) and 11(2))

Total No. of Containers/Packages received by the Carrier:	**Shipper's declared value (see clause 7(1) and 7(2) hereof):**	Received by the Carrier from the Shipper in apparent good order and condition (unless otherwise noted herein) the total number or quantity of Containers or other packages or units indicated in the box opposite entitled "Total No. of Containers/Packages received by the Carrier" for Carriage subject to all the terms and conditions hereof **(Including the Terms and Conditions on the Reverse hereof and the Terms and Conditions of the Carrier's Applicable Tariff)** from the Place of Receipt or the Port of Loading, whichever is applicable, to the Port of Discharge or the Place of Delivery, whichever is applicable. One original Bill of Lading, duly endorsed, must be surrendered by the Merchant to the Carrier in exchange for the Goods or a delivery order. In accepting this Bill of Lading the Merchant expressly accepts and agrees to all its terms and conditions whether printed, stamped or written, or otherwise incorporated, notwithstanding the non-signing of this Bill of Lading by the Merchant. **In Witness whereof** the number of original Bills of Lading stated below all of this tenor and date has been signed, one of which being accomplished the others to stand void.
1		

Movement FCL/FCL	**Currency** USD			
Charge	**Rate**	**Basis**	**WT/MEA/VAL**	**Payment**	**Amount**

Charge	Rate	Basis	WT/MEA/VAL	Payment	Amount
THO	420.00	CTR	1	P	420.00
SEA	1530.00	CTR	1	P	1530.00
BAF	40.00	CTR	1	P	40.00
CAF	6.00	PCT	1530	P	91.80
THD	185.00	CTR	1	C	185.00

Place and Date of Issue:
CORTE MADERA, CA   MAR/05/1998

Freight Payable at: CORTE MADERA, CA	**Number of original Bs/l:** 3/3

**For above named carrier
Hapag-Lloyd (America) Inc.
(as agent)**   *Allen Miller*

Total Freight Prepaid	**Total Freight Collect**	**Total Freight**
2081.80	185.00	2266.80

Non-Negotiable Sea Waybill

Definition

A non-negotiable sea waybill is a transport document covering port-to-port shipments. It is not a title document, is not negotiable and cannot be endorsed.

✔ Key Elements

A completed non-negotiable sea waybill contains the following elements:

1. Name of carrier with a signature identified as that of carrier, or ship's master, or agent for or on behalf of either the carrier or ship's master
2. An indication or notation that the goods have been loaded "on board" or shipped on a named vessel. Also, the date of issuance or date of loading
3. An indication of the port of loading and the port of discharge as specified in the original sales contract or documentary credit
4. A sole original, or if issued in multiple originals, the full set of originals
5. The terms and conditions of carriage or a reference to the terms and conditions of carriage in another source or document
6. In a documentary letter of credit, no indication that the document is subject to a charter party and/or an indication that the named vessel is propelled by sail only
7. Meets any other stipulations of the sales contract or documentary credit

Cautions & Notes for Documentary Letters of Credit

If the document includes the notation "intended vessel" it must also contain an "on board" notation of a named vessel along with the date of loading, even if the named vessel is the same as the intended vessel.

If the document indicates a place where the goods were received by the carrier different from the port of loading, the document must also contain an "on-board" notation indicating the port of loading as named in the documentary letter of credit and the named vessel, along with the date.

If the documentary credit calls for a port-to-port shipment but does not call specifically for a marine bill of lading, the banks will accept a transport document, however named, that contains the above information. Banks will normally accept the following documents under this title: ocean bill of lading, combined transport bill of lading, short form bill of lading, or received for shipment bill of lading, provided it carries the notation "on board."

Because they are not title documents, sea waybills eliminate many of the inconveniences of a bill of lading and offer advantages in situations where the rigid security of a bill of lading is not required. Waybills reduce the opportunity for fraud—although they do by no means eliminate it—and they remove the problems of goods arriving ahead of documents (because they travel with the goods).

Sea waybills are appropriate for shipments between associated companies, for shipments to an agent for sale at destination on an open account basis, and for shipments between companies that have established mutual trust.

DOCUMENTS

Express Cargo Bill

PAGE 2

Hapag-Lloyd

Carrier: Hapag-Lloyd Container Linie GmbH, Hamburg	Multimodal Transport or Port to Port Shipment

Shipper:
ABC WINE COMPANY
1234 SPAIN STREET
SONOMA, CA 96476

Hapag-Lloyd Reference: 10347784

ECB-No.: HLCUOAK980300071

Export References:
USS-NL-000-008

C.H.B.NO: 5118

Consignee:
DELAHAY WINE ENTERPRISES, LTD.
HAZELDONK 1408 - 1412
NL 4386 LH BREDA
THE NETHERLANDS

Forwarding Agent: F.M.C.NO: 0087
NALDUZAK ASSOCIATES, INC.
5088A DIAMOND HEIGHTS BLVD.
SAN FRANCISCO, CA 94131-1605

Consignee's Reference:

Notify Address (Carrier not responsible for failure to notify):
DELAHAY WINE ENTERPRISES, LTD.
HAZELDONK 1408 - 1412
NL 4386 LH BREDA
THE NETHERLANDS

Place of Receipt:

Pre-Carriage by:	**Place of Receipt by Pre-Carrier:**	**Place of Delivery:**

Ocean Vessel: KOELN EXPRESS 06E07	**Port of Loading:** OAKLAND, CA	
Port of Discharge: ROTTERDAM	**Place of Delivery by On-Carrier:**	

Container Nos.; Seal Nos.; Marks and Nos.	Number and Kind of Packages; Description of Goods	Gross Weight (kg)	Measurement (cbm)
HLCU 4073300 SEAL: 2902455 PO-DS: 3327-04G PO-C1: EL100093	1 X 40' CONTAINER SAID TO CONTAIN: 1246 CS CALIFORNIA WINES LESS THAN 14% ALCOHOL COMMODITY: 2204000000	19872 KGM	

SHIPPED ON BOARD DATE: MAR/06/1998
PORT OF LOADING: OAKLAND, CA
VESSEL NAME: KOELN EXPRESS

SHIPMENT PURSUANT TO SC NO. 98-500
SHIPPER'S LOAD, STOWAGE AND COUNT
FREIGHT COLLECT
PROTECT AGAINST EXTREME TEMPERATURES
THESE COMMODITIES LICENSED BY THE U.S. FOR ULTIMATE DESTINATION
THE NETHERLANDS.   DIVERSION CONTRARY TO U.S. LAW PROHIBITED.

Above Particulars as declared by Shipper. Without responsibility or warranty as to correctness by carrier.

RECEIPT

Total No. of Containers/Packages received by the Carrier:	Shipper's declared value (see clause 7(1) and 7(2) hereof):
1	

RECEIVED by the Carrier from the Shipper in apparent good order and condition (unless otherwise noted herein) the total number or quantity of Containers or other packages or units indicated in the box opposite entitled "Total No. of Containers/Packages received by the Carrier" for Carriage subject to all the terms and conditions hereof (INCLUDING THE TERMS AND CONDITIONS ON THE REVERSE HEREOF AND THE TERMS AND CONDITIONS OF THE CARRIER'S APPLICABLE TARIFF) from the Place of Receipt or the Port of Loading, whichever is applicable, to the Port of Discharge or the Place of Delivery, whichever is applicable. In accepting this Express Cargo Bill the Merchant expressly accepts and agrees to all its terms and conditions whether printed, stamped or written, or otherwise incorporated, notwithstanding the non-signing of this Express Cargo Bill by the Merchant.

Movement		FCL/FCL		Currency USD	
Charge	Rate	Basis	WT/MEA/VAL	Payment	Amount
THO	500.00	CTR	1	C	500.00
SEA	1701.00	CTR	1	C	1701.00
BAF	80.00	CTR	1	C	80.00
CAF	21.00	PCT	1701	C	357.21
THO	343.00	CTR	1	C	167.33

Place and Date of Issue:
CORTE MADERA, CA MAR/05/1998

Freight Payable at:
BARKING, U.K.

For above named carrier
Hapag-Lloyd (America) Inc.
(as agent)

Total Freight Prepaid	Total Freight Collect	Total Freight
	2805.54	2805.54

Express Cargo Bill · Not Negotiable

90116743

Multimodal (Combined) Transport Document

Definition

A multimodal transport document is a bill of lading covering two or more modes of transport, such as shipping by rail and by sea.

✔ Key Elements

A completed multimodal transport document contains the following elements:

1. Name of carrier or multimodal transport operator with a signature identified as that of carrier, transport operator, or ship's master, or agent for or on behalf of either the carrier, transport operator, or ship's master

2. An indication that the shipment has been "dispatched," "taken in charge," or "loaded on board," along with a date

3. Indication of the place of receipt of the shipment that may be different from the place of actual loading "on board" and the place of delivery of the shipment, which may be different from the place of discharge

4. A sole original, or if issued in multiple originals, the full set of originals

5. The terms and conditions of carriage or a reference to the terms and conditions of carriage in another source or document other than the multimodal transport document

6. In a documentary letter of credit, no indication that the document is subject to a charter party and/ or an indication that the named vessel is propelled by sail only

7. Meets any other stipulations of the sales contract or documentary letter of credit

Cautions & Notes for Documentary Letters of Credit

In multimodal situations the contract of carriage and liability is for a combined transport from the place of shipment to the place of delivery. Thus, the document evidences receipt of goods and not shipment on board.

The date of issuance of the document is deemed to be the date of dispatch unless there is a specific date of dispatch, taking in charge, or loading on board, in which case the latter date is deemed to be the date of dispatch.

Even if a documentary letter of credit prohibits transshipment, banks will accept a multimodal transport document that indicates that transshipment will or may take place, provided that the entire carriage is covered by one transport document.

A combined transport document issued by a freight forwarder is acceptable unless the documentary letter of credit stipulates otherwise or unless the credit specifically calls for a "marine bill of lading." The issuing freight forwarder accepts carrier responsibility for performance of the entire contract of carriage and liability for loss or damage wherever and however it occurs.

As a rule, multimodal transport documents are not negotiable instruments.

Bill of Lading   PAGE 2   **Hapag-Lloyd**

Carrier:
Hapag-Lloyd Container Linie GmbH, Hamburg   Multimodal Transport or Port to Port Shipment

Shipper:	Hapag-Lloyd Reference:	B/L-No.:
WILSON COMMODITIES INTERNATIONAL 100 MEADOWCREEK DRIVE CORTE MADERA, CA 94125	10347484	HLCUOAK980204041

Export References:
REF#156008
REF#156008
C.H.B.NO: 12330

Consignee or Order:	Forwarding Agent: F.M.C.NO: 0953
ZAIDNERS INTERNATIONAL B.V. POSTBUS 27 4870 AA ETTEN-LEUR THE NETHERLANDS	NALDUZAK ASSOCIATES, INC. 5088A DIAMOND HEIGHTS BLVD. SAN FRANCISCO, CA 94131-1605 Consignee's Reference:

Notify Address (Carrier not responsible for failure to notify; see clause 20 (1) hereof):	Place of Receipt:
GARCIA ROTTERDAM B.V. POSTBUS 425 3200 AK SPIJKENISSE THE NTHERLANDS	FRESNO, CA

Pre-Carriage by:	Place of Receipt by Pre-Carrier: FRESNO, CA	Place of Delivery:
Ocean Vessel: 23E06	Port of Loading:	
ROTTERDAM EXPRESS	OAKLAND, CA	
Port of Discharge:	Place of Delivery by On-Carrier:	
ROTTERDAM		

Container Nos., Seal Nos.; Marks and Nos.	Number and Kind of Packages; Description of Goods	Gross Weight (kg)	Measurement (cbm)
HLXU 4787302 SEAL: 3814	1 40' HC REEFER CONTAINER STC: 791 CARTONS OF RASPBERRIES SEEDLESS COMMODITY: 0811000003 MAINTAIN TEMPERATURE AT -18.0 CELSIUS OR LOWER	42857LBS	

SHIPPED ON BOARD DATE: FEB/17/1998
PORT OF LOADING: OAKLAND, CA
VESSEL NAME: CAPE HENRY

CARGO STOWED UNDER REFRIGERATION
SHIPPER'S LOAD, STOWAGE AND COUNT
FREIGHT COLLECT
THESE COMMODITIES, TECHNOLOGY OR SOFTWARE WERE EXPORTED FROM
THE UNITED STATES IN ACCORDANCE WITH THE EXPORT ADMINISTRATION
REGULATIONS. DIVERSION CONTRARY TO U.S. LAW PROHIBITED. NLR

Above Particulars as declared by Shipper. Without responsibility or warranty as to correctness by carrier (see clause 11(1) and 11(2))   ORIGINAL

Total No. of Containers/Packages received by the Carrier:	Shipper's declared value (see clause 7(1) and 7(2) hereof):				Received by the Carrier from the Shipper in apparent good order and condition (unless otherwise noted herein) the total number or quantity of Containers or other packages or units indicated in the box opposite entitled "Total No. of Containers/Packages received by the Carrier" for Carriage subject to all the terms and conditions hereof **(Including the Terms and Conditions on the Reverse hereof and the Terms and Conditions of the Carrier's Applicable Tariff)** from the Place of Receipt or the Port of Loading, whichever is applicable, to the Port of Discharge or the Place of Delivery, whichever is applicable. One original Bill of Lading, duly endorsed, must be surrendered by the Merchant to the Carrier in exchange for the Goods or a delivery order. In accepting this Bill of Lading the Merchant expressly accepts and agrees to all its terms and conditions whether printed, stamped or written, or otherwise incorporated, notwithstanding the non-signing of this Bill of Lading by the Merchant.
			1		
Movement FCL/FCL	Currency USD				

Charge	Rate	Basis	WT/MEA/VAL	Payment	Amount
OLF	490.00	CTR	1	C	490.00
THO	500.00	CTR	1	C	500.00
SEA	3805.00	CTR	1	C	3805.00
BAF	80.00	CTR	1	C	80.00
CAF	21.00	PCT	3805	C	799.05
THO	343.00	CTR	1	C	170.12

In Witness whereof the number of original Bills of Lading stated below all of this tenor and date has been signed, one of which being accomplished the others to stand void.

Place and Date of Issue: CORTE MADERA, CA FEB/23/1998	
Freight Payable at: DESTINATION	Number of original Bs/l: 3/3

For above named carrier
Hapag-Lloyd (America) Inc.
(as agent)   *Allen Miller*

Total Freight Prepaid	Total Freight Collect	Total Freight
	5844.17	5844.17

90116741

Air Transport Document (Air Waybill)

Definition

An air waybill is a non-negotiable transport document covering transport of cargo from airport to airport.

✔ Key Elements

A completed air waybill contains the following elements:

1. Name of carrier with a signature identified as that of carrier or named agent for or on behalf of the carrier
2. An indication that the goods have been accepted for carriage. Also, the date of issuance or date of loading
3. In a documentary letter of credit, an indication of the actual date of dispatch if required by the documentary letter of credit, or, if the actual date of dispatch is not required by the credit, the issuance date of the document is deemed to be the date of shipment
4. An indication of the airport of departure and airport of destination
5. Appears on its face to be the original for consignor/shipper
6. The terms and conditions of carriage or a reference to the terms and conditions of carriage in another source or document
7. Meets any other stipulations of the sales contract or documentary letter of credit

Cautions & Notes for Documentary Letters of Credit

Information contained in the "for carrier use only" box concerning flight number and date are not considered to be the actual flight number and date.

Since air waybills are issued in three originals—one for the issuing carrier, one for the consignee (buyer), and one for the shipper (seller)—a documentary credit should not require presentation in more than one original. Nor should it call for a "full set of original air waybills."

The air waybill is not a negotiable document. It indicates only acceptance of goods for carriage.

The air waybill must name a consignee (who can be the buyer), and it should not be required to be issued "to order" and/or "to be endorsed." Since it is not negotiable, and it does not evidence title to the goods, in order to maintain some control of goods not paid for by cash in advance, sellers often consign air shipments to their sales agents, or freight forwarders' agents in the buyer's country.

The air waybill should not be required to indicate an "actual flight date" since IATA regulations specify that reservations requested by the shipper shall not be inserted under "Flight/Date."

Definitions

Master Air Waybill A shipper's contract of carriage with an airline.

House Air Waybill A shipper's contract of carriage with the logistics firm.

085 | BSL | **7260 2751**   **085-7260-2751**

Shipper's Name and Address | Shipper's account Number | NOT NEGOTIABLE

AIR WAYBILL

swissair ✚

SWISS EXPORT LTD
AIRFREIGHT DIVISION
ZUERICH

AIR CONSIGNMENT NOTE — Issued by: Swiss Air Transport Co., Ltd., Zurich, Switzerland
Member of IATA (International Air Transport Association)

Copies 1, 2 and 3 of this Air Waybill are originals and have the same validity

Consignee's Name and Address | Consignee's account Number

IMPORT KONTOR
VIENNA

Phone: 633 7876

It is agreed that the goods described herein are accepted in apparent good order and condition (except as noted) for carriage SUBJECT O THE CONDITIONS OF CONTRACT ON THE REVERSE HEREOF. THE SHIPPER'S ATTENTION IS DRAWN TO THE NOTICE CONCERNING CARRIERS' LIMITATION OF LIABILITY. Shipper may increase such limitation of liability by declaring a higher value for carriage and paying a supplemental charge if required.

Issuing Carrier's Agent Name and City | Accounting information

FORWARDING LTD
BASLE

Agent's IATA Code | Account No.
81-4 0000

Airport of Departure (Addr. of the Carrier) and requested Routing
BSL-VIE

to	By first Carrier	Routing and Destination	to	by	to	by	Currency	CHGS Code	WT/VAL PPD COLL	Other PPD COLL	Declared Value for Carriage	Declared Value for Customs
VIE	SWISSAIR						SFR		CO PP		NVD	

Airport of Destination	Flight/Date	For Carrier Use only Flight/Date	Amount of Insurance	INSURANCE - If carrier offers insurance and such insurance is requested in accordance with conditions on reverse hereof, indicate amount to be insured in figures in box marked amount of insurance.
VIENNA	SR436/8.7.			

Handling Information

No of Pieces RCP	Gross Weight	kg lb	Rate Class / Commodity Item No.	Chargeable Weight	Rate / Charge	Total	Nature and Quantity of Goods (incl. Dimensions or Volume)
8	200,6	K	C 6750	201	1.90	381.90	CHEMICALS NOT RESTRICTED CONTRACT No 100-15-2
8	200,6						

Prepaid	Weight Charge	Collect	Other Charges
	381.90		AWA 15.00

Valuation Charge

Tax

| Total other Charges Due Agent |
| 15.00 |

Shipper certifies that the particulars on the face hereof are correct and that insofar as any part of the consignment contains dangerous goods, such part is properly described by name and is in proper condition for carriage by air according to the applicable Dangerous Goods Regulations.

Total other Charges Due Carrier

SWISS EXPORT LTD / p.o. Forwarding LTD

Signature of Shipper or his Agent

Total Prepaid	Total Collect
15.00	381.90

Currency Conversion Rates | cc charges in Dest. Currency
07.07.   BASLE   Forwarding LTD

Executed on (Date) at (Place) Signature of Issuing Carrier or its Agent

Charges at Destination | Total collect Charges

For Carrier's Use only at Destination

085-7260 2751

No. 3 - ORIGINAL for SHIPPER

Form 30.301
Printed in the Fed. Rep. Germany - Bartsch Verlag, Munich-Ottobrunn 600j (III)

D O C U M E N T S

Insurance Document (or Certificate)

Definition

A document indicating the type and amount of insurance coverage in force on a particular shipment. In documentary credit transactions the insurance document is used to assure the consignee that insurance is provided to cover loss of or damage to cargo while in transit.

✔ Key Elements

A completed insurance document includes the following elements:

1. The name of the insurance company
2. Policy number
3. Description of the merchandise insured
4. Points of origin and destination of the shipment. Coverage is indicated by the terms of sale. For example, for goods sold "FOB," coverage commences once the cargo, is on board the vessel and continues until the consignee takes possession at either the seaport or in-land port of destination.
5. Conditions of coverage, exclusions, and deductible, if applicable.
6. A signature by the insurance carrier, underwriter or agent for same
7. Indication that the cover is effective at the latest from the date of loading of the goods on board a transport vessel or the taking in charge of the goods by the carrier, as indicated by the transport document (bill of lading, etc.)
8. Statement of the sum insured
9. In a documentary letter of credit, specifies coverage for at least 110 percent of either: (a) the CIF or CIP value of the shipment, if such can be determined from the various documents on their face, otherwise, (b) the amount of the payment, acceptance or negotiation specified in the documentary credit, or (c) the gross amount of the commercial invoice
10. Is presented as the sole original, or if issued in more than one original, all the originals

Cautions & Notes

In documentary credit transactions the insurance currency should be consistent with the currency of the documentary credit.

Documentary credit transactions indicating CIF (Cost Insurance Freight) or CIP (Carriage and Insurance Paid) pricing should list an insurance document in their required documentation.

"Cover notes" issued by insurance brokers (as opposed to insurance companies, underwriters, or their agents) are not accepted in letter of credit transactions unless authorized specifically by the credit.

In Case of Loss or Shortfall

The consignee should always note on the delivery document any damage or shortfall prior to signing for receipt of the goods. The consignee has the responsibility to make reasonable efforts to minimize loss. This includes steps to prevent further damage to the shipment. Expenses incurred in such efforts are almost universally collectible under the insurance policy. Prompt notice of loss is essential.

The original copy of the insurance certificate is a negotiable document and is required in the filing of a claim.

Copies of documents necessary to support an insurance claim include the insurance policy or certificate, bill of lading, invoice, packing list, and a survey report (usually prepared by a claims agent).

DOCUMENTS

$ _____
(sum insured)

No. 473301

CERTIFICATE OF MARINE INSURANCE

WASHINGTON INTERNATIONAL INSURANCE COMPANY
300 PARK BOULEVARD, SUITE 500, ITASCA, IL 60143-2625

This is to Certify, *That on the* _____ day of _____ 19____ , this Company

insured under Policy No. _____ made for

for the sum of _____ Dollars,

on _____

Valued at sum insured. Shipped on board the S/S or M/S _____ and/or following
steamer or steamers

at and from _____ , via _____
(Initial Point of Shipment)   (Port of Shipment)

to _____ and it is understood and agreed, that in case of loss, the same
(Port or Place of Destination)

is payable to the order of _____ on surrender of this Certificate which
conveys the right of collecting any such loss as fully as if the property were covered by a special policy direct to the holder hereof, and free from any liability for unpaid premiums. This certificate is subject to all the terms of the open policy, provided however, that the rights of a bona fide holder of this certificate for value shall not be prejudiced by any terms of the open policy which are in conflict with the terms of this certificate.

SPECIAL CONDITIONS   **MARKS & NUMBERS**

NEW MERCHANDISE shipped subject to an UNDER DECK bill of lading insured–
    Against all risks of physical loss or damage from any external cause, irrespective of percentage, excepting those excluded by the F.C. & S., Nuclear Exclusion and S.R. & C.C. Warranties, arising during transportation between the points of shipment and of destination named herein.
    The above conditions apply only to New Approved Commodities, properly packed for export, as listed in the Master Policy to which this Certificate is made a part of. Commodities such as, but not limited to, Automobiles, Household Goods and Personal Effects, Wines, Liquors, Beer and Similar Spirits, are subject to further conditions and/or warranties of the policy.
    Non-approved commodities are subject to the F.P.A. conditions of the Master Policy unless broader conditions have been approved by these underwriters prior to attachment of risk and so endorsed hereon.

DEDUCTIBLE	COUNTRY CODE

USED MERCHANDISE AND/OR ON DECK SHIPMENTS insured–
    Warranted free of particular average unless caused by the vessel being stranded, sunk, burnt, on fire or in collision, but including risk of jettison and/or washing overboard, irrespective of percentage.

TERMS AND CONDITIONS—SEE ALSO BACK HEREOF

WAREHOUSE TO WAREHOUSE: This insurance attaches from the time the goods leave the Warehouse and/or Store at the place named in the Policy for the commencement of the transit and continues during the ordinary course of transit, including customary transhipment if any, until the goods are discharged overside from the overseas vessel at the final port. Thereafter the insurance continues whilst the goods are in transit and/or awaiting transit until delivered to final warehouse at the destination named in the Policy or until the expiry of 15 days (or 30 days if the destination to which the goods are insured is outside the limits of the port) whichever shall first occur. The time limits referred to above to be reckoned from midnight of the day on which the discharge overside of the goods hereby insured from the overseas vessel is completed. Held covered at a premium to be arranged in the event of transhipment, if any, other than as above and/or in the event of delay in transit arising from circumstances beyond the control of the Assured.
    NOTE–IT IS NECESSARY FOR THE ASSURED TO GIVE PROMPT NOTICE TO THESE ASSURERS WHEN THEY BECOME AWARE OF AN EVENT FOR WHICH THEY ARE "HELD COVERED" UNDER THIS POLICY AND THE RIGHT TO SUCH COVER IS DEPENDENT ON COMPLIANCE WITH THIS OBLIGATION.
    PERILS CLAUSE: Touching the adventures and perils which this Assurer is contented to bear and takes upon itself, they are of the seas, fires, assailing thieves, jettisons, barratry of the masters and mariners, and all other like perils, losses and misfortunes that have or shall come to the hurt, detriment or damage of the said goods and merchandise, or any part thereof, except as may be otherwise provided for herein or endorsed hereon.
    SHORE CLAUSE: Where this insurance by its terms covers while on docks, wharves or elsewhere on shore, and/or during land transportation, it shall include the risks of collision, derailment, overturning or other accident to the conveyance, fire, lightning, sprinkler leakage, cyclones, hurricanes, earthquakes, floods (meaning the rising of navigable waters), and/or collapse or subsidence of docks or wharves, even though the insurance be otherwise F.P.A.
    BOTH TO BLAME CLAUSE: Where goods are shipped under a Bill of Lading containing the so-called "Both to Blame Collision" Clause, these Assurers agree as to all losses covered by this insurance, to indemnify the Assured for this Policy's proportion of any amount (not exceeding the amount insured) which the Assured may be legally bound to pay to the shipowners under such clause. In the event that such liability is asserted the Assured agrees to notify these Assurers who shall have the right at their own cost and expense to defend the Assured against such claim.
    MACHINERY CLAUSE: When the property insured under this Policy includes a machine consisting when complete for sale or use of several parts, then in case of loss or damage covered by this insurance to any part of such machine, these Assurers shall be liable only for the proportion of the insured value of the part lost or damaged, or at the Assured's option, for the cost and expense, including labor and forwarding charges, of replacing or repairing the lost or damaged part; but in no event shall these Assurers be liable for more than the insured value of the complete machine.
    LABELS CLAUSE: In case of damage affecting labels, capsules or wrappers, these Assurers, if liable therefor under the terms of this policy, shall not be liable for more than an amount sufficient to pay the cost of new labels, capsules or wrappers, and the cost of reconditioning the goods, but in no event shall these Assurers be liable for more than the insured value of the damaged merchandise.
    DELAY CLAUSE: Warranted free of claim for loss of market or inherent vice or nature of the subject matter insured or for loss, damage or deterioration arising from delay, whether caused by a peril insured against or otherwise.
    AMERICAN INSTITUTE CLAUSES: This insurance, in addition to the foregoing, is also subject to the following American Institute Cargo Clauses, current forms:

1. MARINE EXTENSION CLAUSES	4. CARRIER	7. INCHMAREE	10. SOUTH AMERICA 60 DAY CLAUSE
2. DEVIATION	5. BILL OF LADING, ETC.	8. CONSTRUCTIVE TOTAL LOSS	11. S.R. & C.C. ENDORSEMENT
3. CRAFT, ETC.	6. EXPLOSION	9. GENERAL AVERAGE	12. WAR RISK INSURANCE

PARAMOUNT WARRANTIES: THE FOLLOWING WARRANTIES SHALL BE PARAMOUNT AND SHALL NOT BE MODIFIED OR SUPERSEDED BY ANY OTHER PROVISION INCLUDED HEREIN OR STAMPED OR ENDORSED HEREON UNLESS SUCH OTHER PROVISION REFERS SPECIFICALLY TO THE RISKS EXCLUDED BY THESE WARRANTIES AND EXPRESSLY ASSUMES THE SAID RISKS:
    F.C. & S.: Notwithstanding anything herein contained to the contrary, this insurance is warranted free from capture, seizure, arrest, restraint, detainment, confiscation, preemption, requisition or nationalization, and the consequences thereof or any attempt thereat, whether in time of peace or war and whether lawful or otherwise; also warranted free, whether in time of peace or war, from all loss, damage or expense caused by any weapon of war employing atomic or nuclear fission and/or fusion or other reaction or radioactive force or matter or by any mine or torpedo, also warranted free from all consequences of hostilities or warlike operations (whether there be a declaration of war or not), but this warranty shall not exclude collision or contact with aircraft, rockets or similar missiles or with any fixed or floating object (other than a mine or torpedo), stranding, heavy weather, fire or explosion unless caused directly (and independently of the nature of the voyage or service which the vessel concerned or, in the case of a collision, any other vessel involved therein, is performing) by a hostile act by or against a belligerent power; and for the purposes of this warranty "power" includes any authority maintaining naval, military or air forces in association with a power.
    Further warranted free from the consequences of civil war, revolution, rebellion, insurrection, or civil strife arising therefrom, or piracy.
    NUCLEAR EXCLUSION: Notwithstanding anything to the contrary herein, it is hereby understood and agreed that this Policy shall not apply to any loss, damage or expense due to or arising out of, whether directly or indirectly, nuclear reaction, radiation, or radioactive contamination, regardless of how it was caused. However, subject to all provisions of this Policy, if this Policy insures against fire, then direct physical damage to the property insured located within the United States or Puerto Rico by fire directly caused by the above excluded perils, is insured, provided that the nuclear reaction, radiation, or radioactive contamination was not caused, whether directly or indirectly, by any of the perils excluded by the F.C. & S. Warranty of this Policy.
    Nothing in this clause shall be construed to cover any loss, damage, liability or expense caused by nuclear reaction, radiation or radioactive contamination arising directly or indirectly from the fire mentioned above.
    S.R. & C.C. Warranted free of loss or damage caused by or resulting from:
    (a) strikes, lockouts, labor disturbances, riots, civil commotions, or the acts of any person or persons taking part in any such occurrences or disorders,
    (b) vandalism, sabotage or malicious act, which shall be deemed also to encompass the act or acts of one or more persons, whether or not agents of a sovereign power, carried out for political, terroristic or ideological purposes and whether any loss, damage or expense resulting therefrom is accidental or intentional.
    TIME FOR SUIT: No suit or action against this Assurer for the recovery of any claim by virtue of this insurance shall be sustained in any Court of Law or Equity unless commenced within one (1) year from the time loss occurred, or, if such limitation is not valid by the law of the place where the policy is issued, within the shortest contractual period of limitation permitted by such law.

This Certificate is issued in Original and Duplicate, one of which being accomplished the other to stand null and void.   To support a claim local Revenue Laws may require this certificate to be stamped.

Not transferable unless countersigned

Countersigned _____

Paul D. Amstutz   *James P. Sheehy*
President   Assistant Treasurer

ORIGINAL

ADDITIONAL CONDITIONS AND
INSTRUCTIONS TO CLAIMANTS ON REVERSE SIDE   W-13FF 6/97

DOCUMENTS

Certificate of Origin

Definition

A document issued by a certifying authority stating the country of origin of goods.

✔ Key Elements

A certificate of origin should include the following elements:

1. Key details (typically consignor, consignee, and description of goods) regarding the shipment. Also, such details to be in conformity with other documents (e.g., documentary credit, commercial invoice)
2. A statement of origin of the goods
3. The name, signature and/or stamp or seal of the certifying authority

A NAFTA Certificate of Origin includes the following elements:

1. Name and address of exporter
2. Blanket period of shipment (for multiple shipments of identical goods for a specified period of up to one year)
3. Name and address of importer
4. Name and address of producer
5. Description of goods
6. Harmonized System tariff classification number up to six digits
7. Preference criteria (one of six criteria of rules of origin of the goods)
8. Indication of whether the exporter is the producer of the goods
9. Regional Value Content indication
10. Country of origin of goods
11. Exporter company name, date and authorized signature

Cautions & Notes

If you are the buyer (importer) the import authority of your country may require a certificate of origin. If so, make certain that you require it of the seller in the form and content as specified by your country's customs authority.

A certificate of origin can be the key document required for obtaining special (reduced) tariff rates for imports from countries listed as beneficiaries to programs such as the GSP (Generalized Systems of Preferences) NAFTA (North American Free Trade Area).

In a documentary letter of credit buyers should avoid the use of such terms as "first class," "well-known," "qualified," "independent," "official," "competent," or "local" when referring to the certifying authority. It is preferable to name the required certifying authority. Use of vague terminology will result in the bank's acceptance of any relevant document that appears "on its face" to be in compliance with the documentary credit, so long as it was not issued and signed by the beneficiary (seller).

In certain countries the certificate of origin is prepared by the seller (beneficiary to the documentary credit) on a standard form and then certified (with a signature, stamp or seal) by the certifying authority.

Certifying authorities most often used are city and regional chambers of commerce and chambers of commerce and industry.

Exporteur Exportateur Esportatore Exporter MUELLER AG Birsstrasse 26 4132 Muttenz / Switzerland	Nr. No. 201884
Empfänger Destinataire Destinatario Consignee ADILMA TRADING CORPORATION 27, Nihonbashi, Chiyoda-Ku TOKYO 125 / Japan	URSPRUNGSZEUGNIS CERTIFICAT D'ORIGINE CERTIFICATO D'ORIGINE CERTIFICATE OF ORIGIN SCHWEIZERISCHE EIDGENOSSENSCHAFT CONFÉDÉRATION SUISSE CONFEDERAZIONE SVIZZERA SWISS CONFEDERATION

	Ursprungsstaat Pays d'origine Paese d'origine SWITZERLAND Country of origin
Angaben über die Beförderung (Ausfüllung freigestellt) Informations relatives au transport (mention facultative) Informazioni riguardanti il trasporto (indicazione facoltativa) Particulars of transport (optional declaration)	Bemerkungen Observations Osservazioni Observations LETTER OF CREDIT NR. 064204

Zeichen, Nummern, Anzahl und Art der Packstücke; Warenbezeichnung Marques, numéros, nombre et nature des colis; désignation des marchandises Marche, numeri, numero e natura dei colli; designazione delle merci Marks, numbers, number and kind of packages; description of the goods	Nettogewicht Poids net Peso netto Net weight kg. l. m³ etc./ecc.
ADILMA TRADING 6 cases CYLINDER- VIA TOKYO PRESS NR. 1-6 COMPLETELY ORDER 0-535/1 ASSEMBLED	12'140,0 kg
	Bruttogewicht Poids brut Peso lordo Gross weight 12'860,0 kg

Die unterzeichnete Handelskammer bescheinigt den Ursprung oben bezeichneter Ware
La Chambre de commerce soussignée certifie l'origine des marchandises désignées ci-dessus
La sottoscritta Camera di commercio certifica l'origine delle merci summenzionate
The undersigned Chamber of commerce certifies the origin of the above mentioned goods

Basel, 2 6. 04.

Basler Handelskammer
Chambre de Commerce de Bâle
Camera di Commercio di Basilea
Basle Chamber of Commerce

DOCUMENTS

Inspection Certificate

Definition

A document issued by an authority indicating that goods have been inspected (typically according to a set of industry, customer, government, or carrier specifications) prior to shipment and the results of the inspection.

Inspection certificates are generally obtained from neutral testing organizations (e.g., a government entity or independent service company). In some cases the inspection certificate can come from the manufacturer or shipper, but not from the forwarder or logistics firm.

✔ Key Elements

An inspection certificate should include the following elements:

1. Key details (typically consignor, consignee, and description of goods) regarding the shipment. Also, such details to be in conformity with other documents (e.g., documentary credit, commercial invoice, etc.)
2. Date of the inspection
3. Statement of sampling methodology
4. Statement of the results of the inspection
5. The name, signature and/or stamp or seal of the inspecting entity

Cautions & Notes

In the case of certain countries and certain commodities the inspection certificate must be issued by an appropriate government entity.

In a documentary letter of credit buyers should avoid the use of such terms as "first class," "well-known," "qualified," "independent," "official," "competent," or "local" when referring to an acceptable inspection authority. It is preferable to agree beforehand as to a specific inspection organization or entity and for the buyer to name the required certifying organization or entity in the documentary credit.

Use of vague terminology (as above) will result in the bank's acceptance of any relevant document that appears "on its face" to be in compliance with the documentary credit, so long as it was not issued by the beneficiary (seller).

DOCUMENTS

•SGS•SGS•SGS•SGS•SGS•SGS•SGS•SGS•SGS•SGS•SGS•SGS•SGS•SGS•SGS•SGS•SGS•SGS•SGS•SGS•SGS•SGS•SGS•

⊕SGS   SGS Supervise (Suisse) S.A.

May 10, 19..

Hardstrasse 1
Postfach 4149
CH-4002 Basel
Tel. (+41-61) 271 36 11
Fax (+41-61) 271 40 48
Telex : 962 457 SGS

Certificate No 1407/ 012488

BUYER	:	TA PING CO. LTD. YACHT BUILDING
		18-5, HARBOUR STREET, TAIPEI, TAIWAN
SELLER	:	SWISS EXPORT LTD. AIRFREIGHT DIVISION
		8008 ZUERICH,SWITZERLAND
LETTER OF CREDIT NBR.	:	FB-03-45786-9
GOODS	:	MACHINERY PARTS, as designated below
CONTRACT NBR.	:	FA12345WO79PE
IMPORT PERMIT NUMBER	:	TW-2395-497-0006, as declared
SERVICES REQUIRED	:	FINAL PRE-SHIPMENT INSPECTION

This is to certify that, at buyers' request and based on the specifications submitted to us, we have inspected the following goods:

1. MATERIAL DESIGNATION
   1 LOT ACCESSORIES AND SPARE PARTS FOR FOOD PROCESSING MACHINERY, as detailed in seller's commercial invoice and corresponding packing list both dated April 29, 19

2. INSPECTIONS PERFORMED AND FINDINGS
   - 2.1. Material identification for conformity with the specifications submitted to us.
   - 2.2. Visual inspection on workmanship, finish and condition.
   - 2.3. Quantitative and completeness checks.
   - 2.4. Dimensional checks at random, where applicable.
   - 2.5. Packing inspection: The packing, consisting of 5 plywood cases, is considered adequate to ship the goods by air to Taipei under normal conditions of transport and handling.
   - 2.6. Marking inspection: The shipping marks include: **SWISS EXPORT 0405/1-5**
   - 2.7. Loading details as per Air Waybill No. BSL 122077 issued by PANALPINA LTD BASLE-AIRPORT on 4 MAY ..

3. INSPECTION RESULTS AND CONCLUSION
   Based on the inspections performed, we certify the goods to be new, of good workmanship and finish, free from apparent damage or defect, and that the shipment is fully in compliance with the contract requirements in specification, quantity, quality, proper packing and marking.

5. DATE AND PLACE OF INSPECTION
   April 30, 19.. on seller's premises in Zurich, Switzerland with subsequent review of loading details.

This certificate is evidence of and reports on our findings at the time and place of inspection. It does not release buyers or sellers from their contractual obligations.

SGS SUPERVISE (SUISSE) SA
BASLE OFFICE, SWITZERLAND

As Member of SOCIETE GENERALE
DE SURVEILLANCE S.A. (SGS)
Geneva, Switzerland

•SGS•SGS•SGS•SGS•SGS•SGS•SGS•SGS•SGS•SGS•SGS•SGS•SGS•SGS•SGS•SGS•SGS•SGS•SGS•SGS•SGS•SGS•SGS•

DOCUMENTS

Regional Trade Pact Import/Export Declaration

Definition

A standardized export/import document used in common by members of a regional trade group containing compliance, administrative and statistical information.

Issued By

This document is typically issued by the exporter/seller.

✔ Key Elements

The typical trade pact import/export declaration contains the following elements:

1. Name and address of exporter/seller/consignor
2. Name and address of importer/buyer/consignee
3. Description and value of the goods
4. A statement of origin of the goods
5. Country of destination of the goods
6. Carrier and means of transport
7. Other compliance, administrative and statistical information

Cautions & Notes

This document is used as an export declaration when exporting from any trade pact member country to a non-member country and as both an import and export declaration when transporting goods across country borders within the trade group.

Because of its standardized format, this document is often linked to a computer system for the electronic transfer of information to export and import authorities within the trade group.

The EU (European Union) SAD (Single Administrative Document)

This document is a prime example of a regional trade pact import/export declaration. It was established by the European Community Council in 1988 with the goal of standardizing customs documentation and simplifying international transactions.

This particular document is used as an import/export declaration and also for the declaration of goods in transit within EU and EFTA (European Free Trade Area) countries. It may be submitted by computer directly to the customs authorities in all the 15 EU member nations.

Countries outside of the EU have shown interest in using the SAD and some have already adopted the format for their import documentation (e.g., Bulgaria).

THIS SET OF FORMS IS PRINTED ON NCR PAPER. IF COMPLETING BY HAND, WRITE IN BLOCK LETTERS, USING A BALLPOINT PEN AND APPLY MAXIMUM PRESSURE WITH THE SET RESTING ON A FIRM SURFACE.

HANDLE WITH CARE

A OFFICE OF DISPATCH/EXPORT

EUROPEAN COMMUNITY   1 2 3 4 5 6 7

1

Copy for the country of dispatch/export

1 DECLARATION

2 Consignor/*Exporter*   No

3 Forms | 4 Loading lists

5 Items | 6 Total packages | 7 Reference number

8 Consignee   No

9 Person responsible for financial settlement   No

10 *Country first destin.* | 11 *Trading country* | 13 *CAP*

14 Declarant/*Representative*   No

15 Country of despatch/*export* | 15 C disp. /exp. Code a| b| | 17 Country destin. Code a| b|

16 Country of origin | 17 Country of destination

18 Identity and nationality of means of transport at departure | 19 Ctr. | 20 Delivery terms

21 Identity and nationality of active means of transport crossing the border | 22 Currency and total amount invoiced | 23 Exchange rate | 24 Nature of transaction

25 Mode of transport at the border | 26 Inland mode of transport | 27 Place of loading | 28 Financial and banking data

29 Office of exit | 30 Location of goods

1

31 Packages and description of goods | Marks and numbers — Container No(s) — Number and kind

32 Item No | 33 Commodity Code

34 Country origin Code a| b| | 35 Gross mass (kg)

37 PROCEDURE | 38 Net mass (kg) | 39 *Quota*

40 Summary declaration/Previous document

41 Supplementary units

44 Additional information/ Documents produced/ Certificates and authorisations

A.I. Code

46 Statistical value

47 Calculation of taxes	Type	Tax base	Rate	Amount	MP
		Total:			

48 Deferred payment | 49 Identification of warehouse

B ACCOUNTING DETAILS

50 Principal   No | Signature: | C OFFICE OF DEPARTURE

51 Intended offices of transit (and country) | represented by
Place and date:

52 Guarantee   not valid for | Code | 53 Office of destination (and country)

D   CONTROL BY OFFICE OF DEPARTURE | Stamp: | 54 Place and date:

Result:

Seals affixed: Number:

Identity:

Time limit (date):

Signature:

Signature and name of declarant/representative:

C88 (1-8)

DOCUMENTS

Shipper's Export Declaration (SED)

Definition

A document prepared by the shipper and presented to a government authority specifying goods exported along with their quantities, weight, value, and destination.

✔ Key Elements

Each country has its own export declaration form. Certain elements are likely to be required in the SED for all countries. The shipper's export declaration typically includes the following elements:

1. Name and address of seller
2. Name and address of buyer
3. Date of issuance
4. Export license number (if required, based upon country of export requirements and goods exported)
5. Country of origin of the goods shipped
6. Country of final destination of the goods
7. Quantity and description of the goods
8. Country of export statistical classification number (some countries do not require this information for shipments under a certain level)
9. Shipping details including: weight of the goods, number of packages, and shipping marks and numbers

Cautions & Notes

The shipper's export declaration is used by a nation's customs authority to control exports and compile trade statistics.

An SED is usually not required by the buyer in a documentary letter of credit transaction unless the buyer is responsible for export formalities.

Many nations impose strict controls on exports (e.g., high technology, armaments and drugs) and use the SED as a means of export control. Because many exports can be diverted to "unfriendly" nations and individuals, it is considered the responsibility of the exporter to know his cargo, destination, customer, end-use, and end-user.

Electronic Filing

Some nations (such as the United States) are in the process of instituting new procedures that will require exporters to submit their Shipper's Export Declarations electronically. This involves using a computer with a modem and specially designed forms software.

DOCUMENTS

U.S. DEPARTMENT OF COMMERCE ☼ U.S. CENSUS BUREAU ⋂ Economics and Statistics Administration ☼ BUREAU OF EXPORT ADMINISTRATION

FORM **7525-V** (7-25-2000)   **SHIPPER ÍS EXPORT DECLARATION**   OMB No. 0607-0152

1a. U.S. PRINCIPAL PARTY IN INTEREST (USPPI) *(Complete name and address)*

ZIP CODE

2. DATE OF EXPORTATION

3. TRANSPORTATION REFERENCE NO.

b. USPPI EIN (IRS) OR ID NO.

c. PARTIES TO TRANSACTION
☐ Related   ☐ Non-related

4a. ULTIMATE CONSIGNEE *(Complete name and address)*

b. INTERMEDIATE CONSIGNEE *(Complete name and address)*

5. FORWARDING AGENT *(Complete name and address)*

6. POINT (STATE) OF ORIGIN OR FTZ NO.

7. COUNTRY OF ULTIMATE DESTINATION

8. LOADING PIER *(Vessel only)*

9. METHOD OF TRANSPORTATION *(Specify)*

14. CARRIER IDENTIFICATION CODE

15. SHIPMENT REFERENCE NO.

10. EXPORTING CARRIER

11. PORT OF EXPORT

16. ENTRY NUMBER

17. HAZARDOUS MATERIALS
☐ Yes   ☐ No

12. PORT OF UNLOADING *(Vessel and air only)*

13. CONTAINERIZED *(Vessel only)*
☐ Yes   ☐ No

18. IN BOND CODE

19. ROUTED EXPORT TRANSACTION
☐ Yes   ☐ No

20. SCHEDULE B DESCRIPTION OF COMMODITIES *(Use columns 22ñ24)*

D/F or M (21)	SCHEDULE B NUMBER (22)	QUANTITY ñ SCHEDULE B UNIT(S) (23)	SHIPPING WEIGHT *(Kilograms)* (24)	VIN/PRODUCT NUMBER/ VEHICLE TITLE NUMBER (25)	VALUE (U.S. dollars, omit cents) *(Selling price or cost if not sold)* (26)

27. LICENSE NO./LICENSE EXCEPTION SYMBOL/AUTHORIZATION

28. ECCN *(When required)*

29. Duly authorized officer or employee

The USPPI authorizes the forwarder named above to act as forwarding agent for export control and customs purposes.

30. I certify that all statements made and all information contained herein are true and correct and that I have read and understand the instructions for preparation of this document, set forth in the **"Correct Way to Fill Out the Shipper ís Export Declaration."** I understand that civil and criminal penalties, including forfeiture and sale, may be imposed for making false or fraudulent statements herein, failing to provide the requested information or for violation of U.S. laws on exportation (13 U.S.C. Sec. 305; 22 U.S.C. Sec. 401; 18 U.S.C. Sec. 1001; 50 U.S.C. App. 2410).

Signature

Confidential ñ For use solely for official purposes authorized by the Secretary of Commerce (13 U.S.C. 301 (g)).

Title

Export shipments are subject to inspection by U.S. Customs Service and/or Office of Export Enforcement.

Date

31. AUTHENTICATION *(When required)*

Telephone No. *(Include Area Code)*

E-mail address

This form may be printed by private parties provided it conforms to the official form. For sale by the Superintendent of Documents, Government Printing Office, Washington, DC 20402, and local Customs District Directors. The **"Correct Way to Fill Out the Shipper ís Export Declaration"** is available from the U.S. Census Bureau, Washington, DC 20233.

DOCUMENTS

Packing List

Definition

A packing list is a document prepared by the shipper listing the kinds and quantities of merchandise in a particular shipment.

A copy of the packing list is often attached to the shipment itself and another copy sent directly to the consignee to assist in checking the shipment when received. Also called a bill of parcels.

✔ Key Elements

The packing list includes the following elements:

1. Name and address of seller
2. Name and address of buyer
3. Date of issuance
4. Invoice number
5. Order or contract number
6. Quantity and description of the goods
7. Shipping details including: weight of the goods, number of packages, and shipping marks and numbers
8. Quantity and description of contents of each package, carton, crate or container
9. Any other information as required in the sales contract or documentary credit (e.g., country of origin)

Cautions & Notes

The packing list is a more detailed version of the commercial invoice but without price information. The type of each container is identified, as well as its individual weight and measurements. The packing list is attached to the outside of its respective container in a waterproof envelope marked "Packing List" or "Packing List Enclosed," and is immediately available to authorities in both the countries of export and import.

Although not required in all transactions, it is required by some countries and some buyers.

DOCUMENTS

NOTES

DOCUMENTS

Key Words in 8 Languages

English	German	French	Spanish
aboard	an Bord	à bord	a bordo
accept	annehmen	accepter	aceptar
acceptable	annehmbar	acceptable	aceptable, admisible, de calidad suficiente
acceptance	Annahme, Empfang	acceptation	aceptación
acceptance, by	durch Akzeptleistung, Akzeptierung	par acceptation	mediante aceptación
accident	Unfall	accident	accidente
account	Konto, Rechnung	compte	cuenta
account number	Kontonummer	numéro de compte	número de cuenta
accounts payable	Verbindlichkeiten	comptes fournisseurs	cuentas de proveedores
accounts receivable	Forderungen	compte clients	cuentas a clientes
acknowledgement	Bestätigung	reconnaissance	reconocimiento
acknowledge-ment of receipt	Empfangsbestätigung, Empfangsanzeige	accusé de réception, reçu	acuse de recibo
Act of God	höhere Gewalt	force majeure	fuerza mayor, caso fortuito (sobre el valor)
ad valorem	ad valorem	ad valorem	ad valorem
ad valorem duty	Wertzoll	droits de douane proportionnels	derecho aduanero "ad valorem"
addendum	Nachtrag, Anhang	avenant, clause additionne	cláusula adicional
address	Anschrift, Adresse	adresse	dirección, domicilio
adjustment	Anpassung, Berichtigung	ajustement	reajuste, corrección
admission tempo-raire/temporary admission (ATA)	vorübergehende Einfuhr	admission temporaire (ATA)	admisión temporal

Key Words in 8 Languages

Italian	Portuguese (Br)	Japanese	Chinese
a bordo	a bordo	乗船 （する）	上船（车、飞机）
accettare	aceitar	受け取る	接受，承兑
accettabile	aceitável, admissível	受け入れられる	可接受的，可承兑的
mediante accettazione	aceitação	引き受け	承兑，认付
mediante accettazione	por, mediante a aceitação	承諾する	接受，接收
infortunio, sinistro	acidente	事故	突发事件，事故
conto	conta	顧客，口座	帐目，帐户
numero del conto	número de(a) conta	客先番号	账号
debiti verso fornitori, conto fornitori	conta(s) a pagar	未払勘定	应付帐款
conto clienti, crediti da clienti	conta(s) a receber	受取勘定	应收帐款
riconoscimento	confirmação	承認書	承认，确认
accusa, di ricevuta, avviso di ricevimento	confirmação, notificação de recebimento	領収書	回执，收悉
causa di forza maggiore	caso fortuito	不可抗力	不可抗拒力，天灾
ad valorem	ad valorem	従価の	按值，从价征收
dazio ad valorem	direitos aduaneiros ad valorem	従価税	从价课税
appendice	adendo, anexo	付録	附约
indirizzo	endereço	住所	地址
aggiustamento	acomodação, liquidação, retificação	調整／調停	调整
temporanea importazione	admissão temporária (ATA)	仮輸入許可	临时许可进口／货物暂准通关证制度 (ATA)

KEY WORDS

English	German	French	Spanish
admitted	zugestanden, anerkannt	agréé	a cuerdo
advance payment	Vorauszahlung, Anzahlung	paiement anticipé	pago por adelantado
advice	Anzeige	avis, notification	aviso, notificación
advice note	Versandanzeige	note de crédit	aviso de abono bancario
advice of fate	Benachrichtigung (über den Stand der Angelegenheit)	avis de destin	aviso de resultados de gestión
advice, credit	Gutschriftanzeige	avis de crédit	aviso de crédito
advice, debit	Belastungsanzeige	avis de débit	aviso de débito
against all risks	gegen alle Gefahren	tous risques	a todo riesgo
agency	Agentur	agence	agencia
agent	Agent	agent	agente
agent, commissioned	Kommissionär	commissionnaire	comisionista
agent, forwarding	Spediteur	transitaire	transitario, agente expedidor
agent, purchasing	Einkaufsagent	courtier	agente de compras
agreement	Vereinbarung, Vertrag, Abkommen	accord, convention	acuerdo, convenio
air	Luft	aérien	aéreo
air cargo	Luftfracht	cargo aérien	carga aérea
air freight	Luftfrachtkosten	fret aérien	flete aéreo
air mail	Luftpost	envoyer par avion	correo aéreo
air waybill (AWB)	Luftfrachtbrief	lettre de transport aérien (LTA)	conocimiento (de transporte) aéreo, guía aérea
airport-to-airport	Verlade- bis - Bestimmungsflughafen	aéroport à aéroport	de aeropuerto a aeropuerto
all	alles	tous	todo
all risks	alle Risiken	tous risques	a todo riesgo

Italian	Portuguese (Br)	Japanese	Chinese
autorizzato, concordato	admitido, aceito	輸入許可済み	承认
pagamento anticipato	pagamento antecipado	前払い金	预付款项
avviso	aviso	通知	通知，通知书
avviso, lettera di avviso, notifica	aviso de recebimento	通知書	通告单，通知书
avviso d'esito	notificação bancária sobre status de cobrança pendente		出险事故通知，通知托收结果
avviso de credito	aviso de crédito	入金通知	贷记报单
avviso di debito	aviso de débito	借記通知	借记报单
contro tutti I rischi	contra todos os riscos	全危険負担	综合险
agenzia	agência, órgão	代理店	代理
agente	agente	代理人	代理人，代理商
commissionario	agente comissionado	委託販売人	代理佣金
spedizioniere	agente transitário, de transporte	運送業者	运送代理商，货运代理
agente degli acquisti	agente de compras	購買担当者	采购代理商
accordo, contratto	acordo, contrato	契約	协议
aereo	ar, aéreo	飛行機；空気	航空
carico aereo	carga aérea	空輸貨物	航空货物
trasporto aereo, merci trasportate via aerea	frete aéreo	航空貨物	航空运费
posta aerea	via aérea	航空郵便物	航空邮件
lettera di trasporto aereo	conhecimento de embarque aéreo (AWB)	航空貨物運送状	航空货运单 (AWB)
da un aeroporto a un altro aeroporto	de aeroporto a aeroporto	空港から空港まで	机场对机场
tutto	tudo	全部／全体／全て	所有，全部
tutti i rischi	todos os riscos	オールリスク	综合险保险

KEY WORDS

English	German	French	Spanish
all risks insurance policy	Gesamtversicherungsp olice	police asssurance tous risques	póliza de seguro a todo riesgo
allowance	Zuschuss Beihilfe, Unterstüfzung	indemnité, allocation	asignación, subsidio, subvención
amend, to	ändern	amender	modificar, enmendar
amendment	Anderung	amendement, modification	modificación, enmienda
amount	Betrag, Summe	montant, somme	montante, cantidad
annual	jährlich	annuel	anual
antidumping	Antidumping	anti-dumping	antidúmping
antidumping duty	Antidumpingzoll	taxe anti-dumping	tasa de antidúmping
apologize	um Entschuldigung bitten	présenter ses excuses	disculparse, excusarse, pedir disculpas
apology	Entschuldigung	excuse	disculpa
applicant	Antragssteller	demandeur, candidat	solicitante
application	Antrag	dossier de candidature, bulletin de demande	solicitud
application for a credit	Kreditantrag	demande de crédit	solicitud de un crédito
arbitration	Schlichtung, Schiedsgerichtsbarkeit	arbitrage	arbitraje
arbitration agreement	Schiedsvertrag	accord d'arbitrage	acuerdo de arbitraje
arbitration clause	Schieds(gerichts)klausel	clause d'arbitrage	cláusula arbitral
arrangement	Abmachung, Vergleich	accord, arrangment	arreglo, medida, disposiciones
arrival	Ankunft	arrivée	llegada
arrival date	Ankunftsdatum	date d'arrivée	fecha de llegada
arrival notice	Ankunftsbestätigung	bon d'arrivée	aviso de llegada de mercancías

Italian	Portuguese (Br)	Japanese	Chinese
polizza di assicurazione cotro tutti i rischi	apólice de seguro contra todos os riscos	オールリスク保険	综合险保险单
indennità, assegnazione	abatimento, benefício, concessão, pensão	支給額；許容額	津贴，减价，补贴
modificare	aditar, alterar	改める	改正，修正
modifica, rettifica	alteração, modificação	改正	修改，订正单
ammontare, mentante	valor, quantia, soma	金額／額	量
annuale, annuo	anual	年次／年間	年鉴
antidumping	antidumping	ダンピング防止	反倾销
dazio doganale antidumping	imposto contra o dumping	ダンピング防止関税	反倾销税
chiedere scusa	desculpar-se, pedir desculpas	謝る／詫び	道歉
scusa	desculpas	詫び	道歉
richiedente	candidato, requerente, solicitante	申込者	申请人
domanda	pedido, solicitação, requerimento	申込書	申请单
domanda di credito	solicitação de crédito	掛売勘定を申し込む	信用证申请
arbitrato	arbitragem	仲裁	仲裁
compromesso arbitrale	acordo de arbitragem	仲裁契約	仲裁协议
clausola compromissoria	cláusula arbitral, de arbitragem	仲裁条項	仲裁条款
accordo, misura, disposizione	acordo, contrato	手配、準備；配列、配置	安排
arrivo	chegada	着荷	到达
data d'arrivo	data de chegada	到着日	到达日期
avviso di ricevimento	aviso de chegada	着荷通知	到货通知，到港通知

KEY WORDS

KEY WORDS

English	German	French	Spanish
as is	Abbedingen der Haftung für einen bestimmten Zweck	en l'état	tal cual, en el estado que está
ASAP (as soon as possible)	möglichst schnell	dès que possible	lo antes posible, tan pronto como sea posible
assessment	Veranlagung, Festsetzung, Schätzung	évaluation, estimation, appréciation	evaluación, estimación, apreciación
assessment of charges	Kostenvoranschlag	évaluation des frais	valoración de cargos, valoración de gastos
assessment of loss	Verlustermittlung, Aktivposten, Aktiva	évaluation des pertes	valoración de pérdidas
assets	Vermögenswerte	actifs, avoirs, biens	activos
assign, to	abtreten	céder	asignar, ceder, trasladar, traspasar
assignee	Zessionar	cessionnaire	apoderado, cesionario, sucesor
assignment	Zession, Abtretung, Auftrag, Aufgabe	cession	asignación, cesión, traspaso, atribución
assignor	Zedent	cédant	asignante, cedente, cesionista
ATA carnet		carnet ATA	Tarjeta de admisión temporal
attachment	Beschlagnahme	saisie	incautación, embargo
attorney	Rechtsanwalt	avocat	abogado, letrado, representante, abogado
attorney in fact (power of attorney)	Vollmacht	pouvoir de représentation	poder notarial
availability	Verfügbarkeit	disponibilité	disponibilidad
available	benutzbar, verfügbar	disponible, utilisable, réalisable	disponible, utilizable
available by	benutzbar durch	utilisable par	utilizable mediante...,
average	Havarie	avaries	avería, pérdida
average, general	grosse Havarie	avarie commune, grosse avarie	avería común, gruesa

Italian	Portuguese (Br)	Japanese	Chinese
nello stato in cui trovasi	como em, tal qual	現状のままで	按货样，按现状
il più presto possibile	assim que possível, o mais rápido possível	早急に／至急	尽快
accertamento, valutazione	avaliação, determinação, verificação	評価	评估
valutazione delle spese	avaliação, determinação das despesas	評価された費用	费用的评估
valutazione di un sinistro	avaliação, determinação do(s) prejuízo(s)	損害査定額	损失的评估
attività	ativo, patrimônio global	資産	资产
cedere, trasferire	ceder, transferir, trasladar	割当てる／指定する	分配，指定，转让
cessionario	cessionário, sucessor, procurador	譲受人	代理人，受让人
trasferimento, cessione (es. atto di cessione)	cessão, transferência, traslado	譲渡	产权转让
cedente	cedente, nomeador	譲渡人	让与人
carnet doganale	carnet ATA	ATA　カルネ	官方证明信件
pignoramento, sequestro	anexo	添付	官方证明信件
procuratore	advogado, procurador, representante legal	弁護士	律师，代理人
procura notarile	procurador (poder judicial)	委任状	代理人，私人律师
disponibilità	disponibilidade	有用性	可用性，有效性
disponibile, utilzzabile	disponível	有効／利用可能／使用可能	可用的，有效的
utilizzabile mediante	disponível por	～で入手可能な	通过…加以利用，由…提供
avaria	avarias, danos	平均	海损
avaria comune/generale	avarias grossas, comuns	共同海損	共同海损

KEY WORDS

English	German	French	Spanish
average, particular	besondere Havarie	avarie particulière	avería particular
award (a contract), to	(einen) Zuschlag erteilen	adjuger un marché	adjudicar un contrato
back order	unerledigter Auftrag	commande en souffrance	pedido pendiente, pedido atrasado
backdated	rückdatieren	antidaté	con efectos retroactivos
balance due	Restschuld, geschuldeter Betrag	solde du	saldo debido
balance on current account	Leistungsbilanz, Bilanz der laufenden Posten	balance des paiements courants	balanza o saldo de cuenta corriente
balance, credit	Habensaldo, Kreditsaldo	solde créditeur	saldo acreedor
balance, debit	Sollsaldo, Passivsaldo	solde débiteur	saldo deudor, débito
bank	Bank	banque	banco
bank charges	Bankgebühren	commissions, frais divers de banque	gastos bancarios diversos, comisiones
bank confirmation	Bankbestätigung	confirmation bancaire	confirmación bancaria
bank draft	Banktratte	traite bancaire	efecto bancario, instrumento
bank transfer	Banküberweisung	virement bancaire	transferencia bancaria
bank wire	Clearingnetz	virement télégraphique	transferencia bancaria
bank, accepting	akzeptierende Bank	banque acceptante	banco aceptador, banco aceptante
bank, buyer's	Käuferbank	banque d'acheteur	banco del comprador
bank, confirming	bestätigende Bank	banque confirmatrice	banco confirmador
bank, paying	zahlende Bank	banque chargée du réglement	banco pagador
bank, presenting	vorlegende Bank	banque présentatrice	banco presentador
bank, seller's	Verkäuferbank	banque vendeuse	banco del vendedor
banker	Bankier	banquier	banquero, banco

Italian	Portuguese (Br)	Japanese	Chinese
avaria particolare	avaria(s) simples, particular(es)	単独海損	单独海损
aggiudicare un contratto	adjudicar (um contrato)	（人）に請け負わせる	裁决（合同）给…
ordine arretrato	pedido pendente, em atraso	バックオーダー／入荷待ち	延期交货
retrodatare	antedatado, retroativo	前の日付にする	追溯到过去某日期
saldo dovuto	saldo devedor, saldo a pagar	不足額	结欠金额
saldo di unconto corrente	saldo da conta corrente	経常収支尻	经常项目收支
saldo creditore	saldo credor	貸方残高	贷方余额
saldo debitore	saldo devedor	借方残高	借方余额
banca	banco	銀行	银行
commissioni bancarie	encargos, tarifas bancários(as)	銀行手数料	银行手续费
conferma bancaria	confirmação bancária	銀行の承認	银行确认
stima giornaliera del credito bancario	saque bancário, letra de câmbio	銀行手形	银行汇票
bonifico bancario	transferência bancária	銀行振込	银行转帐，银行划拨
bonifico telegrafico	transferência bancária	電信送金	银行电报
banca accettante	banco aceitante (de carta de crédito)	引受銀行	承兑银行
banca del compratore	banco do comprador	買い手銀行	买方银行
banca confermante	banco confirmador	確認銀行	保兑银行
banca pagante	banco pagador	支払銀行	付帐银行
banca presentatrice	banco apresentante	提示銀行	兑换银行
banca del venditore	banco do vendedor	売り手銀行	卖方银行
banchiere	banqueiro, bancário	銀行業者	银行家

English	German	French	Spanish
bargain, a	Gelegenheitskauf, Ausverkauf	soldes, occasions	rebajas
bargain, to	handeln	marchander, négocier	regatear
barter	Tauschgeschäft, Tausch (Warenaustausch)	troc, échange	trueque, compensación
bay	Bucht	baie	bahía
bearer, to	(zum) Inhaber	au porteur	al portador
beneficiary	Begünstigter	bénéficiaire	beneficiario
bid	Gebot, Angebot	offre, enchère	puja, oferta
bid, to	bieten, anbieten	faire une offre	hacer una oferta, pujar
bidder	Anbieter, Bieter	offrant, enchérisseur	postor
bill	Bescheinigung, Wechsel, Rechnung	effet, traite, billet	factura, giro, letra, efecto de comercio
bill for charges	Rechnung	états des frais	cuenta de gastos
bill for collection	Inkassowechsel	effet à l'encaissement	efecto al cobro
bill of entry	Zollerklärung	déclaration en douane	declaración de aduanas hecha por importador
bill of exchange	Wechsel	lettre de change	letra de cambio
bill of lading	Seefrachtbrief, Konnossement	connaissement, nantissement	conocimiento de embarque
bill of lading, air	Luftfrachtbrief	connaissement aérien	conocimiento de embarque aéreo
bill of lading, claused	Konnossement mit Vorbehalt	connaissement clausé	conocimiento con cláusula adicional
bill of lading, clean	reines Konnossement	connaissement net	conocimiento limpio
bill of lading, clean onboard	reines Bordkonnossement	connaissement net à bord	conocimiento a bordo limpio
bill of lading, combined	Sammelkonnossement	connaissement de transport combiné	conocimiento de embarque combinado
bill of lading, multimodal	kombiniertes Konnossement	connaissement multimodal	conocimiento de embarque multimodal

KEY WORDS

Italian	Portuguese (Br)	Japanese	Chinese
affare, svendita	acordo, pechincha	安売り	交易
contrattare, negoziare, trattare sul prezzo	negociar, regatear	交渉する	讲价，谈判
baratto	permutar, trocar	物々交換	物物交换
baia	baía	入江	海湾
al portatore	ao portador	持参人払い	持票人
beneficiario (dir.), ordinatario (banc.)	beneficiário(a)	受益者	受益人
offerta, bando d'appalto	oferta, concorrência	入札	投标
fare un'offerta	oferecer, leiloar	入札する	出价
offerente, concorrente	lançador, licitante	入札者	出价人，投标人
conto, titolo, cambiale	fatura, nota, conta, título bancário	請求書	帐单，票据
conto delle spese	nota de débito	料金表	费用的帐单
titolo di incasso	letra para cobrança	取立手形	托收票据
bolletta d'entrata doganale	declaração de entrada de mercadorias	税関申告書	报关单
cambiale, tratta	letra de câmbio	為替手形	汇票
polizza di carico (P/C)	conhecimento de embarque	船荷証券	提货单
polizza di carico aereo	conhecimento de embarque aéreo	航空貨物受取証	航空提货单
polizza di carico sporca	conhecimento de embarque clausulado	条項付き船荷証券	附条款提单，附条件提单
polizza di carico netta	conhecimento de embarque limpo	無故障船荷証券	清洁提单
polizza di carico pulita a bordo	conhecimento de embarque limpo a bordo	無故障船積み船荷証券	随车清洁提单
polizza di carico combinata	conhecimento de embarque combinado	複合運送証券	联运提单
polizza di carico multimodale	conhecimento de embarque multimodal, B/L multimodal	複合船荷証券	多种方式联运提单

English	German	French	Spanish
bill of lading, negotiable	Orderkonnossement	connaissement négociable	conocimiento de embarque negociable
bill of lading, non-negotiable	nicht übertragbares Konnossement	connaissement intransmissible	conocimiento no negociable
bill of lading, ocean	Bordkonnossement	connaissement maritime	conocimiento de embarque marítimo, conocimiento de embarque a la orden
bill of lading, onboard	An-Bord-Konnossement	connaissement à bord	conocimiento a bordo
bill of lading, received	Übernahme-Konnossement	connaissement reçu à quai	conocimiento recibido en muelle
bill of lading, received for shipment	Konnossement 'empfangen zur Vershiffung'	connaissement reçu pour embarquement	conocimiento recibido para embarque
bill of lading, straight	Orderkonnossement	connaissement nominatif	conocimiento nominativo
bill of lading, through	Durch(fracht) konnossement	connaissement direct	conocimiento directo
bill of parcels		liste de colis expédiés	listado de la mercancía
bill of sale	Kassenbon	acte de vente	factura, comprobante o documento de venta
bill, outstanding	nicht beglichene Rechnung, offene Rechnung	facture en souffrance, non réglée	factura pendiente
bill-to party	Rechnungsempfänger	facture à la partie	parte a facturar
binder	Versicherungsschein	engagement	póliza de seguros provisional, nota de cobertura
bond	Obligation, Garantie, Verpflichtungsschein	obligation, engagement, contrat	obligación, caución, contrato
bond, bearer	Inhaberschuldver-schreibung	obligation au porteur	obligación al portador

Italian	Portuguese (Br)	Japanese	Chinese
polizza di carico negoziabile	conhecimento de embarque negociável, B/L negociável	譲渡可能船荷証券	流通提单，可转让提单
polizza di carico non negoziabile	conhecimento de embarque não negociável B/L não negociável	非流通船荷証券	不流通提单，不可转让提单
polizza di carico per trasporto oceanico	conhecimento de embarque marítimo	船荷証券	船货提单
polizza di caricoper merce a bordo	conhecimento de embarque a bordo	船積み船荷証券	随车携带提单
polizza di carico 'ricevuto per imbarco'	conhecimento de embarque recebido	受取船荷証券	收到提单
polizza di carico ricevuto per l'imbarco	conhecimento de embarque acreditador de recepção de mercadorias para sua carga	受取船荷証券	待装船运提单
polizza di carico nominativa	conhecimento de embarque nominativo	記名式船荷証券	记名提单
polizza di carico diretta	conhecimento de embarque corrido	通し船荷証券	全程提单
bolla di consegna	lista de mercadorias	貨物証券	装运明细单，发票
atto di vendita	nota, comprovante de venda de venda	売買証書	卖据，所有权转移证书
titolo insoluto	título, fatura a receber	未払い手形	未尝票据
fatturare	título nominal	請求書送付先	接受票据方
polizza d'assicurazione provvisoria	contrato provisório de seguro, contrato provisório	仮保険証	临时合同，临时保险单
titolo, obbligazione, garanzia	título, garantia	債券	债券
obbligazione al portatore	portador de ação	無記名債券	不记名债券

English	German	French	Spanish
bond, under	unter Zollverschluss	sous régime de douane	bajo régimen de aduana, sometido a despacho aduanero
bonded (goods in bond)	unter Zolllagerschluss	marchandises sous douane	mercancias en almacén aduanero
bonded stores	Zolllager	magasin sous douane	provisiones en depósito
bonded terminal		terminal sous douane	terminal en depósito
bonded warehouse	Zolllager	entrepôt sous douane	almacén general de depósito, depósito aduanero
book (an order), to	Auftrag erteilen	enregistrer (une commande)	contabilizar (un pedido)
booking	buchen	retenir (le fret)	reserva, inscripción
breach of contract	Vertragsverletzung, Vertragsbruch	rupture de contrat	ruptura de contrato
break bulk	Verteilung des Sammelguts	dégroupage	traccionamiento de carga
break bulk cargo	Sammelgut	marchandises diverses	carga fraccionada
breakage	Bruch	casse	destrozo, ruptura
bribe	Bestechungsgeld	pot-de-vin	soborno
broker	Makler	courtier	broker, agente de bolsa, corredor, comisionista
broker, customs	Zollspediteur	commissionnaire en douane, agent	agente de aduana
broker, insurance	Versicherungsmakler	courtier d'assurance	corredor de seguro
budget	Haushalt, Etat, Budget	budget	presupuesto preventivo
bulk cargo	Massengut	cargaison de vrac	carga (mento) a granel
bulk transport	Massengut-Transport	transport en vraq	transporte a granel
bunker adjustment factor (BAF)	Zuschlag für Bunkerung	surtaxe de soutage	factor de ajuste por combustible

Italian	Portuguese (Br)	Japanese	Chinese
in custodia doganale	(mercadorias) em garantia, em depósito (temporariamente)	保税中	保兑，未完税扣存关栈
merce depositata non sdoganata	produtos retidos, armazenados na alfândega (até pagamento de impostos)	保税倉庫留置の商品	以债券作保证的，存入保税仓库的
provviste di bordo	armazéns alfandegados	保税船舶用品	保税仓库
terminale doganale autorizzata	terminal alfandegado	保税ターミナル	保税码头
magazzino doganale	depósito alfandegado	保税倉庫	保税仓库
contabilizzare	contabilizar, registrar (um pedido)	注文する	预订，登记
prenotazione	reserva	貨物運送引受け	预订
inadempienza, inadempimento contrattuale	violação de contrato	違約する	违约，违反合同
frazionamento di carico alla rinfusa	fragmentar, descarregar	船荷を下ろす	开始卸货；零担
carico alla rinfusa da frazionare	carga fracionada, fragmentada	船荷を下ろす	零碎装卸货物，普通货物
rottura e/o danni	indenização, desconto por danos	破損	破损
tangente, bustarella	subornar	贈賄	贿赂
mediatore, intermediario, sensale	corretor	仲介業者	经纪人
spedizioniere doganale	despachante aduaneiro	税関貨物取扱人	报关经纪人
mediatore di assicurazione	corretor de seguros	保険仲介人	保险经纪人
previsione, bilancio	orçamento	予算	预算
carico alla rinfusa	carga a granel	散荷	散装货
trasporto alla rinfusa	transporte a granel	船荷運送	散装运输，整批运输
coefficiente di adeguamento per il bunker	fator de ajuste de combustível	バンカー調整係数	燃油调整因素

English	German	French	Spanish
business	Geschäftswelt, Wirtschaft	affaires, business	negocio, empresa
business entity	Geschäftsentität	entité commerciale	entidad comercial
business name	Firma, Gegenstand der Gesellschaft	raison sociale	razón social
business opportunity	Marktlücke	créneau commercial	oportunidad comercial, de negocio
business plan	Geschäftsplan	projet d'entreprise	planes económicos, comerciales
business trip	Geschäftsreise	voyage d'affaires	viaje de negocios
buy	kaufen	acheter	comprar
buyer	Käufer	acheteur	comprador
cancel, to	rückgängig machen, für ungültig erklären	annuler, résilier	cancelar, anular, rescindir
capital	Kapital	capital, capitaux	capital
cargo	Fracht, Ladung	cargaison	carga, cargamento
cargo insurance	Frachtversicherung, Ladungsversicherung	assurance faculté	seguro de carga
cargo, break bulk	Sammelgut	marchandises diverses	carga fraccionada
cargo, general	Stückgut	marchandises générales	carga mixta, mercancías varias
cargo, unitized	unitizierte Ladung	cargaison sous forme d'unité de charge	cargamento unitarizado (bajo forma de unidad de carga)
carnet	Carnet	carnet	carné
carnet/ATA Carnet	Carnet für vorübergehende Einfuhr	carnet ATA	carné ATA
carriage	Fracht Porto	port, transport	portes, transporte
carrier	Frachtführer	transporteur	transportador, porteador
carrier, common	Frachtführer (gewerbsmässiger)	transporteur général	transportador general

KEY WORDS

KEY WORDS

Italian	Portuguese (Br)	Japanese	Chinese
affari, commercio	negócio(s), empresa, assunto, profissão	ビジネス / 仕事 / 取引	商业
entità aziendale	entidade comercial	企業実体	企业单位，营业单位
nome dell'azienda, ragione sociale	nome comercial, razão social	商号	企业名称，商号
possibilità di realizzare un affare	oportunidade comercial	ビジネスチャンス / 商機	商业机会，商机
programma di gestione aziendale	plano econômico, comercial	経営計画	商务计划
viaggio per affari	viagem de negócios	出張	商务旅行
comprare, acquistare	comprar	買う	购买
compratore	comprador	購入者	购买者，采购员
annullare, risolvere, rescindere	cancelar	取り消す	取消
capitale	capital	資本	资本
carico	carga	積み荷	货物
assicurazione del carico	seguro da carga, mercadoria	積荷保険	货物保险
carico alla rinfusa da frazionare	carga fracionada, fragmentada	積荷を下ろす	零担货物货物
carico di merci varie	carga mista	一般貨物	普通货物
carico unitizzato	carga unificada	ユニタイズド貨物	成套货物
carnet	carnê	無関税許可書	官方证明信件
carnet ATA	carnê / carnê ATA	カルネ	官方证明信件 / ATA Carnet
trasporto, porto	transporte, frete, transporte	運賃	运费，搬运费
vettore, trasportatore	transportador, transportadora	キャリヤー	运载工
vettore generico/ordinario	transportador(a) público(a)	一般通信事業者	承运商

KEY WORDS

English	German	French	Spanish
cartage	Fuhrlohn	camionnage	empresa de transporte por carretera, transportista
cash	Bargeld	espèces, numéraire, liquide	numerario, efectivo, liquido, caja
cash against documents (CAD)	Zahlung gegen Dokumente	comptant contre document	pago contra documentos
cash terms	Barzahlung	condition au comptant	condiciones de pago al contado
cash with order (CWO)	Zahlung bei Auftragserteilung	comptant à la commande	pagado a la orden
certificate	Zeugnis, Zertifikat	certificat	certificado
certificate of inspection	Inspektionszertifikat	certificat d'inspection	certificado de inspección
certificate of insurance	Versicherungszertifikat	certificat d'assurance	certificado de seguro
certificate of origin	Ursprungszeugnis	certificat d'origine	certificado de origen
certificate, health	Gesundheits-bescheinigung	certificat sanitaire, certificat de santé	certificado de sanidad
certification	Beglaubigung	attestation	certificación, atestación
CFR Cost and Freight (named port of destination)	CFR Kosten und Fracht (... benannter Bestimmungshafen)	CFR cout et fret (... port de destination convenu)	CFR coste y flete (...puerto de destino convenido)
charge card	Debetkarte	carte de crédit	tarjeta de débito
charge(s)	Kosten, Gebühren, Fracht	frais, prix, droits, redevances	gasto(s), precio, derecho
chargeable weight	Taxgewicht	poids taxé	peso imputable
charges collect (cc)	unfrei, unfrankiert	frais dus	gastos por cobrar
charges prepaid	franko	frais payés	gastos pagados
check	Scheck	chèque	cheque

KEY WORDS

Italian	Portuguese (Br)	Japanese	Chinese
spese di trasporto a mezzo carri	transporte intermunicipal rodoviário (em reboques ou caminhões)	荷車運送	货车运输
contante, pronta cassa	dinheiro (em espécie), ativo disponível	現金	现金
pagamento contro documenti	pagamento contra apresentação de documento	書類引換現金払い	凭单据付现
condizioni per pagamento in contanti	condições de pagamento a vista	現金支払条件	现金术语
pagamento all'ordine	pagamento contra o pedido	現金注文	定货付现，认购即付
certificato	certificado	証明書	证明书
certificato d'ispezione	certificado de inspeção	検査証明書	检验证书
certificato di assicurazione	certificado de seguro	保険証明書	保险证书
certificato d'origine	certificado de origem	原産地証明書	原产地证明书
certificato di sana costituzione, certificato medico	certificado de saúde	健康証明書	健康证书
certificazione	certificação	証明	举证，证明
CFR costo e nolo (... porto di destinazione convenuto)	CFR custo e frete pagos até¶ (... porto de destino)	CFR 運賃込 (... 指定仕向港)	CFR 成本加运费 (... 指定目的港口)
carta di addebito	cartão de débito	クレジットカード	信用卡，签帐卡
spese, onere, addebito	encargo(s), despesa(s), gasto(s)	料金	费用
peso addebitabile	peso cobrável	課税可能重量	收费重量
spese assegnate/da incassare	encargos, despesas a cobrar	運賃着払い	费用收集
spese prepagate	despesas pagas, encargos pagos	前納の料金	预付费用
assegno bancario	cheque	小切手	支票

K E Y   W O R D S

English	German	French	Spanish
check, certified	bestätigter Scheck	chèque certifié	cheque conformado
CIF Cost, Insurance and Freight (...named port of destination)	CIF Kosten, Versicherung und Fracht (...benannter Bestimmungshafen)	CIF coût, assurance et frêt (...porte de destination convenu)	CIF coste, seguro y flete (...puerto de destino convenido)
CIP Carriage and Insurance Paid To (...named place of destination)	CIP Frachtfrei versichert (...Benannter Bestimmungsort)	CIP port payé, assurance comprise (...lieu de destination convenu)	CIP transporte y seguro pagados hasta (...lugar de destino)
claim	Forderung, Anspruch, Reklamation	demande, créance, réclamation	reclamación, demanda
claim, insurance	Versicherungsanspruch	réclamation	reclamación de seguro
claim, submission of a	Anmeldung eines Anspruchs, Inanspruchnahme (der Garantie)	présentation d'une demande	presentación de una reclamación
class or kind (of merchandise)	Warenkategorie	classe ou type (de marchandise)	clase o tipo (de mercancías)
classification	Klassizierung	nomenclature	clasificación
classify, to	klassifizieren	déterminer l'espèce tarifaire	clasificar
clause(s)	Klausel, Bestimmung, Bedingung	clause, stipulation, disposition, article	cláusula, artículo, pacto, disposición
clause, contract	Vertragbestimmung	clause d'un contrat	cláusula de un contrato
clause, standard	Standardklausel	clause type	cláusula tipo
claused	unrein	avec réserve	con reservas
clean	vorbehaltlos, uneingeschränkt	net	limpio, neto
cleared, customs	zollabgefertigt, verzollt	dédouané	despachado de aduanas
clearance, customs	Zollabfertigung	dédouanement	despacho de aduanas
client	Kunde	client	cliente
close a sale	einen Verkauf abschließen	conclure une vente	cerrar un trato de venta

Italian	Portuguese (Br)	Japanese	Chinese
assegno bancario a copertura garantita	cheque visado	支払保証小切手	保付支票
CIF costo, assicurazione e nolo (...porto di destinazione convenuto)	CIF - custo, seguro e frete pagos até (... porto de destino)	CIF 運賃保険料込 （... 指定仕向港）	CIF 成本、保险费加运费（... 指定目的港）
CIP trasporto e assicurazione pagati fino a (...luogo di destinazione convenuto)	CIP transporte e seguro pagos, incluídos até (... local de destino)	CIP 輸送費保険料込 （... 指定仕向地）	CIP 运费、保险费，付至（... 目的地名）
domanda, reclamo	reclamação, reivindicação, demanda	請求する	索赔
dichiarazione di sinistro	reivindicação de indenização por sinistro	保険金請求	保险索赔
presentazione di una domanda	instauração de uma ação de reclamação ou demanda	請求する	要求索赔
classe, categoria	classe ou tipo (de mercadoria(s))	種類	或者种类 class(商品的)
classificazione	classificação	分類	分类类别
classificare	classificar	分類する	分类
clausola	cláusula(s)	条項	条款
clausola contrattuale	cláusula contratual	契約条項	合同条款
clausola tipo	cláusula normal, padrão	基準条項	标准条款
Sporco, con riserva	clausulado(a), com reservas	条項付き	条款
senza riserve, netto	limpo(a)	無故障	清洁
sdoganato	desembaraçao na alfândega	税関を通過	进行结关
sdoganamento	desembaraço aduaneiro	通関手続き	结关
cliente	cliente	クライアント	顾客
concludere un affare	fechar uma venda	取引を成立させる	关闭销售

English	German	French	Spanish
collect on delivery (COD)	Barzahlung bei Lieferung	paiement à la livraison	pago contra reembolso
collection order	Inkassoauftrag	ordre d'encaissement	orden de cobro
collection, documentary	dokumentäres Inkasso	encaissement documentaire	cobro documentario
combined transport (CT)	kombinierter Transport	transport combiné (TC)	transporte combinado (TC)
commercial invoice	Handelsrechnung	facture commerciale	factura comercial
commercial sample	Warenmuster	échantillion	muestra comercial
commission, sales	Verkaufsprovision	commission sur vente	comisión sobre ventas
commodity	Ware, Handelsware, Rohstoff	produit, marchandise, denrée	mercancía, producto
company	Gesellschaft, Firma, Unternehmen	société, compagnie, entreprise	compañía, empresa, sociedad
company, insurance	Versicherungs- gesellschaft	compagnie d'assurances	compañía de seguros, compañía aseguradora
compensation	Ausgleich	rémunération	compensación
complaint	Klage, Beschwerde, Reklamation	réclamation, litige	reclamación, litigio
comply, to	entsprechen, entsprochen	satisfaire, satisfait à	satisfacer, satisfecho cumplir, cumplido con
compromise	Kompromiss	compromis	compromiso
computer	Computer	ordinateur	ordenador, computadora
confirm, to	bestätigen	confirmer	confirmar, declarar, afirmar, ratificar
confirmed	bestätigt	confirmé	confirmado
congratulations	Glückwunsch	félicitations	felicitaciones
consign, to	in Konsignation geben, abschicken	expédier	consignar, remitir, enviar

KEY WORDS

Italian	Portuguese (Br)	Japanese	Chinese
da pagare alla consegna, contrassegno	entrega contra reembolso	代金引換払い	货到收款
ordine d'incasso s	ordem de cobrança	手形取立指図書	托收委托书
incasso documentario	cobrança documentária	荷為替手形取り立て	单据托收
trasporto combinato (TC)	transporte combinado (TC)	複合輸送	联运
fattura commerciale	fatura comercial	商業送り状	商业发票
campione commerciale	amostra comercial	商品サンプル	商品试样
provvigione sulle vendite	comissão de venda	売上手数料	回扣
derrata, materia prima, merce	artigo, bem, produto	商品	日用品
compagnia, società, impresa	companhia, empresa, sociedade	会社	公司
compagnia di assicurazione	companhia de seguros, seguradora	保険会社	保险公司
rimunerazione	compensação	報酬	补偿
reclamo, protesta, querela	reclamação, queixa	訴状	抱怨
soddisfare, adempiere	ater-se a, cumprir, obedecer	応じる	顺从
compromesso	concessão mútua, compromisso	譲歩する	妥协
computer, calcolatore, elaboratore	computador	コンピュータ	计算机
confermare	confirmar	確認する	确认
confermato	confirmado	確認済みの	保兑；证实的
congratulazioni, complimenti	congratulações, cumprimento	おめでとう	祝贺
consegnare	consignar	委託する	托运

English	German	French	Spanish
consignee	Empfänger	destinataire, consignataire	consignatario, destinatario
consignment	Sendung, Warensendung	expédition, envoi	expedición, envío
consignor	Absender	expéditeur, consignateur	expedidor, consignador, remitente
consolidate goods, to	(eine) Sammelladung zusammenstellen	grouper des marchandises	agrupar o consolidar mercancias
consolidation	Sammelladung	groupage	agrupamiento
consolidator	Sammelladungs-spediteur	groupeur	agrupador, consolidador
consular invoice	Konsularfaktura	facture consulaire	factura consular
container	Container	conteneur	contenedor
container load	Container-Fracht	lot de marchandises suffisant pour remplir un conteneur	carga del contenedor
container ship	Container-Schiff	navire porte-conteneurs	buque de contenedores
container, air freight	Luftfracht-Container	conteneur pour fret aérien	contenedor para carga aérea
container, ocean freight	Seefracht-Container	conteneur pour fret maritime	contenedor para transporte marítimo
containerization	Verfrachtung in einen Container	mise en conteneurs	transporte en contenedores
contents	Inhalt	contenu	contenido
contract	Vertrag	contrat	contrato, acuerdo
contract of carriage	Frachtführervertrag	contrat de transport	contrato de transporte
contract term	Vertragsbedingung	durée d'un contrat	duración del contrato
contract terms	Vertragsbedingungen	clause d'un contrat	cláusulas de un contrato
contract, draft	Vertragsentwurf	projet de contrat	precontrato
contract, sales	Kaufvertrag	contrat de vente	contrato de compraventa
copy(ies)	Kopie	exemplaire, copie	copia(s)

KEY WORDS

Italian	Portuguese (Br)	Japanese	Chinese
destinatario, consegnatario	consignatário	荷受人	受货人
spedizione, invio	carregamento, consignação	出荷	托付
mittente, speditore	consignador	荷送人	发货人
consolidare le merci	consolidar	連結する	集中
consolidamento	consolidação	連結	集中
consolidatore, operatore di groupage	consolidador	統合整理者	并装业者，混载业者
fattura consolare	fatura consular	領事送り状	领事发票
contenitore	contêiner	コンテナ	集装箱
carico del container	carga para a capacidade do contêiner	コンテナロード	集装箱装载
nave portacontainer	navio para transporte de contêineres	コンテナ船	集装箱货船
container per il trasporto aereo	contêiner de carga aérea	航空貨物コンテナ	空运集装箱
Container per trasporto marittimo	contêiner de carga marítima	海上運賃コンテナ	海运集装箱
spedizione e trasporto in container	conteinerização	コンテナ輸送	货柜运输
contenuto	conteúdo	コンテンツ/内容	内容
contratto	contrato	契約	合同
contratto di trasporto	contrato de transporte	運送契約	运费合同
durata del contratto	prazo do contrato	契約期間	合同术语
clausole (condizioni) del contratto	termos do contrato	契約条件	合同术语
bozza di contratto	minuta de contrato	契約案	合同草案
contratto di vendita	contrato de venda(s)	販売契約	销售合同
copia(e), esemplare	cópia(s), via(s)	コピー	复制

KEY WORDS

English	German	French	Spanish
copyright	Urheberrecht, Verlagsrecht	droit d'auteur, droits de reproduction	derechos de reproducción/autor
cost(s)	Kosten	coût, frais	gasto(s), costo(s)
costs, total	Gesamtkosten	coût total	gastos totales
counteroffer	Gegenangebot	contre-offre	contraoferta
country of destination	Bestimmungsland	pays destinataire	país de destino
country of origin	Ursprungsland	pays d'origine	país de origen
courier	Kurier	transporteur	mensajero
courier service	Kurierdienst	messagerie express	servicio de mensajería
coverage	Deckung	couverture, portée, protection	cobertura, alcance, garantía, protección
CPT Carriage Paid To (...named place of destination)	CPT Frachtfrei (...Benannter Bestimmungsort)	CPT port payé jusqu'à (...lieu de destination convenu)	CPT transporte pagado hasta (...lugar de destino convenido)
credit	Kredit	crédit	crédito
credit application	Akkreditiver öffnungsauftrag	demande d'ouverture de crédit	solicitud de apertura de crédito
credit card	Kreditkarte	carte de crédit	tarjeta de crédito
credit card expiration date	Kreditkarte-Verfalldatum	date limite d'une carte de crédit	fecha de caducidad de la tarjeta de crédito
credit card number	Kreditkartennummer	numéro de carte de crédit	número de la tarjeta de crédito
credit, acceptance	Akzeptkredit	acceptation de crédit	crédito de aceptación
credit, advise of	Kreditavis	note de crédit	notificación de disponibilidad de crédito
credit, amendment of the	Kreditänderung	amendemant de crédit	modificación del crédito
credit, confirmed irrevocable	bestätigtes unwiderrufliches Akkreditiv	crédit confirmé irrévocable	crédito irrevocable confirmado
credit, date of	Akkreditivdatum	date de crédit	fecha del crédito

Italian	Portuguese (Br)	Japanese	Chinese
diritti d'autore	direitos autorais, direitos de reprodução	著作権	版权
costo(i)	custo(s), despesa(s)	コスト	成本
costi totali	custo(s), despesa(s) total(is)	総費用	总成本
controfferta	contra-oferta	逆提案	还盘
paese di destinazione	país de destino	出向国	目的国
paese d 'origine	país de origem	原産国	生产国
corriere	emissário, mensageiro, courier	配達する	送急件的人
servizio di corriere	serviço de emissário, de courier	国際宅配便	送急件服务
copertura	cobertura	担保 （保険）	保险总额
CPT trasporto pagato a (...luogo di destinazione convenuto)	CPT transporte pago até (... local de destino)	輸送費込 （... 指定仕向地）	运费，支付到目的地的 (... 地名)
credito	crédito	信用	贷方
richiesta di apertura di credito	solicitação de crédito	借入申込書	贷款申请
carta di credito	cartão de crédito	クレジットカード	信用卡
data di scadenza della carta di credito	data de validade do cartão de crédito	クレジットカード有効期限	信用卡有效期
numero della carta di credito	número do cartão de crédito	クレジットカード番号	信用卡号
credito di accettazione	aceitação de crédito	引受条件付き信用	承兑信贷
nota di credito	assessoria de crédito	入金通知	贷方建议
revisione del credito	aditamento, ajuste de crédito	信用状の変更	贷款修正
credito confermato irrevocabile	crédito irrevogável confirmado	確認取消不能信用	不可取消贷款
data del credito	data do crédito	信用状開始日	贷款日期

KEY WORDS

English	German	French	Spanish
credit, documentary (letter of)	Dokumentenakkreditiv	lettre de crédit documentaire	carta de crédito documentario
credit, irrevocable	unwiderrufliches Akkreditiv	crédit irrévocable	crédito irrevocable
currency adjustment factor / charge (CAF or CAC)	Währungszuschlag	surcharge monétaire	recargo por ajustes cambiarios
currency of payment	Zahlungswährung	monnaie de paiement	moneda de pago
customer	Kunde	client	cliente
customs bond	Zollkaution	marchandises en entrepôt sous douane	fianza aduanera
customs broker	Zollspediteur	commissionnaire ou agent en douane	agente o corredor de aduanas
customs clearance	Zollabfertigung	formalités douanières, dédouanement	trámite aduanero, despacho aduanal
customs declaration	Zollerklärung	déclaration en douane	declaración aduanera
customs entry	Zollanmeldung	déclaration en douane	declaración o entrada de aduana
DAF Delivered at Frontier (...named place)	DAF geliefert Grenze (...genannter Bestimmungsort)	DAF rendu frontière (...lieu convenu)	DAF entreda en frontera (...lugar convenido)
damage	Schaden	dommage	daño, perjuicio, siniestro
damage to goods	Warenbeschädigung	dommage aux marchandises	daños de las mercancías
damages, to claim	Schadenersatzverlangen	réclamer une indemnité	reclamar una indemnización
data	Daten, Information	donnée, information	datos, información
date	Datum, Zeitangabe	date	fecha
date of arrival	Ankunftsdatum	date d'arrivée	fecha de llegada
date of issuance	Ausstellungsdatum	date d'émission	fecha de emisión

Italian	Portuguese (Br)	Japanese	Chinese
lettera di credito documentario	crédito documentário (carta de)	荷為替信用状	信用记录（文件）
credito irrevocabile	crédito irrevogável	取引不能信用状	不能可消贷款
coefficiente di adeguamento monetario	fator de ajuste de moeda	通貨調整料	币值调整因素
valuta di pagamento	moeda de pagamento	支払通貨	支付货币
cliente	cliente	取引先	消费者
vincolo doganale	cauções alfandegárias	関税支払保証書	进口税合同
spedizioniere doganale	despachante aduaneiro	税関貨物取扱人	报关行
formalità doganali, sdoganamento	desembaraço aduaneiro, alfandegário	通関手続き	海关放行
dichiarazione doganale	declaração aduaneira, alfandegária	税関申告	海关申报单
dichiarazione in dogana	declaração aduaneira de entrada de mercadorias (feita pelo importador)	通関申告	海关登记
DAF reso frontiera (...luogo convenuto)	DAF entrega na fronteira (... local)	DAF 国境渡し条件	DAF 边界交货（... 指定地点）
danno	avaria, dano, prejuízo, sinistro	損害	损害
danno alla merce	avaria nos produtos, nas mercadorias	貨物の損害	对商品的损害
richiedere un risarcimento	reclamar danos e prejuízos	損害賠償金を要求する	赔偿金索赔
dati	dados	データ	数据
data	data	日付	日期
data d'arrivo	data de chegada	納期を請け合う	到达日期
data di emissione	data de emissão	発行日	发出日期

KEY WORDS

English	German	French	Spanish
date of shipment	Verschiffungsdatum	date d'embarquement	fecha de embarque
date, acceptance	Annahmedatum	date d'acceptation	fecha de aceptación
date, expiry	Verfalldatum	date de validité	fecha de vencimiento
DDP Delivered Duty Paid (named place of destination)	DDP geliefert verzollt (... genannter Bestimmungsort)	DDP rendu droits acquittés (... lieu de destination convenu)	DDP entregada derechos pagados (... lugar de destino convenido)
DDU Delivered Duty Unpaid (named place of destination)	DDP geliefert unverzollt (... genannter Bestimmungsort)	DDP rendu droits non acquittés (... lieu de destination convenu)	DDU entregada derechos no pagados (... lugar de destino convenido)
debit	Belastung	débit	débito
debt	Schuld	dette	deuda, oblagación
decision	Entscheidung	décision	decisión
decision maker	Entscheidender	décideur	responsable de decidir
declaration	Erklärung	déclaration en douane	declaración
declared value	Verzollungswert	valeur déclarée	valor declarado
declared value for carriage	Deklarationswert für Fracht	valeur déclarée pour transport	valor declarado para el transportista
declared value for customs	Verzollungswert	valeur déclarée en douane	valor declarado en aduanas
delay	Verzögerung, Verzug	retard	demora, retraso
delayed	verzögerte	retardé	retrasado
delivered	geliefert	(de)livré	entregado
delivery	Aus Lieferung, Übergabe	livraison, délivrance, émise	entrega
delivery date	Liefertermin	date de livraison	fecha de entrega
demand for payment	Mahnbescheid, Zahlungsaufforderung	mise en demeure	intimación de pago, requerimiento de pago
demurrage (charges)	Überliegegeld	(indemnités de) surestaries	(gastos de) sobreestadías, demoras
departure date	Abfahrtsdatum	date de départ	fecha de salida
deposit	Einlage, Guthaben	dépôt	depósito

Italian	Portuguese (Br)	Japanese	Chinese
data d'imbarco	data de embarque	出荷予定日	装运日期
data di accettazione	data de aceitação	承諾	承诺日期
data di scadenza	data de validade	有効期限	期满日
DDP reso sdoganato (... luogo di destinazione convenuto)	DDP com entrega e impostos pagos até (... local de destino)	DDP 関税込持込渡 （.. 指定仕向地）	DDP 完税后交货 (.. 指定目的地)
DDP reso non sdoganato (... luogo di destinazione convenuto)	DDU com entrega e impostos a pagar em (... local de destino)	DDU 関税抜き持込渡 （... 指定仕向地）	DDU 完税前交货 (.. 指定目的地)
addebito	débito	借方	借方
debito	divida consolidada	借金	债务
decisione	decisão	決定	决定
decisore	tomador de decisões	意思決定者	决策人
dichiarazione	declaração	積出申告	申报单
valore dichiarato	valor declarado	公示価格	申报价格
valore dichiarato del porto	valor declarado para transporte	輸送用公示価格	申报价格以确定运费
valore dichiarato per la dogana	valor declarado na alfândega	公示価格	向海关申报价格
ritardo	atraso	遅れる	延迟
ritardato, rinviato, differito	atrasado	遅延した	延时的
consegnato	entregue	配達費込みの	运费包括在内的
consegna	entrega	配達	交货
data di consegna	data de entrega	配送日	交货日期
intimazione di pagamento	demanda, solicitação de pagamento	支払請求	付款要求
controstallìe (indennità)	sobrestada, demurrage	滞船料	逾期费
data di partenza	data de partida	搭乗日	开船日期
deposito, versamento	depósito	預金	保证金

KEY WORDS

KEY WORDS

English	German	French	Spanish
depot	Lager	entrepôt	bodega, almacén, depósito para distribución, almacén central
DEQ Delivered Ex Quay (...named port of destination)	DEQ geliefert ab Kai (...genannter Bestimmungshafen)	DEQ rendu à quai (...port de destination convenu)	DEQ entregada en muelle (...puerto de destino convenido)
DES Delivered Ex Ship (...named port of destination)	DES geliefert ab Schiff (...genannter Bestimmungshafen)	DES rendu ex ship (...port de destination convenu)	DES entregada sobre buque (...puerto de destino convenido)
destination	Bestimmungsort, Lieferort	lieu de livraison, destination	(lugar de) destino, destinación
disclosure	Offenlegung, Enthüllung, Aufdeckung	divulagation, donner communication	divulgación, revelación
discount (on goods)	Preisnachlass, Diskont	rabais, escompte	descuento (sobre la mercancía)
discrepancies	Abweichungen	irrégularités	discrepancias
dispatch (goods)	Ware versenden	expédier	envío, despacho
dispute	widerlegen	dirrérend, litige	conflicto, litigio, controversia, diferencia
document	Dokument	document	documento
document, combined transport	Dokument des kombinierten Transports	document de transport combiné	documento de transporte combinado
document, negotiable	übertragbares Dokument	document négociable	documento negociable
Document, Single Administrative (SAD)	Einheitspapier	Document Administratif Unique	documento único aduanero
documentary credit	Dokumentenakkreditiv	crédit documentaire	crédito documentario
documentation	Dokumentation	documentation	documentación
documents against acceptance (D/A)	Dokumente gegen Akzept	(remise des) document contre acceptation	(entrega de) documentos contra aceptación

KEY WORDS

Italian	Portuguese (Br)	Japanese	Chinese
deposit, magazzino, parco di deposito, stazione merci	depósito	デポー	仓库
DEQ reso banchina (...porto di destinazione convenuto)	DEQ entrega no cais (... porto de destino)	DEQ 埠頭持込渡（...指定仕向港）	DEQ 目的港码头交货（..指定目的港）
DES reso exship (...porto di destinazione convenuto)	DES entrega no navio em (... porto de destino)	DES 本船持込渡（...指定仕向港）	DES 目的港船上交货（...指定目的港口）
destinazione	destino	宛て先	目的地
informazione, rivelazione divulgazione (es. del bilancio)	revelação, descoberta	公開	透漏
sconto (sul prezzo delle merci)	desconto, dedução	割引	折扣
discrepanze, divergenze	discrepâncias	過不足	偏差
spedire (merci)	despachar, enviar (produtos)	発送する	发送（商品）
controversia, lite, vertenza	disputa, litígio	論争	争论
documento	documento	ドキュメント	文件
documento di trasporto combinàto	documento de transporte combinado	複合運送証券	联合运输文件
documento negoziabile	documento, título negociável	譲渡可能書類	可谈判文件
documento unico amministrativo	Documento Aduaneiro Único	単回投与書類	单一管理文件 (SAD)
credito documentario	crédito documentário	荷為替信用状	贷款文件
documentazione	documentação	ドキュメンティション	文件
documenti contro accettazione	entrega de documentos contra aceitação	引渡書類渡し	承兑交单托收

KEY WORDS

English	German	French	Spanish
documents against payment (D/P)	Dokumente gegen Zahlung	(remise des) document contre paiement	(entrega de) documentos contra pago
draft	Tratte, Wechsel	traite	giro, letra
draft at tenor	Datowechsel	traite à échéance	letra a vencimiento, giro
draft, (30) days sight	(30) Tage Nachsichttratte	traite à (30) jours de vue	giro, letra a (30) días vista
draft, claused	unreine Tratte	effet avec réserve	letra con reservas
draft, clean	reine Tratte	effet sans réserve	letra limpia
draft, sight	Sichttratte	traite à vue	giro, letra a vista
draft, usance	Usancetratte	traite à échéance	letra de cambio con vencimiento común
drawee	Bezogener	tiré	girado, librador
drawer	Aussteller	tireur	girador, librador
due	fällig, (das) Geschuldete	dû, exigible, échu	exigible, dado, derechos
due, past	überfällig	en souffrance	vencido y no pagado
duties, import	Einfuhrabgaben, Importzölle	droits d'entrée	derechos de entrada
duty	Zoll, Steure, Pflicht, Obliegenheit, Abgabe, Zölle	droit(s) de douane	derecho(s) de aduana, derecho, impuesto derechos, impuestos
duty free	zollfrei	exempt de droits (de douane)	libre de impuestos (aduaneros)
electronic funds transfer (EFT)	elektronischer Zahlungsverkehr	transfert électronique de fonds (TEF)	transferencia electrónica de fondos
e-mail	E-Mail	messagerie électronique	correo electrónico, e-mail
endorsement	Ubertragung, Indossierung	endossement, avenant	endorso, póliza
endorser	Indossant	endosseur	endosante
entry	Eingang	déclaration en douane	entrada, admisión

Italian	Portuguese (Br)	Japanese	Chinese
documenti contro pagamento	documentos contra pagamento	代金引換書類渡し	付款交单托收
tratta	saque	ドラフト	汇票
tratta a scadenza	título pagável de acordo com seus próprios termos	手形の支払期間	汇票期限副本
tratta a (30) giorni vista	título pagável a (30) dias da apresentação	(30)日の参着為替	(30) 天汇票
tratta sporca, con riserva	letra de câmbio clasulada	条件付き手形	汇票条款
tratta libera	letra de câmbio sem garantia	普通為替	光本汇票
tratta a vista	letra de câmbio a vista	参着為替	可见汇票
tratta a tempo vista	título pagável em prazo estabelecido pelo costume local	手形支払猶予期間	票据期限
trassato	sacado	手形名宛人	付款人
traente (di un assegno)	sacador	振出人	发票人
scaduto, esigibile	a vencer	デュー	应付款
in sofferenza	vencido e não pago	不渡り	过去应付款
diritti d'importazione	imposto de importação	輸入税	进口关税
dazio, diritto, i doganale (i)	imposto	関税	关税
esente da diritti (doganali)	livre de impostos	無税	免税
trasferimento elettronico di fondi	transferência eletrônica de fundos	電子資金取引	电子资金过户
posta elettronica	e-mail	電子メール	电子邮件
girata, clausola	endosso	裏書き	背书
girante	endossante	譲渡人	背书人
dichiarazione	entrada	通関手続き	报关

KEY WORDS

English	German	French	Spanish
entry documents	Zollantrag	documents de déclaration en douane	documentos de admisión
entry for consumption	Zollantrag auf Abfertigung zum freien Verkehr	entrée pour consommation	admisión para consumo
estimate	Schätzung	estimation	estimación, previsión, presupuesto
estimated date of arrival	voraussichtlicher Abfahrtstermin	date d'arrivée prévue	fecha de llegada estimada
estimated date of departure	voraussichtlicher Ankunftstermin	date de départ prévue	fecha de salida estimada
exchange rate	Wechselkurs	taux de change	tipo de cambio
expense(s)	Koste(n), Spese(n)	frais	gasto(s)
expiry date	Verfalltag, Ablauftermin	date d'éxpiration, de péremption	fecha de vencimiento
export	Ausfuhr, Export	exportation	exportación
export charges	Ausfuhrkosten	frais d'exportation	gastos de exportación
export declaration	Ausfuhrerklärung	déclaration d'export	declaración de exportación
export license	Ausfuhrerlaubnis	licence d'exportation	licencia/permiso de exportación
export permit	Ausfuhrlizenz, Exportlizenz	permis d'exportation	permiso/licencia de exportación
exporter	Exporteur	exportateur	exportador
FAS Free Alongside Ship (named port of shipment)	FAS frei Langsseite Schiff (... benannter Verschiffungshafen)	FAS franco le long du navire (... port d'embarquement convenu)	FAS libre al costado del buque (... puerto de carga convenido)
fax	Telefax	télécopie	fax, facsímil
FCA Free Carrier (...named place)	FCA frei Frachtführer (...benannter Ort)	FCA franco transporteur (...lieu convenu)	FCA franco transportista (...lugar convenido)
fee(s)	Gebühr, Taxe(n)	droit, taxe	derechos, impuesto, tasa(s), tarifas
final payment	Endzahlung	paiement final	pago final, último plazo, último pago

KEY WORDS

Italian	Portuguese (Br)	Japanese	Chinese
documenti di dichiarazione	documentos de entrada	記入文書	报关文件
bolletta doganale per merci da consumo	admissão, entrada para consumo	輸入申告書	消费品报关手续
stima, stima, previsione (es. previsioni di spesa)	estimativa, orçamento	予測	评估
data prevista di arrivo	data prevista de chegada	到着予定日	预计到岸日期
data prevista di partenza	data prevista de partida	出発予定日	预计开船日期
corso del combio, rata di cambio	taxa de câmbio	為替レート	汇率
spese	despesa(s)	費用	支出
data di scadenza	data de vencimento	満了日	期满日
esportazione	exportação	輸出	出口
spese d'esportazione	taxas de exportação	輸出手数料	出口费用
dichiarazione d'esportazione	declaração de exportação	輸出申告	出口申报单
licenza d'espotazione	licença de exportação	輸出承認	出口许可
permesso d'esportazione	permissão de exportação	輸出許可書	出口许可
esportatore	exportador	輸出業者	出口商
FAS franco lungo bordo (... porto di imbarco convenuto)	FAS Livre ao Lado do Navio (... porto de embarque)	FAS船側渡し	FAS 船边交货 (.. 指定装运港)
fax	fax	ファックス	传真
FCA franco vettore (...luogo convenuto)	FCA livre no transportador (... local)	FCA運送人渡し	FCA 货交承运人 (... 指定地点)
onorario, diritti	taxa, pagamento, taxa de entrada, salário, honorários	料金	费用
ultimo pagamento	pagamento final	最終払い	最终付款

English	German	French	Spanish
fine	Geldstrafe	amende	multa
firm commitment	feste Zusage	engagement ferme	compromiso en firme
FOB Free On Board (named port of shipment)	FOB frei an Bord (... benannter Verschiffungshafen)	FOB Franco bord (port d'embarquement convenu)	FOB franco a bordo (... puerto de embarque convenido)
force majeure	höhere Gewalt	force majeure	fuerza mayor
foreign exchange	Devisen	devises	cambio exterior
foreign exchange rate	Devisenkurs	taux de change	tipo de cambio de divisas
foreign trade zone	Außenhandelszone	zone franche	zona franca
forwarder	Spediteur	transporteur, chargeur, expéditeur	transportista, embarcador, expedidor de carga
forwarding instructions	Versandinstruktionen	instructions d'expédition	instrucciones de expedición
fragile	zerbrechlich	fragile	frágil
freight	Fracht	fret	flete
freight all kinds (FAK)	Fracht (für Güter) aller Art	fret pour tous genres (de marchandises)	carga de toda clase
freight bill	Frachtbrief	état du tarif de transport	carta de porte, albarán, nota de expedición, nota del flete
freight charges	Frachtkosten	tarif du transport marchandise	gastos de transporte
freight collect	unfrei	fret payable à l'arrivée	portes debidos
freight forwarder	Spediteur	expéditeur, transporteur	transportista, expedidor de carga
freight prepaid	Fracht im voraus bezahlt	frét payé	flete prepagado, flete pagado en origen
freight rate	Frachtrate	taux de fret	tasa de flete, cuota de flete
full container load (FCL)	Voll-Containerladung	conteneur complet	(carga por) contenedor completo
full set	voller Satz	jeu de documents complet	juego completo

Italian	Portuguese (Br)	Japanese	Chinese
multa (es. pagare una multa)	multa	ファイン	罚金
impegno fermo	compromisso firme	確約	公司承担义务
FOB franco a bordo (... porto di imbarco convenuto)	FOB Livre a Bordo (... porto de embarque)	FOB本船渡し	FOB 装运港船上交货 (... 指定装运港)
forza maggiore	força maior	不可抗力	不可抗力
cambio estero	câmbio exterior	外為	外币兑换
cambio	taxa de câmbio exterior	外国為替相場	汇率
punto franco, zona franca, zona di libero scambio	zona de comércio exterior	外国貿易地域	对外贸易地区
spedizioniere	despachante	運送業者	代运人
istruzioni per la spedizione	instruções de despacho	運送指図書	货物发送细则
fragile, delicato	frágil	虚弱な	易碎的
nolo	frete	運送貨物	运费
nolo per ogni tipo (di merci)	fretes de todo o tipo (FAK)	品目無差別で	所有种类运费 (FAK)
certificato di imbarco	nota de frete	運賃勘定	运费单
spese di trasporto	despesas de frete	運送料	货运收费
nolo assegnato, spese a carico del destinatario	frete a pagar	荷受人払い運賃	运费向收货人索取
spedizioniere	despachante aduaneiro	運送会社	运输代理人
nolo prepagato	frete pré-pago	運賃前払い	预付运费
rata di nolo	taxa de frete	運賃率	货运价格
contenitore a carico completo	carga total do container	フルコンテナ？ロード	集装箱整箱货物 (FCL)
set completo, tutti	conjunto completo (de documentos)	フルセット	全套

KEY WORDS

English	German	French	Spanish
full truckload	komplette Wagenladung	wagon complet	carga plena del camión
general average (g/a)	grosse Havarie	avarie commune	avería común, gruesa
general cargo	Stückgut	marchandises générales, marchandises diverses	carga mixta, mercancías varias
global business	globales Geschäft	affaires globales	negocios a nivel mundial
global market	globaler Markt	marché global	mercado mundial, mercado global
good faith	guter Glaube	bonne foi	buena fe
goods	Waren, Güter	marchandises, produits, biens	mercancías, productos, bienes
goods, dutiable	verzollbare Güter	biens soumis à droit de douane	mercancías sujetas a impuestos
guarantee	Garantie, Sicherheit, Bürgschaft	garantie	garantía, aval
guarantee, to	garantieren	garantir	garantizar, avalar
handling charges	Ladekosten	frais de mautention	gastos por gestión/ tramitación
hazardous goods	gefährliche Güter	produits dangereux	bienes peligrosos
hazardous materials	Gefahrstoffe	matériel dangereux	materiales peligrosos
house air waybill (HAWB)	Hausluftfrachtbrief (des Spediteurs)	émise par transitaire	guía aérea emitida por un expedidor de carga
import	Import	importation	importación
import authority	Importstelle	autorités d'importation	autoridades de importación
import declaration	Importerklärung	déclaration d'importation	declaración de importación
import duty	Importzölle, Einfuhrzölle	droits d'entrée à l'importation	aranceles
import license	Importlizenz, Einfuhrlizenz	licence d'importation	licencia/permiso de importación

Italian	Portuguese (Br)	Japanese	Chinese
carico completo di camion	carga total do caminhão	トラック1台分の積荷	货车满载
avaria comune/generale	média geral	共同海損	一般平均值
carico di merci varie	carga geral	一般貨物	一般的货物
affari globali	empresa, negócios internacional(s), global(is), mundial(is)	世界ビジネス	全球商业
mercato globale	mercado global	世界市場	全球市场
buona fede	boa fé	誠実な	真诚
merce, prodotti, beni	produtos	貨物	商品
merci soggete a dazio	produtos taxáveis	課税品目	应纳关税的商品
garanzia	garantia	保証	保证
garantire, fornire garanzia	garantir	保証する	保证
spese di movimentazione, costi di trasporto interno	custo de manuseio, tratamento	手数料	装卸费
merce pericolose	produtos perigosos	危険貨物	危险品
materiali pericolosi	materiais perigosos	危険物	危险材料
lettera di trasporto aereo emessa da un consolidatore	conhecimento de embarque de frete aéreo consolidado	混載業者発行の航空貨物運送状	空运分提单 (HAWB)
importazione	importar	輸入	进口
autorità per l'importazione	autoridade de importação	輸入権限	进口当局
dichiarazione d'importazione	declaração de importação	輸入申告	进口申报单
dazio d'importazione	imposto de importação	輸入税	进口税
licensa d'importazione	licença de importação	輸入許可書／輸入承認書	进口许可

English	German	French	Spanish
import quota(s)	Einfuhrquoten	contingent d'importation	cuota de importación
import, to	importieren, einführen	importer	importar
importer	Importeur	importateur	importador
in bond	unter Zollverschluss	en entrepôt sous douane	en garantía
in bond shipment	Sendung unter Zollverschluss	expédition en entrepôt sous douane	en depósito, en admisión temporal
information	Information	informations	informaciones
inspection	Inspektion	contrôle	inspección
inspection service	Kontrollservice	servoce de contrôle	servicio de inspecciones
inspection, agricultural	Landwirtschafts-überprüfung	contrôle agricole	inspección agrícola
inspection, customs	Zollkontrolle	contrôle douanier	inspección aduanera
instruction(s)	Anweisung(en)	instruction(s)	instrucción(es)
instrument, negotiable	übertragbares Wertpapier	document négociable	documento negociable
insurance	Versicherung	assurance	seguro
insurance agent	Versicherungsagent	courtier	agente de seguros
insurance certificate	Versicherungszertifikat	certificat d'assurance	certificado de seguro
insurance claim	Anspruch auf Versicherungsleistung	sinistre	reclamación, demanda de seguro
insurance policy	Versicherungspolice	police d'assurance	póliza de seguros
insurance, all risk	Versicherung gegen alle Risiken	assurance tous risques	seguro a todo riesgo
insurance, cargo	Frachtversicherung, Ladungsversicherung	assurance faculté	seguro de carga
insurance, war risk	Kriegsgefahrversicherung	assurance de guerre	seguro de riesgo de guerra
insured	versichert	assuré	asegurado
insured value	versicherter Wert	valeur assurée	valor asegurado

KEY WORDS

Italian	Portuguese (Br)	Japanese	Chinese
quota d'importazione	quotas de importação	輸入割当て	进口限额
importare	importar	輸入先	进口到
importatore	importador	輸入業者	进口商
soggetto a vincolo doganale, in deposito doganale	em garantia	倉庫渡し	关栈保留中
spedizione franco deposito doganale	carga de importação ou exportação já desembaraçada	保税出荷	关栈保留出货
informazioni	informações	情報	信息
ispezione, esame, verifica	inspeção	検査	检验
servizio d'ispezione	serviço de inspeção	検査サービス	检验程序
ispezione agricola	inspeção agrícola	農業検査	农业检验
controllo doganale	inspeção aduaneira	税関検査	海关检验
istruzione(i), disposizione(i), avvertenza(e), direttiva(e)	instruções	指示	指令
effetto negoziabile	instrumento negociável	譲渡可能証券	可转让的仪器
assicurazione	seguro	保険	保险
agente di assicurazione	agente de seguro	保険代理店	保险代理
certificato di assicurazione	certificado de seguro	保険証明書	保险凭证
richiesta di risarcimento	reclamação de seguro	保険金請求	保险索赔
polizza di assicurazione	apólice de seguro	保険契約	保险政策
assicurazione contro tutti I rischi	seguro contra todos os riscos	オールリスク保険	保全险
assicurazione merci/facoltà	seguro de carga	貨物保険	货物保险
assicurazione contro il rischio della guerra	seguro contra risco de guerra	戦争傷害保険	战争险
assicurato, sottoscrittore	segurado	保険付きの	保户
valore assicurato	valor segurado	保険価額	保险价值

KEY WORDS

English	German	French	Spanish
insurer	Versicherer	assureur	asegurador, aseguradora
intermodal	kombiniert	intermodal	combinado
intermodal transport	intermodaler Transport	transport intermodal	transporte intermodal
inventory	Liste, Inventurliste, Lagerbestand	stock, inventaire	inventario
invoice	Rechnung	facture	factura
invoice number	Rechnungsnummer	numéro de facture	número de factura
invoice, commercial	Handelsrechnung	facture commerciale	factura comercial
invoice, consular	Konsularfaktura	facture consulaire	factura consular
invoice, proforma	Pro-Forma-Rechnung	facture pro forma	factura pro forma
invoice, signed	unterschriebene Rechnung	facture visée	factura firmada
issuance	Ausgabe	émission	emisión
issuance date	Ausgabedatum	date d'émission	fecha de emisión
joint venture	Joint-Venture	entreprise commune	joint venture, empresa conjunta
label(s)	Etikett(en)	étiquette	etiqueta(s)
label, to	etikettieren	étiqueter	etiquetar
late	spät	en retard	tarde
law	Gesetz, Recht, Gesetzgebung	loi, législation, droit	ley, leyes, legislación, derecho
law suit	Verfahren, Prozess	procès juridique	pleito, litigio
legal entity	Rechtspersönlichkeit	personne morale	entidad jurídica
less thancontainer load (LCL)	Teil-Containerladung	charge incompléte du conteneur	menos de contenedor completo
less than truck load (LTL)	LkW-Stückgut	camion incomplet	menos de camión completo

Italian	Portuguese (Br)	Japanese	Chinese
assicuratore, persona che assicura	companhia de seguro	保険加入者	承保人
intermodale	intermodal	複合	联合运输的
trasporto intermodale	transporte intermodal	複合輸送	联合运输
inventario, rimanenze di magazzino	estoque	在庫	存货
fattura	fatura	インボイス	发票
numero della fattura	número da fatura	送り状番号	发票号码
fattura commerciale	fatura comercial	商業送り状	商业发票
fattura consolare	fatura consular	領事送り状	领事签证的发票
fattura pro forma	fatura pro forma	見積送り状	形式发票
fattura firmata	fatura assinada	署名インボイス	签署发票
emissione	emissão	発行	发行
data di emissione	data de emissão	発行日付	发行日期
joint venture	empreendimento conjunto	共同事業	合资企业
etichetta(e) (es. etichetta del prezzo)	rótulo(s)	ラベル	标号
etichettare, contrassegnare (es. carico contrassegnato)	rotular	名付ける	标签贴于…
tardo (es. a ora tarda), avanzato, inoltrato	tarde, atrasado	遅い	迟到
legge(i), diritto	lei, Direito	法律	法律
causa, azione legale, processo civile, querela	ação judicial	告訴	（律）诉讼
persona giuridica	pessoa jurídica (entidade com personalidade jurídica)	合法的な組織	法人实体
carico incompleto del contenitore (di groupage)	menos que a carga do contêiner	貨物 (LCL)	少于集装箱装载 (LCL)
camion a carico parziale	menos que a carga do caminhão	貨物 (LTL)	少于卡车装载 (LTL)

KEY WORDS

English	German	French	Spanish
letter	Brief, Schreiben	lettre, requête	carta, petición
letter of credit	Akkreditiv, Kreditbrief	lettre de crédit	carta de crédito
liability	Verbindlichkeit, Haftung, Verantwortung	responsabilité, obligation, passif	responsabilidad, pasivo, obligación
license	Bewilligung, Erlaubnis	licence	licencia, permiso, autorización
licensee	Lizenznehmer, Lizenzinhaber, Konzessionsinhaber	concessionnaire	concesionario, licenciatario
licensor	Lizenzgeber, Konzessionsgeber	concédant	cedente, otorgante, licenciador
load, to	laden	charger	cargar
logistics	Logistik	logistique	logística
logistics, integrated	vernetzte Logistik	logistique intégrée	logística integrada
loss, constructive total	konstruktiver Totalverlust	perte censée etre totale	pérdida estimada ser total
mandatory	zwingend, obligatorisch	impératif, obligatoire	inderogable, imperativo, obligatorio
manifest, cargo	Frachtliste, Ladungsverzeichnis	manifeste de bord	manifiesto, guia de carga
market	Markt	marché	mercado
market, domestic	Binnenmarkt	marché intérieur	mercado nacional
market, foreign	Auslandsmarkt	marché extérieur, marché international	mercado internacional, exterior
marks	Marken	marques	marcas
measurement(s)	Abmessung(en)	mesure	medida(s)
merchandise	Ware, Güter	marchandise	mercancía, mercadería
minimum price	Mindestpreis	prix minimal	precio mínimo
money	Geld, Münze, Geldmittel, Kapital	argent, numéraire, monnaie légale	dinero, liquido, moneda legal
multimodal	multimodaler, kombiniert	multimodal	combinado/a, multimodal

Italian	Portuguese (Br)	Japanese	Chinese
lettera	carta, letra	レター	信件
lettera di credito	carta de crédito	銀行信用状	信用证
responsabilità, impegni (finanziari)	obrigação, responsabilidade legal	責任保険	责任
licenza	licença	ライセンス	许可证
concessionario, licenziatario	licenciado	ライセンシー	领有许可证者
chi concede o emette licenze	licenciante	実施許諾者	认可证颁发者
caricare (es. caricare una nave di merci)	carregar	積む	装载于…
logistica	logística	ロジスティックス	后勤
logistica integrata	logística integrada	集中兵站	后勤综合
perdita totale equivalente	perda total implícita	準全損	拟定全损
imperativa, obbligatorio	obrigatório	必須の	强制性
manifesto di carico	manifesto de carga	積荷目録	货物舱单
mercato	mercado	マーケット	市场
mercato interno	mercado doméstico	国内市場	国内市场
mercato estero	mercado exterior	海外市場	国外市场
segnalazioni	marcas	マーク寸法	标记
misura(e)	medida(s)	寸法	测量
merce	mercadoria(s)	商業化する	商品
prezzo minimo	preço mínimo	最低価格	最低价格
denaro, moneta, capitale	dinheiro	金額	金额
multimodale	multimodal	多モードの	多方式

K
E
Y

W
O
R
D
S

English	German	French	Spanish
multimodal transport	multimodaler Transport	transport multimodal	transporte multimodal
name	Name	nom	nombre
negligence	Fahrlässigkeit, Nachlässigkeit	omission, négligence	omisión, negligencia
negotiable	negozierbar	négociable	negociable
negotiable instrument	übertragbares Wertpapier	document négociable	documento negociable
negotiated price	verhandelter Preis	prix négocié	precio negociado
net	Netto	net	neto
net amount due	fälliger Nettobetrag	montant échu net	importe neto debido
net price	Nettopreis	prix net	precio neto
never	nie	jamais	nunca
next month	nächster Monat	le mois prochain	el mes siguiente, el próximo mes
next week	nächste Woche	la semaine prochaine	la semana que viene, la próxima semana
next year	nächstes Jahr	l'année prochaine	el año que viene
no	nein	non	no
nondisclosure agreement (NDA)	Geheimhaltungsvsertrag	accord de non révélation	acuerdo/pacto/convenio de confidencialidad/ buena fe
non negotiable	nicht negozierbar	non-négociable	no negociable
notice	Notiz, Nachricht, Benachrichtigung	avis	aviso, anuncio
notification	Mitteilung, Bekanntmachung, Notifizierung	avis, déclaration, notification	notificación, declaracion
null and void	null und nichtig, rechtsunwirksam	nul et non avenu	nulo y sin valor, nulo de pleno derecho
ocean	Ozean	océan	mar
ocean bill of lading	Bordkonnossement	connaissement maritime	conocimiento de embarque a la orden
offer	Angebot	offre	oferta

KEY WORDS

Italian	Portuguese (Br)	Japanese	Chinese
trasporto multimodale	transporte multimodal	複合一貫輸送	多式联运
nome	nome	名前	名称
negligenza, colpa	negligência	無頓着	疏忽
negoziabile	negociável	交渉できる	可通过谈判解决
effetto negoziabile	instrumento negociável	流通証券	可流通票据
prezzo negoziato	preço negociado	交渉価格	仅付价格
netto	líquido	ネット	净价
importo netto dovuto	valor líquido devido	正味支払金	应付净总值
prezzo netto	preço líquido	正価	纯价格
mai	nunca	以前に～したことがない	决不
il mese prossimo	no próximo mês	来月	下个月
la settimana prossima	na próxima semana	来週	下星期
anno prossimo	no próximo ano	来年	明年
No	não	なし	没有
accordo di segreto industriale	acordo de confidencialidade	機密保持契約	保密协议 (NDA)
non negoziabile	não negociável	交渉のできない	不可协商的
avviso, notifica, avvertenza	aviso, advertência	通告	通告
notificazione, comunicazione	notificação	通告	通告
nullo, nullo e non valido, privo di valore legale	nulo e anulado	無効	无效的
oceano	oceano	オーシャン	海洋
polizza di carico oceanico	conhecimento de embarque marítimo	船荷証券	海运提单
offerta	oferta	勧める	提案，出价

KEY WORDS

English	German	French	Spanish
on time	rechtzeitig	à l'heure	a tiempo, puntual
open account	offene Rechnung, Kontokorrent	compte courant	cuenta abierta
open policy	laufende Versicherung	police ouverte	póliza abierta
opportunity	Gelegenheit	occasion	oportunidad
order	Auftrag, Bestellung, Order	commande, ordre	pedido, orden
order, to	bestellen	commander	ordenar, pedir
order, to cancel an	einen Auftrag stornieren	annuler une commande	cancelar un pedido
order, to place an	einen Auftrag erteilen	passer une commande	entregar un pedido
original documents	Originaldokumente	original d'un document	documentos originales
overcharge	Überlastung, Überladung	surcharge	recargo
packing	Verpackung, Packmaterial	emballage	embalaje, envase, empaquetado
packing cost	Verpackungskosten	frais d'emballage	gastos de embalaje
packing list	Packliste	liste de colisage	lista de empaquetado
packing materials	Verpackungsmaterialien	matériel d'emballage	materiales de embalaje
packing, export	Exportverpackung	emballage pour l'exportation	embalaje para exportaciones
partial delivery	Teillieferung	livraison partielle	entrega parcial
particular average	besondere Havarie	avaries particulières	avería particular
partner	Partner, Teilhaber	associé, partenaire	asociado
partnership	Partnerschaft, Personengesellschaft	partenariat, société de personnes	asociado, sasociación
past due	überfällig	en souffrance	vencido y no pagado
pay at sight, to	bei Sicht zahlen	payer à vue	pagar a la vista
pay at tenor, to	zahlen	payer à échéance	pagar a vencimiento
pay in advance, to	vorauszahlen	payer à l'avance	pagar con anticipación

Italian	Portuguese (Br)	Japanese	Chinese
puntualmente, in orario	na hora	時間とおりに	准时
conto aperto	conta aberta, sem restrições	オープン勘定	未清结的帐目，往来帐户
polizza aperta	apólice aberta	予定保険	开放政策
opportunità, occasione	oportunidade	機会	机会，时机
ordine, mandato, ordinazione	pedido, ordem	命令	订购
ordinare, commissionare	pedir, solicitar, fazer pedido	注文する	订购于…
cancellare, annullare un' ordine	cancelar um pedido	注文の取り消し	取消订购
passare un ordine	colocar, fazer um pedido	注文する	订货
documenti in originale	documentos originais	原始文書	原始文件
sovraccarico, sovrapprezzo	preço excessivo, sobretaxa	値段を高く請求	滥开（账目）
imballaggio, confezione	empacotamento, embalagem, fechamento	梱包	包装
spese di imballaggio	custo de embalagem	包装費	包装成本
distinta colli, lista di imballaggio	lista de embalagem	パッキングリスト	包装单
materiali da imballaggio	materiais de embalagem	梱包材	包装材料
imballaggio destinato all'esportazione	embalagem para exportação	輸出包装	出口包装
consegna parziale	entrega parcial	分割出荷	分期交货
avaria particolare	perda ou avaria particular	分損担保	单独海损
partner, socio	sócio, parceiro	パートナー	合作者
associazione, società (di persone)	sociedade	パートナーシップ	合作关系
scaduto, in sofferenza	vencido	期日経過	赊欠的金额
pagare a vista	pagar contra apresentação	一覧払い	见票即付于…
pagare ad una scadenza	efetuar pagamento conforme indicado no documento	テナーで払う	限期付款于…
pagare anticipatamente	pagar antecipadamente	先払い	预先支付于…

KEY WORDS

English	German	French	Spanish
pay in installments, to	in Raten zahlen an	payer à tempérament	pagar a plazos
pay, to	zahlen, bezahlen	payer	pagar
payee	Wechselnehmer, Begünstigter	bénéficiare, preneur d'un effet	beneficiario, tomador de una letra
payer	Zahler	payeur	pagador
payment	Zahlung	paiement, versement	pago
payment at sight	Zahlung bei Sicht	paiement à vue	pago a la vista
payment in advance	vorauszahlbar	paiement à l'avance	pago anticipado
phytosanitary inspection certificate	phytosanitäre zertifikate	certificat de contrôle phztosanitaire	certificado de inspección fitosanitaria
point of origin	Ursprungsort	point d'origine	punto de origen
policy, insurance	Versicherungspolice	police d'assurance	póliza de seguro
port	Hafen	port	puerto
port facilities	Hafenanlage	installations portuaires	instalaciones del puerto
port of departure	Abgangshafen	port de départ	puerto de salida
port of destination	Bestimmungshafen	port de destination	puerto de destino
port of entry	Eingangshafen	port d'arrivée	puerto de entrada
power of attorney	Vollmacht	procuration écrite	poder para pleitos
prepaid charges	franko	frais payés	gastos pagados
price	Preis, Kurs	prix	precio
price adjustment	Abschöpfung	ajustement des prix	ajuste del precio
price schedule	Preisliste	tarif	lista de precios
price, fixed selling	festgelegter Verkaufspreis	prix imposé	precio fijado
price, offered	Preisangebot	prix offert	precio ofrecido
principal	Auftraggeber, Lieferant, Hauptperson	cédant, donneur d'ordrel	principal, ordenante, concedente
problem	Problem	problème	problema, dificultad

Italian	Portuguese (Br)	Japanese	Chinese
pagare a rate	pagar a prestação	月賦で払う	分期支付于…
pagare	pagar	支払う	支付于…
beneficiario, creditore	recebedor	払受人	收款人
pagatore, soggetto pagante	pagador	支払人	付款人
pagamento, versamento	pagamento	支払い	付款
pagamento a vista	pagamento a vista	一覧払い	见票即付于…
pagamento anticipato	pagamento antecipado	前払い	预付
certificato d'ispezione fitosanitaria	certificado de inspeção fitossanitária	植物衛生の検査証明書	植物检疫证书
punto di origine	ponto de origem	原産地	起源地
polizza di assicurazione	apólice de seguro	保険証券	保险政策
porto	porto	ポート	港口
attrezzature portuali	instalações portuárias	港湾施設	港口设施
porto di partenza	porto de saída	出帆港	离港处
porto di destinazione	porto de destino	仕向港	到港点
porto d'entrata	porto de entrada	輸入港	港口入口处
procura	procuração, poder	委任権	委托权
spese prepagate	despesas prépagas	前納料	预先付讫的费用
prezzo	preço	価格	价格
riallineamento dei prezzi	ajuste de preço	価格調整	调整价格
lista dei prezzi	lista de preços	価格表	价格计划表
prezzo imposto	preço fixo	固定価格	固定的价格
prezzo offerto	preço oferecido	売り出し価格	提供的价格
ordinante, concedente	principal	主役	负责人
problema, difficoltà	problema	問題	问题

English	German	French	Spanish
product	Produkt	produit	producto
profit(s)	Gewinn(e)	bénéfices, profit	beneficio, ganancia, utilidad
proof of receipt	Empfangsbeweis	récépissé	comprobante de recepción
proposal	Angebot	proposition	propuesta
protest	Protest, Einspruch	protêt, rapport, procès-verbal	protesta, rechazo, reporte, proceso verbal
prototype	Prototyp	prototype	prototipo
purchase	Kauf, Ankauf, Einkauf	achat	compra
purchase order	Bestellung	commande d'achat	pedido de compra, orden de compra
purchaser	Einkäufer	acheteur	comprador
quality, acceptable	akzeptable Qualität	qualité acceptable	calidad aceptable
quality, good	gute Qualität	bonne qualité	buena calidad
quality, poor	schlechte Qualität	mauvaise qualité	poca calidad
quota	Quote	contingent	cuota
quote	Zitat	citation	cita
rail car	Wagon	wagon de chemin de fer	vehículo ferroviario
rail waybill	Bahnfrachtbrief	lettre de voiture ferroviaire	resguardo de transporte por tren
rate	Kurs, Tarif, Zinssatz	taux, cours, tarif	tasa, tarifa, indice
rate, duty	Zollsatz	taxe douanière	tasa de derechos
receipt	Quittung	reçu, récépissé	recibo, resguardo, talón
regulation(s), customs	Vorschriften, Regeln (Zollordnung)	réglements (des douanes)	reglamento aduanero
reject	ablehnen	rejeter	rechazar
remittance	Überweisung	versement	remesa, giro
representative	Vertreter	représentant	representante

Italian	Portuguese (Br)	Japanese	Chinese
prodotto	produto	製品	产品
profitto, guadagno, utile	lucro(s)	利益	利润
prova di ricevimento	comprovação recebimento	領収証明書	收据证明
porposta	proposta	提案	提议
protesta, riserva, protesto	protesto	主張する	抗议
prototipo	protótipo	プロトタイプ	原型
acquisto	compra	購入する	购买
ordine d'acquisto	ordem de compra	注文書	购买定单
acquirente, compratore	comprador	購入者	买方
qualità accettabile	qualidade aceitável	合格品質	可接受质量
buona qualità	boa qualidade	良質	优质
qualità scadente	má qualidade	質が悪い	劣质
contingente doganale	cota	クォータ	限额
quotazione	cotação, cotação de preço	引用	报价
carrozza, vagone ferroviario	carro, veículo ferroviário	軌道車	机动轨道车
polizza di carico ferroviario	conhecimento de embarque ferroviário	鉄道建設法案	铁路运货单
tasso, tariffa, tassa	preço, taxa, valor, alíquota	レート	比率
aliquota doganale	alíquota de imposto, taxa alfandegária	通関料	税率
ricevuta, ricevimento	recibo, comprovante	領収書	收据
regolamento doganale	regulamentações alfandegárias	関税規則	进口税规章
rifiutare	recusar, rejeitar	拒否	拒绝
rimessa	pagamento, transferência de dinheiro	送金	汇款额
rappresentante	representante	代理人	代表

English	German	French	Spanish
request for bid	Ausschreibung	demande d'offre	petición de oferta
request for proposal (RFP)	Aufforderung zur Angebotsabgabe	demande d'offre (RFP)	petición de propuestas (RFP)
request for quotation (RFQ)	Aufforderung zur Angebotsabgabe	demande de cotation	petición de presupuesto
requirements	Bedingungen	conditions, exigences	requisitos
return, to (send back)	zurückgeben, zurücksenden	renvoyer, retourner	retornar, devolver
revenue(s)	Einkommen	revenu, rapport, recettes	ingresos, reporte
review, to	überprüfen	réviser	revisar, controlar, examinar
right	Recht, Anspruch	droit	derecho, privilegio
risk	Risiko	risque	riesgo
road waybill	Straßenfrachtbrief	feuille de voiture	conocimiento de embarque terrestre
route	Weg, Strecke	itinéraire, route	itinerario, ruta
rule(s)	Regel, Vorschrift, Norm, Bestimmung	règle, norme, principe	regla, norma, principio, artículo
sale	Verkäuf, Umsatz	vente, chiffre d'affaires	venta, compraventa
sample(s) with no commercial value	Muster ohne Wert	échantillon sans valeur commerciale	muestra(s) sin valor comercial
schedule	Fahrplan, Zeitplan	horaire, programme	horario, programa
sea	Meer	mer	mar
sea waybill	Seefrachtbrief	permis de navigation	conocimiento de embarque marítimo
seizure, customs	Pfändung, Zollbeschlagnahme	saisie douanière	embargo, confiscación en aduanas
sell	verkaufen	vendre	vender
seller	Verkäufer	vendeur	vendedor
ship	Schiff	navire	buque

KEY WORDS

Italian	Portuguese (Br)	Japanese	Chinese
sollecitare l'offerta	pedidos de ofertas ou lances	入札要求	投标要求
sollecitazione di proposta (RFP	requisição formal de proposta (RFP)	提案要求	提议要求（RFP)
sollecitazione di quotazione	requisição formal de cotação	見積依頼書	报价要求 (RFQ)
condizioni, requisiti	requisitos, necessidades	要求	需求，必要条件
rispedire, rimandare, restituire	devolver	戻る	（退还）利润
entrata(e), reddito(i)	receita(s)	収益	收入
rassegnare	revisar, estudar, examinar, pesquisar, rever	再検討する	回顾
diritto	direito, correto, privilégio	権利	权力
rischio	risco	危険	风险
lettera di trasporto stradale	conhecimento de carga rodoviária	道貨物運送状	公路运货单
itinerario, percorso	rota	輸送	路线
regola, norma	regra	ルール	规则
vendita	liquidação, promoção, venda	セール	销售
campione(i) senza valore commerciale	amostra(s) sem valor comercial	商品価値のない標本	毫无商业价值的样品
programma, orario, calendario	programação, horário, planejamento, anexo	スケジュール	时间表，进度表
mare	mar	海	海洋
lettera di trasporto via mare	conhecimento de embarque marítimo	海貨物運送状	海运单
sequestro doganale, confisca	confisco, apreensão alfandegário(a)	関税の差し押さえ	海关没收
vendire	vender	販売	出售
venditore	vendedor	売り方	卖主
nave	navio, nau	シップ	船

English	German	French	Spanish
ship, to	absenden, verschiffen	expédier	despachar, enviar
shipment	Sendung, Verschiffung	expédition, embarquement	expedición, despacho, embarque
shipper	Befrachter, Verlader, Absender	expéditeur, chargeur	expedidor, remitente, cargador, embarcador
shipper's letter of instruction	Anweisungen des Befrachters	lettre d'instruction pour le chargement	carta de instrucciones del expedidor/ embarcador
shipping company	Rederei	compagnie maritime	empresa naviera o marítima
shipping line	Reederei, Schifffahrtsgesellschaft	compagnie de navigation	compañia naviera, línea marítima
shortage	Fehlmenge, Manko	manquant	menoscabo, faltante, escasez
signature	Unterschrift	signature	firma, rúbrica
sold	verkauft	vendu	vendido
specifications	Lastenheft, Vorgaben	cahier des charges, spécifications	especificaciones, pliego de condiciones
statement	Erklärung, Ausführung, Kontoauszug	déclaration, constat, décompte, état	declaración, constancia, extracto de cuenta, estado
storage	Lagerung	stockage, entreposage	almacenamiento, almacenaje, depósito
storage charges	Lagerkosten	frais de stockage	gastos de depósito/ almacenaje
store, to	aufbewahren, lagern	stocker	almacenar, depositar
stow, to	verstauen	arrimer	arrumar, estibar, almacenar
supplier	Lieferant, Hersteller	fournisseur	proveedor, abastecedor
surcharge	Zuschlag, Aufgeld	surtaxe, surcharge	recargo, sobretasa
tariff	Tarif, Preis	tarif	tarifa, arancel
tariff schedule	Tariftabelle	barème des tarifes, liste tarifaire	indice de tarifa, arancel
tax	Steuer, Abgabe	impôt, taxe	impuesto

Italian	Portuguese (Br)	Japanese	Chinese
spedire, inviare	despachar, enviar	乗船する	装运
spedizione, invio, imbarco	carga, carregamento	出荷	装船，出货
speditore, caricatore	expedidor, despachante, transportador	荷送人	托运人，. 装货者，货主
dichiarazione dello speditore	carta de instruções do expedidor	荷送人信用指図書	托运人信函通知书
compagnia di navigazione, società di navigazione	companhia navieira	船会社	航运公司
compagnia di navigazione, linea marittima	linha de transporte marítimo	船会社	航运线
mancante, insufficienza, ammanco	falta, deficiência	不足	不足，缺乏
firma	assinatura	署名	签名
venduto	vendido	特定関税金利	特别税率
specificazioni, capitolato	especificações	仕様書	说明书，规格
dichiarazione, prospetto	declaração, demonstração, demonstrativo	決算報告	陈述，声明
magazzinaggio, stoccaggio	armazenamento	保管	存储
spese di magazzinaggio	custo de armazenamento	倉敷料	存储费用
immagazzinare, stoccare	armazenar	保管する	存储
stivare, mettere nella stiva	armazenar	積み込む	装载
fornitore	fornecedor	供給者	供给者，厂商
sovrimposta, sovrattassa	acréscimo, sobretaxa	割り増し料金	额外费
tariffa	tarifa	関税	关税
tabella della tariffa	pauta aduaneira	関税表	关税时间表
imposta, tassa	taxa, imposto	税金	税收

K E Y   W O R D S

English	German	French	Spanish
tax, value added (VAT)	Mehrwertsteuer	taxe à valeur ajoutée (TVA)	impuesto sobre el valor añadido (IVA)
telephone	Telefon	téléphone	teléfono
terms and conditions	Bedingungen	conditions	condiciones
terms of a contract	Vertragsbedingungen	clauses d'un contrat	cláusulas de un contrato
terms of payment	Zahlungsbedingungen	conditions de paiement	condiciones de pago
thank you	Danke	merci	gracias
third-party	Dritter	tiers	terceros
today	heute	aujourd'hui	hoy
tomorrow	morgen	demain	mañana
total cost	Gesamtkosten	coût total	gasto/coste total
trade barrier	Handelshemmnis	barrière douanière	arancel aduanero
trailer	Anhänger	remorque	(carro de) remolque, trailer
transaction	Transaktion, Geschäft	opération, transaction	transacción, operación, negocio
transaction value	Verkehrswert	valeur de transaction	valor de la transacción
transport	Transport	transport	transporte
transport documents	Beförderungspapiere	documents de transport	documentos de transporte
transport, air	Lufttransport	transport aérien	transporte aéreo
transport, ocean	Transport per Schiff	transport maritime	transporte marítimo, transporte transoceánico
transport, rail	Transport per Bahn	transport ferroviaire	transporte ferroviario
transport, road	Transport per LkW	transport routier	transporte por carretera
transportation	Transport	transport	transporte
under deck	unter Deck	sous pont	bajo cubierta
unit	Einheit	unité	unidad

Italian	Portuguese (Br)	Japanese	Chinese
imposta sul valore aggiunto (IVA)	imposto acrescentado ao valor (IAV)	付加価値税	増値税 (VAT)
telefono	telefone	電話	电话
termini e condizioni	termos e condições	諸条件	条款与条件
clausole contrattuali	termos de um contrato	契約条件	合同条款
condizioni di pagamento	condições, termos de pagamento	支払条件	付款条款
grazie	obrigado(a)	ありがとうございます	谢谢你
terzo	terceiro	第三者	第三方
oggi	hoje	今日	今天
domani	amanhã	明日	明天
costo totale	custo total	總原価計算	总成本
barriera agli scambi	barreira comercial	貿易障壁	贸易壁垒
rimorchio	reboque, trailer	トレーラ	拖车
transazione, operazione commerciale	transação	取引	交易，处理
valore della transazione	valor da transação	取引額	交易价值
trasporto	transporte	輸送	运输
documenti di trasporto	documentos de transporte	運送書類	运输单据
trasporto aereo	transporte aéreo	航空輸送	航空运输
trasporto oceanico	transporte marítimo	海上輸送	海洋运输
trasporti ferroviari	transporte ferroviário	鉄道輸送	轨道运输
trasporto stradale	transporte rodoviário	道路輸送	道路运输
trasporto	transporte	輸送	运输
sotto ponte	sob o deque	甲板下	在甲板下
unità	unidade	一団	单元

KEY WORDS

KEY
WORDS

English	German	French	Spanish
unit cost	Stückkosten	cout unitaire	coste unitario
unit load	Ladungseinheit	unité de charge, charge unitaire	unidad de carga, carga unitaria
unit price	Stückpreis	prix unitaire	precio unitario
valid	gültig	valable	válido, vigente
valuation	Bewertung	évaluation	tasación, valoración
value	Wert, Valuta	valeur	valor
vessel	Schiff, Dampger	navire, bateau	buque, nave, barco
vessel, container	Container-Schiff	navire porte-conteneurs	buque transportador de contenedores
vessel, ocean	Frachtschiff	navire de haute mer	buque de navegación oceánica, buque
visa	Aufenthaltserlaubnis	visa	visado
visa, consular	Aufenthaltserlaubnis	consulaire	visado consular
volume	Volumen	volume	volumen
warehouse	Lagerhaus	entrepôt, dépôt	almacén, depósito
warehouse charges	Lagerkosten	frais de magasinage	gastos de depósito
warehouse, bonded	Zollager	entrepôt en douane	almacén aduanero, depósito de aduana
warranty	Garantie, Zusicherung	garantie, autorisation	garantía, autorización
waybill	Frachtbrief	lettre de voiture, feuille de voiture	carta de porte, guia de carga
weight, gross	Bruttogewicht	poids brut	peso bruto
weight, net	Nettogewicht	poids net	peso neto
with average	mit Havarie	avec avaries	con avería
with particular average (WPA)	mit besonderer Havarie	avec avarie particulière	con avería particular
yes	ja	oui	sí

KEY WORDS

Italian	Portuguese (Br)	Japanese	Chinese
costo unitario	custo unitário	単位原価	单位成本
unità di carico, carico unitario	unidade de carga	航空貨物コンテナー	单元装载设备 (ULD)
prezzo unitario	preço unitário	単価	单价
valido, valevole	válido, vigente	有効	有效的
valutazione	avaliação	評価額	估价
valore, valuta	valor	値；価値	价值
nave	navio, embarcação	船舶	船舶
nave portacontainer	navio para (transporte de) contêineres	コンテナ船	集装箱船
nave di lungo corso, nave di linea transoceanica	navio	外航船	远洋船舶
visto	visto	査証 / ビザ	签证
visto consolare	visto consular, do consulado	領事査証	领事签证
volume	volume	容積 / 体積	体积
magazzino, deposito	depósito, armazém	倉庫	仓库
spese di immagazzinaggio	custos de armazenagem	倉庫料	仓库费
deposito/magazzino doganale	armazém alfandegado	保税倉庫	有担保的仓库
garanzia, autorizzazione	garantia	保証	保证，担保，授权
lettera di vettura, bollettino di spedizione	conhecimento de embarque	ウエービル	运货单
peso lordo	peso bruto	総重量	毛重
peso netto	peso líquido	正味重量	净重
avaria inclusa	com avaria(s)	海損担保	平均
avaria particolare inclusa	com avaria(s) particular(es)	単独海損担保	单独海损
sì	sim	はい	是

KEY WORDS

NOTES

World Airports by IATA Code

List 1 of 2:
IATA Code...Airport/location...Country

Notes

1. The following is a list of more than 10,000 three-letter IATA (International Air Transport Association) codes and their respective locations.
2. IATA codes are primarily used to identify airports, but are also used to identify transshipment, pick-up and delivery locations; cities; bus and train stations; as well as harbors and ports.
3. Approximately ten percent of these locations are major international airports. The balance are municipal and remote airfields and other locations.
4. Locations in the U.S., Canada, and Australia generally have a two-letter state or province notation (e.g., CA for California).
5. Global location codes are added, reassigned, or deleted at the rate of approximately ten to twelve per month. This list is current as of January 2002.
6. For the most up-to-date information, refer to www.iata.org.

Abbreviations

AAF	Army Air Field
AFB	Air Force Base
AFS	Air Force Station
AHP	Army Heliport
Arpt	Airport
CGS	Coast Guard Station
Cnty	County
Fld	Field
HP	Heliport
HVC	Hovercraft Terminal
Int'l	International
Is	Island
Mt	Mount
NAS	Naval Air Station
PT	Point
RR Stn.	Railway Station/Service
RAF	Royal Air Force
SPB	Sea Plane Base
Stn	Station
Svc	Service
USAF	United States Air Force

A

Code	Airport/location	Country
AAA	Anaa	F. Polynesia
AAB	Arrabury	Australia
AAC	Al Arish	Egypt
AAD	Ad-Dabbah	Sudan
AAE	Annaba	Algeria
AAF	Apalachicola Municipal, FL.	USA
AAG	Arapoti	Brazil
AAH	Aachen/Merzbruck	Germany
AAI	Arraias	Brazil
AAJ	Awaradam/Cayana Arpt	Suriname
AAK	Aranulka	Kiribati
AAL	Aalborg/Civil/Military	Denmark
AAM	Mala Mala	S. Africa
AAN	Al Ain Int'l	UAE
AAO	Anaco	Venezuela
AAP	Houston/Andrau Airpark, TX	USA
AAQ	Anaapa	Russia
AAR	Aarhus/Tirstrup	Denmark
AAS	Apalapsili	Indonesia
AAT	Altay	China
AAU	Asau	Samoa
AAV	Alah	Philippines
AAW	Abbottabad	Pakistan
AAX	Araxa	Brazil
AAY	Al Ghayclah	Yemen
AAZ	Quetzaltenanac	Guatemala
ABA	Abakan	Russia
ABB	Abingdon/RAF	UK
ABD	Abadan	Iran
ABE	Allentown/Lehigh Int'l, PA	USA
ABF	Abaiang	Kiribati
ABG	Abingdon	Australia
ABH	Alpha	Australia
ABI	Abilene Municipal, TX	USA
ABJ	Abidjan	Côte D'Ivoire
ABK	Kabri Dar	Ethiopia
ABL	Ambler, AK	USA
ABM	Barnaga	Australia
ABN	Alnina	Suriname
ABO	Aboisso	Côte D'Ivoire
ABP	Atkamba	Papua New Guinea
ABQ	Albuquerque Int'l, NM	USA
ABR	Aberdeen Municipal, SD	USA
ABS	Abu Simbel	Egypt
ABT	Al-Baha/Al-Aqiq	Saudi Arabia
ABU	Atambua	Indonesia
ABV	Abuja Int'l	Nigeria
ABW	Abau	Papua New Guinea
ABX	Albury	Australia
ABY	Albany, GA	USA
ABZ	Aberdeen/Dyce	UK
ACA	Acapulco/G. Alvarez Int'l.	Mexico
ACB	Bellaire/Antrim County, MI	USA
ACC	Accra/Kotoka	Ghana
ACD	Acandi	Colombia
ACE	Lanzarote	Spain
ACH	Altenirhein	Switzerland
ACI	Alderney	UK
ACK	Nantucket, MA	USA
ACL	Aguaclara	Colombia
ACM	Arica	Colombia
ACN	Ciudad Acuna Int'l	Mexico
ACO	Ascona	Switzerland
ACR	Araracuara	Colombia
ACS	Achinsk	Russia
ACT	Waco, TX	USA
ACU	Achutupo	Panama
ACV	Arcata, CA	USA
ACY	Atlantic City, NJ	USA
ADA	Adana/Sakirpasa	Turkey
ADB	Izmir/Adnan Menderes	Turkey
ADC	Altenburg	Germany
ADD	Addis Ababa/Bole	Ethiopia
ADE	Aden Int'l	Yemen
ADF	Adiyaman/Incirlik	Turkey
ADG	Adrian/Lenawee County, MI	USA
ADH	Aidan	Russia
ADI	Aranclis	Namibia
ADJ	Amman/Marka (Civil)	Jordan
ADK	Adak Is/NAS, AK.	USA
ADL	Adelaide	Australia
ADM	Ardmore, OK	USA
ADN	Andes	Colombia
ADO	Andamooka	Australia
ADP	Anuradhapura	Sri Lanka
ADQ	Kodiak Arpt, AK	USA
ADR	Andrews, SC	USA
ADS	Dallas, TX.	USA
ADT	Ada, OK.	USA
ADU	Arclabil	Iran
ADV	Andover	UK
ADW	Camp Springs, MD.	USA
ADX	St Andrews/Leuchars	UK
ADY	Alidays	S. Africa
ADZ	San Andres Is	Colombia
AEA	Abernama Atoll	Kiribati
AED	Aleneva, AK	USA
AEG	Aek Godang	Indonesia
AEH	Abecher	Chad
AEK	Aseki	Papua New Guinea
AEL	Albert Lea, MN	USA
AEO	Aioun El Atrouss	Mauritania
AEP	Buenos Aires/Newbery	Argentina
AER	Adler/Sochi	Russia
AES	Aalesund/Vigra	Norway
AET	Allakaket, AK	USA
AEX	Alexandria, LA.	USA
AEY	Akureyri	Iceland
AFA	San Rafael	Argentina
AFD	Port Alfred	S. Africa
AFF	Colorado Springs, USAF Academy, CO	USA
AFI	Amalfi	Colombia
AFL	Alta Floresta	Brazil
AFN	Jaffrey/Municipal, NH	USA
AFO	Afton/Municipal, WY	USA
AFR	Afore	Papua New Guinea
AFT	Afutara/Atutara	Solomon Is
AFW	Dallas/Fort Worth, TX	USA
AFY	Afyon	Turkey
AGA	Agadir/Agadir Almassira	Morocco
AGB	Augsburg, Muehlhausen	Germany
AGC	Pittsburgh/Allegheny, PA	USA
AGD	Anggi	Indonesia
AGE	Wangerooge/Fluglplatz	Germany
AGF	Agen/La Garenne	France
AGG	Angorarn	Papua New Guinea
AGH	Helsingborg	Sweden

AIRPORTS

Code	Location	Country
AGI	Wageningen	Suriname
AGJ	Aguni	Japan
AGK	Kagua	Papua New Guinea
AGL	Wanigela	Papua New Guinea
AGM	Tasiilaq	Greenland
AGN	Angoon, AK	USA
AGO	Magnolia/Municipal, AK	USA
AGP	Malaga	Spain
AGQ	Agrinion	Greece
AGR	Agra/Kheria	India
AGS	Augusta, GA	USA
AGT	Ciudad del Este	Paraguay
AGU	Aguascalientes	Mexico
AGV	Acarigua	Venezuela
AGW	Agnew	Australia
AGX	Agatti Is.	India
AGY	Argyle Downs	Australia
AGZ	Aggeneys	S. Africa
AHA	Okinawa/Naha AFB	Japan
AHB	Ablitia	Saudi Arabia
AHC	Amedee/AAF, CA	USA
AHD	Ardmore/Downtown, OK	USA
AHE	Ahe	F. Polynesia
AHF	Arapahoe/Municipal, NE	USA
AHH	Amery/Municipal, WI	USA
AHI	Amahai	Indonesia
AHL	Aishaiton	Guyana
AHN	Athens, GA.	USA
AHO	Alghero	Italy
AHS	Ahuas	Honduras
AHT	Amchitka, AK	USA
AHU	Al Hoceima	Morocco
AHY	Ambatolahy	Madagascar
AHZ	Alpe D Huez	France
AIA	Alliance, NE	USA
AIB	Anita Bay, AK	USA
AIC	Airok	Marshall Is
AID	Anderson/Municipal, IN	USA
AIE	Aiome	Papua New Guinea
AIF	Assis	Brazil
AIG	Yalinga	Central African Rep
AII	Alisabieh	Djibouti
AIK	Aiken/Municipal, SC	USA
AIL	Ailigandi	Panama
AIM	Ailuk Is	Marshall Is
AIN	Wainwright, AK	USA
AIO	Atlantic, IA	USA
AIP	Ailinglapalap Is	Marshall Is
AIR	Aripuana	Brazil
AIS	Arorae Is	Kiribati
AIT	Aitutaki	Cook Is
AIU	Atiu Is	Cook Is
AIV	Aliceville, AL	USA
AIW	Ai-Ais	Namibia
AIY	Atlantic City/Bader Field, NJ	USA
AIZ	Kaiser/Lake Ozark, MO	USA
AJA	Ajaccio/Campo Dell Oro	France
AJF	Jouf	Saudi Arabia
AJI	Agri/Agri	Turkey
AJJ	Akioujt	Mauritania
AJL	Aizawi	India
AJN	Anjouan/Ouant	Comoros
AJO	Aljouf	Yemen
AJR	Arvidsiaur	Sweden
AJS	Abreojos	Mexico
AJU	Aracap	Brazil
AJY	Agades/Manu Dayak	Niger
AKA	Ankang	China
AKB	Atka, AK	USA
AKC	Akron/Fulton Int'l, OH	USA
AKD	Akola	India
AKE	Akieni	Gabon
AKF	Kufrah	Libya
AKG	Anguganak	Papua New Guinea
AKH	Gastonia, NC	USA
AKI	Akiak, AK	USA
AKJ	Asahikawa/Akhiolk SPB	Japan
AKK	Akhiok, AK	USA
AKL	Auckland	New Zealand
AKM	Zakouma	Chad
AKN	King Salmon, AK	USA
AKO	Akron, CO	USA
AKP	Anaktuvuk, AK	USA
AKQ	Astraksetra	Indonesia
AKR	Akure	Nigeria
AKS	Auki/Gwaunaru'u	Solomon Is
AKT	Akrotiri	Cyprus
AKU	Aksu	China
AKV	Akulivik, QC	Canada
AKW	Klawock, AK	USA
AKX	Aktyubinsk	Kazakstan
AKY	Sittwe/Civil	Myanmar
ALA	Almaty	Kazakstan
ALB	Albany, NY	USA
ALC	Alicante	Spain
ALD	Alerta	Peru
ALE	Alpine, TX	USA
ALF	Alta/Lufthavn	Norway
ALG	Algiers-Houari Boumediene	Algeria
ALH	Albany	Australia
ALI	Alice, TX	USA
ALJ	Alexander Bay/Koftdoorn	S. Africa
ALK	Asela	Ethiopia
ALL	Albenga	Italy
ALM	Alamogordo, NM	USA
ALN	Alton, IL	USA
ALO	Waterloo, IA	USA
ALP	Aleppo/Nejrab	Syria
ALQ	Alegrete/Federal	Brazil
ALR	Alexandra	New Zealand
ALS	Alamosa, CO	USA
ALT	Alenquer	Brazil
ALU	Alula	Somalia
ALV	Andorra La Vella	Andorra
ALW	Walla Walla, WA	USA
ALX	Alexander City, AL	USA
ALY	Alexandria/Nouzha	Egypt
ALZ	Alitak/SPB, AK	USA
AMA	Amarillo, TX.	USA
AMB	Ambilobe	Madagascar
AMC	Am Timan	Chad
AMD	Ahmadabad	India
AME	Alto Molocue	Mozambique
AMF	Ama	Papua New Guinea
AMG	Amboin	Papua New Guinea
AMH	Arba Mintch	Ethiopia
AMI	Mataram/Selaparang	Indonesia
AMJ	Almenara	Brazil
AMK	Durango/Animas Airpark, CO	USA
AML	Puerto Armuellas	Panama
AMM	Amman/Queen Alia Int'l	Jordan
AMN	Alma/Gratiot Com Municipality, MI	USA
AMO	Mao	Chad
AMP	Ampanihy	Madagascar
AMQ	Ambon/Pattimura	Indonesia
AMR	Arno	Marshall Is
AMS	Amsterdam/Schiphol	Netherlands
AMT	Amata	Australia
AMU	Amanab	Papua New Guinea
AMV	Amderma	Russia
AMW	Ames, IA	USA
AMX	Ammaroo	Australia
AMY	Ambatomainty	Madagascar
AMZ	Ardmore	New Zealand
ANA	Anaheim, CA	USA
ANB	Anniston, AL	USA
ANC	Anchorage Int'l, AK	USA
AND	Anderson, SC	USA
ANE	Angers/Marce.	France
ANF	Antofagasta/Cerro Moreno	Chile
ANG	Angouleme	France
ANH	Anuha Is	Solomon Is
ANI	Aniak, AK	USA
ANJ	Zanaga	Congo, DR
ANK	Ankara/Etimesgut	Turkey
ANL	Andulo	Angola
ANM	Antalaha/Antsirabato	Madagascar
ANN	Annette Is, AK	USA
ANO	Angoche	Mozambique
ANP	Annapolis/Lee, MD	USA
ANQ	Angola, IN	USA
ANR	Antwerp/Deurne	Belgium
ANS	Andahuaylas	Peru
ANT	St Anton	Austria
ANU	V.C. Bird Int'l	Antigua & Barbuda
ANV	Anvik, AK	USA
ANW	Ainsworth, NE	USA
ANX	Andenes	Norway
ANY	Anthony, KS.	USA
ANZ	Angus Downs	Australia
AOA	Aroa	Papua New Guinea
AOB	Annanberg	Papua New Guinea
AOD	Abou Deia	Chad
AOE	Eskisehir/Anadolu Univ.	Turkey
AOG	Anshan.	China
AOH	Lima, OH	USA
AOI	Ancona/Falconara	Italy
AOJ	Aomori	Japan
AOK	Karpathos	Greece
AOL	Paso De Los Libres	Argentina
AON	Arona	Papua New Guinea
AOO	Altoona, PA	USA
AOR	Mor Setar	Malaysia
AOS	Amook, AK	USA
AOT	Aosta/Corrado Gex	Italy
AOU	Attopeu	Laos
APA	Denver, CO	USA
APB	Apolo	Bolivia
APC	Napa, CA.	USA
APE	San Juan Aposento	Peru
APF	Naples, FL	USA
APG	Aberdeen, MD	USA
APH	Bowling Green, VA	USA
API	Apiay	Colombia
APK	Apataki	F. Polynesia
APL	Nampula	Mozambique
APN	Alpena, MI	USA
APO	Apartacto	Colombia
APP	Asapa	Papua New Guinea
APQ	Arapiraca	Brazil
APR	April River	Papua New Guinea
APS	Anapolis.	Brazil
APT	Jasper/Marion County, TN	USA
APU	Apucarana	Brazil
APV	Apple Valley, CA	USA
APW	Apia/Faleolo	Samoa
APX	Arapongas	Brazil
APY	Alto Parnatiba	Brazil
APZ	Zapala	Argentina
AQA	Araraquara	Brazil
AQB	Quiche/Quiche Arpt	Guatemala
AQG	Anqing	China
AQI	Qaisumah	Saudi Arabia
AQJ	Aqaba	Jordan
AQM	Ariquernes	Brazil
AQP	Arequipa/Rodriguez Ballon	Peru
AQQ	Apalachicola, FL.	USA
AQS	Saqani	Fiji
AQY	Alyeska, AK.	USA
ARA	New Iberia, LA	USA
ARB	Ann Arbor, MI	USA
ARC	Arctic Village, AK	USA
ARD	Alor Is	Indonesia
ARE	Arecilbo	Puerto Rico
ARF	Acaricuara	Colombia
ARG	Walnut Ridge, AR	USA
ARH	Arkhan,elsk	Russia
ARI	Anica/Chacalluta	Chile
ARJ	Arso	Indonesia
ARK	Arusha	Tanzania
ARL	Arty	Burkina Faso
ARM	Armidale	Australia
ARN	Stockholm/Arlanda	Sweden
ARO	Arboletas	Colombia
ARP	Aragip	Papua New Guinea
ARQ	Arauquita	Colombia

ARR	Alto Rio Senguerr	Argentina
ARS	Aragarcas	Brazil
ART	Watertown, NY	USA
ARU	Aracatuba	Brazil
ARV	Minocqua, WI.	USA
ARW	Arad	Romania
ARX	Asbury Park, NJ.	USA
ARY	Ararat	Australia
ARZ	N'Zeto	Angola
ASA	Assab	Eritrea
ASB	Ashgabat	Turkmenistan
ASC	Ascension	Bolivia
ASD	Andros Town	Bahamas
ASE	Aspen, CO	USA
ASF	Astrakhan	Russia
ASG	Ashburton	New Zealand
ASH	Nashua, NH	USA
ASI	Georgetown	St. Helena
ASJ	Amami O Shima	Japan
ASK	Yamoussoukro	Côte D'ivoire
ASL	Marshall, TX	USA
ASM	Asmara Int'l	Eritrea
ASN	Talladega, AL	USA
ASO	Asosa	Ethiopia
ASP	Alice Springs	Australia
ASQ	Austin, NV.	USA
ASR	Kayseri	Turkey
AST	Astoria, OR.	USA
ASU	Asuncion/Silvio Pettirossi	Paraguay
ASV	Amboseli	Kenya
ASW	Aswan	Egypt
ASX	Ashland, WI	USA
ASY	Ashley, ND	USA
ASZ	Asirim	Papua New Guinea
ATA	Anta	Peru
ATB	Atbara	Seychelles
ATC	Arthur's Town	Bahamas
ATD	Atoifi	Solomon Is
ATE	Antlers, OK.	USA
ATF	Ambato/Chachoan	Ecuador
ATG	Attock	Pakistan
ATH	Athens-Eleftherios Venizelos Int'l	Greece
ATI	Artigas	Uruguay
ATJ	Antsirabe	Madagascar
ATK	Atqasuk, AK	USA
ATL	Atlanta/Hartsfield, GA	USA
ATM	Altamira	Brazil
ATN	Namatanai	Papua New Guinea
ATO	Athens/Ohio University, OH	USA
ATP	Aitape/Airstrip	Papua New Guinea
ATQ	Amritsar/Raja Sansi	India
ATR	Atar/Mouakchott	Mauritania
ATS	Artesia, NM	USA
ATT	Atmautluak, AK	USA
ATU	Attu Is/Casco Cove, AK	USA
ATV	Ati	Chad
ATW	Appleton, WI	USA
ATX	Atbasar	Kazakhstan
ATY	Watertown, SD	USA
ATZ	Assiut	Egypt
AUA	Aruba/Reina Beatrix	Aruba
AUB	Itauba	Brazil
AUC	Arauca	Colombia
AUD	Augustus Downs	Australia
AUE	Abu Rudeis	Egypt
AUF	Auxerre/Auxerre Branches	France
AUG	Augusta, ME	USA
AUH	Abu Dhabi Int'l	UAE
AUI	Aua Is	Papua New Guinea
AUJ	Ambunti	Papua New Guinea
AUK	Alakanuk, AK	USA
AUL	Aur Is	Marshall Is
AUM	Austin, MN	USA
AUN	Auburn, CA	USA
AUO	Auburn, AL.	USA
AUP	Agaun	Papua New Guinea
AUQ	Atuona	F. Polynesia

AUR	Aurillac	France
AUS	Austin, TX	USA
AUT	Atauro	Indonesia
AUU	Aurukun Mission	Australia
AUV	Aurno.	Papua New Guinea
AUW	Wausau, WI.	USA
AUX	Araguaina	Brazil
AUY	Aneityum	Vanuatu
AUZ	Aurora/Municipal, IL.	USA
AVB	Aviano	Italy
AVF	Avoriaz	France
AVG	Auvergne	Australia
AVI	Ciego De Avila	Cuba
AVK	Arvaikheer	Mongolia
AVL	Asheville/Municipal, NC	USA
AVN	Avignon/Avignon-Caum	France
AVO	Avon Park/Municipal, FL	USA
AVP	Scranton, OH	USA
AVU	Avu Avu	Solomon Is
AVV	Avalon	Australia
AVW	Tucson/Avra Valley, AZ	USA
AVX	Avalon, CA	USA
AWA	Awassa	Ethiopia
AWB	Awaba	Papua New Guinea
AWD	Aniwa	Vanuatu
AWE	Alowe	Gabon
AWG	Washington, IA	USA
AWH	Awareh	Ethiopia
AWI	Wainwright, AK	USA
AWK	Wake Is	Wake/Midway Is
AWM	W Memphis/Municipal, AR	USA
AWN	Afton Downs	Australia
AWO	Arlington, WA	USA
AWP	Austral Downs	Australia
AWR	Awar	Papua New Guinea
AWZ	Ahwaz	Iran
AXA	Anguilla/Wallblake	Anguilla
AXB	Alexandria Bay, NY	USA
AXC	Aramac	Australia
AXD	Alexandroupolis-Demokritos	Greece
AXE	Xanxere	Brazil
AXG	Algona, IA	USA
AXK	Ataq	Yemen
AXL	Alexandria	Australia
AXM	Armenia/El Eden	Colombia
AXN	Alexandria, MN.	USA
AXP	Spring Point	Bahamas
AXR	Arutua	F. Polynesia
AXS	Altus/Municipal, OK	USA
AXT	Akita.	Japan
AXU	Axurn	Ethiopia
AXV	Wapakoneta/Armstrong, OH	USA
AXX	Angel Fire, NM	USA
AYA	Ayapel	Colombia
AYC	Ayacucho	Colombia
AYD	Alroy Downs	Australia
AYE	Fort Devens, MA	USA
AYG	Yaguara	Colombia
AYH	Alconbury/RAF	UK
AYI	Yan.	Colombia
AYK	Arkalyk.	Kazakhstan
AYL	Anthony Lagoon	Australia
AYN	Anyang	China
AYO	Ayoias	Paraguay
AYP	Ayacucho/Yanamilla	Peru
AYQ	Ayers Rock/COnnellan	Australia
AYR	Ayr	Australia
AYS	Waycross/Ware County, GA	USA
AYT	Antalya	Turkey
AYU	Aiyura	Papua New Guinea
AYW	Ayawasi	Indonesia
AYZ	Amityville/Zahns, NY	USA
AZB	Amazon Bay	Papua New Guinea
AZD	Yazd.	Iran
AZG	Apatzingan	Mexico
AZI	Abu Dhalbi/Bateen	UAE
AZN	Andizhan.	Uzbekistan
AZO	Kalamazoo, MI	USA
AZP	Mexico City/Atizapan	Mexico

AZR	Adrar	Algeria
AZT	Zapatoca	Colombia
AZZ	Ambriz	Andorra

B

BAA	Bialla	Papua New Guinea
BAB	Beale/AFB, CA	USA
BAC	Barranca De Upia	Colombia
BAD	Barksdale/AFB, LA	USA
BAE	Barcelonnette	France
BAF	Westfield/Barnes, MA	USA
BAG	Baguic,/Loakan	Philippines
BAH	Bahrain/Int'l	Bahrain
BAI	Buenos Aires	Costa Rica
BAJ	Bali	Papua New Guinea
BAK	Baku	Azerbaijan
BAL	Batman	Turkey
BAM	Battle Mountain, NV	USA
BAN	Basongo	Congo, DR
BAO	Ban Mak Khaen/Udorn	Thailand
BAP	Baibara	Papua New Guinea
BAQ	Barranquilla/E Cortissoz	Colombia
BAR	Baker/AAF, AK	USA
BAS	Balalae	Solomon Is
BAT	Barretos	Brazil
BAU	Bauru	Brazil
BAV	Baotou	China
BAW	Biawonque	Gabon
BAX	Barnaul	Russia
BAY	Baia Mare	Romania
BAZ	Barbelos	Brazil
BBA	Balmaceda/Teniente Vicial	Chile
BBB	Benson/Municipal, MN.	USA
BBC	Bay City, TX	USA
BBD	Brady/Curtis Fld, TX	USA
BBE	Big Bell	Australia
BBF	Burlington, MA	USA
BBG	Butaritari	kiribati
BBH	Barth	Germany
BBI	Bhubaneswar	India
BBJ	Bitiburg Air Base	Germany
BBK	Kasane	Botswana
BBL	Babolsar	Iran
BBM	Battambang	Cambodia
BBN	Bario	Malaysia
BBO	Berbera	Somalia
BBP	Bembridge	UK
BBQ	Barbuda	Antigua & Barbuda
BBR	Basse Terre/Baillif	Gaudeloupe
BBS	Blackbushe	UK
BBT	Berberati	Central African Rep
BBU	Bucharest/Baneasa	Romania
BBV	Bereby	Côte D'Ivoire
BBW	Broken Bow Municipal, NE	USA
BBX	Blue Bell/Wings Fld, PA	USA
BBY	Bambari	Central African Rep
BBZ	Zambezi	Zambia
BCA	Baracoa	Cuba
BCB	Virginia Tech Arpt, VA	USA
BCC	Bear Creek, AK	USA
BCD	Bacolod	Philippines
BCE	Bryce Canyon, UT	USA
BCF	Bouca	Central African Rep
BCG	Bemichi	Guyana
BCH	Baucau/English Madeira	Indonesia
BCI	Barcaidine	Australia
BCJ	Baca Grande, CO	USA
BCK	Bolwarra	Australia
BCL	Barra Colorado	Costa Rica
BCM	Bacau	Romania
BCN	Barcelona	Spain
BCO	Jinka	Ethiopia
BCP	Bambu	Papua New Guinea
BCQ	Brack	Libya
BCR	Boca Do Acre	Brazil

A I R P O R T S

Code	Location
BCS	Belle Chasse/Southern Seaplane, LA . . . . USA
BCT	Boca Raton/Public, FL . . . . . USA
BCU	Bauchi . . . . Nigeria
BCV	Belmopan. . . . . Belize
BCW	Benguera Is . . . . Mozambique
BCX	Beloreck . . . . Russia
BCY	Buichi . . . . Ethiopia
BCZ	Bickerton Is . . . . Australia
BDA	Hamilton/Int'l. . . . . Bermuda
BDB	Bundaberg . . . . Australia
BDC	Barra Do COrda . . . . Brazil
BDD	Badu Is . . . . Australia
BDE	Baudette/Int'l, MN . . . . USA
BDF	Bradford/Rinkenberg, IL . . . . USA
BDG	Blanding, UT . . . . USA
BDH	Bandar Lengeh . . . . Iran
BDI	Bird Is . . . . Seychelles
BDJ	Banjarmasin/Sjamsudin Noor . . . . Indonesia
BDK	Bondoukou/Soko . . . Côte D'Ivoire
BDL	Hartford/Bradley Int'l, CT . . . USA
BDM	Bandirma . . . . Turkey
BDN	Badin/Talhar . . . . Pakistan
BDO	Bandung/Husein Sastranegara . . . . Indonesia
BDP	Elhadrapur . . . . Nepal
BDQ	Vadodara . . . . India
BDR	Bridgeport/Sikorsky Memorial, CT . . . . USA
BDS	Brindisi/Papola Casale . . . . . Italy
BDT	Gbadolite . . . . Congo, DR
BDU	Bardufoss . . . . Norway
BDV	Moba . . . . Congo, DR
BDW	Bedford Downs . . . . Australia
BDX	Broadus, MT . . . . USA
BDY	Bandon/State, OR . . . . USA
BDZ	Baindoung . . Papua New Guinea
BEA	Bereina . . . . . Papua New Guinea
BEB	Benbecula . . . . UK
BEC	Wichita, KS. . . . . USA
BED	Bedford/Hanscom Fld, MA . USA
BEE	Beagle Bay . . . . Australia
BEF	Bluefields . . . . Netherlands
BEG	Belgrade/Becigrad . . . Yugoslavia
BEH	Benton Harbor/Ross Fld, MI. USA
BEI	Beica. . . . . Ethiopia
BEJ	Berau . . . . Indonesia
BEK	careh. . . . . India
BEL	Belem/Val De Cans . . . . . . Brazil
BEN	Benghazi/Benina Intl . . . . . . Libya
BEO	Newcastle/Belmont . . . . Australia
BEP	Beliary. . . . . India
BEQ	Bury St Edmunds/Honington . UK
BES	Brest/Guipavas . . . . France
BET	Bethel, AK . . . . USA
BEU	Bedourie. . . . . Australia
BEV	Beer Sheba . . . . Israel
BEW	Beira . . . . Mozambique
BEX	Benson/RAF. . . . . UK
BEY	Beirut/Int'l . . . . Lebanon
BEZ	Beru . . . . Kiribati
BFB	Blue Fox Bay, AK. . . . . USA
BFC	Bloomfield . . . . Australia
BFD	Bradford, PA. . . . . USA
BFE	Bielefeid . . . . Germany
BFF	Scottsbluff, Heilig Fld, NE . . . USA
BFG	Bullfrog Basin, UT . . . . USA
BFH	Curitiba./Bacacher; . . . . . . Brazil
BFI	Seattle, Boeing Fld, WA . . . . USA
BFJ	Ba . . . . Fiji
BFK	Denver/Buckley ANGB, CO . USA
BFL	Bakersfield/Meadows Fld, CA . . . . USA
BFM	Mobile/Dwntwn Arpt, AL. . . . USA
BFN	Bloemfontein Int'l . . . . South Africa
BFO	Buffalo Range . . . . Zimbabwe
BFP	Beaver Falls Arpt, PA . . . . . USA
BFQ	Bahia Pinas . . . . Panama
BFR	Bedford, IN. . . . . USA
BFS	Belfast/Belfast Int'l Arpt . . . . UK

Code	Location
BFT	Beaufort/County, SC . . . . . . USA
BFU	Bengbu . . . . China
BFV	Buri Ram . . . . Thailand
BFW	Silver Bay, MN . . . . USA
BFX	Bafoussarn . . . . Cameroon
BFZ	Bedford/Thurleigh (Military). . UK
BGA	Bucaramanga/Palo Negro . . . . Colombia
BGB	Booue . . . . Gabon
BGC	Braganca . . . . Portugal
BGD	Hutchinson County Arpt, TX . USA
BGE	Bainbridge/Decatur County, GA . . . . USA
BGF	Bangui . . . . Central African Rep
BGG	Bongouanou. . . . . Chile
BGH	Boghe/Abbaye. . . . . . . Mauritania
BGI	Bridgetown/Grantley Adams Int'l . . . . Barbados
BGJ	Borgarfiordur Eystri . . . . . Iceland
BGK	Big Creek . . . . Belize
BGL	Baglung . . . . Nepal
BGM	Binghamton, NY. . . . . USA
BGN	Brueggen/R.A.F. . . . . . . Germany
BGO	Bergen/Flesland . . . . Norway
BGP	Bongo . . . . Gabon
BGQ	Big Lake, AK. . . . . USA
BGR	Bangor Int'l Arpt, ME . . . . . . USA
BGS	Big Spring, Webb/AFB, TX . USA
BGT	Bagdad, AZ . . . . USA
BGU	Bangassou . . Central African Rep
BGV	Bento Goncalves . . . . Brazil
BGW	Baghdad/Al Muthana . . . . . . Iraq
BGX	Bage . . . . Brazil
BGY	Milan/Milano/Ono Al Serio. . . Italy
BGZ	Braga. . . . . Portugal
BHA	Bahia De Caraquez . . . . Ecuador
BHB	Bar Harbour, ME. . . . . USA
BHC	Bhurban/Bhurban HP . . . Pakistan
BHD	Belfast/Belfast City Arpt . . . . . UK
BHE	Blenheim. . . . . New Zealand
BHF	Bahia Cupica . Cocos (Keeling) Is
BHG	Brus Laguna . . . . Honduras
BHH	Bisha . . . . Saudi Arabia
BHI	Bahia Blanca/Comandante . . . . Argentina
BHJ	Bhuj/Rudra Mata . . . . India
BHK	Bukhara. . . . . Uzbekistan
BHL	Bahla Angeles . . . . Mexico
BHM	Birmingham/Int'l, AL. . . . . . . USA
BHN	Beinan. . . . . Yemen
BHO	Bhopal. . . . . India
BHP	Bhojpur . . . . Nepal
BHQ	Broken Hill. . . . . Australia
BHR	Bharatpur . . . . Nepal
BHS	Bathurst/Raglan . . . . Australia
BHT	Brighton Downs . . . . Australia
BHU	Bhavnagar . . . . India
BHV	Bahawaipur . . . . Pakistan
BHW	Sargodha/Bhagatanwala . . . . Pakistan
BHX	Birmingham/Int'l . . . . UK
BHY	Beil-tai . . . . China
BIA	Bastia/Poretta . . . . France
BIB	Baidoa . . . . Somalia
BIC	Big Creek, AK. . . . . USA
BID	Block Is, RI . . . . USA
BIE	Beatrice, NE . . . . USA
BIF	Biggs/AAF, TX. . . . . USA
BIG	Big Delta/Intermediate Fld, AK . . . . USA
BIH	Bishop, CA . . . . USA
BII	Bikini Atoll/Enyu Airfield . . . . Marshall Is
BIJ	Biliau . . . . . . Papua New Guinea
BIK	Biak/Mokmer . . . . . . Indonesia
BIL	Billings/Int'l, MT. . . . . USA
BIM	Bimini/Int'l . . . . Bahamas
BIN	Bamiyan . . . . Afghanistan
BIO	Bilbao . . . . Spain
BIP	Bulimba . . . . Australia
BIQ	Biarritz/Biarritz Parme . . . . France

Code	Location
BIR	Biratnagar . . . . Nepal
BIS	Bismarck, ND . . . . USA
BIT	Baitadi . . . . Nepal
BIU	Bildudalur . . . . Iceland
BIV	Bria. . . . . Costa Rica
BIW	Billiluna. . . . . Australia
BIX	Keesler/AFB, MS. . . . . USA
BIY	Bisho . . . . South Africa
BIZ	Bimin . . . . . . Papua New Guinea
BJA	Bejaia . . . . Algeria
BJB	Bopord. . . . . Iran
BJC	Broomfield/Jeffco, CO . . . . . USA
BJD	Bakkafjordur . . . . Iceland
BJF	Batsfjord. . . . . Norway
BJG	Bolaang . . . . Indonesia
BJH	Bajhang . . . . Nepal
BJI	Bemidji, MN. . . . . USA
BJJ	Wooster/Wayne Cnty. Arpt, OH . . . . USA
BJK	Berijina . . . . Indonesia
BJL	Banjul/Yundum Int'l . The Gambia
BJM	Bujumbura/Int'l . . . . Burundi
BJN	Bajone . . . . Mozambique
BJO	Bermejo . . . . Bolivia
BJP	Braganca Paulista . . . . Brazil
BJR	Bahar Dar . . . . Ethiopia
BJU	Bajura Arpt . . . . Nepal
BJV	Bodrum./Milas Arpt. . . . . . . Turkey
BJW	Bajawa. . . . . Indonesia
BJX	Lecin/Guanajuato/Del Bajic . . . . Mexico
BJY	Belgrade/Batapica . . . Yugoslavia
BJZ	Baclajoz/Talaveral La Real . Spain
BKA	Moscow/Bykovo . . . . Russia
BKB	Bikaner. . . . . India
BKC	Buckland, AK. . . . . USA
BKD	Breckenridge/Stephens Cnty., TX . . . . USA
BKE	Baker/Baker Mncpl Arpt, OR, ... USA
BKF	Brooks Lake, AK. . . . . USA
BKH	Kekaha/Barking Sands, HI . USA
BKI	Kota Kinabalu . . . . Malaysia
BKJ	Boke. . . . . Guinea
BKK	Bangkok/Int'l . . . . Thailand
BKL	Cleveland, Burke Arpt, OH . USA
BKM	Bakalalan. . . . . Malaysia
BKN	Birni Nkoni . . . . Niger
BKO	Bamako . . . . Mali
BKP	Barkly Downs . . . . Australia
BKQ	Blackall . . . . Australia
BKR	Bokoro . . . . Chad
BKS	Bengkulu/Padangkemiling . . . . Indonesia
BKT	Blackstone/AAF, VA . . . . . . USA
BKU	Betioky . . . . Madagascar
BKV	Brooksville, FL. . . . . USA
BKW	Beckley, WV . . . . USA
BKX	Brookings, SD . . . . USA
BKY	Bukavu/Kamenbe . . . . Congo, DR
BKZ	Bukoba . . . . Tanzania
BLA	Barcelona . . . . Venezuela
BLB	Balboa . . . . Panama
BLC	Bali . . . . Cameroon
BLD	Boulder City, CO . . . . USA
BLE	Boriange/Dala . . . . Sweden
BLF	Bluefield, Mercer County Arpt, WV . . . . USA
BLG	Belaga . . . . Malaysia
BLH	Blythe Arpt, CA . . . . USA
BLI	Bellingham/Int'l Arpt, WA . . . USA
BLJ	Batna . . . . Algeria
BLK	Blackpool. . . . . UK
BLL	Billund/Lufthavn . . . . . . Denmark
BLM	Belmar-Farmdale, NJ . . . . . USA
BLN	Benalla . . . . Australia
BLO	Blonduos . . . . Iceland
BLP	Bellavista . . . . Peru
BLQ	Bologna/Gugllelmo Marconi . Italy
BLR	Bangalore,/Hindustan . . . . . India
BLS	Bollon. . . . . Australia

BLT .. Blackwater ... Australia
BLU .. Blue Canyon, CA ... USA
BLV .. Scott/AFB, IL ... USA
BLW .. Waimanalo/Bellows Fld, HI .. USA
BLX .. Belluno ... Italy
BLY .. Belmullet ... Ireland
BLZ .. Blantyre/Chileka ... Malawi
BMA . Stockholm/Bromma ... Sweden
BMB . Bumba ... Congo, DR
BMC . Brigham City, UT ... USA
BMD . Belo ... Madagascar
BME . Broome ... Australia
BMF .. Bakourna ... Central African Rep
BMG . Bloomington, IN ... USA
BMH . Bomai ... Papua New Guinea
BMI .. Bloomington/Normal, IL ... USA
BMJ .. Baramita ... Guyana
BMK . Borkum ... Germany
BML .. Berlin Municipal Arpt, NH ... USA
BMM . Bitam ... Gabon
BMN . Bamerny ... Iraq
BMO . Bhamo ... Myanmar
BMP . Brampton Is ... Australia
BMQ . Bamburi ... Kenya
BMR . Baitrum ... Germany
BMS . Brumado ... Brazil
BMT .. Beaumont/Municipal, TX ... USA
BMU . Bima ... Indonesia
BMV . Banmethuot/Phung-Duc . Vietnam
BMW . Bordj Badji Mokintar ... Algeria
BMX . Big Mountain, AK ... USA
BMY . Belep Is ... New Caledonia
BMZ .. Bamu ... Papua New Guinea
BNA .. Nashville/Int'l, TN ... USA
BNB .. Boende ... Congo, DR
BNC .. Beni ... Congo, DR
BND .. Bandar Abbas ... Iran
BNE .. Brisbane/Int'l ... Australia
BNF .. Warm Spring Bay/SPB, AK . USA
BNG . Banning, CA ... USA
BNH .. Hartford/Barnes, CT ... USA
BNI ... Benin City ... Nigeria
BNJ .. Cologne/Bann/Off-line Pt ... Germany
BNK .. Ballina ... Australia
BNL .. Barnwell, SC ... USA
BNM . Bodinumu ... Papua New Guinea
BNN .. Bronnoysund/Bronnoy .. Norway
BNO . Burns Municipal Arpt, OR ... USA
BNP .. Bannu ... Pakistan
BNQ . Baganga ... Philippines
BNR .. Banfora ... Burkina Faso
BNS .. Barinas ... Venezuela
BNT .. Bundi ... Papua New Guinea
BNU .. Biumenau ... Brazil
BNV .. Boana ... Papua New Guinea
BNW . Boone Municipal, IA ... USA
BNX .. Banja Luka . .Bosnia Hercegovina
BNY .. Bellona ... Solomon Is
BNZ .. Banz ... Papua New Guinea
BOA .. Boma ... Congo, DR
BOB . Bora Bora/Motu-mute F. Polynesia
BOC . Bocas Del Tore, ... Panama
BOD . Bordeaux/Merignac ... France
BOE .. Boundji ... Congo, DR
BOF .. Bolling/AFB, DC ... USA
BOG . Bogota/Eldorado ... Colombia
BOH . Bournemouth/Int'l ... UK
BOI .. Boise, Boise Air Terminal, ID ... USA
BOJ .. Bourgas ... Bulgaria
BOK . Brookings, OR ... USA
BOL .. Bally Kelly ... UK
BOM . Mumbai ... India
BON . Bonaire/Int'l. Netherlands Antilles
BOO . Bodo ... Norway
BOP .. Bouar ... Central African Rep
BOQ . Boku ... Papua New Guinea
BOR . Belfort/Fontaine ... France
BOS .. Boston/Logan Int'l, MA ... USA
BOT .. Boset ... Papua New Guinea
BOU .. Bourges ... France
BOV .. Boang ... Papua New Guinea
BOW . Bartow Municipal, FL ... USA
BOX .. Borroloola ... Australia
BOY .. Bobo Dioulasso/Borgo ... Burkina Faso
BOZ .. Bozoum ... Central African Rep
BPA .. Bethpage/Grumman, NY ... USA
BPB .. Boridi ... Papua New Guinea
BPC .. Bamenda ... Cameroon
BPD .. Bapi ... Papua New Guinea
BPE .. Bagan ... Myanmar
BPF .. Batuna Aerodrome .. Solomon Is
BPG .. Barra Do Garcas ... Brazil
BPH .. Bislig ... Philippines
BPI ... Big Piney, WY ... USA
BPK .. Mountain Home, AR ... USA
BPN .. Balikipapan/Sepingan . Indonesia
BPS .. Porto Seguro ... Brazil
BPT .. Beaumont, TX ... USA
BPU .. Beppu ... Japan
BPX .. Bangda ... China
BPY .. Besalampy ... Madagascar
BQA .. Baler ... Philippines
BQB .. Busselton/Busselton Arpt ... Australia
BQE .. Bubaque ... Guinea Bissau
BQH .. London/Biggin Hill ... UK
BQI ... Bagani ... Namibia
BQK .. Brunswick/Glynco, GA ... USA
BQL .. Boulia ... Australia
BQN .. Aguadilla/Borinquen . Puerto Rico
BQO .. Bouna/Tehini ... Côte D'Ivoire
BQQ .. Barra ... Brazil
BQS .. Blagoveschensk ... Russia
BQT .. Brest ... Belarus
BQU .. Bequia Arpt ... St. Vincent & Grenadines
BQV .. Gustavus/Bartlett SPB, AK .. USA
BQW . Balgo Hills ... Australia
BRA .. Barreiras ... Brazil
BRB .. Barreirinhas ... Brazil
BRC .. San Carlos DeBariloche/Int'l ... Argentina
BRD .. Brainerd, MN ... USA
BRE .. Bremen ... Germany
BRF .. Bradford ... UK
BRG .. Whitesburg/Municipal, KY ... USA
BRH .. Brahman ... Papua New Guinea
BRI ... Bari/Palese Macchie ... Italy
BRJ .. Bright ... Australia
BRK .. Bourke ... Australia
BRL .. Burlington, IA ... USA
BRM . Barquisimeto ... Venezuela
BRN .. Berne/Belp ... Switzerland
BRO .. Brownsville/Int'l, TX ... USA
BRP .. Biaru ... Papua New Guinea
BRQ .. Brno/Turany ... Czech Rep
BRR .. Barra/North Bay ... UK
BRS .. Bristol/Lulsgate ... UK
BRT .. Bathurst Is ... Australia
BRU .. Brussels/National ... Belgium
BRV .. Bremerhaven ... Germany
BRW . Barrow/Metro., AK ... USA
BRX .. Barahona ... Dominican Rep
BRY .. Bardstown/Samuels Fld, KY ... USA
BRZ .. Borotou ... Côte D'Ivoire
BSA .. Bossaso ... Somalia
BSB .. Brasilia/Int'l ... Brazil
BSC .. Bahia Solano ... Colombia
BSD .. Baoshan ... China
BSE .. Sematan ... Malaysia
BSF .. Bradshaw/AAF, HI ... USA
BSG .. Bata ... Equatorial Guinea
BSH .. Brighton ... UK
BSI ... Blairsville, PA ... USA
BSJ .. Bairnsdale ... Australia
BSK .. Biskra ... Algeria
BSL .. Basel/Mulhouse ... Switzerland
BSN .. Bossangoa .. Central African Rep
BSO . Basco ... Philippines
BSP . Bensbach .. Papua New Guinea
BSQ . Bisbee/Municipal, AZ ... USA
BSR . Basra/Int'l ... Iraq
BSS . Balsas ... Brazil
BST .. Bost ... Afghanistan
BSU . Basankusu ... Congo, DR
BSV . Besakoa ... Madagascar
BSW . Boswell Bay, AK ... USA
BSX . Bassein ... Myanmar
BSY . Bardera ... Somalia
BSZ .. Bartletts, AK ... USA
BTA .. Bertoua ... Cameroon
BTB . Betou ... Congo, DR
BTC . Batticaloa ... Sri Lanka
BTD . Brunette Downs ... Australia
BTE .. Bonthe ... Sierra Leone
BTF .. Bountiful, UT ... USA
BTG . Batangafo .. Central African Rep
BTH . Batam/HaNadirr, ... Indonesia
BTI .. Barter Is, AK ... USA
BTJ .. Banda Aceh/Blang Bintang ... Indonesia
BTK . Bratsk ... Russia
BTL .. Battle Creek/Kellogg, MI ... USA
BTM . Butte, Mooney Arpt, MT ... USA
BTN . Bennettsville, SC ... USA
BTO . Botopasie ... Suriname
BTP .. Butler/Graham Fld, PA ... USA
BTQ . Butare ... Rwanda
BTR . Baton Rouge/Ryan Fld, LA . USA
BTS .. Bratislava/Ivanka ... Slovakia
BTT .. Bettles Arpt, AK ... USA
BTU . Bintulu ... Malaysia
BTV .. Burlington/Int'l, VT ... USA
BTW . BaLicin ... Indonesia
BTX .. Betoota ... Australia
BTY .. Beatty, NV ... USA
BTZ .. Bursa ... Turkey
BUA . Buka ... Papua New Guinea
BUB . Burwell/Municipal, NE ... USA
BUC . Burketown ... Australia
BUD . Budapest/Ferihegy ... Hungary
BUF . Buffalo Int'l Arpt, NY ... USA
BUG . Benguela/GV Deslandes . Angola
BUI .. Bokondini ... Indonesia
BUJ .. Boussaada ... Algeria
BUK . Albuq ... Yemen
BUL . Bulolo ... Papua New Guinea
BUM . Butler, MO ... USA
BUN . Buenaventura ... Colombia
BUO . Burao ... Somalia
BUP . Bhatinda ... India
BUQ . Bulawayo ... Zimbabwe
BUR . Burbank, CA ... USA
BUS . Batumi ... Georgia
BUT . Burtonwood ... UK
BUU . Buyo ... Côte D'Ivoire
BUV . Bella Union ... Uruguay
BUW . Baubau/Beto Ambiri ... Indonesia
BUY . Bunbury ... Australia
BUZ . Bushehr ... Iran
BVA .. Beauvais ... France
BVB . Boa Vista ... Brazil
BVC . Boa Vista/Rabil ... Cape Verde Is
BVD . Beaver Inlet/Sea Port, AK .. USA
BVE . Brive-La-Gaillarde/Laroche ... France
BVF .. Bua/Dama ... Fiji
BVG . Berlevag ... Norway
BVH . Vilhena ... Brazil
BVI . Birdsville ... Australia
BVK . Huacaraje ... Bolivia
BVL .. Baures ... Bolivia
BVM . Belmonte ... Brazil
BVO . Bartlesville, OK ... USA
BVP . Bolovip ... Papua New Guinea
BVR . Brava ... Cape Verde Is
BVS . Breves ... Brazil
BVU . Beluga, AK ... USA
BVW . Batavia Downs ... Australia

AIRPORTS

Code	Location	Country/Region
BVX	Batesvilie,/Municipal	Australia
BVY	Beverly, MA	USA
BVZ	Beverley Springs	Australia
BWA	Bhairawa	Nepal
BWB	Barrow Is	Australia
BWC	Brawley, CA	USA
BWD	Brownwood, TX	USA
BWE	Braunschweig	Germany
BWF	Barrow-In-Furness/Walney Isl	UK
BWG	Bowling Green, KY	USA
BWH	Butterworth	Malaysia
BWI	Baltimore, MD	USA
BWJ	Bawan	Papua New Guinea
BWK	Bol	Croatia
BWL	Backwell, OK	USA
BWM	Bowman, ND	USA
BWN	Bandar Seri Begawan	Brunei
BWO	Balakovo	Russia
BWP	Bewani	Papua New Guinea
BWQ	Brewarrina	Australia
BWS	Blaine, WA	USA
BWT	Burnie/Burnie Wynyard	Australia
BWU	Bankstown	Australia
BWY	Woodbridge	UK
BXA	Bogalusa/George R Carr, LA	USA
BXB	Babo	Indonesia
BXC	Boxborough, MA	USA
BXD	Bade	Indonesia
BXE	Bakel	Senegal
BXH	Balhash	Kazakstan
BXI	Boundiali	Côte D'Ivoire
BXJ	Burundai	Kazakstan
BXK	Buckeye, AZ	USA
BXL	Blue Lagoon	Fiji
BXM	Batom	Indonesia
BXN	Bodrum/Imisk Arpt	Turkey
BXR	Barn	Iran
BXS	Borrego Springs, CA	USA
BXT	Bontang	Indonesia
BXU	Butuan	Philippines
BXV	Breiddalsvilk	Iceland
BXX	Borama	Somalia
BXZ	Bunsil	Papua New Guinea
BYA	Boundary, AK	USA
BYB	Dibaa	Oman
BYC	Yacuiba	Bolivia
BYD	Beidah	Yemen
BYG	Buffalo, WY	USA
BYH	Blytheville/AFB, AR	USA
BYI	Burley, ID	USA
BYK	Bouake	Côte D'Ivoire
BYL	Bella Yeila	Liberia
BYM	Bayamo/C.M. de Cespedes	Cuba
BYN	Bayankhongor	Mongolia
BYQ	Bunyu	Indonesia
BYR	Laeso Is Arpt	Denmark
BYS	Fort Irwin/AAF, CA	USA
BYT	Bantry	Ireland
BYU	Bayreuth	Germany
BYW	Blakely Is, WA	USA
BYX	Baniyala	Australia
BZA	Bonanza/San Pedro	Netherlands
BZB	Bazaruto Is	Mozambique
BZC	Buzios	Brazil
BZD	Balranald	Australia
BZE	Belize City/Goldson Int'l	Belize
BZG	Bydgoszcz	Poland
BZH	Bumi Hills	Zimbabwe
BZI	Balikesir	Turkey
BZK	Briansk	Russia
BZL	Barisal	Bangladesh
BZM	Bergen Op Zoom	Netherlands
BZN	Bozeman, MT	USA
BZO	Boizano	Italy
BZP	Bizant	Australia
BZR	Beziers/Vias	France
BZS	Washington/Buzzards Pt S., DC	USA

Code	Location	Country/Region
BZT	Brazoria/Hinkles Ferry, TX	USA
BZU	Buta	Congo, DR
BZV	Brazzaville/Maya-Maya	Congo, DR
BZY	Beitsy	Macau
BZZ	RAF Brize Norton	UK

C

CAA	Catacamas	Honduras
CAB	Cabinda	Angola
CAC	Cascavel	Brazil
CAD	Cadillac, MI	USA
CAE	Columbia, SC	USA
CAF	Carauari	Brazil
CAG	Cagliari/Elmas	Italy
CAH	Ca Mau	Vietnam
CAI	Cairo/Int'l	Egypt
CAJ	Canaima	Venezuela
CAK	Akron, OH	USA
CAL	Campbeltown/Machrihanish	UK
CAM	Camiri	Bolivia
CAN	Guangzhou	China
CAO	Clayton, NM	USA
CAP	Cap Haitien	Haiti
CAQ	Caucasia	Colombia
CAR	Caribou, ME	USA
CAS	Casablanca/Anfa	Morocco
CAT	Cat Is	Bahamas
CAU	Caruaru	Brazil
CAV	Cazombo	Andorra
CAW	Campos/B. Lisandro	Brazil
CAX	Carlisle	UK
CAY	Cayenne/Rochambeau	F. Guiana
CAZ	Cobar	Australia
CBA	Corner Bay, AK	USA
CBB	Cochabamba/J Wilsterman	Bolivia
CBC	Cherrabun	Australia
CBD	Car Niconar	India
CBE	Cumberland/Wiley Ford, MD	USA
CBF	Council Bluffs, IA	USA
CBG	Cambridge, MN	UK
CBH	Bechar	Algeria
CBI	Cape Barren Is	Australia
CBJ	Cabo Rojo	Dominican Rep
CBK	Colby/Municipal, KS	USA
CBL	Ciudad Boliva	Venezuela
CBM	Columbus/AFB, MS	USA
CBN	Cirebon/Penggung	Indonesia
CBO	Cotabato/Awang	Philippines
CBP	Coirribra	Portugal
CBQ	Calabar	Nigeria
CBR	Canberra	Australia
CBS	Cabimas/Oro Negro	Venezuela
CBT	Catumbela	Andorra
CBU	Cottbus/Flugplatz	Germany
CBV	Coban	Guatemala
CBW	Campo Mourac	Brazil
CBX	Condobolin	Australia
CBY	Canobie	Australia
CBZ	Cabin Creek, AK	USA
CCA	Chaffee/AFB, AR	USA
CCB	Upland/Cable, CA	USA
CCC	Cayo Coco	Cuba
CCD	Los Angeles/Century City, CA	USA
CCE	St Martin/Grand Case	Gaudeloupe
CCF	Carcassonne/Salvaza	France
CCG	Crane County Arpt, TX	USA
CCH	Chile Chico	Chile
CCI	Concordia	Brazil
CCJ	Calicut	India
CCK	Cocos Iss	Cocos (Keeling) Is
CCL	Chinchilla	Australia
CCM	Cricluma	Brazil

Code	Location	Country/Region
CCN	Chakcharan	Afghanistan
CCO	Carimagua	Colombia
CCP	Concepcion/Carriel Sur	Chile
CCQ	Cachoeira	Brazil
CCR	Concord, CA	USA
CCS	Caracas/Simon Bolivar	Venezuela
CCT	Colonia Catriel	Argentina
CCU	Calcutta/N. S. Chandra	India
CCV	Craig Cove	Vanuatu
CCW	Cowell	Australia
CCX	Caceres	Brazil
CCY	Charles City, IA	USA
CCZ	Chub Cay	Bahamas
CDA	Cooinda	Australia
CDB	Cold Bay, AK	USA
CDC	Cedar City, UT	USA
CDD	Cauquira	Honduras
CDE	Caledonia	Panama
CDF	Cortina d'Ampezzo/Fiames	Italy
CDG	Paris/Charles De Gaulle	France
CDH	Camden, AR	USA
CDI	Cachoeiro Itapernirim	Brazil
CDJ	Conceicao Do Araguaia	Brazil
CDK	CedarKey/Lewis, FL	USA
CDL	Candle, AK	USA
CDN	Camden/Woodward Fld, SC	USA
CDO	Cradock	S. Africa
CDP	Cuddapain	India
CDQ	Croydon	Australia
CDR	Chadron, NE	USA
CDS	Childress, TX	USA
CDU	Camden	Australia
CDV	Cordova, AK	USA
CDW	Caldwell, NJ	USA
CDY	Cagayan De Sulu	Philippines
CEA	Wichita/Cessna Aircraft Fld, KS	USA
CEB	Cebu	Philippines
CEC	Crescent City, CA	USA
CED	Ceduna	Australia
CEE	Cherepovets	Russia
CEF	Chicopee/Westover Arpt, MA	USA
CEG	Chester	UK
CEH	Chelinda	Malawi
CEI	Chiang Rai	Thailand
CEJ	Chernigov	Ukraine
CEK	Chelyabinsk	Russia
CEL	Cape Eleuthera	Bahamas
CEM	Central, AK	USA
CEN	Ciudad Obregon	Mexico
CEO	Waco Kungo	Angola
CEP	Concepcion	Bolivia
CEQ	Cannes/Mandelieu	France
CER	Cherbourg/Maupertus	France
CES	Cessnock	Australia
CET	Cholet/Le Pontreau	France
CEU	Clemson, SC	USA
CEV	Connersville/Mettle Fld, IN	USA
CEW	Crestview, FL	USA
CEX	Chena Hot Springs, AK	USA
CEY	Murray/Calloway County, KY	USA
CEZ	Cortez, CO	USA
CFA	Coffee Point, AK	USA
CFC	Cacador	Brazil
CFD	Bryan/Coulter Fld, TX	USA
CFE	Clermont-Ferrand/Aulriat	France
CFF	Cafunfo	Angola
CFG	Cienfuegos	Cuba
CFH	Clifton Hills	Australia
CFI	Camfield	Australia
CFN	Donegal	Ireland
CFO	Confreza	Brazil
CFP	Carpentaria Downs	Australia
CFQ	Creston, BC	Canada
CFR	Caen/Carpiquet	France
CFS	Coffs Harbour	Australia
CFT	Clitton/Morenci, AZ	USA

CFU	Kerkyra/Corfu/Ioannis	.... Greece
CFV	Coffeyvifle, KS	USA
CGA	Craig/SPB, AK	USA
CGB	Cuiaba/M. Rondon	Brazil
CGC	Cape Gloucester	Papua New Guinea
CGD	Changde	China
CGE	Cambridge, MD	USA
CGF	Cleveland, OH	USA
CGG	Casiguran	Philippines
CGH	Sao Paulo/Congonhas	Brazil
CGI	Cape Girardeau, MO	USA
CGJ	Chingola	Zambia
CGK	Jakarta/Soekarno Int'l	Indonesia
CGM	Camiguin/Mamoajao	Philippines
CGN	Cologne/Cologne/Bonn	Germany
CGO	Zhengzhou	China
CGP	Chittagong/Patenga	Bangladesh
CGQ	Changchun	China
CGR	Campo Grande/Int'l	Brazil
CGS	College Park, MD	USA
CGT	Chinguitti	Mauritania
CGU	Ciudad Guayana	Venezuela
CGV	Caiguna	Australia
CGX	Chicago, IL	USA
CGY	Cagayan De Oro/Lumbia	Philippines
CGZ	Casa Grande/Municipal, AZ	USA
CHA	Chattanooga, TN	USA
CHB	Chilas	Pakistan
CHC	Christchurch	New Zealand
CHD	Williams/AFB, AZ	USA
CHE	Caherciveen/Reenroe	Ireland
CHF	Chinhae	S. Korea
CHG	Chaoyang/Chaoyang Arpt	China
CHH	Chachapoyas	Peru
CHI	Chicago, IL	USA
CHJ	Chipinge	Zimbabwe
CHK	Chickasha/Municipal, OK	USA
CHL	Challis, ID	USA
CHM	Chimbote	Peru
CHN	Chongju/Air Base	S. Korea
CHO	Charlottesville, VA	USA
CHP	Circle Hot Springs, AK	USA
CHQ	Souda/Khania	Greece
CHR	Chateauroux	France
CHS	Charleston/AFB, SC	USA
CHT	Chatham Is/Karewa	New Zealand
CHU	Chuathbaluk, AK	USA
CHV	Chaves	Portugal
CHW	Jiuquan	China
CHX	Changuinola	Panama
CHY	Choiseul Bay	Solomon Is
CHZ	Chiloquin/State, OR	USA
CIA	Rome/Roma/Ciampino	Italy
CIB	Catalina Is, CA	USA
CIC	Chico, CA	USA
CID	Cedar Rapids, IA	USA
CIE	Collie	Australia
CIF	Chifeng	China
CIG	Craig/Craig-Molfat, CO	USA
CIH	Changzhi	China
CIJ	Cobija/E. Beltram	Bolivia
CIK	Chalkyitsik, AK	USA
CIL	Council/Melsing Creek, AK	USA
CIM	Cimitarra	Colombia
CIN	Carroll, IA	USA
CIO	Concepcion/MCAL Lopez	Paraguay
CIP	Chipata	Zambia
CIQ	Chiquimula	Guatemala
CIR	Cairo, IL	USA
CIS	Canton Is	Kiribati
CIT	Shirrikent	Kazakstan
CIU	Sault Ste Marie, MI	USA
CIV	Chomley, AK	USA
CIW	Canouan Is	St. Vincent & Grenadines
CIX	Chiclayo/Connel Ruiz	Peru

CIY	Comiso	Italy
CIZ	Coan	Brazil
CJA	Cajamarca	Peru
CJB	Coimbatore/Peelamedu	India
CJC	Calama/El Loa	Chile
CJD	Candilejas	Colombia
CJH	Chilko Lake, BC	Canada
CJJ	Cheong Ju City Arpt	S. Korea
CJL	Chitral	Pakistan
CJM	Chumphon Arpt	Thailand
CJN	El Cajon, CA	USA
CJS	Ciudad Juarez/A. Gonzaiez	Mexico
CJU	Cheju/Cheju Int'l Arpt	S. Korea.
CKA	Cherokee/Kegelman AF, OK	USA
CKB	Clarksburg, WV	USA
CKC	Cherkassy	Ukraine
CKD	Crooked Creek, AK	USA
CKE	Clear Lake, CA	USA
CKG	Chongqing	China
CKH	Chokurdah	Russia
CKI	Croker Is	Australia
CKK	Cherokee, AR	USA
CKL	Chkalovsky	Russia
CKM	Clarksdale/Fletcher Fld, MS	USA
CKN	Crookston, MN	USA
CKO	Comelio Procopio	Brazil
CKR	Crane Is, WA	USA
CKS	Carajas	Brazil
CKT	Sarakhs	Iran
CKU	Cordova/City, AK	USA
CKV	Clarksville, TN	USA
CKX	Chicken, AK	USA
CKY	Conakry	Guinea
CKZ	Canakkaie	Turkey
CLA	Comilla	Bangladesh
CLB	Castlebar	Ireland
CLC	Clearlake/Metroport, TX	USA
CLD	Carlsbad, CA	USA
CLE	Cleveland, OH	USA
CLF	Coltishall	UK
CLG	Coalinga, CA	USA
CLH	Coolah	Australia
CLI	Clintonville, WI	USA
CLJ	Cluj/Napoca	Romania
CLK	Clinton/Municipal, OK	USA
CLL	College Stn, TX	USA
CLM	Port Angeles, WA	USA
CLN	Carolina	Brazil
CLO	Cali/Alfonso B. Aragon	Colombia
CLP	Clarks Point, AK	USA
CLQ	Colima	Myanmar
CLR	Calipatria, CA	USA
CLS	Chehalis/Centralia, WA	USA
CLT	Charlotte, NC	USA
CLU	Columbus Municipal, IN	USA
CLV	Caldas Novas	Brazil
CLW	Clearwater/Executive, FL	USA
CLX	Clorinda	Argentina
CLY	Calvi/Ste Catherine	France
CLZ	Calabozo	Venezuela
CMA	Cunnamuila	Australia
CMB	Colombo/Bandaranayake	Sri Lanka
CMC	Camocim	Brazil
CMD	Cootamundra	Australia
CME	Ciudad Del Carmen	Mexico
CMF	Chambery/Aix-Les-Bains	France
CMG	Corumba/Int'l	Brazil
CMH	Columbus, OH	USA
CMI	Champaign, IL	USA
CMJ	Chi Mei	Taiwan
CMK	Club Makokola	Malawi
CML	Camooweal	Australia
CMM	Carmelita	Guatemala
CMN	Casablanca/Mohamed V	Morocco
CMO	Obbia	Somalia
CMP	Santana Do Araguaia	Brazil
CMQ	Clermont	Australia

CMR	Coirnar/Colmar-Houssen	France
CMS	Scusciuban	Somalia
CMT	Cameta	Brazil
CMU	Kundiawa	Papua New Guinea
CMV	Coromandel	New Zealand
CMW	Camaguey/Ign Agramonte	Cuba
CMX	Hancock, MI	USA
CMY	Sparta/AAF, WI	USA
CMZ	Caia	Mozambique
CNA	Cananea	Mexico
CNB	Coonamble	Australia
CNC	Coconut Is	Australia
CND	Constanta/Kogainiceanu	Romania
CNE	Canon City, CO	USA
CNF	Belo Horizonte/T. Neves	Brazil
CNG	Cognac/Chateau Bernard	France
CNH	Claremont/Municipal, NH	USA
CNI	Changhai	China
CNJ	Cloncurry	Australia
CNK	Concordia, KS	USA
CNL	Sindal/Flyveplads	Denmark
CNM	Carlsbad, NM	USA
CNN	Chulman	Russia
CNO	Chino, CA	USA
CNP	Neerlerit Inaat	Greenland
CNQ	Corrientes/Camba Punta	Argentina
CNR	Chanaral	Chile
CNS	Cairns, CA	Australia
CNT	Charata	Argentina
CNU	Chanute, KS	USA
CNV	Canavieiras	Brazil
CNW	Waco/James Connall, TX	USA
CNX	Chiang Mai/Int'l	Thailand
CNY	Moab, UT	USA
CNZ	Cangamba	Angola
COA	Columbia, CA	USA
COB	Coolibah	Australia
COC	Concordia	Argentina
COD	Cody, WY	USA
COE	Coeur D'Alene, ID	USA
COF	Cocoa/AFB, FL	USA
COG	Condoto/Mandinga	Colombia
COH	Cooch Behar	India
COI	Cocoa/Merritt Is, FL	USA
COJ	Coonabarabran	Australia
COK	Cochin	India
COL	Colt Is	UK
COM	Coleman, TX	USA
CON	Concord, NH	USA
COO	Cotonou/Cadjehoun	Benin
COP	Cooperstown, NY	USA
COQ	Choibalsan	Mongolia
COR	Cordoba/Pajas Blancas	Argentina
COS	Colorado Springs, CO	USA
COT	Cotulla, TX	USA
COU	Columbia, MO	USA
COV	Covilha	Portugal
COW	Coquimbo	Chile
COX	Congo Town	Bahamas
COY	Coolawanyah	Australia
COZ	Constanza	Dominican Rep
CPA	Cape Palmas/A. Tubman	Liberia
CPB	Capurgana	Colombia
CPC	San Martin Del-os Andes	Argentina
CPD	Coober Pedy	Australia
CPE	Campeche/Campeche Int'l	Mexico
CPF	Cepu	Indonesia
CPG	Carmen De Patagones	Argentina
CPH	Copenhagen/Kastrup	Denmark
CPI	Cape Orford	Papua New Guinea
CPL	Chaparral	Colombia
CPM	Compton, CA	USA
CPN	Cape Rodney	Papua New Guinea

AIRPORTS

Code	Location	Country/Region
CPO	Copiapo/Chamonate	Chile
CPQ	Campinas/Int'l	Brazil
CPR	Casper, WY	USA
CPS	St Louis, IL	USA
CPT	Cape Town Int'l	S. Africa
CPU	Cururupu	Brazil
CPV	Campina Grande/J. Suassuna	Brazil
CPX	Culebra	Puerto Rico
CQA	Canarana/Canarana Arpt	Brazil
CQF	Calais	France
CQN	Chattanooga/Daisy, TN	USA
CQP	Cape Flattery	Australia
CQS	Costa Marques	Brazil
CQT	Caquetania	Colombia
CQV	Colville Municipal, WA	USA
CQX	Chatham Municipal, MA	USA
CRA	Craiciva	Romania
CRB	Collarenebri	Australia
CRC	Cartago	Colombia
CRD	Comodoro Rivadavia	Argentina
CRE	Myrtle Beach, SC	USA
CRF	Carnot	Central African Rep
CRG	Jacksonville, FL	USA
CRH	Cherribah	Australia
CRI	Crooked Is	Bahamas
CRJ	Coorabie	Australia
CRK	Luzon Is/Clark Field	Philippines
CRL	Brussels	Belgium
CRM	Catarman/National	Philippines
CRN	Cromarty	UK
CRO	Corcoran, CA	USA
CRP	Corpus Christi, TX	USA
CRQ	Caravelas	Brazil
CRR	Ceres	Argentina
CRS	Corsicana, TX	USA
CRT	Crossett/Municipal, AR	USA
CRU	Carriacou Is	Grenada
CRV	Crotone	Italy
CRW	Charleston, WV	USA
CRX	Corinth/Roscoe Turner, MS	USA
CRY	Cariton Hill	Australia
CRZ	Chardzhou	Turkmenistan
CSA	Colonsay Is	UK
CSB	Caransebes	Romania
CSC	Canas	Costa Rica
CSD	Cresswell Downs	Australia
CSE	Crested Butte, CO	USA
CSF	Creil/AFB	France
CSG	Columbus Metropolitan, GA	USA
CSI	Casino	Australia
CSJ	Cape St Jacques	Vietnam
CSK	Cap Skirring	Senegal
CSL	San Luis Obispo/AAF, CA	USA
CSM	Clinton, OK	USA
CSN	Carson City, NV	USA
CSO	Cochstedt	Germany
CSP	Cape Spencer/Coast Guard HP, AK	USA
CSQ	Creston, IA	USA
CSR	Casuarito	Colombia
CSS	Cassilandia	Brazil
CST	Castaway	Fiji
CSU	Santa Cruz Do Sul	Brazil
CSV	Crossville, TN	USA
CSW	Colorado do Oeste	Brazil
CSX	Changsha	China
CSY	Cheboksary	Russia
CTA	Catania/Fontanarossa	Italy
CTB	Cut Bank, MT	USA
CTC	Catamarca	Argentina
CTD	Chitre	Panama
CTE	Carti	Panama
CTF	Coatepeque	Guatemala
CTG	Cartagena/Rafael Nunez	Colombia
CTH	Coatesville, PA	USA
CTI	Cuito Cuanavale	Angola
CTK	Canton, SD	USA
CTL	Charleville	Australia
CTM	Cheturnal	Mexico
CTN	Cookitown	Australia
CTO	Calverton, NY	USA
CTP	Carutapera	Brazil
CTQ	Santa Vitoria/Do Palmar	Brazil
CTR	Cattle Creek	Australia
CTS	Sapporo/Chitose	Japan
CTT	Le Castellet	France
CTU	Chengdu	China
CTW	Cottonwood, AZ	USA
CTX	Cortland, NY	USA
CTY	Cross City, FL	USA
CTZ	Clinton/Sampson County, NC	USA
CUA	Ciudad Constitucion	Mexico
CUB	Columbia, SC	USA
CUC	Cucuta/Camilo Dazo	Colombia
CUD	Caloundra	Australia
CUE	Cuenca	Ecuador
CUF	Cuneo/Levaldigi	Italy
CUG	Cudal	Australia
CUH	Cushing/Municipal, OK	USA
CUI	Currillo	Colombia
CUJ	Culion	Philippines
CUK	Caye Caulker	Belize
CUL	Cuhacan/F.D. Bachigualato	Mexico
CUM	Cumana	Venezuela
CUN	Cancun	Mexico
CUO	Caruru	Colombia
CUP	Carupano	Venezuela
CUQ	Coen	Australia
CUR	Curacao/Halo	Netherlands Antilles
CUS	Columbus/Municipal, NM	USA
CUT	Cutral	Argentina
CUU	Chihuahua/G.F. Villalobos	Mexico
CUV	Casigua	Venezuela
CUW	Cube CoveAK	USA
CUX	Corpus Christi/Cuddihy Fld, TX	USA
CUY	Cue	Australia
CUZ	Cuzio/Velazco Astete	Peru
CVA	Pittsburgh/Civic HP, PA	USA
CVB	Chungribu	Papua New Guinea
CVC	Cleve	Australia
CVE	Covenas	Colombia
CVF	Courchevel	France
CVG	Cincinnati, KY	USA
CVH	Caviahue	Argentina
CVI	Caleta Olivia	Argentina
CVJ	Cuernavaca	Mexico
CVL	Cape Vogel	Papua New Guinea
CVM	Ciudad Victoria	Mexico
CVN	Clovis/Municipal, NM	USA
CVO	Albany, OR	USA
CVQ	Carnarvon	Australia
CVR	Culver City/Hughes, CA	USA
CVS	Clovis/AFB, NM	USA
CVT	Coventry/Baginton	UK
CVU	Corvo Is	Portugal
CWA	Mosinee, WI	USA
CWB	Curitiba/Afonso Pena	Brazil
CWC	Chernovtsy	Ukraine
CWF	Chenault Airpark, LA	USA
CWG	Callaway Gardens, GA	USA
CWI	Clinton, IA	USA
CWL	Cardiff	UK
CWO	Ft Wolter/AAF, TX	USA
CWP	Campbellpore	Pakistan
CWR	Cowarie	Australia
CWS	Center Is, WA	USA
CWT	Cowra	Australia
CWW	Corowa	Australia
CXA	Caicara De Oro	Venezuela
CXB	Cox's Bazar	Bangladesh
CXC	Chitina Arpt, AK	USA
CXF	Coldfoot, AK	USA
CXH	Vancouver/Coal Harbour, BC	Canada
CXI	Christmas Is	Kiribati
CXJ	Camas Do Sul/C.D. Bugres	Brazil
CXL	Calexico/Int'l, CA	USA
CXN	Candala	Somalia
CXO	Conroe, TX	USA
CXP	Cilacap/Tunggul Wuiung	Indonesia
CXQ	Christmas Creek	Australia
CXT	Charters Towers	Australia
CXY	Cat Cays	Bahamas
CYA	Les Cayes	Haiti
CYB	Cayman Brac	Cayman Is
CYC	Caye Chapel	Belize
CYE	Crystal Lake, PA	USA
CYF	Chefornak/SPB, AK	USA
CYG	Corryong	Australia
CYI	Chiayi	Taiwan
CYL	Coyoles	Honduras
CYM	Chatham/SPB, AK	USA
CYO	Cayo Largo Del Sur	Cuba
CYP	Calbayog	Philippines
CYR	Colonia	Uruguay
CYS	Cheyenne, WY	USA
CYT	Yakataga/Intermediate, AK	USA
CYU	Cuyo	Philippines
CYX	Cherskiy	Russia
CYZ	Cauayan	Philippines
CZA	Chichen Itza	Mexico
CZB	Cruz Alta/Carios Ruhl	Brazil
CZC	Copper Centre, AK	USA
CZD	Cozad Municipal, NE	USA
CZE	Coro	Venezuela
CZF	Cape Romanzof, AK	USA
CZH	Corozal	Belize
CZJ	Corazon De Jesus	Panama
CZK	Cascade Locks, OR	USA
CZL	Constantine	Algeria
CZM	Cozumel	Mexico
CZN	Chisana/Chisana Fld, AK	USA
CZO	Chistochina, AK	USA
CZP	Cape Pole, AK	USA
CZS	Cruzeiro Do Sul/Campo Int'l	Brazil
CZT	Carrizo Springs, TX	USA
CZU	Corozal	Colombia
CZW	Czestochowa	Poland
CZX	Changzhou	China
CZY	Cluny	Australia
CZZ	Campo, CA	USA

D

DAA	Fort Belvoir/Davison/AAF, VA	USA
DAB	Daytona Beach/Regional, FL	USA
DAC	Dhaka/Zia Int'l	Bangladesh
DAD	Da Nang	Vietnam
DAE	Daparizo	India
DAF	Daup	Papua New Guinea
DAG	Barstow-Daggett, CA	USA
DAH	Dathina	Yemen
DAI	Darjeelino	India
DAJ	Dauan Is	Australia
DAK	Dakhla Oasis/Dakhla	Egypt
DAL	Dallas, TX	USA
DAM	Damascus/Int'l	Syria
DAN	Danville, VA	USA
DAP	Darchula	Nepal
DAR	Dar Es Salaam/Int'l	Tanzania
DAS	Great Bear Lake, NT	Canada
DAT	Datong	China
DAU	Daru	Papua New Guinea
DAV	David/Enrique Maiek	Panama
DAX	Daxian	China
DAY	Dayton, OH	USA
DAZ	Darwaz	Afghanistan
DBA	Dalbandin	Pakistan

DBD .. Dhanbad ... India
DBM . Debra Marcos ... Ethiopia
DBN .. Dublin/Municipal, GA ... USA
DBO . Dubbo ... Australia
DBP .. Debepare ... Papua New Guinea
DBQ . Dubuque, IA ... USA
DBS .. Dubois, ID ... USA
DBT .. Debra Tabor ... Ethiopia
DBV .. Dubrovnik ... Croatia
DBY .. Dallby ... Australia
DCA .. Washington D.C. ... USA
DCF .. Dominica/Cane Field .. Dominica
DCI ... Decimomannu/Ratsu ... Italy
DCK .. Dahl Creek/Dahl Creek Arpt, AK ... USA
DCM . Castres/Mazamet ... France
DCR .. Decatur/Decatur Hi-Way, IN . USA
DCS .. Doncaster/Finningley ... UK
DCT .. Duncan Town ... Bahamas
DCU .. Decatur, AL ... USA
DDC .. Dodge City, KS ... USA
DDG . Dandong ... China
DDI ... Daydream Is ... Australia
DDL .. ACARS ... n/a
DDM . Dodoirna ... Papua New Guinea
DDN .. Delta Downs ... Australia
DDP .. Dorado/Dorado Beach ... Puerto Rico
DDU .. Dadu ... Pakistan
DEA .. Dera Ghazi Khan ... Pakistan
DEB .. Debrecen ... Hungary
DEC .. Decatur, IL ... USA
DED .. Dehra Dun ... India
DEE .. Deering, Deering Arpt, AK .. USA
DEH .. Decorah, IA ... USA
DEI ... Denis Is ... Seychelles
DEL .. Delhi/Indira Gandhi Inti ... India
DEM . Dembidollo ... Ethiopia
DEN .. Denver, CO ... USA
DEO .. Dearborn/Hyatt Regency HP, MI ... USA
DEP .. Deparizo ... India
DER .. Derim ... Papua New Guinea
DES .. Desroches ... Seychelles
DET .. Detroit, MI ... USA
DEZ .. Deirezzor/Al Jafrah ... Syria
DFI ... Defiance, OH ... USA
DFP .. Drumduff ... Australia
DFW . Fort Worth, TX ... USA
DGA . Dangriga ... Belize
DGB . Danger Bay, AK ... USA
DGC . Degalthbur ... Ethiopia
DGD . Dalgaranga ... Australia
DGE .. Mudgee ... Australia
DGF .. Douglas Lake, BC ... Canada
DGG . Daugo ... Papua New Guinea
DGL .. Douglas Municipal, AZ ... USA
DGM . Dongguan ... China
DGN . Dahigren/NAF, VA ... USA
DGO . Durango/Guadalupe Victoria ... Mexico
DGP .. Daugavpils ... Latvia
DGR . Dargaville ... New Zealand
DGT .. Dumaguete ... Philippines
DGU . Dedougou ... Burkina Faso
DGW . Douglas, WY ... USA
DHA .. Dhahran ... Saudi Arabia
DHD .. Durham Downs ... Australia
DHF .. Abu Dhabi/Al Dhafra Military Arpt ... UAE
DHI ... Dhangarhi ... Nepal
DHL .. Dhala ... Yemen
DHM . Dharamsala/Gaggal Arpt ... India
DHN .. Dothan, AL ... USA
DHR .. Den Helder/De Kooy ... Netherlands
DHT .. Dalhart, TX ... USA
DIB ... Dibrugarn/Chabua ... India
DIC ... Dili ... Congo, DR
DIE ... Antsiranana/Arrachart ... Madagascar
DIG ... Dicling ... China
DIJ ... Dijon ... France
DIK ... Dickinson, ND ... USA
DIL ... Dili/Comoro ... Indonesia
DIM ... Dimbokro/Ville ... Côte D'Ivoire
DIN ... Dien Sien Phu/Gialam ... Vietnam
DIO ... Diomede Is, AK ... USA
DIP ... Diapaga ... Burkina Faso
DIQ ... Divinopolis ... Brazil
DIR ... Dire Dawa/Aba Tenna D Yilma ... Ethiopia
DIS ... Loubomo ... Congo, DR
DIU ... Diu ... India
DIV ... Divo ... Côte D'Ivoire
DIX ... Phila. Nexrad, PA ... USA
DIY ... Diyarbakir ... Turkey
DJA .. Djougou ... Benin
DJB .. Jambi/Sultan Taha Syarifudn ... Indonesia
DJE .. Djerba/Zarzis ... Tunisia
DJG .. Djanet ... Algeria
DJJ ... Jayapura/Sentani ... Indonesia
DJM .. Djambala ... Congo, DR
DJN .. Delta Junction, AK ... USA
DJO .. Daloa ... Côte D'Ivoire
DJU .. Djupivogur ... Iceland
DKI ... Dunk Is ... Australia
DKK .. Dunkirk, NY ... USA
DKR .. Dakar/Yoff ... Senegal
DKS .. Dikson ... Russia
DKV .. Docker River ... Australia
DKX .. Knoxville Downtown, TN ... USA
DLA .. Douala ... Cameroon
DLB .. Dalbertis ... Papua New Guinea
DLC .. Dalian ... China
DLD .. Geilo/Dagali ... Norway
DLE .. Dote/Tavaux ... France
DLF .. Del Rio/AFB, TX ... USA
DLG .. Dillingharn/Municipal, AK ... USA
DLH .. Duluth, MN ... USA
DLI ... Dalat/Lienkinang ... Vietnam
DLJ .. Batna ... Algeria
DLK .. Dulkaninna ... Australia
DLL .. Dillon, SC ... USA
DLM .. Dataman ... Turkey
DLN .. Dillon, MT ... USA
DLO .. Dolorni, AK ... USA
DLS .. The Dalles, OR ... USA
DLU .. Dali City/Dali ... China
DLV .. Delissaville ... Australia
DLY .. Dillons Bay ... Vanuatu
DLZ .. Dalanzadgad ... Mongolia
DMA .. Tucson/AFB, AZ ... USA
DMB .. Zhambyl ... Kazakstan
DMD .. Doomadgee ... Australia
DME .. Moscow/Domodedovo ... Russia
DMM . Dammarn/King Fahad ... Saudi Arabia
DMN .. Deming, NM ... USA
DMO .. Sedalia, MO ... USA
DMR .. Dharnar ... Yemen
DMT .. Diarnantino ... Brazil
DMU .. Dimapur ... India
DMX .. Des Moines Nexrad, IA ... USA
DNA .. Okinawa/Kadena AFB ... Japan
DNB .. Dunbar ... Australia
DNC .. Danane ... Côte D'Ivoire
DND .. Dundee/Riverside ... UK
DNE .. Dallas North Arpt, TX ... USA
DNF .. Derna/Martuba ... Libya
DNG .. Doongan ... Australia
DNH .. Dunhuang ... China
DNI ... Wad Medani ... Somalia
DNK .. Dnepropetrovsk ... Ukraine
DNL .. Augusta, GA ... USA
DNM .. Denham ... Australia
DNN .. Dalton/Municipal, GA ... USA
DNO .. Dianopolis ... Brazil
DNP .. Dang ... Nepal
DNQ .. Deniliquin ... Australia
DNR .. Dinard ... France
DNS . Denison, IA ... USA
DNT . Santa Ana / HP, CA ... USA
DNU . Dinangat ... Papua New Guinea
DNV . Danville/Vermilion County, IL ... USA
DNX . Dinder/Galegu ... Sudan
DNZ . Denizli/Cardak ... Turkey
DOA . Doany ... Madagascar
DOB . Dobo/Dobo Arpt ... Indonesia
DOC . Dornoch ... UK
DOD . Dodoma ... Tanzania
DOE . Djoemoe ... Suriname
DOF . Dora Bay, AK ... USA
DOG . Dongola ... Sudan
DOH . Doha Int'l Arpt ... Qatar
DOI .. Doini ... Papua New Guinea
DOK . Donetsk ... Ukraine
DOL . Deauville/St Gatien ... France
DOM . Dominica/Melville Hail ... Oman
DON . Dos Lagunas ... Guatemala
DOO . Dorobisoro .. Papua New Guinea
DOP . Dolpa ... Nepal
DOR . Dori ... Burkina Faso
DOS . Dios ... Papua New Guinea
DOU . Dourados ... Brazil
DOV . Dover/AFB, DE ... USA
DOX . Dongara ... Australia
DPA .. West Chicago, IL ... USA
DPC . Data Processing Ctr ... n/a
DPE . Dieppe/Saint Aubin ... France
DPG . Dugway/AAF, UT ... USA
DPI .. Dipolog ... Philippines
DPO . Devonpori ... Australia
DPS . Denpasar, Bali/N. Rai .. Indonesia
DPU . Dumpu ... Papua New Guinea
DRA . Mercury, NV ... USA
DRB . Derby ... Australia
DRC . Dinco ... Angola
DRD . Dorunda Stn ... Australia
DRE . Drummond Is, MI ... USA
DRF . Drift River, AK ... USA
DRG . Deering, AK ... USA
DRH . Dabra ... Indonesia
DRI .. De Ridder/Beauregard Parish, LA ... USA
DRJ .. Drietabbetje ... Suriname
DRM . Drama ... Greece
DRN . Dirranbandi ... Australia
DRO . Durango, CO ... USA
DRR . Durrie ... Australia
DRS . Dresden/Klotzsche ... Germany
DRT . Del Rio, TX ... USA
DRU . Drummond, MT ... USA
DRW . Darwin Arpt ... Australia
DRY . Drysdale River ... Australia
DSC . Dschang ... Cameroon
DSD . La Desirade ... Gaudeloupe
DSE . Dessie/Combolcha ... Ethiopia
DSG . Dilasag ... Philippines
DSI .. Destin, FL ... USA
DSK . Dera Ismail Khan ... Pakistan
DSL .. Daru ... Sierra Leone
DSM . Des Moines, IA ... USA
DSN . Dongsheng ... China
DSV . Dansville, NY ... USA
DTA .. Delta, UT ... USA
DTD . Datadawai ... Indonesia
DTE .. Dael/Camarines Norte ... Philippines
DTH . Death Valley, CA ... USA
DTL .. Detroit Lakes/Municipal, MN ... USA
DTM . Dortmund/Wickede ... Germany
DTN . Shreveport, LA ... USA
DTO . Denton Municipal Arpt, TX .. USA
DTR . Decatur Is, WA ... USA
DTS .. Destin, Ft Walton Beach, FL USA
DTW . Detroit, MI ... USA
DTX .. Detroit Nexrad, MI ... USA
DUA . Durant/Eaker, OK ... USA
DUB . Dublin ... Ireland

A I R P O R T S

DUC	Duncan/Halliburton, OK	USA
DUD	Dunedin	New Zealand
DUE	Dunce	Angola
DUF	Duck/Pine Is Arpt, OK	USA
DUG	Douglas, AZ	USA
DUI	Duisburg	Germany
DUJ	Dubois/Jefferson County, PA	
		USA
DUK	Dukuduk	S. Africa
DUM	Dumai	Indonesia
DUN	Dundas	Greenland
DUR	Durban/Durban Int'l	S. Africa
DUS	Duesseldorf	Germany
DUT	Dutch Harbor/Emergency Fld, AK	USA
DVA	Deva	Romania
DVL	Devils Lake, ND	USA
DVN	Davenport, IA	USA
DVO	Davao	Philippines
DVP	Davenport Downs	Australia
DVR	Daly River	Australia
DVT	Phoenix, AZ	USA
DWA	Dwangwa	Malawi
DWB	Soalaia	Madagascar
DWF	Daylon/Wright/AFB	USA
DWH	Houston, TX	USA
DWN	Oklahoma City/Dntwn, OK	USA
DWS	Orlando/Walt Disney World, FL	USA
DXA	Deux Alpes	France
DXB	Dubai	UAE
DXD	Dixie	Australia
DXR	Danbury, CT	USA
DYA	Dysart	Australia
DYG	Dayong	China
DYL	Doylestown	Australia
DYM	Diamantina Lakes	Australia
DYR	Anadyr	Russia
DYS	Abilene/Dyess/AFB, TX	USA
DYU	Dushanbe	Australia
DYW	Daly Waters	Australia
DZA	Dzaoudzi	Mayotte
DZN	Zhezkazgan/Zhezhazgan	Kazakstan
DZO	Durazno	Uruguay
DZU	Dazu	China

E

EAA	Eagle, Eagle Arpt, AK	USA
EAB	Abbse	Yemen
EAE	Ernae	Vanuatu
EAM	Nelran	Saudi Arabia
EAN	Wheatland/Phifer Fld, WY	USA
EAR	Kearney, NE	USA
EAS	San Sebastian	Spain
EAT	Wenatchee, WA	USA
EAU	Eau Claire, WI	USA
EAX	Pleasant Nexrad, MO	USA
EBA	Elba Is/Marina Di Campe	Italy
EBB	Entebbe	Uganda
EBD	El Obeid	Sudan
EBG	El Bagre	Colombia
EBJ	Esbjerg	Denmark
EBM	El Borma	Tunisia
EBN	Ebadon	Marshall Is
EBO	Ebon/Ebon Arpt	Marshall Is
EBR	Baton Rouge/Downtown, LA	USA
EBS	Webster City, IA	USA
EBU	St Etienne/Boutheon	France
EBW	Ebolowa	Cameroon
ECA	East Tawas, MI	USA
ECG	Elizabeth City, NC	USA
ECH	Echuca	Australia
ECN	Ercan	Cyprus
ECO	El Encanto	Colombia

ECR	El Charco	Colombia
ECS	Newcastle/Mondell, WY	USA
EDA	Edna Bay, AK	USA
EDB	Eldebba	Sudan
EDD	Erldunda	Australia
EDE	Edenton/Municipal, NC	USA
EDF	Anchorage/Elmendorl/AFB, AK	USA
EDG	Edgewood/Weide/AAF, MD	USA
EDI	Edinburgh/Turnhouse	UK
EDK	El Dorado, KS	USA
EDL	Eldoret	Kenya
EDM	La Roche/Les Ajoncs	France
EDO	Edremit/Korfez	Turkey
EDQ	Erandique	Honduras
EDR	Edward River	Australia
EDW	Edwards/AFB, CA	USA
EED	Needles, CA	USA
EEK	Eek, AK	USA
EEN	Brattleboro, VT	USA
EEO	Meeker, Meeker Arpt, CO	USA
EET	Alabaster, Shelby County, AL	USA
EEW	Neenah, WI	USA
EFB	Eight Fathom Bight, AK	USA
EFC	Belle Fourche, SD	USA
EFD	Ellington, TX	USA
EFG	Efogi	Papua New Guinea
EFK	Newport, VT	USA
EFL	Kefalhnia/Argostolion	Greece
EFO	East Fork, AK	USA
EFW	Jefferson/Municipal, IA	USA
EGA	Engati	Papua New Guinea
EGC	Bergerac/Roumanieres	France
EGE	Vail, CO	USA
EGI	Valparaiso, FL	USA
EGL	Negrielli	Ethiopia
EGM	Sege	Sweden
EGN	Geneina	Sudan
EGO	Belgorod	Russia
EGP	Eagle Pass/Maverick, TX	USA
EGS	Egilsstadir	Iceland
EGV	Eagle River, WI	USA
EGX	Egegik, AK	USA
EHL	El Bolson	Argentina
EHM	Cape Newenham, AK	USA
EHR	Henderson City, KY	USA
EHT	East Hartford/Rentschler, CT	USA
EIA	Eia/Popondetta	Papua New Guinea
EIB	Eisenach	Germany
EIE	Eniseysk	Russia
EIH	Einasieigh	Australia
EIL	Fairbanks/Eielson/AFB, AK	USA
EIN	Eindhoven	Netherlands
EIS	Beef Is	Virgin Is (British)
EIY	Ein Yahav	Israel
EJA	Barrancabermeia/Vrgs	Colombia
EJH	Wedjh	Saudi Arabia
EKA	Eureka/Murray Fld, CA	USA
EKB	Ekibastuz	Kazakstan
EKD	Elkedra	Australia
EKE	Ekereku	Guyana
EKI	Elkhart/Municipal, IN	USA
EKN	Elkins, WV	USA
EKO	Elko, NV	USA
EKT	Eskilstuna	Sweden
EKX	Elizabethtown, KY	USA
ELA	Eagle Lake, TX	USA
ELB	El Banco/San Bernado	Colombia
ELC	Elcho Is	Australia
ELD	El Dorado, AR	USA
ELE	El Real	Panama
ELF	El Fasher	Somalia
ELG	El Golea	Algeria
ELH	North Eleuthera/Int'l	Bahamas
ELI	Elim, AK	USA
ELJ	El Recreo	Colombia
ELK	Elk City/Municipal, OK	USA

ELL	Ellisras	S. Africa
ELM	Elmira, NY	USA
ELN	Ellensburg, WA	USA
ELO	Eldorado	Argentina
ELP	El Paso, TX	USA
ELQ	Gassim	Saudi Arabia
ELR	Elelim	Indonesia
ELS	East London	S. Africa
ELT	Tour Sinai City	Egypt
ELU	El Oued	Algeria
ELV	Elfin Cove/SPB, AK	USA
ELW	Ellamar, AK	USA
ELX	El Tigre	Venezuela
ELY	Ely, NV	USA
ELZ	Wellsville, NY	USA
EMA	Nottingham	UK
EMB	San Francisco/Embarcadero, CA	USA
EMD	Emerald	Australia
EME	Ernden	Germany
EMG	Empangeni	S. Africa
EMI	Emirau	Papua New Guinea
EMK	Emmonak, AK	USA
EMM	Kemerer, WY	USA
EMN	Nema	Mauritania
EMO	Emo	Papua New Guinea
EMP	Emporia, KS	USA
EMS	Embessa	Papua New Guinea
EMT	El Monte, CA	USA
EMX	El Maiten	Argentina
EMY	El Minya	Egypt
ENA	Kenai, AK	USA
ENB	Eneabba West	Australia
ENC	Nancy/Essey	France
END	Enid/AFB, OK	USA
ENE	Ende	Indonesia
ENF	Enontekiö	Finland
ENH	Enshi	China
ENI	El Nido	Philippines
ENJ	El Naranjo	Guatemala
ENK	Enniskillen/St Angelo	UK
ENL	Centralia/Municipal, IL	USA
ENN	Nenana, AK	USA
ENO	Encarnacion	Paraguay
ENQ	Coronel E Solo Cano AB	Honduras
ENS	Enschede/Twente	Netherlands
ENT	Enewetak Is	Marshall Is
ENU	Enugu	Nigeria
ENV	Wendover, UT	USA
ENW	Kenosha, WI	USA
ENX	Albany Nexrad, NY	USA
ENY	Yan'an	China
EOH	Medellin/E. O. Herrera	Colombia
EOI	Eday	UK
EOK	Keokuk, IA	USA
EOR	El Dorado	Venezuela
EOS	Neosho, MO	USA
EOZ	Elorza	Venezuela
EPG	Weeping Water/Browns, NE	USA
EPH	Ephrata, WA	USA
EPI	Epi	Vanuatu
EPK	Episkopi	Cyprus
EPL	Epinal/Mirecourt	France
EPN	Epena	Congo, DR
EPO	Eastport, ME	USA
EPR	Esperance	Australia
EPS	El Portillo	Dominican Rep
EPT	Eliptarnin	Papua New Guinea
EPZ	Santa Teresa, NM	USA
EQS	Esquel	Argentina
EQY	Monroe, Monroe Arpt, NC	USA
ERA	Erigavo	Somalia
ERB	Ernabella	Australia
ERC	Erzincan	Turkey
ERD	Berdyansk	Ukraine
ERE	Erave	Papua New Guinea
ERF	Erfurt/Bindersleben	Germany
ERH	Errachidla	Morocco
ERI	Erie, PA	USA
ERM	Erechim/C. Kraemer	Brazil

ERN . . Eirunepe . . . . Brazil
ERO . . Eldred Rock/Coast Guard, AK
. . . . USA
ERR . . Errol, NH . . . . USA
ERS . . Windhoek/Eros . . . . Namibia
ERT . . Erdenet . . . . Mongolia
ERU . . Erume . . . . . . Papua New Guinea
ERV . . Kerrville, TX . . . . USA
ERZ . . Erzurum . . . . Turkey
ESA . . Esa'Ala . . . . . Papua New Guinea
ESB . . Ankara/Esenboga . . . . Turkey
ESC . . Escanaba, MI . . . . USA
ESD . . Eastsound/Orcas Is, WA . . . . USA
ESE . . Ensenada . . . . Mexico
ESF . . Alexandria, LA . . . . USA
ESG . . Mariscal Estigarribia . . . Paraguay
ESH . . Shoreham By Sea/Shoreham . UK
ESI . . . Espinosa . . . . Brazil
ESK . . Eskisehir . . . . Turkey
ESL . . . Elista . . . . Russia
ESM . . Esmeraidas . . . . Ecuador
ESN . . Easton, MD . . . . USA
ESO . . Espanola, NM . . . . USA
ESP . . East Stroudsburg/B. Pocono, PA
. . . . USA
ESR . . El Salvador . . . . Chile
ESS . . Essen . . . . Germany
EST . . Estherville, IA . . . . USA
ESU . . Essaouira . . . . Morocco
ESW . . Easton/State, WA . . . . USA
ESX . . Las Vegas Nexrad, NV . . . . . USA
ETB . . West Send, WI . . . . USA
ETD . . Etadunna . . . . Australia
ETE . . Genda Wuha . . . . Ethiopia
ETH . . Elat/J. Hozman . . . . Israel
ETN . . Eastland/Municipal, TX . . . . . USA
ETR . . Esltree . . . . UK
ETS . . Enterprise/Municipal, AL . . . . USA
ETZ . . Metz/Nancy/Lorraine . . . . . France
EUA . . Eua/Kaufana . . . . Tonga
EUC . . Eucla . . . . Australia
EUE . . Eureka . . . . USA
EUF . . Eufaula . . . . USA
EUG . . Eugene, OR . . . . USA
EUM . . Neumuenster . . . . Germany
EUN . . Laayoune/Hassan I . . . . Morocco
EUO . . Paratebueno . . . . Colombia
EUX . . St Eustatius . . Netherlands Antilles
EVA . . Evadale/Landing Strip, TX . . USA
EVE . . Harstad-Narvik/Evenes . Norway
EVG . . Sveg . . . . Sweden
EVH . . Evans Head . . . . Australia
EVM . . Eveleth, MN . . . . USA
EVN . . Yerevan . . . . Armenia
EVO . . Eva Downs . . . . Australia
EVV . . Evansville, IN . . . . USA
EVW . . Evanston, WY . . . . USA
EVX . . Evreux . . . . France
EWB . . Fail River, MA . . . . USA
EWE . . Ewer . . . . Indonesia
EWI . . Enarotali . . . . Indonesia
EWK . . Newton, KS . . . . USA
EWN . . New Bern, NC . . . . USA
EWO . . Ewo . . . . Congo, DR
EWR . . Newark, NJ . . . . USA
EWX . . San Antonio Nexrad, TX . . . . USA
EWY . . Newbury/Greenham/RAF . . . . UK
EXI . . . Excursion Inlet/SPB, AK . . . . USA
EXM . . Exmouth Gulf . . . . Australia
EXT . . Exeter Arpt . . . . UK
EYE . . Indianapolis, Eagle Creek, IN
. . . . USA
EYL . . Yelimane . . . . Mali
EYP . . El Yopal . . . . Colombia
EYR . . Yerington, NV . . . . USA
EYS . . Eflye Springs . . . . Kenya
EYW . . Key West, FL . . . . USA
EZE . . Buenos Aires/Ministro Pistarini
. . . . Argentina
EZF . . Shannon Arpt, VA . . . . USA
EZS . . Elazig . . . . Turkey

F

FAA . . Faranah . . . . Guinea
FAB . . Farnborough . . . . UK
FAC . . Faaite . . . . F. Polynesia
FAE . . Faroe Iss/Vagar . . . Faroe Islands
FAF . . Feiker/AAF, VA . . . . USA
FAG . . Fagurholsmyri . . . . Iceland
FAH . . Farah . . . . Afghanistan
FAI . . . Fairbanks Int'l, AK . . . . USA
FAJ . . Fajardo . . . . Puerto Rico
FAK . . False Is, AK . . . . USA
FAL . . Roma/Falcon State, TX . . . . . USA
FAM . . Farmington, MO . . . . USA
FAN . . Farsund/Lista . . . . Norway
FAO . . Faro . . . . Portugal
FAQ . . Freida River . . Papua New Guinea
FAR . . Fargo, ND . . . . USA
FAS . . Faskrudsfjordur . . . . Iceland
FAT . . Fresno, CA . . . . USA
FAV . . Fakarava . . . . F. Polynesia
FAY . . Fayetteville, NC . . . . USA
FBD . . Faizabad . . . . Afghanistan
FBE . . Francisco Beltrao . . . . Brazil
FBG . . Fort Bragg/AAF, NC . . . . . . USA
FBK . . Fairbanks/Ft Wainwright, AK . USA
FBL . . Faribault/Municipal, MN . . . . USA
FBM . . Lubumbashi/Luano . . Congo, DR
FBR . . Fort Bridger, WY . . . . USA
FBU . . Oslo/Fornebu . . . . Norway
FBY . . Fairbury/Municipal, NE . . . . . USA
FCA . . Kalispell, MT . . . . USA
FCB . . Ficksburg . . . . S. Africa
FCH . . Fresno-Chandler, CA . . . . . . USA
FCM . . Minneapolis, Flying Cloud Arpt,
MN . . . . USA
FCO . . Rome/Roma/Fiumicino . . . . . Italy
FCS . . Colorado Springs/AAF, CO . . USA
FCT . . Yakima/Firing Center/AAF,
WA . . . . USA
FCX . . Roanoke Nexrad, VA . . . . . . USA
FCY . . Forrest City/Municipal, AR . . . USA
FDE . . Forde/Bringeland . . . . Norway
FDF . . Fort De France/Lamentin
. . . . Martinique
FDH . . Friedrichshafen . . . . Germany
FDK . . Frederick, MD . . . . USA
FDR . . Frederick, OK . . . . USA
FDU . . Bandundu . . . . Congo, DR
FDY . . Findlay, OH . . . . USA
FEA . . Fetlar . . . . UK
FEB . . Sanfebagar . . . . Nepal
FEC . . Feira De Santana . . . . Brazil
FEG . . Fercana . . . . Uzbekistan
FEJ . . Feijo . . . . Brazil
FEK . . Ferkessedougou . . . Côte D'Ivoire
FEL . . Fuerstenfeldbruck . . . . . Germany
FEN . . Fernando De Noronha . . . Brazil
FEP . . Freeport/Albertus, IL . . . . . . USA
FER . . Fercusons Gulf . . . . Kenya
FET . . Fremont, NE . . . . USA
FEW . . Cheyenne/AFB, WY . . . . USA
FEZ . . Fez/Sars . . . . Morocco
FFA . . Kill Devil Hills/First Flight,
NC . . . . USA
FFC . . Atlanta, Falcon Fld, GA . . . . . USA
FFD . . Fairford/RAF . . . . UK
FFL . . Fairfield, IA . . . . USA
FFM . . Fergus Falls, MN . . . . USA
FFO . . Dayton/AFB, OH . . . . USA
FFT . . Frankfort, KY . . . . USA
FFU . . Furtaeulu . . . . Chile
FFZ . . Mesa/Falcon Fld, AZ . . . . . . USA
FGD . . Fderik . . . . Mauritania
FGI . . . Apia/Fagali I . . . . Samoa
FGL . . Fox Glacier . . . . New Zealand
FGU . . Fangatau . . . . F. Polynesia

FHR . Friday Harbor Arpt, WA . . . . USA
FHU . Libby/AAF, AZ . . . . USA
FHZ . Fakahina . . . . F. Polynesia
FIC . . Fire Cove, AK . . . . USA
FID . . Fishers Is, NY . . . . USA
FIE . . Fair Isle . . . . UK
FIG . . Fria . . . . Guinea
FIH . . Kinshasa/N'Djili . . . . . Congo, DR
FIK . . Finke . . . . Australia
FIL . . . Fillmore/Municipal, UT . . . . . USA
FIN . . Finschhafen . Papua New Guinea
FIT . . . Fitchburg Municipal, MA . . . . USA
FIV . . Five Finger, AK . . . . USA
FIZ . . Fitzroy Crossing . . . . Australia
FJR . . Fujairah Int'l Arpt . . . . UAE
FKB . Karlsruhe/Baden Baden
. . . . Germany
FKH . Fakenham/Sculthorp/RAF
. . . . Georgia
FKI . . Kisangani . . . . Congo, DR
FKJ . . Fukui . . . . Japan
FKL . . Franklin, PA . . . . USA
FKN . . Franklin Municipal, VA . . . . . USA
FKQ . . Fak Fak/Torea . . . . Indonesia
FKS . . Fukushima Arpt . . . . Japan
FLA . . Florencia, CO . . . . USA
FLB . . Floriano . . . . Brazil
FLC . . Falls Creek . . . . Australia
FLD . . Fond Du Lac Arpt, WI . . . . . . USA
FLE . . Fort Lee/AAF, VA . . . . USA
FLF . . Flensburg/Schaferhaus
. . . . Germany
FLG . . Flagstaff/Pulliam Arpt, AZ . . . USA
FLH . . Flotta . . . . UK
FLI . . . Flateyri . . . . Iceland
FLJ . . Falls Bay, AK . . . . USA
FLL . . Fort Lauderdale Int'l, FL . . . . USA
FLM . . Filadelfia . . . . Paraguay
FLN . . Florianopolis . . . . Brazil
FLO . . Florence Regional Arpt, SC . USA
FLP . . Flippin . . . . Australia
FLR . . Florence/Peretola . . . . Italy
FLS . . Flinders Is . . . . Australia
FLT . . Flat, AK . . . . USA
FLU . . Flushing, NY . . . . USA
FLV . . Sherman/AAF, KS . . . . USA
FLW . . Flores Is/Santa Cruz . . . Portugal
FLX . . Fallon/Municipal, NV . . . . . . USA
FLY . . Finley . . . . Australia
FMA . . Formosa . . . . Argentina
FMC . . Five Mile, AK . . . . USA
FME . . Tipton/AAF, MD . . . . USA
FMG . . Flaminoo . . . . Costa Rica
FMH . . Otis/AFB, MA . . . . USA
FMI . . . Kalemie . . . . Congo, DR
FMN . . Farmington Municipal, NM . . USA
FMO . . Muenster . . . . Germany
FMS . . Fort Madison, IA . . . . USA
FMY . . Fort Myers, FL . . . . USA
FNA . . Freetown . . . . Sierra Leone
FNB . . Neulbrandenburg . . . . . Germany
FNC . . Funchal/Madeira . . . . Portugal
FNE . . Fane . . . . Papua New Guinea
FNG . . Fada N'Gourma . . . Burkina Faso
FNH . . Fincha . . . . Ethiopia
FNI . . . Nimes/Garons . . . . France
FNJ . . Pyongyang/Sunan . . . . . N. Korea
FNK . . Fin Creek, AK . . . . USA
FNL . . Fort Collins, CO . . . . USA
FNR . . Funter Bay/SPB, AK . . . . . . USA
FNT . . Flint Int'l Arpt, MI . . . . USA
FOA . . Foula . . . . UK
FOB . . Fort Bragg, CA . . . . USA
FOC . . Fuzhou . . . . China
FOD . . Fort Dodge, IA . . . . USA
FOE . . Forbes/AFB, KS . . . . USA
FOG . . Foggia . . . . Italy
FOK . . Westhampton, NY . . . . USA
FOM . . Foumban . . . . Cameroon
FON . . Fortuna . . . . Costa Rica
FOO . . Numfoor . . . . Indonesia

Code	Airport	Location
FOP	Forest Park/Morris/AAF, GA	USA
FOR	Fortaleza/Pinto Martins	Brazil
FOS	Forrest	Australia
FOT	Forster	Australia
FOU	Fougamou	Gabon
FOX	Fox, AK	USA
FOY	Foya	Liberia
FPO	Freeport	Bahamas
FPR	Fort Pierce Int'l, FL	USA
FPY	Perry-Foley, FL	USA
FRA	Frankfurt/Int'l	Germany
FRB	Forbes	Australia
FRC	Franca	Brazil
FRE	Fera Is	Solomon Is
FRF	Frankfurt AFB	Germany
FRG	Farmingdale, NY	USA
FRH	French Lick, IN	USA
FRI	Marshall/AAF, KS	USA
FRJ	Frejus	France
FRK	Fregate Is	Seychelles
FRL	Forli/Luigi Ridolfi	Italy
FRM	Fairmont, MN	USA
FRN	Bryant/AAF, AK	USA
FRO	Floro	Norway
FRP	Fresh Water Bay, AK	USA
FRQ	Feramin	Papua New Guinea
FRR	Front Royal/Warren County, VA	USA
FRS	Flores/Santa Elena	Guatemala
FRT	Frutillar	Chile
FRU	Bishkek	Kyrgyzstan
FRW	Francistown	Botswana
FRY	Fryeburg, ME	USA
FRZ	Fritziar	Germany
FSC	Figari	France
FSD	Sioux Falls, SD	USA
FSI	Henry Post/AAF, OK	USA
FSK	Forl Scott, KS	USA
FSL	Fossil Downs	Australia
FSM	Fort Smith Municipal, AR	USA
FSN	Fort Sheridan/AAF, IL	USA
FSP	St Pierre . St. Pierre and Miquelon
FSS	Kinloss/RAF	UK
FST	Fort Stockton, TX	USA
FSU	Fort Sumner, NM	USA
FSW	Fort Madison, IA	USA
FTA	Futuna Is Arpt	Vanuatu
FTG	Denver Nexrad, CO	USA
FTI	Fitiuta	American Samoa
FTK	Godman/AAF, KY	USA
FTL	Fortuna Ledge, AK	USA
FTU	Fort Dauphin	Madagascar
FTW	Fort Worth, TX	USA
FTX	Owando	Congo, DR
FTY	Fulton County, GA	USA
FUB	Fulleborn	Papua New Guinea
FUE	Fuerteventura	Spain
FUG	Fuyang	China
FUJ	Fukue	Japan
FUK	Fukuoka	Japan
FUL	Fullerton Municipal, CA	USA
FUM	Fuma	Papua New Guinea
FUN	Funafuti Atol Int'l	Tuvalu
FUO	Fucishan	China
FUT	Futuna Is	Wallis and Futuna Is
FVE	Frenchville, N Aroostook, ME	USA
FVL	Flora Valley/Flora Valey	Australia
FVR	Forrest River Arpt	Australia
FVX	Farmville, VA	USA
FWA	Fort Wayne Int'l, IN	USA
FWD	Ft Worth, TX	USA
FWH	Carswell/AFB, TX	USA
FWL	Farewell, AK	USA
FWM	Fort William/ HPHP	UK
FWN	Sussex, Sussex Arpt, NJ	USA
FWS	Dfw Nexrad, TX	USA
FXE	Fort Lauderdale Executive, FL	USA
FXM	Flaxman Is, AK	USA
FXO	Cuamba	Mozambique

Code	Airport	Location
FXY	Forest City/Municipal, IA	USA
FYM	Fayetteville/Municipal, TN	USA
FYN	Fuyun	China
FYT	Faya	Chad
FYU	Fort Yukon, AK	USA
FYV	Fayetteville Municipal, AR	USA
FZO	Bristol/Filton	UK

G

GAA	Guarrial	Colombia
GAB	Gabbs, NV	USA
GAC	Gracias	Honduras
GAD	Gadsden/Municipal, AL	USA
GAE	Gabes	Tunisia
GAF	Gafsa/Ksar	Tunisia
GAG	Gage, OK	USA
GAH	Gayndah	Australia
GAI	Gaithersburg, MD	USA
GAJ	Yamagata/Junmachi	Japan
GAK	Gakona, AK	USA
GAL	Galena, AK	USA
GAM	Gambell, AK	USA
GAN	Gan Is/Gan/Seenu	Maldives
GAO	Guantanamo/Los Canos	Cuba
GAP	Gusap	Papua New Guinea
GAQ	Gao	Mali
GAR	Garaina	Papua New Guinea
GAS	Garissa	Kenya
GAT	Gap/Tallard	France
GAU	Gauhati/Borlhar	India
GAV	Gag Is	Indonesia
GAW	Gangaw	Myanmar
GAX	Gamba	Gabon
GAY	Gaya	India
GAZ	Guasopa	Papua New Guinea
GBA	Big Bay	Vanuatu
GBB	Gara Djebilet	Algeria
GBC	Gasuke	Papua New Guinea
GBD	Great Bend, KS	USA
GBE	Gaborone/Sir Seretse Khama Int'l	Botswana
GBF	Negarbo	Papua New Guinea
GBG	Galesburg, GBG	USA
GBH	Galbraith Lake, AK	USA
GBI	Grand Bahama/Aux Ab	Bahamas
GBJ	Marie Galante/Les Bases	Gaudeloupe
GBK	Gbangbatok	Sierra Leone
GBL	Goulburn Is	Australia
GBM	Garbaharey	Somalia
GBN	Gila Bend/AAF, AZ	USA
GBO	Baltimore-Greenbelt, MD	USA
GBP	Gamboola	Australia
GBR	Great Barrington, MA	USA
GBS	Port Fitzroy	New Zealand
GBU	Khashm El Girba	Somalia
GBV	Gibb River	Australia
GBZ	Great Barrier Is	New Zealand
GCA	Guacamaya	Colombia
GCC	Campbell County Arpt, WY	USA
GCI	Guernsey	UK
GCJ	Johannesburg/Grand Central	S. Africa
GCK	Garden City, KS	USA
GCM	Grand Cayman Is Int'l	Cayman Is
GCN	Grand Canyon Natl. Park, AZ	USA
GCY	Greenville/Municipal, TN	USA
GDA	Gounda	Central African Rep
GDC	Greenville/Donaldson Cntr, SC	USA
GDD	Gordon Downs	Australia
GDE	Gode/Iddidole	Ethiopia
GDG	Magelagachi	Russia
GDH	Golden Horn/SPB, AK	USA
GDI	Gordil	Central African Rep

Code	Airport	Location
GDJ	Gandajika	Congo, DR
GDL	Guadalajara/Miguel Hidal	Mexico
GDM	Gardner/Municipal, MA	USA
GDN	Gdansk-Rebiechowo	Poland
GDO	Guasdualito/Vare Maria	Venezuela
GDP	Guadalupe	Brazil
GDQ	Gondar	Ethiopia
GDT	Grand Turk Is	Turks & Caicos Is
GDV	Glendive, MT	USA
GDW	Gladwin, MI	USA
GDX	Magadan	Russia
GDZ	Gelenclzilk	Russia
GEA	Noumea/MagentaNew Caledonia
GEB	Gebe	Indonesia
GEC	Geatkale	Cyprus
GED	Georgetown, DE	USA
GEE	George Town	Australia
GEF	Geva Airstrip	Solomon Is
GEG	Spokane Int'l Arpt, WA	USA
GEI	Green Iss	Papua New Guinea
GEK	Ganes Creek, AK	USA
GEL	Santo Angelo/Sepe Tiaraju	Brazil
GEO	Georgetown/Cheddi Jagan Int'l	Guyana
GER	Nueva Gerona/Rafael Cabrera	Cuba
GES	General Safflos/Buayan	Philippines
GET	Geraldton	Australia
GEV	Gallivare	Sweden
GEW	Gewoia	Papua New Guinea
GEX	Geelong	Australia
GEY	Greybull, WY	USA
GFA	Malmstrom/AFB, MT	USA
GFB	Togiak Fish, AK	USA
GFD	Greenfeid/Pope Fld, IN	USA
GFE	Grenfell	Australia
GFF	Griffith	Australia
GFK	Grand Forks Int'l, ND	USA
GFL	Glens Falls, NY	USA
GFN	Grafton	Australia
GFO	Bartica	Guyana
GFR	Granville	France
GFY	Grootfontein	Namibia
GGB	Golden Gate Bridge, CA	USA
GGC	Lumbala	Angola
GGD	Gregory Downs	Australia
GGE	Georgetown, SC	USA
GGG	Gladewater, TX	USA
GGL	Gilgal	Colombia
GGN	Gagnoa	Côte D'Ivoire
GGO	Guiglo	Côte D'Ivoire
GGR	Garoe	Somalia
GGS	Gobernador Gregores	Argentina
GGT	George Town/Exurna Int'l	Bahamas
GGW	Glasgow Int'l Arpt, MT	USA
GHA	Ghardaia Nournerate	Algeria
GHB	Governors Harbour	Bahamas
GHC	Great Harbour	Bahamas
GHD	Ghimbi	Ethiopia
GHE	Garachine	Panama
GHF	Gebelstacit	Germany
GHK	Gush Katif	Israel
GHM	Centerville MunicipalTN	USA
GHN	Guanghan	China
GHT	Ghat	Libya
GHU	Gualeguaychu	Argentina
GHW	Glenwood Asos, MN	USA
GIB	Gibraltar North Front	Gibraltar
GIC	Boigu Is	Australia
GID	Gitega	Benin
GIF	Winter Haven/Gilbert Fld, FL	USA
GIG	Rio De Janeiro Int'l	Brazil
GII	Siguin	Guinea
GIL	Gilgit	Pakistan
GIM	Miele Mimbale	Gabon
GIR	Girardot	Colombia

AIRPORTS

GIS	Gisborne	New Zealand
GIT	Geita	Tanzania
GIY	Giyani	S. Africa
GIZ	Gizan	Saudi Arabia
GJA	Guanaja	Honduras
GJL	Jijel Achouat	Algeria
GJM	Gualara-Mirim	Brazil
GJR	Gjogur	Iceland
GJT	Grand Junction/Walker Fld, CO	USA
GKA	Goroka	Papua New Guinea
GKE	Geilenkirchen	Germany
GKH	Gorkha	Nepal
GKL	Great Keppel Is	Australia
GKN	Gulkana Arpt, AK	USA
GKO	Kongoboumba	Gabon
GKT	Gatlinburg, TN	USA
GLA	Glasgow/Int'l	UK
GLC	Geladi	Ethiopia
GLD	Goodland, Renner Fld, KS	USA
GLE	Gainesville/Municipal, TX	USA
GLF	Golfito	Costa Rica
GLG	Glengyie	Australia
GLH	Greenville, MS	USA
GLI	Glen Innes	Australia
GLK	Galcaio	Somalia
GLL	Gol/Klanten	Norway
GLM	Gienormiston	Australia
GLN	Goulimime	Morocco
GLO	Gloucester/Staverton Private	UK
GLP	Guigubip	Papua New Guinea
GLQ	Glennallen, AK	USA
GLR	Gaylord, Otsego County, MI.	USA
GLS	Galveston, Scholes Fld, TX	USA
GLT	Gladstone	Australia
GLV	Golovin, AK	USA
GLW	Glasgow/Municipal, KY	USA
GLX	Galela/Gamarmalamu	Indonesia
GLY	Goldsworthy	Australia
GLZ	Breda/Gilze-Rijen	Netherlands
GMA	Gemena	Congo, DR
GMB	Gambela	Ethiopia
GMC	Guerima	Colombia
GME	Gomel	Belarus
GMI	Gasmata Is.	Papua New Guinea
GMM	Gamboma	Congo, DR
GMN	Greymouth	New Zealand
GMR	Gambier Is	F. Polynesia
GMS	Guimaraes	Brazil
GMT	Granite Mountain, AK	USA
GMU	Greenville, SC	USA
GMV	Monument Valley, UT	USA
GMY	Rheindahlen	Germany
GNA	Grodna	Belarus
GNB	Grenoble/Saint Geoirs	France
GND	Grenada/Point Saline Int'l	Grenada
GNE	Ghent/Industrie-Zone	Belgium
GNG	Gooding, ID	USA
GNI	Green Is	Taiwan
GNM	Guanambi	Brazil
GNN	Ghinnir	Ethiopia
GNR	General Roca	Argentina
GNS	Gunungsitoli/Binaka	Indonesia
GNT	Grants-Milan, NM	USA
GNU	Goodnews Bay, AK	USA
GNV	Gainesville, FL	USA
GNZ	Ghanzi	Botswana
GOA	Genoa/Cristoforo Colombo	Italy
GOB	Goba	Ethiopia
GOC	Gora	Papua New Guinea
GOE	Gonalia	Papua New Guinea
GOF	Goodfellow/AFB, TX	USA
GOG	Golbabis	Namibia
GOH	Nuuk	Greenland
GOI	Goa/Dabolim	India
GOJ	Nizhniy Novgorod	Russia
GOK	Guthrie, OK	USA
GOL	Gold Beach/State, OR	USA
GOM	Goma	Congo, DR
GON	New London, CT	USA
GOO	Goondiwindi	Australia
GOP	Gorakhpur	India
GOQ	Golmud	China
GOR	Gore	Ethiopia
GOS	Gosford	Australia
GOT	Goteborg/Landvetter	Sweden
GOU	Garoua	Cameroon
GOV	Gove/Nhulunbuy	Australia
GOY	Gal Oya/Amparai	Sri Lanka
GOZ	Gorna Orechovitsa	Bulgaria
GPA	Araxos/Patrai	Greece
GPB	Guarapuava/Tancredo Thornaz Faria	Brazil
GPI	Guapi	Colombia
GPL	Guapiles	Costa Rica
GPN	Garden Point	Australia
GPO	General Pico	Argentina
GPS	Galapagos Is/Baltra	Ecuador
GPT	Biloxi Regional Arpt, MS	USA
GPZ	Grand Rapids, MN	USA
GQJ	Machrihanish/RAF	UK
GQQ	Galion, OH	USA
GRA	Gamarra	Colombia
GRB	Green Bay, Austin Straubel Int'l Arpt, WI	USA
GRC	Grand Cess	Liberia
GRD	Greenwood County Arpt, SC	USA
GRE	Greenville/Municipal, IL	USA
GRF	Ft. Lewis Gray/AAF, WA	USA
GRG	Gardez	Afghanistan
GRH	Garuahi	Papua New Guinea
GRI	Grand Is, NE	USA
GRJ	George	S. Africa
GRK	Ft. Hood Gray/AAF, TX	USA
GRL	Garasa	Papua New Guinea
GRM	Grand Marais Municipal, MN	USA
GRN	Gordon Municipal, NE	USA
GRO	Gerona/Costa Brava	Spain
GRP	Gurupi	Brazil
GRQ	Groningen/Eelde	Netherlands
GRR	Kent County Int'l Arpt, MI	USA
GRS	Grosseto/Baccarini	Italy
GRT	Guirat	Pakistan
GRU	Sao Paulo/Guarulhos Int'l	Brazil
GRV	Groznyj	Russia
GRW	Graciosa Is	Portugal
GRX	Granada	Spain
GRY	Grimsey	Iceland
GRZ	Graz/Thalerhof	Austria
GSA	Long Pasia	Malaysia
GSB	Seymour Johnson/AFB, NC	USA
GSC	Gascoyne Junction	Australia
GSE	Gothenburg/Saeve	Sweden
GSH	Goshen Municipal Arpt, IN	USA
GSI	Guadalcanal	Solomon Is
GSL	Taltheilei Narrows, NT	Canada
GSM	Gheshm	Iran
GSN	Mount Gunson	Australia
GSO	Piedmont Triad/Int'l, NC	USA
GSP	Greenville, SC	USA
GSQ	Shark El Oweinat	Egypt
GSR	Gardo	Somalia
GSS	Sabi Sabi	S. Africa
GST	Gustavus, AK	USA
GSU	Gedaref	Somalia
GSY	Grimsby/Binbrook	UK
GTA	Gatokae Aerodrom	Solomon Is
GTB	Genting	Malaysia
GTC	Green Turtle	Bahamas
GTE	Groote Eylandt/Alyangula	Australia
GTF	Great Falls Int'l Arpt, MT	USA
GTG	Grantsburg/Municipal, WI	USA
GTI	Guettin	Germany
GTK	SungeiTekai	Malaysia
GTN	Mount Cook/Glentanner	New Zealand
GTO	Gorontalo/Tolotio	Indonesia
GTR	Columbus, MS	USA
GTS	Granites	Australia
GTT	Georgetown	Australia
GTW	Zlin/Holesov	Czech Rep
GTY	Gettysburg, PA	USA
GUA	Guatemala City/La Aurora	Guatemala
GUB	Guerrero Negro	Mexico
GUC	Gunnison, CO	USA
GUD	Goundam	Mali
GUE	Guriaso	Papua New Guinea
GUF	Gulf Shores/Edwards, AL	USA
GUG	Guari	Papua New Guinea
GUH	Gunnedah	Australia
GUI	Guiria	Venezuela
GUJ	Guaratingueta	Brazil
GUL	Goulburn	Australia
GUM	Guam/A.B. Won Pat Infl	Guam
GUN	Montgomery/Gunter/AFB, AL	USA
GUO	Gualaco	Honduras
GUP	Gallup Municipal Arpt, NM	USA
GUQ	Guanare	Venezuela
GUR	Alotau/Gurney	Papua New Guinea
GUS	Grissom/AFB, IN	USA
GUT	Guetersloh	Germany
GUU	Grundarfjordur	Iceland
GUV	Mougulu	Papua New Guinea
GUW	Atyrau	Kazakstan
GUX	Guna	India
GUY	Guymon, OK	USA
GUZ	Guarapari	Brazil
GVA	Geneva Cointrin	Switzerland
GVE	Gordonsville/Municipal, VA	USA
GVI	Green River	Papua New Guinea
GVL	Gainesville/Gilmer Memorial, GA	USA
GVP	Greenvale	Australia
GVR	Governador Valadares	Brazil
GVT	Greenville Majors, TX	USA
GVW	Kansas City, Richards-Gebaur Arpt, MO	USA
GVX	Gavie/Sandviken AFB	Sweden
GWA	Gwa	Myanmar
GWD	Gwadar	Pakistan
GWE	Gweru	Zimbabwe
GWL	Gwalior	India
GWN	Gnarowein	Papua New Guinea
GWO	Greenwood/Leflore, MS	USA
GWS	Glenwood Springs, CO	USA
GWT	Westerland/Sylt	Germany
GWV	Glendale,WV	USA
GWW	Berlin/RAF Gatow	Germany
GWY	Galway Cammore	Ireland
GXF	Seiyun	Yemen
GXG	Negage	Andorra
GXH	Mildenhall/NAF	UK
GXQ	Coyhaique/Ten. Vidal	Chile
GXX	Yagoua	Cameroon
GXY	Greeley/Weld County, CO	USA
GYA	Guayaramerin	Bolivia
GYE	Guayaquil/Simon Bolivar	Ecuador
GYI	Gisenyi	Rwanda
GYL	Argyle	Australia
GYM	Guaymas	Mexico
GYN	Goiania/Santa Genoveva	Brazil
GYP	Gympie	Australia
GYR	Goodyear Municipal, AZ	USA
GYY	Gary Regional, IN	USA
GZA	Gaza Strip/Gaza Int'l	Occupied Palestinian Ter
GZH	Evergreen, Middleton Fld, AL	USA
GZI	Ghazni	Afghanistan
GZM	Gozo	Malta
GZO	Gizo/Nusatope	Solomon Is

H

Code	Location	Country
HAA	Hasvik	Norway
HAB	Hamilton/Marion County, AL.	USA
HAC	Hachijo Jima	Japan
HAD	Halmstad/AFB	Sweden
HAE	Havasupai, AZ	USA
HAF	Half Moon, CA	USA
HAH	Moroni/Prince Said Ibrahim Int'l	Comoros
HAI	Three Rivers/Dr Haines, MI	USA
HAJ	Hanover	Germany
HAK	Haikou	China
HAL	Halah	Namibia
HAM	Hamburg/Fuhlsbuettel	Germany
HAN	Hanoi/Noibai	Vietnam
HAO	Hamilton, OH	USA
HAP	Long Is	Australia
HAQ	Hanimaadhoo	Maldives
HAR	Harrisburg Skyport, PA	USA
HAS	Hail	Saudi Arabia
HAT	Heathlands	Australia
HAU	Haugesund/Karmoy	Norway
HAV	Havana/Jose Marti Int'l	Cuba
HAW	Haverfordwest	UK
HAX	Muskogee/Hatbox Fld, OK.	USA
HAY	Haycock, AK	USA
HAZ	Hatzfeldthaven	Papua New Guinea
HBA	Hobart Arpt	Australia
HBB	Hobbs/Industrial Airpark, NM	USA
HBC	Hanus Bay, AK.	USA
HBE	Alexandria/Borg El Arab	Egypt
HBG	Hattiesburg, MS.	USA
HBH	Hobart Bay, AK	USA
HBI	Harbour Is	Bahamas
HBL	Babelegi/ HP	S. Africa
HBN	Phu-bon	Vietnam
HBO	Humboldt Municipal, NE	USA
HBR	Hobart Municipal Arpt, OK.	USA
HBT	Hafr Albatin	Saudi Arabia
HBX	Hubli	India
HCA	Big Spring/Howard Cnty, TX	USA
HCB	Shoal Cove, AK	USA
HCC	Hudson/Columbia Cnty, NY	USA
HCM	Eil	Somalia
HCN	Hengchun	Taiwan
HCQ	Halls Creek	Australia
HCR	Holy Cross, AK	USA
HCS	Johannesburg/HP	S. Africa
HCW	Cheraw, SC	USA
HDA	Hidden Falls, AK	USA
HDB	Heidelberg	Germany
HDD	Hyderabad	Pakistan
HDE	Brewster Fld Arpt, NE	USA
HDF	Heringsdorf	Germany
HDH	Oahu/Dillingham Airfield, HI.	USA
HDM	Hamadan	Iran
HDN	Hayden/Yampa Valley, CO	USA
HDO	Hondo, TX	USA
HDQ	Atlanta/Headquarters	n/a
HDS	Hoedspruit	S. Africa
HDY	Hat Yai	Thailand
HEA	Herat	Afghanistan
HEB	Henzada	Myanmar
HED	Herendeen, AK	USA
HEE	Helena/Thompson-Robbins, AR	USA
HEH	Heho	Myanmar
HEI	Hettinger Municipal Arpt, ND	USA
HEK	Heihe	China
HEL	Helsinki/Vantaa	Finland
HEM	Helsinki/Malmi	Finland
HEN	Hendon	UK
HEO	Haeloao	Papua New Guinea
HER	Heraklion/Iraklio	Greece
HES	Hermiston/State, OR	USA
HET	Hohhot	China
HEW	Athens/Athinai/Hellinikon	Greece
HEX	Santo Domingo/Herrera	Dominican Rep
HEY	Hanchey/AHP, AL	USA
HEZ	Natchez/Hardy-Anders, MS	USA
HFA	Haifa/U Michaeli	Israel
HFD	Hartford-Brainard Arpt, CT	USA
HFE	Hefei	China
HFF	Mackall/AAF, NC	USA
HFN	Hornafjordur	Iceland
HFS	Hagfors	Sweden
HFT	Hammerfest	Norway
HGA	Hargeisa	Somalia
HGD	Hughenden	Australia
HGH	Hangzhou	China
HGL	Helgoland	Germany
HGN	Mae Hong Son	Thailand
HGO	Korhogo	Côte D'Ivoire
HGR	Hagerstown, MD	USA
HGS	Freetown/Hastings	Sierra Leone
HGT	Jolon/Hunter/AAF, CA	USA
HGU	Mount Hagen/Kagamuga	Papua New Guinea
HGX	HuStn/GlvStn Nexrad, TX	USA
HGZ	Hogatza, AK	USA
HHE	Hachinohe AB	Japan
HHF	Canadian/Hemphill, TX	USA
HHH	Hilton Head, SC	USA
HHI	Wheeler/AFB, HI	USA
HHN	Hahn	Germany
HHP	Hong Kong / HP	Hong Kong
HHQ	Hua Hin	Thailand
HHR	Hawthorne, CA	USA
HHZ	Hikueru	F. Polynesia
HIB	Chisholm-Hibbing Arpt, MN	USA
HIC	Pretoria/iscor HP	S. Africa
HID	Horn Is	Australia
HIE	Whitefield, NH	USA
HIF	Hill/AFB, UT	USA
HIG	Highbury	Australia
HIH	Hook Is	Australia
HII	Lake Havasu City, AZ	USA
HIJ	Hiroshima/Int'l	Japan
HIK	Hickam/AFB, HI	USA
HIL	Shillavo	Ethiopia
HIN	Chinju/Sacheon	S. Korea
HIO	Hillsboro, OR	USA
HIP	Headingly	Australia
HIR	Honiara/Henderson	Solomon Is
HIS	Hayman Is	Australia
HIT	Hivaro	Papua New Guinea
HIW	Hiroshima/Hiroshima West	Japan
HIX	Hiva Oa	F. Polynesia
HJR	Khajuraho	India
HJT	Khujirt	Mongolia
HKA	Blytheville Municipal, AR	USA
HKB	Healy Lake, AK	USA
HKD	Hakodate	Japan
HKG	Hong Kong Int'l	Hong Kong
HKK	Hokitika	New Zealand
HKN	Hoskins	Papua New Guinea
HKS	Jackson, Hawkins Fld, MS	USA
HKT	Phuket/Int'l	Thailand
HKV	Haskovo	Bulgaria
HKY	Hickory, NC	USA
HLA	Lanseria	S. Africa
HLB	Batesville/Hillenbrand, IN	USA
HLC	Hill City, KS	USA
HLD	Hailar	China
HLF	Hultsfred/AFB	Sweden
HLG	Wheeling, WV	USA
HLH	Ulanhot	China
HLI	Hollister, CA	USA
HLJ	Shauliaj	Lithuania
HLL	Hillside	Australia
HLM	Holland/Park Township, MI	USA
HLN	Heiena, MT	USA
HLP	Jakarta/Halim Penclana Kusuma	Indonesia
HLR	Ft. Hood/AAF, TX	USA
HLS	St Helens	Australia
HLT	Hamilton	Australia
HLU	Houailou	New Caledonia
HLV	Helenvaie	Australia
HLW	Hluhluwe	S. Africa
HLX	Hillsville, VA	USA
HLY	Holyhead	UK
HLZ	Hamilton	New Zealand
HMA	Malmo/Malmo City HVC.	Sweden
HME	Hassi-Messaoud	Algeria
HMG	Hermannsburg	Australia
HMI	Hami	China
HMJ	Khmeinitskiy	Ukraine
HMM	Hamilton/Ravalli County, MT	USA
HMN	Holloman/AFB, NM	USA
HMO	Hermosillo/Gen Pesqueira Garcia	Mexico
HMR	Hamar/Hamar Arpt	Norway
HMS	Hanford, WA	USA
HMT	Hemet/Ryan Fld, CA	USA
HMV	Hemavan	Sweden
HNA	Moriolka/Hanamaki	Japan
HNB	Huntingburg, IN	USA
HNC	Hatteras, NC	USA
HND	Tokyo/Haneda	Japan
HNE	Tahneta Pass Lodge, AK	USA
HNG	Hienghene	New Caledonia
HNH	Hoonah, AK	USA
HNI	Heiweni	Papua New Guinea
HNK	Hinchinbrook Is	Australia
HNL	Honolulu/Int'l, HI	USA
HNM	Hana, HI	USA
HNN	Honinabi	Papua New Guinea
HNO	Hercegnovi	Yugoslavia
HNS	Haines Arpt, AK	USA
HNX	Hanna, WY	USA
HNY	Hengyang	China
HOA	Hola	Kenya
HOB	Hobbs, NM	USA
HOC	Komako	Papua New Guinea
HOD	Hodeidah/Hodeidah Arpt	Yemen
HOE	Houeisay	Laos
HOF	Hofuf/Al Hasa	Saudi Arabia
HOG	Holguir/Frank Pais	Cuba
HOH	Hohenems	Austria
HOI	Hao Is	F. Polynesia
HOK	Hooker Creek	Australia
HOL	Holikachu, AK	USA
HOM	Homer Arpt, AK	USA
HON	Huron, SD	USA
HOO	Quanduc/Nhon Co	Vietnam
HOP	Campbell/AAF, KY	USA
HOQ	Hof	Germany
HOR	Horta	Portugal
HOS	Chos Malal/Oscar Reguera	Argentina
HOT	Hot Springs, AR	USA
HOU	Houston, Hobby Arpt, TX	USA
HOV	Orsta-Volda/Hovden	Norway
HOW	Ft. Kobbe/Howard AFB	Panama
HOX	Homalin	Myanmar
HOY	Hoy Is	UK
HPA	Ha'Apai/Salote Pilolevu	Tonga
HPB	Hooper Bay, AK	USA
HPE	Hope Vale	Australia
HPH	Haiphong/Catbi	Vietnam
HPN	Westchester County, NY	USA
HPR	Pretoria/Central Hpr	S. Africa
HPT	Hampton/Municipal, IA	USA
HPV	Kauai Is/Princeville, HI	USA
HPY	Baytown, TX	USA
HQM	Hoquiam, WA	USA
HRA	Mansehra	Pakistan
HRB	Harbin	China
HRC	Zhairem	Kazakstan

HRD . .	Harstad	Norway
HRE . .	Harare Kutsaga	Zimbabwe
HRG . .	Hurghada	Egypt
HRJ . .	Chaurjlnari	Nepal
HRK . .	Kharkov	Ukraine
HRL . .	Harlingen/Valley Int'l, TX	USA
HRM . .	Hassi R Mel/Tilrempt	Algeria
HRN . .	Heron Is / HP	Australia
HRO . .	Harrison, AR	USA
HRR . .	Herrera	Colombia
HRS . .	Harrismith	S. Africa
HRT . .	Harrogate/Linton-On-Ouse . . .	UK
HRY . .	Henbury	Australia
HRZ . .	Horizontina	Brazil
HSB . .	Harrisburg/Raleigh, NC	USA
HSC . .	Shaoguan	China
HSE . .	Hatteras, Mitchell Fld, NC . . .	USA
HSG . .	Saga	Japan
HSH . .	Las Vegas/Henderson Sky Harbor, NV	USA
HSI . .	Hastings Municipal, NE	USA
HSL . .	Huslia, AK	USA
HSM . .	Horsham	Australia
HSN . .	Zhoushan	China
HSP . .	Hot Springs/Ingalls, VA . . .	USA
HSS . .	Hissar	India
HST . .	Homestead/AFB, FL	USA
HSV . .	Huntsville, AL	USA
HSZ . .	Hsinchu	Taiwan
HTA . .	Chita	Russia
HTB . .	Terre-de-Bas	Gaudeloupe
HTF . .	Hatfeild	UK
HTG . .	Hatanga	Russia
HTH . .	Hawthorne, NV	USA
HTI . .	Hamilton Is	Australia
HTL . .	Houghton Lake, MI	USA
HTN . .	Hotan	China
HTO . .	East Hampton, NY	USA
HTR . .	Hateruma	Japan
HTS . .	Huntington, WV	USA
HTU . .	Hopetoun	Australia
HTV . .	Huntsville, TX	USA
HTW .	Chesapeake/Huntington County, OH	USA
HTZ . .	Hato Corozal	Colombia
HUA . .	Huntsville/Redstone/AAF . . .	USA
HUB . .	Humbert River	Australia
HUC . .	Humacao/Humacao Arpt	Puerto Rico
HUD . .	Humboldt, IA	USA
HUE . .	Humera	Ethiopia
HUF . .	Terre Haute, IN	USA
HUG . .	Huelnuetenango	Guatemala
HUH . .	Huahine/Flying Boat	French Polynesia
HUI . .	Hue/Phu Bai	Vietnam
HUJ . .	Hugo, OK	USA
HUK . .	Hukuntsi	Botswana
HUL . .	Houlton Int'l, ME	USA
HUM . .	Houma-Terrebonne, LA	USA
HUN . .	Hualien	Taiwan
HUQ . .	Houn	Libya
HUS . .	Hughes/Municipal, AK	USA
HUT . .	Hutchinsen, KS	USA
HUU . .	Huanuco	Peru
HUV . .	Hudiksvall	Sweden
HUX . .	Huatulco	Mexico
HUY . .	Humberside	UK
HUZ . .	Huizinou	China
HVA . .	Analalava	Madagascar
HVB . .	Hervey Bay	Australia
HVD . .	Khovd	Mongolia
HVE . .	Hanksville/Intermediate, UT .	USA
HVG . .	Honningsvag/Valan	Norway
HVK . .	Holmavik	Iceland
HVM .	Hvammstangi	Iceland
HVN . .	Tweed-New Haven, CT	USA
HVR . .	Havre City-County, MT	USA
HVS . .	Hartsville, SC	USA
HWA .	Hawabango .	Papua New Guinea
HWD .	Hayward Air Terminal, CA . .	USA

HWI . .	Hawk Inlet/SPB, AK	USA
HWK .	Hawker/Wilpena Pound .	Australia
HWN .	Hwange Nat Park	Zimbabwe
HWO .	Hollywood-North Perry, FL . . .	USA
HWV .	Shirley, Brookhaven Arpt, NY	USA
HXX . .	Hay	Australia
HYA . .	Hyannis-Barnstable, MA . . .	USA
HYC . .	High Wycombe (MOD)	UK
HYD . .	Hyderabad/Begumpet	India
HYF . .	Hayfields	Papua New Guinea
HYG . .	Hydaburg/SPB, AK	USA
HYL . .	Hollis/SPB, AK	USA
HYN . .	Huangyan	China
HYR . .	Hayward Municipal, WI	USA
HYS . .	Hays/Municipal, KS	USA
HYV . .	Hyvinkää	Finland
HZB . .	Hazebrouck, Merville/Calonne	France
HZG . .	Harlzhong	China
HZK . .	Husavik	Iceland
HZL . .	HazletonPA	USA
HZV . .	Hazyview	S. Africa

I

IAA . .	Igarka	Russia
IAB . .	Mcconnell/AFB, KS	USA
IAD . .	Dulles Int'l, DC	USA
IAG . .	Niagara Falls Int'l, NY	USA
IAH . .	Houston George Bush Int'l, TX	USA
IAM . .	In Amenas	Algeria
IAN . .	Kiana/Bob Barker Memorial, AK	USA
IAQ . .	Bahregan	Iran
IAR . .	Yaroslavl	Russia
IAS . .	Iasi	Romania
IAT . .	IATA Traffic Svcs	n/a
IAU . .	Iaura	Papua New Guinea
IBA . .	Ibadan/(NAW)	Nigeria
IBE . .	Ibague	Colombia
IBI . .	Iboki	Papua New Guinea
IBO . .	Illbo	Mozambique
IBP . .	Iberia	Peru
IBZ . .	Ibiza	Spain
ICA . .	Icabaru	Venezuela
ICI . .	Cicia	Fiji
ICK . .	Nieuw Nickerie	Suriname
ICL . .	Clarinda, IA	USA
ICO . .	Sicogon Is	Philippines
ICR . .	Nicaro	Cuba
ICT . .	Wichita Mid-Continent, KS . .	USA
ICY . .	Icy Bay, AK	USA
IDA . .	Idaho Falls, Fanning Fld, ID .	USA
IDB . .	Idre	Sweden
IDF . .	Idiofa	Congo, DR
IDG . .	Ida Grove/Municipal, IA	USA
IDI . .	Indiana, PA	USA
IDK . .	Indulkana	Australia
IDN . .	Indagen	Papua New Guinea
IDO . .	Santa Isabel do Morro	Brazil
IDP . .	Independence, KS	USA
IDR . .	Indore	India
IDY . .	Ile d'Yeu	France
IEG . .	Zielona Gora/Babimost . . .	Poland
IEJ . .	Lejima	Japan
IEN . .	Pine Ridge, SD	USA
IEV . .	Kiev/Zhulhany	Ukraine
IFA . .	Iowa Falls, IA	USA
IFF . .	Iffley	Australia
IFJ . .	Isafjordur	Iceland
IFL . .	Innisfail	Australia
IFN . .	Isfahan	Iran
IFO . .	Ivanci-Frankovsk	Ukraine
IFP . .	Bullhead City/Int'l, AZ	USA
IGA . .	Inagua	Bahamas
IGB . .	Ingeniero Jacobacci . .	Argentina

IGC . .	Charleston/AFB, SC	USA
IGE . .	Iguela	Gabon
IGG . .	Igiugig, AK	USA
IGH . .	Ingham	Australia
IGM . .	Kingman, AZ	USA
IGN . .	Iligan/Maria Cristina . .	Philippines
IGO . .	Chigorodo	Colombia
IGR . .	Iguazu/Cataratas	Argentina
IGU . .	Iguassu Falls/Cataratas	Brazil
IGX . .	Chapel Hill/Williams, NC . . .	USA
IHA . .	Niihama	Japan
IHN . .	Oishn	Yemen
IHO . .	Ithosy	Madagascar
IHU . .	Ihu	Papua New Guinea
IIA . .	Inishmaian	Ireland
IIN . .	Nishinoomote	Japan
IIS . .	Nissan Is . .	Papua New Guinea
IJD . .	Willimantic/Windham, CT . . .	USA
IJK . .	Izhevsk	Russia
IJU . .	Ijui/J.Batista Bos Filho	Brazil
IJX . .	Jacksonville, IL	USA
IKB . .	Wilkesboro/Wilkes County, NC	USA
IKI . .	Iki	Japan
IKK . .	Kankakee, IL	USA
IKL . .	Ikela	Congo, DR
IKO . .	Nikolski/AFS, AK	USA
IKP . .	Inkerman	Australia
IKR . .	Kirtland/AFB, NM	USA
IKS . .	Tiksi	Russia
IKT . .	Irkutsk	Russia
ILA . .	Illaga	Indonesia
ILB . .	Ilha Solteira	Brazil
ILE . .	Killeen/Municipal, TX	USA
ILF . .	Ilford, MB	Canada
ILG . .	Wilmington, DE	USA
ILH . .	Illishern/Illis Airbase . . .	Germany
ILI . .	Iliamna Arpt, AK	USA
ILK . .	Ilaka	Madagascar
ILL . .	Willmar, MN	USA
ILM . .	Wilmington, New Hanover Int'l, NC	USA
ILN . .	Wilmington, Airborne Airpark, OH	USA
ILO . .	Ioilo/Mandurriao . .	Philippines
ILP . .	Ile Des Pins	New Caledonia
ILQ . .	Ilo	Peru
ILR . .	Iiorin	Nigeria
ILU . .	Kilaguni	Kenya
ILX . .	Ileg	Papua New Guinea
ILY . .	Islay/Glenegedaie	UK
ILZ . .	Zilina	Slovakia
IMA . .	Iamalele	Papua New Guinea
IMB . .	Imbaimadai	Guyana
IMD . .	Imonda . . .	Papua New Guinea
IMF . .	Imphal/Mun	India
IMG . .	Inhaminga	Mozambique
IMI . .	Ine Is	Marshall Is
IMK . .	Simikot	Nepal
IML . .	Imperial Municipal, NE	USA
IMM . .	Immokalee, FL	USA
IMN . .	Imane	Papua New Guinea
IMO . .	Zemio	Central African Rep
IMP . .	Imperatriz	Brazil
IMT . .	Iron Mountain, MI	USA
IMZ . .	Nimroz	Afghanistan
INA . .	Inta	Russia
INB . .	Independence	Belize
INC . .	Yinchuan	China
IND . .	Indianapolis Int'l, IN	USA
INE . .	Chinde	Mozambique
INF . .	In Guezzam	Algeria
ING . .	Lago Argentina	Argentina
INH . .	Inhambane	Mozambique
INI . .	Nis	Yugoslavia
INJ . .	Injune	Australia
INK . .	Wink, TX	USA
INL . .	Int'l Falls, MN	USA
INM . .	Innamiricka	Australia
INN . .	Innsbruck/Kranebitten . . .	Austria
INO . .	Inongo	Congo, DR

INQ . . Inisheer . . . . Ireland
INR . . . Sault Ste Marie/Kincheloe/AFB, MI . . . . USA
INS . . . Indian Springs, NV . . . . USA
INT . . . Winston Salem, NC . . . . USA
INU . . . Nauru Arpt . . . . Nauru
INV . . . Inverness/Dalcross . . . . UK
INW . . Winslow Municipal, AZ . . . . . USA
INX . . . Inanwatan . . . . Indonesia
INY . . . Inyati . . . . S. Africa
INZ . . . In Salah North . . . . Algeria
IOA . . Ioannina . . . . Greece
IOK . . Iokea . . . . Papua New Guinea
IOM . . Isle Of Man/Ronaldsway . . . . . UK
ION . . Imptondo . . . . Congo, DR
IOP . . . Ioma . . . . Papua New Guinea
IOR . . Inishmore/Kilronan . . . . Ireland
IOU . . Ile Ouen . . . . New Caledonia
IOW . . Iowa City Municipal, IA . . . . . USA
IPA . . . Ipota . . . . Vanuatu
IPC . . . Easter Is/Mataveri inE . . . . . . Chile
IPE . . . Ipil . . . . Philippines
IPG . . . Ipiranga . . . . Brazil
IPH . . . Ipoh . . . . Malaysia
IPI . . . . Ipiales/San Luis . . . . Colombia
IPL . . . Imperial County, CA . . . . USA
IPN . . . Ipatinga/Usiminas . . . . Brazil
IPT . . . Williamsport, PA . . . . USA
IPU . . . Ipiau . . . . Brazil
IPW . . Ipswich . . . . UK
IQM . . Cierno . . . . China
IQN . . Qingyang . . . . China
IQQ . . Iquique/Cavancha . . . . Chile
IQT . . . Iquitos/CF, Secada . . . . Peru
IRA . . . KiraKira . . . . Solomon Is
IRB . . . Iraan/Municipal, TX . . . . USA
IRC . . . Circle/Circle City, AK . . . . USA
IRD . . . Ishurdi . . . . Bangladesh
IRE . . . Irece . . . . Brazil
IRG . . Lockhart River . . . . Australia
IRI . . . Iringa/Nduli . . . . Tanzania
IRJ . . . La Riola . . . . Argentina
IRK . . . Kirksvite Municipal, MO . . . . USA
IRN . . . Iriona . . . . Honduras
IRO . . Birao . . . . Central African Rep
IRP . . . Isro/Matari . . . . Congo, DR
IRS . . . Sturgis/Kirsch Municipal, MI . USA
ISA . . . Mount Isa . . . . Australia
ISB . . . Islamabad Int'l . . . . Pakistan
ISC . . . Isles Of Scilly-St Marys . . . . . . UK
ISD . . . Iscuande . . . . Colombia
ISE . . . Isparta . . . . Turkey
ISG . . . Ishigalki . . . . Japan
ISH . . . Ischia . . . . Italy
ISI . . . . Isisford . . . . Australia
ISJ . . . Isla Mujeres . . . . Mexico
ISK . . . Nasik/Gandhinagar . . . . India
ISL . . . Isabel Pass, AK . . . . USA
ISM . . Kissimmee/Municipal, FL . . . USA
ISN . . . Williston/Sloulin Fld Int'l, ND . USA
ISO . . . Kinston-Stallings, NC . . . . . . USA
ISP . . . Long Is MacArthur, NY . . . . . USA
ISQ . . . Manistique, MI . . . . USA
ISS . . . Wiscasset, ME . . . . USA
IST . . . Istanbul/Ataturk . . . . Turkey
ISW . . Wisconsin Rapids, WI . . . . . . USA
ITA . . . Itacoatiara . . . . Brazil
ITB . . . Itaituba . . . . Brazil
ITE . . . Itubera . . . . Brazil
ITH . . . Ithaca, NY . . . . USA
ITI . . . . Itambacuri . . . . Brazil
ITJ . . . Itaiai . . . . Brazil
ITK . . . Tokarna . . . . . Papua New Guinea
ITM . . . Osaka/Itami . . . . Japan
ITN . . . Itaburia . . . . Brazil
ITO . . . Hilo Int'l, HI . . . . USA
ITP . . . Itaperuna . . . . Brazil
ITQ . . . Itaqui . . . . Brazil
ITR . . . Itumbiara . . . . Brazil
IUE . . . Niue Is/Hanan . . . . Niue Is
IUL . . . Ilu . . . . Indonesia
IUM . . . Summit Lake, BC . . . . Canada
IUS . . . Inus . . . . Papua New Guinea
IVA . . . Ambanja . . . . Madagascar
IVC . . . Invercargill . . . . New Zealand
IVG . . . Ivangrad . . . . Yugoslavia
IVH . . . Ivishak, AK . . . . USA
IVL . . . Ivalo . . . . Finland
IVO . . . Chivoo . . . . Colombia
IVR . . . Inverell . . . . Australia
IVW . . Inverway . . . . Australia
IWA . . Ivanova . . . . Russia
IWD . . Ironwood/Gogebic County, MI . . . . USA
IWH . . Lawn Hill . . . . Australia
IWI . . . Wiscasset, ME . . . . USA
IWJ . . . Iwami . . . . Japan
IWO . . Iwo Jima Vol/Airbase . . . . Japan
IWS . . Lakeside, TX . . . . USA
IXA . . . Agartala/Singerbhil . . . . India
IXB . . . Bagdogra . . . . India
IXC . . . Chandigarh . . . . India
IXD . . . Allahabad/Bamrauli . . . . India
IXE . . . Mangalore/Balpe . . . . India
IXG . . . Belgaum/Sambre . . . . India
IXH . . . Kailashahar . . . . India
IXI . . . . Lilabari . . . . India
IXJ . . . Jammu/Satwari . . . . India
IXK . . . Keshod . . . . India
IXL . . . Leh . . . . India
IXM . . . Madurai . . . . India
IXN . . . Khowai . . . . India
IXP . . . Pathankot . . . . India
IXQ . . . Kamalpur . . . . India
IXR . . . Ranchi . . . . India
IXS . . . Silchar/Kumbhirgram . . . . . . India
IXT . . . Pasighat . . . . India
IXU . . . Aurangabad/Chikkalthana . India
IXV . . . Along . . . . India
IXW . . Jamshedpur/Sonari . . . . India
IXY . . . Kandla . . . . India
IXZ . . . Port Blair . . . . India
IYK . . . Inyokern, CA . . . . USA
IZG . . . Fryeburg, Eastern Slopes Regional Arpt, ME . . . . USA
IZO . . . Izumo . . . . Japan
IZT . . . Ixtepec . . . . Mexico

J

JAA . . Jalalabad . . . . Afghanistan
JAB . . Jabiru . . . . Australia
JAC . . Jackson Hole, WY . . . . USA
JAD . . Jandakot . . . . Australia
JAE . . Atlanta/Technology Park, GA . . . . USA
JAF . . . JaUna/Kankesanturai . . Sri Lanka
JAG . . Jacobabad . . . . Pakistan
JAH . . Aubagne/Agora Helipad . . France
JAI . . . Jaipur/Sanganeer . . . . India
JAJ . . . Atlanta/Perimeter Mall, GA . . USA
JAK . . Jacmel . . . . Haiti
JAL . . . Jalapa . . . . Mexico
JAM . . Jambol . . . . Bulgaria
JAN . . Jackson Int'l, MS . . . . USA
JAO . . Atlanta/Beaver Ruin, GA . . . . USA
JAP . . Punta Renes . . . . Costa Rica
JAQ . . Jacquinot Bay . . . . Papua New Guinea
JAS . . Jasper/County, TX . . . . USA
JAT . . Jabot . . . . Marshall Is
JAU . . Jaula . . . . Peru
JAV . . . Ilulissat . . . . Greenland
JAX . . Jacksonville Int'l, FL . . . . USA
JBC . . Boston / HP, MA . . . . USA
JBK . . Berkeley, CA . . . . USA
JBP . . Los Angeles/Commerce Bus. Plaza, CA . . . . USA
JBR . . Jonesboro, AR . . . . USA
JBS . . Pleasanton/Hacienda Bus-Park HP, CA . . . . USA
JBT . . Bethel/City Landing, AK . . . . USA
JCA . . Cannes/Croisette HP . . . . France
JCB . . Joacaba . . . . Brazil
JCC . . San Francisco/China Basin HP, CA . . . . USA
JCD . . St Croix Is/Downtown HP . . . . Virgin Is (US)
JCH . . Qasigiannguit . . . . Greenland
JCI . . . Kansas City/Johnson Industrial, MO . . . . USA
JCJ . . Cheju/Chu Ja HP . . . . . . S. Korea
JCK . . Julia Creek . . . . Australia
JCM . . Jacobina . . . . Brazil
JCN . . Incheon / HP . . . . S. Korea
JCO . . Cominc / HP . . . . Malta
JCR . . Jacareacanga . . . . Brazil
JCT . . Junction, TX . . . . USA
JCU . . Ceuta/Ceuta HP . . . . Spain
JCX . . Los Angeles/Citicorp Plaza HP, CA . . . . USA
JCY . . Johnson, TX . . . . USA
JDF . . Juiz De Fora/Francisco De Assis . . . . Brazil
JDH . . Jodhpur . . . . India
JDM . . Miami/Downtown HP, FL . . . USA
JDN . . Jordan, MT . . . . USA
JDO . . Juazeiro Do Norte/Regional Do Carin . . . . Brazil
JDP . . Paris / HP . . . . France
JDT . . Minneapolis/Downtown HP . USA
JDX . . Houston/Cntrl Bus. District, TX . . . . USA
JDY . . Downey / HP, CA . . . . USA
JDZ . . Jingdezhen . . . . China
JED . . Jeddah/King Abdul Aziz Int'l Arpt . . . . Saudi Arabia
JEE . . Jeremie . . . . Haiti
JEF . . Jefferson City, MO . . . . USA
JEG . . Aasiaat . . . . Greenland
JEJ . . Jeh . . . . Marshall Is
JEM . . Emeryville / HP, CA . . . . USA
JEQ . . Jequie . . . . Brazil
JER . . Jersey . . . . UK
JEV . . Eviry HP . . . . France
JFK . . Kennedy Int'l, NY . . . . USA
JFM . . Fremantle/ HP . . . . Australia
JFN . . Jefferson/Ashtabula, OH . . . USA
JFR . . Paamiut . . . . Greenland
JGA . . Jamnagar/Govardhanpur . . India
JGB . . Jagdaipur . . . . India
JGC . . Grand Canyon / HP, AZ . . . . USA
JGE . . Geoie HP . . . . S. Korea
JGL . . Atlanta/Galleria, GA . . . . USA
JGN . . Jiayuguan . . . . China
JGO . . Oeqertarsuaq . . . . Greenland
JGP . . Houston/Greenway Plaza HP, TX . . . . USA
JGQ . Houston/Transco Twr Galleria, TX . . . . USA
JGR . . Groennedal/ HP . . . . . Greenland
JGX . . Glendale / HP, CA . . . . USA
JHB . . Johor Bahru/Sultan Ismail Int'l . . . . Malaysia
JHC . . Garden City/Is HP, NY . . . . . USA
JHE . . Helsingborg/ HP . . . . Sweden
JHG . . Jinghong/Gasa . . . . China
JHM . . Kapalua, HI . . . . USA
JHN . . Nanchang . . . . China
JHQ . . Shute Harbour HP . . . . . Australia
JHS . . Sisimiut . . . . Greenland
JHW . . Jamestown, NY . . . . USA
JHY . . Cambridge/Hyatt Regency HP, MA . . . . USA
JI0 . . . Ontario/Int'l HP, CA . . . . USA
JIA . . . Juina . . . . Brazil
JIB . . . Djibouti/Ambouli . . . Côte D'Ivoire
JID . . . Los Angeles/City Of Industry HP, CA . . . . USA

AIRPORTS

JIJ	Jijig/Jigiga	Ethiopia
JIK	Ikaria Is/Ikaria	Greece
JIL	Jilin	China
JIM	Jimma	Ethiopia
JIN	Jinja	Uganda
JIP	Jpjapa	Ecuador
JIR	Jin	Nepal
JIU	Jiujiang	China
JIW	Jiwani	Pakistan
JJI	Juanjui	Peru
JJN	Jinjiang	China
JJU	Qaqortoq / HP	Greenland
JKG	Jonkoping/Axamo	Sweden
JKH	Chios/Khios	Greece
JKL	Jackson/Carroll, KY	USA
JKR	Janakpur	Nepal
JKV	Jacksonville, TX	USA
JLA	Cooper Lodge/Quartz Creek, AK	USA
JLB	Long Beach / HP, CA	USA
JLD	Landskrona/ HP	Sweden
JLH	Arlington Heights/US AHP, IL	USA
JLN	Joplin, MO	USA
JLO	Jesolo	Italy
JLP	Juan Les Pins	France
JLR	Jalbalpur	India
JLS	Jales	Brazil
JLX	Los Angeles/Union Stn HP, CA	USA
JMA	Houston/Marriot Astrodome, TX	USA
JMB	Jamba	Angola
JMC	Sausalito/Marin County, CA	USA
JMD	Dallas/Market Centre HP, TX	USA
JMH	Schaumburg/Marriott HP, IL	USA
JMK	Mikonos	Greece
JMM	Malmo/Malmo Harbour HP	Sweden
JMN	Mankato/Municipal HP, MN	USA
JMO	Jornsom	Nepal
JMS	Jamestown, ND	USA
JMU	Jiarnusi	China
JMY	Freetown/Mammy Yoko HP	Sierra Leone
JNA	Januaria	Brazil
JNB	Johannesburg Int'l	S. Africa
JNG	Jining	China
JNH	Dallas/North Park Inn HP, TX	USA
JNI	Junin	Argentina
JNN	Nanortalik	Greenland
JNP	Newport Beach / HP, CA	USA
JNS	Narsaq/ HP	Greenland
JNU	Juneau Int'l, AK	USA
JNW	Newport, OR	USA
JNX	Naxos	Greece
JNZ	Jinzhou	China
JOC	Santa Ana/Centerport HP, CA	USA
JOE	Joensuu	Finland
JOG	Yogyakarta/Adisutjipto	Indonesia
JOH	Port Saint Johns	S. Africa
JOI	Joinville/Cubatao	Brazil
JOK	Josrikar-Cia	Russia
JOL	Jolo	Philippines
JOM	Njornbe	Tanzania
JON	Johnston Is	Wake/Midway Is
JOP	Josephstaal	Papua New Guinea
JOR	Orange/The City HP, CA	USA
JOS	Jos	Nigeria
JOT	Joliet Municipal, IL	USA
JPA	Joato Pessoa/Castro Pinto	Brazil
JPD	Pasadena / HP, CA	USA
JPN	Washington/Pentagon Army, DC	USA
JPR	Ji-Parana	Brazil
JPT	Houston/Park Ten HP, TX	USA
JPU	Paris/La Defense HP	France
JQE	Jaque	Panama

JRA	New York/West 30th St HP, NY	USA
JRB	New York/Downtown Manhattan HP, NY	USA
JRC	Rochester/Municipal HP, MN	USA
JRD	Riverside / HP, CA	USA
JRE	New York/East 60th Street HP, NY	USA
JRH	Jorhat/Rowriah	India
JRK	Arsuk	Greenland
JRN	Juruena	Brazil
JRO	Kilimanjaro	Tanzania
JRS	Jerusalem	Occupied Palestinian Ter
JSA	Jaisalmer	India
JSD	Stratford/Sikorsky HP, CT	USA
JSG	San Rafael HP, CA	USA
JSH	Sitia	Greece
JSI	Skiathos Is	Greece
JSK	Saint Cloud HP, MN	USA
JSL	Atlantic City/Steel Pier HP, NJ	USA
JSM	Jose De San Martin	Argentina
JSN	Los Angeles/Sherman Oaks HP, CA	USA
JSO	Sodertalje/Sodertalje HP	Sweden
JSP	Cheju/Sogwipo HP	S. Korea
JSR	Jessore	Bangladesh
JSS	Spetsai Is	Gaudeloupe
JST	Johnstown-Cambria, PA	USA
JSU	Manihsoq / HP	Greenland
JSY	Syros Is	Greece
JSZ	Saint Tropez / HP	France
JTI	Jalai	Brazil
JTO	Thousand Oaks / HP, CA	USA
JTR	Thira	Greece
JTY	Astypalaia Is	Greece
JUA	Juara	Brazil
JUB	Juba	Sudan
JUC	Los Angeles/Universal City HP, CA	USA
JUI	Juist	Germany
JUJ	Jujuy/El Cadilial	Argentina
JUL	Juliaca	Peru
JUM	Jumia	Nepal
JUN	Jundah	Australia
JUO	Jurado	Colombia
JUP	Upland/Cable HP, CA	USA
JUR	Jurien Bay	Australia
JUT	Juticalpa	Honduras
JUV	Upernavik/ HP	Greenland
JUZ	Juzhou	China
JVA	Ankavandra	Madagascar
JVI	Manville/Kupper, NJ	USA
JVL	Janesville, WI	USA
JWA	Jwaneng	Botswana
JWC	Los Angeles/Warner Cntr Bus. Plaza, CA	USA
JWH	Houston/Westchase Hilton HP, TX	USA
JWL	Houston/Woodlawns, TX	USA
JXN	Jackson-Reynolds Municipal, MI	USA
JYO	Leesburg/Godfrey, VA	USA
JYV	Jyvaskyla	Finland

K

KAA	Kasama	Zambia
KAB	Kariba	Zimbabwe
KAC	Kameshli	Syria
KAD	Kaduna	Nigeria
KAE	Kake/SPB, AK	USA
KAF	Karato	Papua New Guinea
KAG	Kangnung/Air Base	S. Korea
KAH	Melbourne HP	Australia

KAI	Kaieteur	Guyana
KAJ	Kajaani	Finland
KAK	Kar	Papua New Guinea
KAL	Kallag, AK	USA
KAM	Kamaran Is	Yemen
KAN	Kano/Aminu Kano Int'l	Nigeria
KAO	Kuusamo	Finland
KAP	Kapanga	Congo, DR
KAQ	Kamulai	Papua New Guinea
KAR	Kamarang	Guyana
KAS	Karasburg	Namibia
KAT	Kaitaia	New Zealand
KAU	Kauhava	Finland
KAV	Kavanayen	Venezuela
KAW	Kawthaung	Myanmar
KAX	Kalbarri	Australia
KAY	Wakaya Is	Fiji
KAZ	Kau	Indonesia
KBA	Kabala	Sierra Leone
KBB	Kirkimbie	Australia
KBC	Birch Creek, AK	USA
KBD	Kimberley Downs	Australia
KBE	Bell Is/Hot Springs SPB, AK	USA
KBF	Karubaga	Indonesia
KBG	Kabaiega Falls	Uganda
KBH	Kalat	Pakistan
KBI	Kribi	Cameroon
KBJ	Kings Canyon	Australia
KBK	Klag Bay, AK	USA
KBL	Kabul/Khwaja Rawash	Afghanistan
KBM	Kabwurn	Papua New Guinea
KBN	Kabinda	Congo, DR
KBO	Kabalo	Congo, DR
KBP	Kiev/Borispol	Ukraine
KBQ	Kasungu	Malawi
KBR	Kota Bharu/Pengkalan Chepa	Malaysia
KBS	Bo	Sierra Leone
KBT	Kaben	Marshall Is
KBU	Kotabaru	Indonesia
KBV	Krabi	Thailand
KBW	Chignik, Chignik Bay, AK	USA
KBX	Kambuaya	Indonesia
KBY	Streaky Bay	Australia
KBZ	Kaikoura	New Zealand
KCA	Kucla	China
KCB	Kasikasirna/Tepoe Airstrip	Suriname
KCC	Coffman Cove, AK	USA
KCD	Kamur	Indonesia
KCE	Collinsville	Australia
KCF	Kadanwari	Pakistan
KCG	Chignik, Fisheries, AK	USA
KCH	Kuching	Malaysia
KCI	Kon	Indonesia
KCJ	Komaio	Papua New Guinea
KCK	Kansas City/Fairfax, KS	USA
KCL	Chignik/Lagoon, AK	USA
KCM	Kahramanmaras	Turkey
KCN	Chernofski/SPB, AK	USA
KCO	Kocaeli/Cengiz Topel	Turkey
KCP	Kamenets-Podolskiy	Ukraine
KCQ	Chignik, AK	USA
KCR	Colorado Creek, AK	USA
KCS	Kings Creek Stn	Australia
KCU	Masindi	Uganda
KCZ	Kochi	Japan
KDA	Kolda	Senegal
KDB	Kambaida	Australia
KDC	Kandi	Benin
KDD	Khuzdar	Pakistan
KDE	Koroba	Papua New Guinea
KDF	Kouba	Algeria
KDG	Kardjali	Bulgaria
KDH	Kandahar	Afghanistan
KDI	Kendan/Wolter Monginsidi	Indonesia
KDJ	N'Djole	Gabon
KDK	Kodiak/Municipal, AK	USA
KDL	Kardla	Estonia

AIRPORTS

Code	Airport	Country
KDM	Kaadedhclhoo	Maldives
KDN	Ndende	Gabon
KDO	Kadhdhoo	Maldives
KDP	Kandep	Papua New Guinea
KDQ	Kamberatoro	Papua New Guinea
KDR	Kandrian	Papua New Guinea
KDS	Kamaran Downs	Australia
KDU	Skardu	Pakistan
KDV	Kandavu	Fiji
KEA	Keisah	Indonesia
KEB	Nanwalek, AK	USA
KEC	Kasenga	Congo, DR
KED	Kaedi	Mauritania
KEE	Kelle	Congo, DR
KEF	Reykjavik Int'l	Iceland
KEG	Keglsugi	Papua New Guinea
KEH	Kenmore Air Harbor, WA	USA
KEi	Kepi	Indonesia
KEJ	Kemerovo	Russia
KEK	Ekwok, AK	USA
KEL	Kiel/Holtenau Civilian	Germany
KEM	Kemi/Tornio	Finland
KEN	Kenema	Sierra Leone
KEO	Odienne	Côte D'Ivoire
KEP	Nepalganj	Nepal
KEQ	Kebar	Indonesia
KER	Kerman	Iran
KES	Kelsey, MB	Canada
KET	Keng Tung	Myanmar
KEU	Kelly Bar, AK	USA
KEV	Kuorevesi/Halli	Finland
KEW	Keewaywin, ON	Canada
KEX	Kanabea	Papua New Guinea
KEY	Kericho	Kenya
KFA	Kiffa	Mauritania
KFG	Kalkurung	Australia
KFP	False Pass, AK	USA
KFS	Kastamonu	Turkey
KGA	Kananga	Congo, DR
KGB	Konge	Papua New Guinea
KGC	Kingscote	Australia
KGD	Kaliningrad	Russia
KGE	Kagau	Solomon Is
KGF	Karaganda	Kazakstan
KGG	Kedougou	Senegal
KGH	Yongai	Papua New Guinea
KGI	Kalgoorlie	Australia
KGJ	Karonga	Malawi
KGK	New Koliganek, AK	USA
KGL	Kigali/Gregoire Kayibanda	Rwanda
KGM	Kungum	Papua New Guinea
KGN	Kasongo Lunda	Congo, DR
KGO	Kirovograd	Ukraine
KGP	Kogalym Int'l	Russia
KGR	Kulgera	Australia
KGS	Kos	Greece
KGU	Keningau	Malaysia
KGW	Kagi	Papua New Guinea
KGX	Grayling, AK	USA
KGY	Kingaroy	Australia
KGZ	Glacier Creek, AK	USA
KHA	Khaneh	Iran
KHC	Kerch	Ukraine
KHD	Khorramabad	Iran
KHE	Kherson	Ukraine
KHG	Kashi	China
KHH	Kaohsiung/Int'l	Taiwan
KHI	Karachi/Quaid-E-Azam Int'l	Pakistan
KHJ	Kauhajoki	Finland
KHK	Khark Is	Iran
KHL	Khulna	Bangladesh
KHM	Khamti	Myanmar
KHN	Nanchang	China
KHO	Khoka Moya	S. Africa
KHR	Kharkhorin	Mongolia
KHS	Khasab	Oman
KHT	Khost	Afghanistan
KHU	Kremenchug	Ukraine
KHV	Khaloarovsk/Novyy	Russia
KHW	Khwai River Lodge	Botswana
KIA	Kaiapit	Papua New Guinea
KIB	Ivanof Bay/SPB, AK	USA
KIC	King City, Mesa Del Rey, CA	USA
KID	Kristianstad/Everod	Sweden
KIE	Kieta/Aropa	Papua New Guinea
KIF	Kingfisher Lake, ON	Canada
KIG	Koinghaas	S. Africa
KIH	Kish Is	Iran
KIJ	Niigata	Japan
KIK	Kirkuk	Iraq
KIL	Kilwa	Congo, DR
KIM	Kimberley	S. Africa
KIN	Kingston/Norman Manley	Jamaica
KIO	Kili Is	Marshall Is
KIP	Wichita Falls/Kickapoo, KS	USA
KIQ	Kira	Papua New Guinea
KIR	Kerry	Ireland
KIS	Kisumu	Kenya
KIT	Kithira	Greece
KIV	Chisinau	Moldova, Republic of
KIW	Kitwe/Southdowns	Zambia
KIX	Osaka/Kansai Int'l	Japan
KIY	Kilwa	Tanzania
KIZ	Kikinonda	Papua New Guinea
KJA	Krasnoiarsk	Russia
KJK	Kortrijk/Wevelgem	Belgium
KJP	Kerama	Japan
KJU	Kamiraba	Papua New Guinea
KKA	Koyuk, AK	USA
KKB	Kitoi Bay/SPB, AK	USA
KKC	Khon Kaen	Thailand
KKD	Kokoda	Papua New Guinea
KKE	Kerikeri	New Zealand
KKF	Kagvik Creek, AK	USA
KKG	Konawaruk	Guyana
KKH	Kongiganak, AK	USA
KKI	Akiachak/SPB, AK	USA
KKJ	Kita Kyushu/Kokura	S. Korea
KKK	Kalakalket/AFS, AK	USA
KKL	Karluk Lake SPB, AK	USA
KKM	Lop Bun	Thailand
KKN	Kirkenes/Hoeybuktmoen	Norway
KKO	Kaikohe	New Zealand
KKP	Koolburra	Australia
KKR	Kaukura Atoll	F. Polynesia
KKT	Kentland, IN	USA
KKU	Ekuk, AK	USA
KKW	Kikwit	Congo, DR
KKX	Kikaiga Shima	Japan
KKY	Kilkenny	Ireland
KKZ	Koh Kong	Cambodia
KLA	Kampala	Uganda
KLB	Kalabo	Zambia
KLC	Kaolack	Senegal
KLD	Kalinin/Migalovo	Russia
KLE	Kaele	Cameroon
KLF	Kaluga	Russia
KLG	Kalskag/Municipal, AK	USA
KLH	Kolhapur	India
KLI	Kota Koli	Congo, DR
KLJ	Klaipeda	Lithuania
KLK	Kalokol	Kenya
KLL	Levelock, AK	USA
KLN	Larsen/SPB, AK	USA
KLO	Kalibo	Philippines
KLP	Kelp Bay, AK	USA
KLQ	Keluang	Indonesia
KLR	Kalmar	Sweden
KLS	Kelso, Longview, WA	USA
KLT	Kaiserslautern	Germany
KLU	Klagenfurt	Austria
KLV	Karlovy Vary	Czech Rep
KLW	Klawock, AK	USA
KLX	Kalamata	Greece
KLY	Kalima	Congo, DR
KLZ	Kleinzee	S. Africa
KMA	Kerema	Papua New Guinea
KMB	Koinambe	Papua New Guinea
KMC	King Khalid Military	Saudi Arabia
KMD	Mandji	Gabon
KME	Kamembe	Rwanda
KMF	Kamina	Papua New Guinea
KMG	Kunming	China
KMH	Kuruman	S. Africa
KMI	Miyazaki	Japan
KMJ	Kumamoto	Japan
KMK	Makabana	Congo, DR
KML	Kamileroi	Australia
KMM	Kimam	Indonesia
KMN	Kamina	Congo, DR
KMO	Manolkotak/SPB, AK	USA
KMP	Keetmanshoop/J.G.H. Van Der Wath	Namibia
KMQ	Konnatsu	Japan
KMR	Karinnui	Papua New Guinea
KMS	Kumasi	Ghana
KMT	Kampot	Cambodia
KMU	Kismayu	Somalia
KMV	Kalemyo	Myanmar
KMW	Kostroma	Russia
KMX	Khamis Mushat	Saudi Arabia
KMY	Moser Bay, AK	USA
KMZ	Kaorna	Zambia
KNA	Vina del Mar	Chile
KNB	Kanab, UT	USA
KNC	Ji'An	China
KND	Kindu	Congo, DR
KNE	Kanainj	Papua New Guinea
KNF	Kings Lynn/Marham/RAF	UK
KNG	Kaimana/Utarom	Indonesia
KNH	Kinmen/Shang-Yi	Taiwan
KNI	Katanning	Australia
KNJ	Kindamba	Congo, DR
KNK	Kakhonak, AK	USA
KNL	Kelanoa	Papua New Guinea
KNM	Kaniama	Congo, DR
KNN	Kankan	Guinea
KNO	Knokke/Het Zoute	Belgium
KNP	Capanda	Angola
KNQ	Kone	New Caledonia
KNR	Kangan/Jam	Iran
KNS	King Is	Australia
KNT	Kennett Municipal, MO	USA
KNU	Kanpur	India
KNV	Knights Inlet, BC	Canada
KNW	New Stuyahok, AK	USA
KNX	Kununurra	Australia
KNY	Kinoosao, SK	Canada
KNZ	Kenieba	Mali
KOA	Kona/Keahole, HI	USA
KOB	Koutaba	Cameroon
KOC	Koumac	New Caledonia
KOD	Kotabangun	Indonesia
KOE	Kupang/El Tari	Indonesia
KOF	Komatipoort	S. Africa
KOG	Khong	Laos
KOH	Koolatah	Australia
KOI	Kirkwall	UK
KOJ	Kagoshima	Japan
KOK	Kokkola/Pietarsaari/Kruunupyy	Finland
KOL	Kounnala	Central African Rep
KOM	Korno-Manda	Papua New Guinea
KON	Kontum	Vietnam
KOO	Kongolo	Congo, DR
KOP	Nakhon Phanom	Thailand
KOQ	Koethen	Germany
KOR	Kokoro	Papua New Guinea
KOS	Sihanoukville	Cambodia
KOT	Kotlik, AK	USA
KOU	Koulamoutou	Gabon
KOV	Kokshetau	Kazakstan
KOW	Ganzhou	China
KOX	Kokonao/Timuka	Indonesia
KOY	Olga Bay/SPB, AK	USA
KOZ	Ouzinkie/SPB, AK	USA
KPA	Koplago	Papua New Guinea

A I R P O R T S

Code	Location	Country
KPB	Point Baker/SPB, AK	USA
KPC	Port Clarence, AK	USA
KPD	King Of Prussia, PA	USA
KPE	Yapsiei	Papua New Guinea
KPG	Kurupung	Guyana
KPH	Pauloff Harbor/SPB, AK	USA
KPI	Kapit	Malaysia
KPK	Parks/SPB, AK	USA
KPM	Kompiam	Papua New Guinea
KPN	Kipnulk, AK	USA
KPO	Pohang/Air Base	S. Korea
KPP	Kalpowar	Australia
KPR	Port Williams/SPB, AK	USA
KPS	Kempsey	Australia
KPT	Jackpot, NV	USA
KPV	Perryville/SPB, AK	USA
KPY	Port Bailey/SPB, AK	USA
KQA	Akutan, AK	USA
KQB	Koonibba	Australia
KQL	Kol	Papua New Guinea
KRA	Kerang	Australia
KRB	Karumba	Australia
KRC	Kerinci/Depati Parbo	Indonesia
KRD	Kurundi	Australia
KRE	Kirundo	Benin
KRF	Kramfors/Flygplats	Sweden
KRG	Karasabai	Guyana
KRH	Redhill	UK
KRI	Kikori	Papua New Guinea
KRJ	Karawari	Papua New Guinea
KRK	Krakow	Poland
KRL	Korla	China
KRM	Karanambo	Guyana
KRN	Kiruna	Sweden
KRO	Kurgan	Russia
KRP	Karup/Military	Denmark
KRQ	Kramatorsk	Ukraine
KRR	Krasnodar	Russia
KRS	Kristiansand/Kjevik	Norway
KRT	Khartoum/Civil	Sudan
KRU	Kerau	Papua New Guinea
KRV	Kerio Valley	Kenya
KRW	Turkmanbashi	Turkmenistan
KRX	Kar Kar	Papua New Guinea
KRY	Karamay	China
KRZ	Kiri	Congo, DR
KSA	Kosrae	Micronesia
KSB	Kasanombe	Papua New Guinea
KSC	Kosice/Barca	Slovakia
KSD	Karlstad/Flygplats	Sweden
KSE	Kasese	Uganda
KSF	Kassel/Calden	Germany
KSG	Kisengan	Papua New Guinea
KSH	Kermanshah	Iran
KSI	Kissidougou	Guinea
KSJ	Kasos Is	Greece
KSK	Karlskoga	Sweden
KSL	Kassala	Sudan
KSM	Saint Marys, AK	USA
KSN	Kostanay	Kazakstan
KSO	Kastoria/Aristotelis	Greece
KSP	Kosipe	Papua New Guinea
KSQ	Karshi	Uzbekistan
KSR	Sanoy River, AK	USA
KSS	Skasso	Mali
KST	Kosti	Sudan
KSU	Kristiansund/Kvernberget	Norway
KSV	Springvale	Australia
KSW	Kiryat Shmona	Israel
KSX	Yasuru	Papua New Guinea
KSY	Kars	Turkey
KSZ	Kotlas	Russia
KTA	Karratha	Australia
KTB	Thorne Bay, AK	USA
KTC	Katiola	Côte D'Ivoire
KTD	Kitadaito Is	Japan
KTE	Kerteh	Malaysia
KTF	Takalka	New Zealand
KTG	Ketapang/Rahadi Usmaman	Indonesia

Code	Location	Country
KTH	Tikchik/SPB, AK	USA
KTI	Kratie	Cambodia
KTK	Kanua	Papua New Guinea
KTL	Kitale	Kenya
KTM	Kathmandu/Tribhuvan	Nepal
KTN	Ketchikan/Int'l, AK	USA
KTO	Kato	Guyana
KTP	Kingston/Tinson	Jamaica
KTQ	Kitee	Finland
KTR	Katherine/Tindal	Australia
KTS	Teller Mission, Brevig Mission, AK	USA
KTT	Kittilä	Finland
KTU	Kota	India
KTV	Kamarata	Venezuela
KTW	Katowice/Pyrzowice	Poland
KTX	Koutiala	Mali
KTZ	Kwun Tong	Hong Kong
KUA	Kuantan	Malaysia
KUB	Koala Belait	Brunei
KUC	Kuria	Kiribati
KUD	Kudat	Malaysia
KUE	Kukundu	Solomon Is
KUF	Samara	Russia
KUG	Kubin Is	Australia
KUH	Kushiro	Japan
KUI	Kawau Is	New Zealand
KUJ	Kushimoto	Japan
KUK	Kasigluk, AK	USA
KUL	Kuala Lumpur/Kuala Lumpur Infl	Malaysia
KUM	Yakushima	Japan
KUN	Kaunas/Int'l	Lithuania
KUO	Kuopio	Finland
KUP	Kupiano	Papua New Guinea
KUQ	Kuri	Papua New Guinea
KUR	Kuran-O-Munjan	Afghanistan
KUS	Kulusuk	Greenland
KUT	Kutaisi	Georgia
KUU	Kulu/Shuntar	India
KUV	Kunsan/Air Base	S. Korea
KUW	Kugururok River, AK	USA
KUY	Kamusi/Kamusi Arpt	Papua New Guinea
KUZ	Kusan/Air Base	S. Korea
KVA	Kavala/Megas Alexandros	Greece
KVB	Skovde	Sweden
KVC	King Cove, AK	USA
KVD	Gyancizha	Azerbaijan
KVE	Kitava	Papua New Guinea
KVG	Kavieng	Papua New Guinea
KVK	Kirovsk	Russia
KVL	Kivalina, AK	USA
KVU	Korolevu	Fiji
KVX	Kirov	Russia
KWA	Kwajalein	Marshall Is
KWB	Karimunjawa	Indonesia
KWD	Kawadjia	Central African Rep
KWE	Guiyang	China
KWF	Waterfall/SPS, AK	USA
KWG	Krivoy Rog	Ukraine
KWH	Khwahan	Afghanistan
KWI	Kuwait Int'l	Kuwait
KWJ	Kwangju/Air Base	S. Korea
KWK	Kwigillingok, AK	USA
KWL	Guilin	China
KWM	Kowanyama	Australia
KWN	Quinhagak/Kwinhagak, AK	USA
KWO	Kawito	Papua New Guinea
KWP	Village/SPB, AK	USA
KWR	Kwai Harbour	Solomon Is
KWS	Kwailabesi Aerodrom	Solomon Is
KWT	Kwethluk, AK	USA
KWU	Mansion House	New Zealand
KWV	Kurwina	Papua New Guinea
KWX	Kiwai Is	Papua New Guinea
KWY	Kiwayu	Kenya
KWZ	Kolwezi	Congo, DR
KXA	Kasaan SPB, AK	USA
KXE	Klerksdorp	S. Africa

Code	Location	Country
KXF	Koro Is	Fiji
KXK	Kornsornolsk Na Amure	Russia
KXR	Karoola	Papua New Guinea
KYA	Konya	Turkey
KYB	Yangoonabie	Australia
KYD	Orchid Is	Taiwan
KYE	Tripoli/Kleyate	Lebanon
KYF	Yeelirrie	Australia
KYI	Yalata Mission	Australia
KYK	Karuk, AK	USA
KYL	Key Largo/Port Largo, FL	USA
KYN	Milton Keynes	UK
KYO	Tampa/Topp Of Tampa, FL	USA
KYP	Kyaukpyu	Myanmar
KYS	Kayes	Mali
KYT	Kyauktaw	Myanmar
KYU	Koyukuk, AK	USA
KYX	Yalumet	Papua New Guinea
KYZ	Kyzyl	Russia
KZB	Zachar Bay/SPB, AK	USA
KZC	Kompong-Chhna	Cambodia
KZD	Krakor	Cambodia
KZF	Kaintiba	Papua New Guinea
KZG	Kitzingen	Germany
KZH	Kizhuyak, AK	USA
KZI	Kozani/Philippos	Greece
KZK	Kompong Thorn	Cambodia
KZN	Kazan	Russia
KZO	Kzyl-Orda	Kazakstan
KZS	Kastelorizo	Greece

L

LAA	Lamar Municipal, CO	USA
LAB	Lablab	Papua New Guinea
LAC	Pulau Layang-Layang Is	Malaysia
LAD	Luanda/4 de Fevereiro	Angola
LAE	Lae/Nadzab	Papua New Guinea
LAF	Lafayette-Purdue, IN	USA
LAG	La Guaira	Venezuela
LAH	Labuha/Taliabu	Indonesia
LAI	Lannion/Servel	France
LAJ	Lages	Brazil
LAK	Aklavik, NT	Canada
LAL	Lakeland, FL	USA
LAM	Los Alamos, NM	USA
LAN	Lansing, MI	USA
LAO	Laoag	Philippines
LAP	La Paz/Leon	Mexico
LAQ	Beida/La Braq	Libya
LAR	Laramie, WY	USA
LAS	Las Vegas, NV	USA
LAT	La Unbe	Colombia
LAU	Lamu	Kenya
LAV	Lalomalava	Samoa
LAW	Lawton, OK	USA
LAX	Los Angeles Int'l, CA	USA
LAY	Ladysmith	S. Africa
LAZ	Bom Jesus Da Lapa	Brazil
LBA	Leeds Bradford/Yeadon	UK
LBB	Lubbock Int'l, TX	USA
LBC	Luebeck/Blankensee	Germany
LBD	Khudzhand	Tajikistan
LBE	Latrobe, PA	USA
LBF	North Platte, NE	USA
LBG	Paris/Le Bourget	France
LBH	Sydney/Palm Beach SPB	Australia
LBI	Albi/Le Sequestre	France
LBJ	Labuan Bajo/Mutiara	Indonesia
LBK	Liboi	Kenya
LBL	Liberal/Municipal, KS	USA
LBM	Lualbo	Mozambique
LBN	Lake Baringo	Kenya
LBO	Lusambo	Congo, DR
LBP	Long Banga	Malaysia
LBQ	Lambarene	Gabon

AIRPORTS

Code	Airport	Location
LBR	Labrea	Brazil
LBS	Labasa	Fiji
LBT	Lumberton, NC	USA
LBU	Labuan	Malaysia
LBV	Libreville	Gabon
LBW	Long Bawan/Juvai Semaring	Indonesia
LBX	Lubang	Philippines
LBY	La Baule/Montoir	France
LBZ	Lukapa	Angola
LCA	Larnaca	Cyprus
LCB	Pontes e Lacerda	Brazil
LCC	Lecce/Galatina	Italy
LCD	Louis Trichardt	S. Africa
LCE	La Ceiba/Goloson Int'l.	Honduras
LCF	Rio Dulce/Las Vegas.	Guatemala
LCG	La Coruna	Spain
LCH	Lake Charles, LA	USA
LCI	Laconia, NH	USA
LCJ	Lodz/Lodz Lublinek	Poland
LCK	Rickenbacker, OH	USA
LCL	La Colorna	Cuba
LCM	La Cumbre	Argentina
LCN	Balcanoona	Australia
LCO	Lague	Congo
LCP	Loncopue	Argentina
LCR	La Chorrera	Colombia
LCS	Las Canas	Costa Rica
LCV	Lucca	Italy
LCY	London/London City Arpt	UK
LDA	Maida	India
LDB	Londrina	Brazil
LDC	Lindernan Is	Australia
LDE	Lourdes/Tarbes	France
LDH	Lord Howe Is	Australia
LDI	Lindi/Kikwetu	Tanzania
LDJ	Linden, NJ	USA
LDK	Lidkoping/Hovby	Sweden
LDM	Ludington/Mason Cnty, MI	USA
LDN	Lamidanda	Nepal
LDO	Ladouanie	Suriname
LDR	Lodar	Yemen
LDS	Leeds, MT	USA
LDU	Lahad Datu	Malaysia
LDV	Landivisiau	France
LDW	Lansdowne	Australia
LDX	St Laurent du Maroni	F. Guiana
LDY	Londonderry/Eglinton	UK
LDZ	Londolozi	S. Africa
LEA	Learmonth	Australia
LEB	Hanover, NH	USA
LEC	Lencois/Chapada Diamantina	Brazil
LED	St Petersburg/Pulkovo	Russia
LEE	Leesburg, FL	USA
LEF	Lebakeng	Lesotho
LEG	Aleg	Mauritania
LEH	Le Havre/Octeville	France
LEI	Almeria	Spain
LEJ	Leipzig/Halle	Germany
LEK	Labe	Guinea
LEL	Lake Evella	Australia
LEM	Lemmon, SD	USA
LEN	Leon	Spain
LEO	Leconi	Gabon
LEP	Leopoldina	Brazil
LEQ	Lands End	UK
LER	Leinster	Australia
LES	Lesobeng	Lesotho
LET	Leticia/Gen. A.V. Cobo	Colombia
LEU	Seo De Urgel/Aeroport De La Seu	Spain
LEV	Bureta/Levuka Airfield	Fiji
LEW	Auburn, ME	USA
LEX	Lexington-Blue Grass, KY	USA
LEY	Lelystad	Netherlands
LEZ	La Esperanza	Honduras
LFI	Langley/AFB, VA	USA
LFK	Nacogdoches, TX	USA
LFN	Louisburg, NC	USA
LFO	Kelafo/Callaf/Kelafo	Ethiopia
LFP	Lakefield	Australia
LFR	La Fria	Venezuela
LFT	Lafayette, LA	USA
LFW	Lome/Tokoin	Togo
LGA	New York-La Guardia, NY	USA
LGB	Long Beach, CA	USA
LGC	La Grange/Calloway, GA	USA
LGD	La Grande, OR	USA
LGE	Lake Gregory	Australia
LGF	Laguna/AAF, AZ	USA
LGG	Liege/Bierset	Belgium
LGH	Leigh Creek	Australia
LGI	Deadmans Cay	Bahamas
LGK	Langkawi	Malaysia
LGL	Long Lellang	Malaysia
LGM	Laiagam	Papua New Guinea
LGN	Linga Linga	Papua New Guinea
LGO	Langeoog	Germany
LGP	Legaspi	Philippines
LGQ	Lago Agrio	Ecuador
LGR	Cochrane	Chile
LGS	Malargue	Argentina
LGT	Las Gaviotas	Colombia
LGU	Logan, UT	USA
LGW	London/Gatwick	UK
LGX	Lugh Ganane	Somalia
LGY	Lagunillas	Venezuela
LGZ	Leguizamo	Colombia
LHA	Lahr	Germany
LHB	Lost Harbor, AK	USA
LHD	Lake Hood/SPB, AK	USA
LHE	Lahore	Pakistan
LHG	Lightning Ridge	Australia
LHI	Lereh	Indonesia
LHK	Guanghua	China
LHN	Lishan	Taiwan
LHP	Lehu	Papua New Guinea
LHQ	Lancaster, Fairfield County Arpt, OH	USA
LHR	London/Heathrow	UK
LHS	Las Heras	Argentina
LHV	Lock Haven, PA	USA
LHW	Lanzhou	China
LHX	La Junta, CO	USA
LIA	Liangping	China
LIB	Limbunya	Australia
LIC	Limon Municipal, CO	USA
LID	Leiden/Valkenburg	Netherlands
LIE	Libenge	Congo, DR
LIF	Lifou	New Caledonia
LIG	Limoges/Bellegarde	France
LIH	Kauai Is/Lihue, HI	USA
LII	Mulia	Indonesia
LIJ	Long Is, AK	USA
LIK	Likiep Is	Marshall Is
LIL	Lille/Lesquin	France
LIM	Lima/J Chavez Int'l	Peru
LIN	Milan/Linate	Italy
LIO	Limon	Costa Rica
LIP	Lins	Brazil
LIQ	Lisala	Congo, DR
LIR	Liberia	Costa Rica
LIS	Lisboa Portela	Portugal
LIT	Little Rock, AR	USA
LIU	Linosa HP	Italy
LIV	Livengood, AK	USA
LIW	Loikaw	Myanmar
LIX	Likoma Is	Malawi
LIY	Wright/AAF, GA	USA
LIZ	Loring/AFB, ME	USA
LJA	Lodja	Congo, DR
LJC	Louisville/Intercontinental, KY	USA
LJG	Lijiang City/Lijiang	China
LJN	Lake Jackson, TX	USA
LJU	Ljubljana/Brnik	Slovenia
LKA	Larantuka	Indonesia
LKB	Lakeba	Fiji
LKC	Lekana	Congo, DR
LKD	Lakeland Downs	Australia
LKE	Lake Union SPB, WA	USA
LKG	Lokichoggio	Kenya
LKI	Duluth/Lakeside USAF, MN	USA
LKK	Kulik Lake, AK	USA
LKL	Lakselv/Banak	Norway
LKN	Leknes	Norway
LKO	Lucknow/Amausi	India
LKP	Lake Placid, NY	USA
LKR	Las Khoreh	Somalia
LKS	LakesideTX	USA
LKT	Lakota	Côte D'Ivoire
LKU	Lake Rudolf	Kenya
LKV	Lakeview, OR	USA
LKY	Lake Manyara	Tanzania
LKZ	Brandon/Lakenheath/RAF	UK
LLA	Lulea/Kallax	Sweden
LLE	Malelane	S. Africa
LLG	Chillagoe	Australia
LLH	Las Limas	Honduras
LLI	Lalibela	Ethiopia
LLL	Lissadell	Australia
LLM	Long Lama	Malaysia
LLN	Kelila	Indonesia
LLP	Linda Downs	Australia
LLQ	Monticello, AR	USA
LLS	Las Lomitas	Argentina
LLU	Alluitsup Paa	Greenland
LLW	Lilongwe Int'l	Malawi
LLX	Lyndonville, VT	USA
LLY	Mount Holly, NJ	USA
LMA	Lake Minchumina, AK	USA
LMB	Salima	Malawi
LMC	Lamacarena	Colombia
LMD	Los Menucos	Argentina
LME	Le Mans/Arnage	France
LMG	Lamassa	Papua New Guinea
LMH	Limon	Honduras
LMI	Lumi	Papua New Guinea
LMK	Limerick	Ireland
LML	Lae Is	Marshall Is
LMM	Los Mochis/Federal	Mexico
LMN	Limbang	Malaysia
LMO	Lossiernouth/RAF	UK
LMP	Lampedusa	Italy
LMQ	Marsa Brega	Libya
LMR	Lime Acres	S. Africa
LMS	Louisville, MS	USA
LMT	Klamath Falls Int'l, OR	USA
LMX	Lopez De Micay	Colombia
LMY	Lake Murray	Papua New Guinea
LMZ	Palma	Mozambique
LNA	West Palm Beach, FL	USA
LNB	Lamen Bay	Vanuatu
LNC	Lengbati	Papua New Guinea
LND	Lander, WY	USA
LNE	Lonorore	Vanuatu
LNF	Munbil	Papua New Guinea
LNG	Lese	Papua New Guinea
LNH	Lake/NASh	Australia
LNI	Lonely/Dew Stn, AK	USA
LNK	Lincoln, NE	USA
LNM	Langimar	Papua New Guinea
LNN	Willoughby, OH	USA
LNO	Leonora	Australia
LNP	Wise, VA	USA
LNQ	Loani	Papua New Guinea
LNR	Lone Rock, WI	USA
LNS	Lancaster, PA	USA
LNV	Lihir Is	Papua New Guinea
LNX	Smolensk	Russia
LNY	Lanai City, HI	USA
LNZ	Linz/Hoersching	Austria
LOA	Lorraine	Australia
LOB	Los Andes	Chile
LOC	Lock	Australia
LOD	Longana	Vanuatu
LOE	Loei	Thailand
LOF	Loen	Marshall Is
LOG	Longview, WA	USA
LOH	Loja	Ecuador
LOI	Lontras/Helmuth Baungartem	Brazil

LOK . . Lodwar . . . . Kenya
LOL . . Lovelock, NV . . . . USA
LOM . Lagos de Moreno . . . . Mexico
LOO . . Laghouat-L'Mekrareg . . . . Algeria
LOQ . . Lobatse . . . . Botswana
LOR . . Ft. Rucker-Army HP, AL . . . . USA
LOS . . Lagos/Murtala Muhammed . . . . Nigeria
LOT . . Chicago Nexrad, IL . . . . USA
LOU . . Louisville, KY . . . . USA
LOV . . Monclova . . . . Mexico
LOW . Louisa, VA . . . . USA
LOX . . Los Tablones . . . . Guatemala
LOY . . Loyangalani . . . . Kenya
LOZ . . London, KY . . . . USA
LPA . . Las Palmas . . . . Spain
LPB . . La Paz/El Alto . . . . Bolivia
LPC . . Lompoc, CA . . . . USA
LPD . . La Pedrera . . . . Colombia
LPE . . La Primavera . . . . Colombia
LPG . . La Plata . . . . Argentina
LPH . . Lochgliphead / HP . . . . UK
LPI . . . Linkoping . . . . Sweden
LPJ . . Pijiguaos . . . . Venezuela
LPK . . Lipetsk . . . . Russia
LPL . . Liverpool/Speke . . . . UK
LPM . . Lamap . . . . Vanuatu
LPN . . Leron Plains . Papua New Guinea
LPO . . Laporte/Municipal, IN . . . . . . USA
LPP . . Lappeenranta . . . . Finland
LPQ . . Luang Prabang . . . . Laos
LPS . . Lopez Is, WA . . . . USA
LPT . . Lampang . . . . Thailand
LPU . . Long Apung . . . . Indonesia
LPW . Little Port Walter, AK . . . . USA
LPX . . Liepaya/Int'l . . . . Latvia
LPY . . Le Puy/Loudes . . . . France
LQK . . Pickens, SC . . . . USA
LQM . Puerto Leguizamo . . . . . Colombia
LQN . . Qala Nau . . . . Afghanistan
LRA . . Larisa . . . . Greece
LRB . . Leribe . . . . Lesotho
LRC . . Laarbruch/RAF . . . . Germany
LRD . . Laredo Int'l, TX . . . . USA
LRE . . Longreach . . . . Australia
LRF . . Little Rock/AFB, AR . . . . USA
LRG . . Lora Lai . . . . Pakistan
LRH . . La Rochelle/Laleu . . . . France
LRI . . . Lorica . . . . Colombia
LRJ . . Lemars/Municipal, IA . . . . . . USA
LRK . . Lincoln Rock/Cst Guard, AK . . . . USA
LRL . . Niamtougou/Lama-Kara . . . . Togo
LRM . . La Romana . . . . . Dominican Rep
LRN . . Larson/AFB, WA . . . . USA
LRO . . Lathrop/Sharpe/AAF, CA . . . USA
LRQ . . Laurie River, MB . . . . Canada
LRR . . Lar . . . . Iran
LRS . . Leros . . . . Greece
LRT . . Lorient/Lann Bilhoue . . . . . France
LRU . . Las Cruces Int'l, NM . . . . USA
LRV . . Los Roques . . . . Venezuela
LRX . . Elko Nexrad, NV . . . . USA
LSA . . Losuia . . . . . . Papua New Guinea
LSB . . Lordsburg, NM . . . . USA
LSC . . La Serena/La Florida . . . . Chile
LSD . . Creech/AAF, KY . . . . USA
LSE . . La Crosse, WI . . . . USA
LSF . . Lawson/AAF, GA . . . . USA
LSH . . Lashio . . . . Myanmar
LSI . . . Shetland Iss . . . . UK
LSJ . . Long Is . . . . . Papua New Guinea
LSK . . Lusk, WY . . . . USA
LSL . . Los Chiles . . . . Costa Rica
LSM . . Long Semado/Lawas . . Malaysia
LSN . . Los Banos, CA . . . . USA
LSO . . Les Sables/Talmont . . . . . . France
LSP . . Las Piedras/Josefa Camejo . . . . Venezuela
LSQ . . Los Angeles . . . . Chile
LSR . . Lost River, AK . . . . USA
LSS . . Terre-de-Haut . . . . . . Gaudeloupe
LST . . Launceston . . . . Australia
LSU . . Long Sukang . . . . Malaysia
LSV . . Nellis/AFB, NV . . . . USA
LSW . . Lhoksumawe/Malikussaleh . . . . Indonesia
LSX . . Lhok Sukon . . . . Indonesia
LSY . . Lismore . . . . Australia
LSZ . . Mali Losinj . . . . Croatia
LTA . . . Tzaneen/Letaba . . . . S. Africa
LTB . . . Latrobe . . . . Australia
LTC . . . Lai . . . . Chad
LTD . . . Ghadames . . . . Libya
LTF . . . Leitre . . . . Papua New Guinea
LTG . . Langtang . . . . Nepal
LTH . . . Lathrop Wells, NV . . . . USA
LTI . . . Altai . . . . Mongolia
LTK . . . Latakia . . . . Syria
LTL . . . Lastourville . . . . Gabon
LTM . . Lethem . . . . Guyana
LTN . . . London/Luton Int'l Arpt . . . . . . UK
LTO . . . Loreto . . . . Mexico
LTP . . . Lyndhurst . . . . Australia
LTQ . . Paris/Le Touquet . . . . France
LTR . . . Letterkenny . . . . Ireland
LTS . . . Altus/AFB, OK . . . . USA
LTT . . . Saint Tropez/La Mole . . . . . France
LTV . . . Lotusvaie . . . . Australia
LTW . . Leonardtown/St Marys County, MD . . . . USA
LTX . . . Wilmington Nexrad, NC . . . . . USA
LUA . . Lukla . . . . Nepal
LUB . . Lumid Pau . . . . Guyana
LUC . . Laucata Is . . . . Fiji
LUD . . Luderitz . . . . Namibia
LUE . . Lucenec . . . . Slovakia
LUF . . Luke/AFB, AZ . . . . USA
LUG . . Lugano . . . . Switzerland
LUH . . Ludhiana . . . . India
LUI . . . La Union . . . . Honduras
LUJ . . Lusikisiki . . . . S. Africa
LUK . . Cincinnati, OH . . . . USA
LUL . . Laurel/Hester/Noble Fld, MS . . . . USA
LUM . . Luxi/Mangshi . . . . China
LUN . . Lusaka . . . . Zambia
LUO . . Luena . . . . Angola
LUP . . Kalaupapa, HI . . . . USA
LUQ . . San Luis . . . . Argentina
LUR . . Cape Lisburne, AK . . . . USA
LUS . . Lusanga . . . . Congo, DR
LUT . . Laura Stn . . . . Australia
LUU . . Laura . . . . Australia
LUV . . Langgur . . . . Indonesia
LUW . . Luwuk/Bubung . . . . Indonesia
LUX . . Luxembourg . . . . Luxembourg
LUY . . Lushoto . . . . Tanzania
LUZ . . Lushan . . . . China
LVA . . Laval/Entrammes . . . . France
LVB . . Uvramento/Dos Galpoes . . Brazil
LVD . . Lime Village, AK . . . . USA
LVI . . . Livingstone . . . . Zambia
LVK . . Livermore, CA . . . . USA
LVL . . . Lawrenceville, VA . . . . USA
LVM . . Livingston, MT . . . . USA
LVO . . Laverlon . . . . Australia
LVP . . . Lavan . . . . Iran
LVS . . . Las Vegas, NM . . . . USA
LVX . . . Louisville Nexrad, KY . . . . USA
LWA . . Lwbak . . . . Philippines
LWB . . Lewisburg, WV . . . . USA
LWC . . Lawrence, KS . . . . USA
LWE . . Lewoleba . . . . Indonesia
LWI . . . Lowai . . . . Papua New Guinea
LWK . . Shetland Iss, Lerwick/Tingwall . . . . UK
LWL . . Wells/Harriet Fld, NV . . . . USA
LWM . . Lawrence, MA . . . . USA
LWN . . Gyoumri . . . . Armenia
LWO . . Lvov/Snilow . . . . Ukraine
LWR . . Leeuwarden . . . . Netherlands
LWS . Lewiston, ID . . . . USA
LWT . Lewistown, MT . . . . USA
LWV . Lawreneeville, IL . . . . USA
LWY . Lawas . . . . Malaysia
LXA . . Lhasa . . . . China
LXG . Luang Namtha . . . . Laos
LXI . . . Linxi . . . . China
LXN . . Lexington, NE . . . . USA
LXR . . Luxor . . . . Egypt
LXS . . Lemnos . . . . Greece
LXU . . Lukulu . . . . Zambia
LXV . . Leadville, CO . . . . USA
LYA . . Luoyang . . . . China
LYB . . Little Cayman . . . . Cayman Is
LYC . . Lycksele . . . . Sweden
LYE . . Lyneham/RAF . . . . UK
LYG . . Lianyungang . . . . China
LYH . . Lynchburg, VA . . . . USA
LYI . . . Linyi . . . . China
LYK . . Lunyuk . . . . Indonesia
LYN . . Lyon/Bron . . . . France
LYO . . Lyons, KS . . . . USA
LYP . . Faisalabad . . . . Pakistan
LYR . . Longyearbyen/Svalbard . . . . . Svalbard and Jan Mayen Is
LYS . . Lyon-Satolas . . . . France
LYT . . Lady Elliot Is . . . . Australia
LYU . . Ely, MN . . . . USA
LYX . . Lydd/Lydd Int'l . . . . UK
LZA . . Luiza . . . . Congo, DR
LZC . . Lazaro Cardenas . . . . Mexico
LZD . . Lanzhou/Lanzhoudong . . . China
LZH . . Liuzhou . . . . China
LZI . . . Luozi . . . . Congo, DR
LZK . . North Little Rock, AR . . . . . . USA
LZM . Luzamba . . . . Angola
LZO . . Luzhou . . . . China
LZR . . Lizard Is . . . . Australia

M

MAA . Chennai . . . . India
MAB . Maraba . . . . Brazil
MAC . Macon/Smart, GA . . . . USA
MAD . Madrid/Barajas . . . . Spain
MAE . Madera, CA . . . . USA
MAF . Midland Int'l, TX . . . . USA
MAG . Madang . . . . Papua New Guinea
MAH . Menorea . . . . Spain
MAI . . Mangochi . . . . Malawi
MAJ . Majuro/Amata Kabua Int'l . . . . Marshall Is
MAK . Malakal . . . . Sudan
MAL . Mangole . . . . Indonesia
MAM . Matamoros . . . . Mexico
MAN . Manchester/Ringway . . . . UK
MAO . Manaus-Eduardo Gomes Int'l . . . . Brazil
MAP . Mamai . . . . . Papua New Guinea
MAQ . Mae Sot . . . . Thailand
MAR . Maracailbo/La Chwila. Venezuela
MAS . Manus Is . . . Papua New Guinea
MAT . Matadi . . . . Congo, DR
MAU . Maupiti . . . . F. Polynesia
MAV . Maloelap Is . . . . Marshall Is
MAW . Malden, MO . . . . USA
MAX . Matam . . . . Senegal
MAY . Mangrove Cay . . . . Bahamas
MAZ . Mayaguez/Eugenic M De Hostos . . . . Puerto Rico
MBA . Mombasa/Moi Int'l . . . . Kenya
MBB . Marble Bar . . . . Australia
MBC . Mbigou . . . . Gabon
MBD . Mmabatho/Int'l . . . . S. Africa
MBE . Monbetsu . . . . Japan
MBF . Mount Buffalo . . . . Australia
MBG . Mobridge Municipal, SD . . . USA
MBH . Maryborough . . . . Australia

A
I
R
P
O
R
T
S

Code	Airport	Location
MBI	Mbeya	Tanzania
MBJ	Montego Bay/Sangster Int'l	Jamaica
MBK	Matupa	Brazil
MBL	Manistee/Blacker, MI	USA
MBM	Mikambati	S. Africa
MBN	Mt Barnett	Australia
MBO	Mamburao	Philippines
MBP	Moyobamba	Peru
MBQ	Mbarara	Uganda
MBR	Mbout	Mauritania
MBS	Bay City, MI	USA
MBT	Masbate	Philippines
MBU	Mbambanakira	Solomon Is
MBV	Masa	Papua New Guinea
MBW	Moorabbin	Australia
MBX	Maribor/Slivnica	Slovenia
MBY	Moberly, MO	USA
MBZ	Maues	Brazil
MCA	Macenta	Guinea
MCB	Mccomb, MS	USA
MCC	Mcclellan/AFB, CA	USA
MCD	Mackinac Is, MI	USA
MCE	Merced, CA	USA
MCF	MacDill/AFB, FL	USA
MCG	Mcgrath, AK	USA
MCH	Machala	Ecuador
MCI	Kansas City Int'l, MO	USA
MCJ	Maicao	Colombia
MCK	Mccook, NE	USA
MCL	Mt Mckinley, AK	USA
MCM	Monte Carlo/ HP	Monaco
MCN	Macon, GA	USA
MCO	Orlando Int'l, FL	USA
MCP	Macapa/Int'l	Brazil
MCQ	Miskolc	Hungary
MCR	Melchor De Menco	Guatemala
MCS	Monte Caseros/Seelb	Argentina
MCT	Muscat	Oman
MCU	Montlucon/Gueret (Lepaud)	France
MCV	Mcarthur River	Australia
MCW	Mason City, IA	USA
MCX	Makhachkala	Russia
MCY	Sunshine Coast/Maroochydore	Australia
MCZ	Maceio/Palmares	Brazil
MDA	Martindale/AAF, TX	USA
MDB	Melinda	Belize
MDC	Manado/Samratulangi	Indonesia
MDD	Midland Airpark, TX	USA
MDE	Medellin/Jose Marie Cordova	Colombia
MDF	Medford, WI	USA
MDG	Muclarijiang	China
MDH	Carbondale, IL	USA
MDI	Makurdi	Nigeria
MDJ	Madras, OR	USA
MDK	Mbandaka	Congo, DR
MDL	Mandalay/Annisaton	Myanmar
MDM	Munduku	Papua New Guinea
MDN	Jefferson Proving Grnd., IN	USA
MDO	Middleton Is, AK	USA
MDP	Mindiptana	Indonesia
MDQ	Mar Del Plata	Argentina
MDR	Medfra, AK	USA
MDS	Middle Caicos	Turks & Caicos Is
MDT	Harrisburg Int'l, PA	USA
MDU	Mendi	Papua New Guinea
MDV	Medouneu	Gabon
MDW	Chicago/Midway, IL	USA
MDX	Mereedes	Argentina
MDY	Midway Is/Sand Is Field	U.S. Minor Outlying Islands
MDZ	Mendoza/El Plumerillo	Argentina
MEA	Macae	Brazil
MEB	Melbourne/Essendon	Australia
MEC	Manta	Ecuador
MED	Madinah/Mohammad Bin Abdulaziz	Saudi Arabia
MEE	Mare	New Caledonia
MEG	Malange	Angola
MEH	Mehamn	Norway
MEI	Meridian, MS	USA
MEJ	Meadville, PA	USA
MEK	Meknes	Morocco
MEL	Melbourne	Australia
MEM	Memphis Int'l, TN	USA
MEN	Mende/Brenoux	France
MEO	Manteo/Dare County Regional, NC	USA
MEP	Mersing	Malaysia
MEQ	Meulaboh/Seunagan	Indonesia
MER	Merced-Castle/AFB, CA	USA
MES	Medan/Polonia	Indonesia
MET	Moreton	Australia
MEU	Monte Dourado	Brazil
MEV	Minden/Douglas County, NV	USA
MEW	Mwelka	Congo, DR
MEX	Mexico City/Juarez Int'l	Mexico
MEY	Meghauli	Nepal
MEZ	Messina	S. Africa
MFA	Mafia	Tanzania
MFB	MonFt	Colombia
MFC	Mafeteng	Lesotho
MFD	Mansfield, OH	USA
MFE	Mcallen, TX	USA
MFF	Moanda	Gabon
MFG	Muzaffarabad	Pakistan
MFH	Mesquite, NV	USA
MFI	Marshfield, WI	USA
MFJ	Moala	Fiji
MFK	Matsu	Taiwan
MFL	Mount Full Stop	Australia
MFM	Macau	Macau
MFN	Milford Sound	New Zealand
MFO	Manguna	Papua New Guinea
MFP	Manners Creek	Australia
MFQ	Maradi	Niger
MFR	Medford, OR	USA
MFS	Miraflores	Colombia
MFT	Machu Picchu	Peru
MFU	Mfuwe	Zambia
MFV	Melfa, VA	USA
MFW	Magaruque	Mozambique
MFX	Meribel	France
MFY	Mayfa'ah	Yemen
MFZ	Mesalia/Sandino	Papua New Guinea
MGA	Managua	Nicaragua
MGB	Mount Gambier	Australia
MGC	Michigan City, IN	USA
MGE	Marietta/AFB, GA	USA
MGF	Maringa	Brazil
MGG	Margarima	Papua New Guinea
MGH	Margate	Australia
MGI	Matagorda/AFB, TX	USA
MGJ	Montgomery, NY	USA
MGK	Mong Ton	Myanmar
MGL	Dusseldorf/Monchen-Gladbach	Germany
MGM	Montgomery, AL	USA
MGN	Magangue/Baracoa	Colombia
MGO	Manega	Gabon
MGP	Manga	Papua New Guinea
MGQ	Mogadishu/Int'l	Somalia
MGR	Moultrie/Thornasville, GA	USA
MGS	Mangaia Is	Cook Is
MGT	Milingimbi	Australia
MGU	Manaung	Myanmar
MGV	Margaret River	Australia
MGW	Morgantown, WV	USA
MGX	Moabi	Australia
MGY	Dayton, OH	USA
MGZ	Myeik	Myanmar
MHA	Mahdia	Guyana
MHB	Auckland	New Zealand
MHC	Macmahon Camp 4	Australia
MHD	Mashad	Iran
MHE	Mitchell, SD	USA
MHF	Morichal	Colombia
MHG	Marinheim	Germany
MHH	Marsh Harbour/Int'l	Bahamas
MHI	Musha	Djibouti
MHJ	Misrak Gashamo	Ethiopia
MHK	Manhattan, KS	USA
MHL	Marshall/Memorial, MO	USA
MHM	Minchumina/Intermediate, AK	USA
MHN	Mullen, NE	USA
MHO	Mount House	Australia
MHP	Minsk/Minsk Int'l	Belarus
MHQ	Mariehamn/Aland Is	Finland
MHR	Mather/AFB, CA	USA
MHS	Mount Shasta, CA	USA
MHT	Manchester, NH	USA
MHU	Mount Hotham	Australia
MHV	Mojave, CA	USA
MHW	Monteagudo	Bolivia
MHX	Manihiki Is	Cook Is
MHY	Morehead	Papua New Guinea
MHZ	Mildenhall/RAF	UK
MIA	Miami Int'l, FL	USA
MIB	Minot/AFB, ND	USA
MIC	Minneapolis-Crystal, MN	USA
MID	Merida/Rejon	Mexico
MIE	Muncie, IN	USA
MIF	Monahans/Roy Hurd, TX	USA
MIG	Munich/Neubiberg Ab	Germany
MIH	Mitchell Plateau	Australia
MII	Marilia/Dr Gastao Vidigal	Brazil
MIJ	Mili Is	Marshall Is
MIK	Mikkeli	Finland
MIM	Merimbula	Australia
MIN	Minnipa	Saudi Arabia
MIO	Miami, FL	USA
MIP	Mitspeh Ramon	Israel
MIQ	Omaha/Millard, NE	USA
MIR	Monastir/Int'l	Tunisia
MIS	Misima Is	Papua New Guinea
MIT	Shatter, CA	USA
MIU	Maiduguri	Nigeria
MIV	Miliville, NJ	USA
MIW	Marshalltown, IA	USA
MIX	Miriti	Colombia
MIY	Mittiebah	Australia
MIZ	Mainoru	Australia
MJA	Manja	Madagascar
MJB	Mejit Is	Marshall Is
MJC	Man	Côte D'Ivoire
MJD	Mohenjodaro	Pakistan
MJE	Majkin	Marshall Is
MJF	Mosjoen/Kjaerstad	Norway
MJG	Mayajigua	Cuba
MJH	Malma	Saudi Arabia
MJI	Mitiga	Libya
MJJ	Moki	Papua New Guinea
MJK	Monkey Mia/Shark Bay	Australia
MJL	Mouila	Gabon
MJM	Mbuji Mayi	Congo, DR
MJN	Majunga/Amborovy	Madagascar
MJO	Mount Etjo Lodge	Namibia
MJP	Manjinnup	Australia
MJQ	Jackson, MN	USA
MJR	Miramar	Argentina
MJS	Maganja Da Costa	Mozambique
MJT	Mytilene	Greece
MJU	Mamuju	Indonesia
MJV	Murcia/San Javier	Spain
MJW	Mahenye	Zimbabwe
MJX	Toms River/Robert J Miller, NJ	
MJY	Mangunjaya	Indonesia
MJZ	Mirnyj	Russia
MKA	Marianske Lazne	Czech Rep
MKB	Mekambo	Gabon
MKC	Kansas City/Downtown, MO	USA
MKD	Chagni	Ethiopia
MKE	Milwaukee, WI	USA
MKF	Mckenna/AAF, OH	USA
MKG	Muskegon, MI	USA

AIRPORTS

Code	Location	Country
MKH	Mokhotlong	Lesotho
MKI	M'Boki	Central African Rep
MKJ	Makoua	Congo, DR
MKK	Hoolehua-Molokai, HI	USA
MKL	Jackson, TN	USA
MKM	Mukah	Malaysia
MKN	Malekolon	Papua New Guinea
MKO	Muskogee, OK	USA
MKP	Makemo	F. Polynesia
MKQ	Merauke/Mopah	Indonesia
MKR	Meekatharra	Australia
MKS	Mekane Selam	Ethiopia
MKT	Mankato, MN	USA
MKU	Makokou	Gabon
MKV	Mt Cavenagh	Australia
MKW	Manokwari/Rendani	Indonesia
MKX	Mukalla	Yemen
MKY	Mackay	Australia
MKZ	Malacca	Malaysia
MLA	Malta Int'l	Malta
MLB	Melbourne Int'l, FL	USA
MLC	McAlester, OK	USA
MLD	Malad City, ID	USA
MLE	Male/Int'l	Maldives
MLF	Milford, UT	USA
MLG	Malang	Indonesia
MLH	Basel/Mulhouse	Switzerland
MLI	Quad-City, IL	USA
MLJ	Milledgeville, GA	USA
MLK	Malta, MT	USA
MLL	Marshall, AK	USA
MLM	Morelia	Mexico
MLN	Melilla	Spain
MLO	Milos	Greece
MLP	Malabang	Philippines
MLQ	Malalaua	Papua New Guinea
MLR	Millicent	Australia
MLS	Milles City, MT	USA
MLT	Millinocket, ME	USA
MLU	Monroe, LA	USA
MLV	Merluna	Australia
MLW	Monrovia/Sprigg Payne	Liberia
MLX	Malatya	Turkey
MLY	Manley Hot Springs, AK	USA
MLZ	Melo	Uruguay
MMB	Memanbetsu	Japan
MMC	Ciudad Mante	Mexico
MMD	Minami Daito	Japan
MME	Teesside	UK
MMF	Marnte	Cameroon
MMG	Mount Magnet	Australia
MMH	Mammoth Lakes, CA	USA
MMI	Athens, TN	USA
MMJ	Matsumoto	Japan
MMK	Murmansk	Russia
MML	Marshall, MN	USA
MMM	Middlemount	Australia
MMN	Stow, MA	USA
MMO	Maio	Cape Verde Is
MMP	Mompos	Colombia
MMQ	Mbala	Zambia
MMR	Camp Maybry AHP, TX	USA
MMS	Marks/Selts, MS	USA
MMT	Columbia, SC	USA
MMU	Morristown, NJ	USA
MMV	Mal	Papua New Guinea
MMW	Moma	New Zealand
MMX	Malmo/Sturup	Sweden
MMY	Miyake Jima/Hirara	Japan
MMZ	Maimana	Afghanistan
MNA	Melangguane	Indonesia
MNB	Moanda	Congo, DR
MNC	Nacala	Mozambique
MND	Medina	Colombia
MNE	Mungeranie	Australia
MNF	Mana Is	Fiji
MNG	Maningrida	Australia
MNH	Minnenya	Sri Lanka
MNI	Montserrat/Bramble	Montserrat
MNJ	Mananjary	Madagascar
MNK	Maiana	Kiribati
MNL	Manila/Int'l	Philippines
MNM	Menominee, MI	USA
MNN	Marion, OH	USA
MNO	Manono	Congo, DR
MNP	Maron	Papua New Guinea
MNQ	Monto	Australia
MNR	Mongu	Zambia
MNS	Mansa	Zambia
MNT	Minto, AK	USA
MNU	Maulmyine	Myanmar
MNV	Mountain Valley	Australia
MNW	Macdonald Downs	Australia
MNX	Manicore	Brazil
MNY	Mono	Solomon Is
MNZ	Manassas, VA	USA
MOA	Moa/Orestes Acosta	Chile
MOB	Mabile, AL	USA
MOC	Montes Claros	Brazil
MOD	Modesto, CA	USA
MOE	Momeik	Myanmar
MOF	Maumere/Waioti	Indonesia
MOG	Mong Hsat	Myanmar
MOH	Mohanban	India
MOI	Mitiaro Is	Cook Is
MOJ	Moengo	Suriname
MOK	Mankono	Côte D'Ivoire
MOL	Molde	Norway
MOM	Moudieria	Mauritania
MON	Mount Cook	New Zealand
MOO	Moomba	Australia
MOP	Mount Pleasant, MI	USA
MOQ	Morondava	Madagascar
MOR	Morristown, TN	USA
MOS	Moses Point, AK	USA
MOT	Minot Int'l, ND	USA
MOU	Mountain Village, AK	USA
MOV	Moranbah	Australia
MOX	Morris, MN	USA
MOY	Monterrey	Colombia
MOZ	Moorea/Ternae	F. Polynesia
MPA	Mpacha	Namibia
MPB	Miami/SPB, FL	USA
MPC	Muko-Muko	Indonesia
MPD	Mirpur Khas	Pakistan
MPE	Madison/Griswold, CT	USA
MPF	Mapoda	Papua New Guinea
MPG	Makini	Papua New Guinea
MPH	Caticlan/Malay	Philippines
MPI	Mannitupo	Panama
MPJ	Morrilton, AR	USA
MPK	Mokpo	S. Korea
MPL	Montpellier/Frejorgues	France
MPM	Maputo Int'l	Mozambique
MPN	Mount Pleasant	Falkand Is
MPO	Mt Pocono, PA	USA
MPP	Mulatupo	Panama
MPQ	Maan	Jordan
MPR	Mcpherson, KS	USA
MPS	Mount Pleasant, TX	USA
MPT	Maliana	Indonesia
MPU	Mapua	Papua New Guinea
MPV	Barre, VT	USA
MPW	Mariupol	Ukraine
MPX	Miyanmin	Papua New Guinea
MPY	Maripasoula	F. Guiana
MPZ	Mt Pleasant, IA	USA
MQA	Mandora	Australia
MQC	Miquelon	St. Pierre and Miquelon
MQD	Maquinchao	Argentina
MQE	Marqua	Australia
MQF	Magnitogorsk	Russia
MQG	Midgard	Namibia
MQH	Minacu	Brazil
MQI	Quincy, MA	USA
MQJ	Balikesir/Merkez	Turkey
MQK	San Matias	Bolivia
MQM	Monida, MT	USA
MQN	Mo I Rana/Rossvoll	Norway
MQO	Moundou	Chad
MQR	Mosquera	Colombia
MQS	Mustique Is	St. Vincent & Grenadines
MQT	Marquette, MI	USA
MQU	Mariquita	Colombia
MQW	Mc Rae, GA	USA
MQX	Makale	Ethiopia
MQY	Smyrna, TN	USA
MRA	Misurata	Libya
MRB	Martinsburg, WV	USA
MRC	Columbia, TN	USA
MRD	Merida/A Carnevalli	Venezuela
MRE	Mara Lodges	Kenya
MRF	Marfa, TX	USA
MRG	Mareeba	Australia
MRH	May River	Papua New Guinea
MRI	Anchorage, AK	USA
MRJ	Mareala	Honduras
MRK	Marco Is, FL	USA
MRL	Miners Lake	Australia
MRM	Manare	Papua New Guinea
MRN	Morganton/Lenoir, NC	USA
MRO	Masterton	New Zealand
MRP	Marla	Australia
MRQ	Marinduque	Philippines
MRR	Macara	Ecuador
MRS	Marseille/Marignane	France
MRT	Moroak	Australia
MRU	Mauritius/Int'l	Mauritius
MRV	Minerainye Vody	Russia
MRW	Maribo/Lufthavn	Denmark
MRX	Bandar Mahshahr	Iran
MRY	Monterey, CA	USA
MRZ	Moree	Australia
MSA	Muskrat Dam, ON	Canada
MSB	Marigot/SPB	Gaudeloupe
MSC	Mesa/Falcon Fld, AZ	USA
MSD	Mt Pleasant, UT	USA
MSE	Manston/Kent Int'l	UK
MSF	Mount Swan	Australia
MSG	Matsaile	Lesotho
MSH	Masirah	Oman
MSI	Masalembo	Indonesia
MSJ	Misawa	Japan
MSK	Mastic Point	Bahamas
MSL	Florence, AL	USA
MSM	Masi Manimba	Congo, DR
MSN	Madison, WI	USA
MSO	Missoula Int'l, MT	USA
MSP	Minneapolis-St Paul Int'l, MN	USA
MSQ	Minsk Int'l	Belarus
MSR	Mus	Turkey
MSS	Massena, NY	USA
MST	Maastricht/Aachen	Netherlands
MSU	Maseru/Moshoeshoe Int'l	Lesotho
MSV	Monticello/Int'l, NY	USA
MSW	Massawa	Eritrea
MSX	Mossendjo	Congo, DR
MSY	New Orleans Int'l, LA	USA
MSZ	Narnibe	Angola
MTA	Matamata	New Zealand
MTB	Monte Libano, CO	Colombia
MTC	Mt Clemens, MI	USA
MTD	Mt Sandford	Australia
MTE	Monte Alegre	Brazil
MTF	Mizan Teferi	Ethiopia
MTG	Mato Grosso	Brazil
MTH	Marathon, FL	USA
MTI	Mosteiros	Cape Verde Is
MTJ	Montrose, CO	USA
MTK	Makin Is	Kiribati
MTL	Maitland	Australia
MTM	Metlakatia/SPB, AK	USA
MTN	Baltimore, MD	USA
MTO	Mattoon, IL	USA
MTP	Montauk, NY	USA
MTQ	Mitchell	Australia
MTR	Monteria/S. Jeronimo	Colombia
MTS	Manzini/Int'l	Swaziland
MTT	Minatitlan	Mexico

MTU	Montepuez	Mozambique
MTV	Mota Lava	Vanuatu
MTW	Manitowoc, WI	USA
MTX	Fairbanks, AK	USA
MTY	Monterrey	Mexico
MTZ	Masada	Israel
MUA	Munda	Solomon Is
MUB	Maun	Botswana
MUC	Munich	Germany
MUD	Mueda	Mozambique
MUE	Kamuela, HI	USA
MUF	Muting	Indonesia
MUG	Mulege	Mexico
MUH	Mersa Matruh	Egypt
MUI	Muir/AAF, PA	USA
MUJ	Mui	Ethiopia
MUK	Mauke Is	Cook Is
MUL	Moultrie, GA	USA
MUM	Mumias	Kenya
MUN	Maturin/Quiriquire	Venezuela
MUO	Mountain Home/AFB, ID	USA
MUP	Mulga Park	Australia
MUQ	Muccan	Australia
MUR	Marudi	Malaysia
MUS	Marcus Is	Japan
MUT	Muscatine, IA	USA
MUU	Mount Union, PA	USA
MUV	Philadelphia/Mustin Alf, PA	USA
MUW	Mascara	Algeria
MUX	Multan	Pakistan
MUY	Mouyiondzi	Congo
MUZ	Musoma	Tanzania
MVA	Myvatn/Reykiahlid	Iceland
MVB	Franceville/Mvengue	Gabon
MVC	Monroeville, AL	USA
MVD	Montevideo/Carrasco	Uruguay
MVE	Montevideo, MN	USA
MVF	Mossoro/Dixsept Rosado	Brazil
MVG	Mevang	Gabon
MVH	Macksville	Australia
MVI	Manetai	Papua New Guinea
MVJ	Mandeville/Mariboro	Jamaica
MVK	Mulka	Australia
MVL	Morrisville, VT	USA
MVM	Kayenta, AZ	USA
MVN	Mt Vernon, IL	USA
MVO	Mongo	Chad
MVP	Mitu	Colombia
MVQ	Mogilev	Belarus
MVR	Maroua/Salam	Cameroon
MVS	Mucuri	Brazil
MVT	Mataiva	F. Polynesia
MVU	Musigrave	Australia
MVV	Megeve	France
MVW	Mount Vernon, WA	USA
MVX	Minvoul	Gabon
MVY	Martha's Vineyard, MA	USA
MVZ	Masvingo	Zimbabwe
MWA	Marion, IL	USA
MWB	Morawa	Australia
MWC	Milwaukee, WI	USA
MWD	Mianwali	Pakistan
MWE	Merowe	Sudan
MWF	Malewo	Vanuatu
MWG	Marawaka	Papua New Guinea
MWH	Moses Lake, WA	USA
MWI	Maramuni	Papua New Guinea
MWJ	Matthews Ridge	Guyana
MWK	Matak	Indonesia
MWL	Mineral Wells, TX	USA
MWM	Windom, MN	USA
MWN	Mwadui	Tanzania
MWO	Middletown, OH	USA
MWP	Mountain	Nepal
MWQ	Magwe	Myanmar
MWR	Motswari Airfield	S. Africa
MWS	Mount Wilson, CA	USA
MWT	Moolawatana	Australia
MWU	Mussau	Papua New Guinea
MWV	Mundulkiri	Cambodia
MWY	Miranda Downs	Australia
MWZ	Mwanza	Tanzania
MXA	Manila/Municipal, AR	USA
MXB	Masamba	Indonesia
MXC	Monticello, UT	USA
MXD	Marion Downs	Australia
MXE	Maxton, NC	USA
MXF	Maxwell/AFB, AL	USA
MXG	Marlborough, MA	USA
MXH	Moro	Papua New Guinea
MXI	Mati	Philippines
MXJ	Minna	Nigeria
MXK	Mindik	Papua New Guinea
MXL	Mexicali	Mexico
MXM	Morombe	Madagascar
MXN	Morlaix/Ploujean	France
MXO	Monticello, IA	USA
MXP	Milan//Malpensa	Italy
MXQ	Mitichell River	Australia
MXR	Mirgorod	Ukraine
MXS	Maota Savaii Is	Samoa
MXT	Maintirano	Madagascar
MXU	Mullewa	Australia
MXV	Moron	Mongolia
MXW	Mandalgobi	Mongolia
MXX	Mora	Sweden
MXY	McCarthy, AK	USA
MXZ	Meixian	China
MYA	Moruya	Australia
MYB	Mayoumba	Gabon
MYC	Maracay	Venezuela
MYD	Malindi	Kenya
MYE	Miyakojima	Japan
MYF	San Diego, CA	USA
MYG	Mayaguana	Bahamas
MYH	Marble Canyon, AZ	USA
MYI	Murray Is	Australia
MYJ	Matsuyama	Japan
MYK	May Creek, AK	USA
MYL	Mccall, ID	USA
MYM	Monkey Mountain	Guyana
MYN	Marelb	Yemen
MYO	Myroodah	Australia
MYP	Mary	Turkmenistan
MYQ	Mysore	India
MYR	Myrtle Beach/AFB, SC	USA
MYS	Moyale	Ethiopia
MYT	Myitkyina	Myanmar
MYU	Mekoryuk/Ellis Fld, AK	USA
MYV	Marysville, CA	USA
MYW	Mtwara	Tanzania
MYX	Menyamya	Papua New Guinea
MYY	Miri	Malaysia
MYZ	Monkey Bay	Malawi
MZA	Muzattarnagar	India
MZB	Mocimboa Praia	Mozambique
MZC	Mitzic	Gabon
MZD	Mendez	Ecuador
MZE	Manatee	Belize
MZF	Mzamba (Wild Coast Sun)	S. Africa
MZG	Makung	Taiwan
MZH	Merzifon	Turkey
MZI	Mopti	Mali
MZJ	Marana, AZ	USA
MZK	Marakei	Kiribati
MZL	Manizales/Santaguida	Colombia
MZM	Metz/Frescaty	France
MZN	Minj	Papua New Guinea
MZO	Manzanillo/Sierra Maestra	Cuba
MZP	Motueka	New Zealand
MZQ	Mkuze	S. Africa
MZR	Mazar-I-Sharif	Afghanistan
MZS	Mostyn	Malaysia
MZT	Mazatian/Gen Ralael Bueina	Mexico
MZU	Muzaffarpur	India
MZV	Mulu	Malaysia
MZX	Mena	Ethiopia
MZY	Mossel Bay	S. Africa
MZZ	Marion, IN	USA

N

NAA	Narrabri	Australia
NAB	Albany/NAS, GA	USA
NAC	Naracoorte	Australia
NAD	Macanal	Colombia
NAE	Natitingou	Benin
NAF	Banaina	Indonesia
NAG	Nagpur/Sonegaon	India
NAH	Naha	Indonesia
NAI	Annat	Guyana
NAJ	Nalkinichevan	Azerbaijan
NAK	Nakhon Ratchasima	Thailand
NAL	Nalchik	Russia
NAM	Namlea	Indonesia
NAN	Nandi/Int'l	Fiji
NAO	Nanchong	China
NAP	Naples/Capodichino	Italy
NAQ	Qaanaaq	Greenland
NAR	Nare	Colombia
NAS	Nassau/Int'l	Bahamas
NAT	Natal/Augusto Severo	Brazil
NAU	Napuka Is	F. Polynesia
NAV	Nevsehir	Turkey
NAW	Narathiwat	Thailand
NAX	Barbers Point, HI	USA
NAY	Beijing/Nanyuan	China
NBA	Nambaiyufa	Papua New Guinea
NBB	Barrancominas	Colombia
NBC	Naberevnye Chelny	Russia
NBE	Dallas/NAS, TX	USA
NBG	New Orleans/NAS, LA	USA
NBH	Narnbucca Heads	Australia
NBJ	Barin/NAS, AL	USA
NBL	San Bias	Panama
NBO	Nairobi/Jorno Kenyatta Int'l	Kenya
NBP	New York/Battery Pk, NY	USA
NBQ	Kings Bay/NAS, GA	USA
NBR	Nambour	Australia
NBU	Glenview/NAS, IL	USA
NBV	Cana Brava	Brazil
NBW	Guantanamo/NAS	Cuba
NBX	Nabire	Indonesia
NCA	North Caicos	Turks & Caicos Is
NCE	Nice	France
NCG	Nueva Casas Grandes	Mexico
NCH	Nachingwea	Tanzania
NCI	Necocli	Colombia
NCL	Newcastle	UK
NCN	New Chenega, AK	USA
NCO	Quonset Point/NAS, RI	USA
NCP	Luzonis/NAS	Philippines
NCR	San Carlos	Netherlands
NCS	Newcastle	S. Africa
NCT	Nicoya/Guanacaste	Costa Rica
NCU	Nukus	Uzbekistan
NCY	Annecy	France
NDA	Bandanatra	Indonesia
NDB	Nouadhilbou	Mauritania
NDC	Nanded	India
NDD	Sumbe	Angola
NDE	Mandera	Kenya
NDF	Ndalatandos	Angola
NDG	Qiqihar	China
NDI	Namudi	Papua New Guinea
NDJ	Ndjamena	Tonga
NDK	Namdrik Is	Marshall Is
NDL	Ndele	Central African Rep
NDM	Mendi	Ethiopia
NDN	Nadunumu	Papua New Guinea
NDP	Pensacola/NAS, FL	USA
NDR	Nador	Morocco
NDS	Sandstone	Australia
NDU	Rundu	Namibia
NDV	Anacostia/USN HP, DC	USA
NDY	Sanday	UK

NDZ Nordholz-Spieka ... Germany
NEA Glynco/NAS, GA ... USA
NEC Necochea ... Argentina
NED Winner, SD ... USA
NEF Neftekamsk ... Russia
NEG Negril ... Jamaica
NEJ Nejjo ... Ethiopia
NEK Nelkernt ... Ethiopia
NEL Lakehurst, NJ ... USA
NEN Whitehouse, FL ... USA
NER Neryungri ... Russia
NES New York/E. 34 St Landing, NY ... USA
NET New Bight ... Bahamas
NEU Sam Neua ... Laos
NEV Nevis/Newcastle ... St. Kitts and Nevis
NEW New Orleans, LA ... USA
NEX Charleston Nise, SC ... USA
NFB Detroit NAF, MI ... USA
NFG Nefteyugansk ... Russia
NFL Fallon/NAS, NV ... USA
NFO Niuafo'ou/Mata'aho ... Tonga
NFR Nafoora ... Libya
NFW Ft. Worth/NAS, TX ... USA
NGA Young ... Australia
NGB Ningbo ... China
NGC Grand Canyon/North Rim, AZ ... USA
NGD Anegada ... Virgin Is (British)
NGE Ngaoundere ... Cameroon
NGI Ngau Is ... Fiji
NGL Ngala ... S. Africa
NGM Guam/Agana/NAS ... Guam
NGN Nargana ... Panama
NGO Nagoya/Koniaki AFS ... Japan
NGP Corpus Christi/NAS, TX ... USA
NGR Ningerum ... Papua New Guinea
NGS Nagasaki ... Japan
NGU Norfolk/NAS, VA ... USA
NGV Ngiva ... Angola
NGW Corpus Christi/NAS, TX ... USA
NGX Manang ... Nepal
NGZ Alameda/NAS, CA ... USA
NHA Nha Trang ... Vietnam
NHD Minhad Ab/Military ... UAE
NHF New Halfa ... Somalia
NHK Patuxent River/NAS, MD ... USA
NHS Nushki ... Pakistan
NHT Northolt/RAF ... UK
NHV Nuku Hiva ... F. Polynesia
NHX Foley, AL ... USA
NHZ Brunswick/NAS, ME ... USA
NIA Nimba ... Liberia
NIB Nikolai, AK ... USA
NIC Nicosia ... Cyprus
NID China Lake/NAS, CA ... USA
NIE Niblack, AK ... USA
NIF Nifty ... Australia
NIG Nikunau ... Kiribati
NIK Mokolo Koba ... Senegal
NIM Niamey/Diori Hamani ... Niger
NIN Ninilchik, AK ... USA
NIO Niolki ... Congo, DR
NIP Jacksonvill/NAS, FL ... USA
NIR Beeville/NAS, TX ... USA
NIS Simberi Is ... Papua New Guinea
NIT Niort/Souche ... France
NIX Nioro ... Mali
NJA Atsugi/NAS ... Japan
NJC Nizhnevartovsk ... Russia
NJK El Centro/NAF, CA ... USA
NKA Nkan ... Gabon
NKB Noonkanbah ... Australia
NKC Nouakchott ... Mauritania
NKD Sinalk ... Indonesia
NKG Nanking ... China
NKI Naukiti, AK ... USA
NKL Nkolo ... Congo, DR
NKN Nankina ... Papua New Guinea
NKS Nkongsamba ... Cameroon
NKT Cherry Point/MCAS, NC ... USA
NKU Nkaus ... Lesotho
NKV Nichen Cove, AK ... USA
NKX Miramar/NAS, CA ... USA
NKY Nkayi/Yokangassi ... Congo, DR
NLA Ndola ... Zambia
NLC Lemoore/NAS, CA ... USA
NLD Nuevo Laredo/Int'l ... Mexico
NLE Niles, MI ... USA
NLF Darnley Is ... Australia
NLG Nelson Lagoon, AK ... USA
NLK Norfolk Is ... Norfolk Is
NLL Nullagine ... Australia
NLO Kinshasa/N'Dolo ... Congo, DR
NLP Neispruit ... S. Africa
NLS Nicholson ... Australia
NLU Mexico City/Santa Lucia ... Mexico
NLV Nikolaev ... Ukraine
NMA Namangan ... Uzbekistan
NMB Daman ... India
NMC Norman's Cay ... Bahamas
NME Nightmute, AK ... USA
NMG San Miguel ... Panama
NMM Meridian/NAS, MS ... USA
NMN Nomane ... Papua New Guinea
NMP New Moon ... Australia
NMR Nappa Merry ... Australia
NMS Namsang ... Myanmar
NMT Namtu ... Myanmar
NMU Namu ... Marshall Is
NNA Kenitra/NAF ... Morocco
NNB Santa Ana ... Solomon Is
NND Nangade ... Mozambique
NNG Nanning ... China
NNI Narnutoni ... Namibia
NNK Naknek, AK ... USA
NNL Nondalton, AK ... USA
NNM Naryan-Mar ... Russia
NNR Spiddal/Connemara ... Ireland
NNT Nan ... Thailand
NNU Nanuque ... Brazil
NNX Nunukan ... Indonesia
NNY Nanyang ... China
NNZ Point Sur, CA ... USA
NOA Nowra ... Australia
NOB Nosara Beach ... Costa Rica
NOC Knock Int'l ... Ireland
NOD Norden ... Germany
NOE Norddeich ... Germany
NOG Nogales ... Mexico
NOH Chicago/NAS, IL ... USA
NOI Novoirossijsk ... Russia
NOJ Nojabrxsk ... Russia
NOK Nova Xavantina ... Brazil
NOL Nakolik River, AK ... USA
NOM Nomad River Papua New Guinea
NON Nonouti ... Kiribati
NOO Naoro ... Papua New Guinea
NOP Mactan Is ... Philippines
NOR Nordfjordur ... Iceland
NOS Nossi-be/Fascene ... Madagascar
NOT Novato, CA ... USA
NOU Nourrea/Tontouta New Caledonia
NOV Huambo ... Andorra
NOW Port Angeles., WA ... USA
NOZ Novokuzinetsk ... Russia
NPA Pensacola/NAS, FL ... USA
NPE Napier-Hastings ... New Zealand
NPG Nipa ... Papua New Guinea
NPH Nephi, UT ... USA
NPL New Plymouth ... New Zealand
NPO Nangapinoh ... Indonesia
NPP Napperby ... Australia
NPT Newport/State, TI ... USA
NPU San Pedro Uraba ... Colombia
NQA Memphis/NAS, TN ... USA
NQI Kingsville/NAS, TX ... USA
NQL Niquelandia ... Brazil
NQT Nottingham ... UK
NQU Nuqui ... Colombia
NQX Key West/NAS, FL ... USA
NQY Newquay-St Mawgan ... UK
NRA Narrandera ... Australia
NRB Mayport/NAF, FL ... USA
NRC Crows Landing/NAS, CA ... USA
NRD Norderney ... Germany
NRE Namrole ... Indonesia
NRG Narrogin ... Australia
NRI Shangri-la, OK ... USA
NRK Norrkoping/Kungsangen ... Sweden
NRL North Ronaldsay ... UK
NRM Nara ... Mali
NRQ N'Fliquinha ... Angola
NRR Roosevelt/NAS ... Puerto Rico
NRS Imperial Beach/NAF, CA ... USA
NRT Tokyo/Narita ... Japan
NRV Guam/USCG Shore St ... Guam
NRY Newry ... Australia
NSA Noosa ... Australia
NSB Bimini/North SPB ... Bahamas
NSE Milton, FL ... USA
NSF Andrews/NAF, MD ... USA
NSH Now Shahr ... Iran
NSI Yaaunde/Nsimalen ... Cameroon
NSK Noril'sk ... Russia
NSM Norseman ... Australia
NSN Nelson ... New Zealand
NSO Scone ... Australia
NSP Sangley Point/NAF ... Philippines
NST Nakhon Si Thammarat ... Thailand
NSV Noosaville ... Australia
NSX N. Sound/Virgin Gorda/ Hovercraft/Launch Pt ... Virgin Is (British)
NSY Sigonella/NAF ... Italy
NTA Natadola ... Fiji
NTB Notodden ... Norway
NTC Santa Carolina ... Mozambique
NTD Point Mugu/NAS, CA ... USA
NTE Nantes ... France
NTG Nantong ... China
NTI Bintuni ... Indonesia
NTJ Manti, UT ... USA
NTL Newcastle/Williamtown ... Australia
NTM Miracema Do Norte ... Brazil
NTN Normanton ... Australia
NTO Santo Antao ... Cape Verde Is
NTR Monterrey/Aeropuerto Del None ... Mexico
NTT Niuatoputapu/Kuini Lavenia ... Tonga
NTU Oceana/NAS, VA ... USA
NTX Natuna Ranai ... Indonesia
NTY Sun City/Pilansberg ... S. Africa
NUB Numbulwar ... Australia
NUC San Clemente/NAF, CA ... USA
NUD En Nahud ... Somalia
NUE Nuernberg ... Germany
NUG Nuguria ... Papua New Guinea
NUH Nunchia ... Colombia
NUI Nuiqsut, AK ... USA
NUK Nukutavake ... F. Polynesia
NUL Nulato, AK ... USA
NUN Saufley/NAS, FL ... USA
NUP Nunapitchuk, AK ... USA
NUQ Mountain View, CA ... USA
NUR Nullarbor ... Australia
NUS Norsup ... Vanuatu
NUT Nutuve ... Papua New Guinea
NUU Nakuru ... Kenya
NUW Whidbey Is/NAS, WA ... USA
NUX Novy Urengoy ... Russia
NVA Neiva/La Marguita ... Colombia
NVD Nevada, MO ... USA
NVG Nueva Guinea ... Netherlands
NVK Narvik/Framnes ... Norway
NVP Novo Aripuana ... Brazil
NVR Novgorod ... Russia
NVS Nevers ... France
NVT Navegantes ... Brazil
NVY Neyveli ... India

AIRPORTS

NWA . Moheli . . . . . Comoros
NWH . Newport, NH . . . . . USA
NWI . . Norwich . . . . . UK
NWP . Argentia, NS. . . . . Canada
NWS . New York/Pier 11/SPB, NY . . USA
NWT . Nowata . . . . . Papua New Guinea
NWU . Bermuda/NAS . . . . . Bermuda
NXP . . Twenty-Nine Palms, Marine Corps Air-Ground Combat Cntr, CA . . . . USA
NXX . . Willow Grove/NAS, PA . . . . . USA
NYC . . New York, NY. . . . . USA
NYE . . Nyeri . . . . . Kenya
NYG . . Quantico-MCAF, VA . . . . . USA
NYI . . . Sunyani. . . . . Ghana
NYK . . Nanyuki . . . . . Kenya
NYL . . Yuma/MCAS, AZ . . . . . USA
NYM . Nadym . . . . . Russia
NYN . . Nyingan . . . . . Australia
NYO . . Stockholm/Skavsta . . . . . Sweden
NYU . . Nyaung-u . . . . . Myanmar
NZA . . Nzagi . . . . . Angola
NZC . . Cecil/NAS, FL . . . . . USA
NZE . . Nzerekore. . . . . Guinea
NZO . . Nzola. . . . . Kenya
NZW . South Weymouth, MA . . . . . USA
NZY . . North Is/NAS, CA. . . . . USA

O

OAG . . Orange/Springhill . . . . . Australia
OAJ . . Jacksonville, NC . . . . . USA
OAK . . Oakland Int'l, CA . . . . . USA
OAL . . Cacoal . . . . . Brazil
OAM . Oamaru . . . . . New Zealand
OAN . . Olanchito . . . . . Honduras
OAR . . Fritzsche/AAF, CA . . . . . USA
OAX . . Oaxaca. . . . . Mexico
OBA . . Oban. . . . . Australia
OBC . Obock. . . . . Djibouti
OBD . Obano . . . . . Indonesia
OBE . . Okeechobee, FL . . . . . USA
OBF . . Oberpfaffenhofen . . . . . Germany
OBI . . Odibos . . . . . Brazil
OBK . Northbrook, IL . . . . . USA
OBL . . Zoersel . . . . . Belgium
OBM . Morobe . . . . . Papua New Guinea
OBN . Oban/Connei . . . . . UK
OBO . Obihiro . . . . . Japan
OBS . . Aubenas/Vals-Lanas . . . . . France
OBT . . Oakland, MD . . . . . USA
OBU . Kobuk, AK . . . . . USA
OBX . . Obo. . . . . Papua New Guinea
OBY . . Ittoqqortoormiit. . . . . Greenland
OCA . Ocean Reef, FL . . . . . USA
OCC . Coca. . . . . Ecuador
OCE . . Ocean City, MD . . . . . USA
OCF . . Ocala, FL . . . . . USA
OCH . Lufkin, TX . . . . . USA
OCI . . Oceanic, AK . . . . . USA
OCJ . . Ocho Rios/Boscobel . . . . Jamaica
OCN . Oceanside, CA . . . . . USA
OCV . . Ocana/Aguasclaras . . . Colombia
OCW . Washington, NC . . . . . USA
ODA . . Ouadda . . . . Central African Rep
ODB . Cordoba. . . . . Spain
ODD . Oodnadatta . . . . . Australia
ODE . . Odense/Beldringe . . . . . Denmark
ODH . Odiham/RAF . . . . . UK
ODJ . . Ouanda Dialle . . . . . Central African Rep
ODL . . Cordillo Downs . . . . . Australia
ODN . Long Seridan . . . . . Malaysia
ODR . Ord River . . . . . Australia
ODS . . Odessa/Central . . . . . Ukraine
ODW . Oak Harbor, WA. . . . . USA
ODX . . Ord/Sharp Fld, NE. . . . . USA
ODY . . Oudoni . . . . . Laos
OEA . . Vincennes/Oneal, IN . . . . . USA
OEC . . Ocussi. . . . . Indonesia
OEL . . Orel . . . . . Russia
OEM . . Paloemeu/Vincent Fayks . . . . . Suriname
OEO . . Osceola, WI . . . . . USA
OER . . Ornskoldsvik. . . . . Sweden
OES . . San Antonio Oeste . . . . Argentina
OFF . . Offutt/AFB, NE . . . . . USA
OFI . . . Ouango Fitini . . . . . Côte D'Ivoire
OFJ . . Olafsfjordur . . . . . Iceland
OFK . . Norfolk, NE . . . . . USA
OFP . . Ashland, VA . . . . . USA
OFU . . Ofu. . . . . American Samoa
OGA . . Ogallala/Searle Fld, NE . . . . . USA
OGB . . Orangeburg, SC . . . . . USA
OGD . . Ogden, UT . . . . . USA
OGE . . Ogeranang . . Papua New Guinea
OGG . . Kahului, HI . . . . . USA
OGL . . Ogle. . . . . Guyana
OGN . . Yonaguni Jima . . . . . Japan
OGO . . Abengourou . . . . . Côte D'Ivoire
OGR . . Bonger . . . . . Chad
OGS . . Ogdensburg Int'l, NY. . . . . USA
OGV . . Ongava Game Reserve Namibia
OGX . . Ouargla . . . . . Algeria
OGZ . . Vladikavkaz. . . . . Russia
OHA . . Ohakea/RAF . . . . . New Zealand
OHC . . Northeast Cape/AFS, AK . . . USA
OHD . . Ohrid . . . . . Macedonia
OHI . . . Oshakati . . . . . Namibia
OHO . . Okhotsk. . . . . Russia
OHP . . Oban/ HP . . . . . UK
OHR . . Wylk Auf Foehr . . . . . Germany
OHT . . Kohat. . . . . Pakistan
OHX . . Nashville Nexrad, TN. . . . . USA
OIA . . . Ourilandia . . . . . Brazil
OIC . . . Norwich/Eaten . . . . . Australia
OIL . . . Oil City, PA. . . . . USA
OIM . . Oshima . . . . . Japan
OIR . . . Okushiri . . . . . Japan
OIT . . . Oita . . . . . Japan
OJC . . Kansas City Exec, KS . . . . . USA
OKA . . Okinawa/Naha . . . . . Japan
OKB . . Orchid Beach/Fraser Is . Australia
OKC . . Oklahoma City, OK . . . . . USA
OKD . . Sapporo/Okadarna . . . . . Japan
OKE . . Okino Erabu . . . . . Japan
OKF . . Okaukuejo. . . . . Namibia
OKG . . Okoyo . . . . . Congo, DR
OKH . . Oakham/Cottesmor/RAF . . . . UK
OKI . . . Oki Is . . . . . Japan
OKJ . . Okayama . . . . . Japan
OKK . . Kokorno, IN. . . . . USA
OKL . . Oksibil . . . . . Indonesia
OKM . . Okmulgee, OK . . . . . USA
OKN . . Okondja . . . . . Gabon
OKO . . Tokyo/Yokota AFB . . . . . Japan
OKP . . Oksapimin. . . Papua New Guinea
OKQ . . Okaba . . . . . Indonesia
OKR . . Yorke Is . . . . . Australia
OKS . . Oshkosh, NE . . . . . USA
OKT . . Oktiabrskij . . . . . Russia
OKU . . Mokuti Lodge . . . . . Namibia
OKV . . Winchester, VA . . . . . USA
OKX . . NY City Nexrad, NY . . . . . USA
OKY . . Oakey . . . . . Australia
OLA . . Orland . . . . . Norway
OLB . . Olbia/Costa Smeraida . . . . . Italy
OLD . . Old Town, ME . . . . . USA
OLE . . Olean, NY . . . . . USA
OLF . . Wolf Point Int'l, MT . . . . . USA
OLH . . Old Harbor/SPB, AK . . . . . USA
OLI . . . Olafsvik/Rif . . . . . Iceland
OLJ . . Olpoi . . . . . Vanuatu
OLM . . Olympia, WA. . . . . USA
OLN . . Colonia Sarmiento . . . . Argentina
OLO . . Olomouc . . . . . Czech Rep
OLP . . Olympic Dam . . . . . Australia
OLQ . . Olsobip . . . . . Papua New Guinea
OLS . . Nogales Int'l, AZ. . . . . USA
OLU . Columbus, NE. . . . . USA
OLV . . Olive Branch, MS . . . . . USA
OLY . . Olney, IL. . . . . USA
OLZ . . Oelwen, IA. . . . . USA
OMA . Omaha, NE . . . . . USA
OMB . Omboue . . . . . Gabon
OMC . Ormoc . . . . . Philippines
OMD . Oranjemund . . . . . Namibia
OME . Nome, AK . . . . . USA
OMF . Mafraq/King Hussein (RJAF) . . . . . Jordan
OMG . Omega. . . . . Namibia
OMH . Urmieh . . . . . Iran
OMJ . Omura . . . . . Japan
OMK . Omak, WA . . . . . USA
OML . Ornkalai . . . . Papua New Guinea
OMM . Marmul. . . . . Oman
OMN . Osmanabad . . . . . India
OMO . Mostar . . . . . Bosnia Hercegovina
OMR . Oradea. . . . . Romania
OMS . Omsk . . . . . Russia
OMY . Oddor Meanche . . . . . Cambodia
ONA . Winona, MN. . . . . USA
ONB . Ononge . . . . Papua New Guinea
OND . Ondangwa . . . . . Namibia
ONE . Onepusu . . . . . Solomon Is
ONG . Mornington . . . . . Australia
ONH . Oneonta/Municipal, NY . . . . USA
ONI . . Moanamani . . . . . Indonesia
ONJ . Odate Noshiro. . . . . Japan
ONL . O'Neill, NE . . . . . USA
ONM . Socorro, NM . . . . . USA
ONN . Onion Bay, AK. . . . . USA
ONO . Ontario, OR . . . . . USA
ONP . Newport, OR . . . . . USA
ONQ . Zonguldak . . . . . Turkey
ONR . Monkira . . . . . Australia
ONS . Onslow. . . . . Australia
ONT . Ontario Int'l, CA. . . . . USA
ONU . Ono I Lau . . . . . Fiji
ONX . Colon . . . . . Panama
ONY . Olney, TX . . . . . USA
OOA . Oskaloosa, IA . . . . . USA
OOL . Gold Coast . . . . . Australia
OOM . Cooma. . . . . Australia
OOR . Mooraberree . . . . . Australia
OOT . Onotoa. . . . . Kiribati
OPA . Kopasker. . . . . Iceland
OPB . Open Bay . . Papua New Guinea
OPF . Miami-Opa Locka, FL. . . . . USA
OPI . . Oenpeili . . . . . Australia
OPL . Opelousas, LA . . . . . USA
OPO . Porto. . . . . Portugal
OPS . Sinop . . . . . Brazil
OPU . Balimo . . . . . Papua New Guinea
OPW . Opuwa. . . . . Namibia
ORA . Oran. . . . . Argentina
ORB . Orebro . . . . . Sweden
ORC . Orocue. . . . . Colombia
ORD . Chicago/O'Hare Int'l, IL . . . . USA
ORE . Orange, MA. . . . . USA
ORF . Norfolk Int'l, VA . . . . . USA
ORG . Paramaribo/Zorg En Hoop . . . . . Suriname
ORH . Worcester, MA. . . . . USA
ORI . . Port Lions/SPB, AK. . . . . USA
ORJ . Orinduik . . . . . Guyana
ORK . Cork . . . . . Ireland
ORL . Orlando Exec, FL . . . . . USA
ORM . Northampton . . . . . Georgia
ORN . Oran/Es Senia . . . . . Algeria
ORO . Yoro . . . . . Honduras
ORP . Orapa. . . . . Botswana
ORQ . Norwalk / HP, CT. . . . . USA
ORR . Yorketown . . . . . Australia
ORS . Orpheus Is Resort/Waterport . . . . . Australia
ORT . Northway, AK . . . . . USA
ORU . Oruro . . . . . Bolivia
ORV . Noorvik/Curtis Memorial, AK USA
ORW . Ormara . . . . . Pakistan

ORX	Oriximina	Brazil
ORY	Paris/Orly	France
ORZ	Orange Walk	Belize
OSB	Osage Beach, MD	USA
OSC	Wurtsmith/AFB, MI	USA
OSD	Ostersund/Froesoe	Sweden
OSE	Omora	Papua New Guinea
OSG	Ossima	Papua New Guinea
OSH	Oshkosh, WI	USA
OSI	Osijek	Croatia
OSK	Oskarshamn	Sweden
OSL	Oslo/Gardermoen	Norway
OSM	Mosul	Iraq
OSN	Osan/Air Base	S. Korea
OSP	Slupsk/Recizikowo	Poland
OSR	Ostrava/Mosnov	Czech Rep
OSS	Osh	Kyrgyzstan
OST	Ostend	Belgium
OSU	Colurribus, OH	USA
OSW	Orsk	Russia
OSX	Kosciusko/Attala County, MS	USA
OSY	Namsos/Lufthavn	Norway
OSZ	Koszalin	Poland
OTA	Mota	Ethiopia
OTC	Bol	Chad
OTD	Contadora	Panama
OTG	Worthington, MN	USA
OTH	North Bend, OR	USA
OTI	Morotai Is	Indonesia
OTJ	Otjiwarongo	Namibia
OTL	Boutilimit	Mauritania
OTM	Ottumwa, IA	USA
OTN	Oaktown, IN	USA
OTO	Otto/Vor, NM	USA
OTP	Bucharest/Otopeni Int'l	Romania
OTR	Coto 47	Costa Rica
OTS	Anacortes, WA	USA
OTU	Otu	Colombia
OTY	Oria	Papua New Guinea
OTZ	Kotzebue, AK	USA
OUA	Ouagadougou/Aeroport	Burkina Faso
OUD	Oujda/Les Angades	Morocco
OUE	Ouesso	Cocos (Keeling) Is
OUG	Ouahigouya	Burkina Faso
OUH	Ouctshoorn	S. Africa
OUI	Ban Houei	Laos
OUK	Outer Skerries	UK
OUL	Oulu	Finland
OUM	Oum Hadjer	Chad
OUN	Norman, OK	USA
OUR	Batouri	Cameroon
OUS	Ourinhos	Brazil
OUT	Bousso	Chad
OUU	Ouanga	Gabon
OUZ	Zouerate	Mauritania
OVA	Bekily	Madagascar
OVB	Novosibirsk	Russia
OVD	Asturias	Spain
OVE	Oroville, CA	USA
OVL	Ovalle	Chile
OVS	Boscobel, WI	USA
OWA	Owatonna, MN	USA
OWB	Owensboro, KY	USA
OWD	Norwood, MA	USA
OWE	Owendo	Gabon
OWK	Norridgewock, ME	USA
OWY	Owyhee, NV	USA
OXB	Bissau/Osvaldo Vieira	Guinea Bissau
OXC	Oxford, CT	USA
OXD	Oxford, OH	USA
OXF	Oxford/Kidlington	UK
OXO	Orientos	Australia
OXR	Oxnard, CA	USA
OXV	Knoxville, IA	USA
OXY	Morney	Australia
OYA	Goya	Argentina
OYE	Oyem	Gabon
OYG	Moyo	Uganda
OYK	Ciapoclue	Brazil

OYL	Moyale	Kenya
OYN	Ouyen	Australia
OYO	Tres Arroyos	Argentina
OYP	St Georges de Ioyapock	French Guiana
OYS	Yosemite Ntl Park, CA	USA
OZA	Ozona, TX	USA
OZC	Ozamis City/Labo	Philippines
OZH	Zaporozhye	Ukraine
OZI	Codazzi	Colombia
OZP	Moron	Spain
OZR	Cairns/AAF, AL	USA
OZZ	Ouarzazate	Morocco

P

PAA	Pa-an	Myanmar
PAB	Bilaspur	India
PAC	Panama City/Paitilia	Panama
PAD	Paderborn/Lippstadt	Germany
PAE	Everett, WA	USA
PAF	Pakulha	Uganda
PAG	Pagadian	Philippines
PAH	Paducah, KY	USA
PAI	Pailin	Cambodia
PAJ	Para Chinar	Pakistan
PAK	Hanapepe/Port Allen, HI	USA
PAL	Palanquero	Colombia
PAM	Tyndall/AFB, FL	USA
PAN	Pattani	Thailand
PAO	Palo Alto, CA	USA
PAP	Port Au Prince	Haiti
PAQ	Palmer, AK	USA
PAS	Paros	Greece
PAT	Patna	India
PAU	Pauk	Myanmar
PAV	Paulo Afonso	Brazil
PAW	Pambwa	Papua New Guinea
PAX	Port De Paix	Haiti
PAY	Pamol	Malaysia
PAZ	Poza Rica/Tajin	Mexico
PBA	Barrow/Point Barrow, AK	USA
PBB	Paranaiba	Brazil
PBC	Puebla/Huejotsingo	Mexico
PBD	Porbandar	India
PBE	Puerto Berrio	Colombia
PBF	Pine Bluff, AR	USA
PBG	Plattsburgh/AFB, NY	USA
PBH	Paro	Bhutan
PBI	West Palm Beach, FL	USA
PBJ	Paama	Vanuatu
PBK	Pack Creek, AK	USA
PBL	Puerto Cabello	Venezuela
PBM	Paramaribo/Zandenj Int'l	Suriname
PBN	Porto Amboim	Angola
PBO	Paraburdoo	Australia
PBP	Punta Istilta	Costa Rica
PBQ	Pimenta Bueno	Brazil
PBR	Puerto Barrios	Guatemala
PDS	Patong Beach	Thailand
PBU	Putao	Myanmar
PBV	Porto Dos Gauchos	Brazil
PBW	Palibelo	Indonesia
PBX	Porto Alegre Do Norte	Brazil
PBZ	Plettenberg Bay	S. Africa
PCA	Portage Creek, AK	USA
PCB	Pondok Cabe	Indonesia
PCC	Puerto Rico	Colombia
PCD	Prairie Du Chien, WI	USA
PCE	Painter Creek, AK	USA
PCG	Paso Calballos	Guatemala
PCH	Palacios	Honduras
PCK	Porcupine Creek, AK	USA
PCL	Pucallpa/Capitan Rolden	Peru
PCM	Playa del Carmen	Mexico
PCN	Picton/Koromiko	New Zealand
PCO	Punta Colorada	Mexico

PCP	Principe	Sao Tome and Principe
PCR	Puerto Carreno	Colombia
PCS	Picos	Brazil
PCT	Princeton, NJ	USA
PCU	Picayune, MS	USA
PCV	Dunta Chivato	Mexico
PDA	Puerto Ininda	Colombia
PDB	Pedro Bay, AK	USA
PDC	Mueo	New Caledonia
PDE	Panclie Pandie	Australia
PDF	Prado	Brazil
PDG	Padang/Tabing	Indonesia
PDI	Pindiu	Papua New Guinea
PDK	Atlanta, GA	USA
PDL	Ponta Delgada/Nordela	Portugal
PDN	Parndana	Australia
PDO	Pendopo	Indonesia
PDP	Punta Del Este	Uruguay
PDR	Presidente Dutra/Mun	Brazil
PDS	Piedras Negras	Mexico
PDT	Pendleton, OR	USA
PDU	Paysandu	Uruguay
PDV	Plovcliv	Bulgaria
PDX	Portland Int'l, OR	USA
PDZ	Pedernales	Venezuela
PEA	Penneshaw	Australia
PEB	Pebane	Mozambique
PEC	Pelican/SPB, AK	USA
PEE	Perm	Russia
PEF	Peenemuende	Germany
PEG	Perugia/Sant Egidio	Italy
PEH	Pehuajo	Argentina
PEI	Pereira/Matecana	Colombia
PEK	Beijing	China
PEL	Pelaneng	Lesotho
PEM	Puerto Madonado	Peru
PEN	Penang Int'l	Malaysia
PEO	Penn Yan, NY	USA
PEP	Peppimenarti	Australia
PEQ	Pecos City, TX	USA
PER	Perth	Australia
PES	Petrozavodsk	Russia
PET	Pelotas/Federal	Brazil
PEU	Puerto Lempira	Honduras
PEW	Peshawar	Pakistan
PEX	Pechora	Russia
PEY	Pencing	Australia
PEZ	Penza	Russia
PFA	Pat Warren, AK	USA
PFB	Passo Fundo	Brazil
PFC	Pacific City, OR	USA
PFD	Port Frederick, AK	USA
PFJ	Patreksfjordur	Iceland
PFN	Panama City, FL	USA
PFO	Paphos Int'l	Cyprus
PFR	Ilebo	Congo, DR
PGA	Page, AZ	USA
PGB	Pangoa	Papua New Guinea
PGC	Petersburg, WV	USA
PGD	Punta Gorda, FL	USA
PGE	Yegepa	Papua New Guinea
PGF	Perpignan/Llabanere	France
PGG	Progresso	Brazil
PGH	Pantnagar	India
PGI	Chitato	Angola
PGK	Pangkalpinang	Indonesia
PGL	Pascagoula, MS	USA
PGM	Port Graham, AK	USA
PGN	Pangia	Papua New Guinea
PGO	Pagosa Springs, CO	USA
PGP	Porto Alegre	Sao Tome and Principe
PGR	Paragould/Mun	Australia
PGS	Peach Springs, AZ	USA
PGV	Greenville, NC	USA
PGX	Perigueux/Bassillac	France
PGZ	Ponta Grossa/Sant'Ana	Brazil
PHA	Phan Rang	Vietnam
PHB	Parnailba/Santos Dumont	Brazil
PHC	Port Harcourt	Nigeria

AIRPORTS

Code	Location	Country
PHD	New Philadelphia, OH	USA
PHE	Port Hedland	Australia
PHF	Hampton, VA	USA
PHH	Phan Thiet	Vietnam
PHI	Pinheiro	Brazil
PHJ	Porl Hunter	Australia
PHK	Pahokee, FL	USA
PHL	Philadelphia Int'l, PA	USA
PHM	Boeblingen	Germany
PHN	Port Huron Int'l, MI	USA
PHO	Point Hope, AK	USA
PHP	Philip, SD	USA
PHR	Pacific Harbor	Fiji
PHS	Phitsanulok	Thailand
PHT	Paris, TN	USA
PHU	Phu Vinh	Vietnam
PHW	Phalaborwa	S. Africa
PHX	Phoenix Int'l, AZ	USA
PHZ	Phi Phi Is	Thailand
PIA	Peoria, IL	USA
PIB	Laurel, MS	USA
PIC	Pine Cay	Turks & Caicos Is
PID	Nassau/Paradise Is	Bahamas
PIE	St Petersburg- Clearwater Int'l, FL	USA
PIF	Pingtung	Taiwan
PIG	Pitinga	Brazil
PIH	Pocatello, ID	USA
PII	Fairbanks/Phillips Fld, AK	USA
PIK	Glasgow	UK
PIL	Pilar	Paraguay
PIM	Pine Mountain, GA	USA
PIN	Parintins	Brazil
PIO	Pisco	Peru
PIP	Pilot Point, AK	USA
PIQ	Pipillipai	Guyana
PIR	Pierre, SD	USA
PIS	Poitiers/Biard	France
PIT	Pittsburgh Int'l, PA	USA
PIU	Ptura	Peru
PIV	Pirapora	Brazil
PIW	Pilkwitonei, MB	Canada
PIX	Pico Is	Portugal
PIZ	Point Lay, AK	USA
PJB	Payson, AZ	USA
PJC	Pedro Juan Caballero	Paraguay
PJG	Panjgur	Pakistan
PJM	Puerto Jimenez	Costa Rica
PJS	Port San Juan, AK	USA
PJZ	Puerto Juarez	Mexico
PKA	Napaskiak/SPB, AK	USA
PKB	Parkersburg, WV	USA
PKC	Petropavlovsk-Kamchats	Russia
PKD	Park Rapids, MN	USA
PKE	Parkes	Australia
PKF	Park Falls, WI	USA
PKG	Pangkor	Malaysia
PKH	Porto Cheli Kheli/Alexion.	Greece
PKJ	Playa Grande	Guatemala
PKK	Palkokku	Myanmar
PKL	Pakatoa Is.	New Zealand
PKM	Port Kaiturna	Guyana
PKN	Pangkalanbuun	Indonesia
PKO	Parakou	Benin
PKP	Puka Puka	F. Polynesia
PKR	Pokhara	Nepal
PKS	Paksane	Laos
PKT	Port Keats	Australia
PKU	Pekanbaru/Simpang Tiga	Indonesia
PKV	Pskov	Russia
PKW	Selebi-Phikwe	Botswana
PKY	Palangkaraya	Indonesia
PKZ	Pakse	Laos
PLA	Planaclas	Colombia
PLB	Plattsburgh, NY	USA
PLC	Pianeta Rica	Colombia
PLD	Playa Samara	Costa Rica
PLE	Paiela	Papua New Guinea
PLF	Pala	Chad
PLG	La Plagne	France
PLH	Plymouth	UK
PLI	Palm Is. St. Vincent & Grenadines	
PLJ	Placencia	Belize
PLL	Ponta Pelada	Brazil
PLM	Palembang/Mahmud Badaruddin II	Indonesia
PLN	Pellston, MI	USA
PLO	Port Lincoln	Australia
PLP	La Palma	Panama
PLQ	Palanga	Italy
PLR	Pell City, AK	USA
PLS	Providenciales/Int'l	Turks & Caicos Is
PLT	Plato	Colombia
PLU	Belo Horizonte/Parnpulha	Brazil
PLV	Poll	Ukraine
PLW	Palu/Mutiara	Indonesia
PLX	Semipalatinsk	Kazakstan
PLY	Plymouth, IN	USA
PLZ	Port Elizabeth	S. Africa
PMA	Pemba/Wawi	Tanzania
PMB	Pembina/Intermediate, ND	USA
PMC	Puerto Moritt/Tepual	Chile
PMD	Palmdale, CA	USA
PME	Portsmouth	UK
PMF	Milan/Milano/Parma	Italy
PMG	Ponta Pora/Int'l	Brazil
PMH	Portsmouth, OH	USA
PMI	Palma Mallorca	Spain
PMK	Palm Is.	Australia
PML	Port Moller/AFS, AK	USA
PMM	Phanom Sarakham	Thailand
PMN	Pumani	Papua New Guinea
PMO	Palermo/Punta Raisi	Italy
PMP	Pimaga	Papua New Guinea
PMQ	Perito Moreno	Argentina
PMR	Palmerston North	New Zealand
PMS	Palmyra	Syria
PMT	Paramakotoi	Guyana
PMU	Paimiut/SPB, AK	USA
PMV	Porlarnar	Venezuela
PMW	Palmas	Brazil
PMX	Palmer, MA	USA
PMY	Puerto Madryn/El Tehuelche	Argentina
PMZ	Palmar/Palmar Sur	Costa Rica
PNA	Pamplona	Spain
PNB	Porto Nacional	Brazil
PNC	Ponca City, OK	USA
PND	Punta Gorda	Belize
PNE	Philadelphia, PA	USA
PNF	Peterson's Point, AK	USA
PNG	Paranagua	Brazil
PNH	Phnom Penh/Pochentong	Cambodia
PNI	Pohnpei	Micronesia
PNK	Pontianak/Supadio	Indonesia
PNL	Pantelleria	Italy
PNM	Princeton, MN	USA
PNN	Princeton, ME	USA
PNO	Pinotepa Nacional	Mexico
PNP	Popondetta/Girua	Papua New Guinea
PNQ	Poona/Lohegaon	India
PNR	Pointe-Noire	Congo, DR
PNS	Pensacola, FL	USA
PNT	Puerto Natales/Teniente J. Gallardo	Chile
PNU	Panguitch, UT	USA
PNV	Panevezys	Lithuania
PNX	Sherman-Denison, TX	USA
PNY	Pondicherry	India
PNZ	Petrolina/Int'l	Brazil
POA	Porto Alegre/Salgado Filhe	Brazil
POB	Pope/AFB, NC	USA
POC	La Verne, CA	USA
POD	Podor	Senegal
POE	Polk/AAF, LA	USA
POF	Poplar Bluff, MO	USA
POG	Port Gentil	Gabon
POH	Pocahontas, IA	USA
POI	Potosi	Bolivia
POJ	Patos De Minas	Brazil
POL	Pemba	Mozambique
POM	Port Moresby/Int'l	Papua New Guinea
PON	Poptun	Guatemala
POO	Pocos De Calclas	Brazil
POP	Puerto Plata/La Union	Dominican Rep
POQ	Polk Inlet, AK	USA
POR	Pori	Finland
POS	Port Of Spain	Trinidad and Tobago
POT	Port Antonio/Ken Jones	Jamaica
POU	Poughkeepsie, NY	USA
POV	Presov	Slovakia
POW	Portoroz/Secovlje	Slovenia
POX	Paris/Paris Cergy Pontoise	France
POY	Lovell, WY	USA
POZ	Pozan/Lawica	Poland
PPA	Pampa/Perry Lefors Fld, TX	USA
PPB	Presidente Prudente/A. De Barros	Brazil
PPC	Prospect Creek, AK	USA
PPD	Humacao/Palmas Del Mar	Puerto Rico
PPE	Puerto Penasco	Mexico
PPF	Parsons, KS	USA
PPG	Pago Pago/Int'l	American Samoa
PPH	Peraitepuy	Venezuela
PPI	Port Pirie	Australia
PPJ	Pulau Panlang	Indonesia
PPK	Petropavlovsk	Kazakhstan
PPL	Phaplu	Nepal
PPM	Pompano Beach, FL	USA
PPN	Popayan/Machangara	Colombia
PPO	Powell Point	Bahamas
PPP	Proserpine	Australia
PPQ	Paraparaumu	New Zealand
PPR	Pasir Pangarayan	Indonesia
PPS	Puerto Princesa	Philippines
PPT	Papeete/Faaa	F. Polynesia
PPU	Papun	Myanmar
PPV	Port Protection, AK	USA
PPW	Papa Westray	UK
PPX	Param	Papua New Guinea
PPY	Pouso Alegre	Brazil
PPZ	Puerto Paez	Venezuela
PQC	Phu Quoc/Duong Dang	Vietnam
PQI	Presque Isle, ME	USA
PQL	Pascagoula, Lott Int'l Arpt, MS	USA
PQM	Palenque	Mexico
PQQ	Port Macquarie	Australia
PQS	Pilot Stn, AK	USA
PRA	Parana	Argentina
PRB	Paso Robles, CA	USA
PRC	Prescott, AZ	USA
PRD	Pardoo	Australia
PRE	Pore	Colombia
PRF	Port Johnson	Australia
PRG	Prague/Ruzyne	Czech Rep
PRH	Phrae	Thailand
PRI	Praslin Is	Seychelles
PRJ	Capri	Italy
PRK	Prieska	S. Africa
PRL	Port Oceanic, AK	USA
PRM	Portimao	Portugal
PRN	Pristina	Yugoslavia
PRO	Perry, IA	USA
PRP	Propriano	France
PRQ	Pres. Roque Saenz Pena	Argentina
PRR	Paruima	Guyana
PRS	Parasi	Solomon Is
PRT	Point Retreat/Coast Guard HP, AK	USA
PRU	Prome	Myanmar
PRV	Prerov	Czech Rep
PRW	Prentice, WI	USA
PRX	Paris, TX	USA

AIRPORTS

Code	Airport	Country
PRY	Pretoria	S. Africa
PRZ	Prineville, OR	USA
PSA	Florence/Pisa/Gal Galilei	Italy
PSB	Bellefonte, PA	USA
PSC	Pasco, WA	USA
PSD	Port Said	Egypt
PSE	Ponce/Mercedita	Puerto Rico
PSF	Pittsfield, MA	USA
PSG	Petersburg, AK	USA
PSH	St Peter	Germany
PSI	Pasni	Pakistan
PSJ	Poso/Kasiguncu	Indonesia
PSK	Dublin, VA	USA
PSL	Perth/Scone	UK
PSM	Pease/AFB, NH	USA
PSN	Palestine, TX	USA
PSO	Pasto/Cano	Colombia
PSP	Palm Springs, CA	USA
PSQ	Philadelphia/SPB, PA	USA
PSR	Pescara/Liberi	Italy
PSS	Posadas	Argentina
PST	Preston	Cuba
PSU	Putussibau	Indonesia
PSV	Papa Stour	UK
PSW	Passos	Brazil
PSX	Palaclos, TX	USA
PSY	Port Stanley	Falkand Is
PSZ	Puerto Suarez	Somalia
PTA	Port Alsworth, AK	USA
PTB	Petersburg, VA	USA
PTC	Port Alice, AK	USA
PTD	Port Alexander, AK	USA
PTE	Port Stephens	Australia
PTF	Malololailal	Fiji
PTG	Pietersburg	S. Africa
PTH	Port Heiden, AK	USA
PTI	Port Douglas	Australia
PTJ	Portland	Australia
PTK	Pontiac, MI	USA
PTL	Port Armstrong, AK	USA
PTM	Palmanto	Venezuela
PTN	Morgan City/Municipal HP, LA	USA
PTO	Pato Branco	Brazil
PTP	Pointe A Pitre/Le Raizet	Gaudeloupe
PTR	Pleasant Harbour, AK	USA
PTS	Pittsburg, KS	USA
PTT	Pratt Municipal, KS	USA
PTU	Platinum, AK	USA
PTV	Porterville, CA	USA
PTW	Pottstown, PA	USA
PTX	Pitalito	Colombia
PTY	Panama City/Tocumen Int'l	Panama
PTZ	Pastaza	Ecuador
PUA	Puas	Papua New Guinea
PUB	Pueblo, CO	USA
PUC	Price, UT	USA
PUD	Puerto Deseado	Argentina
PUE	Puerto Obaldia	Panama
PUF	Pau/Uzein	France
PUG	Port Augusta	Australia
PUH	Pochutla	Mexico
PUI	Pureni	Papua New Guinea
PUJ	Punta Cana	Dominican Rep
PUK	Pukarua	F. Polynesia
PUL	Poulsbo, WA	USA
PUM	Pomala	Indonesia
PUN	Punia	Congo, DR
PUO	Prudhoe Bay, AK	USA
PUP	Po	Burkina Faso
PUQ	Punta Arenas/Pres Ibanez	Chile
PUR	Puerto Rico	Somalia
PUS	Pusan/Kimhae Int'l Arpt	S. Korea
PUT	Puttaparthi/Puttaprathe	India
PUU	Puerto Asis	Colombia
PUV	Pourn	New Caledonia
PUW	Pullman, WA	USA
PUX	Puerto Varas	Chile
PUY	Pula	Croatia
PUZ	Puerto Cabezas	Netherlands
PVA	Providencia	Colombia
PVC	Provincetown, MA	USA
PVD	Providence, RI	USA
PVE	El Porvenir	Panama
PVF	Placerville, CA	USA
PVG	Shanghai/Pu Dong	China
PVH	Porto Velho/Belmonte	Brazil
PVI	Paranavai	Brazil
PVK	Preveza/Lefkas/Aktion	Greece
PVN	Pleven	Bulgaria
PVO	Portoviejo	Ecuador
PVR	Puerto Vallarta/Ordaz	Mexico
PVS	Providemya	Russia
PVU	Provo, UT	USA
PVW	Plainview, TX	USA
PVX	Provedenia	Russia
PVY	Pope Vanoy, AK	USA
PVZ	Painesville, OH	USA
PWA	Oklahoma City, OK	USA
PWD	Plentywood, MT	USA
PWE	Pevek	Russia
PWI	Pawi/Beles	Ethiopia
PWK	Chicago/Pal-Waukee, IL	USA
PWL	Purwokerto	Indonesia
PWM	Portland Int'l, ME	USA
PWN	Pitts Town	Bahamas
PWO	Pweto	Congo, DR
PWQ	Pavloclar	Kazakstan
PWR	Port Walter, AK	USA
PWT	Bremerton, WA	USA
PXL	Polacca, AZ	USA
PXM	Puerto Escondido	Myanmar
PXO	Porto Santo	Portugal
PXU	Pleiku	Vietnam
PYA	Puerto Boyaca	Colombia
PYB	Jeypore	India
PYC	Playon Chico	Panama
PYE	Penrhyn Island	Cook Is
PYH	Puerto Ayacucho	Venezuela
PYJ	Polyarnyl	Russia
PYL	Perry/SPB, AK	USA
PYM	Plymouth, MA	USA
PYN	Payan	Colombia
PYO	Putumayo	Ecuador
PYR	Pyrgos/Andravida	Greece
PYV	Yaviza	Panama
PYX	Pattaya	Thailand
PZA	Paz De Ariporo/Casanare	Colombia
PZB	Pietermaritzburg	S. Africa
PZE	Penzance/ HP	UK
PZH	Zhob	Pakistan
PZK	Puka Puka Is/Attol	Cook Is
PZL	Phinda/Zulu Inyaia	S. Africa
PZO	Puerto Ordaz	Venezuela
PZQ	Presque Isle/Rogers, MI	USA
PZU	Port Sudan	Sudan
PZY	Piestany	Slovakia

Q

Code	Airport	Country
QAC	Castro	Brazil
QAD	Pordenone	Italy
QAE	Arzew	Algeria
QAG	El Ghazaciuet	Algeria
QAH	Alcantara	Brazil
QAI	Aime	France
QAJ	Ajman City	UAE
QAK	Barbacena	Brazil
QAL	Alessandria	Italy
QAM	Amiens/Glisy	France
QAN	Nedroma	Algeria
QAO	Agrigento	Italy
QAP	Apapa	Nigeria
QAQ	L'Aquila	Italy
QAR	Arnhem/Bus Svc	Netherlands
QAS	Ech Cheliff	Algeria
QAT	Abeokuta	Nigeria
QAU	Bebedouro	Brazil
QAV	Benjamin Constant	Brazil
QAW	Anniston/Ft Mcclellan Bus Trml, AL	USA
QAX	Alaa	Nigeria
QAY	Alba lufla	Romania
QAZ	Zakopane	Poland
QBA	Budva	Yugoslavia
QBB	BelAbbes	Algeria
QBC	Bella Coola, BC	Canada
QBD	Barra Do Pirai	Brazil
QBE	Bega/Off-line Pt	Australia
QBF	Vail Van Svc, CO	USA
QBG	Pancevo	Yugoslavia
QBH	Levaliois	France
QBI	Bitola	Macedonia
QBJ	Bordj-Bou-Arreri	Algeria
QBK	Betim	Brazil
QBL	Bani-walid	Libya
QBM	Bourg-St Maurice	France
QBN	Barra Mansa	Brazil
QBO	Bochum	Germany
QBP	Ain Beida	Algeria
QBQ	Besancon	France
QBR	Bandar Khomeini	Iran
QBS	Brescia	Italy
QBT	Bettioua	Algeria
QBU	Bauchi	Nigeria
QBV	Benevento	Italy
QBW	Batemans Bay	Australia
QBX	Sobral	Brazil
QBY	Bistrita/Nasaud	Romania
QBZ	Bouira	Algeria
QCA	Makkah	Saudi Arabia
QCB	Chiba City	Japan
QCC	Camacari	Brazil
QCD	Campo Born	Brazil
QCE	Copper Mountain/Van Svc, CO	USA
QCF	Birigui	Brazil
QCG	Cataguases	Brazil
QCH	Colatina	Brazil
QCI	Playa deLos Cristianos	Spain
QCJ	Botucatu	Brazil
QCK	Cabo Frio	Brazil
QCL	Caltanissetta	Italy
QCM	Como	Italy
QCN	Canela	Brazil
QCO	Colon	Chile
QCP	Currais Novos	Brazil
QCQ	Caraguatatuba	Brazil
QCR	Curitibanos	Brazil
QCS	Cosenza	Italy
QCT	Bacita	Nigeria
QCU	Akunnaaq	Greenland
QCV	Guarulhos	Brazil
QCW	Wilton, CT/Off-line Pt	USA
QCX	Sao Caetano Do Sul	Brazil
QCY	Coningsby/RAF	UK
QCZ	Catanzaro	Italy
QDA	Charqueada	Brazil
QDB	Cachoeira Do Sul	Brazil
QDC	Dracena	Brazil
QDD	Botosani	Romania
QDE	Catanduva	Brazil
QDF	Conselheiro Lafaiete	Brazil
QDG	Ostro Weikopolski	Poland
QDH	Ashford/Int'l RR Stn	UK
QDI	Dornbirn	Austria
QDJ	Djelfa	Algeria
QDK	Chattanooga/Greyhound Bus Svc, TN	USA
QDN	Eden	Australia
QDO	Icoaraci	Brazil
QDP	Dom Pedrito	Brazil
QDQ	Duque De Caxias	Brazil
QDR	Dera'a	Syria
QDS	Itajuba	Brazil
QDT	Sedrata	Algeria
QDU	Dusseldorf/Stn	Germany

AIRPORTS

QDV . Jundiai . . . . Brazil	QGY . Gyor . . . . Hungary	QKA . Cachoeirinha . . . . Brazil
QDW . Diadema . . . . Brazil	QGZ . Yokkaichi . . . . Japan	QKB . Breckenridge/Van Svc, CO . USA
QDX . Damierta . . . . Egypt	QHA . Hasselt . . . . Belgium	QKC . Karaj . . . . Iran
QDY . Andong . . . . S. Korea	QHB . Piracicaba . . . . Brazil	QKD . Elk . . . . Poland
QDZ . Saida . . . . Algeria	QHC . Rolandia . . . . Brazil	QKE . Kabwe . . . . Zambia
QEA . Teramo . . . . Italy	QHD . Hahnweide/RR . . . . Germany	QKF . Kirefeld . . . . Germany
QEB . Maebashi . . . . Japan	QHE . Sato Bento Do Sul . . . . . Brazil	QKG . Chalkis . . . . Greece
QEC . Elmarj City . . . . Libya	QHF . Saa Sebastiao Do Cai . . . . Brazil	QKH . Kharian . . . . Pakistan
QED . Medea . . . . Algeria	QHG . Sete Lagoas . . . . Brazil	QKI . Kielce . . . . Poland
QEE . Ebeye . . . . Marshall Is	QHH . El Harrouche . . . . Algeria	QKJ . Khenchela . . . . Algeria
QEF . Egeisbach . . . . Germany	QHI . Chonburi . . . . Thailand	QKK . Karasjok . . . . Norway
QEG . Ribera Grande . . . . Portugal	QHJ . Hjoerring/Bus Svc . . . . . Denmark	QKL . Cologne/Stn . . . . Germany
QEH . El Hadjar . . . . Algeria	QHK . Shahrkord . . . . Iran	QKM . Gurni City . . . . S. Korea
QEI . Crailsheim . . . . Germany	QHL . Castanhal . . . . Brazil	QKN . Kairouan . . . . Tunisia
QEJ . Elgarhbolli . . . . Libya	QHM . Hama . . . . Syria	QKO . Khoms . . . . Libya
QEK . El Mahalla El Kobra . . . . . Egypt	QHN . Taguatinga . . . . Brazil	QKP . Kruger National Park . . . S. Africa
QEL . Wellington . . . . Australia	QHO . Oak Brook, IL/Off-line Pt . . . USA	QKQ . Anklam . . . . Germany
QEM . Elmanzala . . . . Egypt	QHP . Taubate . . . . Brazil	QKR . Kourou . . . . F. Guiana
QEN . SITA . . . . -	QHQ . Cham . . . . Germany	QKS . Keystone/Van Svc, CO . . . . USA
QEO . Bielsko-Baila . . . . Poland	QHR . Harar . . . . Ethiopia	QKT . Kangaamiut . . . . Greenland
QEP . Tarnobrzeg . . . . Poland	QHS . Horns . . . . Syria	QKU . Cologne/RR . . . . Germany
QEQ . Embrach . . . . Switzerland	QHT . Terezopolis . . . . Brazil	QKV . Osaka/Off-line Pt . . . . Japan
QER . Shehr . . . . Yemen	QHU . Husum . . . . Germany	QKW . Kanazawa . . . . Japan
QES . SITA . . . . -	QHV . Novo Hamburgo . . . . Brazil	QKX . Kautokeino . . . . Norway
QET . Taedok . . . . S. Korea	QHW . Brooklyn, NJ . . . . USA	QKY . Wakayama . . . . Japan
QEU . Parnamirim . . . . Brazil	QHX . Sohag . . . . Egypt	QKZ . Konstanz . . . . Germany
QEV . Courbevoie . . . . France	QHY . Hachioji City . . . . Japan	QLA . Lasham . . . . UK
QEW . Nottingham . . . . UK	QHZ . Hoofddorp . . . . Netherlands	QLB . Lajeado . . . . Brazil
QEX . Emmerich . . . . Germany	QIA . Itauna . . . . Brazil	QLC . Gilwice . . . . Poland
QEY . Qeqertarsuatsiaat . . . . Greenland	QIB . Ibiruba/Off-line Pt . . . . . . Brazil	QLD . Blida . . . . Algeria
QEZ . Pomezia . . . . Italy	QIC . Siracusa . . . . Italy	QLE . Leeton/Bus Svc . . . . . . Australia
QFA . Aalsmeer . . . . Netherlands	QID . Tres Coracoes . . . . Brazil	QLF . Lahti . . . . Finland
QFB . Freburg . . . . Germany	QIE . Istres . . . . France	QLG . Landshut . . . . Germany
QFC . Creteil . . . . France	QIF . Isleworth . . . . UK	QLH . Kelsterbach . . . . Germany
QFD . Boufarik . . . . Algeria	QIG . Iguatu . . . . Brazil	QLI . Limassol . . . . Cyprus
QFE . Ft. Benning, GA . . . . USA	QIH . Tres Rios . . . . Brazil	QLJ . Lucerne . . . . Switzerland
QFF . Brooklyn, NJ . . . . USA	QII . Lindau . . . . Germany	QLK . El Kala . . . . Algeria
QFG . Eqalugaiarsuit . . . . . . Greenland	QIJ . Gijon . . . . Spain	QLL . Sao Leopoldo . . . . Brazil
QFH . Frederkshavn/Bus Svc . Denmark	QIK . Ikoyi . . . . Norway	QLM . La Munoza . . . . Spain
QFI . Iginniarfik . . . . Greenland	QIL . Sig . . . . Algeria	QLN . Sulmona . . . . Italy
QFJ . Alluitsup Paa . . . . Greenland	QIM . Ain Mlila . . . . Algeria	QLO . Loerrach . . . . Germany
QFK . Selje/Harbour . . . . Norway	QIN . Mersin . . . . Turkey	QLP . La Spezia . . . . Italy
QFL . Freilassing . . . . Germany	QIO . Ain Temouchent . . . . . . Algeria	QLQ . Lerida . . . . Spain
QFM . Meet Ghamr . . . . Egypt	QIP . Simbach . . . . Germany	QLR . Leiria . . . . Portugal
QFN . Narsaq Kujalleq . . . . . Greenland	QIQ . Rio Claro . . . . Brazil	QLS . Lausanne . . . . Switzerland
QFO . Duxford . . . . UK	QIR . Irbid/Off-line Pt . . . . Jordan	QLT . Latina . . . . Italy
QFQ . Maloy/Harbour . . . . Norway	QIS . Mito . . . . Japan	QLU . Lublin . . . . Poland
QFR . Frosinone . . . . Italy	QIT . Itapetinga . . . . Brazil	QLV . Olivos . . . . Argentina
QFS . Sao Francisco . . . . Brazil	QIU . Ciucladela . . . . Spain	QLW . Lavras . . . . Brazil
QFT . Qassiarsulk . . . . Greenland	QIV . Ismailia . . . . Egypt	QLX . Lauterach . . . . Austria
QFU . Corralejo . . . . Spain	QIW . Umm Alquwain . . . . UAE	QLY . Playa Blanca . . . . Spain
QFV . Bergen/Harbour Pier . . . . Norway	QIX . Quixada . . . . Brazil	QLZ . Ikast/Bus Svc . . . . Denmark
QFW . Ft. Washington, PA/Off-line Pt	QIY . Beclarra Is . . . . Australia	QMA . Matanzas . . . . Cuba
. . . . USA	QIZ . Bizerte . . . . India	QMB . Panambi . . . . Brazil
QFX . Igaliku . . . . Chile	QJA . Jaragua Do Sul . . . . Brazil	QMC . Mairipora . . . . Brazil
QFY . Fukuyama . . . . Japan	QJB . Jubail . . . . Saudi Arabia	QMD . Madaba . . . . Jordan
QFZ . Saarbruecken/HBF RR . Germany	QJC . Thimbu . . . . Bhutan	QME . Messina . . . . Italy
QGA . Guaira . . . . Brazil	QJD . Jindaloyne . . . . Australia	QMF . Mafra . . . . Brazil
QGB . Limeira . . . . Brazil	QJE . Kitsissuarsuit . . . . Greenland	QMG . Maghnia . . . . Algeria
QGC . Lencois Paulista . . . . Brazil	QJF . Atammik . . . . Greenland	QMH . Cum El Bouaghi . . . . Algeria
QGD . Monte Alegre . . . . Brazil	QJG . Itilleq . . . . Greenland	QMI . Mogi Das Cruzes . . . . Brazil
QGE . Guelma . . . . Algeria	QJH . Gassimiut . . . . Greenland	QMJ . Masjed Soleyman . . . . Iran
QGF . Monte Negro . . . . Brazil	QJI . ikarniut . . . . Greenland	QMK . Niacornaarsuk . . . . Greenland
QGG . Agedabia . . . . Libya	QJJ . Dalton/FlightLink Bus Svc, GA	QML . Mirpur . . . . Pakistan
QGH . Gherian . . . . Libya	. . . . USA	QMM . Marina Di Massa . . . . Italy
QGI . Ilha Do Governador . . . . . . Brazil	QJK . Ajaokuta . . . . Nigeria	QMN . Mbabane/Off-line Pt/(DCA HQ)
QGJ . Nova Friburgo . . . . Brazil	QJL . Kjoellefjord . . . . Norway	. . . . Swaziland
QGK . Palmares . . . . Brazil	QJM . Brusque . . . . Brazil	QMO . Mons . . . . Belgium
QGL . St Gallen . . . . Switzerland	QJN . Jounieh . . . . Lebanon	QMP . Macon/FlightLink Bus Svc, GA
QGM . Cheighourn Laid . . . . Algeria	QJO . Campos Do Jorclao . . . . . . Brazil	. . . . USA
QGN . Tarragona . . . . Spain	QJP . Puchon City . . . . S. Korea	QMQ . Murzuq . . . . Libya
QGO . Gorizia . . . . Italy	QJQ . Jal Edib . . . . Lebanon	QMR . Marsala . . . . Italy
QGP . Garanhuns . . . . Brazil	QJR . La Junquera . . . . Spain	QMS . Masan . . . . S. Korea
QGQ . Attu . . . . Greenland	QJS . Saelby . . . . Denmark	QMT . Mostaganem . . . . Algeria
QGR . Kangerluk . . . . Greenland	QJT . Napasoq/Off-line Pt . . . Greenland	QMU . Moutiers . . . . France
QGS . Alagoinhas . . . . Brazil	QJU . Jullundur . . . . India	QMV . Montvale, NJ . . . . USA
QGT . Moriguchi . . . . Japan	QJV . Skagen/Limousine Svc . Denmark	QMW . Mohammadia . . . . Algeria
QGU . Gifu AB . . . . Japan	QJW . Kjellerup/Bus Svc . . . . . Denmark	QMZ . Mainz . . . . Germany
QGV . Frankfurt/Neu Isenburg . Germany	QJX . Nong Khai . . . . Thailand	QNA . Ballina . . . . Australia
QGW . Neustadt/Glawe . . . . . . Germany	QJY . Kolobrzeg/Bus Svc . . . . . Poland	QNB . Anand . . . . India
QGX . Gerga . . . . Egypt	QJZ . Nantes/RR . . . . France	QNC . Neuchatel . . . . Switzerland

QND	NoviSad	Yugoslavia
QNE	Rio Negrinho	Brazil
QNF	Faridabad	India
QNG	Nagano	Japan
QNH	Canoinhas	Brazil
QNI	Onitsha	Norway
QNJ	Annemasse	France
QNK	Nsukka	Norway
QNL	Neuilly-Sur-Seine	France
QNM	Namur	Belgium
QNN	Marina	Nigeria
QNO	Ascoli Piceno	Italy
QNP	Ayja Napa	Cyprus
QNQ	Malmo Town	Sweden
QNR	Santa Cruz Rio Pardo	Brazil
QNS	Canoas	Brazil
QNT	Niteroi	Brazil
QNU	Nuoro	Italy
QNV	Novalguacu	Brazil
QNW	Nawanshahar	India
QNX	Macon	France
QNY	New York/Marine Air Terminal, NY	USA
QNZ	Nara City	Japan
QOA	Mococa	Brazil
QOB	Ansbach/Katterbach	Germany
QOC	Osasco	Brazil
QOD	Osvaldo Cruz/Off-line Pt	Brazil
QOE	Noervenich	Germany
QOF	Kiev/Darnitsa Bus Stn	Ukraine
QOG	Homburg	Germany
QOH	Kiev/Hotel Rus Bus Stn	Ukraine
QOI	Cotia	Brazil
QOJ	Sac Borja	Brazil
QOK	Oeksfjord	Norway
QOL	Collo	Algeria
QOM	Ornlya	Japan
QON	Arlon	Belgium
QOO	Otsu City	Japan
QOP	Codroipo	Italy
QOQ	Saarloq	Greenland
QOR	Ordu	Turkey
QOS	Oristano	Italy
QOT	Otaru	Japan
QOU	Oued Rhiou	Algeria
QOV	Comuna Providencia	Chile
QOW	Owerri	Nigeria
QOX	Memmingen	Germany
QOY	Lorriza	Poland
QOZ	Oued Zenati	Algeria
QPA	Padova	Italy
QPB	Campobasso	Italy
QPC	Plock	Poland
QPD	Pinar Del Rio	Colombia
QPE	Petropolis	Brazil
QPF	Pompeia	Brazil
QPG	Singapore/Paya Lebar	Seychelles
QPH	Palapye	Botswana
QPI	Palmira	Colombia
QPJ	Pecs	Hungary
QPK	Strausberg	Germany
QPL	Ploiesti	Romania
QPM	Opoie	Poland
QPN	Piatra Neamt	Romania
QPO	Potenza	Italy
QPP	Berlin	Germany
QPQ	Pinamar	Argentina
QPR	Prato	Italy
QPS	Pirassununga/Off-line Pt	Brazil
QPU	Porto Uniao	Brazil
QPV	PerisheR Valley/Bus Svc	Australia
QPW	Kangaiatsiaq	Greenland
QPZ	Piacenza	Italy
QQA	Britrail Rail Zone A	UK
QQB	Britrail Rail Zone B	UK
QQC	Britrail Rail Zone C	UK
QQD	Dover/RR	UK
QQE	Britrail Rail Zone E	UK
QQF	Britrail Rail Zone F	UK
QQG	Britrail Rail Zone G	UK
QQH	Harwich/RR	UK
QQI	Britrail Rail Zone I	UK
QQJ	Britrail Rail Zone J	UK
QQK	London Kings Cross/RR	UK
QQL	Britrail Rail Zone L	UK
QQM	Manchester Piccadilly/RR	UK
QQN	Birminaham-New Street/RR	UK
QQO	Britrail Rail Zone O	UK
QQP	London-Paddington/RR	UK
QQR	Ramsgate/RR	UK
QQS	Britrail Rail Zone S	UK
QQT	Britrail Rail Zone T	UK
QQU	London Euston/RR	UK
QQV	Britrail Rail Zone V	UK
QQW	London/London-Waterloo	UK
QQX	Bath/RR	UK
QQY	York/RR	UK
QQZ	Britrail Rail Zone Z	Georgia
QRA	Johannesburg/Randgermiston	S. Africa
QRB	Ravensburg	Germany
QRC	Rancagua	Chile
QRD	Andradas	Brazil
QRE	Carazinho	Brazil
QRF	Bragado	Argentina
QRG	Ragusa	Italy
QRH	Rotterdam/Central Stn	Netherlands
QRI	Rize	East Timor
QRJ	Cariacica	Brazil
QRK	Aricos	Brazil
QRL	Marbella	Spain
QRM	Narromine	Australia
QRN	Muroran	Japan
QRO	Queretaro	Myanmar
QRP	Gramado	Brazil
QRQ	Marmaris	Turkey
QRR	Warren	Australia
QRS	Resita	Romania
QRT	Rieti	Italy
QRU	Rio Do Sul	Brazil
QRV	Arras	France
QRW	Warn	Nigeria
QRX	Narooma	Australia
QRY	Ikerasaarsuk	Greenland
QRZ	Resende	Brazil
QSA	Sabadell	Spain
QSB	Sac Bernardo Do Campo	Brazil
QSC	Sac Carlos	Brazil
QSD	Sac Goncad	Brazil
QSE	Santo Andre	Brazil
QSF	Setif	Algeria
QSG	Sonderborg	Denmark
QSH	Seeheim	Germany
QSI	Moshi	Tanzania
QSJ	Sao Joao Del Rei	Brazil
QSK	Souk Ahras	Algeria
QSL	Suru-Lere	Nigeria
QSM	Uetersen/Off-line Pt	Germany
QSN	San Nicolas Ban	Cuba
QSO	Sousse	Tunisia
QSP	Reserved/Network Service Code	
QSQ	Sidon	Lebanon
QSR	Salerno	Italy
QSS	Sassan	Italy
QST	Izmil	Turkey
QSU	Mansoura	Egypt
QSV	Sovata	Romania
QSW	Sweida	Syria
QSX	New Amsterdam	Guyana
QSY	Ruedesheim/Off-line Pt	Germany
QSZ	Shizijoka City	Japan
QTC	Caserta	Italy
QTD	Timbauba	Brazil
QTE	Sac Goncalo Amarante	Brazil
QTF	Qatif	Saudi Arabia
QTG	Tupi Paulista	Brazil
QTH	Thredbo/Bus Svc	Australia
QTI	Termini Imere	Italy
QTJ	Chartres	France
QTK	Rothenburg/Off-line Pt.	Germany
QTL	Caratinga	Brazil
QTM	Tomakomaj	Japan
QTN	San Antonjo	Chile
QTO	Skitube/Bus Svc	Australia
QTP	Tana	Norway
QTR	Tartous	Syria
QTS	Englewood, CO/Off-line Pt.	USA
QTT	Tanta	Egypt
QTU	Itu	Brazil
QTW	Taejon	S. Korea
QTX	Arbatax	Italy
QTY	Tsu	Japan
QTZ	Coatzacoalcos	Mexico
QUA	Puttgarden	Germany
QUB	Ubari	Libya
QUC	Puerto la Cruz	Venezuela
QUD	Damanhour	Egypt
QUE	Qullissat	Greenland
QUF	Tallinn/Pirita Harbour	Estonia
QUG	Chichester Goodwood	UK
QUH	Shebeen El Korn	Egypt
QUI	Chuquicamata	Chile
QUJ	Uijongbu	S. Korea
QUL	Ulm	Germany
QUM	Qum	Iran
QUN	Chun Chon City/Air Base	S. Korea
QUO	Uyo	Nigeria
QUP	Saqqaq	Greenland
QUQ	Caceres	Spain
QUR	Muriae	Brazil
QUS	Gusau	Nigeria
QUT	Utsunomiya AB	Japan
QUU	Chung-Mu City	S. Korea
QUV	Aappilattoq	Greenland
QUW	Ammassivik	Greenland
QUX	Caudebec en Caux	France
QUY	Wyton/RAF	UK
QUZ	Puerto de la Luz	Spain
QVA	Varese	Italy
QVB	Uniao Da Vitoria	Brazil
QVC	Vicosa	Brazil
QVD	Salo	Finland
QVE	Forssa	Finland
QVF	Karkkila	Finland
QVG	Vilgenis	France
QVH	Vila Velha	Brazil
QVI	Valbonne	France
QVJ	Vraidebria	Bulgaria
QVK	Valkeakoski	Finland
QVL	Victoria Is	Nigeria
QVM	Hämeenlinna	Finland
QVN	Avellino	Italy
QVO	Havoeysund	Norway
QVP	Avare	Brazil
QVQ	Verden	Germany
QVR	Volta Redonda	Brazil
QVS	Tervakoski	Finland
QVT	Riihimäki	Finland
QVU	Vaduz	Liechtenstein
QVV	Heinola	Finland
QVW	Kotka	Finland
QVX	Ghazaouet	Algeria
QVY	Kouvola/Bus Stn	Finland
QVZ	Hamina	Finland
QWA	Oshawa, ON	Canada
QWB	Berlin/HBF Railway Svc	Germany
QWC	Berlin/Berlin Zoo	Germany
QWD	Mittenwaid	Germany
QWE	Berlin/Fredrichstr. Railway Svc	Germany
QWF	Ft. Collins Bus Svc, CO	USA
QWG	Charlotte/Wilgrove Air Park, NC	USA
QWH	Loveland Bus Svc, CO	USA
QWI	Schleswig	Germany
QWJ	Americana	Brazil
QWK	Wloclawek	Poland
QWL	Crankenback Villeage/Bus Svc	Australia
QWM	Longmont Bus Svc, CO	USA
QWN	Astorga	Brazil
QWO	Holstelbro/Bus Svc	Denmark

A
I
R
P
O
R
T
S

QWP	Winter Park/Van Svc, CO	USA
QWQ	Struer/Bus Svc	Denmark
QWR	Donauwoerth	Germany
QWS	Nowy Targ	Poland
QWT	Talavera de la Reina	Spain
QWU	Wuerzburg	Germany
QWV	Valevo	Yugoslavia
QWW	Navalmoral de a Mata	Spain
QWX	Merida	Spain
QWY	Albany/Bus Svc, NY	USA
QWZ	Best/Bus Svc	Netherlands
QXB	Aix-en-Provence	France
QXC	Caxias	Brazil
QXD	Cachoeiro Itapemirim	Brazil
QXE	Sora	Italy
QXF	Vestbjerg/Bus Svc	Denmark
QXG	Angers/RR	France
QXH	Schoenhagen	Germany
QXI	Loviisa	Finland
QXJ	Porvoo	Finland
QXK	St. Genis/Bus Svc	France
QXN	SITA Network	
QXO	Tokyo	Japan
QXP	Struga	Macedonia
QXQ	Stalowa Wola	Poland
QXR	Radom	Poland
QXS	SITA Aircom	-
QXT	SITA Network	-
QXV	Svendborg/RR	Denmark
QXW	Alfenas	Brazil
QXZ	Woergi/Bus Svc	Austria
QYA	Anyang	S. Korea
QYB	Yaba	Nigeria
QYC	Drachten/Bus Svc	Netherlands
QYD	Gdynia	Poland
QYE	Enschede/RR	Netherlands
QYF	German Railways Zone F/RR Germany	
QYG	Germany/RR	Germany
QYH	Hengelo/RR	Netherlands
QYI	Hilversum/RR	Netherlands
QYJ	German Railways Zone J/RR Germany	
QYK	Koyang	Kuwait
QYL	Almelo/RR	Netherlands
QYM	Amersfoort/RR	Netherlands
QYN	Byron Bay	Australia
QYO	Olsztyin	Poland
QYP	Apeldoorn/RR	Netherlands
QYQ	Sulsted/Bus Svc	Denmark
QYR	Troyes	France
QYS	Yasoudj	Netherlands
QYT	Paterswolde/Bus Svc Netherlands	
QYV	Deventer/RR	Netherlands
QYW	Cannes/Vieux Port	France
QYY	Bialystok	Poland
QYZ	Heerenveen/Bus Svc	Netherlands
QZA	Zarqa	Jordan
QZB	Zermatt	Switzerland
QZC	Smiggin Holes/Bus Svc	Australia
QZD	Szeged	Hungary
QZE	Mont Louis	France
QZF	Font Romeu	France
QZG	La Llagone	France
QZH	Les Angles	France
QZI	Tizi Ouzou	Algeria
QZJ	Loimaa	Finland
QZK	Mantsala	Finland
QZL	Zliten	Libya
QZM	Bullocks Flat/Bus Svc	Australia
QZN	Relizane	Algeria
QZO	Arezzo	Italy
QZP	GC Apollo, ON/Off-line Pt	Canada
QZQ	Zahleh	Lebanon
QZR	Aprilia	Italy
QZS	Soeroeya	Norway
QZT	Zawia Town	Libya
QZU	Rauma	Finland
QZV	Roissy-en-France	France
QZZ	Zagazeeg	Egypt

R

RAA	Rakanda	Papua New Guinea
RAB	Rabaui/Tokua Papua New Guinea	
RAC	Racine, WI	USA
RAD	Tortola/Road Town Virgin Is (British)	
RAE	Arar	Saudi Arabia
RAG	Raglan	New Zealand
RAH	Rafha	Saudi Arabia
RAI	Praia/Francisco Mendes Cape Verde Is	
RAJ	Raikot/Civil	India
RAK	Marrakeeh/Menara	Morocco
RAL	Riverside, CA	USA
RAM	Ramingining	Australia
RAN	Ravenna/La Spreta	Italy
RAO	Ribeirao Preto/Leite Lopes	Brazil
RAP	Rapid City, SD	USA
RAQ	Raha/Sugimanuru	Indonesia
RAR	Rarotonga	Cook Is
RAS	Rasht	Iran
RAT	Raduzhnyi	Russia
RAU	Rangpur	Bangladesh
RAV	Cravo None	Colombia
RAW	Arawa	Papua New Guinea
RAX	Oram	Papua New Guinea
RAY	Rothesay / HP	UK
RAZ	Rawala Kot	Pakistan
RBA	Rabat/Sale	Morocco
RBB	Borba	Brazil
RBC	Robinvale	Australia
RBD	Dallas-Redbird, TX	USA
RBE	Ratanakiri	Cambodia
RBF	Big Bear, CA	USA
RBG	Roseburg, OR	USA
RBH	Brooks Lodge, AK	USA
RBI	Rabi	Fiji
RBJ	Rebun	Japan
RBK	Rancho, CA	USA
RBL	Red Bluff, CA	USA
RBM	Straubing/Wallmuhle	Germany
RBN	Ft. Jelferson, FL	USA
RBO	Robore	Bolivia
RBP	Rabaraba	Papua New Guinea
RBQ	Rurrenabaque	Bolivia
RBR	Rio Branco/Pres. Medici	Brazil
RBS	Orbost	Australia
RBT	Marsabit	Kenya
RBU	Roebourne	Australia
RBV	Ramata	Solomon Is
RBY	Ruby, AK	USA
RCA	Ellsworth/AFB, SD	USA
RCB	Richards Bay	S. Africa
RCE	Roche Harbor, WA	USA
RCH	Riohacha	Colombia
RCK	Rockdale/Coffield, TX	USA
RCL	Redcliffe	Vanuatu
RCM	Richmond	Australia
RCN	American River	Australia
RCO	RocheFt./Saint Agnant	France
RCQ	Reconquista	Argentina
RCR	Rochester, IN	USA
RCS	Rochester	UK
RCT	Reed City, MI	USA
RCU	Rio Cuarto	Argentina
RCY	Rum Cay	Bahamas
RDA	Rockhampton Downs	Australia
RDB	Red Dog, AK	USA
RDC	Redencao	Brazil
RDD	Redding, CA	USA
RDE	Mercley	Indonesia
RDG	Reading, PA	USA
RDK	Red Oak, IA	USA
RDM	Redmond, OR	USA
RDR	Grand Forks/AFB, ND	USA

RDS	Rincon de los Sauces	Argentina
RDT	Richard Toll	Senegal
RDU	Raleigh-Durham Int'l, NC	USA
RDV	Red Devil, AK	USA
RDZ	Rodez/Marcillac	France
REA	Reaci	F. Polynesia
REB	Rechlin	Germany
REC	Recife/Guararapes Int'l	Brazil
RED	Red Lodge, MT	USA
REE	Reese/AFB, TX	USA
REG	Reggio Calabria/Tito Menniti	Italy
REH	Rehoboth Beach, DE	USA
REI	Regina	F. Guiana
REL	Trelew	Argentina
REN	Orenburg	Russia
REO	Rome, OR	USA
REP	Siern Reap	Cambodia
RER	Retallnuleu/Base Aerea Del Sur Guatemala	
RES	Resistencia	Argentina
RET	Rost/Stollport	Norway
REU	Reus	Spain
REW	Rewa	India
REX	Reynosa/Gen Lucio Blanco Mexico	
REY	Reyes	Bolivia
REZ	Resende	Brazil
RFA	Rafai	Central African Rep
RFD	Rockford, IL	USA
RFG	Refugio/Rooke Fld, TX	USA
RFK	Anguilla/Rollang Fld, MS	USA
RFN	Raufarhofn	Iceland
RFP	Raiatea	F. Polynesia
RFR	Rio Frio	Costa Rica
RFS	Rosita	Netherlands
RGA	Rio Grande	Argentina
RGE	Porgera	Papua New Guinea
RGH	Balurghat	India
RGI	Rangiroa	F. Polynesia
RGL	Rio Gallegos Int'l	Argentina
RGN	Yangon/Mingaladon	Myanmar
RGR	Ranger, TX	USA
RGT	Rengat/Japura	Jamaica
RGX	Reno Nexrad, NV	USA
RHA	Reykholar	Iceland
RHD	Rio Hondo	Argentina
RHE	Reims	France
RHG	Ruhengeri	Rwanda
RHI	Rhinelander, WI	USA
RHL	Roy Hill	Australia
RHO	Rhodes/Diagoras/Paradisi Greece	
RHP	Ramechhap	Nepal
RHV	San Jose, CA	USA
RIA	Santa Maria/Base Aerea	Brazil
RIB	Riberalta/Gen Buech	Bolivia
RIC	Richmond Int'l, VA	USA
RID	Richmond, IN	USA
RIE	Rice Lake, WI	USA
RIF	Richfield/Reynolds, UT	USA
RIG	Rio Grande	Brazil
RIJ	Rioja	Peru
RIK	Carrillo	Costa Rica
RIL	Rifle, CO	USA
RIM	Rodriguez De Men	Peru
RIN	Ringi Cove	Solomon Is
RIR	Riverside, CA	USA
RIS	Rishin	Japan
RIT	Rio Tigre	Panama
RIV	March/AFB, CA	USA
RIW	Riverton, WY	USA
RIX	Riga/Int'l	Latvia
RIY	Riyan Mulkalla	Yemen
RIZ	Rio Aizucar	Panama
RJA	Rajahmundry	India
RJB	Rajbiraj	Nepal
RJH	Raishahi	Bangladesh
RJI	Rajouri	India
RJK	Rijelka	Croatia
RJN	Rafsanian	Iran
RKC	Yreka, CA	USA

RKD Rockland, ME ... USA
RKE Copenhagen/Roskilde . Denmark
RKH Rock Hill, SC ... USA
RKI Rokot ... Indonesia
RKO Spora ... Indonesia
RKP Rockport, TX ... USA
RKR Poteau/Robert S Kerr, OK ... USA
RKS Rock Springs, WY ... USA
RKT Ras Al Khaimah Int'l ... UAE
RKU Yule Is/Kairuku ... Papua New Guinea
RKV Reykjavik Domestic ... Iceland
RKW Rockwood/Municipal, TN ... USA
RKY Rokeby ... Australia
RLA Rolla/National, MO ... USA
RLD Richland, WA ... USA
RLG Rostock-Laage/Laane . Germany
RLI Anniston/Reilly AHP, AL ... USA
RLP Rosella Plains ... Australia
RLT Arlit ... Niger
RLU Bornite, AK ... USA
RLX Charleston, WV ... USA
RMA Roma ... Australia
RMB Buraimi ... Oman
RMC Rockford/Machesney, IL ... USA
RMD Ramagundarn ... India
RME Griffiss/AFB, NY ... USA
RMG Rome, GA ... USA
RMI Rimini/Miramare ... Italy
RMK Renmark ... Australia
RML Colombo/Ratmalana ... Sri Lanka
RMN Rurriginae ... Papua New Guinea
RMP Rampart, AK ... USA
RMS Ramstein ... Germany
RNB Ronneby/Kallinge ... Sweden
RNC Mcminnville, TN ... USA
RND Randolph/AFB, TX ... USA
RNE Roanne/Renaison ... France
RNG Rangely, CO ... USA
RNH New Richmond, WI ... USA
RNI Corn Is ... Netherlands
RNJ Yororijima ... Japan
RNL Rennell ... Solomon Is
RNN Bornholm/Ronne ... Denmark
RNO Reno Int'l, NV ... USA
RNP Rongelap Is ... Marshall Is
RNR Robinson River ... Papua New Guinea
RNS Rennes/St Jacques ... France
RNT Renton, WA ... USA
RNU Ranau ... Malaysia
RNZ Rensselaer, IN ... USA
ROA Roanoke, VA ... USA
ROB Monrovia/Roberts Int'l ... Liberia
ROC Rochester Int'l, NY ... USA
ROD Roberlson ... S. Africa
ROG Rogers, AR ... USA
ROH Robinhood ... Australia
ROI Roi Et Arpt ... Thailand
ROK Rockhampton ... Australia
ROL Roosevelt, UT ... USA
RON Rondon ... Colombia
ROO Rondonopolis ... Brazil
ROP Rota ... Northern Mariana Is
ROR Koror/Airai ... Palau
ROS Rosario/Fisherton ... Argentina
ROT Rotorua ... New Zealand
ROU Rousse ... Bulgaria
ROV Rostov ... Russia
ROW Roswell, NM ... USA
ROX Roseau/Municipal, MN ... USA
ROY Rio Mayo ... Argentina
RPA Rolpa ... Nepal
RPB Roper Bar ... Australia
RPE Sabine Pass, TX ... USA
RPM Ngukurr ... Australia
RPN Rosh Pina ... Israel
RPR Raipur ... India
RPV Roper Valley ... Australia
RPX Roundup, MT ... USA
RRE Marree ... Australia
RRF Tampa Bay Exec., FL ... USA
RRG Rodriguesis ... Mauritius
RRI Barora ... Solomon Is
RRK Rourkela ... India
RRL Merrill/Municipal, WI ... USA
RRM Marromeu ... Mozambique
RRN Serra Norte ... Brazil
RRO Sorrento ... Italy
RRS Poros ... Norway
RRT Warroad, MN ... USA
RRV Robinson River ... Australia
RSA Santa Rosa ... Argentina
RSB Poseberth ... Australia
RSD Rock Sound/S Eleuthera ... Bahamas
RSE Sydney/Au-Rose Bay .. Australia
RSG Serra Pelada ... Brazil
RSH Russian/SPB, AK ... USA
RSI Rio Sidra ... Panama
RSJ Rosario/SPB, AK ... USA
RSK Ransiki ... Indonesia
RSL Russell, KS ... USA
RSN Ruston, LA ... USA
RSP Raspberry Strait, AK ... USA
RSS Roseires, SD ... USA
RST Rochester, MN ... USA
RSU Yosu ... S. Korea
RSW Ft. Myers Int'l, FL ... USA
RSX Rouses Point, NY ... USA
RTA Rotuma Is ... Fiji
RTB Roatan ... Honduras
RTC Ratinagiri ... India
RTD Rotunda, FL ... USA
RTE Marguerite Bay, AK ... USA
RTG Ruteng ... Indonesia
RTI Roti ... Indonesia
RTL Spirit Lake, IA ... USA
RTM Rotterdam/Zestienhoven ... Netherlands
RTN Raton, NM ... USA
RTP Rutland Plains ... Australia
RTS Rottnest Is ... Australia
RTW Saratov ... Russia
RTX Portland Nexrad, OR ... USA
RTY Merty ... Australia
RUA Anua ... Uganda
RUE Russellville/Municipal, AR ... USA
RUF Yurut ... Indonesia
RUG Rugao ... China
RUH Riyadh/King Khaled Int'l ... Saudi Arabia
RUI Ruidoso/Municipal, NM ... USA
RUK Rukumkot ... Nepal
RUM Rumjatar ... Nepal
RUN St Denis de la Reunion Reunion Is
RUP Rupsi ... India
RUR Rurutu ... F. Polynesia
RUS Marau Sound ... Solomon Is
RUT Rutland, VT ... USA
RUU Ruti ... Papua New Guinea
RUV Rubelsanto ... Guatemala
RUY Copan ... Honduras
RVA Farafangana ... Madagascar
RVC Rivercess ... Liberia
RVD Rio Verde ... Brazil
RVE Saravena ... Colombia
RVH St Petersburg/Rzhevka ... Russia
RVN Rovaniemi ... Finland
RVO Reivilo ... S. Africa
RVR Green River, UT ... USA
RVS Tulsa, OK ... USA
RVY Rivera ... Uruguay
RWB Rowan Bay, AK ... USA
RWF Redwood Falls, MN ... USA
RWI Rocky Mount, NC ... USA
RWL Rawlins, WY ... USA
RWN Rovirio ... Ukraine
RWP Rawalpindi ... Pakistan
RXA Raudha ... Yemen
RXS Roxas City ... Philippines
RYB Rybirisk ... Russia
RYK Rahim Yar Khan ... Pakistan
RYN Royan/Medis ... France
RYO Rio Turbio ... Argentina
RYV Watertown, WI ... USA
RZA Santa Cruz ... Argentina
RZE Rzeszow/Jasionka ... Poland
RZH Lancaster/Quartz Hill, CA .. USA
RZN Ryazan ... Russia
RZR Ramsar ... Iran
RZZ Roanoke Rapids, NC ... USA

S

SAA Saratoga/Shively, WY ... USA
SAB Saba Is ... Netherlands Antilles
SAC Sacramento Exec, CA ... USA
SAD Safford, AZ ... USA
SAE Sangir ... Indonesia
SAF Santa Fe, NM ... USA
SAG Sagwon, AK ... USA
SAH Sana'a/Sana'a Int'l ... Yemen
SAI San Marino ... San Marino
SAJ Sirajganj ... Bangladesh
SAK Saudarkrokur/Comalapa Int'l ... Iceland
SAL San Salvador ... El Salvador
SAM Salamo ... Papua New Guinea
SAN San Diego Int'l, CA ... USA
SAP San Pedro Sula/RMorales ... Honduras
SAQ San Andros ... Bahamas
SAR Sparta/ComMunicipality, IL . USA
SAS Salton City, CA ... USA
SAT San Antonio Int'l, TX ... USA
SAU Sawu ... Indonesia
SAV Savannah Int'l, GA ... USA
SAW Sabiha Gokcen ... Turkey
SAX Sambu ... Panama
SAY Siena ... Italy
SAZ Sasstown ... Liberia
SBA Santa Barbara, CA ... USA
SBB Santa Barbara Ba ... Venezuela
SBC Selbang ... Papua New Guinea
SBD Norton/AFB, CA ... USA
SBE Suabi ... Papua New Guinea
SBF Sardeh Band ... Afghanistan
SBG Sabang/Cut Bau ... Indonesia
SBH St Barthelemy ... Gaudeloupe
SBI Koundara/Sambailo ... Guinea
SBJ Sao Mateus ... Brazil
SBK St Brieuc/Tremuson ... Eritrea
SBL Santa Aria/Yacuma ... Bolivia
SBM Sheboygan, WI ... USA
SBN South Bend, IN ... USA
SBO Salina, UT ... USA
SBP San Luis Obispo, CA ... USA
SBQ Sibi ... Pakistan
SBR Saibai Is ... Australia
SBS Steamboat Springs, CO ... USA
SBT San Bernardino/Tri-City, CA . USA
SBU Springbok ... S. Africa
SBV Sabah ... Papua New Guinea
SBW Sibu ... Malaysia
SBX Shelby, MT ... USA
SBY Salisbury, MD ... USA
SBZ Sibiu ... Romania
SCA Santa Catalina ... Colombia
SCB Scribner/State, NE ... USA
SCC Deadhorse, AK ... USA
SCD Suiaco ... Honduras
SCE State College, PA ... USA
SCG Spring Creek ... Australia
SCH Schenectady, NY ... USA
SCI San Cristobal ... Venezuela
SCJ Smith Cove, AK ... USA
SCK Stockton, CA ... USA
SCL Santiago/Arturo M. Benitez . Chile
SCM Scammon Bay/SPB, AK ... USA

Code	Airport	Location
SCN	Saarbruecken/Ensheim	Germany
SCO	Aktau	Kazakstan
SCP	St Crepin	Eritrea
SCQ	Santiago De Compostela	Spain
SCR	Scranton/Municipal, PA	USA
SCS	Shetland Iss/Scatsta	UK
SCT	Socotra	Yemen
SCU	Santiago/Antonio Maceo	Cuba
SCV	Suceava/Salcea	Romania
SCW	SyklyvKar	Russia
SCX	Salina Cruz	Mexico
SCY	San Cristobal/Arpt	Ecuador
SCZ	Santa Cruz	Solomon Is
SDA	Baghdad/Saddam Int'l	Iraq
SDB	Saldanha Bay	S. Africa
SDC	Sandcreek	Guyana
SDD	Lubango	Angola
SDE	Santiago Del Estero	Argentina
SDF	Louisville, KY	USA
SDG	Sanandaj	Iran
SDH	Santa Rosa Copan	Honduras
SDI	Saidor	Papua New Guinea
SDJ	Sendai	Japan
SDK	Sandakan	Malaysia
SDL	Sundsvall	Sweden
SDM	San Diego/Brown Fld, CA	USA
SDN	Sandane/Anda	Norway
SDO	Ryotsu Sado Is	Japan
SDP	Sand Point/Municipal, AK	USA
SDQ	Santo Domingo	Dominican Rep
SDR	Santander	Spain
SDS	Sado Shima	Japan
SDT	Saidu Sharif	Pakistan
SDU	Rio De Janeiro/S. Dumont	Brazil
SDV	Tel Aviv Yafo/Sde Dov	Israel
SDW	Sandwip	Bangladesh
SDX	Sedona, AZ	USA
SDY	Sidney-Richland, MT	USA
SEA	Seattle, WA	USA
SEB	Sebha	Libya
SEC	Serre Chevalier	Eritrea
SED	Sedom/Min'hat Hashnayim	Israel
SEE	San Diego-Gillespie, CA	USA
SEG	Selinsgrove, PA	USA
SEH	Senggeh	Indonesia
SEI	Senhor Do Bonfirn	Brazil
SEJ	Seyclisfjordur	Iceland
SEK	Ksar Es Souk	Morocco
SEL	Seoul/Kimp'O Int'l Arpt	S. Korea
SEM	Craig/AFB, AL	USA
SEN	Southend	UK
SEO	Seguela	Côte D'Ivoire
SEP	Stephenville, TX	USA
SEQ	Sungai Pakning	Indonesia
SER	Seymour/Freeman Municipal, IN	USA
SES	Selma/Selfield, AL	USA
SET	San Esteban	Honduras
SEU	Seronera	Tanzania
SEV	Severodoneck	Ukraine
SEW	Siwa	Egypt
SEX	Sembach	Germany
SEY	Selibaby	Mauritania
SEZ	Mahe Is	Seychelles
SFA	Sfax/Sfax El Maou	Tunisia
SFB	Sanford, FL	USA
SFC	St Francois	Gaudeloupe
SFD	San Fernando De Apure	Venezuela
SFE	San Fernando	Philippines
SFF	Spokane, WA	USA
SFG	St Martin/Esperance	Gaudeloupe
SFH	San Felipe	Mexico
SFI	Safi	Morocco
SFJ	Kangerlussuaq	Greenland
SFK	Soure	Brazil
SFL	Sao Filipe	Cape Verde Is
SFM	Sanford, ME	USA
SFN	Santa Fe	Argentina
SFO	San Francisco Int'l, CA	USA
SFP	Surfers Paradise	Australia
SFQ	Sanliurfa	Turkey
SFR	San Fernando, CA	USA
SFS	Subic Bay/Int'l Airpt	Philippines
SFT	Skelleftea	Sweden
SFU	Safia	Papua New Guinea
SFV	Santa Fe Do Sul	Brazil
SFW	Santa Fe	Panama
SFX	San Felix	Venezuela
SFZ	Smithfield/North Central, RI	USA
SGA	Sheghnan	Afghanistan
SGB	Singaua	Papua New Guinea
SGC	Surgut	Russia
SGD	Sonderborg/Lufthavn	Denmark
SGE	Siegen/Segerland Arpt	Germany
SGF	Springfield, MO	USA
SGG	Simanggang	Malaysia
SGH	Springfield, OH	USA
SGI	Sargodha/Sargodha Arpt	Pakistan
SGJ	Sagarai	Papua New Guinea
SGK	Sangapi	Papua New Guinea
SGL	Manila/Sangley Pt/NAS	Philippines
SGM	San Ignacio	Mexico
SGN	Ho Chi Minh	Vietnam
SGO	St George	Australia
SGP	Shay Gap	Australia
SGQ	Sanggata	Indonesia
SGR	Houston-SugarLand, TX	USA
SGS	Santa Sanga	Philippines
SGT	Stuttgart, AR	USA
SGU	Saint George/Municipal, UT	USA
SGV	Sierra Grande	Argentina
SGW	Saginaw Bay, AK	USA
SGX	Songea	Tanzania
SGY	Skagway/Municipal, AK	USA
SGZ	Songkhla	Thailand
SHA	Shanghai/Hongqiao	China
SHB	Nakashibetsu	Japan
SHC	Indaselassie	Ethiopia
SHD	Staunton, VA	USA
SHE	Shenyang	China
SHF	Shanhaiguan	China
SHG	Shungnak, AK	USA
SHH	Shishmaref, AK	USA
SHI	Shimojishima	Japan
SHJ	Sharjah Int'l	UAE
SHK	Sehonghong	Lesotho
SHL	Shillong	India
SHM	Shirahama	Japan
SHN	Shelton, WA	USA
SHO	Sokcho/Solak	S. Korea
SHP	Qinhuangdao	China
SHQ	Southport	Australia
SHR	Sheridan, WY	USA
SHS	Shashi	China
SHT	Shepparton	Australia
SHU	Smith Point	Australia
SHV	Shreveport, LA	USA
SHW	Sharurah	Saudi Arabia
SHX	Shageluk, AK	USA
SHY	Shinyanga	Tanzania
SHZ	Seshutes	Lesotho
SIA	Xi An	China
SIB	Sibiti	Colombia
SIC	Sinop/Sinop Arpt	Turkey
SID	Sal/Amilcar Cabrai Int'l	Cape Verde Is
SIE	Sines	Portugal
SIF	Simara	Nepal
SIG	San Juan/Isla Grande	Puerto Rico
SIH	Silgadi Doti	Nepal
SII	Sidi Ifni	Morocco
SIJ	Siglufjordur	Iceland
SIK	Sikeston/Memorial, MO	USA
SIL	Sila	Papua New Guinea
SIM	Simbas	Papua New Guinea
SIN	Singapore	Singapore
SIO	Smithton	Australia
SIP	Simferopol	Ukraine
SIQ	Singkep/Dabo	Indonesia
SIR	Sion	Switzerland
SIS	Sishen	S. Africa
SIT	Sitka, AK	USA
SIU	Siuna	Netherlands
SIV	Sullivan/County, IN	USA
SIW	Sibisa	Indonesia
SIX	Singleton	Australia
SIY	Montague, CA	USA
SIZ	Sissano	Papua New Guinea
SJA	San Juan	Peru
SJB	San Joacluin	Bolivia
SJC	San Jose Int'l, CA	USA
SJD	San Jose Cabo/Los Cabos	Mexico
SJE	San Jose Del Gua	Colombia
SJF	Kangerlussuaq	Greenland
SJF	St John Is	Virgin Is (US)
SJG	San Pedro Jagua	Colombia
SJI	San Jose/Meguire Fld	Philippines
SJJ	Saraievo/Butmir	Bosnia Hercegovina
SJK	Sao Jose Dos Campos	Brazil
SJL	Sao Gabriel/Da Cachoeira	Brazil
SJM	San Juan	Dominican Rep
SJN	St Johns, AZ	USA
SJO	San Jose/Juan Santamaria Int'l	Costa Rica
SJP	Sap Jose Do Rio Preto	Brazil
SJQ	Sesheke	Zambia
SJR	San Juan D Ur	Colombia
SJS	San Jose	Bolivia
SJT	San Angelo, TX	USA
SJU	San Juan Int'l, PR	USA
SJV	San Javier	Bolivia
SJW	Shijiazhuang/Daguocun	China
SJX	Sartaneja	Belize
SJY	Seinäjoki/Ilmajoki	Finland
SJZ	Sao Jorge Is	Portugal
SKA	Fairchild/AFB, WA	USA
SKB	St Kitts/Gldn Rck	St. Kitts and Nevis
SKC	Suki	Papua New Guinea
SKD	Samarkand	Uzbekistan
SKE	Skien	Norway
SKF	Kelly/AFB, TX	USA
SKG	Thessaloniki/Makedonia	Greece
SKH	Surkhet	Nepal
SKI	Skikda	Algeria
SKJ	Sitkinak Is/CGS, AK	USA
SKK	Shaktoolik, AK	USA
SKL	Isle Of Skye/Broadford	UK
SKM	Skeldon	Guyana
SKN	Stokmarknes/Skagen	Norway
SKO	Sokoto	Nigeria
SKP	Skople	Macedonia
SKQ	Sekakes	Lesotho
SKR	Shakiso	Ethiopia
SKS	Vojens/Skrydstrup/Military	Denmark
SKT	Sialkot	Pakistan
SKU	Skiros	Greece
SKV	Santa Katarina/Mount Sinai	Egypt
SKW	Skwentna/Intermediate, AK	USA
SKX	Saransk	Russia
SKY	Sandusky/G. Sandusky, OH	USA
SKZ	Sukkur	Pakistan
SLA	Salta/Gen Belgrano	Argentina
SLB	Storm Lake, IA	USA
SLC	Salt Lake City Int'l, UT	USA
SLD	Sliac	Slovakia
SLE	Salem, OR	USA
SLF	Sulayel	Saudi Arabia
SLG	Siloam Springs/Smith Fld, AR	USA
SLH	Sola	Vanuatu
SLI	Solwezi	Zambia
SLJ	Chandler/Stellar Air Park, AZ	USA
SLK	Saranac Lake, NY	USA
SLL	Salatah	Oman
SLM	Salamanca/Matacan	Spain
SLN	Salina, KS	USA

Code	Airport	Country
SLO	Salem-Leckrone, IL	USA
SLP	San Lus Potosi	Mexico
SLQ	Sleetmute, AK	USA
SLR	Sulphur Springs, TX	USA
SLS	Silistra	Bulgaria
SLT	Salida, CO	USA
SLU	St Lucia/Vigie	St. Lucia
SLV	Simia	India
SLW	Saltillo	Mexico
SLX	Salt Cay	Tonga
SLY	Salehard	Russia
SLZ	Sao Luiz/Mal. C. Machado	Brazil
SMA	Santa Maria/Vila Do Porto	Portugal
SMB	Cerro Sombrero	Chile
SMC	Santa Maria	Colombia
SMD	Ft. Wayne/Smith Fld, IN	USA
SME	Somerset/Pulaski County, KY	USA
SMF	Sacramento, CA	USA
SMG	Santa Maria	Peru
SMH	Sapmanga	Papua New Guinea
SMI	Samos	Greece
SMJ	Sim	Papua New Guinea
SMK	St Michael, AK	USA
SML	Stella Maris/Estate Airstrip	Bahamas
SMM	Serrporna	Malaysia
SMN	Salmon, AK	USA
SMO	Santa Monica, CA	USA
SMP	Stockholm	Papua New Guinea
SMQ	Sampit	Indonesia
SMR	Santa Marta/S. Bolivar	Colombia
SMS	Sainte Marie	Madagascar
SMT	Sun Moon Lake	Taiwan
SMU	Sheep Mountain, ID	USA
SMV	St Moritz/Samedan	Switzerland
SMW	Smara	Morocco
SMX	Santa Maria, CA	USA
SMY	Simenti	Senegal
SMZ	Stoelmans Eiland	Suriname
SNA	Santa Ana, CA	USA
SNB	Snake Bay	Australia
SNC	Salinas	Ecuador
SND	Seno	Laos
SNE	Sao Nicolau/Prgca	Cape Verde Is
SNF	San Felipe	Venezuela
SNG	San Ignacio De Velasco	Bolivia
SNH	Stanthorpe	Australia
SNI	Sinoe/R.E. Murray	Liberia
SNJ	San Julian	Cuba
SNK	Snyder/Winston Fld, TX	USA
SNL	Shawnee/Municipal, OK	USA
SNM	San Ignacio De M	Bolivia
SNN	Shannon	Ireland
SNO	Sakon Nakhon	Thailand
SNP	St Paul Is, AK	USA
SNQ	San Quintin	Mexico
SNR	St Nazaire/Montoir	France
SNS	Salinas, CA	USA
SNT	Sabana De Torres	Colombia
SNU	Santa Clara	Cuba
SNV	Santa Eiena	Venezuela
SNW	Thandwe	Myanmar
SNX	Sabana De Mar	Dominican Rep
SNY	Sidney, NE	USA
SNZ	Santa Cruz	Brazil
SOA	Soc Trang	Vietnam
SOB	Saarmelleek/Srmhk/Btn	Hungary
SOC	Solo City/Adi Surnarmo	Indonesia
SOD	Sorocaba	Brazil
SOE	Souanke	Congo
SOF	Sofia	Bulgaria
SOG	Sogndal	Norway
SOH	Solita	Colombia
SOI	South Molle Is	Australia
SOJ	Sorkjosen	Norway
SOK	Semongkong	Lesotho
SOL	Solomon, AK	USA
SOM	San Tome/El Tigre	Venezuela
SON	Espiritu Santo/Pekoa	Vanuatu
SOO	Soderhamn	Sweden
SOP	Southern Pines/Pinehurst, NC	USA
SOQ	Sorong/Jefman	Indonesia
SOR	X Thaurah	Syria
SOT	Sodankyla	Finland
SOU	Southampton	UK
SOV	Seldovia, AK	USA
SOW	Show Low, AZ	USA
SOX	Sogamoso	Colombia
SOY	Stronsay	UK
SOZ	Soienzara	France
SPA	Spartanburg Memorial, SC	USA
SPB	St Thomas/SPB	Virgin Is (US)
SPC	Santa Cruiz De La Palma	Spain
SPD	Saidpur	Bangladesh
SPE	Sepulot	Malaysia
SPF	Spearfish, SD	USA
SPG	St Petersburg, FL	USA
SPH	Sopu	Papua New Guinea
SPI	Springfield, IL	USA
SPJ	Sparta	Greece
SPL	Schiphol	Netherlands
SPM	Spangdahlem	Germany
SPN	Saipan/Int'l	Northern Mariana Is
SPO	San Pabio	Spain
SPP	Menongue	Angola
SPQ	San Pedro/Catalina SPB, CA	USA
SPR	San Pedro	Belize
SPS	Sheppard/AFB, TX	USA
SPT	Sipitang	Malaysia
SPU	Split	Croatia
SPV	Sepik Plains	Papua New Guinea
SPW	Spencer, IA	USA
SPX	Houston/Spaceland, TX	USA
SPY	San Pedro	Côte D'Ivoire
SPZ	Springdale/Springdale Municipal, AR	USA
SQA	Santa Ynez, CA	USA
SQB	Santa Ana	Colombia
SQC	Southern Cross	Australia
SQD	Sinop	Turkey
SQE	San Luis De Pale	Colombia
SQF	Solano	Colombia
SQG	Sintang	Indonesia
SQH	Son-La/Na-San	Vietnam
SQI	Sterling Rockfalls, IL	USA
SQJ	Shehdi	Ethiopia
SQK	Sidi Barani	Egypt
SQL	San Carlos, CA	USA
SQM	Sao Miguel Araguaia	Brazil
SQN	Sanana	Indonesia
SQO	Storurnan/Gunnarn	Sweden
SQP	Starcke	Australia
SQQ	Siauliai/Int'l	Lithuania
SQR	Soroako	Indonesia
SQS	San Ignacio/Matthew Spain	Belize
SQT	Samarai Is/China Straits Airstrip	Papua New Guinea
SQU	Saposcia	Peru
SQV	Sequim/Valley Arpt, WA	USA
SQW	Skive/Skive Arpt	Denmark
SQX	Sao Miguel Do Oeste	Brazil
SQY	Sao Lourenco Do Sul	Brazil
SQZ	Scampton/RAF Stn	UK
SRA	Santa Rosa	Brazil
SRB	Santa Rosa	Bolivia
SRC	Searcy, AR	USA
SRD	San Ramon	Bolivia
SRE	Sucre	Bolivia
SRF	Hamilton/AAF, CA	USA
SRG	Semarang/Achmad Uani	Indonesia
SRH	Sarh	Chad
SRI	Samarinda/Temindung	Indonesia
SRJ	San Borja/Capitan G Q Guardia	Bolivia
SRK	Sierra Leone	Sierra Leone
SRL	Santa Rosalia	Mexico
SRM	Sandringham	Australia
SRN	Strahan	Australia
SRO	Santana Ramos	Colombia
SRP	Stord/Stord Airporl	Norway
SRQ	Sarasota, FL	USA
SRR	Stradbroke Is	Australia
SRS	San Marcos	Colombia
SRT	Soroti	Uganda
SRU	Santa Cruz/Skypark, CA	USA
SRV	Stony River, AK	USA
SRW	Salisbury/Rowan County, NC	USA
SRX	Sert	Libya
SRY	Sary/Dashte Naz	Iran
SRZ	Santa Cruz/El Trompillo	Bolivia
SSA	Salvador/Arpt Luis R. Magalhaes	Brazil
SSB	St Croix Is/SPB	Virgin Is (US)
SSC	Shaw/AFB, SC	USA
SSD	San Felipe	Colombia
SSE	Sholapur	India
SSF	San Antonio, TX	USA
SSG	Malabo/Santa Isabel	Equatorial Guinea
SSH	Sharm El Sheikh/Ophira	Egypt
SSI	Brunswick, GA	USA
SSJ	Sandnessjoen/Stokka	Norway
SSK	Sturt Creek	Australia
SSL	Santa Rosalia	Colombia
SSN	Seoul/Seoul Air Base	S. Korea
SSO	Sac, Lourenco	Brazil
SSP	Silver Plains	Australia
SSQ	La Sarre, QC	Canada
SSR	Sara	Vanuatu
SSS	Siassi	Papua New Guinea
SST	Santa Teresita	Argentina
SSU	White Sulphur Sprng, WV	USA
SSV	Siasi	Philippines
SSW	Stuart Is, WA	USA
SSX	Samsun	Turkey
SSY	M'Banza Congo	Angola
SSZ	Santos	Brazil
STA	Stauning/Lufthavn	Denmark
STB	Santa Barbara Ed/L Dlcias	Venezuela
STC	St Cloud, MN	USA
STD	Santo Domingo	Venezuela
STE	Stevens Point, WI	USA
STF	Stephen Is	Australia
STG	St George Is, AK	USA
STH	Strathmore	Australia
STI	Santiago/Mun	Dominican Rep
STJ	St Joseph, MO	USA
STK	Sterling/Crosson Fld, CO	USA
STL	St Louis Int'l, MO	USA
STM	Santarem/Eduardo Gomes	Brazil
STN	London/Stansted	UK
STP	St Paul-Dwntnw, MN	USA
STQ	St Marys, PA	USA
STR	Stuttgart/Echterdingen	Germany
STS	Santa Rosa, CA	USA
STT	St Thomas Is	Virgin Is (US)
STU	Santa Cruz	Belize
STV	Surat	India
STW	Stavropol	Russia
STX	St Croix Is	Virgin Is (US)
STY	Saito	Uruguay
STZ	Santa Terezinha/Confresa	Brazil
SUA	Stuart/Witham Fld, FL	USA
SUB	Surabaya/Juanda	Indonesia
SUC	Sundance/Schloredt, WY	USA
SUD	Stroud, OK	USA
SUE	Sturgeon Bay, WI	USA
SUF	Lamezia-Terme/S Eufernia	Italy
SUG	Surigao	Philippines
SUH	Sur	Oman
SUI	Sukhumi/Babusheri	Georgia
SUJ	Satu Mare	Romania
SUK	Samchok	S. Korea
SUL	Sui	Pakistan
SUM	Surnter/Municipal, SC	USA
SUN	Hailey, ID	USA
SUO	Sun River, OR	USA
SUP	Sumeneo/Trunojoyo	Indonesia

Code	Location	Country
SUQ	Sucua	Ecuador
SUR	Summer Beaver, ON	Canada
SUS	St Louis-Spirit Of St Louis, MO	USA
SUT	Sumbawanga	Tanzania
SUU	Travis/AFB, CA	USA
SUV	Suva/Nausori	Fiji
SUW	Superior/Richard 1 Bong, WI	USA
SUX	Sioux City, IA	USA
SUY	Sudureyri	Iceland
SUZ	Suria	Papua New Guinea
SVA	Savoonga, AK	USA
SVB	Sambava	Madagascar
SVC	Silver City, NM	USA
SVD	St Vincent/E.-T. Joshua	St. Vincent & Grenadines
SVE	Susanville, CA	USA
SVF	Save	Benin
SVG	Stavanger/Sola	Norway
SVH	Statesville/Municipal, NC	USA
SVI	San Vicente	Colombia
SVJ	Svolvaer/Helle	Norway
SVK	Silver Creek	Belize
SVL	Savonlinna	Finland
SVM	St Paul's Mission	Australia
SVN	Hunter/AAF, GA	USA
SVO	Moscow	Russia
SVP	Kuito	Angola
SVQ	Sevilla	Spain
SVR	Svay Rieng	Cambodia
SVS	Stevens Village, AK	USA
SVT	Savuti	Botswana
SVU	Savusavu	Fiji
SVV	San Salvador De	Venezuela
SVW	Sparrevohn/AFS, AK	USA
SVX	Ekaterinburg	Russia
SVY	Savo	Solomon Is
SVZ	San Antonio	Venezuela
SWA	Shantou	China
SWB	Shaw River	Australia
SWC	Stawell	Australia
SWD	Seward, AK	USA
SWE	Siwea	Papua New Guinea
SWF	Newburgh, NY	USA
SWG	Satwag	Papua New Guinea
SWH	Swan Hill	Australia
SWI	Swindon	UK
SWJ	South West Bay	Vanuatu
SWK	Milan/Milano/Segrate	Italy
SWL	Spanish Wells	Bahamas
SWM	Suia-Missu	Brazil
SWN	Sahiwal	Pakistan
SWO	Stillwater, OK	USA
SWP	Swakopmund	Namibia
SWQ	Sumbawa/Brang Bidji	Indonesia
SWR	Silur	Papua New Guinea
SWS	Swansea	UK
SWT	Strzhewoi	Russia
SWU	Su Won City/Su Won Arpt	S. Korea
SWV	Shikarpur	Pakistan
SWW	Sweetwater, TX	USA
SWX	Shakawe	Botswana
SWY	Sitiawan	Malaysia
SWZ	Sydney/Sydney West	Australia
SXA	Sialum	Papua New Guinea
SXB	Strasbourg/Entzineim	France
SXC	Catalina Is, CA	USA
SXD	Sophia Antipolis	France
SXE	Sale	Australia
SXF	Berlin/Schoenefeld	Germany
SXG	Senanga	Zambia
SXH	Sehuiea	Papua New Guinea
SXI	Sirri Is	Iran
SXJ	Shanshan	China
SXK	Saumlaki	Indonesia
SXL	Sligo	Ireland
SXM	St Maarten/Princ. Juliana	Netherlands Antilles
SXN	Sua pan	Botswana
SXO	Sao Felix Do Araguaia	Brazil

Code	Location	Country
SXP	Sheldon Point/Sheldon SPB, AK	USA
SXQ	Soldotna, AK	USA
SXR	Srinagar	India
SXS	Sahabat 16	Malaysia
SXT	Taman Negara	Malaysia
SXU	Soddu	Ethiopia
SXV	Salem	India
SXW	Sauren	Papua New Guinea
SXX	Sao Fefix DO Xingu	Brazil
SXY	Sidney, NY	USA
SXZ	Slirt	Turkey
SYA	Shemya/Shemya/AFB, AK	USA
SYB	Seal Bay, AK	USA
SYC	Shiringayoc	Peru
SYD	Sydney	Australia
SYE	Sadah	Yemen
SYF	Silva Bay, BC	Canada
SYG	Svalbard/Spitsberg	Norway
SYH	Syangboche	Nepal
SYI	Shelbyville/Bomar Fld, AK	USA
SYJ	Sirjan	Iran
SYK	Stykkisholmur	Iceland
SYL	San Miguel/Roberts/AAF, CA	USA
SYM	Simao	China
SYN	Stanton/Carleton, MN	USA
SYO	Shonai	Japan
SYP	Santiago	Panama
SYQ	San Jose/Tobias Bolanos Intl	Costa Rica
SYR	Syracuse Int'l, NY	USA
SYS	Sunchon/Yosu	S. Korea
SYT	Saint Yan/Charolais Bourgogne	France
SYU	Sue Is/Warraber Is	Australia
SYV	Sylvester, GA	USA
SYW	Sehwen Sharif	Pakistan
SYX	Sanya	China
SYY	Stornoway	UK
SYZ	Shiraz	Iran
SZA	Soyo	Angola
SZB	Kuala Lumpur/Sultan Alodul Aziz Shah	Malaysia
SZC	Santa Cruz/Guanacaste	Costa Rica
SZD	Sheffield	UK
SZE	Semera/Semera Arpt	Ethiopia
SZF	Samsun/Carsamba	Turkey
SZG	Salzburg	Austria
SZH	Senipah	Indonesia
SZI	Zaisan	Kazakstan
SZJ	Siguanea	Cuba
SZK	Skukuza	S. Africa
SZL	Whiteman/AFB, MO	USA
SZM	Sesnem	Namibia
SZN	Santa Barbara, CA	USA
SZO	Shanzinou	China
SZP	Santa Paula, CA	USA
SZQ	Saenz Pena	Argentina
SZR	Stara Zagora	Bulgaria
SZS	Stewart Is	New Zealand
SZT	S.Cristobal del- Casas/San Cristobal Arpt	Mexico
SZU	Segou	Mali
SZV	Suzhou	China
SZW	Schwerin/Parchim Arpt	Germany
SZX	Shenzhen	China
SZY	Szymany/Mazury	Poland
SZZ	Szczecin/Goleniow	Poland

T

Code	Location	Country
TAA	Tarapaina	Solomon Is
TAB	Tobago	Trinidad and Tobago
TAC	Tacloban/D1. Rornualdez	Philippines
TAD	Trinidad, CO	USA
TAE	Taegu/Air Base	S. Korea

Code	Location	Country
TAG	Tagbilaran	Philippines
TAH	Tanna	Vanuatu
TAI	Taiz/AlJanad	Yemen
TAJ	Aitape/Tadji	Papua New Guinea
TAK	Takamatsu	Japan
TAL	Tanana, AK	USA
TAM	Tampico/Gen F Javier Mina	Mexico
TAN	Tangalooma	Australia
TAO	Oingdao	China
TAP	Tapachula Int'l	Mexico
TAQ	Tarcoola	Australia
TAR	Taranto/M. A. Grottag	Italy
TAS	Tashkent	Uzbekistan
TAT	Tatry/Poprad	Slovakia
TAU	Tauramena	Colombia
TAV	Tau	American Samoa
TAW	Tacuarembo	Uruguay
TAX	Taliabu	Indonesia
TAY	Tartu/Raadi	Estonia
TAZ	Tashauz	Turkmenistan
TBA	Tabibuga	Papua New Guinea
TBB	Tuy Hoa	Vietnam
TBC	Tuba City, AZ	USA
TBD	Timbiqui	Colombia
TBE	Timbunke	Papua New Guinea
TBF	Tabiteuea North	Kiribati
TBG	Tabubil	Papua New Guinea
TBH	Tablas	Philippines
TBI	The Bight	Bahamas
TBJ	Tabarka/7 Novembre	Tunisia
TBK	Timber Creek	Australia
TBL	Tableland	Australia
TBM	Tumbang Samba	Indonesia
TBN	Forney/AAF, MO	USA
TBO	Talbora	Tanzania
TBP	Tumbes	Peru
TBQ	Tarabo	Papua New Guinea
TBR	Statesboro/Municipal, GA	USA
TBS	Tbilisi/Novo Alexeyevka	Georgia
TBT	Tabatinga/Int'l	Brazil
TBU	Nuku'Alofa/Fija'Arnotu International	Tonga
TBV	Tabal	Marshall Is
TBW	Tambov	Russia
TBX	Taabo	Côte D'Ivoire
TBY	Tsabong	Botswana
TBZ	Tabriz	Iran
TCA	Tennant Creek	Australia
TCB	Treasure Cay	Bahamas
TCC	Tucumcari, NM	USA
TCD	Tarapaca	Colombia
TCE	Tuicea	Romania
TCF	Tocoa	Honduras
TCG	Tacheng	China
TCH	Tehibanga	Gabon
TCJ	Torembi Arpt	Papua New Guinea
TCK	Tinboli Arpt	Papua New Guinea
TCL	Tuscaloosa, AL	USA
TCM	McChord/AFB, WA	USA
TCN	Tehuacan	Mexico
TCO	Turnaco/La Florida	Colombia
TCP	Taba/Talba Int'l	Egypt
TCQ	Tacna	Peru
TCR	Tuticorin	India
TCS	Truth Or Consequences, NM	USA
TCT	Takotna, AK	USA
TCU	Thaba Nchu	S. Africa
TCV	Tete	Mozambique
TCW	Tocurnwal	Australia
TCX	Tabas	Iran
TCY	Terrace Bay	Namibia
TDA	Trinidad	Colombia
TDB	Tetabedi	Papua New Guinea
TDD	Trinidad	Bolivia
TDG	Tandag	Philippines
TDJ	Tadjoura	Djibouti
TDK	Taldy-Kurgan	Kazakstan
TDL	Tandil	Argentina
TDN	Thecia/Thecia Stn	Australia
TDO	Toledo, WA	USA

TDR	Theodore	Australia
TDT	Tanda Tula	S. Africa
TDV	Tanandava	Madagascar
TDW	Annarillo/Tradewind, TX	USA
TDZ	Toledo, OH	USA
TEA	Tela	Honduras
TEB	Teterboro, NJ	USA
TEC	Telemaco Borba	Brazil
TED	Thisted/Lufthavn	Denmark
TEE	Tbessa	Algeria
TEF	Teller	Australia
TEG	Tenkodogo	Burkina Faso
TEH	Tetlin, AK	USA
TEI	Tezu	India
TEK	Tatitlek, AK	USA
TEL	Telupid	Malaysia
TEM	Temora	Australia
TEN	Tongren	China
TEO	Terapo	Papua New Guinea
TEP	Teptelp	Papua New Guinea
TEQ	TeKirdag/Corlu	Turkey
TER	Terceira Is/Laies	Portugal
TES	Tessenei	Eritrea
TET	Tete/Matunda	Mozambique
TEU	Te Anau/Manapouri	New Zealand
TEX	Telluride, CO	USA
TEY	Thingeyn	Iceland
TEZ	Tezpur/Salonibari	India
TFA	Tilfalmin	Papua New Guinea
TFF	Tete	Brazil
TFI	Tufl	Papua New Guinea
TFL	Teofilo Otoni	Brazil
TFM	Telefornin	Papua New Guinea
TFN	Tenerife	Spain
TFR	Ramadan	Ecuador
TFS	Tenerife Sur	Spain
TFT	Taftan	Pakistan
TFX	Great Falls Nexrad, MT	USA
TFY	Tarlaya	Morocco
TGA	Tengah	Singapore
TGB	Tagloita	Philippines
TGD	Poelgorica,/Golubovci	Yugoslavia
TGE	Tuskegee/Sharpe Fld, AL	USA
TGF	Tignes	France
TGG	Kuala Terengganu/Sultan Mahmood	Malaysia
TGH	Tongoa	Vanuatu
TGI	Tinge Maria	Peru
TGJ	Tiga	New Caledonia
TGL	Tagula	Papua New Guinea
TGM	Tirgu Mures	Romania
TGN	Traralgon/La Trobe Regional	Australia
TGO	Tongliao	China
TGQ	Tangara da Serra	Brazil
TGR	Touggourt	Algeria
TGS	Chokwe	Mozambique
TGT	Tanga	Tanzania
TGU	Tegucigalpa/Toncontin	Honduras
TGV	Targovishte	Bulgaria
TGX	Tingrela	Côte D'Ivoire
TGZ	Tuxtla Gutierrez/Llano San Juan	Mexico
THA	Tullahoma/Northern, TN	USA
THB	Thalba-Tselka	Lesotho
THC	Tchien	Liberia
THE	Teresina	Brazil
THF	Berlin/Tempelhof	Germany
THG	Thangool	Australia
THH	Taharoa	New Zealand
THI	Tichitt	Mauritania
THK	Thakhek	Laos
THL	Tachilek	Myanmar
THM	Thompsonfield, MO	USA
THN	Trollhattan/Private	Sweden
THO	Thorshofn	Iceland
THP	Thermopolis/Hot Springs, WY	USA
THR	Tehran-Mehrabad	Iran
THS	Sukinothai	Thailand
THT	Tamchakett	Mauritania

THU	Pituffik	Greenland
THV	York, PA	USA
THY	Thohoyandou	S. Africa
THZ	Tahoua	Niger
TIA	Tirana/Rinas	Albania
TIB	Tibu	Colombia
TIC	Tinak Is	Marshall Is
TID	Tiaret	Algeria
TIE	Tippi	Ethiopia
TIF	Taif	Saudi Arabia
TIG	Tingwon	Papua New Guinea
TIH	Tikehau Atoll	F. Polynesia
TII	Tirinkot	Afghanistan
TIJ	Tijuana/Rodriguez	Mexico
TIK	Tinker/AFB, OK	USA
TIL	Inverlake, AB	Canada
TIM	Tembagapura/Timika	Indonesia
TIN	Tindouf	Algeria
TIO	Tilin	Myanmar
TIP	Tripoli/Int'l	Libya
TIQ	Tinian	Northern Mariana Is
TIR	Tirupati	India
TIS	Thursday Is	Australia
TIU	Timaru	New Zealand
TIV	Tivat	Yugoslavia
TIW	Tacoma-Narrows, WA	USA
TIX	Titusville, FL	USA
TIY	Tidjikia	Mauritania
TIZ	Tari	Papua New Guinea
TJA	Tarija	Bolivia
TJB	Tanjung Balai	Indonesia
TJC	Ticantiki	Panama
TJG	Tanjung Warukin	Indonesia
TJH	Toyooka/Tapma	Japan
TJI	Trujillo/Capiro	Honduras
TJK	Tokat	Turkey
TJM	Tyumen	Russia
TJN	Takume	F. Polynesia
TJQ	Tanjung Pandan/Bulutumbang	Indonesia
TJS	Tanjung Selor	Indonesia
TJV	Thanjavur	India
TKA	Talkeetna, AK	USA
TKB	Tekadu	Papua New Guinea
TKC	Tiko	Cameroon
TKD	Takoradi	Ghana
TKE	Tenakee Springs/Tenakee SPB, AK	USA
TKF	Truckee, CA	USA
TKG	Bandar Lampung/Branti	Indonesia
TKH	Takhli	Thailand
TKI	Tokeen, AK	USA
TKK	Truk	Micronesia
TKL	Taku Lodge/Taku SPB, AK	USA
TKM	Tikal/El Peten	Guatemala
TKN	Tokunoshima	Japan
TKO	Tlokoeng	Lesotho
TKP	Takapoto	F. Polynesia
TKQ	Kigoma	Tanzania
TKR	Thakurgaon	Bangladesh
TKS	Tokushima AB	Japan
TKT	Tak	Thailand
TKU	Turku	Finland
TKV	Tatakoto	F. Polynesia
TKW	Tekin	Papua New Guinea
TKX	Takaroa	F. Polynesia
TKY	Turkey Creek	Australia
TKZ	Tokoroa	New Zealand
TLA	Teller, AK	USA
TLB	Tarbela	Pakistan
TLC	Toluca	Mexico
TLD	Tuli Lodge	Botswana
TLE	Tulear	Madagascar
TLF	Telida, AK	USA
TLG	Tulagi Is	Solomon Is
TLH	Tallahassee, FL	USA
TLI	Tolitoli/Lalos	Indonesia
TLJ	Tatalina/Tatalina AFS, AK	USA
TLK	Taiknafjordur	Iceland
TLL	Tallinn/Ulemiste	Estonia

TLM	Tlemcen/Zenata	Algeria
TLN	Toulon/Hyeres	France
TLO	Tol	Papua New Guinea
TLP	Tumolbil	Papua New Guinea
TLR	Tulare, CA	USA
TLS	Toulouse/Blagnac	France
TLT	Tuluksak, AK	USA
TLU	Tolu	Colombia
TLV	Tel Aviv-Ben Gurion Int'l	Israel
TLW	Talasea	Papua New Guinea
TLX	Talca	Chile
TLZ	Catalao	Brazil
TMA	Tifton/Henry Tift Myers, GA	USA
TMB	Miami Exec, FL	USA
TMC	Tambolaka	Indonesia
TMD	Timbedra	Mauritania
TME	Tame	Colombia
TMG	Tomanggong	Malaysia
TMH	Tanah Merah/Tanah Merah	Indonesia
TMI	Tumling Tar	Nepal
TMJ	Termez	Uzbekistan
TMK	Tarnky	Vietnam
TML	Tamale	Ghana
TMM	Tamatave	Madagascar
TMN	Tamana Is	Kiribati
TMO	Tumeremo	Venezuela
TMP	Tampere/Pirkkala	Finland
TMQ	Tambao	Burkina Faso
TMR	Tamanrasset/Aguemar	Algeria
TMS	Sao Tome Is	Sao Tome and Principe
TMT	Trombetas	Brazil
TMU	Tambor	Costa Rica
TMW	Tamworth	Australia
TMX	Timimoun	Algeria
TMY	Tiom	Indonesia
TMZ	Thames	New Zealand
TNA	Jinan	China
TNB	Tanah Grogot	Indonesia
TNC	Tin City/AFS, AK	USA
TND	Trinidad	Cuba
TNE	Tanegashima	Japan
TNF	Toussus Le Noble	France
TNG	Tangier/Boukhalef	Morocco
TNH	Tonghua/Tonghua Liuhe	China
TNI	Satna	India
TNJ	Tanjung Pinang/Kidjang	Indonesia
TNK	Tununak, AK	USA
TNL	Ternopol	Laos
TNM	Teniente R. Marsh	Antarctica
TNN	Tainan	Taiwan
TNO	Tamarindo	Costa Rica
TNP	Twentynine Palms, CA	USA
TNQ	Teraina	Kiribati
TNR	Antananarivo	Madagascar
TNS	Tungsten, NT	Canada
TNT	Miami/Dade Collier, FL	USA
TNU	Newton, IA	USA
TNV	Tabuaeran	Kiribati
TNX	Stung Treng	Cambodia
TOA	Torrance, CA	USA
TOB	Tobruk	Libya
TOC	Toccoa, GA	USA
TOD	Tioman	Malaysia
TOE	Tozeur/Nefta	Tunisia
TOG	Togiak Village, AK	USA
TOH	Torres/Torres Airstrip	Vanuatu
TOI	Troy, AL	USA
TOJ	Madrid/Torrejon AFB	Spain
TOK	Torokina	Papua New Guinea
TOL	Toledo, OH	USA
TOM	Tombouctou	Mali
TON	Tonu	Papua New Guinea
TOO	San Vito	Costa Rica
TOP	Topeka, KS	USA
TOQ	Tocopilla/Barriles	Chile
TOR	Torrington, WY	USA
TOS	Tromso/Langnes	Norway
TOT	Totness/Coronie	Suriname

A I R P O R T S

TOU	Touho	New Caledonia
TOV	Tortola/West End SPB	Virgin Is (British)
TOW	Toledo	Brazil
TOX	Tobolsk	Russia
TOY	Toyama	Japan
TOZ	Touba/Mahana	Côte D'Ivoire
TPA	Tampa Int'l, FL	USA
TPC	Tarapoa	Ecuador
TPE	Taipei/Chiang Kai Shek	Taiwan
TPF	Tampa/Peter O'Knight, FL	USA
TPG	Taiping	Malaysia
TPH	Tonopah, NV	USA
TPI	Tapini	Papua New Guinea
TPJ	Tapiejung	Nepal
TPK	Tapaktuan	Indonesia
TPL	Temple/Draughon-Miller, TX	USA
TPN	Tiputini	Ecuador
TPO	Tanalian Point, AK	USA
TPP	Tarapoto	Peru
TPQ	Tepic	Mexico
TPR	Tom Price	Australia
TPS	Trapani/Birgi	Italy
TPT	Tapeta	Iran
TPU	Tikapur	Nepal
TQE	Tekamah, Tekamah Municipal Arpt, NE	USA
TQN	Taluqan	Afghanistan
TQR	San Domino Is	Italy
TQS	Tres Esquinas	Colombia
TRA	Taramaprina/Tarama	Japan
TRB	Turbo/Gonzalo	Colombia
TRC	Torreon	Mexico
TRD	Trondheim/Vaernes	Norway
TRE	Tiree	UK
TRF	Oslo/Sandefjord	Norway
TRG	Tauranga	New Zealand
TRH	Trona, CA	USA
TRI	Bristol, TN	USA
TRJ	Tarakbits	Papua New Guinea
TRK	Tarakan	Indonesia
TRL	Terrell, TX	USA
TRM	Palm Springs-Thermal, CA	USA
TRN	Turin/Citta Di Torino	Italy
TRO	Taree	Australia
TRP	Tree Point/Cst Guard Heliport, AK	USA
TRQ	Tarauaca	Brazil
TRR	Trincomalee/China Bay	Sri Lanka
TRS	Trieste/Dei Legionari	Italy
TRT	Tremonton, UT	USA
TRU	Trujillo	Peru
TRV	Trivandrum/Int'l	India
TRW	Tarawa/Bonriki	Kiribati
TRX	Trenton/Memorial, MO	USA
TRY	Tororo	Uganda
TRZ	Tiruchirapally/Civil	India
TSA	Taipei/Sung Shan	Taiwan
TSB	Tsumeb	Namibia
TSC	Taisha	Ecuador
TSD	Tshipise	S. Africa
TSE	Astana	Kazakstan
TSF	Venice/Treviso	Italy
TSG	Tanacross/Intermediate, AK	USA
TSH	Tshikapa	Congo, DR
TSI	Tsili Tsili	Papua New Guinea
TSJ	Tsushima	Japan
TSK	Taskul	Papua New Guinea
TSL	Tarnuin	Myanmar
TSM	Taos, NM	USA
TSN	Tiarijin	China
TSO	Isles Of Scilly/Tresco	UK
TSP	Tehachapi/Kern County, CA	USA
TSQ	Torres	Brazil
TSR	Timisoara	Romania
TSS	New York/E. 34th St Heiliport, NY	
TST	Trang	Thailand
TSU	Tabiteuea South	Kiribati
TSV	Townsville	Australia
TSW	Tsewi	Papua New Guinea

TSX	Tanjung Santan	Indonesia
TSY	Tasikmalaya/Cibeureum	Indonesia
TSZ	Tsetserleg	Mongolia
TTA	Tan Tan	Morocco
TTB	Tortoli/Arbatax	Italy
TTC	Taltal	Chile
TTD	Portland-Troutdale, OR	USA
TTE	Ternate/Babullah	Indonesia
TTG	Tartagal	Argentina
TTH	Thurnrait	Oman
TTI	Tetiaroa Is	F. Polynesia
TTJ	Tottori	Japan
TTK	Tottenham Hale Stn	UK
TTL	Turtle Is	Fiji
TTM	Tablon De Tamara	Colombia
TTN	Trenton, NJ	USA
TTO	Britton/Municipal, SD	USA
TTQ	Tortuquero	Costa Rica
TTR	Tana Toraja	Indonesia
TTS	Tsaratanana	Madagascar
TTT	Taitung	Taiwan
TTU	Tetuan/Sania Ramel	Morocco
TUA	Tulcan	Ecuador
TUB	Tubuai	F. Polynesia
TUC	Tueuman/Benj Matienzo	Argentina
TUD	Tambacounda	Senegal
TUE	Tupile	Panama
TUF	Tours/St Symphorien	France
TUG	Tuguegarao	Philippines
TUH	Tullahoma/Arnold AFS, TN	USA
TUI	Turaif	Saudi Arabia
TUJ	Turn	Ethiopia
TUK	Turbat	Pakistan
TUL	Tulsa Int'l, OK	USA
TUM	Tumut	Australia
TUN	Tunis/Carthage	Tunisia
TUO	Taupo	New Zealand
TUP	Tupelo, MS	USA
TUQ	Tougan	Burkina Faso
TUR	Tucurui	Brazil
TUS	Tucson Int'l, AZ	USA
TUT	Tauta	Papua New Guinea
TUU	Tabuk	Saudi Arabia
TUV	Tucupita	Venezuela
TUW	Tubala	Panama
TUX	Tumbler Ridge, BC	Canada
TUY	Tulum	Mexico
TUZ	Tucuma	Brazil
TVA	Morafenobe	Madagascar
TVC	Traverse City, MI	USA
TVF	Thief River Falls/Regional, MN	USA
TVI	Thornasville/Municipal, GA	USA
TVL	South Lake Tahoe, CA	USA
TVR	Vicksburg, Tallulah Rgnl. Arpt, LA	USA
TVU	Taveuni/Matei	Fiji
TVY	Dawe	Myanmar
TWA	Twin Hills, AK	USA
TWB	Toowoomba	Australia
TWD	Port Townsend, WA	USA
TWE	Taylor, AK	USA
TWF	Twin Falls, ID	USA
TWH	Catalina Is/Two Harbors, CA	USA
TWM	Two Harbors, MN	USA
TWN	Tewantin	Australia
TWP	Torwood	Australia
TWT	Tawitawi	Philippines
TWU	Tawau	Malaysia
TWX	Topeka Nexrad, KS	USA
TWY	Tawa	Papua New Guinea
TWZ	Mount Cook/Pulkalki/Twizel	New Zealand
TXF	Te ixeira de Freitas	Brazil
TXG	Taichung	Taiwan
TXK	Texarkana, AR	USA
TXL	Berlin/Tegel	Germany
TXM	Terninabuan	Indonesia
TXN	Tunxl	China

TXR	Tanbar	Australia
TXU	Tabou	Côte D'Ivoire
TYA	Tula	Russia
TYB	Tibooburra	Australia
TYD	Tyncia	Russia
TYE	Tyonek, AK	USA
TYF	Torsby/Torsby Arpt	Sweden
TYG	Thylungra	Australia
TYL	Talara	Peru
TYM	Staniel Cay	Bahamas
TYN	Taiyuan	China
TYP	Tobermorey	Australia
TYR	Tyler, TX	USA
TYS	Knoxville, TN	USA
TYT	Treinta-y-Tres	Uruguay
TYZ	Taylor, AZ	USA
TZA	Belize City/Mun	Belize
TZL	Tuzia/Tuzla Int'l	Bosnia Hercegovina
TZM	Tizimin	Mexico
TZN	South Andros	Bahamas
TZX	Trabzon	Turkey

U

UAC	San Luis Rio Colorado	Mexico
UAE	Mount Aue	Papua New Guinea
UAH	Lia Hulka	F. Polynesia
UAI	Suai	Indonesia
UAK	Narsarsuaq	Greenland
UAL	Luau	Andorra
UAM	Guam/Anderson AFB	Guam
UAO	Aurora State Arpt, OR	USA
UAP	Lia Pou	F. Polynesia
UAQ	San Juan	Argentina
UAS	Sarnburu	Kenya
UAX	Uaxactun	Guatemala
UBA	Uberaba	Brazil
UBB	Mabuiag Is	Australia
UBI	Buin	Papua New Guinea
UBJ	Ube	Japan
UBP	Ubon Ratchathani	Thailand
UBR	Ubrub	Indonesia
UBS	Columbus/Lowrides County, MS	USA
UBT	Ubatuba	Brazil
UBU	Kalumburu	Australia
UCA	Utica, NY	USA
UCC	Yucca Flat, NV	USA
UCE	Eunice, LA	USA
UCK	Lutsk	Ukraine
UCN	Buchanan	Liberia
UCT	Ukhta	Russia
UCY	Union City/Everett-Stewart, TN	USA
UDA	Unclarra	Australia
UDD	Palm Springs/Bermuda Dunes, CA	USA
UDE	Uden/Volkel	Netherlands
UDI	Uberlandia/Eduardo Gomes	Brazil
UDJ	Uzhgorod	Ukraine
UDN	Udine/Airfield	Italy
UDO	Udomxay	Laos
UDR	Udaipur/Dabok	India
UEE	Queenstown	Australia
UEL	Quelimane	Mozambique
UEO	Kumejima	Japan
UES	Waukesha, WI	USA
UET	Quetta	Pakistan
UEX	Grand Is Nexrad, NE	USA
UFA	Ufa	Russia
UGA	Bulgan	Mongolia
UGB	Pilot Point/Ugashik Bay, AK	USA
UGC	Urgench	Uzbekistan
UGI	Uganik, AK	USA
UGN	Chicago-Waukegan, IL	USA
UGO	Uige	Andorra

UGS.. Ugashik, AK.............. USA
UGU.. Zugapa................Indonesia
UHE.. Uherske Hradiste ... Czech Rep
UHF.. Upper Heyford/RAF .... UK
UIB.. Quibdo.............. Colombia
UIH.. Qui Nhon .... Vietnam
UII ... Utila................ Honduras
UIK... Ust-Llimsk............. Russia
UIL... Quillayute, WA .... USA
UIN... Quincy, IL .... USA
UIO... Quito/Mariscal Sucr.....Ecuador
UIP... Quimper/Pluguffan ...... France
UIQ... Quine Hill .... Vanuatu
UIR... Quirincli............. Australia
UIT... Jaluit Is .... Marshall Is
UIZ... Utica/Berz-Macomb, MI .... USA
UJE.. Ujae Is............ Marshall Is
UKA.. Ukunda .... Kenya
UKB.. Kobe..................Japan
UKI.. Ukiah, CA............... USA
UKK.. Ust-Kamenogorsk.... Kazakstan
UKN.. Waukon/Municipal, IA...... USA
UKR.. Mukeiras................ Yemen
UKT.. Quakertown/Upper Bucks, PA
.... USA
UKU.. Nuku ...... Papua New Guinea
UKX.. Ust-Kut .... Russia
UKY.. Kyoto...................Japan
ULA.. San Julian..............Argentina
ULB.. Ulei/Los Cerrillos .... Vanuatu
ULC.. Santiago ....Chile
ULD.. Ulundi .... S. Africa
ULE.. Sule ...... Papua New Guinea
ULG.. Ulgit................. Mongolia
ULI.. Ulithi.................Micronesia
ULL.. Mull .... UK
ULM.. New Ulm, MN .... USA
ULN.. Ulaaribaatar/Buyant Uhaa
.... Mongolia
ULO.. Ulaangom .... Mongolia
ULP.. Quilpie ....Australia
ULQ.. Tulua/Farfan ....Colombia
ULS.. Mulatos ....Colombia
ULU.. Gulu .... Uganda
ULX.. Ulusaba .... S. Africa
ULY.. Ulyanovsk............. Russia
ULZ.. Liliastai .... Mongolia
UMA.. Punta De Maisi.......Colombia
UMB.. Umnak Is/North Shore, AK.. USA
UMC.. Umba ...... Papua New Guinea
UMD.. Uummannaq ....Greenland
UME.. Umea/Flygplats ....Sweden
UMI.. Quincemil ....Peru
UMM.. Summit, AK .... USA
UMR.. Woomera ....Australia
UMT.. Umiat, AK............... USA
UMU.. Umuarama/Ernesto Geisel. Brazil
UMY.. Sumy.................Ukraine
UNC.. Unguia ....Colombia
UND.. Kunduz ....Afghanistan
UNE.. Gachas Nek........... Lesotho
UNG.. Kiunga ...... Papua New Guinea
UNI.. Union IslSt. Vincent & Grenadines
UNK.. Unalakleet, AK............ USA
UNN.. Ranong................Thailand
UNO.. West Plains Municipal Arpt, MO
.... USA
UNR.. Underkhaan .... Mongolia
UNS.. Umnak Is/Umnak, AK....... USA
UNT.. Unst Shetland Iss .... UK
UNU.. Juneau/Dodge County, AK.. USA
UNV.. State College, PA.......... USA
UOL.. Buol.................Indonesia
UON.. Muong Sai .... Laos
UOS.. Sewanee/Franklin County, TN
.... USA
UOX.. Oxford/University-Oxford, MS
.... USA
UPA.. Punta Alegre ....Colombia
UPC.. Puerto La Cruz........... Spain
UPF.. Pforheim.............. Germany

UPG.. Ujung Pandang/Hasanudin
.... Indonesia
UPL.. Upala................ Costa Rica
UPN.. Uruapan .... Mexico
UPP.. Upolu Point, HI ....USA
UPR.. Uplara .... Papua New Guinea
UPV.. Upavon .... UK
UQE.. Queen, AK .... USA
URA.. Uralsk ....Kazakstan
URB.. Urubupunga/Ernesto Pochier
.... Brazil
URC.. Urumqi ....China
URD.. Burg Feuerstein ....Germany
URE.. Kuressaare .... Estonia
URG.. Uruguaiana/Ruben Berta .. Brazil
URI.. Uribe .... Colombia
URJ.. Uraj .... Russia
URM.. Uriman ....Venezuela
URN.. Urgoon ....Afghanistan
URO.. Rouen/Boos ....France
URR.. Urrao .... Colombia
URS.. Kursk .... Russia
URT.. Surat Thani .... Thailand
URU.. Uroubi ....Papua New Guinea
URY.. Gurayat ....Saudi Arabia
URZ.. Unuzgan ....Afghanistan
USC.. Union South Carolina, SC ...USA
USH.. Ushuaia/Islas Malvinas Argentina
USI.. Mabaruma .... Guyana
USK.. Usinsk .... Russia
USL.. Useless Loop .... Australia
USM.. Koh Sannui .... Thailand
USN.. Uisan .... S. Korea
USO.. Usino ......Papua New Guinea
USQ.. Usak .... Turkey
USS.. Sancti Spiritus .... Cuba
UST.. St Augustine, FL...........USA
USU.. Busuanga .... Philippines
UTA.. Mutare .... Zimbabwe
UTB.. Muttaburra .... Australia
UTC.. Utrecht/Soesterberg Netherlands
UTD.. Nutwood Downs .... Australia
UTE.. Butterworth .... S. Africa
UTG.. Outhing .... Iceland
UTH.. Udon Thani .... Thailand
UTI.. Kouvola/Utti .... Finland
UTK.. Utirik Is............. Marshall Is
UTL.. Torremolinos ....Spain
UTN.. Upington .... S. Africa
UTO.. Indian Mountain AFS, AK ....USA
UTP.. Utapato .... Thailand
UTR.. Uttaradit................ Thailand
UTS.. Huntsville, TX ....USA
UTT.. Urntata .... S. Africa
UTU.. Ustupo................. Panama
UTW.. Queenstown .... S. Africa
UUA.. Buguima .... Russia
UUD.. Ulan-Ude .... Russia
UUK.. Kuparuk, AK .... USA
UUN.. Baruun-Urt ....Mongolia
UUS.. Yuzhno-Sakhalinsk...... Russia
UUU.. Manumu ...... Papua New Guinea
UVA.. Uvaide/Garner Fld, TX......USA
UVE.. Ouvea .... New Caledonia
UVF.. St Lucia/Hewanorra .... St. Lucia
UVL.. Kharga ....Egypt
UVO.. Llvol........Papua New Guinea
UWA.. Ware, MA .... USA
UWE.. Wiesbaden ....Germany
UWP.. Wuppertal ....Germany
UYL.. Nyala .... Somalia
UYN.. Yulin ....China
UZC.. Uzice/Ponikve...... Yugoslavia
UZH.. Unayzah ....Saudi Arabia
UZU.. Cunuzu Cuatia .... Argentina

V

VAA.. Vaasa.................. Finland
VAB.. Yavarate..............Colombia
VAC.. Varrelbusch........... Germany
VAD.. Moody/AFB, GA .... USA
VAF.. Valence/Chalpeuil........ France
VAG.. Varginha/M. B. Trompowsky Brazil
VAH.. Vallegrande .... Bolivia
VAI.. Vanimo .... Papua New Guinea
VAK.. Chevak, AK .... USA
VAL.. Vaienca .... Brazil
VAN.. Van .... Turkey
VAO.. Suavanao Airstrip ....Solomon Is
VAP.. Valparaiso .... Chile
VAR.. Varna .... Bulgaria
VAS.. Sivas..................Turkey
VAT.. Vatomandry....... Madagascar
VAU.. Vatulkoula .... Fiji
VAV.. Vava'u/Lupepau'u........ Tonga
VAW.. Vandoe................. Norway
VAY.. Mount Holly, South Jersey, NJ
.... USA
VAZ.. Val D'Isere .... France
VBG.. Vandenberg/AFB, CA ..... USA
VBS.. Brescia/Montichiari .... Italy
VBV.. Vanuabalavu .... Fiji
VBY.. Visby/Flygplats .... Sweden
VCA.. Can Tho .... Vietnam
VCB.. View Cove, AK .... USA
VCC.. Limbe .... Cameroon
VCD.. Victoria River Downs .. Australia
VCE.. Venice/Marco Polo .... Italy
VCF.. Valcheta .... Argentina
VCH.. Vichadero .... Uruguay
VCP.. Sao Paud/Viracopos....... Brazil
VCR.. Carora .... Vanuatu
VCT.. Victoria, TX.............. USA
VCV.. George/AFB, CA.......... USA
VDA.. Ovda .... Israel
VDB.. Fagernes/Valdres ....Norway
VDC.. Vitoria Da Conquista ....Brazil
VDD.. Vienna/Danubelpier Hov . Austria
VDE.. Valverde/Hierro .... Spain
VDI.. Vidalia/Municipal, GA ...... USA
VDM.. Viedma................ Argentina
VDP.. Valle De Pascua ..... Venezuela
VDR.. Villa Dolores........... Argentina
VDS.. Vadso .... Norway
VDU.. Refugio/O'Connor Oilfield, TX
.... USA
VDZ.. Valdez/Municipal, AK ...... USA
VEE.. Venetie, AK .... USA
VEG.. Mailkwalk.............. Guyana
VEJ.. Vejle .... Denmark
VEL.. Vernal, UT .... USA
VER.. Veracruz/Las Bajadas ... Mexico
VEV.. Barakorna ....Solomon Is
VEX.. Tioga/Municipal, ND....... USA
VEY.. Vestmannaeyjar .... Iceland
VFA.. Victoria Falls .... Zimbabwe
VGA.. Vijayawada .... India
VGD.. Vologoda..............Russia
VGG.. Vangrieng .... Laos
VGO.. Vigo .... Spain
VGS.. General Villegas ...... Argentina
VGT.. Las Vegas/North Air Terminal, NV
.... USA
VGZ.. Villagarzon .... Colombia
VHC.. Saurimo .... Angola
VHM.. Vilhelmina .... Sweden
VHN.. Van Horn/Cullberson County, TX
.... USA
VHY.. Vichy/Charmeil .... France
VHZ.. Vahitahi .... F. Polynesia
VIA.. Videira .... Brazil
VIB.. Villa Constitucion........ Mexico

VIC ... Vicenza ... Italy
VID ... Vidin ... Bulgaria
VIE ... Vienna Int'l ... Austria
VIG ... El Vigia ... Venezuela
VIH ... Vichy, MO ... USA
VII ... Vinh City ... Vietnam
VIJ ... Virgin Gorda ... Virgin Is (British)
VIK ... Kavik/Airstrip, AK ... USA
VIL ... Dakhla ... Morocco
VIN ... Vinnica ... Ukraine
VIQ ... Viqueque ... Indonesia
VIR ... Durban/Virginia ... S. Africa
VIS ... Visalia, CA ... USA
VIT ... Vitoria ... Spain
VIU ... Viru/Viru Harbour ... Solomon Is
VIV ... Vivigani ... Papua New Guinea
VIX ... Vitoria/Euroo Sales ... Brazil
VJB ... Xai Xai ... Mozambique
VJI ... Abingdon/Virginia Highlands, VA ... USA
VJQ ... Gurue ... Mozambique
VKG ... Rach Gia ... Vietnam
VKO ... Moscow/Vnukovo ... Russia
VKS ... Vicksburg, MS ... USA
VKT ... Vorkuta ... Russia
VKW ... West Kavik, AK ... USA
VLA ... Vandalia, IL ... USA
VLC ... Valencia ... Spain
VLD ... Valdosta, GA ... USA
VLE ... Valle, AZ ... Australia
VLG ... Villa Gesell ... Argentina
VLI ... Port Vila/Bauerfield ... Vanuatu
VLK ... Volgodonsk ... Russia
VLL ... Valladolid ... Spain
VLM ... Villamontes ... Bolivia
VLN ... Valencia ... Venezuela
VLO ... Vallejo/Stolport, CA ... USA
VLP ... Vila Rica/Mun ... Brazil
VLR ... Vallenar ... Chile
VLS ... Valesdir ... Vanuatu
VLU ... Velikiye Luki ... Russia
VLV ... Valera/Carvajal ... Venezuela
VME ... Villa Mercedes ... Argentina
VMI ... Vallemi/INC ... Paraguay
VMU ... Baimuru ... Papua New Guinea
VNA ... Saravane ... Laos
VNC ... Venice, FL ... USA
VND ... Vangaindrano ... Madagascar
VNE ... Vannes/Meucon ... Eritrea
VNG ... Viengxay ... Laos
VNO ... Vilnius/Int'l ... Lithuania
VNR ... Vanrook ... Australia
VNS ... Varanasi ... India
VNX ... Vilanculos ... Mozambique
VNY ... Los Angeles-Van Nuys, CA ... USA
VOG ... Volgograd ... Russia
VOH ... Vohemar ... Madagascar
VOI ... Voinjama ... Liberia
VOK ... Camp Douglas, WI ... USA
VOL ... Volos/Nea Anchialos ... Greece
VOT ... Votuporanga ... Brazil
VOZ ... Voronezh ... Russia
VPC ... Cartersville, GA ... USA
VPE ... Ongiva ... Angola
VPN ... Vopnafjordur ... Iceland
VPS ... Elglin/AFB, FL ... USA
VPY ... Chimoio ... Mozambique
VPZ ... Valparaiso, IN ... USA
VQN ... Volens, VA ... USA
VQS ... Vieques ... Puerto Rico
VRA ... Varadero/Juan Gualberto Gomez ... Cuba
VRB ... Vero Beach, FL ... USA
VRC ... Virac ... Philippines
VRE ... Vredendal ... S. Africa
VRK ... Varkaus ... Finland
VRL ... Vila Real ... Portugal
VRN ... Verona/Villafranca ... Italy
VRS ... Versailles, MO ... USA
VRU ... Vryburg ... S. Africa
VRX ... Vermillion Area, LA ... USA
VRY ... Vaeroy/Stolport ... Norway
VSA ... Villahermosa/Capitan Carlos Perez ... Mexico
VSE ... Viseu ... Portugal
VSF ... Springfield, VT ... USA
VSG ... Lugansk ... Ukraine
VSO ... Phuoclong ... Vietnam
VST ... Vasteras/Hasslo ... Sweden
VTA ... Victoria ... Honduras
VTB ... Vitebsk ... Belarus
VTE ... Vientiane/Wattav ... Laos
VTF ... Vatulele ... Fiji
VTG ... Vung Tau ... Vietnam
VTL ... Vittel ... Eritrea
VTN ... Valentine, NE ... USA
VTU ... Las Tunas ... Cuba
VTX ... Los Angeles Nexrad, CA ... USA
VTZ ... Vishakhapatnam ... India
VUO ... Vancouver, Pearson Airpark, WA ... USA
VUP ... Valledupar ... Colombia
VUS ... Velikij Ustyug ... Russia
VUW ... Eugene Is, LA ... USA
VVB ... Mahanoro ... Madagascar
VVC ... Villavicencio/La Vanguardia ... Colombia
VVI ... Santa Cruz/Viru Viru Int'l ... Bolivia
VVK ... Vastervik ... Sweden
VVO ... Vladivostok ... Russia
VVZ ... Illizi ... Algeria
VXC ... Lichinga ... Mozambique
VXE ... Sao Vicente/San Pedro ... Cape Verde Is
VXO ... Vaxjo ... Sweden
VYD ... Vryheid ... S. Africa
VYS ... Peru/Illinois Valley Regional, IL ... USA

W

WAA ... Wales, AK ... USA
WAB ... Wabag ... Papua New Guinea
WAC ... Waca ... Ethiopia
WAD ... Andriamena ... Madagascar
WAE ... Wadi Ad Dawasir ... Saudi Arabia
WAF ... Wana ... Pakistan
WAG ... Wanganui ... New Zealand
WAH ... Wahpeton, ND ... USA
WAI ... Antsohihy ... Madagascar
WAJ ... Wawoi Falls ... Papua New Guinea
WAK ... Ankazoabo ... Madagascar
WAL ... Wallops Is, VA ... USA
WAM ... Ambatondrazalka ... Madagascar
WAN ... Waverney ... Australia
WAO ... Wabo ... Papua New Guinea
WAP ... Alto Palena ... Chile
WAQ ... Antsalova ... Madagascar
WAR ... Waris ... Indonesia
WAT ... Waterford ... Ireland
WAU ... Wauchope ... Australia
WAV ... Wave Hill/Kalkgurung ... Australia
WAW ... Warszawa-Okecie ... Poland
WAX ... Zwara ... Libya
WAY ... Waynesburg/Green County, PA ... USA
WAZ ... Warwick ... Australia
WBA ... Wahai ... Indonesia
WBB ... Stebbins, AK ... USA
WBC ... Wapolu ... Papua New Guinea
WBD ... Befandriana ... Madagascar
WBE ... Bealanana ... Madagascar
WBG ... Schieswig-Jagel ... Germany
WBI ... Boulder/Broker Inn, CO ... USA
WBM ... Wapenamanda ... Papua New Guinea
WBN ... Woburn/Cummings Park, MA ... USA
WBO ... Beroroha ... Madagascar
WBQ ... Beaver, AK ... USA
WBR ... Big Rapids, MI ... USA
WBU ... Boulder/Metro, CO ... USA
WBW ... Wilkes-Barre/Wyoming Valle, PA ... USA
WCA ... Castro/Gamboa ... Chile
WCH ... Chaiten ... Chile
WCR ... Chandalar, AK ... USA
WDA ... Wadi Ain ... Yemen
WDB ... Deep Bay, AK ... USA
WDG ... Enid, OK ... USA
WDH ... Windhoek/H. Kutako Int'l Namibia
WDI ... Wondai ... Australia
WDN ... Waldron Is, WA ... USA
WDR ... Winder, GA ... USA
WDT ... Woensdrecht ... Netherlands
WDY ... Kodiak, AK ... USA
WEA ... Weatherford/Parker County, TX ... USA
WED ... Wedau ... Papua New Guinea
WEE ... Weifang ... China
WEH ... Weihai ... China
WEI ... Weipa ... Australia
WEL ... Welkorn ... S. Africa
WEM ... West Malling ... UK
WEP ... Wearn ... Papua New Guinea
WES ... Weasua ... Iran
WET ... Wagethe ... Indonesia
WEW ... Wee Waa ... Australia
WEX ... Wexford/Castlebridge ... Ireland
WEY ... West Yellowstone, MT ... USA
WFB ... Ketchikan/Waterfront SPB, AK ... USA
WFI ... Fianarantsoa ... Madagascar
WFK ... Frenchville, ME ... USA
WGA ... Wagga Wagga/Forrest Hill ... Australia
WGB ... Bahawainagar ... Pakistan
WGC ... Warrangal ... India
WGE ... Walgett ... Australia
WGL ... Isle Baltra ... Ecuador
WGN ... Waitangi ... New Zealand
WGO ... Winchester/Municipal, VA ... USA
WGP ... Waingapu/Mau Hau ... Indonesia
WGT ... Wangaratta ... Australia
WGU ... Wagau ... Papua New Guinea
WGY ... Wagny ... Gabon
WHD ... Hyder/SPB, AK ... USA
WHF ... Wadi Halfa ... Somalia
WHH ... Boulder/Hiltons Har H, CO ... USA
WHK ... Whakatane ... New Zealand
WHL ... Welshpool ... Australia
WHO ... Franz Josef ... New Zealand
WHP ... Los Angeles/Whiteman, CA ... USA
WHS ... Whalsay ... UK
WHT ... Wharton, TX ... USA
WHU ... Wuhu ... China
WIC ... Wick ... UK
WID ... Wildenrath ... Germany
WIE ... Wiesbaden/Air Base ... Germany
WIH ... Walaba ... Vanuatu
WIK ... Surfdale ... New Zealand
WIL ... Nairobi/Wilson ... Kenya
WIN ... Winton ... Australia
WIO ... Wilcannia ... Australia
WIR ... Wairoa ... New Zealand
WIT ... Wittenoom ... Australia
WIU ... Witu ... Papua New Guinea
WJA ... Woja ... Marshall Is
WJF ... Lancaster, CA ... USA
WJR ... Wajir ... Kenya
WJU ... Wonju ... S. Korea
WKA ... Wanaka ... New Zealand
WKB ... Warracknabeal ... Australia
WKI ... Hwange ... Zimbabwe
WKJ ... Wakkanai/Hokkaido ... Japan
WKK ... Aleknagik, AK ... USA
WKL ... Waikoloa/Waikoloa Arpt, HI ... USA
WKN ... Wakunai ... Papua New Guinea
WKR ... Walker's Cay ... Bahamas
WLA ... Walial ... Australia

WLB	Labouchere Bay, AK	USA
WLC	Walcha	Australia
WLD	Winfield, KS	USA
WLG	Wellington/Int'l	New Zealand
WLI	Wollogorang	Australia
WLK	Selawilk, AK	USA
WLM	Waltham, MA	USA
WLN	Little Naukati, AK	USA
WLO	Waterloo	Australia
WLR	Loring, AK	USA
WLS	Wallis Is.	Wallis and Futuna Is
WLW	Willows/Glenn County, CA	USA
WMA	Mandritsara	Madagascar
WMB	Warmarnboof	Australia
WMC	Winnemucca, NV	USA
WMD	Mandabe	Madagascar
WME	Mount Keith	Australia
WMH	Mountain Home, AR	USA
WMK	Meyers Chuck/SPB, AK	USA
WML	Malaimbandy	Madagascar
WMN	Maroantsetra	Madagascar
WMO	White Mountain, AK	USA
WMP	Mampikony	Madagascar
WMR	Mananara	Madagascar
WMV	Madirovalo	Madagascar
WMX	Wamena	Indonesia
WNA	Napakiak/SPB, AK	USA
WNC	Nichen Cove/SPB, AK	USA
WND	Windarra	Australia
WNE	Wora Na Ye	Gabon
WNN	Wunnummin Lake, ON	Canada
WNP	Naga	Philippines
WNR	Windorah	Australia
WNS	Nawabshah	Pakistan
WNU	Wanurna	Papua New Guinea
WNZ	Werizinou	China
WOA	Wonenara	Papua New Guinea
WOB	Suttonheath/Woodbridge/RAF	UK
WOD	Wood River, AK	USA
WOE	Woensdrecht/AB	Netherlands
WOG	Woodgreen	Australia
WOI	Wologissi	Liberia
WOK	Wonken	Venezuela
WOL	Wollongong	Australia
WON	Wondoola	Australia
WOO	Woodchopper, AK	USA
WOT	Wonan	Taiwan
WOW	Willow, AK	USA
WPA	Puerto Aisen	Chile
WPB	Port Berge	Madagascar
WPC	Pincher Creek, AB	Canada
WPK	Wrotham Park	Australia
WPL	Powell Lake, BC	Canada
WPM	Wipim	Papua New Guinea
WPO	Paonia/North Fork Valley, CO	USA
WPR	Porvenir	Chile
WPS	Persepolis	Iran
WPU	Puerto Williams	Chile
WRA	Warder	Ethiopia
WRB	Robins/AFB, GA	USA
WRE	Whangarei	New Zealand
WRG	Wrangell/SPB, AK	USA
WRH	Wrench Creek, AK	USA
WRI	Mcguire/AFB, NJ	USA
WRL	Worland, WY	USA
WRO	Wroclaw/Strachowice	Poland
WRW	Warrawagine	Australia
WRY	Westray	UK
WSA	Wasua	Papua New Guinea
WSB	Steamboat Bay/SPB, AK	USA
WSD	White Sands/Condron/AAF, NM	
		USA
WSE	Santa Cecilia	Ecuador
WSF	Sarichef, AK	USA
WSG	Washington/County, PA	USA
WSH	Shirley/Brookhaven, NY	USA
WSJ	San Juan/SPB, AK	USA
WSM	Wiseman, AK	USA
WSN	South Naknek, AK	USA
WSO	Washabo	Suriname
WSP	Waspam	Netherlands

WSR	Wasior	Indonesia
WST	Westerly, RI	USA
WSU	Wasu	Papua New Guinea
WSX	Westsound, WA	USA
WSY	Airlie Beach/Whitsunday Airstrip	
		Australia
WSZ	Westport	New Zealand
WTA	Tarnbohorano	Madagascar
WTC	New York/World Trade Center, NY	
		USA
WTD	West End	Bahamas
WTE	Wotje Is	Marshall Is
WTK	Noatak, AK	USA
WTL	Tuntutuliak, AK	USA
WTN	Waddington/RAF Stn	UK
WTO	Wotho Is	Marshall Is
WTP	Woitape	Papua New Guinea
WTR	White River, AZ	USA
WTS	Tsiroanomandidy	Madagascar
WTT	Wantoat	Papua New Guinea
WTZ	Whitianga	New Zealand
WUD	Wudinna	Australia
WUG	Wau	Papua New Guinea
WUH	Wuhan	China
WUM	Wasum	Papua New Guinea
WUN	Wiluna	Australia
WUS	Wuyishan	China
WUU	Wau	Sudan
WUV	Wuvulu Is	Papua New Guinea
WUX	Wuxi	China
WUZ	Wuzhou/Changzhoudao	China
WVB	Walvis Bay/Rooikop	Namibia
WVI	Watsonville, CA	USA
WVK	Manakara	Madagascar
WVL	Waterville/Robert Lafleur, ME	USA
WVN	Wilhelmshaven	Germany
WWA	Wasilia, AK	USA
WWD	Wildwood/Cape May County, NJ	
		USA
WWI	Woodie Woodie	Australia
WWK	Wewak/Boram	
		Papua New Guinea
WWP	Whale Pass, AK	USA
WWR	West Woodward, OK	USA
WWS	Wildwood/USAF HP, AK	USA
WWT	Newtok, AK	USA
WWY	West Wyalong	Australia
WXF	Braintree/Wether Fld/RAF	UK
WXN	Wanxian	China
WYA	Whyalla	Australia
WYB	Yes Bay/SPB, AK	USA
WYE	Yengema	Sierra Leone
WYN	Wyndharn	Australia
WYS	West Yellowstone, MT	USA
WZY	Nassau/Seaplane Base	Bahamas
XAB	Abbeville	France

X

XAC	Arcachon/Teste de Buch.	France
XAD	Churchill/RR, MB	Canada
XAG	Agde/Off-line Pt	France
XAH	Silkeborg/RR Stn.	Denmark
XAI	Aix Les Bains	France
XAJ	Hirlshals/Bus Svc	Denmark
XAK	Herning/RR	Denmark
XAL	Alamos	Mexico
XAM	Amboise	France
XAN	Alencon	France
XAP	Chapeco	Brazil
XAQ	Broenclersev/Bus Svc	Denmark
XAR	Aribinda	Burkina Faso
XAS	Ales	France
XAT	Antibes	France
XAU	Saul	F. Guiana
XAV	Alberville	France
XAW	Capreol/RR, ON	Canada
XAX	Montreal/Dorval RR, QC	Canada

XAY	Xayabury	Laos
XAZ	Campbellton/RR, NB	Canada
XBA	Bareges	France
XBB	Blubber Bay, BC	Canada
XBC	Briancon	France
XBE	Bearskin Lake, ON	Canada
XBF	Bellegarde	France
XBG	Bogande	Burkina Faso
XBH	Bethune	France
XBI	Bourg D'Oisans	France
XBJ	Birjand	Iran
XBK	Bourg En Bresse	France
XBL	Buno Bedelle	Ethiopia
XBM	Beaulieu Sur Mer	France
XBN	Biniguni	Papua New Guinea
XBO	Boulsa	Burkina Faso
XBP	La Baule Les Pins	France
XBQ	Blois	France
XBR	Brockville, ON	Canada
XBS	Boulogne Sur Mer	France
XBT	Boulogne Billancourt	France
XBU	Banyuls Sur Mer	France
XBV	Beaune	France
XBW	Killineq, QC	Canada
XBX	Bernay	France
XBY	Bayonne	France
XBZ	Bandol	France
XCB	Cambrai	France
XCC	Creusot Montceau MON	France
XCD	Chalon Sur Saone	France
XCE	Cerbere	France
XCF	Chamonix Mont Blanc	France
XCG	Cagnes Sur Mer	France
XCH	Christmas Is	Christmas Is
XCI	Chambord/RR, QC	Canada
XCJ	Marigot	Gaudeloupe
XCK	St Die	France
XCL	Cluff Lake, SK	Canada
XCM	Chatham, ON	Canada
XCN	Coron	Philippines
XCO	Colac	Australia
XCP	Compiegne/Margny	France
XCQ	Chamrousse	France
XCR	Chalons Sur Marne	France
XCS	Caussade	France
XCT	La Ciotat	France
XCU	Collioure/Off-line Pt	France
XCV	Chantilly	France
XCW	Chaumont	France
XCX	Chatellerault/Targe	France
XCY	Chateau Thierry	France
XCZ	Charleville Mezieres	France
XDA	Dax/Seyresse	France
XDB	Lille/Lille Europe Rail Svc	France
XDC	Dives Cabourg	France
XDD	Gaspe/RR, QC	Canada
XDE	Diebougou	Burkina Faso
XDG	Halifax/RR. NS	Canada
XDH	Jasper/RR, AB	Canada
XDI	Digne	France
XDJ	Djibo	Burkina Faso
XDK	Dunkerque/Ghyvelde	France
XDL	Chandler/RR, QC	Canada
XDM	Drummondville/RR, QC	
		Canada
XDN	Douai	France
XDO	Grande-Riviere/RR, QC	
		Canada
XDP	Moncton/RR, NB	Canada
XDQ	London/RR, ON	Canada
XDR	Dreux	France
XDS	Ottawa/RR, ON	Canada
XDT	Paris/C.de G. ITGV Rail Sve	
		France
XDU	Hervey/RR, QC	Canada
XDV	Prince George/RR, BC	
		Canada
XDW	Prince Rupert/RR, BC	
		Canada
XDX	Sarnia/RR, ON	Canada
XDY	Sudbury/Jet RR, ON	Canada

Code	Location	Country
XDZ	The Pas/RR, MB	Canada
XEA	Vancouver/RR, BC	Canada
XEB	Evian Les Bains	France
XEC	Windsor/RR, ON	Canada
XED	Disneyland Paris-RR	France
XEE	Lac Edouard/RR, QC	Canada
XEF	Winnipeg/RR, MB	Canada
XEG	Kingston/RR, ON	Canada
XEH	Ladysmith/RR, BC	Canada
XEI	Tsukuba	Japan
XEJ	Langford/RR, BC	Canada
XEK	Melville/RR, SK	Canada
XEL	New Carlisle/RR, QC	Canada
XEM	New Richmond/RR, QC	Canada
XEN	Xingcheng	China
XEO	Ocatsut/Harbour	Greenland
XEP	Epernay	France
XEQ	Tasiuasaq/Harbour	Greenland
XER	Strasbourg/Bus Svc	France
XES	Lake Geneva/Municipal, WI	USA
XET	Karisruhe/Baden Baden/Bus Svc	Germany
XEX	Paris/Aerogare des Invalides	France
XEY	Miramichi/RR, NB	Canada
XFA	Lille/Lille Flanders Rail Svc	France
XFB	Fontainebieau	France
XFC	Fredericton Junction/RR, NB	Canada
XFD	Stratford/RR, ON	Canada
XFE	Parent/RR, QC	Canada
XFF	Calais/Frethun RR	France
XFG	Perce/RR, QC	Canada
XFI	Port-Daniel/RR, QC	Canada
XFK	Senneterre/RR, QC	Canada
XFL	Shawinigan/RR, QC	Canada
XFM	Shawinigan/RR, BC	Canada
XFN	Xiangan	China
XFO	Taschereau/RR, QC	Canada
XFQ	Weymont/RR, QC	Canada
XFS	Alexandria/RR, ON	Canada
XFV	Brantford/RR, ON	Canada
XFW	Hamburg/Finkenwerder	Germany
XFX	Foix	France
XFY	Quebec/Sainte-Foy Rail Svc, QC	Canada
XFZ	Quebec/Charny, QC	Canada
XGA	Gaoua	Burkina Faso
XGB	Paris/Gare Montparnasse	France
XGF	St Gervais Le Fayet	France
XGG	Gorom-Gorom	Burkina Faso
XGJ	Cobourg/RR, ON	Canada
XGK	Coteau/RR, QC	Canada
XGL	Granville Lake, MB	Canada
XGM	Grantham/RR	UK
XGN	Xangongo	Angola
XGO	Santiago	Brazil
XGR	Kangiqsualuijuaq, QC	Canada
XGT	Gueret/Saint Laurent	France
XGV	St Gilles Croix De Vie	France
XGW	Gananoque/RR, ON	Canada
XGY	Grimsby/RR, ON	Canada
XHE	Hyeres	France
XHM	Georgetown/RR, ON	Canada
XHR	Timbo/Ott-Line Point	Brazil
XHS	Chemainus/RR, BC	Canada
XHU	Huntingdon/RR	UK
XHY	Hendaye	France
XI0	St Marys/RR, ON	Canada
XIA	Guelph/RR, ON	Canada
XIB	Ingersoll/RR, ON	Canada
XIC	Xichang	China
XID	Maxvifle/RR, ON	Canada
XIE	Xienglorn	Laos
XIF	Napanee/RR, ON	Canada
XIG	Xinguara/Mun	Brazil
XII	Prescott/RR, ON	Canada
XIL	Xilinhot	China
XIM	Saint Hyacinthe/RR, QC	Canada
XIN	Xingning	China

Code	Location	Country
XIP	Woodstock/RR, ON	Canada
XIQ	Ilimanaq/Harbour	Greenland
XIS	Dionisio Cerqueira	Brazil
XIY	Xi An/Xianyang	China
XJE	Vojens/RR	Denmark
XJL	Joliette/RR, QC	Canada
XJQ	Jonquiere/RR, QC	Canada
XJT	Tours/RR	France
XJZ	St Jean De Luz	France
XKA	Kantchari	Burkina Faso
XKH	Xieng Khouang	Laos
XKL	Kuala Lumpur/KUL Sentral Rail	Malaysia
XKO	Kemano, BC	Canada
XKS	Kasabonika, ON	Canada
XKT	Kennedy Town	Hong Kong
XKU	Kusadasi	Turkey
XKV	Sackville/RR, NB	Canada
XKY	Kaya	Burkina Faso
XLA	La Bastide Puylaurent	France
XLB	Lac Brochet, MB	Canada
XLC	Fictious Point/Off-line Pt	USA
XLD	Landerneau	France
XLE	Lens	France
XLF	Leaf Bay, QB	Canada
XLG	Lognes	France
XLH	Luchon	France
XLI	St Louis	France
XLJ	Quebec/Quebec Stn Rail Svc, QC	Canada
XLK	Quebec/Levis Rail Svc, QC	Canada
XLM	Montreal/St. Lambert Rail Svc, QC	Canada
XLN	Laon/Chambry	France
XLO	Long Xuyen	Vietnam
XLP	Matapedia/RR, QC	Canada
XLQ	Toronto/Guildwood Rail Svc, ON	Canada
XLR	Libourne/Artiques de Lussac	France
XLS	St Louis	Senegal
XLT	Ax Les Thermes	France
XLU	Leo	Burkina Faso
XLV	Niagara Falls/RR, ON	Canada
XLW	Lernwerder	Germany
XLX	Lisieux	France
XLY	Aldershot/RR, ON	Canada
XLZ	Truro/RR, NS	Canada
XMA	Maramag	Philippines
XMB	M'Bahiakro	Côte D'Ivoire
XMC	Mallacoota	Australia
XMD	Madison, SD	USA
XME	Maubeuge	France
XMF	Montbelliard	France
XMG	Mahendranagar	Nepal
XMH	Manihi	F. Polynesia
XMI	Masasi	Tanzania
XMJ	Mont De Marsan	France
XMK	Montelimar	France
XML	Minlaton	Australia
XMM	Monaco Monte Carlo	France
XMN	Xiamen	China
XMO	Modane	France
XMP	Maemillan Pass, YT	Canada
XMQ	Morzine	France
XMR	Marmande/Off-line Pt	France
XMS	Macas	Ecuador
XMT	Menton	France
XMU	Moulin Sur Allier	France
XMV	Pichanal	Argentina
XMW	Montauban	France
XMX	Ledesma	Argentina
XMY	Yam Is	Australia
XMZ	Macclesfield/RR	UK
XNA	Fayetteville/Northwest Arkansas, AR	USA
XNE	Newport (Gwent)/RR	UK
XNG	Quang Ngai	Vietnam
XNK	Newark Northgate/RR	UK

Code	Location	Country
XNM	Nottingham/RR	UK
XNN	Xining	China
XNO	Northallerton/RR	UK
XNR	Aalbenraa/Bus Svc	Denmark
XNS	Ansan	Kuwait
XNT	Xingtai	China
XNU	Nouna	Burkina Faso
XNV	Nuneaton/RR	UK
XOE	Sao Jose	Brazil
XOG	Orange	France
XOK	Oakville/Rail Svc, ON	Canada
XON	Carleton/RR, QC	Canada
XOP	Poitiers/RR	France
XOS	Mosconi	Argentina
XOX	Cheonan	Kuwait
XOY	Aulnoye	France
XPA	Pama	Burkina Faso
XPB	Parksville/RR, BC	Canada
XPD	San Pedro	Argentina
XPF	Penrith/RR	UK
XPG	Paris/Gare du Nord RR	France
XPH	Port Hope/RR, ON	Canada
XPK	Pukatawagan, MB	Canada
XPL	Comayagua/Palmerola Air Base	Honduras
XPM	Pontorson Mt St Michel	France
XPN	Brampton/RR, ON	Canada
XPP	Poplar River, MB	Canada
XPR	Pine Ridge, SD	USA
XPS	Provins	France
XPT	Preston/RR	UK
XPU	West Kuparuk, AK	USA
XPV	Port Vendres	France
XPW	Didcot Parkway/RR	UK
XPX	Pointe-aux-Trembles/RR, QC	Canada
XPZ	Saint-Tropez/Harbour	France
XQB	Basingstoke/RR	UK
XQD	Bedford/RR	UK
XQG	Berwick/RR	UK
XQH	Nottingham/RR	UK
XQI	Nottingham/RR Stn.	UK
XQL	Lancaster/RR	UK
XQM	Market Harborough/RR Stn.	UK
XQP	Quepos	Costa Rica
XQT	Lichfield T.V./RR Stn.	UK
XQU	Qualicurn, BC	Canada
XQW	Motherwell/RR Stn.	UK
XQY	St Quentin en Yvelines	France
XRA	Graasten/Bus Svc	Denmark
XRB	Ararangua	Brazil
XRC	Runcom/RR Stn.	UK
XRE	Reading	UK
XRG	Rugeley T.V./RR Stn.	UK
XRI	Riom	France
XRM	Armentieres	France
XRN	Redon	France
XRO	La Roche Sur Yon	France
XRP	Riviere-a-Pierre/RR Stn., QC	Canada
XRR	Ross River, YT	Canada
XRS	Les Ares	France
XRT	Rambouillet	France
XRU	Rugby/RR Stn.	UK
XRX	Roubaix	France
XRY	Jerez De La Frontera/La Parra	Spain
XSA	Sinoe/AFC	Liberia
XSB	St Malo	France
XSC	South Caicos/Int'l	Turks & Caicos Is
XSD	Tonopah/Test Range, NV	USA
XSE	Sebba	Burkina Faso
XSF	Sens	France
XSG	St Omer	France
XSH	Tours/RR Stn.	France
XSI	South Indian Lake, MB	Canada
XSJ	St Quentin	France
XSK	St Raphael	France
XSL	Sarlat/Domme	France

AIRPORTS

XSM . . St Marys, MD . . . . USA
XSN . . Sallanches . . . . France
XSO . . Siocon. . . . . Philippines
XSP . . Singapore/Seletar . . . . Singapore
XSQ . . Selestat . . . . France
XSR . . Salisbury/RR Stn. . . . . UK
XSS . . Soissons . . . . France
XST . . Saintes . . . . France
XSU . . Saumur . . . . France
XSV . . Senlis . . . . France
XSW . . Sedan . . . . France
XSX . . Seclin . . . . France
XSY . . Sete. . . . . France
XSZ . . Setubal . . . . Portugal
XTB . . Tarbes/Laloubere. . . . . France
XTC . . St Claude . . . . France
XTE . . La Tour De Carol . . . . France
XTG . . Thargomindah . . . . Australia
XTH . . Thionvifle . . . . France
XTK . . Thirsk/RR Stn. . . . . UK
XTL . . Tadoule Lake, MB . . . . . Canada
XTN . . Tourcoing . . . . France
XTO . . Taroom . . . . Australia
XTR . . Tara . . . . Australia
XTS . . Thonon Les Bains . . . . . . France
XTT . . Paris/Etoile . . . . France
XTU . . Tulle . . . . France
XTY . . Strathroy/RR Stn., ON . . . Canada
XUY . . Auray . . . . France
XUZ . . Xuzhou . . . . China
XVA . . Stockport/RR Stn. . . . . UK
XVB . . Stafford/RR Stn. . . . . UK
XVC . . Crewe/RR Stn. . . . . UK
XVD . . Vendome . . . . France
XVE . . Versailles . . . . France
XVF . . Villefranche Sur Saone . . . France
XVG . . Darlington/RR Stn. . . . . UK
XVH . . Peterborough/RR Stn. . . . . . UK
XVI . . Vienne . . . . France
XVJ . . Stevenage/RR Stn. . . . . UK
XVL . . Vinh Long . . . . Vietnam
XVN . . Verdun . . . . France
XVO . . Vesoul . . . . France
XVP . . Villepinte . . . . France
XVR . . Valloire . . . . France
XVS . . Valenciennes/RR Stn. . . . . France
XVT . . Vitre . . . . France
XVU . . Durham/RR Stn. . . . . UK
XVV . . Belleville/RR Stn., ON . . . Canada
XVW . . Wolverhampton-RR. . . . . UK
XVX . . Vejle/RR Stn. . . . . Denmark
XVZ . . Vierzon . . . . France
XWA . . Watford/RR Stn., ON . . . . Canada
XWB . . Stirling/RR Stn. . . . . UK
XWD . . Wakefield Westgate/RR Stn. . UK
XWE . . Wellingborough/RR Stn. . . . . UK
XWH . . Stoke on Trent/RR Stn. . . . . UK
XWI . . Wigan N.W./RR Stn. . . . . . . UK
XWN . . Warrington B.Q./RR Stn. . . . . UK
XWO . . Woking/RR Stn. . . . . UK
XWS . . Swindon/RR Stn. . . . . UK
XWY . . Wyoming/RR Stn., ON . . Canada
XXB . . Bhadohi . . . . India
XXF . . Scenic Flight . . . . . New Zealand
XXH . . Helicopter Scenic . New Zealand
XXP . . Potsdam . . . . Germany
XXS . . Skiplane Scenic. . . . New Zealand
XYA . . Yandina. . . . . Solomon Is
XYD . . Lyon/Lyon Part-Dieu Rail Svc
. . . . France
XYE . . Ye . . . . Myanmar
XYL . . Lyon/Lyon Perrache Rail Svc
. . . . France
XYR . . Yellow River . Papua New Guinea
XYT . . Toulouse/Montaudran . . . France
XYV . . Lyon/Lyon Satolas Rail Svc
. . . . France
XZA . . Zabre . . . . Burkina Faso
XZB . . Casselman/RR Stn., ON . Canada
XZC . . Glencoe/RR Stn., ON . . . Canada
XZK . . Amherst/RR Stn., NS . . . . Canada

XZL . . Edmonton/RR Stn., AB . . Canada
XZP . . Pass (Generic), QC . . . . . Canada
XZR . . Rail (Generic), QC . . . . . . Canada
XZY . . Alzey . . . . Germany

Y

YAA . . Anahim Lake, BC . . . . . . Canada
YAB . . Arctic Bay, NU . . . . Canada
YAC . . Cat Lake, ON . . . . Canada
YAD . . Moose Lake, MB . . . . Canada
YAE . . Alta Lake, BC . . . . Canada
YAF . . Asbestos Hill, QC . . . . . . Canada
YAG . . Ft. Frances/Mun, ON . . . . Canada
YAH . . La Grande, QC. . . . . Canada
YAI . . Chillan . . . . Chile
YAJ . . Lyall Harbour, BC . . . . . . Canada
YAK . . Yakutat, AK . . . . USA
YAL . . Alert Bay, BC . . . . Canada
YAM . . Sault Ste Marie, ON . . . . Canada
YAN . . Yangambi . . . . Congo, DR
YAO . . Yaounde/Yaciunde Arpt
. . . . Cameroon
YAP . . Yap. . . . . Micronesia
YAQ . . Maple Bay, BC . . . . Canada
YAR . . Lagrande 3, QC . . . . Canada
YAS . . Yasawa Is . . . . Fiji
YAT . . Attawapiskat, ON . . . . . . Canada
YAU . . Kattiniq/Donaldson Lak, QC
. . . . Canada
YAV . . Miners Bay, BC . . . . Canada
YAW . . Shearwater, NS. . . . . Canada
YAX . . Angling Lake, ON . . . . . . Canada
YAY . . St Anthony, NF . . . . Canada
YAZ . . Tofino, BC . . . . Canada
YBA . . Banff, AB. . . . . Canada
YBB . . Pelly Bay, NU . . . . Canada
YBC . . Baie Comeau, QC. . . . . . Canada
YBD . . New Westminster, BC . . Canada
YBE . . Uranium City, SK . . . . . . Canada
YBF . . Bamfield, BC . . . . Canada
YBG . . Bagotville, QC . . . . Canada
YBH . . Bull Harbour, BC . . . . . . Canada
YBI . . Black Tickle, NF . . . . Canada
YBJ . . Bale Johan Beetz, QC . . Canada
YBK . . Baker Lake, NT. . . . . Canada
YBL . . Campbell River, BC. . . . . Canada
YBM . . Bronson Creek, BC . . . . . Canada
YBN . . Borden, ON . . . . Canada
YBO . . Bobquinn Lake, BC . . . . . Canada
YBP . . Yibin. . . . . China
YBQ . . Telegraph Harbour, BC . . Canada
YBR . . Brandon, MB . . . . Canada
YBS . . Opapamiska Lake/Musselwhite,
ON . . . . Canada
YBT . . Brochet, MB . . . . Canada
YBU . . Nipawin, SK . . . . Canada
YBV . . Berens River, MB . . . . . . Canada
YBW . . Springbank, AB . . . . Canada
YBX . . Blanc Sablon, QC . . . . . . Canada
YBY . . Bonnyville, AB . . . . Canada
YBZ . . Toronto/Downtown RR Stn., ON
. . . . Canada
YCA . . Courtenay, BC . . . . Canada
YCB . . Cambridge Bay, NT . . . . Canada
YCC . . Cornwall/Regional, ON . . Canada
YCD . . Nanaimo, BC . . . . Canada
YCE . . Centralia, ON . . . . Canada
YCF . . Cortes Bay, BC. . . . . Canada
YCG . . Castlegar, BC . . . . Canada
YCH . . Miramichi, NB . . . . Canada
YCI . . Caribou Is, ON . . . . Canada
YCJ . . Cape St James, BC . . . . . Canada
YCK . . Colville Lake, NT . . . . Canada
YCL . . Charlo, NB . . . . Canada
YCM . . St Catharines, ON . . . . . Canada
YCN . . Cochrane, ON . . . . Canada
YCO . . Coppermine, NU . . . . . . Canada

YCP . . Blue River, BC . . . . Canada
YCQ . . Chetwynd, BC. . . . . Canada
YCR . . Cross Lake, MB . . . . Canada
YCS . . Chesterfield Inlet, NU . . . Canada
YCT . . Coronation, AB . . . . Canada
YCV . . Cartierville, QC . . . . Canada
YCW . . Chilliwack, BC. . . . . Canada
YCX . . Gagetown, NB . . . . Canada
YCY . . Clyde River, NU. . . . . . . Canada
YCZ . . Fairmount Springs, BC. . Canada
YDA . . Dawson, YT. . . . . Canada
YDB . . Burwash Landings, YT. . Canada
YDC . . Drayton Valley, AB . . . . . Canada
YDE . . Paradise River, NF . . . . . Canada
YDF . . Deer Lake, NF. . . . . Canada
YDG . . Djgby, NS. . . . . Canada
YDH . . Daniels Harbour, NF. . . . Canada
YDI . . Davis Inlet, NF. . . . . Canada
YDJ . . Hatchet Lake, SK . . . . . . Canada
YDK . . Main Duck Is, ON . . . . . . Canada
YDL . . Dease Lake, BC . . . . Canada
YDN . . Dauphin, MB. . . . . Canada
YDO . . Dolbeau/St Methode, QC Canada
YDP . . Nain, NF. . . . . Canada
YDQ . . Dawson Creek, BC. . . . . Canada
YDR . . Broadview, SK. . . . . Canada
YDS . . Desolation Sound, BC . . Canada
YDT . . Vancouver/Boundary Bay, BC
. . . . Canada
YDU . . Kasba Lake, NT . . . . Canada
YDV . . Bloodvein, MB. . . . . Canada
YDW . . Obre Lake, NT . . . . Canada
YDX . . Doc Creek, BC . . . . Canada
YEC . . Yechon/Air Base . . . . . . S. Korea
YED . . Edmonton Namao, AB . . Canada
YEG . . Edmonton Int'l, AB . . . . . Canada
YEI . . Bursa . . . . Turkey
YEK . . Arviat, NU . . . . Canada
YEL . . Elliot Lake, ON. . . . . Canada
YEM . . Manitowaning/East Manitoulin,
ON . . . . Canada
YEN . . Estevan, SK . . . . Canada
YEO . . Yeovilton-RNAS. . . . . UK
YEP . . Estevan Point, BC . . . . . . Canada
YEQ . . Yenkis . . . . . . Papua New Guinea
YER . . Ft. Severn, ON . . . . Canada
YET . . Edson, AB . . . . Canada
YEU . . Eureka, MB . . . . Canada
YEV . . Inuvik, NT. . . . . Canada
YEY . . Amos, QC . . . . Canada
YFA . . Ft. Albany, ON. . . . . Canada
YFB . . Iqaluit, NT . . . . Canada
YFC . . Fredericton, NB. . . . . Canada
YFE . . Forestville, QC. . . . . Canada
YFG . . Fontanges, QC . . . . Canada
YFH . . Ft. Hope, ON . . . . Canada
YFJ . . Snare Lake, NT. . . . . Canada
YFL . . Ft. Reliance, NT. . . . . Canada
YFO . . Flin Flon, MB . . . . Canada
YFR . . Ft. Resolution, NT . . . . . . Canada
YFS . . Ft. Simpson, NT . . . . Canada
YFT . . Makkovik Arpt . . . . Canada
YFX . . Fox Harbour (St Lewis), NG
. . . . Canada
YGA . . Gagnon, QC . . . . Canada
YGB . . Gillies Bay, BC. . . . . Canada
YGC . . Grande Cache, AB. . . . . Canada
YGE . . Gorge Harbor, BC. . . . . . Canada
YGG . . Ganges Harbor, BC . . . . Canada
YGH . . Ft. Good Hope, NT . . . . . Canada
YGJ . . Yonago/Miho. . . . . Japan
YGK . . Kingston, ON. . . . . Canada
YGL . . La Grande, QC . . . . Canada
YGM . . Gimli, MB . . . . Canada
YGN . . Greenway Sound, BC . . Canada
YGO . . Gods Narrows, MB. . . . . Canada
YGP . . Gaspe, QC . . . . Canada
YGQ . . Geraldton, ON. . . . . Canada
YGR . . Iles De La MadeleineQC Canada
YGS . . Germansen, BC . . . . Canada
YGT . . Igloolik, BC . . . . Canada

A I R P O R T S

Code	Location	Country
YGV	Havre St Pierre, QC	Canada
YGW	Kuujjuarapik, QC	Canada
YGX	Gillam, MB	Canada
YGY	Deception, QC	Canada
YGZ	Grise Fiord, NU	Canada
YHA	Port Hope Simpson, NF	Canada
YHB	Hudson Bay, SK	Canada
YHC	Hakai Pass, BC	Canada
YHD	Dryden, ON	Canada
YHE	Hope, BC	Canada
YHF	Hearst, OH	Canada
YHG	Charlottetown, NF	Canada
YHH	Campbell River/Harbor SPB, BC	Canada
YHI	Holman, NT	Canada
YHK	Gjoa Haven, NU	Canada
YHM	Hamilton, ON	Canada
YHN	Hornepayne, ON	Canada
YHO	Hopedale, NF	Canada
YHP	Poplar Hill, ON	Canada
YHR	Chevery, QC	Canada
YHS	Secheit, BC	Canada
YHT	Haines Junction, YT	Canada
YHU	Montreal-St. Hubert, QC	Canada
YHY	Hay River, NT	Canada
YHZ	Halifax Int'l, NS	Canada
YIB	Atikokan, ON	Canada
YIF	Pakuashipi, QC	Canada
YIG	Big Bay Marina, BC	Canada
YIH	Yichang, QC	China
YIK	Ivujivik, QC	Canada
YIN	Yining	China
YIO	Pond Inlet, NU	Canada
YIP	Detroit-Willow Run, MI	USA
YIV	Is Lake, MB	Canada
YIW	Yiwu	China
YJF	Ft. Liard, NT	Canada
YJN	St Jean, QC	Canada
YJO	Johnny Mountain, BC	Canada
YJP	Jasper-Hinton, AB	Canada
YJT	Stephenville, NF	Canada
YKA	Kamloops. BC	Canada
YKC	Collins Bay, SK	Canada
YKD	Kincardine, ON	Canada
YKE	Knee Lake, MB	Canada
YKF	Kitchener, ON	Canada
YKG	Kangirsuk, QC	Canada
YKI	Kennosao Lake, MB	Canada
YKJ	Key Lake, SK	Canada
YKK	Kitkatla, BC	Canada
YKL	Schefferville, QC	Canada
YKM	Yakima, WA	USA
YKN	Yankton/Chan Gurney, SD	USA
YKQ	Waskaganish, QC	Canada
YKS	Yakutsk	Russia
YKT	Kierritu, BC	Canada
YKU	Chisasibi, QC	Canada
YKX	Kirkland Lake, ON	Canada
YKY	Kindersley, SK	Canada
YKZ	Toronto Buttonville, ON	Canada
YLA	Langara, BC	Canada
YLB	Lac Biche, AB	Canada
YLC	Kimmirut, NT	Canada
YLD	Chapleau, ON	Canada
YLE	Wha Ti/Lac La Martre, NT	Canada
YLF	LaForges, QC	Canada
YLG	Yalgoo	Australia
YLH	Lansdowne House, ON	Canada
YLI	Ylivieska	Finland
YLJ	Meadow Lake, SK	Canada
YLL	Lloydminister, AB	Canada
YLM	Clinton Creek, YT	Canada
YLN	Yilan	China
YLO	Shilo-YLP Mingan, MB	Canada
YLP	Mingan, QC	Canada
YLQ	La Tuclue, QC	Canada
YLR	Leaf Rapids, MB	Canada
YLS	Lebel-Sur-Quevillon, QC	Canada
YLT	Alert, NU	Canada
YLW	Kelowna, BC	Canada

Code	Location	Country
YLX	Long Point, ON	Canada
YMA	Mayo, YT	Canada
YMB	Merritt, BC	Canada
YMC	Maricourt Airstrip, QC	Canada
YMD	Mould Bay, NT	Canada
YME	Matane, QC	Canada
YMF	Montagne Harbor, BC	Canada
YMG	Manitouwadge, ON	Canada
YMH	Mary's Harbour, NF	Canada
YMI	Minaki, ON	Canada
YMJ	Moose Jaw, SK	Canada
YML	Murray Bay, QC	Canada
YMM	Ft. Mcmurray, AB	Canada
YMN	Makkovik, NF	Canada
YMO	Moosonee, ON	Canada
YMP	Port McNeil, BC	Canada
YMR	Merry Is, BC	Canada
YMS	Yurimaguas	Peru
YMT	Chibougamau, QC	Canada
YMW	Maniwaki, QC	Canada
YMX	Montreal/Mirabel, QC	Canada
YMY	Montreal/Downtown RR Stn., QC	Canada
YNA	Natashquan, QC	Canada
YNB	Yanbu	Saudi Arabia
YNC	Wemindpi, QC	Canada
YND	Gatineati, ON	Canada
YNE	Norway House, MB	Canada
YNF	Corner Brook/Deer Lake, NF	Canada
YNG	Youngstown, OH	USA
YNH	Hudson's Hope, BC	Canada
YNI	Nitchequon, QC	Canada
YNJ	Yanji	China
YNK	Nootka Sound, BC	Canada
YNL	Points North Landing, SK	Canada
YNM	Matagami, QC	Canada
YNO	North Spirit Lake, ON	Canada
YNR	Arnes, MB	Canada
YNS	Nemiscau, QC	Canada
YNT	Yantai/Laishan	China
YNZ	Yancheng	China
YOA	Ekati, NT	Canada
YOC	Old Crow, YT	Canada
YOD	Cold Lake, AB	Canada
YOE	Falher, AB	Canada
YOG	Ogoki, ON	Canada
YOH	Oxford House, MB	Canada
YOJ	High Level, AB	Canada
YOK	Yokohama	Japan
YOL	Yola	Nigeria
YOO	Oshawa, ON	Canada
YOP	Rainbow Lake, AB	Canada
YOS	Owen Sound/Billy Bishop Regional, ON	Canada
YOT	Yotvata	Israel
YOW	Ottawa Int'l, ON	Canada
YOY	Valcartier, QC	Canada
YPA	Prince Albert,SK	Canada
YPB	Port Allberni, BC	Canada
YPC	Paulatuk, NT	Canada
YPD	Parry Sound, ON	Canada
YPE	Peace River, AB	Canada
YPF	Esquimalt, BC	Canada
YPG	Portage La Prairie, MB	Canada
YPH	Inulkjualk, QC	Canada
YPI	Port Simpson, BC	Canada
YPJ	Aupaluk, QC	Canada
YPL	Pickle Lake, MB	Canada
YPM	Pikangikum, ON	Canada
YPN	Port Menier, MB	Canada
YPO	Peawanuck, ON	Canada
YPP	Pine Point, NT	Canada
YPQ	Peterborough, ON	Canada
YPR	Prince Rupert, BC	Canada
YPS	Port Hawkesbury, NS	Canada
YPT	Pender Harbor, BC	Canada
YPW	Powell River, BC	Canada
YPX	Povungnituk, QC	Canada
YPY	Ft. Chipewyan, AB	Canada
YPZ	Burns Lake, BC	Canada

Code	Location	Country
YQA	Muskoka, ON	Canada
YQB	Quebec, QC	Canada
YQC	Quaqtaq, QC	Canada
YQD	The Pas, MB	Canada
YQE	Kimberley, BC	Canada
YQF	Red Deer, AB	Canada
YQG	Windsor, ON	Canada
YQH	Watson Lake, YT	Canada
YQI	Yarmouth, NS	Canada
YQK	Kenora, ON	Canada
YQL	Lethbridge, AB	Canada
YQM	Moncton, NB	Canada
YQN	Nakina, ON	Canada
YQQ	Comox, BC	Canada
YQR	Regina, SK	Canada
YQS	St Thomas/Pembroke Area, ON	Canada
YQT	Thunder Bay, ON	Canada
YQU	Grande Prairie, AB	Canada
YQV	Yorkton, SK	Canada
YQW	North Battleford, SK	Canada
YQX	Gander Int'l, NF	Canada
YQY	Sydney, NS	Canada
YQZ	Ouesnel, BC	Canada
YRA	Rae Lakes, NT	Canada
YRB	Resolute, NT	Canada
YRD	Dean River, BC	Canada
YRE	Resolution Is, NU	Canada
YRF	Cartwright, NF	Canada
YRG	Rigolet, NF	Canada
YRI	Riviere Du Loup, QC	Canada
YRJ	Roberval, QC	Canada
YRL	Red Lake, ON	Canada
YRM	Rocky Mountain House, AB	Canada
YRN	Rivers Inlet, BC	Canada
YRO	Ottawa/Rockcliffe St, ON	Canada
YRQ	Trois-Rivieres, QC	Canada
YRR	Stuart Is, BC	Canada
YRS	Red Sucker Lake, MB	Canada
YRT	Rankin Inlet, NT	Canada
YRV	Revelstoke, BC	Canada
YSA	Sable Is, NS	Canada
YSB	Sudbury, ON	Canada
YSC	Sherbrooke, QC	Canada
YSD	Suffield, AB	Canada
YSE	Squamish, BC	Canada
YSF	Stony Rapids, SK	Canada
YSG	Lutselke/Snowdrift, NT	Canada
YSH	Smith Falls, ON	Canada
YSI	Sans Souci, ON	Canada
YSJ	Saint John, NB	Canada
YSK	Sanikiluaq, NU	Canada
YSL	St Leonard, NB	Canada
YSM	Ft. Smith, NT	Canada
YSN	Salmon Arm, BC	Canada
YSO	Postville, NF	Canada
YSP	Marathon, ON	Canada
YSQ	Spring Is, BC	Canada
YSR	Nanisivik, NU	Canada
YSS	Slate Is, ON	Canada
YST	Ste Therese Point, MB	Canada
YSU	Summerside, PE	Canada
YSV	Saglek, NF	Canada
YSX	Shearwater, BC	Canada
YSY	Sachs Harbour, NT	Canada
YSZ	Squirrel Cove, BC	Canada
YTA	Pembroke, ON	Canada
YTB	Hartley Bay, BC	Canada
YTC	Sturdee, BC	Canada
YTD	Thicket Portage, MB	Canada
YTE	Cape Dorset, NT	Canada
YTF	Alma, QC	Canada
YTG	Sullivan Say, BC	Canada
YTH	Thompson, MB	Canada
YTI	Triple Is, BC	Canada
YTJ	Terrace Bay, ON	Canada
YTK	Tuiugak, QC	Canada
YTL	Big Trout, ON	Canada
YTN	Riviere Au Tonnerre, QC	Canada
YTO	Guildwood/Toronto, ON	Canada

AIRPORTS

Code	Location	Country
YTP	Tofino/Seaplane Base, BC	Canada
YTQ	Tasiujuaq, QC	Canada
YTR	Trenton, ON	Canada
YTS	Timmins, ON	Canada
YTT	Tisdale, SK	Canada
YTU	Tasu, BC	Canada
YTX	Telegraph Creek, BC	Canada
YTZ	Toronto/Toronto Is, ON	Canada
YUA	Yuanmou	China
YUB	Tukloyaktuk, NT	Canada
YUD	Urniujaq, QC	Canada
YUE	Yuendurnu	Australia
YUL	Montreal Int'l, QC	Canada
YUM	Yuma Int'l, AZ	USA
YUT	Repulse Bay, NU	Canada
YUX	Hall Beach, NU	Canada
YUY	Rouyn, QC	Canada
YVA	Moroni/Iconi	Comoros
YVB	Bonaventure, QC	Canada
YVC	La Ronge, SK	Canada
YVD	Yeva	Papua New Guinea
YVE	Vernon, BC	Canada
YVG	Vermilion, AB	Canada
YVM	Qikiqtarjuaq, NU	Canada
YVO	Val D'Or, QC	Canada
YVP	Kuujjuaq, QC	Canada
YVQ	Norman Wells, NT	Canada
YVR	Vancouver Int'l, BC	Canada
YVT	Buffalo Narrows, SK	Canada
YVV	Wiarton, ON	Canada
YVZ	Deer Lake, ON	Canada
YWA	Petawawa, ON	Canada
YWB	Kangiqsujuaq, QC	Canada
YWF	Halifax/Dwtown Waterfront HP, NS	Canada
YWG	Winnipeg Int'l, MB	Canada
YWH	Victoria Harbour, BC	Canada
YWJ	Deline, NT	Canada
YWK	Wabush, NF	Canada
YWL	Williams Lake, BC	Canada
YWM	Williams Harbour, NF	Canada
YWN	Winisk, ON	Canada
YWO	Lupin, NT	Canada
YWP	Welbequie, ON	Canada
YWQ	Chute-Des-Passes, QC	Canada
YWR	White River, ON	Canada
YWS	Whistler, BC	Canada
YWV	Wainwright Arpt, AB	Canada
YWY	Wrigley, NT	Canada
YXC	Cranbrook, BC	Canada
YXD	Edmonton, AB	Canada
YXE	Saskatoon, SK	Canada
YXF	Snake River, YT	Canada
YXH	Medicine Hat, AB	Canada
YXI	Kilialoe, ON	Canada
YXJ	Fort St John, BC	Canada
YXK	Rimouski, QC	Canada
YXL	Sioux Lookout, ON	Canada
YXN	Whale Cove, NU	Canada
YXP	Pangnirtung, NU	Canada
YXQ	Beaver Creek, YT	Canada
YXR	Earlton, ON	Canada
YXS	Prince George, BC	Canada
YXT	Terrace, BC	Canada
YXU	London, ON	Canada
YXX	Abbotsford, BC	Canada
YXY	Withehorse, YT	Canada
YXZ	Wawa, ON	Canada
YY	Clyde, NT	Canada
YYA	Big Bay Yacht Club, BC	Canada
YYB	North Bay, ON	Canada
YYC	Calgary Int'l, AB	Canada
YYD	Smithers, BC	Canada
YYE	Ft. Nelson, BC	Canada
YYF	Penticton, BC	Canada
YYG	Charlottetown, PE	Canada
YYH	Spence Bay Arpt, NU	Canada
YYI	Rivers, MB	Canada
YYJ	Victoria Int'l, BC	Canada
YYL	Lynn Lake, MB	Canada
YYM	Cowley, AB	Canada
YYN	Swift Current, SK	Canada
YYQ	Churchill, MB	Canada
YYR	Goose, NF	Canada
YYT	St. John's, NF	Canada
YYU	Kapuskasing, ON	Canada
YYW	Armstrong, ON	Canada
YYY	Mont Joli, QC	Canada
YYZ	Toronto-Pearson Int'l., ON	Canada
YZA	Ashcrott, BC	Canada
YZC	Beatton River, BC	Canada
YZE	Gore Bay, ON	Canada
YZF	Yellowknife, NT	Canada
YZG	Salluit, QC	Canada
YZH	Slave Lake, AB	Canada
YZM	Buchans, NF	Canada
YZP	Sandspit, BC	Canada
YZR	Sarnia, ON	Canada
YZS	Coral Harbour, NT	Canada
YZT	Port Hardy, BC	Canada
YZU	Whitecourt, AB	Canada
YZV	Sept-Iles, QC	Canada
YZW	Teslin, YT	Canada
YZX	Greenwood, NS	Canada
YZY	Mackenzie, BC	Canada

Z

Code	Location	Country
ZAA	Alice Arm, BC	Canada
ZAB	Boukadir	Algeria
ZAC	York Landing	Mongolia
ZAD	Zadar	Croatia
ZAE	El Eulma	Algeria
ZAF	Arles/RR Stn	France
ZAG	Zagreb/Pleso	Croatia
ZAH	Zahedan	Iran
ZAI	Embarcacion	Argentina
ZAJ	Zaranj	Afghanistan
ZAK	Chiusa/Klausen/Bus Stn	Italy
ZAL	Valdivia/Pichoy	Chile
ZAM	Zamboanga	Philippines
ZAN	Aghios Nicolaos	Greece
ZAO	Cahors/Laberande	France
ZAP	Appenzell	Switzerland
ZAQ	Nuremberg/HBF Railway Svc	Germany
ZAR	Zaria	Nigeria
ZAS	Arenshausen/RR Stn.	Germany
ZAT	Zhaotong	China
ZAU	Aue/RR Stn.	Germany
ZAV	Aveiro	Portugal
ZAW	Nyikobing Mors/Bus Svc	Denmark
ZAX	Angermuende/RR Stn.	Germany
ZAY	Antwerp/De Keyserlei Bus Stn	Belgium
ZAZ	Zaragoza	Spain
ZBA	Basel/Mulhouse/German Railway Svc	Switzerland
ZBB	Esbjerg/RR Stn.	Denmark
ZBC	Birmingham/Colmore Row Bus Stn	UK
ZBD	Bad Brambach/RR Stn.	Germany
ZBE	Zabreh/Dolni Benesov	Czech Rep
ZBF	Bathurst, NB	Canada
ZBG	Elblag	Poland
ZBH	Severac Le Chateau/RR Stn.	France
ZBI	Berriane	Algeria
ZBJ	Fredericia/RR Stn.	Denmark
ZBK	Zabljak	Yugoslavia
ZBL	Biloela	Australia
ZBM	Bromont, QC	Canada
ZBN	Bozen/Bus Stn	Italy
ZBO	Bowen	Australia
ZBP	Baltimore/Baltimore Rail, MD	USA
ZBQ	Odense/RR Stn.	Denmark
ZBR	Chah-Bahar	Iran
ZBS	Mesa/Bus Svc, AZ	USA
ZBT	Kolding/RR Stn.	Denmark
ZBU	Aarhus/Limousine Svc	Denmark
ZBV	Vail/Eagle/Beaver Creek Van Svc, CO	USA
ZBW	Atibaia	Brazil
ZBX	Szombathely	Hungary
ZBY	Sayaboury	Laos
ZBZ	Bad Saizurigen/RR Stn.	Germany
ZCA	Amsberg	Germany
ZCB	Aschaffenburg	Germany
ZCC	Baden-Baden	Germany
ZCD	Bamberg/Off-line Pt	Germany
ZCE	Berchtesgaden	Germany
ZCF	Bergheim (Cologne)	Germany
ZCG	Bergisch Gladbach	Germany
ZCH	Bergkamen/Off-line Pt	Germany
ZCI	Bocholt	Germany
ZCJ	Bottrop	Germany
ZCK	Bruehl	Germany
ZCL	Zacatecas/La Calera	Mexico
ZCM	Castrop-Rauxel	Germany
ZCN	Celle	Germany
ZCO	Temuco	Chile
ZCP	Coburg	Germany
ZCQ	Curico	Chile
ZCR	Dachau	Germany
ZCS	Darmstact	Germany
ZCT	Delmenhorst	Germany
ZCU	Detmold	Germany
ZCV	Dinslaken	Germany
ZCW	Dormagen	Germany
ZCX	Dorsten	Germany
ZCY	Dueren	Germany
ZCZ	Erlangen	Germany
ZDA	Aarau	Switzerland
ZDB	Adelboden	Switzerland
ZDC	Aiale	Switzerland
ZDD	Arbon	Switzerland
ZDE	Arosa	Switzerland
ZDF	Nablus	West Bank
ZDG	Baden	Switzerland
ZDH	Basel/Mulhouse/SBB Railway Svc	Switzerland
ZDI	Bellinzona	Switzerland
ZDJ	Berne	Switzerland
ZDK	Biel/Bienne	Switzerland
ZDL	Brig	Switzerland
ZDM	Ramallah	West Bank
ZDN	Brno/Bus Svc	Czech Rep
ZDO	Buchs SG	Switzerland
ZDP	Burgdorf	Switzerland
ZDQ	Champery	Switzerland
ZDR	Chateau-d-Oex	Switzerland
ZDS	Chasso	Switzerland
ZDT	Chur	Switzerland
ZDU	Dundee/ScotRail	UK
ZDV	Davos	Switzerland
ZDW	Delemont	Switzerland
ZDX	Dietikon	Switzerland
ZDY	Gaza Strip	Occupied Palestinian Ter
ZDZ	Einsiedeln	Switzerland
ZEA	Eschweiler	Germany
ZEB	Esslingen	Germany
ZEC	Secunda	S. Africa
ZED	Euskirchen	Germany
ZEE	Fulda	Germany
ZEF	Fuerth	Germany
ZEG	Senggo	Indonesia
ZEH	Garbsen	Germany
ZEI	Garmisch-Partenkirchen	Germany
ZEJ	Gelsenkirchen	Germany
ZEK	Gladbeck	Germany
ZEL	Bella Bella, BC	Canada
ZEM	East Main, QC	Canada
ZEN	Zenag	Papua New Guinea
ZEO	Savi Ragha	Pakistan

Code	Location	Country
ZEP	London/Victoria Railway Stn	UK
ZEQ	Dewsbury/Bus Stn	UK
ZER	Zero	India
ZES	Goeppingen	Germany
ZET	Goslar	Germany
ZEU	Goettingen	Germany
ZEV	Grevenbroich	Germany
ZEW	Gummersbach	Germany
ZEX	Guetersloh	Germany
ZEY	Hagen	Germany
ZEZ	Hameln	Germany
ZFA	Faro, YT	Canada
ZFB	Old Ft. Bay, QC	Canada
ZFC	Bradford/Bus Stn	UK
ZFD	Fond Du Lac, SK	Canada
ZFE	Beltsville, MO/Off-line Pt	USA
ZFF	Tulsa/Off-Line Pt (Fedex), OK	USA
ZFG	Sheffield/Bus Svc	UK
ZFH	Milton Keynes/Bus Svc	UK
ZFI	Chesterfield/Bus Svc	UK
ZFJ	Rennes/Gare de Rennes	France
ZFL	South Trout Lake, ON	Canada
ZFM	Ft. Mcpherson, NT	Canada
ZFN	Tulita/Ft. Norman, NT	Canada
ZFO	Franconia, VA	
ZFP	Veszprern	Hungary
ZFQ	Bordeaux/Gare de Bordeaux	France
ZFR	Frankfurt/Oder/RR Stn	Germany
ZFS	Sabre-Tech, FL	USA
ZFT	Ft. Lauderdale/RR Stn., FL	USA
ZFV	Philadelphia/Philadelphia Rail, P	USA
ZFW	Fairview, AB	Canada
ZFZ	Buffalo/Buffalo Depew RR, NY	USA
ZGA	Gera/RR Stn	Germany
ZGB	Nottingham/Bus Svc	UK
ZGC	Lanzhou/Zhongchuan	China
ZGD	Groton/New London Rail, CT USA	
ZGE	Goerlitz/RR Stn	Germany
ZGF	Grand Forks, BC	Canada
ZGG	Glasgow/ScotRail	UK
ZGH	Copenhagen/RR Stn	Denmark
ZGI	Gods River, MB	Canada
ZGJ	Brugge	Belgium
ZGK	Leuven	Belgium
ZGL	South Galway	Australia
ZGM	Ngoma	Zambia
ZGN	Gutenfuerst/RR Stn	Germany
ZGO	Gotha/RR Stn	Germany
ZGP	Mechelen	Belgium
ZGQ	Tournai	Belgium
ZGR	Little Grand Rapids, MB	Canada
ZGS	Gethsemani, QC	Canada
ZGT	Gerstungen/RR Stn	Germany
ZGU	Gaua	Vanuatu
ZGV	Wavre	Belgium
ZGW	Greifswald/RR Stn	Germany
ZGX	Viborg/RR Stn	Denmark
ZHA	Zhanjiang	China
ZHB	Engelberg	Switzerland
ZHC	Philadelphia/N Philadelphia Rail Stn, PA	USA
ZHD	Fluelen	Switzerland
ZHE	Frauenfeld	Switzerland
ZHF	Fribourg	Switzerland
ZHG	Glarus	Switzerland
ZHH	Gossau SG	Switzerland
ZHI	Grenchen	Switzerland
ZHJ	Grindelwald	Switzerland
ZHK	Gstaad	Switzerland
ZHL	Heerbrugg	Switzerland
ZHM	Shamshernagar	Bangladesh
ZHN	Herzogenbuchsee	Switzerland
ZHO	Houston/Bus Stn, BC	Canada
ZHP	High Prairie, AB	Canada
ZHQ	Halberstadt/RR Stn	Germany
ZHR	Kandersteg	Switzerland
ZHS	Klosters	Switzerland

Code	Location	Country
ZHT	Geneva-Cornavin/RR Stn	Switzerland
ZHU	Kreuzlingen	Switzerland
ZHV	La Chaux-de-Fonds	Switzerland
ZHW	Langenthal	Switzerland
ZHX	Tubarao	Brazil
ZHY	Geneva Aeroport/RR Stn	Switzerland
ZHZ	Halle/RR Stn	Germany
ZIA	Trento	Italy
ZIB	Nyborg/RR Stn	Denmark
ZIC	Victoria	Chile
ZID	Aarhus/Bus Svc	Denmark
ZIG	Ziguinchor	Senegal
ZIH	Ixtapa/Zihuatanejo/Int'l	Mexico
ZIJ	Sjaelland/RR Stn	Denmark
ZIM	Odense/Bus Svc	Denmark
ZIN	Interlaken	Switzerland
ZIO	Solingen-Ohligs/RR Stn	Germany
ZIR	Randers/RR Stn	Denmark
ZIS	Zhongshan	China
ZIT	Zittau/RR Stn	Germany
ZIV	Inverness/ScotRail	UK
ZJA	Le Locle	Switzerland
ZJC	Lenzburg	Switzerland
ZJD	Lenzerheide/Lai	Switzerland
ZJG	Jenpeg, MB	Canada
ZJH	Aarhus/RR Stn	Denmark
ZJI	Locarno	Switzerland
ZJL	Lyss	Switzerland
ZJM	Martigny	Switzerland
ZJN	Swan River, MB	Canada
ZJO	San Jose/Bus Svc, CA	USA
ZJP	Montreux	Switzerland
ZJQ	Morges	Switzerland
ZJS	Jena/RR Stn	Germany
ZJU	Olten	Switzerland
ZJV	Pontresina	Switzerland
ZJW	Rapperswil	Switzerland
ZJZ	Rorschach	Switzerland
ZKA	Sargans	Switzerland
ZKB	Kasaba Bay	Zambia
ZKC	Sarnen	Switzerland
ZKD	Moscow/Leningradsky RR Stn	Russia
ZKE	Kaschechewan, ON	Canada
ZKF	St Margrethen	Switzerland
ZKG	Kegaska, QC	Canada
ZKH	St Moritz	Switzerland
ZKI	Saas Fee	Switzerland
ZKJ	Schaffhausen	Switzerland
ZKK	Schwyz	Switzerland
ZKL	Steenkool	Indonesia
ZKM	Sette Cama	Gabon
ZKN	Skive/RR Stn	Denmark
ZKO	Sierre/Siders	Switzerland
ZKP	Kasompe	Zambia
ZKQ	Kotor	Yugoslavia
ZKR	Karlovasi	Greece
ZKS	Solothurn	Switzerland
ZKT	Komotini	Greece
ZKU	Sursee	Switzerland
ZKV	Thalwil	Switzerland
ZKW	Wetzikon	Switzerland
ZKX	Uzwil	Switzerland
ZKY	Verbier	Switzerland
ZKZ	Vevey	Switzerland
ZLA	Villars	Switzerland
ZLB	Visp	Switzerland
ZLC	Waedenswil/Off-line Pt	Switzerland
ZLD	Weinfelden	Switzerland
ZLE	Wengen	Switzerland
ZLF	Wettingen	Switzerland
ZLG	El Gouera	Mauritania
ZLH	Wil	Switzerland
ZLI	Winterthur	Switzerland
ZLJ	Yverdon	Switzerland
ZLK	St Petersburg/Moscovskiy Railway Stn	Russia
ZLL	Zofingen	Switzerland

Code	Location	Country
ZLM	Zug	Switzerland
ZLN	Le Mans/RR Stn	France
ZLO	Manzanillo	Mexico
ZLP	Zurich/HBF Railway Svc	Switzerland
ZLQ	Zurich	Switzerland
ZLR	Linares	Chile
ZLS	Liverpool Street Stn/RR Stn	UK
ZLT	La Tabatiere, QC	Canada
ZLU	Ludwigslust/RR Stn	Germany
ZLX	London/British Rail Terminal	UK
ZLY	Albany/Allbany NY Rail, NY	USA
ZLZ	Leeds/Bus Svc	UK
ZMA	Mansfield/Bus Svc	UK
ZMB	Hamburg/RR Stn	Germany
ZMD	Sena Madureira	Brazil
ZME	Newark/Metropark Rail, NJ	USA
ZMG	Magdeburg/RR Stn	Germany
ZMH	108 Mile Ranch, BC	Canada
ZMI	Naples/Mergellina Railway Svc	Italy
ZML	Milwaukee/Rail Svc., WI	USA
ZMM	Zamora	Mexico
ZMO	Modena/Bus Stn	Italy
ZMP	Manchester/Manchester Bus Stn	UK
ZMR	Meran/Bus Stn	Italy
ZMS	Florence/S.M. Novella Rail.Svc	Italy
ZMT	Masset, BC	Canada
ZMU	Munich/HBF Railway Svc	Germany
ZMV	Melville, NY/Off-line Pt	USA
ZNA	Nanaimo/Harbour, BC	Canada
ZNB	Hamm	Germany
ZNC	Nyac, AK	USA
ZND	Zinder	Niger
ZNE	Newman	Australia
ZNF	Hanau	Germany
ZNG	Negginan, MB	Canada
ZNH	Hettlingen	Germany
ZNI	Heidenheim	Germany
ZNJ	Heilbronn	Germany
ZNK	Herford	Germany
ZNL	Herne	Germany
ZNM	Herten	Germany
ZNN	Hilden	Germany
ZNO	Hildesheim	Germany
ZNP	Huerth	Germany
ZNQ	Ingolstadt	Germany
ZNR	Iserlohn	Germany
ZNS	Kempten	Germany
ZNT	Kerpen	Germany
ZNU	Namu, BC	Canada
ZNV	Koblenz	Germany
ZNW	Limburg	Germany
ZNX	Lagenfeld	Germany
ZNY	Langenhagen	Germany
ZNZ	Zanzibar/Kisauni	Tanzania
ZOA	Level	Germany
ZOB	Lippstadt	Germany
ZOC	Luedenscheid	Germany
ZOD	Ludwigsburg	Germany
ZOE	Ludwigshafen	Germany
ZOF	Ocean Falls, BC	Canada
ZOG	Lueneburg/RR Stn	Germany
ZOH	Luenen	Germany
ZOI	Marburg An Der Lahn	Germany
ZOJ	Marl	Germany
ZOK	Meerbusch	Germany
ZOL	Menden	Germany
ZOM	Minden	Germany
ZON	Moers	Germany
ZOO	Muelhefm An Der Ruhr	Germany
ZOP	Neunkirchen/Ott^line Pt	Germany
ZOQ	Neuss	Germany
ZOR	Neustadt-Weinstrasse	Germany
ZOS	Osorno/Canal Balo	Chile
ZOT	Neu-Ulm	Germany
ZOU	Neuwied	Germany
ZOV	Norderstedt	Germany

AIRPORTS

ZOW . Nordhorn . . . . Germany	ZRU . . Boston/Boston RT128 Rail, MA	ZUS. . Dutch Rail Zone 20/Rail Svc
ZOX . . Oberammergau. . . . . . . Germany	. . . . USA	. . . . Netherlands
ZOY . . Oberhausen . . . . Germany	ZRV . . Providence/Providence Rail, RI	ZUT. . Dutch Rail Zone 21/Rail Svc
ZOZ . . Offerfbach . . . . Germany	. . . . USA	. . . . Netherlands
ZPA . . Offenburg. . . . . Germany	ZRW . .Rastatt/Bus Svc . . . . . . .Germany	ZUU . Dutch Rail Zone 22/Rail Svc
ZPB . . Sachigo Lake, ON . . . . . . Canada	ZRX . . Riesa/RR Stn. . . . . .Germany	. . . . Netherlands
ZPC . . Pucon . . . . .Chile	ZRZ . .Washington/New Carrolton RR,	ZUV . . Dutch Rail Zone 23/Rail Svc
ZPD . . Oldenburg . . . . Germany	DC . . . . USA	. . . . Netherlands
ZPE . . Osnabrueck/RR Stn. . . . Germany	ZSA . .San Salvador . . . . Bahamas	ZUW . Dutch Rail Zone 24/Rail Svc
ZPF . . Passau . . . . Germany	ZSB . .Salzburg/German Railway Svc	. . . . Netherlands
ZPG . . Peine . . . . Germany	. . . . Austria	ZUX . . Dutch Rail Zone 25/Rail Svc
ZPH . . Zephyrhills, FL . . . . USA	ZSC . .Schoena/RR Stn. . . . . . .Germany	. . . . Netherlands
ZPI . . . Pirmasens . . . . Germany	ZSD . .Schwanheide/RR Stn. . .Germany	ZUY . . Dutch Rail Zone 26/Rail Svc
ZPJ . . Ratingen . . . . Germany	ZSE . .St Pierre dela Reunion .Reunion Is	. . . . Netherlands
ZPK . . Ravensburg . . . . Germany	ZSF . .Springfield, MA RR . . . . . . .USA	ZUZ. . Dutch Rail Zone 27/Rail Svc
ZPL . . Recklinghausen. . . . . . . Germany	ZSG . .Sonneberg/RR Stn. . . . .Germany	. . . . Netherlands
ZPM . . Regensburg/RR Stn. . . . Germany	ZSH . .Santa Fe/Bus Stn, NM . . . . .USA	ZVA . . Miandrivazo. . . . . Madagascar
ZPN . . Remscheid/Offline Pt . . Germany	ZSI . . .Sassnitz/RR Stn. . . . . . .Germany	ZVE . . New Haven/New Haven Rail, CT
ZPO . . Pine House, SK . . . . Canada	ZSJ . . .Sandy Lake, ON. . . . . . . .Canada	. . . . USA
ZPP . . Reutlingen . . . . Germany	ZSK . .Pasewalk/RR Stn. . . . . .Germany	ZVG . . Springvale . . . . .Australia
ZPQ . . Rheine/Bentlage . . . . . . Germany	ZSL . .Sligo/Bus Stn . . . . Ireland	ZVH. . . Veldhoven/RR Stn. . . .Netherlands
ZPR . . Rosenheim . . . . Germany	ZSM . .Santa Clara/Bus Svc, CA . . .USA	ZVK . . Savannakhet . . . . Laos
ZPS . . Ruesselsheim . . . . Germany	ZSN . .Stendal/RR Stn. . . . . . . .Germany	ZVL . . Dutch Rail Zone 01/Rail Svc
ZPT . . Saarlouis. . . . . Germany	ZSO . .Suhl/RR Stn. . . . . .Germany	. . . . Netherlands
ZPU . . Salzgitter. . . . . Germany	ZSP . .St Paul, QC . . . . .Canada	ZVM . Hanover/Messe-BF Railway Svc
ZPV . . Schwaebisch Gmuend/Off-line Pt	ZSQ . .Salzwedel/RR Stn. . . . . .Germany	. . . . Germany
. . . . Germany	ZSR . .Schwerin/RR Stn. . . . . .Germany	ZVN. . Dutch Rail Zone 03/Rail Svc
ZPW . . Schweinfurt . . . . Germany	ZSS . .Sassandra. . . . . .Côte D'Ivoire	. . . . Netherlands
ZPX . . Schwerte . . . . Germany	ZST . .Stewart, BC. . . . . .Canada	ZVO. . Dutch Rail Zone 04/Rail Svc
ZPY . . Siegburg. . . . . Germany	ZSU . .Dessau/RR Stn. . . . . . . .Germany	. . . . Netherlands
ZPZ . . Sindelfingen/Off-line Pt . Germany	ZSV . .St Louis/Rail Svc., MO . . . . .USA	ZVP . . Dutch Rail Zone 05/Rail Svc
ZQA . . Singen . . . . Germany	ZSW . .Prince Rupert/SealCove, BC	. . . . Netherlands
ZQB . . Solingen . . . . Germany	. . . . Canada	ZVQ . . Dutch Rail Zone 06/Rail Svc
ZQC . . Speyer . . . . Germany	ZSX . .Straisund/RR Stn. . . . . . .Germany	. . . . Netherlands
ZQD . . Stade . . . . Germany	ZSY . .Scottsdale/Bus Svc, AZ. . . . .USA	ZVR . . Hanover/HBF Railway Svc
ZQE . . Stolberg . . . . Germany	ZSZ . .Swakopmund/RR Stn. . . Namibia	. . . . Germany
ZQF . . Trier . . . . Germany	ZTA. .Tureira . . . . .F. Polynesia	ZVS . . Dutch Rail Zone 08/Rail Svc
ZQG . . Troisdorf . . . . Germany	ZTB . .Tete-a-La Baleine, QC . . .Canada	. . . . Netherlands
ZQH . . Tuebingen . . . . Germany	ZTC . . Turin/Bus Svc . . . . Italy	ZVT . . Dutch Rail Zone 09/Rail Svc
ZQI . . . Unna . . . . Germany	ZTD . .Schenectady/Schenectady Rail,	. . . . Netherlands
ZQJ . . Velbert . . . . Germany	NY . . . . USA	ZVU . . Dutch Rail Zone 10/Rail Svc
ZQK . . Viersen . . . . Germany	ZTE . . Rochester/Rochester NY Rail	. . . . Netherlands
ZQL . . Villingen-Schwenningen Germany	. . . . USA	ZVV . . Dutch Rail Zone 11/Rail Svc
ZQM . . Voelklingen. . . . . Germany	ZTF. . .Westchester County/	. . . . Netherlands
ZQN . . Queenstown/Frankton	Stamford RR Stn., NY . . . . . .USA	ZVW . . Dutch Rail Zone 12/Rail Svc
. . . . New Zealand	ZTG . .Aalborg/RR Stn. . . . . . . .Denmark	. . . . Netherlands
ZQO . . Waiblingen . . . . .Germany	ZTH . .Zakinthos Is . . . . Greece	ZVX . . Dutch Rail Zone 13/Rail Svc
ZQP . . Wesel . . . . Germany	ZTJ . .Princeton/Princeton JT Rail, NJ	. . . . Netherlands
ZQQ . . Wetzlar . . . . Germany	. . . . USA	ZVY . . Dutch Rail Zone 14/Rail Svc
ZQR . . Witten . . . . Germany	ZTK . .Thun . . . . .Switzerland	. . . . Netherlands
ZQS . . Queen Charlotte Is, BC . . Canada	ZTL . .Telluride/Bus Stn, CO . . . . .USA	ZVZ . . Dutch Rail Zone 15/Rail Svc
ZQT . . Wolfenbuettel . . . . Germany	ZTM . .Shamattawa, MB . . . . . . .Canada	. . . . Netherlands
ZQU . . Wolfsburg/Off-line Pt . . . Germany	ZTN . .Philadelphia/Trenton RR Stn., PA	ZWA . Andapa . . . . Madagascar
ZQV . . Worms . . . . Germany	. . . . USA	ZWB . Hampton/Williamsburg Rail, VA
ZQW . Zweibruecken . . . . Germany	ZTO . .Boston/Boston South Rail, MA	. . . . USA
ZQX . . Nias. . . . . .Indonesia	. . . . USA	ZWD . Warnemuende/RR Stn. . . . Germany
ZRA . . Atlantic City/Rail Svc., NJ . . . USA	ZTP . .Itapetininga . . . . Brazil	ZWG . Weingarten . . . . Germany
ZRB . . Frankfurt/HBF Railway Svc	ZTR . .Zhitomir . . . . .Ukraine	ZWH . Windhoek/RR Stn. . . . . . . Namibia
. . . . Germany	ZTS . .Tahsis, BC. . . . . .Canada	ZWI . . Wilmington/Wilmington Rail, DE
ZRC . . San Pedro de Alcantara/Bus Stn	ZTT. . .Cottbus/RR Stn. . . . . . . .Germany	. . . . USA
. . . . Spain	ZTW . .Tsuen Wan/RR Stn. . .Hong Kong	ZWK . Suwalki. . . . . Poland
ZRD . . Richmond/Richmond VA Rail, VA	ZTY . . Boston/BKBAY Rail, MA . . . .USA	ZWL . Wollaston Lake, SK. . . . . Canada
. . . . USA	ZTZ . .Chemnitz/RR Stn. . . . . . .Germany	ZWM . Wismar/RR Stn. . . . . Germany
ZRE . . Rethymno. . . . . .Greece	ZUA . . Utica/Utica NY Rail. . . . . USA	ZWN . Wittenberg/RR Stn. . . . . Germany
ZRF . . Rockford/Park & Ride Bus Svc., IL	ZUC . . Ignace, ON . . . . .Canada	ZWO . Dutch Rail Zone 02/Rail Svc
. . . . USA	ZUD . .Ancud . . . . Chile	. . . . Netherlands
ZRG . . Bratislava/Bus Svc . . . . . Slovakia	ZUE . . Zuenoula . . . . .Côte D'Ivoire	ZWP . West Palm Beach/RR Stn., FL
ZRH . . Zurich . . . . Switzerland	ZUG . .Harrisburg/Rail, PA. . . . . . . .USA	. . . . USA
ZRI . . . Serui/Yendosa . . . . . . .Indonesia	ZUH . .Zhuhai/Zhuhai Arpt . . . . . .China	ZWQ . Dutch Rail Zone 07/Rail Svc
ZRJ . . Round Lake, ON . . . . . . Canada	ZUL . .Zilfi. . . . . .Saudi Arabia	. . . . Netherlands
ZRK . . Rockford/Van Galder Bus	ZUM . .Churchill Falls, NF . . . . . .Canada	ZWS . Stuttgart/RR Stn. . . . . . . Germany
Terminal, IL. . . . . USA	ZUN . .Chicago/Union Railway Svc, IL	ZWT . Wittenberg/RR Stn. . . . . Germany
ZRL . . Lancaster/Lancaster PA RR Stn.	. . . . USA	ZWU . Washington/Washington DC
. . . . USA	ZUO . . Dutch Rail Zone 16/Rail Svc	RR Stn. . . . . USA
ZRM. . Sarmi . . . . .Indonesia	. . . . Netherlands	ZWW. Hampton/Newport News Rail,
ZRN . . Nyon. . . . . Switzerland	ZUP . .Dutch Rail Zone 17/Rail Svc	VA. . . . . USA
ZRO . . Reggio Nell Emilia/Bus Svc . .Italy	. . . . Netherlands	ZWX . Dutch Rail Zone 28/Rail Svc
ZRP . . Newark/Newark NJ Rail . . . .USA	ZUQ . .Dutch Rail Zone 18/Rail Svc	. . . . Netherlands
ZRS . . Zurs/Lech/Flexenpass HP	. . . . Netherlands	ZWY . Dutch Rail Zone 29/Rail Svc
. . . . Austria	ZUR . .Dutch Rail Zone 19/Rail Svc	. . . . Netherlands
ZRT . . Hartford/Hartford CT Rail . . . USA	. . . . Netherlands	

A I R P O R T S

ZWZ . . Dutch Rail Zone 30/Rail Svc
. . . . Netherlands
ZXA . . Aberdeen/ScotRail . . . . UK
ZXB . . Jan Mayen
. . . . Svalbard and Jan Mayen Is
ZXC . . Bangsiund . . . . Norway
ZXD . . Vikna . . . . Norway
ZXE . . Edinburgh/ScotRail . . . . UK
ZXF . . Roervik . . . . Norway
ZXG . . Gravik . . . . Norway
ZXH . . Soerfjord . . . . Norway
ZXI . . Roeddey . . . . Norway
ZXJ . . Fore . . . . Norway
ZXK . . Baasmo . . . . Norway
ZXL . . Skjerstad . . . . Norway
ZXM . . Rognan . . . . Norway
ZXN . . Leka . . . . Norway
ZXO . . Fauske . . . . Norway
ZXP . . Perth/ScotRail . . . . UK
ZXQ . . Solstad . . . . Norway

ZXR . . Hemnes . . . . Norway
ZXS . . Buffalo/Exchange St Railway
Svc., NY . . . . USA
ZYA . . Amsterdam/RR Stn. . Netherlands
ZYC . . Gizycio . . . . Poland
ZYE . . Eindhoven/RR Stn. . . Netherlands
ZYH . . The Hague/Holland Spoor
RR Stn. . . . . Netherlands
ZYI . . Zunyi . . . . China
ZYL . . Syllnet/Civil . . . . Bangladesh
ZYM . . Arnhem/RR Stn. . . . . Netherlands
ZYO . . Roosendaal/RR Stn. . Netherlands
ZYP . . New York/Penn Rail, NY . . . . USA
ZYQ . . Syracuse/NY Rail, NY . . . . . USA
ZYR . . Brussels/Midi Railway Stn
. . . . Belgium
ZYT . . Maastricht/RR Stn. . . Netherlands
ZYU . . Utrecht/RR Stn . . . . . . Netherlands
ZYZ . . Antwerp . . . . Belgium
ZZA . . Azzazga . . . . Algeria

ZZB . . Barka . . . . Algeria
ZZC . . Cherchell . . . . Algeria
ZZD . . Dra El Mizan . . . . Algeria
ZZE . . Uzice . . . . Yugoslavia
ZZF . . Mystery Flight . . . . Australia
ZZH . . Cranzahl/RR Stn. . . . . . Germany
ZZI . . Elite Mystery Night . . . . Australia
ZZJ . . Mystery Night . . . . Australia
ZZK . . Khemis Miliana . . . . Algeria
ZZL . . Larba Nath Iraten . . . . Algeria
ZZM . . Borcj Menatiel . . . . Algeria
ZZP . . Pozarevac . . . . Yugoslavia
ZZQ . . Cheung Sha Wan . . . Hong Kong
ZZR . . Kherrata . . . . Algeria
ZZS . . M'Sila . . . . Algeria
ZZT . . Taher . . . . Algeria
ZZU . . Mzuzu . . . . Malawi
ZZV . . Zanesville, OH . . . . USA

World Airports by Airport

List 2 of 2:
Airport/Location...Country...IATA Code

Notes

1. The following is a list of more than 10,000 airports and locations worldwide and their three-letter IATA (International Air Transport Association) codes.
2. IATA codes are primarily used to identify airports, but are also used to identify transshipment, pick-up and delivery locations; cities; bus and train stations; as well as harbors and ports.
3. Approximately ten percent of these locations are major international airports. The balance are municipal and remote airfields and other locations.
4. Locations in the U.S., Canada, and Australia generally have a two-letter state or province notation (e.g., CA for California).
5. Global location codes are added, reassigned, or deleted at the rate of approximately ten to twelve per month. This list is current as of January 2002.
6. For the most up-to-date information, refer to www.iata.org.

Abbreviations

AAF	Army Air Field
AFB	Air Force Base
AFS	Air Force Station
AHP	Army Heliport
Arpt	Airport
CGS	Coast Guard Station
Cnty	County
Fld	Field
HP	Heliport
HVC	Hovercraft Terminal
Int'l	International
Is	Island
Mt	Mount
NAS	Naval Air Station
PT	Point
RR Stn.	Railway Station/Service
RAF	Royal Air Force
SPB	Sea Plane Base
Stn	Station
Svc	Service
USAF	United States Air Force

A

Albina	Suriname	ABN
108 Mile Ranch, BC	Canada	ZMH
Aachen/Merzbruck	Germany	AAH
Aalbenraa/Bus Svc	Denmark	XNR
Aalborg/Civil/Military	Denmark	AAL
Aalborg/RR Stn.	Denmark	ZTG
Aalesund/Vigra	Norway	AES
Aalsmeer	Netherlands	QFA
Aappilattoq	Greenland	QUV
Aarau	Switzerland	ZDA
Aarhus/Bus Svc	Denmark	ZID
Aarhus/Limousine Svc	Denmark	ZBU
Aarhus/RR Stn.	Denmark	ZJH
Aarhus/Tirstrup	Denmark	AAR
Aasiaat	Greenland	JEG
Abadan	Iran	ABD
Abaiang	Kiribati	ABF
Abakan	Russia	ABA
Abau	Papua New Guinea	ABW
Abbeville	France	XAB
Abbotsford, BC	Canada	YXX
Abbottabad	Pakistan	AAW
Abbse	Yemen	EAB
Abecher	Chad	AEH
Abengourou	Côte D'Ivoire	OGO
Abeokuta	Nigeria	QAT
Aberdeen Municipal, SD	USA	ABR
Aberdeen, MD	USA	APG
Aberdeen/Dyce	UK	ABZ
Aberdeen/ScotRail	UK	ZXA
Abernama Atoll	Kiribati	AEA
Abidjan	Côte D'Ivoire	ABJ
Abilene Municipal, TX	USA	ABI
Abilene/Dyess/AFB, TX	USA	DYS
Abingdon	Australia	ABG
Abingdon/RAF	UK	ABB
Abingdon/Virginia Highlands, VA	USA	VJI
Ablitia	Saudi Arabia	AHB
Aboisso	Côte D'Ivoire	ABO
Abou Deia	Chad	AOD
Abreojos	Mexico	AJS
Abu Dhabi Int'l	UAE	AUH
Abu Dhabi/Al Dhafra Military Arpt	UAE	DHF
Abu Dhalbi/Bateen	UAE	AZI
Abu Rudeis	Egypt	AUE
Abu Simbel	Egypt	ABS
Abuja Int'l	Nigeria	ABV
Acandi	Colombia	ACD
Acapulco/G. Alvarez Int'l	Mexico	ACA
Acaricuara	Colombia	ARF
Acarigua	Venezuela	AGV
ACARS	n/a	DDL
Accra/Kotoka	Ghana	ACC
Achinsk	Russia	ACS
Achutupo	Panama	ACU
Ad-Dabbah	Sudan	AAD
Ada, OK	USA	ADT
Adak Is/NAS, AK	USA	ADK
Adana/Sakirpasa	Turkey	ADA
Addis Ababa/Bole	Ethiopia	ADD
Adelaide	Australia	ADL

Adelboden	Switzerland	ZDB
Aden Int'l	Yemen	ADE
Adiyaman/Incirlik	Turkey	ADF
Adler/Sochi	Russia	AER
Adrar	Algeria	AZR
Adrian/Lenawee County, MI	USA	ADG
Aek Godang	Indonesia	AEG
Afore	Papua New Guinea	AFR
Afton Downs	Australia	AWN
Afton/Municipal, WY	USA	AFO
Afutara/Atutara	Solomon Is	AFT
Afyon	Turkey	AFY
Agades/Manu Dayak	Niger	AJY
Agadir/Agadir Almassira	Morocco	AGA
Agartala/Singerbhil	India	IXA
Agatti Is	India	AGX
Agaun	Papua New Guinea	AUP
Agde/Off-line Pt	France	XAG
Agedabia	Libya	QGG
Agen/La Garenne	France	AGF
Aggeneys	S. Africa	AGZ
Aghios Nicolaos	Greece	ZAN
Agnew	Australia	AGW
Agra/Kheria	India	AGR
Agri/Agri	Turkey	AJI
Agrigento	Italy	QAO
Agrinion	Greece	AGQ
Aguaclara	Colombia	ACL
Aguadilla/Borinquen	Puerto Rico	BQN
Aguascalientes	Mexico	AGU
Aguni	Japan	AGJ
Ahe	F. Polynesia	AHE
Ahmadabad	India	AMD
Ahuas	Honduras	AHS
Ahwaz	Iran	AWZ
Ai-Ais	Namibia	AIW
Aiale	Switzerland	ZDC
Aiamosa, CO	USA	ALS
Aidan	Russia	ADH
Aljouf	Yemen	AJO
Aiken/Municipal, SC	USA	AIK
Ailigandi	Panama	AIL
Ailinglapalap Is	Marshall Is	AIP
Ailuk Is	Marshall Is	AIM
Aime	France	QAI
Ain Beida	Algeria	QBP
Ain Mlila	Algeria	QIM
Ain Temouchent	Algeria	QIO
Ainsworth, NE	USA	ANW
Aiome	Papua New Guinea	AIE
Aioun El Atrouss	Mauritania	AEO
Airlie Beach/Whitsunday Airstrip	Australia	WSY
Airok	Marshall Is	AIC
Aishaiton	Guyana	AHL
Aitape/Airstrip	Papua New Guinea	ATP
Aitape/Tadji	Papua New Guinea	TAJ
Aitutaki	Cook Is	AIT
Aix Les Bains	France	XAI
Aix-en-Provence	France	QXB
Aiyura	Papua New Guinea	AYU
Aizawi	India	AJL
Ajaccio/Campo Dell Oro	France	AJA
Ajaokuta	Nigeria	QJK
Ajman City	UAE	QAJ
Akhiok, AK	USA	AKK

Column 1	Column 2	Column 3
Akiachak/SPB, AK . . . . .USA . . . KKI	**Algiers-Houari Boumediene**	Amery/Municipal, WI . . . . . . USA . . AHH
Akiak, AK . . . . .USA . . . AKI	. . . . Algeria . . ALG	Ames, IA . . . . USA . .AMW
Akieni . . . . .Gabon . . AKE	Algona, IA. . . . . USA . .AXG	Amherst/RR Stn., NS . . . Canada. . .XZK
Akioujt . . . . .Mauritania . . AJJ	Alicante . . . . Spain . . ALC	Amiens/Glisy . . . . France. . QAM
Akita . . . . Japan . . AXT	Alice Arm, BC . . . . Canada . . ZAA	Amityville/Zahns, NY . . . . . USA. . . AYZ
Aklavik, NT . . . . .Canada . . LAK	Alice Springs . . . . .Australia . . ASP	Amman/Marka (Civil) . . . Jordan. . .ADJ
Akola . . . . India . . AKD	Alice, TX . . . . USA . . ALI	Amman/Queen Alia Int'l. . . Jordan. .AMM
Akron, CO . . . . USA . .AKO	Aliceville, AL . . . . USA . . AIV	Ammaroo . . . . .Australia. . AMX
Akron, OH . . . . .USA . . CAK	Alidays . . . . S. Africa . .ADY	Ammassivik . . . . .Greenland. .QUW
Akron/Fulton Int'l, OH . . . . .USA . . AKC	Alitak/SPB, AK . . . . USA . . ALZ	Amook, AK . . . . USA. . . AOS
Akrotiri . . . . Cyprus . . AKT	Allahabad/Bamrauli . . . . . India . . .IXD	Amos, QC . . . . Canada. . .YEY
Aksu . . . . .China . . AKU	Allakaket, AK. . . . . USA . . AET	Ampanihy . . . . Madagascar. . AMP
Aktau . . . . .Kazakstan . . SCO	Allentown/Lehigh Int'l, PA . . USA . . ABE	Amritsar/Raja Sansi. . . . . . .India. . .ATQ
Aktyubinsk . . . . .Kazakstan . . AKX	Alliance, NE . . . . USA . . AIA	Amsberg . . . . Germany. . ZCA
Akulivik, QC . . . . .Canada . . AKV	Alluitsup Paa . . . . Greenland . . LLU	Amsterdam/RR Stn. Netherlands. . .ZYA
Akunnaaq . . . . Greenland . .QCU	Alluitsup Paa . . . . Greenland . . QFJ	**Amsterdam**/Schiphol
Akure . . . . Nigeria . . AKR	**Alma**, QC . . . . Canada . . YTF	. . . . Netherlands. . AMS
Akureyri . . . . Iceland . . AEY	**Alma**/Gratiot ComMunicipality,	Anaa . . . . .F. Polynesia. . AAA
Akutan, AK . . . . .USA . .KQA	MI . . . . USA . . AMN	Anaapa . . . . Russia. . AAQ
Al Ain Int'l . . . . .UAE . . AAN	Almaty . . . . Kazakstan . . ALA	Anaco . . . . .Venezuela. . AAO
Al Arish . . . . .Egypt . . AAC	Almelo/RR . . . . .Netherlands . .QYL	Anacortes, WA . . . . USA. . .OTS
Al Ghayclah . . . . .Yemen . . AAY	Almenara . . . . .Brazil . .AMJ	Anacostia/USN HP, DC . . . USA. . NDV
Al Hoceima . . . . .Morocco . .AHU	Almeria . . . . Spain . . .LEI	Anadyr . . . . Russia. . DYR
Al-Baha/Al-Aqiq . . Saudi Arabia . . ABT	Along . . . . India . . .IXV	Anaheim, CA . . . . USA. . ANA
Alaa . . . . Nigeria . . QAX	Alor Is . . . . Indonesia . .ARD	Anahim Lake, BC . . . Canada. . .YAA
Alabaster, Shelby County, AL	**Alotau**/Gurney	Anaktuvuk, AK . . . . USA. . .AKP
. . . . .USA . . .EET	. . . . Papua New Guinea . GUR	Analalava . . . . Madagascar. . .HVA
Alagoinhas . . . . .Brazil . .QGS	Alowe . . . . Gabon . .AWE	Anand . . . . India. . QNB
Alah. . . . . Philippines . .AAV	Alpe D Huez . . . . France . . AHZ	Anapolis . . . . Brazil. . .APS
Alakanuk, AK . . . . .USA . . AUK	Alpena, MI . . . . USA . .APN	Anchorage Int'l, AK . . . . . . USA. . ANC
Alameda/NAS, CA . . . . . . .USA . . NGZ	Alpha . . . . .Australia . .ABH	Anchorage, AK . . . . USA. . .MRI
Alamogordo, NM. . . . . . . .USA . . ALM	Alpine, TX. . . . . USA . . ALE	**Anchorage**/Elmendorf/AFB, AK
Alamos . . . . .Mexico . . XAL	Alroy Downs . . . . .Australia . . AYD	. . . . USA. . .EDF
Alba Iufla . . . . .Romania . . QAY	Alta Floresta . . . . .Brazil . . AFL	Ancona/Falconara . . . . .Italy. . .AOI
Albany . . . . .Australia . . ALH	Alta Lake, BC . . . . Canada . . YAE	Ancud . . . . .Chile. . ZUD
Albany Nexrad, NY . . . . . .USA . . ENX	Alta/Lufthavn. . . . . .Norway . . ALF	Andahuaylas . . . . Peru. . ANS
Albany, GA . . . . .USA . . ABY	Altai . . . . Mongolia . . LTI	Andamooka . . . . .Australia. . ADO
Albany, NY . . . . .USA . . ALB	Altamira . . . . .Brazil . . ATM	Andapa . . . . Madagascar. . ZWA
Albany, OR . . . . .USA . . CVO	Altay . . . . China . . AAT	Andenes . . . . .Norway. . ANX
Albany/Allbany NY Rail, NY .USA . . .ZLY	Altenburg. . . . . Germany . . ADC	Anderson, SC . . . . USA. . AND
Albany/Bus Svc, NY . . . . . .USA . . QWY	Altenirhein . . . . Switzerland . . ACH	Anderson/Municipal, IN . . . USA. . AID
Albany/NAS, GA . . . . .USA . . NAB	Alto Molocue . . . .Mozambique . . AME	Andes . . . . .Colombia. . ADN
Albenga . . . . Italy . . .ALL	Alto Palena . . . . .Chile . . WAP	Andizhan . . . . Uzbekistan. . AZN
Albert Lea, MN . . . . .USA . . AEL	Alto Parnatiba . . . . .Brazil . . APY	Andong . . . . .S. Korea. . QDY
Alberwille . . . . .France . . XAV	Alto Rio Senguerr . . Argentina . .ARR	Andorra La Vella . . . . . . Andorra. . ALV
Albi/Le Sequestre . . . . . .France . . LBI	Alton, IL . . . . USA . . ALN	Andover . . . . UK. . ADV
Albuq . . . . .Yemen . . BUK	Altoona, PA . . . . USA . . AOO	Andradas . . . . .Brazil. . QRD
Albuquerque Int'l, NM . . .USA . . ABQ	Altus/AFB, OK . . . . USA . . LTS	Andrews, SC . . . . USA. . ADR
Albury . . . . .Australia . . ABX	Altus/Municipal, OK . . . . . . USA . . AXS	Andrews/NAF, MD . . . . .USA. . .NSF
Alcantara . . . . .Brazil . .QAH	Alula . . . . Somalia . . ALU	Andriamena . . . . Madagascar. . WAD
Alconbury/RAF. . . . . .UK . . AYH	Alyeska, AK . . . . USA . .AQY	Andros Town . . . . .Bahamas. . ASD
Alderney . . . . .UK . . .ACI	Alzey . . . . Germany . . XZY	Andulo. . . . . Angola. .ANL
Aldershot/RR Stn., ON .Canada . . .XLY	Am Timan . . . . .Chad . .AMC	Anegada . . . . . . Virgin Is (British). . NGD
Aleg. . . . . .Mauritania . . LEG	Ama . . . . . . Papua New Guinea . .AMF	Aneityum . . . . .Vanuatu. . AUY
Alegrete/Federal . . . . . . .Brazil . . ALQ	Amahai . . . . Indonesia . . AHI	Angel Fire, NM . . . . USA. . .AXX
Aleknagik, AK. . . . . .USA . . WKK	Amalfi . . . . Colombia . .AFI	Angermuende/RR Stn.Germany. . .ZAX
Alencon . . . . .France . . XAN	Amami O Shima . . . . . .Japan . . ASJ	Angers/Marce. . . . . France. . ANE
Aleneva, AK. . . . . .USA . . AED	Amanab . . Papua New Guinea . . AMU	Angers/RR . . . . France. . QXG
Alenquer . . . . .Brazil . .ALT	Amarillo, TX . . . . USA . . AMA	Anggi . . . . Indonesia. . AGD
Aleppo/Nejrab. . . . . Syria . . ALP	Amata . . . . .Australia . . AMT	Angling Lake, ON . . . Canada. . .YAX
Alert Bay, BC . . . . .Canada . .YAL	**Amazon Bay**Papua New Guinea . . AZB	Angoche . . . . .Mozambique. . ANO
Alert, NU . . . . .Canada . . YLT	Ambanja . . . . Madagascar . .IVA	Angola, IN . . . . USA. . ANQ
Alerta . . . . .Peru . . ALD	Ambato/Chachoan . . . . Ecuador . . ATF	Angoon, AK . . . . USA. . AGN
Ales . . . . .France . . XAS	Ambatolahy . . . . . . Madagascar . . AHY	Angorarn . . Papua New Guinea. . AGG
Alessandria . . . . .Italy . . QAL	Ambatomainty . . . . . Madagascar . . AMY	Angouleme . . . . France. . ANG
Alexander Bay/Koftdoorn	Ambatondrazalka Madagascar . . WAM	Anguganak Papua New Guinea. . AKG
. . . . S. Africa . .ALJ	Ambilobe . . . . Madagascar . . AMB	Anguilla/Rollang Fld, MS . . USA. . .RFK
Alexander City, AL . . . . . .USA . . ALX	Ambler, AK. . . . . USA . . ABL	Anguilla/Wallblake . . . . . Anguilla. . .AXA
Alexandra . . . . New Zealand . . ALR	Amboin . . . . Papua New Guinea . AMG	Angus Downs . . . . .Australia. . ANZ
Alexandria . . . . Australia . . AXL	Amboise . . . . France . . XAM	Aniak, AK . . . . USA. . . ANI
Alexandria Bay, NY . . . . . .USA . . AXB	Ambon/Pattimura . . . . . Indonesia . . AMQ	Anica/Chacalluta . . . . .Chile. . . ARI
Alexandria, LA . . . . .USA . . AEX	Amboseli . . . . .Kenya . . ASV	Anita Bay, AK . . . . USA. . . AIB
Alexandria, LA . . . . .USA . . .ESF	Ambriz . . . . Andorra . . AZZ	Aniwa . . . . .Vanuatu. . AWD
Alexandria, MN . . . . .USA . . AXN	Ambunti . . . Papua New Guinea . . AUJ	Anjouan/Ouant. . . . . Comoros. . .AJN
Alexandria/Borg El Arab .Egypt . . HBE	Amchitka, AK . . . . USA . . AHT	Ankang . . . . .China. . AKA
Alexandria/Nouzha . . . . . .Egypt . . ALY	Amderma . . . . Russia . . AMV	Ankara/Esenboga . . . . . . Turkey. . .ESB
Alexandria/RR Stn., ON.Canada . .XFS	Amedee/AAF, CA . . . . USA . . AHC	Ankara/Etimesgut. . . . . . . Turkey. . ANK
Alexandroupolis-Demokritos . .	American River . . . . . .Australia . . RCN	Ankavandra . . . . Madagascar. . JVA
. . . . .Greece . . AXD	Americana . . . . .Brazil . . QWJ	Ankazoabo . . . . Madagascar. . WAK
Alfenas. . . . . .Brazil . . QXW	Amersfoort/RR . . . .Netherlands . . QYM	Anklam . . . . Germany. . QKQ
Alghero . . . . .Italy . . AHO		Ann Arbor, MI . . . . USA. . ARB

Annaba	Algeria	AAE
Annanberg	Papua New Guinea	AOB
Annapolis/Lee, MD	USA	ANP
Annarillo/Tradewind, TX	USA	TDW
Annat	Guyana	NAI
Annecy	France	NCY
Annemasse	France	QNJ
Annette Is, AK	USA	ANN
Anniston, AL	USA	ANB
Anniston/Ft Mcclellan Bus Trml, AL		
	USA	QAW
Anniston/Reilly AHP, AL	USA	RLI
Anqing	China	AQG
Ansan	Kuwait	XNS
Ansbach/Katterbach	Germany	QOB
Anshan	China	AOG
Anta	Peru	ATA
Antalaha/Antsirabato		
	Madagascar	ANM
Antalya	Turkey	AYT
Antananarivo	Madagascar	TNR
Anthony Lagoon	Australia	AYL
Anthony, KS	USA	ANY
Antibes	France	XAT
Antlers, OK	USA	ATE
Antofagasta/Cerro Moreno Chile	ANF
Antsalova	Madagascar	WAQ
Antsirabe	Madagascar	ATJ
Antsiranana/Arrachart		
	Madagascar	DIE
Antsohihy	Madagascar	WAI
Antwerp	Belgium	ZYZ
Antwerp/De Keyserlei Bus Stn		
	Belgium	ZAY
Antwerp/Deurne	Belgium	ANR
Anua	Uganda	RUA
Anuha Is	Solomon Is	ANH
Anuradhapura	Sri Lanka	ADP
Anvik, AK	USA	ANV
Anyang	China	AYN
Anyang	S. Korea	QYA
Aomori	Japan	AOJ
Aosta/Corrado Gex	Italy	AOT
Apalachicola Municipal, FL USA	AAF
Apalachicola, FL	USA	AQQ
Apalapsili	Indonesia	AAS
Apapa	Nigeria	QAP
Apartacto	Colombia	APO
Apataki	F. Polynesia	APK
Apatzingan	Mexico	AZG
Apeldoorn/RR	Netherlands	QYP
Apia/Fagali I	Samoa	FGI
Apia/Faleolo	Samoa	APW
Apiay	Colombia	API
Apolo	Bolivia	APB
Appenzell	Switzerland	ZAP
Apple Valley, CA	USA	APV
Appleton, WI	USA	ATW
April River	Papua New Guinea	APR
Aprilia	Italy	QZR
Apucarana	Brazil	APU
Aqaba	Jordan	AQJ
Aracap	Brazil	AJU
Aracatuba	Brazil	ARU
Arad	Romania	ARW
Aragarcas	Brazil	ARS
Aragip	Papua New Guinea	ARP
Araguaina	Brazil	AUX
Aramac	Australia	AXC
Aranclis	Namibia	ADI
Aranulka	Kiribati	AAK
Arapahoe/Municipal, NE	USA	AHF
Arapiraca	Brazil	APQ
Arapongas	Brazil	APX
Arapoti	Brazil	AAG
Arar	Saudi Arabia	RAE
Araracuara	Colombia	ACR
Ararangua	Brazil	XRB
Araraquara	Brazil	AQA
Ararat	Australia	ARY
Arauca	Colombia	AUC

Arauquita	Colombia	ARQ
Arawa	Papua New Guinea	RAW
Araxa	Brazil	AAX
Araxos/Patrai	Greece	GPA
Arba Mintch	Ethiopia	AMH
Arbatax	Italy	QTX
Arboletas	Colombia	ARO
Arbon	Switzerland	ZDD
Arcachon/Teste de Buch France	XAC
Arcata, CA	USA	ACV
Arclabil	Iran	ADU
Arctic Bay, NU	Canada	YAB
Arctic Village, AK	USA	ARC
Ardmore	New Zealand	AMZ
Ardmore, OK	USA	ADM
Ardmore/Downtown, OK	USA	AHD
Arecilbo	Puerto Rico	ARE
Arenshausen/RR Stn.	Germany	ZAS
Arequipa/Rodriguez Ballon	Peru	AQP
Arezzo	Italy	QZO
Argentia, NS	Canada	NWP
Argyle	Australia	GYL
Argyle Downs	Australia	AGY
Aribinda	Burkina Faso	XAR
Arica	Colombia	ACM
Aricos	Brazil	QRK
Aripuana	Brazil	AIR
Ariquernes	Brazil	AQM
Arkalyk	Kazakstan	AYK
Arkhanelsk	Russia	ARH
Arles/RR Stn.	France	ZAF
Arlington Heights/US AHP, IL		
	USA	JLH
Arlington, WA	USA	AWO
Arlit	Niger	RLT
Arlon	Belgium	QON
Armenia/El Eden	Colombia	AXM
Armentieres	France	XRM
Armidale	Australia	ARM
Armstrong, ON	Canada	YYW
Arnes, MB	Canada	YNR
Arnhem/Bus Svc	Netherlands	QAR
Arnhem/RR Stn.	Netherlands	ZYM
Arno	Marshall Is	AMR
Aroa	Papua New Guinea	AOA
Arona	Papua New Guinea	AON
Arorae Is	Kiribati	AIS
Arosa	Switzerland	ZDE
Arrabury	Australia	AAB
Arraias	Brazil	AAI
Arras	France	QRV
Arso	Indonesia	ARJ
Arsuk	Greenland	JRK
Artesia, NM	USA	ATS
Arthur's Town	Bahamas	ATC
Artigas	Uruguay	ATI
Arty	Burkina Faso	ARL
Aruba/Reina Beatrix	Aruba	AUA
Arusha	Tanzania	ARK
Arutua	F. Polynesia	AXR
Arvaikheer	Mongolia	AVK
Arviat, NU	Canada	YEK
Arvidsiaur	Sweden	AJR
Arzew	Algeria	QAE
Asahikawa/Akhiolk SPB	Japan	AKJ
Asapa	Papua New Guinea	APP
Asau	Samoa	AAU
Asbestos Hill, QC	Canada	YAF
Asbury Park, NJ	USA	ARX
Ascension	Bolivia	ASC
Aschaffenburg	Germany	ZCB
Ascoli Piceno	Italy	QNO
Ascona	Switzerland	ACO
Aseki	Papua New Guinea	AEK
Asela	Ethiopia	ALK
Ashburton	New Zealand	ASG
Ashcrott, BC	Canada	YZA
Asheville/Municipal, NC	USA	AVL
Ashford/Int'l RR	UK	QDH
Ashgabat	Turkmenistan	ASB
Ashland, VA	USA	OFP

Ashland, WI	USA	ASX
Ashley, ND	USA	ASY
Asirim	Papua New Guinea	ASZ
Asmara/Int'l Arpt.	Eritrea	ASM
Asosa	Ethiopia	ASO
Aspen, CO	USA	ASE
Assab	Eritrea	ASA
Assis	Brazil	AIF
Assiut	Egypt	ATZ
Astana	Kazakstan	TSE
Astorga	Brazil	QWN
Astoria, OR	USA	AST
Astrakhan	Russia	ASF
Astraksetra	Indonesia	AKQ
Asturias	Spain	OVD
Astypalaia Is	Greece	JTY
Asuncion/Silvio Pettirossi		
	Paraguay	ASU
Aswan	Egypt	ASW
Atambua	Indonesia	ABU
Atammik	Greenland	QJF
Ataq	Yemen	AXK
Atar/Mouakchott	Mauritania	ATR
Atauro	Indonesia	AUT
Atbara	Seychelles	ATB
Atbasar	Kazakstan	ATX
Athens, GA	USA	AHN
Athens, TN	USA	MMI
Athens-Eleftherios Venizelos		
Int'l	Greece	ATH
Athens/Athinai/Hellinikon Greece	HEW
Athens/Ohio University, OH	USA	ATO
Ati	Chad	ATV
Atibaia	Brazil	ZBW
Atikokan, ON	Canada	YIB
Atiu Is	Cook Is	AIU
Atka, AK	USA	AKB
Atkamba	Papua New Guinea	ABP
Atlanta, Falcon Fld, GA	USA	FFC
Atlanta, GA	USA	PDK
Atlanta/Beaver Ruin, GA	USA	JAO
Atlanta/Galleria, GA	USA	JGL
Atlanta/Hartsfield, GA	USA	ATL
Atlanta/Headquarters	USA	HDQ
Atlanta/Perimeter Mall, GA	USA	JAJ
Atlanta/Technology Park, GA		
	USA	JAE
Atlantic City, NJ	USA	ACY
Atlantic City/Bader Fld, NJ	USA	AIY
Atlantic City/Rail Svc., NJ	USA	ZRA
Atlantic City/Steel Pier HP, NJ		
	USA	JSL
Atlantic, IA	USA	AIO
Atmautluak, AK	USA	ATT
Atoifi	Solomon Is	ATD
Atqasuk, AK	USA	ATK
Atsugi/NAS	Japan	NJA
Attawapiskat, ON	Canada	YAT
Attock	Pakistan	ATG
Attopeu	Laos	AOU
Attu	Greenland	QGQ
Attu Is/Casco Cove, AK	USA	ATU
Atuona	F. Polynesia	AUQ
Atyrau	Kazakstan	GUW
Aua Is	Papua New Guinea	AUI
Aubagne/Agora Helipad	France	JAH
Aubenas/Vals-Lanas	France	OBS
Auburn, AL	USA	AUO
Auburn, CA	USA	AUN
Auburn, ME	USA	LEW
Auckland	New Zealand	AKL
Auckland	New Zealand	MHB
Aue/RR Stn.	Germany	ZAU
Augsburg, Muehlhausen		
	Germany	AGB
Augusta, GA	USA	AGS
Augusta, GA	USA	DNL
Augusta, ME	USA	AUG
Augustus Downs	Australia	AUD
Auki/Gwaunaru'u	Solomon Is	AKS
Aulnoye	France	XOY

A I R P O R T S

Aupaluk, QC . . . . Canada . . .YPJ
Aur Is . . . . Marshall Is . . AUL
Aurangabad/Chikkalthana India . . .IXU
Auray . . . . France . . XUY
Aurillac . . . . France . . AUR
Aurno . . . . . Papua New Guinea . . AUV
Aurora State Arpt, OR . . . . USA . . UAO
Aurora/Municipal, IL . . . . . . .USA . . AUZ
Aurukun Mission . . . . Australia . . AUU
Austin, MN. . . . . .USA . .AUM
Austin, NV . . . . .USA . . ASQ
Austin, TX . . . . .USA . . AUS
Austral Downs. . . . . . Australia . . AWP
Auvergne . . . . Australia . . AVG
Auxerre/Auxerre Branches
. . . . France . . AUF
Avalon . . . . Australia . . AVV
Avalon, CA . . . . .USA . . AVX
Avare . . . . Brazil . . QVP
Aveiro . . . . Portugal . . ZAV
Avellino . . . . Italy . . QVN
Aviano . . . . Italy . . AVB
Avignon/Avignon-Caum .France . . AVN
Avon Park/Municipal, FL . .USA . . AVO
Avoriaz . . . . .France . . AVF
Avu Avu . . . . Solomon Is . . AVU
Awaba . . . . Papua New Guinea . . AWB
Awar . . . . . . Papua New Guinea . . AWR
Awaradam/Cayana Arpt
. . . . Suriname . . AAJ
Awareh. . . . . Ethiopia . .AWH
Awassa . . . . Ethiopia . . AWA
Ax Les Thermes . . . . . .France . . XLT
Axurn . . . . Ethiopia . . AXU
Ayacucho . . . . Colombia . . AYC
Ayacucho/Yanamilla. . . . . . .Peru . . AYP
Ayapel . . . . Colombia . . AYA
Ayawasi . . . . Indonesia . . AYW
Ayers Rock/Connellan. Australia . . AYQ
Ayja Napa . . . . Cyprus . . QNP
Ayoias . . . . Paraguay . . AYO
Ayr . . . . Australia . . AYR
Azzazga . . . . .Algeria . . ZZA

B

Ba . . . . Fiji . . BFJ
Baasmo . . . . Norway . . ZXK
Babelegi/ HP . . . . S. Africa . . HBL
Babo . . . . Indonesia . . BXB
Babolsar . . . . Iran . . BBL
Baca Grande, CO . . . . . . .USA . . BCJ
Bacau . . . . Romania . .BCM
Bacita . . . . Nigeria . . QCT
Backwell, OK . . . . .USA . . BWL
Baclajoz/Talaveral La Real.Spain . .BJZ
Bacolod . . . . Philippines . . BCD
Bad Brambach/RR Stn.
. . . . Germany . . ZBD
Bad Saizurigen/RR Stn.
. . . . Germany . . ZBZ
Bade . . . . Indonesia . . BXD
Baden . . . . .Switzerland . . ZDG
Baden-Baden . . . . Germany . . ZCC
Badin/Talhar. . . . . Pakistan . . BDN
Badu Is . . . . Australia . . BDD
Bafoussarn . . . . Cameroon . . BFX
Bagan . . . . Myanmar . . BPE
Baganga . . . . Philippines . . BNQ
Bagani . . . . Namibia . .BQI
Bagdad, AZ . . . . .USA . . BGT
Bagdogra . . . . India . . IXB
Bage . . . . Brazil . . BGX
Baghdad/Al Muthana . . . . Iraq . . BGW
Baghdad/Saddam Int'l . . . . . Iraq . . SDA
Baglung . . . . Nepal . . BGL
Bagotville, QC . . . . .Canada . . YBG
Baguic,/Loakan . . . . . Philippines . . BAG

Bahar Dar . . . . Ethiopia . . BJR
Bahawainagar . . . . Pakistan . . WGB
Bahawaipur. . . . . Pakistan . . BHV
Bahia Blanca/Comandante
. . . . Argentina . . BHI
Bahia Cupica Cocos (Keeling) Is . . BHF
Bahia De Caraquez . . Ecuador . .BHA
Bahia Pinas. . . . . Panama . . BFQ
Bahia Solano . . . . Colombia . . BSC
Bahla Angeles . . . . Mexico . . BHL
Bahrain/Int'l . . . . Bahrain . .BAH
Bahregan . . . . Iran . . IAQ
Baia Mare. . . . . Romania . . BAY
Baibara . . . . Papua New Guinea . . BAP
Baidoa . . . . Somalia . .BIB
Baie Comeau, QC . . . . Canada . . YBC
Baimuru . . Papua New Guinea . . VMU
Bainbridge/Decatur County, GA
. . . . USA . .BGE
Baindoung Papua New Guinea . . BDZ
Bairnsdale . . . . Australia . . BSJ
Baitadi . . . . Nepal . . BIT
Baitrum . . . . Germany . . BMR
Bajawa . . . . Indonesia . . BJW
Bajhang . . . . Nepal . . BJH
Bajone . . . . Mozambique . . BJN
Bajura Arpt . . . . Nepal . . BJU
Bakalalan . . . . Malaysia . . BKM
Bakel . . . . Senegal . . BXE
Baker Lake, NT. . . . . . Canada . . YBK
Baker, Baker Municipal Arpt, OR
. . . . USA . . BKE
Baker/AAF, AK . . . . USA . . BAR
Bakersfield/Meadows Fld, CA
. . . . USA . . BFL
Bakkafjordur . . . . Iceland . . BJD
Bakourna . . Central African Rep .BMF
Baku . . . . Azerbaijan . . BAK
Balakovo . . . . Russia . . BWO
Balalae . . . . Solomon Is . . BAS
Balboa . . . . Panama . . BLB
Balcanoona . . . . Australia . . LCN
Bale Johan Beetz, QC Canada . . YBJ
Baler . . . . Philippines . . BQA
Balgo Hills . . . . Australia . . BQW
Balhash . . . . Kazakstan . . BXH
Bali. . . . . . . Papua New Guinea . . BAJ
Bali. . . . . Cameroon . . BLC
BaLicin . . . . Indonesia . . BTW
Balikesir . . . . Turkey . . BZI
Balikesir/Merkez . . . . .Turkey . . MQJ
Balikipapan/Sepingan
. . . . Indonesia . . BPN
Balimo . . . . Papua New Guinea . . OPU
Ballina . . . . Australia . . BNK
Ballina . . . . Australia . . QNA
Bally Kelly . . . . .UK . . BOL
Balmaceda/Teniente Vicial. Chile . . BBA
Balranald . . . . Australia . . BZD
Balsas . . . . Brazil . . BSS
Baltimore, MD. . . . . USA . . BWI
Baltimore, MD. . . . . USA . . MTN
Baltimore-Greenbelt, MD. . USA . . GBO
Baltimore/Baltimore Rail, MD
. . . . USA . . ZBP
Balurghat . . . . India . . RGH
Bamako . . . . Mali . . BKO
Bambari . . . . Central African Rep . . BBY
Bamberg/Off-line Pt. . Germany . .ZCD
Bambu . . . Papua New Guinea . . BCP
Bamburi . . . . Kenya . . BMQ
Bamenda . . . . Cameroon . . BPC
Bamerny. . . . . Iraq . . BMN
Bamfield, BC . . . . Canada . . YBF
Bamiyan . . . . Afghanistan . . BIN
Bamu . . . . . Papua New Guinea . . BMZ
Ban Houei . . . . Laos . . OUI
Ban Mak Khaen/Udorn Thailand . . BAO
Banaina . . . . Indonesia . . NAF
Banda Aceh/Blang Bintang
. . . . Indonesia . . BTJ

Bandanatra . . . . Indonesia,. . NDA
Bandar Abbas . . . . .Iran.. BND
Bandar Khomeini . . . . .Iran.. QBR
Bandar Lampung/Branti
. . . . Indonesia. . TKG
Bandar Lengeh . . . . .Iran.. BDH
Bandar Mahshahr . . . . . . .Iran.. MRX
Bandar Seri Begawan . Brunei. . BWN
Bandirma . . . . Turkey. . BDM
Bandol . . . . France. . XBZ
Bandon/State, OR . . . . USA. . BDY
Bandundu . . . . Congo, DR. . FDU
Bandung/Husein Sastranegara
. . . . Indonesia. . BDO
Banff, AB. . . . . Canada. . YBA
Banfora . . . . Burkina Faso. . BNR
Bangalore/Hindustan . . . . India. . BLR
Bangassou Central African Rep. . BGU
Bangda . . . . China. . BPX
Bangkok Int'l . . . . Thailand. . BKK
Bangor Int'l Arpt, ME . . . USA. . BGR
Bangsiund . . . . Norway. . ZXC
Bangui. . . . . Central African Rep.. BGF
Bani-walid . . . . Libya. . QBL
Baniyala . . . . Australia. . BYX
Banja Luka Bosnia Hercegovina. . BNX
Banjarmasin/Sjamsudin Noor
. . . . Indonesia. .BDJ
Banjul/Yundum Int'l The Gambia. . BJL
Bankstown . . . . Australia. . BWU
Banmethuot/Phung-Duc
. . . . Vietnam. . BMV
Banning, CA. . . . . USA. . BNG
Bannu . . . . Pakistan. . BNP
Bantry . . . . Ireland.. BYT
Banyuls Sur Mer . . . . . France.. XBU
Banz . . . . . Papua New Guinea.. BNZ
Baoshan . . . . China.. BSD
Baotou . . . . China.. BAV
Bapi . . . . Papua New Guinea.. BPD
Bar Harbour, ME . . . . . USA.. BHB
Baracoa . . . . Cuba.. BCA
Barahona . . . . . .Dominican Rep.. BRX
Barakorna . . . . Solomon Is.. VEV
Baramita. . . . . Guyana.. BMJ
Barbacena . . . . Brazil.. QAK
Barbelos . . . . Brazil.. BAZ
Barbers Point, HI . . . . . USA.. NAX
Barbuda . . . . Antigua & Barbuda.. BBQ
Barcaidine . . . . .Australia.. BCI
Barcelona . . . . Spain.. BCN
Barcelona . . . . Venezuela..BLA
Barcelonnette . . . . France.. BAE
Bardera . . . . Somalia..BSY
Bardstown/Samuels Fld, KY
. . . . USA.. BRY
Bardufoss . . . . Norway.. BDU
Bareges . . . . France.. XBA
Bari/Palese Macchie . . . . . . Italy.. BRI
Barin/NAS, AL. . . . . USA.. NBJ
Barinas . . . . Venezuela.. BNS
Bario . . . . Malaysia.. BBN
Barisal . . . . Bangladesh.. BZL
Barka . . . . .Algeria.. ZZB
Barkly Downs . . . . Australia.. BKP
Barksdale/AFB, LA . . . . . USA.. BAD
Barn . . . . Iran.. BXR
Barnaga . . . . .Australia.. ABM
Barnaul . . . . Russia.. BAX
Barnwell, SC . . . . USA.. BNL
Barora . . . . Solomon Is.. RRI
Barquisimeto . . . . . . Venezuela.. BRM
Barra . . . . Brazil.. BQQ
Barra Colorado . . . Costa Rica.. BCL
Barra Do Corda . . . . . . Brazil.. BDC
Barra Do Garcas . . . . . . Brazil.. BPG
Barra Do Pirai . . . . Brazil.. QBD
Barra Mansa . . . . Brazil.. QBN
Barra/North Bay . . . . .UK.. BRR
Barranca De Upia . . .Colombia.. BAC
Barrancabermeia/Vrgs Colombia. . . EJA

Barrancominas . . . . . Colombia . . NBB	Bearskin Lake, ON . . . Canada . . XBE	Beltsville, MO/Off-line Pt. . . . USA. . . ZFE
Barranquilla/E Cortissoz	Beatrice, NE. . . . . USA . . BIE	Beluga, AK . . . . USA. . BVU
. . . . Colombia . . BAQ	Beatton River, BC . . . . Canada . . YZC	Bembridge . . . . UK. . BBP
Barre, VT . . . . USA . . MPV	Beatty, NV. . . . . USA . . BTY	Bemichi. . . . . Guyana. . BCG
Barreiras . . . . Brazil . . BRA	Beaufort/County, SC . . . . . . USA . . BFT	Bemidji, MN . . . . USA. . . BJI
Barreirinhas . . . . Brazil . . BRB	Beaulieu Sur Mer . . . . . France . . XBM	Benalla . . . . .Australia. . BLN
Barretos . . . . Brazil . . BAT	Beaumont, TX . . . . USA . . BPT	Benbecula . . . . UK. . BEB
Barrow Is . . . . Australia . .BWB	Beaumont/Municipal, TX . . . USA . .BMT	Benevento . . . . Italy. . QBV
Barrow-In-Furness/Walney Isl.	Beaune . . . . France . . XBV	Bengbu . . . . China. . BFU
. . . . UK . . BWF	Beauvais . . . . France . . BVA	Benghazi/Benina Intl . . . . . Libya. . BEN
Barrow/Metro., AK . . . . USA. . BRW	Beaver Creek, YT . . . . Canada . . YXQ	Bengkulu/Padangkemiling
Barrow/Point Barrow, AK . . . USA . . PBA	Beaver Falls Arpt, PA . . . . . USA . . BFP	. . . . Indonesia. . BKS
Barstow-Daggett, CA. . . . . .USA . . DAG	Beaver Inlet/Sea Port, AK . USA . . BVD	Benguela/GV Deslandes Angola. . BUG
Barter Is, AK . . . . USA. . . BTI	Beaver, AK . . . . USA . . WBQ	Benguera Is . . . . . .Mozambique. . BCW
Barth . . . . Germany . . BBH	Bebedouro . . . . .Brazil . . QAU	Beni . . . . Congo, DR. . BNC
Bartica . . . . .Guyana . . GFO	Bechar . . . . Algeria . CBH	Benin City . . . . Nigeria. . BNI
Bartlesville, OK . . . . USA . . BVO	Beckley, WV . . . . USA . . BKW	Benjamin Constant . . . . . . Brazil. . QAV
Bartletts, AK . . . . USA . . BSZ	Beclarra Is . . . . Australia . . QIY	Bennettsville, SC . . . . USA. . BTN
Bartow Municipal, FL. . . . .USA . . BOW	Bedford Downs . . . . . . Australia . BDW	Bensbach . . Papua New Guinea. . BSP
Baruun-Urt . . . . Mongolia . . UUN	Bedford, IN. . . . . USA . . BFR	Benson/Municipal, MN . . . . USA. . BBB
Basankusu . . . . Congo, DR . . BSU	Bedford/Hanscom Fld, MA . USA . . BED	Benson/RAF . . . . UK. . BEX
Basco . . . . Philippines . . BSO	Bedford/RR Stn. . . . . .UK . . XQD	Bento Goncalves . . . . Brazil. . BGV
Basel/Mulhouse. . . . . Switzerland . . BSL	Bedford/Thurleigh (Military) . .UK . . BFZ	Benton Harbor/Ross Fld, MI
Basel/Mulhouse. . . . . Switzerland . .MLH	Bedourie . . . . Australia . . BEU	. . . . USA. . BEH
Basel/Mulhouse/German Railway	Beef Is. . . . . Virgin Is (British) . . EIS	Beppu . . . . .Japan. . BPU
Svc. . . . . Switzerland . . ZBA	Beer Sheba . . . . Israel . . BEV	Bequia Arpt
Basel/Mulhouse/SBB Railway	Beeville/NAS, TX . . . . USA . . NIR	. . . . St. Vincent & Grenadines. . BQU
Svc. . . . . Switzerland . . ZDH	Befandriana . . . . . Madagascar . WBD	Berau . . . . Indonesia. . BEJ
Basingstoke/RR Stn. . . . . . UK . . XQB	Bega/Off-line Pt. . . . . . . Australia . .QBE	Berbera . . . . Somalia. . BBO
Basongo . . . . Congo, DR . . BAN	Beica . . . . Ethiopia . .BEI	Berberati . . . Central African Rep. . BBT
Basra/Int'l . . . . Iraq . . BSR	Beida/La Braq . . . . .Libya . .LAQ	Berchtesgaden . . . . . . Germany. . ZCE
Basse Terre/Baillif . Gaudeloupe . . BBR	Beidah . . . . Yemen . . BYD	Berdyansk . . . . Ukraine. . ERD
Bassein . . . . Myanmar . . BSX	Beijing . . . . China . . PEK	Bereby . . . . Côte D'Ivoire. . BBV
Bastia/Poretta . . . . .France . . . BIA	Beijing/Nanyuan . . . . China . . NAY	Bereina . . . . Papua New Guinea. . BEA
Bata . . . . Equatorial Guinea . . BSG	Beil-tai . . . . China . . BHY	Berens River, MB . . . . . Canada. . YBV
Batam/HaNadirr, . . . Indonesia . . BTH	Beinan . . . . Yemen . . BHN	Bergen Op Zoom . . Netherlands. . BZM
Batangafo . . Central African Rep . . BTG	Beira . . . . Mozambique . BEW	Bergen/Flesland . . . . Norway. . BGO
Batavia Downs . . . . . . Australia . .BVW	Beirut/Int'l . . . . .Lebanon . . BEY	Bergen/Harbour Pier . . . Norway. .QFV
Batemans Bay . . . . . . Australia . . QBW	Beitsy . . . . Macau . . BZY	Bergerac/Roumanieres . . France. . EGC
Batesvilie,/Municipal . Australia . . BVX	Bejaia . . . . Algeria . . BJA	Bergheim (Cologne) . . Germany. . ZCF
Batesville/Hillenbrand, IN . .USA . . HLB	Bekily . . . . Madagascar . . OVA	Bergisch Gladbach . Germany. . ZCG
Bath/RR . . . . UK . .QQX	BelAbbes . . . . Algeria . QBB	Bergkamen/Off-line Pt. Germany. . ZCH
Bathurst Is . . . . Australia . . BRT	Belaga. . . . . Malaysia . . BLG	Berijina . . . . Indonesia. .BJK
Bathurst, NB . . . . .Canada . . ZBF	Belem/Val De Cans . . . . . . Brazil . . BEL	Berkeley, CA . . . . USA. . JBK
Bathurst/Raglan . . . . . . Australia . . BHS	Belep Is . . . . New Caledonia . . BMY	Berlevag . . . . Norway. . BVG
Batman . . . . Turkey . . BAL	Belfast/Belfast City Arpt . . . . .UK . . BHD	Berlin . . . . Germany. . QPP
Batna . . . . Algeria . .BLJ	Belfast/Belfast Int'l Arpt. . . . . .UK . . BFS	Berlin Municipal Arpt, NH USA. . BML
Batna . . . . Algeria . .DLJ	Belfort/Fontaine . . . . France . . BOR	Berlin/Berlin Zoo Railway Sta
Batom . . . . Indonesia . . BXM	Belgaum/Sambre . . . . India . . IXG	. . . . Germany. .QWC
Baton Rouge/Downtown, LA	Belgorod . . . . Russia . EGO	Berlin/Fredrichstr. Railway Sta
. . . . .USA . . EBR	Belgrade/Batapica . Yugoslavia . . BJY	. . . . Germany. . QWE
Baton Rouge/Ryan Fld, LA.USA . . BTR	Belgrade/Becigrad . Yugoslavia . . BEG	Berlin/HBF Railway Sta
Batouri . . . . Cameroon . .OUR	Beliary . . . . India . . BEP	. . . . Germany. .QWB
Batsfjord . . . . Norway . .BJF	Belize City/Goldson Int'l. . Belize . . BZE	Berlin/RAF Gatow . . Germany. GWW
Battambang . . . . Cambodia . . BBM	Belize City/Mun . . . . Belize . TZA	Berlin/Schoenefeld . . . Germany. . . SXF
Batticaloa . . . . Sri Lanka . . BTC	Bell Is/Hot Springs SPB, AK	Berlin/Tegel . . . . Germany. . . TXL
Battle Creek/Kellogg, MI. . .USA . . BTL	. . . . USA . . KBE	Berlin/Tempelhof . . . . . Germany. . THF
Battle Mountain, NV . . . . . .USA . . BAM	Bella Bella, BC . . . . Canada . . ZEL	Bermejo . . . . Bolivia. . BJO
Batumi . . . . .Georgia . . BUS	Bella Coola, BC . . . . Canada . . QBC	Bermuda/NAS . . . . . . Bermuda. . NWU
Batuna Aerodrome Solomon Is. . BPF	Bella Union . . . . Uruguay . . BUV	Bernay . . . . France. .XBX
Baubau/Beto Ambiri . . Indonesia . . BUW	Bella Yeila . . . . Liberia . . BYL	Berne . . . . Switzerland. .ZDJ
Baucau/English Madeira	Bellaire/Antrim County, MI . USA . .ACB	Berne/Belp . . . . Switzerland. . BRN
. . . . Indonesia . . BCH	Bellavista . . . . Peru . . BLP	Beroroha . . . . Madagascar. .WBO
Bauchi . . . . Nigeria . . BCU	Belle Chasse/Southern	Berriane . . . . Algeria. . . ZBI
Bauchi . . . . Nigeria . . QBU	Seaplane, LA. . . . . USA . . BCS	Bertoua . . . . Cameroon. . . BTA
Baudette/Int'l, MN. . . . . . . .USA . . BDE	Belle Fourche, SD . . . . . . USA . . EFC	Beru . . . . Kiribati. . BEZ
Baures . . . . Bolivia . . BVL	Bellefonte, PA . . . . USA . . PSB	Berwick/RR Stn. . . . . UK. . XQG
Bauru . . . . Brazil . . BAU	Bellegarde . . . . France . XBF	Besakoa . . . . Madagascar. . BSV
Bawan . . . . .Papua New Guinea . . BWJ	Belleville/RR Stn., ON . Canada . . XVV	Besalampy . . . . Madagascar. . BPY
Bay City, MI . . . . .USA . . MBS	Bellingham/Int'l Arpt, WA. . USA . . BLI	Besancon . . . . France. . QBQ
Bay City, TX. . . . . .USA . . BBC	Bellinzona . . . . Switzerland . . ZDI	Best/Bus Svc. . . . . . Netherlands. . QWZ
Bayamo/C.M. de CespedesCuba . BYM	Bellona . . . . Solomon Is . . BNY	Bethel, AK . . . . USA. . BET
Bayankhongor. . . . . . . Mongolia . . BYN	Belluno . . . . Italy . . BLX	Bethel/City Landing, AK . . .USA. . . JBT
Bayonne . . . . .France . . XBY	Belmar-Farmdale, NJ . . . . USA . . BLM	Bethpage/Grumman, NY . . . USA. . BPA
Bayreuth . . . . Germany . . BYU	Belmonte . . . . .Brazil . . BVM	Bethune . . . . France. .XBH
Baytown, TX . . . . .USA . . HPY	Belmopan . . . . Belize . . BCV	Betim . . . . Brazil. . QBK
Bazaruto Is . . . . . . Mozambique . . BZB	Belmullet . . . . Ireland . . BLY	Betioky . . . . Madagascar. . BKU
Beagle Bay . . . . Australia . . BEE	Belo . . . . Madagascar . BMD	Betoota . . . . .Australia. . BTX
Bealanana. . . . . . .Madagascar . .WBE	Belo Horizonte/Parnpulha Brazil . . PLU	Betou . . . . Congo, DR. . .BTB
Beale/AFB, CA. . . . . .USA . . BAB	Belo Horizonte/T. Neves . .Brazil . . CNF	Bettioua . . . . Algeria. . QBT
Bear Creek, AK . . . . .USA . . BCC	Beloreck . . . . Russia . .BCX	Bettles Arpt, AK . . . . USA. . BTT

Airport	Location	Code
Beverley Springs	Australia	BVZ
Beverly, MA	USA	BVY
Bewani	Papua New Guinea	BWP
Beziers/Vias	France	BZR
Bhadohi	India	XXB
Bhairawa	Nepal	BWA
Bhamo	Myanmar	BMO
Bharatpur	Nepal	BHR
Bhatinda	India	BUP
Bhavnagar	India	BHU
Bhojpur	Nepal	BHP
Bhopal	India	BHO
Bhubaneswar	India	BBI
Bhuj/Rudra Mata	India	BHJ
Bhurban/Bhurban HP	Pakistan	BHC
Biak/Mokmer	Indonesia	BIK
Bialla	Papua New Guinea	BAA
Bialystok	Poland	QYY
Biarritz/Biarritz Parme	France	BIQ
Biaru	Papua New Guinea	BRP
Biawonque	Gabon	BAW
Bickerton Is	Australia	BCZ
Biel/Bienne	Switzerland	ZDK
Bielefeld	Germany	BFE
Bielsko-Baila	Poland	QEO
Big Bay	Vanuatu	GBA
Big Bay Marina, BC	Canada	YIG
Big Bay Yacht Club, BC	Canada	YYA
Big Bear, CA	USA	RBF
Big Bell	Australia	BBE
Big Creek	Belize	BGK
Big Creek, AK	USA	BIC
Big Delta/Intermediate Fld, AK	USA	BIG
Big Lake, AK	USA	BGQ
Big Mountain, AK	USA	BMX
Big Piney, WY	USA	BPI
Big Rapids, MI	USA	WBR
Big Spring, Webb/AFB, TX	USA	BGS
Big Spring/Howard County, TX	USA	HCA
Big Trout, ON	Canada	YTL
Biggs/AAF, TX	USA	BIF
Bikaner	India	BKB
Bikini Atoll/Enyu Airfield	Marshall Is	BII
Bilaspur	India	PAB
Bilbao	Spain	BIO
Bildudalur	Iceland	BIU
Biliau	Papua New Guinea	BIJ
Billiluna	Australia	BIW
Billings/Int'l, MT	USA	BIL
Billund/Lufthavn	Denmark	BLL
Biloela	Australia	ZBL
Biloxi Regional Arpt, MS	USA	GPT
Bima	Indonesia	BMU
Bimin	Papua New Guinea	BIZ
Bimini/Int'l	Bahamas	BIM
Bimini/North SPB	Bahamas	NSB
Binghamton, NY	USA	BGM
Biniguni	Papua New Guinea	XBN
Bintulu	Malaysia	BTU
Bintuni	Indonesia	NTI
Birao	Central African Rep	IRO
Biratnagar	Nepal	BIR
Birch Creek, AK	USA	KBC
Bird Is	Seychelles	BDI
Birdsville	Australia	BVI
Birigui	Brazil	QCF
Birjand	Iran	XBJ
Birmingham-New Street/RR	UK	QQN
Birmingham/Colmore Row Bus Stn	UK	ZBC
Birmingham/Int'l	UK	BHX
Birmingham/Int'l, AL	USA	BHM
Birni Nkoni	Niger	BKN
Bisbee/Municipal, AZ	USA	BSQ
Bisha	Saudi Arabia	BHH
Bishkek	Kyrgyzstan	FRU
Bisho	South Africa	BIY
Bishop, CA	USA	BIH
Biskra	Algeria	BSK
Bislig	Philippines	BPH
Bismarck, ND	USA	BIS
Bissau/Osvaldo Vieira	Guinea Bissau	OXB
Bistrita/Nasaud	Romania	QBY
Bitam	Gabon	BMM
Bitburg Air Base	Germany	BBJ
Bitola	Macedonia	QBI
Biumenau	Brazil	BNU
Bizant	Australia	BZP
Bizerte	India	QIZ
Black Tickle, NF	Canada	YBI
Blackall	Australia	BKQ
Blackbushe	UK	BBS
Blackpool	UK	BLK
Blackstone/AAF, VA	USA	BKT
Blackwater	Australia	BLT
Blagoveschensk	Russia	BQS
Blaine, WA	USA	BWS
Blairsville, PA	USA	BSI
Blakely Is, WA	USA	BYW
Blanc Sablon, QC	Canada	YBX
Blanding, UT	USA	BDG
Blantyre/Chileka	Malawi	BLZ
Blenheim	New Zealand	BHE
Blida	Algeria	QLD
Block Is, RI	USA	BID
Bloemfontein Int'l	South Africa	BFN
Blois	France	XBQ
Blonduos	Iceland	BLO
Bloodvein, MB	Canada	YDV
Bloomfield	Australia	BFC
Bloomington, IN	USA	BMG
Bloomington/Normal, IL	USA	BMI
Blubber Bay, BC	Canada	XBB
Blue Bell/Wings Fld, PA	USA	BBX
Blue Canyon, CA	USA	BLU
Blue Fox Bay, AK	USA	BFB
Blue Lagoon	Fiji	BXL
Blue River, BC	Canada	YCP
Bluefield/Mercer County Arpt, WV	USA	BLF
Bluefields	Netherlands	BEF
Blythe Arpt, CA	USA	BLH
Blytheville Municipal, AR	USA	HKA
Blytheville/AFB, AR	USA	BYH
Bo	Sierra Leone	KBS
Boa Vista	Brazil	BVB
Boa Vista/Rabil	Cape Verde Is	BVC
Boana	Papua New Guinea	BNV
Boang	Papua New Guinea	BOV
Bobo Dioulasso/Borgo	Burkina Faso	BOY
Bobquinn Lake, BC	Canada	YBO
Boca Do Acre	Brazil	BCR
Boca Raton/Public, FL	USA	BCT
Bocas Del Tore	Panama	BOC
Bocholt	Germany	ZCI
Bochum	Germany	QBO
Bodinumu	Papua New Guinea	BNM
Bodo	Norway	BOO
Bodrum,/Milas Arpt	Turkey	BJV
Bodrum/Imisk Arpt	Turkey	BXN
Boeblingen	'. Germany	PHM
Boende	Congo, DR	BNB
Bogalusa/George R Carr, LA	USA	BXA
Bogande	Burkina Faso	XBG
Boghe/Abbaye	Mauritania	BGH
Bogota/Eldorado	Colombia	BOG
Boigu Is	Australia	GIC
Boise/Boise Air Terminal, ID	USA	BOI
Boizano	Italy	BZO
Boke	Guinea	BKJ
Bokondini	Indonesia	BUI
Bokoro	Chad	BKR
Boku	Papua New Guinea	BOQ
Bol	Croatia	BWK
Bol	Chad	OTC
Bolaang	Indonesia	BJG
Bolling/AFB, DC	USA	BOF
Bollon	Australia	BLS
Bologna/Gugliemo Marconi Italy		BLQ
Bolovip	Papua New Guinea	BVP
Bolwarra	Australia	BCK
Bom Jesus Da Lapa	Brazil	LAZ
Boma	Congo, DR	BOA
Bomai	Papua New Guinea	BMH
Bonaire/Int'l. Netherlands Antilles		BON
Bonanza/San Pedro Netherlands		BZA
Bonaventure, QC	Canada	YVB
Bondaukou/Soko	Côte D'Ivoire	BDK
Bonger	Chad	OGR
Bongo	Gabon	BGP
Bongouanou	Chile	BGG
Bonnyville, AB	Canada	YBY
Bontang	Indonesia	BXT
Bonthe	Sierra Leone	BTE
Boone Municipal, IA	USA	BNW
Booue	Gabon	BGB
Bopord	Iran	BJB
Bora Bora/Motu-mute	F. Polynesia	BOB
Borama	Somalia	BXX
Borba	Brazil	RBB
Borcj Menatiel	Algeria	ZZM
Bordeaux/Gare de Bordeaux	France	ZFQ
Bordeaux/Merignac	France	BOD
Borden, ON	Canada	YBN
Bordj Badji Mokintar	Algeria	BMW
Bordj-Bou-Arreri	Algeria	QBJ
Borgarfiordur Eystri	Iceland	BGJ
Boriange/Dala	Sweden	BLE
Boridi	Papua New Guinea	BPB
Borkum	Germany	BMK
Bornholm/Ronne	Denmark	RNN
Bornite, AK	USA	RLU
Borotou	Côte D'Ivoire	BRZ
Borrego Springs, CA	USA	BXS
Borroloola	Australia	BOX
Boscobel, WI	USA	OVS
Boset	Papua New Guinea	BOT
Bossangoa	Central African Rep.	BSN
Bossaso	Somalia	BSA
Bost	Afghanistan	BST
Boston/HP, MA	USA	JBC
Boston/BKBAY Rail, MA	USA	ZTY
Boston/Boston RT128 Rail, MA	USA	ZRU
Boston/Boston South Rail, MA	USA	ZTO
Boston/Logan Int'l, MA	USA	BOS
Boswell Bay, AK	USA	BSW
Botopasie	Suriname	BTO
Botosani	Romania	QDD
Bottrop	Germany	ZCJ
Botucatu	Brazil	QCJ
Bouake	Côte D'Ivoire	BYK
Bouar	Central African Rep.	BOP
Bouca	Central African Rep.	BCF
Boufarik	Algeria	QFD
Bouira	Algeria	QBZ
Boukadir	Algeria	ZAB
Boulder City, CO	USA	BLD
Boulder/Broker Inn, CO	USA	WBI
Boulder/Hiltons Har H, CO	USA	WHH
Boulder/Metro, CO	USA	WBU
Boulia	Australia	BQL
Boulogne Billancourt	France	XBT
Boulogne Sur Mer	France	XBS
Boulsa	Burkina Faso	XBO
Bouna/Tehini	Côte D'Ivoire	BQO
Boundary, AK	USA	BYA
Boundiali	Côte D'Ivoire	BXI
Boundji	Congo, DR	BOE
Bountiful, UT	USA	BTF
Bourg D'Oisans	France	XBI
Bourg En Bresse	France	XBK
Bourg-St Maurice	France	QBM
Bourgas	Bulgaria	BOJ

AIRPORTS

Bourges. . . . . .France . . BOU	Britrail Rail Zone G . . . . .UK . QQG	Buguima . . . . Russia. . UUA
Bourke . . . . Australia. . BRK	Britrail Rail Zone I . . . . .UK . . QQI	Buichi . . . . Ethiopia. . BCY
Bournemouth/Int'l . . . . .UK . .BOH	Britrail Rail Zone J . . . . .UK . QQJ	Buin . . . . . . Papua New Guinea. . . UBI
Boussaada . . . . .Algeria . . BUJ	Britrail Rail Zone L . . . . . . .UK . QQL	Bujumbura/Int'l . . . . Burundi. . BJM
Bousso . . . . Chad . . OUT	Britrail Rail Zone O . . . . . . .UK . QQO	Buka . . . . Papua New Guinea. . BUA
Boutilimit . . . . .Mauritania. . OTL	Britrail Rail Zone S . . . . . . .UK . QQS	Bukavu/Kamenbe . . Congo, DR. .BKY
Bowen . . . . Australia. . ZBO	Britrail Rail Zone T . . . . . . .UK . QQT	Bukhara . . . . Uzbekistan. . BHK
Bowling Green, KY . . . . . .USA. . BWG	Britrail Rail Zone V . . . . . . .UK . QQV	Bukoba . . . . Tanzania. . .BKZ
Bowling Green, VA . . . . . . .USA. . APH	Britrail Rail Zone Z . . . . Georgia . .QQZ	Bulawayo . . . . Zimbabwe. . BUQ
Bowman, ND. . . . . .USA. . BWM	Britton/Municipal, SD . . . . USA . . TTO	Bulgan . . . . Mongolia. . UGA
Boxborough, MA . . . . .USA. . BXC	Brive-La-Gaillarde/Laroche	Bulimba . . . . Australia. . BIP
Bozeman, MT . . . . .USA. . BZN	. . . . France . . BVE	Bull Harbour, BC . . . . Canada. . YBH
Bozen/Bus Stn. . . . . Italy . . ZBN	Brize Norton/RAF. . . . . .UK . . BZZ	Bullfrog Basin, UT . . . . . . .USA. . BFG
Bozoum . . . .Central African Rep . . BOZ	Brno/Bus Svc . . . . .Czech Rep . . ZDN	Bullhead City/Int'l, AZ . . . . .USA. . . IFP
Brack . . . . Libya. . BCQ	Brno/Turany . . . . .Czech Rep . . BRQ	Bullocks Flat/Bus Svc .Australia. .QZM
Bradford . . . . .UK . . BRF	Broadus, MT . . . . USA . .BDX	Bulolo . . . . . Papua New Guinea. . .BUL
Bradford, PA. . . . . .USA. . BFD	Broadview, SK. . . . . Canada . .YDR	Bumba . . . . Congo, DR. . BMB
Bradford/Bus Stn . . . . .UK . . ZFC	Brochet, MB. . . . . Canada . . YBT	Bumi Hills . . . . Zimbabwe. . BZH
Bradford/Rinkenberg, IL . . .USA. . BDF	Brockville, ON. . . . . . . Canada . .XBR	Bunbury . . . . Australia. . BUY
Bradshaw/AAF, HI . . . . . . .USA. . BSF	Broenclersev/Bus Svc Denmark . .XAQ	Bundaberg . . . . .Australia. . BDB
Brady/Curtis Fld, TX . . . . . . .USA. . BBD	Broken Bow Municipal, NE	Bundi . . . . . . Papua New Guinea. . .BNT
Braga . . . . Portugal . . BGZ	. . . . USA . . BBW	Buno Bedelle . . . . Ethiopia. . .XBL
Bragado . . . . Argentina . .QRF	Broken Hill . . . . Australia. . BHQ	Bunsil . . . . . Papua New Guinea. . .BXZ
Braganca . . . . Portugal . . BGC	Bromont, QC . . . . Canada . . ZBM	Bunyu . . . . Indonesia. . BYQ
Braganca Paulista . . . . . . Brazil. . .BJP	Bronnoysund/Bronnoy .Norway . . BNN	Buol . . . . Indonesia. . UOL
Brahman . . . . . .Papua New Guinea . . BRH	Bronson Creek, BC. . . Canada . . YBM	Buraimi . . . . .Oman. . RMB
Brainerd, MN . . . . .USA. . BRD	Brookings, OR . . . . USA . . BOK	Burao . . . . Somalia. . BUO
Braintree/Wether Fld/RAF . . .UK . . WXF	Brookings, SD . . . . USA . . BKX	Burbank, CA. . . . . .USA. . BUR
Brampton Is . . . . Australia. . BMP	Brooklyn, NJ . . . . USA . . QFF	Bureta/Levuka Airfield . . . . . .Fiji. . . LEV
Brampton/RR Stn., ON .Canada . . XPN	Brooklyn, NJ . . . . USA . .QHW	Burg Feuerstein . . . . . .Germany. . URD
Brandon, MB. . . . . .Canada . . YBR	Brooks Lake, AK . . . . . . USA . . BKF	Burgdorf . . . . Switzerland. . .ZDP
Brandon/Lakenheath/RAF. . . .UK . . LKZ	Brooks Lodge, AK . . . . . USA . .RBH	Buri Ram . . . . Thailand. . .BFV
Brantford/RR Stn., ON . .Canada . . XFV	Brooksville, FL . . . . USA . . BKV	Burketown . . . . .Australia. . BUC
Brasilia/Int'l . . . . Brazil. . BSB	Broome. . . . . Australia. . BME	Burley, ID. . . . . .USA. . . BYI
Bratislava/Bus Svc. . . . . Slovakia . . ZRG	Broomfield/Jeffco, CO . . . USA . . BJC	Burlington, IA . . . . .USA. . .BRL
Bratislava/Ivanka . . . . . Slovakia . . BTS	Brownsville/Int'l, TX . . . . USA . . BRO	Burlington, MA . . . . .USA. . .BBF
Bratsk. . . . . Russia. . BTK	Brownwood, TX . . . . USA . . BWD	Burlington/Int'l, VT. . . . . . . .USA. . .BTV
Brattleboro, VT. . . . . .USA. . EEN	Brueggen/R.A.F. . . . . . . Germany . .BGN	Burnie/Burnie Wynyard .Australia. . BWT
Braunschweig . . . . Germany . . BWE	Bruehl . . . . Germany . . ZCK	Burns Lake, BC. . . . . . Canada. . .YPZ
Brava . . . . Cape Verde Is . . BVR	Brugge . . . . Belgium . . ZGJ	Burns Municipal Arpt, OR USA. . BNO
Brawley, CA. . . . . .USA. . BWC	Brumado . . . . Brazil. . BMS	Bursa . . . . Turkey. . .BTZ
Brazoria/Hinkles Ferry, TX . .USA. . BZT	Brunette Downs . . . . . . Australia. . BTD	Bursa . . . . Turkey. . . YEI
Brazzaville/Maya-Maya	Brunswick, GA . . . . USA . . . SSI	Burtonwood . . . . .UK . . .BUT
. . . . Congo, DR . . BZV	Brunswick/Glynco, GA . . . USA . . BQK	Burundai . . . . Kazakstan. . .BXJ
Breckenridge/Stephens County,	Brunswick/NAS, ME. . . . . USA . .NHZ	Burwash Landings, YT Canada. . YDB
TX. . . . . .USA. . BKD	Brus Laguna. . . . . . .Honduras . . BHG	Burwell/Municipal, NE. . . . .USA. . BUB
Breckenridge/Van Svc, CO USA . . QKB	Brusque . . . . Brazil. . QJM	Bury St Edmunds/Honington UK . . BEQ
Breda/Gilze-Rijen . . Netherlands . . GLZ	Brussels . . . . Belgium . . CRL	Bushehr . . . . Iran. . .BUZ
Breiddalsvilk . . . . Iceland . . BXV	Brussels/Midi Railway Stn	Bussellton/Bussellton Arpt
Bremen . . . . Germany . . BRE	. . . . Belgium . . ZYR	. . . . Australia. . BQB
Bremerhaven. . . . . . . Germany . . BRV	Brussels/National . . . . . . Belgium . .BRU	Busuanga . . . . .Philippines. . USU
Bremerton, WA . . . . .USA. . PWT	Bryan/Coulter Fld, TX . . . . USA . .CFD	Buta . . . . Congo, DR. . BZU
Brescia . . . . Italy . . QBS	Bryant/AAF, AK . . . . USA . .FRN	Butare . . . . Rwanda.. BTQ
Brescia/Montichiari . . . . Italy . . VBS	Bryce Canyon, UT . . . . . USA . . BCE	Butaritari . . . . Kiribati. . BBG
Brest . . . . Belarus . . BQT	Bua/Dama. . . . . Fiji . . BVF	Butler, MO. . . . . .USA. . BUM
Brest/Guipavas . . . . France . . BES	Bubaque . . . . . Guinea Bissau . .BQE	Butler/Graham Fld, PA. . . . .USA. . .BTP
Breves . . . . Brazil. . BVS	Bucaramanga/Palo Negro	Butte/Mooney Arpt, MT . . . .USA. . BTM
Brewarrina . . . . Australia. . BWQ	. . . . Colombia . . BGA	Butterworth . . . . Malaysia. . BWH
Brewster Fld Arpt, NE . . . . .USA. . HDE	Buchanan . . . . Liberia . . UCN	Butterworth . . . . .S. Africa.. UTE
Bria . . . . Costa Rica . . BIV	Buchans, NF . . . . Canada . . YZM	Butuan . . . . .Philippines. . BXU
Briancon . . . . France . . XBC	Bucharest/Baneasa . . . Romania . . BBU	Buyo. . . . . Côte D'Ivoire. . BUU
Briansk . . . . Russia. . BZK	Bucharest/Otopeni Int'l Romania . . OTP	Buzios . . . . Brazil. . BZC
Bridgeport/Sikorsky Memorial,	Buchs SG . . . . Switzerland . . ZDO	Bydgoszcz . . . . Poland.. BZG
CT. . . . . .USA. . BDR	Buckeye, AZ . . . . USA . . BXK	Byron Bay . . . . .Australia. . QYN
Bridgetown/Grantley Adams Int'l	Buckland, AK . . . . USA . .BKC	
. . . . Barbados . .BGI	Budapest/Ferihegy . . . .Hungary . . BUD	
Brig . . . . .Switzerland. . ZDL	Budva . . . . Yugoslavia . . QBA	
Brigham City, UT . . . . .USA. .BMC	Buenaventura . . . . Colombia . . BUN	**C**
Bright . . . . Australia. . BRJ	Buenos Aires . . . . . . .Costa Rica . . BAI	
Brighton . . . . .UK . . BSH	Buenos Aires/Ministro Pistarini	
Brighton Downs . . . . . . Australia. . BHT	. . . . Argentina . . EZE	Ca Mau . . . . Vietnam. . CAH
Brindisi/Papola Casale . . . . Italy . . BDS	Buenos Aires/Newbery	Cabimas/Oro Negro . Venezuela. . CBS
Brisbane/Int'l. . . . . Australia. . BNE	. . . . Argentina . . AEP	Cabin Creek, AK . . . . .USA. . CBZ
Bristol, TN . . . . .USA. . TRI	Buffalo Int'l Arpt, NY . . . . USA . . BUF	Cabinda . . . . Angola. . CAB
Bristol/Filton . . . . .UK . . FZO	Buffalo Narrows, SK. . Canada . . YVT	Cabo Frio . . . . Brazil. . QCK
Bristol/Lulsgate. . . . . .UK . . BRS	Buffalo Range . . . . . Zimbabwe . .BFO	Cabo Rojo . . . . .Dominican Rep. . .CBJ
Britrail Rail Zone A . . . . . .UK . .QQA	Buffalo, WY . . . . USA . .BYG	Cacador . . . . Brazil. . CFC
Britrail Rail Zone B . . . . . .UK . .QQB	Buffalo/Buffalo Depew RR, NY	Caceres . . . . Brazil. . CCX
Britrail Rail Zone C . . . . . .UK . .QQC	. . . . USA . . ZFZ	Caceres . . . . Spain.. QUU
Britrail Rail Zone E . . . . . .UK . .QQE	Buffalo/Exchange St Railway	Cachoeira . . . . Brazil. . CCQ
Britrail Rail Zone F . . . . . .UK . .QQF	Svc., NY . . . . USA . . ZXS	Cachoeira Do Sul . . . . . Brazil. . QDB

AIRPORTS

Cachoeirinha . . . . Brazil . . QKA	Campo Born . . . . Brazil . QCD	Cariton Hill . . . . Australia . . CRY
Cachoeiro Itapemirim . . . Brazil . . QXD	Campo Grande/Int'l . . . . . Brazil . . CGR	Carleton/RR Stn., QC . . Canada . . XON
Cachoeiro Itapernirim . . Brazil . . CDI	Campo Mourac . . . . Brazil . CBW	Carlisle . . . . UK . . CAX
Cacoal . . . . Brazil . . OAL	Campo, CA . . . . USA . . CZZ	Carlsbad, CA . . . . USA . . CLD
Cadillac, MI . . . . USA . . CAD	Campobasso . . . . Italy . . QPB	Carmelita . . . . Guatemala . . CMM
Caen/Carpiquet . . . . France . . CFR	Campos Do Jorclao . . . . . Brazil . . QJO	**Carmen De Patagones**
Cafunfo . . . . Angola . . CFF	Campos/B. Lisandro . . . . Brazil . CAW	. . . . Argentina . . CPG
Cagayan De Oro/Lumbia	Can Tho . . . . Vietnam . . VCA	Carnarvon . . . . Australia . . CVQ
. . . . Philippines . . CGY	Cana Brava . . . . Brazil . . NBV	Carnot . . . . . Central African Rep . . CRF
Cagayan De Sulu . . Philippines . . CDY	Canadian/Hemphill, TX . . . USA . . HHF	Carolina . . . . Brazil . . CLN
Cagliari/Elmas . . . . Italy . . CAG	Canaima . . . . Venezuela . . CAJ	Carora . . . . Vanuatu . . VCR
Cagnes Sur Mer . . . . . . France . . XCG	Canakkaie . . . . Turkey . . CKZ	Carpentaria Downs . . . Australia . . CFP
Caherciveen/Reenroe . . Ireland . . CHE	Cananea . . . . Mexico . . CNA	Carriacou Is . . . . Grenada . . CRU
Cahors/Laberande . . . . . France . . ZAO	Canarana/Canarana Arpt . . Brazil . . CQA	Carrillo . . . . Costa Rica . . RIK
Caia . . . . Mozambique . . CMZ	Canas . . . . Costa Rica . . CSC	Carrizo Springs, TX . . . . . USA . . CZT
Caicara De Oro . . . . . Venezuela . . CXA	Canavieiras . . . . Brazil . . CNV	Carroll, IA . . . . USA . . CIN
Caiguna . . . . Australia . . CGV	Canberra . . . . Australia . . CBR	Carson City, NV. . . . . USA . . CSN
Cairns, CA . . . . Australia . . CNS	Cancun . . . . Mexico . . CUN	Carswell/AFB, TX. . . . . . . USA . . FWH
Cairns/AAF, AL . . . . USA . . OZR	Candala . . . . Somalia . . CXN	Cartagena/Rafael Nunez
Cairo, IL . . . . USA . . CIR	Candilejas . . . . Colombia . CJD	. . . . Colombia . . CTG
Cairo/Int'l . . . . Egypt . . CAI	Candle, AK . . . . USA . CDL	Cartago . . . . Colombia . . CRC
Cajamarca . . . . Peru . . CJA	Canela . . . . Brazil . . QCN	Cartersville, GA . . . . USA . . VPC
Calabar . . . . Nigeria . . CBQ	Cangamba . . . . Angola . . CNZ	Carti . . . . Panama . . CTE
Calabozo . . . . Venezuela . . CLZ	Cannes/Croisette HP . . . France . . JCA	Cartierville, QC . . . . Canada . . YCV
Calais . . . . France . . CQF	Cannes/Mandelieu . . . . . France . CEQ	Cartwright, NF . . . . Canada . . YRF
Calais/Frethun RR Stn. . . . France . . XFF	Cannes/Vieux Port . . . . . France . QYW	Caruaru . . . . Brazil . . CAU
Calama/El Loa . . . . Chile . . CJC	Canoas . . . . Brazil . . QNS	Carupano . . . . Venezuela . . CUP
Calbayog . . . . Philippines . . CYP	Canobie . . . . Australia . . CBY	Caruru . . . . Colombia . . CUO
Calcutta/N. S. Chandra . . . India . . CCU	Canoinhas . . . . Brazil . . QNH	Carutapera . . . . Brazil . . CTP
Caldas Novas . . . . Brazil . . CLV	Canon City, CO. . . . . USA . . CNE	Casa Grande/Mncpl, AZ . . USA . . CGZ
Caldwell, NJ . . . . USA . . CDW	**Canouan Is**	Casablanca/Anfa. . . . . Morocco . . CAS
Caledonia . . . . Panama . . CDE	. . . . St. Vincent & Grenadines . . CIW	**Casablanca**/Mohamed V
Caleta Olivia. . . . . Argentina . . CVI	Canton Is . . . . Kiribati . . CIS	. . . . Morocco . . CMN
Calexico/Int'l, CA . . . . USA . . CXL	Canton, SD . . . . USA . . CTK	Cascade Locks, OR. . . . . . USA . . CZK
Calgary Int'l, AB . . . . Canada . . YYC	Cap Haitien . . . . Haiti . . CAP	Cascavel . . . . Brazil . . CAC
Cali/Alfonso B. Aragon Colombia . . CLO	Cap Skirring . . . . Senegal . . CSK	Caserta . . . . Italy . . QTC
Calicut . . . . India . . CCJ	Capanda . . . . Angola . . KNP	Casigua . . . . Venezuela . . CUV
Calipatria, CA . . . . USA . . CLR	Cape Barren Is . . . . Australia . . CBI	Casiguran . . . . Philippines . . CGG
Callaway Gardens, GA . . . USA . . CWG	Cape Dorset, NT. . . . . . Canada . . YTE	Casino . . . . Australia . . CSI
Caloundra . . . . Australia . . CUD	Cape Eleuthera . . . . . Bahamas . . CEL	Casper, WY . . . . USA . . CPR
Caltanissetta . . . . Italy . . QCL	Cape Flattery . . . . Australia . . CQP	Casselman/RR Stn., ON Canada . . XZB
Calverton, NY . . . . USA . . CTO	Cape Girardeau, MO. . . . . USA . . CGI	Cassilandia . . . . Brazil . . CSS
Calvi/Ste Catherine . . . . . France . . CLY	**Cape Gloucester**	Castanhal . . . . Brazil . . QHL
Camacari . . . . Brazil . . QCC	. . . . Papua New Guinea . . CGC	Castaway . . . . Fiji . . CST
Camaguey/Ign Agramonte	Cape Lisburne, AK . . . . . . USA . . LUR	Castlebar . . . . Ireland . . CLB
. . . . Cuba . CMW	Cape Newenham, AK . . . . USA . EHM	Castlegar, BC. . . . . Canada . . YCG
Camas Do Sul/C.D. BugresBrazil . . CXJ	Cape Orford Papua New Guinea . . CPI	Castres/Mazamet. . . . . . . France . DCM
Cambrai . . . . France . . XCB	Cape Palmas/A. Tubman Liberia . . CPA	Castro . . . . Brazil . . QAC
Cambridge Bay, NT . . . Canada . . YCB	Cape Pole, AK. . . . . USA . . CZP	Castro/Gamboa . . . . Chile . WCA
Cambridge, MD . . . . USA . . CGE	**Cape Rodney**	Castrop-Rauxel . . . . . . Germany . . ZCM
Cambridge, MN . . . . UK . . CBG	. . . . Papua New Guinea . . CPN	Casuarito . . . . Colombia . . CSR
Cambridge/Hyatt Regency HP,	Cape Romanzof, AK . . . . . USA . . CZF	Cat Cays . . . . Bahamas . . CXY
MA . . . . USA . . JHY	**Cape Spencer**/Coast Guard HP,	Cat Is . . . . Bahamas . . CAT
Camden . . . . Australia . . CDU	AK. . . . . USA . . CSP	Cat Lake, ON . . . . Canada . . YAC
Camden, AR . . . . USA . . CDH	Cape St Jacques . . . . . Vietnam . . CSJ	Catacamas . . . . Honduras . . CAA
Camden/Woodward Fld, SC USA . . CDN	Cape St James, BC. . . . Canada . . YCJ	Cataguases . . . . Brazil . . QCG
Cameta . . . . Brazil . . CMT	Cape Town Int'l . . . . S. Africa . . CPT	Catalao . . . . Brazil . . TLZ
Camfieid . . . . Australia . . CFI	Cape Vogel Papua New Guinea . . CVL	Catalina Is, CA. . . . . USA . . CIB
Camiguin/Mamoajao Philippines . . CGM	Capreol/RR Stn., ON . . . Canada . . XAW	Catalina Is, CA. . . . . USA . . SXC
Camiri . . . . Bolivia . . CAM	Capri . . . . Italy . . PRJ	**Catalina Is**/Two Harbors, CA
Camocim . . . . Brazil . CMC	Capurgana . . . . Colombia . . CPB	. . . . USA . . TWH
Camooweal . . . . Australia . . CML	Caquetania . . . . Colombia . . CQT	Catamarca . . . . Argentina . . CTC
Camp Douglas, WI . . . . . USA . . VOK	Car Niconar. . . . . India . . CBD	Catanduva . . . . Brazil . . QDE
Camp Maybry AHP, TX . . . USA . . MMR	Caracas/Simon Bolivar	Catania/Fontanarossa . . . . Italy. . . CTA
Camp Springs, MD. . . . . . USA . . ADW	. . . . Venezuela . . CCS	Catanzaro . . . . Italy. . QCZ
Campbell County Arpt, WY	Caraguatatuba . . . . Brazil . . QCQ	Catarman/National. . . Philippines . . CRM
. . . . USA . . GCC	Carajas . . . . Brazil . . CKS	Caticlan/Malay . . . . . . Philippines . . MPH
Campbell River, BC . . Canada . . YBL	Caransebes . . . . Romania . . CSB	Cattle Creek . . . . Australia . . CTR
Campbell River/Harbor SPB,	Caratinga . . . . Brazil . . QTL	Catumbela . . . . Andorra . . CBT
BC . . . . Canada . . YHH	Carauari . . . . Brazil . . CAF	Cauayan . . . . Philippines . . CYZ
Campbell/AAF, KY . . . . . USA . . HOP	Caravelas . . . . Brazil . . CRQ	Caucasia . . . . Colombia . . CAQ
Campbellpore . . . . Pakistan . . CWP	Carazinho . . . . Brazil . . QRE	Caudebec en Caux . . . France . . QUX
Campbellton/RR Stn., NB	Carbondale, IL . . . . USA . MDH	Cauquira . . . . Honduras . . CDD
. . . . Canada . . XAZ	Carcassonne/Salvaza . . France . . CCF	Caussade . . . . France . . XCS
Campbeltown/Machrihanish	Cardiff. . . . . UK . CWL	Caviahue . . . . Argentina . . CVH
. . . . UK . . CAL	careh . . . . India . . BEK	Caxias . . . . Brazil . . QXC
Campeche/Campeche Int'l	Cariacica . . . . Brazil . . QRJ	Caye Caulker . . . . Belize. . CUK
. . . . Mexico . . CPE	Caribou Is, ON . . . . Canada . . YCI	Caye Chapel . . . . Belize. . CYC
Campina Grande/J. Suassuna	Caribou, ME. . . . . USA . . CAR	Cayenne/Rochambeau . . . .
. . . . Brazil . . CPV	Carimagua . . . . Colombia . . CCO	. . . . French Guiana . . CAY
Campinas/Int'l . . . . Brazil . . CPQ	Carlsbad, NM. . . . . USA . . CNM	Cayman Brac . . . . . . Cayman Is. . . CYB

A I R P O R T S

Cayo Coco . . . . Cuba . . CCC
Cayo Largo Del Sur . . . . . Cuba . . CYO
Cazombo . . . . Andorra . . CAV
Cebu . . . . Philippines . . CEB
Cecil/NAS, FL . . . . USA . . NZC
Cedar City, UT . . . . USA . . CDC
Cedar Rapids, IA . . . . USA . . CID
CedarKey/Lewis, FL . . . . USA . . CDK
Ceduna . . . . Australia . . CED
Celle . . . . Germany . . ZCN
Center Is, WA . . . . USA . . CWS
Centerville/Mncpl Arpt, TN .USA . GHM
New York, NY . . . . USA . . NYC
Central, AK . . . . USA . . CEM
Centralia, ON . . . . .Canada . . YCE
Centralia/Municipal, IL . . . .USA . . ENL
Cepu . . . . Indonesia . . CPF
Cerbere . . . . .France . . XCE
Ceres . . . . Argentina . . CRR
Cerro Sombrero . . . . Chile . . SMB
Cessnock . . . . Australia . . CES
Ceuta/Ceuta HP . . . . .Spain . . JCU
Chachapoyas . . . . .Peru . . CHH
Chadron, NE . . . . USA . . CDR
Chaffee/AFB, AR . . . . .USA . . CCA
Chagni . . . . Ethiopia . . MKD
Chah-Bahar . . . . Iran . . ZBR
Chaiten . . . . Chile . WCH
Chakcharan . . . . . . Afghanistan . . CCN
Chalkis . . . . Greece . .QKG
Chalkyitsik, AK . . . . .USA . . CIK
Challis, ID . . . . USA . . CHL
Chalon Sur Saone . . . . .France . XCD
Chalons Sur Marne . . . .France . XCR
Cham . . . . Germany . . QHQ
Chambery/Aix-Les-Bains France . CMF
Chambord/RR Stn., QC .Canada . . XCI
Chamonix Mont Blanc .France . XCF
Champaign, IL . . . . USA . . CMI
Champery . . . . .Switzerland . ZDQ
Chamrousse . . . . .France . XCQ
Chanaral . . . . Chile . . CNR
Chandalar, AK . . . . .USA . WCR
Chandigarh . . . . India . . IXC
Chandler/RR Stn., QC . .Canada . XDL
Chandler/Stellar Air Park, AZ
. . . . .USA . . SLJ
Changchun . . . . .China . CGQ
Changde . . . . .China . CGD
Changhai . . . . .China . . CNI
Changsha . . . . .China . CSX
Changuinola . . . . Panama . CHX
Changzi . . . . .China . . CIH
Changzhou . . . . .China . CZX
Chantilly . . . . .France . XCV
Chanute, KS . . . . .USA . CNU
Chaoyang/Chaoyang Arpt China . CHG
Chaparral . . . . Colombia . CPL
Chapeco . . . . Brazil . XAP
Chapel Hill/Williams, NC . .USA . . IGX
Chapleau, ON . . . . .Canada . YLD
Charata . . . . Argentina . CNT
Chardzhou . . . . . . Turkmenistan . CRZ
Charles City, IA . . . . .USA . CCY
Charleston Nise, SC. . . . . .USA . . NEX
Charleston, WV . . . . .USA . CRW
Charleston, WV . . . . .USA . RLX
Charleston/AFB, SC . . . . .USA . CHS
Charleston/AFB, SC . . . . .USA . . IGC
Charleville . . . . Australia . CTL
Charleville Mezieres . . .France . XCZ
Charlo, NB . . . . .Canada . YCL
Charlotte, NC . . . . .USA . .CLT
Charlotte/Wilgrove Air Park, NC
. . . . .USA . QWG
Charlottesville, VA . . . . . .USA . CHO
Charlottetown, NF. . . . .Canada . YHG
Charlottetown, PE. . . . .Canada . YYG
Charqueada . . . . Brazil . QDA
Charters Towers . . . . . Australia . CXT
Chartres . . . . .France . . QTJ

Chasso . . . . Switzerland . ZDS
Chateau Thierry . . . . France . XCY
Chateau-d-Oex. . . . . Switzerland . ZDR
Chateauroux. . . . . France . CHR
Chatellerault/Targe . . . . . France . XCX
Chatham Is/KarewaNew Zealand . CHT
Chatham Municipal, MA . USA . CQX
Chatham, ON . . . . Canada . XCM
Chatham/SPB, AK. . . . . . . USA . CYM
Chattanooga, TN . . . . USA . CHA
Chattanooga/Daisy, TN . . . USA . CQN
Chattanooga/Greyhound Bus
Svc, TN . . . . USA . QDK
Chaumont . . . . France . XCW
Chaurjlnari . . . . Nepal . HRJ
Chaves . . . . Portugal . CHV
Cheboksary . . . . Russia . CSY
Chefornak/SPB, AK . . . . . . USA . CYF
Chehalis/Centralia, WA. . . USA . CLS
Cheighourn Laid . . . . . . Algeria . QGM
Cheju/Cheju Int'l Arpt. . . . S. Korea . CJU
Cheju/Chu Ja HP . . . . . S. Korea . JCJ
Cheju/Sogwipo HP . . . . S. Korea . JSP
Cheinda . . . . Malawi . CEH
Chelyabinsk . . . . Russia . CEK
Chemainus/RR Stn., BC Canada . XHS
Chemnitz/RR Stn. . . . . . Germany . ZTZ
Chena Hot Springs, AK. . USA . CEX
Chenault Airpark, LA . . . . USA . CWF
Chengdu . . . . China . CTU
Chennai . . . . India . MAA
Cheonan . . . . Kuwait . XOX
Cheong Ju City/Arpt . S. Korea . CJJ
Cheraw, SC . . . . USA . HCW
Cherbourg/Maupertus . . France . CER
Cherchell . . . . Algeria . ZZC
Cherepovets . . . . Russia . CEE
Cherkassy . . . . Ukraine . CKC
Chernigov . . . . Ukraine . CEJ
Chernofski/SPB, AK. . . . . USA . KCN
Chernovtsy . . . . Ukraine . CWC
Cherokee, AR . . . . USA . CKK
Cherokee/Kegelman AF, OKUSA . CKA
Cherrabun . . . . Australia . CBC
Cherribah . . . . Australia . CRH
Cherry Point/MCAS, NC . . USA . NKT
Cherskiy . . . . Russia . CYX
Chesapeake/Huntington Cnty, OH
. . . . USA . HTW
Chester . . . . UK . CEG
Chesterfield Inlet, NU. Canada . . YCS
Chesterfield/Bus Svc . . . . . .UK . . ZFI
Cheturnal . . . . Mexico . CTM
Chetwynd, BC. . . . . Canada . YCQ
Cheung Sha Wan . . Hong Kong . ZZQ
Chevak, AK. . . . . USA . VAK
Chevery, QC . . . . Canada . YHR
Cheyenne, WY . . . . USA . CYS
Cheyenne/AFB, WY . . . . . USA . FEW
Chi Mei . . . . Taiwan . CMJ
Chiang Mai/Int'l . . . . . . Thailand . CNX
Chiang Rai . . . . Thailand . . CEI
Chiayi . . . . Taiwan . . CYI
Chiba City . . . . Japan . QCB
Chibougamau, QC . . . Canada . YMT
Chicago Nexrad, IL . . . . . USA . LOT
Chicago, IL. . . . . USA . CGX
Chicago, IL. . . . . USA . . CHI
Chicago-Waukegan, IL . . USA . UGN
Chicago/NAS, IL . . . . USA . NOH
Chicago/O'Hare Int'l, IL. . . USA . ORD
Chicago/Pal-Waukee, IL . . . USA . PWK
Chicago/Union Railway Svc, IL
. . . . USA . ZUN
Chichen Itza . . . . Mexico . CZA
Chichester Goodwood . . . .UK . QUG
Chickasha/Municipal, OK . USA . CHK
Chicken, AK. . . . . USA . CKX
Chiclayo/Connel Ruiz . . . . Peru . . CIX
Chico, CA . . . . USA . . CIC

Chicopee/Westover Arpt, MA
. . . . USA. . .CEF
Chifeng . . . . .China. . . CIF
Chignik, AK . . . . USA. . KCQ
Chignik, Chignik Bay, AK . . USA. . KBW
Chignik, Fisheries, AK . . . . . USA. . KCG
Chignik/Lagoon, AK . . . . . . USA. .KCL
Chigorodo . . . . .Colombia. . IGO
Chihuahua/G.F. Villalobos
. . . . .Mexico. . CUU
Chilas . . . . Pakistan. . CHB
Childress, TX . . . . USA. . CDS
Chile Chico . . . . .Chile. . CCH
Chilko Lake, BC . . . . . . Canada. . CJH
Chillagoe . . . . .Australia. .LLG
Chillan . . . . .Chile. . YAI
Chilliwack, BC. . . . . . . Canada. . YCW
Chiloquin/State, OR . . . . . USA. . CHZ
Chimbote . . . . Peru. . CHM
Chimoio . . . . .Mozambique. . VPY
China Lake/NAS, CA . . . . . USA. . NID
Chinchilla . . . . .Australia. . CCL
Chinde . . . . .Mozambique. . INE
Chingola . . . . Zambia. . CGJ
Chinguitti . . . . Mauritania. . CGT
Chinhae . . . . .S. Korea. . CHF
Chinju/Sacheon . . . . . .S. Korea. . . HIN
Chino, CA . . . . USA. . CNO
Chios/Khios. . . . . .Greece. . JKH
Chipata . . . . Zambia. . CIP
Chipinge . . . . .Zimbabwe. . CHJ
Chiquimula . . . . Guatemala. . CIQ
Chisana/Chisana Fld, AK . . USA. . CZN
Chisasibi, QC . . . . Canada. . YKU
Chisholm-Hibbing Arpt, MN
. . . . USA. . HIB
Chisinau . . . . Moldova. . KIV
Chistochina, AK . . . . USA. . CZO
Chita . . . . .Russia. .HTA
Chitato. . . . . .Angola. . PGI
Chitina Arpt, AK . . . . USA. . CXC
Chitral . . . . Pakistan. . CJL
Chitre . . . . .Panama. . CTD
Chittagong/PatengaBangladesh . CGP
Chiusa/Klausen/Bus Stn . . Italy. .ZAK
Chivoo . . . . .Colombia. . IVO
Chkalovsky . . . . .Russia. .CKL
Choibalsan . . . . Mongolia. . COQ
Choiseul Bay. . . . . . Solomon Is.. . CHY
Chokurdah . . . . .Russia. . CKH
Chokwe . . . . .Mozambique. .TGS
Cholet/Le Pontreau . . . . . France.. CET
Chomley, AK . . . . USA. . CIV
Chonburi . . . . .Thailand. . QHI
Chongju/Air Base . . . . .S. Korea. . CHN
Chongqing . . . . .China. . CKG
Chos Malal/Oscar Reguera
. . . . .Argentina. . HOS
Christchurch . . . New Zealand. . CHC
Christmas Creek . . . . .Australia. . CXQ
Christmas Is . . . . Kiribati. . CXI
Christmas Is . . . . Christmas Is.. XCH
Chuathbaluk, AK . . . . USA. . CHU
Chub Cay . . . . .Bahamas. . CCZ
Chulman . . . . Russia. . CNN
Chumphon Arpt . . . . . .Thailand. . CJM
Chun Chon City/Air Base
. . . . .S. Korea. . QUN
Chung-Mu City . . . . . .S. Korea. . QUU
Chungribu . Papua New Guinea. . CVB
Chuquicamata . . . . .Chile. . QUI
Chur . . . . Switzerland. .ZDT
Churchill Falls, NF . . . . Canada. . ZUM
Churchill, MB. . . . . Canada. . YYQ
Churchill/RR Stn., MB . . Canada. . XAD
Chute-Des-Passes, QC
. . . . Canada. .YWQ
Ciapoclue . . . . Brazil. . OYK
Cicia . . . . .Fiji. . . ICI
Ciego De Avila . . . . Cuba. . AVI
Cienfuegos . . . . Cuba. . CFG

AIRPORTS

Cierno . . . . .China . . IQM	Coen . . . . Australia . CUQ	Comuna Providencia . . . .Chile. . QOV
Cilacap/Tunggul Wuiung	Coeur D'Alene, ID . . . . USA . . COE	Conakry . . . . .Guinea. . CKY
. . . . .Indonesia . . CXP	Coffee Point, AK. . . . . USA . CFA	Conceicao Do Araguaia Brazil. . .CDJ
Cimitarra . . . . Colombia . . CIM	Coffeyvifle, KS . . . . USA . CFV	Concepcion . . . . Bolivia. . .CEP
Cincinnati, KY . . . . .USA . . CVG	Coffman Cove, AK. . . . . . . USA . KCC	Concepcion/Carriel Sur . . .Chile. . CCP
Cincinnati, OH . . . . .USA . . LUK	Coffs Harbour . . . . . . .Australia . CFS	Concepcion/MCAL Lopez
Circle Hot Springs, AK . . .USA . . CHP	Cognac/Chateau Bernard	. . . . .Paraguay. . CIO
Circle/Circle City, AK. . . . .USA . . IRC	. . . . France . CNG	Concord, CA . . . . .USA. . CCR
Cirebon/Penggung. . . Indonesia . CBN	Coimbatore/Peelamedu . . India . . CJB	Concord, NH . . . . USA. . CON
Ciucladela. . . . . .Spain . .QIU	Coirnar/Colmar-Houssen France . CMR	Concordia . . . . Brazil. . CCI
Ciudad Acuna Int'l . . . . .Mexico. .ACN	Coirribra. . . . . Portugal. .CBP	Concordia . . . . .Argentina. . COC
Ciudad Boliva . . . . . .Venezuela . . CBL	Colac . . . . Australia . XCO	Concordia, KS . . . . .USA. . CNK
Ciudad Constitucion . . Mexico . .CUA	Colatina . . . . .Brazil . QCH	Condobolin . . . . .Australia. . CBX
Ciudad Del Carmen . . . Mexico . CME	Colby/Municipal, KS . . . . . USA . .CBK	Condoto/Mandinga . . .Colombia. . COG
Ciudad del Este . . . . Paraguay . . AGT	Cold Bay, AK . . . . USA . CDB	Confreza . . . . Brazil. . CFO
Ciudad Guayana . . . .Venezuela . .CGU	Cold Lake, AB . . . . Canada . YOD	Congo Town . . . . . . .Bahamas. . COX
Ciudad Juarez/A. Gonzaiez	Coldfoot, AK . . . . USA . CXF	Coningsby/RAF. . . . . .UK. . QCY
. . . . Mexico . . CJS	Coleman, TX . . . . USA . COM	Connersville/Mettle Fld, IN USA. . CEV
Ciudad Mante . . . . Mexico . MMC	Colima . . . . Myanmar . .CLQ	Conroe, TX . . . . .USA. . CXO
Ciudad Obregon . . . . . . Mexico . . CEN	Collarenebri . . . . .Australia . .CRB	Conselheiro Lafaiete . . Brazil. . QDF
Ciudad Victoria . . . . Mexico . CVM	College Park, MD. . . . . . . USA . CGS	Constanta/Kogainiceanu
Claremont/Municipal, NH . .USA . .CNH	College Stn, TX. . . . . USA . CLL	. . . . .Romania. . CND
Clarinda, IA . . . . .USA . . ICL	Collie . . . . Australia . .CIE	Constantine . . . . .Algeria. . CZL
Clarks Point, AK . . . . . . .USA . . CLP	Collins Bay, SK. . . . . . . Canada . YKC	Constanza . . . . . .Dominican Rep. . COZ
Clarksburg, WV . . . . .USA . . CKB	Collinsville . . . . Australia . KCE	Contadora . . . . .Panama. . OTD
Clarksdale/Fletcher Fld, MS USA . CKM	Collioure/Off-line Pt. . . France . XCU	Coober Pedy . . . . .Australia. . CPD
Clarksville, TN . . . . .USA . . CKV	Collo . . . . Algeria . QOL	Cooch Behar . . . . .India. . COH
Clayton, NM . . . . .USA . . CAO	Cologne/Bonn/Off-line Pt	Cooinda . . . . .Australia. . CDA
Clear Lake, CA . . . . .USA . . CKE	. . . . .Germany . . BNJ	Cookitown . . . . .Australia. . CTN
Clearlake/Metroport, TX. . . .USA . . CLC	Cologne/Cologne/Bonn Mtrpltn.	Coolah . . . . .Australia. . CLH
Clearwater/Executive, FL . .USA . . CLW	. . . . .Germany . CGN	Coolawanyah . . . . . . .Australia. . COY
Clemson, SC. . . . . .USA . . CEU	Cologne/RR . . . . .Germany . QKU	Coolibah . . . . .Australia. . COB
Clermont . . . . Australia . CMQ	Cologne/Stn. . . . . .Germany . .QKL	Cooma . . . . .Australia. .OOM
Clermont-Ferrand/Aulriat.France . . CFE	Colombo/Bandaranayake	Coonabarabran . . . . . .Australia. . COJ
Cleve . . . . Australia . CVC	. . . . Sri Lanka . CMB	Coonamble . . . . .Australia. . CNB
Cleveland, Burke Arpt, OH .USA . . BKL	Colombo/Ratmalana. . Sri Lanka . .RML	Cooper Lodge/Quartz Creek,
Cleveland, OH . . . . .USA . . CGF	Colon . . . . Panama . ONX	AK. . . . . .USA. . JLA
Cleveland, OH . . . . .USA . . CLE	Colon . . . . .Chile . QCO	Cooperstown, NY. . . . . . . .USA. . COP
Clifton Hills . . . . Australia . CFH	Colonia . . . . Uruguay . CYR	Coorabie . . . . .Australia. . CRJ
Clinton Creek, YT . . . . .Canada . . YLM	Colonia Catriel . . . . . . Argentina . CCT	Cootamundra . . . . .Australia. . CMD
Clinton, IA . . . . .USA . . CWI	Colonia Sarmiento . . Argentina . OLN	Copan . . . . Honduras. . RUY
Clinton, OK. . . . . .USA . .CSM	Colonsay Is . . . . .UK . CSA	Copenhagen/Kastrup . Denmark. . CPH
Clinton/Municipal, OK . . . .USA . . CLK	Colorado Creek, AK . . . . USA . KCR	Copenhagen/RR Stn. . Denmark. . ZGH
Clinton/Sampson County, NC	Colorado do Oeste . . . . .Brazil . CSW	Copenhagen/Roskilde Denmark. .RKE
. . . . USA . . CTZ	Colorado Springs, CO. . . USA . COS	Copiapo/Chamonate . . . .Chile. . CPO
Clintonville, WI. . . . . .USA . . CLI	Colorado Springs/USAF Academy, CO	Copper Centre, AK. . . . . .USA. . CZC
Clitton/Morenci, AZ . . . . . .USA . . CFT	. . . . USA . . AFF	Copper Mountain/Van Svc, CO
Cloncurry . . . . Australia . CNJ	Colorado Springs/AAF, COUSA . . FCS	. . . . .USA. . QCE
Clorinda. . . . . Argentina . . CLX	Colt Is . . . . .UK . .COL	Coppermine, NU. . . . . . Canada. . YCO
Clovis/AFB, NM. . . . . .USA . . CVS	Coltishall . . . . .UK . . CLF	Coquimbo . . . . .Chile. .COW
Clovis/Municipal, NM . . . . .USA . . CVN	Columbia, CA . . . . USA . COA	Coral Harbour, NT . . . . Canada. . YZS
Club Makokola . . . . . . .Malawi . .CMK	Columbia, MO. . . . . USA . COU	Corazon De Jesus . . . Panama. . CZJ
Cluff Lake, SK . . . . . . .Canada . . XCL	Columbia, SC . . . . USA . CAE	Corcoran, CA. . . . . .USA. . CRO
Cluj/Napoca . . . . .Romania . .CLJ	Columbia, SC . . . . USA . CUB	Cordillo Downs . . . . . .Australia. . ODL
Cluny . . . . Australia . . CZY	Columbia, SC . . . . USA . MMT	Cordoba . . . . Spain. . ODB
Clyde River, NU . . . . . . .Canada . . YCY	Columbia, TN . . . . USA . MRC	Cordoba/Pajas Blancas
Clyde, NT . . . . .Canada . . . YY	Columbus Metropolitan, GA	. . . . .Argentina. . COR
Coalinga, CA. . . . . .USA . . CLG	. . . . USA . CSG	Cordova, AK. . . . . .USA. . CDV
Coan . . . . Brazil . . CIZ	Columbus Municipal, IN . USA . CLU	Cordova/City, AK . . . . .USA. . CKU
Coatepeque . . . . Guatemala . CTF	Columbus, MS . . . . USA . GTR	Corinth/Roscoe Turner, MS. USA. . CRX
Coatesville, PA. . . . . .USA . . CTH	Columbus, NE. . . . . USA . OLU	Cork . . . . Ireland. . ORK
Coatzacoalcos . . . . Mexico . QTZ	Columbus, OH . . . . USA . CMH	Corn Is. . . . . Netherlands. . RNI
Coban . . . . Guatemala . CBV	Columbus/AFB, MS . . . . . USA . CBM	Corner Bay, AK . . . . .USA. . CBA
Cobar . . . . Australia . CAZ	Columbus/Lowrides County, MS	Corner Brook/Deer Lake, NF
Cobija/E. Beltram . . . . . Bolivia . . CIJ	. . . . USA . .UBS	. . . . Canada. . YNF
Cobourg/RR Stn., ON. . .Canada . . XGJ	Columbus/Municipal, NM . USA . .CUS	Cornwall/Regional, ON . Canada. . YCC
Coburg. . . . . .Germany . ZCP	Colurribus, OH . . . . USA . OSU	Coro . . . . Venezuela. . CZE
Coca . . . . .Ecuador . .OCC	Colville Lake, NT . . . . . Canada . YCK	Coromandel. . . . . . New Zealand. . CMV
Cochabamba/J Wilsterman	Colville Municipal, WA. . . USA . CQV	Coron . . . . Philippines. . XCN
. . . . Bolivia . . CBB	Comayagua/Palmerola Air Base	Coronation, AB . . . . Canada. . YCT
Cochin . . . . India . .COK	. . . . Honduras. . XPL	Coronel E Solo Cano AB . . . .
Cochrane . . . . Chile . LGR	Comelio Procopio. . . . . .Brazil . CKO	. . . . Honduras. . ENQ
Cochrane, ON . . . . . . .Canada . . YCN	Comilla . . . . .Bangladesh . CLA	Corowa . . . . .Australia. . CWW
Cochstedt . . . . .Germany . . CSO	Cominc / HP. . . . . .Malta . JCO	Corozal . . . . Belize. . CZH
Cocoa/AFB, FL . . . . .USA . .COF	Comiso . . . . Italy . .CIY	Corozal . . . . Colombia. . CZU
Cocoa/Merritt Is, FL. . . . . .USA . .COI	Como . . . . Italy . QCM	Corpus Christi, TX . . . . . . .USA. . CRP
Coconut Is . . . . Australia . CNC	Comodoro Rivadavia	Corpus Christi/Cuddihy Fld,
Cocos Iss . . .Cocos (Keeling) Is . .CCK	. . . . .Argentina . CRD	TX . . . . .USA. . CUX
Codazzi . . . . Colombia . .OZI	Comox, BC. . . . . Canada . YQQ	Corpus Christi/NAS, TX . .USA. . NGP
Codroipo . . . . Italy . QOP	Compiegne/Margny . . . . France . XCP	Corpus Christi/NAS, TX . .USA. .NGW
Cody, WY . . . . .USA . . COD	Compton, CA . . . . USA . CPM	Corralejo. . . . . Spain. . QFU

AIRPORTS

Corrientes/Camba PuntaArgentina		CNQ
Corryong	Australia	CYG
Corsicana, TX	USA	CRS
Cortes Bay, BC	Canada	YCF
Cortez, CO	USA	CEZ
Cortina d'Ampezzo/Fiames	Italy	CDF
Cortland, NY	USA	CTX
Corumba/Int'l	Brazil	CMG
Corvo Is	Portugal	CVU
Cosenza	Italy	QCS
Costa Marques	Brazil	CQS
Cotabato/Awang	Philippines	CBO
Coteau/RR Stn., QC	Canada	XGK
Cotia	Brazil	QOI
Coto 47	Costa Rica	OTR
Cotonou/Cadjehoun	Benin	COO
Cottbus/Flugplatz	Germany	CBU
Cottbus/RR Stn.	Germany	ZTT
Cottonwood, AZ	USA	CTW
Cotulla, TX	USA	COT
Council Bluffs, IA	USA	CBF
Council/Melsing Creek, AK	USA	CIL
Courbevoie	France	QEV
Courchevel	France	CVF
Courtenay, BC	Canada	YCA
Covenas	Colombia	CVE
Coventry/Baginton	UK	CVT
Covilha	Portugal	COV
Cowarie	Australia	CWR
Cowell	Australia	CCW
Cowley, AB	Canada	YYM
Cowra	Australia	CWT
Cox's Bazar	Bangladesh	CXB
Coyhaique/Ten. Vidal	Chile	GXQ
Coyoles	Honduras	CYL
Cozad Municipal, NE	USA	CZD
Cozumel	Mexico	CZM
Cradock	S. Africa	CDO
Craiciva	Romania	CRA
Craig Cove	Vanuatu	CCV
Craig/AFB, AL	USA	SEM
Craig/Craig-Molfat, CO	USA	CIG
Craig/SPB, AK	USA	CGA
Crailsheim	Germany	QEI
Cranbrook, BC	Canada	YXC
Crane County Arpt, TX	USA	CCG
Crane Is, WA	USA	CKR
Crankenback Villeage/		
Bus Svc	Australia	QWL
Cranzahl/RR Stn.	Germany	ZZH
Cravo None	Colombia	RAV
Creech/AAF, KY	USA	LSD
Creil/AFB	France	CSF
Crescent City, CA	USA	CEC
Cresswell Downs	Australia	CSD
Crested Butte, CO	USA	CSE
Creston, BC	Canada	CFQ
Creston, IA	USA	CSQ
Crestview, FL	USA	CEW
Creteil	France	QFC
Creusot Montceau Mont		
	France	XCC
Crewe/RR Stn.	UK	XVC
Cricluma	Brazil	CCM
Croker Is	Australia	CKI
Cromarty	UK	CRN
Crooked Creek, AK	USA	CKD
Crooked Is	Bahamas	CRI
Crookston, MN	USA	CKN
Cross City, FL	USA	CTY
Cross Lake, MB	Canada	YCR
Crossett/Municipal, AR	USA	CRT
Crossville, TN	USA	CSV
Crotone	Italy	CRV
Crows Landing/NAS, CA	USA	NRC
Croydon	Australia	CDQ
Cruz Alta/Carios Ruhl	Brazil	CZB
Cruzeiro Do Sul/Campo Int'l		
	Brazil	CZS
Crystal Lake, PA	USA	CYE
Cuamba	Mozambique	FXO

Cube Cove	AK	USA	CUW
Cucuta/Camilo Dazo	Colombia	CUC
Cudal	Australia	CUG
Cuddapain	India	CDP
Cue	Australia	CUY
Cuenca	Ecuador	CUE
Cuernavaca	Mexico	CVJ
Cuhacan/F.D. Bachigualato		
	Mexico	CUL
Cuiaba/M. Rondon	Brazil	CGB
Cuito Cuanavale	Angola	CTI
Culebra	Puerto Rico	CPX
Culion	Philippines	CUJ
Culver City/Hughes, CA	USA	CVR
Cum El Bouaghi	Algeria	QMH
Cumana	Venezuela	CUM
Cumberland/Wiley Ford, MD		
	USA	CBE
Cuneo/Levaldigi	Italy	CUF
Cunnamuila	Australia	CMA
Cunuzu Cuatia	Argentina	UZU
Curacao/Halo		
	Netherlands Antilles	CUR
Curico	Chile	ZCQ
Curitiba./Bacacher;	Brazil	BFH
Curitiba/Afonso Pena	Brazil	CWB
Curitibanos	Brazil	QCR
Currais Novos	Brazil	QCP
Currillo	Colombia	CUI
Cururupu	Brazil	CPU
Cushing/Municipal, OK	USA	CUH
Cut Bank, MT	USA	CTB
Cutral	Argentina	CUT
Cuyo	Philippines	CYU
Cuzio/Velazco Astete	Peru	CUZ
Czestochowa	Poland	CZW

D

Da Nang	Vietnam	DAD
Dabra	Indonesia	DRH
Dachau	Germany	ZCR
Dadu	Pakistan	DDU
Dael/Camarines Norte		
	Philippines	DTE
Dahigren/NAF, VA	USA	DGN
Dahl Creek/Dahl Creek Arpt, AK		
	USA	DCK
Dakar/Yoff	Senegal	DKR
Dakhla	Morocco	VIL
Dakhla Oasis/Dakhla	Egypt	DAK
Dalanzadgad	Mongolia	DLZ
Dalat/Lienkinang	Vietnam	DLI
Dalbandin	Pakistan	DBA
Dalbertis	Papua New Guinea	DLB
Dalgaranga	Australia	DGD
Dalhart, TX	USA	DHT
Dali City/Dali	China	DLU
Dalian	China	DLC
Dallas North Arpt, TX	USA	DNE
Dallas, TX	USA	ADS
Dallas, TX	USA	DAL
Dallas/DFW Redbird, TX	USA	RBD
Dallas/Fort Worth, TX	USA	AFW
Dallas/Market Centre HP, TX	USA	JMD
Dallas/NAS, TX	USA	NBE
Dallas/North Park Inn HP, TX	USA	JNH
Dallby	Australia	DBY
Daloa	Côte D'Ivoire	DJO
Dalton/FlightLink Bus Svc, GA		
	USA	QJJ
Dalton/Municipal, GA	USA	DNN
Daly River	Australia	DVR
Daly Waters	Australia	DYW
Daman	India	NMB
Damanhour	Egypt	QUD
Damascus/Int'l	Syria	DAM
Damierta	Egypt	QDX

Dammarn/King Fahad		
	Saudi Arabia	DMM
Danane	Côte D'Ivoire	DNC
Danbury, CT	USA	DXR
Dandong	China	DDG
Dang	Nepal	DNP
Danger Bay, AK	USA	DGB
Dangriga	Belize	DGA
Daniels Harbour, NF	Canada	YDH
Dansville, NY	USA	DSV
Danville, VA	USA	DAN
Danville/Vermilion County, IL	USA	DNV
Daparizo	India	DAE
Dar Es Salaam/Int'l	Tanzania	DAR
Darchula	Nepal	DAP
Dargaville	New Zealand	DGR
Darjeelino	India	DAI
Darlington/RR Stn.	UK	XVG
Darmstact	Germany	ZCS
Darnley Is	Australia	NLF
Daru	Papua New Guinea	DAU
Daru	Sierra Leone	DSL
Darwaz	Afghanistan	DAZ
Darwin Arpt	Australia	DRW
Data Processing Ctr	n/a	DPC
Datadawai	Indonesia	DTD
Dataman	Turkey	DLM
Dathina	Yemen	DAH
Datong	China	DAT
Dauan Is	Australia	DAJ
Daugavpils	Latvia	DGP
Daugo	Papua New Guinea	DGG
Daup	Papua New Guinea	DAF
Dauphin, MB	Canada	YDN
Davao	Philippines	DVO
Davenport Downs	Australia	DVP
Davenport, IA	USA	DVN
David/Enrique Maiek	Panama	DAV
Davis Inlet, NF	Canada	YDI
Davos	Switzerland	ZDV
Dawe	Myanmar	TVY
Dawson Creek, BC	Canada	YDQ
Dawson, YT	Canada	YDA
Dax/Seyresse	France	XDA
Daxian	China	DAX
Daydream Is	Australia	DDI
Daylon/Wright/AFB	USA	DWF
Dayong	China	DYG
Dayton, OH	USA	DAY
Dayton, OH	USA	MGY
Dayton/AFB, OH	USA	FFO
Daytona Beach/Regional, FL		
	USA	DAB
Dazu	China	DZU
De Ridder/Beauregard Parish,		
LA	USA	DRI
Deadhorse, AK	USA	SCC
Deadmans Cay	Bahamas	LGI
Dean River, BC	Canada	YRD
Dearborn/Hyatt Regency HP, MI		
	USA	DEO
Dease Lake, BC	Canada	YDL
Death Valley, CA	USA	DTH
Deauville/St Gatien	France	DOL
Debepare	Papua New Guinea	DBP
Debra Marcos	Ethiopia	DBM
Debra Tabor	Ethiopia	DBT
Debrecen	Hungary	DEB
Decatur Is, WA	USA	DTR
Decatur, AL	USA	DCU
Decatur, IL	USA	DEC
Decatur/Decatur Hi-Way, IN	USA	DCR
Deception, QC	Canada	YGY
Decimomannu/Ratsu	Italy	DCI
Decorah, IA	USA	DEH
Dedougou	Burkina Faso	DGU
Deep Bay, AK	USA	WDB
Deer Lake, NF	Canada	YDF
Deer Lake, ON	Canada	YVZ
Deering, AK	USA	DRG
Deering, Deering Arpt, AK	USA	DEE

Defiance, OH ... USA ... DFI
Degalthbur ... Ethiopia .. DGC
Dehra Dun ... India .. DED
Deirezzor/Al Jafrah ... Syria .. DEZ
Del Rio, TX ... USA .. DRT
Del Rio/AFB, TX ... USA .. DLF
Delemont ... Switzerland .. ZDW
Delhi/Indira Gandhi Int'l ... India .. DEL
Deline, NT ... Canada .. YWJ
Delissaville ... Australia .. DLV
Delmenhorst ... Germany .. ZCT
Delta Downs ... Australia .. DDN
Delta Junction, AK ... USA .. DJN
Delta, UT ... USA .. DTA
Dembidollo ... Ethiopia .. DEM
Deming, NM ... USA .. DMN
Den Helder/De Kooy ... Netherlands .. DHR
Denham ... Australia .. DNM
Deniliquin ... Australia .. DNQ
Denis Is ... Seychelles ... DEI
Denison, IA ... USA .. DNS
Denizli/Cardak ... Turkey .. DNZ
Denpasar, Bali/N. Rai ... Indonesia .. DPS
Denton/Municipal Arpt, TX .. USA .. DTO
Denver Nexrad, CO ... USA .. FTG
Denver, CO ... USA .. APA
Denver, CO ... USA .. DEN
Denver/Buckley ANGB, CO.USA .. BFK
Deparizo ... India .. DEP
Dera Ghazi Khan ... Pakistan .. DEA
Dera Ismail Khan ... Pakistan .. DSK
Dera'a ... Syria .. QDR
Derby ... Australia .. DRB
Derim ... Papua New Guinea .. DER
Derna/Martuba ... Libya .. DNF
Des Moines Nexrad, IA ... USA .. DMX
Des Moines, IA ... USA .. DSM
Desolation Sound, BC.Canada .. YDS
Desroches ... Seychelles .. DES
Dessau/RR Stn. ... Germany .. ZSU
Dessie/Combolcha ... Ethiopia .. DSE
Destin, FL ... USA ... DSI
Destin, Ft Walton Beach, FL USA ... DTS
Detmold ... Germany .. ZCU
Detroit Lakes/Municipal, MN ... USA .. DTL
Detroit NAF, MI ... USA .. NFB
Detroit Nexrad, MI ... USA .. DTX
Detroit, MI ... USA .. DET
Detroit, MI ... USA .. DTW
Detroit-Willow Run, MI ... USA ... YIP
Deux Alpes ... France .. DXA
Deva ... Romania .. DVA
Deventer/RR ... Netherlands .. QYV
Devils Lake, ND ... USA .. DVL
Devonpori ... Australia .. DPO
Dewsbury/Bus Stn ... UK .. ZEQ
Dfw Nexrad, TX ... USA .. FWS
Dhahran ... Saudi Arabia .. DHA
Dhaka/Zia Int'l ... Bangladesh .. DAC
Dhala ... Yemen .. DHL
Dhanbad ... India .. DBD
Dhangarhi ... Nepal .. DHI
Dharamsala/Gaggal Arpt . India .. DHM
Dharnar ... Yemen .. DMR
Diadema ... Brazil . QDW
Diamantina Lakes ... Australia .. DYM
Dianopolis ... Brazil .. DNO
Diapaga ... Burkina Faso ... DIP
Diarnantino ... Brazil .. DMT
Dibaa ... Oman .. BYB
Dibrugarn/Chabua ... India .. DIB
Dickinson, ND ... USA .. DIK
Dicling ... China ... DIG
Didcot Parkway/RR Stn. ... UK .. XPW
Diebougou ... Burkina Faso .. XDE
Dien Sien Phu/Gialam .Vietnam ... DIN
Dieppe/Saint Aubin ... France .. DPE
Dietikon ... Switzerland .. ZDX

Digne ... France ... XDI
Dijon ... France ... DIJ
Dikson ... Russia .. DKS
Dilasag ... Philippines . DSG
Dili ... Congo, DR .. DIC
Dili/Comoro ... Indonesia ... DIL
Dillingharn/Municipal, AK . USA .. DLG
Dillon, MT ... USA .. DLN
Dillon, SC ... USA .. DLL
Dillons Bay ... Vanuatu .. DLY
Dimapur ... India . DMU
Dimbokro/Ville ... Côte D'Ivoire .. DIM
Dinangat .. Papua New Guinea . DNU
Dinard ... France . DNR
Dinco ... Angola . DRC
Dinder/Galegu ... Sudan .. DNX
Dinslaken ... Germany .. ZCV
Diomede Is, AK ... USA .. DIO
Dionisio Cerqueira ... Brazil ... XIS
Dios ... Papua New Guinea . DOS
Dipolog ... Philippines ... DPI
Dire Dawa/Aba Tenna D Yilma ... Ethiopia .. DIR
Dirranbandi ... Australia . DRN
Disneyland Paris-RR .. France .. XED
Diu ... India .. DIU
Dives Cabourg ... France .. XDC
Divinopolis ... Brazil .. DIQ
Divo ... Côte D'Ivoire ... DIV
Dixie ... Australia .. DXD
Diyarbakir ... Turkey ... DIY
Djambala ... Congo, DR .. DJM
Djanet ... Algeria .. DJG
Djelfa ... Algeria .. QDJ
Djerba/Zarzis ... Tunisia .. DJE
Djgby, NS ... Canada . YDG
Djibo ... Burkina Faso .. XDJ
Djibouti/Ambouli .. Côte D'Ivoire ... JIB
Djoemoe ... Suriname . DOE
Djougou ... Benin .. DJA
Djupivogur ... Iceland .. DJU
Dnepropetrovsk ... Ukraine . DNK
Doany ... Madagascar . DOA
Dobo/Dobo Arpt ... Indonesia . DOB
Doc Creek, BC ... Canada .. YDX
Docker River ... Australia .. DKV
Dodge City, KS ... USA . DDC
Dodoirna .. Papua New Guinea . DDM
Dodoma ... Tanzania . DOD
Doha/Int'l Arpt ... Qatar . DOH
Doini ... Papua New Guinea .. DOI
Dolbeau/St Methode, QC ... Canada . YDO
Dolorni, AK ... USA .. DLO
Dolpa ... Nepal . DOP
Dom Pedrito ... Brazil . QDP
Dominica/Cane Field . Dominica .. DCF
Dominica/Melville Hail ... Oman . DOM
Donauwoerth ... Germany . QWR
Doncaster/Finningley ... UK .. DCS
Donegal ... Ireland . CFN
Donetsk ... Ukraine . DOK
Dongara ... Australia . DOX
Dongguan ... China . DGM
Dongola ... Sudan . DOG
Dongsheng ... China .. DSN
Doomadgee ... Australia . DMD
Doongan ... Australia . DNG
Dora Bay, AK ... USA .. DOF
Dorado/Dorado Beach ... Puerto Rico .. DDP
Dori ... Burkina Faso . DOR
Dormagen ... Germany . ZCW
Dornbirn ... Austria .. QDI
Dornoch ... UK . DOC
Dorobisoro Papua New Guinea . DOO
Dorsten ... Germany .. ZCX
Dortmund/Wickede .. Germany . DTM
Dorunda Stn ... Australia . DRD
Dos Lagunas ... Guatemala . DON
Dote/Tavaux ... France .. DLE

Dothan, AL ... USA .. DHN
Douai ... France .. XDN
Douala ... Cameroon .. DLA
Douglas Lake, BC ... Canada .. DGF
Douglas Municipal, AZ ... USA .. DGL
Douglas, AZ ... USA .. DUG
Douglas, WY ... USA .. DGW
Dourados ... Brazil .. DOU
Dover/AFB, DE ... USA .. DOV
Dover/RR ... UK .. QQD
Downey/HP, CA ... USA ... JDY
Doylestown ... Australia ... DYL
Dra El Mizan ... Algeria ... ZZD
Dracena ... Brazil .. QDC
Drachten/Bus Svc . Netherlands .. QYC
Drama ... Greece .. DRM
Drayton Valley, AB ... Canada .. YDC
Dresden/Klotzsche ... Germany .. DRS
Dreux ... France .. XDR
Drietabbetje ... Suriname ... DRJ
Drift River, AK ... USA ... DRF
Drumduff ... Australia ... DFP
Drummond Is, MI ... USA .. DRE
Drummond, MT ... USA .. DRU
Drummondville/RR Stn., QC ... Canada .. XDM
Dryden, ON ... Canada .. YHD
Drysdale River ... Australia .. DRY
Dschang ... Cameroon .. DSC
Dubai ... UAE .. DXB
Dubbo ... Australia .. DBO
Dublin ... Ireland .. DUB
Dublin, VA ... USA ... PSK
Dublin/Municipal, GA ... USA .. DBN
Dubois, ID ... USA .. DBS
Dubois/Jefferson County, PA ... USA ... DUJ
Dubrovnik ... Croatia .. DBV
Dubuque, IA ... USA .. DBQ
Duck/Pine Is Arpt, OK ... USA .. DUF
Dueren ... Germany ... ZCY
Duesseldorf ... Germany .. DUS
Dugway/AAF, UT ... USA .. DPG
Duisburg ... Germany ... DUI
Dukuduk ... S. Africa .. DUK
Dulkaninna ... Australia ... DLK
Dulles Int'l, DC ... USA ... IAD
Duluth, MN ... USA .. DLH
Duluth/Lakeside USAF, MN USA ... LKI
Dumaguete ... Philippines .. DGT
Dumai ... Indonesia .. DUM
Dumpu ... Papua New Guinea .. DPU
Dunbar ... Australia .. DNB
Duncan Town ... Bahamas .. DCT
Duncan/Halliburton, OK ... USA .. DUC
Dunce ... Angola .. DUE
Dundas ... Greenland .. DUN
Dundee/Riverside ... UK .. DND
Dundee/ScotRail ... UK .. ZDU
Dunedin ... New Zealand .. DUD
Dunhuang ... China .. DNH
Dunk Is ... Australia ... DKI
Dunkerque/Ghyvelde ... France .. XDK
Dunkirk, NY ... USA .. DKK
Dunta Chivato ... Mexico ... PCV
Duque De Caxias ... Brazil .. QDQ
Durango, CO ... USA .. DRO
Durango/Animas Airpark, CO ... USA .. AMK
Durango/Guadalupe Victoria ... Mexico .. DGO
Durant/Eaker, OK ... USA .. DUA
Durazno ... Uruguay .. DZO
Durban/Durban Int'l ... S. Africa .. DUR
Durban/Virginia ... S. Africa ... VIR
Durham Downs ... Australia .. DHD
Durham/RR Stn. ... UK .. XVU
Durrie ... Australia .. DRR
Dushanbe ... Australia .. DYU
Dusseldorf/Monchen-Gladbach ... Germany .. MGL

AIRPORTS

Dusseldorf/Stn . . . . . . Germany . . QDU	**East Hartford**/Rentschler, CT . . . . USA . . EHT	**El Minya** . . . . Egypt. . EMY
Dutch Harbor/Emergency Fld, AK . . . . USA . . DUT	**East London** . . . . S. Africa . . ELS	**El Monte**, CA . . . . USA . . EMT
Dutch Rail Zone 01/Rail Service . . . . Netherlands . . .ZVL	**East Main**, QC . . . . Canada . .ZEM	**El Naranjo** . . . . Guatemala. . ENJ
Dutch Rail Zone 02/Rail Service . . . . Netherlands . ZWO	**East Stroudsburg**/B. Pocono, PA. . . . . USA . . ESP	**El Nido**. . . . . Philippines. . ENI **El Obeid** . . . . Sudan. . EBD
Dutch Rail Zone 03/Rail Service . . . . Netherlands . . ZVN	**East Tawas**, MI . . . . USA . .ECA	**El Oued** . . . . Algeria. . ELU
Dutch Rail Zone 04/Rail Service . . . . Netherlands . . ZVO	**Easter Is**/Mataveri inE. . . . .Chile . . .IPC	**El Paso**, TX . . . . .USA . . ELP
Dutch Rail Zone 05/Rail Service . . . . Netherlands . . ZVP	**Eastland**/Municipal, TX. . . . USA . . ETN	**El Portillo** . . . . .Dominican Rep. . EPS
Dutch Rail Zone 06/Rail Service . . . . Netherlands . . ZVQ	**Easton**, MD . . . . USA . .ESN	**El Porvenir** . . . . Panama. . PVE
Dutch Rail Zone 07/Rail Service . . . . Netherlands . . ZWQ	**Easton**/State, WA. . . . . USA . . ESW	**El Real** . . . . Panama. . ELE
Dutch Rail Zone 08/Rail Service . . . . Netherlands . . ZVS	**Eastport**, ME . . . . USA . . EPO	**El Recreo** . . . . Colombia. . ELJ
Dutch Rail Zone 09/Rail Service . . . . Netherlands . .ZVT	**Eastsound**/Orcas Is, WA . . USA . . ESD	**El Salvador** . . . . Chile. . ESR
Dutch Rail Zone 10/Rail Service . . . . Netherlands . ZVU	**Eau Claire**, WI . . . . .USA . .EAU	**El Tigre** . . . . Venezuela. . ELX
Dutch Rail Zone 11/Rail Service . . . . Netherlands . . ZVV	**Ebadon** . . . . Marshall Is . . EBN	**El Vigia** . . . . Venezuela. . VIG
Dutch Rail Zone 12/Rail Service . . . . Netherlands . .ZVW	**Ebeye** . . . . Marshall Is . . QEE	**Elat**/J. Hozman . . . . Israel. . ETH
Dutch Rail Zone 13/Rail Service . . . . Netherlands . . ZVX	**Ebolowa** . . . . Cameroon . EBW	**Elazig** . . . . Turkey. . EZS
Dutch Rail Zone 14/Rail Service . . . . Netherlands . ZVY	**Ebon**/Ebon Arpt . . . . . Marshall Is . . EBO	**Elblag**. . . . . Poland. . ZBG
Dutch Rail Zone 15/Rail Service . . . . Netherlands . . ZVZ	**Ech Cheliff**. . . . . Algeria . . QAS	**Elcho Is**. . . . . Australia. . ELC
Dutch Rail Zone 16/Rail Service . . . . Netherlands . . ZUO	**Echuca** . . . . Australia . .ECH	**Eldebba**. . . . . Sudan. . EDB
Dutch Rail Zone 17/Rail Service . . . . Netherlands . . ZUP	**Eday** . . . . .UK . . EOI	**Eldorado**. . . . . .Argentina. . ELO
Dutch Rail Zone 18/Rail Service . . . . Netherlands . .ZUQ	**Eden** . . . . .Australia . QDN	**Eldoret**. . . . . Kenya. . EDL
Dutch Rail Zone 19/Rail Service . . . . Netherlands . . ZUR	**Edenton**/Municipal, NC . . . USA . . EDE	**Eldred Rock**/Coast Guard, AK . . . . USA. . ERO
Dutch Rail Zone 20/Rail Service . . . . Netherlands . . ZUS	**Edgewood**/Weide/AAF, MD USA . . EDG	**Elelim**. . . . . Indonesia. . ELR
Dutch Rail Zone 21/Rail Service . . . . Netherlands . . ZUT	**Edinburgh**/ScotRail . . . . . . .UK . . ZXE	**Elfin Cove**/SPB, AK. . . . . . USA. . ELV
Dutch Rail Zone 22/Rail Service . . . . Netherlands . . ZUU	**Edinburgh**/Turnhouse. . . . . .UK . . .EDI	**Elgarhbolli** . . . . Libya. . QEJ
Dutch Rail Zone 23/Rail Service . . . . Netherlands . . ZUV	**Edmonton Int'l**, AB. . . . Canada . . YEG	**Elglin**/AFB, FL. . . . . .USA. . VPS
Dutch Rail Zone 24/Rail Service . . . . Netherlands . .ZUW	**Edmonton Namao**, AB Canada . YED	**Elhadrapur** . . . . .Nepal. . BDP
Dutch Rail Zone 25/Rail Service . . . . Netherlands . . ZUX	**Edmonton**, AB . . . . Canada . . YXD	**Elim**, AK . . . . USA. . .ELI
Dutch Rail Zone 26/Rail Service . . . . Netherlands . ZUY	**Edmonton**/RR Stn., AB. Canada . . XZL	**Eliptarnin** . . Papua New Guinea. . EPT
Dutch Rail Zone 27/Rail Service . . . . Netherlands . ZUZ	**Edna Bay**, AK . . . . USA . .EDA	**Elista** . . . . Russia. . ESL
Dutch Rail Zone 28/Rail Service . . . . Netherlands . .ZWX	**Edremit**/Korfez. . . . . .Turkey . EDO	**Elite Mystery Night** . .Australia. . ZZI
Dutch Rail Zone 29/Rail Service . . . . Netherlands . .ZWY	**Edson**, AB . . . . Canada . . YET	**Elizabeth City**, NC . . . . . .USA. . ECG
Dutch Rail Zone 30/Rail Service . . . . Netherlands . . ZWZ	**Edward River** . . . . .Australia . EDR	**Elizabethtown**, KY . . . . . . USA. . EKX
Duxford . . . . .UK . . QFO	**Edwards**/AFB, CA. . . . . . . USA . EDW	**Elk**. . . . . Poland. . QKD
Dwangwa . . . . .Malawi . DWA	**Eek**, AK . . . . USA . . EEK	**Elk City**/Municipal, OK . . . USA. . ELK
Dysart. . . . . Australia . . DYA	**Eflye Springs** . . . . .Kenya . EYS	**Elkedra** . . . . .Australia. . EKD
Dzaoudzi . . . . .Mayotte . DZA	**Efogi** . . . . Papua New Guinea . EFG	**Elkhart**/Municipal, IN . . . . . USA. . EKI
	Egegik, AK. . . . . USA . . EGX	**Elkins**, WV. . . . . .USA. . EKN
	Egeisbach . . . . Germany . QEF	**Elko Nexrad**, NV . . . . .USA. . LRX
	Egilsstadir . . . . Iceland . EGS	**Elko**, NV. . . . . USA. . EKO
	El Ghazaciuet . . . . Algeria . QAG	**Ellamar**, AK. . . . . .USA. . ELW
	El Harrouche . . . . Algeria . QHH	**Ellensburg**, WA . . . . .USA. . ELN
	El Yopal . . . . Colombia . EYP	**Ellington**, TX. . . . . .USA. . EFD
E	**Eia**/Popondetta . . . . Papua New Guinea . . .EIA	**Elliot Lake**, ON . . . . Canada. . YEL **Ellisras** . . . . .S. Africa. . ELL
	Elba Is/Marina Di Campe . . . Italy . EBA	**Ellsworth**/AFB, SD. . . . . . .USA. . RCA
	Eight Fathom Bight, AK . . USA . . EFB	**Elmanzala**. . . . . Egypt. . QEM
	Eil. . . . . Somalia . HCM	**Elmarj City** . . . . Libya. . QEC
Eagle Lake, TX. . . . . .USA. . ELA	**Ein Yahav**. . . . . Israel . . EIY	**Elmira**, NY. . . . . USA. . ELM
Eagle Pass/Maverick, TX . .USA. . EGP	**Einasieigh** . . . . Australia . .EIH	**Elorza** . . . . Venezuela. . EOZ
Eagle River, WI. . . . . .USA. . EGV	**Eindhoven** . . . . .Netherlands . .EIN	**Ely**, MN. . . . . .USA. . LYU
Eagle, Eagle Arpt, AK . . . . .USA. . EAA	**Eindhoven**/RR Stn . . Netherlands . ZYE	**Ely**, NV . . . . .USA. . ELY
Earlton, ON . . . . .Canada. . YXR	**Einsiedeln** . . . . Switzerland . ZDZ	**Embarcacion** . . . . .Argentina. . ZAI
East Fork, AK . . . . .USA. . EFO	**Eirunepe** . . . . .Brazil . ERN	**Embessa**. . . Papua New Guinea. . EMS
East Hampton, NY . . . . . . .USA. . HTO	**Eisenach** . . . . Germany . .EIB	**Embrach** . . . . .Switzerland. . QEQ
	Ekaterinburg. . . . . Russia . . SVX	**Emerald** . . . . .Australia. . EMD
	Ekati, NT. . . . . Canada . .YOA	**Emeryville**/HP, CA. . . . . . . USA. . JEM
	Ekereku . . . . Guyana . EKE	**Emirau** . . . . Papua New Guinea. . EMI
	Ekibastuz . . . . Kazakstan . . EKB	**Emmerich**. . . . . .Germany. . QEX
	Ekuk, AK. . . . . USA . .KKU	**Emmonak**, AK . . . . .USA. . EMK
	Ekwok, AK . . . . USA . . KEK	**Emo** . . . . Papua New Guinea. . EMO
	El Bagre . . . . Colombia . EBG	**Empangeni** . . . . .S. Africa. . EMG
	El Banco/San BernadoColombia . ELB	**Emporia**, KS . . . . .USA. . EMP
	El Bolson . . . . Argentina . EHL	**En Nahud** . . . . Somalia. . NUD
	El Borma . . . . Tunisia . EBM	**Enarotali** . . . . Indonesia. . EWI
	El Cajon, CA . . . . USA . CJN	**Encarnacion** . . . . .Paraguay. . ENO
	El Centro/NAF, CA . . . . . USA . NJK	**Ende**. . . . . Indonesia. . ENE
	El Charco . . . . Colombia . ECR	**Eneabba West**. . . . . . . .Australia. . ENB
	El Dorado. . . . . Venezuela . EOR	**Enewetak Is** . . . . . . .Marshall Is. . ENT
	El Dorado, AR . . . . USA . ELD	**Engati** . . . . . . Papua New Guinea. . EGA
	El Dorado, KS . . . . USA . EDK	**Engelberg**. . . . . Switzerland. . ZHB
	El Encanto . . . . Colombia . ECO	**Englewood**, CO/Off-line Pt . USA. . .QTS
	El Eulma . . . . Algeria . ZAE	**Enid**, OK . . . . USA. . WDG
	El Fasher . . . . Somalia . ELF	**Enid**/AFB, OK . . . . .USA. . END
	El Golea . . . . Algeria . ELG	**Eniseysk**. . . . . Russia. . . EIE
	El Gouera . . . . Mauritania . ZLG	**Enniskillen**/St Angelo . . . . . UK.. ENK
	El Hadjar . . . . Algeria . QEH	**Enontekiö** . . . . .Finland. . .ENF
	El Kala . . . . Algeria . QLK	**Enschede**/RR. . . . . Netherlands. . QYE
	El Mahalla El Kobra . . . . Egypt . QEK	**Enschede**/Twente . Netherlands.. .ENS
	El Maiten . . . . Argentina . EMX	**Ensenada** . . . . .Mexico. . ESE

**A
I
R
P
O
R
T
S**

Enshi	China	ENH
Entebbe	Uganda	EBB
Enterprise/Municipal, AL	USA	ETS
Enugu	Nigeria	ENU
Epena	Congo, DR	EPN
Epernay	France	XEP
Ephrata, WA	USA	EPH
Epi	Vanuatu	EPI
Epinal/Mirecourt	France	EPL
Episkopi	Cyprus	EPK
Eqalugaiarsuit	Greenland	QFG
Erandique	Honduras	EDQ
Erave	Papua New Guinea	ERE
Ercan	Cyprus	ECN
Erdenet	Mongolia	ERT
Erechim/C. Kraemer	Brazil	ERM
Erfurt/Bindersleben	Germany	ERF
Erie, PA	USA	ERI
Erigavo	Somalia	ERA
Erlangen	Germany	ZCZ
Erldunda	Australia	EDD
Ernabella	Australia	ERB
Ernae	Vanuatu	EAE
Ernden	Germany	EME
Errachidla	Morocco	ERH
Errol, NH	USA	ERR
Erume	Papua New Guinea	ERU
Erzincan	Turkey	ERC
Erzurum	Turkey	ERZ
Esa'Ala	Papua New Guinea	ESA
Esbjerg	Denmark	EBJ
Esbjerg/RR Stn.	Denmark	ZBB
Escanaba, MI	USA	ESC
Eschweiler	Germany	ZEA
Eskilstuna	Sweden	EKT
Eskisehir	Turkey	ESK
Eskisehir/Anadolu Univ.	Turkey	AOE
Esltree	UK	ETR
Esmeraidas	Ecuador	ESM
Espanola, NM	USA	ESO
Esperance	Australia	EPR
Espinosa	Brazil	ESI
Espiritu Santo/Pekoa	Vanuatu	SON
Esquel	Argentina	EQS
Esquimalt, BC	Canada	YPF
Essaouira	Morocco	ESU
Essen	Germany	ESS
Esslingen	Germany	ZEB
Estevan Point, BC	Canada	YEP
Estevan, SK.	Canada	YEN
Estherville, IA	USA	EST
Etadunna	Australia	ETD
Eua/Kaufana.	Tonga	EUA
Eucla	Australia	EUC
Eufaula.	USA	EUF
Eugene Is, LA	USA	VUW
Eugene, OR.	USA	EUG
Eunice, LA	USA	UCE
Eureka	USA	EUE
Eureka, MB	Canada	YEU
Eureka/Murray Fld, CA	USA	EKA
Euskirchen	Germany	ZED
Eva Downs	Australia	EVO
Evadale/Landing Strip, TX	USA	EVA
Evans Head	Australia	EVH
Evanston, WY	USA	EVW
Evansville, IN	USA	EVV
Eveleth, MN.	USA	EVM
Everett, WA	USA	PAE
Evergreen, Middleton Fld, AL		
	USA	GZH
Evian Les Bains	France	XEB
Eviry/HP	France	JEV
Evreux	France	EVX
Ewer	Indonesia	EWE
Ewo	Congo, DR	EWO
Excursion Inlet/SPB, AK	USA	EXI
Exeter Arpt	UK	EXT
Exmouth Gulf	Australia	EXM

F

Faaite	F. Polynesia	FAC
Fada N'Gourma	Burkina Faso	FNG
Fagernes/Valdres	Norway	VDB
Fagurholsmyri	Iceland	FAG
Fail River, MA	USA	EWB
Fair Isle	UK	FIE
Fairbanks/Int'l Arpt, AK	USA	FAI
Fairbanks, AK	USA	MTX
Fairbanks/Eielson/AFB, AK	USA	EIL
Fairbanks/Ft Wainwright, AK	USA	FBK
Fairbanks/Phillips Fld, AK	USA	PII
Fairbury/Municipal, NE.	USA	FBY
Fairchild/AFB, WA.	USA	SKA
Fairfield, IA.	USA	FFL
Fairford/RAF	UK	FFD
Fairmont, MN	USA	FRM
Fairmount Springs, BC		
	Canada	YCZ
Fairview, AB.	Canada	ZFW
Faisalabad	Pakistan	LYP
Faizabad	Afghanistan	FBD
Fajardo	Puerto Rico	FAJ
Fak Fak/Torea.	Indonesia	FKQ
Fakahina	F. Polynesia	FHZ
Fakarava	F. Polynesia	FAV
Fakenham/Sculthorp/RAF		
	Georgia	FKH
Falher, AB.	Canada	YOE
Fallon/Municipal, NV	USA	FLX
Fallon/NAS, NV	USA	NFL
Falls Bay, AK	USA	FLJ
Falls Creek	Australia	FLC
False Is, AK	USA	FAK
False Pass, AK	USA	KFP
Fane	Papua New Guinea	FNE
Fangatau	F. Polynesia	FGU
Farafangana	Madagascar	RVA
Farah	Afghanistan	FAH
Faranah	Guinea	FAA
Farewell, AK	USA	FWL
Fargo, ND	USA	FAR
Faribault/Municipal, MN.	USA	FBL
Faridabad	India	QNF
Farmingdale, NY	USA	FRG
Farmington Municipal, NM		
	USA	FMN
Farmington, MO.	USA	FAM
Farmville, VA	USA	FVX
Farnborough	UK	FAB
Faro	Portugal	FAO
Faro, YT	Canada	ZFA
Faroe Iss/Vagar	Faroe Islands	FAE
Farsund/Lista.	Norway	FAN
Faskrudsfjordur	Iceland	FAS
Fauske	Norway	ZXO
Faya	Chad	FYT
Fayetteville Municipal, AR		
	USA	FYV
Fayetteville, NC	USA	FAY
Fayetteville/Municipal, TN.	USA	FYM
Fayetteville/Northwest Arkansas, AR.	USA	XNA
Fderik	Mauritania	FGD
Feijo	Brazil	FEJ
Feiker/AAF, VA	USA	FAF
Feira De Santana.	Brazil	FEC
Fera Is	Solomon Is	FRE
Feramin	Papua New Guinea	FRQ
Fercana	Uzbekistan	FEG
Fercusons Gulf	Kenya	FER
Fergus Falls, MN	USA	FFM
Ferkessedougou	Côte D'Ivoire	FEK
Fernando De Noronha	Brazil	FEN
Fetlar	UK	FEA
Fez/Sais	Morocco	FEZ

Fianarantsoa	Madagascar	WFI
Ficksburg	S. Africa	FCB
Figari	France	FSC
Filadelfia	Paraguay	FLM
Fillmore/Municipal, UT	USA	FIL
Fin Creek, AK.	USA	FNK
Fincha	Ethiopia	FNH
Findlay, OH	USA	FDY
Finke	Australia	FIK
Finley	Australia	FLY
Finschhafen	Papua New Guinea	FIN
Fire Cove, AK.	USA	FIC
Fishers Is, NY	USA	FID
Fitchburg Municipal, MA	USA	FIT
Fitiuta	American Samoa	FTI
Fitzroy Crossing	Australia	FIZ
Five Finger, AK.	USA	FIV
Five Mile, AK.	USA	FMC
Flagstaff/Pulliam Fld, AZ	USA	FLG
Flaminoo	Costa Rica	FMG
Flat, AK.	USA	FLT
Flateyri	Iceland	FLI
Flaxman Is, AK	USA	FXM
Flensburg/Schaferhaus	Germany	FLF
Flin Flon, MB	Canada	YFO
Flinders Is	Australia	FLS
Flint Int'l Arpt, MI	USA	FNT
Flippin	Australia	FLP
Flora Valley/Flora Vale	Australia	FVL
Florence Regional Arpt, SC		
	USA	FLO
Florence, AL.	USA	MSL
Florence/Peretola.	Italy	FLR
Florence/Pisa/Gal Galilei.	Italy	PSA
Florence/S.M. Novella Rail.Svc	Italy	ZMS
Florencia, CO	USA	FLA
Flores Is/Santa Cruz	Portugal	FLW
Flores/Santa Elena.	Guatemala	FRS
Floriano	Brazil	FLB
Florianopolis	Brazil	FLN
Floro.	Norway	FRO
Flotta	UK	FLH
Fluelen	Switzerland	ZHD
Flushing, NY	USA	FLU
Foggia	Italy	FOG
Foix	France	XFX
Foley, AL	USA	NHX
Fond Du Lac Arpt, WI	USA	FLD
Fond Du Lac, SK	Canada	ZFD
Font Romeu	France	QZF
Fontainebieau.	France	XFB
Fontanges, QC	Canada	YFG
Forbes	Australia	FRB
Forbes/AFB, KS	USA	FOE
Forde/Bringeland	Norway	FDE
Fore	Norway	ZXJ
Forest City/Municipal, IA	USA	FXY
Forest Park/Morris/AAF, GA	USA	FOP
Forestville, QC	Canada	YFE
Forl Scott, KS	USA	FSK
Forli/Luigi Ridolfi.	Italy	FRL
Formosa	Argentina	FMA
Forney/AAF, MO.	USA	TBN
Forrest.	Australia	FOS
Forrest City/Municipal, AR.	USA	FCY
Forrest River Arpt.	Australia	FVR
Forssa	Finland	QVE
Forster.	Australia	FOT
Fort Belvoir/Davison/AAF, VA		
	USA	DAA
Fort Bragg, CA	USA	FOB
Fort Bragg/AAF, NC	USA	FBG
Fort Bridger, WY	USA	FBR
Fort Collins, CO	USA	FNL
Fort Dauphin	Madagascar	FTU
Fort De France/Lamentin		
	Martinique	FDF
Fort Devens, MA.	USA	AYE
Fort Dodge, IA.	USA	FOD

AIRPORTS

Fort Irwin/AAF, CA . . . . USA . . BYS	Friday Harbor Arpt, WA. . . USA . . FHR	Gage, OK. . . . . USA . . GAG
Fort Lauderdale/Executive, FL	Friedrichshafen . . . . . Germany . . FDH	Gagetown, NB . . . . Canada. . . YCX
. . . . USA . . FXE	Fritziar . . . . Germany . . FRZ	Gagnoa . . . . Côte D'Ivoire. . GGN
Fort Lauderdale Int'l, FL. . .USA . . FLL	Fritzsche/AAF, CA. . . . . . . USA . . OAR	Gagnon, QC . . . . Canada. . YGA
Fort Lee/AAF, VA . . . . USA . . FLE	Front Royal/Warren County, VA	Gainesville, FL. . . . . USA . . GNV
Fort Madison, IA . . . . USA . . FMS	. . . . USA . . FRR	Gainesville/Gilmer Memorial,
Fort Madison, IA . . . . USA . . FSW	Frosinone . . . . Italy . QFR	GA . . . . USA . . GVL
Fort Myers, FL . . . . USA . . FMY	Frutillar . . . . Chile . . FRT	Gainesville/Municipal, TX. . USA. . . GLE
Fort Pierce Int'l, FL. . . . . USA . . FPR	Fryeburg, Eastern Slopes	Gaithersburg, MD. . . . . USA . . GAI
Fort Sheridan/AAF, IL . . . . .USA . . FSN	Regional Arpt, ME. . . . . . USA . . IZG	Gakona, AK . . . . USA . . GAK
Fort Smith Municipal, AR.USA . . FSM	Fryeburg, ME. . . . . USA . . FRY	Gal Oya/Amparai . . . Sri Lanka. . GOY
Fort St John, BC . . . . .Canada . . YXJ	Ft Wolter/AAF, TX . . . . . . USA . CWO	Galapagos Is/Baltra . . .Ecuador. . GPS
Fort Stockton, TX . . . . USA . . FST	Ft Worth, TX. . . . . USA . . FWD	Galbraith Lake, AK. . . . . . . USA . . GBH
Fort Sumner, NM. . . . . USA . . FSU	Ft. Albany, ON . . . . . . Canada . . YFA	Galcaio . . . . Somalia. . GLK
Fort Wayne/Mncpl/Baer Fld, IN	Ft. Benning, GA . . . . USA . . QFE	Galela/Gamarmalamu Indonesia. . .GLX
. . . . USA . . FWA	Ft. Chipewyan, AB. . . . Canada . . YPY	Galena, AK . . . . USA . . GAL
Fort William/ HPHP . . . . .UK . FWM	Ft. Collins Bus Svc, CO. . . USA . QWF	Galesburg, GBG . . . . USA . . GBG
Fort Worth, TX . . . . .USA . . DFW	Ft. Frances/Mun, ON . . Canada . . YAG	Galion, OH . . . . USA . .GQQ
Fort Worth, TX . . . . USA . . FTW	Ft. Good Hope, NT . . . Canada . . YGH	Gallivare . . . . .Sweden. . GEV
Fort Yukon, AK. . . . . USA . . FYU	Ft. Hood Gray/AAF, TX . . . USA . . GRK	Gallup Municipal Arpt, NMUSA . . GUP
Fortaleza/Pinto Martins . . . .Brazil. . FOR	Ft. Hood/AAF, TX. . . . . . . USA . . HLR	Galveston, Scholes Fld, TX USA . .GLS
Fortuna . . . . Costa Rica. . FON	Ft. Hope, ON . . . . Canada . . YFH	Galway Cammore . . . . . Ireland. . GWY
Fortuna Ledge, AK. . . . . . . USA . . FTL	Ft. Jelferson, FL. . . . . . . USA . .RBN	Gamarra . . . . .Colombia. . GRA
Fossil Downs . . . . Australia. . FSL	Ft. Kobbe/Howard AFB	Gamba. . . . . Gabon. . GAX
Fougamou . . . . .Gabon. . FOU	. . . . Panama . .HOW	Gambela . . . . Ethiopia. . GMB
Foula. . . . . UK. . FOA	Ft. Lauderdale/RR Stn., FL USA . . ZFT	Gambell, AK. . . . . USA . . GAM
Foumban . . . . Cameroon. . FOM	Ft. Lewis Gray/AAF, WA . . USA . . GRF	Gambier Is . . . . F. Polynesia. GMR
Fox Glacier . . . . . . New Zealand . . FGL	Ft. Liard, NT. . . . . Canada . . YJF	Gamboma . . . . Congo, DR. GMM
Fox Harbour (St Lewis), NG	Ft. Mcmurray, AB. . . . . Canada . . YMM	Gamboola . . . . .Australia. . GBP
. . . . .Canada. .YFX	Ft. Mcpherson, NT. . . . Canada . . ZFM	Gan Is/Gan/Seenu . . Maldives. . GAN
Fox, AK. . . . . USA . . FOX	Ft. Myers/SW Florida Reg, FLUSA RSW	Gananoque/RR Stn., ON
Foya . . . . Liberia. . FOY	Ft. Nelson, BC. . . . . Canada . . YYE	. . . . Canada. .XGW
Franca . . . . Brazil. . FRC	Ft. Reliance, NT . . . . . . Canada . . YFL	Gandajika . . . . Congo, DR. . GDJ
Franceville/Mvengue. . . . .Gabon . . MVB	Ft. Resolution, NT . . . . Canada . . YFR	Gander Int'l, NF . . . . Canada. . YQX
Francisco Beltrao . . . . . Brazil. . FBE	Ft. Rucker/Ozark/Army HP, AL	Ganes Creek, AK . . . . USA . . GEK
Francistown . . . . Botswana. . FRW	. . . . USA . .LOR	Gangaw . . . . .Myanmar. . GAW
Franconia, VA. . . . . .USA . . ZFO	Ft. Severn, ON . . . . Canada . . YER	Ganges Harbor, BC . . Canada. . YGG
Frankfort, KY . . . . .USA . . FFT	Ft. Simpson, NT . . . . . . Canada . . YFS	Ganzhou . . . . China. .KOW
Frankfurt AFB . . . . . . Germany . .FRF	Ft. Smith, NT. . . . . Canada . . YSM	Gao. . . . . Mali. . GAQ
Frankfurt/HBF Railway Svc	Ft. Washington, PA/Off-line Pt	Gaoua . . . . .Burkina Faso. . XGA
. . . . Germany . . ZRB	. . . . USA . QFW	Gap/Tallard. . . . . .France. . .GAT
Frankfurt/Int'l. . . . . Germany . . FRA	Ft. Wayne/Smith Fld, IN . . USA . . SMD	Gara Djebilet . . . . Algeria. . GBB
Frankfurt/Neu Isenburg	Ft. Worth/NAS, TX. . . . . . USA . . NFW	Garachine. . . . . .Panama. . GHE
. . . . Germany . .QGV	Fucishan . . . . China . .FUO	Garaina . . Papua New Guinea. . GAR
Frankfurt/Oder/RR Stn.	Fuerstenfeldbruck . . Germany . . FEL	Garanhuns . . . . Brazil. . QGP
. . . . Germany . . ZFR	Fuerteventura . . . . Spain . . FUE	Garasa . . . . Papua New Guinea. . GRL
Franklin Municipal, VA . . .USA . . FKN	Fuerth . . . . Germany . . ZEF	Garbaharey . . . . Somalia. . GBM
Franklin, PA. . . . . USA . .FKL	Fujairah/Int'l Arpt . . . . . . UAE . . FJR	Garbsen . . . . Germany. . ZEH
Franz Josef . . . . . New Zealand . WHO	Fukue . . . . .Japan . . FUJ	Garden City, KS. . . . . USA . . GCK
Frauenfeld . . . . .Switzerland. . ZHE	Fukui . . . . .Japan . . FKJ	Garden City/Is HP, NY . . . USA. . . JHC
Freburg . . . . Germany . . QFB	Fukuoka . . . . .Japan . . FUK	Garden Point. . . . . . . .Australia. . GPN
Fredericia/RR Stn. . . . .Denmark . . ZBJ	Fukushima Arpt . . . . . . .Japan . . FKS	Gardez . . . . .Afghanistan. . GRG
Frederick, MD. . . . . .USA . . FDK	Fukuyama . . . . .Japan . . QFY	Gardner/Municipal, MA . . . USA. .GDM
Frederick, OK. . . . . USA . . FDR	Fulda . . . . Germany . . ZEE	Gardo. . . . . Somalia. . GSR
Fredericton Junction/RR Stn.,	Fulleborn . . Papua New Guinea . . FUB	Garissa . . . . Kenya. . GAS
NB . . . . .Canada. . XFC	Fullerton Municipal, CA . USA . . FUL	Garmisch-Partenkirchen
Fredericton, NB . . . . . . .Canada. . YFC	Fulton County, GA. . . . . . USA . . FTY	. . . . Germany. . . ZEI
Frederkshavn/Bus Svc	Fuma . . . . . Papua New Guinea . . FUM	Garoe. . . . . Somalia. . GGR
. . . . .Denmark . . QFH	Funafuti Atol Int'l . . . . . .Tuvalu . . FUN	Garoua . . . . .Cameroon. . GOU
Freeport. . . . . Bahamas . . FPO	Funchal/Madeira . . . . . . Portugal . . FNC	Garuahi . . . . Papua New Guinea. . GRH
Freeport/Albertus, IL . . . . .USA . . FEP	Funter Bay/SPB, AK. . . . . USA . .FNR	Gary Regional, IN. . . . . USA. . . GYY
Freetown . . . . .Sierra Leone . . FNA	Furtaeulu . . . . .Chile . . FFU	Gascoyne Junction . .Australia. . GSC
Freetown/Hastings .Sierra Leone . . HGS	Futuna Is . . Wallis and Futuna Is . . FUT	Gasmata Is. Papua New Guinea. . GMI
Freetown/Mammy Yoko HP	Futuna Is Arpt . . . . Vanuatu . . FTA	Gaspe, QC . . . . Canada. . YGP
. . . . .Sierra Leone . . JMY	Fuyang . . . . China . .FUG	Gaspe/RR Stn., QC . . . . Canada. . XDD
Fregate Is . . . . Seychelles . . FRK	Fuyun . . . . China . . FYN	Gassim . . . . Saudi Arabia. .ELQ
Freida River	Fuzhou . . . . China . .FOC	Gassimiut . . . . .Greenland. . QJH
. . . . .Papua New Guinea . . FAQ		Gastonia, NC . . . . USA . . AKH
Freilassing . . . . Germany . . QFL		Gasuke . . . . Papua New Guinea. . GBC
Frejus . . . . .France. .FRJ		Gatineati, ON . . . . Canada. . YND
Fremantle/ HP . . . . Australia. . JFM	# G	Gatlinburg, TN . . . . USA. . . GKT
Fremont, NE . . . . .USA . . FET		Gatokae Aerodrom Solomon Is.. .GTA
French Lick, IN . . . . .USA . . FRH	Gabbs, NV . . . . USA . . GAB	Gaua . . . . Vanuatu. . ZGU
Frenchville, ME . . . . .USA . .WFK	Gabes . . . . Tunisia . .GAE	Gauhati/Borlhar . . . . .India. . GAU
Frenchville, N Aroostook, ME	Gaborone/Sir Seretse	Gavie/Sandviken AFB . . Sweden. . GVX
. . . . .USA . .FVE	Khama Int'l . . . . .Botswana . .GBE	Gaya . . . . India. . GAY
Fresh Water Bay, AK . . . .USA . . FRP	Gachas Nek . . . . Lesotho . UNE	Gaylord, Otsego County, MI
Fresno, CA . . . . USA . . FAT	Gadsden/Municipal, AL . . . USA . . GAD	. . . . USA. . . GLR
Fresno-Chandler, CA. . . . .USA . . FCH	Gafsa/Ksar . . . . Tunisia . .GAF	Gayndah . . . . .Australia. . GAH
Fria . . . . Guinea. . FIG	Gag Is . . . . Indonesia . .GAV	Gaza Strip
Fribourg. . . . . .Switzerland . . ZHF		. . . . . Occupied Palestinian Ter. . .ZDY

Gaza Strip/Gaza Int'l ... Occupied Palestinian Ter. . GZA
Gbadolite ... Congo, DR . . BDT
Gbangbatok ... Sierra Leone . . GBK
GC Apollo, ON/Off-line Pt ... Canada . . QZP
Gdansk/Rebiechowo ... Poland . . GDN
Gdynia ... Poland . . QYD
Geatkale ... Cyprus . . GEC
Gebe ... Indonesia . . GEB
Gebelstacit ... Germany . . GHF
Gedaref ... Somalia . . GSU
Geelong ... Australia . . GEX
Geilenkirchen ... Germany . . GKE
Geilo/Dagali ... Norway . . DLD
Geita ... Tanzania . . . GIT
Geladi ... Ethiopia . . GLC
Gelenclzilk ... Russia . . GDZ
Gelsenkirchen ... Germany . . . ZEJ
Gemena ... Congo, DR . GMA
Genda Wuha ... Ethiopia . . . ETE
Geneina ... Sudan . . EGN
General Pico ... Argentina . . GPO
General Roca ... Argentina . . GNR
General Safflos/Buayan ... Philippines . . GES
General Villegas ... Argentina . . VGS
Geneva Aeroport/RR Stn. ... Switzerland . . ZHY
Geneva Cointrin ... Switzerland . . GVA
Geneva-Cornavin/RR Stn. ... Switzerland . . ZHT
Genoa/Cristoforo Colombo . Italy . . GOA
Genting ... Malaysia . . GTB
Geoie HP ... S. Korea . . JGE
George ... S. Africa . . GRJ
George Town ... Australia . . GEE
George Town/Exurna Int'l ... Bahamas . . GGT
George/AFB, CA ... USA . . VCV
Georgetown ... St. Helena . . . ASI
Georgetown ... Australia . . GTT
Georgetown, DE ... USA . . GED
Georgetown, SC ... USA . . GGE
Georgetown/Cheddi Jagan Int'l ... Guyana . . GEO
Georgetown/RR Stn., ON ... Canada . . XHM
Gera/RR Stn. ... Germany . . ZGA
Geraldton ... Australia . . GET
Geraldton, ON ... Canada . . YGQ
Gerga ... Egypt . . QGX
German Railways Zone F/RR ... Germany . . QYF
German Railways Zone J/RR ... Germany . . QYJ
Germansen, BC ... Canada . . YGS
Germany/RR ... Germany . . QYG
Gerona/Costa Brava ... Spain . . GRO
Gerstungen/RR Stn. . Germany . . ZGT
Gethsemani, QC ... Canada . . ZGS
Gettysburg, PA ... USA . . GTY
Geva Airstrip ... Solomon Is . . GEF
Gewoia ... Papua New Guinea . GEW
Ghadames ... Libya . . . LTD
Ghanzi ... Botswana . . GNZ
Ghardaia Nournerate . Algeria . . GHA
Ghat ... Libya . . GHT
Ghazaouet ... Algeria . . QVX
Ghazni ... Afghanistan . . . GZI
Ghent/Industrie-Zone . . Belgium . . GNE
Gherian ... Libya . . QGH
Gheshm ... Iran . . GSM
Ghimbi ... Ethiopia . . GHD
Ghinnir ... Ethiopia . . GNN
Gibb River ... Australia . . GBV
Gibraltar/North Front . . Gibraltar . . . GIB
Gienormiston ... Australia . . GLM
Gifu AB ... Japan . QGU
Gijon ... Spain . . . QIJ
Gila Bend/AAF, AZ ... USA . . GBN
Gilgal ... Colombia . GGL
Gilgit ... Pakistan . . . GIL
Gillam, MB ... Canada . . YGX
Gillies Bay, BC ... Canada . . YGB
Gilwice ... Poland . . QLC
Gimli, MB ... Canada . YGM
Girardot ... Colombia . . GIR
Gisborne ... New Zealand . . GIS
Gisenyi ... Rwanda . . GYI
Gitega ... Benin . . GID
Giyani ... S. Africa . . GIY
Gizan ... Saudi Arabia . . GIZ
Gizo/Nusatope ... Solomon Is . GZO
Gizycio ... Poland . . ZYC
Gjoa Haven, NU ... Canada . . YHK
Gjogur ... Iceland . . GJR
Glacier Creek, AK ... USA . . KGZ
Gladbeck ... Germany . . ZEK
Gladewater, TX ... USA . GGG
Gladstone ... Australia . . GLT
Gladwin, MI ... USA . GDW
Glarus ... Switzerland . ZHG
Glasgow ... UK . . . PIK
Glasgow Int'l Arpt, MT ... USA . GGW
Glasgow/Int'l ... UK . . GLA
Glasgow/Municipal, KY ... USA . GLW
Glasgow/ScotRail ... UK . ZGG
Glen Innes ... Australia . . . GLI
Glencoe/RR Stn., ON . . Canada . . XZC
Glendale / HP, CA ... USA . . JGX
Glendale, WV ... USA . GWV
Glendive, MT ... USA . GDV
Glengyie ... Australia . GLG
Glennallen, AK ... USA . GLQ
Glens Falls, NY ... USA . GFL
Glenview/NAS, IL ... USA . NBU
Glenwood Asos, MN ... USA . GHW
Glenwood Springs, CO . . USA . GWS
Gloucester/Staverton Private UK . GLO
Glynco/NAS, GA ... USA . . NEA
Gnarowein. Papua New Guinea . GWN
Goa/Dabolim ... India . . GOI
Goba ... Ethiopia . GOB
Gobernador Gregores ... Argentina . GGS
Gode/Iddidole ... Ethiopia . GDE
Godman/AAF, KY ... USA . . FTK
Gods Narrows, MB ... Canada . YGO
Gods River, MB ... Canada . . ZGI
Goeppingen ... Germany . . ZES
Goerlitz/RR Stn. ... Germany . . ZGE
Goettingen ... Germany . . ZEU
Goiania/Santa Genoveva . . Brazil . GYN
Gol/Klanten ... Norway . . GLL
Golbabis ... Namibia . GOG
Gold Beach/State, OR ... USA . GOL
Gold Coast ... Australia . OOL
Golden Gate Bridge, CA . . USA . GGB
Golden Horn/SPB, AK ... USA . GDH
Goldsworthy ... Australia . . GLY
Golfito ... Costa Rica . . GLF
Golmud ... China . GOQ
Golovin, AK ... USA . . GLV
Goma ... Congo, DR . GOM
Gomel ... Belarus . GME
Gonalia ... Papua New Guinea . GOE
Gondar ... Ethiopia . GDQ
Goodfellow/AFB, TX ... USA . GOF
Gooding, ID ... USA . GNG
Goodland, Renner Fld, KS . USA . . GLD
Goodnews Bay, AK ... USA . GNU
Goodyear Municipal, AZ . USA . . GYR
Goondiwindi ... Australia . GOO
Goose, NF ... Canada . . YYR
Gora ... Papua New Guinea . GOC
Gorakhpur ... India . GOP
Gordil ... Central African Rep . . GDI
Gordon Downs ... Australia . GDD
Gordon Municipal, NE ... USA . GRN
Gordonsville/Municipal, VA ... USA . . GVE
Gore ... Ethiopia . . GOR
Gore Bay, ON ... Canada . . YZE
Gorge Harbor, BC ... Canada . . YGE
Gorizia ... Italy . . QGO
Gorkha ... Nepal . . GKH
Gorna Orechovitsa ... Bulgaria . . GOZ
Goroka ... Papua New Guinea . . GKA
Gorom-Gorom ... Burkina Faso . . XGG
Gorontalo/Tolotio ... Indonesia . . GTO
Gosford ... Australia . . GOS
Goshen Municipal Arpt, IN USA . . GSH
Goslar ... Germany . . . ZET
Gossau SG ... Switzerland . . ZHH
Goteborg/Landvetter ... Sweden . . GOT
Gotha/RR Stn. ... Germany . . ZGO
Gothenburg/Saeve ... Sweden . . GSE
Goulburn ... Australia . . GUL
Goulburn Is ... Australia . . GBL
Goulimime ... Morocco . . GLN
Gounda ... Central African Rep . . GDA
Goundam ... Mali . . GUD
Gove/Nhulunbuy ... Australia . . GOV
Governador Valadares . . Brazil . . GVR
Governors Harbour . Bahamas . . GHB
Goya ... Argentina . . OYA
Gozo ... Malta . . GZM
Graasten/Bus Svc ... Denmark . . . XRA
Gracias ... Honduras . . GAC
Graciosa Is ... Portugal . . GRW
Grafton ... Australia . . GFN
Gramado ... Brazil . . QRP
Granada ... Spain . . GRX
Grand Bahama/Aux Ab ... Bahamas . . . GBI
Grand Canyon/HP, AZ ... USA . . JGC
Grand Canyon National Park, AZ ... USA . . GCN
Grand Canyon/North Rim, AZ ... USA . . NGC
Grand Cayman Is Int'l ... Cayman Is . . GCM
Grand Cess ... Liberia . . GRC
Grand Forks Int'l, ND ... USA . . GFK
Grand Forks, BC ... Canada . . ZGF
Grand Forks/AFB, ND ... USA . . RDR
Grand Is Nexrad, NE ... USA . . . UEX
Grand Is, NE ... USA . . . GRI
Grand Junction/Walker Fld, CO ... USA . . . GJT
Grand Marais/Municipal, MN ... USA . . GRM
Grand Rapids, MN ... USA . . GPZ
Grand Rapids/Kent County Int'l Arpt, MI ... USA . . GRR
Grand Turk Is . Turks & Caicos Is . . GDT
Grande Cache, AB ... Canada . . YGC
Grande Prairie, AB ... Canada . . YQU
Grande-Riviere/RR Stn., QC ... Canada . . XDO
Granite Mountain, AK ... USA . . GMT
Granites ... Australia . . GTS
Grantham/RR Stn. ... UK . . XGM
Grants-Milan, NM ... USA . . GNT
Grantsburg/Municipal, WI . USA . . GTG
Granville ... France . . GFR
Granville Lake, MB ... Canada . . . XGL
Gravik ... Norway . . ZXG
Grayling, AK ... USA . . KGX
Graz/Thalerhof ... Austria . . GRZ
Great Barrier Is . . New Zealand . . GBZ
Great Barrington, MA ... USA . . GBR
Great Bear Lake, NT ... Canada . . DAS
Great Bend, KS ... USA . . GBD
Great Falls Int'l Arpt, MT ... USA . . . GTF
Great Falls Nexrad, MT ... USA . . . TFX
Great Harbour ... Bahamas . . GHC
Great Keppel Is ... Australia . . GKL
Greeley/Weld County, CO . . USA . . GXY
Green Bay, Austin Straubel Int'l, WI ... USA . . GRB
Green Is ... Taiwan . . . GNI

AIRPORTS

Green Iss...Papua New Guinea...GEI
Green River/Papua New Guinea...GVI
Green River, UT.........USA..RVR
Green Turtle........Bahamas..GTC
Greenfeid/Pope Fld, IN ....USA..GFD
Greenvale........Australia..GVP
Greenville Majors, TX...USA..GVT
Greenville, MS.........USA..GLH
Greenville, NC.........USA..PGV
Greenville, SC.........USA..GMU
Greenville, SC.........USA..GSP
Greenville/Donaldson Center,
SC.........USA..GDC
Greenville/Municipal, IL...USA..GRE
Greenville/Municipal, TN...USA..GCY
Greenway Sound, BC .Canada..YGN
Greenwood County Arpt, SC
.........USA..GRD
Greenwood, NS......Canada..YZX
Greenwood/Leflore, MS ...USA..GWO
Gregory Downs.....Australia..GGD
Greifswald/RR Stn...Germany..ZGW
Grenada/Point Saline Int'l
.........Grenada..GND
Grenchen.........Switzerland...ZHI
Grenfell.........Australia..GFE
Grenoble/Saint Geoirs...France..GNB
Grevenbroich.........Germany..ZEV
Greybull, WY.........USA..GEY
Greymouth......New Zealand..GMN
Griffiss/AFB, NY.........USA..RME
Griffith.........Australia..GFF
Grimsby/Binbrook........UK..GSY
Grimsby/RR Stn., ON...Canada..XGY
Grimsey.........Iceland..GRY
Grindelwald......Switzerland..ZHJ
Grise Fiord, NU......Canada..YGZ
Grissom/AFB, IN.........USA..GUS
Grodna.........Belarus..GNA
Groennedal/ HP....Greenland..JGR
Groningen/Eelde..Netherlands..GRQ
Groote Eylandt/Alyangula
.........Australia..GTE
Grootfontein.........Namibia..GFY
Grosseto/Baccarini........Italy..GRS
Groton/New London Rail, CT
.........USA..ZGD
Groznyj.........Russia..GRV
Grundarfjordur.......Iceland..GUU
Gstaad.........Switzerland..ZHK
Guacamaya........Colombia..GCA
Guadalajara/Miguel Hidal
.........Mexico..GDL
Guadalcanal......Solomon Is...GSI
Guadalupe.........Brazil..GDP
Guaira.........Brazil..QGA
Gualaco.........Honduras..GUO
Gualara-Mirim.........Brazil..GJM
Gualeguaychu.......Argentina..GHU
Guam/A.B. Won Pat Infl ..Guam..GUM
Guam/Agana/NAS.....Guam..NGM
Guam/Anderson AFB....Guam..UAM
Guam/USCG Shore St....Guam..NRV
Guanaja.........Honduras..GJA
Guanambi.........Brazil..GNM
Guanare.........Venezuela..GUQ
Guanghan.........China..GHN
Guanghua.........China..LHK
Guangzhou.........China..CAN
Guantanamo/Los Canos .Cuba..GAO
Guantanamo/NAS.......Cuba..NBW
Guapi.........Colombia..GPI
Guapiles.........Costa Rica..GPL
Guarapari.........Brazil..GUZ
Guarapuava/Tancredo
Thornaz Faria.........Brazil..GPB
Guaratingueta.........Brazil..GUJ
Guari.........Papua New Guinea..GUG
Guarrial.........Colombia..GAA
Guarulhos.........Brazil..QCV

Guasdualito/Vare Maria
.........Venezuela . GDO
Guasopa .. Papua New Guinea ..GAZ
Guatemala City/La Aurora
.........Guatemala . GUA
Guayaquil/Simon Bolivar
.........Ecuador . GYE
Guayaramerin.........Bolivia . GYA
Guaymas.........Mexico . GYM
Guelma.........Algeria . QGE
Guelph/RR Stn., ON ...Canada...XIA
Gueret/Saint Laurent...France..XGT
Guerima.........Colombia . GMC
Guernsey.........UK . GCI
Guerrero Negro......Mexico . GUB
Guetersloh.........Germany . GUT
Guetersloh.........Germany . ZEX
Guettin.........Germany . GTI
Guiglo.....Côte D'Ivoire . GGO
Guigubip .. Papua New Guinea..GLP
Guildwood/Toronto, ON Canada..YTO
Guilin.........China . KWL
Guimaraes.........Brazil . GMS
Guirat.........Pakistan . GRT
Guiria.........Venezuela . GUI
Guiyang.........China . KWE
Gulf Shores/Edwards, AL . USA . GUF
Gulkana Arpt, AK.......USA . GKN
Gulu.........Uganda . ULU
Gummersbach.........Germany . ZEW
Guna.........India . GUX
Gunnedah.........Australia . GUH
Gunnison, CO.........USA . GUC
Gunungsitoli/Binaka .Indonesia . GNS
Gurayat.........Saudi Arabia . URY
Guriaso....Papua New Guinea . GUE
Gurni City.........S. Korea . QKM
Gurue.........Mozambique . VJQ
Gurupi.........Brazil . GRP
Gusap....Papua New Guinea . GAP
Gusau.........Nigeria . QUS
Gush Katif.........Israel . GHK
Gustavus, AK.........USA . GST
Gustavus/Bartlett SPB, AK. USA . BQV
Gutenfuerst/RR Stn...Germany . ZGN
Guthrie, OK.........USA . GOK
Guymon, OK.........USA . GUY
Gwa.........Myanmar . GWA
Gwadar.........Pakistan . GWD
Gwalior.........India . GWL
Gweru.........Zimbabwe . GWE
Gyancizha.........Azerbaijan . KVD
Gympie.........Australia . GYP
Gyor.........Hungary . QGY
Gyoumri.........Armenia . LWN

H

Ha'Apai/Salote Pilolevu ... Tonga . HPA
Hachijo Jima.........Japan . HAC
Hachinohe AB.........Japan . HHE
Hachioji City.........Japan . QHY
Haeloao .. Papua New Guinea . HEO
Hafr Albatin......Saudi Arabia . HBT
Hagen.........Germany . ZEY
Hagerstown, MD.........USA . HGR
Hagfors.........Sweden . HFS
Hahn.........Germany . HHN
Hahnweide/RR.........Germany . QHD
Haifa/U Michaeli.........Israel . HFA
Haikou.........China . HAK
Hail.........Saudi Arabia . HAS
Hailar.........China . HLD
Hailey, ID.........USA . SUN
Haines Arpt, AK.........USA . HNS
Haines Junction, YT .. Canada . YHT
Haiphong/Catbi.......Vietnam . HPH
Hakai Pass, BC.......Canada . YHC

Hakodate.........Japan...HKD
Halah.........Namibia...HAL
Halberstadt/RR Stn...Germany..ZHQ
Half Moon, CA.........USA..HAF
Halifax/Int'l Arpt, NS....Canada..YHZ
Halifax/Dwtown Waterfront HP,
NS.........Canada..YWF
Halifax/RR Stn.. NS...Canada..XDG
Hall Beach, NU.........Canada..YUX
Halle/RR Stn.........Germany..ZHZ
Halls Creek.........Australia..HCQ
Halmstad/AFB.........Sweden..HAD
Hama.........Syria..QHM
Hamadan.........Iran..HDM
Hamar/Hamar Arpt...Norway...HMR
Hamburg/Finkenwerder
.........Germany..XFW
Hamburg/Fuhlsbuettel.Germany..HAM
Hamburg/RR Stn.........Germany..ZMB
Hämeenlinna.........Finland..QVM
Hameln.........Germany..ZEZ
Hami.........China..HMI
Hamilton.........Australia..HLT
Hamilton......New Zealand..HLZ
Hamilton Is.........Australia..HTI
Hamilton, OH.........USA..HAO
Hamilton, ON.........Canada..YHM
Hamilton/AAF, CA.........USA...SRF
Hamilton/Int'l.........Bermuda..BDA
Hamilton/Marion County, AL
.........USA..HAB
Hamilton/Ravalli County, MT
.........USA..HMM
Hamina.........Finland..QVZ
Hamm.........Germany..ZNB
Hammerfest.........Norway..HFT
Hampton, VA.........USA..PHF
Hampton/Municipal, IA.....USA..HPT
Hampton/Newport News Rail, VA
.........USA..ZWW
Hampton/Williamsburg Rail, VA
.........USA..ZWB
Hana, HI.........USA..HNM
Hanapepe/Port Allen, HI ...USA..PAK
Hanau.........Germany...ZNF
Hanchey/AHP, AL.........USA..HEY
Hancock, MI.........USA..CMX
Hanford, WA.........USA..HMS
Hangzhou.........China..HGH
Hanimaadhoo......Maldives..HAQ
Hanksville/Intermediate, UT
.........USA..HVE
Hanna, WY.........USA..HNX
Hanoi/Noibai.........Vietnam..HAN
Hanover.........Germany..HAJ
Hanover, NH.........USA..LEB
Hanover/HBF Railway Svc
.........Germany...ZVR
Hanover/Messe-BF Railway Sev
.........Germany..ZVM
Hanus Bay, AK.........USA..HBC
Hao Is.........F. Polynesia..HOI
Harar.........Ethiopia..QHR
Harare Kutsaga....Zimbabwe..HRE
Harbin.........China..HRB
Harbour Is.........Bahamas..HBI
Hargeisa.........Somalia..HGA
Harlingen/Valley Int'l, TX....USA..HRL
Harlzhong.........China..HZG
Harrisburg/Int'l Arpt, PA...USA..MDT
Harrisburg Skyport, PA ...USA..HAR
Harrisburg/Rail, PA.........USA..ZUG
Harrisburg/Raleigh, NC...USA..HSB
Harrismith.........S. Africa..HRS
Harrison, AR.........USA..HRO
Harrogate/Linton-On-Ouse..UK..HRT
Harstad.........Norway..HRD
Harstad-Narvik/Evenes Norway...EVE
Hartford-Brainard Arpt, CT.USA..HFD
Hartford/Barnes, CT......USA..BNH
Hartford/Bradley Int'l, CT...USA...BDL

A I R P O R T S

Hartford/Hartford CT Rail...USA.. ZRT	Henry Post/AAF, OK...... USA ..FSI	Homalin ....Myanmar.. HOX
Hartley Bay, BC ....Canada.. YTB	Henzada ....Myanmar..HEB	Homburg..........Germany..QOG
Hartsville, SC ....USA.. HVS	Heraklion/Iraklio ....Greece ..HER	Homer Arpt, AK.........USA..HOM
Harwich/RR ....UK. QQH	Herat ....Afghanistan ..HEA	Homestead/AFB, FL ......USA...HST
Haskovo.............Bulgaria.. HKV	Hercegnovi ....Yugoslavia. HNO	Hondo, TX................USA.. HDO
Hasselt ....Belgium. QHA	Herendeen, AK ....USA ..HED	Hong Kong / HP ..Hong Kong.. HHP
Hassi R'Mel/Tilrempt ....Algeria..HRM	Herford ....Germany ..ZNK	Hong Kong Int'l ..Hong Kong.. HKG
Hassi-Messaoud ......Algeria.. HME	Heringsdorf ....Germany ..HDF	Honiara/Henderson . Solomon Is... HIR
Hastings Municipal, NE ..USA.. HSI	Hermannsburg.......Australia. HMG	Honinabi ... Papua New Guinea.. HNN
Hasvik ....Norway.. HAA	Hermiston/State, OR ......USA ..HES	Honningsvag/Valan ... Norway.. HVG
Hat Yai ....Thailand.. HDY	Hermosillo/Gen Pesqueira Garcia	Honolulu/Int'l, HI ....USA.. HNL
Hatanga ....Russia.. HTG	...............Mexico . HMO	Hoofddorp ....Netherlands.. QHZ
Hatchet Lake, SK...Canada.. YDJ	Herne ....Germany.. ZNL	Hook Is ....Australia.. HIH
Hateruma ....Japan.. HTR	Herning/RR Stn......Denmark ..XAK	Hooker Creek ....Australia.. HOK
Hatfeild ....UK.. HTF	Heron Is / HP ....Australia. HRN	Hoolehua/Molokai, HI .....USA.. MKK
Hato Corozal ....Colombia. HTZ	Herrera ....Colombia ..HRR	Hoonah, AK ....USA.. HNH
Hatteras/Mitchell Fld, NC. .USA.. HSE	Herten ....Germany .. ZNM	Hooper Bay, AK.........USA.. HPB
Hatteras, NC.............USA..HNC	Hervey Bay ....Australia .HVB	Hope Vale ....Australia.. HPE
Hattiesburg, MS.........USA..HBG	Hervey/RR Stn., QC. ...Canada .XDU	Hope, BC ....Canada.. YHE
Hatzfeldthaven	Herzogenbuchsee Switzerland ..ZHN	Hopedale, NF ....Canada.. YHO
........Papua New Guinea .. HAZ	Hettinger Municipal Arpt, ND	Hopetoun ....Australia.. HTU
Haugesund/Karmoy ..Norway.. HAU	...............USA ..HEI	Hoquiam, WA ....USA.. HQM
Havana/Jose Marti Int'l ....Cuba.. HAV	Hettlingen ....Germany ..ZNH	Horizontina ....Brazil.. HRZ
Havasupai, AZ ....USA.. HAE	Hickam/AFB, HI ....USA .. HIK	Horn Is..............Australia.. HID
Haverfordwest ....UK.. HAW	Hickory, NC ....USA ..HKY	Hornafjordur ....Iceland.. HFN
Havoeysund ....Norway.. QVO	Hidden Falls, AK ....USA .HDA	Hornepayne, ON.......Canada.. YHN
Havre City-County, MT ...USA.. HVR	Hienghene ..... New Caledonia . HNG	Horns ....Syria.. QHS
Havre St Pierre, QC ....Canada.. YGV	High Level, AB ......Canada .. YOJ	Horsham ....Australia.. HSM
Hawabango Papua New Guinea ..HWA	High Prairie, AB ....Canada ..ZHP	Horta ....Portugal.. HOR
Hawk Inlet/SPB, AK ......USA.. HWI	High Wycombe (MOD) .....UK ..HYC	Hoskins .... Papua New Guinea.. HKN
Hawker/Wilpena Pound Australia . HWK	Highbury ....Australia .. HIG	Hot Springs, AR ....USA.. HOT
Hawthorne, CA...........USA.. HHR	Hikueru ....F. Polynesia ..HHZ	Hot Springs/Ingalls, VA ....USA.. HSP
Hawthorne, NV...........USA.. HTH	Hilden ....Germany ..ZNN	Hotan ....China.. HTN
Hay ....Australia.. HXX	Hildesheim ....Germany ..ZNO	Houailou ....New Caledonia.. HLU
Hay River, NT ....Canada.. YHY	Hill City, KS ....USA ..HLC	Houeisay ....Laos.. HOE
Haycock, AK ....USA.. HAY	Hill/AFB, UT ....USA ..HIF	Houghton Lake, MI ......USA.. HTL
Hayden/Yampa Valley, CO. .USA.. HDN	Hillsboro, OR..........USA ..HIO	Houlton Int'l, ME ....USA.. HUL
Hayfields ..Papua New Guinea .. HYF	Hillside ....Australia ..HLL	Houma-Terrebonne, LA . . USA.. HUM
Hayman Is............Australia.. HIS	Hillsville, VA...........USA ..HLX	Houn ....Libya.. HUQ
Hays/Municipal, KS........USA.. HYS	Hilo Int'l, HI...........USA ..ITO	Houston George Bush Int'l,
Hayward Air Terminal, CA. .USA.. HWD	Hilton Head, SC ....USA .HHH	TX...............USA... IAH
Hayward Municipal, WI ...USA.. HYR	Hilversum/RR .....Netherlands . QYI	Houston/Hobby Arpt, TX . USA.. HOU
Hazebrouck/Merville/Calonne	Hinchinbrook Is........Australia. HNK	Houston, TX ....USA..DWH
.............France .. HZB	Hirlshals/Bus Svc ....Denmark .. XAJ	Houston-SugarLand, TX...USA.. SGR
HazletonPA ....USA.. HZL	Hiroshima/Hiroshima West	Houston/Andrau Airpark, TX
Hazyview ....S. Africa.. HZV	...............Japan . HIW	...............USA..AAP
Headingly ....Australia.. HIP	Hiroshima/Int'l ....Japan ..HIJ	Houston/Bus Stn, BC . . Canada.. ZHO
Healy Lake, AK...........USA.. HKB	Hissar ....India ..HSS	Houston/Central Bus. District,
Hearst, OH. ....Canada.. YHF	Hiva Oa ....F. Polynesia ..HIX	TX ....USA..JDX
Heathlands ....Australia.. HAT	Hivaro .... Papua New Guinea ..HIT	Houston/Greenway Plaza HP,
Heerbrugg........Switzerland .. ZHL	Hjoerring/Bus Svc ....Denmark .QHJ	TX ....USA..JGP
Heerenveen/Bus Svc	Hluhluwe ....S. Africa. HLW	Houston/Marriot Astrodome, TX
.............Netherlands .. QYZ	Ho Chi Minh ....Vietnam . SGN	...............USA..JMA
Hefei ....China.. HFE	Hobart Arpt ....Australia ..HBA	Houston/Park Ten HP, TX . . USA.. JPT
Heho ....Myanmar.. HEH	Hobart Bay, AK ....USA . HBH	Houston/Spaceland, TX ...USA..SPX
Heidelberg ....Germany.. HDB	Hobart Municipal Arpt, OK USA ..HBR	Houston/Transco Twr Galleria, TX
Heidenheim ....Germany .. ZNI	Hobbs, NM............USA . HOB	...............USA..JGQ
Heiena, MT ....USA.. HLN	Hobbs/Industrial Airpark, NM	Houston/Westchase Hilton HP,
Heihe ....China.. HEK	...............USA ..HBB	TX...............USA.. JWH
Heilbronn ....Germany .. ZNJ	Hodeidah/Hodeidah Arpt	Houston/Woodlawns, TX ..USA..JWL
Heinola ....Finland.. QVV	...............Yemen . HOD	Hoy Is.............UK.. HOY
Heiweni ....Papua New Guinea ..HNI	Hoedspruit ....S. Africa. HDS	Hsinchu............Taiwan..HSZ
Helena/Thompson-Robbins, AR	Hof ....Germany . HOQ	Hua Hin ....Thailand.. HHQ
...............USA.. HEE	Hofuf/Al Hasa.. Saudi Arabia ..HOF	Huacaraje ....Bolivia..BVK
Helenvaie ....Australia.. HLV	Hogatza, AK..........USA . HGZ	Huahine/Flying Boat ....
Helgoland ....Germany.. HGL	Hohenems ....Austria. HOH	........French Polynesia.. HUH
Helicopter Scenic New Zealand .. XXH	Hohhot ....China . HET	Hualien ....Taiwan.. HUN
Helsingborg ....Sweden. AGH	Hokitilka ....New Zealand ..HKK	Huambo ....Andorra.. NOV
Helsingborg/ HP ....Sweden.. JHE	Hola ....Kenya . HOA	Huangyan ....China.. HYN
Helsinki/Malmi ....Finland.. HEM	Holguir./Frank Pais .....Cuba . HOG	Huanuco ....Peru.. HUU
Helsinki/Vantaa........Finland.. HEL	Holikachu, AK.........USA . HOL	Huatulco ....Mexico.. HUX
Hemavan ....Sweden..HMV	Holland/Park Township, MI. USA . HLM	Hubli ....India.. HBX
Hemet/Ryan Fld, CA......USA.. HMT	Hollis/SPB, AK.........USA . HYL	Hudiksvall ....Sweden.. HUV
Hemnes ....Norway.. ZXR	Hollister, CA ....USA . HLI	Hudson Bay, SK ......Canada.. YHB
Henbury ....Australia.. HRY	Holloman/AFB, NM.......USA . HMN	Hudson's Hope, BC .. Canada.. YNH
Hendaye ....France.. XHY	Hollywood-North Perry, FL USA . HWO	Hudson/Columbia County, NY
Henderson City, KY ......USA.. EHR	Holman, NT ....Canada . YHI	...............USA..HCC
Hendon ....UK.. HEN	Holmavik ....Iceland . HVK	Hue/Phu Bai..........Vietnam.. HUI
Hengchun ....Taiwan. HCN	Holstelbro/Bus Svc . . Denmark . QWO	Huelnuetenango . . Guatemala.. HUG
Hengelo/RR ....Netherlands.. QYH	Holy Cross, AK.........USA . HCR	Huerth ....Germany..ZNP
Hengyang ....China.. HNY	Holyhead ....UK . HLY	Hughenden ....Australia.. HGD

A
I
R
P
O
R
T
S

Hughes/Municipal, AK . . . . .USA . . HUS
Hugo, OK . . . . .USA . . HUJ
Huizinou . . . . .China . . HUZ
Hukuntsi . . . . Botswana . . HUK
Hultsfred/AFB . . . . Sweden . . HLF
Humacao/Humacao Arpt
. . . . .Puerto Rico . . HUC
Humacao/Palmas Del Mar
. . . . .Puerto Rico . . PPD
Humberside . . . . .UK . . HUY
Humbert River . . . . Australia . . HUB
Humboldt Municipal, NE .USA . .HBO
Humboldt, IA . . . . .USA . .HUD
Humera . . . . .Ethiopia . . HUE
Hunter/AAF, GA. . . . . .USA . . SVN
Huntingburg, IN. . . . . .USA . .HNB
Huntingdon/RR Stn. . . . . . .UK . .XHU
Huntington, WV . . . . .USA . . HTS
Huntsville, AL. . . . . .USA . . HSV
Huntsville, TX. . . . . .USA . . HTV
Huntsville, TX. . . . . .USA . . UTS
Huntsville/Redstone/AAF . .USA . .HUA
Hurghada . . . . .Egypt . .HRG
Huron, SD . . . . .USA . .HON
Husavik . . . . Iceland . . HZK
Huslia, AK . . . . .USA . . HSL
HuStn/GlvStn Nexrad, TX. .USA . .HGX
Husum . . . . Germany . . QHU
Hutchinsen, KS . . . . .USA . . HUT
Hutchinson County Arpt, TX
. . . . .USA . .BGD
Hvammstangi . . . . Iceland . .HVM
Hwange . . . . Zimbabwe . . WKI
Hwange Nat Park . . Zimbabwe . . HWN
Hyannis-Barnstable, MA .USA . . HYA
Hydaburg/SPB, AK. . . . . . . .USA . . HYG
Hyder/SPB, AK . . . . .USA . . WHD
Hyderabad . . . . Pakistan . . HDD
Hyderabad/Begumpet. . . . India . . HYD
Hyeres . . . . .France . . XHE
Hyvinkää . . . . Finland . . HYV

I

Iamalele . . . . .Papua New Guinea . . .IMA
Iasi. . . . . .Romania . . IAS
IATA Traffic Svcs . . . . n/a . . IAT
Iaura . . . . . . .Papua New Guinea . . .IAU
Ibadan/(NAW) . . . . Nigeria . . IBA
Ibague . . . . Colombia . . IBE
Iberia. . . . . .Peru . . IBP
Ibiruba/Off-line Pt . . . . . . Brazil . . QIB
Ibiza . . . . .Spain . . IBZ
Iboki . . . . . . .Papua New Guinea . . . IBI
Icabaru. . . . . .Venezuela . . ICA
Icy Bay, AK . . . . .USA . . ICY
Ida Grove/Municipal, IA . . . .USA . .IDG
Idaho Falls, Fanning Fld, ID USA . . IDA
Iffley . . . . Australia . . IFF
Igloolik, BC . . . . .Canada . . YGT
Ignace, ON . . . . .Canada . .ZUC
Iguela . . . . .Gabon . . IGE
Iiorin . . . . Nigeria . . ILR
Ijui/J.Batista Bos Filho . . . . . Brazil . . IJU
Ikaria Is/Ikaria . . . . Greece . . JIK
ikarniut. . . . . Greenland . . QJI
Ikast/Bus Svc . . . . Denmark . . QLZ
Ikela . . . . .Congo, DR . . IKL
Iki . . . . Japan . . IKI
Ilaka . . . . Madagascar . . ILK
Ile Des Pins . . . . New Caledonia . . ILP
Ile Ouen . . . . New Caledonia . . IOU
Ilebo . . . . .Congo, DR . . PFR
Ileg. . . . . .Papua New Guinea . . ILX
Iles De La Madeleine, QC
. . . . .Canada . . YGR
Ilford, MB . . . . .Canada . . ILF
Ilha Solteira . . . . .Brazil . . ILB

Iliamna Arpt, AK. . . . . USA . . .ILI
Iligan/Maria Cristina . . Philippines . . IGN
Illaga . . . . Indonesia . . ILA
Illbo . . . . Mozambique . . IBO
Illishern/Illis Airbase . . Germany . . ILH
Illizi . . . . Algeria . . VVZ
Ilo . . . . Peru . .ILQ
Ilu . . . . Indonesia . . IUL
Imane . . . . . Papua New Guinea . . IMN
Imbaimadai . . . . Guyana . . IMB
Immokalee, FL . . . . USA . . IMM
Imonda . . . . Papua New Guinea . . IMD
Imperatriz . . . . .Brazil . . IMP
Imperial Beach/NAF, CA. . USA . .NRS
Imperial County, CA . . . . . USA . . IPL
Imperial Municipal, NE . . USA . . IML
Imphal/Mun . . . . India . . IMF
Imptondo . . . . .Congo, DR . . ION
In Amenas . . . . Algeria . . IAM
In Guezzam . . . . Algeria . . INF
In Salah North . . . . Algeria . .INZ
Inagua . . . . Bahamas . . IGA
Inanwatan . . . . Indonesia . . INX
Incheon / HP . . . . S. Korea . .JCN
Indagen . . . Papua New Guinea . . IDN
Indaselassie . . . . Ethiopia . .SHC
Independence . . . . Belize . . INB
Independence, KS . . . . USA . .IDP
Indian Mountain AFS, AK. USA . .UTO
Indian Springs, NV . . . . . . USA . .INS
Indiana, PA. . . . . USA . . IDI
Indianapolis/Int'l Arpt, IN . . USA . . IND
Indianapolis, Eagle Creek, IN
. . . . USA . . EYE
Indore . . . . India . . IDR
Indulkana . . . . Australia . . IDK
Ine Is . . . . Marshall Is . . IMI
Ingeniero Jacobacci Argentina . . IGB
Ingersoll/RR Stn., ON . . Canada . . XIB
Ingham . . . . Australia . . IGH
Ingolstadt . . . . Germany . . ZNQ
Inhambane . . . . . . Mozambique . . INH
Inhaminga . . . . Mozambique . . IMG
Inisheer . . . . Ireland . . INQ
Inishmaian . . . . Ireland . . IIA
Inishmore/Kilronan . . . . . Ireland . . IOR
Injune . . . . Australia . . INJ
Inkerman . . . . Australia . . IKP
Innamiricka . . . . Australia . . INM
Innisfail. . . . . Australia . . IFL
Innsbruck/Kranebitten . . Austria . . INN
Int'l Falls, MN . . . . USA . . INL
Inta . . . . Russia . . INA
Interlaken. . . . . Switzerland . . ZIN
Inulkjualk, QC. . . . . Canada . . YPH
Inus . . . . Papua New Guinea . . IUS
Inuvik, NT . . . . Canada . . YEV
Invercargill . . . . . .New Zealand . . IVC
Inverell . . . . Australia . . IVR
Inverlake, AB . . . . Canada . . TIL
Inverness/Dalcross. . . . . . .UK . . INV
Inverness/ScotRail . . . . . . .UK . . ZIV
Inverway . . . . Australia . . IVW
Inyati . . . . S. Africa . . INY
Inyokern, CA . . . . USA . . IYK
Ioannina . . . . Greece . . IOA
Ioilo/Mandurriao . . . . . Philippines . . ILO
Iokea . . . . Papua New Guinea . . IOK
Iowa City Municipal, IA. . . . USA . . IOW
Iowa Falls, IA. . . . . USA . . IFA
Ipatinga/Usiminas . . . . . . .Brazil . . IPN
Ipiales/San Luis . . . . . . Colombia . . IPI
Ipiau. . . . . .Brazil . . IPU
Ipil . . . . Philippines . . IPE
Ipiranga . . . . .Brazil . . IPG
Ipoh . . . . Malaysia . . IPH
Ipota . . . . Vanuatu . . IPA
Ipswich . . . . .UK . . IPW
Iqaluit, NT. . . . . Canada . . YFB
Iquique/Cavancha. . . . . . . Chile . . IQQ
Iquitos/CF, Secada . . . . . . Peru . .IQT

Iraan/Municipal, TX. . . . . . . .USA. . . IRB
Irbid/Off-line Pt . . . . .Jordan. . . QIR
Irece. . . . . Brazil. . . IRE
Iringa/Nduli . . . . Tanzania. . . IRI
Iriona . . . . Honduras. . . IRN
Irkutsk. . . . . Russia. . . IKT
Iron Mountain, MI . . . . USA. . . IMT
Ironwood/Gogebic County, MI
. . . . USA. . .IWD
Is Lake, MB. . . . . Canada. . . YIV
Isabel Pass, AK. . . . . USA. . .ISL
Isafjordur . . . . .Iceland. . . IFJ
Ischia . . . . Italy. . . ISH
Iscuande . . . . .Colombia. . . ISD
Iserlohn. . . . . Germany. . . ZNR
Isfahan . . . . Iran. . . IFN
Ishigalki . . . . Japan. . . ISG
Ishurdi . . . . Bangladesh. . . IRD
Isisford . . . . .Australia. . . ISI
Isla Mujeres . . . . .Mexico. . . ISJ
Islamabad Int'l . . . . .Pakistan. . . ISB
Islay/Glenegedaie . . . . .UK. . . ILY
Isle Baltra . . . . .Ecuador. . . WGL
Isle Of Man/Ronaldsway . . . UK. . .IOM
Isle Of Skye/Broadford. . . . UK. . . SKL
Isles Of Scilly/St Marys . . . UK. . . ISC
Isles Of Scilly/Tresco . . . . . UK. . .TSO
Isleworth . . . . .UK. . . QIF
Ismailia . . . . Egypt. . . QIV
Isparta . . . . Turkey. . . ISE
Isro/Matari . . . . Congo, DR. . . IRP
Istanbul/Ataturk . . . . Turkey. . . IST
Istres . . . . .France. . . QIE
Itaburia . . . . Brazil. . . ITN
Itacoatiara . . . . Brazil. . .ITA
Itaiai . . . . Brazil. . .ITJ
Itaituba . . . . Brazil. . . ITB
Itajuba . . . . Brazil. . . QDS
Itambacuri . . . . Brazil. . . ITI
Itaperuna . . . . Brazil. . .ITP
Itapetinga . . . . Brazil. . . QIT
Itaqui . . . . Brazil. . . ITQ
Itauba . . . . Brazil. . . AUB
Itauna . . . . Brazil. . . QIA
Ithaca, NY . . . . .USA. . . ITH
Ithosy . . . . Madagascar. . . IHO
Itilleq . . . . Greenland. . . QJG
Ittoqqortoormiit . . . . Greenland. . . OBY
Itu . . . . Brazil. . . QTU
Itubera . . . . Brazil. . . ITE
Itumbiara . . . . Brazil. . . ITR
Ivalo . . . . Finland. . . IVL
Ivanci-Frankovsk . . . . . Ukraine. . . IFO
Ivangrad . . . . .Yugoslavia. . . IVG
Ivanova . . . . Russia. . . IWA
Ivishak, AK . . . . .USA. . . IVH
Iwami . . . . .Japan. . . IWJ
Iwo Jima Vol/Iwo Jima Airbase
. . . . .Japan. . .IWO
Ixtapa/Zihuatanejo/Int'l . . .Mexico. . . ZIH
Ixtepec. . . . . .Mexico. . . IZT
Izhevsk. . . . . Russia. . . IJK
Izmil . . . . Turkey. . .QST
Izmir/Adnan Menderes . . Turkey. . . ADB
Izumo . . . . .Japan. . . IZO

J

Jabiru . . . . .Australia. . .JAB
Jabot . . . . .Marshall Is. . . JAT
Jacareacanga . . . . Brazil. . . JCR
Jackpot, NV . . . . USA. . .KPT
Jackson Hole, WY . . . . USA. . . JAC
Jackson/Int'l Arpt, MS. . . . USA. . . JAN
Jackson/Hawkins Fld, MS. . USA. . . HKS
Jackson, MN . . . . USA. . . MJQ
Jackson, TN . . . . USA. . . MKL

AIRPORTS

Jackson/Reynolds Municipal, MI
...................................USA .. JXN
Jackson/Carroll, KY ......USA .. JKL
Jacksonvill/NAS, FL ......USA .. NIP
Jacksonville/Mtrpltn, FL ...USA .. JAX
Jacksonville/Craig Mncpl FLUSA .CRG
Jacksonville, IL ....USA .. IJX
Jacksonville, NC ....USA .. OAJ
Jacksonville, TX ....USA .. JKV
Jacmel ....Haiti .. JAK
Jacobabad ....Pakistan .. JAG
Jacobina ....Brazil .. JCM
Jacquinot Bay
............Papua New Guinea .. JAQ
Jaffrey/Municipal, NH......USA .. AFN
Jagdaipur ....India .. JGB
Jaipur/Sanganeer ....India .. JAI
Jaisalmer ....India .. JSA
Jakarta/Halim Penclana Kusuma
...................Indonesia .. HLP
Jakarta/Soekarno Int'l. Indonesia .. CGK
Jal Edib ....Lebanon .. QJQ
Jalai ....Brazil .. JTI
Jalalabad.............Afghanistan .. JAA
Jalapa ....Mexico .. JAL
Jalbalpur ....India .. JLR
Jales ....Brazil .. JLS
Jaluit Is ....Marshall Is .. UIT
Jamba ....Angola .. JMB
Jambi/Sultan Taha Syarifudn
...................Indonesia .. DJB
Jambol ....Bulgaria .. JAM
Jamestown, ND ....USA .. JMS
Jamestown, NY ....USA .. JHW
Jammu/Satwari ....India .. IXJ
Jamnagar/Govardhanpur . India .. JGA
Jamshedpur/Sonari......India .. IXW
Jan Mayen
... Svalbard and Jan Mayen Is .. ZXB
Janakpur...............Nepal .. JKR
Jandakot ....Australia .. JAD
Janesville, WI ....USA .. JVL
Januaria................Brazil .. JNA
Jaque ....Panama .. JQE
Jaragua Do Sul.........Brazil .. QJA
Jasper-Hinton, AB ....Canada .. YJP
Jasper/County, TX ....USA .. JAS
Jasper/Marion County, TN ..USA .. APT
Jasper/RR Stn., AB .....Canada .. XDH
Jaula ....Peru .. JAU
JaUna/Kankesanturai ..Sri Lanka .. JAF
Jayapura/Sentani ....Indonesia .. DJJ
Jeddah/King Abdul Aziz Int'l Arpt
...................Saudi Arabia .. JED
Jefferson City, MO ....USA .. JEF
Jefferson Proving Grnd., IN
...................USA . MDN
Jefferson/Ashtabula, OH. ..USA .. JFN
Jefferson/Municipal, IA ...USA .. EFW
Jeh...................Marshall Is .. JEJ
Jena/RR Stn. ....Germany .. ZJS
Jenpeg, MB ....Canada .. ZJG
Jequie ....Brazil .. JEQ
Jeremie ....Haiti .. JEE
Jerez De La Frontera/La Parra
...................Spain . XRY
Jersey ....UK .. JER
Jerusalem
..... Occupied Palestinian Ter .. JRS
Jesolo ....Italy .. JLO
Jessore ....Bangladesh .. JSR
Jeypore ....India .. PYB
Ji'An ....China .. KNC
Ji-Parana ....Brazil .. JPR
Jiarnusi ....China .. JMU
Jiayuguan ....China .. JGN
Jijel Achouat ....Algeria .. GJL
Jijig/Jigiga ....Ethiopia ...JIJ
Jilin ....China ... JIL
Jimma ....Ethiopia .. JIM
Jin ....Nepal .. JIR

Jinan ....China . TNA
Jindaloyne..............Australia .. QJD
Jingdezhen.............China .. JDZ
Jinghong/Gasa ....China .. JHG
Jining ....China .. JNG
Jinja ....Uganda ...JIN
Jinjiang...............China .. JJN
Jinka ....Ethiopia . BCO
Jinzhou................China . JNZ
Jiujiang ....China ... JIU
Jiuquan ....China . CHW
Jiwani ....Pakistan . JIW
Joacaba ....Brazil .. JCB
Joato Pessoa/Castro PintoBrazil .. JPA
Jodhpur ....India .. JDH
Joensuu ....Finland .. JOE
Johannesburg Int'l ... S. Africa .. JNB
Johannesburg/Grand Central
...................S. Africa .. GCJ
Johannesburg/HP ... S. Africa .. QRA
Johnny Mountain, BC Canada .. YJO
Johnson, TX ....USA .. JCY
Johnston Is ... Wake/Midway Is .. JON
Johnstown-Cambria, PA . USA .. JST
Johor Bahru/Sultan Ismail Int'l
...................Malaysia .. JHB
Joinville/Cubatao ....Brazil .. JOI
Joliet Municipal, IL ....USA .. JOT
Joliette/RR Stn., QC ... Canada .. XJL
Jolo ....Philippines .. JOL
Jolon/Hunter/AAF, CA .....USA .. HGT
Jonesboro, AR ....USA .. JBR
Jonkoping/Axamo .... Sweden .. JKG
Jonquiere/RR Stn., QC. Canada .. XJQ
Joplin, MO ....USA .. JLN
Jordan, MT..............USA .. JDN
Jorhat/Rowriah............India .. JRH
Jornsom ....Nepal .. JMO
Jos ....Nigeria .. JOS
Jose De San Martin . Argentina . JSM
Josephstaal Papua New Guinea .. JOP
Josrikar-Ola ....Russia .. JOK
Jouf ....Saudi Arabia .. AJF
Jounieh ....Lebanon .. QJN
Jpjapa ....Ecuador ... JIP
Juan Les Pins ....France .. JLP
Juanjui ....Peru ... JJI
Juara ....Brazil .. JUA
Juazeiro Do Norte/Regional
Do Cariri...............Brazil .. JDO
Juba ....Sudan .. JUB
Jubail ....Saudi Arabia .. QJB
Juina ....Brazil .. JIA
Juist ....Germany ...JUI
Juiz De Fora/Francisco De Assis
...................Brazil .. JDF
Jujuy/El Cadilial ...... Argentina .. JUJ
Julia Creek ....Australia .. JCK
Juliaca ....Peru .. JUL
Jullundur ....India .. QJU
Jumia ....Nepal .. JUM
Junction, TX ....USA .. JCT
Jundah ....Australia .. JUN
Jundiai ....Brazil .. QDV
Juneau/Int'l, AK ....USA .. JNU
Juneau/Dodge County, AK. USA .. UNU
Junin ....Argentina .. JNI
Jurado ....Colombia .. JUO
Jurien Bay ....Australia .. JUR
Juruena ....Brazil .. JRN
Juticalpa ....Honduras .. JUT
Juzhou ....China .. JUZ
Jwaneng ....Botswana ..JWA
Jyvaskyla..............Finland .. JYV

K

Kaadedhclhoo ...... Maldives .. KDM
Kabaiega Falls ....Uganda .. KBG
Kabala ....Sierra Leone .. KBA
Kabalo ....Congo, DR .. KBO
Kaben ....Marshall Is .. KBT
Kabinda ....Congo, DR .. KBN
Kabri Dar ....Ethiopia .. ABK
Kabul/Khwaja Rawash
...................Afghanistan .. KBL
Kabwe ....Zambia .. QKE
Kabwurn ... Papua New Guinea .. KBM
Kadanwari ....Pakistan .. KCF
Kadhdhoo ....Maldives .. KDO
Kaduna ....Nigeria .. KAD
Kaedi ....Mauritania .. KED
Kaele ....Cameroon .. KLE
Kagau ....Solomon Is .. KGE
Kagi ..... Papua New Guinea .. KGW
Kagoshima ....Japan .. KOJ
Kagua ..... Papua New Guinea .. AGK
Kagvik Creek, AK ......USA .. KKF
Kahramanmaras ....Turkey .. KCM
Kahului, HI ....USA .. OGG
Kaiapit ..... Papua New Guinea .. KIA
Kaieteur ....Guyana .. KAI
Kaikohe ....New Zealand .. KKO
Kaikoura ....New Zealand .. KBZ
Kailashahar ....India .. IXH
Kaimana/Utarom .... Indonesia .. KNG
Kaintiba ... Papua New Guinea .. KZF
Kairouan ....Tunisia .. QKN
Kaiser/Lake Ozark, MO ....USA .. AIZ
Kaiserslautern ....Germany .. KLT
Kaitaia ....New Zealand .. KAT
Kajaani ....Finland .. KAJ
Kake/SPB, AK ....USA .. KAE
Kakhonak, AK ....USA .. KNK
Kalabo ....Zambia .. KLB
Kalakalket/AFS, AK ......USA .. KKK
Kalamata ....Greece .. KLX
Kalamazoo, MI ....USA .. AZO
Kalat ....Pakistan .. KBH
Kalaupapa, HI ....USA .. LUP
Kalbarri ....Australia .. KAX
Kalemie ....Congo, DR .. FMI
Kalemyo ....Myanmar .. KMV
Kalgoorlie..............Australia .. KGI
Kalibo ....Philippines .. KLO
Kalima ....Congo, DR .. KLY
Kalinin/Migalovo ....Russia .. KLD
Kaliningrad ....Russia .. KGD
Kalispell, MT ....USA .. FCA
Kalkurung ....Australia .. KFG
Kallag, AK ....USA .. KAL
Kalmar ....Sweden .. KLR
Kalokol ....Kenya .. KLK
Kalpowar ....Australia .. KPP
Kalskag/Municipal, AK .... USA .. KLG
Kaluga ....Russia .. KLF
Kalumburu ....Australia .. UBU
Kamalpur ....India .. IXQ
Kamaran Downs .....Australia .. KDS
Kamaran Is ....Yemen .. KAM
Kamarang ....Guyana .. KAR
Kamarata ....Venezuela .. KTV
Kambaida ....Australia .. KDB
Kamberatoro
............Papua New Guinea .. KDQ
Kambuaya ....Indonesia .. KBX
Kamembe ....Rwanda .. KME
Kamenets-Podolskiy . Ukraine .. KCP
Kameshli ....Syria .. KAC
Kamileroi ....Australia .. KML
Kamina ..... Papua New Guinea .. KMF
Kamina ....Congo, DR .. KMN

Kamiraba...Papua New Guinea .. KJU	**Karlstad**/Flygplats..... Sweden .. KSD	**Kelly Bar**, AK .... USA.. KEU
Kamloops. BC ....Canada.. YKA	**Karluk Lake** SPB, AK..... USA .. KKL	**Kelly**/AFB, TX ....USA...SKF
Kampala .... Uganda .. KLA	**Karonga** .... Malawi ..KGJ	**Kelowna**, BC ....Canada.. YLW
Kampot .... Cambodia .. KMT	**Karoola** ... Papua New Guinea .. KXR	**Kelp Bay**, AK ....USA... KLP
Kamuela, HI ....USA .. MUE	**Karpathos** ....Greece .. AOK	**Kelsey**, MB ....Canada...KES
Kamulai ....Papua New Guinea .. KAQ	**Karratha** ....Australia .. KTA	**Kelso**, Longview, WA .....USA...KLS
Kamur............ Indonesia .. KCD	**Kars**, ...Turkey .. KSY	**Kelsterbach**........... Germany... QLH
Kamusi/Kamusi Arpt	**Karshi** ....Uzbekistan ..KSQ	**Keluang**.......... Indonesia... KLQ
..........Papua New Guinea .. KUY	**Karubaga** ....Indonesia .. KBF	**Kemano**, BC ....Canada.. XKO
Kanab, UT ....USA... KNB	**Karuk**, AK .... USA .. KYK	**Kemerer**, WY ....USA.. EMM
Kanabea ..Papua New Guinea .. KEX	**Karumba** ....Australia .. KRB	**Kemerovo** ....Russia... KEJ
Kanainj.....Papua New Guinea .. KNE	**Karup**/Military ...... Denmark .. KRP	**Kemi**/Tornio ....Finland.. KEM
Kananga ....Congo, DR .. KGA	**Kasaan SPB**, AK ....USA .. KXA	**Kempsey** ....Australia... KPS
Kanazawa .... Japan .. QKW	**Kasaba Bay** ....Zambia .. ZKB	**Kempten** .... Germany...ZNS
Kandahar .... Afghanistan .. KDH	**Kasabonika**, ON...... Canada .. XKS	**Kenai**, AK ....USA... ENA
Kandavu .... Fiji .. KDV	**Kasama** ....Zambia .. KAA	**Kendan**/Wolter Monginsidi
Kandep ..Papua New Guinea .. KDP	**Kasane** ....Botswana .. BBK	.... Indonesia... KDI
Kandersteg........Switzerland .. ZHR	**Kasanombe** Papua New Guinea .. KSB	**Kenema** .... Sierra Leone.. KEN
Kandi .... Benin .. KDC	**Kasba Lake**, NT ...... Canada .. YDU	**Keng Tung** ....Myanmar... KET
Kandla .... India .. IXY	**Kaschechewan**, ON .. Canada .. ZKE	**Kenieba** .... Mali.. KNZ
Kandrian ...Papua New Guinea .. KDR	**Kasenga** ....Congo, DR .. KEC	**Keningau** ....Malaysia... KGU
Kangaamiut .... Greenland .. QKT	**Kasese** .... Uganda .. KSE	**Kenitra**/NAF ....Morocco... NNA
Kangaiatsiaq .... Greenland .. QPW	**Kashi** ....China .. KHG	**Kenmore Air** Harbor, WA ..USA... KEH
Kangan/Jam .... Iran .. KNR	**Kasigluk**, AK ....USA ..KUK	**Kennedy**/Int'l, NY ....USA... JFK
Kangerluk .... Greenland .. QGR	**Kasikasirna**/Tepoe Airstrip	**Kennedy Town** ..... Hong Kong... XKT
Kangerlussuaq .... Greenland .. SFJ	.............Suriname ..KCB	**Kennett Municipal**, MO... USA...KNT
Kangerlussuaq .... Greenland .. SJF	**Kasompe** ....Zambia .. ZKP	**Kennosao Lake**, MB .. Canada... YKI
Kangiqsualuijuaq, QC.Canada .. XGR	**Kasongo Lunda**....Congo, DR .. KGN	**Kenora**, ON............ Canada... YQK
Kangiqsujuaq, QC .....Canada .. YWB	**Kasos Is** ....Greece .. KSJ	**Kenosha**, WI ....USA... ENW
Kangirsuk, QC ....Canada .. YKG	**Kassala**...............Sudan .. KSL	**Kentland**, IN ....USA...KKT
Kangnung/Air Base ... S. Korea .. KAG	**Kassel**/Calden ...... Germany .. KSF	**Keokuk**, IA ....USA... EOK
Kaniama ....Congo, DR .. KNM	**Kastamonu** ....Turkey .. KFS	**Kepi** .... Indonesia... KEi
Kankakee, IL ....USA... IKK	**Kastelorizo** ....Greece .. KZS	**Kerama** ....Japan... KJP
Kankan .... Guinea .. KNN	**Kastoria**/Aristotelis ....Greece .. KSO	**Kerang** ....Australia... KRA
Kano/Aminu Kano Int'l .. Nigeria .. KAN	**Kasungu** ....Malawi .. KBQ	**Kerau** ....Papua New Guinea... KRU
Kanpur .... India .. KNU	**Katanning** ....Australia .. KNI	**Kerch** ....Ukraine... KHC
Kansas City/Johnson Exec, KS	**Katherine**/Tindal .....Australia .. KTR	**Kerema** ....Papua New Guinea... KMA
...............USA .. OJC	**Kathmandu**/Tribhuvan ... Nepal ..KTM	**Kericho** .... Kenya...KEY
Kansas City/Int'l, MO......USA.. MCI	**Katiola** .... Côte D'Ivoire .. KTC	**Kerikeri** .... New Zealand..KKE
Kansas City, Richards-Gebaur	**Kato** ....Guyana .. KTO	**Kerinci**/Depati Parbo. Indonesia... KRC
Arpt, MO ....USA. GVW	**Katowice**/Pyrzowice .... Poland .. KTW	**Kerio Valley** .... Kenya...KRV
Kansas City/Downtown, MO	**Kattiniq**/Donaldson Lak,	**Kerkyra**/I. Kapodistrias . Greece... CFU
...............USA..MKC	QC .... Canada .. YAU	**Kerman** ....Iran... KER
Kansas City/Fairfax, KS ...USA.. KCK	**Kau** .... Indonesia .. KAZ	**Kermanshah** ....Iran... KSH
Kansas City/Johnson Industrial,	**Kauai Is**/Lihue, HI .... USA ..LIH	**Kerpen** ....Germany...ZNT
MO ....USA... JCI	**Kauai Is**/Princeville, HI .... USA .. HPV	**Kerrville**, TX ....USA... ERV
Kantchari ...... Burkina Faso .. XKA	**Kauhajoki** ....Finland .. KHJ	**Kerry** ....Ireland... KIR
Kanua......Papua New Guinea .. KTK	**Kauhava** ....Finland .. KAU	**Kerteh** ....Malaysia...KTE
Kaohsiung/Int'l ....Taiwan .. KHH	**Kaukura Atoll** ... F. Polynesia .. KKR	**Keshod** ....India... IXK
Kaolack .... Senegal .. KLC	**Kaunas**/Int'l. ....Lithuania .. KUN	**Ketapang**/Rahadi Usmaman
Kaorna ....Zambia .. KMZ	**Kautokeino** ....Norway .. QKX	.... Indonesia... KTG
Kapalua, HI ....USA... JHM	**Kavala**/Megas Alexandros	**Ketchikan**/Int'l, AK ....USA...KTN
Kapanga ....Congo, DR .. KAP	............Greece .. KVA	**Ketchikan**/Waterfront SPB, AK
Kapit .... Malaysia .. KPI	**Kavanayen** .... Venezuela .. KAV	.............USA... WFB
Kapuskasing, ON .....Canada .. YYU	**Kavieng** ... Papua New Guinea .. KVG	**Key Lake**, SK ....Canada...YKJ
Kar.......Papua New Guinea .. KAK	**Kavik**/Airstrip, AK ....USA .. VIK	**Key Largo**/Port Largo, FL .. USA...KYL
Kar Kar.....Papua New Guinea .. KRX	**Kawadjia** .. Central African Rep . KWD	**Key West**, FL ....USA... EYW
Karachi/Quaid-E-Azam Int'l	**Kawau Is** ....New Zealand .. KUI	**Key West**/NAS, FL ....USA... NQX
.... Pakistan .. KHI	**Kawito** ... Papua New Guinea .. KWO	**Keystone**/Van Svc, CO ....USA... QKS
Karaganda ....Kazakstan .. KGF	**Kawthaung** ....Myanmar .. KAW	**Khajuraho** ....India... HJR
Karaj ....Iran ..QKC	**Kaya** ....Burkina Faso .. XKY	**Khaloarovsk**/Novyy .... Russia... KHV
Karamay ....China .. KRY	**Kayenta**, AZ .... USA .. MVM	**Khamis Mushat** ..Saudi Arabia... KMX
Karanambo ....Guyana .. KRM	**Kayes** ....Mali .. KYS	**Khamti** ....Myanmar... KHM
Karasabai ....Guyana .. KRG	**Kayseri** ....Turkey .. ASR	**Khaneh** ....Iran... KHA
Karasburg.............Namibia .. KAS	**Kazan** ....Russia .. KZN	**Kharga** ....Egypt...UVL
Karasjok ....Norway .. QKK	**Kearney**, NE .... USA .. EAR	**Kharian** ....Pakistan... QKH
Karato ....Papua New Guinea .. KAF	**Kebar** .... Indonesia .. KEQ	**Khark Is** ....Iran... KHK
Karawari ..Papua New Guinea .. KRJ	**Kedougou** .... Senegal .. KGG	**Kharkhorin** ....Mongolia... KHR
Kardjali .... Bulgaria .. KDG	**Keesler**/AFB, MS ....USA ..BIX	**Kharkov** ....Ukraine... HRK
Kardla................Estonia .. KDL	**Keetmanshoop**/	**Khartoum**/Civil .... Sudan... KRT
Kariba ....Zimbabwe .. KAB	J.G.H. Van Der Wath.. Namibia .. KMP	**Khasab** ....Oman... KHS
Karimunjawa .... Indonesia .. KWB	**Keewaywin**, ON ...... Canada .. KEW	**Khashm El Girba** ..... Somalia... GBU
Karinnui ..Papua New Guinea .. KMR	**Kefalhnia**/Argostolion ... Greece .. EFL	**Khemis Miliana** ....Algeria...ZZK
Karisruhe/Baden Baden/	**Kegaska**, QC .... Canada .. ZKG	**Khenchela** ....Algeria...QKJ
Bus Svc...........Germany ..XET	**Kegisugi** ... Papua New Guinea .. KEG	**Kherrata** ....Algeria...ZZR
Karkkila ....Finland .. QVF	**Keisah** .... Indonesia .. KEA	**Kherson** ....Ukraine... KHE
Karlovasi ....Greece .. ZKR	**Kekaha**/Barking Sands, HI . USA .. BKH	**Khmeinitskiy** ....Ukraine... HMJ
Karlovy Vary ....Czech Rep .. KLV	**Kelafo**/Callaf/Kelafo.... Ethiopia .. LFO	**Khoka Moya** ....S. Africa... KHO
Karlskoga ....Sweden .. KSK	**Kelanoa** ... Papua New Guinea .. KNL	**Khoms** ....Libya... QKO
Karlsruhe/Baden Baden	**Kelila** ....Indonesia .. LLN	**Khon Kaen** ....Thailand... KKC
.............Germany .. FKB	**Kelle** ....Congo, DR .. KEE	**Khong** ....Laos... KOG

Khorramabad	Iran	KHD
Khost	Afghanistan	KHT
Khovd	Mongolia	HVD
Khowai	India	IXN
Khudzhand	Tajikistan	LBD
Khujirt	Mongolia	HJT
Khulna	Bangladesh	KHL
Khuzdar	Pakistan	KDD
Khwahan	Afghanistan	KWH
Khwai River Lodge	Botswana	KHW
Kiana/Bob Barker Memorial, AK		
	USA	IAN
Kiel/Holtenau Civilian	Germany	KEL
Kielce	Poland	QKI
Kierritu, BC	Canada	YKT
Kieta/Aropa	Papua New Guinea	KIE
Kiev/Borispol	Ukraine	KBP
Kiev/Darnitsa Bus Stn	Ukraine	QOF
Kiev/Hotel Rus Bus Stn	Ukraine	QOH
Kiev/Zhulhany	Ukraine	IEV
Kiffa	Mauritania	KFA
Kigali/Gregoire Kayibanda		
	Rwanda	KGL
Kigoma	Tanzania	TKQ
Kikaiga Shima	Japan	KKX
Kikinonda	Papua New Guinea	KIZ
Kikori	Papua New Guinea	KRI
Kikwit	Congo, DR	KKW
Kilaguni	Kenya	ILU
Kili Is	Marshall Is	KIO
Kilialoe, ON	Canada	YXI
Kilimanjaro	Tanzania	JRO
Kilkenny	Ireland	KKY
Kill Devil Hills/First Flight, NC		
	USA	FFA
Killeen/Municipal, TX	USA	ILE
Killineq, QC	Canada	XBW
Kilwa	Congo, DR	KIL
Kilwa	Tanzania	KIY
Kimam	Indonesia	KMM
Kimberley	S. Africa	KIM
Kimberley Downs	Australia	KBD
Kimberley, BC	Canada	YQE
Kimmirut, NT	Canada	YLC
Kincardine, ON	Canada	YKD
Kindamba	Congo, DR	KNJ
Kindersley, SK	Canada	YKY
Kindu	Congo, DR	KND
King City, Mesa Del Rey, CAUSA		KIC
King Cove, AK	USA	KVC
King Is	Australia	KNS
King Khalid Military City		
	Saudi Arabia	KMC
King Of Prussia, PA	USA	KPD
King Salmon, AK	USA	AKN
Kingaroy	Australia	KGY
Kingfisher Lake, ON	Canada	KIF
Kingman, AZ	USA	IGM
Kings Bay/NAS, GA	USA	NBQ
Kings Canyon	Australia	KBJ
Kings Creek Stn	Australia	KCS
Kings Lynn/Marham/RAF	UK	KNF
Kingscote	Australia	KGC
Kingston, ON	Canada	YGK
Kingston/Norman Manley		
	Jamaica	KIN
Kingston/RR Stn., ON	Canada	XEG
Kingston/Tinson	Jamaica	KTP
Kingsville/NAS, TX	USA	NQI
Kinloss/RAF	UK	FSS
Kinmen/Shang-Yi	Taiwan	KNH
Kinoosao, SK	Canada	KNY
Kinshasa/N'Djili	Congo, DR	FIH
Kinshasa/N'Dolo	Congo, DR	NLO
Kinston/Stallings Fld, NC	USA	ISO
Kipnulk, AK	USA	KPN
Kira	Papua New Guinea	KIQ
KiraKira	Solomon Is	IRA
Kirefeld	Germany	QKF
Kiri	Congo, DR	KRZ

Kirkenes/Hoeybuktmoen	Norway	KKN
Kirkimbie	Australia	KBB
Kirkland Lake, ON	Canada	YKX
Kirksvite Municipal, MO	USA	IRK
Kirkuk	Iraq	KIK
Kirkwall	UK	KOI
Kirov	Russia	KVX
Kirovograd	Ukraine	KGO
Kirovsk	Russia	KVK
Kirtland/AFB, NM	USA	IKR
Kiruna	Sweden	KRN
Kirundo	Benin	KRE
Kiryat Shmona	Israel	KSW
Kisangani	Congo, DR	FKI
Kisengan	Papua New Guinea	KSG
Kish Is	Iran	KIH
Kismayu	Somalia	KMU
Kissidougou	Guinea	KSI
Kissimmee/Municipal, FL	USA	ISM
Kisumu	Kenya	KIS
Kita Kyushu/Kokura	S. Korea	KKJ
Kitadaito Is	Japan	KTD
Kitale	Kenya	KTL
Kitava	Papua New Guinea	KVE
Kitchener, ON	Canada	YKF
Kitee	Finland	KTQ
Kithira	Greece	KIT
Kitkatla, BC	Canada	YKK
Kitoi Bay/SPB, AK	USA	KKB
Kitsissuarsuit	Greenland	QJE
Kittilä	Finland	KTT
Kitwe/Southdowns	Zambia	KIW
Kitzingen	Germany	KZG
Kiunga	Kenya	KIU
Kiunga	Papua New Guinea	UNG
Kivalina, AK	USA	KVL
Kiwai Is	Papua New Guinea	KWX
Kiwayu	Kenya	KWY
Kizhuyak, AK	USA	KZH
Kjellerup/Bus Svc	Denmark	QJW
Kjoellefjord	Norway	QJL
Klag Bay, AK	USA	KBK
Klagenfurt	Austria	KLU
Klaipeda	Lithuania	KLJ
Klamath Falls Int'l, OR	USA	LMT
Klawock, AK	USA	AKW
Klawock, AK	USA	KLW
Kleinzee	S. Africa	KLZ
Klerksdorp	S. Africa	KXE
Klosters	Switzerland	ZHS
Knee Lake, MB	Canada	YKE
Knights Inlet, BC	Canada	KNV
Knock Int'l	Ireland	NOC
Knokke/Het Zoute	Belgium	KNO
Knoxville Downtown, TN	USA	DKX
Knoxville, IA	USA	OXV
Knoxville, TN	USA	TYS
Koala Belait	Brunei	KUB
Kobe	Japan	UKB
Koblenz	Germany	ZNV
Kobuk, AK	USA	OBU
Kocaeli/Cengiz Topel	Turkey	KCO
Kochi	Japan	KCZ
Kodiak Arpt, AK	USA	ADQ
Kodiak, AK	USA	WDY
Kodiak/Municipal, AK	USA	KDK
Koethen	Germany	KOQ
Kogalym Int'l	Russia	KGP
Koh Kong	Cambodia	KKZ
Koh Sannui	Thailand	USM
Kohat	Pakistan	OHT
Koinambe	Papua New Guinea	KMB
Koinghaas	S. Africa	KIG
Kokkola/Pietarsaari/Kruunupyy		
	Finland	KOK
Kokoda	Papua New Guinea	KKD
Kokonao/Timuka	Indonesia	KOX
Kokorno, IN	USA	OKK
Kokoro	Papua New Guinea	KOR
Kokshetau	Kazakhstan	KOV
Kol	Papua New Guinea	KQL

Kolda	Senegal	KDA
Kolding/RR Stn	Denmark	ZBT
Kolhapur	India	KLH
Kolobrzeg/Bus Svc	Poland	QJY
Kolwezi	Congo, DR	KWZ
Komaio	Papua New Guinea	KCJ
Komako	Papua New Guinea	HOC
Komatipoort	S. Africa	KOF
Komotini	Greece	ZKT
Kompiam	Papua New Guinea	KPM
Kompong Thorn	Cambodia	KZK
Kompong-Chhna	Cambodia	KZC
Kon	Indonesia	KCI
Kona/Keahole, HI	USA	KOA
Konawaruk	Guyana	KKG
Kone	New Caledonia	KNQ
Konge	Papua New Guinea	KGB
Kongiganak, AK	USA	KKH
Kongoboumba	Gabon	GKO
Kongolo	Congo, DR	KOO
Konnatsu	Japan	KMQ
Konstanz	Germany	QKZ
Kontum	Vietnam	KON
Konya	Turkey	KYA
Koolatah	Australia	KOH
Koolburra	Australia	KKP
Koonibba	Australia	KQB
Kopasker	Iceland	OPA
Koplago	Papua New Guinea	KPA
Korhogo	Côte D'Ivoire	HGO
Korla	China	KRL
Korno-Manda		
	Papua New Guinea	KOM
Kornsornolsk Na Amure		
	Russia	KXK
Koro Is	Fiji	KXF
Koroba	Papua New Guinea	KDE
Korolevu	Fiji	KVU
Koror/Airai	Palau	ROR
Kortrijk/Wevelgem	Belgium	KJK
Kos	Greece	KGS
Kosciusko/Attala County, MS		
	USA	OSX
Kosice/Barca	Slovakia	KSC
Kosipe	Papua New Guinea	KSP
Kosrae	Micronesia	KSA
Kostanay	Kazakstan	KSN
Kosti	Sudan	KST
Kostroma	Russia	KMW
Koszalin	Poland	OSZ
Kota	India	KTU
Kota Bharu/Pengkalan Chepa		
	Malaysia	KBR
Kota Kinabalu	Malaysia	BKI
Kota Koli	Congo, DR	KLI
Kotabangun	Indonesia	KOD
Kotabaru	Indonesia	KBU
Kotka	Finland	QVW
Kotlas	Russia	KSZ
Kotlik, AK	USA	KOT
Kotor	Yugoslavia	ZKQ
Kotzebue, AK	USA	OTZ
Kouba	Algeria	KDF
Koulamoutou	Gabon	KOU
Koumac	New Caledonia	KOC
Koundara/Sambailo	Guinea	SBI
Kounnala	Central African Rep.	KOL
Kourou	F. Guiana	QKR
Koutaba	Cameroon	KOB
Koutiala	Mali	KTX
Kouvola/Bus Stn	Finland	QVY
Kouvola/Utti	Finland	UTI
Kowanyama	Australia	KWM
Koyang	Kuwait	QYK
Koyuk, AK	USA	KKA
Koyukuk, AK	USA	KYU
Kozani/Philippos	Greece	KZI
Krabi	Thailand	KBV
Krakor	Cambodia	KZD
Krakow	Poland	KRK
Kramatorsk	Ukraine	KRQ

AIRPORTS

Kramfors/Flygplats.... Sweden .. KRF
Krasnodar............. Russia .. KRR
Krasnoiarsk........... Russia .. KJA
Kratie .... Cambodia .. KTI
Kremenchug .... Ukraine . KHU
Kreuzlingen ...... Switzerland . ZHU
Kribi .... Cameroon .. KBI
Kristiansand/Kjevik .. Norway .. KRS
Kristianstad/Everod .. Sweden .. KID
Kristiansund/Kvernberget
.... Norway .. KSU
Krivoy Rog .... Ukraine . KWG
Kruger National Park .. S. Africa . QKP
Ksar Es Souk .... Morocco .. SEK
Kuala Lumpur/Kuala Lumpur Infl
.... Malaysia .. KUL
Kuala Lumpur/KUL Sentral Rail
.... Malaysia .. XKL
Kuala Lumpur/Sultan Alodul
Aziz Shah .... Malaysia .. SZB
Kuala Terengganu/
Sultan Mahmood .... Malaysia .. TGG
Kuantan .... Malaysia .. KUA
Kubin Is .... Australia .. KUG
Kuching .... Malaysia .. KCH
Kucla................. China .. KCA
Kudat .... Malaysia .. KUD
Kufrah .... Libya .. AKF
Kugururok River, AK ...USA.. KUW
Kuito .... Angola . SVP
Kukundu .... Solomon Is.. KUE
Kulgera .... Australia .. KGR
Kulik Lake, AK ....USA.. LKK
Kulu/Shuntar .... India .. KUU
Kulusuk .... Greenland.. KUS
Kumamoto .... Japan . KMJ
Kumasi.............. Ghana . KMS
Kumejima .... Japan . UEO
Kundiawa ..Papua New Guinea . CMU
Kunduz .... Afghanistan . UND
Kungum ....Papua New Guinea . KGM
Kunming ....China . KMG
Kunsan/Air Base...... S. Korea . KUV
Kununurra .... Australia .. KNX
Kuopio .... Finland . KUO
Kuorevesi/Halli........ Finland . KEV
Kupang/El Tari....... Indonesia.. KOE
Kuparuk, AK ....USA.. UUK
Kupiano ...Papua New Guinea .. KUP
Kuran-O-Munjan .. Afghanistan .. KUR
Kuressaare .... Estonia . URE
Kurgan .... Russia . KRO
Kuri ....Papua New Guinea . KUQ
Kuria................ Kiribati .. KUC
Kursk .... Russia .. URS
Kuruman .... S. Africa ..KMH
Kurundi .... Australia .. KRD
Kurupung .... Guyana .. KPG
Kurwina ....Papua New Guinea . KWV
Kusadasi............ Turkey .. XKU
Kusan/Air Base ...... S. Korea .. KUZ
Kushimoto .... Japan .. KUJ
Kushiro .... Japan .. KUH
Kutaisi .... Georgia .. KUT
Kuujjuaq, QC ....Canada.. YVP
Kuujjuarapik, QC .....Canada . YGW
Kuusamo............ Finland . KAO
Kuwait Int'l .... Kuwait .. KWI
Kwai Harbour ..... Solomon Is .. KWR
Kwailabesi Aerodrom
.... Solomon Is .. KWS
Kwajalein .... Marshall Is .. KWA
Kwangju/Air Base..... S. Korea . KWJ
Kwethluk, AK ....USA.. KWT
Kwigillingok, AK ....USA.. KWK
Kwun Tong .... Hong Kong . KTZ
Kyauktaw .... Myanmar .. KYT
Kyaulkpyu........... Myanmar .. KYP
Kyoto .... Japan .. UKY
Kyzyl............... Russia .. KYZ
Kzyl-Orda .... Kazakstan .. KZO

L

L'Aquila .... Italy . QAQ
La Bastide Puylaurent France .. XLA
La Baule Les Pins .... France .. XBP
La Baule/Montoir ...... France .. LBY
La Ceiba/Goloson Int'l
.... Honduras .. LCE
La Chaux-de-Fonds Switzerland .. ZHV
La Chorrera........ Colombia .. LCR
La Ciotat .... France .. XCT
La Colorna .... Cuba .. LCL
La Coruna .... Spain .. LCG
La Crosse, WI .... USA .. LSE
La Cumbre .... Argentina . LCM
La Desirade...... Gaudeloupe . DSD
La Esperanza ...... Honduras .. LEZ
La Fria.............. Venezuela . LFR
La Grande, OR .... USA . LGD
La Grande, QC ...... Canada .. YAH
La Grande, QC ...... Canada .. YGL
La Grange/Calloway, GA .. USA . LGC
La Guaira .... Venezuela . LAG
La Junquera .... Spain .. QJR
La Junta, CO .... USA .. LHX
La Llagone .... France . QZG
La Munoza .... Spain . QLM
La Palma .... Panama .. PLP
La Paz/El Alto ....Bolivia . LPB
La Paz/Leon .... Mexico .. LAP
La Pedrera .... Colombia .. LPD
La Plagne .... France .. PLG
La Plata .... Argentina . LPG
La Primavera ...... Colombia .. LPE
La Riola .... Argentina .. IRJ
La Roche Sur Yon .... France .. XRO
La Roche/Les Ajoncs ... France . EDM
La Rochelle/Laleu ..... France .. LRH
La Romana ...... Dominican Rep .. LRM
La Ronge, SK .... Canada . YVC
La Sarre, QC .... Canada .. SSQ
La Serena/La Florida .... Chile .. LSC
La Spezia .... Italy . QLP
La Tabatiere, QC ...... Canada .. ZLT
La Tour De Carol .... France .. XTE
La Tuclue, QC .... Canada .. YLQ
La Unbe .... Colombia .. LAT
La Union .... Honduras .. LUI
La Verne, CA .... USA . POC
Laarbruch/RAF ...... Germany .. LRC
Laayoune/Hassan I. ....Morocco ..EUN
Labasa .... Fiji .. LBS
Labe................. Guinea .. LEK
Lablab ..... Papua New Guinea .. LAB
Labouchere Bay, AK..... USA . WLB
Labrea................. Brazil .. LBR
Labuan .... Malaysia .. LBU
Labuan Bajo/Mutiara . Indonesia .. LBJ
Labuha/Taliabu ...... Indonesia .. LAH
Lac Biche, AB .... Canada . YLB
Lac Brochet, MB ..... Canada .. XLB
Lac Edouard/RR Stn., QC
.... Canada .. XEE
Laconia, NH........... USA . LCI
Ladouanie .... Suriname . LDO
Lady Elliot Is .... Australia .. LYT
Ladysmith .... S. Africa . LAY
Ladysmith/RR Stn., BC Canada .. XEH
Lae Is .... Marshall Is .. LML
Lae/Nadzab Papua New Guinea . LAE
Laeso Is Arpt .... Denmark .. BYR
Lafayette, LA .... USA .. LFT
Lafayette-Purdue, IN...... USA .. LAF
LaForges, QC .... Canada .. YLF
Lagenfeld........... Germany .. ZNX
Lages ....Brazil . LAJ
Laghouat/L'Mekrareg... Algeria . LOO

Lago Agrio ....Ecuador.. LGQ
Lago Argentina ..... Argentina.. ING
Lagos de Moreno ......Mexico.. LOM
Lagos/Murtala Muhammed
.... Nigeria..LOS
Lagrande 3, QC...... Canada.. YAR
Lague .... Congo.. LCO
Laguna/AAF, AZ .... USA.. LGF
Lagunillas .... Venezuela.. LGY
Lahad Datu .... Malaysia.. LDU
Lahore ....Pakistan.. LHE
Lahr .... Germany..LHA
Lahti................Finland.. QLF
Lai.................. Chad.. LTC
Laiagam ... Papua New Guinea.. LGM
Lajeado .... Brazil.. QLB
Lake Baringo .... Kenya.. LBN
Lake Charles, LA ...... USA.. LCH
Lake Evella .... Australia.. LEL
Lake Geneva/Municipal, WI USA.. XES
Lake Gregory ....Australia.. LGE
Lake Havasu City, AZ .... USA... HII
Lake Hood/SPB, AK .... USA.. LHD
Lake Jackson, TX .... USA.. LJN
Lake Manyara .... Tanzania.. LKY
Lake Minchumina, AK.... USA.. LMA
Lake Murray Papua New Guinea.. LMY
Lake Placid, NY........ USA... LKP
Lake Rudolf......... Kenya..LKU
Lake Union SPB, WA ..... USA... LKE
Lake Nash .... Australia.. LNH
Lakeba..................Fiji.. LKB
Lakefield............Australia.. LFP
Lakehurst, NJ .... USA.. NEL
Lakeland Downs ....Australia.. LKD
Lakeland, FL........... USA.. LAL
Lakeside, TX........... USA.. IWS
Lakeside TX........... USA.. LKS
Lakeview, OR.......... USA.. LKV
Lakota .... Côte D'Ivoire.. LKT
Lakselv/Banak .... Norway... LKL
Lalibela .... Ethiopia...LLI
Lalomalava .... Samoa.. LAV
Lamacarena ....Colombia.. LMC
Lamap .... Vanuatu.. LPM
Lamar Municipal, CO ..... USA.. LAA
Lamassa ... Papua New Guinea.. LMG
Lambarene............ Gabon.. LBQ
Lamen Bay .... Vanuatu.. LNB
Lamezia-Terme/S Eufernia Italy.. SUF
Lamidanda............Nepal.. LDN
Lampang ....Thailand.. LPT
Lampedusa............ Italy.. LMP
Lamu .... Kenya..LAU
Lanai City, HI .... USA... LNY
Lancaster, CA .... USA...WJF
Lancaster, Fairfield County Arpt,
OH.................. USA.. LHQ
Lancaster, PA.......... USA... LNS
Lancaster/Lancaster PA Rail USA .. ZRL
Lancaster/Quartz Hill, CA .. USA.. RZH
Lancaster/RR Stn. .... UK.. XQL
Lander, WY .... USA.. LND
Landerneau ....France.. XLD
Landivisiau ....France.. LDV
Lands End .... UK... LEQ
Landshut .... Germany.. QLG
Landskrona/ HP ...... Sweden.. JLD
Langara, BC...........Canada...YLA
Langenhagen .... Germany.. ZNY
Langenthal .... Switzerland.. ZHW
Langeoog............. Germany.. LGO
Langford/RR Stn., BC .. Canada... XEJ
Langgur .... Indonesia.. LUV
Langimar .. Papua New Guinea.. LNM
Langkawi .... Malaysia.. LGK
Langley/AFB, VA .... USA... LFI
Langtang ....Nepal.. LTG
Lannion/Servel ....France... LAI
Lansdowne ....Australia.. LDW

A I R P O R T S

Lansdowne House, ON
.................................Canada .. YLH
Lanseria .... S. Africa .. HLA
Lansing, MI ....USA .. LAN
Lanzarote ....Spain .. ACE
Lanzhou ....China .. LHW
Lanzhou/Lanzhoudong ...China .. LZD
Lanzhou/Zhongchuan ....China .. ZGC
Laoag .... Philippines .. LAO
Laon/Chambry.............France .. XLN
Laporte/Municipal, IN.......USA .. LPO
Lappeenranta .... Finland ..LPP
Lar................................ Iran .. LRR
Laramie, WY ....USA .. LAR
Larantuka .... Indonesia .. LKA
Larba Nath Iraten........Algeria ..ZZL
Laredo/Int'l, TX ....USA .. LRD
Larisa ....Greece .. LRA
Larnaca ....Cyprus .. LCA
Larsen/SPB, AK ....USA .. KLN
Larson/AFB, WA ....USA .. LRN
Las Canas .... Costa Rica .. LCS
Las Cruces/Int'l, NM ....USA .. LRU
Las Gaviotas .... Colombia .. LGT
Las Heras .... Argentina .. LHS
Las Khoreh...............Somalia .. LKR
Las Limas .... Honduras .. LLH
Las Lomitas .... Argentina .. LLS
Las Palmas ....Spain .. LPA
Las Piedras/Josefa Camejo
.... Venezuela ..LSP
Las Tunas ....Cuba .. VTU
Las Vegas Nexrad, NV ....USA .. ESX
Las Vegas, NM ....USA ..LVS
Las Vegas, NV ....USA .. LAS
Las Vegas/Henderson Sky
Harbor, NV ....USA .. HSH
Las Vegas/North Air Terminal, NV
...............................USA .. VGT
Lasham ....UK .. QLA
Lashio .... Myanmar .. LSH
Lastourville ....Gabon .. LTL
Latakia .... Syria ..LTK
Lathrop Wells, NV ....USA ..LTH
Lathrop/Sharpe/AAF, CA ...USA .. LRO
Latina ....Italy .. QLT
Latrobe .... Australia ..LTB
Latrobe, PA ....USA .. LBE
Laucata Is .... Fiji .. LUC
Launceston .... Australia .. LST
Laura .... Australia .. LUU
Laura Stn .... Australia .. LUT
Laurel, MS ....USA .. PIB
Laurel/Hester/Noble Fld, MS
...............................USA .. LUL
Laurie River, MB ....Canada .. LRQ
Lausanne ....Switzerland .. QLS
Lauterach ....Austria .. QLX
Laval/Entrammes ....France ..LVA
Lavan .... Iran ..LVP
Laverton .... Australia ..LVO
Lavras ....Brazil .. QLW
Lawas .... Malaysia .. LWY
Lawn Hill .... Australia .. IWH
Lawrence, KS ....USA .. LWC
Lawrence, MA ....USA .. LWM
Lawrenceville, VA ....USA .. LVL
Lawreneeville, IL.............USA .. LWV
Lawson/AAF, GA.............USA .. LSF
Lawton, OK ....USA .. LAW
Lazaro Cardenas ......Mexico .. LZC
Icoaraci ....Brazil .. QDO
Idiofa ....Congo, DR .. IDF
Idre ....Sweden .. IDB
Le Castellet ....France .. CTT
Le Havre/Octeville ......France .. LEH
Le Locle ....Switzerland .. ZJA
Le Mans/Arnage.........France .. LME
Le Mans/RR Stn............France .. ZLN
Le Puy/Loudes ....France ..LPY
Leadville, CO ....USA ..LXV

Leaf Bay, QB .... Canada .. XLF
Leaf Rapids, MB....... Canada .. YLR
Learmonth............... Australia .. LEA
Lebakeng .... Lesotho .. LEF
Lebel-Sur-Quevillon, QC
.... Canada .. YLS
Lecce/Galatina ....Italy ..LCC
Lecin/Guanajuato/Del Bajic
.... Mexico .. BJX
Leconi ....Gabon .. LEO
Ledesma .... Argentina ..XMX
Leeds Bradford/Yeadon ....UK .. LBA
Leeds, MT.....................USA .. LDS
Leeds/Bus Svc.................UK .. ZLZ
Leesburg, FL ....USA .. LEE
Leesburg/Godfrey, VA ...... USA .. JYO
Leeton/Bus Svc .... Australia .. QLE
Leeuwarden ...... Netherlands .. LWR
Legaspi .... Philippines .. LGP
Leguizamo .... Colombia .. LGZ
Leh .... India .. IXL
Lehu ...... Papua New Guinea .. LHP
Leiden/Valkenburg .Netherlands .. LID
Leigh Creek .... Australia ..LGH
Leinster .... Australia .. LER
Leipzig/Halle .... Germany .. LEJ
Leiria ....Portugal .. QLR
Leitre .... Papua New Guinea ..LTF
Iejima ....Japan .. IEJ
Leka ....Norway .. ZXN
Lekana ....Congo, DR .. LKC
Leknes ....Norway .. LKN
Lelystad ....Netherlands .. LEY
Lemars/Municipal, IA ...... USA .. LRJ
Lemmon, SD ....USA .. LEM
Lemnos ....Greece .. LXS
Lemoore/NAS, CA ....USA .. NLC
Lencois Paulista ....Brazil .. QGC
Lencois/Chapada Diamantina
.... Brazil .. LEC
Lengbati... Papua New Guinea .. LNC
Lens .... France .. XLE
Lenzburg .... Switzerland .. ZJC
Lenzerheide/Lai ... Switzerland .. ZJD
Leo .... Burkina Faso .. XLU
Leon .... Spain .. LEN
Leonardtown/St Marys County,
MD ....SA .. LTW
Leonora .... Australia ..LNO
Leopoldina ....Brazil .. LEP
Lereh .... Indonesia ..LHI
Leribe .... Lesotho .. LRB
Lerida .... Spain .. QLQ
Lernwerder .... Germany ..XLW
Leron Plains
.... Papua New Guinea .. LPN
Leros .... Greece .. LRS
Les Angles .... France .. QZH
Les Ares .... France .. XRS
Les Cayes .... Haiti .. CYA
Les Sables/Talmont .... France .. LSO
Lese .... Papua New Guinea .. LNG
Lesobeng .... Lesotho .. LES
Lethbridge, AB .... Canada .. YQL
Lethem .... Guyana .. LTM
Leticia/Gen. A.V. Cobo Colombia .. LET
Letterkenny .... Ireland .. LTR
Leuven .... Belgium .. ZGK
Levaliois .... France .. QBH
Level .... Germany .. ZOA
Levelock, AK .... USA .. KLL
Lewisburg, WV .... USA .. LWB
Lewiston, ID .... USA .. LWS
Lewistown, MT .... USA .. LWT
Lewoleba .... Indonesia .. LWE
Lexington, NE .... USA .. LXN
Lexington-Blue Grass, KY. USA .. LEX
Igaliku .... Chile .. QFX
Igarka .... Russia .. IAA
Iginniarfik .... Greenland .. QFI
Igiugig, AK .... USA .. IGG

Iguassu Falls/Cataratas.. Brazil... IGU
Iguatu .... Brazil...QIG
Iguazu/Cataratas .....Argentina... IGR
Lhasa ....China...LXA
Lhok Sukon .... Indonesia... LSX
Lhoksumawe/Malikussaleh
.... Indonesia... LSW
Ihu .... Papua New Guinea... IHU
Lia Hulka .... F. Polynesia... UAH
Lia Pou .... F. Polynesia... UAP
Liangping ....China...LIA
Lianyungang ....China...LYG
Libby/AAF, AZ..................USA...FHU
Libenge .... Congo, DR...LIE
Liberal/Municipal, KS....USA...LBL
Liberia .... Costa Rica... LIR
Libourne/Artiques de Lussac
.... France...XLR
Libreville .... Gabon...LBV
Lichfield T.V./RR Stn........ UK...XQT
Lichinga ....Mozambique...VXC
Lidkoping/Hovby......... Sweden...LDK
Liege/Bierset ....Belgium...LGG
Liepaya/Int'l .... Latvia...LPX
Lifou ....New Caledonia... LIF
Lightning Ridge ......Australia...LHG
Lihir Is ...... Papua New Guinea...LNV
Lijiang City/Lijiang ....China...LJG
Likiep Is .... Marshall Is... LIK
Likoma Is .... Malawi...LIX
Lilabari ....India... IXI
Lilboi ....Kenya...LBK
Liliastai .... Mongolia...ULZ
Lille/Lesquin .... France... LIL
Lille/Lille Europe Rail Svc.France... XDB
Lille/Lille Flanders Rail Svc
.... France...XFA
Lilongwe/Int'l .... Malawi...LLW
Lima, OH ....USA... AOH
Lima/J Chavez Int'l ..... Peru... LIM
Limassol ....Cyprus... QLI
Limbang .... Malaysia... LMN
Limbe.................... Cameroon... VCC
Limbunya ....Australia... LIB
Limburg .... Germany...ZNW
Lime Acres .... S. Africa... LMR
Lime Village, AK ....USA... LVD
Limeira ....Brazil... QGB
Limerick .... Ireland... LMK
Limoges/Bellegarde .... France... LIG
Limon .... Costa Rica... LIO
Limon .... Honduras... LMH
Limon Municipal, CO .....USA... LIC
Linares ....Chile...ZLR
Lincoln Rock/Coast Guard, AK
...................................USA...LRK
Lincoln, NE.....................USA...LNK
Linda Downs ....Australia...LLP
Lindau .... Germany...QII
Linden, NJ ....USA...LDJ
Lindernan Is ....Australia... LDC
Lindi/Kikwetu .... Tanzania... LDI
Linga Linga Papua New Guinea... LGN
Linkoping .... Sweden...LPI
Linosa HP ....Italy... LIU
Lins ....Brazil... LIP
Linxi ....China... LXI
Linyi ....China... LYI
Linz/Hoersching .... Austria... LNZ
Lipetsk ....Russia...LPK
Lippstadt .... Germany... ZOB
Lisala .... Congo, DR... LIQ
Lisboa Portela .... Portugal...LIS
Lishan ....Taiwan... LHN
Lisieux .... France...XLX
Lismore ....Australia... LSY
Lissadell ....Australia... LLL
Little Cayman ....Cayman Is.... LYB
Little Grand Rapids, MB
.... Canada... ZGR
Little Naukati, AK ....USA... WLN

A
I
R
P
O
R
T
S

Little Port Walter, AK	USA	LPW
Little Rock, AR	USA	LIT
Little Rock/AFB, AR	USA	LRF
Liuzhou	China	LZH
Livengood, AK	USA	LIV
Livermore, CA	USA	LVK
Liverpool Street Stn/RR Stn, UK		ZLS
Liverpool/Speke	UK	LPL
Livingston, MT	USA	LVM
Livingstone	Zambia	LVI
LIvoi	Papua New Guinea	UVO
Lizard Is	Australia	LZR
Ljubljana/Brnik	Slovenia	LJU
Ikerasaarsuk	Greenland	QRY
Ikoyi	Norway	QIK
Ile d'Yeu	France	IDY
Ilha Do Governador	Brazil	QGI
Ilimanaq/Harbour	Greenland	XIQ
Lloydminister, AB	Canada	YLL
Ilulissat	Greenland	JAV
Inongo	Congo, DR	INO
Loani	Papua New Guinea	LNQ
Lobatse	Botswana	LOQ
Locarno	Switzerland	ZJI
Lochgliphead / HP	UK	LPH
Lock	Australia	LOC
Lock Haven, PA	USA	LHV
Lockhart River	Australia	IRG
Lodar	Yemen	LDR
Lodja	Congo, DR	LJA
Lodwar	Kenya	LOK
Lodz/Lodz Lublinek	Poland	LCJ
Loei	Thailand	LOE
Loen	Marshall Is	LOF
Loerrach	Germany	QLO
Logan, UT	USA	LGU
Lognes	France	XLG
Loikaw	Myanmar	LIW
Loimaa	Finland	QZJ
Loja	Ecuador	LOH
Lokichoggio	Kenya	LKG
loma	Papua New Guinea	IOP
Lome/Tokoin	Togo	LFW
Lompoc, CA	USA	LPC
Loncopue	Argentina	LCP
Londolozi	S. Africa	LDZ
London Euston/RR	UK	QQU
London Kings Cross/RR	UK	QQK
London, KY	USA	LOZ
London, ON	Canada	YXU
London/Paddington/RR	UK	QQP
London/Biggin Hill	UK	BQH
London/British Rail Terminal	UK	ZLX
London/Gatwick Arpt	UK	LGW
London/Heathrow Arpt	UK	LHR
London/London City Arpt	UK	LCY
London/London-Waterloo	UK	QQW
London/Luton Int'l Arpt	UK	LTN
London/RR Stn., ON	Canada	XDQ
London/Stansted	UK	STN
London/Victoria RR Stn	UK	ZEP
Londonderry/Eglinton	UK	LDY
Londrina	Brazil	LDB
Lone Rock, WI	USA	LNR
Lonely/Dew Stn, AK	USA	LNI
Long Apung	Indonesia	LPU
Long Banga	Malaysia	LBP
Long Bawan/Juvai Semaring	Indonesia	LBW
Long Beach/HP, CA	USA	JLB
Long Beach, CA	USA	LGB
Long Is	Australia	HAP
Long Is	Papua New Guinea	LSJ
Long Is MacArthur, NY	USA	ISP
Long Is, AK	USA	LIJ
Long Lama	Malaysia	LLM
Long Lellang	Malaysia	LGL
Long Pasia	Malaysia	GSA
Long Point, ON	Canada	YLX
Long Semado/Lawas	Malaysia	LSM
Long Seridan	Malaysia	ODN

Long Sukang	Malaysia	LSU
Long Xuyen	Vietnam	XLO
Longana	Vanuatu	LOD
Longmont Bus Svc, CO	USA	QWM
Longreach	Australia	LRE
Longview, WA	USA	LOG
Longyearbyen/Svalbard		
Svalbard and Jan Mayen Is		LYR
Lonorore	Vanuatu	LNE
Lontras/Helmuth Baungartem		
	Brazil	LOI
Lop Bun	Thailand	KKM
Lopez De Micay	Colombia	LMX
Lopez Is, WA	USA	LPS
Lora Lai	Pakistan	LRG
Lord Howe Is	Australia	LDH
Lordsburg, NM	USA	LSB
Loreto	Mexico	LTO
Lorica	Colombia	LRI
Lorient/Lann Bilhoue	France	LRT
Loring, AK	USA	WLR
Loring/AFB, ME	USA	LIZ
Lorraine	Australia	LOA
Lorriza	Poland	QOY
Los Alamos, NM	USA	LAM
Los Andes	Chile	LOB
Los Angeles	Chile	LSQ
Los Angeles/Int'l, CA	USA	LAX
Los Angeles/Nexrad, CA	USA	VTX
Los Angeles/Van Nuys, CA		
	USA	VNY
Los Angeles/Century City, CA		
	USA	CCD
Los Angeles/Citicorp Plaza HP, CA		
	USA	JCX
Los Angeles/City Of Industry HP, CA		
	USA	JID
Los Angeles/Commerce Bus. Plaza,		
CA	USA	JBP
Los Angeles/Sherman Oaks HP, CA		
	USA	JSN
Los Angeles/Union Stn HP, CA		
	USA	JLX
Los Angeles/Universal City HP, CA		
	USA	JUC
Los Angeles/Warner Cntr Bus. Plaza,		
CA	USA	JWC
Los Angeles/Whiteman, CA		
	USA	WHP
Los Banos, CA	USA	LSN
Los Chiles	Costa Rica	LSL
Los Menucos	Argentina	LMD
Los Mochis/Federal	Mexico	LMM
Los Roques	Venezuela	LRV
Los Tablones	Guatemala	LOX
Lossiernouth/RAF	UK	LMO
Lost Harbor, AK	USA	LHB
Lost River, AK	USA	LSR
Losuia	Papua New Guinea	LSA
Lotusvaie	Australia	LTV
Loubomo	Congo, DR	DIS
Louis Trichardt	S. Africa	LCD
Louisa, VA	USA	LOW
Louisburg, NC	USA	LFN
Louisville Nexrad, KY	USA	LVX
Louisville, KY	USA	LOU
Louisville, KY	USA	SDF
Louisville, MS	USA	LMS
Louisville/Intercontinental, KY		
	USA	LJC
Lourdes/Tarbes	France	LDE
Loveland Bus Svc, CO	USA	QWH
Lovell, WY	USA	POY
Lovelock, NV	USA	LOL
Loviisa	Finland	QXI
Lowai	Papua New Guinea	LWI
Loyangalani	Kenya	LOY
Itapetininga	Brazil	ZTP
Lualbo	Mozambique	LBM
Luanda/4 de Fevereiro	Angola	LAD
Luang Namtha	Laos	LXG

Luang Prabang	Laos	LPQ
Luau	Andorra	UAL
Lubang	Philippines	LBX
Lubango	Angola	SDD
Lubbock/Int'l, TX	USA	LBB
Lublin	Poland	QLU
Lubumbashi/Luano Congo, DR		FBM
Lucca	Italy	LCV
Lucenec	Slovakia	LUE
Lucerne	Switzerland	QLJ
Luchon	France	XLH
Lucknow/Amausi	India	LKO
Luderitz	Namibia	LUD
Ludhiana	India	LUH
Ludington/Mason County, MI		
	USA	LDM
Ludwigsburg	Germany	ZOD
Ludwigshafen	Germany	ZOE
Ludwigslust/RR Stn.	Germany	ZLU
Luebeck/Blankensee	Germany	LBC
Luedenscheid	Germany	ZOC
Luena	Angola	LUO
Lueneburg/RR Stn.	Germany	ZOG
Luenen	Germany	ZOH
Lufkin, TX	USA	OCH
Lugano	Switzerland	LUG
Lugansk	Ukraine	VSG
Lugh Ganane	Somalia	LGX
Luiza	Congo, DR	LZA
Lukapa	Angola	LBZ
Luke/AFB, AZ	USA	LUF
Lukla	Nepal	LUA
Lukulu	Zambia	LXU
Lulea/Kallax	Sweden	LLA
Lumbala	Angola	GGC
Lumberton, NC	USA	LBT
Lumi	Papua New Guinea	LMI
Lumid Pau	Guyana	LUB
Lunyuk	Indonesia	LYK
Luoyang	China	LYA
Luozi	Congo, DR	LZI
Lupin, NT	Canada	YWO
Lusaka	Zambia	LUN
Lusambo	Congo, DR	LBO
Lusanga	Congo, DR	LUS
Lushan	China	LUZ
Lushoto	Tanzania	LUY
Lusikisiki	S. Africa	LUJ
Lusk, WY	USA	LSK
Lutselke/Snowdrift, NT	Canada	YSG
Lutsk	Ukraine	UCK
Luwuk/Bubung	Indonesia	LUW
Luxembourg	Luxembourg	LUX
Luxi/Mangshi	China	LUM
Luxor	Egypt	LXR
Luzamba	Angola	LZM
Luzhou	China	LZO
Luzon Is/Clark Field	Philippines	CRK
Luzonis/NAS	Philippines	NCP
Ivanof Bay/SPB, AK	USA	KIB
Lvov/Snilow	Ukraine	LWO
Ivujivik, QC	Canada	YIK
Lwbak	Philippines	LWA
Lyall Harbour, BC	Canada	YAJ
Lycksele	Sweden	LYC
Lydd/Lydd Int'l	UK	LYX
Lynchburg, VA	USA	LYH
Lyndhurst	Australia	LTP
Lyndonville, VT	USA	LLX
Lyneham/RAF	UK	LYE
Lynn Lake, MB	Canada	YYL
Lyon-Satolas	France	LYS
Lyon/Bron	France	LYN
Lyon/Lyon Part-Dieu Rail Svc		
	France	XYD
Lyon/Lyon Perrache Rail Svc		
	France	XYL
Lyon/Lyon Satolas Rail SvcFrance		XYV
Lyons, KS	USA	LYO
Lyss	Switzerland	ZJL

AIRPORTS

M

M'Bahiakro . . . . . . .Côte D'Ivoire . . XMB
M'Banza Congo . . . . . . Angola . . SSY
M'Boki . . . . .Central African Rep . . MKI
M'Sila . . . . .Algeria . . ZZS
Maan . . . . .Jordan . .MPQ
Maastricht/Aachen Netherlands . . MST
Maastricht/RR Stn. . Netherlands . .ZYT
Mabaruma . . . . .Guyana . . . USI
Mabile, AL . . . . .USA . MOB
Mabuiag Is . . . . Australia . . UBB
Macae . . . . Brazil . MEA
Macanal . . . . .Colombia . . NAD
Macapa/Int'l . . . . .Brazil . .MCP
Macara . . . . Ecuador . . MRR
Macas . . . . Ecuador . . XMS
Macau . . . . .Macau . .MFM
Macclesfield/RR Stn. . . . . . .UK . XMZ
MacDill/AFB, FL . . . . .USA . .MCF
Macdonald Downs . . Australia . MNW
Maceio/Palmares . . . . . Brazil . .MCZ
Macenta . . . . Guinea . MCA
Machala . . . . Ecuador . MCH
Machrihanish/RAF . . . . . . .UK . GQJ
Machu Picchu . . . . .Peru. . MFT
Mackall/AAF, NC . . . . .USA . . HFF
Mackay . . . . Australia . .MKY
Mackenzie, BC . . . . . . .Canada . . YZY
Mackinac Is, MI . . . . .USA . MCD
Macksville . . . . Australia . .MVH
Macmahon Camp 4 . Australia . MHC
Macon . . . . .France . .QNX
Macon, GA. . . . . .USA . MCN
Macon/FlightLink Bus Svc, GA
. . . . .USA . .QMP
Macon/Smart, GA . . . . .USA . .MAC
Mactan Is . . . . Philippines . NOP
Madaba . . . . .Jordan . QMD
Madang . . . .Papua New Guinea . MAG
Madera, CA . . . . .USA . MAE
Madinah/Mohammad Bin
    Abdulaziz . . . . . . Saudi Arabia . MED
Madirovalo . . . . . . .Madagascar . WMV
Madison, SD . . . . .USA . .XMD
Madison, WI . . . . .USA . .MSN
Madison/Griswold, CT . . . . .USA . MPE
Madras, OR . . . . .USA . MDJ
Madrid/Barajas . . . . .Spain . MAD
Madrid/Torrejon AFB . . . . .Spain . . TOJ
Madurai . . . . India . . IXM
Mae Hong Son . . . . . Thailand . . HGN
Mae Sot . . . . Thailand . MAQ
Maebashi . . . . .Japan . QEB
Maemillan Pass, YT . . .Canada . . XMP
Mafeteng . . . . .Lesotho . .MFC
Mafia . . . . Tanzania . MFA
Mafra . . . . Brazil . QMF
Mafraq/King Hussein (RJAF)
. . . . .Jordan . .OMF
Magadan . . . . .Russia . . GDX
Magangue/Baracoa . . Colombia . MGN
Maganja Da Costa Mozambique . . MJS
Magaruque . . . . . . Mozambique . MFW
Magdeburg/RR Stn. . . . Germany . .ZMG
Magelagachi . . . . .Russia . . GDG
Maghnia . . . . .Algeria . QMG
Magnitogorsk . . . . .Russia . .MQF
Magnolia/Municipal, AK. . . .USA . AGO
Magwe . . . . Myanmar . MWQ
Mahanoro . . . . .Madagascar . . VVB
Mahdia . . . . .Guyana . MHA
Mahe Is . . . . Seychelles . . SEZ
Mahendranagar . . . . Nepal . .XMG
Mahenye . . . . Zimbabwe . .XMJ
Maiana . . . . .Kiribati . MNK
Maicao . . . . .Colombia . .MCJ

Maida . . . . India . .LDA
Maiduguri . . . . Nigeria . . MIU
Mailkwalk . . . . Guyana . . VEG
Maimana . . . . Afghanistan . . MMZ
Main Duck Is, ON. . . . . Canada . .YDK
Mainoru . . . . Australia . . MIZ
Maintirano . . . . . . Madagascar . . MXT
Mainz . . . . Germany . QMZ
Maio . . . . Cape Verde Is .MMO
Mairipora . . . . .Brazil . QMC
Maitland . . . . Australia . .MTL
Majkin . . . . Marshall Is . . MJE
Majunga/Amborovy
. . . . Madagascar . .MJN
Majuro/Amata Kabua Int'l
. . . . .Marshall Is . .MAJ
Makabana . . . . .Congo, DR . KMK
Makale . . . . Ethiopia . MQX
Makemo . . . . F. Polynesia . MKP
Makhachkala . . . . .Russia . MCX
Makin Is . . . . Kiribati . .MTK
Makini . . . . . Papua New Guinea . MPG
Makkah . . . . Saudi Arabia . QCA
Makkovik Arpt . . . . Canada . . YFT
Makkovik, NF. . . . . Canada . . YMN
Makokou . . . . Gabon . MKU
Makoua . . . . .Congo, DR . MKJ
Makung . . . . Taiwan . MZG
Makurdi . . . . Nigeria . . MDI
Mal . . . . Papua New Guinea . MMV
Mala Mala . . . . S. Africa . AAM
Malabang . . . . Philippines . .MLP
Malabo/Santa Isabel
. . . . Equatorial Guinea . . SSG
Malacca . . . . .Malaysia . MKZ
Malad City, ID . . . . USA . MLD
Malaga . . . . Spain . AGP
Malaimbandy . . . . Madagascar . WML
Malakal . . . . .Sudan . MAK
Malalaua . . . Papua New Guinea . MLQ
Malang . . . . Indonesia . MLG
Malange . . . . Angola . MEG
Malargue . . . . Argentina . LGS
Malatya . . . . .Turkey . .MLX
Malden, MO . . . . USA . MAW
Male/Int'l . . . . Maldives . MLE
Malekolon . . Papua New Guinea . MKN
Malelane . . . . S. Africa . LLE
Malewo . . . . .Vanuatu . MWF
Mali Losinj . . . . Croatia . LSZ
Maliana . . . . Indonesia . .MPT
Malindi . . . . .Kenya . MYD
Mallacoota . . . . Australia . XMC
Malma . . . . Saudi Arabia . MJH
Malmo Town . . . . Sweden . QNQ
Malmo/Malmo City HVC
. . . . Sweden . HMA
Malmo/Malmo Harbour HP
. . . . Sweden . JMM
Malmo/Sturup . . . . Sweden . MMX
Malmstrom/AFB, MT . . . . USA . GFA
Maloelap Is . . . . Marshall Is . .MAV
Malololailal . . . . Fiji . . PTF
Maloy/Harbour . . . . . . Norway . QFQ
Malta/Int'l . . . . .Malta . MLA
Malta, MT . . . . USA . MLK
Mamai . . . . . Papua New Guinea . MAP
Mamburao . . . . Philippines . MBO
Mammoth Lakes, CA . . . . USA . MMH
Mampikony . . . . . . Madagascar . WMP
Mamuju . . . . Indonesia . .MJU
Man . . . . Côte D'Ivoire . MJC
Mana Is . . . . Fiji . MNF
Manado/Samratulangi
. . . . Indonesia . MDC
Managua . . . . Nicaragua . MGA
Manakara . . . . Madagascar . WVK
Mananara . . . . Madagascar . WMR
Manang . . . . Nepal . NGX
Mananjary . . . . Madagascar . .MNJ
Manare . . . . Papua New Guinea . MRM

Manassas, VA . . . . USA . MNZ
Manatee . . . . .Belize. . MZE
Manaung . . . . .Myanmar. .MGU
Manaus/Eduardo Gomes Int'l
. . . . .Brazil. .MAO
Manchester Piccadilly/RR. UK . QQM
Manchester, NH . . . . .USA . . MHT
Manchester/Manchester Bus Stn
. . . . .UK . ZMP
Manchester/Ringway . . . . .UK . MAN
Mandabe . . . . Madagascar . WMD
Mandalay/Annisaton . Myanmar. . MDL
Mandalgobi . . . . Mongolia. .MXW
Mandera . . . . Kenya . NDE
Mandeville/Mariboro . .Jamaica . .MVJ
Mandji . . . . Gabon. KMD
Mandora . . . . Australia. .MQA
Mandritsara . . . . . . Madagascar . WMA
Manega . . . . Gabon. .MGO
Manetai . . . . Papua New Guinea. . MVI
Manga . . . . . Papua New Guinea. MGP
Mangaia Is . . . . Cook Is. . MGS
Mangalore/Balpe . . . . . . .India . . IXE
Mangochi . . . . Malawi. . MAI
Mangole . . . . Indonesia. MAL
Mangrove Cay . . . . . . .Bahamas. . MAY
Manguna . . . Papua New Guinea. MFO
Mangunjaya . . . . Indonesia. .MJY
Manhattan, KS . . . . .USA. . MHK
Manicore . . . . Brazil. MNX
Manihi . . . . F. Polynesia. XMH
Manihiki Is . . . . Cook Is. . MHX
Manihsoq / HP . . . . Greenland. .JSU
Manila/Int'l . . . . Philippines. MNL
Manila/Municipal, AR . . . . .USA. MXA
Manila/Sangley Pt/NAS
. . . . .Philippines. .SGL
Maningrida . . . . .Australia. .MNG
Manistee/Blacker, MI . . . . .USA. . MBL
Manistique, MI . . . . .USA. . ISQ
Manitouwadge, ON . . .Canada. YMG
Manitowaning/East Manitoulin,
    ON. . . . . .Canada. . YEM
Manitowoc, WI . . . . .USA. .MTW
Maniwaki, QC . . . . .Canada. .YMW
Manizales/Santaguida
. . . . .Colombia. MZL
Manja . . . . Madagascar. . MJA
Manjinnup . . . . .Australia. .MJP
Mankato, MN . . . . .USA. MKT
Mankato/Municipal HP, MN USA. JMN
Mankono . . . . Côte D'Ivoire. MOK
Manley Hot Springs, AK . . .USA. .MLY
Manners Creek . . . . . . .Australia. .MFP
Mannitupo . . . . Panama. . MPI
Manokwari/Rendani . Indonesia. .MKW
Manolkotak/SPB, AK . . . . .USA. .KMO
Manono . . . . .Congo, DR. MNO
Mansa . . . . Zambia. MNS
Mansehra . . . . Pakistan. . HRA
Mansfield, OH . . . . .USA. . MFD
Mansfield/Bus Svc . . . . . . UK. ZMA
Mansion House . New Zealand. .KWU
Mansoura . . . . Egypt. QSU
Manston/Kent Int'l . . . . UK. . MSE
Manta . . . . .Ecuador. MEC
Manteo/Dare County Regional,
    NC . . . . .USA. MEO
Manti, UT. . . . . .USA. NTJ
Mantsala . . . . Finland. QZK
Manumu . . . Papua New Guinea. UUU
Manus Is . . . Papua New Guinea. MAS
Manville/Kupper, NJ . . . . .USA. . JVI
Manzanillo . . . . Mexico. .ZLO
Manzanillo/Sierra Maestra
. . . . Cuba. MZO
Manzini/Int'l . . . . Swaziland. MTS
Mao. . . . . Chad. AMO
Maota Savaii Is . . . . . . Samoa. MXS
Maple Bay, BC . . . . .Canada. . YAQ
Mapoda . . . .Papua New Guinea. . MPF

AIRPORTS

Mapua	Papua New Guinea	MPU
Maputo Int'l	Mozambique	MPM
Maquinchao	Argentina	MQD
Mar Del Plata	Argentina	MDQ
Mara Lodges	Kenya	MRE
Maraba	Brazil	MAB
Maracailbo/La Chwila	Venezuela	MAR
Maracay	Venezuela	MYC
Maradi	Niger	MFQ
Marakei	Kiribati	MZK
Maramag	Philippines	XMA
Maramuni	Papua New Guinea	MWI
Marana, AZ	USA	MZJ
Marathon, FL	USA	MTH
Marathon, ON	Canada	YSP
Marau Sound	Solomon Is	RUS
Marawaka	Papua New Guinea	MWG
Marbella	Spain	QRL
Marble Bar	Australia	MBB
Marble Canyon, AZ	USA	MYH
Marburg An Der Lahn	Germany	ZOI
March/AFB, CA	USA	RIV
Marco Is, FL	USA	MRK
Marcus Is	Japan	MUS
Mare	New Caledonia	MEE
Mareala	Honduras	MRJ
Mareeba	Australia	MRG
Marelb	Yemen	MYN
Marfa, TX	USA	MRF
Margaret River	Australia	MGV
Margarima	Papua New Guinea	MGG
Margate	Australia	MGH
Marguerite Bay, AK	USA	RTE
Marianske Lazne	Czech Rep	MKA
Maribo/Lufthavn	Denmark	MRW
Maribor/Slivnica	Slovenia	MBX
Maricourt Airstrip, QC	Canada	YMC
Marie Galante/Les Bases	Guadeloupe	GBJ
Mariehamn/Aland Is	Finland	MHQ
Marietta/AFB, GA	USA	MGE
Marigot	Guadeloupe	XCJ
Marigot/SPB	Guadeloupe	MSB
Marilia/Dr Gastao Vidigal	Brazil	MII
Marina	Nigeria	QNN
Marina Di Massa	Italy	QMM
Marinduque	Philippines	MRQ
Maringa	Brazil	MGF
Marinheim	Germany	MHG
Marion Downs	Australia	MXD
Marion, IL	USA	MWA
Marion, IN	USA	MZZ
Marion, OH	USA	MNN
Maripasoula	F. Guiana	MPY
Mariquita	Colombia	MQU
Mariscal Estigarribia	Paraguay	ESG
Mariupol	Ukraine	MPW
Market Harborough/RR Stn. UK		XQM
Marks/Selts, MS	USA	MMS
Marl	Germany	ZOJ
Marla	Australia	MRP
Marlborough, MA	USA	MXG
Marmande/Off-line Pt	France	XMR
Marmaris	Turkey	QRQ
Marmul	Oman	OMM
Marnte	Cameroon	MMF
Maroantsetra	Madagascar	WMN
Maron	Papua New Guinea	MNP
Maroua/Salam	Cameroon	MVR
Marqua	Australia	MQE
Marquette, MI	USA	MQT
Marrakeeh/Menara	Morocco	RAK
Marree	Australia	RRE
Marromeu	Mozambique	RRM
Marsa Brega	Libya	LMQ
Marsabit	Kenya	RBT
Marsala	Italy	QMR
Marseille/Marignane	France	MRS
Marsh Harbour/Int'l	Bahamas	MHH

Marshall, AK	USA	MLL
Marshall, MN	USA	MML
Marshall, TX	USA	ASL
Marshall/AAF, KS	USA	FRI
Marshall/Memorial, MO	USA	MHL
Marshalltown, IA	USA	MIW
Marshfield, WI	USA	MFI
Martha's Vineyard, MA	USA	MVY
Martigny	Switzerland	ZJM
Martindale/AAF, TX	USA	MDA
Martinsburg, WV	USA	MRB
Marudi	Malaysia	MUR
Mary	Turkmenistan	MYP
Mary's Harbour, NF	Canada	YMH
Maryborough	Australia	MBH
Marysville, CA	USA	MYV
Masa	Papua New Guinea	MBV
Masada	Israel	MTZ
Masalembo	Indonesia	MSI
Masamba	Indonesia	MXB
Masan	S. Korea	QMS
Masasi	Tanzania	XMI
Masbate	Philippines	MBT
Mascara	Algeria	MUW
Maseru/Moshoeshoe Int'l	Lesotho	MSU
Mashad	Iran	MHD
Masi Manimba	Congo, DR	MSM
Masindi	Uganda	KCU
Masirah	Oman	MSH
Masjed Soleyman	Iran	QMJ
Mason City, IA	USA	MCW
Massawa	Eritrea	MSW
Massena, NY	USA	MSS
Masset, BC	Canada	ZMT
Masterton	New Zealand	MRO
Mastic Point	Bahamas	MSK
Masvingo	Zimbabwe	MVZ
Matadi	Congo, DR	MAT
Matagami, QC	Canada	YNM
Matagorda/AFB, TX	USA	MGI
Mataiva	F. Polynesia	MVT
Matak	Indonesia	MWK
Matam	Senegal	MAX
Matamata	New Zealand	MTA
Matamoros	Mexico	MAM
Matane, QC	Canada	YME
Matanzas	Cuba	QMA
Matapedia/RR Stn., QC	Canada	XLP
Mataram/Selaparang	Indonesia	AMI
Mather/AFB, CA	USA	MHR
Mati	Philippines	MXI
Mato Grosso	Brazil	MTG
Matsaile	Lesotho	MSG
Matsu	Taiwan	MFK
Matsumoto	Japan	MMJ
Matsuyama	Japan	MYJ
Matthews Ridge	Guyana	MWJ
Mattoon, IL	USA	MTO
Matupa	Brazil	MBK
Maturin/Quiriquire	Venezuela	MUN
Maubeuge	France	XME
Maues	Brazil	MBZ
Mauke Is	Cook Is	MUK
Maulmyine	Myanmar	MNU
Maumere/Waioti	Indonesia	MOF
Maun	Botswana	MUB
Maupiti	F. Polynesia	MAU
Mauritius/Int'l	Mauritius	MRU
Maxton, NC	USA	MXE
Maxvifle/RR Stn., ON	Canada	XID
Maxwell/AFB, AL	USA	MXF
May Creek, AK	USA	MYK
May River	Papua New Guinea	MRH
Mayaguana	Bahamas	MYG
Mayaguez/Eugenic M De Hostos	Puerto Rico	MAZ
Mayajigua	Cuba	MJG
Mayfa'ah	Yemen	MFY
Mayo, YT	Canada	YMA

Mayoumba	Gabon	MYB
Mayport/NAF, FL	USA	NRB
Mazar-I-Sharif	Afghanistan	MZR
Mazatian/Gen Ralael Bueina	Mexico	MZT
Mbabane/Off-line Pt/(DCA HQ)	Swaziland	QMN
Mbala	Zambia	MMQ
Mbambanakira	Solomon Is	MBU
Mbandaka	Congo, DR	MDK
Mbarara	Uganda	MBQ
Mbeya	Tanzania	MBI
Mbigou	Gabon	MBC
Mbout	Mauritania	MBR
Mbuji Mayi	Congo, DR	MJM
Mc Rae, GA	USA	MQW
McAlester, OK	USA	MLC
Mcallen, TX	USA	MFE
Mcarthur River	Australia	MCV
Mccall, ID	USA	MYL
McCarthy, AK	USA	MXY
McChord/AFB, WA	USA	TCM
Mcclellan/AFB, CA	USA	MCC
Mccomb, MS	USA	MCB
Mcconnell/AFB, KS	USA	IAB
Mccook, NE	USA	MCK
Mcgrath, AK	USA	MCG
Mcguire/AFB, NJ	USA	WRI
Mckenna/AAF, OH	USA	MKF
Mcminnville, TN	USA	RNC
Mcpherson, KS	USA	MPR
Meadow Lake, SK	Canada	YLJ
Meadville, PA	USA	MEJ
Mechelen	Belgium	ZGP
Medan/Polonia	Indonesia	MES
Medea	Algeria	QED
Medellin/E. O. Herrera	Colombia	EOH
Medellin/Jose Marie Cordova	Colombia	MDE
Medford, OR	USA	MFR
Medford, WI	USA	MDF
Medfra, AK	USA	MDR
Medicine Hat, AB	Canada	YXH
Medina	Colombia	MND
Medouneu	Gabon	MDV
Meekatharra	Australia	MKR
Meeker, Meeker Arpt, CO	USA	EEO
Meerbusch	Germany	ZOK
Meet Ghamr	Egypt	QFM
Megeve	France	MVV
Meghauli	Nepal	MEY
Mehamn	Norway	MEH
Meixian	China	MXZ
Mejit Is	Marshall Is	MJB
Mekambo	Gabon	MKB
Mekane Selam	Ethiopia	MKS
Meknes	Morocco	MEK
Mekoryak/Ellis Fld, AK	USA	MYU
Melangguane	Indonesia	MNA
Melbourne	Australia	MEL
Melbourne HP	Australia	KAH
Melbourne Int'l, FL	USA	MLB
Melbourne/Essendon	Australia	MEB
Melchor De Menco	Guatemala	MCR
Melfa, VA	USA	MFV
Melilla	Spain	MLN
Melinda	Belize	MDB
Melo	Uruguay	MLZ
Melville, NY/Off-line Pt	USA	ZMV
Melville/RR Stn., SK	Canada	XEK
Memanbetsu	Japan	MMB
Memmingen	Germany	QOX
Memphis/Int'l, TN	USA	MEM
Memphis/NAS, TN	USA	NQA
Mena	Ethiopia	MZX
Mende/Brenoux	France	MEN
Menden	Germany	ZOL
Mendez	Ecuador	MZD
Mendi	Papua New Guinea	MDU
Mendi	Ethiopia	NDM

World Airports by Airport 588 Dictionary of

AIRPORTS

Mendoza/El Plumerillo
. . . . Argentina . . MDZ
Menominee, MI . . . . USA . MNM
Menongue . . . . Angola . . SPP
Menorea . . . . Spain . . MAH
Menton . . . . France . . XMT
Menyamya . . Papua New Guinea . . MYX
Meran/Bus Stn . . . . Italy . . ZMR
Merauke/Mopah . . . . Indonesia . MKQ
Merced, CA . . . . USA . . MCE
Merced-Castle/AFB, CA . . . USA . . MER
Mercley . . . . Indonesia . . RDE
Mercury, NV . . . . USA . . DRA
Mereedes . . . . Argentina . . MDX
Meribel . . . . France . . MFX
Merida . . . . Spain . QWX
Merida/A Carnevalli . . Venezuela . . MRD
Merida/Rejon . . . . Mexico . . MID
Meridian, MS . . . . USA . . . MEI
Meridian/NAS, MS . . . . USA . NMM
Merimbula . . . . Australia . . MIM
Merluna . . . . Australia . . MLV
Merowe . . . . Sudan . MWE
Merrill/Municipal, WI . . . . USA . . RRL
Merritt, BC . . . . Canada . . YMB
Merry Is, BC . . . . Canada . . YMR
Mersa Matruh . . . . Egypt . MUH
Mersin . . . . Turkey . . . QIN
Mersing . . . . Malaysia . . MEP
Merty . . . . Australia . . RTY
Merzifon . . . . Turkey . . MZH
Mesa/Bus Svc, AZ . . . . USA . . ZBS
Mesa/Falcon Fld, AZ . . . . USA . . . FFZ
Mesa/Falcon Fld, AZ . . . . USA . . MSC
Mesalia/Sandino
. . . . Papua New Guinea . . MFZ
Mesquite, NV . . . . USA . . MFH
Messina . . . . S. Africa . . MEZ
Messina . . . . Italy . . QME
Metlakatia/SPB, AK . . . . USA . . MTM
Metz/Frescaty . . . . France . MZM
Metz/Nancy/Lorraine . . . . France . . . ETZ
Meulaboh/Seunagan . Indonesia . . MEQ
Mevang . . . . Gabon . . MVG
Mexicali . . . . Mexico . . MXL
Mexico City/Atizapan . . Mexico . . AZP
Mexico City/Juarez Int'l . Mexico . . MEX
Mexico City/Santa Lucia
. . . . Mexico . . NLU
Meyers Chuck/SPB, AK . . . USA . WMK
Mfuwe . . . . Zambia . . MFU
Miami/Exec, FL . . . . USA . . TMB
Miami/Int'l, FL . . . . USA . . . MIA
Miami, FL . . . . USA . . MIO
Miami-Opa Locka, FL . . . . USA . . OPF
Miami/Dade Collier, FL . . . . USA . . TNT
Miami/Downtown HP, FL . . . . USA . . JDM
Miami/SPB, FL . . . . USA . . MPB
Miandrivazo . . . . Madagascar . . ZVA
Mianwali . . . . Pakistan . MWD
Michigan City, IN . . . . USA . MGC
Middle Caicos Turks & Caicos Is . . MDS
Middlemount . . . . Australia . MMM
Middleton Is, AK . . . . USA . MDO
Middletown, OH . . . . USA . MWO
Midgard . . . . Namibia . MQG
Midland Airpark, TX . . . . USA . MDD
Midland/Int'l, TX . . . . USA . . MAF
Midway Is/Sand Is Field
. . U.S. (Minor Outlying Islands) . . MDY
Miele Mimbale . . . . Gabon . . GIM
Mikambati . . . . S. Africa . MBM
Mikkeli . . . . Finland . . MIK
Mikonos . . . . Greece . . JMK
Milan//Malpensa . . . . Italy . . MXP
Milan/Linate . . . . Italy . . . LIN
Milan/Milano/Ono Al Serio . . Italy . . BGY
Milan/Milano/Parma . . . . Italy . . . PMF
Milan/Milano/Segrate . . . . Italy . . SWK
Mildenhall/NAF . . . . UK . . GXH
Mildenhall/RAF . . . . UK . . MHZ
Milford Sound . . . New Zealand . MFN
Milford, UT . . . . USA . . MLF
Mili Is . . . . Marshall Is . . . MIJ
Milingimbi . . . . Australia . MGT
Miliville, NJ . . . . USA . . MIV
Milledgeville, GA . . . . USA . . MLJ
Milles City, MT . . . . USA . . MLS
Millicent . . . . Australia . . MLR
Millinocket, ME . . . . USA . . MLT
Milos . . . . Greece . MLO
Milton Keynes . . . . UK . . KYN
Milton Keynes/Bus Svc . . . . UK . . ZFH
Milton, FL . . . . USA . . NSE
Milwaukee, WI . . . . USA . . MKE
Milwaukee, WI . . . . USA . MWC
Milwaukee/Rail Svc., WI . . . USA . . ZML
Minacu . . . . Brazil . MQH
Minaki, ON . . . . Canada . . YMI
Minami Daito . . . . Japan . MMD
Minatitlan . . . . Mexico . . MTT
Minchumina/Intermediate, AK
. . . . USA . MHM
Minden . . . . Germany . ZOM
Minden/Douglas County, NV
. . . . USA . . MEV
Mindik . . . . Papua New Guinea . MXK
Mindiptana . . . . Indonesia . MDP
Minerainye Vody . . . . Russia . . MRV
Mineral Wells, TX . . . . USA . MWL
Miners Bay, BC . . . . Canada . . YAV
Miners Lake . . . . Australia . . MRL
Mingan, QC . . . . Canada . . YLP
Minhad Ab/Military . . . . UAE . NHD
Minj . . . . Papua New Guinea . MZN
Minlaton . . . . Australia . . XML
Minna . . . . Nigeria . . MXJ
Minneapolis/Flying Cloud Arpt,
MN . . . . USA . FCM
Minneapolis/Crystal, MN . . USA . . MIC
Minneapolis/St Paul Int'l, MN
. . . . USA . . MSP
Minneapolis/Downtown HP
. . . . USA . . JDT
Minnenya . . . . Sri Lanka . MNH
Minnipa . . . . Saudi Arabia . . MIN
Minocqua, WI . . . . USA . . ARV
Minot Int'l, ND . . . . USA . MOT
Minot/AFB, ND . . . . USA . . MIB
Minsk Int'l . . . . Belarus . MSQ
Minsk/Minsk Int'l . . . . Belarus . MHP
Minto, AK . . . . USA . MNT
Minvoul . . . . Gabon . . MVX
Miquelon
. . . . St. Pierre and Miquelon . MQC
Miracema Do Norte . . . . Brazil . NTM
Miraflores . . . . Colombia . . MFS
Miramar . . . . Argentina . . MJR
Miramar/NAS, CA . . . . USA . . NKX
Miramichi, NB . . . . Canada . . YCH
Miramichi/RR Stn., NB . Canada . . XEY
Miranda Downs . . . . Australia . MWY
Mirgorod . . . . Ukraine . MXR
Miri . . . . Malaysia . . MYY
Miriti . . . . Colombia . . MIX
Mirnyj . . . . Russia . . MJZ
Mirpur . . . . Pakistan . QML
Mirpur Khas . . . . Pakistan . MPD
Misawa . . . . Japan . . MSJ
Misima Is . . Papua New Guinea . . MIS
Miskolc . . . . Hungary . MCQ
Misrak Gashamo . . . . Ethiopia . . MHJ
Missoula/Int'l, MT . . . . USA . MSO
Misurata . . . . Libya . MRA
Mitchell . . . . Australia . MTQ
Mitchell Plateau . . . . Australia . . MIH
Mitchell, SD . . . . USA . MHE
Mitiaro Is . . . . Cook Is . . MOI
Mitichell River . . . . Australia . MXQ
Mitiga . . . . Libya . . . MJI
Mito . . . . Japan . . QIS
Mitspeh Ramon . . . . Israel . . MIP
Mittenwaid . . . . Germany . . QWD
Mittiebah . . . . Australia . . . MIY
Mitu . . . . Colombia . . MVP
Mitzic . . . . Gabon . . MZC
Miyake Jima/Hirara . . . . Japan . . MMY
Miyakojima . . . . Japan . . MYE
Miyanmin . . Papua New Guinea . . MPX
Miyazaki . . . . Japan . . . KMI
Mizan Teferi . . . . Ethiopia . . . MTF
Mkuze . . . . S. Africa . . MZQ
Mmabatho/Int'l . . . . S. Africa . . MBD
Mo I Rana/Rossvoll . . . . Norway . . MQN
Moa/Orestes Acosta . . . . Chile . . MOA
Moab, UT . . . . USA . . CNY
Moabi . . . . Australia . . MGX
Moala . . . . Fiji . . . MFJ
Moanamani . . . . Indonesia . . . ONI
Moanda . . . . Gabon . . . MFF
Moanda . . . . Congo, DR . . MNB
Moba . . . . Congo, DR . . BDV
Moberly, MO . . . . USA . . MBY
Mobile/Dwntwn Arpt, AL . . . USA . . BFM
Mobridge Municipal, SD . USA . . MBG
Mocimboa Praia . . Mozambique . . MZB
Mococa . . . . Brazil . . QOA
Modane . . . . France . . XMO
Modena/Bus Stn . . . . Italy . . ZMO
Modesto, CA . . . . USA . . MOD
Moengo . . . . Suriname . . MOJ
Moers . . . . Germany . . ZON
Mogadishu/Int'l . . . . Somalia . . MGQ
Mogi Das Cruzes . . . . Brazil . . . QMI
Mogilev . . . . Belarus . . MVQ
Mohammadia . . . . Algeria . QMW
Mohanban . . . . India . . MOH
Moheli . . . . Comoros . . NWA
Mohenjodaro . . . . Pakistan . . MJD
Mojave, CA . . . . USA . . MHV
Mokhotlong . . . . Lesotho . . MKH
Moki . . . . Papua New Guinea . . MJJ
Mokolo Koba . . . . Senegal . . . NIK
Mokpo . . . . S. Korea . . MPK
Mokuti Lodge . . . . Namibia . . OKU
Molde . . . . Norway . . MOL
Moma . . . . New Zealand . MMW
Mombasa/Moi Int'l . . . . Kenya . . MBA
Momeik . . . . Myanmar . . MOE
Mompos . . . . Colombia . . MMP
Monaco-Monte Carlo . . France . XMM
Monahans/Roy Hurd, TX . . USA . . MIF
Monastir/Int'l . . . . Tunisia . . . MIR
Monbetsu . . . . Japan . . MBE
Monclova . . . . Mexico . . . LOV
Moncton, NB . . . . Canada . . YQM
Moncton/RR Stn., NB . . Canada . . . XDP
MonFt . . . . Colombia . . MFB
Mong Hsat . . . . Myanmar . . MOG
Mong Ton . . . . Myanmar . . MGK
Mongo . . . . Chad . . MVO
Mongu . . . . Zambia . . MNR
Monida, MT . . . . USA . MQM
Monkey Bay . . . . Malawi . . MYZ
Monkey Mia/Shark Bay
. . . . Australia . . MJK
Monkey Mountain . . . . Guyana . . MYM
Monkira . . . . Australia . . ONR
Mono . . . . Solomon Is . . MNY
Monroe, LA . . . . USA . . MLU
Monroe, Monroe Arpt, NC . . USA . . EQY
Monroeville, AL . . . . USA . . MVC
Monrovia/Roberts Int'l . . . Liberia . . ROB
Monrovia/Sprigg Payne . Liberia . . MLW
Mons . . . . Belgium . . QMO
Mont De Marsan . . . . France . . . XMJ
Mont Joli, QC . . . . Canada . . . YYY
Mont Louis . . . . France . . QZE
Montagne Harbor, BC . Canada . . YMF
Montague, CA . . . . USA . . . SIY
Montauban . . . . France . . XMW
Montauk, NY . . . . USA . . MTP
Montbelliard . . . . France . . XMF

A I R P O R T S

Monte Alegre . . . . Brazil . . MTE	Morombe . . . . Madagascar . MXM	Mountain Home, AR . . . . . USA . WMH
Monte Alegre . . . . Brazil . QGD	Moron . . . . Mongolia . .MXV	Mountain Home/AFB, ID . . USA . .MUO
Monte Carlo/ HP . . . . . . Monaco . MCM	Moron . . . . Spain . .OZP	Mountain Valley . . . . . .Australia . MNV
Monte Caseros/Seelb Argentina . .MCS	Morondava . . . . Madagascar . MOQ	Mountain View, CA . . . . . . USA . NUQ
Monte Dourado . . . . Brazil . .MEU	Moroni/Iconi . . . . Comoros . YVA	Mountain Village, AK. . . . USA . MOU
Monte Libano, CO . . Colombia . .MTB	Moroni/Prince Said Ibrahim In	Moutiers . . . . France. QMU
Monte Negro . . . . Brazil . QGF	. . . . Comoros . HAH	Mouyiondzi . . . . Congo. MUY
Monteagudo . . . . Bolivia. MHW	Morotai Is . . . . Indonesia . .OTI	Moyale . . . . Ethiopia. MYS
Montego Bay/Sangster Int'l	Morrilton, AR. . . . . USA .MPJ	Moyale . . . . Kenya. .OYL
. . . . Jamaica . MBJ	Morris, MN . . . . USA . MOX	Moyo . . . . Uganda. OYG
Montelimar . . . . .France . XMK	Morristown, NJ . . . . USA . MMU	Moyobamba . . . . Peru. MBP
Montepuez . . . . . . Mozambique . .MTU	Morristown, TN. . . . . USA . MOR	Mpacha . . . . .Namibia. MPA
Monterey, CA . . . . USA . MRY	Morrisville, VT. . . . . USA . MVL	Mt Barnett . . . . .Australia. MBN
Monteria/S. Jeronimo . Colombia . .MTR	Moruya . . . . Australia . MYA	Mt Cavenagh . . . . .Australia. MKV
Monterrey . . . . Colombia . .MOY	Morzine . . . . France . XMQ	Mt Clemens, MI . . . . USA. MTC
Monterrey . . . . Mexico . .MTY	Mosconi . . . . Argentina . XOS	Mt Mckinley, AK. . . . . USA. MCL
Monterrey/Aeropuerto Del None	Moscow . . . . Russia . SVO	Mt Pleasant, IA . . . . USA. MPZ
. . . . Mexico . NTR	Moscow/Bykovo . . . . Russia . .BKA	Mt Pleasant, UT. . . . . USA. MSD
Montes Claros . . . . Brazil . MOC	Moscow/Domodedovo . . Russia . DME	Mt Pocono, PA. . . . . USA. MPO
Montevideo, MN . . . . USA . MVE	Moscow/Leningradsky RR Stn.	Mt Sandford . . . . .Australia. MTD
Montevideo/Carrasco . Uruguay . .MVD	. . . . Russia . ZKD	Mt Vernon, IL . . . . USA. MVN
Montgomery, AL . . . . USA. MGM	Moscow/Vnukovo . . . . . . Russia . .VKO	Mtwara . . . . Tanzania. MYW
Montgomery, NY . . . . USA . MGJ	Moser Bay, AK . . . . USA . KMY	Muccan . . . . .Australia. MUQ
Montgomery/Gunter/AFB, AL	Moses Lake, WA. . . . . . . USA . MWH	Muclarijiang . . . . China. .MDG
. . . . .USA . GUN	Moses Point, AK. . . . . . . USA . MOS	Mucuri . . . . Brazil. . MVS
Monticello, AR . . . . USA . LLQ	Moshi . . . . Tanzania . QSI	Mudgee . . . . .Australia. DGE
Monticello, IA . . . . .USA . MXO	Mosinee, WI . . . . USA . CWA	Mueda . . . . .Mozambique. MUD
Monticello, UT . . . . .USA . MXC	Mosjoen/Kjaerstad . . . . .Norway . . MJF	Muelhefm An Der Ruhr
Monticello/Int'l, NY . . . . . . USA . MSV	Mosquera . . . . Colombia . MQR	. . . . Germany. . ZOO
Montlucon/Gueret (Lepaudy)	Mossel Bay . . . . S. Africa .MZY	Muenster . . . . Germany. . FMO
. . . . .France . MCU	Mossendjo . . . . .Congo, DR . .MSX	Mueo . . . . .New Caledonia. PDC
Monto . . . . Australia . MNQ	Mossoro/Dixsept Rosado .Brazil . MVF	Mui . . . . Ethiopia. MUJ
Montpellier/Frejorgues . .France . MPL	Mostaganem. . . . . Algeria . QMT	Muir/AAF, PA . . . . .USA. .MUI
Montreal/Int'l, QC . . . . . . .Canada . YUL	Mostar. . . . . . .Bosnia Hercegovina . OMO	Mukah . . . . Malaysia. MKM
Montreal-St. Hubert, QC	Mosteiros . . . . Cape Verde Is . MTI	Mukalla . . . . Yemen. MKX
. . . . .Canada . YHU	Mostyn . . . . .Malaysia . MZS	Mukeiras . . . . Yemen. UKR
Montreal/Dorval RR Stn., QC	Mosul . . . . Iraq . OSM	Muko-Muko . . . . Indonesia. MPC
. . . . .Canada . . XAX	Mota . . . . Ethiopia . OTA	Mulatos . . . . Colombia. .ULS
Montreal/Downtown RR Stn.,	Mota Lava . . . . Vanuatu .MTV	Mulatupo . . . . Panama. MPP
QC . . . . .Canada . . YMY	Motherwell/RR Stn. . . . . .UK . XQW	Mulege. . . . . Mexico. MUG
Montreal/Mirabel, QC . Canada . .YMX	Motswari Airfield. . . . . . S. Africa . MWR	Mulga Park . . . . .Australia. MUP
Montreal/St. Lambert Rail Svc,	Motueka . . . . .New Zealand . MZP	Mulia . . . . Indonesia. . LII
QC . . . . .Canada . . XLM	Moudieria. . . . . Mauritania . MOM	Mulka . . . . .Australia. MVK
Montreux . . . . .Switzerland . .ZJP	Mougulu . . . Papua New Guinea . GUV	Mull . . . . UK. .ULL
Montrose, CO. . . . . .USA . . MTJ	Mouila . . . . Gabon . MJL	Mullen, NE . . . . USA. MHN
Montserrat/Bramble Montserrat . MNI	Mould Bay, NT. . . . . Canada . YMD	Mullewa . . . . .Australia. MXU
Montvale, NJ. . . . . .USA . QMV	Moulin Sur Allier . . . . . . France . XMU	Multan . . . . .Pakistan. MUX
Monument Valley, UT . . . . .USA . GMV	Moultrie, GA . . . . USA . MUL	Mulu . . . . Malaysia. MZV
Moody/AFB, GA . . . . .USA . . VAD	Moultrie/Thornasville, GA. . USA . MGR	Mumbai . . . . .India. .BOM
Moolawatana . . . . Australia . MWT	Moundou . . . . Chad . MQO	Mumias . . . . Kenya. MUM
Moomba . . . . Australia . MOO	Mount Aue. Papua New Guinea . .UAE	Munbil . . . . . . Papua New Guinea. . .LNF
Moorabbin . . . . Australia . MBW	Mount Buffalo . . . . .Australia . .MBF	Muncie, IN. . . . . USA. . MIE
Mooraberree . . . . Australia . .OOR	Mount Cook . . . . .New Zealand . MON	Munda . . . . Solomon Is. . MUA
Moorea/Ternae . . . . .F. Polynesia .MOZ	Mount Cook/Glentanner	Munduku . . Papua New Guinea. .MDM
Moose Jaw, SK. . . . . . . .Canada . YMJ	. . . . .New Zealand . .GTN	Mundulkiri . . . . Cambodia. MWV
Moose Lake, MB . . . . . .Canada . YAD	Mount Cook/Pulkalki/Twizel	Mungeranie . . . . .Australia. MNE
Moosonee, ON. . . . . . .Canada . .YMO	. . . . .New Zealand . . TWZ	Munich . . . . Germany. MUC
Mopti. . . . . .Mali . .MZI	Mount Etjo Lodge. . . . . Namibia . MJO	Munich/HBF Railway Svc
Mor Setar . . . . Malaysia . AOR	Mount Full Stop. . . . . . .Australia . MFL	. . . . Germany. . ZMU
Mora . . . . Sweden . MXX	Mount Gambier . . . . . . Australia . MGB	Munich/Neubiberg Ab. Germany. .MIG
Morafenobe . . . . .Madagascar . TVA	Mount Gunson . . . . .Australia . GSN	Muong Sai . . . . Laos. .UON
Moranbah . . . . Australia . MOV	Mount Hagen/Kagamuga	Murcia/San Javier. . . . . . . .Spain. . MJV
Morawa . . . . Australia . MWB	. . . . Papua New Guinea . HGU	Muriae . . . . Brazil. QUR
Moree . . . . Australia . MRZ	Mount Holly, NJ . . . . USA . . .LLY	Murmansk . . . . Russia. MMK
Morehead . .Papua New Guinea . MHY	Mount Holly, South Jersey, NJ	Muroran . . . . .Japan. QRN
Morelia. . . . . Mexico . MLM	. . . . USA . . VAY	Murray Bay, QC . . . . . . .Canada . YML
Moreton . . . . Australia . MET	Mount Hotham . . . . . . .Australia . MHU	Murray Is . . . . .Australia. . MYI
Morgan City/Municipal HP, LA	Mount House . . . . .Australia . MHO	Murray/Calloway County, KY
. . . . .USA . . PTN	Mount Isa . . . . .Australia . .ISA	. . . . USA. .CEY
Morganton/Lenoir, NC . . . .USA . .MRN	Mount Keith . . . . Australia . WME	Murzuq . . . . Libya. QMQ
Morgantown, WV. . . . . . . .USA . MGW	Mount Magnet . . . . Australia . MMG	Mus . . . . Turkey. . MSR
Morges. . . . . .Switzerland . ZJQ	Mount Pleasant . . . . Falkand Is . MPN	Muscat. . . . . Oman. MCT
Morichal. . . . . Colombia . MHF	Mount Pleasant, MI . . . . . USA . MOP	Muscatine, IA . . . . USA. MUT
Moriguchi . . . . Japan . . QGT	Mount Pleasant, TX. . . . . . USA . MPS	Musha . . . . Djibouti. . MHI
Moriolka/Hanamaki . . . . . Japan . HNA	Mount Shasta, CA . . . . . . USA . MHS	Musigrave . . . . .Australia. MVU
Morlaix/Ploujean . . . . . . .France . MXN	Mount Swan . . . . Australia . MSF	Muskegon, MI . . . . USA. MKG
Morney . . . . Australia . OXY	Mount Union, PA . . . . USA . MUU	Muskogee, OK. . . . . USA. MKO
Mornington. . . . . Australia . ONG	Mount Vernon, WA. . . . . . USA . MVW	Muskogee/Hatbox Fld, OK. USA . HAX
Moro . . . . . .Papua New Guinea . MXH	Mount Wilson, CA . . . . . . USA . MWS	Muskoka, ON . . . . .Canada. . YQA
Moroak. . . . . Australia . MRT	Mountain . . . . .Nepal . MWP	Muskrat Dam, ON. . . . . .Canada. . MSA
Morobe . . . . . .Papua New Guinea . OBM	Mountain Home, AR . . . . . USA . .BPK	Musoma . . . . Tanzania. . MUZ

AIRPORTS

Mussau	Papua New Guinea	MWU
Mustique Is		
	St. Vincent & Grenadines	MQS
Mutare	Zimbabwe	UTA
Muting	Indonesia	MUF
Muttaburra	Australia	UTB
Muzaffarabad	Pakistan	MFG
Muzaffarpur	India	MZU
Muzattarnagar	India	MZA
Mwadui	Tanzania	MWN
Mwanza	Tanzania	MWZ
Mwelka	Congo, DR	MEW
Myeik	Myanmar	MGZ
Myitkyina	Myanmar	MYT
Myroodah	Australia	MYO
Myrtle Beach, SC	USA	CRE
Myrtle Beach/AFB, SC	USA	MYR
Mysore	India	MYQ
Mystery Flight	Australia	ZZF
Mystery Night	Australia	ZZJ
Mytilene	Greece	MJT
Myvatn/Reykiahlid	Iceland	MVA
Mzamba (Wild Coast Sun)		
	S. Africa	MZF
Mzuzu	Malawi	ZZU

N

N'Djole	Gabon	KDJ
N'Fliquinha	Angola	NRQ
N'Zeto	Angola	ARZ
N. Sound/Virgin Gorda/Hovercraft/		
Launch Pt	Virgin Is (British)	NSX
Naberevnye Chelny	Russia	NBC
Nabire	Indonesia	NBX
Nablus	West Bank	ZDF
Nacala	Mozambique	MNC
Nachingwea	Tanzania	NCH
Nacogdoches, TX	USA	LFK
Nador	Morocco	NDR
Nadunumu	Papua New Guinea	NDN
Nadym	Russia	NYM
Nafoora	Libya	NFR
Naga	Philippines	WNP
Nagano	Japan	QNG
Nagasaki	Japan	NGS
Nagoya/Koniaki AFS	Japan	NGO
Nagpur/Sonegaon	India	NAG
Naha	Indonesia	NAH
Nain, NF	Canada	YDP
Nairobi/Jorno Kenyatta Int'l		
	Kenya	NBO
Nairobi/Wilson	Kenya	WIL
Nakashibetsu	Japan	SHB
Nakhon Phanom	Thailand	KOP
Nakhon Ratchasima	Thailand	NAK
Nakhon Si Thammarat	Thailand	NST
Nakina, ON	Canada	YQN
Naknek, AK	USA	NNK
Nakolik River, AK	USA	NOL
Nakuru	Kenya	NUU
Nalchik	Russia	NAL
Nalkinichevan	Azerbaijan	NAJ
Namangan	Uzbekistan	NMA
Namatanai	Papua New Guinea	ATN
Nambaiyufa	Papua New Guinea	NBA
Nambour	Australia	NBR
Namdrik Is	Marshall Is	NDK
Namlea	Indonesia	NAM
Nampula	Mozambique	APL
Namrole	Indonesia	NRE
Namsang	Myanmar	NMS
Namsos/Lufthavn	Norway	OSY
Namtu	Myanmar	NMT
Namu	Marshall Is	NMU
Namu, BC	Canada	ZNU
Namudi	Papua New Guinea	NDI
Namur	Belgium	QNM

Nan	Thailand	NNT
Nanaimo, BC	Canada	YCD
Nanaimo/Harbour, BC	Canada	ZNA
Nanchang	China	JHN
Nanchang	China	KHN
Nanchong	China	NAO
Nancy/Essey	France	ENC
Nanded	India	NDC
Nandi/Int'l	Fiji	NAN
Nangade	Mozambique	NND
Nangapinoh	Indonesia	NPO
Nanisivik, NU	Canada	YSR
Nankina	Papua New Guinea	NKN
Nanking	China	NKG
Nanning	China	NNG
Nanortalik	Greenland	JNN
Nantes	France	NTE
Nantes/RR	France	QJZ
Nantong	China	NTG
Nantucket, MA	USA	ACK
Nanuque	Brazil	NNU
Nanwalek, AK	USA	KEB
Nanyang	China	NNY
Nanyuki	Kenya	NYK
Naoro	Papua New Guinea	NOO
Napa, CA	USA	APC
Napakiak/SPB, AK	USA	WNA
Napanee/RR Stn., ON	Canada	XIF
Napaskiak/SPB, AK	USA	PKA
Napasoq/Off-line Pt	Greenland	QJT
Napier-Hastings	New Zealand	NPE
Naples, FL	USA	APF
Naples/Capodichino	Italy	NAP
Naples/Mergellina Railway Svc		
	Italy	ZMI
Nappa Merry	Australia	NMR
Napperby	Australia	NPP
Napuka Is	F. Polynesia	NAU
Nara	Mali	NRM
Nara City	Japan	QNZ
Naracoorte	Australia	NAC
Narathiwat	Thailand	NAW
Nare	Colombia	NAR
Nargana	Panama	NGN
Narnbucca Heads	Australia	NBH
Narnibe	Angola	MSZ
Narnutoni	Namibia	NNI
Narooma	Australia	QRX
Narrabri	Australia	NAA
Narrandera	Australia	NRA
Narrogin	Australia	NRG
Narromine	Australia	QRM
Narsaq Kujalleq	Greenland	QFN
Narsaq/ HP	Greenland	JNS
Narsarsuaq	Greenland	UAK
Narvik/Framnes	Norway	NVK
Naryan-Mar	Russia	NNM
Nashua, NH	USA	ASH
Nashville Nexrad, TN	USA	OHX
Nashville/Int'l, TN	USA	BNA
Nasik/Gandhinagar	India	ISK
Nassau/Int'l	Bahamas	NAS
Nassau/Paradise Is	Bahamas	PID
Nassau/Seaplane Base		
	Bahamas	WZY
Natadola	Fiji	NTA
Natal/Augusto Severo	Brazil	NAT
Natashquan, QC	Canada	YNA
Natchez/Hardy-Anders, MS	USA	HEZ
Natitingou	Benin	NAE
Natuna Ranai	Indonesia	NTX
Naukiti, AK	USA	NKI
Nauru Arpt	Nauru	INU
Navalmoral de a Mata	Spain	QWW
Navegantes	Brazil	NVT
Nawabshah	Pakistan	WNS
Nawanshahar	India	QNW
Naxos	Greece	JNX
Ndalatandos	Angola	NDF
Ndele	Central African Rep	NDL
Ndende	Gabon	KDN

Ndjamena	Tonga	NDJ
Ndola	Zambia	NLA
Necochea	Argentina	NEC
Necocli	Colombia	NCI
Nedroma	Algeria	QAN
Needles, CA	USA	EED
Neenah, WI	USA	EEW
Neerlerit Inaat	Greenland	CNP
Neftekamsk	Russia	NEF
Nefteyugansk	Russia	NFG
Negage	Andorra	GXG
Negarbo	Papua New Guinea	GBF
Negginan, MB	Canada	ZNG
Negrielli	Ethiopia	EGL
Negril	Jamaica	NEG
Neispruit	S. Africa	NLP
Neiva/La Marguita	Colombia	NVA
Nejjo	Ethiopia	NEJ
Nelkernt	Ethiopia	NEK
Nellis/AFB, NV	USA	LSV
Nelran	Saudi Arabia	EAM
Nelson	New Zealand	NSN
Nelson Lagoon, AK	USA	NLG
Nema	Mauritania	EMN
Nemiscau, QC	Canada	YNS
Nenana, AK	USA	ENN
Neosho, MO	USA	EOS
Nepalganj	Nepal	KEP
Nephi, UT	USA	NPH
Neryungri	Russia	NER
Neu-Ulm	Germany	ZOT
Neuchatel	Switzerland	QNC
Neuilly-Sur-Seine	France	QNL
Neulbrandenburg	Germany	FNB
Neumuenster	Germany	EUM
Neunkirchen/Off-line Pt	Germany	ZOP
Neuss	Germany	ZOQ
Neustadt-Weinstrasse	Germany	ZOR
Neustadt/Glawe	Germany	QGW
Neuwied	Germany	ZOU
Nevada, MO	USA	NVD
Nevers	France	NVS
Nevis/Newcastle		
	St. Kitts and Nevis	NEV
Nevsehir	Turkey	NAV
New Amsterdam	Guyana	QSX
New Bern, NC	USA	EWN
New Bight	Bahamas	NET
New Carlisle/RR Stn., QC		
	Canada	XEL
New Chenega, AK	USA	NCN
New Halfa	Somalia	NHF
New Haven/New Haven Rail, CT		
	USA	ZVE
New Iberia, LA	USA	ARA
New Koliganek, AK	USA	KGK
New London, CT	USA	GON
New Moon	Australia	NMP
New Orleans Int'l, LA	USA	MSY
New Orleans, LA	USA	NEW
New Orleans/NAS, LA	USA	NBG
New Philadelphia, OH	USA	PHD
New Plymouth	New Zealand	NPL
New Richmond, WI	USA	RNH
New Richmond/RR Stn., QC		
	Canada	XEM
New Stuyahok, AK	USA	KNW
New Ulm, MN	USA	ULM
New Westminster, BC	Canada	YBD
New York/La Guardia, NY	USA	LGA
New York/Battery Pk, NY	USA	NBP
New York/Downtown Manhattan		
HP, NY	USA	JRB
New York/E. 34 St Landing, NY		
	USA	NES
New York/E. 34th St Heiliport, NY		
		TSS
New York/East 60th Street HP, NY		
	USA	JRE
New York/Marine Air Terminal, NY		
	USA	QNY

AIRPORTS

New York/Penn Rail, NY . . . . USA . . ZYP	**Niuatoputapu**/Kuini Lavenia	**Nottingham**/RR Stn. . . . . UK . . . XQI
New York/Pier 11/SPB, NY . .USA . .NWS	. . . . Tonga . . NTT	**Nouadhibou** . . . . Mauritania . . NDB
New York/West 30th St HP, NY	**Niue Is**/Hanan . . . . Niue Is . . .IUE	**Nouakchott** . . . . Mauritania . . NKC
. . . . .USA . . JRA	**Nizhnevartovsk** . . . . . Russia . .NJC	**Noumea**/Magenta
New York/World Trade Center, NY	**Nizhniy Novgorod** . . . . . Russia . .GOJ	. . . . .New Caledonia . . GEA
. . . . .USA . .WTC	**Njornbe** . . . . .Tanzania . JOM	**Nouna** . . . . .Burkina Faso. . XNU
Newark Northgate/RR Stn. . UK . . XNK	**Nkan** . . . . Gabon . .NKA	**Nourrea**/TontoutaNew Caledonia. . NOU
Newark, NJ . . . . .USA . .EWR	**Nkaus** . . . . Lesotho . .NKU	**Nova Friburgo** . . . . Brazil. . QGJ
Newark/Metropark Rail, NJ .USA . .ZME	**Nkayi**/Yokangassi. . . .Congo, DR .NKY	**Nova Xavantina** . . . . . . Brazil. . NOK
Newark/Newark NJ Rail . . . .USA . .ZRP	**Nkolo** . . . . .Congo, DR . NKL	**Novalguacu** . . . . Brazil. . QNV
Newburgh, NY . . . . .USA . . SWF	**Nkongsamba** . . . . . . Cameroon . .NKS	**Novato**, CA . . . . USA. . NOT
Newbury/Greenham/RAF . . UK . .EWY	**Noatak**, AK . . . . USA . WTK	**Novgorod** . . . . .Russia. . NVR
Newcastle . . . . UK . .NCL	**Noervenich** . . . . Germany . QOE	**NoviSad** . . . . .Yugoslavia. . QND
Newcastle . . . . S. Africa . NCS	**Nogales** . . . . Mexico . NOG	**Novo Aripuana** . . . . Brazil. . .NVP
Newcastle/Belmont . . Australia . BEO	**Nogales**/Int'l, AZ . . . . . . USA . OLS	**Novo Hamburgo** . . . . . Brazil. . QHV
Newcastle/Mondell, WY. . . .USA . . ECS	**Nojabrxsk** . . . . Russia . .NOJ	**Novoirossijsk** . . . . .Russia. . NOI
Newcastle/Williamtown Australia. . NTL	**Nomad River**	**Novokuzinetsk** . . . . . . Russia. . NOZ
Newman . . . . Australia . ZNE	. . . . Papua New Guinea . NOM	**Novosibirsk** . . . . Russia. . OVB
Newport (Gwent)/RR Stn. . UK . .XNE	**Nomane** . . . Papua New Guinea . NMN	**Novy Urengoy** . . . . . . .Russia. . NUX
Newport Beach / HP, CA . .USA . . JNP	**Nome**, AK . . . . USA . OME	**Now Shahr** . . . . .Iran. . NSH
Newport, NH . . . . .USA . .NWH	**Nondalton**, AK . . . . USA . .NNL	**Nowata** . . . . Papua New Guinea. . NWT
Newport, OR . . . . .USA . .JNW	**Nong Khai** . . . . Thailand . QJX	**Nowra** . . . . .Australia. . NOA
Newport, OR . . . . .USA . .ONP	**Nonouti** . . . . Kiribati . NON	**Nowy Targ** . . . . .Poland. . QWS
Newport, UT . . . . .USA . . EFK	**Noonkanbah** . . . . .Australia . .NKB	**Nsukka** . . . . Norway. . QNK
Newport/State, RI . . . . .USA . . NPT	**Noorvik**/Curtis Memorial, AK	**Nuernberg** . . . . Germany. . NUE
Newquay-St Mawgan . . . . .UK . .NQY	. . . . USA . .ORV	**Nueva Casas** Grandes. .Mexico. . NCG
Newry . . . . Australia . NRY	**Noosa** . . . . .Australia . .NSA	**Nueva Gerona**/Rafael Cabrera
Newtok, AK . . . . .USA . .WWT	**Noosaville** . . . . .Australia . NSV	. . . . Cuba. . GER
Newton, IA . . . . .USA . . TNU	**Nootka Sound**, BC . . . Canada . .YNK	**Nueva Guinea** . . . . Netherlands. . NVG
Newton, KS . . . . .USA . .EWK	**Norddeich** . . . . Germany . NOE	**Nuevo Laredo**/Int'l. . . . .Mexico. . NLD
Neyveli . . . . India . NVY	**Norden** . . . . Germany . NOD	**Nuguria** . . . Papua New Guinea. . NUG
Ngala . . . . S. Africa . NGL	**Norderney** . . . . Germany . NRD	**Nuiqsut**, AK . . . . USA. . NUI
Ngaoundere . . . . . . Cameroon . NGE	**Norderstedt** . . . . Germany . .ZOV	**Nuku** . . . . Papua New Guinea. . UKU
Ngau Is . . . . Fiji . .NGI	**Nordfjordur** . . . . Iceland . NOR	**Nuku Hiva** . . . . .F. Polynesia. . NHV
Ngiva . . . . Angola . NGV	**Nordholz-Spieka** . . . .Germany . .NDZ	**Nuku'Alofa**/Fija'Arnotu Int'l
Ngoma . . . . Zambia . ZGM	**Nordhorn** . . . . Germany . ZOW	. . . . .Tonga. . .TBU
Ngukurr . . . . Australia . RPM	**Norfolk**/Int'l, VA . . . . USA . .ORF	**Nukus** . . . . Uzbekistan. . NCU
Nha Trang . . . . Vietnam . NHA	**Norfolk Is** . . . . Norfolk Is . NLK	**Nukutavake** . . . . . .F. Polynesia. . NUK
Niacornaarsuk . . . . . Greenland . QMK	**Norfolk**, NE. . . . . .USA . .OFK	**Nulato**, AK. . . . . USA. . NUL
Niagara Falls/Int'l, NY . . . . .USA . . IAG	**Norfolk**/NAS, VA . . . . USA . NGU	**Nullagine** . . . . .Australia. . NLL
Niagara Falls/RR Stn., ON	**Noril'sk** . . . . Russia . .NSK	**Nullarbor** . . . . .Australia. . NUR
. . . . .Canada . .XLV	**Norman Wells**, NT . . . . Canada . .YVQ	**Numbulwar** . . . . .Australia. . NUB
Niamey/Diori Hamani . . . . . Niger . NIM	**Norman**'s Cay . . . . . . Bahamas . NMC	**Numfoor** . . . . Indonesia. . FOO
Niamtougou/Lama-Kara . Togo . .LRL	**Norman**, OK. . . . . USA . OUN	**Nunapitchuk**, AK . . . . . . USA. . NUP
Nias . . . . Indonesia . ZQX	**Normanton** . . . . Australia . NTN	**Nunchia** . . . . .Colombia. . NUH
Niblack, AK . . . . .USA . . NIE	**Norridgewock**, ME. . . . . USA . OWK	**Nuneaton**/RR Stn. . . . . . . UK . .XNV
Nicaro . . . . .Cuba . . ICR	**Norrkoping**/Kungsangen	**Nunukan** . . . . Indonesia. . NNX
Nice . . . . France . NCE	. . . . Sweden . .NRK	**Nuoro** . . . . Italy. . QNU
Nichen Cove, AK . . . . . . .USA . .NKV	**Norseman** . . . . Australia . NSM	**Nuqui** . . . . .Colombia. . NQU
Nichen Cove/SPB, AK. . . .USA . . WNC	**Norsup** . . . . Vanuatu . .NUS	**Nuremberg**/HBF Railway Svc
Nicholson . . . . Australia . NLS	**North Battleford**, SK. . . Canada . YQW	. . . . Germany. . ZAQ
Nicosia . . . . Cyprus . .NIC	**North Bay**, ON. . . . . . . Canada . . YYB	**Nushki** . . . . .Pakistan. . NHS
Nicoya/Guanacaste . Costa Rica . NCT	**North Bend**, OR . . . . USA . .OTH	**Nutuve**. . . . . Papua New Guinea. . NUT
Nieuw Nickerie . . . . . Suriname . .ICK	**North Caicos** Turks & Caicos Is . NCA	**Nutwood Downs** . . . . .Australia. . UTD
Nifty . . . . Australia . NIF	**North Eleuthera**/Int'l . Bahamas . ELH	**Nuuk**. . . . . Greenland. . GOH
Nightmute, AK . . . . .USA . .NME	**North Is**/NAS, CA . . . . . . USA . NZY	**NY City** Nexrad, NY. . . . . . .USA. . OKX
Niigata . . . . Japan . . KIJ	**North Little** Rock, AR. . . . USA . LZK	**Nyac**, AK . . . . USA. . ZNC
Niihama . . . . Japan . . IHA	**North Platte**, NE. . . . . . . USA . LBF	**Nyala** . . . . Somalia. . UYL
Nikolaev. . . . . .Ukraine . NLV	**North Ronaldsay**. . . . . . .UK . .NRL	**Nyaung-u** . . . . .Myanmar. . NYU
Nikolai, AK. . . . . .USA . . NIB	**North Spirit** Lake, ON . Canada . YNO	**Nyborg**/RR Stn. . . . . . Denmark. . ZIB
Nikolski/AFS, AK . . . . . . .USA . . IKO	**Northallerton**/RR Stn. . . . .UK . .XNO	**Nyeri**. . . . . Kenya. .NYE
Nikunau . . . . Kiribati . .NIG	**Northampton** . . . . Georgia . ORM	**Nyikobing Mors**/Bus Svc
Niles, MI . . . . .USA . .NLE	**Northbrook**, IL . . . . USA . OBK	. . . . Denmark. . ZAW
Nimba . . . . Liberia . .NIA	**Northeast Cape**/AFS, AK . USA . OHC	**Nyingan** . . . . .Australia. . NYN
Nimes/Garons . . . . .France . . FNI	**Northolt**/RAF . . . . .UK . .NHT	**Nyon** . . . . Switzerland. . ZRN
Nimroz . . . . Afghanistan . .IMZ	**Northway**, AK . . . . USA . .ORT	**Nzagi** . . . . Angola. . NZA
Ningbo . . . . .China . NGB	**Norton**/AFB, CA. . . . . USA . SBD	**Nzerekore** . . . . .Guinea. .NZE
Ningerum . .Papua New Guinea . NGR	**Norwalk**/HP, CT . . . . USA . ORQ	**Nzola** . . . . Kenya. . NZO
Ninilchik, AK. . . . . .USA . .NIN	**Norway House**, MB . . . Canada . YNE	
Niolki . . . . Congo, DR . .NIO	**Norwich** . . . . .UK . .NWI	
Nioro . . . . Mali . NIX	**Norwich**/Eaten. . . . . . .Australia . . OIC	
Niort/Souche . . . . France . .NIT	**Norwood**, MA . . . . USA . OWD	
Nipa . . . . .Papua New Guinea . NPG	**Nosara Beach** . . . . Costa Rica . NOB	
Nipawin, SK. . . . . .Canada . . YBU	**Nossi-be**/Fascene. Madagascar . NOS	
Niquelandia . . . . Brazil . .NQL	**Notodden** . . . . .Norway. . .NTB	
Nis . . . . Yugoslavia . .INI	**Nottingham** . . . . .UK . EMA	
Nishinoomote . . . . Japan . . .IIN	**Nottingham** . . . . .UK . .NQT	
Nissan Is . . .Papua New Guinea . IIS	**Nottingham** . . . . .UK . QEW	
Nitchequon, QC. . . . . .Canada . .YNI	**Nottingham**/Bus Svc . . . . .UK . ZGB	
Niteroi. . . . . Brazil . QNT	**Nottingham**/RR Stn. . . . . . .UK . XNM	
Niuafo'ou/Mata'aho . . . . Tonga . NFO	**Nottingham**/RR Stn. . . . . . .UK . XQH	

O

		O'Neill, NE. . . . . USA. . ONL
		Oahu/Dillingham Airfield, HI
		. . . . USA. . HDH
		Oak Brook, IL/Off-line Pt . . .USA. .QHO
		Oak Harbor, WA. . . . . USA. .ODW
		Oakey. . . . . .Australia. . OKY
		Oakham/Cottesmor/RAF . . . . UK. . OKH

Oakland Int'l, CA	USA	OAK
Oakland, MD	USA	OBT
Oaktown, IN	USA	OTN
Oakville/Rail Svc, ON	Canada	XOK
Oamaru	New Zealand	OAM
Oaxaca	Mexico	OAX
Oban	Australia	OBA
Oban/HP	UK	OHP
Oban/Connei	UK	OBN
Obano	Indonesia	OBD
Obbia	Somalia	CMO
Oberammergau	Germany	ZOX
Oberhausen	Germany	ZOY
Oberpfaffenhofen	Germany	OBF
Obihiro	Japan	OBO
Obo	Papua New Guinea	OBX
Obock	Djibouti	OBC
Obre Lake, NT	Canada	YDW
Ocala, FL	USA	OCF
Ocana/Aguasclaras	Colombia	OCV
Ocatsut/Harbour	Greenland	XEO
Ocean City, MD	USA	OCE
Ocean Falls, BC	Canada	ZOF
Ocean Reef, FL	USA	OCA
Oceana/NAS, VA	USA	NTU
Oceanic, AK	USA	OCI
Oceanside, CA	USA	OCN
Ocho Rios/Boscobel	Jamaica	OCJ
Ocussi	Indonesia	OEC
Odate Noshiro	Japan	ONJ
Oddor Meanche	Cambodia	OMY
Odense/Beldringe	Denmark	ODE
Odense/Bus Svc	Denmark	ZIM
Odense/RR Stn	Denmark	ZBQ
Odessa/Central	Ukraine	ODS
Odibos	Brazil	OBI
Odienne	Côte D'Ivoire	KEO
Odiham/RAF	UK	ODH
Oeksfjord	Norway	QOK
Oelwen, IA	USA	OLZ
Oenpeili	Australia	OPI
Oeqertarsuaq	Greenland	JGO
Offenburg	Germany	ZPA
Offerfbach	Germany	ZOZ
Offutt/AFB, NE	USA	OFF
Ofu	American Samoa	OFU
Ogallala/Searle Fld, NE	USA	OGA
Ogden, UT	USA	OGD
Ogdensburg Int'l, NY	USA	OGS
Ogeranang	Papua New Guinea	OGE
Ogle	Guyana	OGL
Ogoki, ON	Canada	YOG
Ohakea/RAF	New Zealand	OHA
Ohrid	Macedonia	OHD
Oil City, PA	USA	OIL
Oingdao	China	TAO
Oishn	Yemen	IHN
Oita	Japan	OIT
Okaba	Indonesia	OKQ
Okaukuejo	Namibia	OKF
Okayama	Japan	OKJ
Okeechobee, FL	USA	OBE
Okhotsk	Russia	OHO
Oki Is	Japan	OKI
Okinawa/Kadena AFB	Japan	DNA
Okinawa/Naha	Japan	OKA
Okinawa/Naha AFB	Japan	AHA
Okino Erabu	Japan	OKE
Oklahoma City, OK	USA	OKC
Oklahoma City, OK	USA	PWA
Oklahoma City/Downtown, OK	USA	DWN
Okmulgee, OK	USA	OKM
Okondja	Gabon	OKN
Okoyo	Congo, DR	OKG
Oksapimin	Papua New Guinea	OKP
Oksibil	Indonesia	OKL
Oktiabrskij	Russia	OKT
Okushiri	Japan	OIR
Olafsfjordur	Iceland	OFJ
Olafsvik/Rif	Iceland	OLI

Olanchito	Honduras	OAN
Olbia/Costa Smeraida	Italy	OLB
Old Crow, YT	Canada	YOC
Old Ft. Bay, QC	Canada	ZFB
Old Harbor/SPB, AK	USA	OLH
Old Town, ME	USA	OLD
Oldenburg	Germany	ZPD
Olean, NY	USA	OLE
Olga Bay/SPB, AK	USA	KOY
Olive Branch, MS	USA	OLV
Olivos	Argentina	QLV
Olney, IL	USA	OLY
Olney, TX	USA	ONY
Olomouc	Czech Rep	OLO
Olpoi	Vanuatu	OLJ
Olsobip	Papua New Guinea	OLQ
Olsztyin	Poland	QYO
Olten	Switzerland	ZJU
Olympia, WA	USA	OLM
Olympic Dam	Australia	OLP
Omaha, NE	USA	OMA
Omaha/Millard, NE	USA	MIQ
Omak, WA	USA	OMK
Omboue	Gabon	OMB
Omega	Namibia	OMG
Omora	Papua New Guinea	OSE
Omsk	Russia	OMS
Omura	Japan	OMJ
Ondangwa	Namibia	OND
Oneonta/Municipal, NY	USA	ONH
Onepusu	Solomon Is	ONE
Ongava Game Reserve	Namibia	OGV
Ongiva	Angola	VPE
Onion Bay, AK	USA	ONN
Onitsha	Norway	QNI
Ono I Lau	Fiji	ONU
Ononge	Papua New Guinea	ONB
Onotoa	Kiribati	OOT
Onsiow	Australia	ONS
Ontario Int'l, CA	USA	ONT
Ontario, OR	USA	ONO
Ontario/Int'l HP, CA	USA	JIO
Oodnadatta	Australia	ODD
Opapamiska Lake/Musselwhite, ON	Canada	YBS
Opelousas, LA	USA	OPL
Open Bay	Papua New Guinea	OPB
Opoie	Poland	QPM
Opuwa	Namibia	OPW
Oradea	Romania	OMR
Oram	Papua New Guinea	RAX
Oran	Argentina	ORA
Oran/Es Senia	Algeria	ORN
Orange	France	XOG
Orange Walk	Belize	ORZ
Orange, MA	USA	ORE
Orange/Springhill	Australia	OAG
Orange/The City HP, CA	USA	JOR
Orangeburg, SC	USA	OGB
Oranjemund	Namibia	OMD
Orapa	Botswana	ORP
Orbost	Australia	RBS
Orchid Beach/Fraser Is	Australia	OKB
Orchid Is	Taiwan	KYD
Ord River	Australia	ODR
Ord/Sharp Fld, NE	USA	ODX
Ordu	Turkey	QOR
Orebro	Sweden	ORB
Orel	Russia	OEL
Orenburg	Russia	REN
Oria	Papua New Guinea	OTY
Orientos	Australia	OXO
Orinduik	Guyana	ORJ
Oristano	Italy	QOS
Oriximina	Brazil	ORX
Orland	Norway	OLA
Orlando Exec, FL	USA	ORL
Orlando Int'l, FL	USA	MCO
Orlando/Walt Disney World, FL	USA	DWS

Ormara	Pakistan	ORW
Ormoc	Philippines	OMC
Ornkalai	Papua New Guinea	OML
Ornlya	Japan	QOM
Ornskoldsvik	Sweden	OER
Orocue	Colombia	ORC
Oroville, CA	USA	OVE
Orpheus Is Resort/Waterport	Australia	ORS
Orsk	Russia	OSW
Orsta-Volda/Hovden	Norway	HOV
Oruro	Bolivia	ORU
Osage Beach, MD	USA	OSB
Osaka/Itami	Japan	ITM
Osaka/Kansai Int'l	Japan	KIX
Osaka/Off-line Pt	Japan	QKV
Osan/Air Base	S. Korea	OSN
Osasco	Brazil	QOC
Osceola, WI	USA	OEO
Osh	Kyrgyzstan	OSS
Oshakati	Namibia	OHI
Oshawa, ON	Canada	QWA
Oshawa, ON	Canada	YOO
Oshima	Japan	OIM
Oshkosh, NE	USA	OKS
Oshkosh, WI	USA	OSH
Osijek	Croatia	OSI
Oskaloosa, IA	USA	OOA
Oskarshamn	Sweden	OSK
Oslo/Fornebu	Norway	FBU
Oslo/Gardermoen	Norway	OSL
Oslo/Sandefjord	Norway	TRF
Osmanabad	India	OMN
Osnabrueck/RR Stn	Germany	ZPE
Osorno/Canal Balo	Chile	ZOS
Ossima	Papua New Guinea	OSG
Ostend	Belgium	OST
Ostersund/Froesoe	Sweden	OSD
Ostrava/Mosnov	Czech Rep	OSR
Ostro Weikopolski	Poland	QDG
Osvaldo Cruz/Off-line Pt	Brazil	QOD
Otaru	Japan	QOT
Otis/AFB, MA	USA	FMH
Otjiwarongo	Namibia	OTJ
Otsu City	Japan	QOO
Ottawa Int'l, ON	Canada	YOW
Ottawa/RR Stn., ON	Canada	XDS
Ottawa/Rockcliffe St, ON	Canada	YRO
Otto/Vor, NM	USA	OTO
Ottumwa, IA	USA	OTM
Otu	Colombia	OTU
Ouadda	Central African Rep	ODA
Ouagadougou/Aeroport	Burkina Faso	OUA
Ouahigouya	Burkina Faso	OUG
Ouanda Dialle	Central African Rep	ODJ
Ouanga	Gabon	OUU
Ouango Fitini	Côte D'Ivoire	OFI
Ouargla	Algeria	OGX
Ouarzazate	Morocco	OZZ
Ouctshoorn	S. Africa	OUH
Oudoni	Laos	ODY
Oued Rhiou	Algeria	QOU
Oued Zenati	Algeria	QOZ
Ouesnel, BC	Canada	YQZ
Ouesso	Cocos (Keeling) Is	OUE
Oujda/Les Angades	Morocco	OUD
Oulu	Finland	OUL
Oum Hadjer	Chad	OUM
Ourilandia	Brazil	OIA
Ourinhos	Brazil	OUS
Outer Skerries	UK	OUK
Outhing	Iceland	UTG
Ouvea	New Caledonia	UVE
Ouyen	Australia	OYN
Ouzinkie/SPB, AK	USA	KOZ
Ovalle	Chile	OVL
Ovda	Israel	VDA
Owando	Congo, DR	FTX
Owatonna, MN	USA	OWA

AIRPORTS

Owen Sound/Billy Bishop, ON	Canada	YOS
Owendo	Gabon	OWE
Owensboro, KY	USA	OWB
Owerri	Nigeria	QOW
Owyhee, NV	USA	OWY
Oxford House, MB	Canada	YOH
Oxford, CT	USA	OXC
Oxford, OH	USA	OXD
Oxford/Kidlington	UK	OXF
Oxford/University-Oxford, MS	USA	UOX
Oxnard, CA	USA	OXR
Oyem	Gabon	OYE
Ozamis City/Labo	Philippines	OZC
Ozona, TX	USA	OZA

P

Pa-an	Myanmar	PAA
Paama	Vanuatu	PBJ
Paamiut	Greenland	JFR
Pacific City, OR	USA	PFC
Pacific Harbor	Fiji	PHR
Pack Creek, AK	USA	PBK
Padang/Tabing	Indonesia	PDG
Paderborn/Lippstadt	Germany	PAD
Padova	Italy	QPA
Paducah, KY	USA	PAH
Pagadian	Philippines	PAG
Page, AZ	USA	PGA
Pago Pago/Int'l American Samoa		PPG
Pagosa Springs, CO	USA	PGO
Pahokee, FL	USA	PHK
Paiela	Papua New Guinea	PLE
Pailin	Cambodia	PAI
Paimiut/SPB, AK	USA	PMU
Painesville, OH	USA	PVZ
Painter Creek, AK	USA	PCE
Pakatoa Is	New Zealand	PKL
Paksane	Laos	PKS
Pakse	Laos	PKZ
Pakuashipi, QC	Canada	YIF
Pakulha	Uganda	PAF
Pala	Chad	PLF
Palacios	Honduras	PCH
Palaclos, TX	USA	PSX
Palanga	Italy	PLQ
Palangkaraya	Indonesia	PKY
Palanquero	Colombia	PAL
Palapye	Botswana	QPH
Palembang/Mahmud Badaruddin II	Indonesia	PLM
Palenque	Mexico	PQM
Palermo/Punta Raisi	Italy	PMO
Palestine, TX	USA	PSN
Palibelo	Indonesia	PBW
Palkokku	Myanmar	PKK
Palm Is St. Vincent & Grenadines		PLI
Palm Is	Australia	PMK
Palm Springs, CA	USA	PSP
Palm Springs-Thermal, CA	USA	TRM
Palm Springs/Bermuda Dunes, CA	USA	UDD
Palma	Mozambique	LMZ
Palma Mallorca	Spain	PMI
Palmanto	Venezuela	PTM
Palmar/Palmar Sur	Costa Rica	PMZ
Palmares	Brazil	QGK
Palmas	Brazil	PMW
Palmdale, CA	USA	PMD
Palmer, AK	USA	PAQ
Palmer, MA	USA	PMX
Palmerston North	New Zealand	PMR
Palmira	Colombia	QPI
Palmyra	Syria	PMS
Palo Alto, CA	USA	PAO

Paloemeu/Vincent Fayks	Suriname	OEM
Palu/Mutiara	Indonesia	PLW
Pama	Burkina Faso	XPA
Pambwa	Papua New Guinea	PAW
Pamol	Malaysia	PAY
Pampa/Perry Lefors Fld, TX	USA	PPA
Pamplona	Spain	PNA
Panama City, FL	USA	PFN
Panama City/Paitilia	Panama	PAC
Panama City/Tocumen Int'l	Panama	PTY
Panambi	Brazil	QMB
Pancevo	Yugoslavia	QBG
Panclie Pandie	Australia	PDE
Panevezys	Lithuania	PNV
Pangia	Papua New Guinea	PGN
Pangkalanbuun	Indonesia	PKN
Pangkalpinang/Pangkalpinang	Indonesia	PGK
Pangkor	Malaysia	PKG
Pangnirtung, NU	Canada	YXP
Pangoa	Papua New Guinea	PGB
Panguitch, UT	USA	PNU
Panjgur	Pakistan	PJG
Pantelleria	Italy	PNL
Pantnagar	India	PGH
Paonia/North Fork Valley, CO	USA	WPO
Papa Stour	UK	PSV
Papa Westray	UK	PPW
Papeete/Faaa	F. Polynesia	PPT
Paphos Int'l	Cyprus	PFO
Papun	Myanmar	PPU
Para Chinar	Pakistan	PAJ
Paraburdoo	Australia	PBO
Paradise River, NF.	Canada	YDE
Paragould/Mun	Australia	PGR
Parakou	Benin	PKO
Param	Papua New Guinea	PPX
Paramakotoi	Guyana	PMT
Paramaribo/Zandenj Int'l	Suriname	PBM
Paramaribo/Zorg En Hoop	Suriname	ORG
Parana	Argentina	PRA
Paranagua	Brazil	PNG
Paranaiba	Brazil	PBB
Paranavai	Brazil	PVI
Paraparaumu	New Zealand	PPQ
Parasi	Solomon Is	PRS
Paratebueno	Colombia	EUO
Pardoo	Australia	PRD
Parent/RR Stn., QC	Canada	XFE
Parintins	Brazil	PIN
Paris / HP	France	JDP
Paris, TN	USA	PHT
Paris, TX	USA	PRX
Paris/Aerogare des Invalides	France	XEX
Paris/C.de G. ITGV Rail Sve	France	XDT
Paris/Charles De Gaulle	France	CDG
Paris/Etoile	France	XTT
Paris/Gare du Nord RR Stn.	France	XPG
Paris/Gare Montparnasse	France	XGB
Paris/La Defense HP	France	JPU
Paris/Le Bourget	France	LBG
Paris/Le Touquet	France	LTQ
Paris/Orly	France	ORY
Paris/Paris Cergy Pontoise	France	POX
Park Falls, WI	USA	PKF
Park Rapids, MN	USA	PKD
Parkersburg, WV	USA	PKB
Parkes	Australia	PKE
Parks/SPB, AK	USA	KPK
Parksville/RR Stn., BC	Canada	XPB
Parnailba/Santos Dumont	Brazil	PHB
Parnamirim	Brazil	QEU
Parndana	Australia	PDN
Paro	Bhutan	PBH

Paros	Greece	PAS
Parry Sound, ON	Canada	YPD
Parsons, KS	USA	PPF
Paruima	Guyana	PRR
Pasadena / HP, CA	USA	JPD
Pascagoula, Lott Int'l Arpt, MS	USA	PQL
Pascagoula, MS	USA	PGL
Pasco, WA	USA	PSC
Pasewalk/RR Stn.	Germany	ZSK
Pasighat	India	IXT
Pasir Pangarayan	Indonesia	PPR
Pasni	Pakistan	PSI
Paso Calballos	Guatemala	PCG
Paso De Los Libres	Argentina	AOL
Paso Robles, CA	USA	PRB
Pass (Generic), QC	Canada	XZP
Passau	Germany	ZPF
Passo Fundo	Brazil	PFB
Passos	Brazil	PSW
Pastaza	Ecuador	PTZ
Pasto/Cano	Colombia	PSO
Pat Warren, AK	USA	PFA
Paterswolde/Bus Svc	Netherlands	QYT
Pathankot	India	IXP
Patna	India	PAT
Pato Branco	Brazil	PTO
Patong Beach	Thailand	PBS
Patos De Minas	Brazil	POJ
Patreksfjordur	Iceland	PFJ
Pattani	Thailand	PAN
Pattaya	Thailand	PYX
Patuxent River/NAS, MD.	USA	NHK
Pau/Uzein	France	PUF
Pauk	Myanmar	PAU
Paulatuk, NT.	Canada	YPC
Paulo Afonso	Brazil	PAV
Pauloff Harbor/SPB, AK	USA	KPH
Pavloclar	Kazakstan	PWQ
Pawi/Beles	Ethiopia	PWI
Payan	Colombia	PYN
Paysandu	Uruguay	PDU
Payson, AZ	USA	PJB
Paz De Ariporo/Casanare	Colombia	PZA
Peace River, AB	Canada	YPE
Peach Springs, AZ	USA	PGS
Pease/AFB, NH.	USA	PSM
Peawanuck, ON.	Canada	YPO
Pebane	Mozambique	PEB
Pechora	Russia	PEX
Pecos City, TX	USA	PEQ
Pecs	Hungary	QPJ
Pedernales	Venezuela	PDZ
Pedro Bay, AK	USA	PDB
Pedro Juan Caballero	Paraguay	PJC
Peenemuende	Germany	PEF
Pehuajo	Argentina	PEH
Peine	Germany	ZPG
Pekanbaru/Simpang Tiga	Indonesia	PKU
Pelaneng	Lesotho	PEL
Pelican/SPB, AK	USA	PEC
Pell City, AK	USA	PLR
Pellston, MI.	USA	PLN
Pelly Bay, NU	Canada	YBB
Pelotas/Federal	Brazil	PET
Pemba	Mozambique	POL
Pemba/Wawi	Tanzania	PMA
Pembina/Intermediate, ND	USA	PMB
Pembroke, ON.	Canada	YTA
Penang/Int'l	Malaysia	PEN
Pencing	Australia	PEY
Pender Harbor, BC	Canada	YPT
Pendleton, OR.	USA	PDT
Pendopo	Indonesia	PDO
Penn Yan, NY	USA	PEO
Penneshaw	Australia	PEA
Penrhyn Island	Cook Is.	PYE
Penrith/RR Stn.	UK	XPF

Pensacola, FL............USA . PNS	Picos ....Brazil . PCS	Poelgorica,/Golubovci
Pensacola/NAS, FL ......USA . NDP	Picton/Koromiko ..New Zealand . PCN	...................Yugoslavia.. TGD
Pensacola/NAS, FL ......USA . NPA	Piedmont Triad/Int'l, NC . . USA . GSO	Pohang/Air Base ......S. Korea.. KPO
Penticton, BC ....Canada . . YYF	Piedras Negras ......Mexico . PDS	Pohnpei............Micronesia.. PNI
Penza ....Russia . . PEZ	Pierre, SD ....USA . PIR	Point Baker/SPB, AK ......USA..KPB
Penzance/ HP ....UK . . PZE	Piestany ....Slovakia . PZY	Point Hope, AK ....USA.. PHO
Peoria, IL ....USA . PIA	Pietermaritzburg ....S. Africa . PZB	Point Lay, AK ....USA . PIZ
Peppimenarti ....Australia . . PEP	Pietersburg ....S. Africa . PTG	Point Mugu/NAS, CA ......USA.. NTD
Peraitepuy ....Venezuela . PPH	Pijiguaos ....Venezuela . LPJ	Point Retreat/Coast Guard HP,
Perce/RR Stn., QC . ...Canada . . XFG	Pikangikum, ON......Canada . YPM	AK ....USA..PRT
Pereira/Matecana ....Colombia . . PEI	Pilar ....Paraguay . PIL	Point Sur, CA ....USA.. NNZ
Perigueux/Bassillac ...France . . PGX	Pilkwitonei, MB ......Canada . PIW	Pointe A Pitre/Le Raizet
PerisheR Valley/Bus Svc	Pilot Point, AK.........USA . PIP	.............Gaudeloupe...PTP
................Australia . . QPV	Pilot Point/Ugashik Bay, AKUSA . UGB	Pointe-aux-Trembles/RR Stn.,
Perito Moreno ......Argentina . .PMQ	Pilot Stn, AK ....USA . PQS	QC................Canada.. XPX
Perm ....Russia . . PEE	Pimaga .... Papua New Guinea . PMP	Pointe-Noire ......Congo, DR. . PNR
Perpignan/Llabanere ....France . . PGF	Pimenta Bueno ....Brazil . PBQ	Points North Landing, SK
Perry, IA ....USA . PRO	Pinamar ....Argentina . QPQ	...................Canada..YNL
Perry-Foley, FL.........USA . .FPY	Pinar Del Rio ......Colombia . QPD	Poitiers/Biard ....France. . PIS
Perry/SPB, AK ....USA.. PYL	Pincher Creek, AB.....Canada . WPC	Poitiers/RR Stn. ......France.. XOP
Perryville/SPB, AK ....USA.. KPV	Pindiu ...... Papua New Guinea . .PDI	Pokhara..............Nepal..PKR
Persepolis ....Iran . WPS	Pine Bluff, AR ....USA . PBF	Polacca, AZ ....USA..PXL
Perth ....Australia . . PER	Pine Cay.... Turks & Caicos Is . .PIC	Polk Inlet, AK ....USA.. POQ
Perth/Scone ....UK . .PSL	Pine House, SK ....Canada . ZPO	Polk/AAF, LA ....USA.. POE
Perth/ScotRail ....UK.. ZXP	Pine Mountain, GA .....USA . PIM	Poll ....Ukraine.. PLV
Peru/Illinois Valley Regional, IL	Pine Point, NT........Canada . YPP	Polyarnyl.............Russia.. PYJ
..................USA . VYS	Pine Ridge, SD ....USA . .IEN	Pomala ....Indonesia.. PUM
Perugia/Sant Egidio ......Italy . PEG	Pine Ridge, SD ....USA . XPR	Pomezia ....Italy.. QEZ
Pescara/Liberi...........Italy . . PSR	Pingtung ....Taiwan . . PIF	Pompano Beach, FL ......USA.. PPM
Peshawar ....Pakistan . . PEW	Pinheiro ....Brazil . .PHI	Pompeia ....Brazil..QPF
Petawawa, ON ....Canada . . YWA	Pinotepa Nacional ....Mexico . PNO	Ponca City, OK ....USA.. PNC
Peterborough, ON ......Canada . .YPQ	Pipillipai ....Guyana . PIQ	Ponce/Mercedita ...Puerto Rico.. PSE
Peterborough/RR Stn......UK . . XVH	Piracicaba ....Brazil . QHB	Pond Inlet, NU ....Canada.. YIO
Petersburg, AK.........USA.. PSG	Pirapora ....Brazil . .PIV	Pondicherry............India..PNY
Petersburg, VA.........USA.. PTB	Pirassununga/Off-line Pt ..Brazil . . QPS	Pondok Cabe ......Indonesia.. PCB
Petersburg, WV ....USA.. PGC	Pirmasens ....Germany . .ZPI	Ponta Delgada/NordelaPortugal.. PDL
Peterson's Point, AK ....USA.. PNF	Pisco ....Peru . PIO	Ponta Grossa/Sant'Ana .. Brazil. PGZ
Petrolina/Int'l ....Brazil . PNZ	Pitalito ....Colombia . PTX	Ponta Pelada ....Brazil.. PLL
Petropavlovsk ......Kazakstan . . PPK	Pitinga ....Brazil . PIG	Ponta Pora/Int'l.......Brazil.. PMG
Petropavlovsk-KamchatsRussia.. PKC	Pitts Town ....Bahamas . PWN	Pontes e Lacerda ......Brazil.. LCB
Petropolis ....Brazil . QPE	Pittsburg, KS..........USA . PTS	Pontiac, MI ....USA..PTK
Petrozavodsk ....Russia.. PES	Pittsburgh/Int'l, PA......USA . PIT	Pontianak/Supadio .. Indonesia.. PNK
Pevek ....Russia . . PWE	Pittsburgh/Allegheny, PA.. USA . AGC	Pontorson Mt St MichelFrance. XPM
Pforheim ....Germany . . UPF	Pittsburgh/Civic HP, PA . . USA . CVA	Pontresina ....Switzerland.. ZJV
Phalaborwa ....S. Africa . .PHW	Pittsfield, MA...........USA . PSF	Poona/Lohegaon ....India.. PNQ
Phan Rang ....Vietnam . PHA	Pituffik ....Greenland . THU	Popayan/Machangara.Colombia..PPN
Phan Thiet ....Vietnam . PHH	Placencia ....Belize . PLJ	Pope Vanoy, AK.........USA.. PVY
Phanom Sarakham .. Thailand . PMM	Placerville, CA ....USA . PVF	Pope/AFB, NC..........USA.. POB
Phaplu ....Nepal . .PPL	Plainview, TX...........USA . PVW	Poplar Bluff, MO ....USA..POF
Phi Phi Is ....Thailand . PHZ	Planaclas ....Colombia . PLA	Poplar Hill, ON ....Canada.. YHP
Philadelphia Int'l, PA ...USA.. PHL	Platinum, AK ....USA . PTU	Poplar River, MB.......Canada.. XPP
Philadelphia, PA ......USA.. PNE	Plato ....Colombia . PLT	Popondetta/Girua
Philadelphia/Mustin Alf, PA.USA . MUV	Plattsburgh, NY ....USA . PLB	..........Papua New Guinea.. PNP
Philadelphia/N Philadelphia	Plattsburgh/AFB, NY .....USA . PBG	Poptun ....Guatemala.. PON
RR Stn., PA ....USA.. ZHC	Playa Blanca..........Spain . QLY	Porbandar ....India.. PBD
Philadelphia/Philadelphia Rail, PA	Playa del Carmen .....Mexico . PCM	Porcupine Creek, AK......USA.. PCK
..................USA.. ZFV	Playa de Los Cristianos Spain . QCI	Pordenone ....Italy.. QAD
Philadelphia/SPB, PA ....USA.. PSQ	Playa Grande ......Guatemala . PKJ	Pore ....Colombia.. PRE
Philadelphia/Trenton RR Stn.,	Playa Samara ......Costa Rica . PLD	Porgera .. Papua New Guinea.. RGE
PA ....USA.. ZTN	Playon Chico ....Panama . PYC	Pori ....Finland.. POR
Philip, SD ....USA.. PHP	Pleasant Harbour, AK.... USA . PTR	Porl Hunter ....Australia..PHJ
Phinda/Zulu Inyaia .... S. Africa . .PZL	Pleasant Nexrad, MO .... USA . EAX	Porlarnar ....Venezuela.. PMV
Phitsanulok ....Thailand . PHS	Pleasanton/Hacienda Bus-Park	Poros ....Norway.. RRS
Phnom Penh/Pochentong	HP, CA ....USA . JBS	Port Alexander, AK ......USA..PTD
...............Cambodia . . PNH	Pleiku ....Vietnam . PXU	Port Alfred ....S. Africa.. AFD
Phoenix/Int'l, AZ ....USA.. PHX	Plentywood, MT ....USA . PWD	Port Alice, AK ....USA..PTC
Phoenix, AZ ....USA.. DVT	Plettenberg Bay......S. Africa . PBZ	Port Allberni, BC ......Canada..YPB
Phrae ....Thailand . PRH	Pleven ....Bulgaria . PVN	Port Alsworth, AK ....USA.. PTA
Phu Quoc/Duong Dang.Vietnam . PQC	Plock ....Poland . QPC	Port Angeles, WA ....USA.. CLM
Phu Vinh ....Vietnam . PHU	Ploiesti ....Romania . QPL	Port Angeles., WA ......USA..NOW
Phu-bon ....Vietnam . . HBN	Plovcliv ....Bulgaria . PDV	Port Antonio/Ken Jones
Phuket/Int'l ....Thailand . HKT	Plymouth ....UK . PLH	.................Jamaica..POT
Phuoclong ....Vietnam . VSO	Plymouth, IN ....USA . PLY	Port Armstrong, AK......USA.. PTL
Piacenza ....Italy . QPZ	Plymouth, MA ....USA . PYM	Port Au Prince ....Haiti.. PAP
Pianeta Rica ....Colombia . PLC	Po ....Burkina Faso . PUP	Port Augusta.........Australia.. PUG
Piatra Neamt ....Romania . QPN	Pocahontas, IA ....USA . POH	Port Bailey/SPB, AK ......USA..KPY
Picayune, MS ....USA.. PCU	Pocatello, ID ....USA . .PIH	Port Berge ......Madagascar.. WPB
Pichanal ....Argentina . XMV	Pochutla ....Mexico . PUH	Port Blair ....India.. IXZ
Pickens, SC..........USA.. LQK	Pocos De Calclas ......Brazil . POO	Port Clarence, AK.......USA.. KPC
Pickle Lake, MB......Canada.. YPL	Podor ....Senegal . POD	Port De Paix ....Haiti.. PAX
Pico Is ....Portugal . PIX		Port Douglas ....Australia....PTI

A
I
R
P
O
R
T
S

Port Elizabeth . . . . S. Africa . . .PLZ	Poughkeepsie, NY . . . . . . USA . POU	Puerto Aisen . . . . .Chile.. WPA
Port Fitzroy. . . . . New Zealand . . GBS	Poulsbo, WA . . . . USA . . PUL	Puerto Armuelles . . . .Panama.. AML
Port Frederick, AK . . . . . .USA . . PFD	Pourn . . . . New Caledonia . .PUV	Puerto Asis . . . . .Colombia.. PUU
Port Gentil . . . . .Gabon . .POG	Pouso Alegre . . . . .Brazil . . PPY	Puerto Ayacucho. . . Venezuela . .PYH
Port Graham, AK . . . . .USA .PGM	Povungnituk, QC . . . . . Canada . YPX	Puerto Barrios . . . . Guatemala. .PBR
Port Harcourt . . . . Nigeria . PHC	Powell Lake, BC . . . . Canada . .WPL	Puerto Berrio . . . . .Colombia.. PBE
Port Hardy, BC . . . . . . .Canada . . YZT	Powell Point . . . . Bahamas . .PPO	Puerto Boyaca . . . . .Colombia. .PYA
Port Hawkesbury, NS. .Canada . . YPS	Powell River, BC. . . . . Canada . YPW	Puerto Cabello . . . . . Venezuela. .PBL
Port Hedland . . . . Australia . . PHE	Poza Rica/Tajin . . . . Mexico . . PAZ	Puerto Cabezas . . Netherlands. .PUZ
Port Heiden, AK. . . . . .USA . . PTH	Pozan/Lawica . . . . Poland . .POZ	Puerto Carreno . . . . . . .Colombia. . PCR
Port Hope Simpson, NF.Canada . .YHA	Pozarevac . . . . Yugoslavia . . ZZP	Puerto de la Luz. . . . . Spain . . QUZ
Port Hope/RR Stn., ON .Canada . . XPH	Prado . . . . .Brazil . .PDF	Puerto Deseado . . . .Argentina.. PUD
Port Huron/Int'l, MI. . . . . . .USA . . PHN	Prague/Ruzyne . . . . .Czech Rep . .PRG	Puerto Escondido . . . Myanmar.. PXM
Port Johnson . . . . Australia . . PRF	Praia/Francisco Mendes	Puerto Ininda . . . . .Colombia.. PDA
Port Kaiturna . . . . .Guyana . PKM	. . . . Cape Verde Is . .RAI	Puerto Jimenez . . . . Costa Rica. . PJM
Port Keats. . . . . Australia . . PKT	Prairie Du Chien, WI. . . . USA . .PCD	Puerto Juarez . . . . .Mexico. . PJZ
Port Lincoln . . . . Australia . . PLO	Praslin Is . . . . Seychelles . . PRI	Puerto la Cruz . . . . . . Venezuela. . QUC
Port Lions/SPB, AK . . . . . .USA . . ORI	Prato . . . . .Italy . QPR	Puerto La Cruz . . . . Spain . . UPC
Port Macquarie . . . . . Australia . . PQQ	Pratt Municipal, KS . . . . . USA . . PTT	Puerto Leguizamo. . .Colombia.. LQM
Port McNeil, BC . . . . . . .Canada . . YMP	Prentice, WI. . . . . USA . PRW	Puerto Lempira . . . . Honduras. . PEU
Port Menier, MB . . . . . .Canada . . YPN	Prerov . . . . .Czech Rep . . PRV	Puerto Madonado . . . . . . Peru. . PEM
Port Moller/AFS, AK . . . . .USA . . PML	Pres. Roque Saenz Pena	Puerto Madryn/El Tehuelche
Port Moresby/Int'l	. . . . Argentina . .PRQ	. . . . .Argentina . . PMY
. . . . .Papua New Guinea . .POM	Prescott, AZ. . . . . USA . .PRC	Puerto Moritt/Tepual . . . .Chile.. PMC
Port Oceanic, AK. . . . . . . .USA . . PRL	Prescott/RR Stn., ON . . . Canada . . . XII	Puerto Natales/Teniente J.
Port Of Spain	Presidente Dutra/Mun . .Brazil . .PDR	Gallardo . . . . .Chile.. .PNT
. . . . .Trinidad and Tobago . . POS	Presidente Prudente/	Puerto Obaldia . . . . . . .Panama.. .PUE
Port Pirie . . . . Australia . . PPI	A. De Barros . . . . .Brazil . . PPB	Puerto Ordaz. . . . . . Venezuela. . PZO
Port Protection, AK . . . . . .USA . . PPV	Presov . . . . Slovakia . .POV	Puerto Paez . . . . Venezuela. . PPZ
Port Said . . . . .Egypt . . PSD	Presque Isle, ME . . . . USA . PQI	Puerto Penasco . . . . .Mexico. . PPE
Port Saint Johns. . . . . S. Africa . . JOH	Presque Isle/Rogers, MI . . USA . .PZQ	Puerto Plata/La Union
Port San Juan, AK . . . . . . .USA . . PJS	Preston . . . . Cuba . . PST	. . . . .Dominican Rep. . POP
Port Simpson, BC . . . . .Canada . . YPI	Preston/RR Stn. . . . . .UK . . XPT	Puerto Princesa . . . .Philippines.. PPS
Port Stanley . . . . .Falkand Is . . PSY	Pretoria . . . . S. Africa . PRY	Puerto Rico . . . . .Colombia.. PCC
Port Stephens . . . . Australia . .PTE	Pretoria/Central Hpr . . S. Africa . .HPR	Puerto Rico . . . . Somalia. . PUR
Port Sudan . . . . .Sudan . . PZU	Pretoria/iscor HP . . . . S. Africa . . HIC	Puerto Suarez . . . . Somalia. . PSZ
Port Townsend, WA . . . . . .USA . . TWD	Preveza/Lefkas/Aktion. . .Greece . .PVK	Puerto Vallarta/Ordaz . .Mexico. . PVR
Port Vendres . . . . .France . . XPV	Price, UT. . . . . USA . .PUC	Puerto Varas . . . . .Chile.. PUX
Port Vila/Bauerfield . . . .Vanuatu . . VLI	Prieska . . . . S. Africa . . PRK	Puerto Williams . . . . .Chile.. WPU
Port Walter, AK. . . . . .USA . . PWR	Prince Albert,SK . . . . . Canada . . YPA	Puka Puka . . . . F. Polynesia. .PKP
Port Williams/SPB, AK . . . .USA . . KPR	Prince George, BC . . . . Canada . . YXS	Puka Puka Is/Attol. . . . Cook Is.. PZK
Port-Daniel/RR Stn., QC	Prince George/RR Stn., BC	Pukarua . . . . F. Polynesia. . PUK
. . . . .Canada . . XFI	. . . . Canada . .XDV	Pukatawagan, MB . . . . .Canada.. .XPK
Portage Creek, AK . . . . . .USA . . PCA	Prince Rupert, BC . . . . Canada . YPR	Pula . . . . .Croatia.. PUY
Portage La Prairie, MB Canada . .YPG	Prince Rupert/RR Stn., BC	Pulau Layang-Layang Is
Porterville, CA . . . . .USA . . PTV	. . . . Canada . XDW	. . . . Malaysia. . LAC
Portimao . . . . Portugal . . PRM	Prince Rupert/SealCove, BC	Pulau Panlang . . . . . Indonesia.. PPJ
Portland. . . . . Australia . .PTJ	. . . . Canada . ZSW	Pullman, WA. . . . . .USA . . PUW
Portland Int'l, ME. . . . . . .USA . PWM	Princeton, ME . . . . USA . .PNN	Pumani . . . . Papua New Guinea. . PMN
Portland Int'l, OR . . . . .USA . . PDX	Princeton, MN. . . . . USA . PNM	Punia . . . . Congo, DR. . PUN
Portland Nexrad, OR . . . . .USA . . RTX	Princeton, NJ . . . . USA . .PCT	Punta Alegre . . . . . . .Colombia.. UPA
Portland-Troutdale, OR . .USA . . TTD	Princeton/Princeton JT Rail, NJ	Punta Arenas/Pres Ibanez Chile. .PUQ
Porto. . . . . Portugal . .OPO	. . . . USA . . ZTJ	Punta Cana . . . .Dominican Rep. . PUJ
Porto Alegre	Principe Sao Tome and Principe . . PCP	Punta Colorada . . . . .Mexico. . PCO
. . . . . . .Sao Tome and Principe . . PGP	Prineville, OR . . . . USA . . PRZ	Punta De Maisi. . . . . .Colombia.. UMA
Porto Alegre Do Norte . . Brazil . . PBX	Pristina. . . . . Yugoslavia . . PRN	Punta Del Este. . . . . . Uruguay.. .PDP
Porto Alegre/Salgado FilheBrazil. .POA	Progresso . . . . .Brazil . PGG	Punta Gorda . . . . .Belize. . PND
Porto Amboim . . . . Angola . . PBN	Prome . . . . Myanmar . .PRU	Punta Gorda, FL . . . . .USA . . PGD
Porto Cheli Kheli/Alexion	Propriano. . . . . France . . PRP	Punta Istilta . . . . Costa Rica. . PBP
. . . . Greece . . PKH	Proserpine . . . . Australia . . PPP	Punta Renes . . . . . . Costa Rica. . JAP
Porto Dos Gauchos. . . . Brazil . . PBV	Prospect Creek, AK . . . . . USA . . PPC	Pureni . . . . . Papua New Guinea. . PUI
Porto Nacional . . . . Brazil . . PNB	Provedenia . . . . Russia . . PVX	Purwokerto . . . . Indonesia.. PWL
Porto Santo . . . . Portugal . . PXO	Providemya . . . . Russia . . PVS	Pusan/Kimhae Int'l Arpt .S. Korea. .PUS
Porto Seguro . . . . .Brazil . . BPS	Providence, RI . . . . USA . . PVD	Putao . . . . .Myanmar.. PBU
Porto Uniao . . . . Brazil . . QPU	Providence/Providence Rail, RI	Puttaparthi/Puttaprathe . . India.. .PUT
Porto Velho/Belmonte . . . Brazil . . PVH	. . . . USA . . ZRV	Puttgarden . . . . Germany.. QUA
Portoroz/Secovlje . . . . . Slovenia . . POW	Providencia . . . . Colombia . PVA	Putumayo . . . . .Ecuador.. PYO
Portoviejo . . . . Ecuador . . PVO	Providenciales/Int'l	Putussibau . . . . Indonesia.. PSU
Portsmouth . . . . .UK . . PME	. . . . Turks & Caicos Is . . PLS	Pweto . . . . Congo, DR. . PWO
Portsmouth, OH . . . . .USA . . PMH	Provincetown, MA . . . . . . USA . . PVC	Pyongyang/Sunan. . . . N. Korea.. FNJ
Porvenir. . . . . .Chile . .WPR	Provins . . . . France . . XPS	Pyrgos/Andravida . . . . . Greece...PYR
Porvoo . . . . Finland . . QXJ	Provo, UT. . . . . USA . .PVU	
Posadas. . . . . Argentina . . PSS	Prudhoe Bay, AK . . . . USA . . PUO	
Poseberth . . . . Australia . . RSB	Pskov . . . . Russia . .PKV	
Poso/Kasiguncu . . . . . Indonesia . .PSJ	Ptura . . . . Peru . . PIU	
Postville, NF . . . . .Canada . . YSO	Puas . . . . . . Papua New Guinea . PUA	
Poteau/Robert S Kerr, OK . . .USA . . RKR	Pucallpa/Capitan Rolden . . Peru . . PCL	**Q**
Potenza . . . . .Italy . QPO	Puchon City . . . . S. Korea . QJP	
Potosi . . . . Bolivia . .POI	Pucon . . . . .Chile . ZPC	
Potsdam . . . . Germany . . XXP	Puebla/Huejotsingo . . . . . Mexico . .PBC	Qaanaaq . . . . .Greenland.. NAQ
Pottstown, PA. . . . . .USA . . PTW	Pueblo, CO . . . . USA . .PUB	Qaisumah. . . . . Saudi Arabia. . . AQI
		Qala Nau . . . . .Afghanistan.. LQN
		Qaqortoq/HP . . . . . . .Greenland.. .JJU

A I R P O R T S

Qasigiannguit	Greenland	JCH
Qassiarsulk	Greenland	QFT
Qatif	Saudi Arabia	QTF
Qeqertarsuatsiaat	Greenland	QEY
Qikiqtarjuaq, NU	Canada	YVM
Qingyang	China	IQN
Qinhuangdao	China	SHP
Qiqihar	China	NDG
Quad-City, IL	USA	MLI
Quakertown/Upper Bucks, PA		
	USA	UKT
Qualicurn, BC	Canada	XQU
Quanduc/Nhon Co	Vietnam	HOO
Quang Ngai	Vietnam	XNG
Quantico/NAS, VA	USA	NYG
Quaqtaq, QC	Canada	YQC
Quebec, QC	Canada	YQB
Quebec/Charny, QC	Canada	XFZ
Quebec/Levis Rail Svc, QC		
	Canada	XLK
Quebec/Quebec Stn Rail Svc,		
QC		Can
	Canada	XFY
Queen Charlotte Is, BC	Canada	ZQS
Queen, AK	USA	UQE
Queenstown	Australia	UEE
Queenstown	S. Africa	UTW
Queenstown/Frankton		
	New Zealand	ZQN
Quelimane	Mozambique	UEL
Quepos	Costa Rica	XQP
Queretaro	Myanmar	QRO
Quetta	Pakistan	UET
Quetzaltenanac	Guatemala	AAZ
Qui Nhon	Vietnam	UIH
Quibdo	Colombia	UIB
Quiche/Quiche Arpt	Guatemala	AQB
Quillayute, WA	USA	UIL
Quilpie	Australia	ULP
Quimper/Pluguffan	France	UIP
Quincemil	Peru	UMI
Quincy, IL	USA	UIN
Quincy, MA	USA	MQI
Quine Hill	Vanuatu	UIQ
Quinhagak/Kwinhagak, AK	USA	KWN
Quirincli	Australia	UIR
Quito/Mariscal Sucr	Ecuador	UIO
Quixada	Brazil	QIX
Qullissat	Greenland	QUE
Qum	Iran	QUM
Quonset Point/NAS, RI	USA	NCO

R

Rabaraba	Papua New Guinea	RBP
Rabat/Sale	Morocco	RBA
Rabaui/Tokua		
	Papua New Guinea	RAB
Rabi	Fiji	RBI
Rach Gia	Vietnam	VKG
Racine, WI	USA	RAC
Radom	Poland	QXR
Raduzhnyi	Russia	RAT
Rae Lakes, NT	Canada	YRA
Rafai	Central African Rep	RFA
Rafha	Saudi Arabia	RAH
Rafsanian	Iran	RJN
Raglan	New Zealand	RAG
Ragusa	Italy	QRG
Raha/Sugimanuru	Indonesia	RAQ
Rahim Yar Khan	Pakistan	RYK
Raiatea	F. Polynesia	RFP
Raikot/Civil	India	RAJ
Rail (Generic), QC	Canada	XZR
Rainbow Lake, AB	Canada	YOP
Raipur	India	RPR
Raishahi	Bangladesh	RJH
Rajahmundry	India	RJA

Rajbiraj	Nepal	RJB
Rajouri	India	RJI
Rakanda	Papua New Guinea	RAA
Raleigh-Durham Int'l, NC	USA	RDU
Ramadan	Ecuador	TFR
Ramagundarn	India	RMD
Ramallah	West Bank	ZDM
Ramata	Solomon Is	RBV
Rambouillet	France	XRT
Ramechhap	Nepal	RHP
Ramingining	Australia	RAM
Rampart, AK	USA	RMP
Ramsar	Iran	RZR
Ramsgate/RR	UK	QQR
Ramstein	Germany	RMS
Ranau	Malaysia	RNU
Rancagua	Chile	QRC
Ranchi	India	IXR
Rancho, CA	USA	RBK
Randers/RR Stn.	Denmark	ZIR
Randolph/AFB, TX	USA	RND
Rangely, CO	USA	RNG
Ranger, TX	USA	RGR
Rangiroa	F. Polynesia	RGI
Rangpur	Bangladesh	RAU
Rankin Inlet, NT	Canada	YRT
Ranong	Thailand	UNN
Ransiki	Indonesia	RSK
Rapid City, SD	USA	RAP
Rapperswil	Switzerland	ZJW
Rarotonga	Cook Is	RAR
Ras Al Khaimah Int'l	UAE	RKT
Rasht	Iran	RAS
Raspberry Strait, AK	USA	RSP
Rastatt/Bus Svc	Germany	ZRW
Ratanakiri	Cambodia	RBE
Ratinagiri	India	RTC
Ratingen	Germany	ZPJ
Raton, NM	USA	RTN
Raudha	Yemen	RXA
Raufarhofn	Iceland	RFN
Rauma	Finland	QZU
Ravenna/La Spreta	Italy	RAN
Ravensburg	Germany	QRB
Ravensburg	Germany	ZPK
Rawala Kot	Pakistan	RAZ
Rawalpindi	Pakistan	RWP
Rawlins, WY	USA	RWL
Reaci	F. Polynesia	REA
Reading	UK	XRE
Reading, PA	USA	RDG
Rebun	Japan	RBJ
Rechlin	Germany	REB
Recife/Guararapes Int'l	Brazil	REC
Recklinghausen	Germany	ZPL
Reconquista	Argentina	RCQ
Red Bluff, CA	USA	RBL
Red Deer, AB	Canada	YQF
Red Devil, AK	USA	RDV
Red Dog, AK	USA	RDB
Red Lake, ON	Canada	YRL
Red Lodge, MT	USA	RED
Red Oak, IA	USA	RDK
Red Sucker Lake, MB	Canada	YRS
Redcliffe	Vanuatu	RCL
Redding, CA	USA	RDD
Redencao	Brazil	RDC
Redhill	UK	KRH
Redmond, OR	USA	RDM
Redon	France	XRN
Redwood Falls, MN	USA	RWF
Reed City, MI	USA	RCT
Reese/AFB, TX	USA	REE
Refugio/O'Connor Oilfield, TX		
	USA	VDU
Refugio/Rooke Fld, TX	USA	RFG
Regensburg/RR Stn.	Germany	ZPM
Reggio Calabria/Tito Menniti		
	Italy	REG
Reggio Nell Emilia/Bus Svc	Italy	ZRO
Regina	F. Guiana	REI

Regina, SK	Canada	YQR
Rehoboth Beach, DE	USA	REH
Reims	France	RHE
Reivilo	S. Africa	RVO
Relizane	Algeria	QZN
Remscheid/Offline Pt	Germany	ZPN
Rengat/Japura	Jamaica	RGT
Renmark	Australia	RMK
Rennell	Solomon Is	RNL
Rennes/Gare de Rennes	France	ZFJ
Rennes/St Jacques	France	RNS
Reno Int'l, NV	USA	RNO
Reno Nexrad, NV	USA	RGX
Rensselaer, IN	USA	RNZ
Renton, WA	USA	RNT
Repulse Bay, NU	Canada	YUT
Resende	Brazil	QRZ
Resende	Brazil	REZ
Reserved/Network Service Code-		QSP
Resistencia	Argentina	RES
Resita	Romania	QRS
Resolute, NT	Canada	YRB
Resolution Is, NU	Canada	YRE
RetalInuleu/Base Aerea Del Sur		
	Guatemala	RER
Rethymno	Greece	ZRE
Reus	Spain	REU
Reutlingen	Germany	ZPP
Revelstoke, BC	Canada	YRV
Rewa	India	REW
Reyes	Bolivia	REY
Reykholar	Iceland	RHA
Reykjavik Domestic	Iceland	RKV
Reykjavik Int'l	Iceland	KEF
Reynosa/Gen Lucio Blanco		
	Mexico	REX
Rheindahlen	Germany	GMY
Rheine/Bentlage	Germany	ZPQ
Rhinelander, WI	USA	RHI
Rhodes/Diagoras/Paradisi		
	Greece	RHO
Ribeirao Preto/Leite Lopes		
	Brazil	RAO
Ribera Grande	Portugal	QEG
Riberalta/Gen Buech	Bolivia	RIB
Rice Lake, WI	USA	RIE
Richard Toll	Senegal	RDT
Richards Bay	S. Africa	RCB
Richfield/Reynolds, UT	USA	RIF
Richland, WA	USA	RLD
Richmond	Australia	RCM
Richmond Int'l, VA	USA	RIC
Richmond, IN	USA	RID
Richmond/Richmond VA Rail, VA		
	USA	ZRD
Rickenbacker, OH	USA	LCK
Riesa/RR Stn.	Germany	ZRX
Rieti	Italy	QRT
Rifle, CO	USA	RIL
Riga/Int'l	Latvia	RIX
Rigolet, NF	Canada	YRG
Riihimäki	Finland	QVT
Rijelka	Croatia	RJK
Rimini/Miramare	Italy	RMI
Rimouski, QC	Canada	YXK
Rincon de los Sauces		
	Argentina	RDS
Ringi Cove	Solomon Is	RIN
Rio Aizucar	Panama	RIZ
Rio Branco/Pres. Medici	Brazil	RBR
Rio Claro	Brazil	QIQ
Rio Cuarto	Argentina	RCU
Rio De Janeiro Int'l	Brazil	GIG
Rio De Janeiro/S. Dumont	Brazil	SDU
Rio Do Sul	Brazil	QRU
Rio Dulce/Las Vegas		
	Guatemala	LCF
Rio Frio	Costa Rica	RFR
Rio Gallegos Int'l	Argentina	RGL
Rio Grande	Argentina	RGA
Rio Grande	Brazil	RIG

Rio Hondo	Argentina	RHD
Rio Mayo	Argentina	ROY
Rio Negrinho	Brazil	QNE
Rio Sidra	Panama	RSI
Rio Tigre	Panama	RIT
Rio Turbio	Argentina	RYO
Rio Verde	Brazil	RVD
Riohacha	Colombia	RCH
Rioja	Peru	RIJ
Riom	France	XRI
Rishin	Japan	RIS
Rivera	Uruguay	RVY
Rivercess	Liberia	RVC
Rivers Inlet, BC	Canada	YRN
Rivers, MB	Canada	YYI
Riverside / HP, CA	USA	JRD
Riverside, CA	USA	RAL
Riverside, CA	USA	RIR
Riverton, WY	USA	RIW
Riviere Au Tonnerre, QC		
	Canada	YTN
Riviere Du Loup, QC	Canada	YRI
Riviere-a-Pierre/RR Stn., QC		
	Canada	XRP
Riyadh/King Khaled Int'l		
	Saudi Arabia	RUH
Riyan Mulkalla	Yemen	RIY
Rize	East Timor	QRI
Roanne/Renaison	France	RNE
Roanoke Nexrad, VA	USA	FCX
Roanoke Rapids, NC	USA	RZZ
Roanoke, VA	USA	ROA
Roatan	Honduras	RTB
Roberlson	S. Africa	ROD
Roberval, QC	Canada	YRJ
Robinhood	Australia	ROH
Robins/AFB, GA	USA	WRB
Robinson River		
	Papua New Guinea	RNR
Robinson River	Australia	RRV
Robinvale	Australia	RBC
Robore	Bolivia	RBO
Roche Harbor, WA	USA	RCE
Rochefort/Saint Agnant	France	RCO
Rochester	UK	RCS
Rochester/Int'l, NY	USA	ROC
Rochester, IN	USA	RCR
Rochester, MN	USA	RST
Rochester/Municipal HP, MN		
	USA	JRC
Rochester/Rochester NY Rail		
	USA	ZTE
Rock Hill, SC	USA	RKH
Rock Sound/S Eleuthera		
	Bahamas	RSD
Rock Springs, WY	USA	RKS
Rockdale/Coffield, TX	USA	RCK
Rockford, IL	USA	RFD
Rockford/Machesney, IL	USA	RMC
Rockford/Park & Ride Bus Svc.,		
IL	USA	ZRF
Rockford/Van Galder Bus Terminal,		
IL	USA	ZRK
Rockhampton	Australia	ROK
Rockhampton Downs	Australia	RDA
Rockland, ME	USA	RKD
Rockport, TX	USA	RKP
Rockwood/Municipal, TN	USA	RKW
Rocky Mount, NC	USA	RWI
Rocky Mountain House, AB		
	Canada	YRM
Rodez/Marcillac	France	RDZ
Rodriguesis	Mauritius	RRG
Rodriguez De Men	Peru	RIM
Roebourne	Australia	RBU
Roeddey	Norway	ZXI
Roervik	Norway	ZXF
Rogers, AR	USA	ROG
Rognan	Norway	ZXM
Roi Et Arpt	Thailand	ROI
Roissy-en-France	France	QZV

Rokeby	Australia	RKY
Rokot	Indonesia	RKI
Rolandia	Brazil	QHC
Rolla/National, MO	USA	RLA
Rolpa	Nepal	RPA
Roma	Australia	RMA
Roma/Falcon State, TX	USA	FAL
Rome, GA	USA	RMG
Rome, OR	USA	REO
Rome/Roma/Ciampino	Italy	CIA
Rome/Roma/Fiumicino	Italy	FCO
Rondon	Colombia	RON
Rondonopolis	Brazil	ROO
Rongelap Is	Marshall Is	RNP
Ronneby/Kallinge	Sweden	RNB
Roosendaal/RR Stn.Netherlands		ZYO
Roosevelt, UT	USA	ROL
Roosevelt/NAS	Puerto Rico	NRR
Roper Bar	Australia	RPB
Roper Valley	Australia	RPV
Rorschach	Switzerland	ZJZ
Rosario/Fisherton	Argentina	ROS
Rosario/SPB, AK	USA	RSJ
Roseau/Municipal, MN	USA	ROX
Roseburg, OR	USA	RBG
Roseires, SD	USA	RSS
Rosella Plains	Australia	RLP
Rosenheim	Germany	ZPR
Rosh Pina	Israel	RPN
Rosita	Netherlands	RFS
Ross River, YT	Canada	XRR
Rost/Stollport	Norway	RET
Rostock-Laage/Laane Germany		RLG
Rostov	Russia	ROV
Roswell, NM	USA	ROW
Rota	Northern Mariana Is	ROP
Rothenburg/Off-line Pt Germany		QTK
Rothesay/HP	UK	RAY
Roti	Indonesia	RTI
Rotorua	New Zealand	ROT
Rotterdam/Central Stn		
	Netherlands	QRH
Rotterdam/Zestienhoven		
	Netherlands	RTM
Rottnest Is	Australia	RTS
Rotuma Is	Fiji	RTA
Rotunda, FL	USA	RTD
Roubaix	France	XRX
Rouen/Boos	France	URO
Round Lake, ON	Canada	ZRJ
Roundup, MT	USA	RPX
Rourkela	India	RRK
Rouses Point, NY	USA	RSX
Rousse	Bulgaria	ROU
Rouyn, QC	Canada	YUY
Rovaniemi	Finland	RVN
Rovirio	Ukraine	RWN
Rowan Bay, AK	USA	RWB
Roxas City	Philippines	RXS
Roy Hill	Australia	RHL
Royan/Medis	France	RYN
Rubelsanto	Guatemala	RUV
Ruby, AK	USA	RBY
Ruedesheim/Off-line PtGermany		QSY
Ruesselsheim	Germany	ZPS
Rugao	China	RUG
Rugby/RR Stn.	UK	XRU
Rugeley T.V./RR Stn.	UK	XRG
Ruhengeri	Rwanda	RHG
Ruidoso/Municipal, NM	USA	RUI
Rukumkot	Nepal	RUK
Rum Cay	Bahamas	RCY
Rumjatar	Nepal	RUM
Runcom/RR Stn.	UK	XRC
Rundu	Namibia	NDU
Rupsi	India	RUP
Rurrenabaque	Bolivia	RBQ
Rurriginae	Papua New Guinea	RMN
Rurutu	F. Polynesia	RUR
Russell, KS	USA	RSL
Russellville/Municipal, AR	USA	RUE

Russian/SPB, AK	USA	RSH
Ruston, LA	USA	RSN
Ruteng	Indonesia	RTG
Ruti	Papua New Guinea	RUU
Rutland Plains	Australia	RTP
Rutland, VT	USA	RUT
Ryazan	Russia	RZN
Rybirisk	Russia	RYB
Ryotsu Sado Is	Japan	SDO
Rzeszow/Jasionka	Poland	RZE

S

S.Cristobal del- Casas/San		
Cristobal Arpt	Mexico	SZT
Saa Sebastiao Do Cai	Brazil	QHF
Saarbruecken/EnsheimGermany		SCN
Saarbruecken/HBF RR		
	Germany	QFZ
Saarloq	Greenland	QOQ
Saarlouis	Germany	ZPT
Saarmelleek/Srmhk/BtnHungary		SOB
Saas Fee	Switzerland	ZKI
Saba Is	Netherlands Antilles	SAB
Sabadell	Spain	QSA
Sabah	Papua New Guinea	SBV
Sabana De Mar	Dominican Rep	SNX
Sabana De Torres	Colombia	SNT
Sabang/Cut Bau	Indonesia	SBG
Sabi Sabi	S. Africa	GSS
Sabiha Gokcen	Turkey	SAW
Sabine Pass, TX	USA	RPE
Sable Is, NS	Canada	YSA
Sabre-Tech, FL	USA	ZFS
Sac Bernardo Do CampoBrazil		QSB
Sac Borja	Brazil	QOJ
Sac Carlos	Brazil	QSC
Sac Goncad	Brazil	QSD
Sac Goncalo Amarante	Brazil	QTE
Sac Lourenco	Brazil	SSO
Sachigo Lake, ON	Canada	ZPB
Sachs Harbour, NT	Canada	YSY
Sackville/RR Stn., NB	Canada	XKV
Sacramento Exec, CA	USA	SAC
Sacramento, CA	USA	SMF
Sadah	Yemen	SYE
Sado Shima	Japan	SDS
Saelby	Denmark	QJS
Saenz Pena	Argentina	SZQ
Safford, AZ	USA	SAD
Safi	Morocco	SFI
Safia	Papua New Guinea	SFU
Saga	Japan	HSG
Sagarai	Papua New Guinea	SGJ
Saginaw Bay, AK	USA	SGW
Saglek, NF.	Canada	YSV
Sagwon, AK	USA	SAG
Sahabat 16	Malaysia	SXS
Sahiwal	Pakistan	SWN
Saibai Is	Australia	SBR
Saida	Algeria	QDZ
Saidor	Papua New Guinea	SDI
Saidpur	Bangladesh	SPD
Saidu Sharif	Pakistan	SDT
Saint Cloud/HP, MN	USA	JSK
Saint George/Municipal, UTUSA		SGU
Saint Hyacinthe/RR Stn., QC		
	Canada	XIM
Saint John, NB	Canada	YSJ
Saint Marys, AK	USA	KSM
Saint Tropez / HP	France	JSZ
Saint Tropez/La Mole	France	LTT
Saint Yan/Charolais Bourgogne S		
	France	SYT
Saint-Tropez/Harbour	France	XPZ
Sainte Marie	Madagascar	SMS
Saintes	France	XST

A I R P O R T S

Saipan/Int'l . .Northern Mariana Is . . SPN	San Domino Is . . . . Italy . .TQR	San Tome/El Tigre . . . Venezuela. . SOM
Saito . . . . Uruguay . .STY	San Esteban . . . . .Honduras . . SET	San Vicente . . . . .Colombia. . . SVI
Sakon Nakhon . . . . Thailand . .SNO	San Felipe . . . . Mexico . .SFH	San Vito. . . . . Costa Rica. . TOO
Sal/Amilcar Cabrai Int'l	San Felipe . . . . . . Venezuela . SNF	Sana'a/Sana'a Int'l . . . . . Yemen. . SAH
. . . . Cape Verde Is . . SID	San Felipe . . . . Colombia . SSD	Sanana . . . . Indonesia. . SQN
Salamanca/Matacan . . . . .Spain . .SLM	San Felix . . . . Venezuela . SFX	Sanandaj . . . . .Iran. SDG
Salamo . . . . .Papua New Guinea . . SAM	San Fernando . . . . . .Philippines . . SFE	Sancti Spiritus . . . . Cuba. .USS
Salatah . . . . Oman . .SLL	San Fernando De Apure	Sand Point/Municipal, AK . USA. . .SDP
Saldanha Bay . . . . S. Africa . . SDB	. . . . Venezuela . .SFD	Sandakan . . . . Malaysia. . SDK
Sale . . . . Australia . . SXE	San Fernando, CA. . . . . . USA . SFR	Sandane/Anda . . . . Norway. . SDN
Salehard . . . . Russia . .SLY	San Francisco/Int'l, CA . . USA . .SFO	Sanday . . . . UK. . NDY
Salem . . . . India . . SXV		Sandcreek . . . . Guyana. . SDC
Salem, OR . . . . .USA . .SLE	San Francisco/China Basin HP,	Sandnessjoen/Stokka . Norway. . . SSJ
Salem-Leckrone, IL . . . . .USA . .SLO	CA . . . . USA . .JCC	Sandringham . . . . .Australia. . SRM
Salerno . . . . Italy . .QSR	San Francisco/Embarcadero,	Sandspit, BC . . . . Canada. . .YZP
Salida, CO . . . . .USA . .SLT	CA . . . . USA . EMB	Sandstone . . . . .Australia. . NDS
Salima . . . . Malawi . . LMB	San Ignacio . . . . Mexico . SGM	Sandusky/G. Sandusky, OH
Salina Cruz . . . . Mexico . . SCX	San Ignacio De M . . . . .Bolivia . SNM	. . . . USA . .SKY
Salina, KS . . . . .USA . .SLN	San Ignacio De Velasco Bolivia . SNG	Sandwip . . . . Bangladesh. . SDW
Salina, UT . . . . .USA . .SBO	San Ignacio/Matthew Spain	Sandy Lake, ON . . . . . . .Canada. . . ZSJ
Salinas . . . . Ecuador . . SNC	. . . . Belize . .SQS	Sanfebagar . . . . .Nepal. . .FEB
Salinas, CA . . . . .USA . . SNS	San Javier . . . . .Bolivia . SJV	Sanford, FL . . . . USA. . .SFB
Salisbury, MD . . . . .USA . . SBY	San Joacluin . . . . .Bolivia . SJB	Sanford, ME . . . . USA. . SFM
Salisbury/RR Stn. . . . . .UK . . XSR	San Jose . . . . .Bolivia . SJS	Sangapi. . . . Papua New Guinea. . SGK
Salisbury/Rowan County, NC	San Jose Cabo/Los Cabos	Sanggata . . . . Indonesia. . SGQ
. . . . .USA . .SRW	. . . . Mexico . SJD	Sangir . . . . Indonesia. . SAE
Sallanches . . . . .France . .XSN	San Jose Del Gua . . . Colombia . SJE	Sangley Point/NAF. .Philippines. . .NSP
Salluit, QC . . . . .Canada . .YZG	San Jose/Int'l, CA . . . . . USA . SJC	Sanikiluaq, NU . . . . . .Canada. . .YSK
Salmon Arm, BC . . . . . .Canada . .YSN	San Jose, CA . . . . USA . RHV	Sanliurfa . . . . .Turkey. . SFQ
Salmon, AK . . . . .USA . .SMN	San Jose/Bus Svc, CA . . . . USA . ZJO	Sanoy River, AK . . . . .USA. . .KSR
Salo. . . . . Finland . . QVD	San Jose/Juan Santamaria Int'l	Sans Souci, ON . . . . . .Canada. . . YSI
Salt Cay . . . . Tonga . .SLX	. . . . Costa Rica . SJO	Santa Ana . . . . Solomon Is.. NNB
Salt Lake City/Int'l, UT . . .USA . .SLC	San Jose/Meguire Fld	Santa Ana . . . . .Colombia. . SQB
Salta/Gen Belgrano. . . Argentina . . SLA	. . . . .Philippines . . . SJI	Santa Ana, CA . . . . .USA. . SNA
Saltillo . . . . Mexico . .SLW	San Jose/Tobias Bolanos Intl	Santa Ana/Centerport HP, CA
Salton City, CA. . . . . .USA . . SAS	. . . . Costa Rica . .SYQ	. . . . USA. . JOC
Salvador/Arpt Luis R. Magalhaes	San Juan . . . . Peru . SJA	Santa Aria/Yacuma . . . . . .Bolivia. . .SBL
. . . . Brazil . . SSA	San Juan . . . . . .Dominican Rep . SJM	Santa Barbara Ba. . . Venezuela. . SBB
Salzburg . . . . Austria . . SZG	San Juan . . . . Argentina . UAQ	Santa Barbara Ed/L Dlcias
Salzburg/German Railway Svc	San Juan Aposento . . . . . Peru . APE	. . . . Venezuela. . .STB
. . . . Austria . . ZSB	San Juan D Ur . . . . . . Colombia . SJR	Santa Barbara, CA . . . . . . .USA. . .SBA
Salzgitter. . . . . Germany . . ZPU	San Juan/Int'l, PR . . . . . USA . SJU	Santa Barbara, CA . . . . . . .USA. . .SZN
Salzwedel/RR Stn. . . . Germany . .ZSQ	San Juan/Isla GrandePuerto Rico. . SIG	Santa Carolina . . .Mozambique. . NTC
Sam Neua . . . . Laos . . NEU	San Juan/SPB, AK . . . . . USA . WSJ	Santa Catalina . . . . .Colombia. . SCA
Samara . . . . Russia . . KUF	San Julian . . . . Cuba . SNJ	Santa Cecilia . . . . .Ecuador. . WSE
Samarai Is/China Straits Airstrip .	San Julian . . . . Argentina . ULA	Santa Clara . . . . Cuba. . SNU
. . . . Papua New Guinea . . SQT	San Luis . . . . Argentina . LUQ	Santa Clara/Bus Svc, CA . .USA. . ZSM
Samarinda/Temindung	San Luis De Pale . . . . Colombia . SQE	Santa Cruiz De La PalmaSpain . .SPC
. . . . Indonesia . . . SRI	San Luis Obispo, CA . . . . USA . SBP	Santa Cruz . . . . .Argentina. . .RZA
Samarkand . . . . Uzbekistan . . SKD	San Luis Obispo/AAF, CA . USA . CSL	Santa Cruz . . . . Solomon Is.. SCZ
Sambava . . . . .Madagascar . . SVB	San Luis Rio Colorado Mexico . UAC	Santa Cruz . . . . Brazil. . SNZ
Sambu . . . . Panama . . SAX	San Lus Potosi . . . . . . Mexico . SLP	Santa Cruz . . . . Belize. . STU
Samchok . . . . S. Korea . . SUK	San Marcos . . . . Colombia . SRS	Santa Cruz Do Sul. . . . . . Brazil. . CSU
Samos . . . . Greece . . SMI	San Marino . . . . . . San Marino . . SAI	Santa Cruz Rio Pardo . . Brazil. . QNR
Sampit . . . . Indonesia . .SMQ	San Martin Del-os Andes	Santa Cruz/El Trompillo. . Bolivia. . .SRZ
Samsun . . . . Turkey . . SSX	. . . . Argentina . .CPC	Santa Cruz/Guanacaste
Samsun/Carsamba . . . . . Turkey . .SZF	San Matias . . . . .Bolivia . MQK	. . . . Costa Rica. . .SZC
San Andres Is . . . . . . Colombia . . ADZ	San Miguei/Roberts/AAF, CA	Santa Cruz/Skypark, CA . . .USA. . SRU
San Andros . . . . Bahamas . . SAQ	. . . . USA . SYL	Santa Cruz/Viru Viru Int'l . Bolivia. . VVI
San Angelo, TX . . . . .USA . . SJT	San Miguel . . . . Panama . NMG	Santa Eiena . . . . Venezuela. . .SNV
San Antonio . . . . . . .Venezuela . . SVZ	San Nicolas Ban . . . . . . Cuba . QSN	Santa Fe . . . . Argentina. . .SFN
San Antonio/Int'l, TX . . . . .USA . . .SAT	San Pabio . . . . Spain . SPO	Santa Fe . . . . Panama. . SFW
San Antonio Nexrad, TX . .USA . . EWX	San Pedro . . . . Belize . SPR	Santa Fe Do Sul . . . . Brazil. . SFV
San Antonio Oeste . Argentina . . OES	San Pedro . . . . Côte D'Ivoire . SPY	Santa Fe, NM . . . . .USA. . SAF
San Antonio, TX . . . . .USA . . .SSF	San Pedro . . . . Argentina . XPD	Santa Fe/Bus Stn, NM . . . .USA. . ZSH
San Antonjo . . . . Chile . .QTN	San Pedro de Alcantara	Santa Isabel do Morro . . Brazil. . IDO
San Bernardino/Tri-City, CAUSA . . SBT	/Bus Stn . . . . Spain . .ZRC	Santa Katarina/Mount SinaiEgypt . SKV
San Bias . . . . Panama . . NBL	San Pedro Jagua . . . . Colombia . SJG	Santa Maria . . . . .Colombia. . SMC
San Borja/Capitan G Q Guardia	San Pedro Sula/RMorales	Santa Maria . . . . Peru. . SMG
. . . . Bolivia . .SRJ	. . . . .Honduras . . SAP	Santa Maria, CA . . . . .USA. . SMX
San Carlos . . . . Netherlands . . NCR	San Pedro Uraba . . . . Colombia . .NPU	Santa Maria/Base Aerea . Brazil. . RIA
San Carlos DeBariloche/Int'l	San Pedro/Catalina SPB, CA	Santa Maria/Vila Do Porto
. . . . Argentina . . BRC	. . . . USA . .SPQ	. . . . Portugal. . SMA
San Carlos . . . . .USA . . SQL	San Quintin. . . . . Mexico . SNQ	Santa Marta/S. Bolivar Colombia. . SMR
San Clemente/NAF, CA . .USA . .NUC	San Rafael . . . . Argentina . AFA	Santa Monica, CA . . . . . . .USA. . SMO
San Cristobal . . . . . .Venezuela . . SCI	San Rafael HP, CA . . . . . USA . JSG	Santa Paula, CA . . . . .USA. . SZP
San Cristobal/Arpt . . Ecuador . . SCY	San Ramon . . . . Bolivia . SRD	Santa Rosa . . . . .Argentina. . .RSA
San Diego/Int'l, CA . . . . . .USA . . SAN	San Salvador . . . . . .El Salvador . SAL	Santa Rosa . . . . Brazil. . SRA
San Diego, CA . . . . .USA . . MYF	San Salvador . . . . . . Bahamas . ZSA	Santa Rosa . . . . Bolivia. . SRB
San Diego-Gillespie, CA. .USA . . SEE	San Salvador De . . . Venezuela . SVV	Santa Rosa Copan . Honduras. . SDH
San Diego/Brown Fld, CA . .USA . .SDM	San Sebastian . . . . Spain . . EAS	

A I R P O R T S

Santa Rosa, CA . . . . .USA . . .STS	Sargodha/Bhagatanwala	Seattle, WA . . . . USA. . .SEA
Santa Rosalia . . . . Mexico . . SRL	. . . . Pakistan . BHW	Sebba . . . . .Burkina Faso. . . XSE
Santa Rosalia . . . . . . Colombia . . SSL	Sargodha/Sargodha Arpt	Sebha . . . . Libya. . .SEB
Santa Sanga. . . . . . Philippines . . SGS	. . . . Pakistan . . SGI	Secheit, BC. . . . . Canada. . .YHS
Santa Teresa, NM . . . . . . .USA . . EPZ	Sarh. . . . . Chad . .SRH	Seclin. . . . . France. . . XSX
Santa Teresita . . . . . Argentina . . SST	Sarichef, AK. . . . . USA . .WSF	Secunda . . . . S. Africa. . .ZEC
Santa Terezinha/Confresa	Sarlat/Domme . . . . France . . XSL	Sedalia, MO . . . . USA. .DMO
. . . . Brazil . .STZ	Sarmi. . . . . Indonesia . ZRM	Sedan . . . . France. . XSW
Santa Vitoria/Do Palmar . . Brazil . .CTQ	Sarnburu . . . . .Kenya . UAS	Sedom/Min'hat Hashnayim Israel. . .SED
Santa Ynez, CA . . . . .USA . . SQA	Sarnen . . . . Switzerland . . ZKC	Sedona, AZ. . . . . USA. . .SDX
Santana Do Araguaia . . . . Brazil . .CMP	Sarnia, ON . . . . Canada . .YZR	Sedrata . . . . Algeria. . QDT
Santana Ramos . . . . Colombia . . SRO	Sarnia/RR Stn., ON . . . . . Canada . .XDX	Seeheim . . . . Germany. . QSH
Santander. . . . . .Spain . . SDR	Sartaneja . . . . Belize . . SJX	Sege. . . . . Sweden. . EGM
Santarem/Eduardo Gomes	Sary/Dashte Naz . . . . Iran . . SRY	Segou . . . . Mali. .SZU
. . . . Brazil . . STM	Saskatoon, SK . . . . Canada . . YXE	Seguela . . . . Côte D'Ivoire. . SEO
Santiago . . . . Panama . . SYP	Sassan . . . . Italy . .QSS	Sehonghong . . . . Lesotho. . SHK
Santiago . . . . Chile . .ULC	Sassandra . . . . . . Côte D'Ivoire . . ZSS	Sehuiea . . . . . Papua New Guinea. . SXH
Santiago . . . . Brazil . .XGO	Sassnitz/RR Stn. . . . . . . Germany . . ZSI	Sehwen Sharif . . . . .Pakistan. . SYW
Santiago De Compostela	Sasstown. . . . . Liberia . .SAZ	Seinäjoki/Ilmajoki . . . . . . .Finland. . . SJY
. . . . .Spain . .SCQ	Satna . . . . India . .TNI	Seiyun . . . . Yemen.. GXF
Santiago Del Estero. . Argentina . . SDE	Sato Bento Do Sul . . . . .Brazil . QHE	Sekakes . . . . Lesotho. . SKQ
Santiago/Antonio Maceo . .Cuba . . SCU	Satu Mare . . . . .Romania . . SUJ	Selawilk, AK. . . . . USA. . WLK
Santiago/Arturo M. Benitez	Satwag . . . . . Papua New Guinea . SWG	Selbang . . . . . Papua New Guinea. . SBC
. . . . Chile . . SCL	Saudarkrokur/Comalapa Int'l	Seldovia, AK. . . . . USA. . SOV
Santiago/Mun . . Dominican Rep . . STI	. . . . .Iceland . . SAK	Selebi-Phikwe. . . . . . Botswana. . PKW
Santo Andre . . . . .Brazil . . QSE	Saufley/NAS, FL . . . . .USA . . NUN	Selestat . . . . France. . XSQ
Santo Angelo/Sepe TiarajuBrazil. . GEL	Saul . . . . F. Guiana . . XAU	Selibaby . . . . Mauritania. . SEY
Santo Antao . . . . Cape Verde Is . .NTO	Sault Ste Marie, MI . . . . . USA . . CIU	Selinsgrove, PA. . . . . USA. . SEG
Santo Domingo Dominican Rep . .SDQ	Sault Ste Marie, ON . . . Canada . .YAM	Selje/Harbour . . . . Norway. . QFK
Santo Domingo . . . . . .Venezuela . . STD	Sault Ste Marie/Kincheloe/AFB,	Selma/Selfield, AL . . . . . . USA. . SES
Santo Domingo/Herrera	MI . . . . USA. . INR	Semarang/Achmad Uani
. . . . Dominican Rep . . HEX	Saumlaki . . . . Indonesia . SXK	. . . . Indonesia. . SRG
Santos . . . . Brazil . .SSZ	Saumur . . . . France . XSU	Sematan . . . . Malaysia. .BSE
Sanya . . . . .China . . SYX	Sauren . . . . Papua New Guinea . SXW	Sembach . . . . Germany. .SEX
Sao Caetano Do Sul . . Brazil . .QCX	Saurimo . . . . Angola . .VHC	Semera/Semera Arpt . . . Ethiopia. . SZE
Sao Fefix Do Xingu . . . Brazil . .SXX	Sausalito/HP, CA . . . . . . .USA . .JMC	Semipalatinsk . . . . . . Kazakstan. . PLX
Sao Felix Do Araguaia . . Brazil . .SXO	Savannah Int'l, GA . . . . . . USA . . SAV	Semongkong. . . . . Lesotho. . SOK
Sao Filipe . . . . . Cape Verde Is . .SFL	Savannakhet . . . . .Laos . .ZVK	Sena Madureira . . . . Brazil. .ZMD
Sao Francisco . . . . Brazil . .QFS	Save . . . . Benin . .SVF	Senanga . . . . Zambia. .SXG
Sao Gabriel/Da Cachoeira	Savi Ragha . . . . Pakistan . .ZEO	Sendai . . . . .Japan. .SDJ
. . . . Brazil . .SJL	Savo. . . . . Solomon Is . SVY	Senggeh . . . . Indonesia. .SEH
Sao Joao Del Rei . . . . . Brazil . .QSJ	Savonlinna . . . . Finland . . SVL	Senggo . . . . Indonesia. .ZEG
Sao Jorge Is . . . . Portugal . .SJZ	Savoonga, AK . . . . USA . . SVA	Senhor Do Bonfirn . . . . . Brazil. . SEI
Sao Jose . . . . Brazil . .XOE	Savusavu . . . . Fiji . .SVU	Senipah . . . . Indonesia. .SZH
Sao Jose Dos Campos . .Brazil . .SJK	Savuti . . . . Botswana . .SVT	Senlis . . . . France. .XSV
Sao Leopoldo . . . . Brazil . .QLL	Sawu . . . . Indonesia . .SAU	Senneterre/RR Stn., QC
Sao Lourenco Do Sul . . . Brazil . .SQY	Sayaboury . . . . .Laos . .ZBY	. . . . Canada. . .XFK
Sao Luiz/Mal. C. Machado	Scammon Bay/SPB, AK . . USA . . SCM	Seno . . . . .Laos. . SND
. . . . Brazil . .SLZ	Scampton/RAF Stn. . . . . . . .UK . . SQZ	Sens. . . . . France. .XSF
Sao Mateus . . . . Brazil . .SBJ	Scenic Flight . . . . .New Zealand . . XXF	Seo De Urgel/Aeroport De La Seu
Sao Miguel Araguaia . . . .Brazil . .SQM	Schaffhausen . . . . . Switzerland . . ZKJ	. . . . Spain. . .LEU
Sao Miguel Do Oeste . . . Brazil . .SQX	Schaumburg/Marriott HP, IL	Seoul/Kimp'O Int'l Arpt. . .S. Korea. . . SEL
Sao Nicolau/Prgca	. . . . USA . . JMH	Seoul/Seoul Air Base . . .S. Korea. . .SSN
. . . . Cape Verde Is . . SNE	Schefferville, QC . . . . . Canada . . YKL	Sepik PlainsPapua New Guinea. . SPV
Sao Paud/Viracopos . . . . Brazil . . VCP	Schenectady, NY . . . . .USA . .SCH	Sept-Iles, QC . . . . Canada. . .YZV
Sao Paulo/Congonhas . . Brazil . .CGH	Schenectady/Schenectady Rail,	Sepulot . . . . Malaysia. . SPE
Sao Paulo/Guarulhos Int'l . Brazil . .GRU	NY. . . . . USA . . ZTD	Sequim/Valley Arpt, WA. . . . USA. . SQV
Sao Tome Is	Schieswig-Jagel . . . . Germany . WBG	Seronera . . . . Tanzania. .SEU
. . . . Sao Tome and Principe . . TMS	Schiphol. . . . . .Netherlands . . SPL	Serra Norte . . . . Brazil. . RRN
Sao Vicente/San Pedro	Schleswig . . . . Germany . .QWI	Serra Pelada . . . . Brazil. . RSG
. . . . Cape Verde Is . . VXE	Schoena/RR Stn. . . . . . . Germany . . ZSC	Serre Chevalier . . . . Eritrea. . SEC
Sap Jose Do Rio Preto . . Brazil . .SJP	Schoenhagen . . . . Germany . QXH	Serrporna . . . . Malaysia. .SMM
Sapmanga . . Papua New Guinea . .SMH	Schwaebisch Gmuend/	Sert . . . . Libya. . SRX
Saposcia . . . . .Peru . . SQU	Off-line Pt . . . . Germany . . ZPV	Serui/Yendosa. . . . . Indonesia. . ZRI
Sapporo/Chitose. . . . . Japan . . CTS	Schwanheide/RR Stn. Germany . . ZSD	Sesheke . . . . Zambia. .SJQ
Sapporo/Okadarna . . . . . Japan . .OKD	Schweinfurt . . . . Germany . ZPW	Seshutes . . . . Lesotho. . SHZ
Saqani . . . . Fiji . .AQS	Schwerin/Parchim ArptGermany . SZW	Sesnem . . . . Namibia. . SZM
Saqqaq. . . . . Greenland . . QUP	Schwerin/RR Stn. . . . . . Germany . . ZSR	Sete . . . . France. . XSY
Sara . . . . .Vanuatu . . SSR	Schwerte . . . . Germany . ZPX	Sete Lagoas . . . . Brazil. .QHG
Saraievo/Butmir	Schwyz. . . . . Switzerland . .ZKK	Setif . . . . Algeria. .QSF
. . . . Bosnia Hercegovina . . SJJ	Scone . . . . Australia . NSO	Sette Cama . . . . Gabon. . ZKM
Sarakhs . . . . Iran . . CKT	Scott/AFB, IL . . . . USA . . BLV	Setubal . . . . Portugal. . XSZ
Saranac Lake, NY . . . . . . .USA . . SLK	Scottsbluff, Heilig Fld, NE . USA . . BFF	Severac Le Chateau/RR Stn.
Saransk . . . . .Russia . . SKX	Scottsdale/Bus Svc, AZ. . . USA . . ZSY	. . . . France. . ZBH
Sarasota, FL . . . . .USA . .SRQ	Scranton, OH . . . . USA . . AVP	Severodoneck. . . . . .Ukraine. . SEV
Saratoga/Shively, WY . . . . .USA . .SAA	Scranton/Municipal, PA . . . USA . .SCR	Sevilla . . . . Spain. . SVQ
Saratov . . . . .Russia . .RTW	Scribner/State, NE . . . . . . USA . .SCB	Sewanee/Franklin County, TN
Saravane . . . . Laos . . VNA	Scusciuban . . . . Somalia . .CMS	. . . . USA. . UOS
Saravena . . . . Colombia . . RVE	Seal Bay, AK . . . . USA . . SYB	Seward, AK. . . . . USA. . SWD
Sardeh Band . . . . . Afghanistan . . SBF	Searcy, AR . . . . USA . .SRC	Seyclisfjordur . . . . .Iceland. . SEJ
Sargans . . . . .Switzerland . . ZKA	Seattle/Boeing Fld, WA. . . . USA . . .BFI	

AIRPORTS

Seymour Johnson/AFB, NC	USA . . GSB
Seymour/Freeman Municipal, IN	USA . . SER
Sfax/Sfax El Maou . . . . . . Tunisia . . SFA	
Shageluk, AK . . . . USA . . SHX	
Shahrkord . . . . Iran . . QHK	
Shakawe . . . . Botswana . . SWX	
Shakiso . . . . Ethiopia . . SKR	
Shaktoolik, AK . . . . USA . . SKK	
Shamattawa, MB . . . . . . Canada . . ZTM	
Shamshernagar . . Bangladesh . . ZHM	
Shanghai/Hongqiao . . . . . . China . . SHA	
Shanghai/Pu Dong . . . . China . . PVG	
Shangri-la, OK . . . . USA . . NRI	
Shanhaiguan . . . . China . . SHF	
Shannon . . . . Ireland . . SNN	
Shannon Arpt, VA . . . . . . USA . . EZF	
Shanshan . . . . China . . SXJ	
Shantou . . . . China . . SWA	
Shanzinou . . . . China . . SZO	
Shaoguan . . . . China . . HSC	
Sharjah Int'l . . . . UAE . . SHJ	
Shark El Oweinat . . . . Egypt . . GSQ	
Sharm El Sheikh/Ophira .Egypt . . SSH	
Shararah . . . . Saudi Arabia . SHW	
Shashi . . . . China . . SHS	
Shatter, CA . . . . USA . . MIT	
Shauliaj . . . . Lithuania . . HLJ	
Shaw River . . . . Australia . SWB	
Shaw/AFB, SC . . . . USA . . SSC	
Shawinigan/RR Stn., QC	Canada . . XFL
Shawnee/Municipal, OK . . .USA . . SNL	
Shawnigan/RR Stn., BC	Canada . . XFM
Shay Gap . . . . Australia . . SGP	
Shearwater, BC . . . . Canada . . YSX	
Shearwater, NS . . . . Canada . . YAW	
Shebeen El Korn . . . . Egypt . . QUH	
Sheboygan, WI . . . . USA . . SBM	
Sheep Mountain, ID . . . . . USA . . SMU	
Sheffield . . . . UK . . SZD	
Sheffield/Bus Svc . . . . UK . . ZFG	
Sheghnan . . . . Afghanistan . . SGA	
Shehdi . . . . Ethiopia . . SQJ	
Shehr . . . . Yemen . . QER	
Shelby, MT . . . . USA . . SBX	
Shelbyville/Bomar Fld, AK .USA . . SYI	
Sheldon Point/Sheldon SPB, AK	USA . . SXP
Shelton, WA . . . . USA . . SHN	
Shemya/Shemya/AFB, AK . .USA . . SYA	
Shenyang . . . . China . . SHE	
Shenzhen . . . . China . . SZX	
Sheppard/AFB, TX . . . . . . USA . . SPS	
Shepparton . . . . Australia . . SHT	
Sherbrooke, QC . . . . . . Canada . . YSC	
Sheridan, WY . . . . USA . . SHR	
Sherman-Denison, TX . . USA . . PNX	
Sherman/AAF, KS . . . . . . .USA . . FLV	
Shetland Is . . . . UK . . LSI	
Shetland Is, Lerwick/Tingwall	UK . . LWK
Shetland Iss/Scatsta . . . . . UK . . SCS	
Shijiazhuang/Daguocun. .China . . SJW	
Shikarpur . . . . Pakistan . . SWV	
Shillavo . . . . Ethiopia . . HIL	
Shillong . . . . India . . SHL	
Shilo-YLP Mingan, MB .Canada . . YLO	
Shimojishima . . . . Japan . . SHI	
Shinyanga . . . . Tanzania . . SHY	
Shirahama . . . . Japan . SHM	
Shiraz . . . . Iran . . SYZ	
Shiringayoc . . . . Peru . . SYC	
Shirley, Brookhaven Arpt, NY	USA . . HWV
Shirley/Brookhaven, NY . . . USA . .WSH	
Shirrikent . . . . .Kazakstan . . CIT	
Shishmaref, AK . . . . USA . . SHH	
Shizijoka City . . . . Japan . . QSZ	

Shoal Cove, AK . . . . USA . HCB	
Sholapur . . . . India . . SSE	
Shonai . . . . Japan . SYO	
Shoreham By Sea/Shoreham	UK . ESH
Show Low, AZ . . . . USA . SOW	
Shreveport, LA . . . . USA . DTN	
Shreveport, LA . . . . USA . SHV	
Shungnak, AK . . . . USA . SHG	
Shute Harbour/HP . . . . Australia . JHQ	
Sialkot . . . . Pakistan . . SKT	
Sialum . . . . Papua New Guinea . SXA	
Siasi . . . . Philippines . SSV	
Siassi . . . . Papua New Guinea . SSS	
Siauliai/Int'l . . . . Lithuania . SQQ	
Sibi . . . . Pakistan . SBQ	
Sibisa . . . . Indonesia . SIW	
Sibiti . . . . Colombia . . SIB	
Sibiu . . . . Romania . SBZ	
Sibu . . . . Malaysia . SBW	
Sicogon Is . . . . Philippines . ICO	
Sidi Barani . . . . Egypt . SQK	
Sidi Ifni . . . . Morocco . . SII	
Sidney, NE . . . . USA . SNY	
Sidney, NY . . . . USA . SXY	
Sidney-Richland, MT . . . . USA . SDY	
Sidon . . . . Lebanon . QSQ	
Siegburg . . . . Germany . ZPY	
Siegen/Segerland Arpt Germany . SGE	
Siena . . . . Italy . SAY	
Siern Reap . . . . Cambodia . REP	
Sierra Grande . . . . . . Argentina . SGV	
Sierra Leone . . Sierra Leone . SRK	
Sierre/Siders . . . . . . Switzerland . ZKO	
Sig . . . . Algeria . QIL	
Siglufjordur . . . . Iceland . SIJ	
Sigonella/NAF . . . . Italy . NSY	
Siguanea . . . . Cuba . SZJ	
Siguin . . . . Guinea . GII	
Sihanoukville . . . . . Cambodia . KOS	
Sikeston/Memorial, MO . . . USA . SIK	
Sila . . . . . . Papua New Guinea . SIL	
Silchar/Kumbhirgram . . . . India . IXS	
Silgadi Doti . . . . Nepal . SIH	
Silistra . . . . Bulgaria . SLS	
Silkeborg/RR Stn. . . . . Denmark . XAH	
Siloam Springs/Smith Fld, AR	USA . SLG
Silur . . . . . . Papua New Guinea . SWR	
Silva Bay, BC . . . . Canada . SYF	
Silver Bay, MN . . . . USA . BFW	
Silver City, NM . . . . USA . SVC	
Silver Creek . . . . Belize . SVK	
Silver Plains . . . . Australia . SSP	
Sim . . . . . . Papua New Guinea . SMJ	
Simanggang . . . . Malaysia . SGG	
Simao . . . . China . SYM	
Simara . . . . Nepal . . SIF	
Simbach . . . . Germany . QIP	
Simbas . . . . Papua New Guinea . SIM	
Simberi Is . Papua New Guinea . .NIS	
Simenti . . . . Senegal . .SMY	
Simferopol . . . . Ukraine . . SIP	
Simia . . . . India . SLV	
Simikot . . . . Nepal . IMK	
Sinalk . . . . Indonesia . NKD	
Sindal/Flyveplads . . . . Denmark . CNL	
Sindelfingen/Off-line PtGermany . ZPZ	
Sines . . . . Portugal . . SIE	
Singapore . . . . Singapore . .SIN	
Singapore/Paya Lebar	
	Seychelles . QPG
Singapore/Seletar . . . Singapore . XSP	
Singaua . . Papua New Guinea . SGB	
Singen . . . . Germany . ZQA	
Singkep/Dabo . . . . Indonesia . SIQ	
Singleton . . . . Australia . . SIX	
Sinoe/AFC . . . . Liberia . XSA	
Sinoe/R.E. Murray . . . . . Liberia . SNI	
Sinop . . . . Brazil . OPS	
Sinop . . . . Turkey . SQD	

Sinop/Sinop Arpt . . . . . . Turkey. . . SIC	
Sintang . . . . Indonesia. . SQG	
Siocon . . . . .Philippines. . XSO	
Sion . . . . Switzerland. . . SIR	
Sioux City, IA . . . . USA. . SUX	
Sioux Falls, SD . . . . USA. . FSD	
Sioux Lookout, ON . . . Canada. . YXL	
Sipitang . . . . Malaysia. . SPT	
Siracusa . . . . Italy. . QIC	
Sirajganj . . . . Bangladesh. . SAJ	
Sirjan . . . . Iran. . SYJ	
Sirri Is . . . . Iran. . SXI	
Sishen . . . . S. Africa. . . SIS	
Sisimiut . . . . .Greenland. . JHS	
Sissano . . . . Papua New Guinea. . SIZ	
SITA . . . . -. . QEN	
SITA . . . . -. . QES	
SITA Aircom . . . . -. . QXS	
SITA Network . . . . -. . QXN	
SITA Network . . . . -. . QXT	
Sitia . . . . Greece. . JSH	
Sitiawan . . . . Malaysia. . SWY	
Sitka, AK . . . . USA. . SIT	
Sitkinak Is/CGS, AK . . . . . USA. . SKJ	
Sittwe/Civil. . . . . .Myanmar. . .AKY	
Siuna . . . . Netherlands. . SIU	
Sivas . . . . Turkey. . .VAS	
Siwa . . . . Egypt. . SEW	
Siwea . . . . . . Papua New Guinea. . SWE	
Sjaelland/RR Stn. . . . . . Denmark. . .ZIJ	
Skagen/Limousine Svc Denmark. . .QJV	
Skagway/Municipal, AK . . . USA. . SGY	
Skardu . . . . .Pakistan. . KDU	
Skasso . . . . Mali. . KSS	
Skeldon . . . . Guyana. . SKM	
Skelleftea . . . . Sweden. . SFT	
Skiathos Is . . . . Greece. . JSI	
Skien . . . . Norway. . .SKE	
Skikda . . . . Algeria. . SKI	
Skiplane Scenic . New Zealand. . . XXS	
Skiros . . . . Greece. . SKU	
Skitube/Bus Svc. . . . . . . Australia. . QTO	
Skive/RR Stn. . . . . Denmark. . ZKN	
Skive/Skive Arpt . . . . . Denmark. . SQW	
Skjerstad . . . . Norway. . .ZXL	
Skople . . . . Macedonia. . .SKP	
Skovde . . . . Sweden. . KVB	
Skukuza . . . . S. Africa. . SZK	
Skwentna/Intermediate, AK USA. . SKW	
Slate Is, ON . . . . Canada. . YSS	
Slave Lake, AB . . . . . . Canada. . YZH	
Sleetmute, AK . . . . USA. . SLQ	
Sliac . . . . Slovakia. . SLD	
Sligo . . . . Ireland. . SXL	
Sligo/Bus Stn . . . . Ireland. . ZSL	
Slirt . . . . Turkey. . SXZ	
Slupsk/Recizikowo. . . . . . .Poland. . OSP	
Smara . . . . Morocco. .SMW	
Smiggin Holes/Bus Svc	
	Australia. . QZC
Smith Cove, AK. . . . . USA. . SCJ	
Smith Falls, ON. . . . . Canada. . YSH	
Smith Point . . . . Australia. . SHU	
Smithers, BC . . . . Canada. . YYD	
Smithfield/North Central, RI USA. . SFZ	
Smithton . . . . Australia. . SIO	
Smolensk . . . . Russia. . LNX	
Smyrna, TN. . . . . USA. . MQY	
Snake Bay . . . . .Australia. . SNB	
Snake River, YT . . . . . . Canada. . YXF	
Snare Lake, NT . . . . . . Canada. . YFJ	
Snyder/Winston Fld, TX . . USA. . SNK	
Soalaia . . . . Madagascar. . DWB	
Sobral . . . . Brazil. . QBX	
Soc Trang . . . . Vietnam. . SOA	
Socorro, NM. . . . . USA. .ONM	
Socotra . . . . Yemen. . SCT	
Sodankyla . . . . .Finland. . SOT	
Soddu . . . . Ethiopia. . SXU	
Soderhamn . . . . Sweden. . SOO	

AIRPORTS

Sodertalje/Sodertalje HP .... Sweden . . JSO	**Spokane**/Int'l Arpt, WA .... USA . GEG	**St Omer** .... France . . XSG
Soerfjord .... Norway . . ZXH	**Spokane**, WA .... USA . . SFF	**St Paul Is**, AK .... USA . . SNP
Soeroeya .... Norway . . QZS	**Spora** .... Indonesia . RKO	**St Paul's** Mission ...... Australia . . SVM
Sofia .... Bulgaria . . SOF	**Spring Creek** .... Australia . SCG	**St Paul**, QC .... Canada . . ZSP
Sogamoso .... Colombia . . SOX	**Spring Is**, BC .... Canada . YSQ	**St Paul-Downtown**, MN . . USA . . STP
Sogndal .... Norway . . SOG	**Spring Point** .... Bahamas . AXP	**St Peter** .... Germany . . PSH
Sohag .... Egypt . . QHX	**Springbank**, AB ..... Canada . YBW	**St Petersburg**, FL .... USA . SPG
Soienzara .... France . . SOZ	**Springbok** .... S. Africa . . SBU	**St Petersburg**/Clearwater Int'l,
Soissons .... France . . XSS	**Springdale**/Springdale Municipal,	FL .... USA . . PIE
Sokcho/Solak .... S. Korea . SHO	AR .... USA . SPZ	**St Petersburg**/Moscovskiy
Sokoto .... Nigeria . SKO	**Springfield**, IL .... USA . SPI	Railway Stn ...... Russia . . ZLK
Sola .... Vanuatu . SLH	**Springfield**, MA RR ...... USA . ZSF	**St Petersburg**/Pulkovo . . Russia . . LED
Solano .... Colombia . . SQF	**Springfield**, MO .... USA . SGF	**St Petersburg**/Rzhevka . Russia . . RVH
Soldotna, AK. ....USA . . SXQ	**Springfield**, OH .... USA . SGH	**St Pierre** St. Pierre and Miquelon. . FSP
Solingen .... Germany . . ZQB	**Springfield**, VT .... USA . VSF	**St Pierre dela Reunion**
Solingen-Ohligs/RR Stn.	**Springvale** .... Australia . KSV	.... Reunion Is. . ZSE
.... Germany . . ZIO	**Springvale** .... Australia . . ZVG	**St Quentin** .... France. . XSJ
Solita .... Colombia . . SOH	**Squamish**, BC .... Canada . YSE	**St Quentin en Yvelines** France. . XQY
Solo City/Adi Surnarmo	**Squirrel Cove**, BC .... Canada . YSZ	**St Raphael** .... France. . XSK
.... Indonesia . . SOC	**Srinagar** .... India . . SXR	**St Thomas Is** ...... Virgin Is (US) . . STT
Solomon, AK. ....USA . . SOL	**St Andrews**/Leuchars ......UK . . ADX	**St Thomas**/Pembroke Area, ON
Solothurn ....Switzerland . . ZKS	**St Anthony**, NF .... Canada . . YAY	.... Canada. . YQS
Solstad .... Norway . . ZXQ	**St Anton** .... Austria . . ANT	**St Thomas**/SPB . . . Virgin Is (US). . SPB
Solwezi .... Zambia . . SLI	**St Augustine**, FL .... USA . UST	**St Vincent**/E-T. Joshua
Somerset/Pulaski County, KYUSA . SME	**St Barthelemy** ... Gaudeloupe . SBH	..... St. Vincent & Grenadines. . SVD
Son-La/Na-San .... Vietnam . . SQH	**St Brieuc**/Tremuson ......Eritrea . . SBK	**St. Genis**/Bus Svc ...... France. . QXK
Sonderborg .... Denmark . . QSG	**St Catharines**, ON .... Canada . YCM	**St. John's**, NF .... Canada. . . YYT
Sonderborg/Lufthavn .Denmark . . SGD	**St Claude** .... France . . XTC	**Stade** .... Germany. . ZQD
Songea .... Tanzania . SGX	**St Cloud**, MN .... USA . STC	**Stafford**/RR Stn. .... UK. . XVB
Songkhla .... Thailand . SGZ	**St Crepin** .... Eritrea . . SCP	**Stalowa Wola** .... Poland. . QXQ
Sonneberg/RR Stn. .. Germany . . ZSG	**St Croix Is** ...... Virgin Is (US) . STX	**Staniel Cay** .... Bahamas. . TYM
Sophia Antipolis......France . . SXD	**St Croix Is**/Downtown HP	**Stanthorpe** ....Australia. . SNH
Sopu ...... Papua New Guinea . . SPH	.... Virgin Is (US) . . JCD	**Stanton**/Carleton, MN ...... USA. . SYN
Sora .... Italy . . QXE	**St Croix Is**/SPB . . Virgin Is (US) . . SSB	**Stara Zagora** .... Bulgaria. . SZR
Sorkjosen .... Norway . . SOJ	**St Denis de la Reunion**	**Starcke** ....Australia. . SQP
Soroako .... Indonesia . . SQR	.... Reunion Is . RUN	**State College**, PA .... USA. . SCE
Sorocaba .... Brazil . . SOD	**St Die** .... France . . XCK	**State College**, PA .... USA. . UNV
Sorong/Jefman ...... Indonesia . . SOQ	**St Etienne**/Boutheon . . . France . . EBU	**Statesboro**/Municipal, GA . . USA. . TBR
Soroti .... Uganda . . SRT	**St Eustatius**Netherlands Antilles . . EUX	**Statesville**/Municipal, NC . . USA. . SVH
Sorrento .... Italy . . RRO	**St Francois** ...... Gaudeloupe . SFC	**Stauning**/Lufthavn .... Denmark. . STA
Souanke .... Congo . . SOE	**St Gallen** .... Switzerland . QGL	**Staunton**, VA .... USA. . SHD
Souda/Khania .... Greece . . CHQ	**St George** .... Australia . SGO	**Stavanger**/Sola .... Norway. . SVG
Souk Ahras ....Algeria . . QSK	**St George Is**, AK. .... USA . STG	**Stavropol** .... Russia. . STW
Soure .... Brazil . . SFK	**St Georges de Loyapock**	**Stawell** ....Australia. . SWC
Sousse .... Tunisia . QSO	.... F. Guiana . OYP	**Ste Therese** Point, MB . Canada. . . YST
South Andros ...... Bahamas . . TZN	**St Gervais Le Fayet** ... France . . XGF	**Steamboat Bay**/SPB, AK. . USA. . WSB
South Bend, IN ....USA . . SBN	**St Gilles Croix De Vie** .. France . . XGV	**Steamboat Springs**, CO. . USA. . SBS
South Caicos/Int'l	**St Helens** .... Australia . HLS	**Stebbins**, AK .... USA. . WBB
.... Turks & Caicos Is . . XSC	**St Jean De Luz**....... France . . XJZ	**Steenkool** .... Indonesia. . . ZKL
South Galway .... Australia . . ZGL	**St Jean**, QC .... Canada . YJN	**Stella Maris**/Estate Airstrip
South Indian Lake, MB Canada . . XSI	**St John Is** ...... Virgin Is (US) . SJF	.... Bahamas. . SML
South Lake Tahoe, CA . . USA . . TVL	**St Johns**, AZ .... USA . SJN	**Stendal**/RR Stn. ...... Germany. . . ZSN
South Molle Is .... Australia . . SOI	**St Joseph**, MO .... USA . STJ	**Stephen Is** ....Australia. . STF
South Naknek, AK ....USA . . WSN	**St Kitts**/Gldn Rck	**Stephenville**, NF ...... Canada. . . YJT
South Trout Lake, ON .Canada . . ZFL	.... St. Kitts and Nevis . SKB	**Stephenville**, TX .... USA. . SEP
South West Bay ......Vanuatu . . SWJ	**St Laurent du Maroni**F. Guiana . . LDX	**Sterling Rockfalls**, IL ..... USA. . SQI
South Weymouth, MA ....USA . . NZW	**St Leonard**, NB .... Canada . YSL	**Sterling**/Crosson Fld, CO . . USA. . STK
Southampton..............UK . . SOU	**St Louis** .... France . . XLI	**Stevenage**/RR Stn. .... UK. . XVJ
Southend ....UK . . SEN	**St Louis** .... Senegal . . XLS	**Stevens Point**, WI .... USA. . STE
Southern Cross ..... Australia . . SQC	**St Louis Int'l**, MO .... USA . STL	**Stevens Village**, AK ...... USA. . SVS
Southern Pines/Pinehurst, NC	**St Louis**, IL. .... USA . CPS	**Stewart Is** .... New Zealand. . SZS
............USA . . SOP	**St Louis**-Spirit Of St Louis, MO	**Stewart**, BC .... Canada. . ZST
Southport .... Australia . . SHQ	.... USA . SUS	**Stillwater**, OK .... USA. . SWO
Sovata .... Romania . . QSV	**St Louis**/Rail Svc., MO .... USA . ZSV	**Stirling**/RR Stn. .... UK. . XWB
Soyo .... Angola . . SZA	**St Lucia**/Hewanorra . . St. Lucia . UVF	**Stockholm** . Papua New Guinea. . SMP
Spangdahlem ...... Germany . . SPM	**St Lucia**/Vigie. .... St. Lucia . SLU	**Stockholm**/Arlanda ..... Sweden. . ARN
Spanish Wells ...... Bahamas . . SWL	**St Maarten**/Princ. Juliana	**Stockholm**/Bromma ..... Sweden. . BMA
Sparrevohn/AFS, AK .....USA . . SVW	.... Netherlands Antilles . . SXM	**Stockholm**/Skavsta ..... Sweden. . NYO
Sparta.............. Greece . . SPJ	**St Malo** .... France . . XSB	**Stockport**/RR Stn. .... UK. . XVA
Sparta/AAF, WI ....USA . . CMY	**St Margrethen** .... Switzerland . ZKF	**Stockton**, CA .... USA. . SCK
Sparta/ComMunicipality, IL .USA . . SAR	**St Martin**/Esperance	**Stoelmans Eiland** .... Suriname. . SMZ
Spartanburg Memorial, SCUSA . SPA	.... Gaudeloupe . SFG	**Stoke on Trent**/RR Stn. . . UK. . XWH
Spearfish, SD ....USA . . SPF	**St Martin**/Grand Case	**Stokmarknes**/Skagen . Norway. . SKN
Spence Bay Arpt, NU . .Canada . . YYH	.... Gaudeloupe . .CCE	**Stolberg** .... Germany. . ZQE
Spencer, IA ....USA . . SPW	**St Marys**, MD. .... USA . XSM	**Stony Rapids**, SK ...... Canada. . . YSF
Spetsai Is .... Gaudeloupe . . JSS	**St Marys**, PA .... USA . STQ	**Stony River**, AK. .... USA. . SRV
Speyer .... Germany . . ZQC	**St Marys**/RR Stn., ON . . Canada . . XIO	**Stord**/Stord Arpt .... Norway. . SRP
Spiddal/Connemara ....Ireland . . NNR	**St Michael**, AK .... USA . SMK	**Storm Lake**, IA. .... USA. . SLB
Spirit Lake, IA. ....USA . . RTL	**St Moritz**. .... Switzerland . ZKH	**Stornoway** ....UK. . SYY
Split. .... Croatia . . SPU	**St Moritz**/Samedan . Switzerland . SMV	**Storurnan**/Gunnarn. .. Sweden. . SQO
	St Nazaire/Montoir ..... France . . SNR	**Stow**, MA .... USA. . .MMN

Stradbroke Is . . . . Australia . . SRR
Strahan . . . . Australia . . SRN
Straisund/RR Stn. . . . . . . Germany . . ZSX
Strasbourg/Bus Svc . . . .France . . XER
Strasbourg/Entzineim . . .France . . SXB
Stratford/RR Stn., ON . .Canada . . XFD
Stratford/Sikorsky HP, CT. .USA . . JSD
Strathmore . . . . Australia . . STH
Strathroy/RR Stn., ON . .Canada . . .XTY
Straubing/Wallmuhle . Germany . . RBM
Strausberg . . . . Germany . . QPK
Streaky Bay . . . . Australia . . KBY
Stronsay . . . . .UK . . SOY
Stroud, OK. . . . . .USA . . SUD
Struer/Bus Svc . . . . . . Denmark . . QWQ
Struga . . . . Macedonia . . QXP
Strzhewoi . . . . Russia . . SWT
Stuart Is, BC . . . . Canada . . YRR
Stuart Is, WA. . . . . .USA . . SSW
Stuart/Witham Fld, FL. . . . . . .USA . . SUA
Stung Treng . . . . Cambodia . . TNX
Sturdee, BC. . . . . Canada . . YTC
Sturgeon Bay, WI . . . . .USA . . SUE
Sturgis/Kirsch Municipal, MI USA . . IRS
Sturt Creek. . . . . Australia . . SSK
Stuttgart, AR. . . . . .USA . . SGT
Stuttgart/Echterdingen
. . . . Germany . . STR
Stuttgart/RR Stn. . . . . . Germany . . ZWS
Stykkisholmur. . . . . Iceland . . SYK
Su Won City/Su Won Arpt
. . . . S. Korea . .SWU
Sua pan . . . . Botswana . . SXN
Suabi . . . . Papua New Guinea . . SBE
Suai. . . . . Indonesia . . UAI
Suavanao Airstrip . Solomon Is . . VAO
Subic Bay/Int'l Airpt . Philippines . . .SFS
Suceava/Salcea . . . . . Romania . . SCV
Sucre . . . . Bolivia . . SRE
Sucua . . . . Ecuador . . SUQ
Sudbury, ON . . . . .Canada . . YSB
Sudbury/Jet RR Stn., ON Canada . . XDY
Sudureyri . . . . Iceland . . SUY
Sue Is/Warraber Is . . . . Australia . . SYU
Suffield, AB. . . . . .Canada . . YSD
Suhl/RR Stn. . . . . Germany . . ZSO
Sui . . . . Pakistan . . SUL
Suia-Missu . . . . Brazil . . SWM
Suiaco . . . . Honduras . . SCD
Sukhumi/Babusheri . . .Georgia . . SUI
Suki . . . . . . Papua New Guinea . . SKC
Sukinothai . . . . Thailand . . THS
Sukkur . . . . Pakistan . . SKZ
Sulayel . . . . Saudi Arabia . . SLF
Sule . . . . Papua New Guinea . . ULE
Sullivan Say, BC . . . . . .Canada . . YTG
Sullivan/County, IN. . . . . . .USA . . SIV
Sulmona . . . . Italy . . QLN
Sulphur Springs, TX. . . . . . .USA . . SLR
Sulsted/Bus Svc . . . . . Denmark . . QYQ
Sumbawa/Brang Bidji Indonesia . SWQ
Sumbawanga. . . . . Tanzania . . SUT
Sumbe . . . . Angola . . NDD
Sumeneo/Trunojoyo . . Indonesia . . SUP
Summer Beaver, ON . .Canada . . SUR
Summerside, PE . . . . . .Canada . . YSU
Summit Lake, BC . . . . .Canada . . IUM
Summit, AK. . . . . .USA . . UMM
Sumy . . . . Ukraine . .UMY
Sun City/Pilansberg . . S. Africa . . NTY
Sun Moon Lake. . . . . . .Taiwan . . SMT
Sun River, OR. . . . . .USA . . SUO
Sunchon/Yosu. . . . . S. Korea . . SYS
Sundance/Schloredt, WY . . .USA . . SUC
Sundsvall . . . . Sweden . . SDL
Sungai Pakning . . . . Indonesia . . SEQ
SungeiTekai . . . . Malaysia . . GTK
Sunshine Coast/Maroochydore
. . . . Australia . .MCY
Sunyani . . . . .Ghana . . NYI

Superior/Richard 1 Bong, WI
. . . . USA . SUW
Sur . . . . Oman . .SUH
Surabaya/Juanda . . . . Indonesia . .SUB
Surat . . . . India . . STV
Surat Thani . . . . Thailand . . URT
Surfdale . . . . .New Zealand . . WIK
Surfers Paradise . . . . Australia . . SFP
Surgut. . . . . Russia . . SGC
Suria . . . . . Papua New Guinea . . SUZ
Surigao. . . . . Philippines . . SUG
Surkhet. . . . . Nepal . .SKH
Surnter/Municipal, SC . . . . USA . . SUM
Sursee . . . . Switzerland . .ZKU
Suru-Lere. . . . . Nigeria . . QSL
Susanville, CA . . . . USA . . SVE
Sussex, Sussex Arpt, NJ . . USA . . FWN
Suttonheath/Woodbridge/RAF
. . . . .UK . WOB
Suva/Nausori . . . . Fiji . .SUV
Suwalki . . . . Poland . ZWK
Suzhou . . . . China . . SZV
Svalbard/Spitsberg . . . . .Norway . .SYG
Svay Rieng . . . . Cambodia . . SVR
Sveg . . . . Sweden . .EVG
Svendborg/RR . . . . . . Denmark . .QXV
Svolvaer/Helle . . . . .Norway . . SVJ
Swakopmund . . . . Namibia . . SWP
Swakopmund/RR Stn. . Namibia . .ZSZ
Swan Hill . . . . Australia . . SWH
Swan River, MB . . . . . . Canada . . ZJN
Swansea . . . . .UK . SWS
Sweetwater, TX. . . . . USA . SWW
Sweida . . . . Syria . QSW
Swift Current, SK. . . . . Canada . . YYN
Swindon . . . . .UK . . SWI
Swindon/RR Stn. . . . . .UK . XWS
Syangboche . . . . Nepal . .SYH
Sydney . . . . Australia . . SYD
Sydney, NS. . . . . Canada . .YQY
Sydney/Au-Rose Bay . Australia . . RSE
Sydney/Palm Beach SPB
. . . . Australia . . LBH
Sydney/Sydney West . Australia . . SWZ
SyklyvKar . . . . Russia . . SCW
Syllnet/Civil. . . . . . . Bangladesh . . ZYL
Sylvester, GA . . . . USA . SYV
Syracuse Int'l, NY . . . . . USA . . SYR
Syracuse/NY Rail, NY. . . . . USA . .ZYQ
Syros Is . . . . Greece . . JSY
Szczecin/Goleniow . . . . . .Poland . . SZZ
Szeged . . . . .Hungary . QZD
Szombathely. . . . . . . .Hungary . . ZBX
Szymany/Mazury . . . . . . Poland . . SZY

T

Taabo . . . . Côte D'Ivoire . . TBX
Taba/Talba Int'l . . . . Egypt . . TCP
Tabal . . . . Marshall Is . . TBV
Tabarka/7 Novembre . . . Tunisia . . TBJ
Tabas. . . . . Iran . . TCX
Tabatinga/Int'l . . . . Brazil . . TBT
Tabibuga . . Papua New Guinea . . TBA
Tabiteuea North. . . . . . Kiribati . . TBF
Tabiteuea South . . . . . . Kiribati . . TSU
Tablas . . . . Philippines . . TBH
Tableland . . . . Australia . . TBL
Tablon De Tamara. . . . Colombia . . TTM
Tabou . . . . Côte D'Ivoire . . TXU
Tabriz . . . . Iran . . TBZ
Tabuaeran . . . . Kiribati . . TNV
Tabubil . . . . Papua New Guinea . . TBG
Tabuk . . . . Saudi Arabia . . TUU
Tacheng . . . . China . . TCG
Tachilek . . . . Myanmar . . THL
Tacloban/D1. Rornualdez
. . . . Philippines . . TAC

Tacna . . . . Peru. . TCQ
Tacoma-Narrows, WA. . . . USA. . TIW
Tacuarembo . . . . Uruguay. . TAW
Tadjoura . . . . Djibouti. . TDJ
Tadoule Lake, MB. . . . Canada. . .XTL
Taedok. . . . . S. Korea. . QET
Taegu/Air Base . . . . . . S. Korea. . TAE
Taejon . . . . S. Korea. . QTW
Taftan . . . . Pakistan. . TFT
Tagbilaran . . . . .Philippines. . TAG
Tagloita . . . . .Philippines. . TGB
Taguatinga . . . . Brazil. . QHN
Tagula . . . . . Papua New Guinea. . TGL
Taharoa . . . . New Zealand. . THH
Taher . . . . Algeria. . ZZT
Tahneta Pass Lodge, AK. . USA. . HNE
Tahoua . . . . Niger. . THZ
Tahsis, BC. . . . . Canada. . ZTS
Taichung. . . . . Taiwan. . .TXG
Taif . . . . Saudi Arabia. . .TIF
Taiknafjordur. . . . . Iceland. . TLK
Tainan . . . . Taiwan. . TNN
Taipei/Chiang Kai Shek . Taiwan. . .TPE
Taipei/Sung Shan . . . . Taiwan. . .TSA
Taiping . . . . Malaysia. . .TPG
Taisha . . . . .Ecuador. . TSC
Taitung . . . . Taiwan. . .TTT
Taiyuan . . . . China. . TYN
Taiz/AlJanad . . . . Yemen. . .TAI
Tak . . . . .Thailand. . .TKT
Takalka . . . . New Zealand. . KTF
Takamatsu . . . . Japan. . TAK
Takapoto . . . . F. Polynesia. . TKP
Takaroa . . . . F. Polynesia. . .TKX
Takhli . . . . .Thailand. . .TKH
Takoradi . . . . Ghana. . .TKD
Takotna, AK . . . . USA. . TCT
Taku Lodge/Taku SPB, AK . USA. . TKL
Takume . . . . F. Polynesia. . TJN
Talara . . . . Peru. . TYL
Talasea . . . . . Papua New Guinea. . TLW
Talavera de la Reina . . . Spain. . QWT
Talbora . . . . Tanzania. . TBO
Talca. . . . . .Chile. . .TLX
Taldy-Kurgan . . . . . . Kazakstan. . .TDK
Taliabu . . . . Indonesia. . TAX
Talkeetna, AK. . . . . USA. . .TKA
Talladega, AL. . . . . USA. . ASN
Tallahassee, FL . . . . USA. . .TLH
Tallinn/Pirita Harbour . . . Estonia. . QUF
Tallinn/Ulemiste . . . . . . Estonia. . TLL
Taltal . . . . .Chile. . .TTC
Taltheilei Narrows, NT Canada. . .GSL
Taluqan . . . . .Afghanistan. . TQN
Tamale. . . . . Ghana. . .TML
Taman Negara . . . . . Malaysia. . SXT
Tamana Is . . . . Kiribati. . TMN
Tamanrasset/Aguemar . Algeria. . TMR
Tamarindo . . . . Costa Rica. . TNO
Tamatave . . . . .Madagascar. . TMM
Tambacounda. . . . . . . .Senegal. . TUD
Tambao . . . . Burkina Faso. . TMQ
Tambolaka . . . . Indonesia. . TMC
Tambor . . . . Costa Rica. . TMU
Tambov . . . . Russia. . TBW
Tamchakett . . . . Mauritania. . THT
Tame . . . . .Colombia. . TME
Tampa Bay/Exec., FL . . . .USA. . .RRF
Tampa/Int'l, FL. . . . . USA. . TPA
Tampa/Peter O'Knight, FL . . USA. . TPF
Tampa/Topp Of Tampa, FL . USA. . KYO
Tampere/Pirkkala . . . . . . .Finland. . TMP
Tampico/Gen F Javier Mina
. . . . Mexico. . TAM
Tamworth . . . . .Australia. . TMW
Tan Tan . . . . Morocco. . TTA
Tana . . . . Norway. . .QTP
Tana Toraja. . . . . Indonesia. . TTR
Tanacross/Intermediate, AK USA. . .TSG
Tanah Grogot . . . . . . Indonesia. . .TNB

Tanah Merah/Tanah Merah
.... Indonesia .. TMH
Tanalian Point, AK ......USA .. TPO
Tanana, AK ....USA...TAL
Tanandava ......Madagascar .. TDV
Tanbar .... Australia .. TXR
Tanda Tula.......... S. Africa .. TDT
Tandag .... Philippines .. TDG
Tandil .... Argentina .. TDL
Tanegashima .... Japan .. TNE
Tanga .... Tanzania .. TGT
Tangalooma .... Australia .. TAN
Tangara da Serra ...... Brazil .TGQ
Tangier/Boukhalef..... Morocco .. TNG
Tanjung Balai...... Indonesia .. TJB
Tanjung Pandan/Bulutumbang
.... Indonesia .. TJQ
Tanjung Pinang/KidjangIndonesia .TNJ
Tanjung Santan.... Indonesia .. TSX
Tanjung Selor ...... Indonesia .. TJS
Tanjung Warukin.... Indonesia .. TJG
Tanna ....Vanuatu .. TAH
Tanta ....Egypt .. QTT
Taos, NM ....USA .. TSM
Tapachula Int'l ..... Mexico .. TAP
Tapaktuan .... Indonesia .. TPK
Tapeta .... Iran .TPT
Tapiejung .... Nepal .. TPJ
Tapini ...Papua New Guinea .. TPI
Tara .... Australia .. XTR
Tarabo .....Papua New Guinea .. TBQ
Tarakan .... Indonesia .. TRK
Tarakbits ...Papua New Guinea .. TRJ
Taramaprina/Tarama.... Japan .. TRA
Taranto/M. A. Grottag..... Italy .. TAR
Tarapaca ...... Colombia .. TCD
Tarapaina .... Solomon Is .. TAA
Tarapoa .... Ecuador .. TPC
Tarapoto ....Peru .. TPP
Tarauaca .... Brazil .. TRQ
Tarawa/Bonriki....... Kiribati .. TRW
Tarbela .... Pakistan ..TLB
Tarbes/Laloubere ......France .. XTB
Tarcoola .... Australia .. TAQ
Taree .... Australia .. TRO
Targovishte .... Bulgaria .. TGV
Tari ....Papua New Guinea .. TIZ
Tarija .... Bolivia .. TJA
Tarlaya .... Morocco ..TFY
Tarnbohorano ...Madagascar .. WTA
Tarnky ....Vietnam .. TMK
Tarnobrzeg..........Poland .. QEP
Tarnuin .... Myanmar ..TSL
Taroom .... Australia .. XTO
Tarragona ....Spain .QGN
Tartagal .... Argentina .. TTG
Tartous................ Syria .. QTR
Tartu/Raadi .... Estonia .. TAY
Taschereau/RR Stn., QC
............Canada .. XFO
Tashauz .... Turkmenistan ..TAZ
Tashkent .... Uzbekistan ..TAS
Tasiilaq .... Greenland . AGM
Tasikmalaya/Cibeureum
.... Indonesia .. TSY
Tasiuasaq/Harbour .. Greenland .. XEQ
Tasiujuaq, QC.........Canada .. YTQ
Taskul .....Papua New Guinea .. TSK
Tasu, BC............Canada.. YTU
Tatakoto...........F. Polynesia .. TKV
Tatalina/Tatalina AFS, AK....USA .. TLJ
Tatitlek, AK ....USA.. TEK
Tatry/Poprad .... Slovakia .. TAT
Tau.........American Samoa .. TAV
Taubate .... Brazil .QHP
Taupo .... New Zealand .. TUO
Tauramena .... Colombia .. TAU
Tauranga ...... New Zealand .. TRG
Tauta ......Papua New Guinea .. TUT
Taveuni/Matei .... Fiji .. TVU
Tawa ......Papua New Guinea .. TWY

Tawau ....Malaysia . TWU
Tawitawi .... Philippines .. TWT
Taylor, AK .... USA .. TWE
Taylor, AZ .... USA .. TYZ
Tbessa .... Algeria .. TEE
Tbilisi/Novo Alexeyevka Georgia .. TBS
Tchien .... Liberia ..THC
Te Anau/ManapouriNew Zealand .. TEU
Te ixeira de Freitas......Brazil .. TXF
Teesside................UK . MME
Tegucigalpa/Toncontin
............Honduras ..TGU
Tehachapi/Kern County, CA
............USA . TSP
Tehibanga .... Gabon .. TCH
Tehran-Mehrabad .... Iran .. THR
Tehuacan ....Mexico .. TCN
Tekadu .... Papua New Guinea .. TKB
Tekamah, Tekamah Municipal Arpt,
NE.............USA .. TQE
Tekin ..... Papua New Guinea .. TKW
TeKirdag/Corlu ....Turkey .. TEQ
Tel Aviv Yafo/Sde Dov....Israel .. SDV
Tel Aviv-Ben Gurion Int'l Israel .. TLV
Tela ....Honduras .. TEA
Telefornin ...Papua New Guinea .. TFM
Telegraph Creek, BC . Canada .. YTX
Telegraph Harbour, BCCanada ..YBQ
Telemaco Borba ....Brazil .. TEC
Telida, AK .... USA .. TLF
Teller ....Australia .. TEF
Teller Mission, Brevig Mission, AK
............USA .. KTS
Teller, AK............ USA .. TLA
Telluride, CO .... USA .. TEX
Telluride/Bus Stn, CO ..... USA .. ZTL
Telupid ....Malaysia .. TEL
Tembagapura/Timika . Indonesia .. TIM
Temora .... Australia .. TEM
Temple/Draughon-Miller, TX
............USA .. TPL
Temuco............... Chile . ZCO
Tenakee Springs/Tenakee SPB,
AK.............USA .. TKE
Tenerife .... Spain .. TFN
Tenerife Sur .... Spain .. TFS
Tengah .... Singapore .. TGA
Teniente R. Marsh .....Antarctica .. TNM
Tenkodogo ...... Burkina Faso .. TEG
Tennant Creek .... Australia .. TCA
Teofilo Otoni ....Brazil .. TFL
Tepic .... Mexico .. TPQ
Teptelp .... Papua New Guinea .. TEP
Teraina .... Kiribati .. TNQ
Teramo .... Italy .QEA
Terapo..... Papua New Guinea .. TEO
Terceira Is/Laies ...... Portugal .. TER
Teresina .... Brazil .. THE
Terezopolis ....Brazil .QHT
Termez .... Uzbekistan .. TMJ
Termini Imere .... Italy .QTI
Ternate/Babullah .....Indonesia .. TTE
Terninabuan .... Indonesia ..TXM
Ternopol............... Laos .. TNL
Terrace Bay .... Namibia .. TCY
Terrace Bay, ON .... Canada .. YTJ
Terrace, BC .... Canada .. YXT
Terre Haute, IN .... USA ..HUF
Terre-de-Bas .... Gaudeloupe .. HTB
Terre-de-Haut .... Gaudeloupe .. LSS
Terrell, TX............. USA .. TRL
Tervakoski .... Finland .QVS
Teslin, YT .... Canada .. YZW
Tessenei .... Eritrea .. TES
Tetabedi ... Papua New Guinea .. TDB
Tete ....Mozambique .. TCV
Tete .... Brazil .TFF
Tete-a-La Baleine, QC Canada .. ZTB
Tete/Matunda .....Mozambique .. TET
Teterboro, NJ .... USA .. TEB
Tetiaroa Is .... F. Polynesia .. TTI

Tetlin, AK................ USA...TEH
Tetuan/Sania Ramel... Morocco...TTU
Tewantin ....Australia.. TWN
Texarkana, AR........... USA... TXK
Tezpur/Salonibari ....India... TEZ
Tezu ....India....TEI
Thaba Nchu ....S. Africa.. TCU
Thakhek ....Laos...THK
Thakurgaon .... Bangladesh.. TKR
Thalba-Tselka ....Lesotho.. THB
Thalwil............. Switzerland.. ZKV
Thames .... New Zealand.. TMZ
Thandwe ....Myanmar.. SNW
Thangool ....Australia.. THG
Thanjavur ....India... TJV
Thargomindah ....Australia.. XTG
The Bight ....Bahamas... TBI
The Dalles, OR .... USA...DLS
The Hague/Holland Spoor
RR Stn. ....Netherlands...ZYH
The Pas, MB. ....Canada.. YQD
The Pas/RR Stn., MB ... Canada...XDZ
Thecia/Thecia Stn. ......Australia.. TDN
Theodore ....Australia..TDR
Thermopolis/Hot Springs, WY
.... USA...THP
Thessaloniki/Makedonia
.... Greece.. SKG
Thicket Portage, MB .. Canada...YTD
Thief River Falls/Regional, MN
.... USA... TVF
Thimbu ....Bhutan.. QJC
Thingeyn ....Iceland.. TEY
Thionvifle ....France...XTH
Thira .... Greece... JTR
Thirsk/RR Stn. .... UK...XTK
Thisted/Lufthavn ..... Denmark...TED
Thohoyandou ....S. Africa...THY
Thompson, MB ....Canada...YTH
Thompsonfield, MO...... USA...THM
Thonon Les Bains ..... France... XTS
Thornasville/Municipal, GAUSA...TVI
Thorne Bay, AK........ USA...KTB
Thorshofn ....Iceland.. THO
Thousand Oaks / HP, CA . USA...JTO
Thredbo/Bus Svc ......Australia.. QTH
Three Rivers/Dr Haines, MI USA... HAI
Thun .... Switzerland...ZTK
Thunder Bay, ON ...... Canada...YQT
Thurnrait...........Oman... TTH
Thursday Is ....Australia...TIS
Thylungra ....Australia...TYG
Tiaret .... Algeria... TID
Tiarijin ....China...TSN
Tibooburra ....Australia... TYB
Tibu ....Colombia... TIB
Ticantiki ....Panama... TJC
Tichitt .... Mauritania... THI
Tidjikia............ Mauritania... TIY
Tifton/Henry Tift Myers, GA. USA... TMA
Tiga ....New Caledonia... TGJ
Tignes ....France... TGF
Tijuana/Rodriguez ......Mexico... TIJ
Tikal/El Peten ...... Guatemala... TKM
Tikapur ....Nepal... TPU
Tikchik/SPB, AK .... USA...KTH
Tikehau Atoll...... F. Polynesia... TIH
Tiko .... Cameroon...TKC
Tiksi .... Russia... IKS
Tilfalmin ... Papua New Guinea... TFA
Tilin .... Myanmar... TIO
Timaru .... New Zealand... TIU
Timbauba ....Brazil... QTD
Timbedra .... Mauritania... TMD
Timber Creek ....Australia... TBK
Timbiqui ....Colombia...TBD
Timbo/Off-Line Point ...... Brazil... XHR
Timbunke .. Papua New Guinea... TBE
Timimoun ....Algeria... TMX
Timisoara .... Romania... TSR
Timmins, ON .... Canada...YTS

AIRPORTS

Tin City/AFS, AK . . . USA . . TNC
Tinak Is . . . Marshall Is . . . TIC
Tinboli Arpt Papua New Guinea . . TCK
Tindouf . . . Algeria . . . TIN
Tinge Maria . . . Peru . . . TGI
Tingrela . . . Côte D'Ivoire . . TGX
Tingwon . . . Papua New Guinea . . . TIG
Tinian . . . Northern Mariana Is . . . TIQ
Tinker/AFB, OK . . . USA . . . TIK
Tioga/Municipal, ND . . . USA . . VEX
Tiom . . . Indonesia . . TMY
Tioman . . . Malaysia . . TOD
Tippi . . . Ethiopia . . . TIE
Tipton/AAF, MD . . . USA . . FME
Tiputini . . . Ecuador . . TPN
Tirana/Rinas . . . Albania . . . TIA
Tiree . . . UK . . TRE
Tirgu Mures . . . Romania . . TGM
Tirinkot . . . Afghanistan . . . TII
Tiruchirapally/Civil . . . India . . TRZ
Tirupati . . . India . . . TIR
Tisdale, SK . . . Canada . . . YTT
Titusville, FL . . . USA . . . TIX
Tivat . . . Yugoslavia . . . TIV
Tizi Ouzou . . . Algeria . . . QZI
Tizimin . . . Mexico . . . TZM
Tlemcen/Zenata . . . Algeria . . TLM
Tlokoeng . . . Lesotho . . TKO
Tobago . . . Trinidad and Tobago . . TAB
Tobermorey . . . Australia . . . TYP
Tobolsk . . . Russia . . . TOX
Tobruk . . . Libya . . TOB
Toccoa, GA . . . USA . . TOC
Tocoa . . . Honduras . . TCF
Tocopilla/Barriles . . . Chile . . TOQ
Tocurnwal . . . Australia . . TCW
Tofino, BC . . . Canada . . YAZ
Tofino/Seaplane Base, BC . . . Canada . . . YTP
Togiak Fish, AK . . . USA . . GFB
Togiak Village, AK . . . USA . . TOG
Tokarna . . . Papua New Guinea . . . ITK
Tokat . . . Turkey . . . TJK
Tokeen, AK . . . USA . . . TKI
Tokoroa . . . New Zealand . . TKZ
Tokunoshima . . . Japan . . TKN
Tokushima AB . . . Japan . . TKS
Tokyo . . . Japan . . QXO
Tokyo/Haneda . . . Japan . . HND
Tokyo/Narita . . . Japan . . NRT
Tokyo/Yokota AFB . . . Japan . . OKO
Tol . . . Papua New Guinea . . TLO
Toledo . . . Brazil . . TOW
Toledo, OH . . . USA . . TDZ
Toledo, OH . . . USA . . TOL
Toledo, WA . . . USA . . TDO
Tolitoli/Lalos . . . Indonesia . . . TLI
Tolu . . . Colombia . . TLU
Toluca . . . Mexico . . TLC
Tom Price . . . Australia . . TPR
Tomakomaj . . . Japan . . QTM
Tomanggong . . . Malaysia . . TMG
Tombouctou . . . Mali . . TOM
Toms River/Robert J Miller, NJ . . . USA . . MJX
Tonghua/Tonghua Liuhe . . China . . TNH
Tongliao . . . China . . TGO
Tongoa . . . Vanuatu . . TGH
Tongren . . . China . . TEN
Tonopah, NV . . . USA . . TPH
Tonopah/Test Range, NV . . . USA . . XSD
Tonu . . . Papua New Guinea . . TON
Toowoomba . . . Australia . . TWB
Topeka Nexrad, KS . . . USA . . TWX
Topeka, KS . . . USA . . TOP
Torembi Arpt . . . Papua New Guinea . . . TCJ
Torokina . . . Papua New Guinea . . TOK
Toronto Buttonville, ON . . . Canada . . YKZ
Toronto/Pearson Int'l., ON . . . Canada . . YYZ
Toronto/Downtown RR Stn., ON . . . Canada . . YBZ
Toronto/Guildwood Rail Svc, ON . . . Canada . . XLQ
Toronto/Toronto Is, ON . Canada . . YTZ
Tororo . . . Uganda . . TRY
Torrance, CA . . . USA . . TOA
Torremolinos . . . Spain . . UTL
Torreon . . . Mexico . . TRC
Torres . . . Brazil . . TSQ
Torres/Torres Airstrip . . . Vanuatu . . TOH
Torrington, WY . . . USA . . TOR
Torsby/Torsby Arpt . . . Sweden . . TYF
Tortola/Road Town . . . Virgin Is (British) . . RAD
Tortola/West End SPB . . . Virgin Is (British) . . TOV
Tortoli/Arbatax . . . Italy . . TTB
Tortuquero . . . Costa Rica . . TTQ
Torwood . . . Australia . . TWP
Totness/Coronie . . . Suriname . . TOT
Tottenham Hale Stn. . . . UK . . TTK
Tottori . . . Japan . . TTJ
Touba/Mahana . . . Côte D'Ivoire . . TOZ
Tougan . . . Burkina Faso . . TUQ
Touggourt . . . Algeria . . TGR
Touho . . . New Caledonia . . TOU
Toulon/Hyeres . . . France . . TLN
Toulouse/Blagnac . . . France . . TLS
Toulouse/Montaudran . . France . . XYT
Tour Sinai City . . . Egypt . . ELT
Tourcoing . . . France . . XTN
Tournai . . . Belgium . ZGQ
Tours/RR Stn. . . . France . . XJT
Tours/RR Stn. . . . France . . XSH
Tours/St Symphorien . . . France . . TUF
Toussus Le Noble . . . France . . TNF
Townsville . . . Australia . . TSV
Toyama . . . Japan . . TOY
Toyooka/Tapma . . . Japan . . TJH
Tozeur/Nefta . . . Tunisia . . TOE
Trabzon . . . Turkey . . TZX
Trang . . . Thailand . . TST
Trapani/Birgi . . . Italy . . TPS
Traralgon/La Trobe Regional . . . Australia . . TGN
Traverse City, MI . . . USA . . TVC
Travis/AFB, CA . . . USA . . SUU
Treasure Cay . . . Bahamas . . TCB
Tree Point/Cst Guard Heliport, AK . . . USA . . TRP
Treinta-y-Tres . . . Uruguay . . TYT
Trelew . . . Argentina . . REL
Tremonton, UT . . . USA . . TRT
Trento . . . Italy . . ZIA
Trenton, NJ . . . USA . . TTN
Trenton, ON . . . Canada . . YTR
Trenton/Memorial, MO . . . USA . . TRX
Tres Arroyos . . . Argentina . . OYO
Tres Coracoes . . . Brazil . . QID
Tres Esquinas . . . Colombia . . TQS
Tres Rios . . . Brazil . . QIH
Trier . . . Germany . . ZQF
Trieste/Dei Legionari . . . Italy . . TRS
Trincomalee/China BaySri Lanka . . TRR
Trinidad . . . Colombia . . TDA
Trinidad . . . Bolivia . . TDD
Trinidad . . . Cuba . . TND
Trinidad, CO . . . USA . . TAD
Triple Is, BC . . . Canada . . . YTI
Tripoli/Int'l . . . Libya . . . TIP
Tripoli/Kleyate . . . Lebanon . . KYE
Trivandrum/Int'l . . . India . . TRV
Trois-Rivieres, QC . . . Canada . . YRQ
Troisdorf . . . Germany . ZQG
Trollhattan/Private . . . Sweden . . THN
Trombetas . . . Brazil . . TMT
Tromso/Langnes . . . Norway . . TOS
Trona, CA . . . USA . . TRH
Trondheim/Vaernes . . . Norway . . . TRD
Troy, AL . . . USA . . . TOI
Troyes . . . France . . QYR
Truckee, CA . . . USA . . . TKF
Trujillo . . . Peru . . . TRU
Trujillo/Capiro . . . Honduras . . . TJI
Truk . . . Micronesia . . . TKK
Truro/RR Stn., NS . . . Canada . . . XLZ
Truth Or Consequences, NM . . . USA . . . TCS
Tsabong . . . Botswana . . . TBY
Tsaratanana . . . Madagascar . . . TTS
Tsetserleg . . . Mongolia . . . TSZ
Tsewi . . . Papua New Guinea . . TSW
Tshikapa . . . Congo, DR . . . TSH
Tshipise . . . S. Africa . . TSD
Tsili Tsili . . . Papua New Guinea . . . TSI
Tsiroanomandidy Madagascar . . WTS
Tsu . . . Japan . . . QTY
Tsuen Wan/RR Stn. . Hong Kong . . ZTW
Tsukuba . . . Japan . . . XEI
Tsumeb . . . Namibia . . . TSB
Tsushima . . . Japan . . . TSJ
Tuba City, AZ . . . USA . . . TBC
Tubala . . . Panama . . TUW
Tubarao . . . Brazil . . . ZHX
Tubuai . . . F. Polynesia . . . TUB
Tucson Int'l, AZ . . . USA . . . TUS
Tucson/AFB, AZ . . . USA . . DMA
Tucson/Avra Valley, AZ . . . USA . . AVW
Tucuma . . . Brazil . . . TUZ
Tucumcari, NM . . . USA . . . TCC
Tucupita . . . Venezuela . . . TUV
Tucurui . . . Brazil . . . TUR
Tuebingen . . . Germany . . ZQH
Tueuman/Benj Matienzo . . . Argentina . . TUC
Tufl . . . Papua New Guinea . . . TFI
Tuguegarao . . . Philippines . . TUG
Tuicea . . . Romania . . . TCE
Tuiugak, QC . . . Canada . . . YTK
Tukloyaktuk, NT . . . Canada . . YUB
Tula . . . Russia . . . TYA
Tulagi Is . . . Solomon Is . . . TLG
Tulare, CA . . . USA . . . TLR
Tulcan . . . Ecuador . . . TUA
Tulear . . . Madagascar . . . TLE
Tuli Lodge . . . Botswana . . . TLD
Tulita/Ft. Norman, NT . . . Canada . . . ZFN
Tullahoma/Arnold AFS, TN. USA . . TUH
Tullahoma/Northern, TN . . . USA . . . THA
Tulle . . . France . . . XTU
Tulsa/Int'l, OK . . . USA . . . TUL
Tulsa, OK . . . USA . . . RVS
Tulsa/Off-Line Pt (Fedex), OKUSA . . ZFF
Tulua/Farfan . . . Colombia . . ULQ
Tuluksak, AK . . . USA . . . TLT
Tulum . . . Mexico . . . TUY
Tumbang Samba . . . Indonesia . . TBM
Tumbes . . . Peru . . . TBP
Tumbler Ridge, BC . . . Canada . . . TUX
Tumeremo . . . Venezuela . . TMO
Tumling Tar . . . Nepal . . . TMI
Tumolbil . . . Papua New Guinea . . . TLP
Tumut . . . Australia . . TUM
Tungsten, NT . . . Canada . . . TNS
Tunis/Carthage . . . Tunisia . . TUN
Tuntutuliak, AK . . . USA . . WTL
Tununak, AK . . . USA . . . TNK
Tunxl . . . China . . . TXN
Tupelo, MS . . . USA . . . TUP
Tupi Paulista . . . Brazil . . QTG
Tupile . . . Panama . . . TUE
Turaif . . . Saudi Arabia . . . TUI
Turbat . . . Pakistan . . . TUK
Turbo/Gonzalo . . . Colombia . . . TRB
Tureira . . . F. Polynesia . . . ZTA
Turin/Bus Svc . . . Italy . . . ZTC
Turin/Citta Di Torino . . . Italy . . . TRN
Turkey Creek . . . Australia . . . TKY
Turkmanbashi . . . Turkmenistan . . KRW

AIRPORTS

Turku	Finland	TKU
Turn	Ethiopia	TUJ
Turnaco/La Florida	Colombia	TCO
Turtle Is	Fiji	TTL
Tuscaloosa, AL	USA	TCL
Tuskegee/Sharpe Fld, AL	USA	TGE
Tuticorin	India	TCR
Tuxtia Gutierrez/Llano San Juan		
	Mexico	TGZ
Tuy Hoa	Vietnam	TBB
Tuzia/Tuzla Int'l		
	Bosnia Herzegovina	TZL
Tweed-New Haven, CT	USA	HVN
Twenty-Nine Palms, Marine Corps Air-Ground Combat Center, CA.	USA	NXP
Twentynine Palms, CA	USA	TNP
Twin Falls, ID	USA	TWF
Twin Hills, AK	USA	TWA
Two Harbors, MN	USA	TWM
Tyler, TX	USA	TYR
Tyncia	Russia	TYD
Tyndall/AFB, FL	USA	PAM
Tyonek, AK	USA	TYE
Tyumen	Russia	TJM
Tzaneen/Letaba	S. Africa	LTA

U

Uaxactun	Guatemala	UAX
Ubari	Libya	QUB
Ubatuba	Brazil	UBT
Ube	Japan	UBJ
Uberaba	Brazil	UBA
Uberlandia/Eduardo Gomes	Brazil	UDI
Ubon Ratchathani	Thailand	UBP
Ubrub	Indonesia	UBR
Udaipur/Dabok	India	UDR
Uden/Volkel	Netherlands	UDE
Udine/Airfield	Italy	UDN
Udomxay	Laos	UDO
Udon Thani	Thailand	UTH
Uetersen/Off-line Pt	Germany	QSM
Ufa	Russia	UFA
Uganik, AK	USA	UGI
Ugashik, AK	USA	UGS
Uherske Hradiste	Czech Rep	UHE
Uige	Andorra	UGO
Uijongbu	S. Korea	QUJ
Uisan	S. Korea	USN
Ujae Is	Marshall Is	UJE
Ujung Pandang/Hasanudin		
	Indonesia	UPG
Ukhta	Russia	UCT
Ukiah, CA	USA	UKI
Ukunda	Kenya	UKA
Ulaangom	Mongolia	ULO
Ulaaribaatar/Buyant Uhaa		
	Mongolia	ULN
Ulan-Ude	Russia	UUD
Ulanhot	China	HLH
Ulei/Los Cerrillos	Vanuatu	ULB
Ulgit	Mongolia	ULG
Ulithi	Micronesia	ULI
Ulm	Germany	QUL
Ulundi	S. Africa	ULD
Ulusaba	S. Africa	ULX
Ulyanovsk	Russia	ULY
Umba	Papua New Guinea	UMC
Umea/Flygplats	Sweden	UME
Umiat, AK	USA	UMT
Umm Alquwain	UAE	QIW
Umnak Is/North Shore, AK	USA	UMB
Umnak Is/Umnak, AK	USA	UNS
Umuarama/Ernesto Geisel	Brazil	UMU
Unalakleet, AK	USA	UNK
Unayzah	Saudi Arabia	UZH
Unciarra	Australia	UDA

Underkhaan	Mongolia	UNR
Unguia	Colombia	UNC
Uniao Da Vitoria	Brazil	QVB
Union City/Everett-Stewart, TN		
	USA	UCY
Union Isl		
	St. Vincent & Grenadines	UNI
Union South Carolina, SC	USA	USC
Unna	Germany	ZQI
Unst Shetland Is	UK	UNT
Unuzgan	Afghanistan	URZ
Upala	Costa Rica	UPL
Upavon	UK	UPV
Upernavik/ HP	Greenland	JUV
Upington	S. Africa	UTN
Upland/Cable HP, CA	USA	JUP
Upland/Cable, CA	USA	CCB
Uplara	Papua New Guinea	UPR
Upolu Point, HI	USA	UPP
Upper Heyford/RAF	UK	UHF
Uraj	Russia	URJ
Uralsk	Kazakstan	URA
Uranium City, SK	Canada	YBE
Urgench	Uzbekistan	UGC
Urgoon	Afghanistan	URN
Uribe	Colombia	URI
Uriman	Venezuela	URM
Urmieh	Iran	OMH
Urniujaq, QC	Canada	YUD
Urntata	S. Africa	UTT
Uroubi	Papua New Guinea	URU
Urrao	Colombia	URR
Uruapan	Mexico	UPN
Urubupunga/Ernesto Pochier		
	Brazil	URB
Uruguaiana/Ruben Berta	Brazil	URG
Urumqi	China	URC
Usak	Turkey	USQ
Useless Loop	Australia	USL
Ushuaia/Islas Malvinas	Argentina	USH
Usino	Papua New Guinea	USO
Usinsk	Russia	USK
Ust-Kamenogorsk	Kazakstan	UKK
Ust-Kut	Russia	UKX
Ust-Llimsk	Russia	UIK
Ustupo	Panama	UTU
Utapato	Thailand	UTP
Utica, NY	USA	UCA
Utica/Berz-Macomb, MI	USA	UIZ
Utica/Utica NY Rail	USA	ZUA
Utila	Honduras	UII
Utirik Is	Marshall Is	UTK
Utrecht/RR Stn.	Netherlands	ZYU
Utrecht/Soesterberg	Netherlands	UTC
Utsunomiya AB	Japan	QUT
Uttaradit	Thailand	UTR
Uummannaq	Greenland	UMD
Uvaide/Garner Fld, TX	USA	UVA
Uvramento/Dos Galpoes	Brazil	LVB
Uyo	Nigeria	QUO
Uzhgorod	Ukraine	UDJ
Uzice	Yugoslavia	ZZE
Uzice/Ponikve	Yugoslavia	UZC
Uzwil	Switzerland	ZKX

V

V.C. Bird Int'l		
	Antigua & Barbuda	ANU
Vaasa	Finland	VAA
Vadodara	India	BDQ
Vadso	Norway	VDS
Vaduz	Liechtenstein	QVU
Vaeroy/Stolport	Norway	VRY
Vahitahi	F. Polynesia	VHZ
Vaienca	Brazil	VAL
Valevo	Yugoslavia	QWV
Vail Van Svc, CO	USA	QBF

Vail, CO	USA	EGE
Vail/Eagle/Beaver Creek Van Svc, CO.	USA	ZBV
Val D'Isere	France	VAZ
Val D'Or, QC	Canada	YVO
Valbonne	France	QVI
Valcartier, QC	Canada	YOY
Valcheta	Argentina	VCF
Valdez/Municipal, AK	USA	VDZ
Valdivia/Pichoy	Chile	ZAL
Valdosta, GA	USA	VLD
Valence/Chalpeuil	France	VAF
Valencia	Spain	VLC
Valencia	Venezuela	VLN
Valenciennes/RR Stn.	France	XVS
Valentine, NE	USA	VTN
Valera/Carvajal	Venezuela	VLV
Valesdir	Vanuatu	VLS
Valkeakoski	Finland	QVK
Valladolid	Spain	VLL
Valle De Pascua	Venezuela	VDP
Valle, AZ	Australia	VLE
Valledupar	Colombia	VUP
Vallegrande	Bolivia	VAH
Vallejo/Stolport, CA	USA	VLO
Vallemi/INC	Paraguay	VMI
Vallenar	Chile	VLR
Valloire	France	XVR
Valparaiso	Chile	VAP
Valparaiso, FL	USA	EGI
Valparaiso, IN	USA	VPZ
Valverde/Hierro	Spain	VDE
Van	Turkey	VAN
Van Horn/Cullberson County, TX		
	USA	VHN
Vancouver/Int'l, BC	Canada	YVR
Vancouver, Pearson Airpark, WA		
	USA	VUO
Vancouver/Boundary Bay, BC		
	Canada	YDT
Vancouver/Coal Harbour, BC		
	Canada	CXH
Vancouver/RR Stn., BC	Canada	XEA
Vandalia, IL	USA	VLA
Vandenberg/AFB, CA	USA	VBG
Vandoe	Norway	VAW
Vangaindrano	Madagascar	VND
Vangrieng	Laos	VGG
Vanimo	Papua New Guinea	VAI
Vannes/Meucon	Eritrea	VNE
Vanrook	Australia	VNR
Vanuabalavu	Fiji	VBV
Varadero/Juan Gualberto Gomez		
	Cuba	VRA
Varanasi	India	VNS
Varese	Italy	QVA
Varginha/M. B. Trompowsky	Brazil	VAG
Varkaus	Finland	VRK
Varna	Bulgaria	VAR
Varrelbusch	Germany	VAC
Vasteras/Hasslo	Sweden	VST
Vastervik	Sweden	VVK
Vatomandry	Madagascar	VAT
Vatulele	Fiji	VTF
Vatulkoula	Fiji	VAU
Vava'u/Lupepau'u	Tonga	VAV
Vaxjo	Sweden	VXO
Vejle	Denmark	VEJ
Vejle/RR Stn.	Denmark	XVX
Velbert	Germany	ZQJ
Veldhoven/RR Stn.	Netherlands	ZVH
Velikij Ustyug	Russia	VUS
Velikiye Luki	Russia	VLU
Vendome	France	XVD
Venetie, AK	USA	VEE
Venice, FL	USA	VNC
Venice/Marco Polo	Italy	VCE
Venice/Treviso	Italy	TSF
Veracruz/Las Bajadas	Mexico	VER
Verbier	Switzerland	ZKY
Verden	Germany	QVQ

Verdun . . . . .France . . XVN
Vermilion, AB . . . . .Canada . . YVG
Vermillion Area, LA . . . . . .USA . . VRX
Vernal, UT . . . . .USA . . VEL
Vernon, BC . . . . .Canada . . YVE
Vero Beach, FL. . . . . .USA . . VRB
Verona/Villafranca . . . . Italy . . VRN
Versailles . . . . .France . . XVE
Versailles, MO . . . . .USA . . VRS
Vesoul . . . . .France . . XVO
Vestbjerg/Bus Svc . . . .Denmark . . QXF
Vestmannaeyjar . . . . Iceland . . VEY
Veszprern . . . . Hungary . . ZFP
Vevey . . . . .Switzerland . . ZKZ
Viborg/RR Stn. . . . . .Denmark . ZGX
Vicenza . . . . Italy . . VIC
Vichadero . . . . .Uruguay . . VCH
Vichy, MO. . . . . .USA . . VIH
Vichy/Charmeil . . . . .France . . VHY
Vicksburg, MS . . . . .USA . . VKS
Vicksburg/Tallulah Rgnl. Arpt, LA
. . . . .USA . . TVR
Vicosa . . . . Brazil . QVC
Victoria . . . . .Honduras . . VTA
Victoria . . . . Chile . . ZIC
Victoria Falls . . . . .Zimbabwe . . VFA
Victoria Harbour, BC . .Canada . .YWH
Victoria/Int'l, BC . . . . . . .Canada . . YYJ
Victoria Is . . . . .Nigeria . QVL
Victoria River Downs Australia . .VCD
Victoria, TX . . . . .USA . . VCT
Vidalia/Municipal, GA. . . . . .USA . . VDI
Videira . . . . .Brazil . . VIA
Vidin . . . . .Bulgaria . . VID
Viedma . . . . .Argentina . VDM
Viengxay . . . . Laos . . VNG
Vienna Int'l . . . . .Austria . . VIE
Vienna/Danubelpier Hov .Austria . . VDD
Vienne . . . . .France . . XVI
Vientiane/Wattav . . . . Laos . .VTE
Vieques . . . . .Puerto Rico . . VQS
Viersen. . . . . .Germany . . ZQK
Vierzon. . . . . .France . . XVZ
View Cove, AK . . . . .USA . . VCB
Vigo. . . . . .Spain . .VGO
Vijayawada . . . . India . .VGA
Vikna. . . . . .Norway . .ZXD
Vila Real . . . . .Portugal . . VRL
Vila Rica/Mun . . . . .Brazil . .VLP
Vila Velha . . . . Brazil . QVH
Vilanculos . . . . .Mozambique . . VNX
Vilgenis . . . . .France . .QVG
Vilhelmina. . . . . Sweden . .VHM
Vilhena. . . . . Brazil . .BVH
Villa Constitucion . . . . Mexico . . VIB
Villa Dolores . . . . .Argentina . . VDR
Villa Gesell . . . . .Argentina . .VLG
Villa Mercedes. . . . . . .Argentina . .VME
Villagarzon . . . . .Colombia . .VGZ
Village/SPB, AK . . . . .USA . .KWP
Villahermosa/Capitan
Carlos Perez . . . . Mexico . . VSA
Villamontes . . . . .Bolivia . .VLM
Villars . . . . .Switzerland . . ZLA
Villavicencio/La Vanguardia
. . . . Colombia . .VVC
Villefranche Sur Saone France . . .XVF
Villepinte . . . . .France . . XVP
Villingen-Schwenningen
. . . . .Germany . . ZQL
Vilnius/Int'l . . . . .Lithuania . .VNO
Vina del Mar . . . . Chile . .KNA
Vincennes/Oneal, IN . . . . .USA . . OEA
Vinh City . . . . .Vietnam . . VII
Vinh Long . . . . .Vietnam . .XVL
Vinnica. . . . . .Ukraine . . VIN
Viqueque. . . . . .Indonesia . .VIQ
Virac . . . . .Philippines . .VRC
Virgin Gorda . . Virgin Is (British) . . VIJ
Virginia Tech Arpt, VA. . . . .USA . . BCB
Viru/Viru Harbour . . . . Solomon Is . .VIU

Visalia, CA . . . . USA . . .VIS
Visby/Flygplats. . . . . . . Sweden . .VBY
Viseu . . . . Portugal . .VSE
Vishakhapatnam . . . . India . .VTZ
Visp . . . . .Switzerland . . ZLB
Vitebsk . . . . .Belarus . .VTB
Vitoria Da Conquista . . . .Brazil . .VDC
Vitoria. . . . . Spain . . . VIT
Vitoria/Euroo Sales . . . . . .Brazil . .VIX
Vitre . . . . France . . XVT
Vittel . . . . Eritrea . .VTL
Vivigani . . . Papua New Guinea . . VIV
Vladikavkaz. . . . . Russia . OGZ
Vladivostok . . . . Russia . .VVO
Voelklingen . . . . .Germany . ZQM
Vohemar. . . . . .Madagascar . VOH
Voinjama . . . . Liberia . . VOI
Vojens/RR Stn. . . . . Denmark . XJE
Vojens/Skrydstrup/Military
. . . . Denmark . . SKS
Volens, VA . . . . USA . VQN
Volgodonsk. . . . . Russia . VLK
Volgograd . . . . Russia . VOG
Vologida . . . . Russia . VGD
Volos/Nea Anchialos . . . .Greece . . VOL
Volta Redonda . . . . .Brazil . QVR
Vopnafjordur . . . . .Iceland . .VPN
Vorkuta . . . . .Russia . VKT
Voronezh . . . . Russia . .VOZ
Votuporanga . . . . .Brazil . .VOT
Vraidebria . . . . .Bulgaria . QVJ
Vredendal . . . . S. Africa . .VRE
Vryburg . . . . S. Africa . .VRU
Vryheid . . . . S. Africa . .VYD
Vung Tau . . . . Vietnam . .VTG

W

W Memphis/Municipal, AR USA . AWM
Wabag . . . . . Papua New Guinea . WAB
Wabo . . . . . . Papua New Guinea . WAO
Wabush, NF . . . . Canada . YWK
Waca . . . . Ethiopia . WAC
Waco Kungo. . . . . Angola . CEO
Waco, TX. . . . . USA . .ACT
Waco/James Connall, TX . . USA . CNW
Wad Medani . . . . .Somalia . . DNI
Waddington/RAF Stn . . . . . .UK . WTN
Wadi Ad Dawasir . . Saudi Arabia . WAE
Wadi Ain. . . . . Yemen . WDA
Wadi Halfa. . . . . .Somalia . WHF
Waedenswil/Off-line Pt . . . .
Switzerland . . . . .ZLC
Wagau . . . . . Papua New Guinea . WGU
Wageningen . . . . .Suriname . . AGI
Wagethe . . . . .Indonesia . .WET
Wagga Wagga/Forrest Hill
. . . . Australia . WGA
Wagny . . . . Gabon . WGY
Wahai . . . . .Indonesia . .WBA
Wahpeton, ND. . . . . USA . WAH
Waiblingen . . . . .Germany . ZQO
Waikoloa/Waikoloa Arpt, HI USA . WKL
Waimanalo/Bellows Fld, HI USA . .BLW
Waingapu/Mau Hau . .Indonesia . WGP
Wainwright Arpt, AB. . Canada . YWV
Wainwright, AK. . . . . USA . . AIN
Wainwright, AK. . . . . USA . . AWI
Wairoa . . . . .New Zealand . WIR
Waitangi . . . . .New Zealand . WGN
Wajir . . . . Kenya . WJR
Wakaya Is . . . . Fiji . KAY
Wakayama. . . . . .Japan . .QKY
Wake Is . . . . . . Wake/Midway Is . WAK
Wakefield Westgate/RR Stn. UK . XWD
Wakkanai/Hokkaido . . . . .Japan . .WKJ
Wakunai . . . Papua New Guinea . WKN
Walaba . . . . Vanuatu . WIH

Walcha. . . . . .Australia. . WLC
Waldron Is, WA . . . . USA. .WDN
Wales, AK . . . . USA. . WAA
Walgett . . . . .Australia. .WGE
Walial . . . . .Australia. . WLA
Walker's Cay . . . . .Bahamas. .WKR
Walla Walla, WA. . . . . USA. . ALW
Wallis Is . . . Wallis and Futuna Is. . WLS
Wallops Is, VA . . . . USA. . WAL
Walnut Ridge, AR. . . . . . . USA. . ARG
Waltham, MA . . . . USA. .WLM
Walvis Bay/Rooikop . . .Namibia. . WVB
Wamena . . . . .Indonesia. .WMX
Wana . . . . .Pakistan. . WAF
Wanaka . . . . New Zealand. .WKA
Wanganui . . . . New Zealand. .WAG
Wangaratta . . . . .Australia. .WGT
Wangerooge/FluglplatzGermany . AGE
Wanigela. . . Papua New Guinea. . AGL
Wantoat. . . . Papua New Guinea. . WTT
Wanurna . . . Papua New Guinea. .WNU
Wanxian . . . . China. . WXN
Wapakoneta/Armstrong, OHUSA . .AXV
Wapenamanda
. . . . Papua New Guinea. .WBM
Wapolu . . . Papua New Guinea. .WBC
Warder. . . . . .Ethiopia. .WRA
Ware, MA . . . . USA. . UWA
Waris . . . . .Indonesia. . WAR
Warm Spring Bay/SPB, AK USA. .BNF
Warmarnboof . . . . .Australia. .WMB
Warn. . . . . .Nigeria. . QRW
Warnemuende/RR Stn.Germany . ZWD
Warracknabeal . . . . .Australia. . WKB
Warrangal. . . . . .India. .WGC
Warrawagine . . . . .Australia. WRW
Warren. . . . . .Australia. . QRR
Warrington B.Q./RR Stn. . . . UK. . XWN
Warroad, MN . . . . .USA. . .RRT
Warszawa/Okecie . . . . . .Poland. .WAW
Warwick . . . . .Australia. . WAZ
Washabo. . . . . .Suriname. .WSO
Washington D.C. . . . . USA. . DCA
Washington, IA . . . . USA. .AWG
Washington, NC . . . . USA. . OCW
Washington/Buzzards Pt S., DCUSA . .
BZS
Washington/County, PA . . . USA. .WSG
Washington/New Carrolton RR, DC
. . . . USA. . ZRZ
Washington/Pentagon Army, DC
. . . . .USA. . JPN
Washington/Washington DC Rail
. . . . .USA. . ZWU
Wasilia, AK . . . . USA. .WWA
Wasior . . . . .Indonesia. . WSR
Waskaganish, QC . . . . . Canada. . YKQ
Waspam . . . . .Netherlands. . WSP
Wasu . . . . . . Papua New Guinea. .WSU
Wasua . . . . . Papua New Guinea. .WSA
Wasum . . . . Papua New Guinea. .WUM
Waterfall/SPS, AK . . . . . . USA. . KWF
Waterford . . . . .Ireland. . WAT
Waterloo . . . . .Australia. .WLO
Waterloo, IA . . . . USA. . ALO
Watertown, NY . . . . USA. . ART
Watertown, SD . . . . .USA. . ATY
Watertown, WI . . . . USA. .RYV
Waterville/Robert Lafleur, ME
. . . . USA. . WVL
Watford/RR Stn., ON . . Canada. . XWA
Watson Lake, YT. . . . . . Canada. . YQH
Watsonville, CA. . . . . USA. .WVI
Wau . . . . . . Papua New Guinea. .WUG
Wau . . . . Sudan. .WUU
Wauchope . . . . .Australia. .WAU
Waukesha, WI . . . . USA. . UES
Waukon/Municipal, IA . . . . USA. . UKN
Wausau, WI . . . . .USA. . AUW
Wave Hill/Kalkgurung .Australia. . WAV
Waverney . . . . .Australia. .WAN

Wavre . . . . Belgium . . ZGV
Wawa, ON . . . . .Canada . . YXZ
Wawoi Falls Papua New Guinea . . WAJ
Waycross/Ware County, GA
. . . . .USA . . AYS
Waynesburg/Green County, PA
. . . . .USA . . WAY
Wearn . . . . . . Papua New Guinea . . WEP
Weasua . . . . Iran . . WES
Weatherford/Parker County, TX
. . . . .USA . . WEA
Webster City, IA . . . . .USA . . EBS
Wedau . . . . .Papua New Guinea . . WED
Wedjh . . . . Saudi Arabia . . EJH
Wee Waa . . . . Australia . . WEW
Weeping Water/Browns, NE USA . . EPG
Weifang . . . . .China . . WEE
Weihai . . . . China . . WEH
Weinfelden . . . . .Switzerland . . ZLD
Weingarten . . . . Germany . ZWG
Weipa . . . . Australia . .WEI
Welbequie, ON . . . . . . .Canada . . YWP
Welkorn . . . . S. Africa . . WEL
Wellingborough/RR Stn. . . UK . XWE
Wellington . . . . Australia . . QEL
Wellington/Int'l . . New Zealand . . WLG
Wells/Harriet Fld, NV . . . . .USA . . LWL
Wellsville, NY . . . . .USA . .ELZ
Welshpool . . . . Australia . .WHL
Wemindpi, QC . . . . .Canada . . YNC
Wenatchee, WA . . . . .USA . .EAT
Wendover, UT . . . . .USA . . ENV
Wengen . . . . .Switzerland . .ZLE
Werizinou . . . . .China . .WNZ
Wesel . . . . Germany . ZQP
West Chicago, IL . . . . .USA . . DPA
West End . . . . Bahamas . .WTD
West Kavik, AK . . . . .USA . .VKW
West Kuparuk, AK. . . . . . . .USA . . XPU
West Malling . . . . .UK . WEM
West Palm Beach, FL . . . . .USA . . LNA
West Palm Beach, FL . . . . .USA . . PBI
West Palm Beach/RR Stn., FL
. . . . .USA . . ZWP
West Plains Municipal Arpt,
MO. .USA . . UNO
West Send, WI . . . . .USA . . ETB
West Woodward, OK . . . . .USA . . WWR
West Wyalong . . . . Australia . . WWY
West Yellowstone, MT . . . .USA . . WEY
West Yellowstone, MT . . .USA . . WYS
Westchester County, NY .USA . . HPN
Westchester County/Stamford
RR Stn., NY . . . . .USA . .ZTF
Westerland/Sylt . . . . . Germany . GWT
Westerly, RI . . . . .USA . .WST
Westfield/Barnes, MA . . . .USA . . BAF
Westhampton, NY . . . . . . .USA . . FOK
Westport . . . . New Zealand . . WSZ
Westray . . . . .UK . .WRY
Westsound, WA . . . . .USA . . WSX
Wettingen . . . . .Switzerland . .ZLF
Wetzikon . . . . .Switzerland . . ZKW
Wetzlar. . . . . Germany . ZQQ
Wewak/Boram
. . . . .Papua New Guinea . . WWK
Wexford/Castlebridge . . . Ireland . . WEX
Weymont/RR Stn., QC . .Canada . . XFQ
Wha Ti/Lac La Martre, NT
. . . . .Canada . .YLE
Whakatane . . . . . New Zealand . . WHK
Whale Cove, NU . . . . . . .Canada . . YXN
Whale Pass, AK . . . . .USA . . WWP
Whalsay . . . . .UK . .WHS
Whangarei . . . . . . New Zealand . . WRE
Wharton, TX . . . . .USA . .WHT
Wheatland/Phifer Fld, WY . .USA . . EAN
Wheeler/AFB, HI . . . . .USA . .HHI
Wheeling, WV . . . . .USA . . HLG

Whidbey Is/NAS, WA . . . . . USA . NUW
Whistler, BC. . . . . Canada . . YWS
White Mountain, AK . . . . . USA . WMO
White River, AZ. . . . . USA . WTR
White River, ON . . . . Canada . YWR
White Sands/Condron/AAF, NM
. . . . USA . WSD
White Sulphur Sprng, WV USA . . SSU
Whitecourt, AB . . . . Canada . . YZU
Whitefield, NH. . . . . USA . .HIE
Whitehouse, FL . . . . USA . .NEN
Whiteman/AFB, MO . . . . . . USA . . SZL
Whitesburg/Municipal, KY. USA . BRG
Whitianga . . . . . . .New Zealand . WTZ
Whyalla . . . . .Australia . .WYA
Wiarton, ON. . . . . Canada . YVV
Wichita Falls/Kickapoo, KS
. . . . USA . . KIP
Wichita Mid-Continent, KS
. . . . USA . .ICT
Wichita, KS . . . . USA . BEC
Wichita/Cessna Aircraft Fld, KS
. . . . USA . .CEA
Wick. . . . . .UK . WIC
Wiesbaden . . . . Germany . UWE
Wiesbaden/Air Base. . Germany . . WIE
Wigan N.W./RR Stn. . . . . . . UK . XWI
Wil . . . . Switzerland . ZLH
Wilcannia . . . . Australia . WIO
Wildenrath. . . . . Germany . WID
Wildwood/Cape May County,
NJ . . . . USA .WWD
Wildwood/USAF HP, AK. . . USA . WWS
Wilhelmshaven . . . . . Germany . WVN
Wilkes-Barre/Wyoming Valle,
PA . . . . USA .WBW
Wilkesboro/Wilkes County, NC
. . . . USA . .IKB
Williams Harbour, NF. Canada . YWM
Williams Lake, BC. . . . Canada . .YWL
Williams/AFB, AZ . . . . . . USA . CHD
Williamsport, PA . . . . USA . IPT
Willimantic/Windham, CT . USA . .IJD
Williston/Sloulin Fld Int'l, ND USA . .ISN
Willmar, MN . . . . USA . ILL
Willoughby, OH . . . . USA .LNN
Willow Grove/NAS, PA . . . USA . NXX
Willow, AK . . . . USA .WOW
Willows/Glenn County, CA. USA . WLW
Wilmington Nexrad, NC . USA . LTX
Wilmington, Airborne Airpark, OH
. . . . USA . .ILN
Wilmington, DE . . . . USA . .ILG
Wilmington, New Hanover Int'l,
NC . . . . USA . ILM
Wilmington/Wilmington Rail, DE
. . . . USA . ZWI
Wilton, CT/Off-line Pt. . . . . USA .QCW
Wiluna . . . . Australia . WUN
Winchester, VA . . . . USA . .OKV
Winchester/Municipal, VA . USA .WGO
Windarra . . . . Australia . WND
Winder, GA. . . . . USA . WDR
Windhoek/Eros . . . . . . Namibia . . ERS
Windhoek/H. Kutako Int'l
. . . . Namibia . WDH
Windhoek/RR Stn. . . . . . Namibia . ZWH
Windom, MN . . . . USA .MWM
Windorah. . . . . Australia . WNR
Windsor, ON . . . . Canada . YQG
Windsor/RR Stn., ON . . Canada . .XEC
Winfield, KS. . . . . USA . WLD
Winisk, ON. . . . . Canada . YWN
Wink, TX . . . . USA . . INK
Winnemucca, NV . . . . . . USA . WMC
Winner, SD . . . . USA . NED
Winnipeg/Int'l, MB. . . . . Canada . YWG
Winnipeg/RR Stn., MB . Canada . XEF
Winona, MN . . . . USA . ONA

Winslow Municipal, AZ. . . USA. . .INW
Winston Salem, NC . . . . .USA. . . INT
Winter Haven/Gilbert Fld, FL
. . . . .USA. . . GIF
Winter Park/Van Svc, CO . . USA . . QWP
Winterthur . . . . Switzerland. . . .ZLI
Winton . . . . .Australia. . .WIN
Wipim . . . . . Papua New Guinea. . WPM
Wiscasset, ME. . . . . .USA. . . ISS
Wiscasset, ME. . . . . .USA. . .IWI
Wisconsin Rapids, WI . . USA. . . ISW
Wise, VA. . . . . .USA. . .LNP
Wiseman, AK. . . . . .USA. .WSM
Wismar/RR Stn. . . . . . .Germany. . ZWM
Withehorse, YT . . . . . . .Canada. . .YXY
Witten . . . . .Germany. . ZQR
Wittenberg/RR Stn. . . . .Germany. . ZWT
Wittenberge/RR Stn. . . .Germany. . ZWN
Wittenoom . . . . .Australia. . . WIT
Witu . . . . Papua New Guinea . . WIU
Wloclawek . . . . Poland. .QWK
Woburn/Cummings Park, MA USA . WBN
Woensdrecht. . . . . . .Netherlands. . WDT
Woensdrecht/AB . Netherlands. . WOE
Woergi/Bus Svc . . . . Austria. . QXZ
Woitape . . . . Papua New Guinea. . WTP
Woja . . . . .Marshall Is. . WJA
Woking/RR Stn. . . . . .UK. .XWO
Wolf Point Int'l, MT. . . . . . .USA. . .OLF
Wolfenbuettel . . . . .Germany. . ZQT
Wolfsburg/Off-line Pt . . Germany. . ZQU
Wollaston Lake, SK . . Canada. . ZWL
Wollogorang . . . . .Australia. . .WLI
Wollongong . . . . .Australia. . WOL
Wologissi . . . . Liberia. . .WOI
Wolverhampton/RR . . . . . .UK. . XVW
Wonan . . . . Taiwan. . WOT
Wondai . . . . .Australia. . .WDI
Wondoola . . . . .Australia. . WON
Wonenara . . Papua New Guinea. . WOA
Wonju . . . . S. Korea. . WJU
Wonken . . . . Venezuela. . WOK
Wood River, AK. . . . . .USA. . WOD
Woodbridge. . . . . .UK. . BWY
Woodchopper, AK . . . . USA. . WOO
Woodgreen . . . . .Australia. . WOG
Woodie Woodie . . . . . . .Australia. . WWI
Woodstock/RR Stn., ON Canada. . . XIP
Woomera . . . . .Australia. . UMR
Wooster, Wayne County Arpt, OH
. . . . .USA . . BJJ
Wora Na Ye. . . . . Gabon. . WNE
Worcester, MA . . . . .USA. . ORH
Worland, WY . . . . .USA. . WRL
Worms . . . . .Germany. . ZQV
Worthington, MN . . . . USA. . OTG
Wotho Is . . . . .Marshall Is. . WTO
Wotje Is. . . . . .Marshall Is. . WTE
Wrangell/SPB, AK . . . . USA. . WRG
Wrench Creek, AK . . . . USA. . WRH
Wright/AAF, GA . . . . .USA. . . LIY
Wrigley, NT . . . . Canada. . YWY
Wroclaw/Strachowice . . . Poland. .WRO
Wrotham Park . . . . .Australia. . WPK
Wudinna . . . . .Australia. . WUD
Wuerzburg . . . . .Germany. .QWU
Wuhan . . . . China. . WUH
Wuhu . . . . China. . WHU
Wunnummin Lake, ON Canada. . WNN
Wuppertal . . . . .Germany. . UWP
Wurtsmith/AFB, MI . . . . . .USA. . OSC
Wuvulu Is . . Papua New Guinea. . WUV
Wuxi . . . . .China. . WUX
Wuyishan . . . . China. . WUS
Wuzhou/Changzhoudao. . China. . WUZ
Wylk Auf Foehr . . . . . .Germany. . OHR
Wyndharn. . . . . .Australia. . WYN
Wyoming/RR Stn., ON . Canada. . XWY
Wyton/RAF . . . . .UK. . QUY

X

X Thaurah	Syria	SOR
Xai Xai	Mozambique	VJB
Xangongo	Angola	XGN
Xanxere	Brazil	AXE
Xayabury	Laos	XAY
Xi An	China	SIA
Xi An/Xianyang	China	XIY
Xiamen	China	XMN
Xiangan	China	XFN
Xichang	China	XIC
Xieng Khouang	Laos	XKH
Xienglorn	Laos	XIE
Xilinhot	China	XIL
Xingcheng	China	XEN
Xingning	China	XIN
Xingtai	China	XNT
Xinguara/Mun	Brazil	XIG
Xining	China	XNN
Xuzhou	China	XUZ

Y

Yaaunde/Nsimalen	Cameroon	NSI
Yaba	Nigeria	QYB
Yacuiba	Bolivia	BYC
Yagoua	Cameroon	GXX
Yaguara	Colombia	AYG
Yakatapa/Intermediate, AK	USA	CYT
Yakima, WA	USA	YKM
Yakima/Firing Center/AAF, WA	USA	FCT
Yakushima	Japan	KUM
Yakutat, AK	USA	YAK
Yakutsk	Russia	YKS
Yalata Mission	Australia	KYI
Yalgoo	Australia	YLG
Yalinga	Central African Rep	AIG
Yalumet	Papua New Guinea	KYX
Yam Is	Australia	XMY
Yamagata/Junmachi	Japan	GAJ
Yamoussoukro	Côte D'ivoire	ASK
Yan	Colombia	AYI
Yan'an	China	ENY
Yanbu	Saudi Arabia	YNB
Yancheng	China	YNZ
Yandina	Solomon Is	XYA
Yangambi	Congo, DR	YAN
Yangon/Mingaladon	Myanmar	RGN
Yangoonabie	Australia	KYB
Yanji	China	YNJ
Yankton/Chan Gurney, SD	USA	YKN
Yantai/Laishan	China	YNT
Yaounde/Yaciunde Arpt	Cameroon	YAO
Yap	Micronesia	YAP
Yapsiei	Papua New Guinea	KPE
Yarmouth, NS	Canada	YQI
Yaroslavl	Russia	IAR
Yasawa Is	Fiji	YAS
Yasoudj	Netherlands	QYS
Yasuru	Papua New Guinea	KSX
Yavarate	Colombia	VAB
Yaviza	Panama	PYV
Yazd	Iran	AZD
Ye	Myanmar	XYE
Yechon/Air Base	S. Korea	YEC
Yeelirrie	Australia	KYF
Yegepa	Papua New Guinea	PGE
Yelimane	Mali	EYL
Yellow River	Papua New Guinea	XYR
Yellowknife, NT	Canada	YZF
Yengema	Sierra Leone	WYE
Yenkis	Papua New Guinea	YEQ
Yeovilton	UK	YEO
Yerevan	Armenia	EVN
Yerington, NV	USA	EYR
Yes Bay/SPB, AK	USA	WYB
Yeva	Papua New Guinea	YVD
Yibin	China	YBP
Yichang, QC	China	YIH
Yilan	China	YLN
Yinchuan	China	INC
Yining	China	YIN
Yiwu	China	YIW
Ylivieska	Finland	YLI
Yogyakarta/Adisutjipto	Indonesia	JOG
Yokkaichi	Japan	QGZ
Yokohama	Japan	YOK
Yola	Nigeria	YOL
Yonago/Miho	Japan	YGJ
Yonaguni Jima	Japan	OGN
Yongai	Papua New Guinea	KGH
York Landing	Mongolia	ZAC
York, PA	USA	THV
York/RR	UK	QQY
Yorke Is	Australia	OKR
Yorketown	Australia	ORR
Yorkton, SK	Canada	YQV
Yoro	Honduras	ORO
Yororijima	Japan	RNJ
Yosemite Ntl Park, CA	USA	OYS
Yosu	S. Korea	RSU
Yotvata	Israel	YOT
Young	Australia	NGA
Youngstown, OH	USA	YNG
Yreka, CA	USA	RKC
Yuanmou	China	YUA
Yucca Flat, NV	USA	UCC
Yuendurnu	Australia	YUE
Yule Is/Kairuku	Papua New Guinea	RKU
Yulin	China	UYN
Yuma/Int'l, AZ	USA	YUM
Yuma/MCAS, AZ	USA	NYL
Yurimaguas	Peru	YMS
Yurut	Indonesia	RUF
Yuzhno-Sakhalinsk	Russia	UUS
Yverdon	Switzerland	ZLJ

Z

Zabljak	Yugoslavia	ZBK
Zabre	Burkina Faso	XZA
Zabreh/Dolni Benesov		
	Czech Rep	ZBE
Zacatecas/La Calera	Mexico	ZCL
Zachar Bay/SPB, AK	USA	KZB
Zadar	Croatia	ZAD
Zagazeeg	Egypt	QZZ
Zagreb/Pleso	Croatia	ZAG
Zahedan	Iran	ZAH
Zahleh	Lebanon	QZQ
Zaisan	Kazakstan	SZI
Zakinthos Is	Greece	ZTH
Zakopane	Poland	QAZ
Zakouma	Chad	AKM
Zambezi	Zambia	BBZ
Zamboanga	Philippines	ZAM
Zamora	Mexico	ZMM
Zanaga	Congo, DR	ANJ
Zanesville, OH	USA	ZZV
Zanzibar/Kisauni	Tanzania	ZNZ
Zapala	Argentina	APZ
Zapatoca	Colombia	AZT
Zaporozhye	Ukraine	OZH
Zaragoza	Spain	ZAZ
Zaranj	Afghanistan	ZAJ
Zaria	Nigeria	ZAR
Zarqa	Jordan	QZA
Zawia Town	Libya	QZT
Zemio	Central African Rep	IMO
Zenag	Papua New Guinea	ZEN
Zephyrhills, FL	USA	ZPH
Zermatt	Switzerland	QZB
Zero	India	ZER
Zhairem	Kazakstan	HRC
Zhambyl	Kazakstan	DMB
Zhanjiang	China	ZHA
Zhaotong	China	ZAT
Zhengzhou	China	CGO
Zhezkazgan/Zhezhazgan		
	Kazakstan	DZN
Zhitomir	Ukraine	ZTR
Zhob	Pakistan	PZH
Zhongshan	China	ZIS
Zhoushan	China	HSN
Zhuhai/Zhuhai Arpt	China	ZUH
Zielona Gora/Babimost	Poland	IEG
Ziguinchor	Senegal	ZIG
Zilfi	Saudi Arabia	ZUL
Zilina	Slovakia	ILZ
Zinder	Niger	ZND
Zittau/RR Stn	Germany	ZIT
Zlin/Holesov	Czech Rep	GTW
Zliten	Libya	QZL
Zoersel	Belgium	OBL
Zofingen	Switzerland	ZLL
Zonguldak	Turkey	ONQ
Zouerate	Mauritania	OUZ
Zuenoula	Côte D'ivoire	ZUE
Zug	Switzerland	ZLM
Zugapa	Indonesia	UGU
Zunyi	China	ZYI
Zurich	Switzerland	ZLQ
Zurich	Switzerland	ZRH
Zurich/HBF Railway Svc		
	Switzerland	ZLP
Zurs/Lech/Flexenpass HP		
	Austria	ZRS
Zwara	Libya	WAX
Zweibruecken	Germany	ZQW